Logs

Lesson	pg
2	42
6	61
19	117
21	126
28	157
30	164
31	167
38	202
44	225
46	235
61	307
70	347
82	400
87	424
100	484

Advanced Mathematics

An Incremental Development

Advanced Mathematics

An Incremental Development

John H. Saxon, Jr.

SAXON PUBLISHERS, INC.

Advanced Mathematics
An Incremental Development

Teachers' Edition

Printed in the United States of America

ISBN: 0-939798-38-7

Editor and Production Supervisor: Nancy Warren
Graphic Artists: Andrew Sims and Robert Norris
Compositor: Syntax International Pte., Ltd.
Printer: Rand McNally & Company

Second printing, May 1991

Saxon Publishers, Inc.
1320 W. Lindsey, Suite 100
Norman, Oklahoma 73069

Contents

Preface

This book is the third book in a three-book high school mathematics sequence designed to prepare students for a comprehensive precalculus course. The topics covered in this book are covered so thoroughly and in such depth that many will consider that this book in itself provides an excellent preparation for calculus and that no further preparation is necessary.

The emphasis in the Algebra I book was on providing a foundation in the basic concepts and skills of algebra with special attention to signed numbers, positive and negative exponents, linear equations, and word problems. In the Algebra II book, practice in the topics of Algebra I was provided while middle-level algebra skills were introduced and practiced. In the Algebra II book, emphasis was given to systems of linear equations, quadratic equations, and systems of nonlinear equations. Area and volume problems were in most of the problem sets. Similar triangles were introduced early, and problems involving similar triangles appeared often. Right-triangle trigonometry was introduced at the one-third point and continued in every problem set in the Algebra II book. The types of word problems and their level of difficulty were selected with the aim of automating the use of the fundamental concepts and procedures required in the solutions of word problems.

This book continues the development begun in the Algebra I and Algebra II books. Practice in the fundamental skills of algebra, geometry, and trigonometry is provided while advanced topics are introduced and practiced. Logarithms are introduced early, and three or four problems that involve logarithms or exponentials are contained in every problem set until the end of the book. Emphasis is on the algebra of logarithms. Heavy emphasis is given to all phases of trigonometry to include trigonometric equations, trigonometric identities, and the equations and graphs of sinusoids. Other topics that are covered in depth include matrices, determinants, arithmetic series, geometric series, conic sections, roots of higher-order polynomial equations, and functions, including curve sketching.

Geometric concepts are introduced early, and the vocabulary of geometry is given continued emphasis. Proofs are based on similar figures. The scale factor is emphasized. Congruent polygons are presented as similar polygons whose scale factor is 1. The format for two-column proofs is presented, but paragraph proofs are emphasized since this format is required by most teachers of upper-division mathematics courses. Two or three proofs are required in every problem set for over half the book.

The emphasis on fundamental word problems in the first two books provides the foundation necessary for the in-depth development of rate problems in this book. This, in turn, permits the introduction and automation of the use of the concepts and procedures necessary to solve abstract rate problems. This three-year development of word problem skills and other skills explains the high college board scores attained by students who have completed this series. These students have been carefully led through a program that has automated the use of fundamental skills and ingrained the concepts necessary for success in the higher-order thought pro-cesses required by the word problems of upper-level mathematics and science courses. Use of these books has caused increased enrollment in upper-level mathematics and science courses. Teachers of these courses have remarked on the improved preparation of their "Saxon students."

The problems of this book deal with advanced concepts and are no longer one-step or two-step problems. These problems must be worked repetitively if the use of the concepts they contain is to be automated. **Thus, all the problems in all the problem sets must be worked by every student to get the full effect of the repetition.** This requirement indicates that this book will be for a three- or four-semester course for many students, although some students may be able to complete the book in two semesters.

To the Teacher

At the end of the school year students should be able to pass a comprehensive test on all topics presented in a course. They should retain much of what they have learned. This book was designed with these two goals in mind. Thorough understanding of abstractions and long-term retention are not the end products of short-term intensive study. The understanding of an abstraction occurs slowly. As an abstraction is contemplated and used over a period of time, nuances that were hidden at first become evident. Then more practice leads to even better comprehension. Continued practice ingrains the concepts so that retention is possible.

Since the learning process is often long and slow, students often have difficulty understanding and retaining explanations that are clear to the teacher doing the explaining. **Comprehension of abstractions occurs over a period of time and cannot be forced, even by brilliant explanations.** This means that presentations by teachers who use this book should be abbreviated as much as possible because students learn by doing and learn much less when the teacher is talking. The presentation that is brief and succinct is the most effective. The new topic presented in each lesson will appear in the problem sets for the rest of the book, and the students will comprehend the concept in due time. Most of the class period should be devoted to the homework problems, which concentrate on review. Students should be advised to begin by working the problems that give them the most difficulty because in the classroom they can get help from the teacher and from peers. If the difficult problems are worked in class, the rest can be easily completed later.

This method of teaching is much more effective than giving in-depth explanations that are marginally comprehended and quickly forgotten. To some teachers, a quick explanation followed by a work session where help is available is not as rewarding personally as is doing an outstanding job of "teaching." But we must remind ourselves that our job is to see that the students learn. We have no other purpose. **Since the students learn by doing the problems themselves, the teacher's job is to find some way to ensure that every student completes on time all the problems in every problem set.**

Acknowledgments

I thank Frank Wang for his insight and helpful comments and for his aid in the development of the problem sets. I thank Arlene Jeskey, Patricia Chesnutt, and Arthur Bernhart for their constructive criticism. I thank Beverly Harrell for correcting errors and suggesting improvements. I thank Mark Wang and Cindy Wang for checking the problem sets and the answers. I again thank my graduate physicist friend, Detia Roe, who typed the manuscript and made other contributions. The book would not have been possible without her help.

Norman, Oklahoma
July 1985

John Saxon

REVIEW LESSON A Fractional equations · Radical equations · Linear systems · Exponents and radicals

RLA.A Fractional equations

A good first step in the solution of a fractional equation is to multiply the numerator in each term on both sides of the equation by the least common multiple of the denominators. This will permit the denominators to be eliminated, and the resulting equation can then be solved. Of course, values of the variable that would cause one or more denominators to equal zero are unacceptable as solutions. In the following example, x cannot equal -2 because replacing x with -2 would cause the second denominator to equal zero.

Example RLA.A.1 Solve: $\dfrac{4}{7} + \dfrac{3}{x+2} = \dfrac{5}{3}$

Solution $(x \neq -2)$. We have noted the unacceptable value of the variable. Next we multiply each numerator by $21(x + 2)$, which is the least common multiple of the denominators. Then we cancel the denominators and solve.

$$21(x+2)\cdot\frac{4}{7} + 21(x+2)\cdot\frac{3}{x+2} = 21(x+2)\cdot\frac{5}{3} \qquad \text{multiplied}$$

$$3(x+2)4 + 21\cdot 3 = 7(x+2)5 \qquad \text{canceled}$$

$$12x + 24 + 63 = 35x + 70 \qquad \text{multiplied}$$

$$23x = 17 \qquad \text{simplified}$$

$$\mathbf{x = \frac{17}{23}} \qquad \text{divided}$$

Example RLA.A.2 Solve:

$$\begin{cases} (a) & \dfrac{3}{7}x + \dfrac{2}{5}y = 11 \\ (b) & 0.03x - 0.2y = -0.37 \end{cases}$$

Solution If we multiply the top equation by 35, we can eliminate the denominators. If we multiply the bottom equation by 100, we can make all the numbers in the bottom equation whole numbers.

	MULTIPLYING		SIMPLIFIED EQUATIONS	
(a)	$35\cdot\frac{3}{7}x + 35\cdot\frac{2}{5}y = 35\cdot 11$	$\longrightarrow$	$15x + 14y = 385$	(c)
(b)	$100(0.03x) - 100(0.2y) = 100(-0.37)$	$\longrightarrow$	$3x - 20y = -37$	(d)

Now if we multiply equation (d) by -5, we can add the equations and eliminate x.

$$\begin{array}{llllrl} (c) & 15x + 14y = 385 & \longrightarrow & (1) & \longrightarrow & 15x + 14y = 385 & \text{multiplied by } 1 \\ (d) & 3x - 20y = -37 & \longrightarrow & (-5) & \longrightarrow & -15x + 100y = 185 & \text{multiplied by } -5 \\ & & & & & 114y = 570 & \text{added} \\ & & & & & y = \dfrac{570}{114} & \text{transformed and divided} \\ & & & & & \mathbf{y = 5} & \text{solved} \end{array}$$

Now we use equation (c) to solve for x.

$$\begin{array}{rl} 15x + 14y = 385 & \text{equation } (c) \\ 15x + 14(5) = 385 & \text{substituted 5 for } y \\ 15x + 70 = 385 & \text{multiplied} \\ x = \dfrac{315}{15} & \text{transformed and divided} \\ \mathbf{x = 21} & \text{solved} \end{array}$$

So our solution is the ordered pair **(21, 5).**

RLA.B Radical equations

Radicals in equations can be eliminated by isolating the radical on one side of the equation and then raising both sides of the equation to the power that will eliminate the radical. When the radical is a square root radical, both sides are raised to the second power. When the radical is a cube root radical, both sides are raised to the third power, and so on. **When an equation contains two radicals, it is sometimes necessary to repeat the procedure.**

Example RLA.B.1 Solve: $\sqrt[3]{x-5} - 2 = 2$

Solution We first isolate the radical by adding $+2$ to both sides of the equation. To eliminate the cube root radical, we raise both sides of the equation to the third power. Then we solve the resulting equation.

$$\begin{array}{rl} \sqrt[3]{x-5} = 4 & \text{added } +2 \text{ to both sides} \\ x - 5 = 64 & \text{raised both sides to third power} \\ \mathbf{x = 69} & \text{solved} \end{array}$$

Now we check our answer in the original equation because raising expressions to a power sometimes generates an equation that has spurious solutions.

$$\begin{array}{rl} \sqrt[3]{(69) - 5} = 4 & \text{substituted} \\ \sqrt[3]{64} = 4 & \text{simplified} \\ 4 = 4 & \text{check} \end{array}$$

Example RLA.B.2 Solve: $\sqrt{s-48} + \sqrt{s} = 8$

Solution First we isolate $\sqrt{s-48}$ and square both sides to eliminate this radical.

$$\begin{array}{rl} \sqrt{s-48} = 8 - \sqrt{s} & \text{added } -\sqrt{s} \text{ to both sides} \\ s - 48 = 64 - 16\sqrt{s} + s & \text{squared both sides} \\ -48 = 64 - 16\sqrt{s} & \text{simplified} \end{array}$$

Now we rearrange the equation to isolate $\sqrt{s}$, and then we square both sides of the equation again.

$$-112 = -16\sqrt{s} \qquad \text{rearranged}$$
$$7 = \sqrt{s} \qquad \text{divided both sides by } -16$$
$$\mathbf{49 = s} \qquad \text{squared both sides}$$

We finish by checking our solution in the original equation.

$$\sqrt{(49) - 48} + \sqrt{(49)} = 8 \qquad \text{substituted}$$
$$\sqrt{1} + 7 = 8 \qquad \text{simplified}$$
$$8 = 8 \qquad \text{check}$$

Example RLA.B.3 Solve: $x^{2/3} = 4$

Solution **This problem gives us another example of how we get rid of undesirable exponents.** We want to find the value of x^1 so we raise both sides of the equation to the 3/2 power.

$$(x^{2/3})^{3/2} = 4^{3/2} \qquad \text{raised to 3/2 power}$$
$$\mathbf{x = 8} \qquad \text{simplified}$$

RLA.C Systems of three linear equations

Systems of linear equations can be solved by using either the substitution method or the elimination method. Some systems are most easily solved if both methods are used.

Example RLA.C.1 Solve:

$$\begin{array}{l} (a) \\ (b) \\ (c) \end{array} \begin{cases} 2x + 2y - z = 14 \\ 3x + 3y + z = 16 \\ x - 2y = 0 \end{cases}$$

Solution In this book, systems of equations of three or more unknowns will be designed so that the numbers are easy to handle and so that most of the answers will be integers. These problems are studied to allow practice in the concepts of solving equations, and not for practice in arithmetic. Even though the numbers in these problems are integers, a calculator can often be used to prevent mistakes in arithmetic. For the first step, we solve equation (c) for x and find that $x = 2y$. Then in equations (a) and (b), we replace x with $2y$, simplify, and use elimination to solve for y.

$$\begin{array}{llll} (a) & 2(2y) + 2y - z = 14 \longrightarrow & 6y - z = 14 & \text{substituted } 2y \text{ for } x \\ (b) & 3(2y) + 3y + z = 16 \longrightarrow & \underline{9y + z = 16} & \text{substituted } 2y \text{ for } x \\ & & 15y \quad = 30 & \text{added} \\ & & \mathbf{y \quad = 2} & \text{solved} \end{array}$$

Now we know that $\mathbf{x = 4}$ because equation (c) tells us that $x = 2y$. We finish by using 2 for y and 4 for x in equation (a), and solving for z.

$$2(4) + 2(2) - z = 14 \qquad \text{substituted 2 for } y \text{ and 4 for } x$$
$$12 - z = 14 \qquad \text{simplified}$$
$$\mathbf{z = -2} \qquad \text{solved}$$

Thus, the solution is the ordered triple **(4, 2, −2)**.

Example RLA.C.2 Solve:

$$\begin{cases} x + 2y + z = 4 & (a) \\ 2x - y - z = 0 & (b) \\ 2x - 2y + z = 1 & (c) \end{cases}$$

Solution We decide to begin by eliminating z. Thus, we first add equations (a) and (b) to get equation (d), which has no z term. Now we must use equation (c). We can add equation (c) to either equation (a) or (b) and eliminate z again. We decide to add equation (c) to equation (b).

$$\begin{array}{ll} (a) & x + 2y + z = 4 \\ (b) & 2x - y - z = 0 \\ \hline (d) & 3x + y = 4 \end{array} \qquad \begin{array}{ll} (b) & 2x - y - z = 0 \\ (c) & 2x - 2y + z = 1 \\ \hline (e) & 4x - 3y = 1 \end{array}$$

Now we have the two equations (d) and (e) in the two unknowns x and y. We will use elimination and add equation (e) to the product of equation (d) and 3.

$$\begin{array}{rl} (3)(d) & 9x + 3y = 12 \\ (e) & 4x - 3y = 1 \\ \hline & 13x = 13 \\ & \mathbf{x = 1} \end{array}$$

Now we can use $x = 1$ in either equation (d) or (e) to find y. This time we will do both to show that either procedure will yield the same result.

$$\begin{array}{rl} (d) & 3(1) + y = 4 \\ & 3 + y = 4 \\ & \mathbf{y = 1} \end{array} \qquad \begin{array}{rl} (e) & 4(1) - 3y = 1 \\ & 4 - 3y = 1 \\ & -3y = -3 \\ & \mathbf{y = 1} \end{array}$$

Now we can use $x = 1$ and $y = 1$ in either (a), (b), or (c) to find z. This time we will use all three equations to show that all three will produce the same result.

USING EQUATION (a)	USING EQUATION (b)	USING EQUATION (c)
$(1) + 2(1) + z = 4$	$2(1) - (1) - z = 0$	$2(1) - 2(1) + z = 1$
$1 + 2 + z = 4$	$2 - 1 - z = 0$	$2 - 2 + z = 1$
$3 + z = 4$	$1 - z = 0$	$0 + z = 1$
$\mathbf{z = 1}$	$\mathbf{z = 1}$	$\mathbf{z = 1}$

Thus, the solution is the ordered triple **(1, 1, 1)**.

Example RLA.C.3 Solve:

$$\begin{cases} 2x + 3y = -4 & (a) \\ x - 2z = -3 & (b) \\ 2y - z = -6 & (c) \end{cases}$$

Solution One variable is missing in each equation. We can see this better if we write the equations in expanded form.

$$\begin{array}{lrrrl} (a) & 2x & + 3y & & = -4 \\ (b) & x & & - 2z & = -3 \\ (c) & & 2y & - z & = -6 \end{array}$$

The first step is to combine any two of the equations so that either x, y, or z is eliminated. We could use equations (a) and (b) and eliminate x; or use equations (b) and (c) and eliminate z; or use equations (a) and (c) and eliminate y. We choose to eliminate x, so we add equation (a) to the product of equation (b) and -2.

$$\begin{array}{rl} (a) & 2x + 3y \qquad = -4 \\ (-2)(b) & -2x \qquad + 4z = 6 \\ \hline (d) & \qquad 3y + 4z = 2 \end{array}$$

The resulting equation, (d), has y and z as variables. So does equation (c). We use these equations to eliminate z by adding equation (d) to the product of (4) and equation (c).

$$\begin{array}{rl} (4)(c) & 8y - 4z = -24 \\ (d) & 3y + 4z = 2 \\ \hline & 11y \qquad = -22 \end{array}$$

$$\mathbf{y = -2}$$

Now we replace y with -2 in equation (a) and solve for x. Then we replace y with -2 in equation (c) and solve for z.

$$\begin{array}{rrcrr} (a) & 2x + 3(-2) = -4 & \qquad & (c) & 2(-2) - z = -6 \\ & 2x - 6 = -4 & & & -4 - z = -6 \\ & 2x = 2 & & & -z = -2 \\ & \mathbf{x = 1} & & & \mathbf{z = 2} \end{array}$$

Thus, our solution is the ordered triple **(1, −2, 2)**.

RLA.D Exponents and radicals

When we simplify radical expressions, it is often helpful to replace radicals with parentheses and fractional exponents.

Example RLA.D.1 Simplify: $\sqrt{x^3y}\,\sqrt[4]{xy^3}$

Solution First we replace the radicals with parentheses and fractional exponents and multiply exponents where indicated.

$$(x^3y)^{1/2}(xy^3)^{1/4} = x^{3/2}y^{1/2}x^{1/4}y^{3/4}$$

Now we rearrange the bases and simplify by adding the exponents of like bases.

$$x^{3/2}x^{1/4}y^{1/2}y^{3/4} = \mathbf{x^{7/4}y^{5/4}}$$

Example RLA.D.2 Simplify: $\dfrac{a^{x/2}(y^{2-x})^{1/2}}{a^{3x}y^{-2x}}$

Solution We simplify and write all exponentials in the numerator.

$$a^{x/2}a^{-3x}y^{1-x/2}y^{2x}$$

We finish by adding the exponents of like bases and get

$$\mathbf{a^{-5x/2}y^{(2+3x)/2}}$$

Example RLA.D.3 Simplify: $3\sqrt{\dfrac{3}{2}} - 4\sqrt{\dfrac{2}{3}} + 2\sqrt{24}$

Solution First we change the form of the radicals and use multiplication as necessary to rationalize the denominators.

$$3\frac{\sqrt{3}}{\sqrt{2}}\cdot\frac{\sqrt{2}}{\sqrt{2}} - 4\frac{\sqrt{2}}{\sqrt{3}}\cdot\frac{\sqrt{3}}{\sqrt{3}} + 2\sqrt{4}\sqrt{6}$$

Next we simplify.

$$\frac{3\sqrt{6}}{2} - \frac{4\sqrt{6}}{3} + 4\sqrt{6}$$

We finish by finding a common denominator and adding.

$$\frac{9\sqrt{6}}{6} - \frac{8\sqrt{6}}{6} + \frac{24\sqrt{6}}{6} = \mathbf{\frac{25\sqrt{6}}{6}}$$

Example RLA.D.4 Simplify: $(\sqrt{2} + \sqrt{x})(1 - \sqrt{x})$

Solution We multiply as indicated.

$$\begin{array}{r} \sqrt{2} + \sqrt{x} \\ 1 - \sqrt{x} \\ \hline \sqrt{2} + \sqrt{x} \\ -\sqrt{2x} - x \\ \hline \boldsymbol{\sqrt{2} + (1 - \sqrt{2})\sqrt{x} - x} \end{array}$$

There are three terms in the answer. We note that the coefficient of the second term is the sum $1 - \sqrt{2}$.

Example RLA.D.5 Simplify: $\dfrac{x^{-2} + y^{-2}}{(xy)^{-1}}$

Solution We begin by eliminating the negative exponents and then we add the two expressions in the numerator.

$$\frac{\dfrac{1}{x^2} + \dfrac{1}{y^2}}{\dfrac{1}{xy}} = \frac{\dfrac{y^2 + x^2}{x^2y^2}}{\dfrac{1}{xy}} \qquad \text{added}$$

We finish by multiplying above and below by the reciprocal of the denominator.

$$\frac{\dfrac{y^2 + x^2}{x^2y^2} \cdot \dfrac{xy}{1}}{\dfrac{1}{xy} \cdot \dfrac{xy}{1}} = \mathbf{\frac{x^2 + y^2}{xy}}$$

Problem set A

Problems that compare the values of quantities come in many forms and can be used to provide practice in mathematical reasoning. In these problems, a statement will be made about two quantities *A* and *B*. The correct answer is *A* if quantity *A* is greater and is *B* if quantity *B* is greater. The correct answer is *C* if the quantities are equal and is *D* if insufficient information is provided to determine which quantity is greater.

Compare:

1. *A.* $\dfrac{6 + \frac{3}{4}}{2 - \frac{5}{4}}$ *B.* 3^2

2. $y \neq 0$: *A.* $\dfrac{x + y}{y}$ *B.* $\dfrac{x}{y} + 1$

3. *A.* $\sqrt{\dfrac{1}{4}} + \sqrt{\dfrac{1}{25}}$ *B.* $\sqrt{\dfrac{1}{4} + \dfrac{1}{25}}$

4. If $x < 0$ and $y < 0$, compare: *A.* $x + y$ *B.* $x - y$

5. Twenty percent of the molybdenum fused. If 1420 grams did not fuse, what was the total weight of molybdenum used?

6. The ratio of pusillanimous brave men to oxymorons on the battlefield was 17 to 2. If the total of both on the battlefield was 342, how many were oxymorons?

Solve:

7. $\frac{4}{7} + \frac{3}{x+3} = \frac{5}{3}$

8. $\frac{5}{3} - \frac{2}{x-4} = \frac{1}{2}$

9. $\frac{1}{x-7} + \frac{1}{4} = \frac{1}{3}$

10. $\begin{cases} \frac{3}{7}x + \frac{2}{5}y = 11 \\ 0.03x - 0.2y = -0.37 \end{cases}$

11. $\begin{cases} \frac{2}{3}x + \frac{3}{5}y = 12 \\ 0.1x + 0.02y = 1.1 \end{cases}$

12. $\sqrt[3]{x-5} - 1 = 2$

13. $\sqrt{s-27} + \sqrt{s} = 9$

14. $\sqrt{s-7} + \sqrt{s} = 7$

15. $\begin{cases} 2x + 2y - z = 9 \\ 3x + 3y + z = 16 \\ x - 2y = -1 \end{cases}$

16. $\begin{cases} x - 2y + z = -2 \\ 2x - 2y - z = -3 \\ x + y - 2z = 1 \end{cases}$

17. $\begin{cases} 2x - y + z = 0 \\ 4x + 2y + z = 2 \\ 2x - y - z = -4 \end{cases}$

18. $\begin{cases} 2x + 3y = -1 \\ x - 2z = -3 \\ 2y - z = -4 \end{cases}$

19. $\begin{cases} \frac{x}{2} + \frac{y}{4} = 2 \\ x - \frac{z}{3} = 1 \\ \frac{y}{2} + z = 5 \end{cases}$

20. $\begin{cases} x - y = 1 \\ y - 2z = 1 \\ 3x - 4z = 7 \end{cases}$

Simplify:

21. $\sqrt{x^3y^2}\,\sqrt[4]{xy^3}$

22. $x^{3/4}\sqrt{xy}\,x^{1/2}\sqrt[3]{x^4}$

23. $\dfrac{a^{x/2}(y^{2-x})^{1/2}}{a^{4x}y^{-2x}}$

24. $\dfrac{y^{x+3}y^{x/2-1}z^a}{y^{(x-a)/2}z^{(x-a)/3}}$

25. $2\sqrt{\frac{3}{2}} - 3\sqrt{\frac{2}{3}} + 2\sqrt{24}$

26. $2\sqrt{\frac{7}{3}} - \sqrt{\frac{3}{7}} - 2\sqrt{84}$

27. $(\sqrt{2} - \sqrt{x})(1 - \sqrt{x})$

28. $(\sqrt{3} + \sqrt{x})(\sqrt{3} + \sqrt{x})$

29. $\sqrt{2x}(\sqrt{3x} + \sqrt{x})$

30. $\dfrac{x^{-2} + y^{-2}}{(xy)^{-1}}$

REVIEW LESSON B Complex numbers · Rational denominators · Completing the square · The quadratic formula

RLB.A Complex numbers

In mathematics, we use the letter i to represent the positive square root of -1.

$$i = \sqrt{-1}$$

The square root of -1 is encountered often in the solution of quadratic equations. It may be that i was first used to represent $\sqrt{-1}$ because i can be written with one stroke of the pen (if the dot is neglected) while $\sqrt{-1}$ requires three strokes of the pen. Square roots of negative numbers can be written as the product of a real number and i as we show here.

$$\sqrt{-13} = \sqrt{13(-1)} = \sqrt{13}\sqrt{-1} = \sqrt{13}\,i$$

Since $i = \sqrt{-1}$, then $i^2 = -1$.

$$i^2 = -1 \qquad \text{because} \qquad \sqrt{-1}\sqrt{-1} = -1$$

A complex number is made up of two real numbers a and b and the letter i. If the number with i as a factor is written last as $\boldsymbol{a + bi}$, the complex number is said to be in ***standard form.*** A complex number has a real component a and an imaginary component. In the past, the combination bi was considered to be the imaginary component, but recently more than a few authors have said that the real number b is the imaginary component of the complex number. Note that all of the following numbers are complex numbers in the standard form $a + bi$.

(*a*) $4 + 2i$ (*b*) $3.01 - \frac{\sqrt{2}}{3}i$ (*c*) 4.06 (*d*) $3i$ (*e*) $\frac{\sqrt{13}}{5.6} + \sqrt{2}\,i$

We note that a and b can be any real numbers, including 0, because (*c*) represents $4.06 + 0i$ and (*d*) represents $0 + 3i$.

Example RLB.A.1 Simplify: $3i^3 + 2i^5 - 3i + 2i^2$

Solution First we expand the i terms and pair the i's.

$$3i(ii) + 2i(ii)(ii) - 3i + 2(ii)$$

Now we replace each pair of i's with -1.

$$3i(-1) + 2i(-1)(-1) - 3i + 2(-1)$$

We finish by simplifying and writing the result in standard form.

$$-3i + 2i - 3i - 2 = \mathbf{-2 - 4i}$$

Example RLB.A.2 Simplify: $\sqrt{-3}\sqrt{4} + 3\sqrt{-2}\sqrt{-9} + \sqrt{-16} + \sqrt{16}$

Solution We begin by using the i notation.

$$(\sqrt{3}\,i)(2) + (3\sqrt{2}\,i)(3i) + 4i + 4$$

Now we simplify

$$2\sqrt{3}\,i - 9\sqrt{2} + 4i + 4$$

and finish by grouping the real parts and the imaginary parts.

$$\mathbf{(4 - 9\sqrt{2}) + (2\sqrt{3} + 4)}\boldsymbol{i}$$

RLB.B Rational denominators

It is customary to write numbers with rational denominators. For example, the four numbers

$$(a)\ \frac{2}{\sqrt{3}} \qquad (b)\ \frac{6}{2i} \qquad (c)\ \frac{4 + \sqrt{3}}{2 - 3\sqrt{3}} \qquad (d)\ \frac{2 - i^3 + 2i^5}{-2i + 4}$$

can be written with rational denominators as

$$(a')\ \frac{2\sqrt{3}}{3} \qquad (b')\ -3i \qquad (c')\ \frac{-17 - 14\sqrt{3}}{23} \qquad (d')\ \frac{1}{10} + \frac{4}{5}i$$

The process of converting a denominator to a rational number is called ***rationalizing the denominator.*** In (a) we multiplied above and below by $\sqrt{3}$. In (b) we multiplied above and below by $-i$. We will show the procedure for (c) and (d) in the next two examples.

Example RLB.B.1 Simplify: $\dfrac{4 + \sqrt{3}}{2 - 3\sqrt{3}}$

Solution We remember that **an expression that contains square roots of counting numbers is in simplified form when no radicand has a perfect square (other than 1) as a factor and no radicals are in the denominator.** We can rationalize the denominator if we multiply above and below by $2 + 3\sqrt{3}$, which is the ***conjugate of the denominator.***

$$\frac{4 + \sqrt{3}}{2 - 3\sqrt{3}} \cdot \frac{2 + 3\sqrt{3}}{2 + 3\sqrt{3}}$$

We have two multiplications to perform, one above and one below. Many people find it easier to do these multiplications separately and then to write the answer. We will do this.

$$\begin{array}{rr} \text{ABOVE} & \\ 4 + \sqrt{3} & \\ 2 + 3\sqrt{3} & \\ \hline 8 + 2\sqrt{3} & \\ 12\sqrt{3} + 9 & \\ \hline 17 + 14\sqrt{3} & \end{array} \qquad \begin{array}{l} \text{BELOW} \\ 2 - 3\sqrt{3} \\ 2 + 3\sqrt{3} \\ \hline 4 - 6\sqrt{3} \\ \quad + 6\sqrt{3} - 27 \\ \hline 4 \qquad\quad - 27 = -23 \end{array}$$

Thus, our simplification is

$$\frac{17 + 14\sqrt{3}}{-23} \quad \text{or} \quad \mathbf{\frac{-17 - 14\sqrt{3}}{23}}$$

Example RLB.B.2 Simplify: $\dfrac{2 - i^3 + 2i^5}{-2i + 4}$

Solution First we write both complex numbers in standard form and get

$$\frac{2 + 3i}{4 - 2i}$$

We can change the denominator of this expression to a rational number if we multiply above and below by $4 + 2i$, which is the **conjugate of the denominator.** We have two multiplications indicated, one above and one below. We will use the vertical format for both of the multiplications.

$$\begin{array}{ll}
\text{ABOVE} & \text{BELOW} \\
\begin{array}{l} 2 + 3i \\ 4 + 2i \\ \hline 8 + 12i \\ \quad\;\; 4i + 6i^2 \\ \hline 8 + 16i - 6 \quad = 2 + 16i \end{array} &
\begin{array}{l} 4 - 2i \\ 4 + 2i \\ \hline 16 - 8i \\ \quad\; + 8i - 4i^2 \\ \hline 16 \qquad + 4 \quad = 20 \end{array}
\end{array}$$

Thus, we can write our answer as

$$\frac{2 + 16i}{20} = \frac{1 + 8i}{10}$$

This answer is not in the preferred form of $a + bi$. We can write this complex number in standard form if we write

$$\frac{1}{10} + \frac{4}{5}i$$

RLB.C Completing the square

If a quadratic equation is in the form of the two equations shown here, the solution can be found by taking the square root of both sides of the equation.

(a)	(b)	
$\left(x + \frac{1}{2}\right)^2 = 3$	$(x - 4)^2 = 5$	equation
$x + \frac{1}{2} = \pm\sqrt{3}$	$x - 4 = \pm\sqrt{5}$	square root of both sides
$x = -\frac{1}{2} \pm \sqrt{3}$	$x = 4 \pm \sqrt{5}$	solved for x

The process of rearranging a quadratic equation into the form $(x - h)^2 = p$ is called ***completing the square.*** The basis for this procedure comes from observing the patterns of the coefficients when binomials are squared. Here we give four examples.

(c) $(x + 3)^2 = x^2 + 6x + 9$ (d) $(x - 5)^2 = x^2 - 10x + 25$

(e) $\left(x - \frac{1}{2}\right)^2 = x^2 - x + \frac{1}{4}$ (f) $\left(x + \frac{2}{5}\right)^2 = x^2 + \frac{4}{5}x + \frac{4}{25}$

We note that, in each example, the constant term of the trinomial is a positive number and is the square of one-half the coefficient of the x term in the trinomial. Thus, if we have

$$x^2 + \frac{3}{5}x$$

and want to add a constant so that the result is the square of a binomial, we multiply the coefficient of x by $\frac{1}{2}$ and square the result.

$$\left(\frac{3}{5} \cdot \frac{1}{2}\right)^2 = \frac{9}{100}$$

Now if we add 9/100 to the expression under consideration, we can write the result as the square of a binomial.

$$x^2 + \frac{3}{5}x + \frac{9}{100} \xrightarrow{\text{which can be written as}} \left(x + \frac{3}{10}\right)^2$$

We also note that the constant in the binomial is one-half the coefficient of x in the trinomial.

Example RLB.C.1 Solve $-x + 3x^2 = -5$ by completing the square.

Solution As the first step we write the equation in standard form.

$$3x^2 - x + 5 = 0$$

Then we divide every term by 3 so that the coefficient of x^2 will be 1.

$$x^2 - \frac{1}{3}x + \frac{5}{3} = 0$$

Next we write the parentheses and move the constant term to the right side.

$$\left(x^2 - \frac{1}{3}x \qquad\right) = -\frac{5}{3}$$

Now we multiply the coefficient of x by $\frac{1}{2}$ and square this product.

$$\left(-\frac{1}{3}\cdot\frac{1}{2}\right)^2 = \frac{1}{36}$$

Then we add 1/36 to both sides of the equation.

$$\left(x^2 - \frac{1}{3}x + \frac{1}{36}\right) = -\frac{5}{3} + \frac{1}{36}$$

Now we simplify and solve for x.

$$\left(x - \frac{1}{6}\right)^2 = -\frac{59}{36} \qquad \text{simplified}$$

$$x - \frac{1}{6} = \pm\sqrt{-\frac{59}{36}} \qquad \text{square root of both sides}$$

$$\mathbf{x = \frac{1}{6} \pm \frac{\sqrt{59}}{6}\,i} \qquad \text{solved}$$

RLB.D The quadratic formula

By completing the square, any quadratic equation can be written in the form $(x - h)^2 = p$ and then can be solved by taking the square root of both sides. This process is time-consuming, and it is a little faster to use the quadratic formula. This formula can be derived by completing the square on a general quadratic equation. We begin by writing a general quadratic equation that uses the letters a, b, and c as constants.

$$ax^2 + bx + c = 0$$

Next we give x^2 a unity coefficient by dividing every term by a, and we get

$$x^2 + \frac{b}{a}x + \frac{c}{a} = 0$$

Now we move c/a to the right side and use parentheses on the left side.

$$\left(x^2 + \frac{b}{a}x \qquad\right) = \qquad -\frac{c}{a}$$

Note that we placed the $-c/a$ well to the right of the equals sign. Now we multiply b/a by $\frac{1}{2}$ and square the result.

$$\left(\frac{b}{a}\cdot\frac{1}{2}\right)^2 = \frac{b^2}{4a^2}$$

Next add $b^2/4a^2$ inside the parentheses and also to the other side of the equation. On the right we are careful to place $b^2/4a^2$ in front of $-c/a$.

$$\left(x^2 + \frac{b}{a}x + \frac{b^2}{4a^2}\right) = \frac{b^2}{4a^2} - \frac{c}{a}$$

Next we write the parentheses term as a squared term and combine $b^2/4a^2$ and $-c/a$.

$$\left(x + \frac{b}{2a}\right)^2 = \frac{b^2 - 4ac}{4a^2}$$

Finally, we take the square root of both sides and then solve for x.

$$x + \frac{b}{2a} = \pm\sqrt{\frac{b^2 - 4ac}{4a^2}} \qquad \text{took square roots}$$

$$x = -\frac{b}{2a} \pm \frac{\sqrt{b^2 - 4ac}}{2a} \qquad \text{solved for } x$$

$$x = \frac{-b \pm \sqrt{b^2 - 4ac}}{2a} \qquad \text{added}$$

The derivation of the quadratic formula will be required in future problem sets. This derivation requires only simple algebraic manipulations, and the requirement that a student be able to perform this derivation is not unreasonable.

Example RLB.D.1 Use the quadratic formula to find the roots of the equation $3x^2 - 2x + 5 = 0$.

Solution The formula is

$$x = \frac{-b \pm \sqrt{b^2 - 4ac}}{2a}$$

If we write the given equation just below the general quadratic equation,

$$ax^2 + bx + c = 0 \qquad \text{general equation}$$

$$3x^2 - 2x + 5 = 0 \qquad \text{given equation}$$

we note the following correspondences between the equations.

$$a = 3 \qquad b = -2 \qquad c = 5$$

If we use these numbers for a, b, and c in the quadratic formula, we get

$$x = \frac{-(-2) \pm \sqrt{(-2)^2 - 4(3)(5)}}{2(3)}$$

$$x = \frac{2 \pm \sqrt{-56}}{6}$$

$$\boldsymbol{x = \frac{1}{3} \pm \frac{\sqrt{14}}{3}i}$$

Problem set B

1. Forty percent of those who attended wore red hats. If 1800 of those who attended did not wear red hats, how many did wear red hats?

2. Two animals out of seven believed Chicken Little. If 85 animals did not believe Chicken Little, how many animals were there in all?

Simplify:

3. $3i^4 + 2i^5 + 3i^3 + 2i^2$

4. $\sqrt{-3}\sqrt{4} + 3\sqrt{-2}\sqrt{-9} + \sqrt{-16} + \sqrt{16}$

5. $2i^3 + 3i^2 + 2i - 2\sqrt{2}\,i$

6. $2\sqrt{-2}\sqrt{2} + 3i\sqrt{2} - \sqrt{-2}\sqrt{2}$

7. $\dfrac{2 + i - 2i^3}{2i^3 + 4}$

8. $\dfrac{4 + \sqrt{3}}{2 - 3\sqrt{3}}$

9. $\dfrac{3 - i^2 + 2i^5 - 2}{-2i^3 + 3i}$

Solve by completing the square:

10. $x + 3x^2 = -5$

11. $-2x - 2x^2 = 5$

12. Begin with $ax^2 + bx + c = 0$ and derive the quadratic formula by completing the square.

Use the quadratic formula to solve:

13. $3x^2 + 2x + 5 = 0$

14. $-x = -3x^2 + 4$

15. $-3x = 2x^2 + 7$

16. If $x = 0$, $y > 1$, and $z > 1$, compare: *A.* $2y(x + z)$ *B.* $x(y + z)$

17. If $a = 3$ and $b = \frac{1}{6}$, compare: *A.* $2a - 18b$ *B.* $3a - 36b$

Solve:

18. $\dfrac{2}{x+4} - \dfrac{1}{5} = \dfrac{2}{3}$

19. $\begin{cases} \dfrac{2}{3}x - \dfrac{4}{5}y = 0 \\ 0.02x - 0.1y = -0.76 \end{cases}$

20. $\sqrt{2s - 7} + \sqrt{25} = 7$

21. $\begin{cases} x + 2y - z = 9 \\ x + 3y = 9 \\ 2x - z = 8 \end{cases}$

22. $\begin{cases} x - y + 2z = 7 \\ 2x + y - z = 0 \\ x + 2y + z = 9 \end{cases}$

23. $\begin{cases} \dfrac{x}{2} - \dfrac{y}{3} = \dfrac{5}{6} \\ \dfrac{2x}{3} + \dfrac{z}{5} = \dfrac{11}{5} \\ 0.1y + 0.02z = 0.22 \end{cases}$

24. $\begin{cases} x + y - z = 2 \\ 2x - y + z = 4 \\ 3x + 2y - z = 5 \end{cases}$

Simplify:

25. $x^{2/3}\sqrt[3]{x^2}\,y(x^2y)^{1/5}$

26. $y^{x/2+1}\sqrt{y^a}\,2y^{2a+3}$

27. $2\sqrt{\dfrac{3}{2}} - 4\sqrt{\dfrac{2}{3}} + 3\sqrt{24}$

28. $(\sqrt{2} + \sqrt{x})(\sqrt{2} + \sqrt{x})$

29. $(x^{1/2} + y^{1/2})^2$

30. $\dfrac{a^{-2} + b^{-1}}{a^{-1}b}$

REVIEW LESSON C Sine, cosine, tangent · Angles of elevation and depression · Rectangular and polar coordinates · Coordinate conversion

RLC.A Sine, cosine, and tangent

A right triangle has one right angle and two acute angles. If we select one of the acute angles, we call the ratio of the side opposite this angle to the hypotenuse the ***sine*** of the angle. The ratio of the side adjacent the selected angle to the hypotenuse is called the ***cosine*** of the angle. The ratio of the side opposite the selected angle to the side adjacent the selected angle is called the ***tangent*** of the angle. These ratios are the same for every acute angle whose measure is the same as that of the selected angle. To remember which ratio corresponds to which name requires pure memorization, and mnemonics are helpful for memorizing these ratios. On the right, below, we use the first letters of the words *opposite, hypotenuse,* and *adjacent* to form the first letters of a sentence that is easy to remember.

$$\sin A = \frac{\text{opposite}}{\text{hypotenuse}} \qquad \frac{\text{Oscar}}{\text{had}}$$

$$\cos A = \frac{\text{adjacent}}{\text{hypotenuse}} \qquad \frac{\text{a}}{\text{hold}}$$

$$\tan A = \frac{\text{opposite}}{\text{adjacent}} \qquad \frac{\text{on}}{\text{Arthur}}$$

Thus, if we can remember to write sine, cosine, and tangent in that order and then write "Oscar had a hold on Arthur," we have the definitions memorized. Some people take the first letters of the words sine, opposite, hypotenuse; cosine, adjacent, hypotenuse; tangent, opposite, adjacent to form the expression

Soh Cah Toa

and say that it sounds like an American Indian phrase.

We can use the sine, cosine, and tangent ratios to solve for unknown values in right triangles, as we show in the following examples.

Example RLC.A.1 Find A and B.

Solution We can find A and B by using the sine and cosine of 36°.

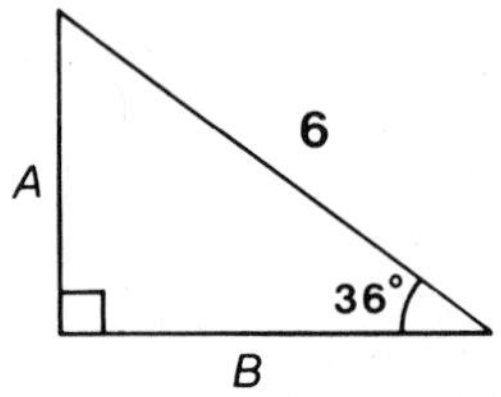

$$\frac{A}{6} = \sin 36^\circ \qquad \frac{B}{6} = \cos 36^\circ$$

$$\text{so} \quad A = 6 \sin 36^\circ \qquad \text{so} \quad B = 6 \cos 36^\circ$$

Next we use the table of trigonometric functions in the appendix to find the values of sin 36° and cos 36° and make these substitutions to get

$$A = 6(0.5878) \qquad B = 6(0.8090)$$

$$\mathbf{A = 3.5268} \qquad \mathbf{B = 4.854}$$

A scientific calculator should be used for these problems, and the tables of trigonometric functions should be used when a scientific calculator is not available. Use your calculator to check the following operations.

$$A = 6 \sin 36° \qquad B = 6 \cos 36°$$
$$\approx 3.5267115 \qquad \approx 4.854102$$
$$\approx 3.53 \qquad \approx 4.85$$

When we use the calculator, we can get the answer without having to write the value of sin 36° as an intermediate step. Also, the calculator answer is accurate to more digits, but we will normally round off answers to a more convenient number, as we did here.

Example RLC.A.2 Find angle M and side x.

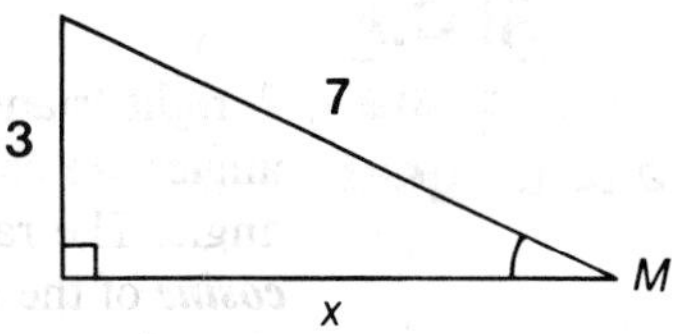

Solution We use the sine ratio to find angle M.

$$\sin M = \frac{3}{7}$$
$$\sin M = 0.4285714$$
$$M = 25.376932°$$
$$\mathbf{M = 25.4°}$$

We used the calculator and then rounded off to a more reasonable number. To find side x, we could use a trigonometric function of 25.4° or we could use the theorem of Pythagoras. We decide to use the theorem of Pythagoras.

$$x^2 + 3^2 = 7^2$$
$$x^2 = 49 - 9$$
$$\mathbf{x = \sqrt{40} \approx 6.32}$$

We used the calculator and rounded off.

RLC.B Angles of elevation and depression

Angles of elevation and **angles of depression** are measured from the horizontal. On the left we show that an angle of elevation is measured ***upward*** from the horizontal, and on the right we show that an angle of depression is measured ***downward*** from the horizontal.

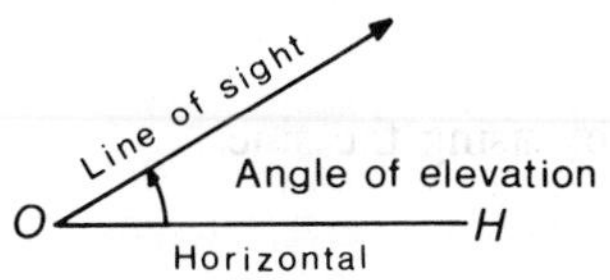

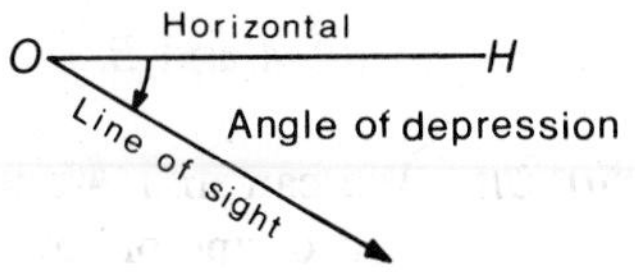

Example RLC.B.1 A man 6 ft tall is 200 ft from a tree, and he measures the angle of elevation to the top of the tree as 11°. How tall is the tree?

Solution **For a problem like this one, a sketch of the problem is very helpful.** This sketch is not drawn to scale.

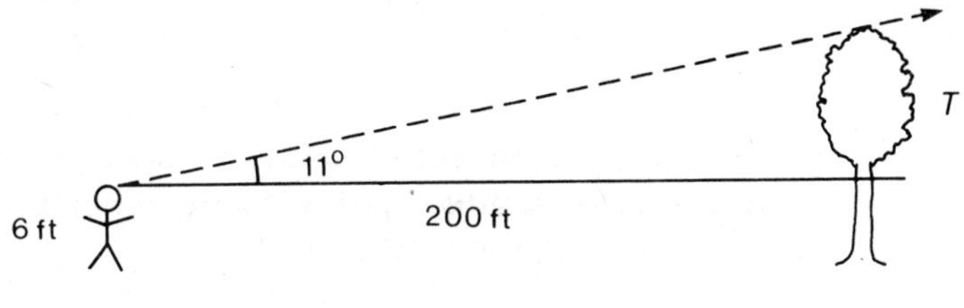

We solve to find T.

$$\frac{T}{200} = \tan 11^\circ$$

$$T = 200 \tan 11^\circ = 38.88$$

The man was 6 ft tall, so the total height of the tree is

$$\text{Height} = 38.88 \text{ ft} + 6 \text{ ft} = \mathbf{44.88 \text{ ft}}$$

Example RLC.B.2 An airplane is flying at an altitude of 3000 ft above the ground. The pilot sights an object on the ground at an angle of depression of 26°. What is the slant range from the airplane to the object?

Solution The angle of depression is 26°, so the angle in the triangle is 90° − 26° = 64°.

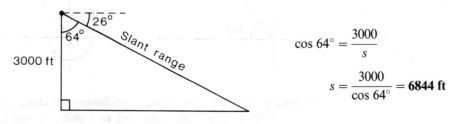

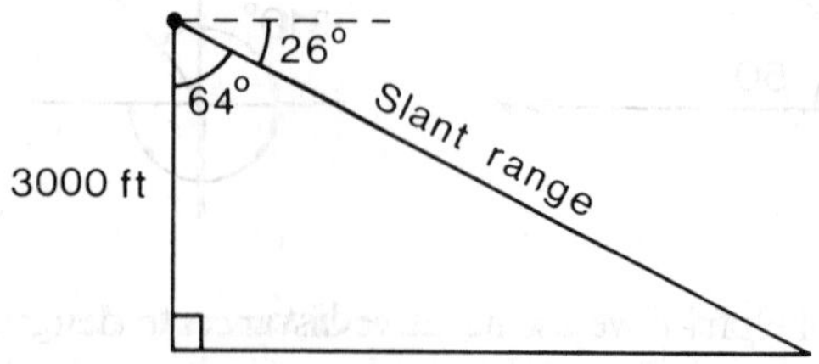

$$\cos 64^\circ = \frac{3000}{s}$$

$$s = \frac{3000}{\cos 64^\circ} = \mathbf{6844 \text{ ft}}$$

We used the calculator to do the arithmetic and rounded off the calculator answer.

RLC.C Rectangular and polar coordinates

The location of a point on a rectangular coordinate system can be designated by using two numbers. One number indicates the distance of the point to the right or the left of the origin, and the other number indicates the distance of the point above or below the origin. We tell which number is which either by writing the numbers as an ordered pair enclosed in parentheses or by writing a letter with each number. **The same notations are used when the numbers are considered to designate two-dimensional vectors. Three-dimensional vectors are customarily identified by using the letters *i*, *j*, and *k*. The letter *i* is used to indicate distances in the *x* direction. The letter *j* is used to indicate distances in the *y* direction, and the letter *k* is used to indicate distances in the *z* direction.** In the Algebra II book, we restricted our study of vectors to two dimensions and used R and U to indicate x distances and y distances, respectively, because we wanted to have the letter i always represent $\sqrt{-1}$. The letter i sometimes has meanings other than $\sqrt{-1}$, and by now we should be sufficiently familiar with its use in complex numbers so that another meaning will not be confusing. Thus, the location of a point 3 units to the left of the origin and 4 units below the origin can be designated by using one of these notations.

$$(-3, -4) \qquad \text{or} \qquad -3i - 4j$$

The notation on the left is an ***ordered pair*** (x, y) and the notation on the right is a ***vector notation*** meaning -3 in the x direction and -4 in the y direction. In this book, we will use the notations interchangeably.

Another method of locating a point is called the method of ***polar coordinates*** and uses a distance and an angle. **Positive angles are measured counterclockwise from the positive *x* axis and negative angles are measured clockwise from the same axis.** If a point is a distance of 6 from the origin at a positive angle of 50°, we can designate the location by using parentheses and an ordered pair of r and θ, as shown on the left, or by giving the distance and then angle, as shown on the right.

$$(6, 50^\circ) \qquad \text{or} \qquad 6\underline{/50^\circ}$$

Measuring counterclockwise 50° from the positive x axis brings one to the same direction as measuring 310° in the clockwise direction, so the point could also be designated by writing either

$$(6, 50^\circ) \qquad \text{or} \qquad 6\underline{/-310^\circ}$$

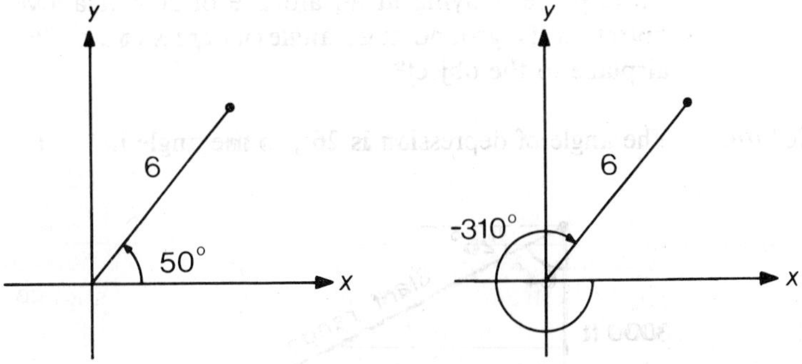

In some problems it is helpful if we use negative distances to designate a point. If we turn through either -130° or $+230^\circ$ **and then back up 6 units,** we find that we are standing on the same point designated in the diagrams above.

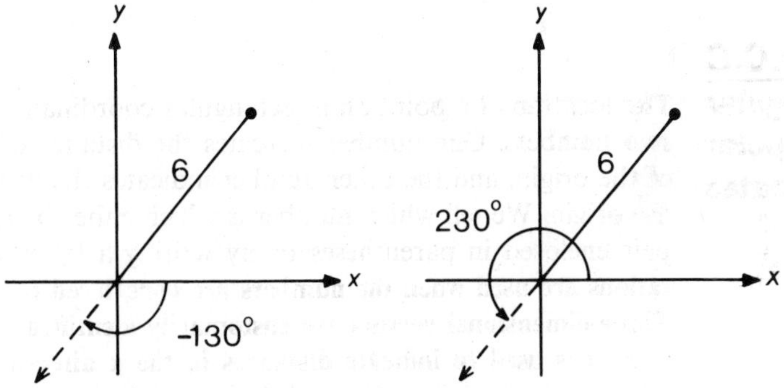

Thus, the point we are discussing can also be designated by writing either

$$-6\underline{/-130^\circ} \qquad \text{or} \qquad -6\underline{/230^\circ}$$

It is less confusing if one can remember to turn through the angle first and then go in the indicated direction for a positive distance and back up when the distance is negative.

RLC.D Coordinate conversion

To convert from rectangular coordinates to polar coordinates, we first draw the diagram. Next we determine the length of hypotenuse of the triangle and the measure of angle. Then we measure the polar angle from the positive x axis.

Example RLC.D.1 Convert $-3i + 2j$ to polar coordinates. Write four forms of the polar coordinates of this point.

Solution On the left we graph the point and draw the triangle. **Note that one side of the triangle is perpendicular to the x axis.**

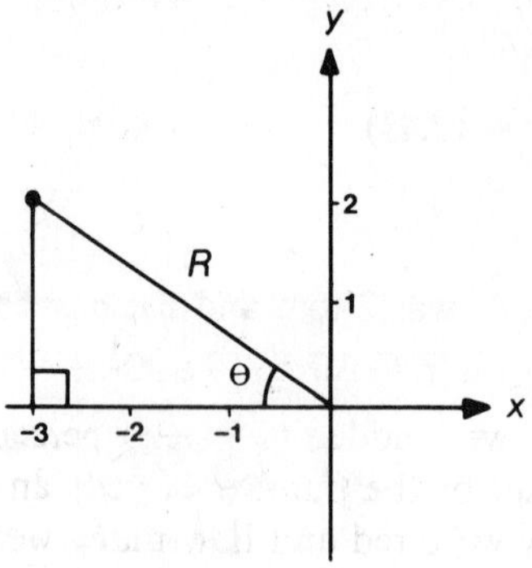

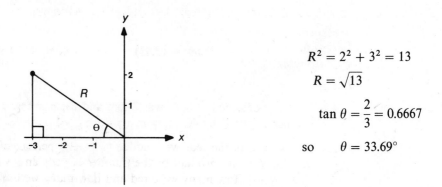

$$R^2 = 2^2 + 3^2 = 13$$
$$R = \sqrt{13}$$
$$\tan\theta = \frac{2}{3} = 0.6667$$
$$\text{so} \qquad \theta = 33.69^\circ$$

On the right, we find that the length of R is $\sqrt{13}$ and that the small angle is 33.69°. If we measure counterclockwise from the x axis, the polar angle is 146.31°; and if we measure clockwise from the positive x axis, the polar angle is 213.69°. If we use negative magnitudes as shown in the right-hand figures, we find the corresponding polar angles are fourth-quadrant angles.

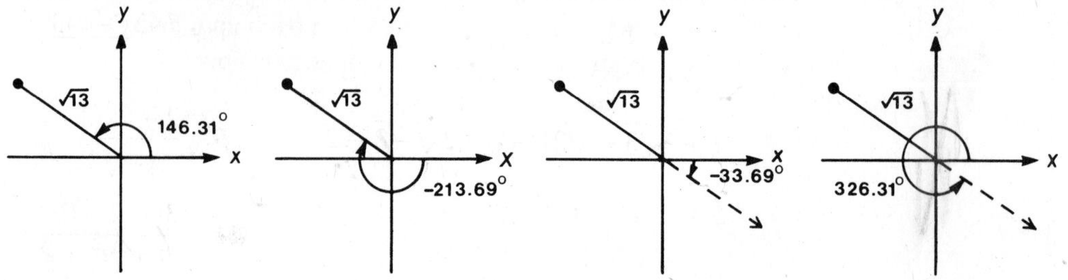

$\sqrt{13}\underline{/146.31^\circ}$ $\qquad$ $\sqrt{13}\underline{/-213.69^\circ}$ $\qquad$ $-\sqrt{13}\underline{/-33.69^\circ}$ $\qquad$ $-\sqrt{13}\underline{/326.31^\circ}$

Example RLC.D.2 Convert $-13\underline{/-253^\circ}$ to rectangular form.

Solution We always draw the angle first, as we show on the left.

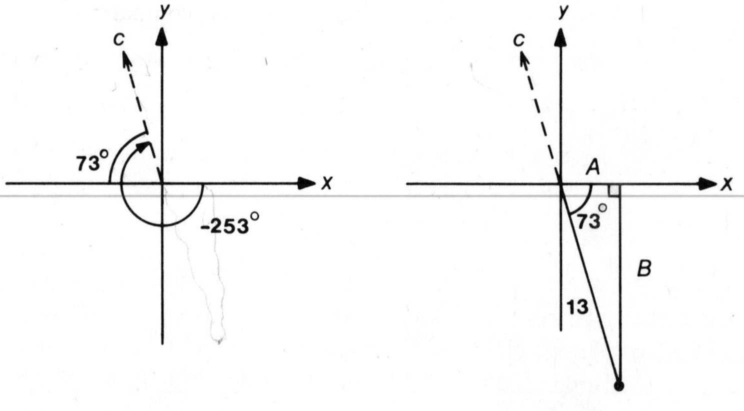

Now, facing in the direction the arrow c is pointing, **we back up 13 units** to locate the designated point. Then we find A and B.

$$A = 13 \cos 73° \qquad B = 13 \sin 73°$$

$$A = 3.80 \qquad B = 12.43$$

Now we can write the rectangular coordinates using either ordered pairs or the letters i and j.

$$\mathbf{(3.80, -12.43)} \quad \text{or} \quad \mathbf{3.80}\boldsymbol{i} - \mathbf{12.43}\boldsymbol{j}$$

Problem set C

1. The ratio of goods to bads was 2 to 5 and the number of bads exceeded twice the number of goods by 40. How many were good and how many were bad?
2. Ten percent of the reds were added to twenty percent of the blues, and the total was 24. Yet, the product of the number of reds and 3 exceeded the number of blues by 20. How many were red and how many were blue?
3. An airplane is flying at an altitude of 5000 ft above the ground. The pilot sights an object on the ground at an angle of depression of 28°. What is the slant range from the airplane to the object?

Convert to polar coordinates:

4. $3.06i - 2.75j$
5. $-2.4i + 7.3j$

Convert to rectangular coordinates:

6. $-8.6\underline{/265°}$
7. $7.42\underline{/-143°}$

Simplify:

8. $\sqrt{-3}\sqrt{3} - \sqrt{2}\,i - \sqrt{-3}\sqrt{-2} - 2$
9. $\dfrac{2 + 2\sqrt{3}}{1 - \sqrt{3}}$
10. $\dfrac{2i^3 - 2i^2 - 1}{i^3 - 2i^4 + 2}$
11. $\dfrac{3i + 2 - 2i^3}{2i - 3i^5 + 2}$

Solve by completing the square:

12. $2x^2 = -x - 5$
13. $2x + 7 = 3x^2$
14. Begin with $ax^2 + bx + c = 0$ and derive the quadratic formula.

Use the quadratic formula to solve:

15. $2x^2 = x - 5$
16. $4 + 3x^2 = -2x$
17. If $0 < x < 10$ and $0 < y < 12$, compare: *A.* x *B.* $y - 2$
18. If $1 < x < 5$ and $1 < y < 5$, compare: *A.* $x - y$ *B.* $y - x$

Solve:

19. $\begin{cases} \dfrac{4}{5}x - \dfrac{2}{3}y = \dfrac{7}{30} \\ 0.01x + 0.1y = 0.03 \end{cases}$
20. $\sqrt{3x - 5} + \sqrt{3x} = 5$
21. $\begin{cases} x + 2y + z = -1 \\ x + z = 3 \\ 3x + y = 4 \end{cases}$
22. $\begin{cases} 2x - y + z = 5 \\ x + y - z = 4 \\ -x + 2y + z = 5 \end{cases}$
23. $\begin{cases} \dfrac{x}{2} - \dfrac{y}{3} = \dfrac{1}{6} \\ \dfrac{x}{3} + \dfrac{2z}{5} = 2\dfrac{3}{5} \\ \dfrac{y}{3} + \dfrac{2z}{3} = 4 \end{cases}$
24. $\begin{cases} x + 2y - z = 7 \\ x - 2z = 2 \\ y + 3z = 5 \end{cases}$

Simplify:

25. $a^2\sqrt[5]{a^3b}(a^2b^4)^{1/3}$

26. $\dfrac{x^{a/2-4}y^{(b-3)/2}}{x^{2a}(y^{1/2})^a}$

27. $3\sqrt{\dfrac{7}{2}}-2\sqrt{\dfrac{2}{7}}+3\sqrt{56}$

28. $(x^{1/2}+y^{1/2})(x^{1/2}-y^{-1/2})$

29. $(\sqrt{2}-x)(2-\sqrt{x})$

30. $\dfrac{x^{-1}+y^{-1}}{x^{-1}y}$

REVIEW LESSON D *Equation of a line · Complex fractions · Abstract equations · Division of polynomials*

RLD.A Equation of a line

A line that is not vertical has a slope and a y intercept.† If you can determine the slope of a line and know where the line crosses the y axis, the line is defined and can be drawn.

If the equation of a line is written in slope-intercept form, the constant term in the equation is the y intercept and the coefficient of x is the slope. The slope is the change in the y coordinate divided by the change in the x coordinate as we move from any point on the line to any other point on the line. The sign of the slope can be determined visually by remembering the following diagrams. **The little man always comes from the left side, as we show here.** He sees the first set of lines as uphill lines with positive slopes and the second set of lines as downhill lines with negative slopes.

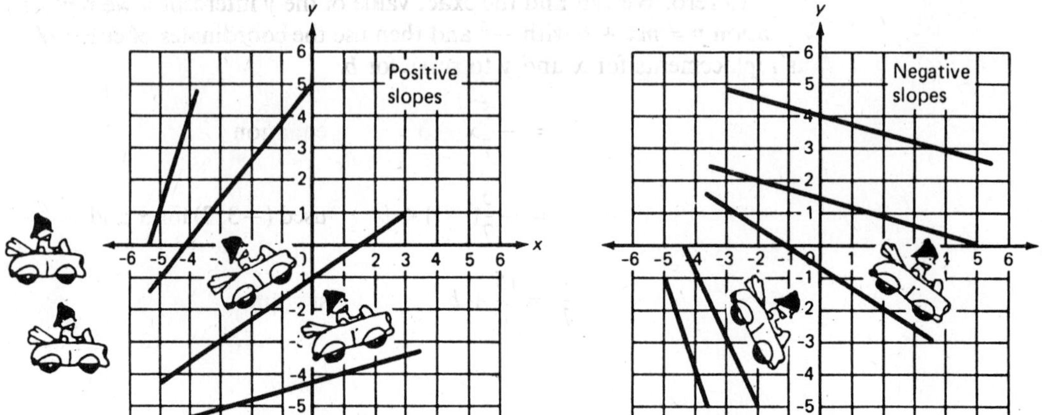

Example RLD.A.1 Find the slope-intercept form of the equation of the line that passes through the points $(-3, 2)$ and $(4, -3)$.

Solution We graph the points and draw the line and a right triangle whose hypotenuse is the segment connecting the points.

† If the line is vertical it has no y intercept. A line that is not vertical and is not horizontal has a y intercept and also has an x intercept. The x intercept will be discussed in a later lesson.

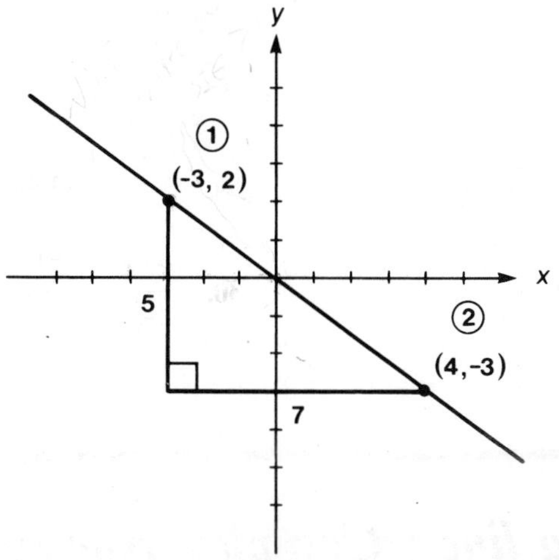

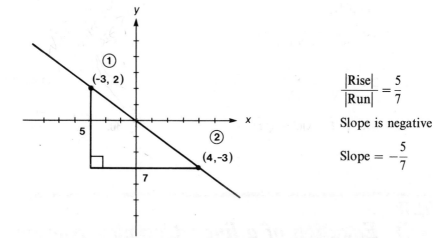

$$\frac{|\text{Rise}|}{|\text{Run}|} = \frac{5}{7}$$

Slope is negative

$$\text{Slope} = -\frac{5}{7}$$

If we move from point 1 to point 2, the y coordinate changes from $+2$ to -3, a change of -5; and the x coordinate changes from -3 to $+4$, a change of $+7$. Thus, the slope is

$$m = \frac{\text{change in } y}{\text{change in } x} = \frac{-5}{+7} = -\frac{5}{7}$$

We get the same result if we move from point 2 to point 1. The y coordinate changes from -3 to $+2$, a change of $+5$; and the x coordinate changes from 4 to -3, a change of -7.

$$m = \frac{\text{change in } y}{\text{change in } x} = \frac{+5}{-7} = -\frac{5}{7}$$

The line appears to cross the y axis near the origin so the y intercept should be a number close to zero. We can find the exact value of the y intercept if we replace m in the linear equation $y = mx + b$ with $-\frac{5}{7}$ and then use the coordinates of either of the given points as replacements for x and y to solve for b.

$$y = -\frac{5}{7}x + b \qquad \text{equation}$$

$$2 = -\frac{5}{7}(-3) + b \qquad \text{used } (-3, 2) \text{ for } x \text{ and } y$$

$$\frac{14}{7} = \frac{15}{7} + b \qquad \text{simplified}$$

$$-\frac{1}{7} = b \qquad \text{solved}$$

We find that b is $-\frac{1}{7}$, so we can write the equation of the line as

$$\mathbf{y = -\frac{5}{7}x - \frac{1}{7}}$$

Example RLD.A.2 Find the equation of the line that passes through the point $(-2, 5)$ and is perpendicular to the line $3y + 4x = 2$.

Solution First we write the given line in slope-intercept form by solving for y.

$$y = -\frac{4}{3}x + \frac{2}{3}$$

A line that is perpendicular to this line would have a slope of $+\frac{3}{4}$ because the slopes of perpendicular lines are negative reciprocals. So we have

$$y = \frac{3}{4}x + b$$

Now we can use $(-2, 5)$ for x and y and solve for b.

$$5 = \frac{3}{4}(-2) + b \qquad \text{used } (-2, 5) \text{ for } x \text{ and } y$$

$$\frac{10}{2} = -\frac{3}{2} + b \qquad \text{simplified}$$

$$\frac{13}{2} = b \qquad \text{solved}$$

Now we have both the slope and the y intercept and can write the equation.

$$\mathbf{y = \frac{3}{4}x + \frac{13}{2}}$$

RLD.B Complex fractions

A complex fraction is a fraction that contains more than one fraction line. Complex fractions are simplified by writing both the numerator and denominator as simple fractions, and then multiplying above and below by the reciprocal of the denominator.

Example RLD.B.1 Simplify: $\dfrac{\dfrac{a}{x^2} + \dfrac{b}{x}}{\dfrac{m}{x^2} + \dfrac{k}{xc}}$

Solution We begin by writing both the numerator and denominator as simple fractions.

$$\frac{\dfrac{a + bx}{x^2}}{\dfrac{mc + kx}{x^2c}}$$

Now we can multiply above and below by the reciprocal of the denominator.

$$\frac{\dfrac{a + bx}{x^2}}{\dfrac{mc + kx}{x^2c}} \cdot \frac{\dfrac{x^2c}{mc + kx}}{\dfrac{x^2c}{mc + kx}} = \mathbf{\frac{c(a + bx)}{mc + kx}}$$

Example RLD.B.2 Simplify: $\dfrac{x}{a + \dfrac{m}{1 + \dfrac{c}{d}}}$

Solution We begin by writing $1 + \dfrac{c}{d}$ as a simple fraction.

$$\frac{x}{a + \dfrac{m}{\dfrac{d + c}{d}}}$$

Now we simplify the triple-decker fraction and get

$$\frac{x}{a+\dfrac{\frac{m}{1}}{\frac{d+c}{d}}\cdot\dfrac{\frac{d}{d+c}}{\frac{d}{d+c}}}=\frac{x}{a+\dfrac{md}{d+c}}$$

Now we add the two terms in the denominator and get

$$\frac{x}{\dfrac{a(d+c)+md}{d+c}}$$

and finish by multiplying above and below by the reciprocal of the denominator.

$$\frac{\frac{x}{1}}{\dfrac{a(d+c)+md}{d+c}}\cdot\frac{\dfrac{d+c}{a(d+c)+md}}{\dfrac{d+c}{a(d+c)+md}}=\mathbf{\frac{x(d+c)}{a(d+c)+md}}$$

RLD.C Abstract equations

Equations composed of variables are sometimes called ***abstract equations.*** Often, it is necessary to rearrange one of these equations.

Example RLD.C.1 Solve $y = v\left(\frac{a}{x}+\frac{b}{mc}\right)$ for c.

Solution As the first step, we use the distributive property to clear the parentheses on the right.

$$y=\frac{va}{x}+\frac{vb}{mc}$$

Next we multiply every numerator by xmc, which is the least common multiple of the denominators.

$$xmc\cdot y = xmc\cdot\frac{va}{x}+xmc\cdot\frac{vb}{mc}$$

Now we can cancel the denominators, and we have left

$$xmcy = mcva + xvb$$

Since we are solving for c, we put all terms with c on one side of the equals sign (either side).

$$xmcy - mcva = xvb$$

Next we factor out c,

$$c(xmy - mva) = xvb$$

and finish by dividing both sides of the equation by the coefficient of c.

$$\frac{c(xmy-mva)}{xmy-mva}=\frac{xvb}{xmy-mva}\longrightarrow c=\mathbf{\frac{xvb}{xmy-mva}}$$

RLD.D Checking division of polynomials

When polynomials are divided, the division can be checked by adding the quotient and the remainder fraction. We demonstrate this procedure in the following example.

Example RLD.D.1 Simplify $\dfrac{x^3 - 2}{x - 1}$ by dividing; then check the result by adding the quotient and the remainder fraction.

Solution First we perform the indicated division and remember to insert $0x^2$ and $0x$ to help with spacing.

$$\begin{array}{r|l} & x^2 + x + 1 \\ \hline x - 1 & x^3 + 0x^2 + 0x - 2 \\ & x^3 - x^2 \\ & \quad\; x^2 + 0x \\ & \quad\; x^2 - x \\ & \qquad\quad x - 2 \\ & \qquad\quad x - 1 \\ & \qquad\quad\;\; -1 \end{array}$$

Thus, we find that

$$\frac{x^3 - 2}{x - 1} = \mathbf{x^2 + x + 1 - \frac{1}{x - 1}}$$

To check, we must write both parts of the answer with a denominator of $x - 1$ so the parts can be added. Thus we must multiply $x^2 + x + 1$ by $(x - 1)$ over $(x - 1)$.

$$(x^2 + x + 1) \cdot \frac{(x - 1)}{(x - 1)} - \frac{1}{x - 1}$$

We perform the multiplication on the left and get

$$\frac{x^3 + x^2 + x - x^2 - x - 1}{x - 1} - \frac{1}{x - 1}$$

and we simplify the numerators and get

$$\frac{\mathbf{x^3 - 2}}{\mathbf{x - 1}} \qquad \textbf{check}$$

Problem set D

1. The ratio of whats to hows was 7 to 3, and thrice the number of hows exceeded twice the number of whats by -40. How many were whats?
2. Fourteen percent of the blues were added to 20 percent of the greens for a total of 54. Also, 5 times the number of blues exceeded twice the number of greens by 100. How many were blue and how many were green?
3. A man stood on the top of a 500-ft building and measured a 20° angle of elevation to an airplane flying at an altitude of 2500 ft. What was the straight-line distance from the man to the airplane?
4. Find the equation of the line that passes through $(-4, 5)$ and $(-6, 3)$.
5. Find the equation of the line that passes through the point $(-2, 5)$ and is perpendicular to the line $2x + 3y = 5$.

Simplify:

6. $\dfrac{\dfrac{x}{a^2}+\dfrac{b}{a}}{\dfrac{1}{a^2}-\dfrac{k}{ac}}$ 7. $\dfrac{p}{m+\dfrac{m}{1+\dfrac{b}{c}}}$ 8. $\dfrac{a}{x+\dfrac{y}{p+\dfrac{m}{c}}}$

9. Solve $y = m\left(\dfrac{a}{x}+\dfrac{b}{mc}\right)$ for c. 10. Solve $x = pm\left(\dfrac{1}{y}+\dfrac{a}{bd}\right)$ for d.

11. Divide $x^3 - 1$ by $x - 2$ and check the result by adding the quotient and the remainder fraction.

Convert to polar coordinates:

12. $-7.08i + 4.2j$ 13. $4.2i - 3j$

Convert to rectangular coordinates:

14. $-15\underline{/-335^\circ}$ 15. $-42\underline{/138^\circ}$

Simplify:

16. $\sqrt{-2}\sqrt{2} - \sqrt{2}\,i - \sqrt{-4} + i$ 17. $\dfrac{3+2\sqrt{3}}{4-12\sqrt{3}}$

18. $\dfrac{2i^2 - 3i + 4i^3}{2i^5 - 3i - 2i^2}$

Solve by completing the square:

19. $3x^2 = -6 - x$ 20. $4x + 7 = 2x^2$

21. Begin with $ax^2 + bx + c = 0$ and derive the quadratic formula.

22. Use the quadratic formula to solve $3x^2 = \dfrac{2}{5}x - 3$.

23. If x, $y + z \neq 0$ and if $x = \dfrac{1}{y+z}$, compare: *A.* $\dfrac{5}{x}$ *B.* $5(y + z)$

24. Given $-10 < z < -1$, compare: *A.* $\dfrac{1}{z^5}$ *B.* $\dfrac{1}{z^4}$

Solve:

25. $\begin{cases} x + 2y - z = -5 \\ 2x - y + z = 11 \\ x + y - z = -2 \end{cases}$ 26. $\begin{cases} 2x - z = 5 \\ 3x + 2y = 13 \\ y - 2z = 0 \end{cases}$

27. $\begin{cases} \dfrac{x}{2} - \dfrac{3y}{4} = \dfrac{5}{2} \\ \dfrac{x}{3} - \dfrac{2z}{5} = -\dfrac{8}{15} \\ 0.4y - 0.05z = -0.95 \end{cases}$

Simplify:

28. $b^2\sqrt[3]{ab^4}(ab^3)^{1/5}$ 29. $\dfrac{x^{a/3-2}y^{(b-2)/3}}{x^{2a}(y^{1/3})^{2a}}$

30. $(2x^{3/4} + y^{-1/2})(2x^{3/4} - y^{-1/2})$

REVIEW LESSON E Review word problems · Addition of vectors

RLE.A Review word problems

Word problems are worked by transforming the written statements into mathematical equations and then solving the equations. **As many variables may be used as are convenient. For a unique solution, we must have as many independent equations as we have variables.**† The variables x, y, and z should be avoided because it is difficult to remember what they represent in a particular problem. Subscripted variables should be used because their meanings are easier to remember.

Word problems tend to be categorized into types according to the different thought processes required to find their solutions. Thus far, we have looked at simple problems whose solutions required the use of at most two variables. In this lesson, we will review the solution of problems that require the use of three variables in three equations. We will also review other types of problems. Some of these problems were selected because they require procedures that have a wide variety of applications. Other problems were selected because they represent types of problems that will be encountered in almost the same forms in chemistry and physics courses.

Example RLE.A.1 The number of blues was 4 less than the sum of the whites and the greens. Also the number of greens equaled the sum of the blues and the whites. How many of each were there if there were twice as many blues as whites?

Solution This problem can be worked by using three equations in three unknowns. We will use N_B, N_W, and N_G as the variables. The three equations are as follows:

(*a*) The number of blues was 4 less than the sum of the whites and the greens.

$$N_B + 4 = N_W + N_G$$

(*b*) The number of greens equaled the sum of the blues and the whites.

$$N_G = N_B + N_W$$

(*c*) There were twice as many blues as whites.

$$N_B = 2N_W$$

Note that in (*a*) we added 4 to the number of blues because there were 4 fewer blues. Also in (*c*) we multiplied the number of whites by 2 to equal the number of blues. When a statement tells how much greater or less a quantity is, addition or multiplication is required so that an equation (statement of equality) may be written. We begin by substituting $2N_W$ for N_B in equations (*a*) and (*b*).

$$\begin{array}{lll} (a)\ (2N_W) + 4 = N_W + N_G & \longrightarrow & N_W - N_G = -4 \\ (b)\ N_G = (2N_W) + N_W & \longrightarrow & -3N_W + N_G = \ \ 0 \\ \hline & & -2N_W \qquad = -4 \\ & & N_W = 2 \end{array}$$

Now N_B equals $2N_W$, so $N_B = 4$; and N_G equals $N_W + N_B$, so $N_G = 6$. Thus

$$\mathbf{N_W = 2 \qquad N_B = 4 \qquad N_G = 6}$$

† This is true for systems of linear equations if the domain for all variables and all coefficients is the set of real numbers.

Example RLE.A.2 The quarters, nickels, and dimes totaled 20, and their value was \$1.90. How many of each kind were there if there were 4 times as many nickels as quarters?

Solution There were 20 coins in all,

$$(a) \quad N_N + N_D + N_Q = 20$$

and their value was \$1.90.

$$(b) \quad 5N_N + 10N_D + 25N_Q = 190$$

There were 4 times as many nickels as quarters.

$$(c) \quad N_N = 4N_Q$$

We begin by using (*c*) to substitute for N_N in (*a*) and (*b*).

$$(a) \quad (4N_Q) + N_D + N_Q = 20 \longrightarrow N_D + 5N_Q = 20 \quad (d)$$

$$(b) \quad 5(4N_Q) + 10N_D + 25N_Q = 190 \longrightarrow 10N_D + 45N_Q = 190 \quad (e)$$

Now we multiply (*d*) by -10 and add to (*e*).

$$(-10)(d) \longrightarrow -10N_D - 50N_Q = -200$$

$$(e) \longrightarrow \underline{10N_D + 45N_Q = 190}$$

$$-5N_Q = -10$$

$$\mathbf{N_Q = 2}$$

$N_N = 4(2) =$ **8**, and since there were 20 in all, **10 were dimes.**

Example RLE.A.3 Reds varied directly as blues squared and inversely as greens. When there were 80 reds, there were 4 blues and 2 greens. How many reds were there when there were 8 blues and 10 greens?

Solution The problem can be worked as a variation problem. This approach is often used in physics books. The first sentence gives us the basic equation.

$$R = \frac{kB^2}{G}$$

where k is a constant. Next we must find k. We replace R with 80, B with 4, and G with 2, and solve for k.

$$80 = \frac{k(4)^2}{2} \longrightarrow k = 10$$

Now we replace k in the basic equation with 10.

$$R = \frac{10B^2}{G}$$

Since we have found k, we can complete the solution. To finish we replace B with 8 and G with 10 and solve for R.

$$R = \frac{10(8)^2}{10} \longrightarrow \mathbf{R = 64}$$

The second method is the ratio method. This approach is often used in chemistry books. The first sentence gives us the basic equation.

$$\frac{R_1}{R_2} = \frac{B_1^2 G_2}{B_2^2 G_1}$$

Now we make the required replacements and solve.

$$\frac{80}{R_2} = \frac{(4)^2(10)}{(8)^2(2)} \longrightarrow \frac{80}{R_2} = \frac{160}{128} \longrightarrow \mathbf{R_2 = 64}$$

Example RLE.A.4 The sum of the digits of a two-digit counting number is 5. When the digits are reversed, the number is 9 greater than the original number. What was the original number?

Solution The counting numbers are the positive integers. The sum of the digits is 5. If we use U for the units digit and T for the tens digit, we get

$$(a) \quad U + T = 5$$

The value of the units digit is U and of the tens digit is $10T$, but when the digits are reversed the values will be $10U$ and T.

ORIGINAL NUMBER		NEW NUMBER MINUS 9
(b) $10T + U$	$=$	$T + 10U - 9$

which simplifies to

$$9T - 9U = -9 \longrightarrow T - U = -1$$

Now we substitute from equation (a) and solve.

$$(5 - U) - U = -1 \quad \text{substituted for } T$$

$$5 - 2U = -1 \quad \text{added}$$

$$-2U = -6 \quad \text{added } -5$$

$$\mathbf{U = 3}$$

Since $U + T = 5$, $\mathbf{T = 2}$ and the original number was **23**.

Example RLE.A.5 To get 1000 gallons (gal) of a mixture that was 56% alcohol, it was necessary to mix some 20% alcohol solution with some 80% alcohol solution. How much of each was required?

Solution We decide to make the statement about alcohol.

$$\text{Alcohol}_1 + \text{alcohol}_2 = \text{alcohol total}$$

Next we use parentheses as mixture containers.

$$(\quad) + (\quad) = (\quad)$$

We pour in some of the first mixture (P_N), and dump in some of the second mixture (D_N) for a total of 1000.

$$(P_N) + \quad (D_N) = \quad (1000)$$

Now we multiply by the proper decimals so that each entry represents alcohol.

$$(a) \quad 0.2(P_N) + 0.8(D_N) = 0.56(1000)$$

This equation has two unknowns so we need another equation, which is

$$(b) \quad P_N + D_N = 1000$$

Now we substitute to solve.

$$0.2(1000 - D_N) + 0.8D_N = 0.56(1000) \quad \text{substituted}$$

$$200 - 0.2D_N + 0.8D_N = 560 \quad \text{multiplied}$$

Now we eliminate the decimals by multiplying by 10.

$$2000 - 2D_N + 8D_N = 5600$$
$$6D_N = 3600$$
$$\mathbf{D_N = 600 \text{ gal of } 80\% \text{ alcohol}}$$

Since the total was 1000 gal, we need **400 gal of 20% alcohol.**

Example RLE.A.6 How many liters of a 64% glycol solution must be added to 77 liters of a 23% glycol solution to get a 42% glycol solution?

Solution The solution to this problem is not difficult if a calculator is used to help with the arithmetic. We will make the statement about glycol and then insert the indicated quantities in the parentheses used as mixture containers.

$$\text{Glycol}_1 + \text{glycol added} = \text{glycol final}$$
$$(77) \quad + \quad (P_N) \quad = (77 + P_N)$$

The mixture entries indicate the amount of mixture. It is important to use symbols such as P_N or D_N for the amount of solution added. **Avoid using G for glycol added because the mixture added was not all glycol.** Next we multiply each of the mixture container entries by the proper decimal number so that the product will equal the amount of glycol for each step.

$$0.23(77) + 0.64(P_N) = 0.42(77 + P_N)$$

We use a calculator to permit a quick solution to this equation.

$$17.71 + 0.64P_N = 32.34 + 0.42P_N \qquad \text{multiplied}$$
$$0.22P_N = 14.63 \qquad \text{rearranged}$$
$$\mathbf{P_N = 66.5 \text{ liters}} \qquad \text{divided}$$

Example RLE.A.7 The weight of the carbon (C) in the container of C_3H_7Cl was 113 grams. What was the total weight of the compound? (C, 12; H, 1; Cl, 35)

Solution This is a ratio problem. The gram atomic weights are given above in parentheses.

Carbon	12 × 3 = 36
Hydrogen	1 × 7 = 7
Chlorine	35 × 1 = 35
Total	78

Thus, the ratio of the carbon to the total weight is 36 to 78, and the carbon weighed 113 grams.

$$\frac{C}{T} = \frac{36}{78} \longrightarrow \frac{113}{T} = \frac{36}{78} \longrightarrow \mathbf{T = 244.8 \text{ grams}}$$

RLE.B Addition of vectors

A vector has both a magnitude and a direction, and a vector can be designated by using either polar coordinates or rectangular coordinates. **Vectors in polar form can be added only if the angles are equal or if they differ by 180°. If the angles are not equal or opposite, the vectors must be rewritten in rectangular form. Then the horizontal components are**

added to find the horizontal component of the resultant, and the vertical components are added to find the vertical component of the resultant.

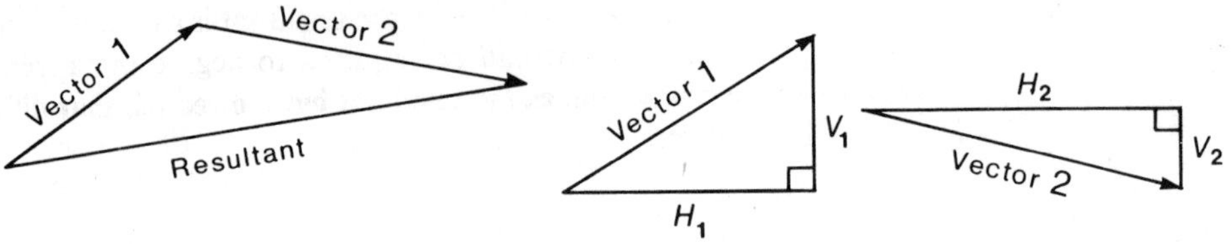

Example RLE.B.1 Find the resultant of $4\underline{/20^\circ} + 7\underline{/-230^\circ}$.

Solution A diagram always helps. We will use calculators to find the components. One component is always $R \sin \theta$ and the other is $R \cos \theta$. Try to develop calculator techniques that will permit a quick and accurate breakdown of vectors.

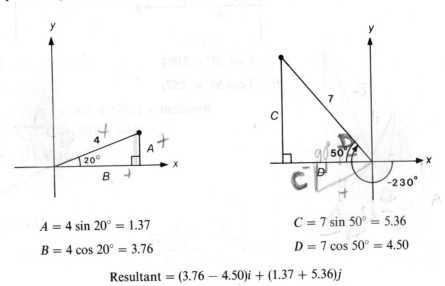

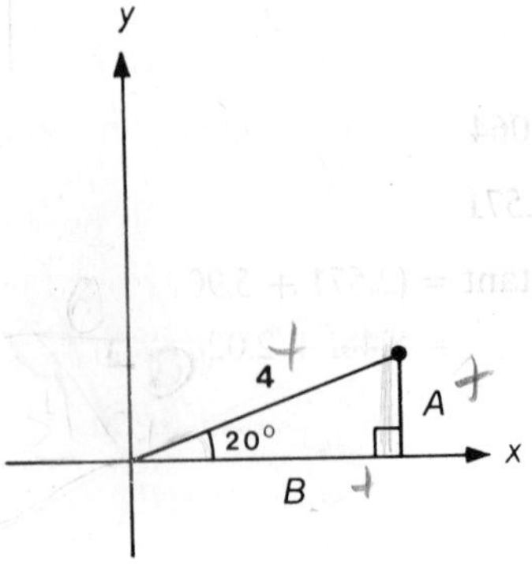

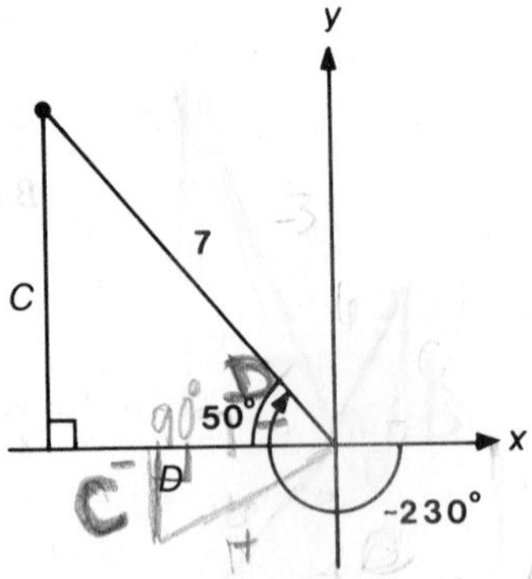

$A = 4 \sin 20^\circ = 1.37$

$B = 4 \cos 20^\circ = 3.76$

$C = 7 \sin 50^\circ = 5.36$

$D = 7 \cos 50^\circ = 4.50$

$$\text{Resultant} = (3.76 - 4.50)i + (1.37 + 5.36)j$$
$$= \mathbf{-0.74i + 6.73j}$$

The resultant can be written in polar form if desired.

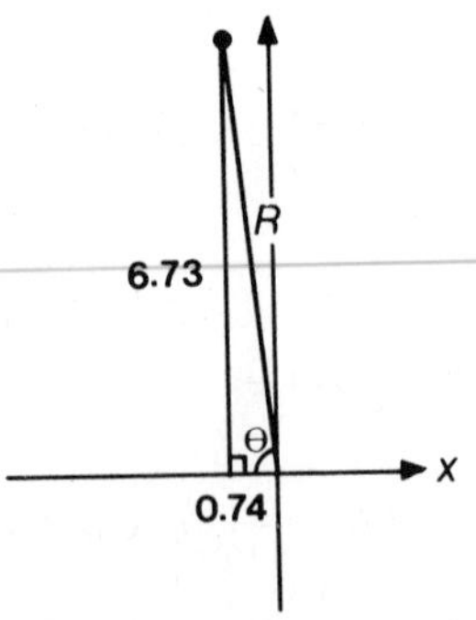

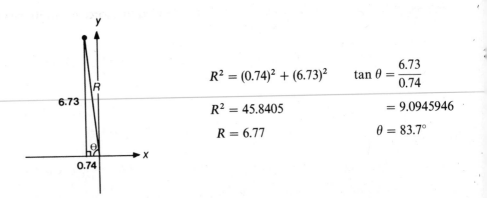

$$R^2 = (0.74)^2 + (6.73)^2 \qquad \tan\theta = \frac{6.73}{0.74}$$

$$R^2 = 45.8405 \qquad = 9.0945946$$

$$R = 6.77 \qquad \theta = 83.7^\circ$$

The polar angle is measured from the positive x axis and is $180^\circ - \theta$, which is

$$180^\circ - 83.73^\circ = 96.27^\circ$$

The resultant can also be written as $\mathbf{6.77\underline{/96.3^\circ}}$.

Example RLE.B.2 The two forces (where lb = pounds) $4\underline{/50^\circ}$ lb and $-6\underline{/170^\circ}$ lb are applied to an object. Find the equilibrant of the forces.

Solution If two forces are applied to a point, the resultant is the sum of the forces. The ***equilibrant*** is the single force that would be required to negate the applied forces. **The equilibrant has the same magnitude as the resultant but a direction that differs by 180°.** First we will find the resultant.

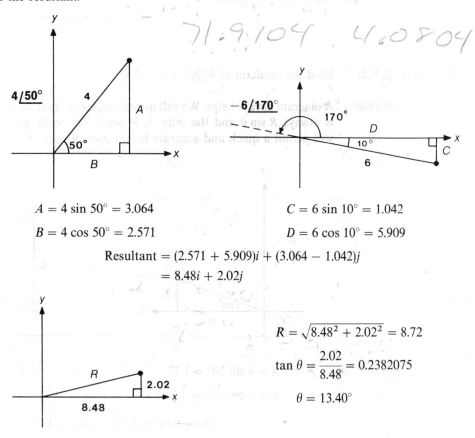

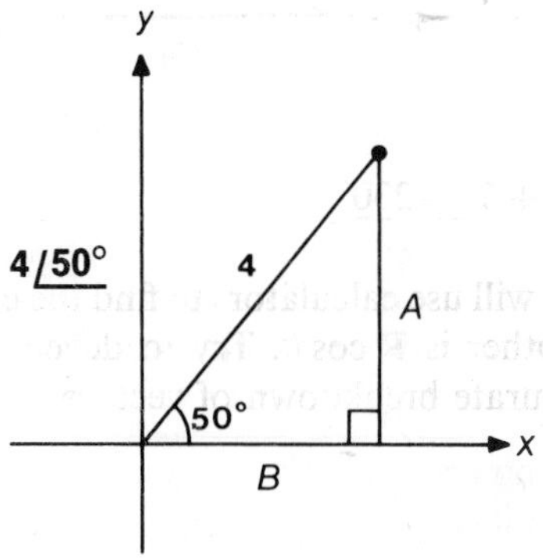

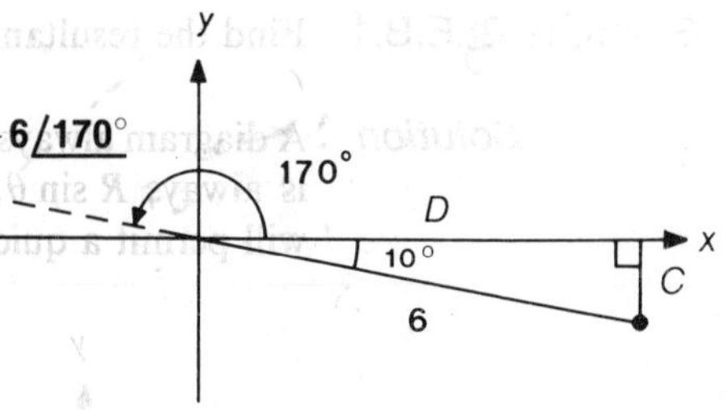

$A = 4 \sin 50^\circ = 3.064$ $\qquad C = 6 \sin 10^\circ = 1.042$

$B = 4 \cos 50^\circ = 2.571$ $\qquad D = 6 \cos 10^\circ = 5.909$

$$\text{Resultant} = (2.571 + 5.909)i + (3.064 - 1.042)j$$
$$= 8.48i + 2.02j$$

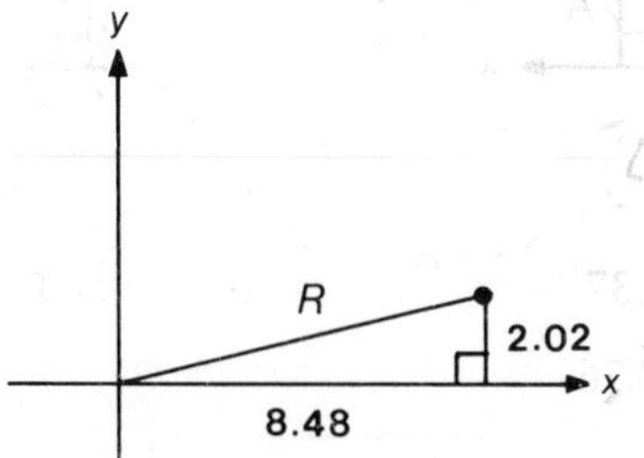

$$R = \sqrt{8.48^2 + 2.02^2} = 8.72$$

$$\tan\theta = \frac{2.02}{8.48} = 0.2382075$$

$$\theta = 13.40^\circ$$

Thus the resultant is $8.48i + 2.02j$, or $8.72\underline{/13.4^\circ}$. The equilibrant is $\mathbf{-8.48i - 2.02j}$, or $\mathbf{-8.72\underline{/13.4^\circ}}$.

Example RLE.B.3 What vector force must be added to a force of $20\underline{/30^\circ}$ newtons to obtain a resultant of $25\underline{/0^\circ}$ newtons?

Solution First we find the horizontal and vertical components of $20\underline{/30^\circ}$.

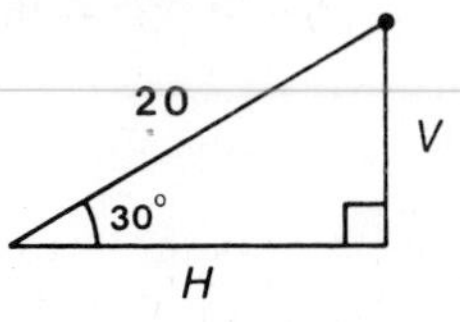

$V = 20 \sin 30^\circ = 10$

$H = 20 \cos 30^\circ = 17.32$ so $20\underline{/30^\circ} = 17.32i + 10j$

Now we wish to add a vector V to $17.32i + 10j$ to get a resultant of $25i + 0j$. This leads to the equation

$$17.32i + 10j + V = 25i + 0j$$

We solve this equation by adding $-17.32i - 10j$ to both sides, and we get

$V = 25i + 0j - 17.32i - 10j$ added to both sides

$\mathbf{V = 7.68i - 10j}$ simplified

If we wish, we can write $7.68i - 10j$ in polar form.

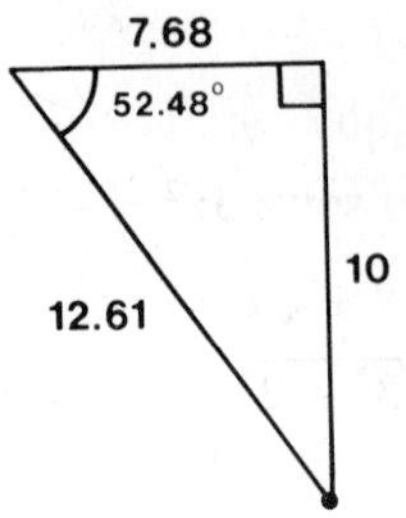

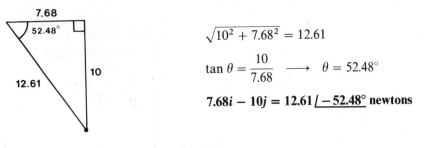

$$\sqrt{10^2 + 7.68^2} = 12.61$$

$$\tan\theta = \frac{10}{7.68} \longrightarrow \theta = 52.48°$$

$$\mathbf{7.68i - 10j = 12.61\underline{/-52.48°}\ newtons}$$

Problem set E

1. The number of blues was 7 less than the sum of the whites and the greens. The number of greens was 1 greater than the sum of the blues and the whites. How many of each kind were there if there were 3 times as many greens as blues?

2. The quarters, nickels, and dimes totaled 20, and their value was \$2.05. How many of each kind were there if there were 3 times as many dimes as quarters?

3. Reds varied directly as blues and inversely as greens squared. When there were 5 reds, there were 2 blues and 4 greens. How many reds were there when there were 4 blues and 4 greens?

4. The sum of the digits of a two-digit counting number is 13. When the digits are reversed, the new number is 45 greater than the original number. What was the original number?

5. How much of a 14% iodine solution should be added to 89 ounces of a 47% iodine solution to get a 29% solution?

6. The weight of the chlorine (Cl) in the container of C_3H_7Cl was 400 grams. What was the total weight of the compound? (C, 12; H, 1; Cl, 35)

7. Find the equation of the line that passes through the point $(-2, 3)$ and is perpendicular to the line $5x - 2y + 4 = 0$.

Simplify:

8. $\dfrac{\dfrac{m^2}{a^2} + \dfrac{7y}{x}}{\dfrac{p^2}{ax} - \dfrac{3}{a^2}}$ 9. $\dfrac{m}{a + \dfrac{b}{1 + \dfrac{c}{d}}}$ 10. $\dfrac{k}{a + \dfrac{b}{x + \dfrac{c}{d}}}$

11. Solve for c: $x = kb\left(\dfrac{1}{c} - \dfrac{a}{x}\right)$ 12. Solve for k: $mc = p\left(\dfrac{a}{cm} + \dfrac{2}{kc}\right)$

13. Divide $x^4 - 2$ by $x^2 - 1$ and check.

14. Find the resultant of: $7\underline{/-200°} + 5\underline{/276°}$

15. Find the equilibrant of: $-14\underline{/130°} + 7\underline{/-30°}$

Simplify:

16. $\sqrt{2}\sqrt{-2} + \sqrt{-3}\sqrt{-3} + \sqrt{-4} - i$ 17. $\dfrac{4 + 2\sqrt{12}}{6 - \sqrt{48}}$

18. $\dfrac{3i^3 - 2i + i^2}{1 - 4i^3}$

Solve by completing the square:

19. $4x^2 = -5 - 2x$

20. $3x + 7 = 4x^2$

21. Derive the quadratic formula.

22. Use the quadratic formula to solve $3x^2 = -4 + 2x$.

23. Compare: *A.* 5 *B.* $\sqrt{9} + \sqrt{16}$

24. Compare: *A.* 5 *B.* $\sqrt{3^2 + 2^2}$

Solve:

25. $\begin{cases} 2x + 2y - z = -1 \\ x + y - 3z = -8 \\ 2x - y + z = 8 \end{cases}$

26. $\begin{cases} 2x - z = 10 \\ y + 2z = -2 \\ 3x - 2y = 8 \end{cases}$

27. $\begin{cases} \dfrac{3}{2}x + \dfrac{4}{3}y = \dfrac{1}{2} \\ -\dfrac{x}{2} + \dfrac{z}{4} = -1 \\ 0.2y - 0.04z = -0.68 \end{cases}$

Simplify:

28. $x^3\sqrt{x^3y}\,(ab^{1/3})^2$

29. $\dfrac{x^{a/2-3}y^{(b-3)/2}}{x^{3a}(y^{1/3})^{2a}}$

30. $(2x^{a/2} + y^{b/2})(2x^{a/2} - y^{b/2})$

REVIEW LESSON F *Nonlinear systems · Factoring exponentials · Sum and difference of two cubes*

RLF.A Nonlinear systems

A nonlinear system of equations contains one or more nonlinear equations. Nonlinear systems are solved by using substitution and elimination just as we do when we solve systems of linear equations. Solving nonlinear systems often involves the solution of a quadratic equation as the final step. These quadratic equations are seldom factorable, and we usually solve them by using the quadratic formula without even trying the factor method of solution.

Example RLF.A.1 Solve:

$$\begin{aligned} &(a) \quad x^2 + y^2 = 9 \qquad \text{(circle)} \\ &(b) \quad y - x = 1 \qquad \text{(line)} \end{aligned}$$

Solution We will begin by solving equation (*b*) for *y* and then we will square both sides.

$$\begin{aligned} y - x &= 1 && \text{equation } (b) \\ y &= x + 1 && \text{solved for } y \\ y^2 &= x^2 + 2x + 1 && \text{squared both sides} \end{aligned}$$

Now we will replace y^2 in equation (a) with $x^2 + 2x + 1$.

$$x^2 + (x^2 + 2x + 1) = 9 \qquad \text{substituted}$$
$$2x^2 + 2x - 8 = 0 \qquad \text{simplified}$$
$$x^2 + x - 4 = 0 \qquad \text{divided by 2}$$

This equation cannot be solved by factoring, so we will use the quadratic formula.

$$x = \frac{-b \pm \sqrt{b^2 - 4ac}}{2a} \longrightarrow x = \frac{-1 \pm \sqrt{1 - 4(1)(-4)}}{2} \longrightarrow x = -\frac{1}{2} \pm \frac{\sqrt{17}}{2}$$

which means $\mathbf{x = -\frac{1}{2} + \frac{\sqrt{17}}{2}}$ and $\mathbf{x = -\frac{1}{2} - \frac{\sqrt{17}}{2}}$

Now we could use either equation (a) or equation (b) to find the values of y. We will use the equation of the line (b) to find y because this equation has no squared terms and is easier to use, and also because the use of the quadratic equation might lead to spurious solutions.

$$y = x + 1 \qquad y = x + 1 \qquad \text{equation } (b)$$
$$y = \left(-\frac{1}{2} + \frac{\sqrt{17}}{2}\right) + 1 \qquad y = \left(-\frac{1}{2} - \frac{\sqrt{17}}{2}\right) + 1 \qquad \text{substituted}$$
$$y = \frac{1}{2} + \frac{\sqrt{17}}{2} \qquad y = \frac{1}{2} - \frac{\sqrt{17}}{2} \qquad \text{simplified}$$

Thus, the ordered pairs of x and y that satisfy the given system are:

$$\mathbf{\left(-\frac{1}{2} + \frac{\sqrt{17}}{2}, \frac{1}{2} + \frac{\sqrt{17}}{2}\right)} \quad \text{and} \quad \mathbf{\left(-\frac{1}{2} - \frac{\sqrt{17}}{2}, \frac{1}{2} - \frac{\sqrt{17}}{2}\right)}$$

The graph of the line and the circle are shown here. We will study the graphs of circles and other conics in later lessons. Here we are concentrating on the algebra of the solutions.

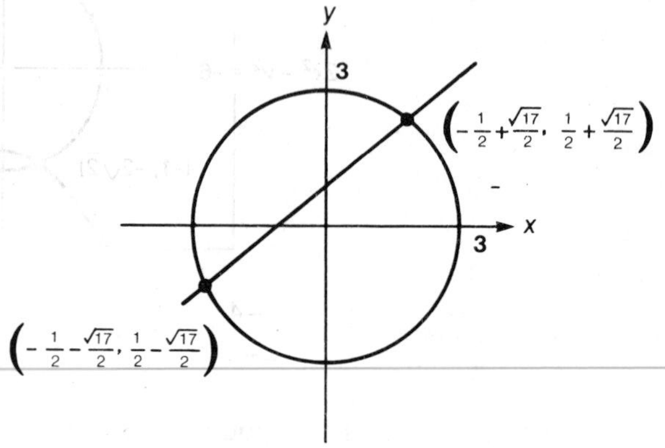

Example RLF.A.2 Solve the system:
$$\begin{cases} (a) & x^2 + y^2 = 9 & \text{(circle)} \\ (b) & 2x^2 - y^2 = -6 & \text{(hyperbola)} \end{cases}$$

Solution This system can be solved by using either substitution or elimination. We must be careful to get all the answers because this circle and hyperbola intersect at four different points. We decide to use elimination. We can eliminate the y^2 terms if we add the equations just as they are. If we do this, we get

$$3x^2 = 3 \qquad \text{added}$$

$$x^2 = 1 \qquad \text{divided by 3}$$

Here we must be careful because this equation has both $+1$ and -1 as solutions.

$$x = \pm\sqrt{1} \longrightarrow x = 1, -1$$

Now we must use these values of x one at a time to solve for y. We will use equation (a) and begin by letting x equal $+1$.

$$(1)^2 + y^2 = 9 \qquad \text{substituted (1) for } x$$

$$y^2 = 8 \qquad \text{added } -1$$

$$y = \pm 2\sqrt{2} \qquad \text{solved}$$

Thus, there are two points of intersection when $x = 1$. So two solutions of our system are

$$(\mathbf{1}, \mathbf{2}\sqrt{\mathbf{2}}) \quad \text{and} \quad (\mathbf{1}, -\mathbf{2}\sqrt{\mathbf{2}})$$

Next, we find the values of y that pair with a value of -1 for x. Again we use equation (a).

$$(-1)^2 + y^2 = 9 \qquad \text{substituted } (-1) \text{ for } x$$

$$y^2 = 8 \qquad \text{added } -1$$

$$y = \pm 2\sqrt{2} \qquad \text{solved}$$

Thus, our other two solutions to the system are

$$(-\mathbf{1}, \mathbf{2}\sqrt{\mathbf{2}}) \quad \text{and} \quad (-\mathbf{1}, -\mathbf{2}\sqrt{\mathbf{2}})$$

Here we show the graphs of the two curves and note that there are four points where the curves intersect. Do not worry about the graphs now. They will be discussed in later lessons.

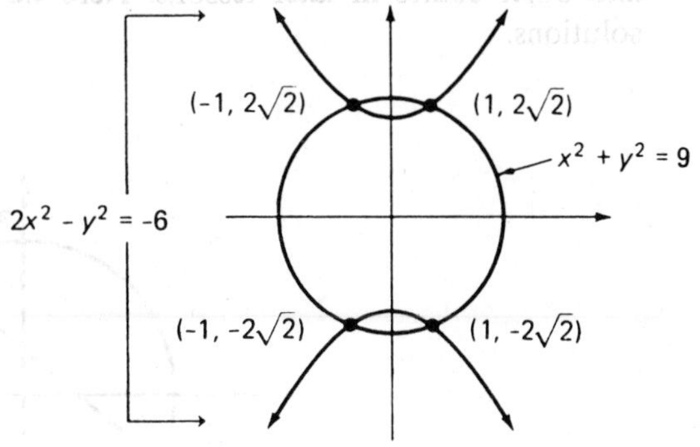

Example RLF.A.3 Solve the system: $\begin{cases} xy = -4 \\ y = -x - 2 \end{cases}$

Solution We decide to use substitution. Thus, in the top equation, we substitute $-x - 2$ for y:

$$x(-x - 2) = -4 \qquad \text{substituted}$$

$$-x^2 - 2x = -4 \qquad \text{multiplied}$$

$$x^2 + 2x - 4 = 0 \qquad \text{rearranged}$$

We will use the quadratic formula to solve this equation.

$$x = \frac{-2 \pm \sqrt{4 - 4(1)(-4)}}{2} = \frac{-2 \pm \sqrt{20}}{2} = -1 \pm \sqrt{5}$$

We find that the values of x that satisfy the equation are $-1 + \sqrt{5}$ and $-1 - \sqrt{5}$. We will use both these values of x in the linear equation and solve for the paired values of y.

$$\begin{array}{ll} \text{IF } x = -1 + \sqrt{5} & \text{IF } x = -1 - \sqrt{5} \\ y = -(-1 + \sqrt{5}) - 2 & y = -(-1 - \sqrt{5}) - 2 \\ y = 1 - \sqrt{5} - 2 & y = 1 + \sqrt{5} - 2 \\ y = -1 - \sqrt{5} & y = -1 + \sqrt{5} \end{array}$$

Thus, the ordered pairs of x and y that satisfy this system of nonlinear equations are

$$\mathbf{(-1 + \sqrt{5}, -1 - \sqrt{5})} \qquad \text{and} \qquad \mathbf{(-1 - \sqrt{5}, -1 + \sqrt{5})}$$

RLF.B Factoring exponentials

Expressions in which a base is raised to a power are often called ***exponential expressions*** or just ***exponentials.*** The word *exponential* also has a more restrictive definition that is explained in Lesson 2. When two quantities are multiplied, each of the quantities is called a ***factor.*** The reverse process is called ***factoring*** because when we factor, we break up an algebraic sum into an indicated product of two or more factors.

Example RLF.B.1 Factor: $3x^{2n+2} + 12x^{3n+3}$

Solution Sometimes it helps if we rewrite exponential expressions whose exponents are complicated. If we do, we get

$$3 \cdot x^n \cdot x^n \cdot x^2 + 3 \cdot 4 \cdot x^n \cdot x^n \cdot x^n \cdot x^3$$

We see that the common factor is $3x^n x^n x^2$. Thus, we can write the expression in factored form as

$$3x^{2n}x^2(1 + 4x^n x) = \mathbf{3x^{2n+2}(1 + 4x^{n+1})}$$

Example RLF.B.2 Simplify: $\dfrac{x^{2a} - y^{2b}}{x^a + y^b}$

Solution We recognize that the numerator is really the difference of two squares and can be factored.

$$\frac{(x^a)^2 - (y^b)^2}{x^a + y^b} = \frac{(x^a + y^b)(x^a - y^b)}{x^a + y^b} = \mathbf{x^a - y^b}$$

RLF.C Sum and difference of two cubes

The sum of two cubes can be factored and the difference of two cubes can be factored.

$$a^3 + b^3 = (a + b)(a^2 - ab + b^2) \qquad a^3 - b^3 = (a - b)(a^2 + ab + b^2)$$

Using the forms for factoring the sum or difference of two cubes is required, and disuse encourages one to forget the factored forms. Yet, if one can remember that $a^3 + b^3$ is divisible by $a + b$ and that $a^3 - b^3$ is divisible by $a - b$, it is possible to do the long divisions to find the other factors, as we show here.

$$\begin{array}{r|l} & a^2 - ab + b^2 \\ \hline a + b & a^3 \qquad\qquad + b^3 \\ & \underline{a^3 + a^2b} \\ & -a^2b \\ & \underline{-a^2b - ab^2} \\ & ab^2 + b^3 \\ & \underline{ab^2 + b^3} \end{array} \qquad \begin{array}{r|l} & a^2 + ab + b^2 \\ \hline a - b & a^3 \qquad\qquad - b^3 \\ & \underline{a^3 - a^2b} \\ & a^2b \\ & \underline{a^2b - ab^2} \\ & ab^2 - b^3 \\ & \underline{ab^2 - b^3} \end{array}$$

Thus, we see that we can factor as follows:

$$(1) \quad a^3 + b^3 = (a + b)(a^2 - ab + b^2)$$
$$(2) \quad a^3 - b^3 = (a - b)(a^2 + ab + b^2)$$

To extend these forms to more complicated expressions, some people find that it is helpful to think F for *first thing* and S for *second thing* instead of a and b. If we do this in the above, we get

$$(1') \quad F^3 + S^3 = (F + S)(F^2 - FS + S^2)$$
$$(2') \quad F^3 - S^3 = (F - S)(F^2 + FS + S^2)$$

Example RLF.C.1 Factor $x^3y^3 - p^3$.

Solution We recognize that this expression can be written as the difference of two cubes:

$$(xy)^3 - (p)^3$$

The first thing that is cubed is xy and the second thing that is cubed is p. If we use form (2′) above,

$$(2') \quad F^3 - S^3 = (F - S)(F^2 + FS + S^2)$$

and replace F with xy and S with p, we can write the given expression in factored form.

$$x^3y^3 - p^3 = \mathbf{(xy - p)(x^2y^2 + xyp + p^2)}$$

Example RLF.C.2 Factor $8m^3y^6 + x^3$.

Solution We recognize this as the sum of two cubes.

$$(2my^2)^3 + (x)^3$$

and note that the first thing that is cubed is $2my^2$ and that the second thing that is cubed is x. Thus, if we use form (1′),

$$(1') \quad F^3 + S^3 = (F + S)(F^2 - FS + S^2)$$

and replace F with $2my^2$ and S with x, we get

$$8m^3y^6 + x^3 = \mathbf{(2my^2 + x)(4m^2y^4 - 2my^2x + x^2)}$$

Problem set F

1. The number of reds was 11 fewer than the sum of the blues and whites. The number of whites was 3 fewer than the sum of the reds and blues. How many of each were there if the number of whites was 1 greater than the number of blues?
2. There were 30 nickels, dimes, and pennies in all, and their value was \$1.35. If there were twice as many pennies as dimes, how many coins of each kind were there?
3. The number of boys varied inversely as the number of teachers and directly as the number of girls squared. When there were 200 boys, there were 10 girls and 20 teachers. How many boys were there when there were 2 teachers and 8 girls?
4. The sum of the digits of a two-digit counting number is 5. When the digits are reversed, the new number is 27 greater than the original number. What are the two numbers?
5. How many liters of a 90% alcohol solution should be mixed with how many liters of a 58% alcohol solution to make 20 liters of a 78% alcohol solution?
6. How many milliliters of a $13\frac{1}{2}$% iodine solution should be mixed with 370 ml of a 6% iodine solution to get a 10% iodine solution?

7. Find the equation of the line that passes through $(-2, 4)$ that is parallel to the line $3x + 2y - 4 = 0$.

Solve:

8. $\begin{cases} x^2 + y^2 = 9 \\ y - x = 1 \end{cases}$
9. $\begin{cases} x^2 + y^2 = 9 \\ 2x^2 - y^2 = -6 \end{cases}$
10. $\begin{cases} xy = -4 \\ y = -x - 2 \end{cases}$

Factor:

11. $8x^6y^3 + p^3$
12. $27x^{12}y^6 - z^9$

Simplify:

13. $\dfrac{\dfrac{n^2}{b^3} + \dfrac{7p}{a}}{\dfrac{r^2}{ba} - \dfrac{4}{b^3}}$
14. $\dfrac{m}{c + \dfrac{f}{2 + \dfrac{g}{h}}}$

15. Solve for x: $k^2 = \dfrac{1}{bc}\left(\dfrac{x}{3} - \dfrac{6y^3}{d}\right)$

16. Divide $x^3 - 3x^2 - 3$ by $x - 2$ and check.

17. Find the equilibrant of: $6\angle -300^\circ + 3\angle 135^\circ$

Simplify:

18. $\sqrt{3}\sqrt{-3} - \sqrt{-2}\sqrt{-2} + \sqrt{-4} + 5i + \sqrt{-3}$

19. $\dfrac{3 + 2\sqrt{12}}{2 - 4\sqrt{48}}$
20. $\dfrac{3i^4 - 2i^2 + i^3}{1 - 3i^2 + \sqrt{-9}}$

Solve by completing the square:

21. $3x^2 = -4 + 3x$
22. $-6x - 9 = 2x^2$

23. If $0 < x < 20$ and $0 < y < 24$, compare: *A.* $\dfrac{x}{y} + 5$ *B.* $\dfrac{y}{x} + 10$

24. If $x \in R$ and $y \in R$, and $y \neq 0$, compare: *A.* $\dfrac{x}{y}$ *B.* $1 + \dfrac{x}{y}$

Solve:

25. $\begin{cases} 2x + 3y - z = 6 \\ 3x - y + z = 1 \\ x + y + z = 1 \end{cases}$
26. $\begin{cases} 2x - z = 1 \\ y + 2z = 7 \\ 3x - y = 5 \end{cases}$

27. $\begin{cases} \dfrac{3}{4}x + \dfrac{5}{2}y = 8 \\ -\dfrac{x}{2} - \dfrac{z}{2} = -\dfrac{5}{2} \\ 0.25y - 0.4z = 0.1 \end{cases}$

Simplify:

28. $x^3\sqrt{x^4y^3}\,(x^3y)^{1/3}$
29. $\dfrac{x^{a/3-2}y^{(b-2)/3}}{x^{2a}(y^{2/3})^a}$

30. $(3x^{a/2} + 2y^{b/3})(2x^{a/2} - 2y^{b/3})$

LESSON 1 Two special triangles

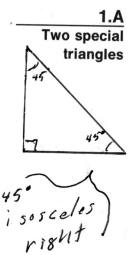

1.A Two special triangles

We have found that the trigonometric ratios that we call the sine, the cosine, and the tangent can be used to help us solve right triangles for unknown sides or angles. We have looked up the values of these ratios in tables of trigonometric functions or have obtained them from a calculator. Often we wish to illustrate something that requires the use of trigonometric concepts but does not require that we use a particular angle. For this purpose mathematicians have found it convenient to use angles whose measure is 30°, 45°, or 60°. The trigonometric functions of these angles can be found by drawing two special triangles; and, thus, calculators or tables are not necessary. The values of the functions found from the triangles are not approximations but are exact.

To find the functions of a 45° angle, we draw a right triangle whose legs are 1 unit long.

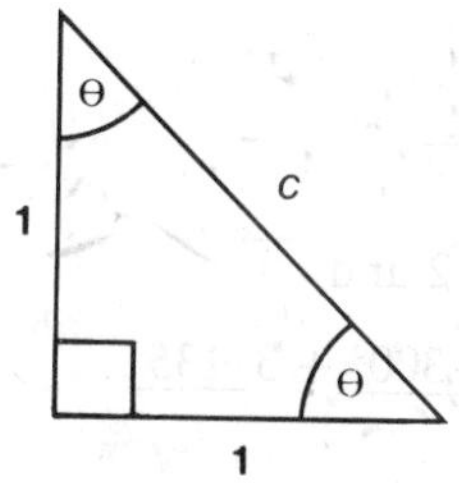

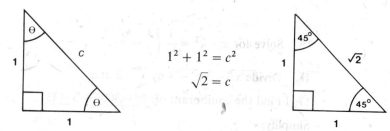

$$1^2 + 1^2 = c^2$$
$$\sqrt{2} = c$$

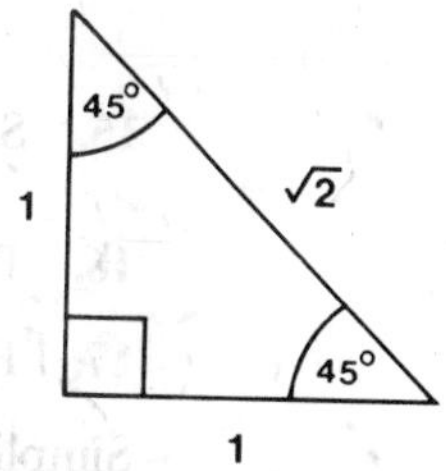

The base angles of an isosceles triangle are equal. Therefore, on the left, the two angles marked θ are equal angles. They are 45° angles because they and the right angle must sum to 180°. We can use the Pythagorean theorem to find out that the length of the hypotenuse is $\sqrt{2}$. We can use the completed triangle to find the sine, cosine, and tangent of 45°.

$$\sin\theta = \frac{\text{opp}}{\text{hyp}} \qquad \sin 45° = \frac{1}{\sqrt{2}}$$

$$\cos\theta = \frac{\text{adj}}{\text{hyp}} \qquad \cos 45° = \frac{1}{\sqrt{2}}$$

$$\tan\theta = \frac{\text{opp}}{\text{adj}} \qquad \tan 45° = \frac{1}{1} = 1$$

To find the functions of 30° and 60°, we begin by drawing an equilateral triangle. The angles in an equilateral triangle are equal angles. Since their sum is 180°, the measure of each angle must be 60°. In a later lesson, we will prove that the bisector of an angle in an equilateral triangle will be perpendicular to the side opposite the angle and will also bisect that side. On the left, we show an equilateral triangle whose sides are 2 units long. We have bisected angle A; and, thus, we have bisected the side opposite angle A. On the right, we discard the lower half of the triangle, and the remaining triangle is a triangle whose sides are 2, 1, and x. Then we use the Pythagorean theorem to solve for x and find that x equals $\sqrt{3}$.

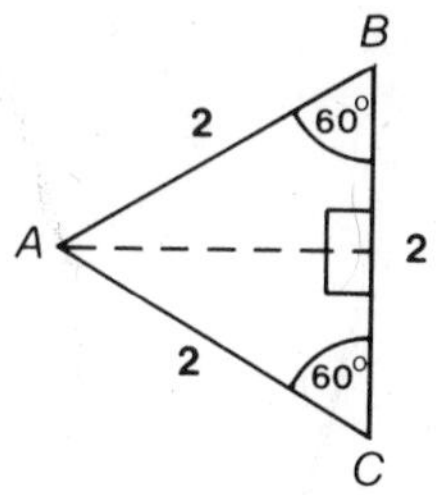

$$2^2 = 1^2 + x^2$$
$$3 = x^2$$
$$\sqrt{3} = x$$

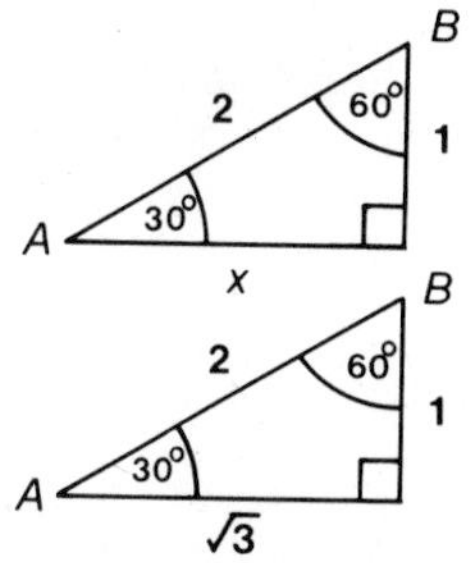

We use this 30°, 60°, 90° triangle to find the sine, cosine, and tangent of 30° and 60°.

$$\sin\theta = \frac{\text{opp}}{\text{hyp}} \qquad \sin 30° = \frac{1}{2} \qquad \sin 60° = \frac{\sqrt{3}}{2}$$

$$\cos\theta = \frac{\text{adj}}{\text{hyp}} \qquad \cos 30° = \frac{\sqrt{3}}{2} \qquad \cos 60° = \frac{1}{2}$$

$$\tan\theta = \frac{\text{opp}}{\text{adj}} \qquad \tan 30° = \frac{1}{\sqrt{3}} \qquad \tan 60° = \sqrt{3}$$

Example 1.A.1 Draw the necessary triangle and find tan 30°.

Solution We draw the triangle and find tan 30°.

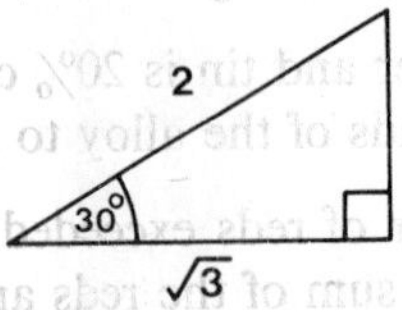

$$\tan\theta = \frac{\text{opp}}{\text{adj}}$$

$$\tan 30° = \frac{1}{\sqrt{3}}$$

It is customary to write answers that do not have a radical in the denominator, so we multiply above and below by $\sqrt{3}$.

$$\frac{1}{\sqrt{3}} \cdot \frac{\sqrt{3}}{\sqrt{3}} = \frac{\sqrt{3}}{3}$$

Some modern authors have suggested that rationalizing the denominator is an unnecessary procedure. Perhaps it is, but we will continue to rationalize denominators for the practice the procedure provides in handling radical expressions.

Example 1.A.2 Draw the necessary triangle and evaluate 7 sin 45°.

Solution We draw the triangle and find sin 45°.

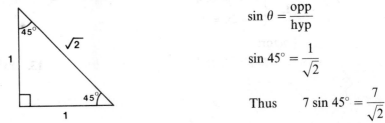

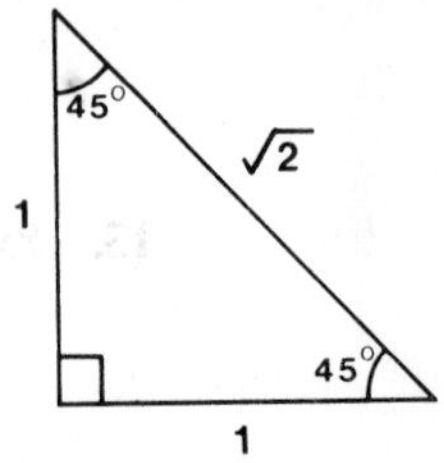

$$\sin\theta = \frac{\text{opp}}{\text{hyp}}$$

$$\sin 45° = \frac{1}{\sqrt{2}}$$

Thus $\quad 7\sin 45° = \frac{7}{\sqrt{2}}$

To finish we multiply above and below by $\sqrt{2}$ to rationalize the denominator.

$$\frac{7}{\sqrt{2}} \cdot \frac{\sqrt{2}}{\sqrt{2}} = \frac{7\sqrt{2}}{2}$$

Example 1.A.3 Draw the necessary triangle and evaluate $4\sqrt{3}\cos 60°$.

Solution First we draw the triangle and find cos 60°.

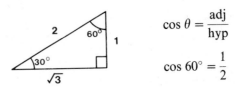

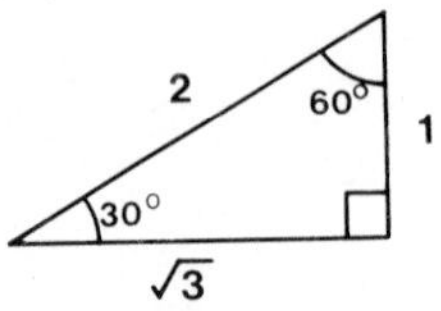

$$\cos\theta = \frac{\text{adj}}{\text{hyp}}$$

$$\cos 60° = \frac{1}{2}$$

To find $4\sqrt{3}\cos 60°$, we multiply by $4\sqrt{3}$.

$$4\sqrt{3}\left(\frac{1}{2}\right) = 2\sqrt{3}$$

Problem set 1

1. The sum of the digits of a two-digit counting number is 12 and the ratio of the units digit to the tens digit is 1 to 2. What is the number?
2. There were 12 nickels, dimes, and quarters whose total value was \$1.55. If the number of nickels exceeded the number of quarters by 1, how many coins of each kind were there?
3. Forty percent of the reds added to 60 percent of the greens numbered 56. If the ratio of the number of reds to the number of greens was 1 to 4, how many were red and how many were green?
4. An alloy of copper and tin is 20% copper. How many pounds of copper must be added to 20 pounds of the alloy to get an alloy that is 50% copper?
5. Twice the number of reds exceeded 3 times the number of blues by 8. The ratio of the reds to the sum of the reds and blues was 5 to 7. How many were red and how many were blue?
6. A pharmacist has 100 ounces of a solution that is $3\frac{1}{2}\%$ iodine and $96\frac{1}{2}\%$ alcohol. How much alcohol should the pharmacist add to get a $1\frac{1}{2}\%$ iodine solution?
7. Find the equation of the line that passes through the point $(-2, 0)$ and is perpendicular to $5x + 3y + 2 = 0$.
8. Draw the necessary triangle and find the exact value of $4 \tan 60°$.
9. Draw the necessary triangle and find the exact value of $6\sqrt{2}\cos 30°$.
10. Draw the necessary triangle and find the exact value of $6\sqrt{3}\sin 45°$.

Solve:

11. $\begin{cases} x^2 + y^2 = 9 \\ y - 2x = 1 \end{cases}$

Factor:

12. $27x^3y^6 + 8p^3$
13. $8x^3y^{12} - 27z^9$

Simplify:

14. $\dfrac{\dfrac{n^3}{b^3} - \dfrac{7p^2}{a}}{\dfrac{s^3}{b^2a} - \dfrac{5t}{b^3a}}$
15. $\dfrac{x}{2y - \dfrac{6z}{3 + \dfrac{s}{t}}}$

16. Solve for y: $s^2 = \dfrac{1}{df}\left(\dfrac{4y}{3} - \dfrac{7x^3}{g}\right)$
17. Divide $x^4 - 6$ by $x^2 - 1$ and check by adding.
18. Find the equilibrant of: $8\underline{/-250°} - 3\underline{/125°}$

Simplify:

19. $\sqrt{3}\sqrt{3}\sqrt{-3} - \sqrt{-2}\sqrt{-2}\sqrt{-2} - 5\sqrt{-9} + 3i$
20. $\dfrac{2 - 3\sqrt{24}}{3 - 2\sqrt{54}}$
21. $\dfrac{3i^3 - 2i^2 - i^5}{2 - 4i^2 + \sqrt{-4}}$

Solve by completing the square:

22. $2x^2 = -3 + 4x$ **23.** $-5x - 8 = 3x^2$

24. If $x > 0$ and $y < 0$, compare: *A.* $x - y$ *B.* $y - x$

25. If $x > 0$ and $y > 0$, compare: *A.* $\frac{x}{y}$ *B.* $\frac{x}{y + 1}$

Solve:

26. $\begin{cases} 2x - 3y + z = -1 \\ x + 3y - z = 4 \\ x - 2y + 2z = 3 \end{cases}$ **27.** $\begin{cases} 2x - y = -1 \\ y + 3z = 9 \\ 3x - z = 1 \end{cases}$ **28.** $\begin{cases} \frac{3}{4}x - \frac{5}{2}z = -2 \\ -\frac{1}{2}x + \frac{3}{2}y = \frac{5}{2} \\ 0.4x + 0.3z = 2.2 \end{cases}$

Simplify:

29. $\dfrac{x^3\sqrt{x^3}\,(yx^2)^{a/3}}{x^a y^{2a}}$ **30.** $(2x^{a/3} - 3z^{2b/3})(3x^{a/2} - 4z^{b/3})$

LESSON 2 *The exponential function*

2.A The exponential function

We call the following expressions ***powers.***

$$3^2 \qquad 4^{10} \qquad 10^5 \qquad 5^{14}$$

The bottom number is called the ***base,*** and the small raised number is called the ***exponent.*** The exponent tells how many times the base is to be used as a factor. The expression 10^2 tells us that 10 is to be used as a factor 2 times, and 10^3 tells us that 10 is to be used as a factor 3 times. But then, what meaning can $10^{2.5}$ have?

$$10^2 = 10 \cdot 10 = 100$$

$$10^{2.5} = ???$$

$$10^3 = 10 \cdot 10 \cdot 10 = 1000$$

It does not mean that 10 should be used as a factor 2.5 times because this makes no sense. From the pattern we see that the expression should have a value between 100 and 1000. The number 2.5 is a rational number, which means it can be written as a fraction. Since the fractional equivalent of 2.5 is 5/2, we can write

$$10^{2.5} = 10^{5/2}$$

If we use our rules for fractional exponents, we can write this as

$$(10^{1/2})^5 \qquad \text{or as} \qquad (10^5)^{1/2}$$

Both these expressions have the same value. We approximate this number by using a calculator and get

$$316.22777$$

Thus, we see that the expression 10^x has a real number value if we replace x with any rational number. This investigation can be extended to demonstrate that the expression 10^x also represents a unique real number for every irrational number replacement of x and thus has a value for all real number values of x, both rational and irrational. Hence, the expression

$$y = 10^x$$

expresses y as a continuous function of x and can be graphed. Of course, the base does not have to be the number 10. Other numbers can be used, as shown by the following equations:

$$y = 2^x \qquad y = 7.5^x \qquad y = (0.62)^x \qquad y = \left(\frac{3}{4}\right)^x$$

A power whose base is a constant and whose exponent contains a variable is a special kind of power that is often called an ***exponential.*** When used with another variable and an equals sign, we can write equations that we call ***exponential equations.*** Some numbers cannot be used as the base of an exponential function (equation). The numbers 0 and 1 are not used as a base because the result would always be the same regardless of the value of the exponent.

$$y = 1^x \longrightarrow y = 1 \qquad \text{for all } x \qquad x \in \{\text{reals}\}$$

$$y = 0^x \longrightarrow y = 0 \qquad \text{for all } x \qquad x \in \{\text{positive reals}\}$$

Negative numbers cannot be used as a base because the y values for some values of x turn out to be complex numbers. For example, suppose we use (-2) as the base:

$y = (-2)^{3/2}$	base is -2
$y = [(-2)^3]^{1/2}$	equivalent expression
$y = \sqrt{-8}$	simplified
$y = 2\sqrt{2}\,i$	simplified

Since we want to define exponential functions to have real number values for all values of x, we see that negative numbers cannot be used as the base of an exponential. Thus, the expression

$$y = b^x$$

has a unique real number value of y for every real number value of x if b is a positive number. If b is a positive number less than 1, the graph of the function decreases as x increases. If b is a positive number greater than 1, the graph of the function increases as x increases.

Example 2.A.1 Graph the function $y = 2^x$.

Solution We make a table and select several positive values and several negative values for x.

x	-3	-2	0	2	3
y					

Now we compute the matching values for y.

If $x = -3$, $\qquad y = 2^{-3} \longrightarrow y = \dfrac{1}{2^3} \longrightarrow y = \dfrac{1}{8}$

If $x = -2$, $\qquad y = 2^{-2} \longrightarrow y = \dfrac{1}{2^2} \longrightarrow y = \dfrac{1}{4}$

If $x = 0$, $\quad y = 2^0 \longrightarrow y = 1$

If $x = 2$, $\quad y = 2^2 \longrightarrow y = 4$

If $x = 3$, $\quad y = 2^3 \longrightarrow y = 8$

Now we complete the table and graph the function.

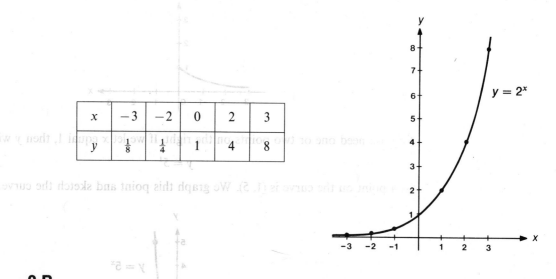

x	-3	-2	0	2	3
y	$\frac{1}{8}$	$\frac{1}{4}$	1	4	8

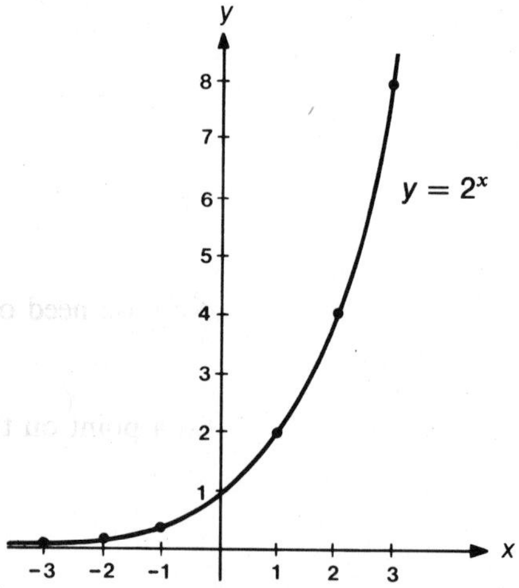

2.B Sketching exponentials

The point-by-point method of graphing exponentials used in the preceding example is laborious and time-consuming, especially when a sketch of the curve is usually all we need. We will begin our investigation of the graphs of exponential functions by looking at functions of the form $y = b^x$. The graphs of these functions "look like" a member of one of the two families of curves shown here.

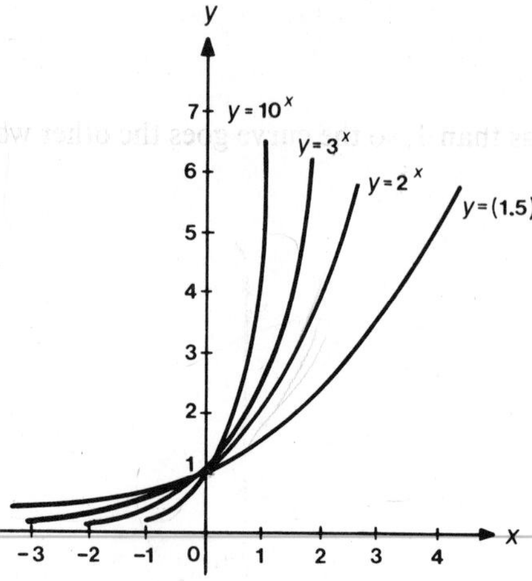

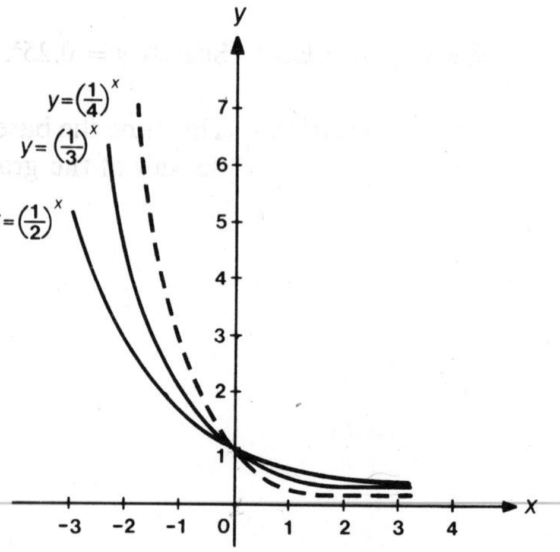

The exponentials graphed in the left-hand figure have a base that is greater than 1, and we note that the value of y increases when x increases. The exponentials graphed in the right-hand figure have a base that is greater than 0 but less than 1. For these curves the value of y increases as the value of x decreases. For curve sketching, it is important to note that every one of the curves passes through the point (0, 1) and that there is very little difference in the graphs of the lower end of the different curves. Thus, it is usually not necessary to find values for the curve on the lower end, and usually the coordinates of one point on the other side will suffice to make a sketch.

Example 2.B.1 Sketch $y = 5^x$.

Solution The base is greater than 1, so y increases as x increases. First we put a couple of values on the horizontal and vertical scales and draw the tail of the graph.

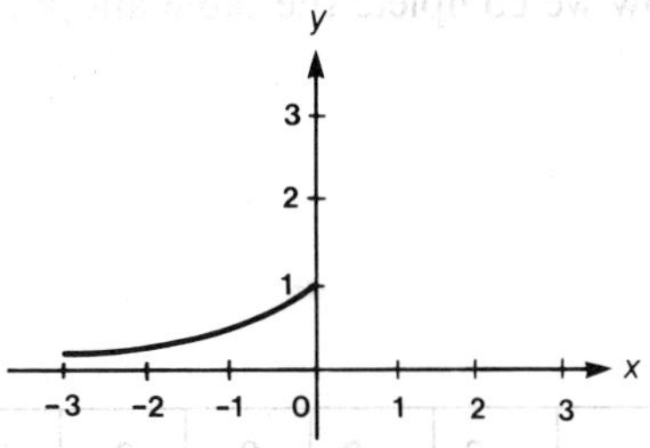

Now we need one or two points on the right. If we let x equal 1, then y will equal 5.

$$y = 5^1$$

So a point on the curve is (1, 5). We graph this point and sketch the curve.

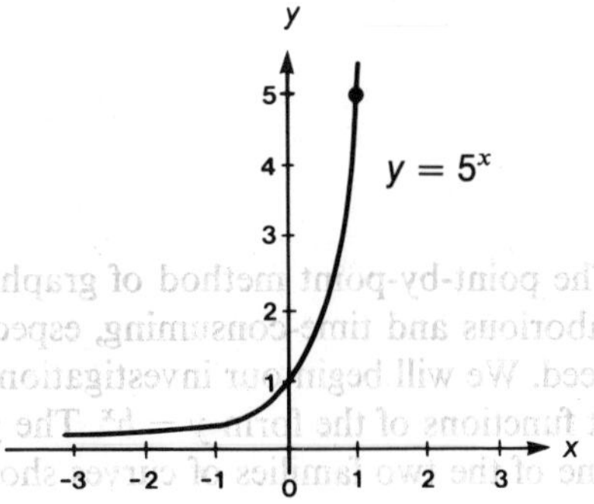

Example 2.B.2 Sketch $y = 0.25^x$.

Solution This time the base is less than 1, so the curve goes the other way. We begin by estimating the tail of the graph.

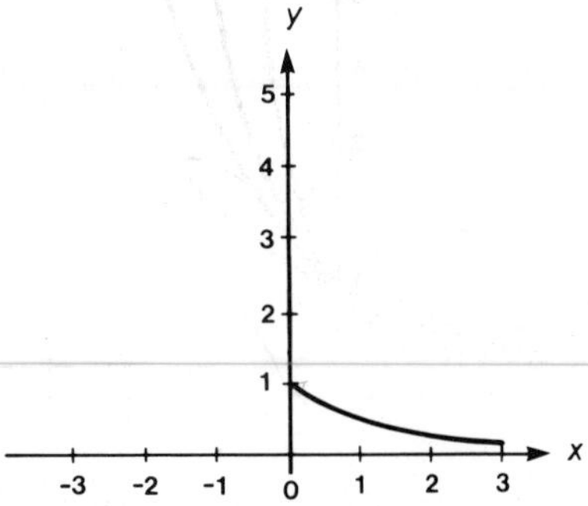

Now we decide to let x equal (a) -1 and (b) -2 and find the paired values of y.

$$(a) \quad y = 0.25^{-1} \longrightarrow y = \frac{1}{0.25} \longrightarrow y = 4$$

$$(b) \quad y = 0.25^{-2} \longrightarrow y = \frac{1}{(0.25)^2} \longrightarrow y = 16$$

The coordinates of (*b*) are $(-2, 16)$. This point falls off of our graph, but now we know the curve goes through $(-1, 4)$ and rises quite rapidly thereafter. This is all we need to know to make our sketch.

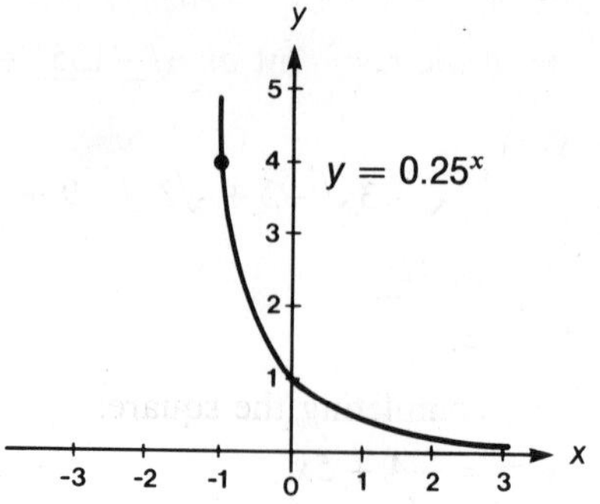

Problem set 2

1. The sum of the digits of a two-digit counting number is 9. When the digits are reversed, the new number is 9 less than the original number. What are the two numbers?

2. There were 35 nickels, dimes, and silver dollars in the pile, and their value was $12.25. How many coins of each kind were there if there were twice as many silver dollars as nickels?

3. How many liters of a solution that is 37% key ingredient should be added to 143 liters of a 73% solution to yield a 51% solution?

4. The number of greens exceeded the sum of the reds and blues by 9. The sum of the blues and greens exceeded 4 times the number of reds by 1. How many of each kind were there if there were 2 more reds than blues?

5. Sam strained and strained but could only garner $7\frac{1}{8}$. If this was only $\frac{2}{7}$ of what he wanted, how much did he want?

6. Find the equation of the line that passes through $(-2, 5)$ that is perpendicular to the line that passes through $(-4, -2)$ and $(5, 7)$.

7. Use the calculator to evaluate: (*a*) 0.6^8 (*b*) 0.04^{-6}

8. Sketch the function $y = 4^x$.

9. Sketch the function $y = (\frac{1}{3})^x$.

10. Draw the required triangle and evaluate $4\sqrt{3}\cos 60°$.

11. Draw the required triangle and evaluate $8 \tan 45°$.

12. Solve: $\begin{cases} xy = 6 \\ x - y = 3 \end{cases}$

Factor:

13. $64a^3b^9 - 8p^3$

14. $27b^9a^6 - 64c^3$

Simplify:

15. $$\frac{\dfrac{a^3}{x^2y} - \dfrac{6m^2}{y^2x}}{\dfrac{l^2}{y^2} - \dfrac{6t}{x^2}}$$

16. $$\frac{3x}{4y - \dfrac{6z}{4 + \dfrac{k}{2l}}}$$

17. Solve for z: $2t = \dfrac{1}{3s^2}\left(\dfrac{5z}{6} - \dfrac{4m}{n}\right)$

18. Divide $x^4 - 2x + 1$ by $x - 2$ and check.

19. Find the resultant of: $6\underline{/-135^\circ} + 4\underline{/130^\circ}$

Simplify:

20. $\sqrt{3}\sqrt{2}\sqrt{-3}\sqrt{-2} + \sqrt{3}\sqrt{-9} + 5\sqrt{-16} - 3i$

21. $\dfrac{3 - 2\sqrt{12}}{1 - 3\sqrt{3}}$

22. $\dfrac{5i^2 - 2i^3 + i^4}{-2i^3 + 4i - \sqrt{-16}}$

Solve by completing the square:

23. $3x^2 = -4 + 5x$

24. $-6x + 9 = 4x^2$

25. If n is a real number, compare: *A.* $n + 1$ *B.* $n - 1$

26. The ratio of a to b is 1. Compare: *A.* a *B.* b

Solve:

27. $\begin{cases} 3x - 2y = 5 \\ y - 3z = -10 \\ 2x - z = -1 \end{cases}$

28. $\begin{cases} \dfrac{1}{5}x - \dfrac{1}{4}y = \dfrac{1}{2} \\ \dfrac{3}{2}y + \dfrac{1}{4}z = -2 \\ 0.1x - 0.5z = -1.5 \end{cases}$

Simplify:

29. $\dfrac{a^{2x}b^{3x}(\sqrt{a^3})^x}{b^{x-y}a}$

30. $(3x^{3a} - 2y^{a/2})(2y^{2a} - x^{2a})$

LESSON 3 Points, lines, and rays · Planes · Angles · Betweenness and assumptions · Triangles

3.A Points, lines, and rays

In our study of mathematics it is interesting to note that we are unable to define some terms, and for this reason these terms are called ***primitive terms.*** The complete meaning of primitive terms is found in the totality of the axioms that use these terms. The words **point, line,** and **plane** are primitive terms. We will explain these terms as best as we can and then will use them to define other terms. We must begin somewhere. Many authors use the word *undefined* instead of the word *primitive;* and these authors say that the words point, line, and plane are ***undefined terms.*** Here we show a series of dots, each one smaller than the dot to its left.

If we continue drawing the dots with each one smaller than the dot to its left, we would finally have a dot so small that it could not be seen without magnification. This dot would still be larger than a mathematical point because a mathematical point is so small that it has no size at all. This is certainly not an exact definition because we have stated what a point is not and we have not said what a point is.

Thus, we see that when we use a dot to mark the location of a mathematical point, the dot is not the point but is the **graph of the point.** We can think of a curve as an unbroken string of mathematical points. A line is a straight curve, and only one line can be drawn through two designated points. If three or more points lie on the same line, we say that the points are ***collinear.*** Because a line is made of mathematical points, a line has no width. When we draw a line with a pencil, the line we draw is a graph of the mathematical line and marks the location of the mathematical line. We sometimes put arrowheads on the ends of graphs of lines to emphasize that the lines continue without end in both directions.

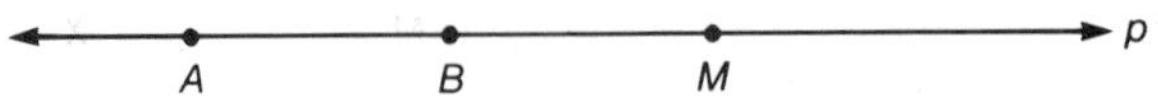

We can name a line by using a single letter (in this case, *p*) or by naming any two points on the line. A commonly used method is to write the letters for two points on the line and to use an overbar with two arrowheads to indicate that the line continues without end in both directions.

$$\overleftrightarrow{AB} \quad \overleftrightarrow{BA} \quad \overleftrightarrow{AM} \quad \overleftrightarrow{MA} \quad \overleftrightarrow{MB} \quad \overleftrightarrow{BM}$$

A ***line segment*** is a part of a line. A line segment contains the endpoints and all points between the endpoints. We will use two letters and an overbar with no arrowheads to name the line segment whose endpoints are the two given points. Thus, we can use either

$$\overline{AB} \quad \text{or} \quad \overline{BA}$$

to name the line segment whose endpoints are A and B. **The length of a line segment is designated by using letters without the overbar.** Thus, the length of line segment AB could be designated by writing either

$$AB \quad \text{or} \quad BA$$

The words ***equal to, greater than,*** and ***less than*** are used to compare numbers. Thus, when we say that one line segment is equal to another line segment, we mean that the number that describes the length of one segment is equal to the number that describes the length of the other line segment. Mathematicians often used the word ***congruent*** to indicate that designated geometric qualities are equal. In the case of line segments, the designated quality is understood to be the length. Thus, if the segments shown here

are of equal length, we could so state by writing that segment $\overline{PQ}$ is congruent to segment $\overline{RS}$ or by writing that length PQ equals length RS.

$\overline{PQ} \cong \overline{RS}$	or we could write	$PQ = RS$
CONGRUENCE OF LINE SEGMENTS		EQUALITY OF LENGTHS

Many authors would say that the measure of one of these segments equals the measure of the other segment. In this book, we will use all of these descriptions. Sometimes we will use the word *congruent* and at other times we will speak of *equal* line segments or of line segments whose *measures* are equal. When we say that line segments are equal, we must remember that we mean that the lengths of the segments are equal.

A ***ray*** is an extension of a segment in one direction. A ray is sometimes called a ***half line.*** The endpoint of a ray is called the ***origin*** of the ray.

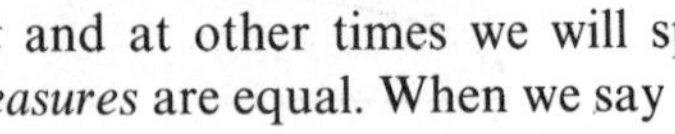

A ray is designated with two letters and a single-arrowhead overbar. The first letter must be the endpoint or origin, and the other letter can be any other point on the ray. Thus we can name the ray on the preceding page by writing either

$$\overrightarrow{TU} \quad \text{or} \quad \overrightarrow{TX}$$

Two rays of opposite directions that lie on the same line (rays that are ***collinear***) and that share a common endpoint are called ***opposite rays.*** Thus, the rays $\overrightarrow{XM}$ and $\overrightarrow{XP}$ are opposite rays, and they are both collinear with line $\overleftrightarrow{MX}$.

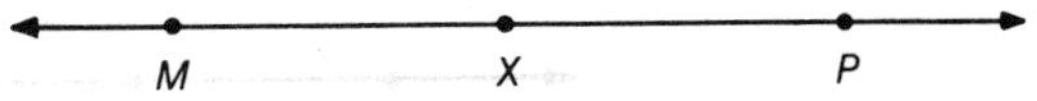

If two geometric figures have points in common, we say that these points are points ***of intersection*** of the figures. We say that the figures intersect each other at these points. If two different lines lie in the same plane and are not parallel, then they intersect in exactly one point. Here we show lines b and e that intersect at point Z.

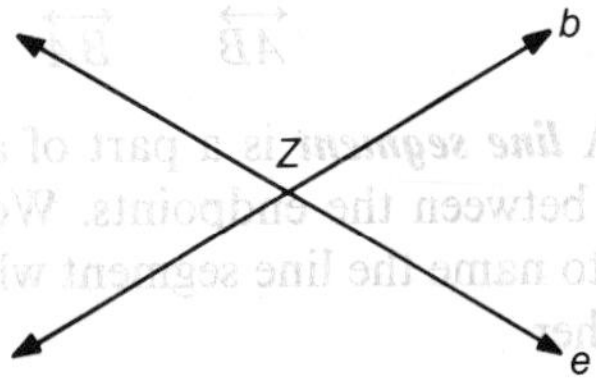

3.B Planes

A mathematical line has no width and continues without end in both directions. A mathematical plane can be thought of as a flat surface like a tabletop that has no thickness and that continues without limit in the two dimensions that define the plane. Although a plane has no edges, we often picture a plane by using a four-sided figure.

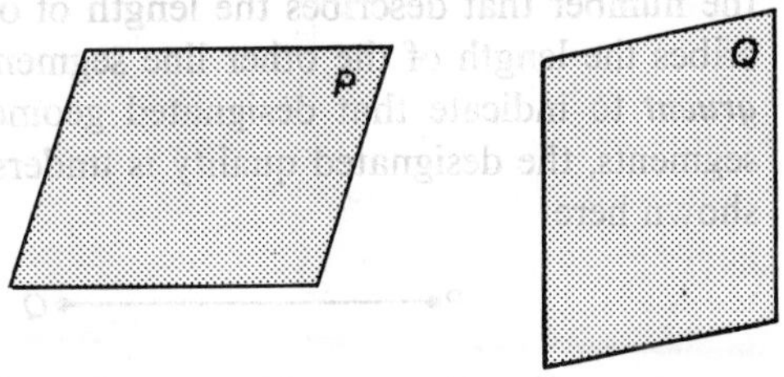

Just as two points determine a line, three noncollinear points determine a plane. As three noncollinear points also determine two intersecting straight lines, we can see that two lines that intersect at one point also determine a plane.

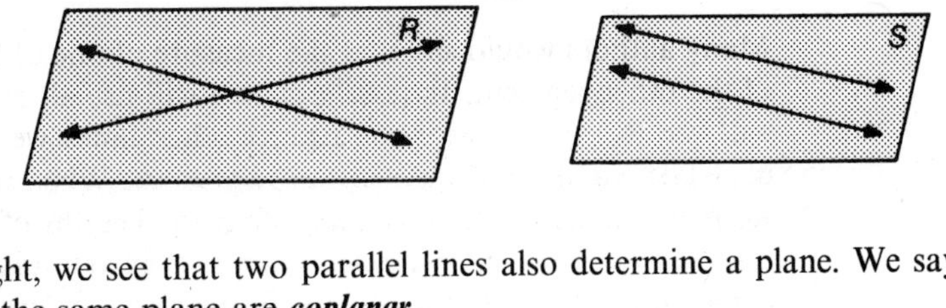

On the right, we see that two parallel lines also determine a plane. We say that lines that lie in the same plane are ***coplanar.***

A line not in a plane is parallel to the plane if the line does not intersect the plane. If a line is not parallel to a plane, the line will intersect the plane and will intersect the plane at only one point. Here we show plane M and line k that lies in the plane. We also show line c that is parallel to the plane and line f that intersects the plane at point P.

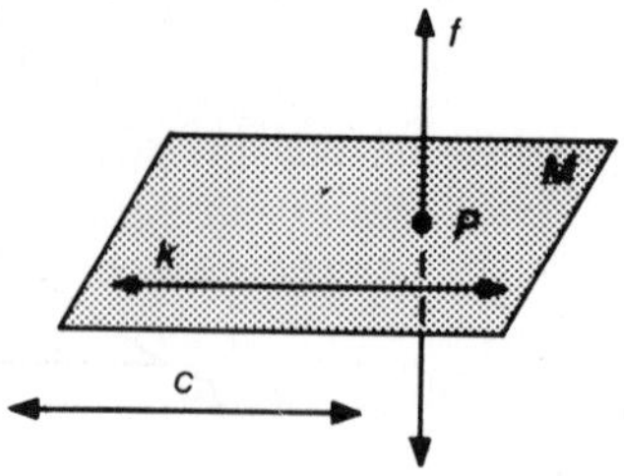

Skew lines are lines that are not in the same plane. Skew lines are never parallel, and they do not intersect. However, saying this is not necessary because if lines are parallel or intersect, they are in the same plane. Thus, lines k and f in the diagram above are skew lines because they are not both in plane M, and they do not form another plane because they are not parallel and they do not intersect.

3.C Angles

There is more than one way to define an angle. An angle can be defined to be the **geometric figure** formed by two rays that have a common endpoint. This definition says that the angle is the set of points that form the rays, and that the measure of the angle is the measure of the opening between the rays. A second definition is that the angle is the **region** bounded by two radii and the arc of a circle. In this definition the measure of the angle is the ratio of the length of the arc to length of the radius.

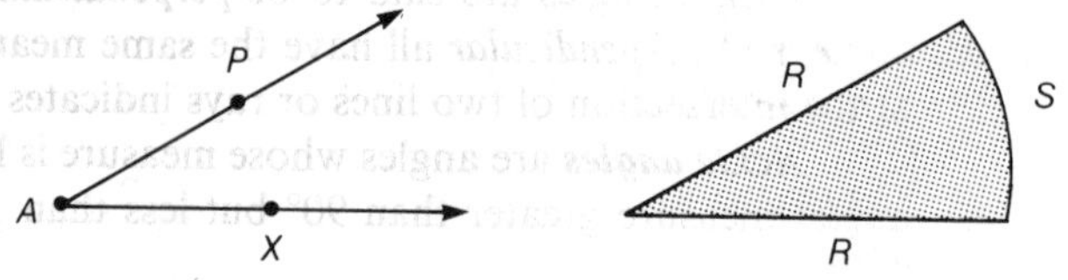

Using the first definition and the figure on the left, we say that the angle is the set of points that form the rays $\overrightarrow{AP}$ and $\overrightarrow{AX}$. Using the second definition of the figure on the right, we say that the angle is the set of points that constitute the shaded region, and that the measure of the angle is S over R. A third definition is that an angle is the **difference in direction** of two intersecting lines. A fourth definition says that an angle is the **rotation of a ray about its endpoint.** This definition is useful in trigonometry. Here we show two angles.

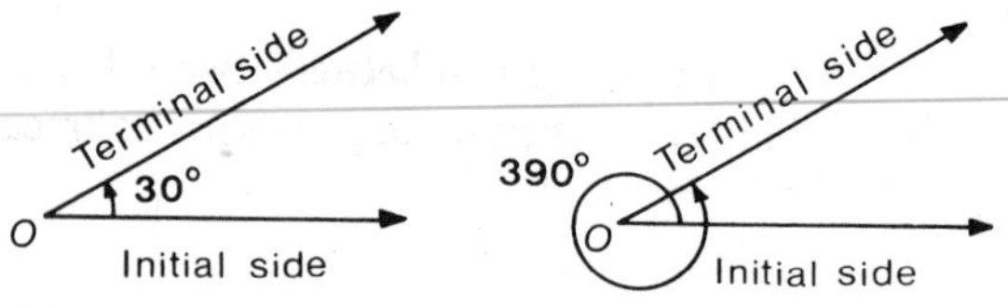

The angle on the left is a 30° angle because the ray was rotated through 30° to get to its terminal position. On the right, the terminal position is the same, but the angle is a 390° angle because the rotation was 390°. Because both angles have the same initial and terminal sides, we say that the angles are ***coterminal.*** We say the measure of the amount of rotation is the measure of the angle. We can name an angle by using a single letter or by using three letters. When we use three letters the first and last letters designate points on the rays, and the center letter designates the common endpoint of the rays, which is called the ***vertex*** of the angle. The angle shown here could be named by using any of the notations shown on the right.

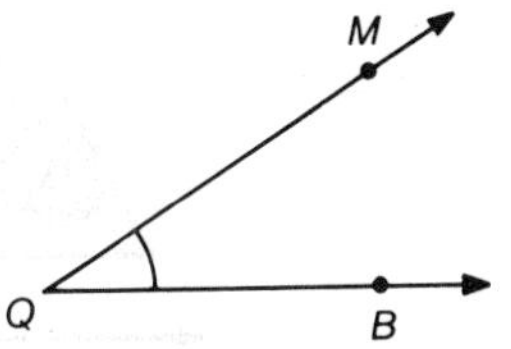

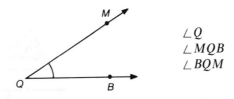

$\angle Q$
$\angle MQB$
$\angle BQM$

When we say that two angles are ***congruent,*** we are saying that the measures of the angles are equal. **Thus, *congruence* of line segments means that the lengths of the segments are equal, and congruence of angles means that the measures of the angles are equal.** If the measure of angle A equals the measure of angle B, we may write

$\angle A \cong \angle B$ or we could write $m\angle A = m\angle B$

CONGRUENCE OF ANGLES — EQUALITY OF ANGLE MEASURE

We will use both of these notations, and, in addition, we will use notations such as

$$\angle A = \angle B \quad \text{and} \quad \angle F = 37°$$

We will remember that when we use these last two notations, the word *measure* is understood. We are stating that the measure of angle A equals the measure of angle B and that the measure of angle F equals 37°.

Right angles have a measure of 90°, and lines, rays, or line segments that intersect at right angles are said to be ***perpendicular*** (⊥). Thus, the words *right angle,* 90° *angle,* and *perpendicular* all have the same meaning. As we show below, a small square at the intersection of two lines or rays indicates that the lines or rays are perpendicular.

Acute angles are angles whose measure is less than 90° but greater than 0°. ***Obtuse angles*** measure greater than 90° but less than 180°. A straight angle has a measure of 180°.

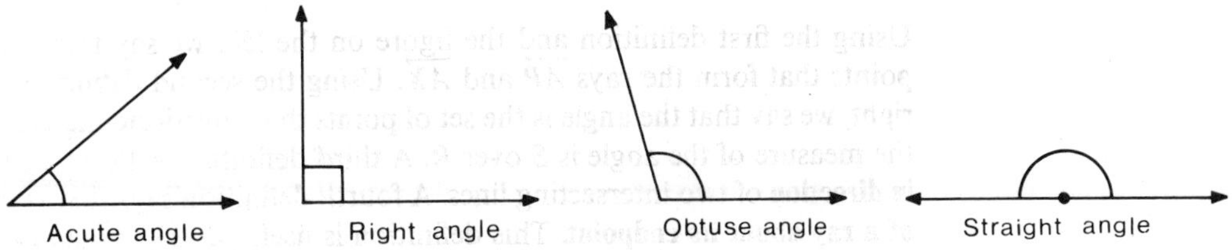

3.D Betweenness, tick marks, assumptions

One point is said to lie **between** two other points only if the points lie on the same line (are collinear). When three points are collinear, one and only one of the points is between the other two.

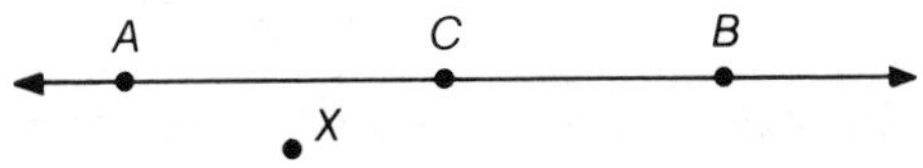

Thus, we can say that point C is between points A and B because point C belongs to the line segment determined by the two points A and B and is not an endpoint of this segment. Point X is not between points A and B because it is not on the same line (is not collinear) that contains points A and B.

We will use "tick marks" on the figures to designate segments of equal length and angles of equal measure.

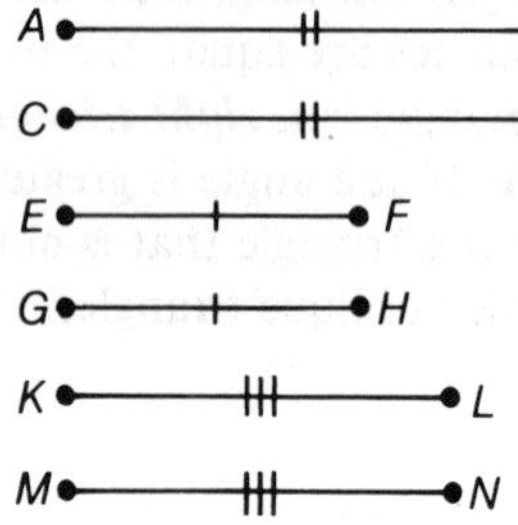

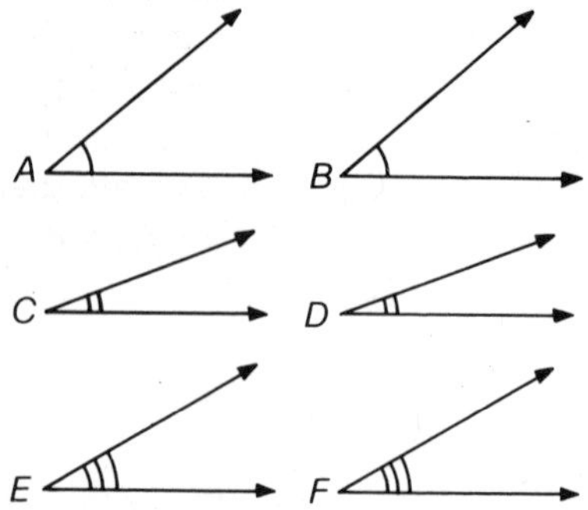

Here we have indicated the following equality of segments: $AB = CD$, $EF = GH$, $KL = MN$. The equality of angles indicated is $\angle A = \angle B$, $\angle C = \angle D$, and $\angle E = \angle F$.

In this book we will introduce the formal proofs of geometry. We will use geometric figures in these proofs. When we do, some assumptions about the figures are permitted and others are not permitted. **It is permitted to assume that a line that appears to be a straight line is a straight line, but it is not permitted to assume that lines that appear to be perpendicular are perpendicular. Further, it is not permitted to assume that one angle or line segment is equal to, greater than, or less than another angle or line segment.** We list some permissible and impermissible assumptions as follows:

Permissible	Not permissible
Straight lines are straight angles	Right angles
Collinearity of points	Equal lengths
Relative location of points	Equal angles
Betweenness of points	Relative size of segments and angles
	Perpendicular or parallel lines

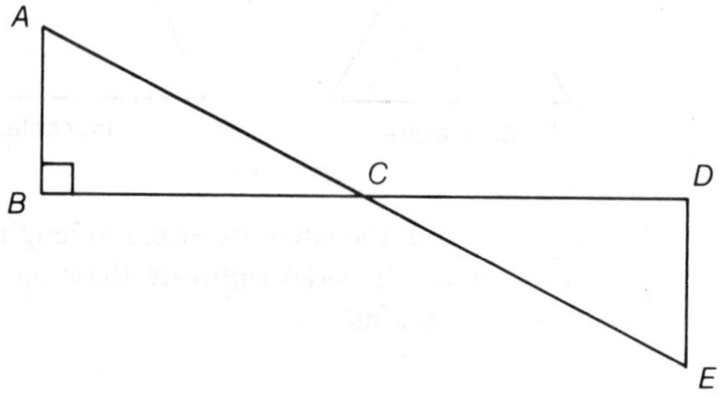

In the figure above we may assume the following:

1. That the four lines shown are straight lines
2. That point C lies on line BD and on line AE

We may not assume:

3. That $\overline{AB}$ and $\overline{DE}$ are of equal length
4. That $\overline{BC}$ and $\overline{CD}$ are of equal length
5. That $\angle D$ is a right angle
6. That $\angle A$ equals $\angle E$
7. That $\overline{AB}$ and $\overline{DE}$ are parallel

3.E Triangles

Triangles have three sides and three angles. Triangles can be classified according to the measures of their angles or according to the lengths of their sides. If all angles are equal, the triangle is ***equiangular.*** If two angles are equal, the triangle is an ***isogonic triangle.*** If one angle is a right angle, the triangle is a ***right triangle.*** If all angles are less than 90°, the triangle is an ***acute triangle.*** If one angle is greater than 90°, the triangle is an ***obtuse triangle.*** An ***oblique triangle*** is a triangle that is not a right triangle. Thus acute triangles and obtuse triangles are also oblique triangles.

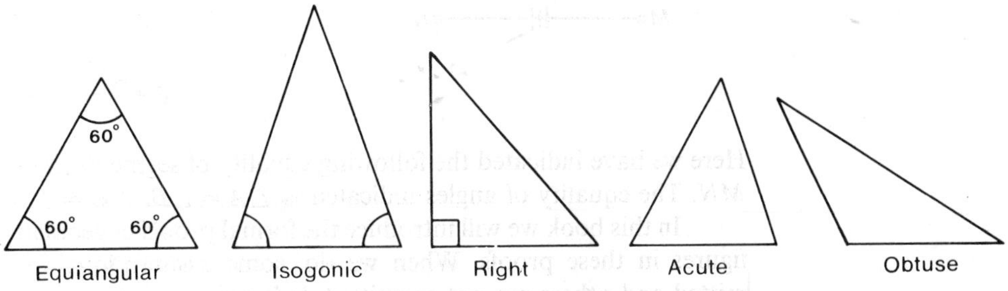

Triangles are also classified according to the relative lengths of the sides. If the sides have equal lengths, the triangle is an ***equilateral triangle.*** If two sides are of equal length, the triangle is an ***isosceles triangle;*** and if no two sides are equal, the triangle is a ***scalene triangle.***

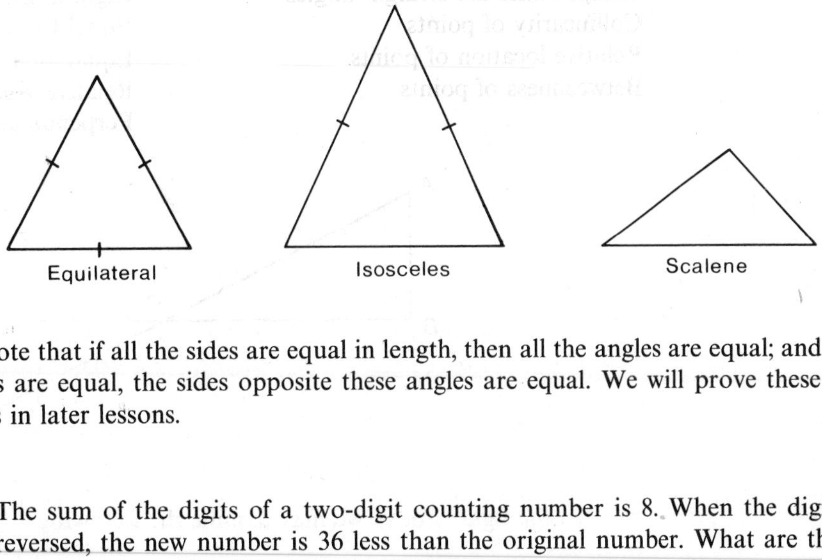

We note that if all the sides are equal in length, then all the angles are equal; and if two angles are equal, the sides opposite these angles are equal. We will prove these statements in later lessons.

Problem set 3

1. The sum of the digits of a two-digit counting number is 8. When the digits are reversed, the new number is 36 less than the original number. What are the two numbers?

2. There were 24 pennies, nickels, and quarters in all, and their total value was \$1.60. How many of each kind of coin was there if the number of nickels equaled the number of pennies?

3. A 27-gallon solution contains 9 gallons of acid and 18 gallons of water. How much water should be added to get a solution that is 25% acid?

4. Twice the sum of the number of blues and greens exceeded the number of reds by only 4. The sum of the reds and blues exceeded the number of greens by 7. How many of each kind were there if there were twice as many reds as there were greens?

5. Robert tried hard but got $4\frac{1}{2}$ times as much as he wanted. If he got a total of $2\frac{1}{5}$, how much did he want?

6. Find the equation of the line that passes through the point $(5, -2)$ and is perpendicular to the line that passes through the points $(-5, 7)$ and $(-8, -2)$.

7. Use the calculator to evaluate: (*a*) $0.5^{1.68}$ (*b*) $1.4^{-2.82}$

8. Sketch the function $y = 3.5^x$.

9. Sketch the function $y = (\frac{1}{2})^x$.

10. Draw the required triangle and evaluate $2\sqrt{2}\sin 60°$.

11. Draw the required triangle and evaluate $4\sqrt{3}\cos 45°$.

12. What do we mean when we say that two line segments are congruent?

13. What is an acute angle?

14. Solve: $\begin{cases} x^2 - 2y^2 = -9 \\ x^2 + y^2 = 18 \end{cases}$

15. Factor: $8x^3b^6 - 27p^3$

Simplify:

16. $\dfrac{\dfrac{b^3}{a^2c} - \dfrac{6m^2}{ac^2}}{\dfrac{x^3}{a^2c} - \dfrac{6y}{c^2}}$

17. $\dfrac{3s}{2m - \dfrac{z}{1 + \dfrac{k}{l}}}$

18. Solve for t: $3z = \dfrac{2m}{n}\left(\dfrac{6s}{t} - \dfrac{4l}{k}\right)$

19. Divide $x^3 - 6x^2 - 3x + 1$ by $x - 2$ and check.

20. Find the equilibrant of: $-4\underline{/-140°} - 6\underline{/150°}$

Simplify:

21. $\sqrt{5}\sqrt{2}\sqrt{-5}\sqrt{-2} + \sqrt{3}\sqrt{-9} + 5\sqrt{-8}\sqrt{2} + 6i$

22. $\dfrac{2 - 3\sqrt{24}}{3 + 2\sqrt{6}}$

23. $\dfrac{6i^3 - 4i^4 - 6i}{-3i^4 - 5i + \sqrt{-25}}$

24. Solve by completing the square: $4x^2 = -5 + 6x$

25. If $a > 0$, $b > 0$, and $\dfrac{a}{b} = 2$, compare: A. a B. b

26. If a and b are real numbers and $\dfrac{a}{b} = 3$, compare: A. a B. b

Solve:

27. $\begin{cases} 3x - 2y + z = -1 \\ x + 2y - z = 9 \\ 2x - y + 2z = 2 \end{cases}$

28. $\begin{cases} \dfrac{1}{2}x - \dfrac{1}{4}y = \dfrac{1}{2} \\ -\dfrac{1}{8}x + \dfrac{1}{4}z = -\dfrac{1}{4} \\ 0.2y - 0.2z = 1 \end{cases}$

Simplify:

29. $\dfrac{x^{3a+2}(\sqrt{x^3})^{2a}}{y^{2a-4}(\sqrt{x})^{2a+1}}$

30. $(6x^{3/2} - 2y^{1/2})(6x^{3/2} + 2y^{1/2})$

LESSON 4 Sums of trigonometric functions

4.A Sums of trigonometric functions

Problems that require the sums of trigonometric functions of 30°, 45°, and 60° provide practice in determining the values of the functions and also provide practice in adding algebraic expressions that contain radicals.

Example 4.A.1 Evaluate $\cos 60° + \sin 45°$.

Solution Drawing the triangles will aid long-term retention of the concepts.

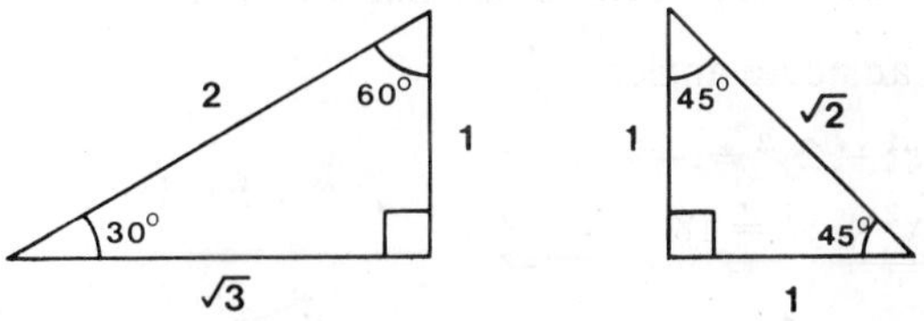

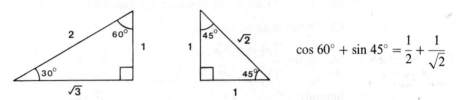

$$\cos 60° + \sin 45° = \frac{1}{2} + \frac{1}{\sqrt{2}}$$

Now we will find a common denominator and add the terms.

$$\frac{\sqrt{2}}{2\sqrt{2}} + \frac{2}{2\sqrt{2}} = \frac{2 + \sqrt{2}}{2\sqrt{2}} \quad \text{added}$$

We finish by multiplying above and below by $\sqrt{2}$.

$$\frac{2 + \sqrt{2}}{2\sqrt{2}} \cdot \frac{\sqrt{2}}{\sqrt{2}} = \frac{2\sqrt{2} + 2}{4} = \mathbf{\frac{\sqrt{2} + 1}{2}}$$

Example 4.A.2 Evaluate $\tan 30° + \cos 45°$.

Solution First we draw the triangles and add the terms.

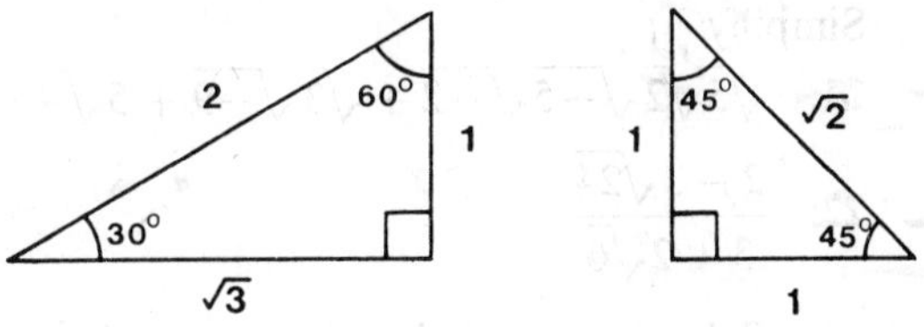

$$\tan 30° + \cos 45° = \frac{1}{\sqrt{3}} + \frac{1}{\sqrt{2}} = \frac{\sqrt{2}}{\sqrt{2}\sqrt{3}} + \frac{\sqrt{3}}{\sqrt{2}\sqrt{3}} = \frac{\sqrt{2} + \sqrt{3}}{\sqrt{6}}$$

We finish by multiplying above and below by $\sqrt{6}$.

$$\frac{\sqrt{2} + \sqrt{3}}{\sqrt{6}} \cdot \frac{\sqrt{6}}{\sqrt{6}} = \mathbf{\frac{2\sqrt{3} + 3\sqrt{2}}{6}}$$

Example 4.A.3 Evaluate $\tan 45° + 2 \tan 30°$.

Solution We draw the triangles to find the functions.

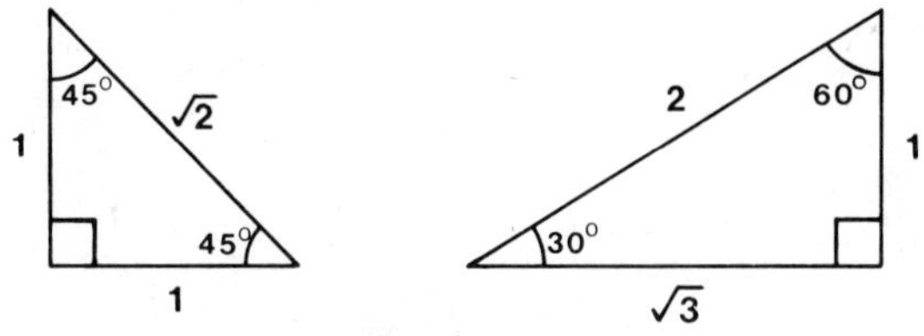

$$\tan 45° + 2 \tan 30° = 1 + 2\left(\frac{1}{\sqrt{3}}\right)$$

Now we find a common denominator and add.

$$\frac{\sqrt{3}}{\sqrt{3}} + \frac{2}{\sqrt{3}} = \frac{\sqrt{3}+2}{\sqrt{3}}$$

Then finish by multiplying above and below by $\sqrt{3}$.

$$\frac{\sqrt{3}+2}{\sqrt{3}} \cdot \frac{\sqrt{3}}{\sqrt{3}} = \frac{\mathbf{3 + 2\sqrt{3}}}{\mathbf{3}}$$

Problem set 4

1. There were 14 dimes, quarters, and half dollars whose total value was \$2.50. How many of each kind of coin was there if the number of quarters equaled the number of half dollars?

2. The sum of the digits of a two-digit counting number is 10. When the digits are reversed, the new number is 36 less than the original number. What are the two numbers?

3. How many ml of a $3\frac{1}{2}\%$ salt solution should be mixed with 176 ml of a $4\frac{3}{4}\%$ salt solution to get a solution that is 4% salt?

4. The total of the numbers of reds and blues was 1 greater than the number of greens. The sum of 3 times the number of reds and twice the number of blues exceeded the number of greens by 9. How many of each color were there if 3 times the number of blues exceeded the number of greens by 2?

5. Sarah looked in every nook and cranny and finally got a measure of $8\frac{1}{4}$. If this was $3\frac{1}{8}$ times the desired measure, what was the desired measure?

6. Find the equation of the line that passes through $(-2, -3)$ and is perpendicular to the line that passes through $(5, 2)$ and $(8, -3)$.

7. Use the calculator to evaluate: (*a*) $5.62^{4.32}$ (*b*) $1.4^{-1.4}$

8. Sketch the function $y = 4.3^x$.

9. Sketch the function $y = \left(\frac{1}{10}\right)^x$.

Evaluate and simplify:

10. $\cos 60° + \sin 45°$

11. $\tan 45° + 2 \tan 30°$

12. $\frac{\sqrt{3}}{2} \tan 30° + \sqrt{2} \cos 60°$

13. $\sqrt{2} \cos 60° + 2 \tan 45°$

14. Solve: $\begin{cases} x^2 + y^2 = 4 \\ 2x + y = 1 \end{cases}$

15. Factor: $27a^6b^9 - 8p^3$

Simplify:

16. $\dfrac{\dfrac{ac^3}{x^3y^2} - \dfrac{6m^3}{x^2y}}{\dfrac{d^2f}{x^2f} - \dfrac{g}{y}}$

17. $\dfrac{2z}{1 - \dfrac{3k}{m - \dfrac{s}{t}}}$

18. Solve for h: $4s = \frac{3z}{m}\left(\frac{1}{2}at^2 - \frac{6m}{h}\right)$

19. Divide $x^5 - 3$ by $x^2 + 1$ and check.

20. Find the equilibrant of: $-6\underline{/30°} + 8\underline{/-140°}$

Simplify:

21. $\sqrt{6}\sqrt{3}\sqrt{-2}\sqrt{-16} + \sqrt{2}\sqrt{-2} - 6\sqrt{-8}\sqrt{2}$

22. $\dfrac{3 - 2\sqrt{18}}{4 + 3\sqrt{8}}$

23. $\dfrac{8i^4 - 4i^3 - 6i}{-3i^3 + 5i - \sqrt{-16}}$

24. Solve by completing the square: $5x^2 = -2x + 6$

25. If $\dfrac{a}{b} = \dfrac{c}{d}$, compare: *A.* ad *B.* $cb - 1$

26. If $a > b$, compare: *A.* $-a$ *B.* $-b$

Solve:

27. $\begin{cases} 2x - 3y + z = -6 \\ x + 2y - z = 1 \\ 3x + y - 2z = -5 \end{cases}$

28. $\begin{cases} \dfrac{1}{5}x + \dfrac{1}{4}z = \dfrac{5}{2} \\ \dfrac{1}{8}y - z = -\dfrac{3}{2} \\ 0.1x + 0.2z = 1.4 \end{cases}$

Simplify:

29. $\dfrac{a^{3z+6}(\sqrt[4]{b^3})^{3z+2}}{b^{3z-2}a^{4z-3}}$

30. $(4x^{1/2} - 2z^{-3/4})(3x^{-1/2} + z^{1/4})$

LESSON 5 *Age problems · Rate problems*

5.A Age problems

Word problems that consider the ages of two or more people now and the ages of the same people at some time in the past or in the future are called ***age problems.*** These problems are uncomplicated, and their solution is straightforward if subscripted variables are used, as we see in the next example.

Example 5.A.1 Ten years ago Thomas was twice as old as Patricia. Five years from now, Thomas will be 10 years older than Patricia. How old are both now?

Solution **The key to this type of problem is the choice of the variables.** We will use P_N for Patricia's age now and T_N for Thomas's age now. Then

$$P_N + 5 = \text{Patricia's age 5 years from now}$$

$$P_N - 10 = \text{Patricia's age 10 years ago}$$

$$T_N + 5 = \text{Thomas's age 5 years from now}$$

$$T_N - 10 = \text{Thomas's age 10 years ago}$$

The first statement was about their ages 10 years ago:

$$(a) \quad T_N - 10 = 2(P_N - 10)$$

The second statement was about their ages 5 years from now:

$$(b) \quad (T_N + 5) - 10 = P_N + 5$$

We simplify the equations and use elimination to solve.

$$\begin{array}{llllll} (a) & T_N - 2P_N = -10 & \longrightarrow & (-1) & \longrightarrow & -T_N + 2P_N = 10 \\ (b) & T_N - P_N = 10 & \longrightarrow & (1) & \longrightarrow & T_N - \ \ P_N = 10 \\ \hline & & & & & \mathbf{P_N = 20} \end{array}$$

If we substitute 20 for P_N in either equation (*a*) or (*b*), we find that the age of Thomas now is **30**.

5.B Rate problems

Forty miles per hour times 2 hours (hr) equals 80 miles (mi). Forty bottles per minute times 2 minutes (min) equals 80 bottles, and 40 cars per hour times 2 hr equals 80 cars.

$$40\frac{\text{mi}}{\cancel{\text{hr}}} \times 2\,\cancel{\text{hr}} = 80\text{ mi} \qquad 40\frac{\text{bottles}}{\cancel{\text{min}}} \times 2\,\cancel{\text{min}} = 80\text{ bottles}$$

$$40\frac{\text{cars}}{\cancel{\text{hr}}} \times 2\,\cancel{\text{hr}} = 80\text{ cars}$$

From this, we see that rate times time does not have to equal distance; it can also equal bottles, cars, or whatever else is the numerator of the rate. Many rate problems have the form

$$R_1t_1 + R_2t_2 = \text{miles, bottles, cars, or whatever}$$

Usually, the problem is stated so that one or both of the rates can be determined. In the next example Joe Frank can wash 3 cars in 5 hr and Myrl can wash 4 cars in 3 hr. These statements allow us to determine both rates by writing the work done over the time.

$$\text{Rate of JF} = \frac{3\text{ cars}}{5\text{ hr}} = \frac{3}{5}\frac{\text{cars}}{\text{hr}} \qquad \text{Rate of Myrl} = \frac{4\text{ cars}}{3\text{ hr}} = \frac{4}{3}\frac{\text{cars}}{\text{hr}}$$

Due to human interaction, the rate of someone working alone would not be the same as that person's rate when he or she works with another person. In these problems, however, we will assume that there is no interaction and that the rates do not change.

Example 5.B.1 Joe Frank can wash 3 cars in 5 hr and Myrl can wash 4 cars in 3 hr. Fifteen cars need to be washed. If Joe Frank works for 2 hr and is then joined by Myrl, how long will Myrl and Joe Frank have to work together to finish washing the 15 cars?

Solution The rates for this problem were found in the preceding paragraph. Now we determine how much Joe Frank accomplished in the 2 hr that he worked alone.

$$\frac{3\text{ cars}}{5\,\cancel{\text{hr}}} \times 2\,\cancel{\text{hr}} = \frac{6}{5}\text{ cars}$$

The total job was 15 cars, so now they have only $13\frac{4}{5}$ cars left to wash. We will use the following equation:

$$R_JT_J + R_MT_M = 13\frac{4}{5}$$

We replace R_J and R_M with the proper rates. Since the times are the same, we can remove the subscripts on the times.

$$\frac{3}{5}T + \frac{4}{3}T = \frac{69}{5}$$

We finish by multiplying every term by 15 and then solving.

$$(15)\frac{3}{5}T + (15)\frac{4}{3}T = (15)\frac{69}{5} \qquad \text{multiplied}$$

$$9T + 20T = 207 \qquad \text{simplified}$$

$$\boldsymbol{T = \frac{207}{29}\ \text{hr}} \qquad \text{solved}$$

Example 5.B.2 Mayha could empty 2 bottles in 3 hr. Working with Wilbur, she found they could empty 4 bottles in 3 hr. What was Wilbur's rate of emptying bottles?

Solution The total work equals the sum of the products of rates and times. The rates are in bottles per hour, and bottles per hour times hours equals bottles. Thus the work unit is bottles:

$$R_M T_M + R_W T_W = \text{bottles}$$

We know that Mayha's rate was two-thirds of a bottle per hour and that the time for each of them was 3 hr. Since the work done was 4 bottles, we can write

$$\frac{2}{3}(3) + R_W(3) = 4 \qquad \text{substituted}$$

$$3R_W = 2 \qquad \text{simplified}$$

$$R_W = \frac{2}{3} \qquad \text{solved}$$

In this problem, the unit of work is bottles and the unit of time is hours, so the units of the rate is bottles per hour

$$\boldsymbol{R_W = \frac{2}{3}\ \frac{\text{bottle}}{\text{hr}}}$$

Example 5.B.3 If 5 workers can do 1 job in 8 days, how many workers would it take to do 3 jobs in 7 days?

Solution This problem is a two-part rate problem, and the rate is in jobs per worker-day.

$$\text{Rate} = \frac{1\ \text{job}}{(5\ \text{workers})(8\ \text{days})} = \frac{1}{40}\ \frac{\text{job}}{\text{worker-day}}$$

When the rate is in two parts, there are four variables in the problem instead of three.

$$\text{Rate} \times \text{workers} \times \text{time} = \text{jobs}$$

We want to solve for workers, so we divide both sides by rate and by time and get

$$\text{Workers} = \frac{\text{jobs}}{\text{rate} \times \text{time}}$$

We finish by substituting:

$$\text{Workers} = \frac{3\ \text{jobs}}{\dfrac{1}{40}\ \dfrac{\text{job}}{\text{worker-day}} \times 7\ \text{days}} = \boldsymbol{17\frac{1}{7}\ \text{workers}}$$

Since the use of a fractional number of workers is impossible, it would be necessary to use 18 workers to ensure that the 3 jobs would be completed in 7 days. Nonetheless, the answer to the problem as stated is $17\frac{1}{7}$ workers.

Example 5.B.4 Mary had 252 gallons (gal) of milk. This would feed 42 infants for 12 days. Then 14 more infants were placed in the nursery and 48 more gallons were provided. How long would the milk last now?

Solution The rate for this problem is milk per infant-day, and the equation is

$$\text{Rate} = \frac{252 \text{ gal}}{42 \times 12 \text{ infant-days}} = \frac{1}{2}\frac{\text{gal}}{\text{infant-day}}$$

and the equation is

$$\text{Rate} \times \text{infants} \times \text{days} = \text{gallons}$$

We want to solve for days, so

$$\text{Days} = \frac{\text{gallons}}{\text{rate} \times \text{infants}} = \frac{(252 + 48) \text{ gal}}{\frac{1}{2}\frac{\text{gal}}{\text{infant-day}} \times 56 \text{ infants}} = 10\frac{5}{7} \text{ days}$$

Problem set 5

1. Five years ago, Orville was twice as old as Wilbur. Five years from now, Orville will be $1\frac{1}{2}$ times as old as Wilbur. How old are both now?

2. Peter can dig 2 holes in 3 hours and Thomas can dig 3 holes in 2 hours. Six holes need to be dug. If Peter digs for 1 hour and then is joined by Thomas, how long will they work together to finish digging the 6 holes?

3. Sandra could build 3 sandcastles in 5 hours. Working with Frederick, she discovered they could build 3 sandcastles in merely 3 hours. What was Frederick's rate of building sandcastles?

4. Six cows can do 1 job in 9 days. How many cows would it take to do 3 jobs in 5 days?

5. The sum of the digits of a two-digit counting number is 14, and the ratio of the tens digit to the units digit is 0.75. What is the number?

6. Find the equation of the line which passes through (3, 1) and is parallel to the line which passes through (−1, 2) and (3, 4).

7. Use the calculator to evaluate: (*a*) $2.61^{5.1}$ (*b*) $2.4^{-2.1}$

8. Sketch the function $y = 2.5^x$.

9. Sketch the function $y = (\frac{1}{3})^x$.

Evaluate and simplify:

10. $\frac{\sqrt{2}}{2}\cos 45° - 2\sin 60°$

11. $\sin 60° - \cos 30°$

12. $\frac{\sqrt{3}}{2}\cos 30° + \frac{1}{2}\sin 30°$

13. $\sqrt{2}\sin 30° - 2\tan 30°$

14. Solve: $\begin{cases} x^2 + y^2 = 9 \\ 2x^2 - y^2 = 6 \end{cases}$

15. Factor: $8x^3y^6 - 27a^6b^9$

Simplify:

16. $\dfrac{\dfrac{b^2c}{x^3y} - \dfrac{6m^2}{x^2y^2}}{\dfrac{mf}{x^3} + \dfrac{h}{y^2}}$

17. $\dfrac{3s}{2 - \dfrac{6l}{m - \dfrac{q}{r}}}$

18. Solve for z: $5s = \dfrac{3k}{m}\left(\dfrac{6t}{z} - \dfrac{4k}{m}\right)$

19. Divide $x^4 - 6x^3 + 7x^2 - 5$ by $x - 2$ and check.

20. Find the equilibrant of: $-5\angle 60° + 10\angle 220°$

Simplify:

21. $\sqrt{2}\sqrt{-2}\sqrt{3}\sqrt{-3} + \sqrt{3}\sqrt{-3} - 7\sqrt{-8}\sqrt{2}$

22. $\dfrac{3 - 2\sqrt{12}}{4 + 3\sqrt{3}}$ **23.** $\dfrac{6i^5 + 4i^3 - 6i}{-3i^3 + 6i - \sqrt{-9}}$

24. Solve by completing the square: $6x^2 = -3x + 8$

25. If $ab > cb$, compare: *A.* a *B.* c

26. If $a + b > c + b$, compare: *A.* a *B.* c

Solve:

27. $\begin{cases} 2x + 2y - z = 8 \\ x - 2y + z = -2 \\ 3x + y + 3z = 1 \end{cases}$ **28.** $\begin{cases} \dfrac{1}{3}x - \dfrac{1}{4}y = 2 \\ \dfrac{1}{6}x + \dfrac{1}{2}z = \dfrac{5}{2} \\ 0.4y + 0.2z = 2 \end{cases}$

Simplify:

29. $\dfrac{a^{2z-3}(\sqrt[4]{b^4})^{4z+8}}{a^{4z+2}b^{2z-3}}$ **30.** $(3x^{1/2} - 2z^{1/4})(3x^{1/2} + 2z^{1/4})$

LESSON 6 The logarithmic form · Logarithmic equations

6.A The logarithmic form of the exponential

We remember that any positive number can be written as a positive base raised to a positive power. We will use the letter N to represent the number and will use the letter b to represent the base. **We will use the letter L to represent the logarithm, which is the exponent.**

$$N = b^L$$

We read this by saying that N equals b to the power L. We could also read this by saying that the logarithm for b to get N is L.

Logarithm for b to get N is L

We abbreviate the word ***logarithm*** with ***log***, and we write this sentence in compact form by writing

$$\log_b N = L$$

We read this as the logarithm of N to the base b equals L. Thus, we see that

$$N = b^L \qquad \text{and} \qquad \log_b N = L$$

are two ways to write the same thing. Since these equations make the same statement and since N is always positive in the exponential form, it must also be positive in the logarithmic form.

Example 6.A.1 Write $4 = 3^y$ in logarithmic form.

Solution We remember that a logarithm is the exponent, and here the exponent is y. Therefore, we begin by writing

$$\log \quad = y$$

Next we indicate the base, which in this case is 3.

$$\log_3 \quad = y$$

Now the only thing left is the number 4. We insert it and have

$$\mathbf{\log_3 4 = y}$$

Example 6.A.2 Write $\log_x 4 = m$ in exponential form.

Solution We see that x is the base and that m is the logarithm, or exponent. Thus, we can write

$$x^m$$

and since 4 is the only symbol we have not used, then what we have written equals 4. Now we have as the exponential form

$$\mathbf{x^m = 4}$$

6.B Logarithmic equations

Both these expressions give us the same information.

$$(a) \quad \log_b N = L \qquad (b) \quad b^L = N$$

Each expression contains the letters b, L, and N. If we designate values for two of these variables, we can solve the equations for the value of the third variable.

Example 6.B.1 Solve $\log_b 8 = 3$.

Solution **We solve logarithmic equations by rewriting them in exponential form.** Then we solve the exponential equation. If we rewrite this equation in exponential form, we get

$$b^3 = 8$$

Now we solve this equation by raising both sides to the $\frac{1}{3}$ power.

$$(b^3)^{1/3} = (8)^{1/3} \longrightarrow \mathbf{b = 2}$$

Example 6.B.2 Solve $\log_b 9 = -\dfrac{1}{2}$.

Solution First we write the equation in exponential form.

$$(a) \quad b^{-1/2} = 9$$

Now we solve by raising both sides to the -2 power:

$$(b^{-1/2})^{-2} = 9^{-2}$$

$$\mathbf{b = \frac{1}{81}}$$

Example 6.B.3 Solve $\log_3 \frac{1}{27} = M$.

Solution We begin by rewriting the equation in exponential form.

$$(a) \quad 3^M = \frac{1}{27}$$

This is a contrived problem and must be recognized as such to be solved without using tables of logarithms or a calculator. The trick is to write the right-hand side as 3 to some power. We remember that 27 can be written as 3^3, so we make this replacement.

$$3^M = \frac{1}{3^3} \qquad \text{replaced 27 with } 3^3$$

Now we invert the right-hand side and get

$$3^M = 3^{-3} \qquad \text{inverted}$$

and this tells us that M equals -3.

$$\mathbf{M = -3} \qquad \text{solved}$$

We say that the problem just worked was contrived because if the problem had been to solve the equation

$$3^M = \frac{1}{15}$$

we could not have found a solution without using tables of logarithms or a calculator because 15 cannot be written as a rational power of 3. Problems such as the one we have just worked provide excellent practice in changing the forms of exponential equations, but it is also helpful to remember that they have been carefully contrived so that an easy solution is possible.

Example 6.B.4 Solve $\log_{1/3} P = -2$.

Solution First we rewrite the equation in exponential form. Then we simplify

$$\left(\frac{1}{3}\right)^{-2} = P \qquad \text{exponential form}$$

$$\frac{1}{3^{-2}} = P \qquad \text{simplified}$$

$$\mathbf{9 = P} \qquad \text{solved}$$

Example 6.B.5 Solve $\log_4 8 = x$.

Solution To solve, we first rewrite the equation in exponential form.

$$4^x = 8$$

Now this contrived problem can be solved if we see that 4 can be written as 2^2, and 8 can be written as 2^3.

$$(2^2)^x = 2^3 \qquad \text{changed form}$$

$$2^{2x} = 2^3 \qquad \text{simplified}$$

$$2x = 3 \qquad \text{equated exponents}$$

$$\mathbf{x = \frac{3}{2}} \qquad \text{solved}$$

Problem set 6

1. Ten years from now Charlotte will be twice as old as Emily will be then. Five years ago Charlotte was 5 times as old as Emily was then. How old are both now?

2. The father can mow the lawn in 30 minutes. His daughter can mow the lawn in 40 minutes. The father works for 10 minutes before the daughter begins to help. How long do they work together to complete the job?

3. The larder contained 360 pounds of food. This would feed the 20 men for 10 days. Then 5 more men staggered into camp. Now how many days would the food supply last?

4. Sarah's speed was 20 mph less than that of Randy. Thus, Randy could travel 325 miles in half the time it took Sarah to travel 450 miles. Find the speeds and times of both.

5. The pressure of a perfect gas was held constant at 450 millimeters of mercury. The volume was 400 liters and the temperature was 1000 kelvins (K). What was the volume when the temperature was increased to 2000 K? *Note:* $\frac{P_1V_1}{T_1} = \frac{P_2V_2}{T_2}$.

6. Sketch the function $y = (3.5)^x$.

Evaluate and simplify:

7. $\frac{\sqrt{3}}{2}\cos 45° - \frac{\sqrt{2}}{2}\sin 60°$

8. $\frac{\sqrt{2}}{2}\tan 45° - \sqrt{3}\tan 30°$

9. $\frac{\sin 60°}{\cos 60°} - \tan 60°$

10. $2\sin 30°\cos 30° - \sin 60°$

11. Write $\log_k 7 = p$ in exponential form.

12. Write $k^p = 7$ in logarithmic form.

Solve:

13. $\log_b 27 = 3$

14. $\log_2 \frac{1}{8} = m$

15. $\log_{1/2} x = -4$

16. Solve: $\begin{cases} 2x^2 - y^2 = 1 \\ y + 2x = 1 \end{cases}$

17. Factor: $64x^{12}y^6 - 27a^6b^9$

18. Simplify: $\dfrac{\dfrac{cd^2}{x^2y^3} - \dfrac{6m^2}{x^2y}}{\dfrac{mf}{xy^2} + \dfrac{h}{y^3}}$

19. Solve for t: $3s = \frac{1}{3p}\left(\frac{6z}{t} - \frac{6q}{r}\right)$

20. Find the equilibrant of: $-4\underline{/130°} - 6\underline{/-220°}$

Simplify:

21. $\sqrt{3}\sqrt{-3}\sqrt{-6}\sqrt{2} + \sqrt{2}\sqrt{3}\sqrt{-2}\sqrt{-3} - 4i$

22. $\frac{4 - 6\sqrt{3}}{2 + 3\sqrt{3}}$

23. $\frac{6i^4 - 4i^3 + 6i}{\sqrt{-16} + 6i - 2i}$

24. Solve by completing the square: $3x = 2x^2 - 8$

25. If $\frac{a}{b} > \frac{c}{b}$, compare: *A.* a *B.* c

26. If $a - b = a + b$, compare: *A.* b *B.* 1

Solve:

27. $\begin{cases} x - 2y + 2z = 4 \\ 2x - y - 2z = 8 \\ x - 2y + z = 3 \end{cases}$

28. $\begin{cases} \frac{1}{3}x + \frac{1}{4}y = 2 \\ \frac{1}{12}x + \frac{1}{3}z = \frac{11}{12} \\ 0.4y - 0.2z = 1.2 \end{cases}$

Simplify:

29. $\dfrac{x^{2a+3}(\sqrt[3]{b^{3a}})^{2a+2}}{x^{3a-2}(b^{2a})^3}$

30. $(2x^{1/3} - 3z^{1/2})(2x^{2/3} + 3z^{1/2})$

LESSON 7 Related angles · Signs of trigonometric functions

7.A Related angles

When we draw the vector $12\underline{/135°}$, we measure the angle from the positive x axis as we show in the left-hand figure.

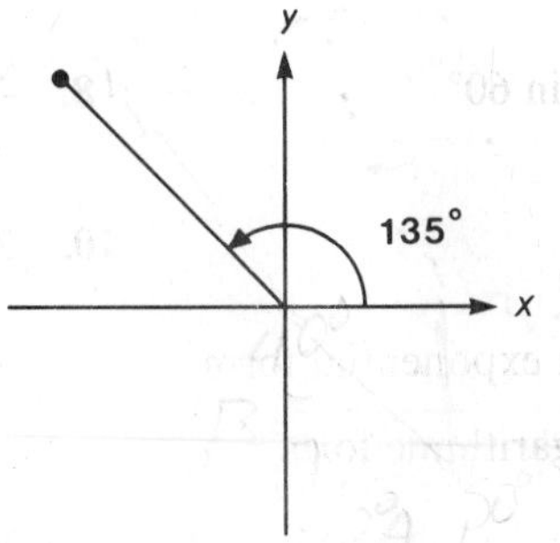

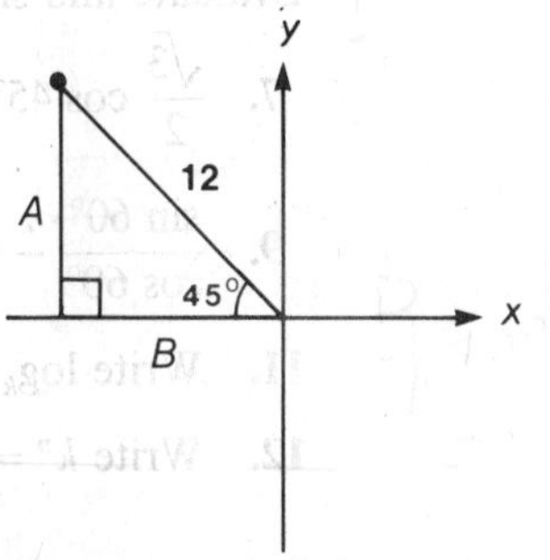

In the right-hand figure, we complete the triangle by drawing a perpendicular from the end of the vector to the x axis. We can find the rectangular coordinates of the vector by solving for A and B.

$$A = 12 \sin 45° \longrightarrow A = 12(0.707) \longrightarrow A = 8.48$$

$$B = 12 \cos 45° \longrightarrow B = 12(0.707) \longrightarrow B = 8.48$$

Thus, we have

$$12\underline{/135°} = -8.48i + 8.48j$$

In this solution, we used the angle 135° to help locate the vector. Then we used the 45° angle to solve the triangle. Many authors call the acute angle between the vector and the x axis the ***related angle.*** In this case, they would say that 45° is the related angle of 135°.

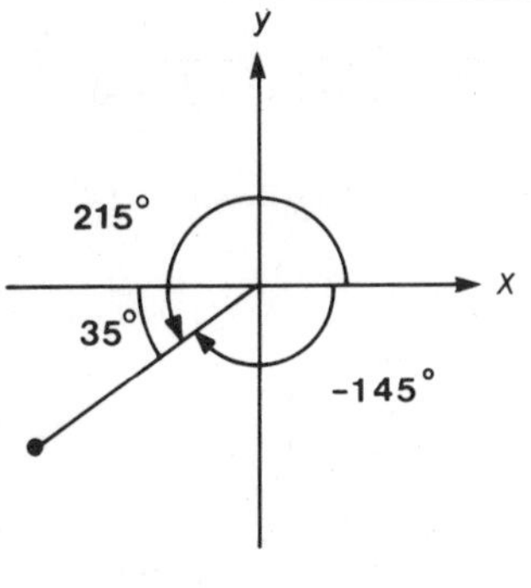

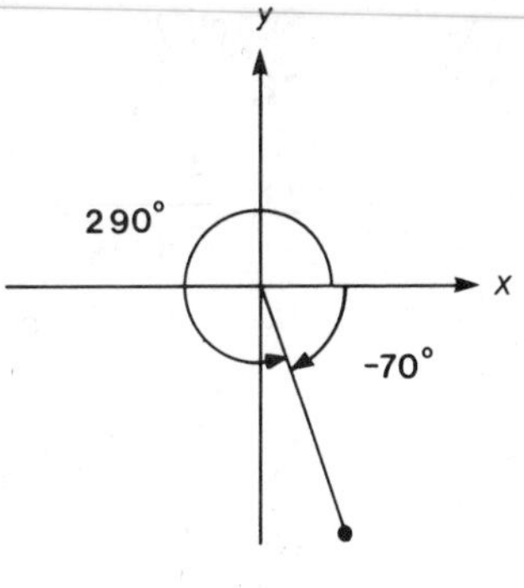

In the left-hand figure on the preceding page, we see that 35° is the related angle of both +215° and −145°. In the right-hand figure, we see that 70° is the related angle of both +290° and −70°. **The related angle is always a positive angle and is the acute angle between the vector and the x axis.**

7.B Signs of trigonometric functions

In the first example in this lesson, we had a vector whose angle was 135°. To find the rectangular components of this vector, we used the related angle, which was 45°, and drew a triangle all sides of which were considered to be positive. We used the sine of 45° and the cosine of 45° to solve this triangle. We did not use the sine of 135° or the cosine of 135°. We will always use this procedure to find the components of vectors.

To discuss trigonometric functions, however, it is necessary to define functions of angles that are not first-quadrant angles. **The absolute value of the function of any angle is the same as that of the related angle, but the sign (+ or −) of the function is determined by the quadrant in which the vector lies.** We determine the sign by considering the signs of the rectangular coordinates of the vector. **The hypotenuse is the length of the vector and is always considered to be positive.** To demonstrate, we will use points whose x coordinates are either +4 or −4 and whose y coordinates are either +3 or −3.

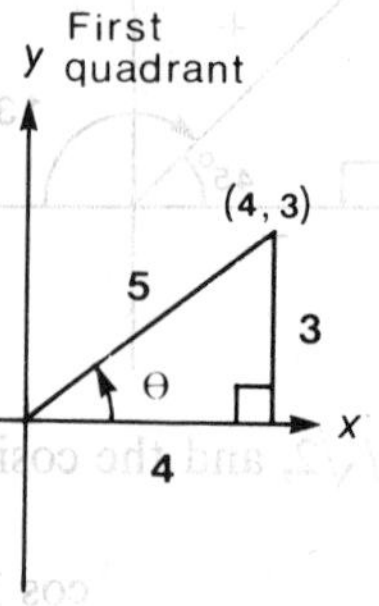

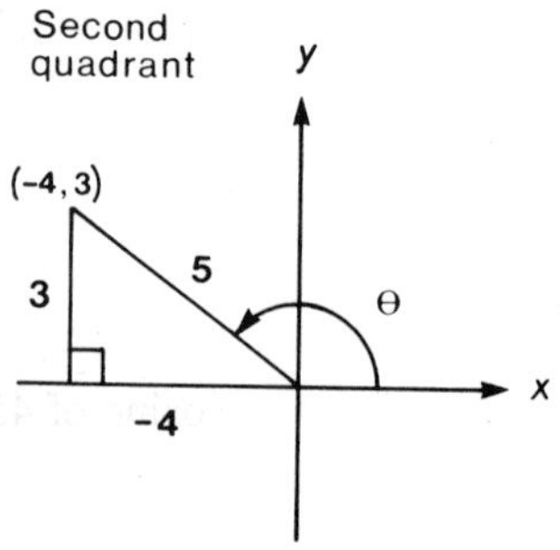

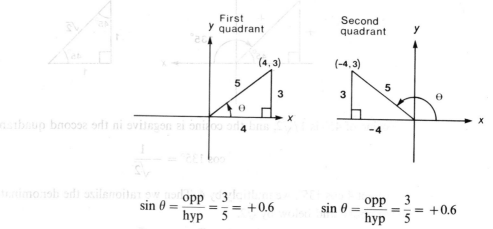

$$\sin\theta = \frac{\text{opp}}{\text{hyp}} = \frac{3}{5} = +0.6 \qquad \sin\theta = \frac{\text{opp}}{\text{hyp}} = \frac{3}{5} = +0.6$$

$$\cos\theta = \frac{\text{adj}}{\text{hyp}} = \frac{4}{5} = +0.8 \qquad \cos\theta = \frac{\text{adj}}{\text{hyp}} = \frac{-4}{5} = -0.8$$

$$\tan\theta = \frac{\text{opp}}{\text{adj}} = \frac{3}{4} = +0.75 \qquad \tan\theta = \frac{\text{opp}}{\text{adj}} = \frac{3}{-4} = -0.75$$

In the first quadrant, we see that the sine, the cosine, and the tangent are all positive. In the second quadrant, the sine is positive and the cosine and tangent are negative.

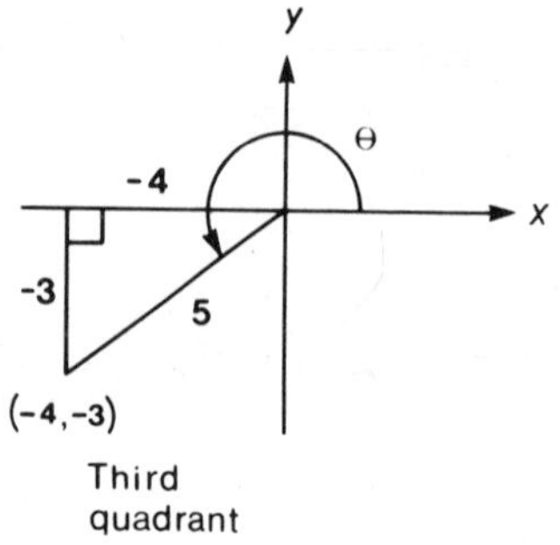

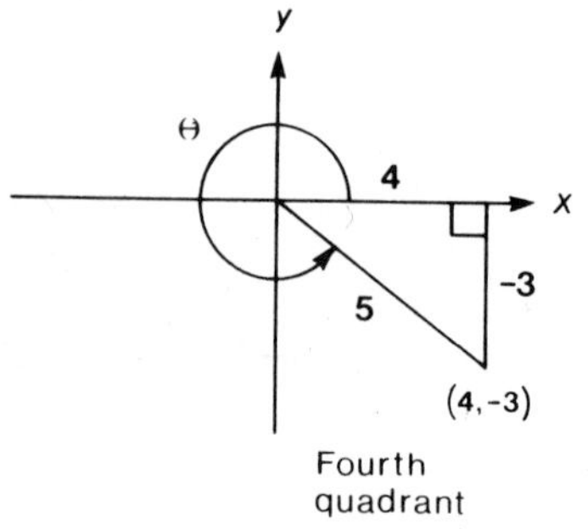

$$\sin\theta = \frac{\text{opp}}{\text{hyp}} = \frac{-3}{5} = -0.6 \qquad \sin\theta = \frac{\text{opp}}{\text{hyp}} = \frac{-3}{5} = -0.6$$

$$\cos\theta = \frac{\text{adj}}{\text{hyp}} = \frac{-4}{5} = -0.8 \qquad \cos\theta = \frac{\text{adj}}{\text{hyp}} = \frac{4}{5} = +0.8$$

$$\tan\theta = \frac{\text{opp}}{\text{adj}} = \frac{-3}{-4} = +0.75 \qquad \tan\theta = \frac{\text{opp}}{\text{adj}} = \frac{-3}{4} = -0.75$$

In the third quadrant, the tangent is positive, and both the sine and the cosine are negative. In the fourth quadrant, the cosine is positive, and both the sine and tangent are negative.

It is important to remember that the sides of a triangle are always positive lengths. We consider negative values only to determine the signs of the functions in the various quadrants.

Example 7.B.1 Evaluate 4 cos 135°.

Solution We sketch the problem and note the related angle.

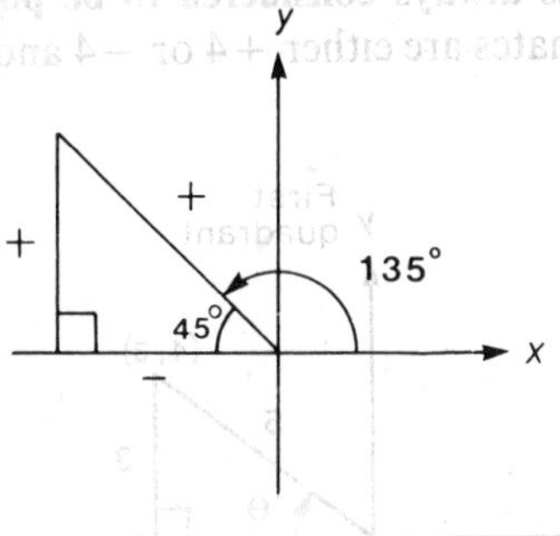

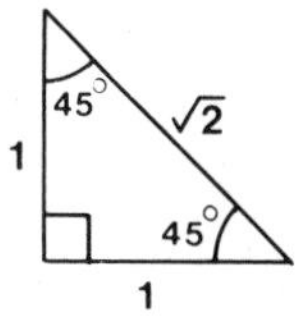

The cosine of 45° is $1/\sqrt{2}$, and the cosine is negative in the second quadrant.

$$\cos 135^\circ = -\frac{1}{\sqrt{2}}$$

Now to get 4 cos 135°, we multiply by 4. Then we rationalize the denominator by multiplying above and below by $\sqrt{2}$.

$$4\left(-\frac{1}{\sqrt{2}}\right)\left(\frac{\sqrt{2}}{\sqrt{2}}\right) = \frac{-4\sqrt{2}}{2} = \mathbf{-2\sqrt{2}}$$

Example 7.B.2 Evaluate $-2\cos(-150^\circ)$.

Solution We sketch the problem and note the related angle.

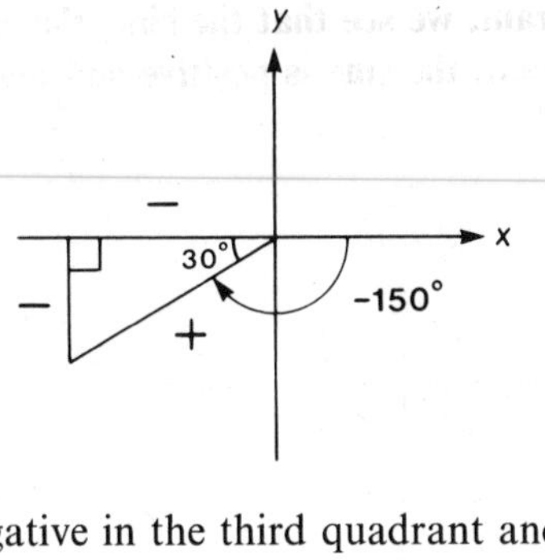

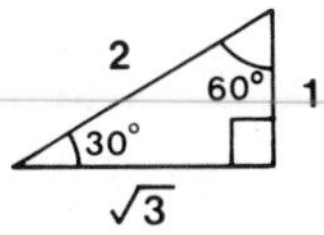

The cosine is negative in the third quadrant and the cosine of 30° is $\sqrt{3}/2$.

$$\cos(-150^\circ) = -\frac{\sqrt{3}}{2}$$

Since we want -2 times this value, we multiply by -2.

$$-2\cos(-150°) = (-2)\left(-\frac{\sqrt{3}}{2}\right) = \sqrt{3}$$

Example 7.B.3 Evaluate $\frac{5}{3}\cos 300°$.

Solution We sketch the problem and note the related angle.

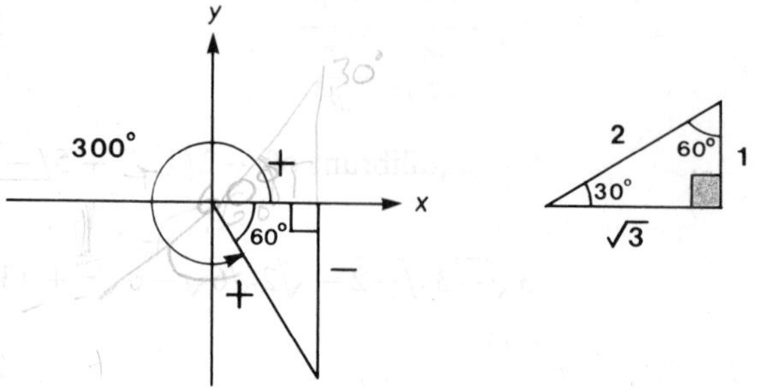

The cosine is positive in the fourth quadrant, and the cosine of 60° is $\frac{1}{2}$.

$$\cos 300° = \frac{1}{2}$$

Since we want $\frac{5}{3}\cos 300°$, we multiply by $\frac{5}{3}$:

$$\frac{5}{3}\cos 300° = \frac{5}{3}\cdot\frac{1}{2} = \mathbf{\frac{5}{6}}$$

Problem set 7

1. Next year George will be twice as old as Marshall will be then. Five years ago George was 8 times as old as Marshall was then. What are their ages now?

2. Marie can eat the entire cake in 10 minutes. Antoinette joins her after 3 minutes, and together they eat the rest of the cake in 4 minutes. How long would it have taken Antoinette to eat the entire cake alone?

3. The tugboat *Brenda Brewer* could go downstream 30 miles in 3 hours, but took 5 hours for the return trip. What was the speed of the current and what was *Brenda*'s speed in calm water?

4. Acorns varied directly as walnuts and inversely as squirrels squared. When there were 28 acorns, there were 7 walnuts and 3 squirrels. How many acorns were there when there were 4 walnuts but only 2 squirrels?

5. Matilda was dismayed when she found out that it would take 2 workers 3 days to do 6 jobs. So she hired 4 more workers. Now how many days will it take all the workers to complete 6 jobs?

6. Sketch the function $y = (\frac{1}{3})^x$.

Draw the triangles and evaluate:

7. $2\sin 135°$

8. $-2\cos(-300°)$

9. $3\cos 300° - \cos 60°$

10. $\sin(-150°) + \frac{\sqrt{3}}{2}\sin 30°$

11. Write $\log_m 8 = n$ in exponential form.

12. Write $7 = 3^k$ in logarithmic form.

Solve:

13. $\log_b 64 = 3$ **14.** $\log_3 \frac{1}{27} = n$ **15.** $\log_{1/2} y = -2$

16. Solve: $\begin{cases} x^2 + y^2 = 16 \\ y - 3x = 4 \end{cases}$ **17.** Factor: $3y^{2n+1} + 12y^{3n+2}$

18. Simplify: $\dfrac{\dfrac{ac^2}{bd^3} - \dfrac{c^3a}{b^2d}}{\dfrac{mn}{b^2d^2} - \dfrac{n}{d^3}}$ **19.** Solve for a: $2t = \dfrac{1}{25}\left(\dfrac{3z}{a} - \dfrac{k}{p}\right)$

20. Find the equilibrant of: $-2\angle 120^\circ + 5\angle -130^\circ$

Simplify:

21. $\sqrt{2}\sqrt{3}\sqrt{-3}\sqrt{-2} - \sqrt{2}\sqrt{6}\sqrt{-6}\sqrt{3} + 13i$

22. $\dfrac{3 - 3\sqrt{2}}{1 + 4\sqrt{2}}$ **23.** $\dfrac{\sqrt{-16}\,i^3 - 4i^2}{1 - \sqrt{-4}}$

24. Solve by completing the square: $4x^2 - 2x = -2$

25. If $x^2 = 9$ and $y^2 = 16$, compare: *A.* x *B.* y

26. If $x^3 = -8$ and $y^3 = -16$, compare: *A.* x *B.* y

27. Solve: $\begin{cases} \frac{1}{5}x - \frac{1}{2}y = -4 \\ 0.1x + 0.2z = 1.3 \\ y - 2z = 2 \end{cases}$

Simplify:

28. $\dfrac{x^{a+3}(\sqrt{x^3})^{a+1}}{x^{3a-2}}$ **29.** $(3x^{1/3} - 6z^{1/2})(3x^{-1/3} + 6z^{-1/2})$

30. Find the equation of the line which passes through $(2, -1)$ and is parallel to $3y - 2x + 1 = 0$.

LESSON 8 Factorial notation · Abstract rate problems

8.A Factorial notation

When we work problems in mathematical probability, it is often necessary to find the product of a number of positive integers such as

(*a*) $4 \cdot 3 \cdot 2 \cdot 1$

(*b*) $12 \cdot 11 \cdot 10 \cdot 9 \cdot 8 \cdot 7 \cdot 6 \cdot 5 \cdot 4 \cdot 3 \cdot 2 \cdot 1$

In these examples, the first factor is an integer, and each succeeding factor is the next smaller integer. This pattern continues, and the number 1 is always the last factor. Rather than write the factors out each time, mathematicians have found it convenient to write the first factor and follow it with an exclamation point. If we do this, the products above could be indicated by writing

(*a*) $4!$ (*b*) $12!$

The exclamation point is read as "factorial." Thus, expression (*a*) is read as "4 factorial" and expression (*b*) as "12 factorial."

Example 8.A.1 Evaluate 5!.

Solution We write out the indicated factors.

$$5! = 5 \cdot 4 \cdot 3 \cdot 2 \cdot 1$$

and, if we multiply, we find that

$$5! = \mathbf{120}$$

Most scientific calculators have a factorial key. Use one of these calculators to calculate 5!. Although these calculators employ scientific notation, the factorial product quickly becomes too large for a calculator to handle. What is the largest factorial your calculator can handle?

Example 8.A.2 Evaluate $\frac{9!}{3! \times 5!}$ without using a calculator.

Solution We write out the factors and simplify.

$$\frac{9 \cdot 8 \cdot 7 \cdot 6 \cdot 5 \cdot 4 \cdot 3 \cdot 2 \cdot 1}{3 \cdot 2 \cdot 1 \cdot 5 \cdot 4 \cdot 3 \cdot 2 \cdot 1}$$

We note that both the numerator and the denominator have $5 \cdot 4 \cdot 3 \cdot 2 \cdot 1$ as factors. We cancel these.

$$\frac{9 \cdot 8 \cdot 7 \cdot 6 \cdot \cancel{5 \cdot 4 \cdot 3 \cdot 2 \cdot 1}}{3 \cdot 2 \cdot 1 \cdot \cancel{5 \cdot 4 \cdot 3 \cdot 2 \cdot 1}}$$

Now the $3 \cdot 2$ below will cancel the 6 above, so we are left with

$$9 \cdot 8 \cdot 7 = \mathbf{504}$$

Example 8.A.3 Evaluate $\frac{14!}{6! \times 11!}$ without using a calculator.

Solution This time we will try a shortcut. We note that 14! can be written with 11! as a factor. Thus, we can write

$$\frac{\overset{7}{\cancel{14}} \cdot 13 \cdot \cancel{12} \cdot \cancel{11!}}{6 \cdot 5 \cdot \cancel{4} \cdot \cancel{3} \cdot \cancel{2} \cdot 1 \cdot \cancel{11!}} = \frac{7 \cdot 13}{30} = \mathbf{\frac{91}{30}}$$

Example 8.A.4 Use the factorial key on a calculator to help evaluate $49 \cdot 48 \cdot 47 \cdot 46$.

Solution There is no key on the calculator for this operation; but, if we multiply above and below by 45!, we get

$$\frac{49 \cdot 48 \cdot 47 \cdot 46 \cdot 45!}{45!} = \frac{49!}{45!}$$

and we can find 49! and 45! on the calculator

$$\frac{49!}{45!} = \frac{6.0828 \times 10^{62}}{1.1962 \times 10^{56}} = \mathbf{5.085 \times 10^6}$$

8.B Abstract rate problems

Rate problems that use letters rather than numbers can be used to enhance our understanding of fundamental concepts. In these problems, it is important to keep track of the units. The fundamental equation in distance-rate problems is rate times time equals distance. On the left, we see how the hours cancel when we multiply 60 miles per hour by 2 hours; and on the right, we see how hours cancel when we multiply m miles per hour by h hours to get a distance of mh miles.

$$\text{Rate} \times \text{time} = \text{distance} \qquad \text{Rate} \times \text{time} = \text{distance}$$

$$60\,\frac{\text{mi}}{\cancel{\text{hr}}} \times 2\,\cancel{\text{hr}} = 120 \text{ mi} \qquad m\,\frac{\text{mi}}{\cancel{\text{hr}}} \times h\,\cancel{\text{hr}} = mh \text{ mi}$$

We use the same statements to see how we handle the units when we divide distance by rate to get time.

$$\text{Time} = \frac{\text{distance}}{\text{rate}} \qquad T = \frac{\text{distance}}{\text{rate}}$$

$$\text{Time} = \frac{120 \text{ mi}}{60\,\dfrac{\text{mi}}{\text{hr}}} = 2 \text{ hr} \qquad T = \frac{mh \text{ mi}}{m\,\dfrac{\text{mi}}{\text{hr}}} = h \text{ hr}$$

Abstract rate problems are usually worked in three steps. The statement of the problem defines two of the components, which allows the third to be calculated. Then a change is made in one or two components and the value of the other is requested. We demonstrate this procedure in the next two examples.

Example 8.B.1 The train traveled m miles at p miles per hour and still got there 1 hour late. How fast should the train have traveled to get there on time?

Solution The first step is to identify the original values of rate, time, and distance.

$$\text{Distance} = m \text{ mi} \qquad \text{Rate} = p\,\frac{\text{mi}}{\text{hr}} \qquad \text{Time} = \frac{\text{distance}}{\text{rate}} = \frac{m \text{ mi}}{p\,\dfrac{\text{mi}}{\text{hr}}} = \frac{m}{p} \text{ hr}$$

To get there on time, the train will have to travel the same distance in 1 hour less. Thus, the new distance will be the same, and the new time will be the old time minus 1 hour.

$$\text{New distance} = m \text{ mi} \qquad \text{New time} = \frac{m}{p} - 1 = \frac{m-p}{p} \text{ hr}$$

To find the new rate, we divide the new distance by the new time. The new distance is the same as the old distance.

$$\text{New rate} = \frac{\text{new distance}}{\text{new time}} = \frac{m \text{ mi}}{\dfrac{m-p}{p} \text{ hr}} = \frac{\mathbf{mp}}{\mathbf{m-p}}\,\frac{\textbf{mi}}{\textbf{hr}}$$

Example 8.B.2 The boat traveled k miles in t hours and was 40 miles short of the goal when the gun went off. If the skipper tried it again, how long would it take to reach the goal if the skipper increased the rate of travel by 10 mph?

Solution The first step is to identify the rate, time, and distance of the first trip.

$$\text{Distance} = k \text{ miles} \qquad \text{Time} = t \text{ hours} \qquad \text{Rate} = \frac{\text{distance}}{\text{time}} = \frac{k}{t}\,\frac{\text{mi}}{\text{hr}}$$

In the next trip, the new distance will be $k + 40$ miles, and the rate will be 10 mph greater than the old rate.

$$\text{New distance} = k + 40 \text{ miles} \qquad \text{New rate} = \frac{k}{t} + 10 = \frac{k + 10t}{t}\,\frac{\text{mi}}{\text{hr}}$$

Now time equals distance divided by rate.

$$\text{Time} = \frac{(k + 40)\text{ mi}}{\dfrac{k + 10t}{t}\,\dfrac{\text{mi}}{\text{hr}}} = \frac{(k + 40)t}{k + 10t}\ \textbf{hours}$$

Problem set 8

1. Seven years from now, Dylan will be 3 times as old as Thomas is now. Dylan's age is twice Thomas's age now. What are their ages now?
2. James can accomplish the entire mission in 20 hours. Irwin joins James after 3 hours. Together they are able to accomplish the mission in 4 hours. How long would it take Irwin to accomplish the mission alone?
3. The bus traveled x miles at p miles per hour and still got there 2 hours late. How fast should the bus have traveled to get there on time?
4. Redig ran for T hours at R miles per hour but ended up 20 miles short of the goal. If he tried again and increased his speed by 5 miles per hour, how long would it take him to reach the goal?
5. Seven workers could do 3 jobs in 5 days. If 3 more workers were hired who worked at the same rate, how long would it take all of them to do 4 jobs?
6. Sketch the function $y = (2.5)^x$.

Draw the triangle and evaluate:

7. $3 \sin 210°$
8. $-2 \sin(-300°)$
9. $2 \cos(-330°) + \sin 60°$
10. $\cos(-150°) + \sqrt{2} \sin 30°$
11. Write $9 = 2^k$ in logarithmic form.

Solve:

12. $\log_c 27 = 3$
13. $\log_2 \frac{1}{16} = m$
14. $\log_{1/4} z = -2$
15. Evaluate $\frac{8!}{2!4!}$ (no calculator).
16. Evaluate $\frac{9!}{3!3!}$ (no calculator).
17. Solve: $\begin{cases} x^2 + y^2 = 4 \\ x^2 - y^2 = 4 \end{cases}$
18. Factor: $4a^{3m+2} - 16a^{3m}$
19. Simplify: $\dfrac{\dfrac{x^2y}{ca^3} - \dfrac{y^3z}{a^2}}{\dfrac{s^2t}{a^2} - \dfrac{r^2z}{a^3c}}$
20. Solve for h: $3z = -\frac{2}{c}\left(\frac{5d}{h} - 2k\right)$
21. Find the equilibrant of: $-3\underline{/200°} - 6\underline{/-140°}$

Simplify:

22. $\dfrac{\sqrt{2}\sqrt{-3}\sqrt{6} + \sqrt{-16} + \sqrt{5}\sqrt{-5}}{1 + \sqrt{-4}\,i^4}$
23. $\dfrac{4 - 3\sqrt{2}}{2 - 2\sqrt{2}}$

24. Solve by completing the square: $5x^2 + 3x + 6 = 0$

25. If $x + y = 7$ and $x - y = 5$, compare: *A.* x *B.* y

26. If $x^2 + y^2 = 25$ and $x = 3$, compare: *A.* y *B.* 0

27. Solve: $\begin{cases} \frac{1}{3}x - \frac{1}{5}z = 1 \\ 0.1x + 0.2y = 1 \\ 2y - z = -1 \end{cases}$

Simplify:

28. $\dfrac{y^{a+2}(\sqrt{y^4})^{2a-1}}{y^{3a+2}}$

29. $(2a^{3/2} - 3b^{-1/2})(4a^{-3/2} + 2b^{3/2})$

30. Divide $x^4 - 3x^3 + 2x - 6$ by $x - 1$ and check.

LESSON 9 Inverse trigonometric functions

9.A Inverse trigonometric functions

The words ***arcsin, arccos,*** and ***arctan*** mean "the angle whose sine is," "the angle whose cosine is," and "the angle whose tangent is," respectively. The notation

$$\arcsin \frac{1}{2} = ?$$

asks for the angle whose sine is $\frac{1}{2}$. There are many angles whose sine is $\frac{1}{2}$, such as 30°, 150°, 390°, 510°, etc. **It is sometimes convenient to have only one answer for the arcsin, and we can do this if we consider only angles in the first and fourth quadrants, for every positive value of the sine is associated with some first-quadrant angle, and every negative value of the sine is associated with some fourth-quadrant angle.**

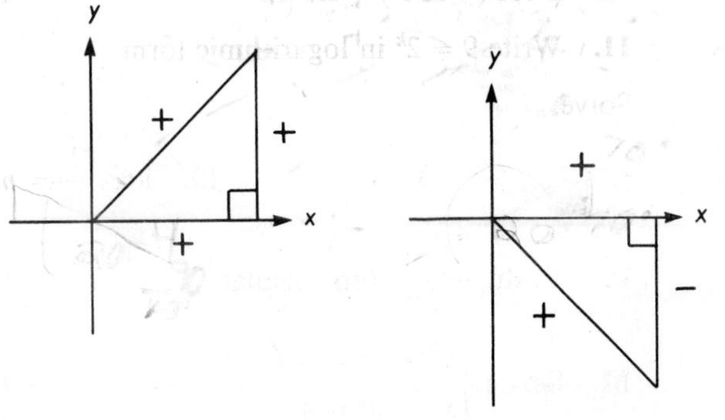

In this book, we will use a lowercase a in arcsin if we are considering multiple angles,

$$\arcsin \frac{1}{2} = 30°, 150°, 390°, 510°, \text{etc.}$$

and a capital A in Arcsin if we are considering only the single angle between 90° and −90° whose sine is the number stated.

$$\text{Arcsin} \frac{1}{2} = 30°$$

The domain for the Arcsin is from -1 to $+1$ and the range is from $-90°$ to $+90°$.

Since there is only one angle for every domain value of the Arcsin, the Arcsin is a function. **We find that every positive and negative value of the tangent is also associated with either a first-quadrant angle or a fourth-quadrant angle, so we also restrict the Arctan to these same two quadrants.** The domain for the Arctan is the real numbers and the range is from $-90°$ to $+90°$.

We cannot use angles in the first and fourth quadrants as the range for the Arccos because the cosine is positive in both these quadrants and we must also provide for negative values of the cosine. Thus we restrict the Arccos to the first and the second quadrants.

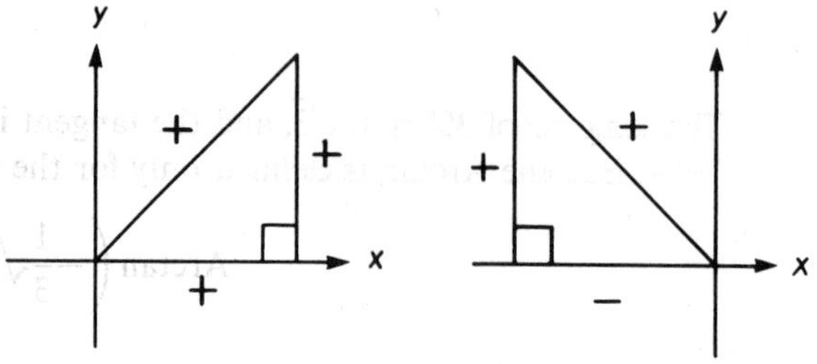

The first quadrant contains all the positive values of the cosine, and the second quadrant contains all the negative values of the cosine. The domain for the Arccos is from -1 to $+1$ and the range is from 0° to 180°.

Example 9.A.1 Evaluate Arcsin $\frac{\sqrt{2}}{2}$.

Solution We are asked to find the first- or fourth-quadrant angle whose sine is the positive number given. We begin by changing the form of the number by multiplying above and below by $\sqrt{2}$.

$$\frac{\sqrt{2}}{2} \cdot \frac{\sqrt{2}}{\sqrt{2}} = \frac{2}{2\sqrt{2}} = \frac{1}{\sqrt{2}}$$

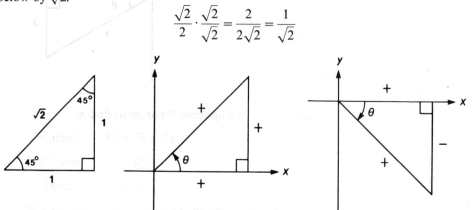

The only angle between $-90°$ and 90° whose sine is $1/\sqrt{2}$ is 45°, so

$$\text{Arcsin}\,\frac{\sqrt{2}}{2} = \mathbf{45°}$$

Example 9.A.2 Evaluate Arctan $(-\frac{1}{3}\sqrt{3})$.

Solution Again we are asked to find a first- or fourth-quadrant angle. We can change the form of the number to a more familiar form if we multiply above and below by $\sqrt{3}$.

$$-\frac{1}{3}\sqrt{3} \cdot \frac{\sqrt{3}}{\sqrt{3}} = \frac{-3}{3\sqrt{3}} = -\frac{1}{\sqrt{3}}$$

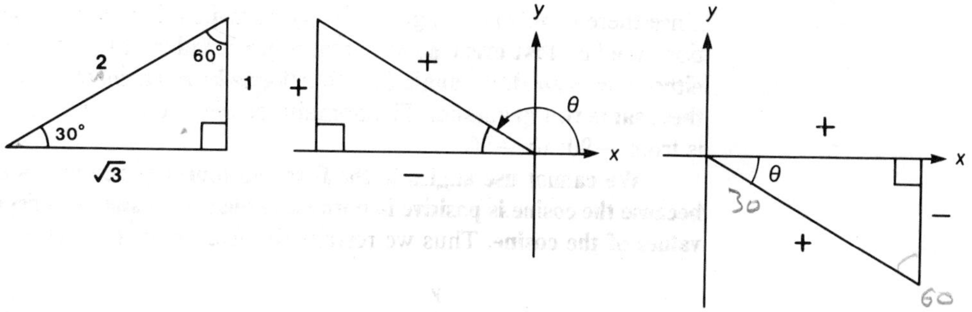

The tangent of 30° is $1/\sqrt{3}$, and the tangent is negative in the second and fourth quadrants. But the Arctan is defined only for the fourth quadrant, so the answer is

$$\text{Arctan}\left(-\frac{1}{3}\sqrt{3}\right) = -30°$$

Example 9.A.3 Evaluate $\cos\left[\text{Arctan}\left(-\frac{3}{5}\right)\right]$.

Solution We are asked to find the cosine of the first- or fourth-quadrant angle whose tangent is $-3/5$. The tangents of fourth-quadrant angles are negative, so this angle is in the fourth quadrant.

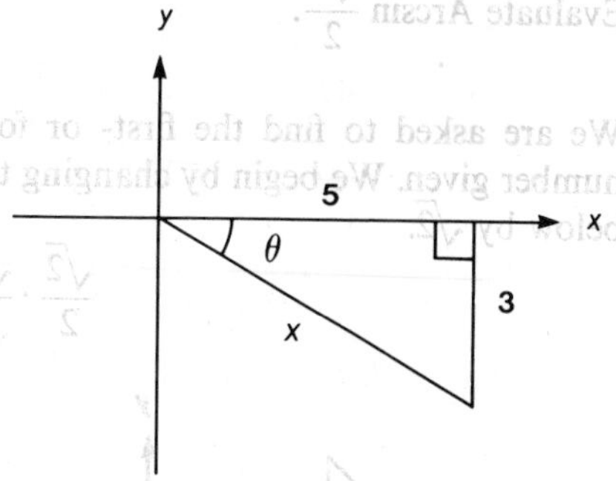

We can use the Pythagorean theorem to find x.

$$x^2 = 5^2 + 3^2 \qquad \text{theorem}$$

$$x^2 = 34 \qquad \text{simplified}$$

$$x = \sqrt{34} \qquad \text{solved}$$

Now we see that the cosine of θ is $5/\sqrt{34}$ so we can write

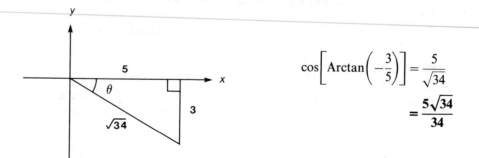

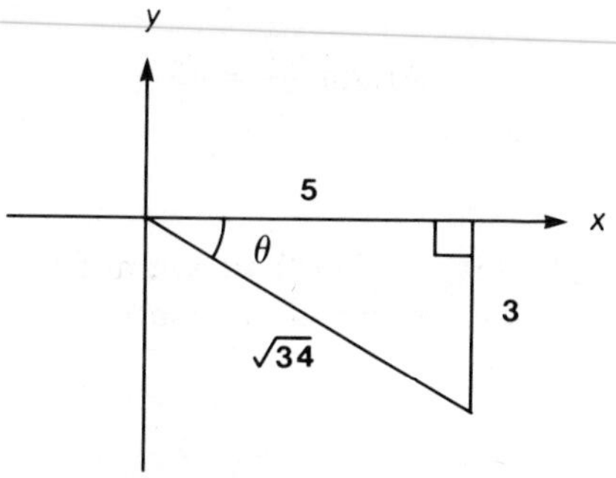

$$\cos\left[\text{Arctan}\left(-\frac{3}{5}\right)\right] = \frac{5}{\sqrt{34}}$$

$$= \frac{5\sqrt{34}}{34}$$

Example 9.A.4 Evaluate $\sin(\text{Arccos } \frac{2}{3})$.

Solution We are asked to find the sine of the first- or second-quadrant angle whose cosine is $\frac{2}{3}$. We have enough information to draw the triangle.

Now we use the Pythagorean theorem to find x.

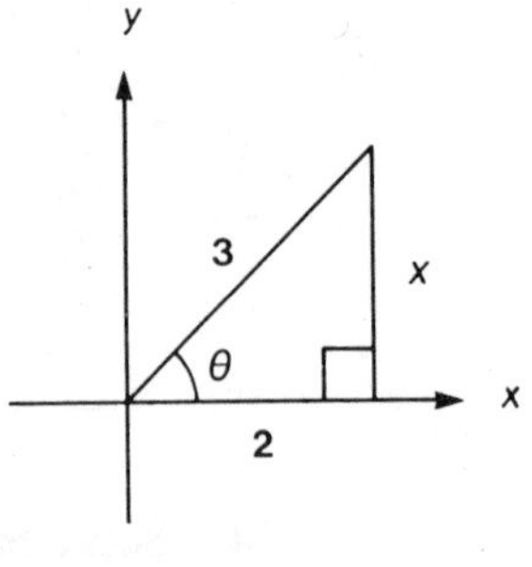

$$3^2 = 2^2 + x^2 \quad \text{theorem}$$
$$5 = x^2 \quad \text{simplified}$$
$$\sqrt{5} = x \quad \text{solved}$$

This means that the sine of θ is $\sqrt{5}/3$, so we have

$$\sin\left(\text{Arccos } \frac{2}{3}\right) = \frac{\sqrt{5}}{3}$$

Problem set 9

1. Ophelia is four-fifths as old as Laertes. Ten years ago, Ophelia was three-fifths as old as Laertes was then. How old will each be 20 years from now?
2. The taskmaster can perform the task in 40 minutes. The apprentice can perform the task in 1 hour. How long will it take both to perform 5 tasks working together if the taskmaster works 1 hour before the apprentice joins in?
3. Mac traveled x miles at p miles per hour and got there 2 hours late. If the distance were increased by 10 miles, how fast would he have to travel to get there on time?
4. Thirty workers could do 6 jobs in 4 days. How many days would it take 20 workers to do 4 jobs?
5. A builder needs many boards $5\frac{1}{2}$ ft long. Boards of this type are sold in multiples of 2 ft from 6 to 24 ft. The builder has a saw. For minimum waste, the boards should be ordered in what lengths?
6. Sketch the function $y = \left(\frac{1}{4}\right)^x$.
7. Evaluate: $\text{Arcsin } \frac{\sqrt{3}}{2}$
8. Evaluate: $\sin\left[\text{Arccos}\left(-\frac{1}{2}\right)\right]$
9. Evaluate: $\cos\left(\text{Arctan } \frac{4}{5}\right)$

Draw the necessary triangle(s) and evaluate:

10. $2 \sin(-300°) + \cos 135°$
11. $-2\sqrt{2} \tan 45° - \sin 45° \cos 45°$

Solve:

12. $\log_a 36 = 2$
13. $\log_3 \frac{1}{81} = n$
14. $\log_{1/3} p = -4$

Evaluate:

15. $\frac{9!}{4!5!}$
16. $\frac{10!}{4!6!}$
17. Solve: $\begin{cases} y^2 - x^2 = 4 \\ y + 3x = 2 \end{cases}$
18. Factor: $16b^{4n+3} + 6b^{4n+2}$

19. Simplify: $\dfrac{2}{6b + \dfrac{3t}{1 + \dfrac{3}{x}}}$

20. Solve for g: $s = \dfrac{5d}{h}\left(\dfrac{1}{2}ag^2 - 2\right)$

21. Find the equilibrant of: $-2\underline{/120^\circ} + 6\underline{/-130^\circ}$

Simplify:

22. $\dfrac{\sqrt{3}\sqrt{-3}\sqrt{2}\sqrt{-2} - \sqrt{-16} + \sqrt{-5}\sqrt{5}}{1 - \sqrt{-16}\,i^2}$

23. $\dfrac{6 - 4\sqrt{3}}{12 - \sqrt{3}}$

24. Solve by completing the square: $6x^2 - 2x + 1 = 0$

25. If $ab = 10$, compare: *A.* a *B.* b

26. If $a > 1$, compare: *A.* a *B.* $\dfrac{1}{a}$

27. Solve: $\begin{cases} \dfrac{1}{4}a - \dfrac{1}{8}b = \dfrac{1}{2} \\ 0.1a + 0.2c = 1 \\ b - 3c = 2 \end{cases}$

28. Simplify: $\dfrac{z^{3+b}(\sqrt{z^3})^{b+1}}{z^b}$

29. Factor: $8x^3y^6 - 27a^3b^9$

30. Find the equation of the line which passes through (1, 2) and is perpendicular to $2y - 4x = 6$.

LESSON 10 Very large and very small fractions · Quadrantal angles

10.A Very large and very small fractions

If the denominator of a fraction is fixed, the value of the fraction is determined by the value of the numerator. The value of fraction (*a*) is 0.002. Fraction (*b*) has the same denominator but has a smaller numerator, so the value of the fraction is the smaller number 0.000002.

$$(a)\ \frac{0.008}{4} = 0.002 \qquad (b)\ \frac{0.000008}{4} = 0.000002$$

If we make the numerator smaller and smaller, the value of the fraction will be smaller and smaller and will get closer and closer to zero. **We say that the value of the fraction**

$$\frac{x}{4}$$

approaches zero as a limit as the value of x gets closer and closer to zero.

If the value of the numerator is fixed, the value of the fraction is determined by the value of the denominator. The value of fraction (*c*) is 500. Fraction (*d*) has the same numerator but has a smaller denominator, and the value of this fraction is 500,000.

$$(c)\ \frac{4}{0.008} = 500 \qquad (d)\ \frac{4}{0.000008} = 500{,}000$$

If we make the denominator smaller and smaller, the value of the fraction will get greater and greater. **We say that the value of the fraction (if x is a positive number)**

$$\frac{4}{x}$$

approaches positive infinity as the value of x gets closer and closer to zero. Of course, if x is a negative number, the fraction gets very large negatively as x gets smaller and smaller. We say that the value of the fraction approaches negative infinity as x approaches zero. When we say that a number approaches positive or negative infinity, we mean that the absolute value of the number gets greater and greater and that the sign of this number is positive or negative, respectively. It is important to realize that there is no particular number that has a value of positive infinity or negative infinity. In the fraction above, we can let the denominator get smaller and smaller and closer to zero, but the denominator can never be equal to zero because division by zero is not defined.

10.B Quadrantal angles

The values of the trigonometric functions of 0°, 90°, 180°, and 270° are sometimes difficult to remember. We can determine the values of these functions if we draw right triangles that have one very small angle. For 0° we can draw the triangle in either the first or the fourth quadrant. We arbitrarily assign a length of 4 to the hypotenuse.

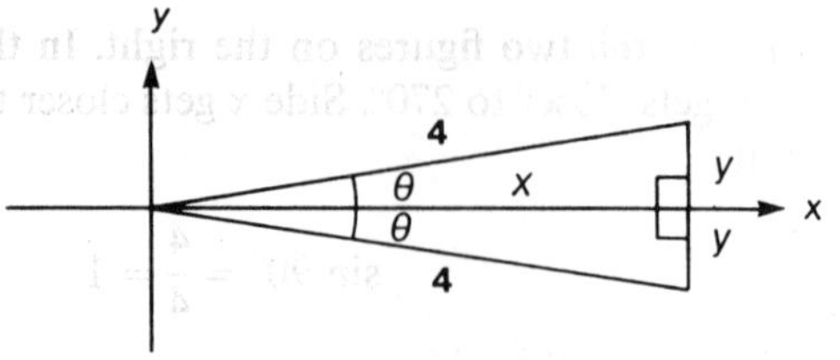

The values of the three functions of the angle θ are:

$$\sin\theta = \frac{y}{4} \qquad \cos\theta = \frac{x}{4} \qquad \tan\theta = \frac{+y}{+x}$$

Now, if we let angle θ get smaller and smaller, we see that the length of side x will get closer and closer to 4 and that the length of side y will get closer and closer to zero. Thus, the values of $\sin\theta$, $\cos\theta$, and $\tan\theta$ get closer and closer to the values shown here.

$$\sin\theta = \frac{0}{4} \qquad \cos\theta = \frac{4}{4} \qquad \tan\theta = \frac{0}{4}$$

Thus,

$$\sin 0° = 0 \qquad \cos 0° = +1 \qquad \tan 0° = 0$$

Now, if we draw small triangles in the second and third quadrants,

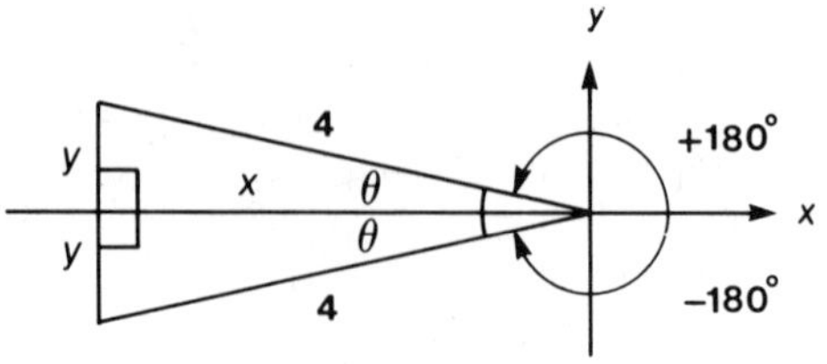

we see that as the angles θ get closer to zero, the lengths of the sides labeled y get closer to zero and the length of side x gets closer and closer to 4. Thus,

$$\sin 180° = \frac{0}{4} = 0 \qquad \cos 180° = \frac{-4}{+4} = -1 \qquad \tan 180° = \frac{0}{-4} = 0$$

To find the values of the trigonometric functions of 90°, we will use the two figures on the left below. As the small angles get closer to 0°, θ gets closer to 90°. Side x then approaches 0 and side y approaches 4. To find the trigonometric functions of 270°, we

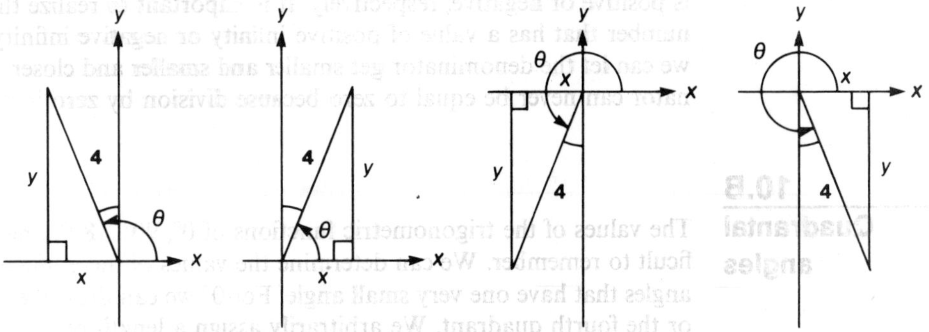

will use the two figures on the right. In these figures, as the small angles get closer to 0°, θ gets closer to 270°. Side x gets closer to 0 and side y gets closer to -4. Thus we can write

$$\sin 90° = \frac{4}{4} = 1 \qquad \cos 90° = \frac{0}{4} = 0$$

$$\sin 270° = \frac{-4}{4} = -1 \qquad \cos 270° = \frac{0}{4} = 0$$

The tangents of 90° and 270° are undefined because their definitions require division by zero, an operation that is undefined. In each of the figures we see that side x approaches 0 as θ gets closer and closer to 90° or 270°, and side y approaches either $+4$ or -4. Thus we get

$$\tan 90° = \frac{\pm 4}{0} \qquad \tan 270° = \frac{\pm 4}{0}$$

Neither of these expressions can be evaluated because we cannot divide by zero.

Example 10.B.1 Draw the triangle and find (*a*) $\sin 180°$ and (*b*) $\cos 180°$.

Solution We draw a small triangle either above or below the negative x axis.

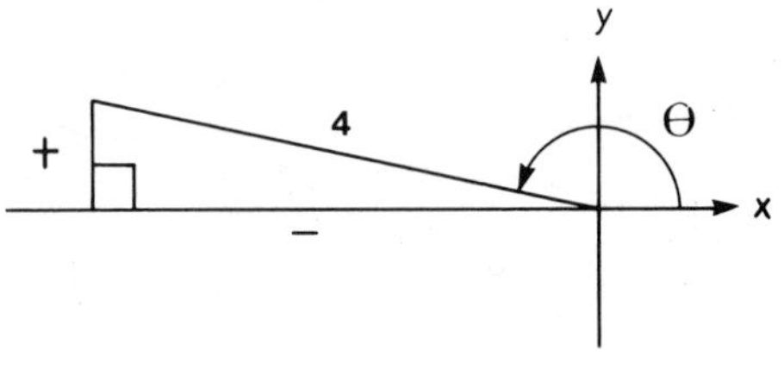

(*a*) $\sin 180° = \frac{0}{4} = \mathbf{0}$

(*b*) $\cos 180° = \frac{-4}{4} = \mathbf{-1}$

Example 10.B.2 Draw the triangle and find (*a*) $4 \sin 270°$ and (*b*) $3 \tan 270°$.

Solution We draw a small triangle near the 270° vector and find the values of the functions.

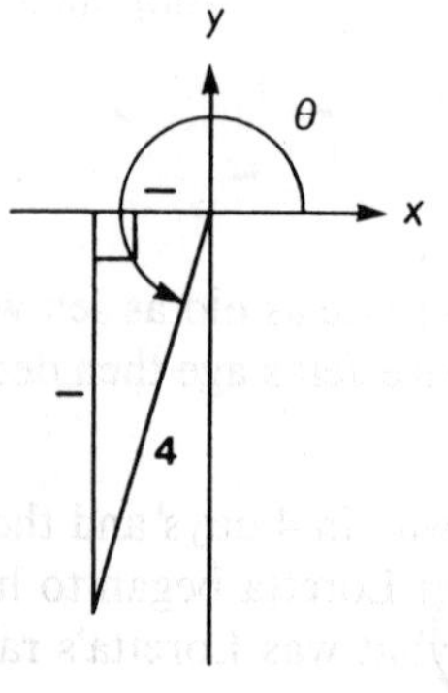

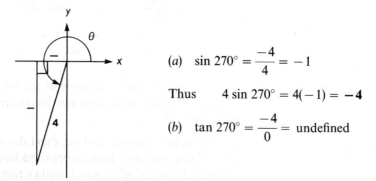

(*a*) $\sin 270° = \dfrac{-4}{4} = -1$

Thus $4 \sin 270° = 4(-1) = \mathbf{-4}$

(*b*) $\tan 270° = \dfrac{-4}{0} =$ undefined

Since tan 270° is undefined, **3 tan 270° is undefined,** and the expression cannot be evaluated.

Example 10.B.3 Draw the triangle and find $3\sqrt{2} \sin 90°$.

Solution We draw the triangle near the 90° vector.

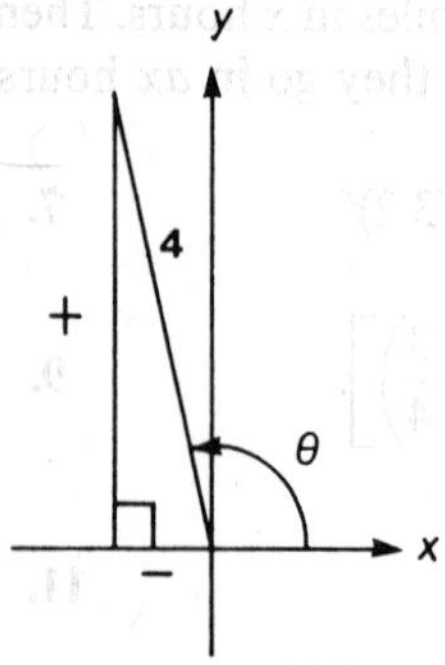

$\sin 90° = \dfrac{4}{4} = 1$

Thus $3\sqrt{2} \sin 90° = 3\sqrt{2}\,(1)$

$= \mathbf{3\sqrt{2}}$

Example 10.B.4 Evaluate $\sin(-135°) + 3\sqrt{2} \cos 180°$.

Solution We use diagrams as necessary.

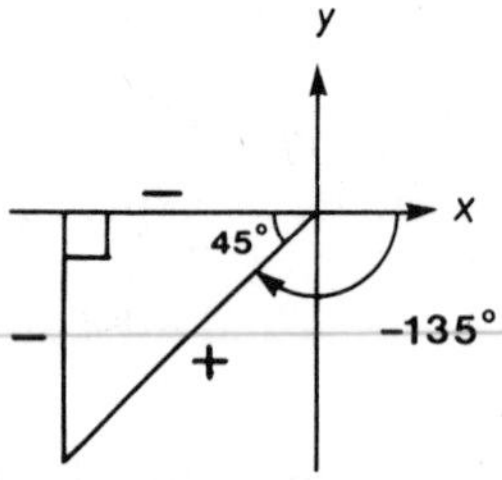

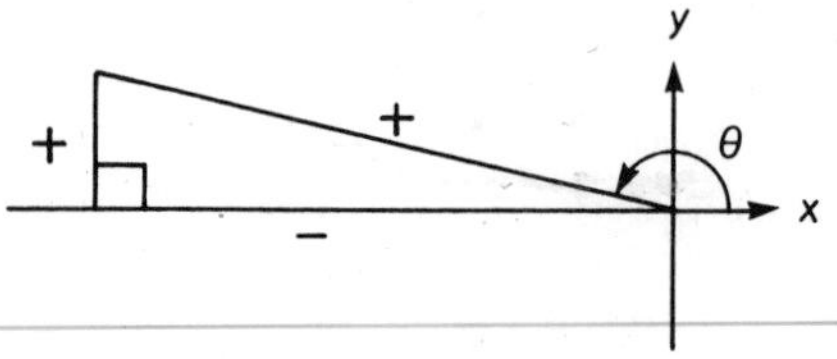

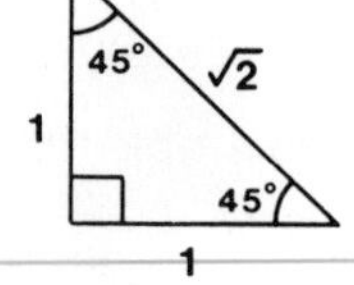

We see that $\sin(-135°) = -\sin 45° = -1/\sqrt{2}$, and that $\cos 180° = -1$. So we have

$$-\frac{1}{\sqrt{2}} + 3\sqrt{2}(-1) \qquad \text{sum of functions}$$

$$= -\frac{\sqrt{2}}{2} - \frac{6\sqrt{2}}{2} \qquad \text{common denominator}$$

$$= \frac{-\sqrt{2} - 6\sqrt{2}}{2} \qquad \text{added}$$

$$= \frac{-7\sqrt{2}}{2} \qquad \text{simplified}$$

Problem set 10

1. Ten years ago Odessa was twice as old as Jeff was then. Ten years from now, twice Odessa's age will equal thrice Jeff's age then decreased by 10. How old will each be 45 years from now?

2. Dennis could build 1 henway in 4 days and the order was for 10 henways. Dennis worked for 1 day and then Loretta began to help. If they worked together for 13 days to finish the order, what was Loretta's rate in henways per day?

3. Aristotle's boat could travel 30 miles downstream in 3 hours but required 5 hours to travel the same distance upstream. What was the speed of the boat in still water and what was the speed of the current?

4. The women all pitched in to do the 10 jobs, and it took 20 women 6 days to do the work. The next time 10 more women volunteered their help. How long would it take the 30 women to complete 20 jobs?

5. Fox and Bob traveled g miles in x hours. Then they increased their speed by p miles per hour. How far could they go in ax hours at the new rate?

6. Sketch the function $y = (3.2)^x$.

7. Evaluate $\text{Arccos}\ \frac{1}{2}$.

8. Evaluate $\cos\left[\text{Arcsin}\left(-\frac{3}{4}\right)\right]$.

9. Evaluate $\tan\left(\text{Arctan}\ \frac{\sqrt{2}}{2}\right)$.

Evaluate:

10. $3\cos(-300°) + \sin 180°$

11. $2\sin 30° \cos 30° - \sin 60° + \cos 90°$

12. $2\sin 180° - 3\cos 90° + \cos 270°$

Solve:

13. $\log_b 49 = 2$

14. $\log_5 \frac{1}{125} = c$

15. $\log_{1/4} k = -3$

Evaluate:

16. $\frac{8!}{2!2!}$

17. $\frac{15!}{8!5!}$

18. Solve: $\begin{cases} x^2 - y^2 = 8 \\ 2x^2 + y^2 = 19 \end{cases}$

19. Factor: $8a^3b^3 - 27c^6d^6$

20. Simplify: $\dfrac{3}{2c + \dfrac{t}{1 + \dfrac{4}{z}}}$

21. Solve for h: $d = \frac{6g}{k}\left(\frac{4t}{h} - \frac{3s}{r}\right)$

22. Find the equilibrant of: $-3\angle 135° + 7\angle -140°$

23. Simplify: $\dfrac{\sqrt{5}\sqrt{-5}\sqrt{6}\sqrt{-6} + \sqrt{-25} - \sqrt{-16}}{-3i^2 - \sqrt{-9}\,i}$

24. Solve by completing the square: $4x^2 + 3x - 2 = 0$

25. If $-x > -y$, compare: *A.* $x + 1$ *B.* y

26. If $2a = b$, compare: *A.* a *B.* b

27. Solve: $\begin{cases} 0.1x - 0.2y = 0.6 \\ \frac{1}{2}x - 2z = 3 \\ y + 3z = 5 \end{cases}$

28. Simplify: $\dfrac{x^{2a+2}(\sqrt{x^3})^{a+2}}{x^{a-2}}$

29. Multiply: $(a^{2a} - b^{1/2})(a^{-2a} + b^{1/2})$

30. Use the calculator to evaluate $(2.6)^{1.52}$.

LESSON 11 *Summation notation*

11.A Summation notation

Summation notation provides a convenient way to designate the sum of a specified list of numbers. The notation consists of a Greek capital letter **sigma** with the ***variable of summation*** indicated below. The least value of the variable of summation is the integer below the sigma, and the greatest value is the integer above the sigma. The expression to the right of the sigma is called a ***typical element*** of the list.

Greatest value → 4
Variable of summation → y
Least value → 1

$$\sum_{y=1}^{4} y^2 \leftarrow \text{Typical element}$$

Here the variable of summation is y, and the typical element is y^2. **The variable will take on the values of the integers above and below $\sum$ and all integers between these numbers.** Thus, the notation above has a value of 30.

$$\sum_{y=1}^{4} y^2 = (1)^2 + (2)^2 + (3)^2 + (4)^2 = 30$$

Any letter can be used for the variable of summation, but the ones that seem to be used most often are x, y, i, j, and k. **Any symbol other than the variable of summation is assumed to be a constant.** Thus, the summation of ik, where i is the variable of summation, is shown here.

$$\sum_{i=2}^{5} ik = 2k + 3k + 4k + 5k = 14k$$

In this example, the letter k is not the variable of summation and is treated as a constant.

Example 11.A.1 Evaluate $\sum_{i=1}^{5} 3$.

Solution In this problem the variable of summation is i, but i is not a factor of the typical element. To make our overall summation notation consistent, we assume an i whose exponent is zero, as

$$\sum_{i=1}^{5} 3i^0$$

Now we can write our sum as

$$\sum_{i=1}^{5} 3i^0 = 3(1)^0 + 3(2)^0 + 3(3)^0 + 3(4)^0 + 3(5)^0 = 15$$

In practice, it is not customary to record the i factors. Instead we let the least and greatest value of the variable of summation tell us that there are five terms in the sum. So we write simply

$$\sum_{i=1}^{5} 3 = 3 + 3 + 3 + 3 + 3 = \mathbf{15}$$

The necessity for this definition of the sum of a constant will become evident in an elementary statistics course.

Example 11.A.2 Evaluate $\sum_{x=1}^{4} 2x$.

Solution The variable of summation is x. If we let x take on the values 1 to 4, we get

$$\sum_{x=1}^{4} 2x = 2 \cdot 1 + 2 \cdot 2 + 2 \cdot 3 + 2 \cdot 4 = \mathbf{20}$$

Example 11.A.3 Evaluate $\sum_{j=0}^{3} \frac{2^j}{j+1}$.

Solution The variable of summation is j and it will take on the values 0, 1, 2, and 3 in turn.

$$\sum_{j=0}^{3} \frac{2^j}{j+1} = \frac{2^0}{0+1} + \frac{2^1}{1+1} + \frac{2^2}{2+1} + \frac{2^3}{3+1} = 1 + 1 + \frac{4}{3} + 2 = \mathbf{\frac{16}{3}}$$

Example 11.A.4 Evaluate $\sum_{y=4}^{6} \frac{1}{y}$.

Solution The variable of summation is y. There are three terms as y takes on the values 4, 5, and 6.

$$\sum_{y=4}^{6} \frac{1}{y} = \frac{1}{4} + \frac{1}{5} + \frac{1}{6} = \mathbf{\frac{37}{60}}$$

Problem set 11

1. Watshas' boat could go 45 miles downstream in 3 hours, but required 5 hours to make the return trip. What was the speed of the boat in still water and what was the speed of the current?

2. The train traveled 100 miles at m miles per hour and still got there 1 hour late. Use the letter m and the number 100 to form an expression for the speed the train should have traveled to arrive on time.

3. A solution is made by mixing V quarts of vinegar and W quarts of water. Write an expression whose value is the percent of the solution that is vinegar.

4. Jeff could complete 4 in 5 hours; but when he worked with Peeto, they could complete 22 in 15 hours. How long would it take Peeto to complete 1 if he worked alone?

5. Fifteen gourmands could put away 45 pounds of food in 2 hours. How many pounds of food could 25 gourmands put away in 10 hours?

6. Sketch the function $y = (\frac{1}{3})^x$.

7. Evaluate: Arctan $\sqrt{3}$

8. Evaluate: $\sin(\text{Arccos } \frac{1}{2})$

9. Evaluate: $\tan[\text{Arcsin } (-\frac{3}{5})]$

Evaluate:

10. $2\cos(-135°) + \sin 180°$

11. $\dfrac{\sin 30°}{\cos 30°} - \cos 180° + \sin 90°$

12. $2\sin 90° \cos 180° - \cos 270°$

13. $\displaystyle\sum_{i=1}^{6} 2$

14. $\displaystyle\sum_{j=2}^{4} \frac{2^j}{1-j}$

Solve:

15. $\log_d 64 = 3$

16. $\log_2 \dfrac{1}{64} = f$

17. $\log_{1/2} p = -3$

18. Evaluate: $\dfrac{9!}{3!2!}$

19. Solve: $\begin{cases} x^2 - y^2 = 4 \\ x + y = 2 \end{cases}$

20. Simplify: $\dfrac{\dfrac{a^2b}{c^2d^3} - \dfrac{fg^2}{cd^3}}{\dfrac{x^2y}{c^2d} + \dfrac{z^3}{cd^3}}$

21. Solve for g: $h = \dfrac{2d}{f}\left(\dfrac{4s}{g} + \dfrac{2s}{r}\right)$

22. Find the equilibrant of: $-2\underline{/140°} + 3\underline{/-120°}$

23. Simplify: $\dfrac{\sqrt{2}\sqrt{-3}\sqrt{-2}\sqrt{3} - \sqrt{-16}}{-4i^3 - \sqrt{-16}\,i}$

24. Solve by completing the square: $3x^2 = -2x + 6$

25. If $\dfrac{a}{b} = \dfrac{c}{d}$, compare: *A*. $\dfrac{a}{c}$ *B*. $\dfrac{b}{d}$

26. If $\dfrac{a}{b} = 4$, compare: *A*. a *B*. $4b$

27. Solve: $\begin{cases} 2x + y - z = 1 \\ x - 2y + z = 0 \\ 3x + y - 2z = -1 \end{cases}$

28. Simplify: $\dfrac{a^{3b+1}(\sqrt{a^3})^{b-1}}{a^{2b+1}}$

29. Factor: $4a^{x+2} - 12a^{x+3}$

30. Find the equation of the line which passes through (2, 2) and is perpendicular to $4x - 2y + 3 = 0$.

LESSON 12 Change in coordinates · The name of a number · Distance formula

12.A Change in coordinates

When we use coordinate geometry, we usually don't encounter expressions such as

$$x_2 - y_1$$

in which the letters are different. Instead, we encounter expressions that contain the same letters but different subscripts.

$$x_1 - x_2 \qquad x_2 - x_1 \qquad y_1 - y_2 \qquad y_2 - y_1$$

These expressions usually represent changes in the values of coordinates as we move from one point to another point. The first entry is the final coordinate, and the last entry is the initial coordinate. If we move one way, the change will be positive. If we move the other way, the change will be negative.

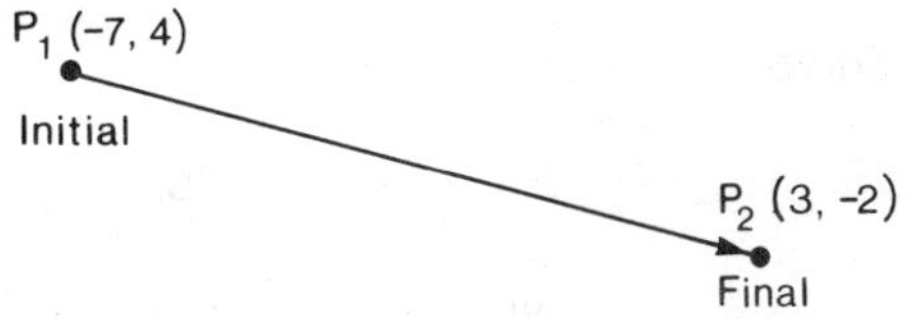

If we move from P_1 (x_1, y_1) to P_2 (x_2, y_2), the x coordinate changes from -7 to 3, a change of $+10$; and the y coordinate changes from 4 to -2, a change of -6. **We use a two-step procedure for determining the change in coordinates. The first step is to write down the final coordinate. Then from this number, we subtract the initial coordinate.**

$$x_2 - x_1 = 3 - (-7) = +10 \qquad \text{and} \qquad y_2 - y_1 = -2 - (4) = -6$$

Now, if we turn around and move from P_2 to P_1, we move the same distance but in the opposite direction.

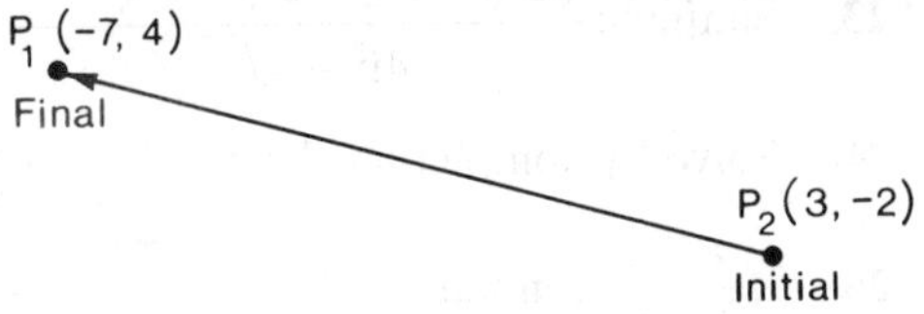

This time the arrowhead is at P_1, so the coordinates of P_1 come first when we write the expressions for the changes in the coordinates.

$$x_1 - x_2 = -7 - (3) = -10 \qquad \text{and} \qquad y_1 - y_2 = 4 - (-2) = +6$$

Thus, notations such as $x_2 - x_1$ and $y_1 - y_2$ represent distances and directions. We can think of each of these notations as representing a **directed distance.**

Example 12.A.1 Given the points $P_1(-3, 2)$ and $P_2(-4, -5)$, what do we represent by (*a*) $-3 - (-4)$ and by (*b*) $-5 - (2)$?

Solution We remember that the first number is the final coordinate.

$$(a) \quad -3 - (-4) \qquad\qquad (b) \quad -5 - (2)$$

Thus, the expression on the left represents the change in the x coordinate when we move from P_2 to P_1, and the expression on the right represents the change in the y coordinate when we move from P_1 to P_2.

Example 12.A.2 If the coordinates of P_1 are $(-3, -2)$ and the coordinates of P_2 are $(-4, -5)$, what do we represent by (*a*) $-4-(-3)$ and by (*b*) $-2-(-5)$?

Solution When we find the change in coordinates, the first number is always the final coordinate. Thus

$$-4-(-3)$$

represents the change in the x coordinate when we move from P_1 to P_2, and

$$-2-(-5)$$

represents the change in the y coordinate when we move from P_2 to P_1.

12.B The name of a number

We will use the symbol ΔC (read "delta C") to mean ***change in coordinate*** and will remember that the final coordinate is written first and the initial coordinate is written last.

$$\Delta C = C_F - C_I$$

The coordinate of a point on the number line gives us the distance and direction from the origin to the graph of the number. We can use arrows that represent changes in coordinates to help us solve some interesting problems about the way numbers are arranged in order.

Example 12.B.1 What is the number whose graph is $\frac{2}{3}$ of the way from 3 to -7?

Solution We always draw a diagram to help prevent mistakes.

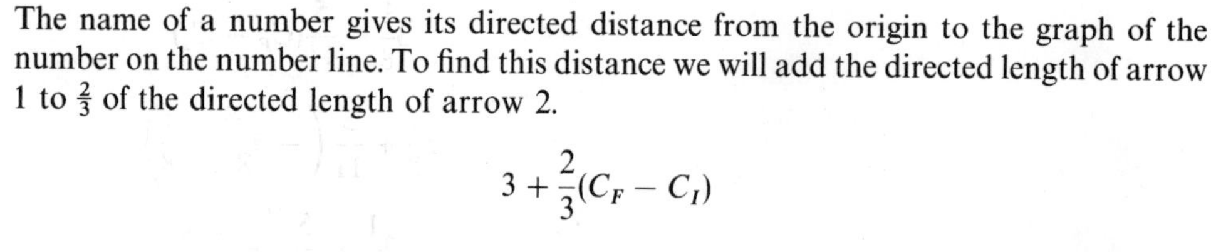

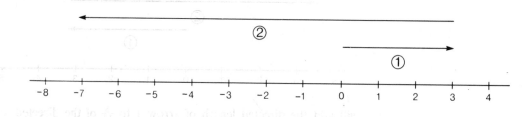

The name of a number gives its directed distance from the origin to the graph of the number on the number line. To find this distance we will add the directed length of arrow 1 to $\frac{2}{3}$ of the directed length of arrow 2.

$$3+\frac{2}{3}(C_F - C_I)$$

$$3+\frac{2}{3}[-7-(3)]$$

$$3+\frac{2}{3}(-10)$$

$$\frac{9}{3}-\frac{20}{3} = \mathbf{-\frac{11}{3}}$$

We note that the numbers could be added easily after 3 had been rewritten as $\frac{9}{3}$.

Example 12.B.2 What is the number that is $\frac{3}{7}$ of the way from -4 to $+9$?

Solution We always draw a diagram when possible.

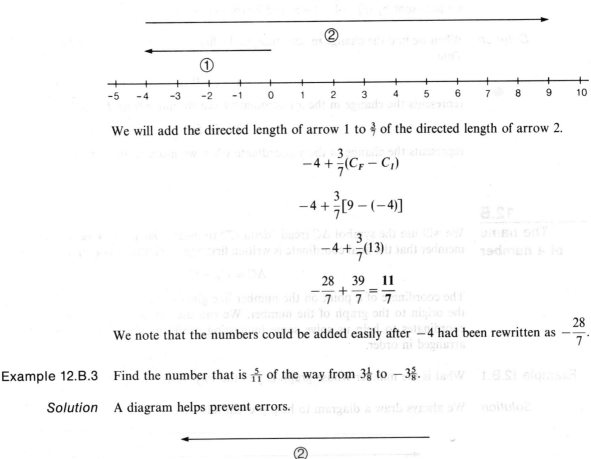

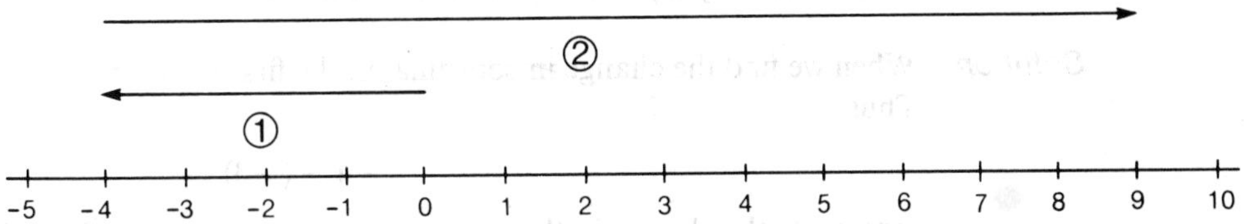

We will add the directed length of arrow 1 to $\frac{3}{7}$ of the directed length of arrow 2.

$$-4 + \frac{3}{7}(C_F - C_I)$$

$$-4 + \frac{3}{7}[9 - (-4)]$$

$$-4 + \frac{3}{7}(13)$$

$$-\frac{28}{7} + \frac{39}{7} = \mathbf{\frac{11}{7}}$$

We note that the numbers could be added easily after -4 had been rewritten as $-\frac{28}{7}$.

Example 12.B.3 Find the number that is $\frac{5}{11}$ of the way from $3\frac{1}{8}$ to $-3\frac{5}{8}$.

Solution A diagram helps prevent errors.

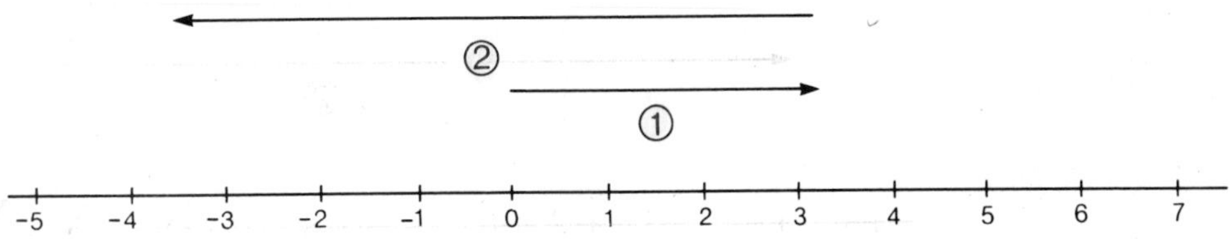

We will add the directed length of arrow 1 to $\frac{5}{11}$ of the directed length of arrow 2.

$$3\frac{1}{8} + \frac{5}{11}(C_F - C_I)$$

$$3\frac{1}{8} + \frac{5}{11}\left(-3\frac{5}{8} - 3\frac{1}{8}\right)$$

$$3\frac{1}{8} + \frac{5}{11}\left(-\frac{27}{4}\right)$$

$$\frac{275}{88} - \frac{270}{88} = \mathbf{\frac{5}{88}}$$

12.C The distance formula

In any right triangle, the square of the length of the hypotenuse equals the sum of the squares of the lengths of the other two sides. The statement of this fact is called the ***Pythagorean theorem.*** The distance between the two points in the figure is the hypotenuse of the right triangle. The length of the horizontal side is the difference of the x

coordinates of the two points, and the length of the vertical side is the difference of the y coordinates of the two points.

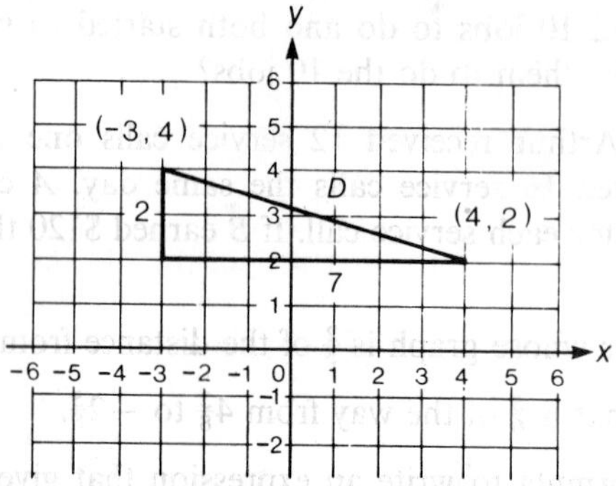

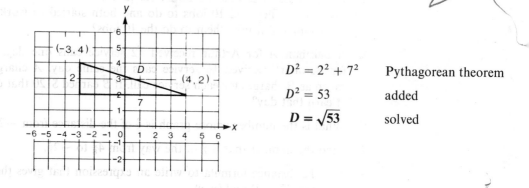

$D^2 = 2^2 + 7^2$ Pythagorean theorem

$D^2 = 53$ added

$D = \sqrt{53}$ solved

The distance formula is a general algebraic statement of the Pythagorean theorem. If we take the square root of both sides, the resulting expression gives the distance between the two points and is called the distance formula.

PYTHAGOREAN THEOREM		DISTANCE FORMULA
$D^2 = (\text{side}_1)^2 + (\text{side}_2)^2$	$\longrightarrow$	$D = \sqrt{(\text{side}_1)^2 + (\text{side}_2)^2}$

The formula doesn't say whether the x side or the y side comes first, and since the coordinates may appear in any order, there are many correct forms of the distance formula. Four of these correct forms are:

$$D = \sqrt{(x_1 - x_2)^2 + (y_2 - y_1)^2} \qquad D = \sqrt{(y_1 - y_2)^2 + (x_2 - x_1)^2}$$

$$D = \sqrt{(y_1 - y_2)^2 + (x_1 - x_2)^2} \qquad D = \sqrt{(x_2 - x_1)^2 + (y_2 - y_1)^2}$$

All that is necessary is that the sum of the squares of the differences in the x coordinates and the differences in the y coordinates appear in some order. We will use the distance formula extensively in our study of conic sections.

Example 12.C.1 Use the distance formula to write an expression that gives the distance between the point $(4, -2)$ and some other point (x, y).

Solution The distance between the points is the square root of the sum of the squares of the lengths of the sides of the triangle. The length of one side is the magnitude of the difference of the x coordinates of the two points. The length of the other side is the magnitude of the difference of the y coordinates of the two points.

$$D = \sqrt{(4 - x)^2 + (-2 - y)^2} \qquad D = \sqrt{(x - 4)^2 + (y + 2)^2}$$

Although the entries appear to be different, when the terms in the radicands are squared, the radicands will be identical. Thus both these expressions give us the distance between $(4, -2)$ and (x, y).

Problem set 12

1. The ratio of reds to blues was 4 to 1, and the ratio of blues to greens was 2 to 1. If there were 55 of them in the bowl, how many were red, how many were green, and how many were blue?

2. Ronk, Keeth, and Renée were average speed eaters and they consumed a total of 20 concoctions in 5 hours. Then they were joined by Sarah and Randy, who were also average speed eaters. How long would it take all 5 of them to consume 14 concoctions?

3. The bunch trotted m miles at z miles per hour and got there 3 hours late. How fast should they have trotted to get there on time?

4. Gregg could do 2 jobs in 5 hours. Jackie was slower, as it took her 6 hours to do just 1 job. They had 10 jobs to do and both started to work at the same time. How long did it take them to do the 10 jobs?

5. Repairman A for Arthur received 12 service calls one day, and repairman B for Bernhart received 16 service calls the same day. A charges three-halves as much as B charges for each service call. If B earned \$120 that day, how much did A earn that day?

6. What is the number whose graph is $\frac{2}{5}$ of the distance from -2 to 6?

7. Find the number that is $\frac{5}{6}$ of the way from $4\frac{3}{8}$ to $-2\frac{5}{8}$.

8. Use the distance formula to write an expression that gives the distance between the point $(2, -1)$ and (x, y).

Evaluate:

9. $\text{Arctan } 1$

10. $\tan\left(\text{Arcsin } \frac{3}{5}\right)$

11. $\cos\left[\text{Arctan }(-3)\right]$

12. $2 \cos 135° - \cos 270°$

13. $3 \cos 60° \sin 30° - \sin 90° \cos 90°$

14. $6 \sin 30° \tan 45° - \cos 270° \sin 90°$

15. $\displaystyle\sum_{i=1}^{7} 3$

16. $\displaystyle\sum_{j=0}^{2} \frac{3^j}{1-2j}$

Solve:

17. $\log_f 125 = 3$

18. $\log_2 \frac{1}{32} = g$

19. $\log_{1/2} p = -2$

20. Evaluate: $\dfrac{10!}{4!2!}$

21. Solve: $\begin{cases} x^2 + y^2 = 10 \\ 2x^2 - y^2 = 17 \end{cases}$

22. Simplify: $\dfrac{\dfrac{x^2y}{cd^2} - \dfrac{z^2}{d^3}}{\dfrac{gh^2}{c^3d} - \dfrac{f}{d^3}}$

23. Solve for x: $\dfrac{y^2}{z} = \dfrac{3s}{r}\left(\dfrac{4t}{x} - \dfrac{3z}{k}\right)$

24. Find the equilibrant of: $-3\underline{/-135°} - 2\underline{/-140°}$

25. Simplify: $\dfrac{\sqrt{-4}\sqrt{5}\sqrt{-5} - \sqrt{-25}}{-2i^3 + \sqrt{-4}}$

26. Compare: A. $\dfrac{x + 2y}{x}$ B. $1 + \dfrac{2y}{x}$

27. If $\dfrac{a}{b} = \dfrac{c}{d}$, compare: A. $\dfrac{a + c}{b + d}$ B. $\dfrac{a}{b}$

28. Solve: $\begin{cases} 0.5x - 0.1y = 0.7 \\ \dfrac{1}{6}y - \dfrac{1}{4}z = -\dfrac{1}{2} \\ x + z = 6 \end{cases}$

29. Solve by completing the square: $2x^2 - 3x = 6$

30. Factor: $8x^3y^6 - 27a^9b^6$

LESSON 13 Angles greater than 360° · Sums of functions · Boats in the river

13.A Angles greater than 360°

In polar coordinates, we measure positive angles counterclockwise from the positive x axis and measure negative angles clockwise from the positive x axis. Thus, the positive x axis is the initial side of the angle.

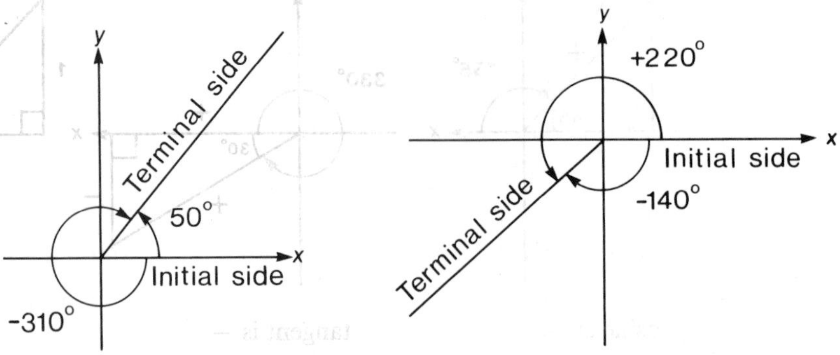

In the left-hand figure, we see that $+50°$ and $-310°$ have the same terminal side, and we say that these angles are ***coterminal angles.*** In the right-hand figure, we see that $+220°$ and $-140°$ are also coterminal angles. For many purposes, we can think of coterminal angles as being the same angle but with a different name. **Angles that differ by multiples of 360° are coterminal angles.**

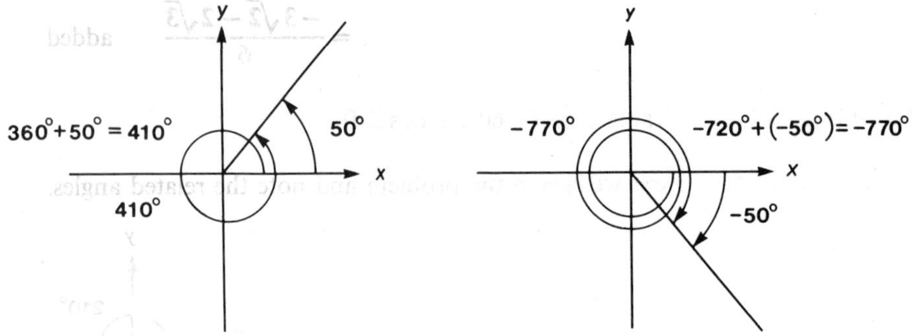

On the left, we see that 50° and 410° are coterminal because 410° is once around for 360° plus 50° more. On the right, we see that $-50°$ and $-770°$ are coterminal because $-770°$ is twice around for $-720°$ plus another $-50°$. Three times around would be 1080°, so angles that differ by 1080° are also coterminal, as are angles that differ by 1440° for four times around, etc.

13.B Sums of functions

Problems that require the addition of functions of angles in all quadrants will provide practice that will lead to greater understanding of the values of functions and will also give practice in simplifying expressions that contain radicals. The three expressions shown here are equivalent expressions.

$$(a)\quad -\frac{1}{\sqrt{2}}-\frac{1}{\sqrt{3}} \qquad (b)\quad -\frac{\sqrt{2}}{2}-\frac{\sqrt{3}}{3} \qquad (c)\quad \frac{-3\sqrt{2}-2\sqrt{3}}{6}$$

Many people prefer expressions that do not have radicals in the denominator. In this case, they would prefer expressions (*b*) and (*c*). In this book, we will combine the parts as in (*c*) because of the practice this procedure provides and not because this form of answer is necessarily more desirable.

Example 13.B.1 Evaluate $\cos 135° + \tan 330°$.

Solution It is always helpful to sketch the problem and note the related angles.

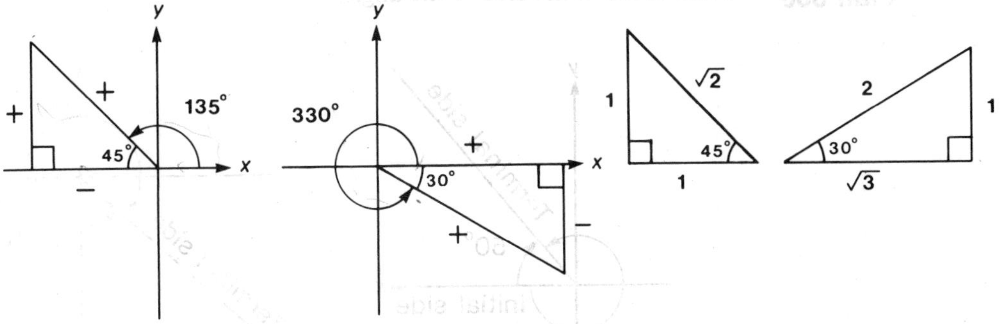

cosine is $-$

$\cos 135° = -\cos 45°$

tangent is $-$

$\tan 330° = -\tan 30°$

$$\cos 135° + \tan 330° = -\frac{1}{\sqrt{2}} - \frac{1}{\sqrt{3}} \qquad \text{sum of functions}$$

$$= -\frac{\sqrt{2}}{2} - \frac{\sqrt{3}}{3} \qquad \text{rationalized denominators}$$

$$= \frac{-3\sqrt{2} - 2\sqrt{3}}{6} \qquad \text{added}$$

Example 13.B.2 Evaluate $\cos(-60°) + \cos 210°$.

Solution First we sketch the problem and note the related angles.

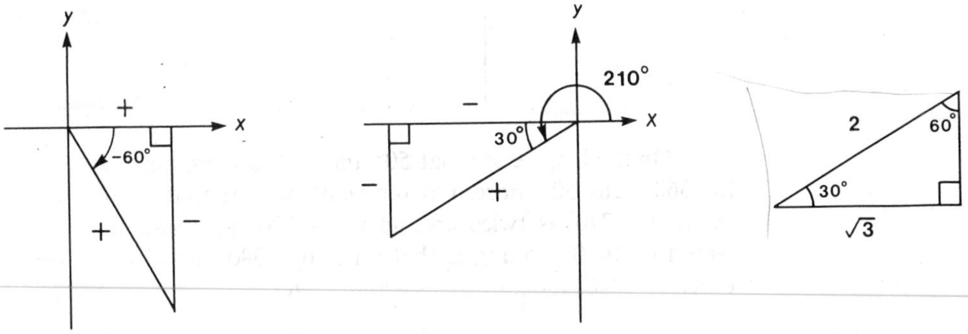

cosine is $+$

$\cos(-60°) = \cos 60°$

cosine is $-$

$\cos 210° = -\cos 30°$

$$\cos(-60°) + \cos 210° = \cos 60° - \cos 30°$$

$$= \frac{1}{2} - \frac{\sqrt{3}}{2} \qquad \text{sum of functions}$$

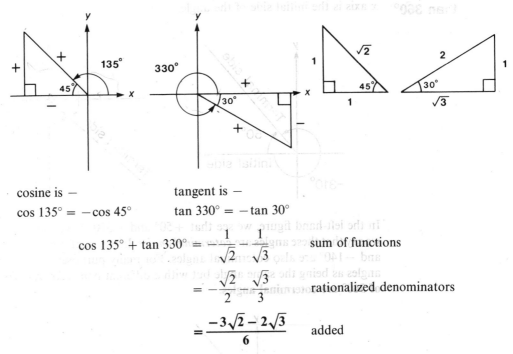

$$= \frac{1 - \sqrt{3}}{2} \qquad \text{added}$$

Example 13.B.3 Evaluate $\cos 570° + \sin(-765°)$.

Solution We begin by reducing the absolute values of the angles 360° at a time until we get an angle whose measure is less than 360°.

$$570° - 360° = 210° \qquad 765° - 360° - 360° = 45°$$

Now we sketch the angles and note the related angles.

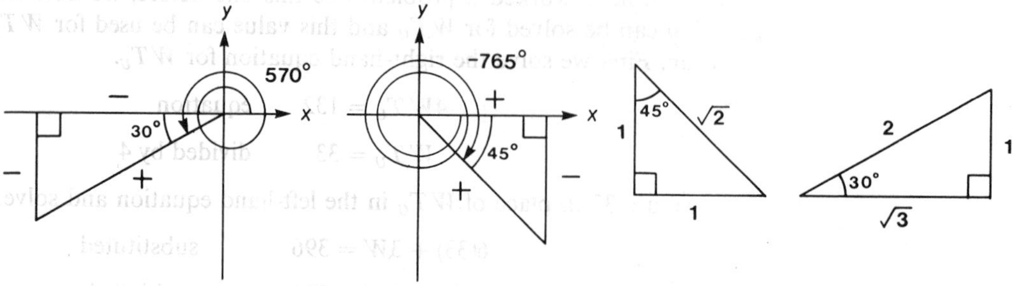

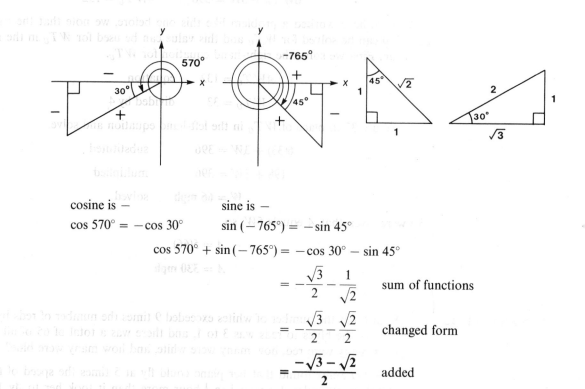

cosine is – sine is –

$\cos 570° = -\cos 30°$ $\sin(-765°) = -\sin 45°$

$$\cos 570° + \sin(-765°) = -\cos 30° - \sin 45°$$

$$= -\frac{\sqrt{3}}{2} - \frac{1}{\sqrt{2}} \qquad \text{sum of functions}$$

$$= -\frac{\sqrt{3}}{2} - \frac{\sqrt{2}}{2} \qquad \text{changed form}$$

$$= \frac{-\sqrt{3} - \sqrt{2}}{2} \qquad \text{added}$$

13.C Boats in the river

We have called problems in which boats traveled distances with and against the current "boat in the river" problems. There is a downstream equation in which the rate is the still-water speed of the boat plus the speed of the water $(B + W)$. There is also an upstream equation where the rate is the still-water speed of the boat minus the speed of the water.

DOWNSTREAM EQUATION	UPSTREAM EQUATION
(a) $(B + W)T_D = D_D$	(b) $(B - W)T_U = D_U$

The same thought process and equations are applicable in problems in which an airplane flies directly against the wind and directly with the wind, as we see in the next example. The setup of this problem is straightforward, but the solution is a little awkward unless a double-variable substitution is used.

Example 13.C.1 One day Selby found that her plane could fly at 5 times the speed of the wind. She flew 396 miles downwind in $\frac{1}{2}$ hour more than it took her to fly 132 miles upwind. What was the speed of her plane and what was the speed of the wind?

Solution First we write the equations. We will use A for the speed of the airplane and W for the speed of the wind.

DOWNWIND EQUATION	UPWIND EQUATION
$(A + W)T_D = D_D$	$(A - W)T_U = D_U$

Now we substitute $5W$ for A, 396 and 132 for the distances, and $T_U + \frac{1}{2}$ for T_D.

$$(5W + W)(T_U + \tfrac{1}{2}) = 396 \qquad (5W - W)T_U = 132$$

Next we multiply and simplify and get

$$6WT_U + 3W = 396 \qquad 4WT_U = 132$$

Now if we have worked a problem like this one before, we note that the right-hand equation can be solved for WT_U and this value can be used for WT_U in the left-hand equation. First we solve the right-hand equation for WT_U.

$4WT_U = 132$	equation
$WT_U = 33$	divided by 4

Now we use 33 in place of WT_U in the left-hand equation and solve.

$6(33) + 3W = 396$	substituted
$198 + 3W = 396$	multiplied
$\mathbf{W = 66}$ **mph**	solved

We were given that A equals $5W$, so

$$A = 5(66)$$

$$\mathbf{A = 330} \textbf{ mph}$$

Problem set 13

1. Four times the number of whites exceeded 9 times the number of reds by 10. The ratio of the blues to reds was 3 to 1, and there was a total of 65 of all 3 colors. How many were red, how many were white, and how many were blue?

2. One day Selby found that her plane could fly at 5 times the speed of the wind. She flew 396 miles downwind in $\frac{1}{2}$ hour more than it took her to fly 132 miles upwind. What was the speed of her plane, and what was the speed of the wind?

3. The safe load a beam can support varies jointly as the width and the square of the depth and inversely as the length. If a 2×8 inch beam 16 feet long is turned so that the width is 2 inches, it can support 2000 pounds. How much weight can the same beam support if it is turned so that the width is 8 inches?

4. Sally could do 3 jobs in 8 hours. When Jack helped, they could do 6 jobs in 4 hours. What was Jack's rate in jobs per hour when he worked alone?

5. The engineer knows that the formula is $T = \sqrt{L/4}$. To get the desired result, she must triple her present value of T. What should she do to the present value of L?

6. What is the number that is $\frac{3}{5}$ of the way from -3 to 9?

7. Find the number that is $\frac{7}{8}$ of the way from $-3\frac{5}{6}$ to $2\frac{1}{6}$.

8. Use the distance formula to write an expression that gives the distance between $(3, -2)$ and (x, y).

Evaluate:

9. $\text{Arctan} \dfrac{1}{\sqrt{3}}$

10. $\cos [\text{Arccos} (-\frac{4}{5})]$

11. $\sin (\text{Arctan } 2)$

12. $\cos 270° + \tan 330°$

13. $\sin(-60°) + \sin 390°$

14. $\tan 570° + \cos(-765°)$

15. $\sum_{j=5}^{6} \frac{2}{j}$

16. $\sum_{n=0}^{3} \frac{3^n}{n+1}$

Solve:

17. $\log_x 64 = 3$

18. $\log_3 \frac{1}{27} = y$

19. $\log_{1/3} K = -3$

20. Evaluate: $\frac{11!}{4!3!}$

21. Solve: $\begin{cases} x^2 + y^2 = 16 \\ 3x + y = 4 \end{cases}$

22. Simplify: $\dfrac{2}{1 + \dfrac{3s}{1 + \dfrac{x}{m}}}$

23. Solve for x: $\frac{t^2}{z} = \frac{3m}{n}\left(\frac{4s}{x} + \frac{3}{4k}\right)$

24. Find the resultant of: $-2\underline{/120°} - 3\underline{/135°}$

25. Simplify: $\dfrac{-\sqrt{-3}\sqrt{3} - \sqrt{2}\sqrt{-3}\sqrt{-6}}{3i^4 - \sqrt{-4}}$

26. If $a < 0$ and $b < 0$, compare: *A.* $a - b$ *B.* $a + b$

27. If $a > 1$, compare: *A.* $\frac{1}{a^3}$ *B.* $\frac{1}{a^4}$

Solve:

28. $\begin{cases} 2x - y + z = 5 \\ x + 2y - z = -1 \\ x + y + 2z = 10 \end{cases}$

29. $\sqrt{2s - 7} + \sqrt{2s} = 7$

30. Divide $x^4 - 2x^3 + 3x + 1$ by $x - 2$.

LESSON 14 The line as a locus · The midpoint formula

14.A The line as a locus

The word ***locus*** is a Latin word which means "place." In mathematics, we use the word *locus* to describe the location of mathematical points. The line, the parabola, the circle, the ellipse, and the hyperbola can all be defined by using the word locus. Here we will investigate the locus definition of a line, and we remember that the word *line* in mathematics usually means a straight line.

> **A line is the locus of all points in a plane that are equidistant from two specified points.**

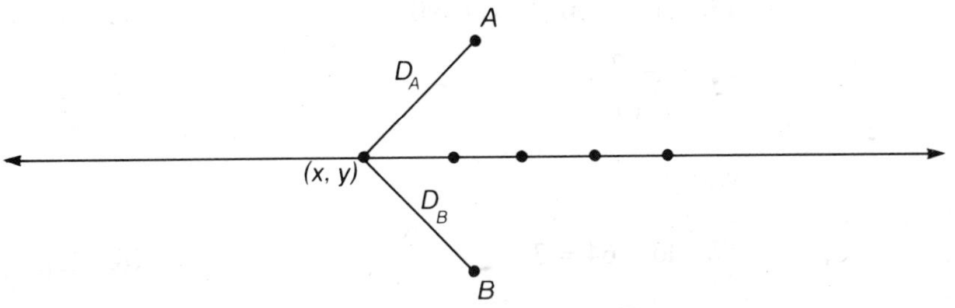

Here we show points A and B and a point (x, y) on a line where D_A equals D_B. The locus of all the points that are equidistant from A and B is the line shown.

Example 14.A.1 Find the equation of the line that is equidistant from the points (4, 2) and $(-2, -3)$.

Solution A sketch of the problem is always helpful. We graph the points, estimate the position of the line, and designate point (x, y) on the line. The distance from this point to the points $(-2, -3)$ and (4, 2) are equal.

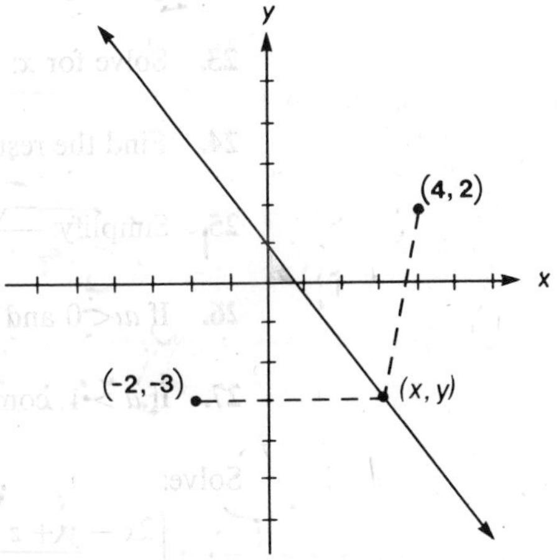

$$\text{Distance from } (x, y) \text{ to } (-2, -3) = \text{distance from } (x, y) \text{ to } (4, 2)$$

There are many forms of the distance formula. We will use two different forms of the distance formula to emphasize that any correct form will suffice.

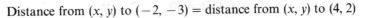

$$\sqrt{[(x) - (-2)]^2 + [(-3) - (y)]^2} = \sqrt{[(4) - (x)]^2 + [(2) - (y)]^2}$$

Now we square both sides to eliminate the radicals, then simplify and get

$$(x + 2)^2 + (-3 - y)^2 = (4 - x)^2 + (2 - y)^2$$

Now we square the terms as indicated and get

$$x^2 + 4x + 4 + 9 + 6y + y^2 = 16 - 8x + x^2 + 4 - 4y + y^2$$

We find an x^2 and a y^2 on both the left side and the right side, and these can be eliminated by adding $-x^2$ and $-y^2$ to both sides.

$$4x + 4 + 9 + 6y = 16 - 8x + 4 - 4y$$

We finish by collecting like terms and writing the equation of the line.

$$\mathbf{12x + 10y - 7 = 0} \qquad \text{simplified}$$

$$y = -\frac{6}{5}x + \frac{7}{10} \qquad \text{slope-intercept form}$$

Example 14.A.2 Find the equation of the line that is equidistant from the points $(0, -4)$ and (5, 2).

Solution First we make a sketch. The distance from (x, y) to $(5, 2)$ must equal the distance from (x, y) to $(0, -4)$.

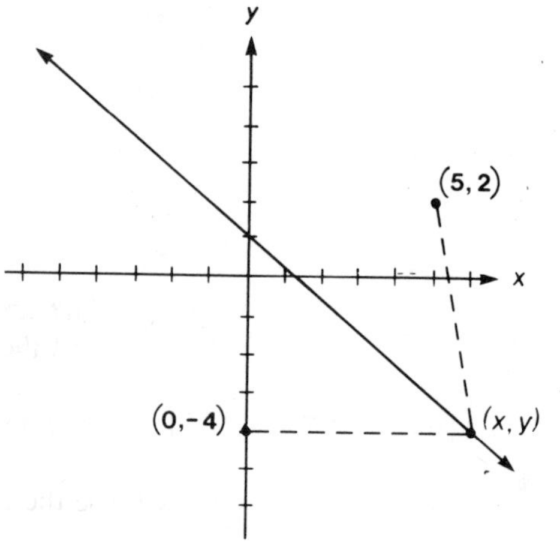

Distance from (x, y) to $(5, 2)$
= distance from (x, y) to $(0, -4)$

Again we will use different forms of the distance equation to emphasize that any one of the forms is correct.

$$\sqrt{[(y) - (2)]^2 + [(5) - (x)]^2} = \sqrt{[(0) - (x)]^2 + [(y) - (-4)]^2}$$

Now we square both sides to eliminate the radicals, simplify, and get

$$(y - 2)^2 + (5 - x)^2 = (0 - x)^2 + (y + 4)^2$$

Now we perform the indicated multiplications and get

$$y^2 - 4y + 4 + 25 - 10x + x^2 = x^2 + y^2 + 8y + 16$$

As the last step, we collect like terms and write the equation.

$$\mathbf{10x + 12y - 13 = 0} \qquad \text{simplified}$$

$$\mathbf{y = -\frac{5}{6}x + \frac{13}{12}} \qquad \text{slope-intercept form}$$

14.B The midpoint formula

There are formulas that can be used to determine the x and y coordinates of the point that lies halfway between two points (x_1, y_1) and (x_2, y_2). These formulas are

$$x = \frac{x_1 + x_2}{2} \qquad \text{and} \qquad y = \frac{y_1 + y_2}{2}$$

We remember that the distance between two points on a number line is the difference in the coordinates of the points, so it seems strange that the signs between x_1 and x_2 and between y_1 and y_2 are plus signs. To find out why, we will look at two points x_1 and x_2 on the number line.

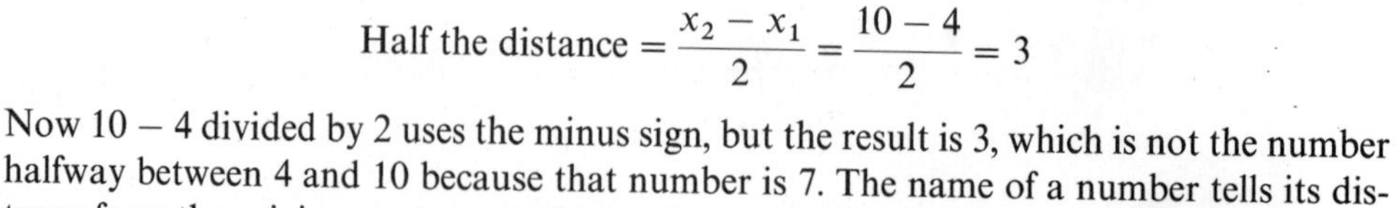

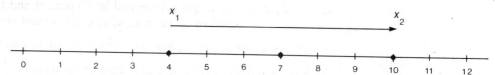

We let x_1 equal 4 and let x_2 equal 10, and we need a formula that will give us the name of the number halfway between. First we find the distance between the points, which is $x_2 - x_1$. To find half this distance, we divide by 2.

$$\text{Half the distance} = \frac{x_2 - x_1}{2} = \frac{10 - 4}{2} = 3$$

Now $10 - 4$ divided by 2 uses the minus sign, but the result is 3, which is not the number halfway between 4 and 10 because that number is 7. The name of a number tells its distance from the origin, so we must add 4 to 3 to get 7. In general, we add the distance from the origin to x_1 to one-half the distance from x_1 to x_2.

$$\text{Distance from the origin} = x_1 + \frac{x_2 - x_1}{2}$$

We can simplify this expression by using a common denominator of 2 and adding the terms.

$$\frac{2x_1}{2} + \frac{x_2}{2} - \frac{x_1}{2} \qquad \text{common denominator}$$

$$\frac{x_1 + x_2}{2} \qquad \text{added}$$

Now the sign between x_1 and x_2 is positive. We see that adding the distance from the origin to x_1 changed the sign between x_1 and x_2 from $-$ to $+$.

Example 14.B.1 Find the coordinates of the point halfway between $(-2, 6)$ and $(4, -10)$.

Solution We will use the two midpoint formulas.

$$x = \frac{x_1 + x_2}{2} \qquad y = \frac{y_1 + y_2}{2}$$

$$x = \frac{(-2) + (4)}{2} = 1 \qquad y = \frac{(6) + (-10)}{2} = -2$$

The coordinates of the midpoint are **(1, −2)**.

Problem set 14

1. The next day Bruce found that his plane could only fly at 4 times the speed of the wind. He flew 400 miles downwind in 1 hour less than it took to fly 300 miles upwind. What was the speed of the plane and what was the speed of the wind?

2. Twenty percent of the number of whites exceeded the number of reds by 10. Also, three-fifths of the number of blues was exactly equal to 3 times the number of reds. How many of each were there if 10 percent of the sum of the reds and blues was 94 less than the number of whites?

3. Francine needed to finish with $3\sqrt{2}$, but her answer was $\frac{2}{\sqrt{6}}$. By what number should she multiply her number to get the answer she needed?

4. If $x^2 + y^2 = 2$ and $x^2 + y^2 = 4$, what is the value of $x^4 - y^4$?

5. If the length of a rectangle is increased by 20 percent and the width of the same rectangle is decreased by 20 percent, what is the percent change in the area?

6. Find the equation of the line that is equidistant from the points (3, 4) and (−2, −1).

7. Find the equation of the line that is equidistant from the points (0, 2) and (5, 3).

8. Find the coordinates of the point halfway between (−3, 6) and (4, 8).

9. What is the number whose graph lies $\frac{2}{9}$ of the way from $-3\frac{3}{7}$ to $4\frac{2}{7}$?

Evaluate:

10. $\text{Arctan}\left(-\frac{1}{3}\sqrt{3}\right)$

11. $\sin\left(\text{Arccos}\,\frac{3}{7}\right)$

12. $\sin(\text{Arctan } 3)$

13. $\cos 90° - \tan 420°$

14. $\sin(-330°) - \cos 495°$

15. $\tan(-135°) + \sin 30° \cos 60°$

16. $\sum_{x=3}^{5} \frac{3}{x+1}$

17. $\sum_{y=-3}^{3} 2y^2$

Solve:

18. $\log_y 27 = 3$ **19.** $\log_2 \frac{1}{64} = t$ **20.** $\log_3 k = -2$

21. Evaluate: $\frac{10!}{4!6!}$ **22.** Solve: $\begin{cases} x^2 - 2y^2 = 6 \\ -x^2 + 3y^2 = 3 \end{cases}$

23. Simplify: $\dfrac{\dfrac{3a^2b}{cd} - \dfrac{d^3}{c^2}}{\dfrac{4s^2t}{c^2d} - \dfrac{l}{d}}$ **24.** Solve for t: $2s = \sqrt{h^2 + 3t}$

25. Find the equilibrant of: $-3\underline{/-135^\circ} + 4\underline{/140^\circ}$

26. Simplify: $\dfrac{-\sqrt{-2}\sqrt{2} + \sqrt{3}\sqrt{-3}\sqrt{-9}}{3i^3 + \sqrt{-9}\,i^3}$

27. If $a > 0$ and $b > 0$, compare: *A.* $a - b$ *B.* $b - a$

28. Solve: $\begin{cases} \frac{1}{4}x - \frac{1}{8}y = 1 \\ 0.3x - 0.2z = 1.2 \\ y - z = 1 \end{cases}$ **29.** Factor: $8x^3y^6 - 27a^3b^9$

30. Multiply: $(6a^{1/2} - b^{-1/2})(3a^{1/2} + b^{1/2})$

LESSON 15 *Fundamental counting principle and permutations · Designated roots*

15.A Fundamental counting principle

The letters A, B, and C can be arranged six different ways. If we put the A first, we can get

A	B	C

and

A	C	B

If we put the B first, we can get

B	A	C

and

B	C	A

If we put the C first, we can get

C	A	B

and

C	B	A

All of the arrangements use the same letters, but the order of the letters is different in each arrangement. We call an arrangement of the members of a set in a definite order a ***permutation*** of the members of the set.

We see that any one of the three letters can be put in the first box.

3		

Now either of the two remaining letters can be put in the second box.

3	2	

And then the last letter goes in the third box.

3	2	1

Thus, any one of the 3 letters can be used first, and any one of the 2 letters that remain can be used second for a total of 3 times 2, or 6, ways. This example is a demonstration of the ***fundamental counting principle.***

> FUNDAMENTAL COUNTING PRINCIPLE
>
> If one choice can be made in A ways and another choice can be made in B ways, then the number of possible choices, in order, is A times B different ways.

If repetition is permitted, the number of possible permutations is even greater. For example, if the letters A, B, and C can be used more than once, then any of the 3 letters can be used in the first, second, or third position for a total of

3	3	3

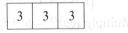

27 possible ways. If we list the ways, we get

AAA	AAB	AAC	ABA	ABB	ABC	ACA	ACB	ACC
BBB	BBA	BBC	BAB	BAA	BAC	BCB	BCA	BCC
CCC	CCB	CCA	CBC	CBB	CBA	CAC	CAB	CAA

The fundamental counting principle can be extended to any number of choices in order. If the first choice can be made in 2 ways, the second choice in 3 ways, the third choice in 5 ways, and the fourth choice in 7 ways, then there are

$$2 \cdot 3 \cdot 5 \cdot 7 = \mathbf{210\ ways}$$

that the choices can be made in order.

Example 15.A.1 How many different ways can the numbers 3, 5, 7, and 8 be arranged in order if no repetition is permitted?

Solution Any one of the 4 numbers can be put in the first box.

4			

Then any one of the remaining 3 numbers can be in the next box,

4	3		

then 2 in the next, and 1 in the last.

4	3	2	1

By the fundamental counting principle, there are

$$4 \cdot 3 \cdot 2 \cdot 1 = \mathbf{24\ ways}$$

that the numbers can be arranged in order. Each of these 24 ways is called a permutation.

Example 15.A.2 How many 4-letter signs can be made from the letters in the word EQUAL if repetition is permitted?

Solution Any one of the 5 letters can be used in any of the positions.

5	5	5	5

$\longrightarrow \quad 5 \cdot 5 \cdot 5 \cdot 5 = \mathbf{625}$

So we have a total of 625 possible arrangements.

Example 15.A.3 A multiple choice quiz has 8 questions, and there are 4 possible answers to each question. How many permutations of the answers are possible?

Solution There are 8 questions and 4 answers are possible to each question.

4	4	4	4	4	4	4	4

$\longrightarrow \quad 4 \cdot 4 \cdot 4 \cdot 4 \cdot 4 \cdot 4 \cdot 4 \cdot 4 = \mathbf{65{,}536}$

Thus, there are 65,536 possible sets of answers to a multiple choice test that has only 8 questions!

Example 15.A.4 How many 3-letter signs can be made from the letters in the word NUMERAL if no repetition is permitted?

Solution This problem is a little different, as only 3 of the 7 letters will be used in each arrangement. So we have only 3 positions, and any one of the 7 letters can be used in the first position.

7		

Now, any one of the 6 that are left can be used in the next position,

7	6	

and any of the 5 that remain can be used in the last box.

7	6	5

$7 \cdot 6 \cdot 5 = \mathbf{210}$

So 210 three-letter permutations of the 7 letters are possible.

15.B Designated roots

The zero factor theorem tells us that, if the product of two or more quantities equals zero, then one of the quantities must equal zero. For example, if we have the equation

$$(x - 4)(x + 7) = 0$$

then either $x - 4$ equals zero or $x + 7$ equals zero. For $x - 4$ to equal zero, x must equal 4; and for $x + 7$ to equal zero, x must equal -7.

$$x - 4 = 0 \qquad x + 7 = 0$$

$$x = 4 \qquad x = -7$$

We can use the reverse of this procedure to write quadratic equations that have designated roots.

Example 15.B.1 Write a quadratic equation whose roots are $-\frac{3}{5}$ and $\frac{1}{2}$.

Solution If the roots are $-\frac{3}{5}$ and $\frac{1}{2}$, the factors are $(x + \frac{3}{5})$ and $(x - \frac{1}{2})$. We write the equation, multiply, and simplify by eliminating the denominators.

$$\left(x+\frac{3}{5}\right)\left(x-\frac{1}{2}\right)=0 \qquad \text{equation}$$

$$x^2+\frac{1}{10}x-\frac{3}{10}=0 \qquad \text{multiplied}$$

$$\mathbf{10x^2+x-3=0} \qquad \text{multiplied by 10}$$

Example 15.B.2 Write a quadratic equation whose roots are $1+\sqrt{2}$ and $1-\sqrt{2}$.

Solution If the roots are as stated, the equation is

$$[x-(1+\sqrt{2})][x-(1-\sqrt{2})]=0$$

The multiplication is easier if we first simplify within the brackets.

$$[x-1-\sqrt{2}][x-1+\sqrt{2}]=0$$

There are nine individual products for this multiplication.

$$x^2-x+\sqrt{2}x-x+1-\sqrt{2}-\sqrt{2}x+\sqrt{2}-2=0$$

Fortunately, this expression can be simplified,

$$x^2-x+\cancel{\sqrt{2}x}-x+1-\cancel{\sqrt{2}}-\cancel{\sqrt{2}x}+\cancel{\sqrt{2}}-2=0$$

and we get

$$\mathbf{x^2-2x-1=0}$$

as our equation whose roots are $1+\sqrt{2}$ and $1-\sqrt{2}$.

Problem set 15

1. Sarah's airplane could fly at 6 times the speed of the wind. She could fly 700 miles upwind in 3 more hours than it took to fly 560 miles downwind. Find the speed of the plane in still air and the speed of the wind.

2. Three men invested \$2000, \$3000, and \$5000, respectively, when they formed a partnership. The profit at the end of the first year was \$1920. How much should the man who invested \$2000 receive if the profits are divided in accordance with the amounts invested?

3. The weather was cold so Jimbo had to use 50 percent of the remaining oil to heat his home that week. If the tank was 3/4 full at the beginning of the week, what fractional part of a full tank did he use that week?

4. Six thousand dollars would suffice for 10 people for 15 days. At the same rate how much money would be required for 20 people for only 5 days?

5. The first leg of the trip was only k miles, and Ralph drove at m miles per hour. He miscalculated because he arrived 2 hours late. If the time allotted for the second leg was the same and the second leg was 10 miles longer, how fast did Ralph have to drive on the second leg to get there on time?

6. How many 4-letter signs can be made from the letters in the word WESTY if repetition is permitted?

7. A true-false quiz has 10 questions. How many permutations of the answers are possible?

8. How many different ways can the letters a, b, c, d be arranged if no repetition is allowed?

9. Find the equation of the line that is equidistant from the points (3, 2) and $(-4, -3)$.

10. Find the coordinates of the point halfway between $(-4, 7)$ and $(3, 2)$.

11. What is the number whose graph is $\frac{3}{7}$ of the way from $-2\frac{2}{5}$ to $3\frac{1}{5}$?

Evaluate:

12. $\text{Arctan}\sqrt{3}$

13. $\sin\left(\text{Arccos}\frac{4}{5}\right)$

14. $\cos\left[\text{Arctan}(-2)\right]$

15. $\sin(-390^\circ) + \cos 495^\circ$

16. $\tan(-495^\circ) - \sin 225^\circ$

17. $\sin 60^\circ \cos 135^\circ - \cos 90^\circ$

18. $\sum_{k=2}^{5}(k^2 - 2)$

Solve:

19. $\log_x 32 = 5$

20. $\log_3 \frac{1}{81} = z$

21. $\log_{1/2} t = -4$

22. Evaluate: $\frac{10!}{3!6!}$

23. Solve: $\begin{cases} x^2 + y^2 = 4 \\ 2x + y = 2 \end{cases}$

24. Simplify: $\dfrac{2}{1 + \dfrac{t}{s - \dfrac{z}{l}}}$

25. Solve for z: $3t = \sqrt{5zt} - 10k$

26. Find the equilibrant of: $-2\underline{/-130^\circ} + 6\underline{/180^\circ}$

27. Simplify: $\dfrac{-\sqrt{3}\sqrt{-3}\sqrt{2}\sqrt{-2} - \sqrt{-6}\sqrt{6}}{4i^3 + \sqrt{-16}\,i}$

28. If $0 < a < 1$, compare: *A.* $\frac{1}{a^2}$ *B.* $\frac{1}{a^3}$

29. Solve: $\begin{cases} x - 2y + z = -2 \\ 2x - y + z = 3 \\ x + y + 2z = 3 \end{cases}$

30. Divide $x^4 - x^3 + x^2 - 1$ by $x - 1$ and check.

LESSON 16 Radian measure of angles

16.A Radian measure of angles

If a length equal to the radius of a circle is measured on the circle itself, the central angle formed is said to measure 1 radian (rad). The measure of the arc is also said to be 1 radian. **We extend this definition to say that the measure of any arc is the same as the measure of its central angle.**

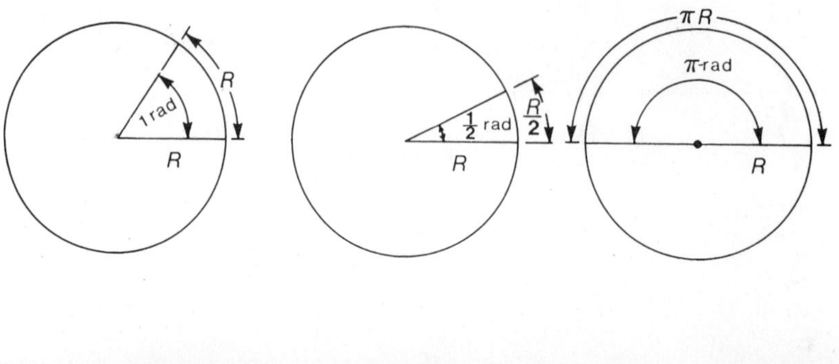

On the preceding page, we see that an arc that is 1 radius long subtends a central angle whose measure is 1 radian. In the center, we see that an arc that is one-half as long as a radius subtends an angle whose measure is $\frac{1}{2}$ radian. On the right, we see that half a circle subtends an angle of π radians. We can remember this by remembering a picture of one of grandmother's pies and a picture of a mathematical π.

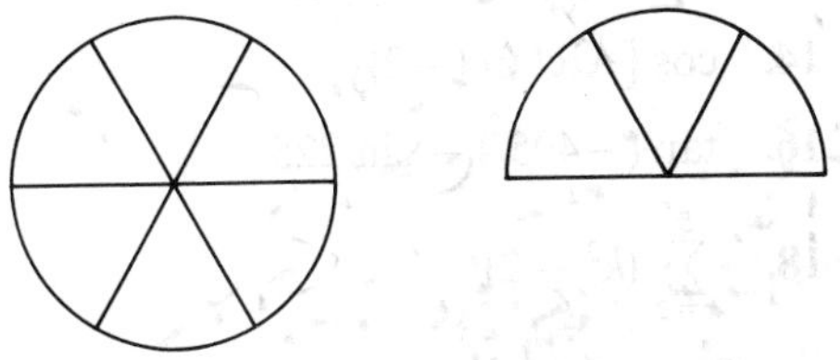

Grandmother's pie   A mathematical pi

This picture helps one remember that π radians is the same measure as 180°. Thus, the unit multipliers necessary to convert degrees to radians and radians to degrees are

$$\frac{\pi \text{ rad}}{180 \text{ deg}} \quad \text{and} \quad \frac{180 \text{ deg}}{\pi \text{ rad}}$$

Unless otherwise designated, angles are always assumed to be measured in radians.

Example 16.A.1 Evaluate $4 \sin \frac{\pi}{4} + \sin\left(-\frac{\pi}{3}\right)$.

Solution If we multiply each of the radian measures by $\frac{180 \text{ deg}}{\pi \text{ rad}}$, we convert the radian measures to degrees.

$$\frac{\cancel{\pi \text{ rad}}}{4} \times \frac{180 \text{ deg}}{\cancel{\pi \text{ rad}}} = 45° \qquad \frac{-\cancel{\pi \text{ rad}}}{3} \times \frac{180 \text{ deg}}{\cancel{\pi \text{ rad}}} = -60°$$

We note that the same numerical result can be achieved if we simply replace π with 180°. Sometimes this shortcut is helpful.

$$\frac{\pi}{4} \longrightarrow \frac{180°}{4} \longrightarrow 45° \qquad -\frac{\pi}{3} \longrightarrow -\frac{180°}{3} \longrightarrow -60°$$

We make these replacements and finish the problem.

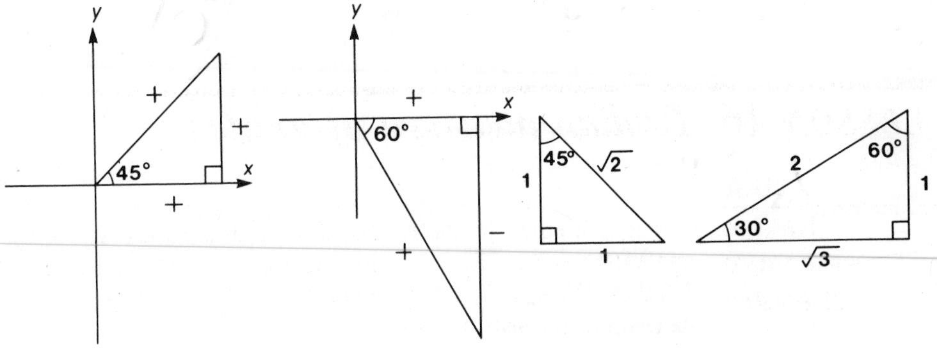

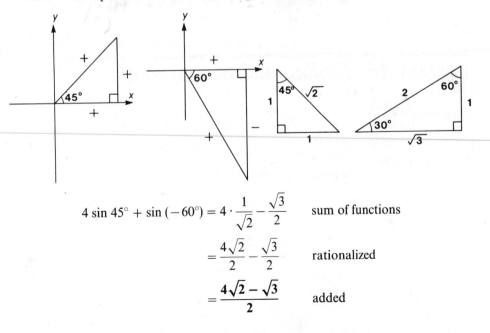

$$\begin{aligned} 4 \sin 45° + \sin(-60°) &= 4 \cdot \frac{1}{\sqrt{2}} - \frac{\sqrt{3}}{2} && \text{sum of functions} \\ &= \frac{4\sqrt{2}}{2} - \frac{\sqrt{3}}{2} && \text{rationalized} \\ &= \mathbf{\frac{4\sqrt{2} - \sqrt{3}}{2}} && \text{added} \end{aligned}$$

It is not necessary to begin by converting radians to degrees, but many people require considerable experience with radian measure before the use of radian measure is comfortable. For those people, the conversion to degrees is a recommended first step.

Example 16.A.2 Evaluate $\sin \dfrac{13\pi}{4} + 3 \cos \dfrac{-5\pi}{3}$.

Solution For both angles we replace π with 180°.

$$\frac{13\pi}{4} \longrightarrow \frac{13(180°)}{4} \longrightarrow 585° \qquad \frac{-5\pi}{3} \longrightarrow \frac{-5(180°)}{3} \longrightarrow -300°$$

Now we use the degree measures, draw the diagrams, and complete the problem.

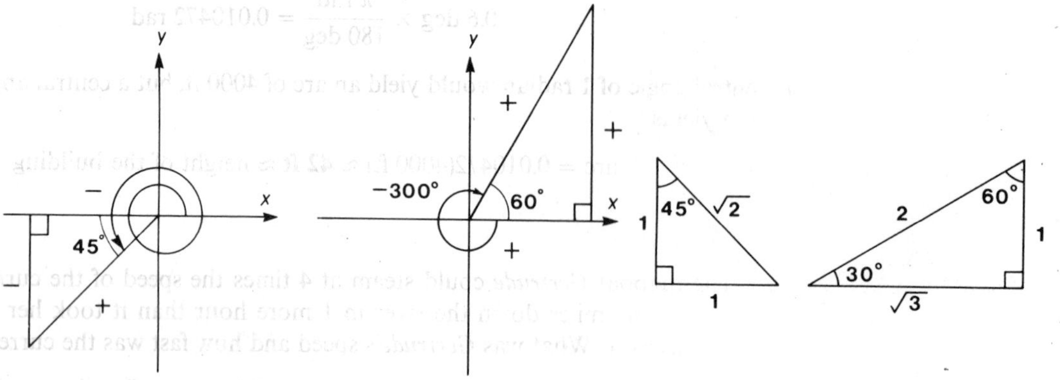

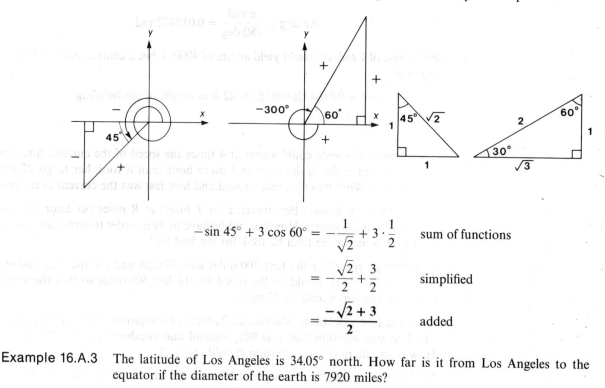

$$-\sin 45° + 3\cos 60° = -\frac{1}{\sqrt{2}} + 3 \cdot \frac{1}{2} \qquad \text{sum of functions}$$

$$= -\frac{\sqrt{2}}{2} + \frac{3}{2} \qquad \text{simplified}$$

$$= \mathbf{\frac{-\sqrt{2} + 3}{2}} \qquad \text{added}$$

Example 16.A.3 The latitude of Los Angeles is 34.05° north. How far is it from Los Angeles to the equator if the diameter of the earth is 7920 miles?

Solution The diameter of the earth is 7920 miles, so the radius is 3960 miles. If the angle were 1 radian, the distance from the equator to LA would be 3960 miles. But the angle is

$$34.05 \text{ deg} \times \frac{\pi \text{ rad}}{180 \text{ deg}} = 0.594 \text{ rad}$$

so the distance is 0.594 times the radius.

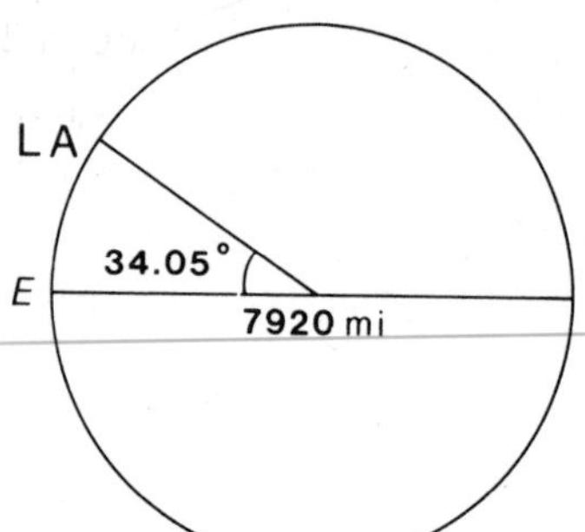

$$\text{Distance} = 0.594(3960) = \mathbf{2352 \text{ miles}}$$

Example 16.A.4 Theo measured the angle between the base of the building and the top of the building and got a reading of 0.6°. If Theo was 4000 ft from the base when the measurement was made, how high was the building?

Solution Even a diagram which is not to scale is helpful.

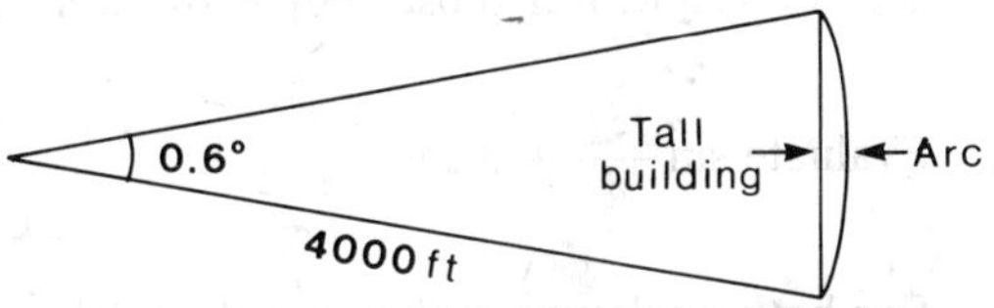

For very small angles, the length of the chord (height of the building) is almost the same as the length of the arc. **The length of the arc is the angle measure in radians times the length of the radius.** As a first step, we convert 0.6° to radians.

$$0.6 \text{ deg} \times \frac{\pi \text{ rad}}{180 \text{ deg}} = 0.010472 \text{ rad}$$

A central angle of 1 radian would yield an arc of 4000 ft, but a central angle of 0.010472 radian yields

$$\text{arc} = 0.010472(4000 \text{ ft}) \approx \mathbf{42\ ft} \approx \text{height of the building}$$

Problem set 16

1. The tugboat *Gertrude* could steam at 4 times the speed of the current. She could make it 60 miles down the river in 1 more hour than it took her to go 27 miles up the river. What was *Gertrude*'s speed and how fast was the current in the river?
2. On the first leg, Ronkie Boy traveled for T hours at R miles per hour. The next leg was 100 miles longer. How fast did he have to fly in order to cover this distance in only P hours more than he took for the first leg?
3. The average speed for the first 300 miles was 60 mph and for the next 200 miles was 20 mph. What should be the speed for the last 500 miles so that the average speed for the trip would be 40 mph?
4. Hortense had a problem. She needed 20 liters of a solution that was 78% alcohol. She had one solution that was 90% alcohol and another that was 75% alcohol. How many liters of each solution should she use?
5. Wilde Oscar worked frantically for 4 hours and called for help because he saw it would take 6 more hours to finish. Calm Sally began to help and they finished the job in 2 more hours. How long would it have taken Sally to do the job alone?
6. How many 5-letter words can be made from the letters in the word LEFTY if repetition is permitted?
7. How many 3-letter signs can be made from the letters in the word HAMLET if no repetition is permitted?
8. Each question on a survey has three possible answers: yes, no, and maybe. The survey has 5 questions. How many possible permutations of responses to the survey are possible?
9. Find the equation of the line that is equidistant from the points (4, 2) and (−4, −3).
10. Find the coordinates of the point halfway between (1, 3) and (6, 5).
11. What is the number whose graph is $\frac{2}{27}$ of the way from $-6\frac{2}{5}$ to $4\frac{2}{5}$?
12. The latitude of Oklahoma City is 35.5° north. How far is it from Oklahoma City to the equator if the diameter of the earth is 7920 miles?

Evaluate:

13. Arctan (-1)

14. $\sin\left(\text{Arctan } \frac{2}{5}\right)$

15. $\cos\left(\text{Arcsin } \frac{3}{4}\right)$

16. $\sin\left(-\frac{13\pi}{6}\right) - \tan\frac{11\pi}{4}$

17. $\sin\frac{\pi}{2}\cos\frac{3\pi}{4} - \tan\frac{\pi}{6}$

18. $\sin\frac{5\pi}{2}\cos\frac{3\pi}{2} - \sin\frac{\pi}{3}$

19. $\sum_{k=-1}^{3} \frac{k^2}{4} - k$

Solve:

20. $\log_x \frac{1}{8} = -3$

21. $\log_2 \frac{1}{16} = s$

22. $\log_{1/3} r = -2$

23. Evaluate: $\frac{11!}{4!5!}$

24. Solve: $\begin{cases} 2y^2 - x^2 = 5 \\ 2y^2 + x^2 = 11 \end{cases}$

25. Simplify: $\frac{z^{2a-3}(\sqrt{z^3})^{a+2}}{z^{2a}z}$

26. Solve for g: $s = x_0 + v_0 t + \frac{1}{2}gt^2$

27. Find the equilibrant of: $-4\underline{/-125°} - 8\underline{/90°}$

28. If $a < 0$, compare: *A.* $\frac{1}{a}$ *B.* $\frac{1}{a^2}$

29. Solve: $\begin{cases} 0.2x - 0.4y = 0.2 \\ \frac{1}{2}x - \frac{1}{4}z = \frac{9}{4} \\ 2y - z = 3 \end{cases}$

30. Factor: $8a^3b^6 - 27x^6y^9$

Before Lesson 17 - Take Test 6

LESSON 17 Similar polygons and the scale factor · Corresponding sides

17.A Similar polygons and the scale factor

The word *similar* comes from the Latin word *similis*, which means "alike" or "of the same kind." We use the word in geometry to describe geometric figures that have the same shape and that look alike. Here we show two quadrilaterals that "look alike" and two triangles that "look alike."

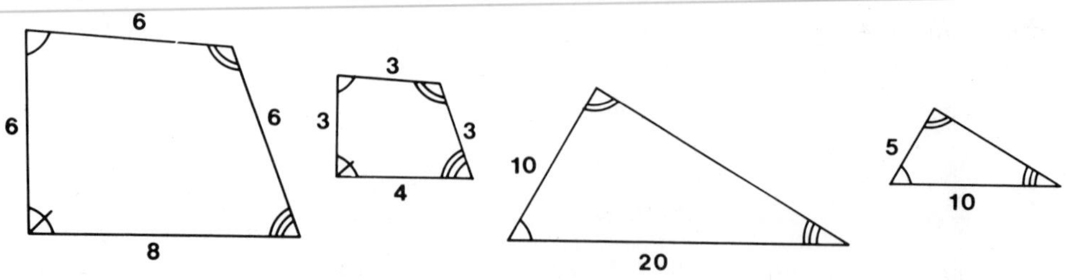

We need a more precise definition than "look alike" so we define *similar polygons* to be polygons in which the corresponding angles are equal and in which the lengths of the

corresponding sides are proportional. Triangles are the only rigid polygons in that only one triangle can be formed from three designated line segments. For triangles only, one part of the definition implies the other. **If three angles in one triangle have the same measures as three angles in another triangle, the triangles are similar and the lengths of the corresponding sides are proportional. Also, if the lengths of the sides in one triangle are proportional to the lengths of the corresponding sides in a second triangle, the triangles are similar and the measures of the corresponding angles are equal.** If we try to prove that these two statements about triangles are true, we find that we cannot do so unless we first assume without proof that at least one other statement is true. Thus, we decide to postulate (assume without proof) that these two statements are true. These postulated properties of triangles make the study of triangles most rewarding, and we will concentrate much of our attention on this fundamental figure of geometry.

In both pairs of polygons on the preceding page the sides in the leftmost figure of each pair are 2 times as long as the corresponding sides in the figures to their right, so the ***scale factor*** (SF, or constant of proportionality) between the small figure and the large figure is 2. If we go from the large figure to the small figure, the scale factor is $\frac{1}{2}$.

Example 17.A.1 Find sides M and P.

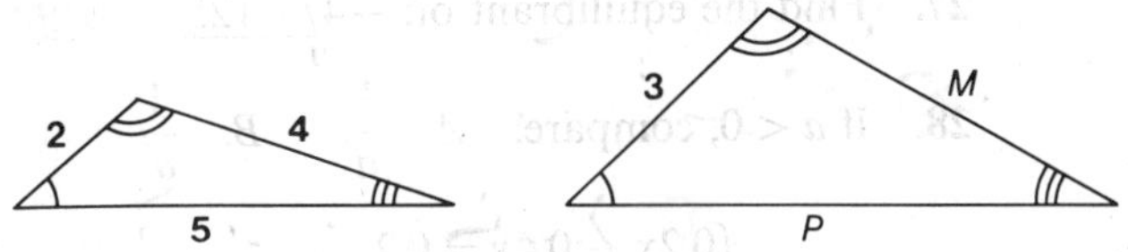

Solution From the tick marks, we can tell that the corresponding angles are equal, so we know that the lengths of the corresponding sides are proportional. Thus, the product of the length of a side from the first triangle and the scale factor gives the length of the corresponding side in the second triangle. We will use the leftmost sides to find the scale factor.

$$2SF = 3 \qquad \text{equation}$$

$$SF = \frac{3}{2} \qquad \text{divided}$$

Thus, $\frac{3}{2}$ times the length of any side of the left triangle gives us the length of the corresponding side of the triangle on the right.

$$5 \times \frac{3}{2} = P \qquad \text{and} \qquad 4 \times \frac{3}{2} = M$$

$$\mathbf{\frac{15}{2} = P} \qquad\qquad \mathbf{6 = M}$$

Example 17.A.2 Find x, y, and z.

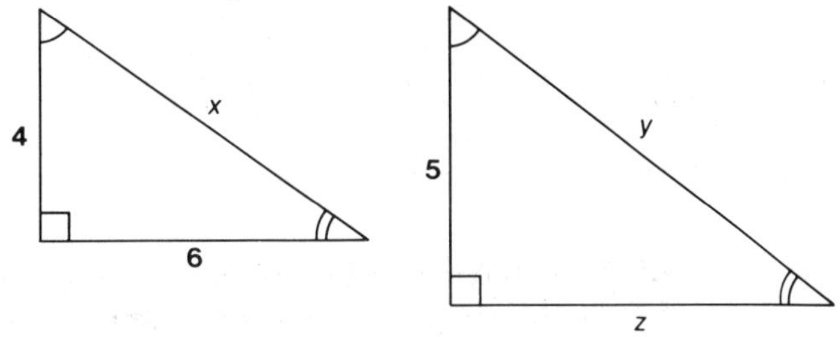

Solution The tick marks tell us that the corresponding angles are equal. Thus, the triangles are similar and the lengths of the corresponding sides are proportional. We begin by using the Pythagorean theorem to find x.

$$x^2 = 4^2 + 6^2 \longrightarrow x = \sqrt{16 + 36} \longrightarrow \mathbf{x = 2\sqrt{13}}$$

Next we find the scale factor.

$$4SF = 5 \longrightarrow SF = \frac{5}{4}$$

We finish by using the scale factor to find the lengths of y and z.

$$6 \times \frac{5}{4} = z \qquad 2\sqrt{13} \times \frac{5}{4} = y$$

$$\mathbf{\frac{15}{2} = z} \qquad \mathbf{\frac{5}{2}\sqrt{13} = y}$$

17.B Corresponding sides and proportions

Sides between corresponding angles in two similar polygons are corresponding sides. Sometimes it is easy to tell which sides are corresponding sides, and writing the proportion is straightforward. If we put the lengths of the sides of the triangle on the left in the numerator, and the lengths of the corresponding sides of the triangle on the right in the denominator, there are three possible ratios, as we show to the right of the figure.

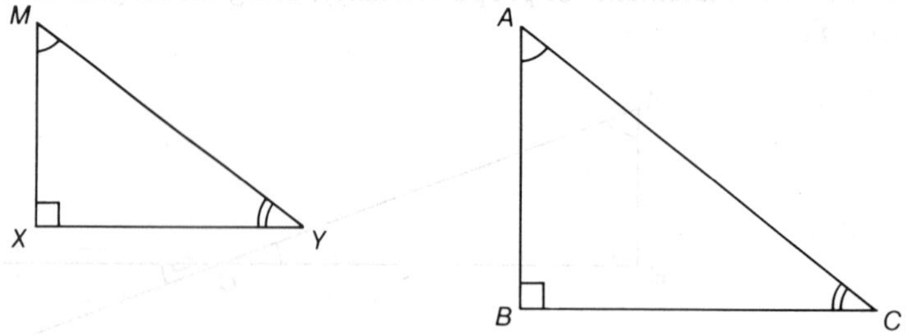

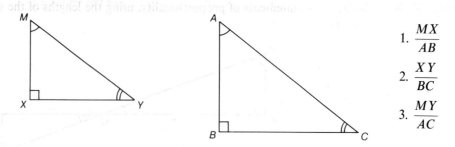

1. $\dfrac{MX}{AB}$
2. $\dfrac{XY}{BC}$
3. $\dfrac{MY}{AC}$

Since the triangles are similar, these ratios are equal, and any two of them may be equated to form a proportion.

$$\frac{MX}{AB} = \frac{XY}{BC} \qquad \frac{MX}{AB} = \frac{MY}{AC} \qquad \frac{XY}{BC} = \frac{MY}{AC}$$

Often, however, the figures are confusing, and it is not easy to determine which sides are corresponding sides, as in the following figure.

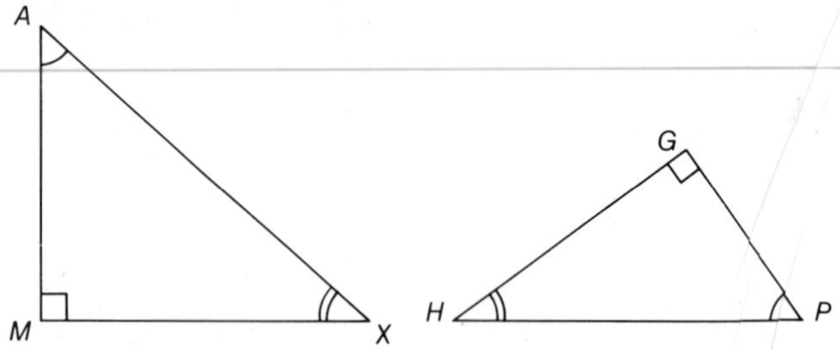

We can see that the angles in one triangle equal the angles in the other triangle, so the triangles are similar and the lengths of the sides are proportional. **If we make the statement of similarity by listing the vertices of equal angles in the same order, the cor-**

responding sides can be determined from this statement. For both triangles, we decide to begin with the single-tick-mark vertex, then the right-angle vertex and then the remaining vertex. Thus, our statement of triangle similarity is

$$\triangle AMX \sim \triangle PGH$$

where the symbol $\sim$ means "is similar to." The corresponding sides are the sides named by the first two letters in each group, the sides named by the last two letters in each group, and the sides named by the first and last letters in each group.

$$\triangle \underline{AM}X \sim \triangle \underline{PG}H \qquad \triangle A\underline{MX} \sim \triangle P\underline{GH} \qquad \triangle \underline{A}M\underline{X} \sim \triangle \underline{P}G\underline{H}$$

Thus, the equal ratios are

$$\frac{AM}{PG} \qquad \frac{MX}{GH} \qquad \frac{AX}{PH}$$

and we can use these ratios to write our statements of proportionality.

$$\frac{AM}{PG} = \frac{MX}{GH} \qquad \frac{AM}{PG} = \frac{AX}{PH} \qquad \frac{MX}{GH} = \frac{AX}{PH}$$

We note from these ratios that corresponding sides of similar triangles are sides that are opposite corresponding angles. In the first ratio, AM and PG are the lengths of the sides opposite the double-tick-mark angles, and MX and GH are lengths of the sides opposite the single-tick-mark angles.

Example 17.B.1 Write three statements of proportionality, using the lengths of the sides of these similar triangles.

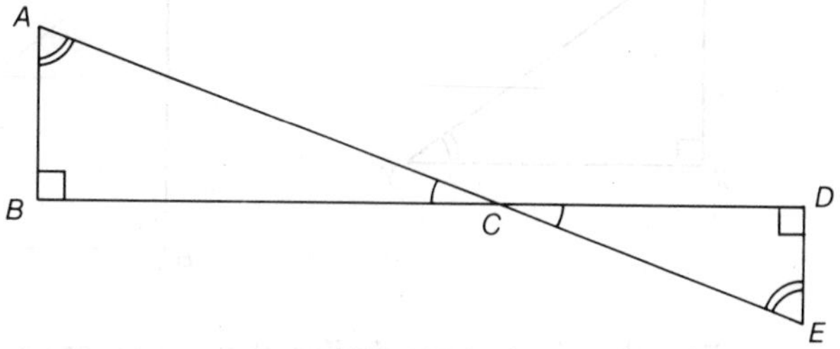

Solution First we write the statement of similarity listing the vertices of equal angles in the same order. We decide to begin with the right-angle vertex, then the vertex at C, and then the remaining vertex.

$$\triangle BCA \sim \triangle DCE$$

Now we can write three statements of proportionality:

$$\frac{BC}{DC} = \frac{CA}{CE} \qquad \frac{BC}{DC} = \frac{BA}{DE} \qquad \frac{CA}{CE} = \frac{BA}{DE}$$

Example 17.B.2 Write three statements of proportionality, using the lengths of the sides of these two triangles.

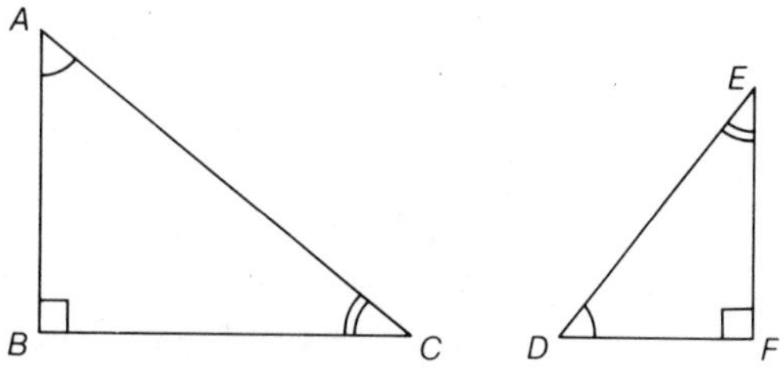

Solution For both triangles, we decide to begin with the right-angle vertex and follow this with the single-tick-mark vertex. So our statement of similarity is

$$\triangle BAC \sim \triangle FDE$$

Now we can write our statements of proportionality.

$$\frac{BA}{FD} = \frac{AC}{DE} \qquad \frac{BA}{FD} = \frac{BC}{FE} \qquad \frac{AC}{DE} = \frac{BC}{FE}$$

Problem set 17

1. The sum of the ages of Gimbel, Farth, and Murk is 90 years. Five years ago, 3 times the sum of the ages of Gimbel and Farth exceeded twice the age of Murk by 50. Five years from now, the sum of the ages of Farth and Murk will exceed the age of Gimbel by 55. How old will each turtle be in 175 years?

2. Krakow and Gadansk could complete 18 jobs in 40 hours. How long would it take Krakow to complete 1 job if Gadansk could complete 5 jobs in 20 hours?

3. The sum of two numbers is 22 and the difference is 6. What is the product of the numbers?

4. Suppose $z = 3y/x$. What happens to the value of z if the value of x is doubled and the value of y is tripled?

5. The ***mean*** of a group of numbers is the sum of the numbers divided by the number of numbers. The ***median*** is the middle number when the numbers are arranged in order of magnitude. If there is an even number of numbers, the median is the number halfway between the two middle numbers. Find the mean and median of 7, 5, 2, 11, 20, and 15.

6. How many 5-letter signs can be made from the word BURGEON if no repetition is permitted?

7. How many 3-digit combinations can be made with the digits 1, 2, 3, 4, 5, and 6 if repetition of digits is permitted?

8. Four chairs are placed against the wall. How many ways can the 7 boys sit in the four chairs if only 4 of them sit at one time?

9. Find a and b.

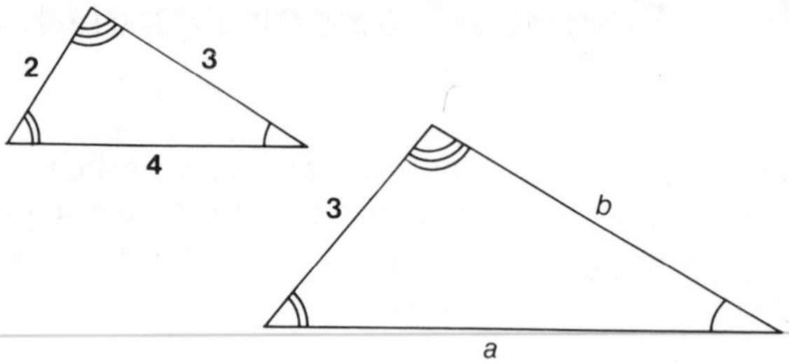

10. Write three statements of proportionality, using the lengths of the sides of these similar triangles.

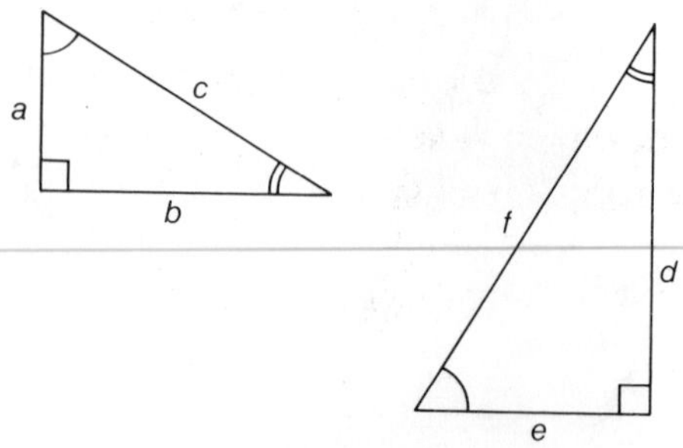

11. Find the equation of the line that is equidistant from the points (6, 4) and (−4, −2).

12. Find the coordinates of the point halfway between (−3, 4) and (6, −2).

13. What is the number whose graph is $\frac{7}{13}$ of the way from $-4\frac{1}{7}$ to $3\frac{2}{7}$?

14. The latitude of Denver is 39.7° north. How far is it from Denver to the equator if the diameter of the earth is 7920 miles?

Evaluate:

15. $\text{Arctan}\left(-\frac{\sqrt{3}}{3}\right)$

16. $\cos\left(\text{Arcsin}\frac{2}{5}\right)$

17. $\sin\left[\text{Arctan}\left(-\frac{2}{3}\right)\right]$

18. $\sin\left(-\frac{\pi}{3}\right)\cos\frac{5\pi}{2} - \tan\left(-\frac{13\pi}{6}\right)$

19. $\sin\frac{\pi}{2}\cos 0 - \sin\frac{7\pi}{6}$

20. $\tan\frac{13\pi}{6} - \sin\frac{\pi}{2}$

21. $\sum_{m=-2}^{2}\frac{(m-2)^2}{3}$

Solve:

22. $\log_a \frac{1}{9} = -2$

23. $\log_3 \frac{1}{27} = k$

24. $\log_{1/4} x = -3$

25. Evaluate: $\frac{12!}{9!3!}$

26. Solve: $\begin{cases} x^2 + y^2 = 9 \\ y - x + 3 = 0 \end{cases}$

27. Solve for t: $rs = \sqrt{qt - \frac{1}{3}h}$

28. Find the equilibrant of: $-5\angle -135^\circ + 6\angle 140^\circ$

29. Solve: $\begin{cases} 2x - y + z = 7 \\ x + 2y - z = 0 \\ x - y + 2z = 9 \end{cases}$

30. Divide $x^3 - 2x^2 + 3x + 4$ by $x - 2$ and check by adding.

LESSON 18 Adjacent, complementary, supplementary, and vertical angles · Forms of linear equations

18.A Adjacent, complementary, supplementary, and vertical angles

Some angle relationships exist by definition and some relationships can be proved. ***Adjacent angles,*** by definition, are angles that have a common vertex and a common side but have no common interior points. Thus, two angles are adjacent if the terminal side of one angle is the initial side of the other angle.

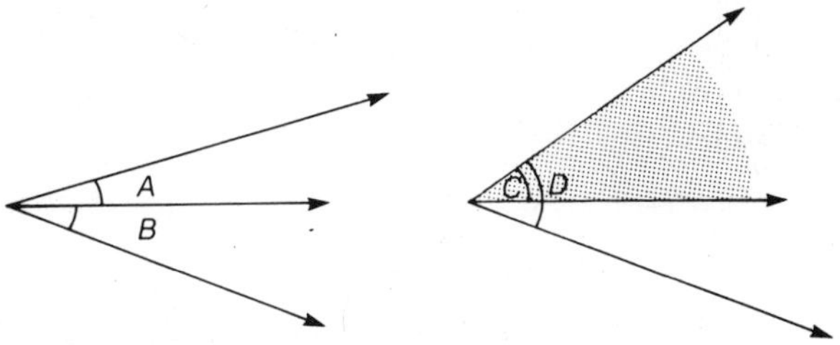

Here angles A and B are adjacent angles, but angles C and D are not adjacent angles because they have common interior points, as indicated by the shaded area in the figure. ***Complementary angles*** are defined to be two angles whose sum is 90°, and ***supplementary angles*** are defined to be two angles whose sum is 180°. In the following diagrams, angles E and F are complementary angles because their sum is 90°, and angles G and H are supplementary angles because their sum is 180°.

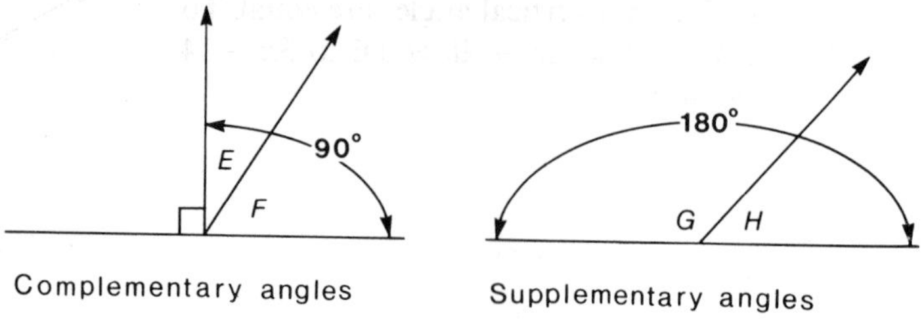

When two lines intersect, two pairs of **vertical angles** are formed. Here angles x and y are vertical angles and angles p and q are vertical angles.

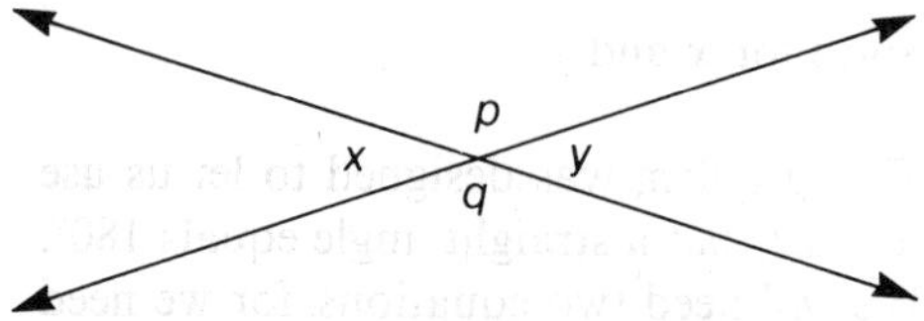

The fact that vertical angles are equal is called a ***theorem*** because we can prove that vertical angles are equal.

Example 18.A.1 Prove that vertical angles are equal.

Solution We begin by drawing two intersecting lines and naming the angles as shown.

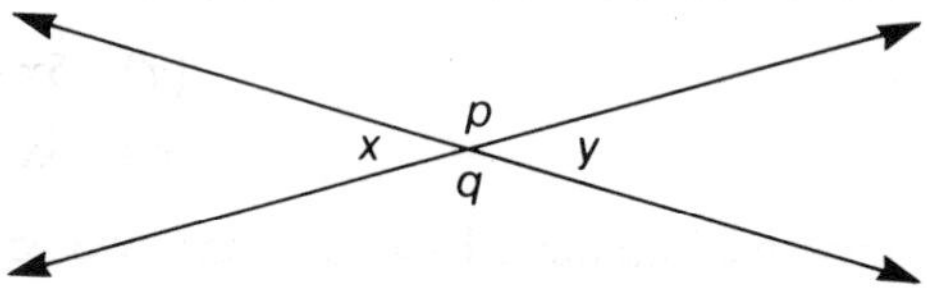

When we do proofs, we must give a reason for each statement. We list the statements on the left and list the reasons on the right.

STATEMENT	REASON
(*a*) $\angle x + \angle p = 180°$	Straight angle equals 180°
(*b*) $\angle p + \angle y = 180°$	Straight angle equals 180°

Now in (*a*), we substitute $\angle p + \angle y$ for 180° and then simplify by adding $-\angle p$ to both sides.

(*c*) $\angle x + \angle p = \angle p + \angle y$	substituted
(*d*) $\angle x = \angle y$	added $-\angle p$ to both sides

This proves that angle x equals angle y. The same procedure can be used to prove that angle p equals angle q.

We have defined a straight angle to equal 180° and a right angle to equal 90°. Now we have proved that vertical angles are equal. Examples like the next two are designed to give us practice in using these statements.

Example 18.A.2 Solve for x.

Solution This problem was designed to let us use the fact that vertical angles are equal. To find x, we set $2x + 28$ equal to $3x - 14$ and solve.

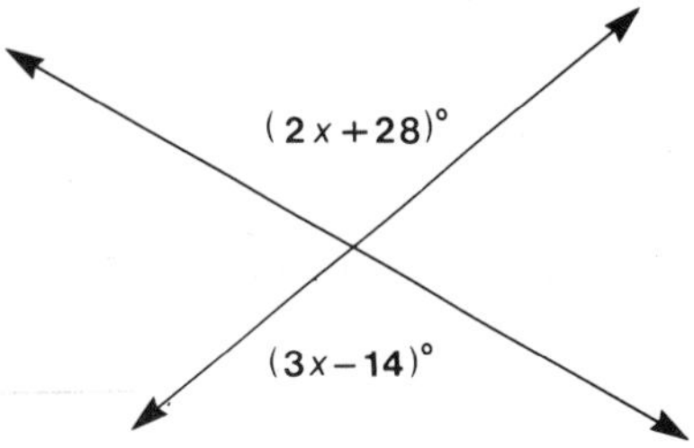

$$\begin{array}{rcll} 2x + 28 &=& 3x - 14 & \\ -2x + 14 &=& -2x + 14 & \text{added } -2x + 14 \\ \hline \mathbf{42} &=& \mathbf{x} & \end{array}$$

Example 18.A.3 Solve for x and y.

Solution This problem was designed to let us use the fact that a straight angle equals 180°. We will need two equations, for we need to solve for both x and y. The equations follow.

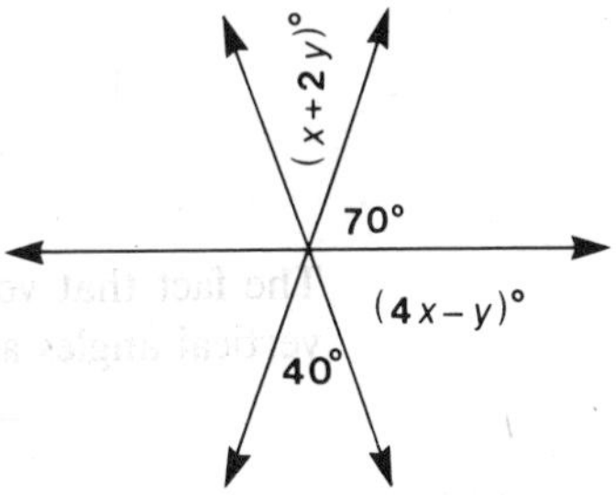

$$\begin{array}{ll} (a) & (4x - y) + 70 + (x + 2y) = 180 \\ (b) & 40 + (4x - y) + 70 = 180 \end{array}$$

Now we simplify the two equations.

$$\begin{array}{ll} (a') & 5x + y = 110 \\ (b') & 4x - y = 70 \end{array}$$

Now we eliminate y by adding the two equations.

$$\begin{array}{rl} 9x = 180 & \text{added} \\ \mathbf{x = 20} & \text{solved} \end{array}$$

From (a'), $y = 110 - 5x$ so $\mathbf{y} = 110 - 100 = \mathbf{10}$.

18.B Forms of linear equations

The slope-intercept equation of the line whose slope is $-\frac{3}{5}$ and whose y intercept is $\frac{11}{5}$ is

$$y = -\frac{3}{5}x + \frac{11}{5}$$

If many lines share a common characteristic, the lines are said to form **a family of lines.** There is an infinite number of lines whose slope is $-\frac{3}{5}$ and an infinite number of lines whose intercept is $\frac{11}{5}$. We show a few members of each of these families in the following figures.

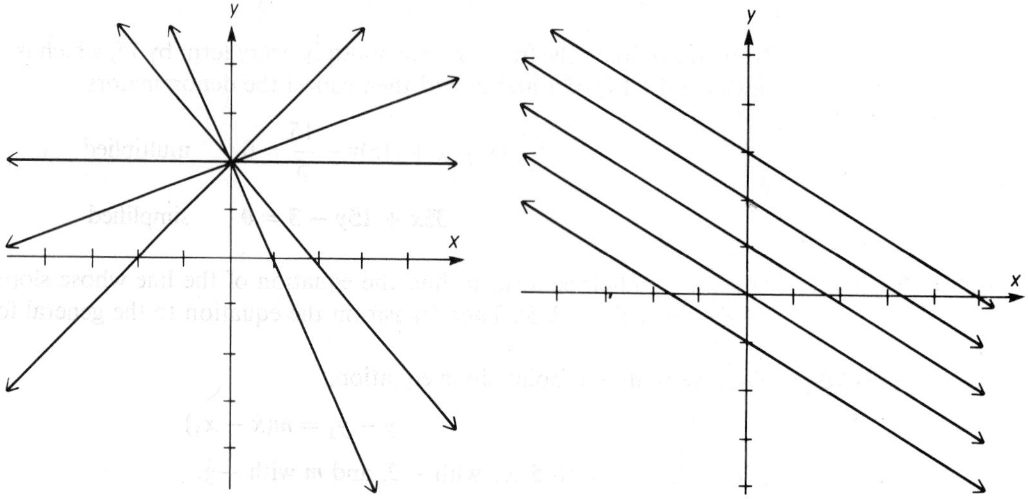

There are other forms of linear equations. Here we show five different forms of the equation on the preceding page.

$$(a)\quad 3x + 5y - 11 = 0 \qquad (b)\quad y = -\frac{3}{5}x + \frac{11}{5} \qquad (c)\quad \frac{x}{\frac{11}{3}} + \frac{y}{\frac{11}{5}} = 1$$

$$(d)\quad y - 1 = -\frac{3}{5}(x - 2) \qquad (e)\quad y - 1 = \frac{-2 - 1}{7 - 2}(x - 2)$$

We have concentrated on form (*b*) because this form is so useful. This form is called the ***slope-intercept form*** because $-\frac{3}{5}$, the first number, is the slope of the line, and $\frac{11}{5}$, the second number, is the y intercept of the line. The other forms have names and are important because each of them has some characteristic that makes the form desirable for some uses. The letters a, b, c, and m are often used to represent the constants in the equations. The names of the different forms and the constants used are as follows:

GENERAL FORM

$$(a)\quad Ax + By + C = 0$$

SLOPE-INTERCEPT FORM

$$(b)\quad y = mx + b$$

DOUBLE-INTERCEPT FORM

$$(c)\quad \frac{x}{a} + \frac{y}{b} = 1$$

POINT-SLOPE FORM

$$(d)\quad y - y_1 = m(x - x_1)$$

TWO-POINT FORM

$$(e)\quad y - y_1 = \frac{y_2 - y_1}{x_2 - x_1}(x - x_1)$$

We will continue to use the slope-intercept form for most applications, but we will practice changing the equations from one form to another form. This practice will help us to recognize the various forms of the equation of a line and will also sharpen a few skills of algebraic manipulation.

Example 18.B.1 Write $y = -\frac{7}{3}x + \frac{1}{5}$ in the general form with integers as the constants.

Solution The general form of the equation is

$$Ax + By + C = 0$$

We need to write the x term first, then the y term, and then the constant. When we do this we get

$$\frac{7}{3}x + y - \frac{1}{5} = 0$$

Now to eliminate the fractions, we multiply every term by 15, which is the least common multiple (LCM) of 3 and 5, and then cancel the denominators.

$$(15)\frac{7}{3}x + (15)y - \frac{15}{5} = 0 \qquad \text{multiplied}$$

$$\mathbf{35x + 15y - 3 = 0} \qquad \text{simplified}$$

Example 18.B.2 Use the point-slope form to find the equation of the line whose slope is $-\frac{1}{3}$ and that passes through $(-2, 5)$. Then transform the equation to the general form.

Solution First we write the point-slope equation,

$$y - y_1 = m(x - x_1)$$

and replace y_1 with 5, x_1 with -2, and m with $-\frac{1}{3}$:

$$y - 5 = -\frac{1}{3}[x - (-2)]$$

Now we simplify and get

$$3y - 15 = -x - 2$$

Then we finish by arranging the result into the general form and get

$$\mathbf{x + 3y - 13 = 0}$$

Example 18.B.3 Write $2x - 3y + 4 = 0$ in the double-intercept form.

Solution The double-intercept form has the constant on the right-hand side of the equals sign, and the constant is always 1. So we add -4 to both sides and then divide by -4. Then we simplify.

$$2x - 3y = -4 \qquad \text{added } -4$$

$$-\frac{x}{2} + \frac{3y}{4} = 1 \qquad \text{divided by } -4$$

Now we rewrite the left side into the required form.

$$\mathbf{\frac{x}{-2} + \frac{y}{\frac{4}{3}} = 1}$$

In this form, the values of the *x* intercept and *y* intercept can be determined by inspection. We see that if we let $x = 0$, y will equal $\frac{4}{3}$, and that if we let $y = 0$, then x will equal -2.

LET $x = 0$	LET $y = 0$
$\frac{0}{-2} + \frac{y}{\frac{4}{3}} = 1$	$\frac{x}{-2} + \frac{0}{\frac{4}{3}} = 1$
so $y = \frac{4}{3}$	so $x = -2$

Thus, the constant under *x* is the *x* intercept, which we call *a*, and the constant under *y* is the *y* intercept, which we call *b*.

Problem set 18

1. Find an angle such that 4 times its complement equals 200°.
2. Find an angle such that 3 times its supplement equals 450°.
3. Roselinda rode her bike for 60 miles at 30 miles per hour and then rode 20 miles at 10 miles per hour. How fast would she have to ride for the next 20 miles to have an average speed of 20 miles per hour for the entire trip?
4. The red-headed wonder boy ran y yards in s seconds. What would his rate be in yards per second if he ran twice as far in 10 more seconds?
5. Queen Wanatonga was frustrated because the men worked so slowly. It took 5 men 10 days to do the first job, and then 3 men quit. How many days would it take the 2 remaining men to do another job the same size?
6. Seven boys were to have their pictures taken three at a time. The photographer had three chairs placed in a row. How many ways could the photographer arrange the boys for their pictures?
7. Prove that vertical angles are equal.
8. Solve for x and y.

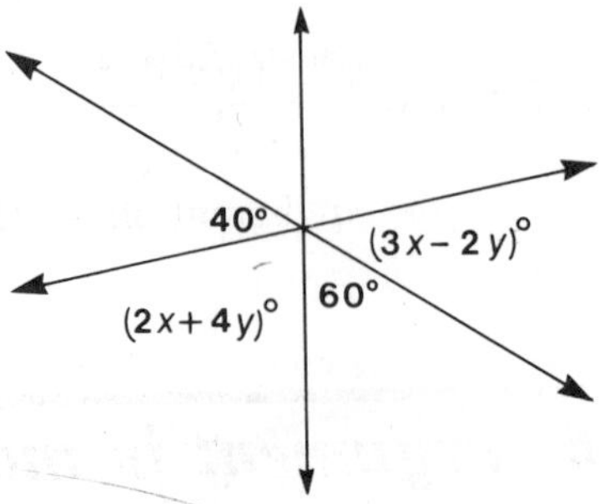

9. Use the point-slope method to find the general form of the equation of the line whose slope is $\frac{1}{2}$ and which passes through $(-2, 3)$.
10. Write $3x - 2y + 6 = 0$ in double-intercept form.
11. Find the lengths of sides p and q.

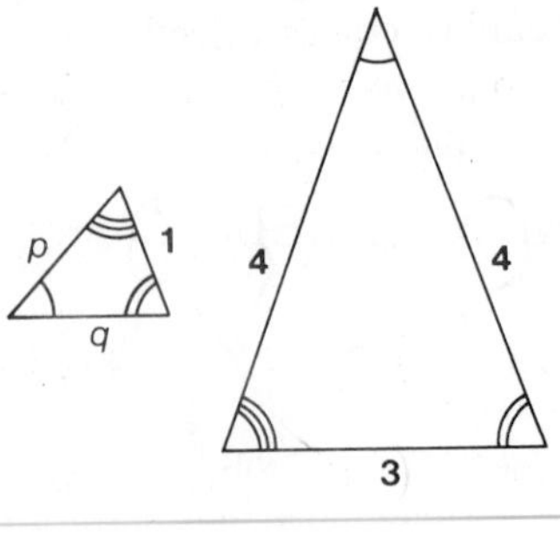

12. Use the lengths of the sides of the triangles to write three different statements of proportionality.

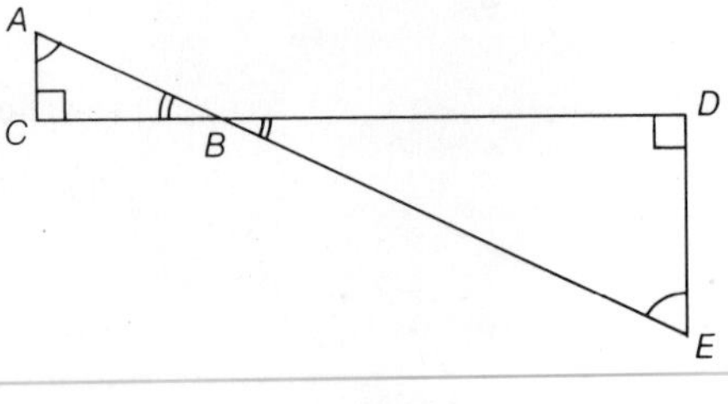

13. Find the equation of the line that is equidistant from the points $(3, 2)$ and $(-4, -3)$.
14. Find the coordinates of the point halfway between $(-2, 6)$ and $(6, 3)$.
15. What is the number whose graph is $\frac{5}{6}$ of the way from $-3\frac{2}{3}$ to $6\frac{1}{3}$?
16. An ant crawls through an arc of 30° along the rim of a grapefruit which is cut in half. If the diameter of the grapefruit is 8 inches, how far did the ant crawl?

Evaluate:

17. $\text{Arcsin}\left(-\dfrac{\sqrt{2}}{2}\right)$

18. $\sin\left[\text{Arccos}\left(-\dfrac{1}{5}\right)\right]$

19. $\sin\left[\text{Arctan}\left(-\dfrac{1}{3}\right)\right]$

20. $\sin\dfrac{\pi}{3}\cos\dfrac{\pi}{3} - \sin\dfrac{\pi}{3}$

21. $\tan\left(-\dfrac{\pi}{4}\right)\cos\dfrac{\pi}{2} + \sin 0$

22. $\cos\left(-\dfrac{13\pi}{6}\right) + \sin\dfrac{13\pi}{6}$

23. $\displaystyle\sum_{p=-1}^{3}\frac{p^2-2}{4}$

Solve:

24. $\log_b \dfrac{1}{27} = -3$

25. $\log_4 \dfrac{1}{64} = k$

26. $\log_{1/3} y = -2$

27. Evaluate: $\dfrac{11!}{6!3!}$

28. Solve: $\begin{cases} x^2 + y^2 = 13 \\ 2x^2 - y^2 = 14 \end{cases}$

29. Simplify: $\dfrac{x^{3a-2}(\sqrt[4]{x^3})^{a-2}}{x^3}$

30. Find the equilibrant of: $-3\angle 35° + 6\angle -40°$

LESSON 19 *The argument in mathematics* · *The laws of logarithms*

19.A The argument in mathematics

Every discipline takes common words and gives them special meanings for use in that discipline. This is also true in mathematics, and the word ***argument*** is a good example. In common usage, an argument refers to a heated discussion. Mathematicians use the word in this context, and they also give the word three other meanings for use in mathematics. The first meaning comes directly from the Latin word *arguere*, which means "to make clear" or "to prove by showing reasons." For this usage, we say that an argument is a connection of statements or reasons intended to establish or refute a given proposition. The second mathematical use is in polar coordinates, where the angle is sometimes called the argument and the length is called the modulus. The third mathematical use of the word argument is to designate the input of a function. A function is a set of ordered pairs, and if the same rule is applied to the first member of each pair to get the second member, the first member can be called the ***argument of the function.*** Here we show three function machines. Each operates on the input in the same way.

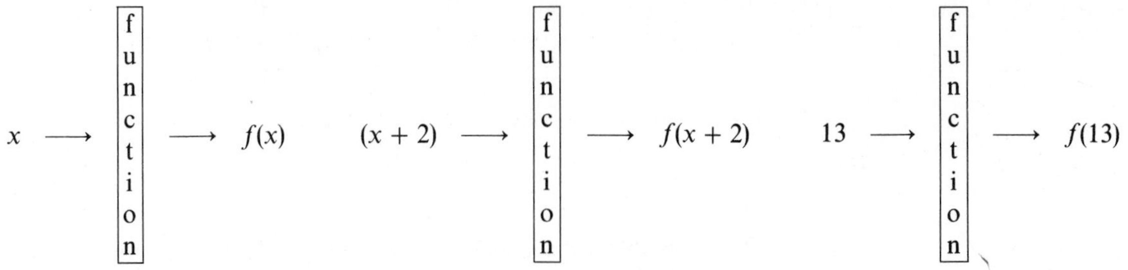

The outputs $f(x)$, $f(x + 2)$, and $f(13)$ tell us that the function machine followed some rule that we designate by the letter f. The inputs (x), $(x + 2)$, and (13) are called **arguments.** If the rule were to take the logarithm of, we would have the following diagrams.

$x \longrightarrow \boxed{\text{log}} \longrightarrow \log x$ $\qquad$ $(x + 2) \longrightarrow \boxed{\text{log}} \longrightarrow \log(x + 2)$ $\qquad$ $13 \longrightarrow \boxed{\text{log}} \longrightarrow \log 13$

$f(x) = \log x$ $\qquad$ $f(x + 2) = \log(x + 2)$ $\qquad$ $f(13) = \log 13$

We use the word argument even if functional notation is not used. In the following expressions, the arguments from left to right are x, $(x + 2)$, and 13, even though these notations do not appear to the left of the equals signs.

$$y = \log x \qquad y = \log (x + 2) \qquad y = \log 13$$

The word argument is used with all functions and especially when discussing trigonometric functions. The arguments in the following trigonometric functions

$$y = \sin x \qquad f(x) = \cos (2x - \pi) \qquad g(\theta) = \tan \left(\frac{\theta}{4} - 30°\right)$$

from left to right are x, $(2x - \pi)$, and $\left(\frac{\theta}{4} - 30°\right)$. If the argument consists of more than a single variable, it is customary to enclose the argument in parentheses to help avoid confusion.

19.B Laws of logarithms

Logarithms are exponents. There are three rules for logarithms, and they can be developed by remembering the rules for exponents. To develop the first rule for logarithms, we remember that 100 equals 10^2 and that 1000 equals 10^3.

$$100 = 10^2 \qquad 1000 = 10^3$$

Thus, if 10 is the base, the logarithm (exponent) necessary to get 100 is 2 and the logarithm (exponent) necessary to get 1000 is 3.

$$\log_{10} 100 = 2 \qquad \log_{10} 1000 = 3$$

If we multiply 10^2 by 10^3, we add the exponents.

$$10^2 \cdot 10^3 = 10^{2+3} = 10^5$$

Thus, we see that the logarithm (exponent) of the product of two exponentials is the sum of the individual logarithms (exponents).

$$\log_{10} (10^2 \cdot 10^3) = \log_{10} 10^2 + \log_{10} 10^3 = 5$$

And, if we use 100 instead of 10^2 and 1000 instead of 10^3, we can write

$$\log_{10} (100 \cdot 1000) = \log_{10} 100 + \log_{10} 1000 = 5$$

From this we can generalize and state the product rule of logarithms. We use N to represent the first number and use M to represent the second number. We will do a formal proof of this rule in a later lesson.

$$\log_b MN = \log_b M + \log_b N$$

This rule tells us that if we encounter an expression that contains the sum of two logarithms, we know that the arguments were multiplied.

Example 19.B.1 Solve $\log_a 4 + \log_a 6 = \log_a (x + 4)$.

Solution On the left-hand side, we have the sum of the logarithm of 4 and the logarithm of 6, and a is the base for both. This means that 6 and 4 are multiplied, so we can write

$$\log_a 24 = \log_a (x + 4)$$

If the logarithms are equal and the bases are equal, then the arguments are equal. So,

$$24 = x + 4 \qquad \text{equal arguments}$$

$$\mathbf{20 = x} \qquad \text{solved}$$

The argument of a logarithmic function must always be a positive number, so the last step in the solution of a problem of this type must be a check to see that the use of the values found for the variable will result in positive arguments. In this problem we have only one value of the variable to check. When 20 is used in $(x + 4)$, we get 24, a positive number. Thus, 20 is an acceptable value of x in this argument.

To find the rule for the quotient of two numbers, we note that when we divide 10^3 by 10^2, the logarithm (exponent) of the denominator is subtracted from the logarithm (exponent) of the numerator.

$$\frac{10^3}{10^2} = 10^{3-2} = 10^1$$

Thus, we can write

$$\log_{10} \frac{10^3}{10^2} = \log_{10} 10^3 - \log_{10} 10^2 = 1$$

If we replace 10^3 with M and 10^2 with N, we can generalize and write the quotient rule as

$$\log_b \frac{M}{N} = \log_b M - \log_b N$$

This rule tells us that if an expression is the difference of two logarithms, then we know that the arguments were divided.

Example 19.B.2 Solve $\log_4 (x + 6) - \log_4 (x - 1) = \log_4 5$.

Solution On the left we see the difference of the logarithms of two expressions and the bases are equal. This tells us that the expressions were divided, so we can write

$$\log_4 \frac{x + 6}{x - 1} = \log_4 5$$

If the logarithms are equal and the bases are equal, then the arguments are equal. We equate the arguments and solve for x.

$$\frac{x + 6}{x - 1} = 5 \qquad \text{equated arguments}$$

$$x + 6 = 5(x - 1) \qquad \text{cross multiplied}$$

$$x + 6 = 5x - 5 \qquad \text{multiplied}$$

$$11 = 4x \qquad \text{simplified}$$

$$\mathbf{\frac{11}{4} = x} \qquad \text{divided}$$

To find the power rule for logarithms, we note that

$$\log_{10} 10^2 = 2$$

because the exponent is the logarithm. If we raise 10^2 to the third power, we get 10^6

$$(10^2)^3 = 10^6$$

and the logarithm of 10^6 is 6. Thus, the log of $(10^2)^3$ is 3 times the logarithm of 10^2. We generalize and state the power rule for logarithms and use M in place of 10^2 and n in place of 3.

$$\log_b M^n = n \log_b M$$

This rule is probably the most useful of the three rules and is the most difficult to remember. The rule is used two different ways. We can turn an exponent into a coefficient, as

$$\log_b x^5 \xrightarrow{\text{equals}} 5 \log_b x$$

and we can go the other way and turn a coefficient into an exponent.

$$5 \log_b x \xrightarrow{\text{equals}} \log_b x^5$$

Example 19.B.3 Solve $3 \log_b x = \log_b 8$.

Solution **On the left we use the power rule to turn the coefficient into an exponent and write**

$$\log_b x^3 = \log_b 8$$

If the logarithms are equal and the bases are equal, then the arguments are equal. We equate the arguments and solve:

$x^3 = 8$ equated arguments

$\mathbf{x = 2}$ solved

Example 19.B.4 Solve $\log_{12} x = \frac{2}{3} \log_{12} 64$.

Solution **This time we change the coefficient on the right-hand side to an exponent and write**

$$\log_{12} x = \log_{12} 64^{2/3}$$

If the logarithms are equal and the bases are equal, then the arguments are equal. We equate the arguments and solve:

$x = 64^{2/3}$ equated arguments

$\mathbf{x = 16}$ solved

Problem set 19

1. Find an angle such that 4 times its complement exceeds its supplement by 60°.
2. The little red airplane could fly at 6 times the speed of the wind. It could fly 700 miles downwind in 1 hour less than it took to fly 600 miles upwind. What was the speed of the little red airplane and what was the speed of the wind?
3. The average speed for the first 45 miles was 15 mph and the average speed for the next 50 miles was 25 mph. What should be the speed for the next 85 miles so that the overall average speed would be 18 mph?

4. The correct mixture for the alloy was 16% tin and 84% copper. How much tin must be added to 410 pounds of the correct mixture to get a mixture that is 18% tin?

5. A cube that measures 4 inches on each side is dipped in red paint. When the paint dries, the cube is cut into 1-inch cubes. How many 1-inch cubes will have no red faces?

6. Twenty books were available for the display of five books in a row. How many different displays were possible?

7. Prove that vertical angles are equal.

8. Solve for x and y.

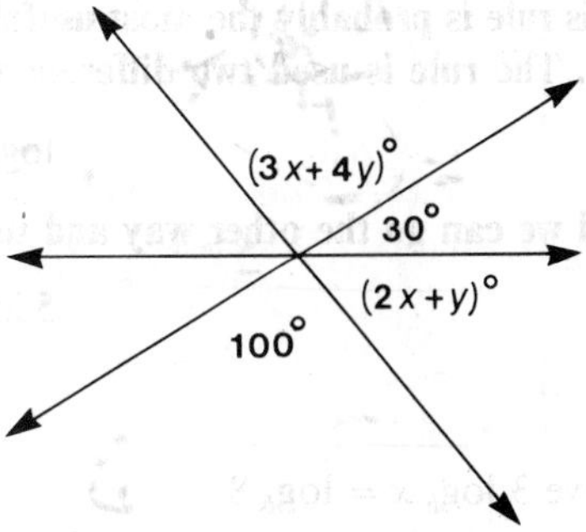

9. Use the point-slope method to find the general form of the equation of the line which has slope $-\frac{1}{3}$ and which passes through $(-3, 4)$.

10. Write $2x - 4y + 5 = 0$ in double-intercept form.

11. Find the lengths of sides a and b.

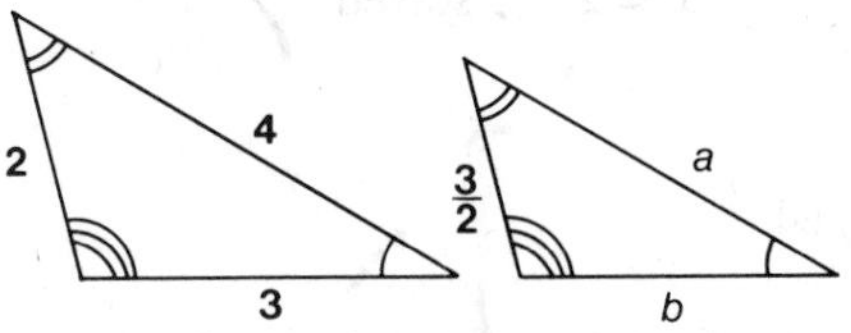

12. The angle of depression from an airplane to an object on the ground is 42°. If the airplane is 7000 feet above the ground, what is the slant range from the airplane to the object?

13. Find the equation of the line that is equidistant from the points $(-4, 2)$ and $(5, 3)$.

14. Find the coordinates of the point halfway between $(-3, 4)$ and $(6, 2)$.

15. What is the number whose graph is $\frac{2}{3}$ of the way from $2\frac{1}{4}$ to $6\frac{3}{4}$?

16. A dog tied by a rope to a pole moves through an angle of 35° along a circular arc. How far did the dog move if the rope is 30 feet in length?

Evaluate:

17. $\text{Arctan}\,(-1)$

18. $\sin\,(\text{Arcsin}\,\frac{1}{2})$

19. $\cos\,[\text{Arctan}\,(-\frac{2}{3})]$

20. $\sin\frac{2\pi}{3}\cos\frac{2\pi}{3} - \sin\frac{4\pi}{3}$

21. $\tan\left(-\frac{3\pi}{4}\right)\cos\frac{\pi}{2} - \sin\frac{\pi}{2}$

22. $\sin\left(-\frac{19\pi}{6}\right) + \sin\frac{13\pi}{6}$

23. $\sum_{j=-2}^{1} \frac{2j-3}{3}$

Solve for x:

24. $\log_a 3 + \log_a 4 = \log_a (x - 2)$

25. $\log_3 (x + 2) - \log_3 (x - 1) = \log_3 4$

26. $3 \log_c x = \log_c 27$

27. $\log_{12} x = \frac{2}{3} \log_{12} 27$

28. Factor: $8x^3y^6 - 27a^3y^9$

29. Solve for z: $2k = \sqrt{3z} - 2p$

30. Solve: $\sqrt{x} + \sqrt{x + 16} = 8$

LESSON 20 Reciprocal functions · Permutation notation

20.A Reciprocal functions

It is convenient to have a name for the reciprocals of the sine, cosine, and tangent. We call these reciprocal functions the cosecant (csc), secant (sec), and cotangent (cot) and define them as follows:

$$\frac{1}{\sin \theta} = \csc \theta \qquad \frac{1}{\cos \theta} = \sec \theta \qquad \frac{1}{\tan \theta} = \cot \theta$$

We can remember the definitions of these ratios if we write the functions vertically and note the pairings.

$$\sin \theta = \frac{\text{opp}}{\text{hyp}}$$

$$\cos \theta = \frac{\text{adj}}{\text{hyp}}$$

$$\tan \theta = \frac{\text{opp}}{\text{adj}}$$

$$\cot \theta = \frac{\text{adj}}{\text{opp}}$$

$$\sec \theta = \frac{\text{hyp}}{\text{adj}}$$

$$\csc \theta = \frac{\text{hyp}}{\text{opp}}$$

We note that the cosecant (csc) is the ratio of the hypotenuse to the side opposite. This is the sine ratio upside-down. We note also that the secant is the cosine ratio upside-down and that the cotangent is the tangent ratio upside-down. If we wanted to, we could use these reciprocal functions to help us solve triangles and add vectors, but we will usually not do so because the sine, cosine, and tangent perform these tasks quite adequately. We will reserve the use of the reciprocal functions to situations where their use is helpful. Problems such as the following will allow us to work with the cotangent, secant, and cosecant so their properties will be as familiar as those of the sine, cosine, and tangent.

Example 20.A.1 Draw the appropriate triangles and evaluate sec 330° + cot 480°.

Solution We draw diagrams and note the related angles.

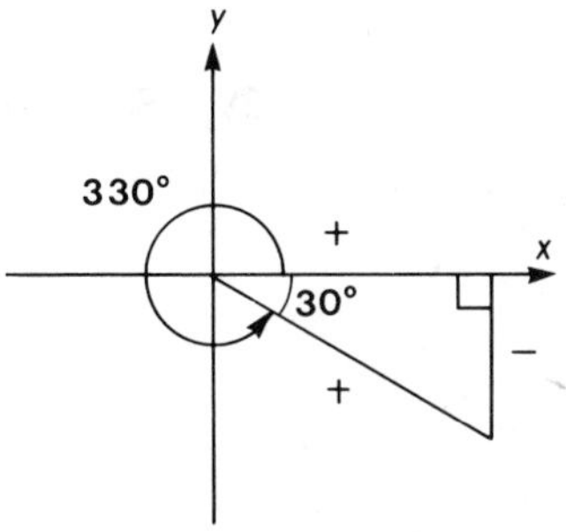

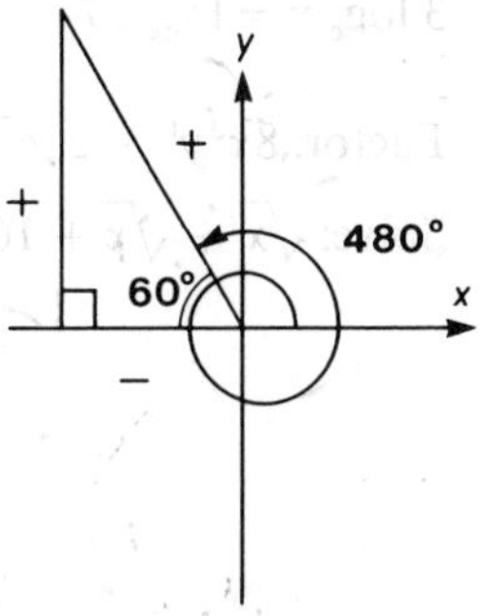

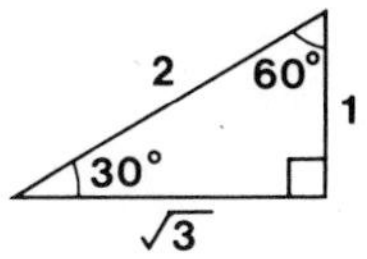

cosine is + so secant is +   tangent is − so cotangent is −

$\sec 330° = \sec 30°$ $\cot 480° = -\cot 60°$

$\cos 30° = \dfrac{\sqrt{3}}{2}$ $\tan 60° = \dfrac{\sqrt{3}}{1}$

so $\sec 30° = \dfrac{2}{\sqrt{3}}$ so $\cot 60° = \dfrac{1}{\sqrt{3}}$

Now we have the values and can add the functions.

$$\sec 330° + \cot 480° = \frac{2}{\sqrt{3}} - \frac{1}{\sqrt{3}} \qquad \text{sum of functions}$$

$$= \frac{1}{\sqrt{3}} \qquad \text{added}$$

$$= \frac{\sqrt{3}}{3} \qquad \text{rationalized}$$

Example 20.A.2 Draw the appropriate triangles and evaluate $\sec \dfrac{11\pi}{4} - \csc \dfrac{5\pi}{2}$.

Solution We draw the diagrams and note the related angles.

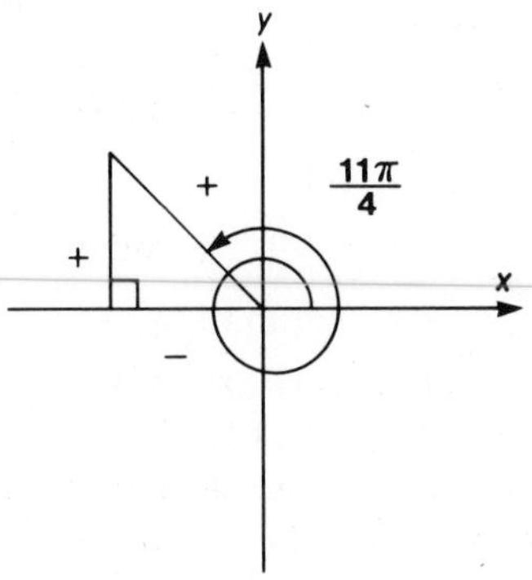

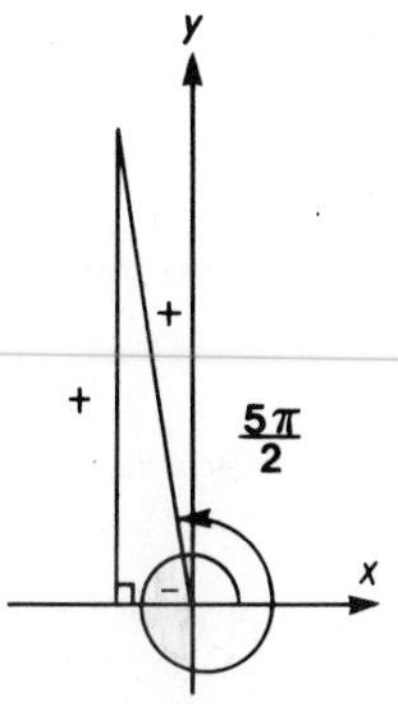

cosine is − so secant is −   sine is + so cosecant is +

$\sec \dfrac{11\pi}{4} = -\sec \dfrac{\pi}{4}$ $\csc \dfrac{5\pi}{2} = \csc \dfrac{\pi}{2}$

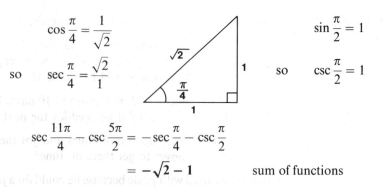

$$\cos\frac{\pi}{4} = \frac{1}{\sqrt{2}}$$

so $$\sec\frac{\pi}{4} = \frac{\sqrt{2}}{1}$$

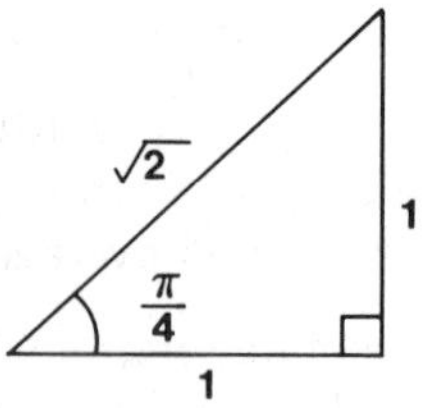

$$\sin\frac{\pi}{2} = 1$$

so $$\csc\frac{\pi}{2} = 1$$

$$\sec\frac{11\pi}{4} - \csc\frac{5\pi}{2} = -\sec\frac{\pi}{4} - \csc\frac{\pi}{2}$$

$$= -\sqrt{2} - 1 \qquad \text{sum of functions}$$

20.B Permutation notation

We have worked specific permutation problems but have avoided the general notation for this type of problem. The concept and the notation are both helpful and are explained in the following example.

Example 20.B.1 How many permutations are there of 22 things taken 6 at a time? Generalize this answer to an expression for n things taken r at a time.

Solution We can put 22 things in the first slot, 21 in the next, 20 in the next, etc., until we have all 6 positions filled.

22	21	20	19	18	17

We see that the first number is 22, the next is 1 less than 22, the next is 2 less than 22, etc.

$$(22) \quad (21) \quad (20) \quad (19) \quad (18) \quad (17)$$
$$(22) \quad (22-1) \quad (22-2) \quad (22-3) \quad (22-4) \quad (22-5)$$

If we use n for 22 and r for 6, the first factor is n, the next is $(n-1)$, the next is $(n-2)$, etc.

$$n(n-1)(n-2)\cdots$$

but the last factor is not $(n-r)$ because $(22-6)$ is 16 and the last entry is 17, which is 1 greater. Thus, we must use $(n-r+1)$ as the last factor. Thus, we write the general expression for the permutation of n things taken r at a time as

$$_nP_r = n(n-1)(n-2)(n-3)\cdots(n-r+1)$$

The notation $_nP_r$ is not the only notation used for the permutation of n things taken r at a time. Some authors use the notation P_r^n and others use $P_{n,r}$ or $P(n, r)$.

Example 20.B.2 Find $_{12}P_4$.

Solution This asks for the number of permutations of 12 things taken 4 at a time. The answer is

$$12 \cdot 11 \cdot 10 \cdot 9$$

Now if we multiply above and below by 8!, we get

$$\frac{12 \cdot 11 \cdot 10 \cdot 9 \cdot 8!}{8!} = \frac{12!}{8!}$$

We can use the calculator to evaluate this expression and we get

$$_{12}P_4 = \mathbf{11{,}880}$$

Problem set 20

1. Find an angle such that 5 times its complement exceeds twice its supplement by 30°.
2. The average speed for the first 36 miles was 12 mph. The average speed for the next 45 miles was 15 mph. What should be the average speed for the next 54 miles so that the overall average would be 15 mph?
3. Four hundred men could do the job in 10 days. Paul had 600 men on the job for 5 days. How many men did he need for the next 5 days to finish the job on time?
4. The airplane flew m miles in h hours and got there 3 hours late. How fast should the plane have flown to get there on time?
5. Bubber strutted with pride because he could do a job in 3 hours that it took Dougan 6 hours to do. Bubber began work at noon and worked for 3 hours and then was joined by Dougan. What time would it be when a total of 4 jobs was completed?
6. Find ${}_{12}P_4$.
7. Find ${}_{13}P_5$.
8. Prove that vertical angles are equal.
9. Solve for x and y.

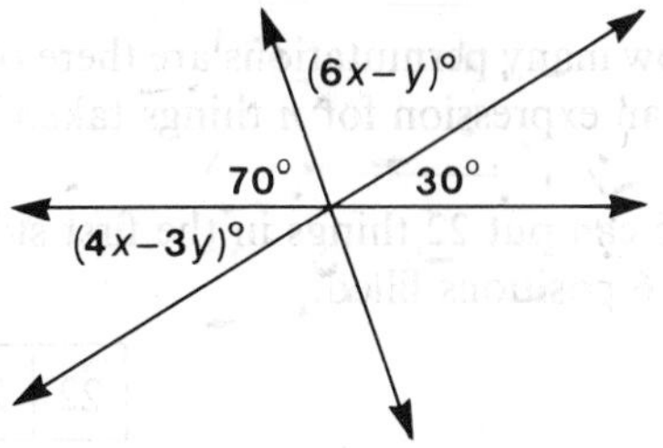

10. Use the point-slope method to find the general form of the equation of the line whose slope is $-\frac{1}{3}$ and which passes through $(-2, 3)$.
11. Write $5x - 3y + 6 = 0$ in double-intercept form.
12. Find the lengths of sides x and y.

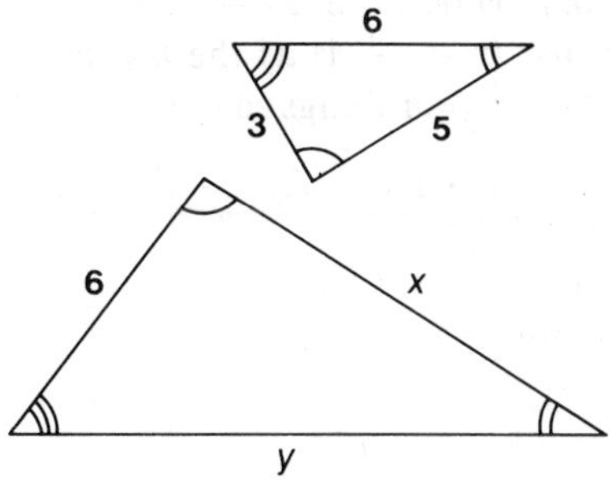

13. The two triangles shown are similar. Use the lengths of the sides of the triangles to write three statements of proportionality.

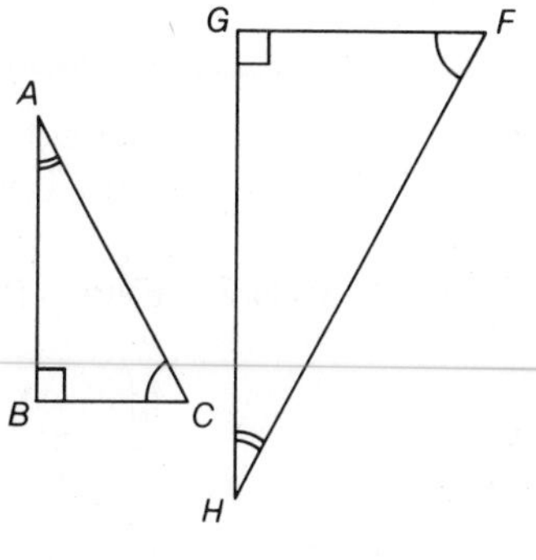

14. Find the equation of the line that is equidistant from the points $(2, 4)$ and $(-4, 6)$.
15. Find the coordinates of the point halfway between $(-3, 4)$ and $(6, -2)$.
16. A mouse scurries through an arc of 50° along the edge of a circular swimming pool. If the swimming pool is 70 feet in diameter, how far did the mouse scurry?

17. What is the number whose graph is $\frac{4}{13}$ of the way from $-3\frac{3}{4}$ to 6?

Evaluate:

18. $\text{Arccos}\left(-\frac{\sqrt{3}}{2}\right)$

19. $\sin\left[\text{Arctan}\left(-\frac{3}{4}\right)\right]$

20. $\cos\left[\text{Arcsin}\left(-\frac{2}{3}\right)\right]$

21. $\sec\left(-\frac{\pi}{3}\right) + \cot\left(-\frac{13\pi}{6}\right)$

22. $\csc(-330°) - \sec 390°$

23. $\sum_{z=-2}^{1} \frac{z^3 - 1}{3}$

Solve for x:

24. $\log_4 2 + \log_4 8 = \log_4 (x + 3)$

25. $\log_3 (x - 2) - \log_3 (x + 1) = \log_3 5$

26. $4 \log_c x = \log_c 81$

27. $\log_{13} x = \frac{3}{4} \log_{13} 16$

28. Solve for h: $gz = \sqrt{4h - ts^3}$

29. Add: $-2\underline{/140°} + 8\underline{/150°}$

30. Simplify: $\dfrac{-\sqrt{3}\sqrt{-3}\sqrt{2}\sqrt{-2} - \sqrt{8}\sqrt{2}}{\sqrt{-16} + 3}$

LESSON 21 Conic sections · Circles · Constants in exponential functions

21.A Conic sections

A *circular cone* is the surface generated by a line when one point on the line is fixed and another point on the line is moved in a circle. The cone has two parts called ***nappes*** that are on either side of the fixed point. If the nappes are cut by a plane, the figures formed by the points of intersection of the cone and the plane are called ***conic sections.*** If the plane is perpendicular to the vertical axis of the cone, the plane will cut only one nappe, and the points of intersection form a ***circle.*** If the plane is tilted slightly, the points of intersection form an ***ellipse.***

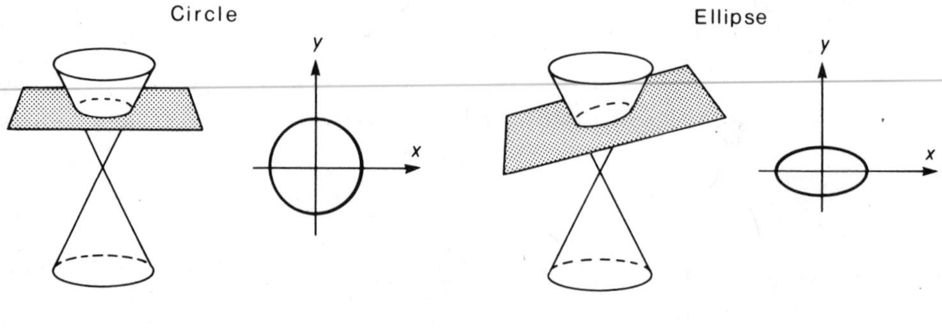

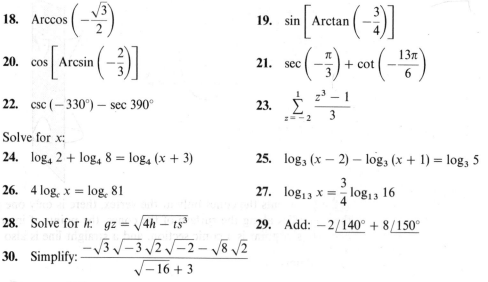

If the plane is tilted even more, the figure formed is a ***parabola.*** If the plane is tilted so that both nappes are cut, a two-part figure called a ***hyperbola*** is formed.

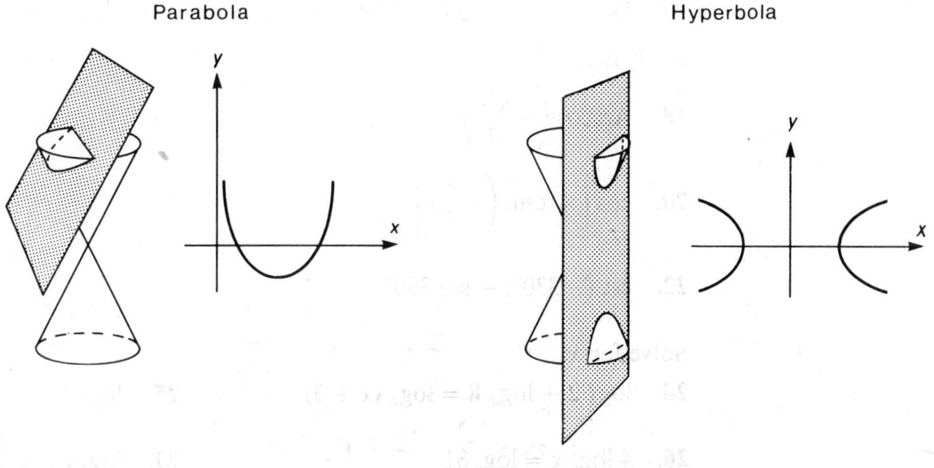

If the plane cuts the cones only at the vertex, there is only one point of intersection. If the plane lies along the surface of the cones, the points of intersection form a straight line. Thus, a point is a conic section, and a straight line is also a conic section.

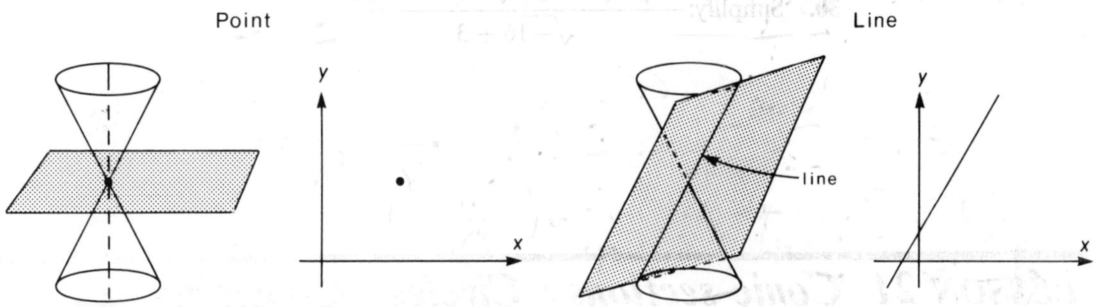

21.B Circles

We remember that a line is the locus of all points in a plane that are equidistant from two given points. We use the distance formula twice to find the equation of a specified line.

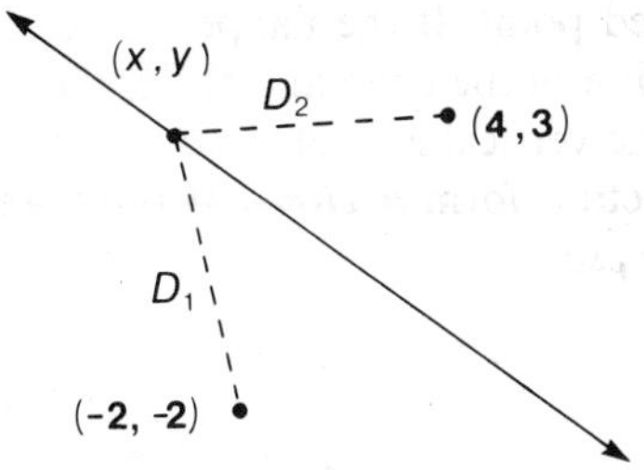

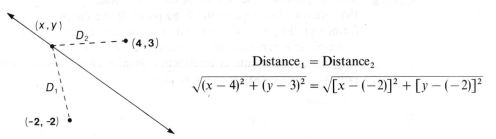

$$\text{Distance}_1 = \text{Distance}_2$$

$$\sqrt{(x-4)^2 + (y-3)^2} = \sqrt{[x-(-2)]^2 + [y-(-2)]^2}$$

A *circle* is the locus of all points in a plane that are equidistant from a point called the center of the circle. Here we show a circle of radius r whose center is $(4, -6)$.

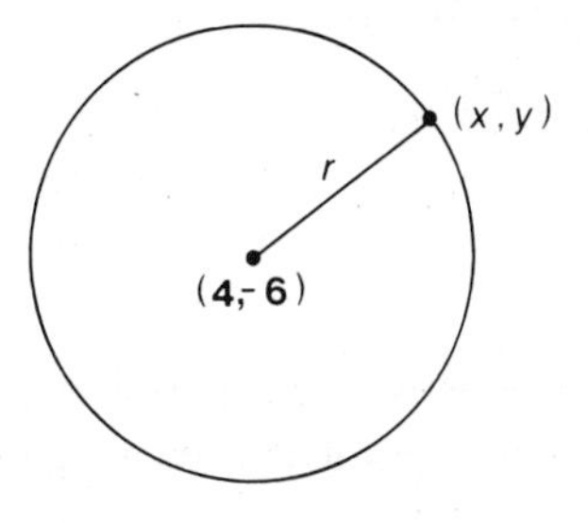

Distance from the center to (x, y) = the radius

$$\sqrt{(x-4)^2 + [y-(-6)]^2} = r$$

Thus, to find the equation of a circle, we have to use the distance equation only once. If the radius of the circle is 5, we can use 5 instead of r and get

$$\sqrt{(x-4)^2 + [y-(-6)]^2} = 5$$

If we square both sides and simplify, we can write the equation of this circle in ***standard form.***

$$(x-4)^2 + (y+6)^2 = 25 \qquad \text{standard form}$$

If we multiply as indicated and collect like terms, we can write the equation in ***general form.***

$$x^2 - 8x + 16 + y^2 + 12y + 36 = 25 \qquad \text{multiplied}$$
$$x^2 + y^2 - 8x + 12y + 27 = 0 \qquad \text{general form}$$

Example 21.B.1 Find the standard form of the equation of a circle whose center is at (h, k) and whose radius is r.

Solution We always use a sketch. When we write the distance equation, we could use either $(x-h)^2$ or $(h-x)^2$. It is customary to write the variable first, and we will follow custom and write

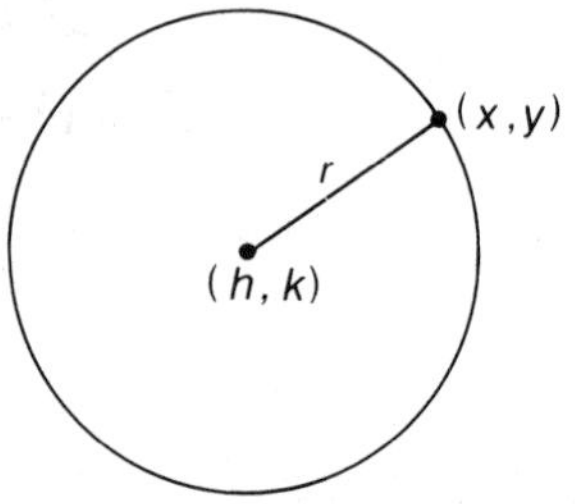

$$\sqrt{(x-h)^2 + (y-k)^2} = r$$

Now we square both sides to eliminate the radical.

$$\mathbf{(x-h)^2 + (y-k)^2 = r^2} \qquad \text{standard form}$$

Example 21.B.2 Find the standard form of the equation of a circle of radius 4 whose center is at $(-3, 3)$. Then write the general form of the equation.

Solution We begin with a sketch. We use the distance formula to describe the distance from $(-3, 3)$ to (x, y).

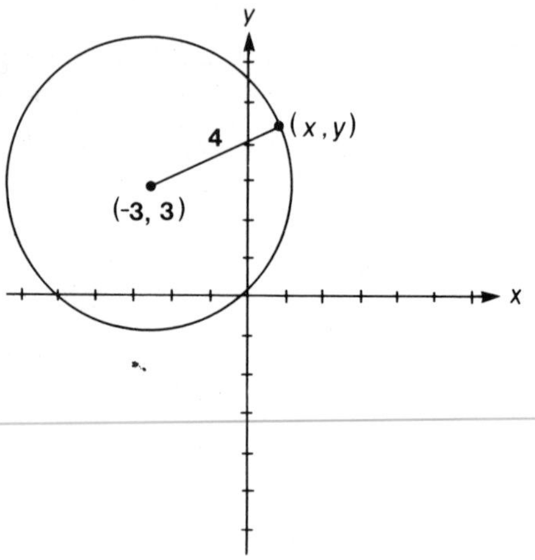

$$\sqrt{[x-(-3)]^2 + [y-(3)]^2} = 4$$

Now we square both sides to eliminate the radical.

$$[x-(-3)]^2 + [y-(3)]^2 = 4^2$$

Then we simplify and get

$$\mathbf{(x+3)^2 + (y-3)^2 = 16} \qquad \text{standard form}$$

Now we perform the indicated multiplications and get

$$x^2 + 6x + 9 + y^2 - 6y + 9 = 16$$

We finish by collecting like terms.

$$x^2 + y^2 + 6x - 6y + 2 = 0 \qquad \text{general form}$$

Example 21.B.3 Write the standard form and the general form of the equation of the circle whose center is the origin and whose radius is r.

Solution We always draw a diagram. Now we use the distance formula to write

$$\sqrt{(x - 0)^2 + (y - 0)^2} = r$$

Again we square both sides to eliminate the radical.

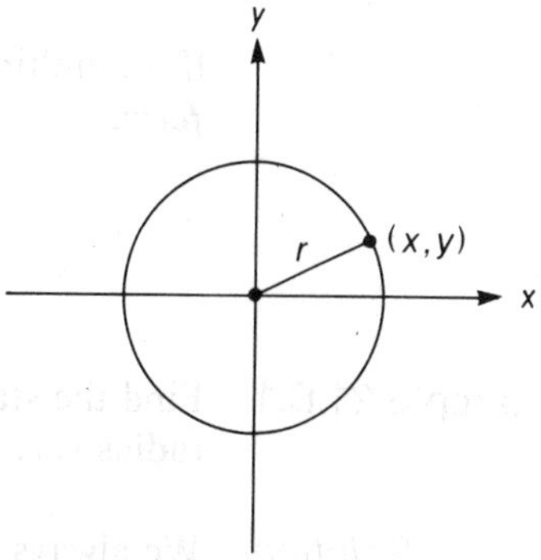

$$x^2 + y^2 = r^2 \qquad \text{standard form}$$

$$x^2 + y^2 - r^2 = 0 \qquad \text{general form}$$

21.C Constants in exponential functions

The following expressions are called ***powers.*** In each of these expressions the exponent is a constant.

(*a*) $y = x^2$ (*b*) $y = -(x - 4)^3$ (*c*) $y = x^{1.2}$ (*d*) $y = (x - 3)^{1/2}$

In exponential functions, the exponent contains a variable and the base can be any positive number except 1. Thus, all of the following are exponential functions:

(*e*) $y = 2.76^x$ (*f*) $y = (\frac{1}{3})^x$ (*g*) $y = 4^{-x}$ (*h*) $y = 0.5^{2x}$ (*i*) $y = 4^{3x+2}$

We have been graphing exponential functions similar to (*e*) and (*f*). They both have a value of 1 when x equals 0, but in (*e*) the value of y increases as x increases, and in (*f*) the value of y decreases as x increases.

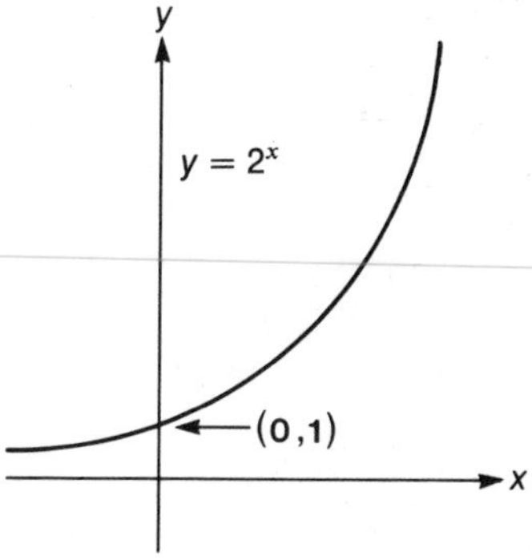

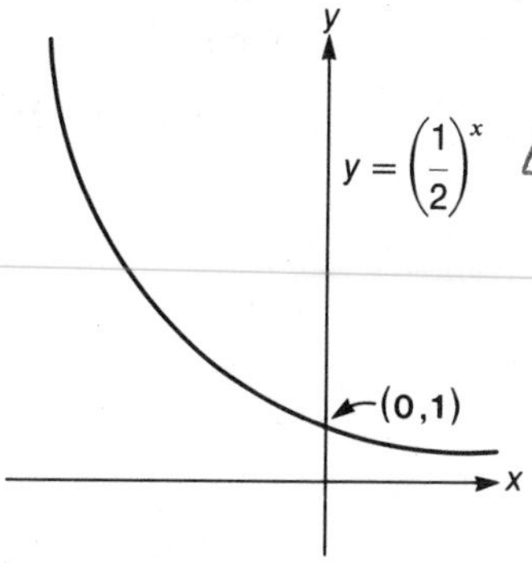

The functions (*g*), (*h*), and (*i*) have the same shape as one of the above with just slight differences. **The trick to graphing one of these functions is to begin by changing the form of the exponential into a form that is more familiar.**

Example 21.C.1 Sketch $y = 3^{-x}$.

Solution When the exponent is negative, it is helpful to write the exponent with a factor of -1. The result is a simple exponential function whose base is $\frac{1}{3}$. It is graphed below on the right.

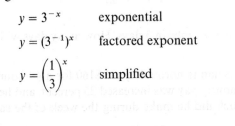

$y = 3^{-x}$ exponential

$y = (3^{-1})^x$ factored exponent

$y = \left(\frac{1}{3}\right)^x$ simplified

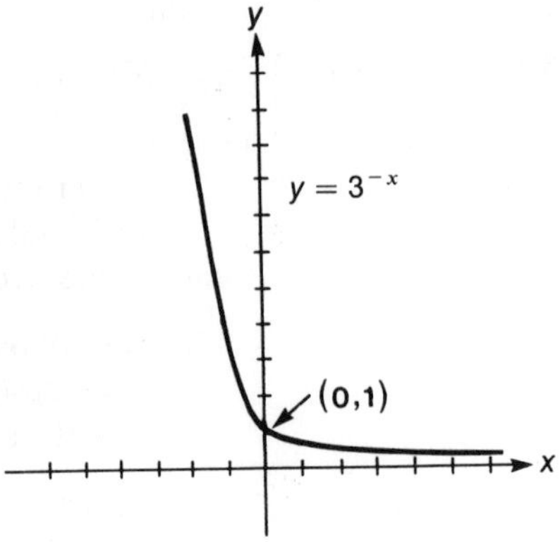

Example 21.C.2 Sketch $y = (\frac{1}{2})^{2x}$.

Solution Again the first step is to work with the exponent. Then we graph the function.

$y = \left(\frac{1}{2}\right)^{2x}$ exponential

$y = \left[\left(\frac{1}{2}\right)^2\right]^x$ factored exponent

$y = \left(\frac{1}{4}\right)^x$ simplified

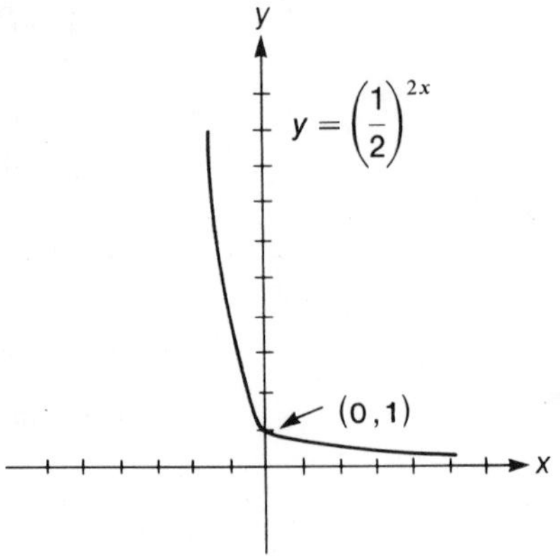

Example 21.C.3 Sketch $y = (\frac{1}{2})^{-x-2}$.

Solution Again we begin by changing the form into a form that is more familiar.

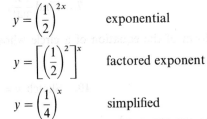

$y = \left(\frac{1}{2}\right)^{-x-2}$ exponential

$y = \left[\left(\frac{1}{2}\right)^{-1}\right]^x\left(\frac{1}{2}\right)^{-2}$ separated

$y = 4 \cdot 2^x$ simplified

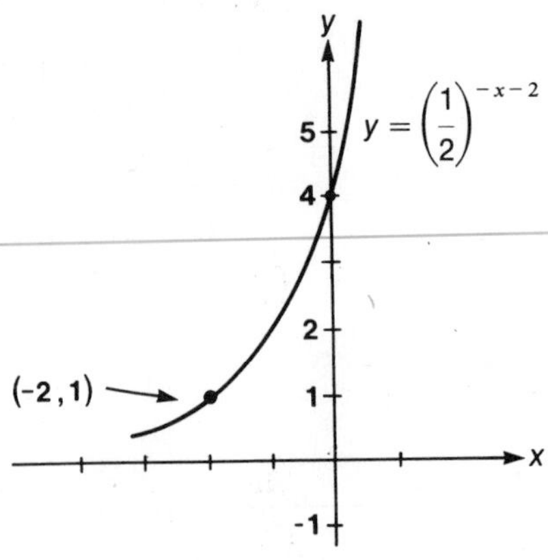

This curve has the same basic shape as $y = 2^x$ except that every y value is multiplied by 4. **It is important to note that if an exponential has a constant in the exponent that is not a coefficient of x, the value of the exponential when $x = 0$ is not 1.** Here we show two other examples of this type of exponential and evaluate each when $x = 0$.

$y = 4^{x+3}$	$y = 3^{2x-3}$	exponential
$y_0 = 4^0 \cdot 4^3$	$y_0 = 3^{2(0)} \cdot 3^{-3}$	let $x = 0$
$y_0 = 64$	$y_0 = \frac{1}{27}$	value of y_0

Problem set 21

1. Five workers can do 7 jobs in 3 days. How many days will it take 10 workers to do 14 jobs?

2. A furniture salesman is normally paid \$160 for a 40-hour week. During the week of the sale, his hourly pay was increased 25 percent, and he was allowed to work 60 hours. How much did he make during the week of the sale?

3. It took Sally 3 hours to go 75 miles downstream, and it took her 5 hours to travel back upstream to her starting position. What was the speed of her boat, and what was the speed of the current in the river?

4. A runner can run 100 yards in 9.8 seconds and 440 yards in 49 seconds. What is the ratio of her average speed in the 440 to her average speed in the 100?

5. Petunia and Petal worked for 5 hours and completed $1\frac{1}{24}$ jobs. If Petal took 12 hours to do 1 job, how long did it take Petunia to do 2 jobs?

6. Find ${}_{10}P_5$.

7. Find $\frac{10!}{3!4!}$.

8. Find the standard form of the equation of a circle whose center is at (3, 4) and whose radius is r.

9. Sketch $y = \left(\frac{1}{2}\right)^{2x}$.

10. Sketch $y = \left(\frac{1}{2}\right)^{x-2}$.

11. Prove that vertical angles are equal.

12. Solve for x and y.

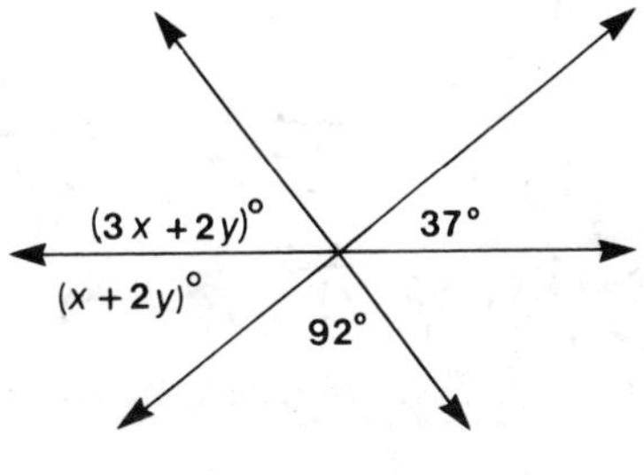

13. Use the point-slope method to find the general form of the equation of the line whose slope is $-\frac{2}{5}$ and which passes through $(-1, 3)$.

14. Write $6x - 5y - 3 = 0$ in double-intercept form.

15. Find the lengths of sides a and b.

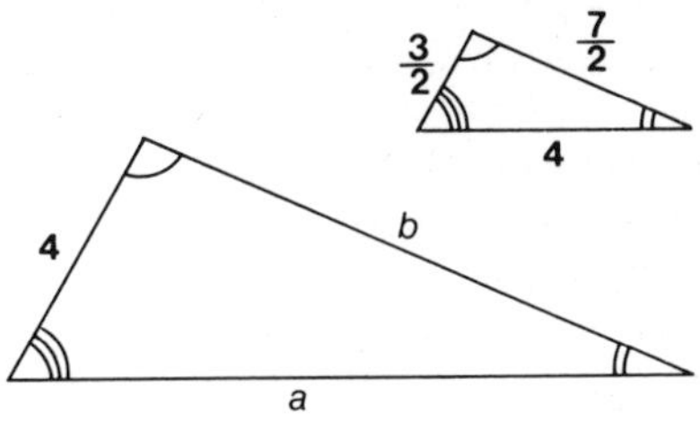

16. Use the lengths of the sides of the triangles in this figure to write three statements of proportionality.

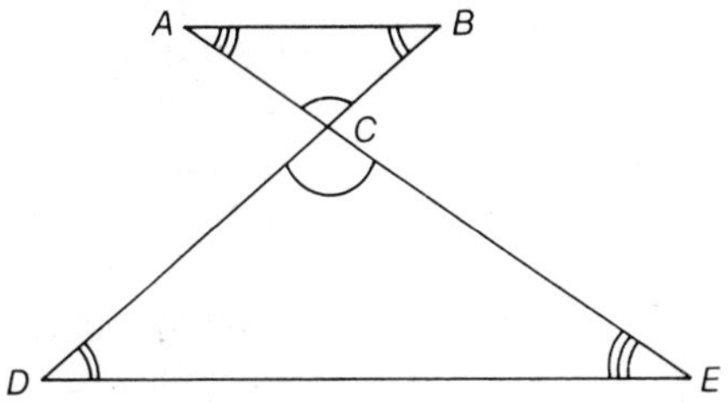

17. Find the equation of the line that is equidistant from the points (1, 4) and (−3, 2).

18. Find the coordinates of the point halfway between (−4, 6) and (8, 4).

19. What is the number whose graph is $\frac{6}{7}$ of the way from $3\frac{1}{2}$ to $6\frac{2}{3}$?

20. A horse runs through an arc of 40° along a circular racetrack. How far did the horse run if the diameter of the racetrack is 3000 feet?

Evaluate:

21. $\text{Arcsin}\left(-\frac{\sqrt{3}}{2}\right)$ 22. $\sin\left[\text{Arccos}\left(-\frac{3}{4}\right)\right]$ 23. $\cos\left[\text{Arcsin}\left(-\frac{4}{5}\right)\right]$

24. $\sec\frac{\pi}{4} - \sin 390°$ 25. $\csc\left(-\frac{\pi}{6}\right) - \cot\left(-\frac{13\pi}{6}\right)$

Solve for x:

26. $2\log_7 x = 4$ 27. $\log_2 (x + 4) - \log_2 (x - 4) = \log_2 5$

28. $4\log_6 x = \log_6 81$ 29. $\log_{14} x = \frac{3}{2}\log_{14} 16$

30. Divide $x^3 - 3x^2 - 2x + 5$ by $x - 3$ and check.

LESSON 22 The unit circle · Graphs of sinusoids

22.A The unit circle

The values of the trigonometric functions of an angle depend on the measure of the angle and do not depend on the size of the triangle. Observe the following right triangles that contain a 27° angle.

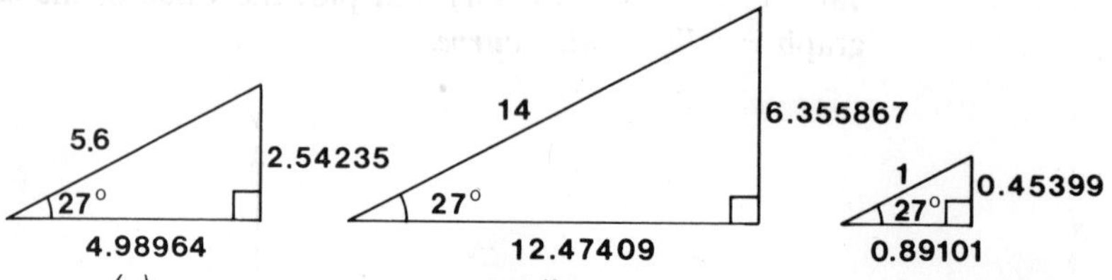

(a) (b) (c)

If we find the sine of each of these 27° angles by writing the ratio of the opposite side to the hypotenuse, we get

(a) $\frac{2.54235}{5.6} = 0.45399$ (b) $\frac{6.355867}{14} = 0.45399$ (c) $\frac{0.45399}{1} = 0.45399$

We note that in the last triangle, the length of the vertical side is the same as the sine of the angle. Now let's find the value of cos 27° for each triangle.

(a) $\frac{4.98964}{5.6} = 0.89101$ (b) $\frac{12.47409}{14} = 0.89101$ (c) $\frac{0.89101}{1} = 0.89101$

Again the answers are the same, but this time in (c) the length of the horizontal side equals the cosine of the angle.

The fact that the sign and the magnitude of the sine and cosine of an angle in any quadrant can be visualized by using right triangles whose hypotenuse equals 1 is of great value. The locus of the end point of the hypotenuse forms a circle that is called the *unit circle*. Here we show several circles and show how they can be used to help us remember the signs of the sine and cosine and the relative magnitudes of the sines and cosines.

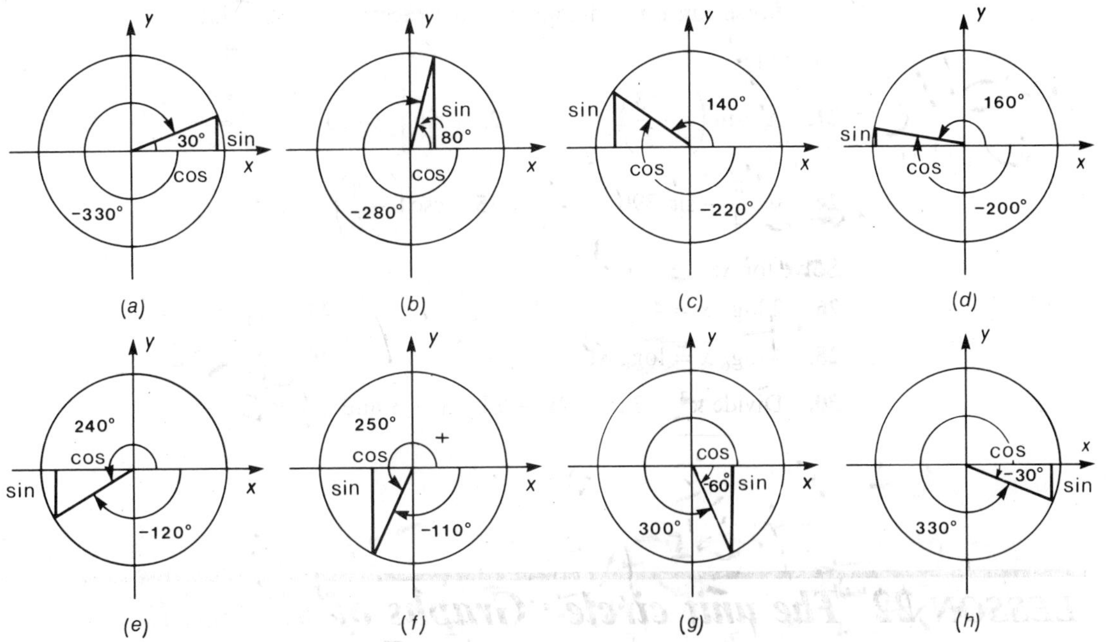

In figures (a) to (d) we note that the length of the vertical side of the triangle equals the sine of the central angle. The sine equals 0 when the central angle is 0°, and increases to 1 as the central angle increases to 90°. Then the sine decreases to 0 as the central angle goes from 90° to 180°. In figures (e) to (h) the value of the sine goes from 0 to -1 and back to 0 as the central angle increases from 180° to 360°. If we plot the value of the sine vertically and plot the value of the central angle θ horizontally, the graph is called a ***sine curve.***

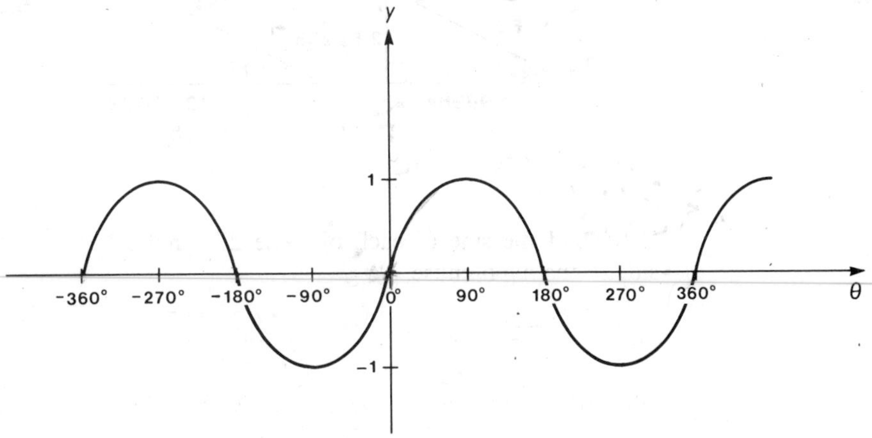

$y = \sin \theta$

If we look at the horizontal sides of the triangles in the unit circles, we see that they represent the values of the cosine. When $\theta = 0°$, the cosine equals 1, and when $\theta = 90°$, the cosine equals 0. Then it decreases to -1 at 180°, goes to 0 at 270°, and returns to 1 at 360°. **A graph of the cosine curve looks exactly like the graph of the sine curve, except the graph of the cosine curve has been shifted horizontally so that it has a y value of $+1$ when $x = 0°$.**

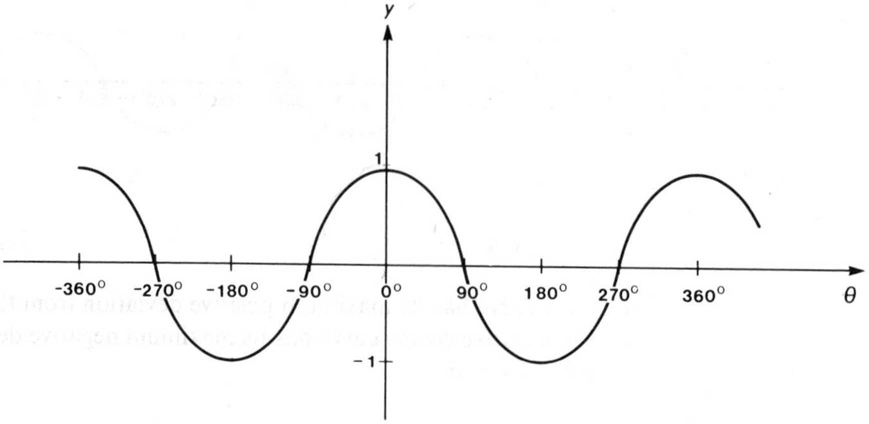

$y = \cos \theta$

22.B Graphs of sinusoids

The Latin suffix *-oid* indicates similarity or likeness. Thus *anthropoid* means "similar to, or like, a man"; *crystalloid* means "similar to, or like, a crystal"; and *planetoid* means "similar to, or like, a planet." In mathematics we use the word ***sinusoid*** to describe a curve that looks like a sine curve. All the following curves are sinusoids. The variables x and θ are often used as the angle variables. We will sometimes use x and sometimes use θ. In these graphs we use θ.

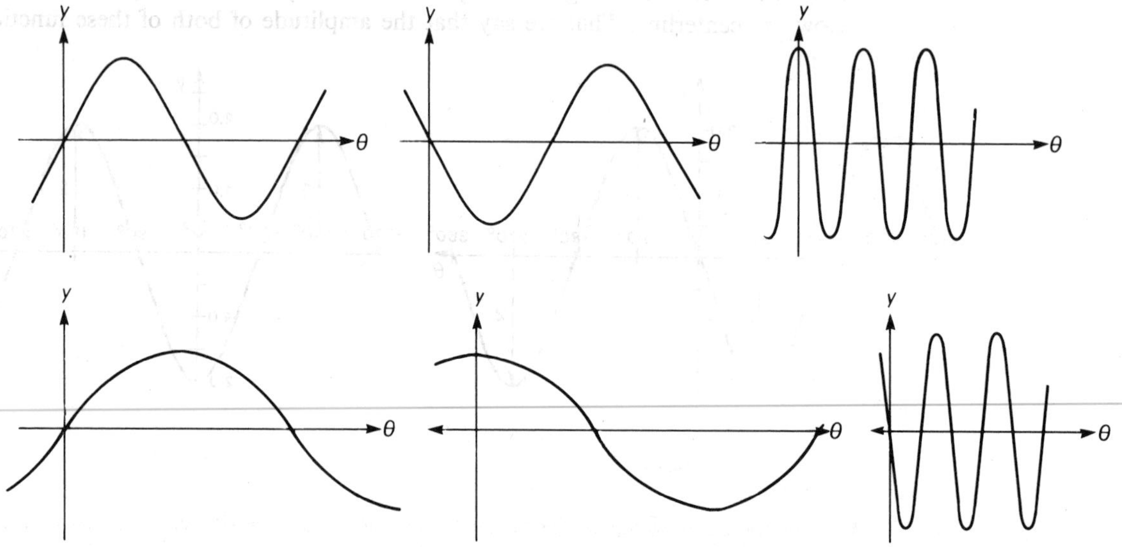

The major differences in the curves are the measure of how much they go above and below the horizontal centerline of the curve, how fast they go up and down, and the value of the curve when θ equals zero. In the graphs above, the zero value of θ occurs at the vertical line on the left end of the graph. The basic sine curve has a value of 0 when θ equals 0 and has an **amplitude** of 1 (goes 1 above and 1 below the centerline).

It completes a full up-and-down cycle of values in 360°, or 2π radians. The negative of the sine curve has the same characteristics, but it begins by going down instead of going up. It is the sine curve inverted.

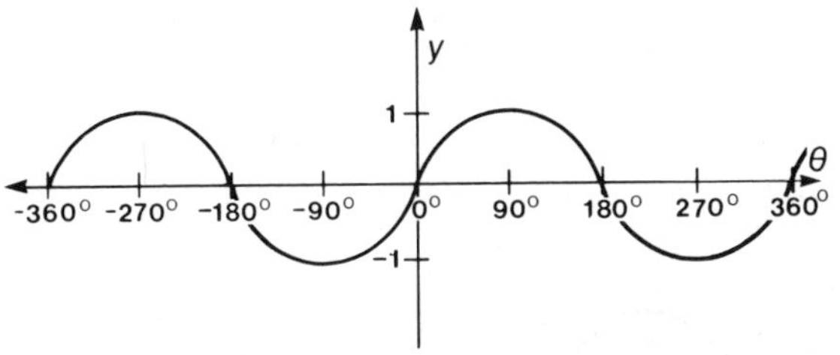

$y = \sin\theta$

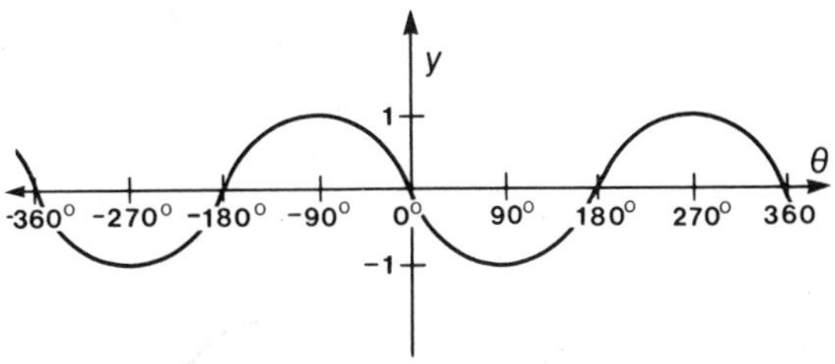

$y = -\sin\theta$

The cosine curve has its maximum positive deviation from the centerline when θ equals zero. The negative cosine curve has its maximum negative deviation from the centerline when θ equals zero.

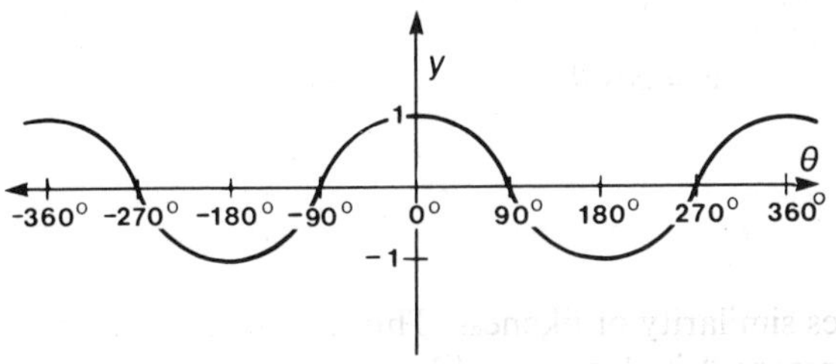

$y = \cos\theta$

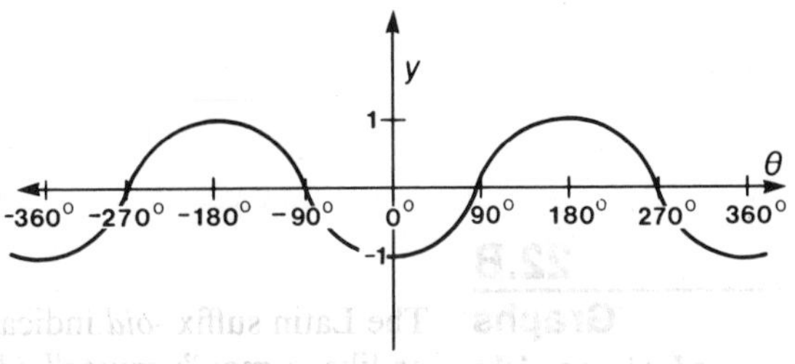

$y = -\cos\theta$

If the function is multiplied by a constant k, the value of the function for any θ is multiplied by k.[†] For example, the graphs of $y = \sin\theta$ and $y = -\cos\theta$ go 1 unit above and below the centerline. The graphs of $y = 2\sin\theta$ and $y = -2\cos\theta$ go 2 units above and below the centerline. Thus we say that the amplitude of both of these functions is 2.

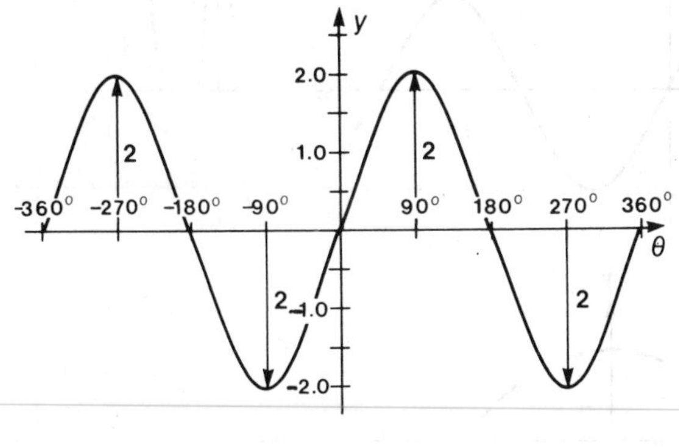

$y = 2\sin\theta$

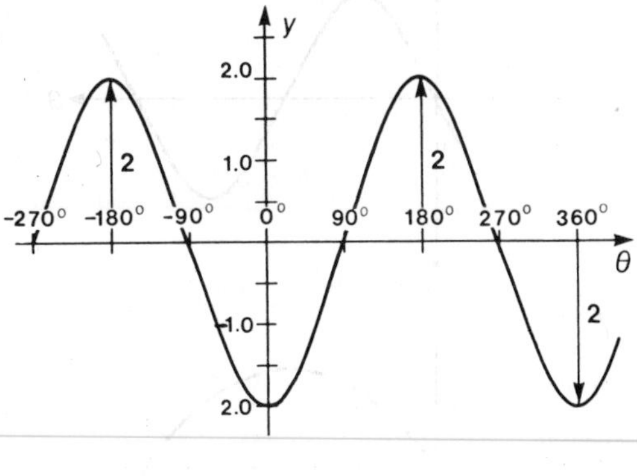

$y = -2\cos\theta$

If a constant c is added to the function, the entire curve is shifted up or down c units. The curve on the left on the next page is shifted up 3 units by the addition of 3, and we note that the equation of the centerline of this curve is $y = 3$. The curve on the right is shifted down 1 unit by the addition of -1, and the equation of the centerline of this

† The $|k|$ is called the amplitude.

curve is $y = -1$. We call these shifts ***vertical translations.*** In neither figure is the centerline the θ axis. The $+\theta$ direction is indicated by the small arrow just above the right end of each graph.

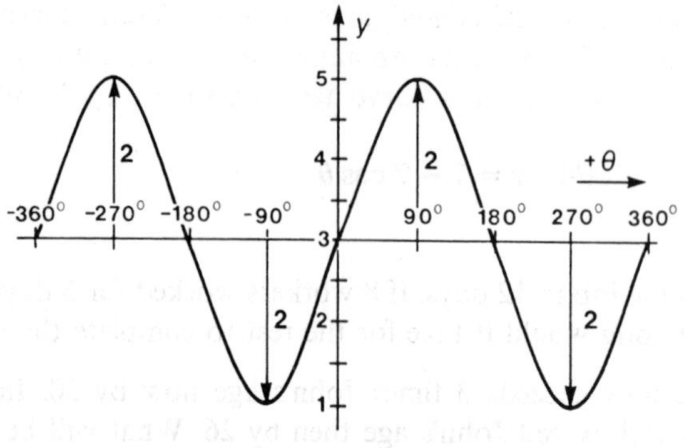

$y = 3 + 2 \sin \theta$

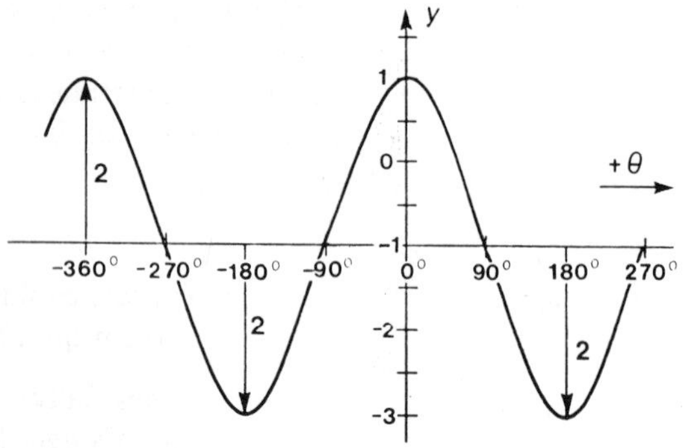

$y = -1 + 2 \cos \theta$

Example 22.B.1 Write the equations of the two sinusoids shown here.

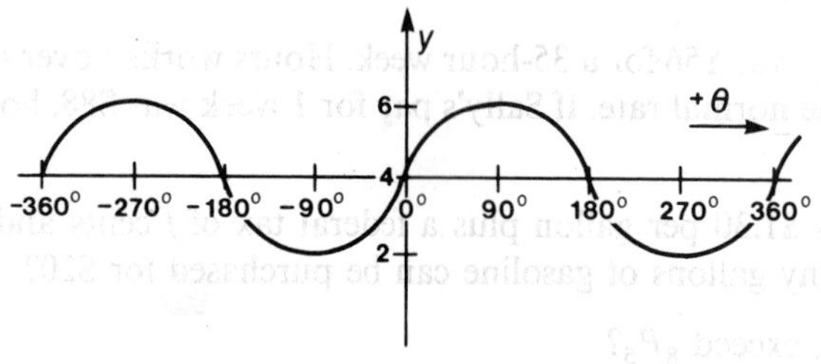

(a)

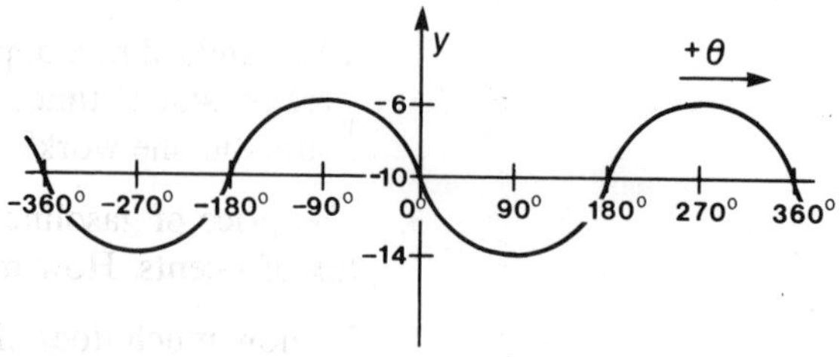

(b)

Solution **Both are sine curves because the value of each curve when θ equals zero is the value of the centerline.** Graph (*a*) begins on the centerline and goes up, so it is a + sine curve. It goes 2 units above and below the centerline, so its amplitude is 2 and it is a +2 sine curve. The centerline is $y = +4$, so the whole curve has been shifted up 4 units. Thus, the equation is

$$(a) \quad y = 4 + 2 \sin \theta$$

Curve (*b*) begins on the centerline so it is a sine curve. It goes down first, so it is a − sine curve. It goes 4 units above and below the centerline, so it has an amplitude of 4 and it is a −4 sine curve. The centerline is $y = -10$, so the whole curve has been shifted down 10 units and the equation is

$$(b) \quad y = -10 - 4 \sin \theta$$

Example 22.B.2 Write the equations of the two sinusoids shown here.

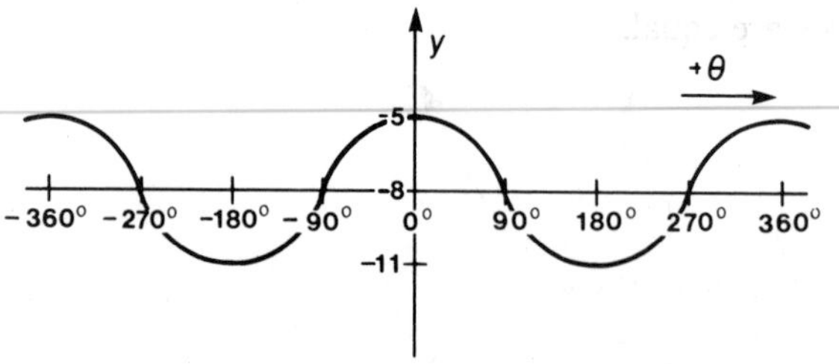

(a)

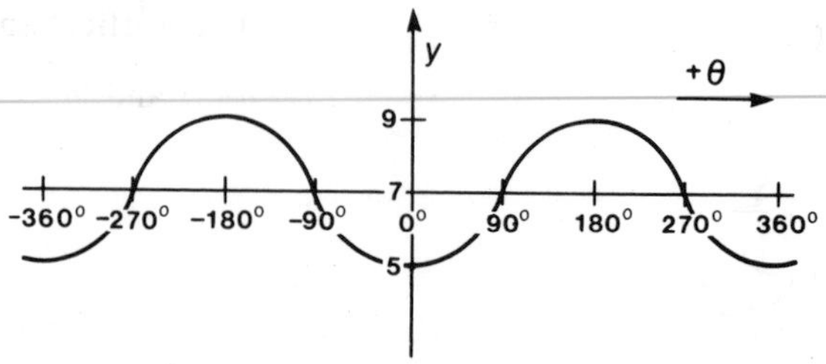

(b)

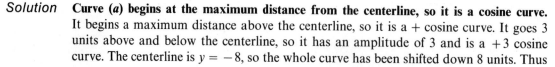

Solution **Curve (*a*) begins at the maximum distance from the centerline, so it is a cosine curve.** It begins a maximum distance above the centerline, so it is a + cosine curve. It goes 3 units above and below the centerline, so it has an amplitude of 3 and is a +3 cosine curve. The centerline is $y = -8$, so the whole curve has been shifted down 8 units. Thus the equation is

$$(a)\quad y = -8 + 3\cos\theta$$

Curve (*b*) begins at a maximum distance from the centerline, so it is a cosine curve. It begins a maximum distance below the centerline, so it is a − cosine curve. It goes 2 units above and below the centerline, so it has an amplitude of 2 and it is a −2 cosine curve. The centerline is $y = +7$, so the whole curve has been shifted up 7 units, and the complete equation is

$$(b)\quad y = 7 - 2\cos\theta$$

Problem set 22

1. Ten workers could do the job in 12 days. If 8 workers worked for 5 days and then half of them quit, how long would it take for the rest to complete the job?

2. Five times Sally's age now exceeds 3 times John's age now by 30. In 10 years, twice Sally's age then will exceed John's age then by 26. What will be their ages 13 years from now?

3. At 9 a.m. an F-foot pole casts an S-length shadow. How long will the shadow of an X-foot pole be?

4. The standard rate of pay was \$56 for a 35-hour week. Hours worked over 40 hours were paid at $1\frac{1}{2}$ times the normal rate. If Sally's pay for 1 week was \$88, how many hours did she work?

5. The price of gasoline is \$1.30 per gallon plus a federal tax of f cents and a state tax of s cents. How many gallons of gasoline can be purchased for \$20?

6. By how much does ${}_8P_6$ exceed ${}_8P_5$?

Write the equations of the following sinusoids.

7.

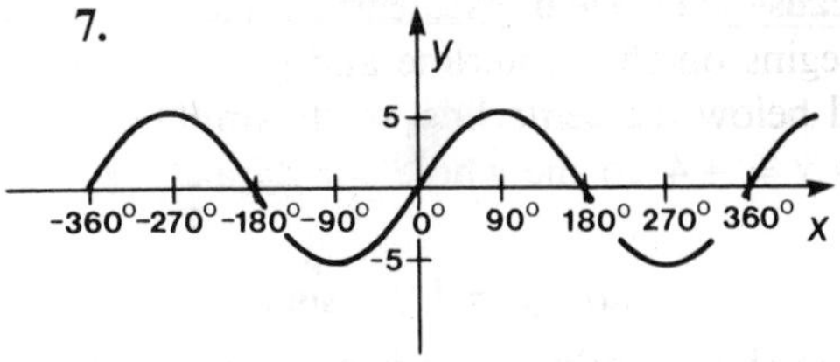

8.

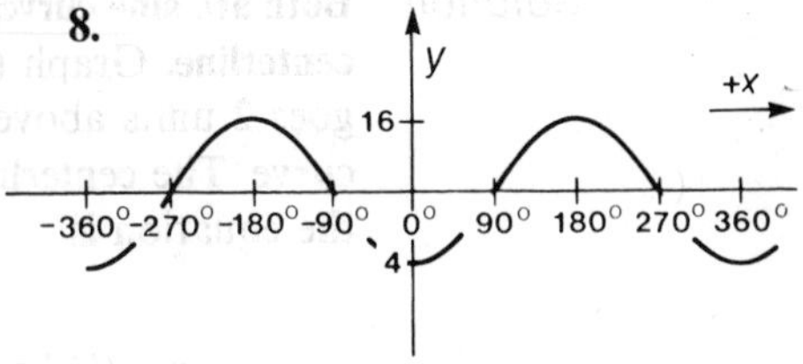

9. Evaluate: $\sum_{i=-1}^{3} i^2 - 3$

10. Find the standard form of the equation of a circle whose center is at $(-2, 3)$ and whose radius is r.

11. Sketch $y = (\frac{1}{3})^{x-1}$.

12. Prove that vertical angles are equal.

13. Solve for a and b.

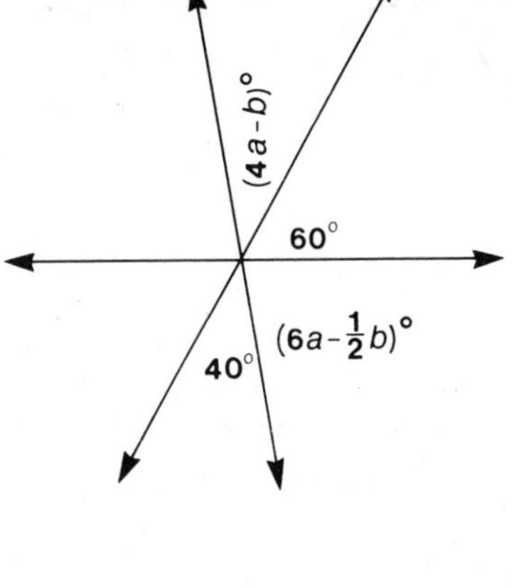

14. Use the point-slope method to find the general form of the equation of the line whose slope is $-\frac{1}{4}$ and which passes through $(-2, 3)$.

15. Find p and q.

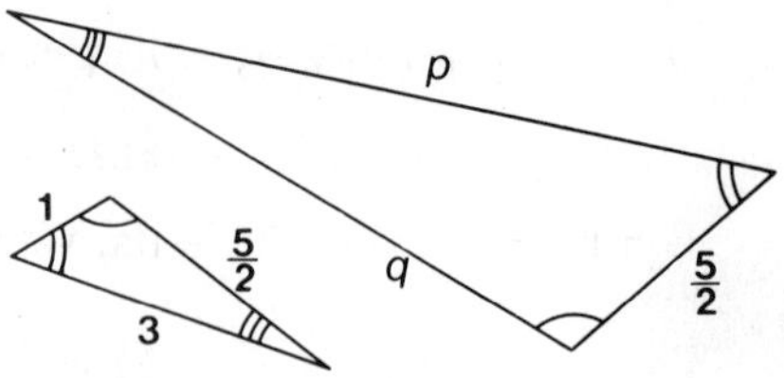

16. If $x < 1$ and $y > 4$, compare: *A.* $x + 1$ *B.* $y - 1$

17. Find the equation of the line that is equidistant from the points $(-3, -2)$ and $(2, 3)$.

18. Find the coordinates of the point halfway between $(-3, 4)$ and $(8, -3)$.

19. What is the number whose graph is $\frac{4}{5}$ of the way from $1\frac{1}{4}$ to $-6\frac{2}{3}$?

20. The jogger ran through an arc of 60° along a circular track whose diameter is 600 yards. How far did the jogger run?

Evaluate:

21. $\text{Arccos}\left(\frac{\sqrt{2}}{2}\right)$

22. $\cos\left[\text{Arcsin}\left(-\frac{4}{5}\right)\right]$

23. $\sin\left(\text{Arctan}\frac{3}{4}\right)$

24. $\csc\left(-\frac{3\pi}{4}\right) + \cos(-390°)$

25. $\sec\left(-\frac{19\pi}{6}\right) + \csc\left(-\frac{\pi}{3}\right)$

Solve for x:

26. $\log_4 8 + \log_4 6 = \log_4 (3x + 2)$

27. $\log_3 (x - 3) - \log_3 (x + 1) = \log_3 12$

28. $\log_x 16 = 4$

29. $\log_{15} x = \frac{2}{3} \log_{15} 8$

30. Solve for t: $\sqrt{3t^2 - 4s} = 5qr$

LESSON 23 Abstract rate problems

23.A Abstract rate problems

Thus far, we have restricted our investigation of abstract rate problems to problems about distances. Problems about price per item and about time to do a job are also interesting rate problems. They are worked in the same way that the distance problems are worked. The first step is to identify the original components. The next step is to note the changes that must be made, and the last step is to solve for the unknown component.

Example 23.A.1 Peter purchased p pencils for d dollars. If the p pencils had cost x more dollars, how many pencils could Peter have purchased for \$20?

Solution The rate for this problem is in pencils per dollar and the equation is

$$\text{Rate} \times \text{money} = \text{pencils}$$

We begin by identifying the initial values of the pencils, the money, and the rate.

$$\text{Pencils} = p \qquad \text{Money} = d \text{ dollars} \qquad \text{Rate} = \frac{p \text{ pencils}}{d \text{ dollar}}$$

If the pencils had cost x more dollars, the values would have been

$$\text{Pencils} = p \qquad \text{Money} = (d + x) \text{ dollars} \qquad \text{Rate} = \frac{p}{d + x}\,\frac{\text{pencils}}{\text{dollar}}$$

Now to find the number of pencils we can buy for \$20, we multiply the rate by \$20.

$$\text{Rate} \times \text{dollars} = \text{pencils} \quad \longrightarrow \quad \frac{p}{d + x}\,\frac{\text{pencils}}{\cancel{\text{dollars}}} \times 20\ \cancel{\text{dollars}} = \mathbf{\frac{20p}{d + x}\ pencils}$$

Example 23.A.2 On an assembly line, m workers worked h hours to produce c articles. If d workers quit, how many hours would the remaining workers have to work to produce the same number of articles?

Solution The rate in this problem is in articles per worker-hour, so the basic equation is

$$\text{Rate} \times \text{workers} \times \text{time} = \text{articles}$$

As the first step, we identify workers, time, articles, and rate.

$$\text{Workers} = m \qquad \text{Time} = h \text{ hours} \qquad \text{Articles} = c$$

$$\text{Rate} = \frac{c}{mh}\,\frac{\text{articles}}{\text{worker-hour}}$$

Now, if d workers quit, we have $m - d$ workers producing c articles at the *same rate*. So

$$\text{Workers} = m - d \qquad \text{Articles} = c \qquad \text{Rate} = \frac{c}{mh}\,\frac{\text{articles}}{\text{worker-hour}}$$

We are asked to find the time. We substitute and solve.

$$\frac{c}{mh}\,\frac{\text{articles}}{\text{worker-hour}} \times (m - d) \text{ workers} \times T \text{ hours} = c \text{ articles} \qquad \text{substituted}$$

$$T = \frac{c\ \cancel{\text{articles}}}{\frac{\cancel{c}}{\cancel{m}h}\,\frac{\cancel{\text{articles}}}{\cancel{\text{worker-hour}}} \times (\cancel{m} - d)\ \cancel{\text{workers}}} \qquad \text{divided}$$

$$T = \mathbf{\frac{mh}{m - d}\ hours} \qquad \text{simplified}$$

Example 23.A.3 Charles had p pounds of food and this would feed m workers for d days. Then 30 more workers showed up. How long would the food feed $m + 30$ workers?

Solution The rate is food per worker-day and the equation is

$$\text{Rate} \times \text{workers} \times \text{time} = \text{food}$$

First we identify the initial components.

Workers $= m$ Time $= d$ days Food $= p$ pounds Rate $= \dfrac{p}{md} \dfrac{\text{pounds}}{\text{worker-day}}$

Now if 30 more workers show up, the components are

Workers $= m + 30$ Food $= p$ pounds Rate $= \dfrac{p}{md} \dfrac{\text{pounds}}{\text{worker-day}}$

We are asked to find the new time.

$$\text{Rate} \times \text{workers} \times \text{time} = \text{food} \longrightarrow \text{Time} = \frac{\text{food}}{\text{workers} \times \text{rate}}$$

Again, we finish by substituting and solving.

$$\text{Time} = \frac{p}{(m + 30)(p/md)} = \frac{\boldsymbol{md}}{\boldsymbol{m + 30}} \textbf{ days}$$

Problem set 23

1. In his search for the fountain, Ponce ambled for 1 year at a leisurely pace and then tripled his pace for the next 10 years. If the total journey was 3100 miles, how far did he amble?

2. In the cookie factory, w workers work h hours to produce c cookies. If m more workers are hired, how many hours would they have to work to produce the same number of cookies?

3. Mom had p pounds of cookies, and this would feed c children for m minutes. Yet n more children showed up. In how many minutes will p pounds of cookies be devoured by the children?

4. The drummer boy purchased d drums for x dollars. If each drum had cost \$5 less, how many drums could the boy have purchased for \$100?

5. If $x = \dfrac{2}{y + z}$, then $\dfrac{6}{x} =$ what?

6. How many four-letter signs can be formed from the letters in the word JUDGE if repetition is not permitted?

7. How many four-digit numbers can be formed from the digits 1, 3, 5, 7, 8, and 9 if repetition is not permitted?

Write the equations of the following sinusoids.

8.

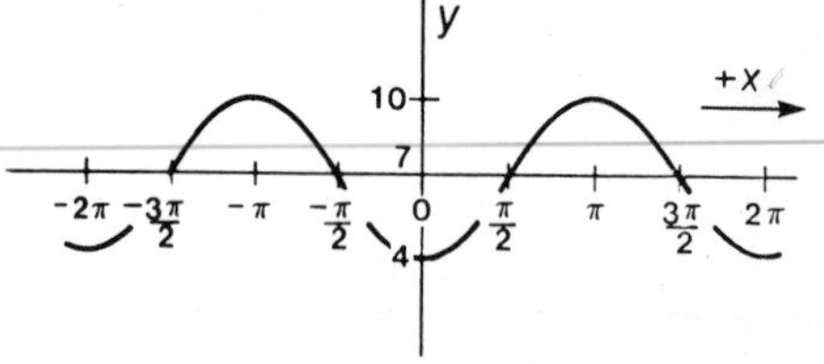

9.

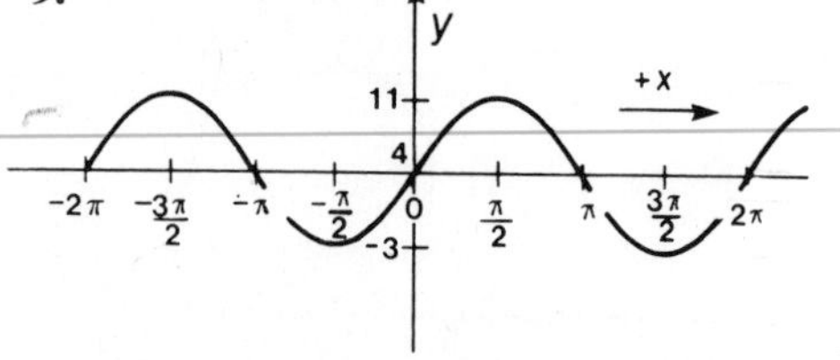

10. Evaluate: $\sum_{n=1}^{3} (n^2 - 2)$

11. Find the standard form of the equation of a circle whose center is (h, k) and whose radius is 5.

12. Sketch $y = 2^{-x-2}$.

13. Prove that vertical angles are equal.

14. Solve for x and y.

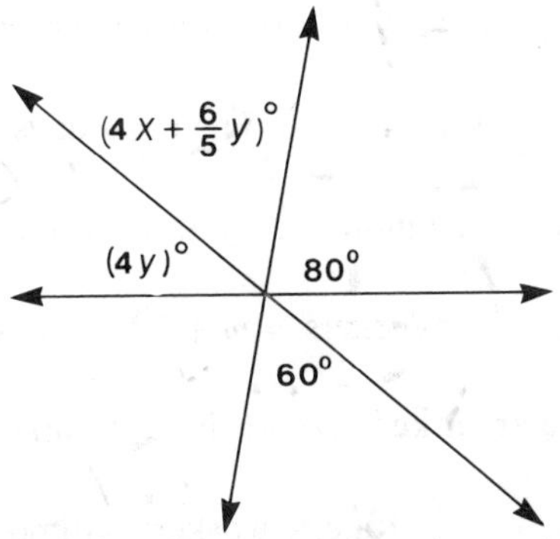

15. Find the lengths of sides a and b.

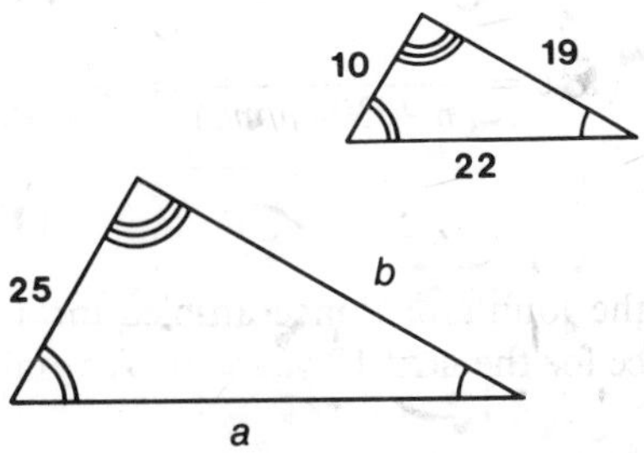

16. The two triangles shown are similar. Use the lengths of the sides of the triangles to write three statements of proportionality.

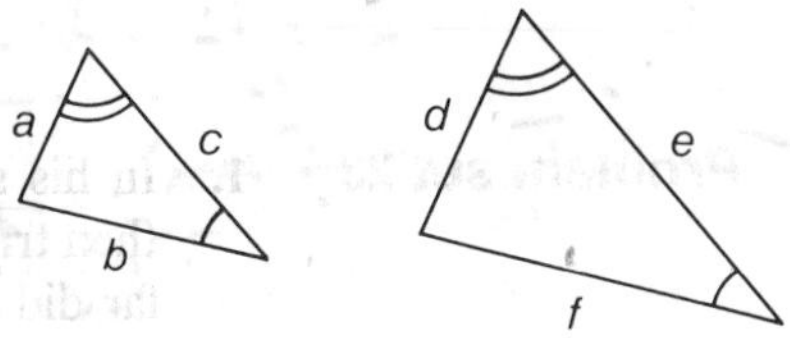

17. Find the equation of the line that is equidistant from the points $(-6, 4)$ and $(0, 8)$. Write the equation in slope-intercept form.

18. Find the coordinates of the point halfway between $(-6, 2)$ and $(7, 4)$.

19. What is the number whose graph is $\frac{1}{5}$ of the way from $2\frac{2}{3}$ to $6\frac{1}{3}$?

20. The tiger trotted through an arc of $\pi/6$ radians along a circular arc of radius 1000 feet. How far did the tiger trot?

Evaluate:

21. $\text{Arcsin}\left(-\frac{1}{2}\right)$ **22.** $\sin\left[\text{Arcsin}\left(-\frac{3}{5}\right)\right]$ **23.** $\cos\left[\text{Arcsin}\left(\frac{4}{5}\right)\right]$

24. $\sec\left(-\frac{7\pi}{6}\right) + \csc\frac{\pi}{3}$ **25.** $\sec\left(-\frac{3\pi}{4}\right) - \cot 90°$

Solve for x:

26. $\log_3 6 + \log_3 3 = \log_3 (4x + 2)$ **27.** $\log_7 (x + 2) - \log_7 (x - 4) = \log_7 2$

28. $2 \log_x 4 = 2$ **29.** $\log_5 (2x + 1) - 2 \log_5 2 = \log_5 3$

30. $\sqrt{x} + \sqrt{x + 9} = 9$

LESSON 24 Conditional permutations

24.A Conditional permutations

Many problems about permutations (arrangements in a definite order) have conditions attached that make finding the solutions challenging. There is no formula that can be used, for the conditions seem to be different each time. We will find, however, that drawing a diagram is helpful, so the use of diagrams is recommended.

Example 24.A.1 How many odd numbers can be formed from the digits 3, 4, and 5 if no repetition of digits is permitted?

Solution We can have one-digit, two-digit, or three-digit odd numbers.

The one-digit odd numbers are 3 and 5 total 2

The last digit in a two-digit odd number is an odd digit. Both 3 and 5 are odd digits, so there are 2 possible odd choices for the last digit.

	2

The other digits may be even or odd, and 2 digits remain that can be used as the first digit.

2	2

$\longrightarrow 2 \cdot 2 = 4$ total 4

For three-digit numbers, we use the same process and get

1	2	2

$\longrightarrow 1 \cdot 2 \cdot 2 = 4$ total 4

grand total 10

Thus, there are **10** possible odd numbers.

Example 24.A.2 Find the number of odd three-digit numbers that are less than 600.

Solution The statement of the problem indicates that repetition of digits is permissible. The 10 digits are 0, 1, 2, 3, 4, 5, 6, 7, 8, 9, and any of the 5 odd digits can be used in the last spot.

		5

The digit 0 cannot be used in the first box because the resulting number would have only two digits. Also 6, 7, 8, or 9 cannot be used in the first box or the number would not be less than 600. Thus, only 1, 2, 3, 4, or 5 can be used in the first box. There are 10 digits possible for the second box, so we have

5	10	5

$\longrightarrow 5 \cdot 10 \cdot 5 = 250$

Thus, there are **250** odd three-digit numbers less than 600.

Example 24.A.3 Five math books and four English books are on a shelf. How many permutations are possible if the math books must be kept together and the English books must be kept together?

Solution If the math books come first, we get

MATH					ENGLISH			
5	4	3	2	1	4	3	2	1

$\longrightarrow 5! \times 4! = 120 \cdot 24 = 2880$

If the English books come first, we get

ENGLISH				MATH				
4	3	2	1	5	4	3	2	1

$\longrightarrow 4! \times 5! = 24 \cdot 120 = 2880$

If we add the two numbers, we get **5760** possible permutations.

Example 24.A.4 How many different four-digit odd numbers can be formed if no repetition of digits is permitted?

Solution The 10 digits are 0, 1, 2, 3, 4, 5, 6, 7, 8, 9, and five digits are even and five are odd. The number must end with an odd digit, so there are 5 choices for the last digit.

			5

A four-digit number cannot begin with 0 because if it did, it would be at most a three-digit number. Thus, there are only 8 choices left for the first digit.

8			5

Zero can be the second digit so there are 8 choices for this digit and 7 choices for the third digit.

8	8	7	5

$\longrightarrow \quad 8 \cdot 8 \cdot 7 \cdot 5 = 2240$

Thus, there are **2240** different four-digit odd numbers.

Example 24.A.5 An elf, a gnome, a fairy, a pixie, and a leprechaun were to sit in a line. How many different ways can they sit if the elf and the gnome insist on sitting next to each other?

Solution Let's begin with the elf and the gnome in the first two seats.

E	G	3	2	1	$\longrightarrow$ $3 \times 2 \times 1 = 6$
G	E	3	2	1	$\longrightarrow$ $3 \times 2 \times 1 = 6$

Now let's put them in the second two seats.

3	E	G	2	1	$\longrightarrow$ $3 \times 2 \times 1 = 6$
3	G	E	2	1	$\longrightarrow$ $3 \times 2 \times 1 = 6$

The other possibilities are

3	2	E	G	1	for 6
3	2	G	E	1	for 6
3	2	1	E	G	for 6
3	2	1	G	E	for 6

There are 8 ways the gnome and elf can sit side by side, and for each of these, there are 6 ways the other 3 little people can sit. Since $6 \times 8 = 48$, there are **48** different ways the people can sit if the elf and the gnome sit next to each other.

Problem set 24

1. On the outbound leg of 24 miles, Paul sauntered at a leisurely pace. Thus he had to double his speed on the way back to complete the trip in 9 hours. How fast did he travel in each direction, and what were the two times?

2. Four thousand liters of solution was available that was 92% alcohol. How many liters of alcohol had to be extracted so that the solution would be only 80% alcohol?

3. In the factory k workers worked f hours to produce c articles. If x workers quit, how long would those that remained have to work to produce $c + 10$ articles?

4. The ratio of greens to blues was 2 to 1, and twice the sum of the number of blues and the number of whites exceeded the number of greens by 10. If there were 35 blues, greens, and whites in all, how many were there of each color?

5. If $k = \dfrac{1}{m + n}$, then $\dfrac{5}{k}$ = what?

6. How many three-digit counting numbers are there that are less than 300 such that all the digits are even?

7. Six math books and three English books are on a shelf. How many ways can they be arranged if the math books are kept together and the English books are kept together?

Write the equations of the following sinusoids.

8.

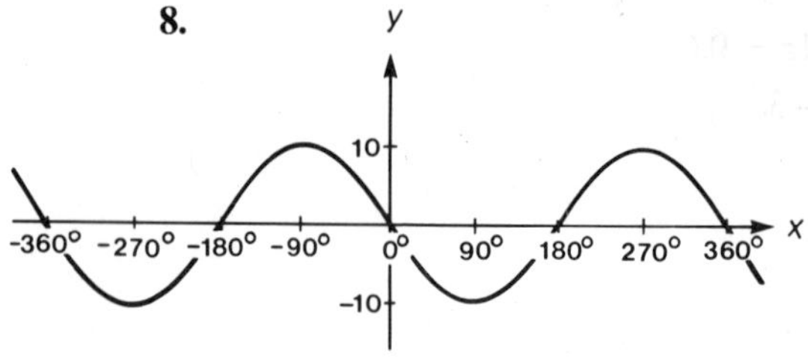

9.

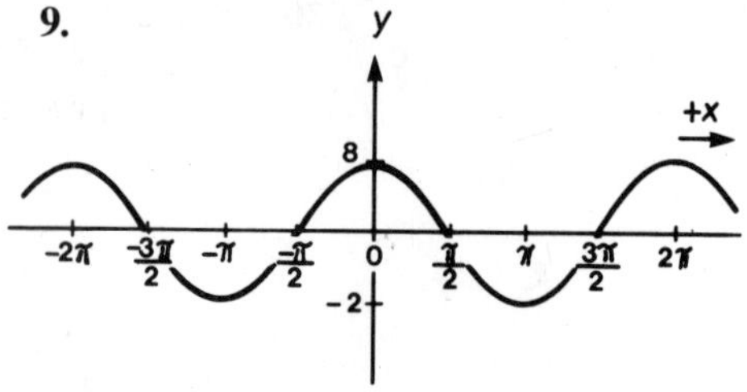

10. Find ${}_6P_3$.

11. Find the standard form of the equation of a circle whose center is (h, k) and whose radius is 5.

12. Sketch $y = (\frac{1}{2})^{-x+1}$.

13. Prove that vertical angles are equal.

14. Solve for x and y.

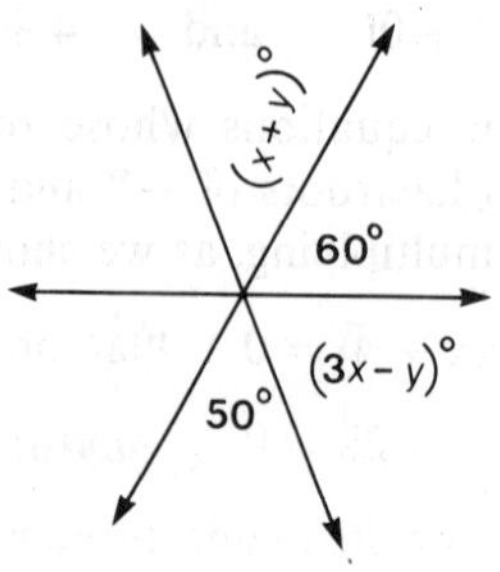

15. Find the lengths of sides m and n.

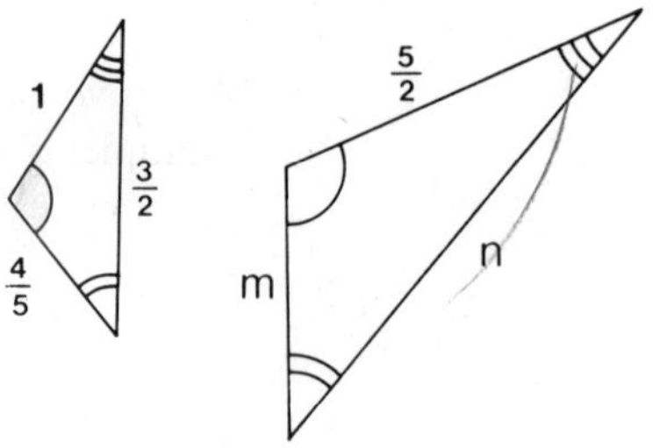

16. If $x < -1$ and $y > 4$, compare: *A.* $x + 5$ *B.* $y - 1$

17. Write $6x - 5y + 7 = 0$ in double-intercept form.

18. Find the equation of the line that is equidistant from the points $(-4, -3)$ and $(4, 6)$.

19. Solve: $\begin{cases} x^2 + y^2 = 5 \\ x + y = 2 \end{cases}$

20. Factor: $x^3y^6 + p^6z^9$

21. Princeton, New Jersey, is 40.5° north of the equator. How many miles is it from Princeton to the equator if the diameter of the earth is 7920 miles?

Evaluate:

22. $\sin\left[\text{Arccos}\left(-\frac{3}{4}\right)\right]$

23. $\sin\left[\text{Arctan}\left(-\frac{2}{3}\right)\right]$

24. $\sec\left(-\frac{19\pi}{6}\right) + \cos 630°$

25. $\csc\frac{3\pi}{4} - \sec\left(-\frac{5\pi}{6}\right)$

Solve for x:

26. $\log_5 7 + \log_5 8 = \log_5 (2x - 4)$

27. $\log_3 (x - 1) - \log_3 x = \log_3 15$

28. $3 \log_c x = \log_c 64$

29. $\frac{3}{4} \log_{10} 10{,}000 = x$

30. Solve: $\begin{cases} \frac{1}{2}x - \frac{1}{3}y = \frac{2}{3} \\ 0.5x - 0.1z = 0.6 \\ y - z = -3 \end{cases}$

LESSON 25 Complex roots · Factoring over the complex numbers

25.A Complex roots

The set of real numbers is a subset of the set of complex numbers. This is easy to remember if we recall that real numbers such as -7 and 4 are complex numbers whose imaginary part is zero and can also be written as

$$-7 + 0i \qquad \text{and} \qquad 4 + 0i$$

We have been writing quadratic equations whose roots have been designated. For example, if a quadratic equation has roots of -7 and $+4$, the equation can be found by writing the factors and then multiplying, as we show here.

$$(x + 7)(x - 4) = 0 \qquad \text{factored form}$$

$$x^2 + 3x - 28 = 0 \qquad \text{multiplied}$$

The same procedure can be used to write quadratic equations whose roots are designated complex numbers whose imaginary parts are not equal to zero. **For quadratic equations with real number coefficients, these complex roots always occur in conjugate pairs.**

Example 25.A.1 Write a quadratic equation whose roots are $1 + 2i$ and $1 - 2i$.

Solution First we write an equation that contains a product of factors.

$$[x - (1 + 2i)][x - (1 - 2i)] = 0$$

Next we simplify the signs within the brackets and get

$$[x - 1 - 2i][x - 1 + 2i] = 0$$

There are nine indicated products which must be summed.

$$x^2 - x + 2xi - x + 1 - 2i - 2xi + 2i - 4i^2 = 0$$

Fortunately, we have $+2xi$ and $-2xi$, which sum to zero, as do the terms $+2i$ and $-2i$. If we remember that i^2 equals -1, we can simplify the above expression and get

$$\mathbf{x^2 - 2x + 5 = 0}$$

as a quadratic equation that has the required roots.

25.B Factoring over the complex numbers

The quadratic polynomial $2x^2 + 6$ can be written as a product of the number 2 and two factors that contain the variable x.

$$2x^2 + 6 = 2(x + \sqrt{3}\,i)(x - \sqrt{3}\,i)$$

If we use the quadratic formula we can find that the roots of the equation $2x^2 + 6 = 0$ are $\pm\sqrt{3}\,i$. These roots can be used to find two of the factors of the polynomial, but we might overlook the constant factor 2. Thus when we use the quadratic formula to find the roots of a quadratic polynomial, we begin by factoring so that the coefficient of x^2 is unity.

Example 25.B.1 Factor $2x^2 + 4x + 8$ over the set of complex numbers.

Solution The wording of the problem tells us that the factors can contain complex numbers. First we factor out the lead coefficient and then set the resulting polynomial equal to 0.

$$2x^2 + 4x + 8 = 2(x^2 + 2x + 4) \longrightarrow x^2 + 2x + 4 = 0$$

Next we use the quadratic formula to find the roots of the resulting polynomial equation.

$$x = \frac{-2 \pm \sqrt{4 - 4(1)(4)}}{2} \longrightarrow x = -1 \pm \sqrt{3}\,i$$

Now the roots of the polynomial equation can be used to write two of the factors of the polynomial, and, from above, the third factor is 2.

$$(2)[x - (-1 + \sqrt{3}\,i)][x - (-1 - \sqrt{3}\,i)] \qquad \text{factors}$$

$$\mathbf{(2)(x + 1 - \sqrt{3}\,i)(x + 1 + \sqrt{3}\,i)} \qquad \text{simplified}$$

Example 25.B.2 Factor $x^2 + 2x - 5$.

Solution Since this polynomial cannot be factored over the integers, we assume that other factors are acceptable. The lead coefficient is 1, so factoring out a constant is not necessary.

$$x^2 + 2x - 5 = 0$$

Now we will use the quadratic formula to find the roots of this equation.

$$x = \frac{-2 \pm \sqrt{4 - 4(1)(-5)}}{2} \qquad \text{quadratic formula}$$

$$= \frac{-2 \pm \sqrt{24}}{2} \qquad \text{simplified}$$

$$= -1 \pm \sqrt{6} \qquad \text{roots}$$

So our roots are $-1 + \sqrt{6}$ and $-1 - \sqrt{6}$. Now we can write the factors of the polynomial.

$$x^2 + 2x - 5 = [x - (-1 + \sqrt{6})][x - (-1 - \sqrt{6})]$$

$$= \mathbf{(x + 1 - \sqrt{6})(x + 1 + \sqrt{6})}$$

Problem set 25

1. On the 36-mile trip to the magic fountain, Alice walked at a brisk pace. On the way back, Alice doubled her pace. If the total trip took 6 hours, how fast did Alice travel on the trip to the magic fountain and on the return trip from the magic fountain?

2. One thousand liters of a solution was available, but the solution was 90% alcohol. Jim needed a solution which was 80% alcohol. How many liters of alcohol had to be extracted so that the solution would be 80% alcohol?

3. The cook had x pounds of food in the storehouse, and this would feed y workers for d days. Then 50 more workers arrived in camp. How many days would the cook's food last since $(y + 50)$ workers must now be fed?

4. The ratio of rubies to emeralds was 3 to 1 and the ratio of emeralds to diamonds was 2 to 1. If there were 18 rubies, emeralds, and diamonds in all, how many of each were there?

5. If $a = \frac{1}{b + c}$, then $\frac{3}{a} = ?$

6. How many three-digit counting numbers are there that are less than 300, such that all the digits are odd?

7. Six literature books and four math books are on a shelf. How many ways can they be arranged if the math books are kept together and the literature books are kept together?

8. Write a quadratic equation whose roots are $2 - 3i$ and $2 + 3i$.

9. Factor $x^2 + 3x + 6$ over the set of complex numbers.

Write the equations of the following sinusoids.

10.

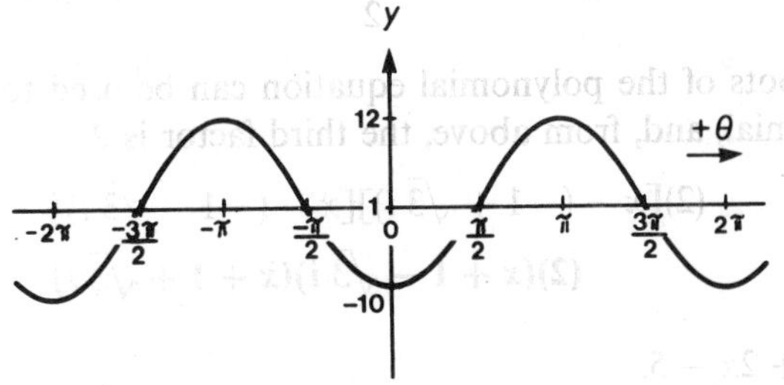

11.

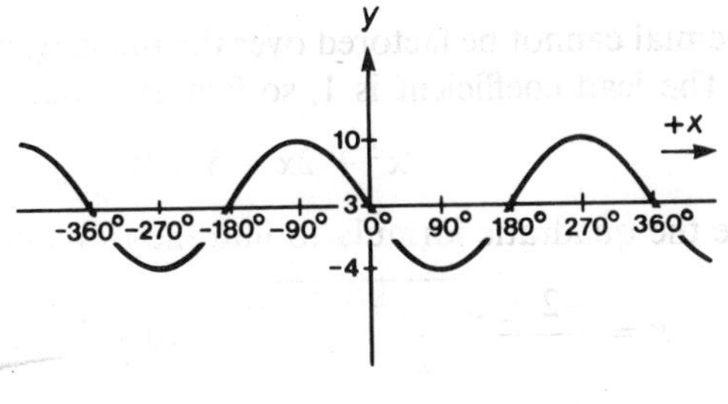

12. Find $_8P_4$.

13. Find the standard form of the equation of a circle whose center is (h, k) and whose radius is 6.

14. Sketch $y = (\frac{1}{3})^{-x+2}$

15. Prove that vertical angles are equal.

16. Solve for x and y.

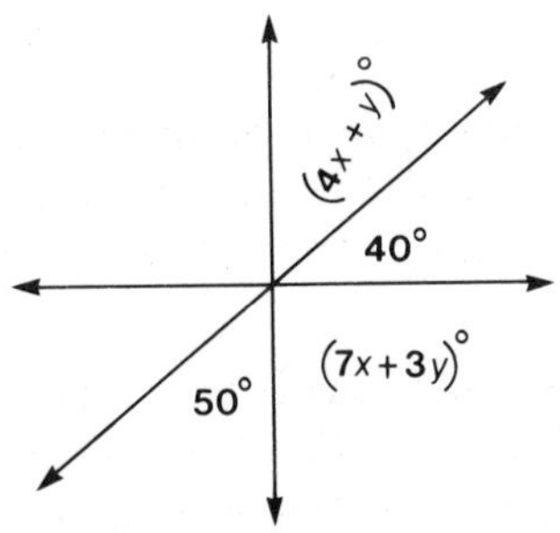

17. Find the lengths of sides m and n.

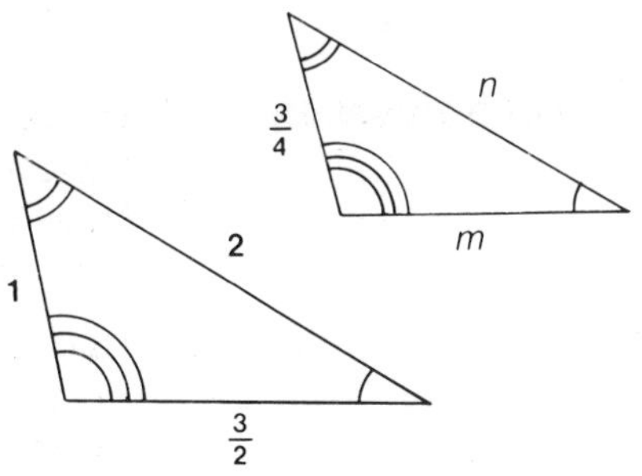

18. Write $2x - 6y - 3 = 0$ in double-intercept form.

19. Find the equation of the line that is equidistant from the points $(-3, 4)$ and $(6, 8)$.

20. What is the number whose graph is $\frac{2}{3}$ of the way from $2\frac{1}{3}$ to $4\frac{2}{3}$?

21. The panther moved 60° along a circular arc of radius 600 meters. How far did the panther move?

Evaluate:

22. $\sin\left[\text{Arccos}\left(-\frac{5}{12}\right)\right]$

23. $\sin\left[\text{Arctan}\left(-\frac{5}{13}\right)\right]$

24. $\cos\left(-\frac{\pi}{4}\right) + \sin\frac{\pi}{4}$

25. $\csc\frac{\pi}{4} - \sec(-45°)$

Solve for x:

26. $\frac{5}{2}\log_4 4 = \log_4(2x - 3)$

27. $\log_3(x + 2) - \log_3 x = \log_3 10$

28. $2\log_c x = \log_c 64$

29. $\log_8 x = \frac{3}{4}\log_8 16$

30. Solve: $\begin{cases} \frac{1}{2}x - \frac{1}{4}y = \frac{3}{2} \\ 0.1y - 0.2z = -1.2 \\ 2x - z = -4 \end{cases}$

LESSON 26 *Similar triangles · More inverse functions*

26.A Similar triangles

Corresponding angles of similar triangles are equal, and the lengths of corresponding sides of similar triangles are proportional. If two angles in one triangle are equal to two angles in a second triangle, the third angles are also equal.

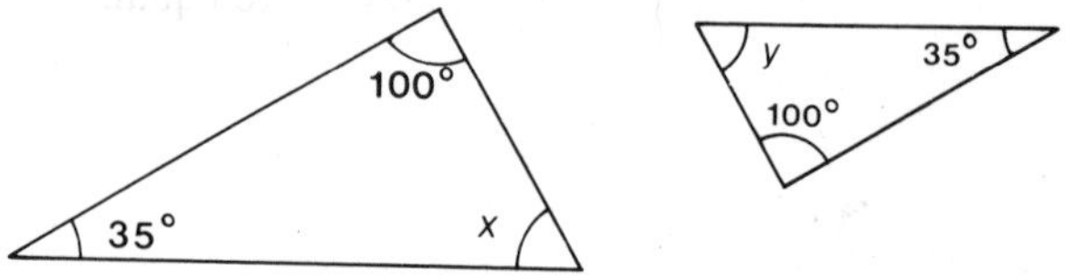

In these triangles the angles x and y are equal angles because the sum of the angles must be 180° in both triangles. This tells us that the triangles are similar and is an illustration of the fact that if two angles in a triangle are equal, the third angles are also equal.

Example 26.A.1 Write three proportions, using the lengths of the sides of the small right triangle and the large right triangle.

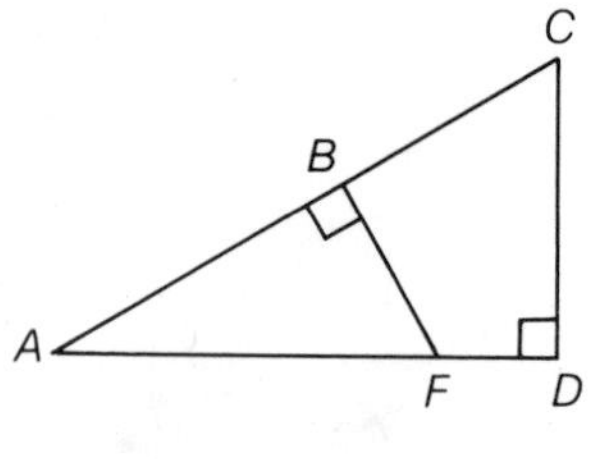

Solution Both triangles contain angle A and both have a right angle. Thus, the third angles are equal, and the triangles are similar. We write the statement of similarity by listing vertex A first and then the right-angle vertex.

$$\triangle ABF \sim \triangle ADC$$

Now we can write the proportions.

$$\frac{AB}{AD} = \frac{BF}{DC} \qquad \frac{AB}{AD} = \frac{AF}{AC} \qquad \frac{BF}{DC} = \frac{AF}{AC}$$

Example 26.A.2 Find the length of segment b.

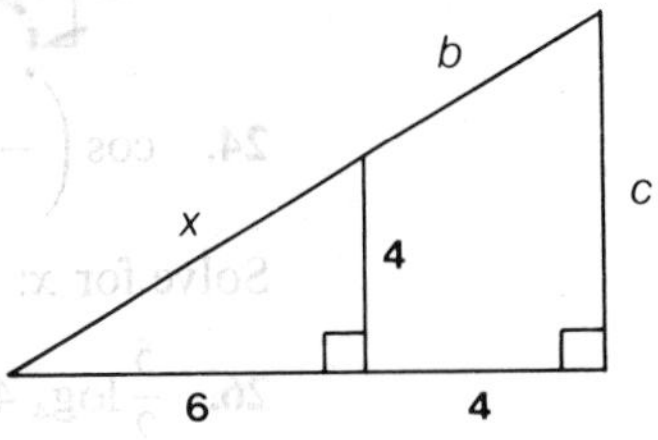

Solution We begin by using the Pythagorean theorem to find x.

$$6^2 + 4^2 = x^2 \longrightarrow \sqrt{52} = x$$
$$\longrightarrow 2\sqrt{13} = x$$

Now we use the long legs and the hypotenuses of both triangles to write a proportion.

$$\frac{x+b}{x} = \frac{6+4}{6}$$

Now we substitute $2\sqrt{13}$ for x and solve.

$$\frac{2\sqrt{13}+b}{2\sqrt{13}} = \frac{10}{6} \qquad \text{substituted}$$
$$12\sqrt{13} + 6b = 20\sqrt{13} \qquad \text{cross multiplied}$$
$$6b = 8\sqrt{13} \qquad \text{added } -12\sqrt{13}$$
$$\mathbf{b = \frac{4\sqrt{13}}{3}} \qquad \text{divided}$$

Example 26.A.3 The shadow of a 6-ft person is 14 ft long at 2 p.m. At the same time, the shadow of a building is 30 ft long. How high is the building?

Solution The sun is far enough away for us to assume that the sun's rays are parallel. Thus, in the picture below, the angles A are equal.

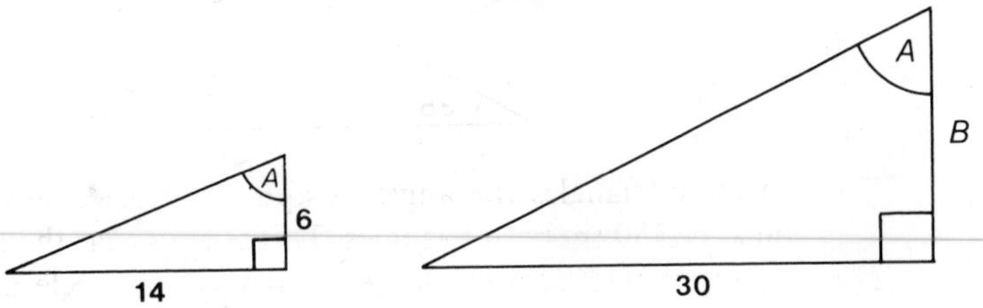

The triangles both have angle A and a right angle. Thus, the third angles are equal and the triangles are similar. We write a proportion to solve for B.

$$\frac{6}{B} = \frac{14}{30} \qquad \text{proportion}$$
$$14B = 6 \cdot 30 \qquad \text{cross multiplied}$$
$$\mathbf{B = 12.9\ ft} \qquad \text{divided}$$

Example 26.A.4 Find the length of sides x and c.

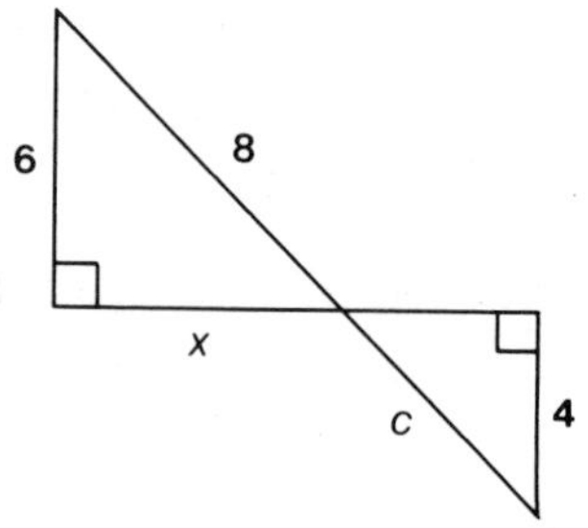

Solution First we use the Pythagorean theorem to solve for x.

$$8^2 = 6^2 + x^2 \quad \text{equation}$$
$$28 = x^2 \quad \text{simplified}$$
$$\mathbf{2\sqrt{7} = x} \quad \text{solved}$$

We could write a proportion to solve for c, but instead we decide to find the scale factor and use it.

$$6SF = 4 \quad \text{equation}$$
$$SF = \frac{2}{3} \quad \text{solved for } SF$$

Thus, the length of each side in the triangle on the right equals the product of $\frac{2}{3}$ and the length of the corresponding side in the triangle on the left.

$$8SF = c \quad \text{equation}$$
$$8\left(\frac{2}{3}\right) = c \quad \text{substituted}$$
$$\mathbf{\frac{16}{3}} = c \quad \text{simplified}$$

26.B More inverse functions

When we look at the notation

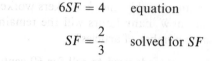

$$\sin\left(\text{Arctan}\,\frac{1}{\sqrt{3}}\right)$$

we remember that the capital A in Arctan restricts us to the first- or fourth-quadrant angle whose tangent is $1/\sqrt{3}$. Thus, the problem simplifies to

$$\sin 30^\circ = \frac{1}{2}$$

Now we will look at another problem that emphasizes the restrictions placed on inverse trigonometric functions to make them single-valued.

Example 26.B.1 Evaluate: Arctan (tan 135°).

Solution This asks for the angle whose tangent is the tangent of 135°. At first glance, one would suspect that the answer is 135°, but let us see. The tangent of 135° is -1.

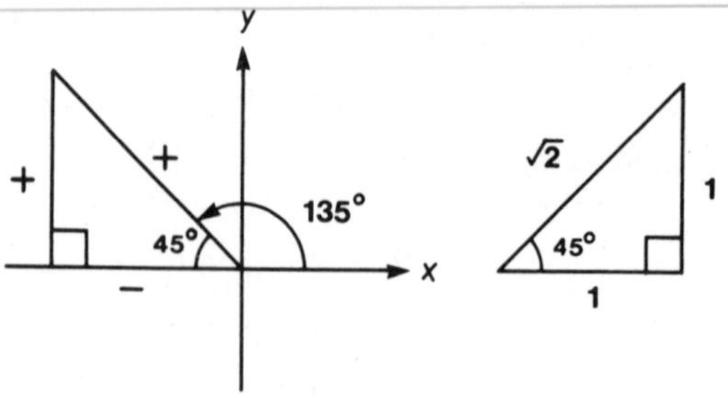

So now we have

$$\text{Arctan}\,(-1)$$

This asks for **the first- or fourth-quadrant** angle whose tangent is -1, and this angle is $-45°$. So we have

$$\text{Arctan}(\tan 135°) = \mathbf{-45°}$$

Problem set 26

1. The still-water speed of the *Faerie Queen* was 4 times the speed of the current in the Lazy River. The *Faerie Queen* can go 100 miles downstream in 1 hour more than she requires to go 30 miles upstream. What is the still-water speed of the *Faerie Queen* and how fast does the Lazy River flow?

2. If m workers can do a job in d days, how long would it take 40 workers to do the same job?

3. On an assembly line, k workers worked d hours to produce x items. If y workers quit, how many hours will the remaining workers have to work to produce the same number of articles?

4. Tomato seeds used to sell for 60 cents per pound. Now a 2-pound package sells for \$1.50. What is the ratio of the old price per pound to the new price per pound?

5. Pencils sell at d dollars for 1 dozen. At this price, what would be the total cost of mc pencils?

6. How many four-digit numbers can be formed from the digits 1, 2, 3, and 4 if 2 and 3 must be next to each other and if repetition is not permitted?

7. How many even three-digit numbers can be formed if the second digit is not 0 and the third digit is not 6? Repetition is permitted.

Write the equations of the following sinusoids.

8. 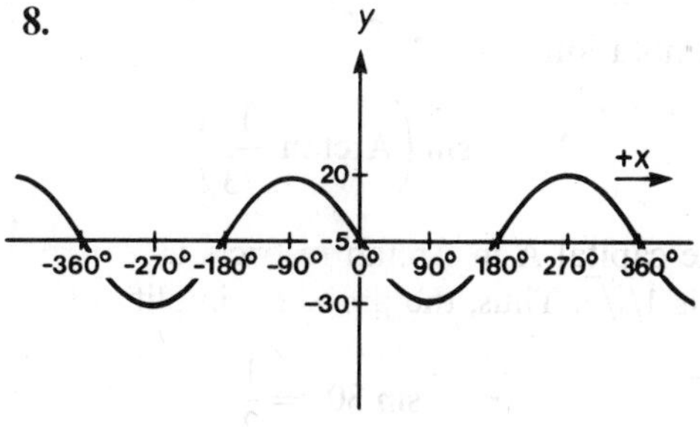

9. 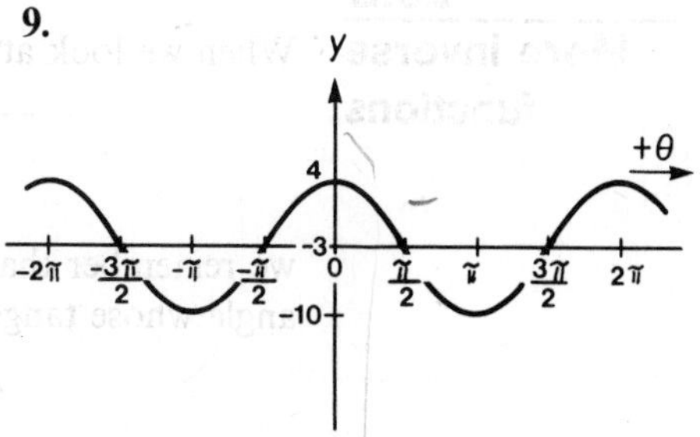

10. Evaluate: $\displaystyle\sum_{k=-1}^{2} \frac{k^2+1}{2}$

11. Find the standard form of the equation of a circle whose radius is 3 and whose center is (2, 1).

12. Sketch $y = \left(\frac{1}{2}\right)^{-x-3}$.

13. Write a quadratic equation whose roots are $3 + 2i$ and $3 - 2i$.

14. Solve for x and y.

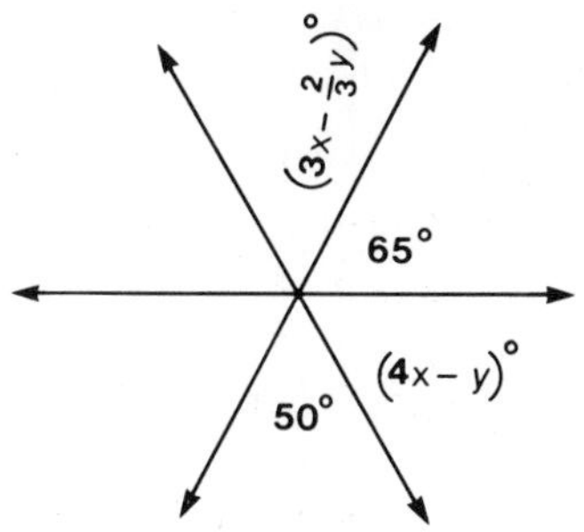

15. Write three proportions, using the sides of the small triangle and the large triangle.

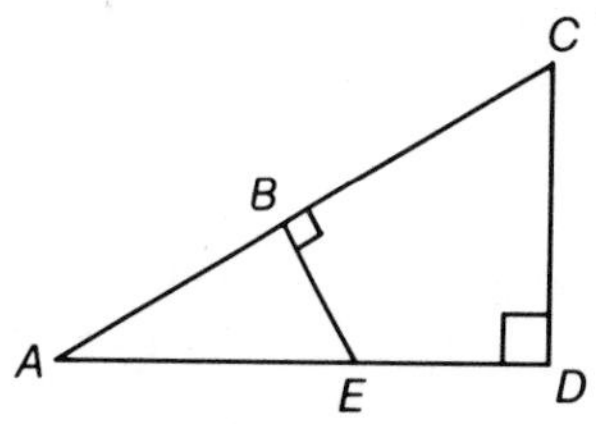

16. Find b.

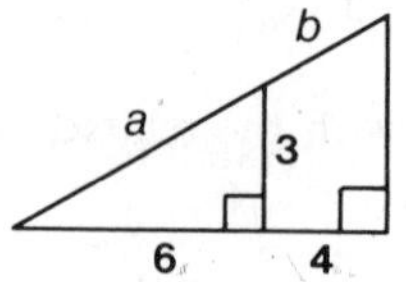

17. The shadow of a 5-foot person is 15 feet at 3 p.m. At the same time the shadow of a building is 30 feet long. How high is the building?

18. Find the equation of the line that is equidistant from the points $(-3, -4)$ and $(3, 2)$. Write the equation in general form.

19. Find the coordinates of the point halfway between $(-4, -2)$ and $(6, 4)$.

20. What is the number whose graph is $\frac{4}{5}$ of the way from $-3\frac{2}{3}$ to $4\frac{1}{4}$?

21. Amy walked through an arc of 40° along the rim of a circular swimming pool 40 feet in diameter. How far did she walk?

Evaluate:

22. $\tan\left[\text{Arcsin}\left(-\frac{3}{4}\right)\right]$

23. $\text{Arctan}(\tan 135°)$

24. $\cot\left(-\frac{3\pi}{4}\right) - \csc\frac{5\pi}{6}$

25. $\sec\frac{13\pi}{6}\cos\frac{13\pi}{6}$

Solve for x:

26. $\log_3 4 + \log_3 5 = \log_3 (4x + 5)$

27. $\log_7 6 - \log_7 (x - 1) = \log_7 3$

28. $3 \log_x 4 = 2$

29. $\log_{15} x = \frac{2}{3}\log_{15} 125$

30. Factor: $8x^3y^6 - 27a^6b^9$

LESSON 27 Powers of trigonometric functions · Perpendicular bisectors

27.A Powers of trigonometric functions

Consider the three notations

$$\sin\theta^2 \qquad (\sin\theta)^2 \qquad \sin^2\theta$$

The left-hand notation is $\sin\theta^2$. If θ equals 30°, then

$$\sin\theta^2 = \sin(30°)^2 = \sin 900 \text{ deg}^2$$

This notation is almost never used because in trigonometry we seldom find a reason to raise the measure of an angle to a power. This leaves us with the two notations

$$(\sin\theta)^2 \qquad \text{and} \qquad \sin^2\theta$$

We often raise trig functions to powers, and we need a notation to so indicate. The notation on the left is unhandy because it requires the use of parentheses. The notation on the right means the same thing and requires only a superscript to denote the power. Thus, we usually prefer this notation but will sometimes use the other notation when required for clarity.

Example 27.A.1 Find (*a*) $\sin^3(-60°)$ and (*b*) $\cot^2 330°$.

Solution First we make the sketches with the related angles.

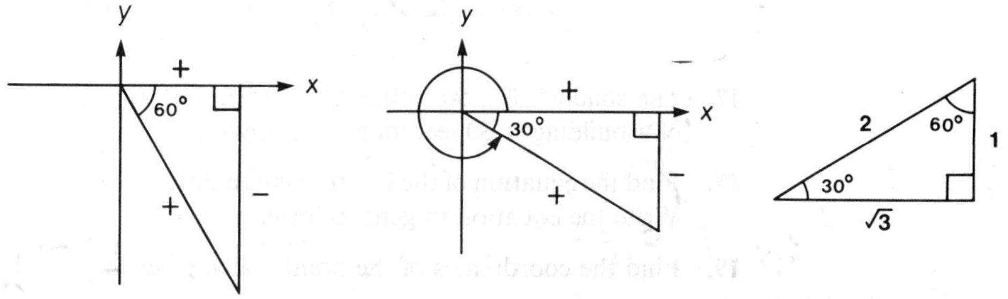

sine is − cotangent is −

$\sin(-60°) = -\sin 60°$ $\cot 330° = -\cot 30°$

$$(a)\quad \sin^3(-60°) = (-\sin 60°)^3 = \left(-\frac{\sqrt{3}}{2}\right)^3 = -\frac{\mathbf{3\sqrt{3}}}{\mathbf{8}}$$

$$(b)\quad \cot^2 330° = (-\cot 30°)^2 = (-\sqrt{3})^2 = \mathbf{3}$$

Example 27.A.2 Evaluate $\csc^2(-405°) - \tan^2 45°$.

Solution First come the diagrams.

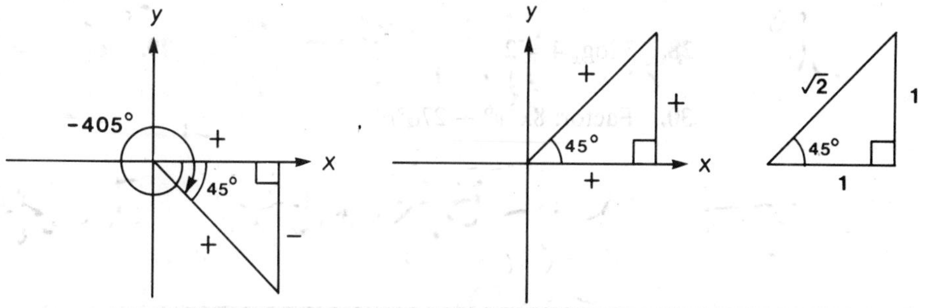

sine and cosecant are − tangent is +

$\csc^2(-405°) = (-\csc 45°)^2$ $\tan^2 45° = (\tan 45°)^2$

$$\csc^2(-405°) - \tan^2 45° = \left(-\frac{\sqrt{2}}{1}\right)^2 - \left(\frac{1}{1}\right)^2 \qquad \text{sum of functions}$$

$$= 2 - 1 \qquad \text{raised to power}$$

$$= \mathbf{1} \qquad \text{added}$$

27.B Perpendicular bisectors

Since Lesson 14, we have been using the locus definition and the distance formula to write the equation of a line that is equidistant from two designated points. This line bisects the line segment that connects the two points and is perpendicular to this segment. There is another way to find the equation of a line that is equidistant from two designated points. We can use the midpoint formula to find the coordinates of the point halfway between the two points. Then we write the equation of the line that passes through this point whose slope is the negative reciprocal of the slope of the segment. We will call this method the ***midpoint formula method*** and will call the other method the ***locus definition method.***

Example 27.B.1 Find the equation of the perpendicular bisector of the line segment whose endpoint coordinates are (4, 2) and (8, −3). Use the midpoint formula method.

Solution First we get a picture of the problem by graphing the points and indicating the position of the perpendicular bisector.

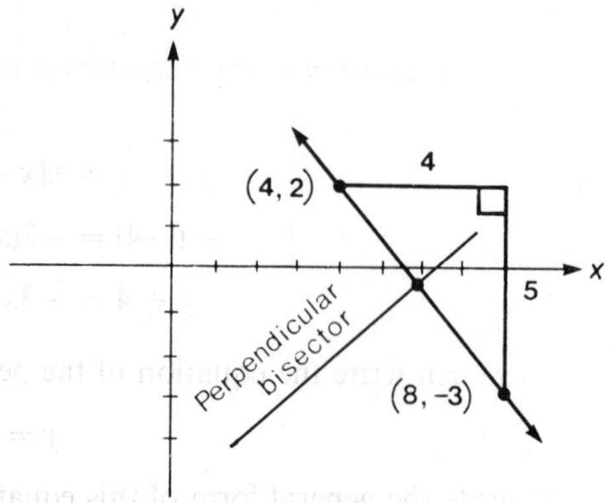

We see that the slope of the line is $-\frac{5}{4}$. Now we need to find the coordinates of the midpoint of the line segment.

$$x_m = \frac{x_1 + x_2}{2} \qquad y_m = \frac{y_1 + y_2}{2}$$

$$x_m = \frac{4 + 8}{2} = 6 \qquad y_m = \frac{2 + (-3)}{2} = -\frac{1}{2}$$

Since the slope of the perpendicular bisector is the negative reciprocal of the slope of the line, the slope of the perpendicular bisector is $\frac{4}{5}$.

$$y = \frac{4}{5}x + b \qquad \text{equation of perpendicular bisector}$$

Now the perpendicular bisector passes through the midpoint of the segment, which is $(6, -\frac{1}{2})$. We use these coordinates for x and y to solve for b.

$$-\frac{1}{2} = \frac{4}{5}(6) + b \qquad \text{substituted}$$

$$-\frac{5}{10} = \frac{48}{10} + b \qquad \text{simplified}$$

$$-5.3 = b \qquad \text{solved}$$

Now we know the intercept and can write the equation of the perpendicular bisector as

$$\mathbf{y = \frac{4}{5}x - 5.3}$$

Example 27.B.2 Write the general form of the perpendicular bisector of the line segment whose endpoints are (4, −3) and (−2, −5). Use the midpoint formula method.

Solution First we must find the equation of the line that passes through these two points. This time we will use the slope formula to find the slope and the point-slope form of the equation. First we use the slope formula.

$$m = \frac{y_2 - y_1}{x_2 - x_1} \longrightarrow m = \frac{-5 - (-3)}{-2 - (4)} \longrightarrow m = \frac{1}{3}$$

Next we find the coordinates of the midpoint.

$$x_m = \frac{x_1 + x_2}{2} \qquad y_m = \frac{y_1 + y_2}{2}$$

$$x_m = \frac{4 + (-2)}{2} = 1 \qquad y_m = \frac{-3 + (-5)}{2} = -4$$

To find the equation of the perpendicular bisector, we use a slope of -3 and the point $(1, -4)$.

$$y - y_1 = m(x - x_1) \qquad \text{equation}$$

$$y - (-4) = -3(x - 1) \qquad \text{substituted}$$

$$y + 4 = -3x + 3 \qquad \text{simplified}$$

Now we can write the equation of the perpendicular bisector as

$$y = -3x - 1$$

If we write the general form of this equation, we get

$$\mathbf{3x + y + 1 = 0}$$

Problem set 27

1. The ratio of the number of reds to the number of blues was 2 to 1, and 5 times the sum of the number of reds and blues exceeded 3 times the number of whites by 12. If there were 4 more whites than blues, how many were red, how many were white, and how many were blue?

2. Francene had two containers of a mixture of alcohol and disinfectant. One was 40% disinfectant and the second was 80% disinfectant. How much of each should be used to get 600 milliliters of a solution that is 50% disinfectant?

3. A recipe calls for 12 ounces of cottage cheese and 6 ounces of cream cheese. If there are 216 calories in 8 ounces of cottage cheese and 106 calories in 1 ounce of cream cheese, how many calories are there in 36 ounces of the mixture?

4. A master painter can paint a house in m days and two workers require W_1 and W_2 days each to paint a house alone. If the master can work as fast as the two workers working together, write an expression for m in terms of W_1 and W_2.

5. Mr. Lynch owns $\frac{3}{7}$ of the business and his share of the profits for the year was \$60,000. Wilbur only owned $\frac{1}{28}$ of the business. What was Wilbur's share of the profits?

6. How many ways can the letters PLAY be arranged in a row given that A cannot be the first letter and Y cannot be the second letter? Repetition is not permitted.

7. How many odd three-digit numbers less than 300 can be found given that the second digit cannot be 2 or 8? Repetition is permitted.

Write the equations of the following sinusoids.

8.

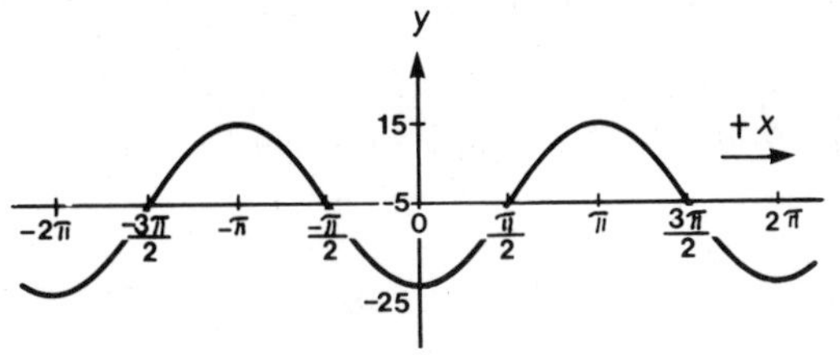

9.

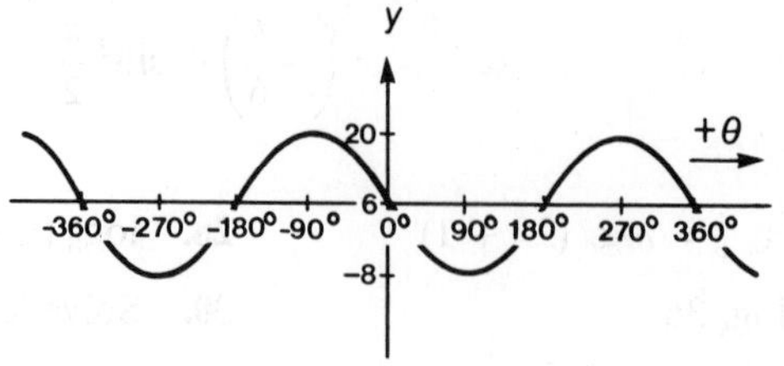

10. Evaluate ${}_4P_3$.

11. Find the standard form of the equation of a circle whose radius is 4 and whose center is (3, 2).

12. Sketch $y = (\frac{1}{2})^{x-3}$.

13. Factor $x^2 - 2x + 3$ over the set of complex numbers.

14. Write three proportions using the lengths of the sides of the small triangle and the large triangle.

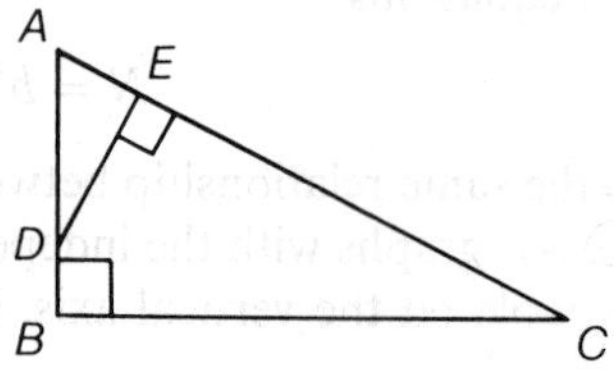

15. A 1-foot-high rock casts a shadow of 2 feet at a given time. At the same time, a person casts a shadow of 13 feet. How tall is the person?

16. Solve for x and y.

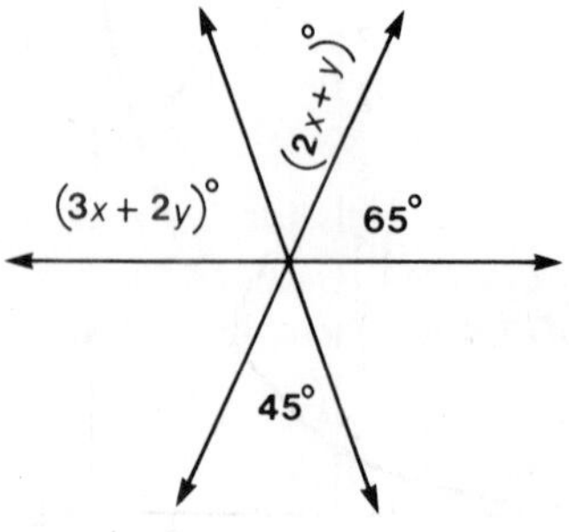

17. Use the midpoint formula method to find the equation of the perpendicular bisector of the line segment whose endpoints are (3, 6) and (8, −4). Write the equation in double-intercept form.

18. Write the equation of the perpendicular bisector of the line segment whose endpoints are (4, −2) and (−2, 6). Use the midpoint formula method.

19. What is the number whose graph is $\frac{2}{9}$ of the way from $-2\frac{1}{5}$ to $3\frac{1}{5}$?

20. Find the equation of the line equidistant from (−2, 1) and (3, 2), using the locus definition method. Write the equation in general form.

21. The latitude of Cambridge is 42.4° north of the equator. If the diameter of the earth is 7920 miles, how far is Cambridge from the equator?

Evaluate:

22. $\sin^3\left(-\frac{\pi}{3}\right)$

23. $\csc^2\frac{9\pi}{4} - \tan^2 45°$

24. Arcsin (sin 150°)

25. $\sin\left[\text{Arccos}\left(-\frac{2}{3}\right)\right]$

26. $\sec^2\left(-\frac{\pi}{6}\right) + \sin^3\frac{\pi}{2}$

Solve for x:

27. $\log_4 5 + \log_4 \frac{1}{5} = \log_4 (2x + 1)$

28. $\log_8 (x - 2) - \log_8 3 = \log_8 16$

29. $2 \log_k x = \log_k 36$

30. Solve for t: $z^3x = \sqrt{2t - 3} + 4$

LESSON 28 The logarithmic function · Development of the rules for logarithms

28.A The logarithmic function

The two equations

$$N = b^L \qquad \text{and} \qquad \log_b N = L$$

express the same relationship between the variables N and L. In mathematics, we prefer to make our graphs with the independent variable on the horizontal axis and the dependent variable on the vertical axis. If $b = 2$ we get these graphs.

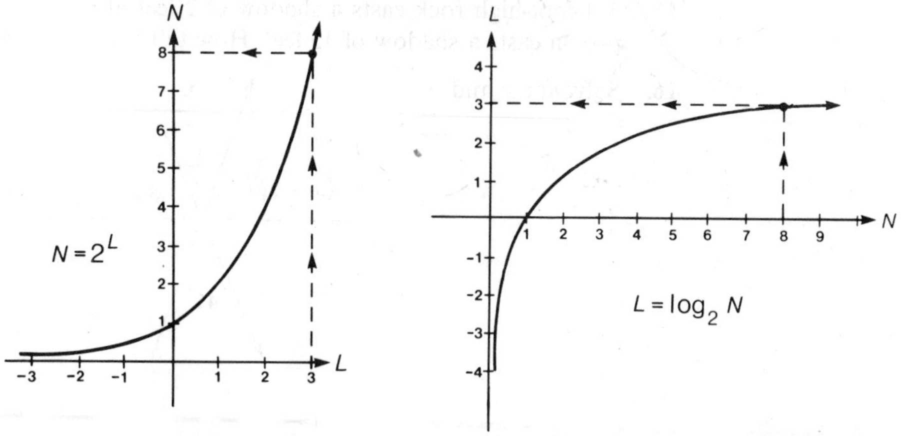

In the figure on the left, we graph the logarithm on the horizontal axis and the number on the vertical axis. Now if we are told that the logarithm is 3, we can use the graph to find that the number is 8. In the figure on the right, we graph the number on the horizontal axis and the logarithm on the vertical axis. We can use this graph to find that if the number is 8, then the logarithm is 3. We see that both graphs give the same information, and that either one can be used, but that if the number (N) is given and we are asked for the logarithm (L), we tend to use

$$\log_b N = L$$

and the graph on the right. If the exponent is given and we are asked for the number, we tend to use the equation

$$N = b^L$$

and use the graph on the left.

28.B Development of the rules for logarithms

It is reasonable for students to be able to demonstrate a development of the three rules for logarithms. We will review the reasoning involved by using 10^2 and 10^3 and noting that

$$\log_{10} 10^2 = 2 \qquad \text{logarithm is 2}$$
$$\log_{10} 10^3 = 3 \qquad \text{logarithm is 3}$$

Further, we note that when we multiply, we add the logarithms.

$$10^3 \cdot 10^2 = 10^{3+2} \qquad \text{so} \qquad \log_{10} 10^3 10^2 = \log_{10} 10^3 + \log_{10} 10^2$$

When we divide, we subtract the logarithms,

$$\frac{10^3}{10^2} = 10^{3-2} \qquad \text{so} \qquad \log_{10} \frac{10^3}{10^2} = \log_{10} 10^3 - \log_{10} 10^2$$

and when we raise to a power, we multiply the logarithm by the power.

$$(10^3)^2 = 10^{3 \cdot 2} \qquad \text{so} \qquad \log_{10} (10^3)^2 = 2 \log_{10} 10^3$$

To develop these ideas in general, we consider that we have two numbers M and N that can be written as a base b to the a power and the same base to the c power.

$$M = b^a \qquad \text{and} \qquad N = b^c$$

So

$$\log_b M = a \qquad \text{and} \qquad \log_b N = c$$

Now we can write the log of the product MN by replacing M with b^a and replacing N with b^c.

$$\log_b MN = \log_b b^a \cdot b^c = \log_b b^{a+c} = a + c$$

But $a + c$ is the log of M plus the log of N, so we have shown that

$$\log_b MN = \log_b M + \log_b N$$

Next we write the log of the quotient M/N.

$$\log_b \frac{M}{N} = \log_b \frac{b^a}{b^c} = \log_b b^{a-c} = a - c$$

But $a - c$ is the log of M minus the log of N, so we have shown that

$$\log_b \frac{M}{N} = \log_b M - \log_b N$$

Lastly, the log of the power $(N)^x$ is

$$\log_b (N)^x = \log_b (b^c)^x = \log_b b^{cx} = cx$$

but this is x times the log of N, so we have shown that

$$\log_b N^x = x \log_b N$$

Problem set 28

1. In a factory, a workers work b hours and produce c articles each day. If d workers quit, how many hours must the remaining workers work to produce the same number of articles each day?

2. Robill can do 2 jobs in 3 days, and Buray can do 5 jobs in 6 days. Robill works for 3 days and then Buray begins to help. How many days will it take to complete a total of 74 jobs?

3. Mugabee thought he was rich because he got paid \$240 for a 40-hour week. The next week he got a 20 percent hourly raise, and in addition he was allowed to work 60 hours. He really celebrated when he saw his paycheck. How much did he get paid?

4. Jimmy smiled, for he had purchased c cats for only d dollars. Then he frowned, for he still had to purchase p parrots and each parrot cost $\frac{7}{4}$ of the cost of 1 cat. How much did he have to pay for his parrots?

5. The nurse was aghast. She knew that G gallons of milk would feed S infants for 11 days, but she had $S + 14$ infants to feed. How many days would K gallons of milk last?

6. How many ways can the letters A, B, C, D, E, and F be arranged in a row 4 at a time if neither A nor C can be first or third and D cannot be fourth? Repetition is permitted.

7. How many ways can 4 geometry books and 3 algebra books be arranged in a row if the geometry books must be kept together and the algebra books must be kept together?

Write the equations of the following sinusoids.

8.

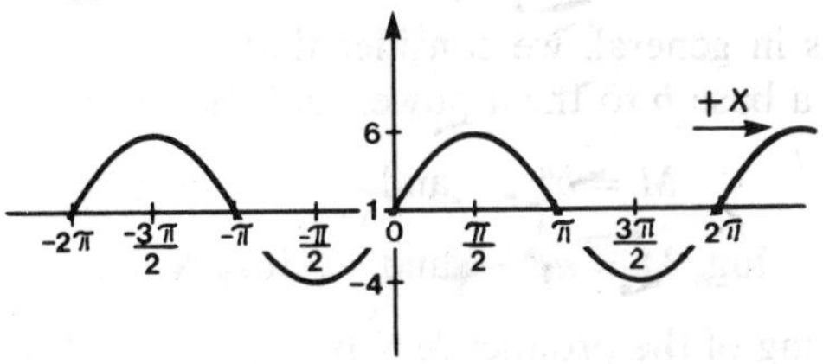

9.

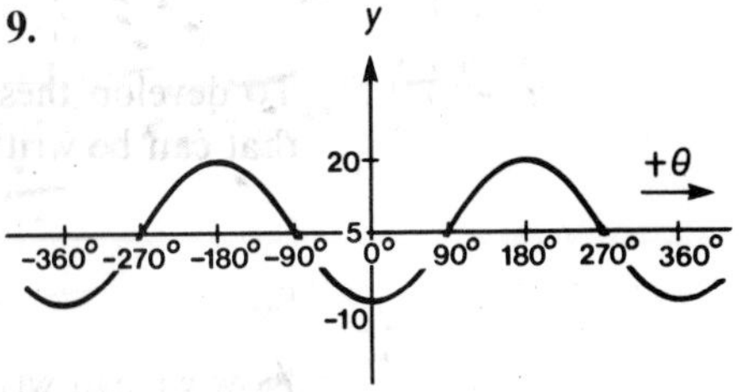

10. Evaluate $\dfrac{7!}{2!3!}$.

11. Find the standard form of the equation of a circle whose radius is 3 and whose center is $(-2, -3)$.

12. Sketch $y = (\frac{1}{2})^{-x+2}$.

13. Write a quadratic equation whose roots are $2 + i$ and $2 - i$.

14. Find a and b.

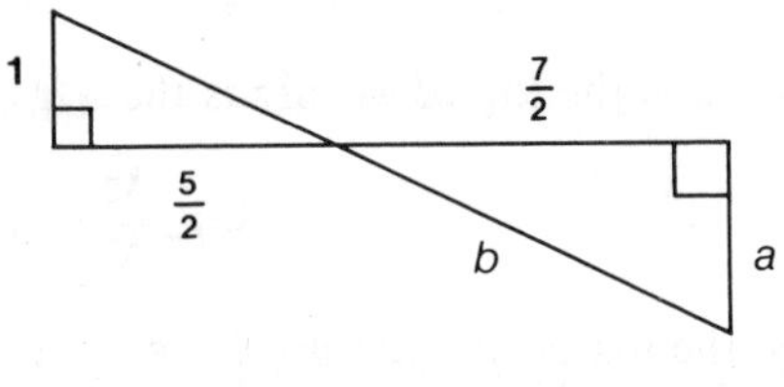

15. A 5-meter-high tree casts a shadow of 12 meters at a given time. At the same time, how long a shadow would a 30-meter-high building cast?

16. Solve for x and y.

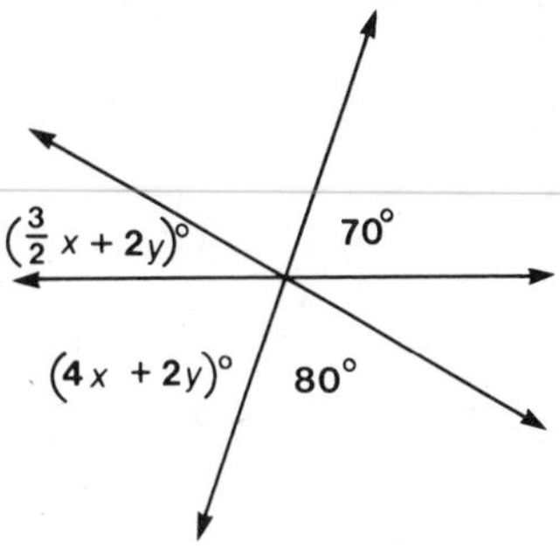

17. Find the equation of the perpendicular bisector of the line segment whose endpoints are $(-2, -4)$ and $(6, 4)$, using the midpoint formula method. Write the equation in general form.

18. Find the equation of the line that is equidistant from the points $(-2, -5)$ and $(3, 4)$, using the midpoint formula method. Write the equation in double-intercept form.

19. What is the number whose graph is $\frac{4}{9}$ of the way from $-3\frac{2}{3}$ to $2\frac{1}{3}$?

20. Write the equation of the line equidistant from $(1, -1)$ and $(2, -6)$, using the midpoint formula method. Write the equation in general form.

21. A rabbit ran through an arc of 0.87 radians along a circular track of radius 200 feet. How many feet did the rabbit run?

Evaluate:

22. $\cos^3\left(-\frac{\pi}{4}\right)$

23. $\sec^2\left(-\frac{13\pi}{6}\right) - \tan^3\frac{\pi}{4}$

24. $\cos\left[\text{Arcsin}\left(-\frac{2}{3}\right)\right]$

25. $\cos\left[\text{Arccos}\left(-\frac{2}{5}\right)\right]$

26. $\csc^2\left(-\frac{\pi}{3}\right) + \sec^2\left(\frac{2\pi}{3}\right)$

Let $M = b^a$ and $N = b^c$.

27. Show why $\log_b MN = \log_b M + \log_b N$.

28. Show why $\log_b (N)^x = x \log_b N$.

29. Show why $\log_b \frac{M}{N} = \log_b M - \log_b N$.

30. Solve for x: $\log_{10}(x - 2) - 2\log_{10} 3 = \log_{10} 4$

LESSON 29 Trigonometric equations

29.A Trigonometric equations

We know that the sine of 45° equals $+1/\sqrt{2}$ and that the sine of 135° also equals $+1/\sqrt{2}$ because the sine is positive in the first and second quadrants.

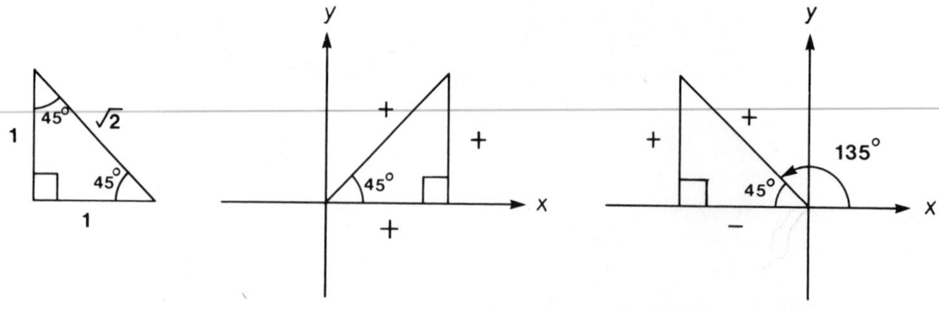

The sine of 405° and the sine of 495° also have a value of $+1/\sqrt{2}$ because these angles are coterminal angles with 45° and 135°. Once around and 45° more equals 405°, and once around and 135° more equals 495°.

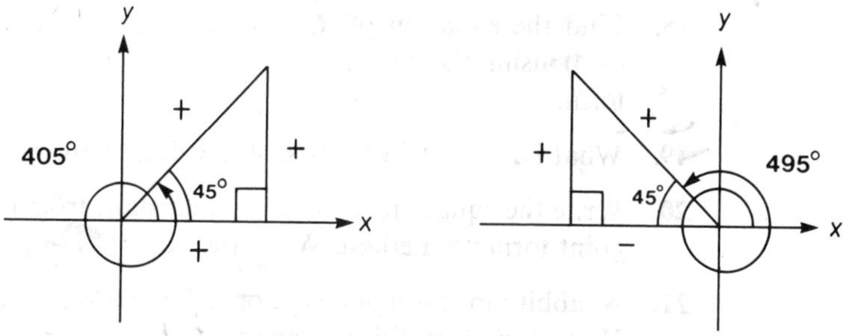

Since twice around, three times around, etc., yield the same result, we find there is an infinite number of angles that have a sine of $1/\sqrt{2}$. If we want to make up a problem that asks which angles have a sine of $1/\sqrt{2}$, and if we wish to restrict the answers to the two angles 45° and 135°, we must make a notation to this effect when we write the problem. We do this by writing

$$0^\circ \le \theta < 360^\circ$$

to the right of the problem. **This notation tells us that θ is an angle greater than or equal to 0° but less than 360°.**

Example 29.A.1 Solve: $\sin\theta = \dfrac{1}{\sqrt{2}} \qquad 0^\circ \le \theta < 360^\circ$

Solution This problem asks for the angles whose sine equals $1/\sqrt{2}$. The problem also states that the angles must lie between 0° and 360°. From the discussion above, we know that the angles that satisfy these requirements are 45° and 135°. So

$$\boldsymbol{\theta = 45^\circ, 135^\circ}$$

Example 29.A.2 Solve: $2 + \sqrt{3}\sec\theta = 0 \qquad 0^\circ \le \theta < 360^\circ$

Solution The notation on the right tells us that the value of θ must be between 0° and 360°. First we solve for $\sec\theta$.

$$\sqrt{3}\sec\theta + 2 = 0 \qquad \text{equation}$$
$$\sqrt{3}\sec\theta = -2 \qquad \text{added } -2 \text{ to both sides}$$
$$\sec\theta = -\frac{2}{\sqrt{3}} \qquad \text{divided by } \sqrt{3}$$

If $\sec\theta$ equals $-2/\sqrt{3}$, then $\cos\theta$ equals $-\sqrt{3}/2$.

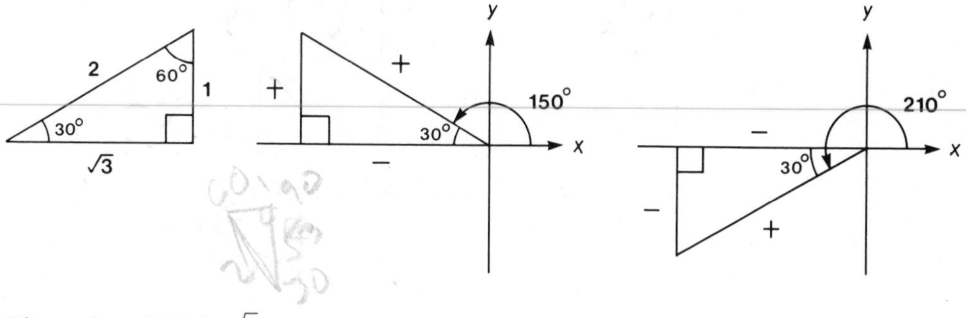

The cosine of 30° is $\sqrt{3}/2$, and the cosine is negative in the second and third quadrants. So the angles are 150° and 210°.

$$\boldsymbol{\theta = 150^\circ, 210^\circ}$$

Example 29.A.3 Solve: $3\sqrt{2} + 3 \csc \theta = 0 \qquad 0° \le \theta < 360°$

Solution We begin by solving the equation for csc θ.

$$3 \csc \theta + 3\sqrt{2} = 0 \qquad \text{equation}$$
$$3 \csc \theta = -3\sqrt{2} \qquad \text{added } -3\sqrt{2} \text{ to both sides}$$
$$\csc \theta = -\sqrt{2} \qquad \text{divided by 3}$$

If $\csc \theta = -\sqrt{2}$, then $\sin \theta = -1/\sqrt{2}$.

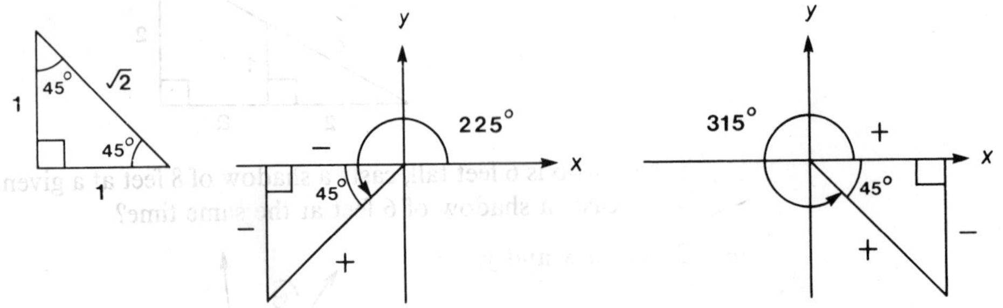

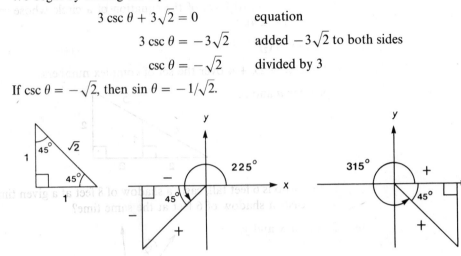

The sine of 45° is $1/\sqrt{2}$, and the sine is negative in the third and fourth quadrants. Thus, the angles that satisfy the given equation are **225°** and **315°**.

Problem set 29

1. The big man could do $\frac{1}{3}$ of a job in 4 hours. The little man could do $\frac{1}{2}$ of a job in 2 hours. If the little man needed to complete 30 jobs and worked for 2 hours alone and then is joined by the big man, how long will it take them both to finish the remaining jobs?
2. Matildabelle found that a quart of milk would serve 4 children or 3 adults. If 16 quarts of milk are available, how much will be left over after 40 children and 12 adults are served?
3. Three times Sally's age now exceeds 5 times John's age now by 15. In 10 years twice Sally's age then will be 20 less than 4 times John's age then. How old will they be 15 years from now?
4. The price of B of the big ones was D dollars. How many big ones could Sam buy for \$6?
5. A bus goes d miles in h hours and gets there 4 hours late. At what speed should the bus have been driven to have arrived on time?
6. How many ways can the digits 1, 2, 3, 4, and 5 be arranged in a row of 3 to form an odd number if repetition is permitted and if 3 cannot be second and 1 cannot be third?
7. How many numbers less than 150 are there such that all the digits are odd?

Write the equations of the following sinusoids.

8.

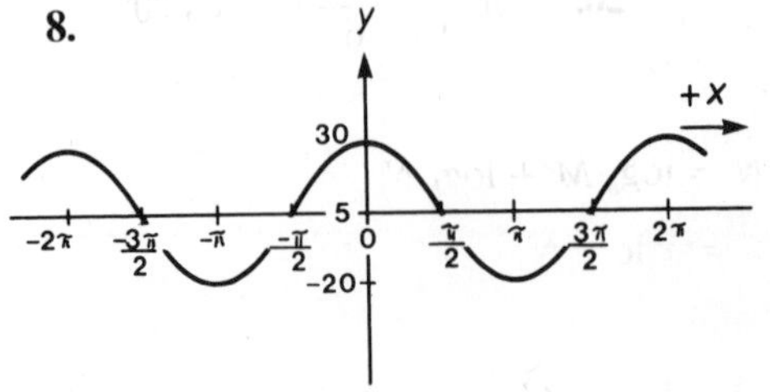

9.

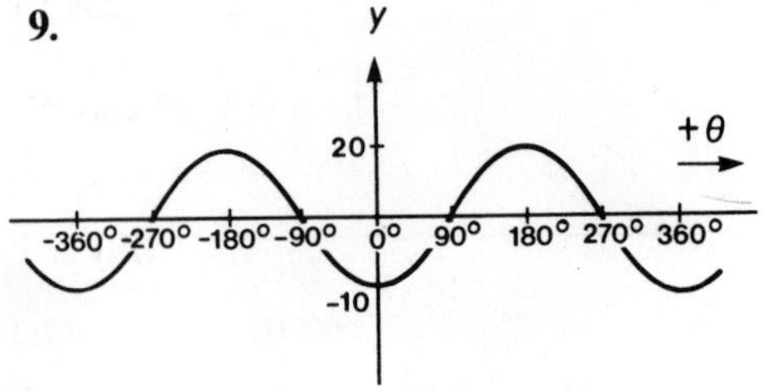

10. Evaluate: $\sum_{p=1}^{3} \frac{p^3 - 2}{p + 1}$

11. Find the standard form of the equation of a circle whose radius is 4 and whose center is $(-2, 4)$.

12. Sketch $y = (\frac{1}{2})^{-x-4}$.

13. Factor $x^2 - 2x + 4$ over the set of complex numbers.

14. Solve for a and b.

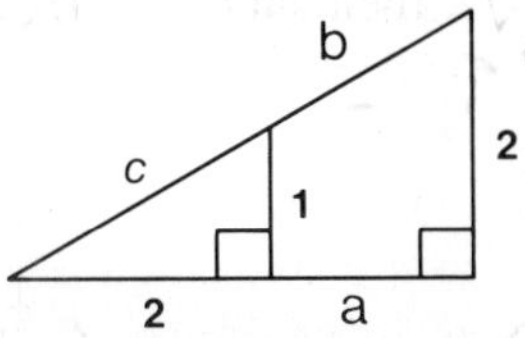

15. Frank, who is 6 feet tall, casts a shadow of 8 feet at a given time. How tall is Cindy if she casts a shadow of 6 feet at the same time?

16. Solve for x and y.

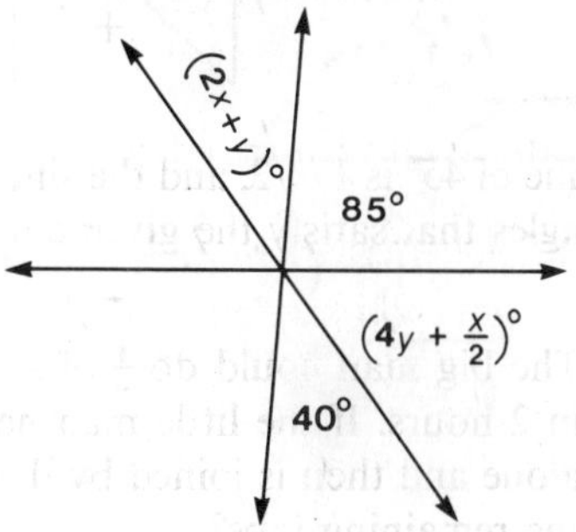

17. Use the midpoint formula method to find the equation of the perpendicular bisector of the line segment whose endpoints are $(-2, 4)$ and $(3, 5)$. Write the equation in general form.

18. Use the locus definition method to write the equation of the line equidistant from $(6, 3)$ and $(3, 2)$. Write the equation in slope-intercept form.

19. A discombobulated man runs through an arc of 80° along a circle of radius 300 meters. How far does he run?

Solve the following equations given that $(0° \le \theta < 360°)$:

20. $\cos\theta = \frac{1}{\sqrt{2}}$ **21.** $-2 + \sqrt{3}\sec\theta = 0$

Evaluate:

22. $\sin^2\frac{\pi}{4} + \cos^2\frac{\pi}{4}$ **23.** $\sec^2\frac{3\pi}{4} - \csc^2\frac{\pi}{4}$ **24.** $\sin\left(\text{Arccos}\,\frac{4}{7}\right)$

25. Arccos (cos 150°) **26.** $\cot^2\left(-\frac{13\pi}{6}\right) - \cos 90°$

Let $M = b^a$ and $N = b^c$.

27. Show why $\log_b MN = \log_b M + \log_b N$

28. Show why $\log_b (N)^x = x \log_b N$

Solve for x:

29. $\log_3 (x - 3) + \log_3 10 = \log_3 22$ **30.** $4 \log_5 3 = \log_5 x$

LESSON 30 Common logarithms and natural logarithms

30.A Common and natural logarithms

We remember that any positive number except 1 can be used as the base of an exponential expression and that the same numbers are the bases of the corresponding logarithmic expressions. We say that the **exponent** is the **logarithm** of the number and that the **number** is the **antilogarithm** of the exponent. Here we use both the exponential form and the logarithmic form to denote that if the base is 10, then 2 is the logarithm of 100 and 100 is the antilogarithm of 2.

$$100 = 10^2 \qquad 2 = \log_{10} 100$$

Logarithms that use 10 as a base are called **common logarithms.** Before slide rules and calculators were invented, most scientific calculations were made by using tables of common logarithms. Common logarithms are still used, and a base of 2 is often used in information theory. The other base most often used is the base e. The number e is an irrational number that is a little greater than 2.71.

$$e = 2.7182818 \cdots$$

Logarithms with a base of e are called **natural logarithms** and are used extensively in calculus, science, engineering, and business.

It is customary to designate that the base is 10 by writing log with no subscript. It is customary to designate that the base is e by using the letters ln with no subscript. Thus,

$$\log 42 \quad \text{means} \quad \log_{10} 42$$
$$\ln 42 \quad \text{means} \quad \log_e 42$$

Tables of logarithms give common logarithms and natural logarithms to four or five places, and calculators are accurate to seven or eight places. When accuracy is desired, logarithms can be obtained from these sources, but since beginners often tend to get lost in the arithmetic of logarithm problems, we will round off logarithms to two decimal places and concentrate on understanding rather than on arithmetic accuracy. Thus, for the time being, the logarithm problems will be designed to permit practice in the algebra of logarithms or will be simplified numerical problems designed to let us study the numerical side of logarithmic computations. In time, we will find that our study of these disparate parts will permit us to understand logarithms better.

Example 30.A.1 Write 2.4 as a power with a base of (*a*) 10, (*b*) e.

Solution The table of logarithms gives us the logarithms (exponents) that allow us to write numbers as powers. We round off the values to two places.

$$(a)\ \mathbf{2.4 = 10^{0.38}} \qquad (b)\ \mathbf{2.4 = e^{0.88}}$$

Example 30.A.2 Find (*a*) log 2.4 and (*b*) ln 2.4.

Solution Log means base 10 and ln means base e, so from the preceding example we have

$$2.4 = 10^{0.38} \quad \text{and} \quad 2.4 = e^{0.88}$$

So we can write

$$(a)\ \mathbf{\log 2.4 = 0.38} \qquad (b)\ \mathbf{\ln 2.4 = 0.88}$$

Example 30.A.3 Write 24,000 as a power with a base of 10.

Solution We begin by writing 24,000 in scientific notation.

$$24{,}000 = 2.4 \times 10^4$$

Now we use the log table to write 2.4 as a power,

$$24{,}000 = 10^{0.38} \times 10^4$$

and we finish by adding the exponents.

$$\mathbf{24{,}000 = 10^{4.38}}$$

Example 30.A.4 Find log 24,000.

Solution From the preceding example,

$$\mathbf{\log 24{,}000 = 4.38}$$

Example 30.A.5 Find log 0.0024.

Solution We begin by writing the number in scientific notation.

$$0.0024 = 2.4 \times 10^{-3}$$

Then we write 2.4 in exponential form and simplify.

$$0.0024 = 10^{0.38} \times 10^{-3}$$
$$= 10^{-2.62}$$

The exponent is the logarithm, so we may write

$$\mathbf{\log 0.0024 = -2.62}$$

Example 30.A.6 Write 24,000 as a power whose base is e.

Solution We first write 24,000 in scientific notation.

$$24{,}000 = 2.4 \times 10^4$$

Next we write 2.4 and 10 as powers whose base is e.

$$24{,}000 = e^{0.88} \times (e^{2.3})^4$$

Finally, we multiply 2.3 by 4 and finish by adding the exponents.

$$\mathbf{24{,}000} = e^{0.88} \times e^{9.2} = \mathbf{e^{10.08}}$$

Problem set 30

1. The first fellow could finish 7 jobs in 3 hours, and the second fellow could finish 8 jobs in 5 hours. How long would they have to work together to finish 59 jobs?
2. Use the letter d and the number 100 as required to write an expression that tells the number of 3-cent stamps that can be purchased for d dollars.
3. At 2 p.m. an F-foot flagpole cast a shadow s feet long. What would be the length in inches of the shadow of a person 5 feet 9 inches tall?
4. A package of raisins weighs 10 ounces. If 3 cups of raisins weighs 1 pound, how many packages will a baker need for a recipe which calls for 15 cups of raisins?
5. A truck went a distance of d miles in m minutes and got there 1 hour late. How fast should the truck have been driven to have arrived on time?
6. How many ways can the letters A, B, C, and D be arranged in a row if B cannot be in the second place and repetition is not allowed?

7. How many numbers are there less than 800 such that all the digits are odd?

Write the equations of the following sinusoids.

8.

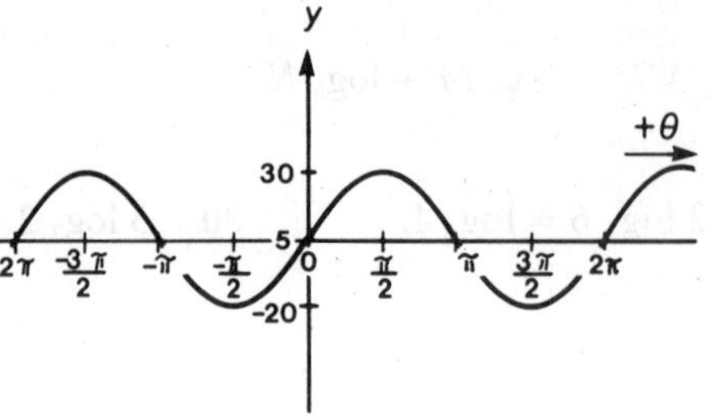

9.

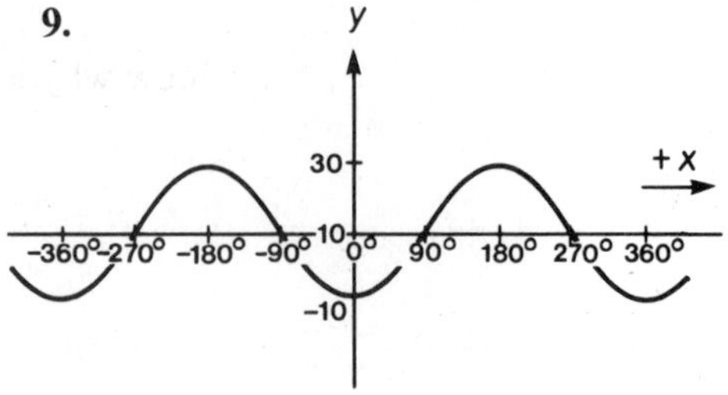

10. Evaluate ${}_5P_2$.

11. Find the standard form of the equation of a circle whose radius is 5 and whose center is $(-3, 2)$.

12. Sketch $y = (\frac{1}{2})^{x+2}$.

13. Write a quadratic equation whose roots are $3 - i$ and $3 + i$.

14. Write three proportions, using the lengths of the sides of the small triangle and the large triangle.

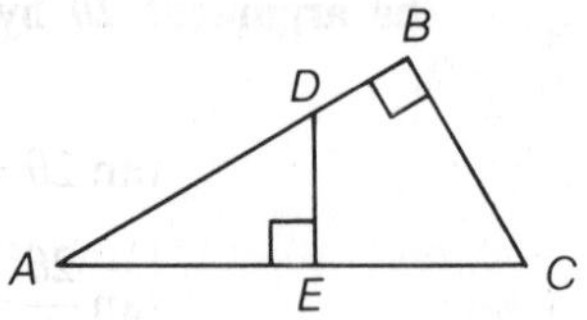

15. A 2-meter-high postbox casts a shadow of 3 meters at 3:00 in the afternoon. At the same time a flagpole casts a shadow of 30 meters. How high is the flagpole?

16. Prove that vertical angles are equal.

17. Find the equation of the perpendicular bisector of the line segment whose endpoints are $(-3, 4)$ and $(6, -2)$, using the locus definition method. Write the equation in general form.

18. A lion ran through an arc of $\pi/3$ radians along a circular path of radius 300 meters. How far did the lion run?

19. Find: (*a*) $\log 3.5$ (*b*) $\ln 3.5$

20. Write 3600 as a power whose base is e.

Solve the following equations given that $(0° \le \theta < 360°)$:

21. $\sin \theta = -\dfrac{\sqrt{3}}{2}$

22. $2 + \sqrt{3} \csc \theta = 0$

Evaluate:

23. $\sin^2 \dfrac{\pi}{6} + \cos^2 \dfrac{\pi}{6}$

24. $\sec^3 0° - \csc^2 \dfrac{5\pi}{6}$

25. $\tan \left[\text{Arcsin} \left(-\dfrac{5}{7} \right) \right]$

26. $\cos \left(\text{Arcsin} \dfrac{3}{4} \right)$

Let $M = b^a$ and $N = b^c$.

27. Show why $\log_b \frac{M}{N} = \log_b M - \log_b N$.

28. Show why $\log_b MN = \log_b M + \log_b N$.

Solve for x:

29. $\log_5 (x + 2) - 2 \log_5 6 = \log_5 1$

30. $3 \log_7 2 = 2 \log_7 3 + \log_7 x$

LESSON 31 The inviolable argument · Arguments in trigonometric equations

31.A The inviolable argument

The word *inviolable* means "safe from violation or profanation and impregnable to assault or trespass." **The argument of a function is inviolable because the arguments cannot be removed from the expression nor changed in form by using standard algebraic techniques. For example, the following procedure is *not* correct because it attempts to change the form of the argument 2θ by the algebraic procedure of dividing both sides of the equation by 2.**

$\tan 2\theta = 1$	equation	
$\tan \frac{2\theta}{2} = \frac{1}{2}$	divided by 2	*NO!*
$\tan \theta = \frac{1}{2}$	simplified	*NO!*

If it is necessary to divide both sides of the equation by 2, it is necessary to divide the whole expression by 2.

$$\frac{\tan 2\theta}{2} = \frac{1}{2} \qquad \text{correct}$$

We must always consider that the argument is a thing or an entity that must be retained in the given form unless changed by substituting an equivalent expression. For instance, if $2\theta - \pi = 4x$, then $4x$ could be substituted for $2\theta - \pi$.

$\cos (2\theta - \pi) = 1$	equation
$\cos 4x = 1$	substituted

Now we can solve this equation for the value of $4x$, but we cannot find the value of x before we find the value of $4x$. We will demonstrate the proper procedure in the following problems.

31.B Arguments in trigonometric equations

When the argument in a trigonometric equation consists of a variable whose coefficient is a number other than 1, the procedure is to solve the equation to find the value of the argument and then solve for the value of the variable.

Example 31.B.1 Solve: $\tan 3\theta - 1 = 0 \qquad 0° \le \theta < 360°$

Solution The first step is to find the value of the argument. Had the equation been written $\tan(3\theta - 1) = 0$, the argument would have been $3\theta - 1$. Because the parentheses were not used, we know that the argument is 3θ. We begin by rearranging the equation.

$$\tan 3\theta = 1 \qquad \text{rearranged}$$

The tangent of 45° is 1, and the tangent is positive in the first and third quadrants.

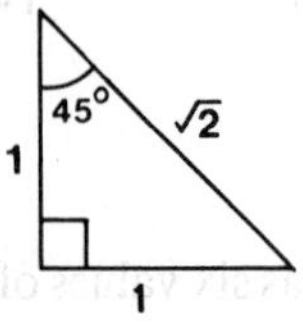

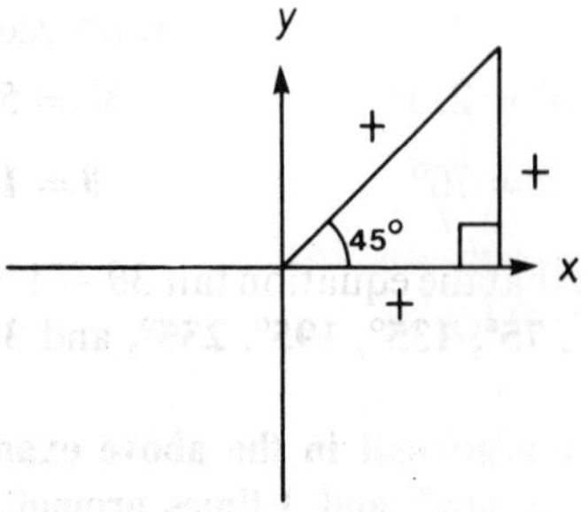

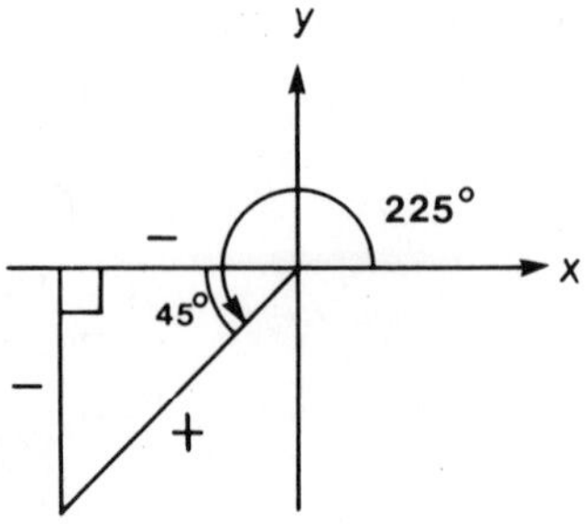

So 3θ equals 45° and 225°. Now we can find θ.

$$3\theta = 45° \qquad 3\theta = 225°$$
$$\theta = 15° \qquad \theta = 75°$$

The statement of the problem asked for all values of θ between 0° and 360°, and thus the values of 3θ are between 0° and 3(360°), or between 0° and 1080°. This means that since 3θ can equal 45°, 3θ can also equal 45° + 360° (once around) and 3θ can equal $45° + 2 \cdot 360°$ (twice around).

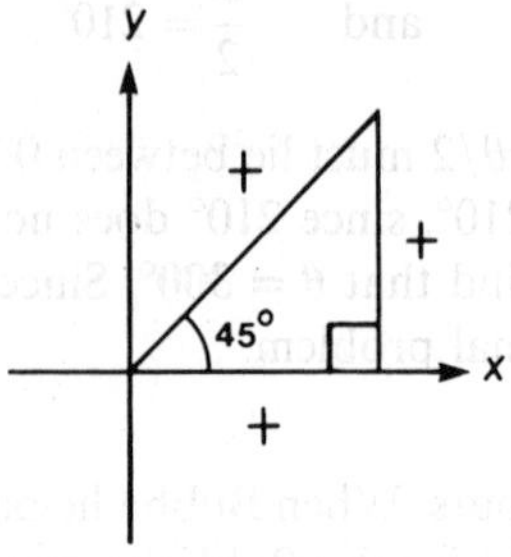

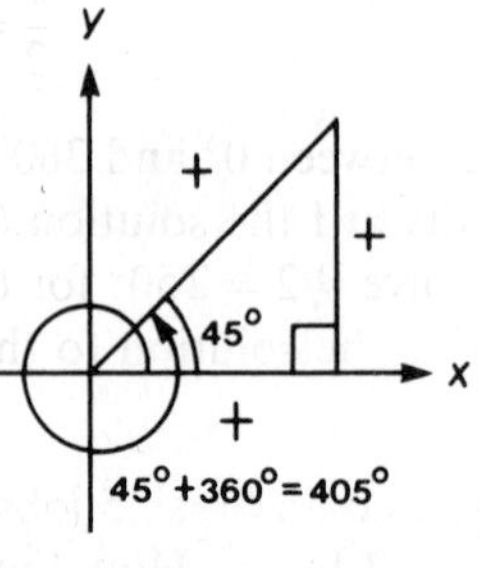

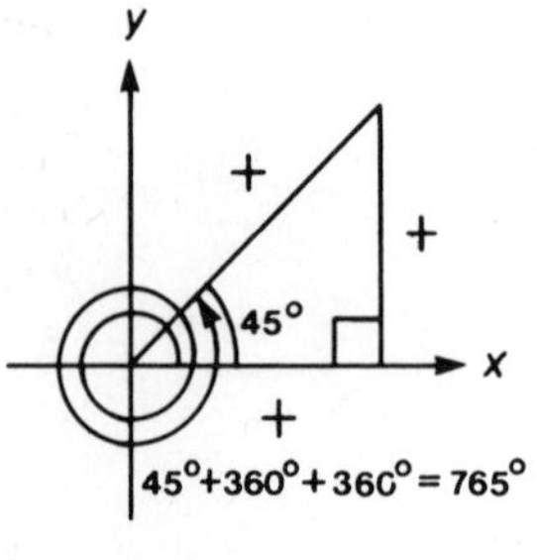

	ONCE AROUND	TWICE AROUND
$3\theta = 45°$	$3\theta = 405°$	$3\theta = 765°$
$\boldsymbol{\theta = 15°}$	$\boldsymbol{\theta = 135°}$	$\boldsymbol{\theta = 255°}$

If we check for 3 times around, we find we begin repeating our answers because 375° is 360° + 15°.

$$3 \text{ times around} = 45° + 3(360°) = 1125°$$
$$3\theta = 1125°$$
$$\theta = 375° \qquad \text{or} \qquad \theta = 15°$$

Now we continue our search for answers and find that 3θ can also equal 225°, 585°, and 945°.

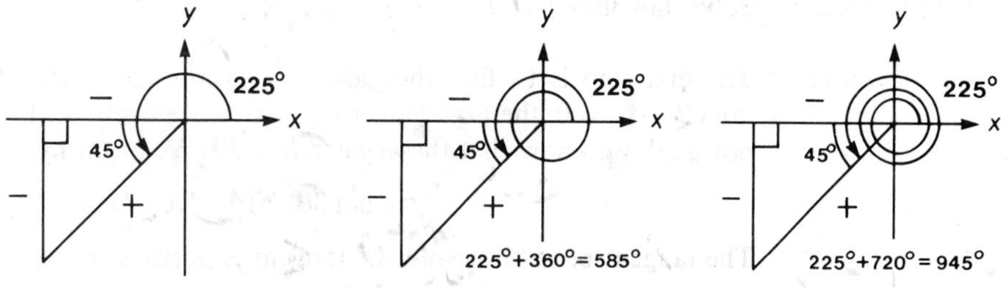

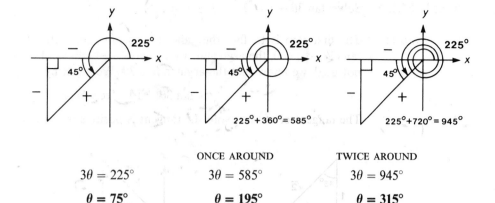

	ONCE AROUND	TWICE AROUND
$3\theta = 225°$	$3\theta = 585°$	$3\theta = 945°$
$\boldsymbol{\theta = 75°}$	$\boldsymbol{\theta = 195°}$	$\boldsymbol{\theta = 315°}$

Thus, we find that the equation $\tan 3\theta - 1 = 0$ has six values of θ that satisfy the equation. They are **15°, 75°, 135°, 195°, 255°,** and **315°.**

Had the argument in the above example been 4θ, we would have had to go once around, twice around, and 3 times around. If the argument had been 5θ, we would have had to go once around, twice around, 3 times around, and 4 times around.

Example 31.B.2 Solve: $\cos \frac{\theta}{2} + \frac{\sqrt{3}}{2} = 0 \qquad 0° \le \theta \le 360°$

Solution The first step is to rearrange to solve for the value of the argument $\frac{\theta}{2}$.

$$\cos \frac{\theta}{2} = -\frac{\sqrt{3}}{2}$$

Thus, $$\frac{\theta}{2} = 150° \qquad \text{and} \qquad \frac{\theta}{2} = 210°$$

θ must lie between 0° and 360°. Thus $\theta/2$ must lie between 0° and $360°/2 = 180°$. Thus we must discard the solution $\theta/2 = 210°$, since 210° does not lie between 0° and 180°. Now we solve $\theta/2 = 150°$ for θ and find that $\boldsymbol{\theta = 300°}$. Since 300° lies between 0° and 360°, **300°** is the solution to the original problem.

Problem set 31

1. Rancie could finish 5 jobs in 4 hours. When Bubba helped, they could complete 12 jobs in 7 hours. How long would it take Bubba to complete 2 jobs if he worked alone?

2. The boy could row at twice the speed of the current in the river. He could row 45 miles downstream in 1 more hour than it took to row 10 miles upstream. How fast was the current and how fast could the boy row?

3. Jimbob worked 40 hours for \$200. The week of the fair he got a 40 percent hourly increase, but because of the extra help, he got to work only 30 hours. What was his paycheck the week of the fair?

4. Sarah bought 50 shares of a company at \$60 per share and 2 months later bought 25 shares at \$56 per share. What price per share should she pay for 25 more shares so that the average price per share would be \$58?

5. A man traveled a distance of D feet in S seconds but got there 2 minutes late. How fast should he have traveled in feet per second to have arrived on time?

6. Given the letters A, B, C, D, E, and F, how many ways can they be arranged in rows of 5 if A is not third and B is fifth? Repetition is allowed.

7. How many numbers less than 500 are there all of whose digits are odd?

Write the equations of the following sinusoids.

8.

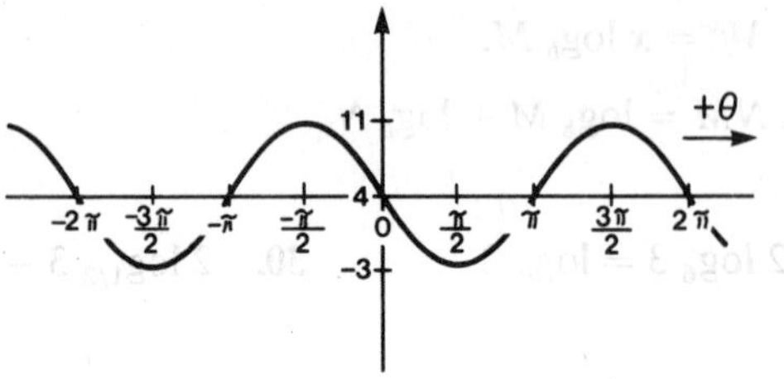

9.

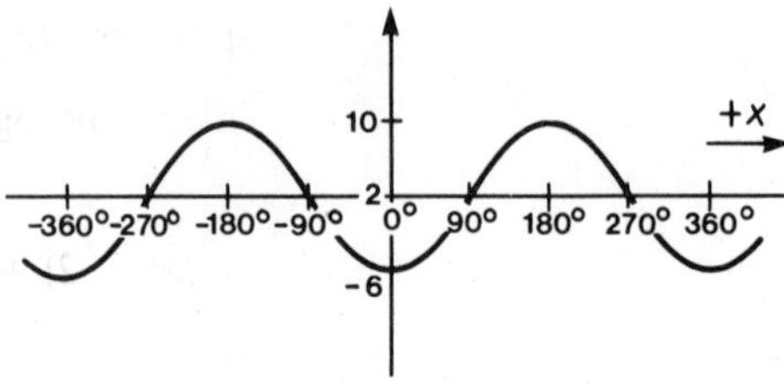

10. Evaluate: $\sum_{k=-1}^{3} (k^3 - 2)$

11. Find the standard form of the equation of a circle whose radius is r and whose center is (h, k).

12. Sketch $y = \left(\frac{1}{2}\right)^{-x+2}$.

13. Factor $x^2 + 4x + 5$ over the set of complex numbers.

14. Find side a.

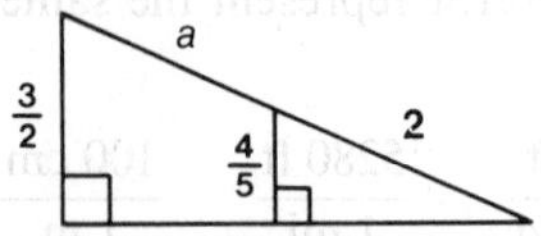

15. Find p.

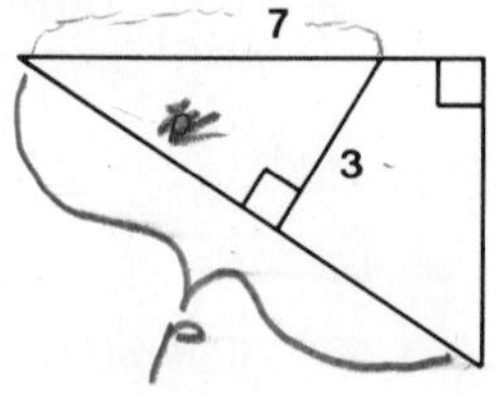

16. A lamppost 4 meters high casts a shadow of 3 meters. The lamppost stands next to a building 12 meters high. How long is the shadow of the building?

17. Use the midpoint formula method to find the equation of the perpendicular bisector of the line segment whose endpoints are $(-4, 8)$ and $(-6, -2)$. Write the equation in slope-intercept form.

18. The latitude of Washington, D.C., is 38.8° north of the equator. If the diameter of the earth is 7920 miles, how far is Washington, D.C., from the equator?

19. Find: (*a*) log 16.3 (*b*) ln 16.3

20. Write 3800 as a power whose base is e.

Solve the following equations given that $(0° \le \theta < 360°)$:

21. $\cos \theta = -\frac{1}{2}$

22. $\tan 3\theta - 1 = 0$

23. $\sin \frac{\theta}{2} + \frac{\sqrt{3}}{2} = 0$

Evaluate:

24. $\sin^2\left(-\frac{\pi}{3}\right) - \cos^2\frac{2\pi}{3}$ **25.** $\csc^2\left(-\frac{13\pi}{6}\right) - \sec^2\frac{19\pi}{6}$

26. Arctan (tan 45°)

Let $M = b^a$ and $N = b^c$.

27. Show why $\log_b M^x = x \log_b M$.

28. Show why $\log_b NM = \log_b M + \log_b N$.

Solve for x:

29. $\log_6 (x - 2) + 2 \log_6 3 = \log_6 2$ **30.** $2 \log_{1/2} 3 - \log_{1/2} (2x - 3) = 1$

LESSON 32 Review of unit multipliers · Angular velocity

32.A Review of unit multipliers

Unit multipliers are so named because they contain units such as feet, meters, hours, and seconds and also because they have a value of 1. In each of the following fractions, the denominator and the numerator represent the same measure and thus the value of each of these fractions is 1.

$$\frac{12 \text{ in}}{1 \text{ ft}} \qquad \frac{3 \text{ ft}}{1 \text{ yd}} \qquad \frac{5280 \text{ ft}}{1 \text{ mi}} \qquad \frac{100 \text{ cm}}{1 \text{ m}} \qquad \frac{1 \text{ liter}}{1000 \text{ cc}}$$

$$\frac{2.54 \text{ cm}}{1 \text{ in}} \qquad \frac{60 \text{ sec}}{1 \text{ min}} \qquad \frac{60 \text{ min}}{1 \text{ hr}} \qquad \frac{24 \text{ hr}}{1 \text{ day}}$$

If any of these fractions is inverted, the value of the fraction will still be 1. Unit multipliers are useful for making unit conversions.

Example 32.A.1 Change 40 miles per hour to meters per second.

Solution First we use unit multipliers to change hours to seconds.

$$\frac{40 \text{ mi}}{1 \cancel{\text{hr}}} \times \frac{1 \cancel{\text{hr}}}{60 \cancel{\text{min}}} \times \frac{1 \cancel{\text{min}}}{60 \text{ sec}}$$

Now we multiply as required to change miles to feet, to inches, to centimeters, to meters.

$$\frac{40 \cancel{\text{mi}}}{1 \cancel{\text{hr}}} \times \frac{1 \cancel{\text{hr}}}{60 \cancel{\text{min}}} \times \frac{1 \cancel{\text{min}}}{60 \text{ sec}} \times \frac{5280 \cancel{\text{ft}}}{1 \cancel{\text{mi}}} \times \frac{12 \cancel{\text{in}}}{1 \cancel{\text{ft}}} \times \frac{2.54 \cancel{\text{cm}}}{1 \cancel{\text{in}}} \times \frac{1 \text{ m}}{100 \cancel{\text{cm}}}$$

The units cancel as shown and our answer is

$$\frac{\mathbf{40 \times 5280 \times 12 \times 2.54}}{\mathbf{60 \times 60 \times 100}} \frac{\mathbf{m}}{\mathbf{sec}}$$

A calculator can be used to reduce this answer to a single decimal number if desired.

32.B Angular velocity

Linear velocity is a vector quantity, as it has both a magnitude and a direction. Angular velocity is the measure of the rate of rotation of an object. The units of angular velocity are some unit of circular measure per unit of time. Some commonly used units of angular velocity are

$$\frac{\text{degrees}}{\text{sec}} \qquad \frac{\text{degrees}}{\text{min}} \qquad \frac{\text{rad}}{\text{sec}} \qquad \frac{\text{rad}}{\text{min}} \qquad \frac{\text{rev}}{\text{sec}} \qquad \frac{\text{rev}}{\text{min}}$$

The velocity of a point on a rotating wheel depends on the rate of rotation and on the distance of the point from the center of the wheel. Consider that the wheel shown here makes 1 revolution (rev) every second.

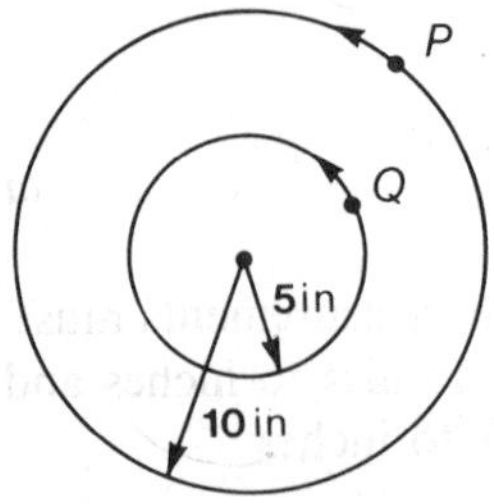

Point P is 10 inches from the center, and in 1 sec it goes all the way around the outside circle which has a circumference of $2\pi R$ inches (in).

$$1 \text{ rotation} = 2(3.14)(10) = 62.8 \text{ in}$$

Point Q has the same rate of turning or angular velocity, but it is closer to the center of rotation, so in 1 sec it travels a different distance.

$$1 \text{ rotation} = 2(3.14)(5) = 31.4 \text{ in}$$

Thus, while the angular velocity of P and Q are the same, their linear velocity is different.

$$\text{Velocity of } P = 62.8 \frac{\text{in}}{\text{sec}} \qquad \text{Velocity of } Q = 31.4 \frac{\text{in}}{\text{sec}}$$

In general, the linear velocity of a point on a rotating body is

$$v = R\omega$$

where ω (omega) is the angular velocity measured in radians per unit time. If the angular velocity is given in revolutions per unit time or degrees per unit time, the revolutions or degrees must be converted to radians in order to calculate linear velocity.

Example 32.B.1 A wheel of a wagon has a radius of 14 inches and is revolving at 40 revolutions per minute (rev/min). How fast is the wagon moving in miles per hour?

Solution **The linear velocity of a point on the rim of the wheel is $R\omega$, where ω is stated in radians per unit time.** Thus, we begin by converting 40 revolutions per minute (rev/min) to radians per minute (rad/min).

$$40 \frac{\text{rev}}{\text{min}} \times 2\pi \frac{\text{rad}}{\text{rev}} = 80\pi \frac{\text{rad}}{\text{min}}$$

Now we can use $v = R\omega$ to find the linear velocity and at the same time convert the answer to miles per hour.

$$v = R\omega = 14\ \cancel{\text{in}} \times 80\pi\ \frac{\text{rad}}{\cancel{\text{min}}} \times \frac{1\ \cancel{\text{ft}}}{12\ \cancel{\text{in}}} \times \frac{1\ \text{mi}}{5280\ \cancel{\text{ft}}} \times \frac{60\ \cancel{\text{min}}}{1\ \text{hr}}$$

$$= \mathbf{\frac{14(80\pi)(60)}{12(5280)}\ \frac{mi}{hr}}$$

Example 32.B.2 An automobile whose wheels are 30 inches in diameter is traveling at 40 mph. What is the angular velocity of the wheels in revolutions per second?

Solution First we solve for ω:

$$v = R\omega \longrightarrow \omega = \frac{v}{R}$$

We will put the numbers we have into this equation and simplify.

$$\omega = \frac{v}{R} = \frac{40\ \frac{\text{mi}}{\text{hr}}}{15\ \text{in}} = \frac{40\ \text{mi}}{15\ \text{hr-in}}$$

All length measurements must be the same. We can convert inches to miles and cancel, or convert miles to inches and cancel. The result will be the same. We decide to convert miles to inches.

$$\omega = \frac{40\ \cancel{\text{mi}}}{15\ \text{hr-}\cancel{\text{in}}} \times \frac{5280\ \cancel{\text{ft}}}{1\ \cancel{\text{mi}}} \times \frac{12\ \cancel{\text{in}}}{1\ \cancel{\text{ft}}} = \frac{40(5280)(12)}{15}\ \frac{}{\text{hr}}$$

This answer is really in radians per hour. Radian measure is dimensionless, and the unit radian is used as a convenience. Thus, the unit radian can be inserted or deleted as is convenient. This is difficult to understand at first and practice with this concept is necessary. In the last step in the preceding example we deleted the unit radian. To finish this problem, we will insert the unit radian.

$$\omega = \frac{40(5280)(12)}{15}\ \frac{\text{rad}}{\text{hr}}$$

Now we finish by using unit multipliers to convert radians per hour to revolutions per second.

$$\omega = \frac{40(5280)(12)}{15}\ \frac{\cancel{\text{rad}}}{\cancel{\text{hr}}} \times \frac{1\ \text{rev}}{2\pi\ \cancel{\text{rad}}} \times \frac{1\ \cancel{\text{hr}}}{60\ \cancel{\text{min}}} \times \frac{1\ \cancel{\text{min}}}{60\ \text{sec}}$$

$$= \mathbf{\frac{40(5280)(12)}{15(60)(60)(2\pi)}\ \frac{rev}{sec}}$$

Problem set 32

1. Mudog can do 8 jobs in 3 days, and Jimmy can do 5 jobs in 2 days. Thirty-nine jobs need to be done. Mudog works 3 days and then Jimmy joins in. How many days will both of them have to work together to complete the 39 jobs?

2. In a factory, m workers work h hours to do j jobs. If p new workers are hired, how many hours will the work force have to work to do j jobs?

3. Find an angle such that 5 times its complement is 30° greater than its supplement.

4. Fast Francie could run Y yards in S seconds. What would her rate be in yards per second if she ran 3 times as far in 20 more seconds?

5. Dillbob converted 2800 francs to dollars at an exchange rate of 350 francs to the dollar. Then he went to another country and converted back to francs at 400 francs to the dollar. What was his profit in francs?

6. If no repetition is permitted, how many ways can the digits 1, 2, 3, 4, 5, and 6 be arranged 4 at a time to form an even number?

7. An automobile whose wheels are 30 inches in diameter is traveling at 50 miles per hour. What is the angular velocity of the wheels in revolutions per second?

Write the equations of the following sinusoids.

8.

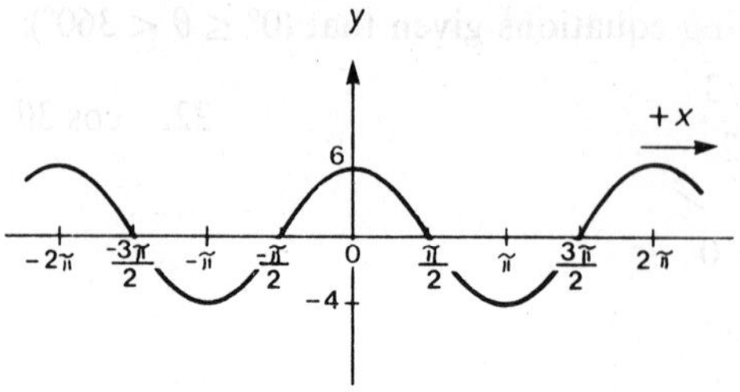

9.

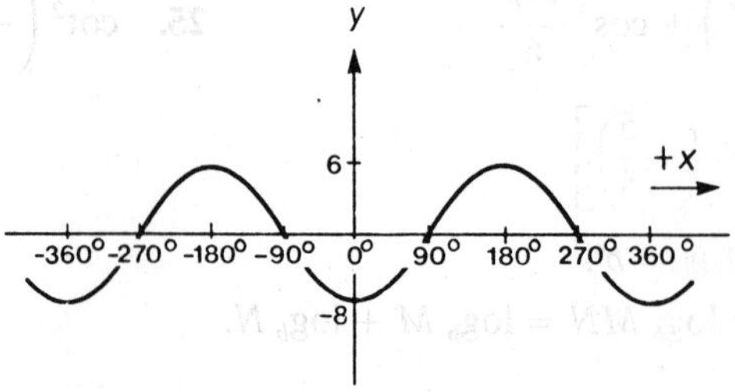

10. Write a quadratic equation whose roots are $-1 + 2\sqrt{2}i$ and $-1 - 2\sqrt{2}i$.

11. Find the standard form of the equation of a circle whose radius is 5 and whose center is (h, k).

12. Sketch $y = (\frac{1}{2})^{-x+2}$.

13. Convert 50 miles per hour to centimeters per minute.

14. Convert 30 liters to cubic inches.

15. Find a and b.

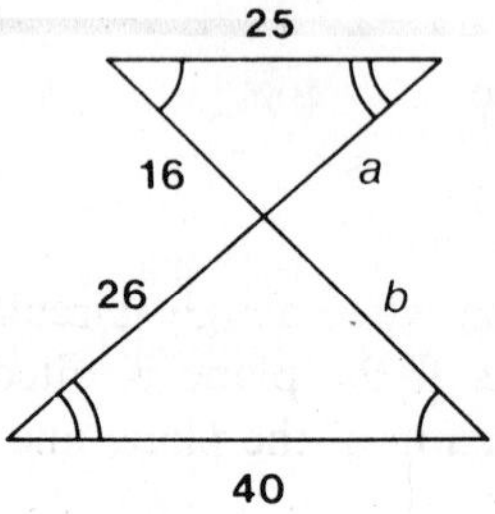

16. A 3-centimeter-high rock casts a shadow of 4 centimeters. At the same time, how many centimeters long is the shadow of a tree that is 6 meters high?

17. Solve for x and y.

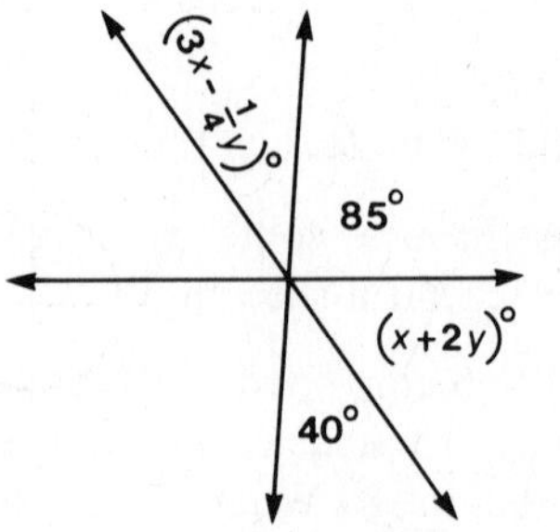

18. Write the equation of the line equidistant from (8, 4) and (−3, 4), using the locus definition method. Write the equation in general form.

19. A horse runs through an arc of 270° along a circular racetrack whose diameter is 4000 meters. How far does the horse run?

20. Write 6200 (*a*) as 10 raised to a power; (*b*) as *e* raised to a power.

Solve the following equations given that $(0° \le \theta < 360°)$:

21. $\sin\theta = -\dfrac{\sqrt{3}}{2}$

22. $\cos 3\theta - 1 = 0$

23. $\sin\dfrac{\theta}{2} - 1 = 0$

Evaluate:

24. $\sec^2\left(-\dfrac{3\pi}{4}\right) + \cos^2\dfrac{13\pi}{6}$

25. $\cot^2\left(-\dfrac{\pi}{3}\right) - \sec^3 0$

26. $\sin\left[\text{Arccos}\left(-\dfrac{5}{8}\right)\right]$

Let $M = b^a$ and $N = b^c$.

27. Show why $\log_b MN = \log_b M + \log_b N$.

Solve for x.

28. $\log_{15} 4 - \log_{15}\dfrac{2}{x} = 2$

29. $2\log_7 4 - \log_7 x = \dfrac{2}{3}\log_7 8$

30. Solve for z: $2t^2 = \sqrt{z-1} + 1$

LESSON 33 Parabolas

33.A Parabolas

A circle is formed when a right circular cone is cut by a plane that is parallel to the base of the cone. If the plane is tilted as shown in the right-hand figure below, the points of intersection of the plane and the cone form a figure called a ***parabola.***

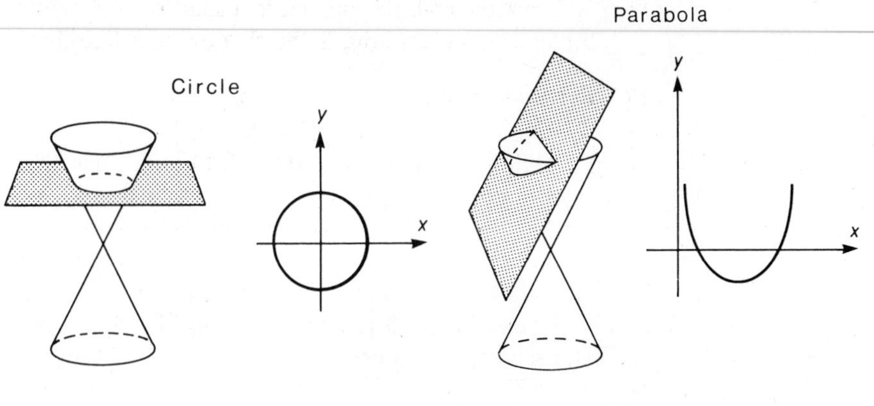

The Greek prefix *syn-* (or *sym-*) means "same" and the Greek word for measure is *metron.* We combine these words to form the English words *symmetric* and *symmetry*, which mean " the same measure." We usually say from where or what we are measuring. The parabolas shown in the figures below are the same measure on both sides of their centerline, and thus we say that parabolas are symmetric about their centerlines. We call the centerline of parabola its ***axis of symmetry.*** We see from these figures that the axis of symmetry of a parabola can be vertical, horizontal, or inclined to the vertical and the horizontal.

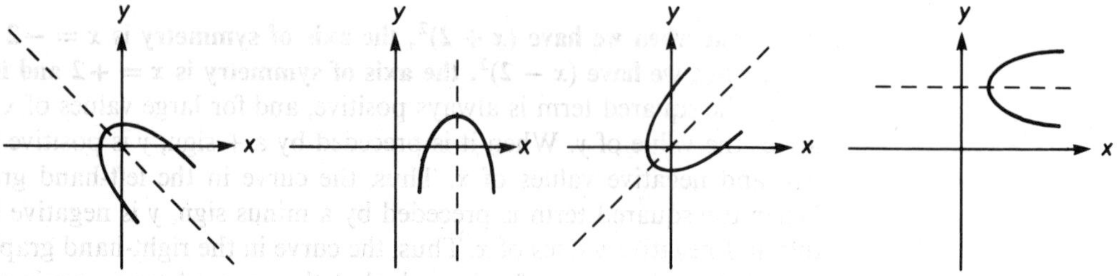

In this book we will concentrate on parabolas whose axes of symmetry are vertical lines. It can be shown that the graph of a quadratic equation in x and y such as

$$y = x^2 + 4x + 1 \qquad \text{or} \qquad y = -x^2 + 4x - 3$$

is symmetric about a vertical line and that the graph either **opens upward** or **opens downward.** If the curve opens upward, the vertex is on the axis of symmetry, and the y coordinate of the vertex is a minimum value. If the curve opens downward, the vertex is on the axis of symmetry, and its y coordinate is a maximum value.

Opens upward

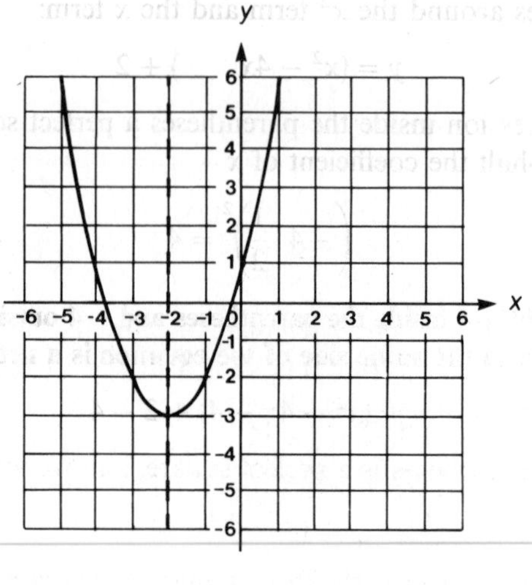

$y = x^2 + 4x + 1$

Open downward

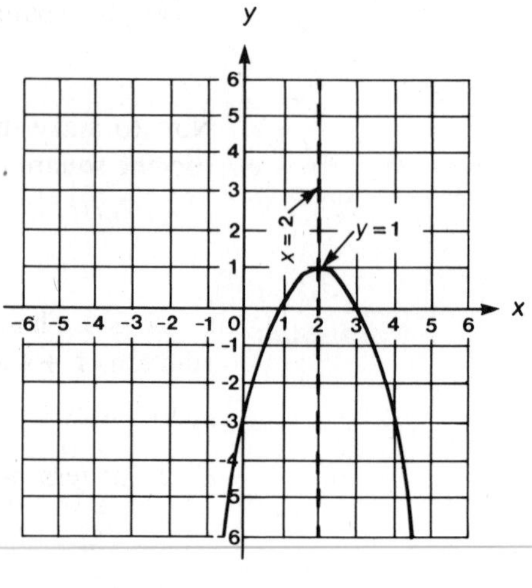

$y = -x^2 + 4x - 3$

These equations could be plotted point by point, but it is easier to change the form of the equation to the form

$$y = a(x - h)^2 + k$$

as we will show in this lesson. We will discover that in this form, we can determine the axis of symmetry, which is the line $x = h$. The coordinates of the vertex are (h, k). If a is greater than zero (is a positive number), the curve opens upward. If a is less than zero (is a negative number), the curve opens downward. If we complete the square on the equations under the graphs in the preceding page, we get

opens upward; vertex at $y = -3$

$$y = +(x + 2)^2 - 3$$

axis of symmetry is $x = -2$

opens downward; vertex at $y = +1$

$$y = -(x - 2)^2 + 1$$

axis of symmetry is $x = +2$

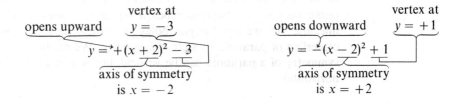

Note that when we have $(x + 2)^2$, the axis of symmetry is $x = -2$ and is not $x = +2$. Also, when we have $(x - 2)^2$, the axis of symmetry is $x = +2$ and is not $x = -2$.

The squared term is always positive, and for large values of x, this term approximates the value of y. When it is preceded by a + sign, y is positive for both large positive and negative values of x. Thus, the curve in the left-hand graph opens upward. When the squared term is preceded by a minus sign, y is negative for both large positive and negative values of x. Thus, the curve in the right-hand graph opens downward.

When the value of x is such that the squared term equals zero, the curve is at a maximum or a minimum point. This is the reason that the y coordinate of the vertex is the constant at the end of the expression.

We will show how to use completing the square as an aid to graphing in the next two examples.

Example 33.A.1 Complete the square to graph $y = x^2 - 4x + 2$.

Solution We want to rearrange the right side of the equation into the form

$$y = (x - h)^2 + k$$

so we place parentheses around the x^2 term and the x term:

$$y = (x^2 - 4x \qquad) + 2$$

Now to make the expression inside the parentheses a perfect square, it is necessary to add the square of one-half the coefficient of x

$$\left(-4 \cdot \frac{1}{2}\right)^2 = 4$$

which is 4. **Thus, we add +4 inside the parentheses and −4 outside the parentheses. This addition of +4 and −4 to the same side of the equation is a net addition of zero.**

$$y = (x^2 - 4x + 4) + 2 - 4$$

Now the term in the parentheses is a perfect square, and we write it as such.

$$y = (x - 2)^2 - 2$$

From this form, we can determine the three things necessary to sketch the curve.

(*a*) Opens upward

(*b*) Axis of symmetry is $x = +2$

(*c*) y coordinate of vertex is -2

$$y = +(x - 2)^2 - 2$$

We use this information to draw the axis of symmetry and the vertex of the curve as we show on the left-hand graph on the next page. Now, if we get one more point on the curve, we can make a sketch. Let's let $x = 4$ in the original equation and solve for y.

$$y = (4)^2 - 4(4) + 2 \qquad \text{substituted}$$

$$y = 16 - 16 + 2 \qquad \text{multiplied}$$

$$y = 2 \qquad \text{simplified}$$

Thus, the point (4, 2) lies on the curve. We remember that the curve is symmetric about the line $x = 2$ and complete the sketch.

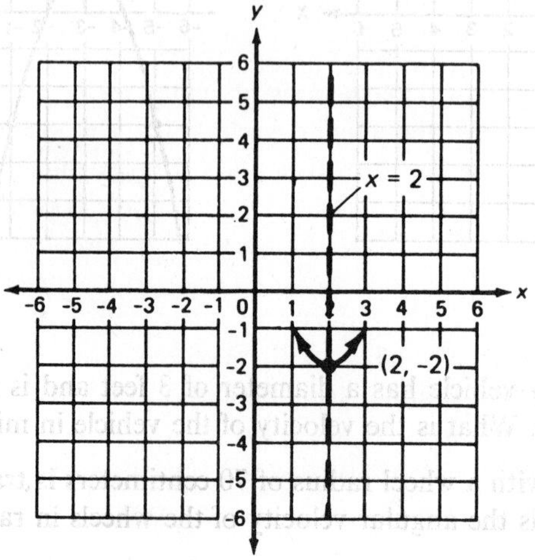

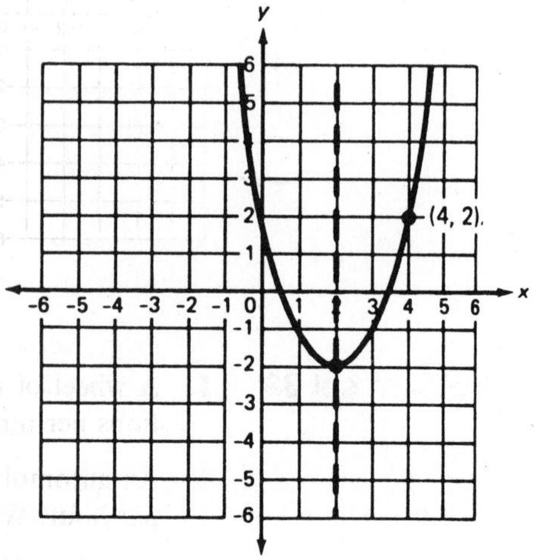

Example 33.A.2 Complete the square to graph $y = -x^2 - 6x - 8$.

Solution **When the coefficient of x^2 is not 1, we begin by factoring the first two terms so that the coefficient of x^2 is 1.**

$$y = -(x^2 + 6x \qquad) - 8 \qquad \text{factored}$$

Now we complete the square inside the parentheses by adding $+9$. **Since the parentheses are preceded by a minus sign, we have really added -9, so we also add $+9$ outside the parentheses.** Then we simplify.

$$y = -(x^2 + 6x + 9) - 8 + 9 \qquad \text{completed the square}$$

$$y = -(x + 3)^2 + 1 \qquad \text{simplified}$$

Now we diagnose the salient features of the graph.

(*a*) Opens downward

(*b*) Axis of symmetry is $x = -3$ $\qquad y = -(x + 3)^2 + 1$

(*c*) y coordinate of vertex is $+1$

On the left-hand graph on the next page we use these facts to begin the curve. To find another point on the curve, we replace x with -1 and find that y equals -3.

$$y = -(-1)^2 - 6(-1) - 8 \qquad \text{substituted}$$

$$y = -1 + 6 - 8 \qquad \text{multiplied}$$

$$y = -3 \qquad \text{simplified}$$

Then we use the point $(-1, -3)$ and symmetry to complete the graph.

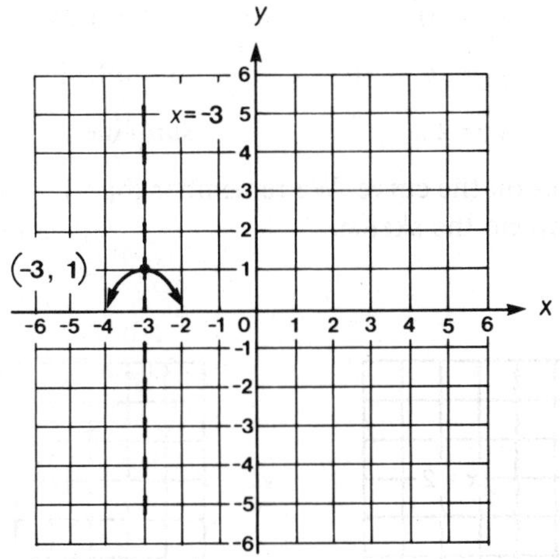

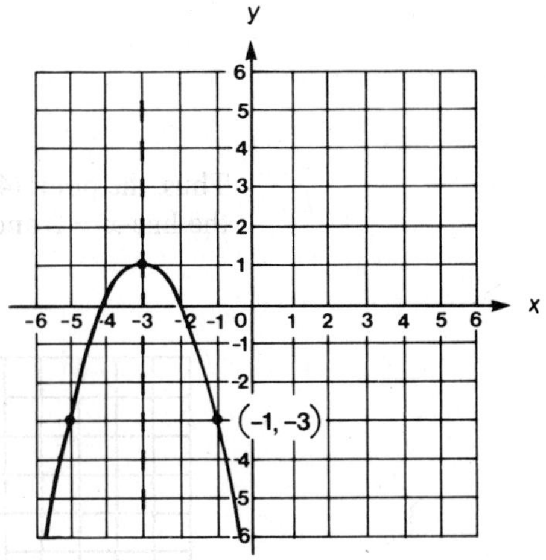

Problem set 33

1. A wheel of a big vehicle has a diameter of 3 feet and is revolving at 30 revolutions per minute. What is the velocity of the vehicle in miles per hour?

2. An automobile with a wheel radius of 70 centimeters is traveling at 30 kilometers per hour. What is the angular velocity of the wheels in radians per minute?

3. Judy flew K miles in h hours but still got there 2 hours late. How fast should she have flown to have arrived on time?

4. The vat contained 40 liters of a 5% salt solution. How many liters of a 20% salt solution should be added to get a solution that is 10% salt?

5. Hortense could complete 1 job in 4 hours while Joe could complete 1 job in 8 hours. If Joe worked for 2 hours and then was joined by Hortense, how long would it take them working together to complete $6\frac{1}{4}$ jobs?

6. How many ways can A, B, C, and D be placed in a row of 3 spaces if B cannot be first and D cannot be second? Repetition is permitted.

7. Factor $x^2 + 3x - 9$ over the set of complex numbers.

Write the equations of the following sinusoids.

8.

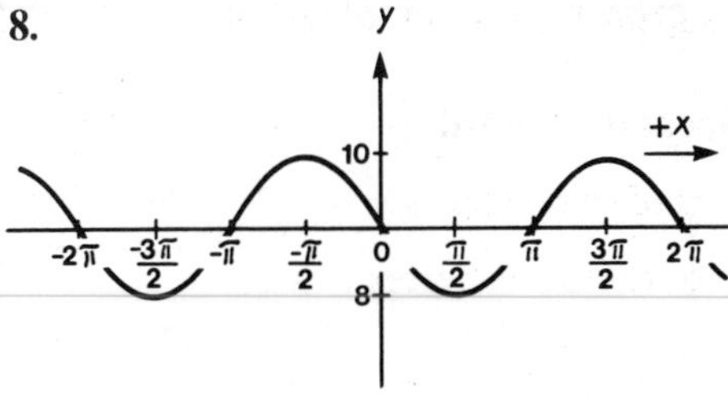

9.

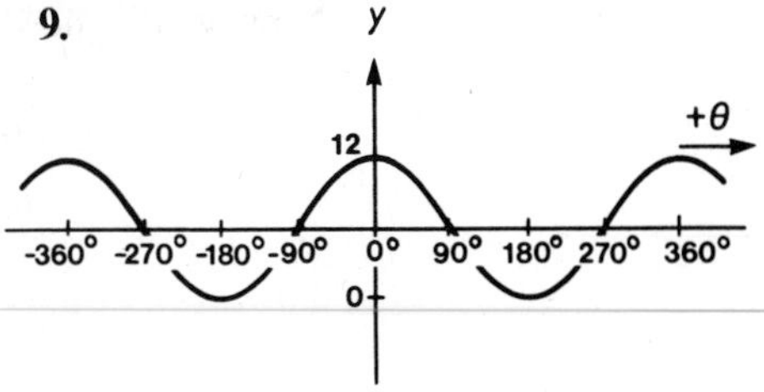

10. Evaluate: $\sum_{k=-3}^{-1} \frac{(k-1)(k+1)}{k}$

11. Find the standard form of the equation of a circle whose radius is 6 and whose center is (3, 2).

12. Complete the square to graph $y = x^2 - 6x + 4$.

13. Complete the square to graph $y = -x^2 - 4x + 6$.

14. Sketch: $y = (2)^{-x-3}$

15. Convert 40 miles per hour to centimeters per second.

16. Convert 12 liters per second to cubic centimeters per hour.

17. Find x.

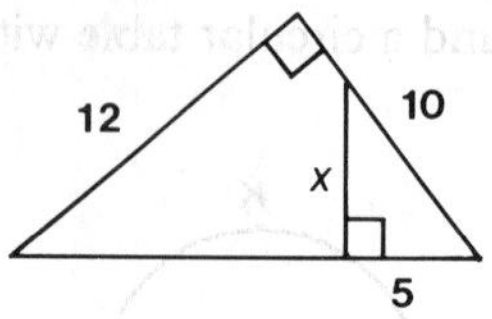

18. A man casts a shadow of 6 meters at a given time. At the same time a 15-meter flagpole casts a shadow of 5 meters. How tall is the man?

19. Solve for x and y.

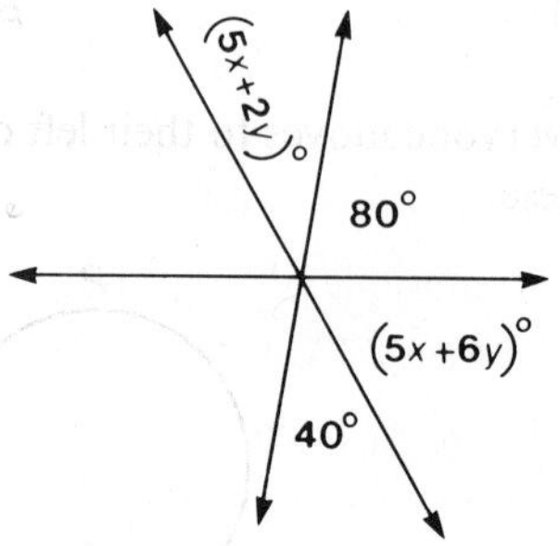

20. Write the equation of the perpendicular bisector of the line segment which joins (4, 6) and (−4, 8). Use the locus definition method and write the equation in slope-intercept form.

21. Write 3100 as (*a*) 10 raised to a power; (*b*) e raised to a power.

Solve the following equations given that ($0° \leq \theta < 360°$):

22. $\cos\theta = -\dfrac{\sqrt{2}}{2}$

23. $\sin 3\theta - \dfrac{1}{2} = 0$

24. $\sec 2\theta - 1 = 0$

Evaluate:

25. $\csc^2\left(-\dfrac{7\pi}{6}\right) + \sec^2\dfrac{7\pi}{6}$

26. $\tan^2\dfrac{19\pi}{6} - \csc^2 90°$

27. $\cos\left[\text{Arcsin}\left(-\dfrac{3}{4}\right)\right]$

28. Let $M = b^a$ and $N = b^c$. Show why $\log_b \dfrac{M}{N} = \log_b M - \log_b N$.

Solve for x:

29. $\log_5 6 - \log_5 \dfrac{1}{x+1} = \log_5 7$

30. $2 \ln 5 - \ln x = \dfrac{3}{4} \ln 16$

LESSON 34 Circular permutations · Distinguishable permutations

34.A Circular permutations

When items are arranged in a circle, there is no first place. Thus, the number of permutations is not as great as if the items were arranged in a line. For instance, if the king, the queen, and the prince sit around a circular table with the queen to the king's left, it would look like this.

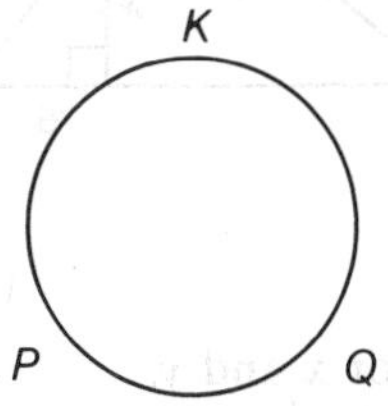

Now, if everyone moves to their left one seat or to their right one seat, it would look like one of these.

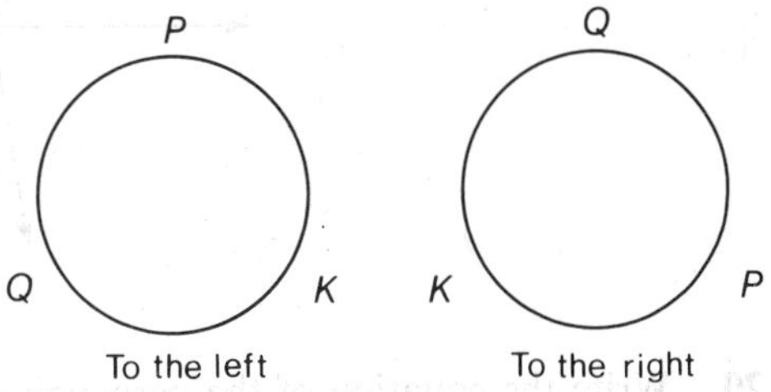

In all three diagrams, the queen is seated on the king's left so all three arrangements are the same. Thus, when three items are arranged in a circle, we consider that there is just one possible entry for the first place instead of the three entries that are possible for the first place of a linear permutation. With three items, the numbers of permutations are

LINEAR PERMUTATIONS

3	2	1

$3 \cdot 2 \cdot 1 = 6$

CIRCULAR PERMUTATIONS

1	2	1

$1 \cdot 2 \cdot 1 = 2$

If we use the letter N to represent the number of objects, we see that there are $N!$ linear permutations but only $(N - 1)!$ circular permutations.

Example 34.A.1 How many ways can 6 different items be arranged in a line and how many ways can 6 different items be arranged in a circle?

Solution For a linear permutation, there are 6 first places, but for a circular permutation, there is only 1 first place. So

LINEAR PERMUTATIONS

6	5	4	3	2	1

$6 \cdot 5 \cdot 4 \cdot 3 \cdot 2 \cdot 1 = \mathbf{720}$

CIRCULAR PERMUTATIONS

1	5	4	3	2	1

$1 \cdot 5 \cdot 4 \cdot 3 \cdot 2 \cdot 1 = \mathbf{120}$

Example 34.A.2 When the chips were down, Ed found that there were 5 chips, and each one was a different color. How many ways could Ed place them (*a*) in a row? (*b*) in a circle?

Solution (*a*) There are 5! linear permutations.

5	4	3	2	1

$\longrightarrow \quad 5 \cdot 4 \cdot 3 \cdot 2 \cdot 1 =$ **120** linear permutations

(*b*) In circular permutations, there is only 1 first position, so we have only $(5 - 1)!$ permutations.

1	4	3	2	1

$\longrightarrow \quad 1 \cdot 4 \cdot 3 \cdot 2 \cdot 1 =$ **24** circular permutations

34.B Distinguishable permutations

If we ask for the number of permutations of the letters in the word *moo*, we have a problem because the two o's look alike. To distinguish between them, we will call them o_1 and o_2 and find

3	2	1

$\longrightarrow \quad 3 \cdot 2 \cdot 1 = 6$

that there are 6 permutations. If we list them, we get

($mo_1o_2 \quad mo_2o_1$) ($o_1mo_2 \quad o_2mo_1$) ($o_1o_2m \quad o_2o_1m$)

Now if we remove the subscripts, we get

(moo moo) (omo omo) (oom oom)

The two permutations in the first oval are exactly alike, and the same is true in the second and third ovals. Thus there are only three permutations that are different. We call permutations that are different **distinguishable permutations.**

There were 3! permutations in all and 2! ways the o's could be arranged. If we divide 3! by 2!, we eliminate the duplications

$$\frac{3!}{2!} = \frac{3 \cdot 2 \cdot 1}{2 \cdot 1} = 3$$

and find that there are only 3 distinguishable permutations. If there are N items and if a of the items are alike, we find that

$$\text{Number of distinguishable permutations} = \frac{N!}{a!}$$

If there are N items and a of one kind, b of another kind, and c of another kind, we find

$$\text{Number of distinguishable permutations} = \frac{N!}{a!b!c!}$$

Example 34.B.1 Jojo has 10 marbles; 3 are red, 3 are blue, and 4 are green. How many distinguishable permutations of the 10 marbles can he form?

Solution There are 10! ways that 10 marbles may be arranged, but we can't tell the reds from one another, the blues from one another, or the greens from one another. Thus, we must divide by 3!, 3!, and 4!.

$$\frac{10!}{3!3!4!} = \frac{10 \cdot \overset{3}{\cancel{9}} \cdot \overset{4}{\cancel{8}} \cdot 7 \cdot \cancel{6} \cdot 5 \cdot \cancel{4 \cdot 3 \cdot 2 \cdot 1}}{\cancel{3} \cdot \cancel{2} \cdot 1 \cdot \cancel{3} \cdot \cancel{2} \cdot 1 \cdot \cancel{4 \cdot 3 \cdot 2 \cdot 1}} = \mathbf{4200}$$

Thus, while there are 10!, or 3,628,800, permutations in all, only 4200 of them are distinguishable.

Example 34.B.2 How many distinguishable permutations can be formed from the letters of the word *nonsense*?

Solution *Nonsense* has 8 letters, so there are 8! permutations. Yet we must divide by 3! because there are three n's, by 2! for the two e's, and again by 2! for the two s's.

$$\frac{8!}{3!2!2!} = \frac{8 \cdot 7 \cdot 6 \cdot 5 \cdot \cancel{4} \cdot \cancel{3} \cdot \cancel{2} \cdot \cancel{1}}{\cancel{3} \cdot \cancel{2} \cdot \cancel{1} \cdot \cancel{2} \cdot 1 \cdot \cancel{2} \cdot 1} = \mathbf{1680}$$

Thus, there are 1680 distinguishable permutations.

Example 34.B.3 How many distinguishable seven-digit numbers can be formed from the digits of 2722424?

Solution There are 7 digits in all, but also four 2's and two 4's, so we have

$$\frac{7!}{4!2!} = \frac{7 \cdot \overset{3}{\cancel{6}} \cdot 5 \cdot \cancel{4} \cdot \cancel{3} \cdot \cancel{2} \cdot \cancel{1}}{\cancel{4} \cdot \cancel{3} \cdot \cancel{2} \cdot \cancel{1} \cdot \cancel{2} \cdot 1} = \mathbf{105}$$

There are 105 distinguishable permutations of 2722424.

Problem set 34

1. The big-wheeled swamp buggy had wheels that were 6 meters in diameter. The swamp buggy was traveling 10 kilometers per hour. What was the angular velocity of the wheels in radians per second?

2. The wheels on the toy car had a diameter of only 1 inch, but they were revolving at 40 radians per second. What was the velocity of the toy car in yards per minute?

3. On the outbound leg of 400 miles, the plane flew at a moderate speed. On the trip back (also 400 miles), the pilot doubled the speed of the plane. How fast did the plane travel on the outbound leg if the total traveling time was 6 hours?

4. There were 2 more reds than there were whites and 1 more red than there were greens. How many of each kind were there if there were 15 reds, whites, and greens in all?

5. Five times the complement of an angle exceeds two times the supplement of the same angle by 60°. What is the measure of the angle?

6. The king, queen, duke, and duchess dined at a circular table. How many seating arrangements are possible?

7. How many distinguishable permutations can be formed from the letters in the word *aberrant*?

8. How many ways can 3 white marbles and 3 red marbles be placed in a row if 2 marbles of the same color cannot be adjacent?

Write the equations of the following sinusoids.

9.

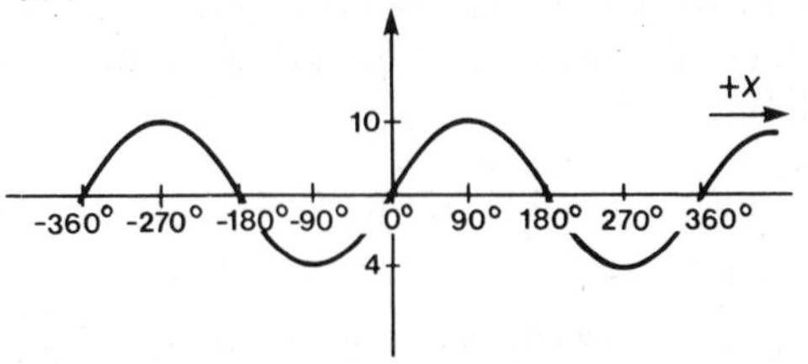

10.

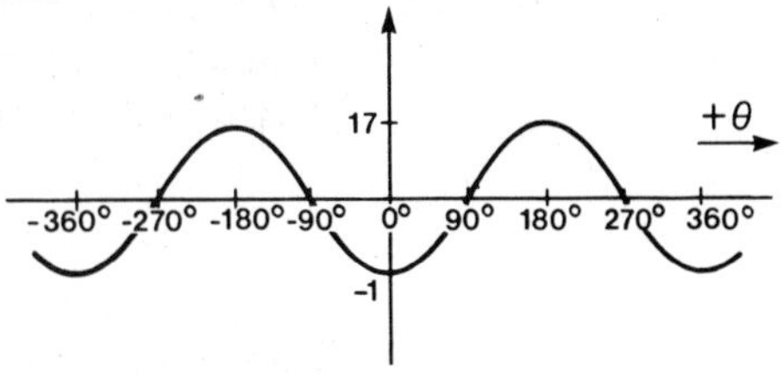

11. Evaluate ${}_7P_3$.

12. Find the standard form of the equation of a circle whose radius is r and whose center is (h, k).

13. Complete the square to graph $y = x^2 - 8x - 2$.

14. Complete the square to graph $y = -x^2 - 10x + 4$.

15. Convert 20 meters per second to miles per hour.

16. Convert 12 liters per hour to cubic inches per minute.

17. Find side K.

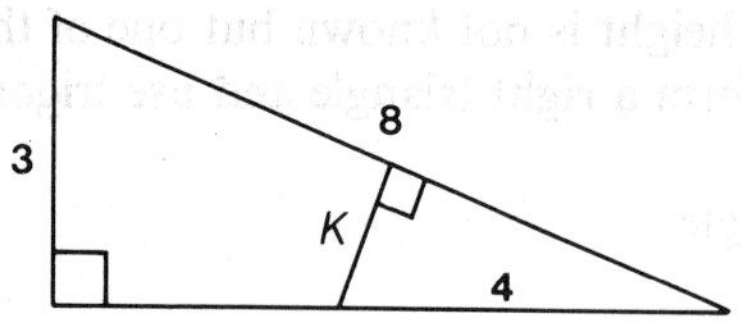

18. A 2-foot-high dog casts a shadow of $\frac{3}{2}$ feet. How long a shadow will a 6-foot-tall man cast at the same time?

19. Solve for x and y.

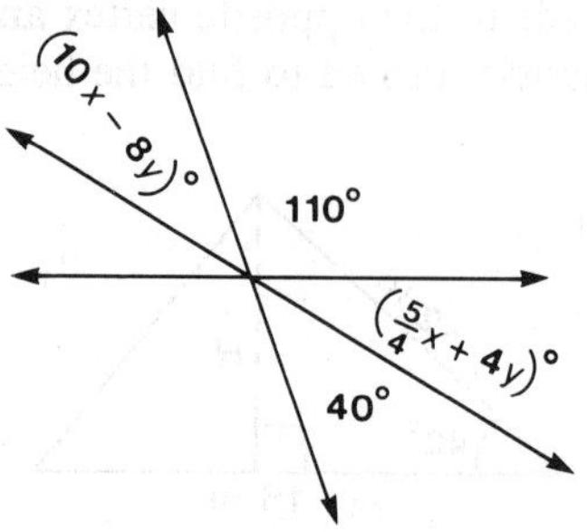

20. Use the midpoint method to write the equation of the perpendicular bisector of the line segment joining the points $(-2, -3)$ and $(4, 3)$. Write the equation in general form.

21. Write 5800 as (*a*) 10 raised to a power; and (*b*) e raised to a power.

Solve the following equations given that $(0° \le \theta < 360°)$:

22. $3 \tan \theta - \sqrt{3} = 0$

23. $\tan 3\theta = \frac{\sqrt{3}}{3}$

24. $\csc 2\theta - 1 = 0$

Evaluate:

25. $\sec^2 \left(-\frac{3\pi}{4}\right) - \cot^2 \frac{7\pi}{6}$

26. $\tan^2 405° - \sin^2 (-330°)$

27. $\tan \left[\text{Arccos} \left(-\frac{4}{5}\right)\right]$

28. Factor $x^2 - 5x + 8$ over the set of complex numbers.

Solve for x:

29. $\log_{18} 12x - 2 \log_{18} 2 = 1$

30. $\frac{2}{3} \ln 8 + 2 \ln 3 = \ln (x + 5)$

LESSON 35 Triangular areas · Areas of sectors · Areas of segments

35.A Triangular areas

The area of any triangle equals one-half the product of the base and the altitude, or height.

$$\text{Area} = \frac{\text{base} \times \text{height}}{2}$$

The **height** of a triangle is the perpendicular distance from the side called the **base** to the opposite vertex. If the height is not known but one of the angles is known, we can draw an auxiliary line to form a right triangle and use trigonometry to find the height.

Example 35.A.1 Find the area of this triangle.

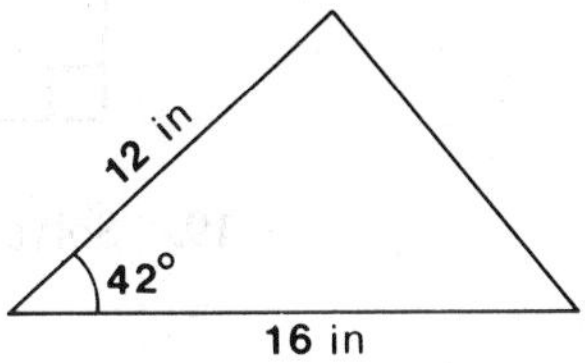

Solution We will draw a perpendicular from the 16-in side to the opposite vertex and use the triangle formed to find the height.

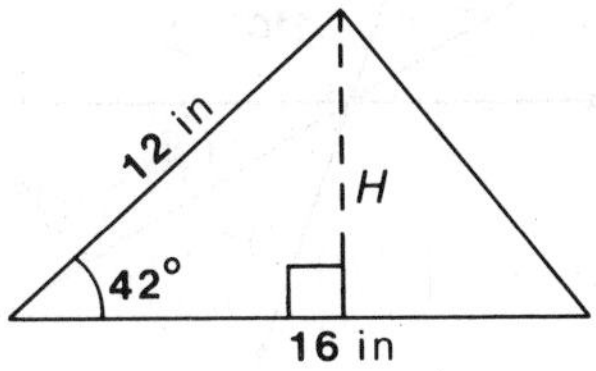

$$\sin 42° = \frac{H}{12}$$

$$H = 12 \sin 42° = 8.03 \text{ in}$$

Now we can use 8.03 for H and find the area.

$$\text{Area} = \frac{B \times H}{2} = \frac{16 \text{ in} \times 8.03 \text{ in}}{2} = \mathbf{64.24\ in^2}$$

Example 35.A.2 Find the area of this triangle.

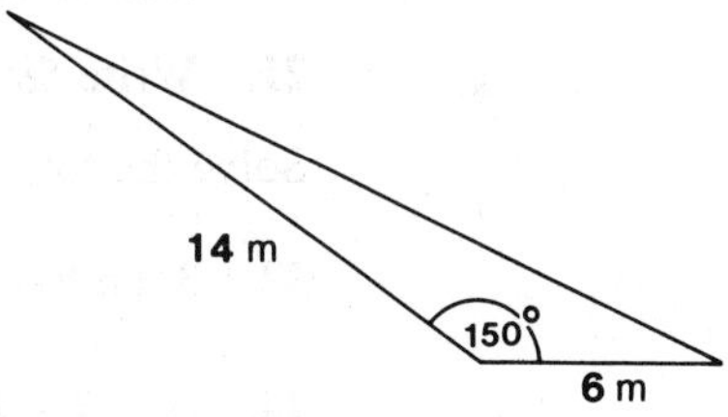

Solution We decide to use the side labeled 6 m as the base. To find the altitude, we must extend this side and erect a perpendicular to the other vertex.

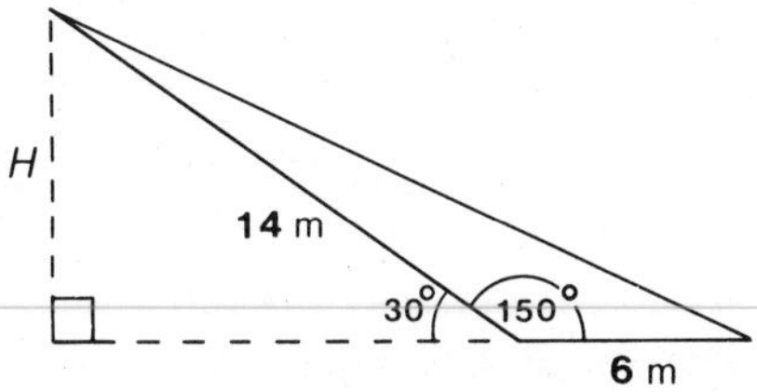

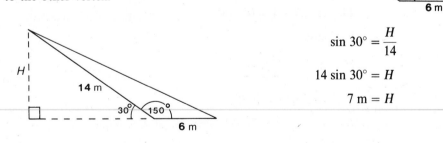

$$\sin 30° = \frac{H}{14}$$

$$14 \sin 30° = H$$

$$7 \text{ m} = H$$

Now we can find the area.

$$\textbf{Area} = \frac{B \times H}{2} = \frac{6 \text{ m} \times 7 \text{ m}}{2} = \mathbf{21\ m^2}$$

Example 35.A.3 Find the area of this trapezoid.

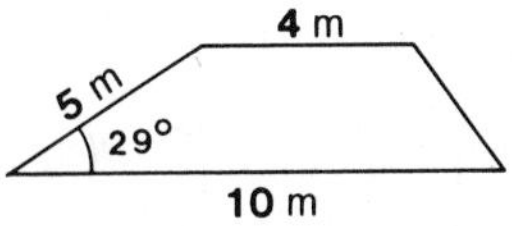

Solution A trapezoid is a four-sided linear figure that has two sides parallel. The parallel sides are called the bases. If we draw auxiliary lines, we can find the distance between the bases and then find the area by dividing the trapezoid into triangles.

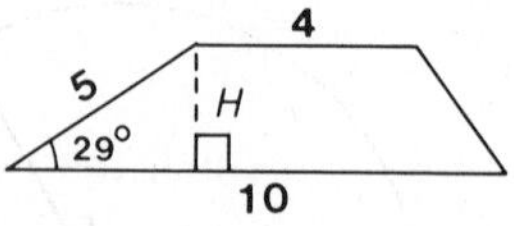

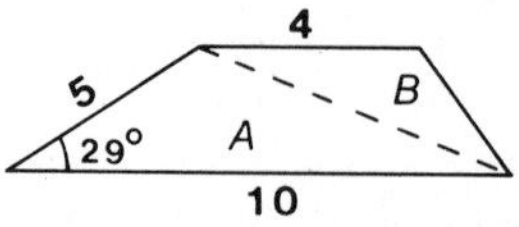

On the left we draw a perpendicular to find the height H, and on the right we draw a diagonal that divides the trapezoid into two triangles A and B. The altitude of both these triangles is H, and the sum of the areas of A and B is the area of the trapezoid.

$$H = 5 \sin 29° \qquad \text{Area } A = \frac{10 \times 2.42}{2} = 12.10 \text{ m}^2$$

$$H = 2.42 \qquad \text{Area } B = \frac{4 \times 2.42}{2} = 4.84 \text{ m}^2$$

$$\text{Total area} = \mathbf{16.94\ m^2}$$

35.B Areas of sectors

We define a ***sector*** of a circle to be the area of the circle bounded by two radii and an arc of the circle. The area of the sector is the fractional part of the total area as determined by the central angle of the sector.

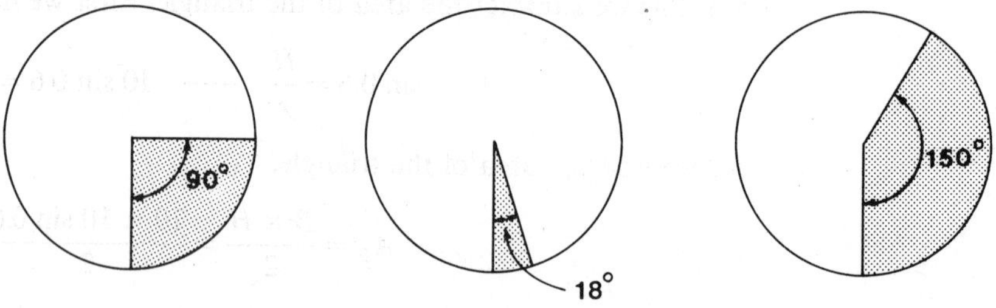

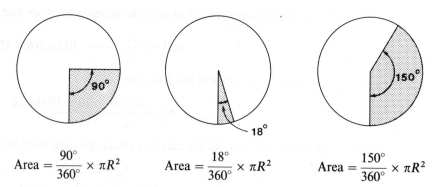

$$\text{Area} = \frac{90°}{360°} \times \pi R^2 \qquad \text{Area} = \frac{18°}{360°} \times \pi R^2 \qquad \text{Area} = \frac{150°}{360°} \times \pi R^2$$

In each case, we see that the area of the sector is the area of the circle multiplied by the fraction formed by the central angle divided by 360°. If the central angle is measured in radians, the procedure is the same except that the fraction is the central angle in radians divided by 2π.

Example 35.B.1 The central angle of a sector of a circle is 0.67 rad. Find the area of the sector if the radius of the circle is 4 ft.

Solution We always use a diagram when possible. First we find the total area of the circle.

$$\text{Total area} = \pi R^2 = \pi(4)^2 = 16\pi \text{ ft}^2$$

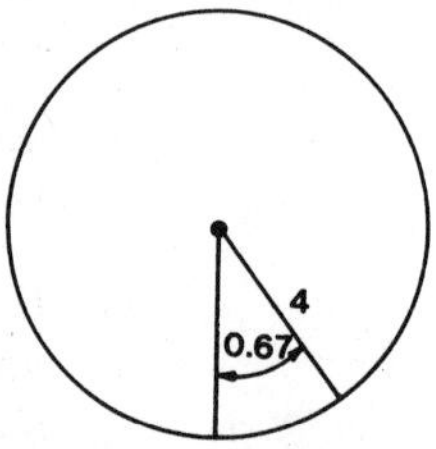

We find the area of the sector by multiplying the total area by $0.67/2\pi$.

$$\text{Area of sector} = (16\pi \text{ ft}^2)\left(\frac{0.67}{2\pi}\right) = \mathbf{5.36\ ft^2}$$

35.C Areas of segments

We define a ***segment*** of a circle to be the area bounded by an arc and the chord that have the same endpoints.

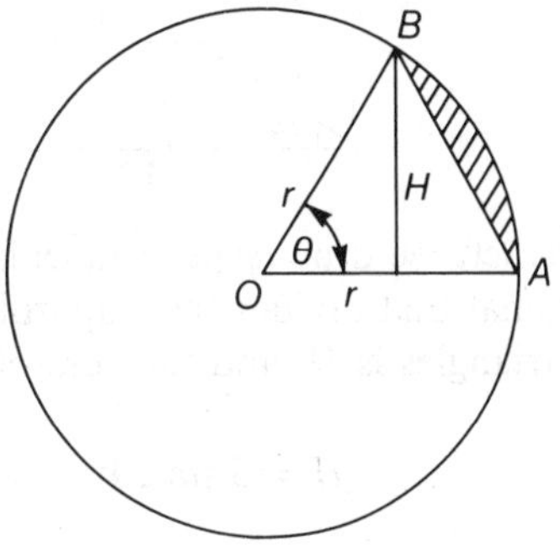

We see that the area of the segment is the area of the sector reduced by the area of triangle OBA. The base of this triangle is r and the altitude H is $r \sin \theta$.

Example 35.C.1 Find the area of the segment shown above if the central angle is 0.6 rad and the radius is 10 ft.

Solution First we find the area of the sector.

$$\text{Area of the sector} = (\pi r^2)\left(\frac{0.6}{2\pi}\right) = \frac{100(0.6)}{2} = 30 \text{ ft}^2$$

From this we subtract the area of the triangle. First we find the altitude H.

$$\sin 0.6 = \frac{H}{r} \longrightarrow 10 \sin 0.6 = H$$

Now we find the area of the triangle.

$$A_{\triangle} = \frac{B \times H}{2} = \frac{10 \times 10 \sin 0.6}{2}$$

When we evaluate, we are careful to have the calculator set to radians.

$$A_{\triangle} = 28.23 \text{ ft}^2$$

So the area of the segment is $30 \text{ ft}^2 - 28.23 \text{ ft}^2 = \mathbf{1.77\ ft^2}$.

Problem set 35

1. The wheels on Susie's car were revolving at 40 revolutions per minute. What was the velocity of the car in centimeters per second if the wheels had a radius of 10 inches?

2. The Formula I car came by at a speed of 260 kilometers per hour. If the wheels had a diameter of 2 feet, what was their angular velocity in revolutions per minute?

3. The ancient one is 40 years older than the youngster. Ten years ago, the age of the ancient one was 20 years greater than 7 times the age of the youngster then. How old are both of them today?

4. Hannibal was paid \$450 for a 30-hour week. He wanted his wages raised 10 percent and wanted to work more hours. His boss gave him the 10 percent hourly raise and increased his weekly hours to 36. What is his weekly paycheck now?

5. The sum of the digits of a two-digit number is 11. If the digits are reversed, the new number is 27 less than the original number. What was the original number?

6. Twelve people sat in a circle. How many distinguishable seating arrangements were possible?

7. How many linear distinguishable permutations can be found by using all the letters in the word *arrogator*?

8. How many three-digit numbers are there such that the first digit is an odd number, the second digit is an even number, and the last digit is an odd number?

9. Find the area of this triangle in square meters. Dimensions are in meters.

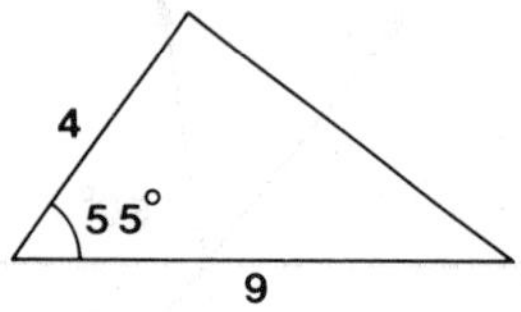

10. Find the area of this triangle in square centimeters. Dimensions are in centimeters.

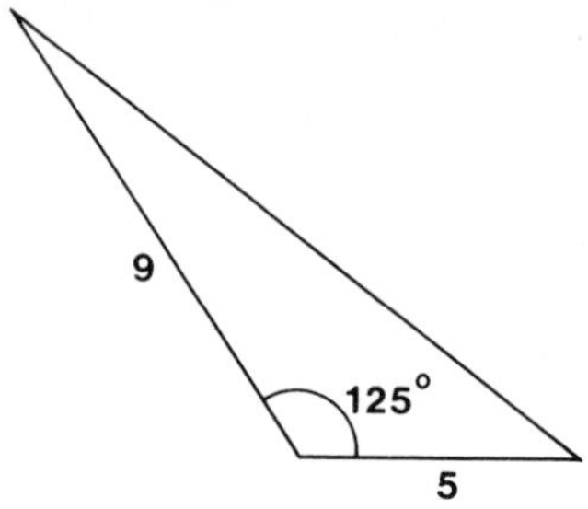

11. Find the area of this trapezoid in square meters.

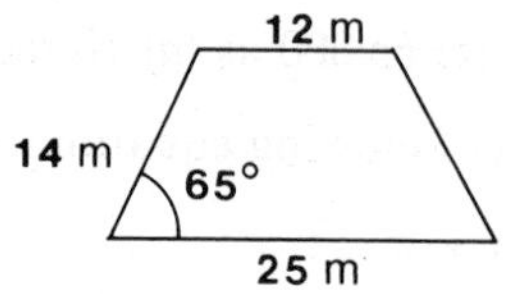

12. The central angle of a sector of a circle is 0.4 radian. Find the area of the sector in square meters if the radius is 5 meters.

13. Find the area in square centimeters of the segment bounded by an arc of measure 60° and the chord joining the endpoints of the arc in a circle of radius 10 feet.

14. Write the equation of the given sinusoid.

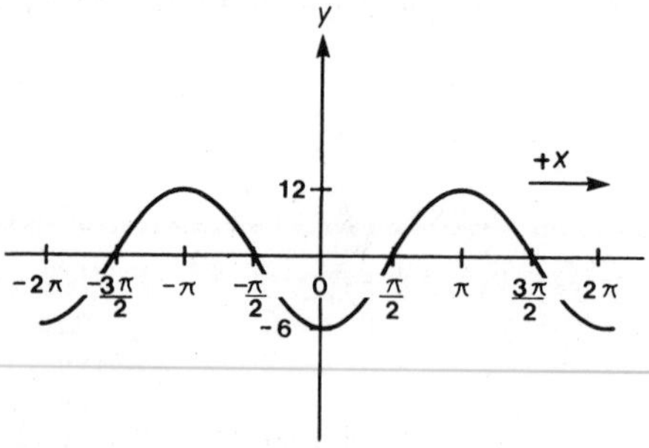

15. Find the standard form of the equation of a circle whose radius is r and whose center is $(4, 5)$.

16. Complete the square to graph $y = x^2 - 4x + 6$.

17. Complete the square to graph $y = -x^2 - 6x + 8$.

18. Convert 70 kilometers per hour to inches per minute.

19. Find a.

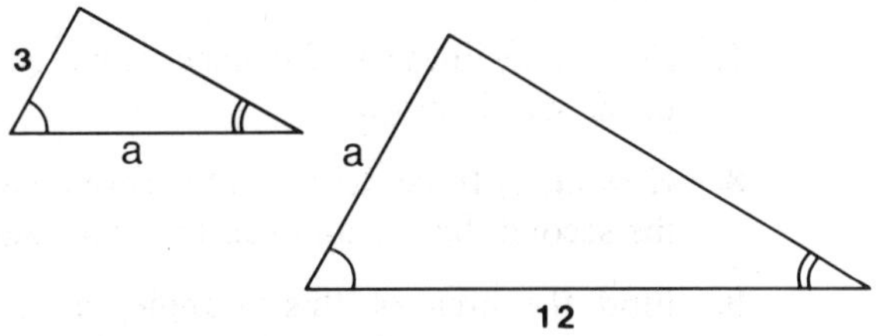

20. Prove that vertical angles are equal.

21. Solve for x and y.

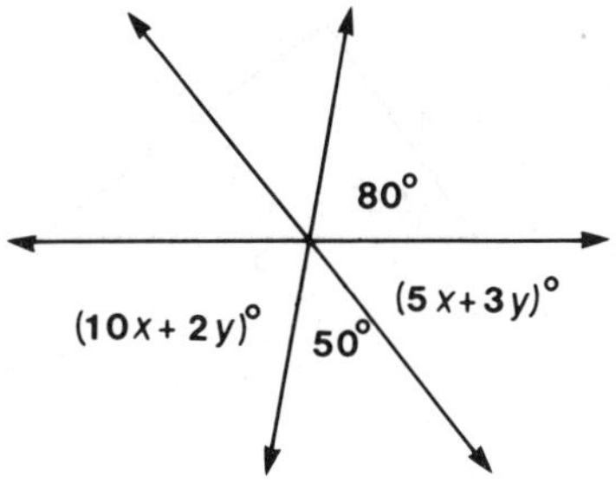

22. Use the locus definition method to write the equation of the line which is equidistant from $(-2, 4)$ and $(-4, -4)$. Write the equation in general form.

23. Write 65,000 as (*a*) 10 raised to a power and (*b*) e raised to a power.

Solve the following equations given that $(0° \leq \theta < 360°)$:

24. $\tan \theta = -1$

25. $\sin 3\theta + \frac{\sqrt{3}}{2} = 0$

26. $\csc 2\theta - 1 = 0$

Evaluate:

27. $\sec^2\left(-\frac{2\pi}{3}\right) - \tan^2 390°$

28. $\sin\left[\text{Arctan}\left(-\frac{2}{3}\right)\right]$

29. Let $M = b^a$ and show $\log_b M^x = x \log_b M$.

30. Solve: $\frac{2}{3}\log_{10} 27 + \log_{10} x = \log_{10} 12$

LESSON 36 *Phase shifts · Period of a sinusoid*

36.A Phase shifts in sinusoids

The basic form of a sinusoid is a repeating curve that deviates the same amount above and below its centerline.

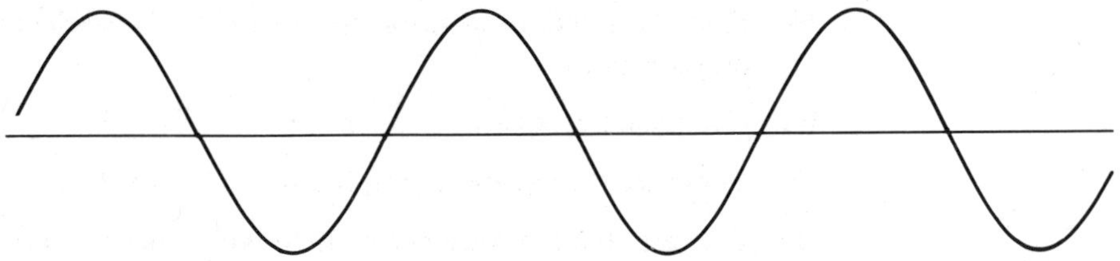

For a given value of the centerline, the equation of a sinusoid whose period is 360° (or 2π radians) is determined by the maximum deviation from the centerline (amplitude); by the value when θ equals 0 (initial value); and by the direction of the change just to the right of the 0 value of θ. A sine curve has an initial value of 0 and increases as θ increases. A $-$ sine curve also has an initial value of 0 but decreases as θ increases. The $+$ cosine curve begins at a maximum value and then decreases, and the $-$ cosine curve begins at a minimum value and then increases.

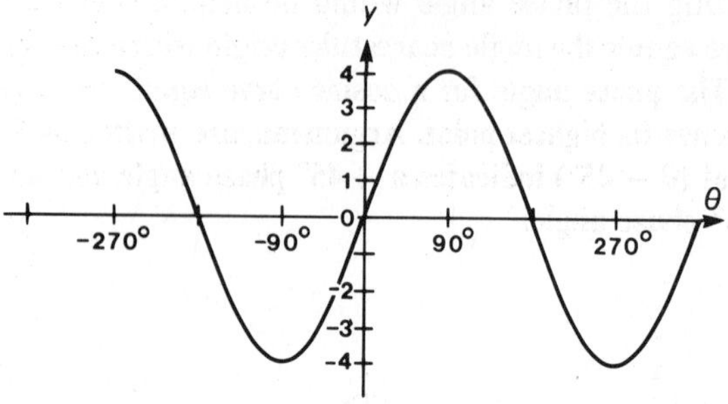

$y = 4 \sin \theta$

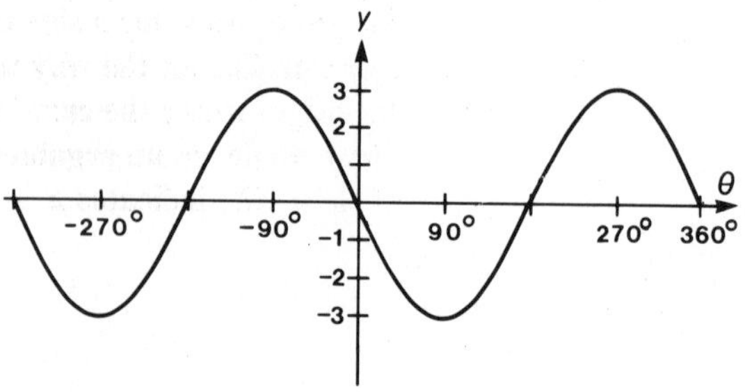

$y = -3 \sin \theta$

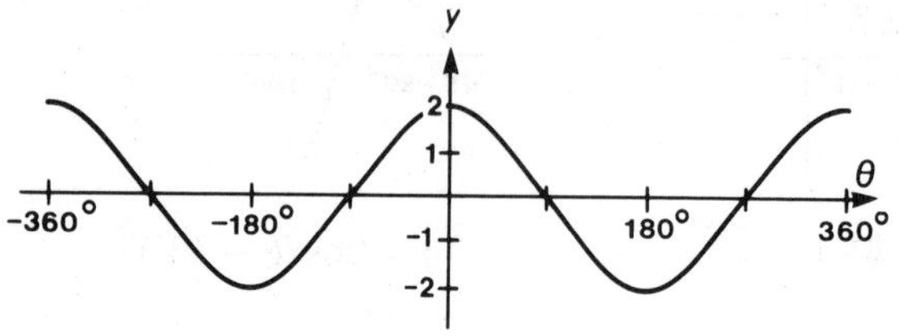

$y = 2 \cos \theta$

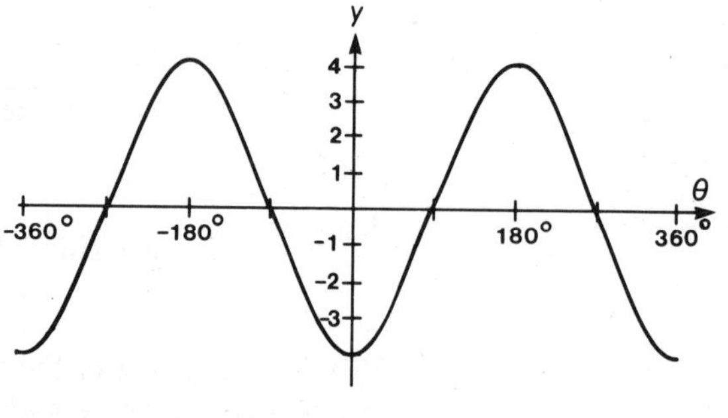

$y = -4 \cos \theta$

The value of the sinusoid does not have to be 0 or its maximum or minimum value when θ equals 0. The initial value can be any value between the maximum value and the minimum value. Observe this curve.

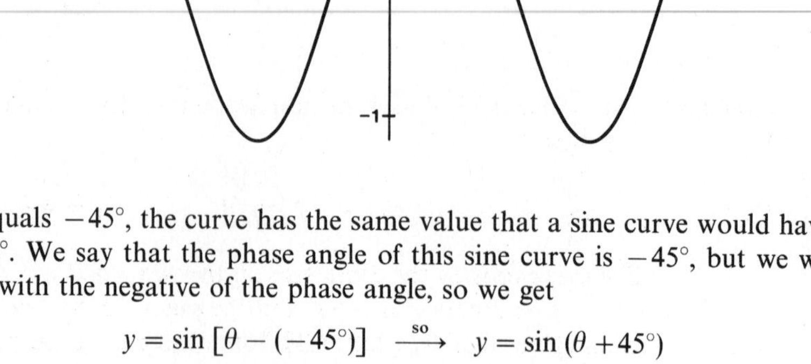

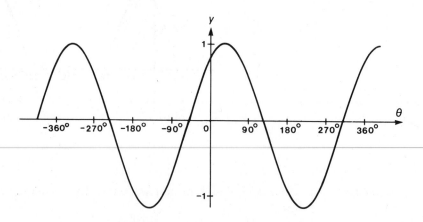

When θ equals $-45°$, the curve has the same value that a sine curve would have when θ equals 0°. We say that the phase angle of this sine curve is $-45°$, but we write the argument with the negative of the phase angle, so we get

$$y = \sin [\theta - (-45°)] \xrightarrow{\text{so}} y = \sin (\theta + 45°)$$

When θ equals $+45°$, the curve has the same value that a cosine curve would have when θ equals 0°, so the equation for this curve as a cosine function with a phase angle is

$$y = \cos[\theta - (45°)] \xrightarrow{\text{so}} y = \cos(\theta - 45°)$$

From this discussion, we see that a positive phase angle means the curve has been shifted to the right and that a negative phase angle means the curve has been shifted to the left. We also see that the concept of phase angle can be confusing and that an automatic procedure for writing the phase angle would be helpful. **Thus we note that the phase angle for a sine curve equals the angle nearest the origin where the curve crosses its centerline on the way up. The phase angle for a cosine curve equals the angle nearest the origin where the curve reaches its highest point. Arguments are written as θ minus the phase angle, so an argument of $(\theta - 45°)$ indicates a $+45°$ phase angle and an argument of $(\theta + 45°)$ indicates a $-45°$ phase angle.**

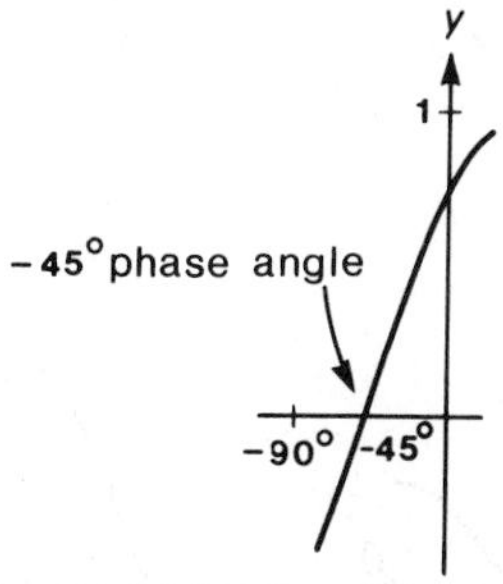

$y = \sin(\theta + 45°)$

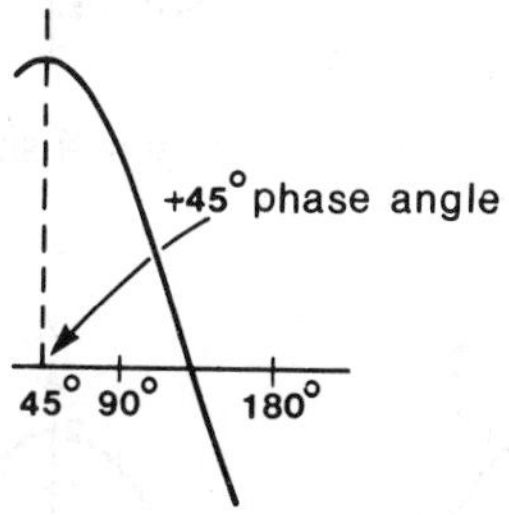

$y = \cos(\theta - 45°)$

Example 36.A.1 Write the equation of the sinusoid shown here as a sine curve with a phase angle and also as a cosine curve with a phase angle.

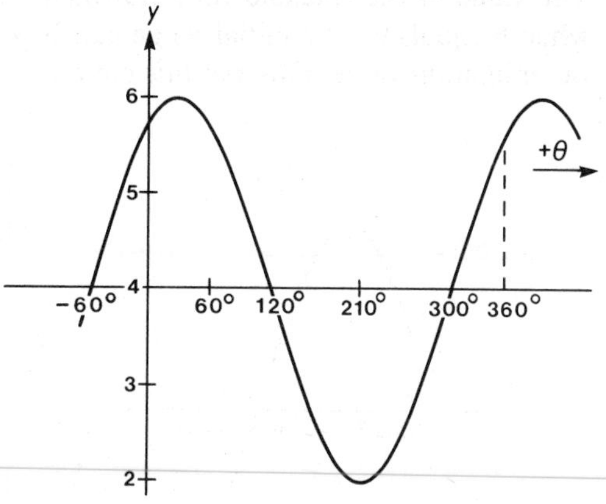

Solution The centerline is 4 and the amplitude is 2. These numbers appear in both forms of the equation.

$$y = 4 + 2\sin(\theta \quad) \qquad y = 4 + 2\cos(\theta \quad)$$

The curve crosses the centerline on the way up at a θ value of $-60°$, so the phase angle for the sine function is $-60°$ and the argument will be $(\theta + 60°)$. The curve has a maximum value when θ equals $+30°$ (our estimate), so the phase angle for the cosine function is $+30^\circ$ and the argument will be $(\theta - 30^\circ)$. Thus our equations are

$$y = 4 + 2 \sin(\theta + 60^\circ) \qquad y = 4 + 2 \cos(\theta - 30^\circ)$$

Example 36.A.2 Write the equation of this function as a sine curve with a phase shift.

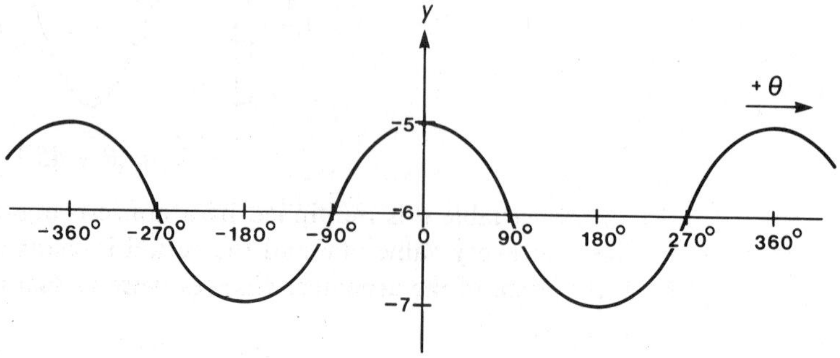

Solution The centerline is -6 and the amplitude is 1, so we begin by writing

$$y = -6 + \sin(\theta \quad\quad)$$

We note that the curve crosses its centerline on its way up when θ equals -90°, so our phase angle is -90°. Now we can write the complete equation and remember that the argument contains the negative of the phase angle.

$$y = -6 + \sin(\theta + 90^\circ)$$

36.B Period of a sinusoid

If the values of the dependent variable of a function repeat periodically as the values of the independent variable increase, the function is called a ***periodic function.*** Sinusoids are periodic functions, since the values of y repeat each time the value of the argument changes 360° or 2π radians. When the argument is a single variable such as θ or x, the change in the argument equals the change in the variable.

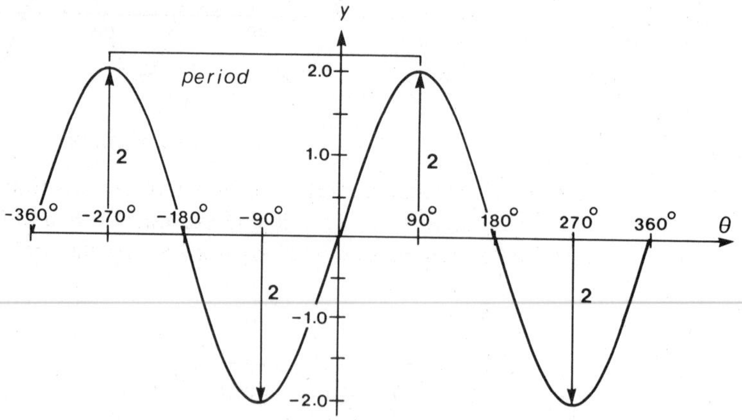

$$y = 2 \sin \theta$$

A phase angle will not change the period of a function. The only effect a phase angle has is to shift the whole curve right or left with respect to the scale on the horizontal axis. If we give the function above a phase angle of -45°, we will shift the function 45° to the left but leave the period unchanged, as the function still completes a full cycle of values as θ changes 360°.

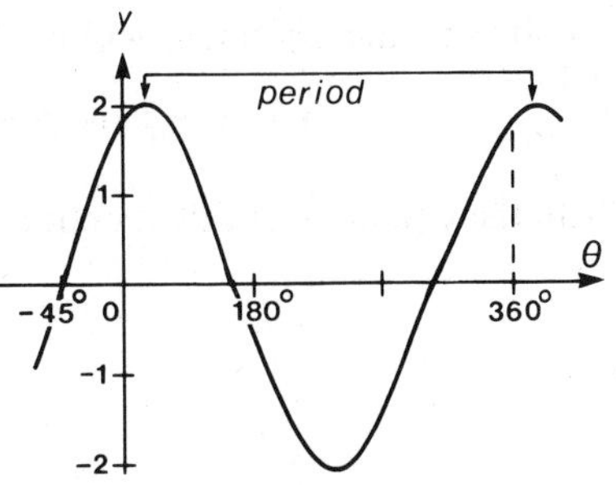

$$y = 2 \sin (\theta + 45°)$$

When the variable θ is multiplied by a nonzero number, the value of the argument is changed for every value of θ and the period is changed. **When the variable is multiplied by 2, the value of the argument changes twice as fast as the change in the variable**

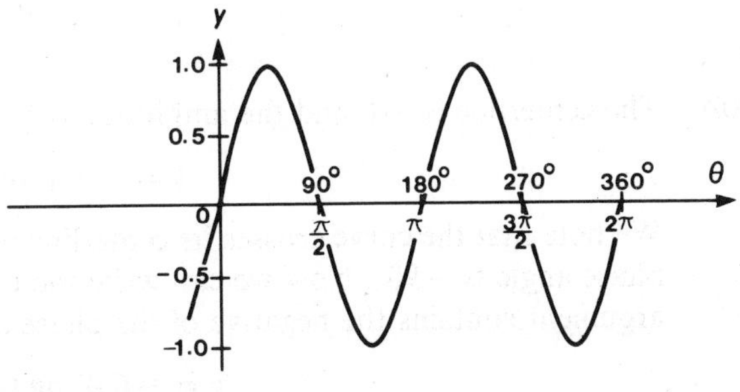

$$y = \sin 2\theta$$

and the function completes a full cycle every time the variable θ goes through 180°. So the period of this function is 180°, or π radians. If the variable is multiplied by 4, the function goes through 4 cycles for every 360° change in the variable, so the period is 90°.

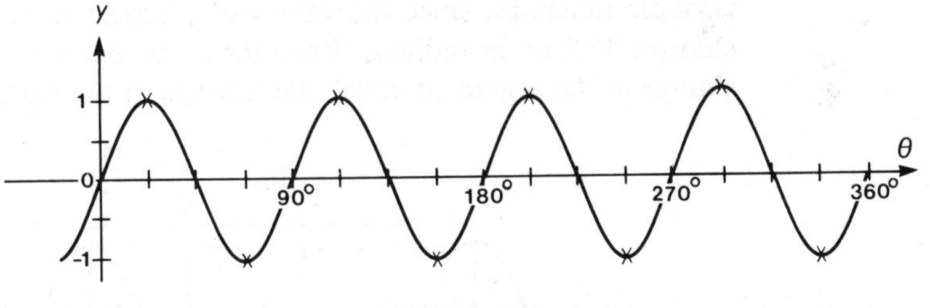

$$y = \sin 4\theta$$

When the variable is multiplied by a number less than 1, the argument changes less for a given change in the variable. **If the variable is multiplied by $\frac{1}{2}$, the argument changes only half as fast as the variable changes, and the period is doubled.**

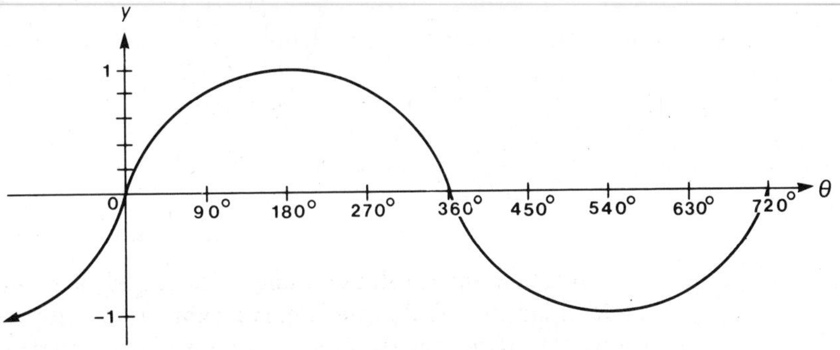

$$y = \sin \frac{\theta}{2}$$

In the same way, when the variable is multiplied by $\frac{1}{4}$, the argument changes only $\frac{1}{4}$ as fast as the variable changes, so the period is 4 times as long. This leads us to the fact that the coefficient of the variable equals 360° divided by the period in degrees or 2π divided by the period in radians.

$$\text{Coefficient} = \frac{360°}{\text{period in degrees}} \quad \text{or} \quad \text{Coefficient} = \frac{2\pi}{\text{period in radians}}$$

Example 36.B.1 Write the equation of the curve.

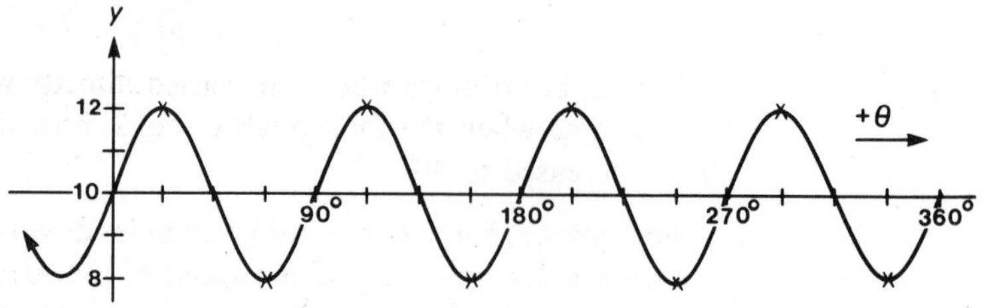

Solution The curve is a sine curve with no phase angle. The centerline is 10 and the amplitude is 2, so we begin by writing

$$y = 10 + 2 \sin k\theta$$

The curve completes a full cycle of values in 90°, so the period is 90°. The coefficient k is 360° divided by the period, so

$$\text{Coefficient } k = \frac{360°}{\text{period}} = \frac{360°}{90°} = 4$$

Thus, the equation we seek is

$$\mathbf{y = 10 + 2 \sin 4\theta}$$

Example 36.B.2 Write the equation of the given curve.

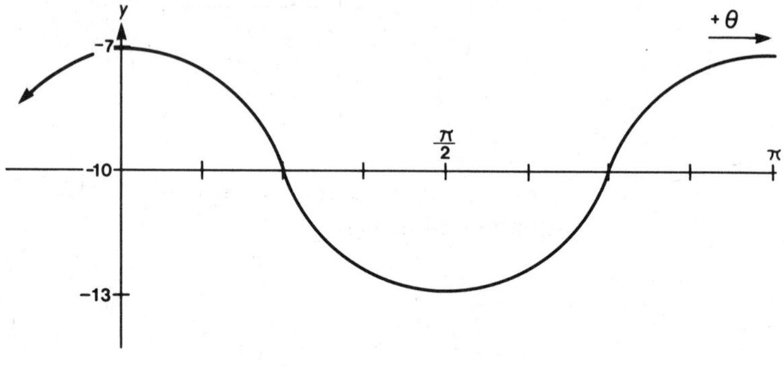

Solution This curve is a cosine curve centered on -10 and it goes up and down 3 units from the centerline. It takes π radians to complete a full cycle, so the coefficient is 2π divided by π, which equals 2. So the equation is as shown.

$$\text{Coefficient} = \frac{2\pi}{\pi} = 2 \quad \text{so} \quad \mathbf{y = -10 + 3 \cos 2\theta}$$

Problem set 36

1. Four hundred radians per minute sounds fast, but the wheels on the tiny car had a radius of only 4 centimeters. What was the velocity of the car in miles per hour?

2. Another little car went by at a speed of 40 kilometers per hour. What was the angular velocity of its wheels in radians per second if the diameter of its wheels was 10 centimeters?

3. The pressure of an ideal gas varies directly as the temperature and inversely as the volume. If the initial pressure, volume, and temperature were 40 atmospheres, 2 liters, and 400 K, what was the pressure if the volume was increased to 4 liters and the temperature increased to 1000 K? Use the following equation:

$$\frac{P_1V_1}{T_1} = \frac{P_2V_2}{T_2}$$

4. The number of boys who came varied directly with the quality of the food. If 100 boys came when the food quality was 2, how many came when the food quality was increased to 40?

5. The tugboat *Mary Beth* could go 24 miles downstream in 1 hour more than it took to go 8 miles upstream. If the speed of the *Mary Beth* in still water was 3 times the speed of the current, what was the still-water speed of the *Mary Beth* and the speed of the current?

6. Six red marbles, 4 blue marbles, and 2 white marbles were arranged in a row. How many distinguishable permutations were possible?

7. How many distinguishable permutations can be made from the letters in the word *distinguishable*?

8. Factor $x^2 - 3x + 4 = 0$ over the set of complex numbers.

Write the equations of the following sinusoids in terms of the sine function.

9.

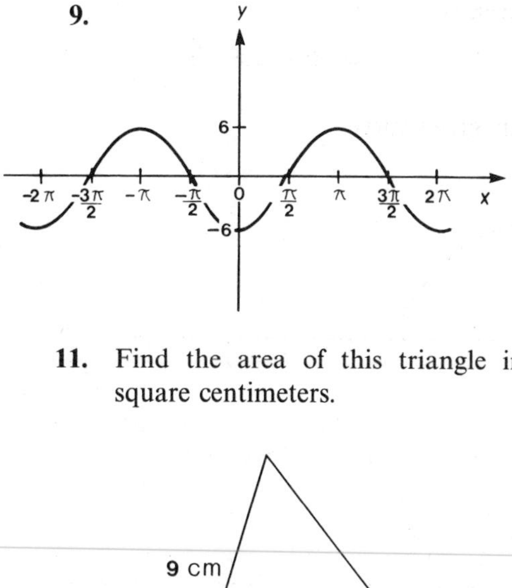

10.

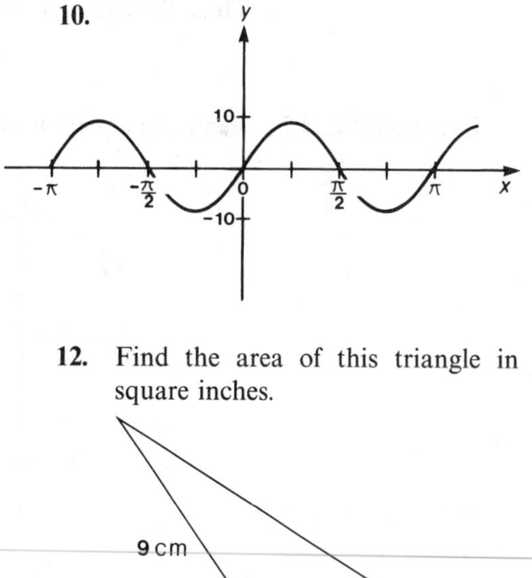

11. Find the area of this triangle in square centimeters.

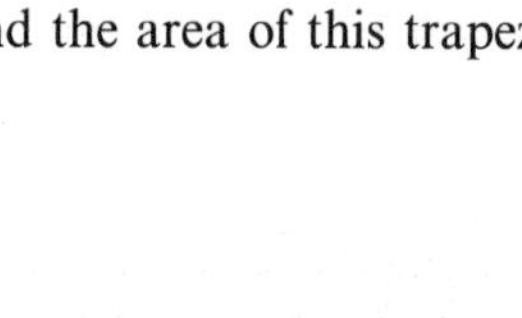

12. Find the area of this triangle in square inches.

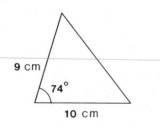

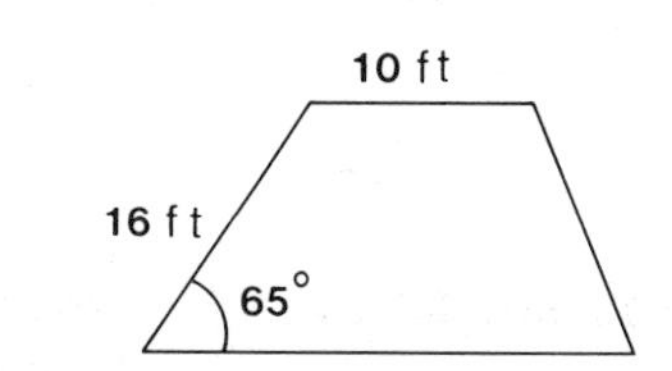

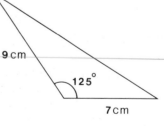

13. Find the area of this trapezoid in square feet.

14. The central angle of a sector of a circle is 0.6 radian. Find the area of the sector in square meters if the radius is 4 meters.

15. Find the area in square centimeters of the segment bounded by an arc of measure 80° and the chord which joins the endpoints of the arc in a circle of radius 10 centimeters.

16. Find the standard form of the equation of a circle whose radius is 5 and whose center is (m, n).

17. Complete the square to graph $y = -x^2 - 4x + 4$.

18. Convert 100 miles per hour to inches per second.

19. Find M.

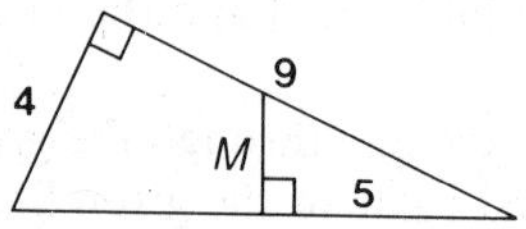

20. The latitude of Charleston is 38.3° north of the equator. If the radius of the earth is 12,000 kilometers, what is the distance from Charleston to the equator in kilometers?

21. Write 10,000 (a) as 10 raised to a power; and (b) as e raised to a power.

22. Use the midpoint formula method to write the equation of the line which is the perpendicular bisector of the line segment whose endpoints are $(-4, -6)$ and $(4, 8)$. Express the equation of the line in slope-intercept form.

Solve the following equations given that $(0° \leq \theta < 360°)$:

23. $2 \cos \theta = 1$

24. $2 \cos 3\theta = 1$

25. $\cot 3\theta = 0$

Evaluate:

26. $\cot^3 \frac{\pi}{4} + \tan^2 480°$

27. $\text{Arctan}\left(\tan \frac{7\pi}{6}\right)$

28. Let $M = b^a$ and $N = b^c$. Show why $\log_b \frac{M}{N} = \log_b M - \log_b N$.

Solve for x.

29. $\frac{3}{4} \log_{1/2} 16 - \log_{1/2} (x - 1) = 2$

30. $\frac{1}{2} \ln 25 + \ln (x + 2) = \ln (2x + 3)$

LESSON 37 Distance from a point to a line · Narrow and wide parabolas

37.A Distance from a point to a line

The distance from a point to a line is measured along the segment perpendicular to the line that connects the point and the line. If we find the equation of the line that contains the perpendicular segment, we can solve for the coordinates of its intersection with the given line. Then the distance formula can be used to find the distance between the point and the point of intersection. This method of solution is rather primitive, but we will use it because its use affords extensive practice with the fundamental concepts of coordinate geometry. The understanding that will accrue from this practice will permit us to understand and appreciate the development of more elegant methods of solution that will be presented in more advanced courses in mathematics. The use of a calculator is recommended to help with the arithmetic of these problems.

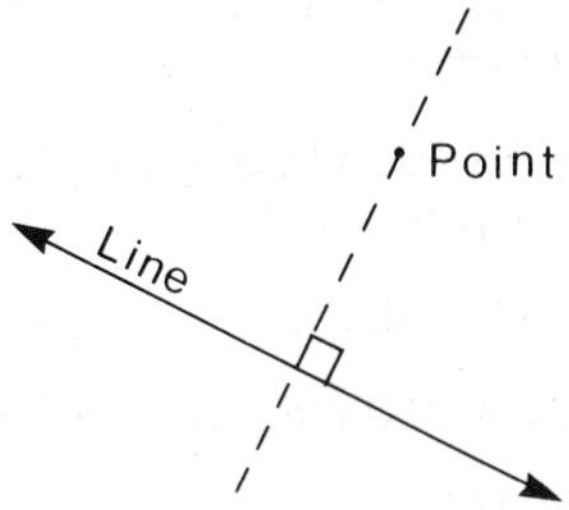

Example 37.A.1 Find the distance between the point $(-3, 5)$ and the line (a) $y = \frac{1}{2}x + 1$.

Solution First we will find the equation of the line through the given point that is perpendicular to the given line. The line perpendicular to the given line has a slope of -2, so

$$y = -2x + b \qquad \text{equation}$$
$$5 = -2(-3) + b \qquad \text{used } (-3, 5)$$
$$-1 = b \qquad \text{solved}$$
$$(b) \quad y = -2x - 1 \qquad \text{completed equation}$$

Now we will use substitution to find the intersection of lines (a) and (b).

$$\frac{1}{2}x + 1 = -2x - 1 \qquad \text{substitution}$$
$$x + 2 = -4x - 2 \qquad \text{multiplied by 2}$$
$$5x = -4 \qquad \text{rearranged}$$
$$x = -\frac{4}{5}$$

Now we use this value of x in equation (b) to find y.

$$y = -2\left(-\frac{4}{5}\right) - 1 \qquad \text{substituted}$$
$$y = \frac{8}{5} - \frac{5}{5} \qquad \text{simplified}$$
$$y = \frac{3}{5}$$

Now we use the distance formula to find the distance between $(-3, 5)$ and $(-0.8, 0.6)$. We use the decimal form of the numbers so we can use a calculator.

$$D = \sqrt{[-3 - (-0.8)]^2 + [5 - (0.6)]^2} \qquad \text{substituted}$$
$$D = \sqrt{(-2.2)^2 + (4.4)^2}$$
$$\mathbf{D = 4.92}$$

Example 37.A.2 Find the distance from $(-1, 5)$ to the line $y = -\frac{1}{3}x + 4$.

Solution First we find the equation of the line that is perpendicular to the given line and that passes through the given point.

$$y = 3x + b \qquad \text{equation}$$

$$5 = 3(-1) + b \longrightarrow b = 8 \qquad \text{used } (-1, 5) \text{ and solved for } b$$

Thus, the perpendicular line is $y = 3x + 8$. Now we substitute to solve for the point of intersection.

$$-\frac{1}{3}x + 4 = 3x + 8 \qquad \text{substituted}$$

$$-x + 12 = 9x + 24 \qquad \text{multiplied by 3}$$

$$x = -1.2 \qquad \text{solved}$$

Now we use the equation of the perpendicular line to find y.

$$y = 3(-1.2) + 8 \longrightarrow y = 4.4$$

Now we use the distance formula to find the distance between $(-1, 5)$ and $(-1.2, 4.4)$.

$$D = \sqrt{[-1 - (-1.2)]^2 + (5 - 4.4)^2}$$

$$D = \sqrt{(0.2)^2 + (0.6)^2}$$

$$\mathbf{D = 0.63}$$

37.B "Narrow" and "wide" parabolas

We remember that when a quadratic equation is written in the form $y = a(x - h)^2 + k$, the sign of a determines whether the graph of the parabola opens up or down. Thus far, we have looked only at equations where the value of a is $+1$ or -1, such as these:

OPENS UPWARD ↓ $y = +(x - 1)^2 + 2$ OPENS DOWNWARD ↓ $y = -(x - 1)^2 + 2$

If the absolute value of a is greater than 1, the graph of the parabola is "narrowed." If the absolute value of a is less than 1, the graph of the parabola is "widened," as we see in the following figures.

GRAPH IS "NARROWER" ↓ $y = -3(x - 1)^2 + 2$ $y = -(x - 1)^2 + 2$ GRAPH IS "WIDER" ↓ $y = -\frac{1}{3}(x - 1)^2 + 2$

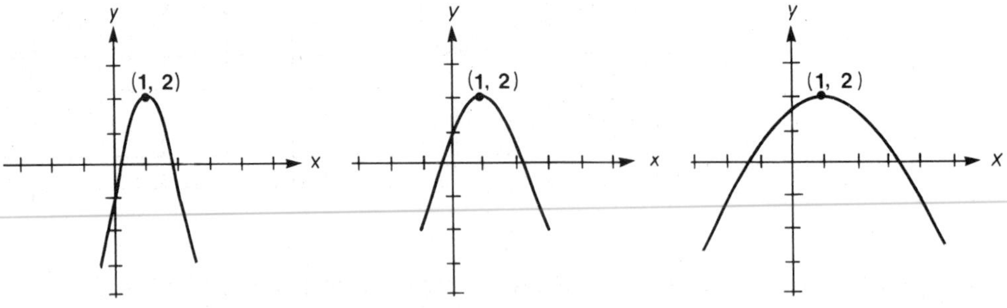

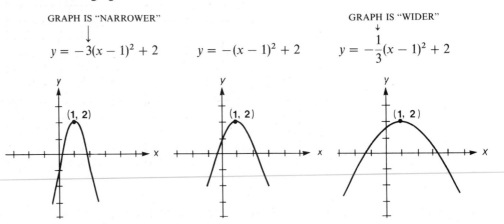

The first step in graphing these parabolas is to write the equation in the form $y = a(x - h)^2 + k$ so that we can determine coordinates of the vertex and determine whether the curve opens up or down. Then the shape of the curve can be determined by finding the coordinates of one more point on the curve. We demonstrate this procedure in the two examples that follow. Note that the procedure for completing the square is just a little more involved because of the necessity of dealing with the nonunity coefficient of the x^2 term.

Example 37.B.1 Complete the square to graph the parabola $3y - x^2 + 2x + 5 = 0$.

Solution We begin by solving the equation for y and we get

$$y = \frac{x^2}{3} - \frac{2}{3}x - \frac{5}{3}$$

Next we factor out $\frac{1}{3}$ from the first two terms so that the coefficient of x^2 will be 1.

$$y = \frac{1}{3}(x^2 - 2x \qquad) - \frac{5}{3}$$

Now we must add +1 inside the parentheses to complete the square. Since the expression within parentheses is multiplied by $\frac{1}{3}$, we have not really added 1 but have added $\frac{1}{3}$ to the right side of the equation. Thus, we must also add $-\frac{1}{3}$ to the right side of the equation.

$$y = \frac{1}{3}(x^2 - 2x + 1) - \frac{5}{3} - \frac{1}{3} \qquad \text{completed the square}$$

$$y = \frac{1}{3}(x - 1)^2 - 2 \qquad \text{simplified}$$

From this form we can see that the equation of the axis of symmetry is $x = +1$ and that the parabola opens upward. The y coordinate of the vertex is -2. To get another point on the curve, we let x equal 4 and find that y equals 1.

$$y = \frac{1}{3}[(4) - 1]^2 - 2 \longrightarrow y = \frac{1}{3}(9) - 2 \longrightarrow y = +1$$

We plot the point (4, 1) and the symmetrical point $(-2, 1)$ and complete the sketch. We note that the coefficient $\frac{1}{3}$ made the curve wider than the parabolas that we have graphed previously.

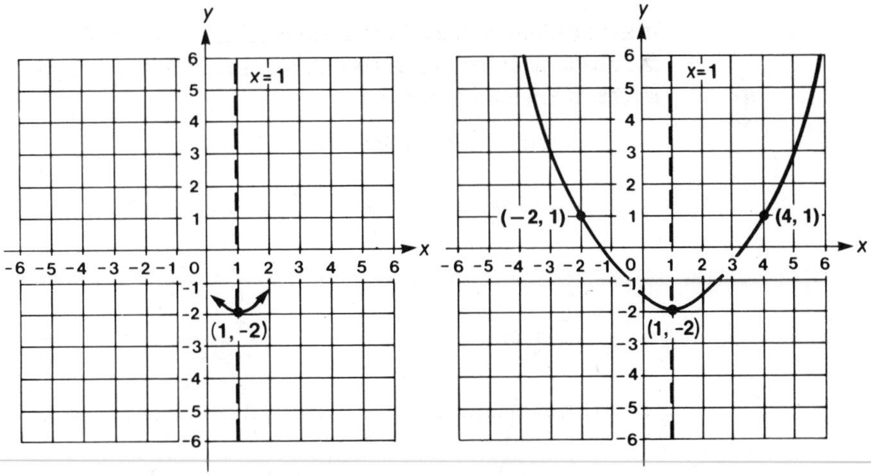

Example 37.B.2 Complete the square to graph the parabola $y + 2x^2 + 12x + 17 = 0$.

Solution As the first step we rearrange the equation to solve for y and get

$$y = -2x^2 - 12x - 17$$

We note that the coefficient of x^2 is not 1. **When the coefficient of x^2 is not 1, we always begin by factoring the first two terms so that the coefficient of x^2 will be 1.** We will factor out -2.

$$y = -2(x^2 + 6x \qquad) - 17$$

Now we add +9 inside the parentheses and note that since the parentheses is multiplied by −2, we have really added −18. Because we have really added −18, we must add +18 also.

$$y = -2(x^2 + 6x + 9) - 17 + 18$$

Now we simplify and analyze.

(*a*) Opens downward

(*b*) Axis of symmetry is $x = -3$ $\qquad y = -2(x + 3)^2 + 1$

(*c*) y coordinate of vertex is $+1$

We use this information to draw the axis of symmetry and the vertex of the curve as we show in the graph on the left below. To get another point, we let x equal −1 in the original equation and find that $y = -7$.

$$y = -2(-1)^2 - 12(-1) - 17 = -2 + 12 - 17 = -7$$

We graph the point (−1, −7) on the right and complete the sketch, remembering that the parabola is symmetric about its center axis.

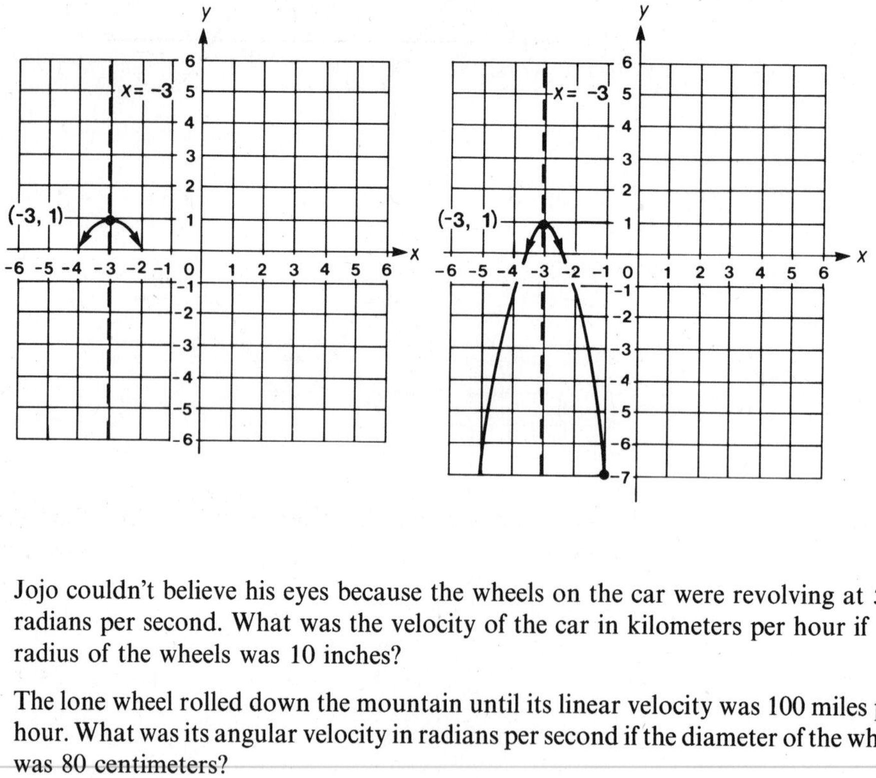

Problem set 37

1. Jojo couldn't believe his eyes because the wheels on the car were revolving at 525 radians per second. What was the velocity of the car in kilometers per hour if the radius of the wheels was 10 inches?

2. The lone wheel rolled down the mountain until its linear velocity was 100 miles per hour. What was its angular velocity in radians per second if the diameter of the wheel was 80 centimeters?

3. The ratio of the number who were impecunious to the number who were truly destitute was 14 to 3. If there were 4420 standing in the line, how many were merely impecunious?

4. Use the ideal gas law

$$\frac{P_1V_1}{T_1} = \frac{P_2V_2}{T_2}$$

to find P_2 if P_1 was 4 atmospheres, V_1 was 5 liters, V_2 was 7 liters, T_1 was 400 K, and T_2 was 500 K.

5. There were 4 in the first group and their average quality was 6. There were 10 in the second group and their average quality was 4. What should the average quality of the last 16 be so that the overall average quality would be 8?

6. There are 5 flags in all. Two are red, 2 are blue, and 1 is yellow. How many different patterns are possible if the flags are displayed vertically on a flagpole?

7. Nine students sat in a row. How many ways could 9 books be distributed if 5 books were of one kind and 4 books were of another kind?

8. How many ways can 5 different birds be arranged in a circle?

9. Find the distance between the point $(-2, 4)$ and the line $y = \frac{1}{2}x - 1$.

10. Complete the square to graph $y = 2x^2 - 8x + 5$.

11. Complete the square to graph $y = -2x^2 - 8x - 4$.

Write the equations of the following sinusoids in terms of the cosine function.

12.

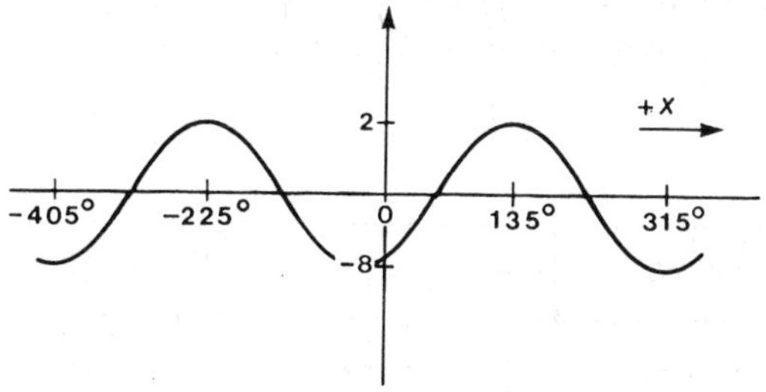

13.

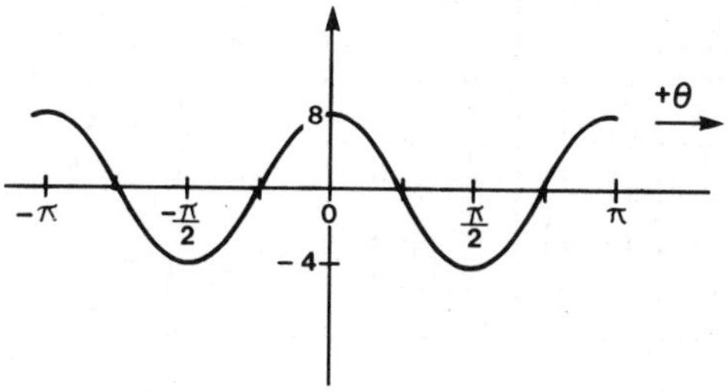

14. Find the area of this triangle in square meters.

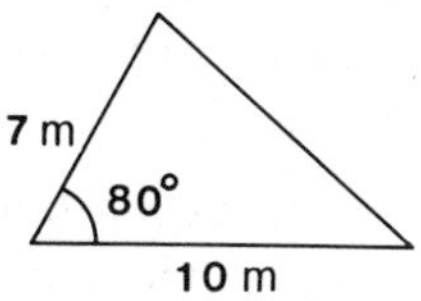

15. Find the area of this trapezoid in square centimeters.

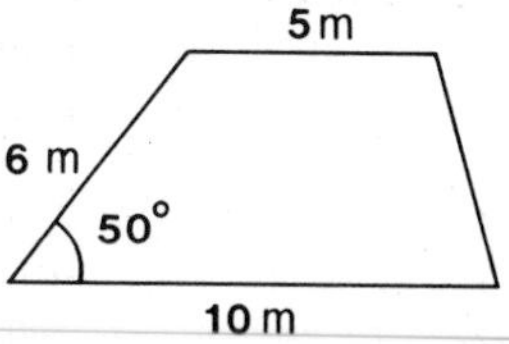

16. The central angle of a sector of a circle is 0.9 radian. Find the area of the sector in square feet if the radius is 1 yard.

17. Find the area in square meters of the segment bounded by an arc of measure 110° and the chord which joins the endpoints of the arc in a circle of radius 50 centimeters.

18. Find the standard form of the equation of a circle whose radius is r and whose center is (h, k).

19. Convert 250 kilometers per second to miles per hour.

20. Solve for b.

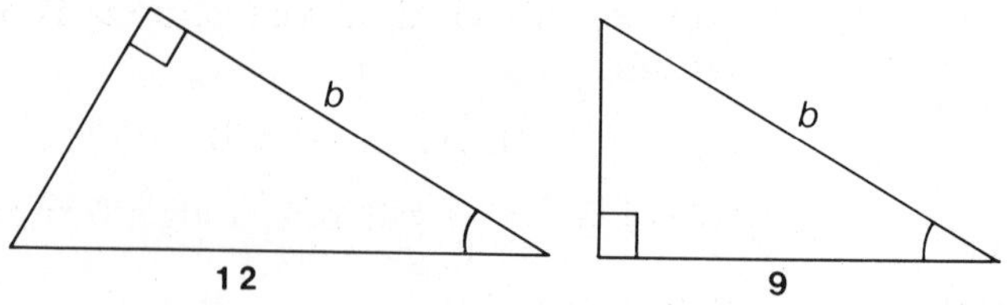

21. Write 20,000 (*a*) as 10 raised to a power; and (*b*) as e raised to a power.

22. Use the locus definition method to write the equation of the line which is the perpendicular bisector of the line segment joining the points $(-2, 3)$ and $(4, 5)$. Express the equation of the line in the general form.

Solve the following equations given that $(0° \le \theta < 360°)$:

23. $2 \cos \theta = \sqrt{3}$ 24. $2 \cos 5\theta - \sqrt{3} = 0$ 25. $\tan 3\theta = 1$

Evaluate:

26. $\sec^2 \frac{3\pi}{4} - 1$ 27. $\tan^2 \frac{3\pi}{4}$ 28. $\cos \left[\text{Arcsin} \left(-\frac{1}{4} \right) \right]$

Solve:

29. $\frac{2}{3} \log_7 27 - \log_7 (x + 2) = \log_7 3$ 30. $\frac{3}{4} \ln 16 - \ln x = \ln 4$

LESSON 38 Advanced logarithm problems · The color of the white house

38.A Advanced logarithm problems

Thus far, we have investigated logarithm problems that can be reduced to one of the two forms shown here.

$$(a)\ \log_4 (x + 2) = \log_4 5 \qquad (b)\ \log_4 (x + 5) = 2$$

In (*a*) the bases are the same, so the logarithm of $x + 2$ equals the logarithm of 5. Thus, $x + 2$ must equal 5.

$$x + 2 = 5$$
$$x = 3$$

We must always check to see that the value of the argument is positive. If we use 3 for x, then

$$(3 + 2) = 5 \quad \text{and 5 is greater than 0}$$

so our argument is a positive number.

The other form is shown in (*b*), where a logarithm on one side equals a constant on the other side. **We solve this type of equation by rewriting it as an exponential equation and then solving the exponential equation.**

$$\log_4 (x + 5) = 2 \qquad \text{logarithmic equation}$$
$$4^2 = x + 5 \qquad \text{exponential equation}$$
$$11 = x \qquad \text{solved}$$

Now we must check to see that using 11 for x will result in a positive argument for the function.

$$\text{Check:} \quad x + 5 > 0 \longrightarrow 11 + 5 > 0 \longrightarrow 16 > 0 \quad \text{check}$$

In this lesson we will look at logarithm problems that are slightly more involved.

Example 38.A.1 Solve $3 \log_{10} x = \log_{10} 16 - \log_{10} 2$.

Solution On the left side we use the power rule and on the right side we use the quotient rule.

$$\log_{10} x^3 = \log_{10} \frac{16}{2} \qquad \text{used rules}$$

$$x^3 = 8 \qquad \text{simplified}$$

$$\mathbf{x = 2} \qquad \text{solved}$$

Example 38.A.2 Solve $\log_7 (x + 1) + \log_7 (x - 5) = 1$.

Solution First we use the product rule.

$$\log_7 (x + 1)(x - 5) = 1$$

Now we rewrite this equation in exponential form. Then we solve the equation.

$$7^1 = (x + 1)(x - 5) \qquad \text{exponential form}$$

$$7 = x^2 - 4x - 5 \qquad \text{multiplied}$$

$$x^2 - 4x - 12 = 0 \qquad \text{rearranged}$$

$$(x - 6)(x + 2) = 0 \qquad \text{factored}$$

$$x = 6, -2 \qquad \text{solved}$$

Now we must check to see that $x + 1$ and $x - 5$ are positive for both 6 and -2.

WHEN $x = 6$

$x + 1 = 7$ and $x - 5 = 1$

Both are greater than 0 so **6** is a solution.

WHEN $x = -2$

$x + 1 = -1$ and $x - 5 = -7$

Thus, -2 is not an acceptable solution for the original equation because its use causes at least one argument to be negative.

Example 38.A.3 Solve $2 \log_3 x - \log_3 (x - 2) = 2$.

Solution We first use the power rule on the first term.

$$\log_3 x^2 - \log_3 (x - 2) = 2$$

Now we use the quotient rule:

$$\log_3 \frac{x^2}{x - 2} = 2$$

Next we rewrite the log equation as an exponential equation and solve.

$$3^2 = \frac{x^2}{x - 2} \qquad \text{exponential form}$$

$$9x - 18 = x^2 \qquad \text{simplified}$$

$$x^2 - 9x + 18 = 0 \qquad \text{rearranged}$$

$$(x - 3)(x - 6) = 0 \qquad \text{factored}$$

$$\mathbf{x = 3, 6} \qquad \text{solved}$$

Since both x and $x - 2$ are positive when $x = 6$ or $x = 3$, both these numbers are solutions.

38.B The color of the white house

The color of the white house is white, and the color of the red house is red. The notation

$$5^{\log_5 14}$$

makes a statement that is just as easy to understand. We read this statement as 5 raised to the power that 5 must be raised to in order to get 14. If we raise 5 to that power, the answer will certainly be 14.

$$5^{\log_5 14} = 14$$

The value of the left-hand expression below is $5x^2$ because it is read as y raised to the exponent y must be raised to in order to get $5x^2$, and the right-hand expression is read as 17 raised to the exponent 17 must be raised to in order to get 6, so its value is 6.

$$y^{\log_y 5x^2} \qquad 17^{\log_{17} 6}$$

Example 38.B.1 Simplify $42^{\log_{42} 5}$.

Solution We read this as 42 raised to the exponent that 42 must be raised to in order to get 5. So the answer is

$$\mathbf{5}$$

Example 38.B.2 Simplify $9^{\log_3 5}$.

Solution This is a trick problem because we must recognize that 9 can be written as 3^2. Thus, we get

$$3^{2 \log_3 5}$$

which we rewrite as

$$3^{\log_3 5^2}$$

and the answer is $\mathbf{5^2}$, or **25**.

Example 38.B.3 Simplify $10^{4 \log_{10} \sqrt{3}}$.

Solution This time we must write $\sqrt{3}$ as $3^{1/2}$ and also use the power rule for logarithms.

$10^{\log_{10} (3^{1/2})^4}$	simplified
$10^{\log_{10} 3^2}$	multiplied
$\mathbf{3^2}$	solution

Example 38.B.4 Simplify $3^{\log_3 4 + \log_3 5}$.

Solution First we use the product rule of logs and get

$3^{\log_3 20}$	used product rule
20	solution

Problem set 38

1. The wheel was rolling along at 400 radians per second. What was its velocity in miles per hour if the radius was 1 foot?

2. The truck was going 40 kilometers per hour and its wheels had 16-inch diameters. What was the angular velocity of the wheels in revolutions per minute?

3. Henry could buy $4x + 4$ pencils for $2y$ dollars. How many pencils could he buy for \$10?

4. How many gallons of an 80% solvent solution should be mixed with how many gallons of a 20% solvent solution to get 50 gallons of a 56% solvent solution?

5. Uncle Wilbur could do 2 jobs in 3 days and Cousin Harriet could do 4 jobs in 7 days. Cousin Harriet worked for 3 days before Uncle Wilbur joined in. How long would they have to work together to complete a total of 8 jobs?

6. How many permutations of the letters in the word *vertical* begin with three vowels?

7. How many distinguishable permutations can be formed from the letters in the word *different*?

8. Tom is a member of a club that has 10 members. How many ways can a president, a vice president, and a secretary be chosen if Tom is not to be president?

9. Find the distance between the point (2, 1) and the line $y = 2x - 1$.

10. Complete the square to graph $y - 3x^2 + 6x - 5 = 0$.

11. Complete the square to graph $y = 2x^2 + 4x + 3$.

Write the equations of the following sinusoids in terms of the sine function.

12.

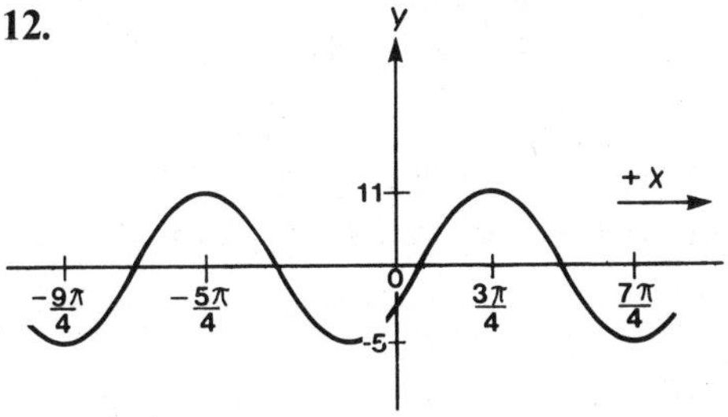

13.

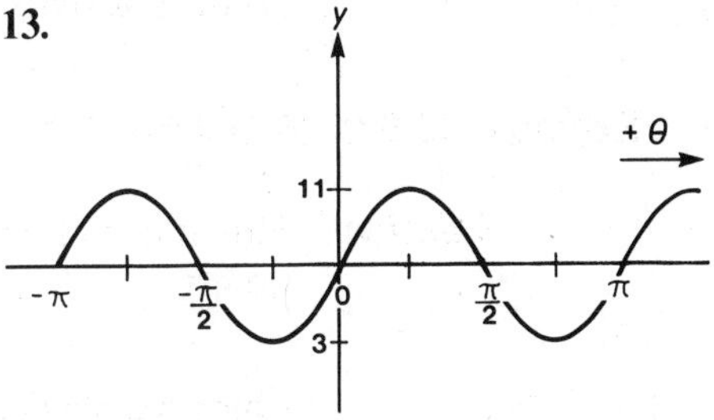

14. Find the area of this triangle in square centimeters. Note that the dimensions are given in meters.

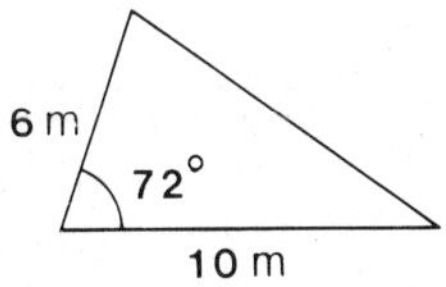

15. Find the area of this trapezoid in square centimeters. Dimensions are in meters.

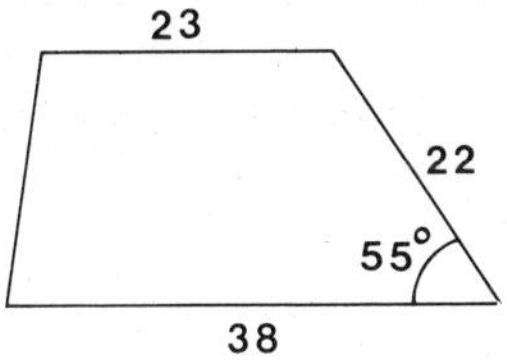

16. Factor $x^2 - 3x + 4$ over the set of complex numbers.

17. Find the area in square meters of the segment bounded by an arc of measure 120° and the chord which joins the endpoints of the arc in a circle of radius 100 centimeters.

18. Find the standard form of the equation of a circle whose radius is 10 and whose center is (3, 2).

19. Convert 30 centimeters per second to kilometers per hour.

20. Solve for C.

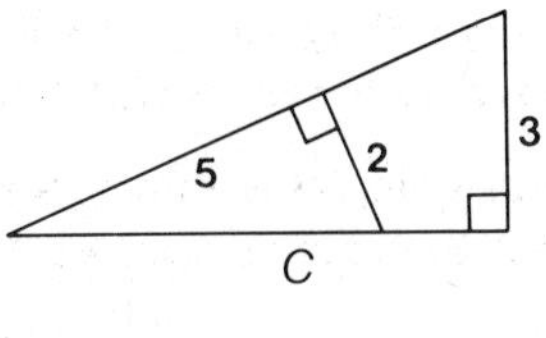

Simplify:

21. $43^{\log_{43} 6}$

22. $2^{\log_2 5 + \log_2 6}$

Solve the following equations given that ($0° \le \theta < 360°$):

23. $\sqrt{3} \tan \theta = 1$

24. $\sqrt{3} \tan 3\theta = 1$

Evaluate:

25. $\sin^2 \dfrac{7\pi}{6} + \cos^2 210°$

26. $\dfrac{1}{\sec \dfrac{13\pi}{6}} - \cos \dfrac{13\pi}{6}$

27. $\sin (\text{Arcsin } \tfrac{3}{4})$

Solve for x:

28. $2 \log_5 x = \log_5 18 - \log_5 2$

29. $\log_4 (x - 1) + \log_4 (x + 2) = 1$

30. $\log_4 x - \log_4 (2x - 1) = 1$

LESSON 39 Factorable trigonometric equations · Loss of roots caused by division

39.A Factorable trigonometric equations

Both the quadratic equations shown below can be solved by factoring.

$$(a) \quad x^2 - 1 = 0 \qquad (b) \quad x^2 + x = 0$$

Equation (a) factors into the product of a sum and a difference. Equation (b) can be solved if we begin by factoring out an x.

$$(x + 1)(x - 1) = 0 \qquad x(x + 1) = 0$$

$$x = -1, 1 \qquad x = 0, -1$$

We can make up some interesting trigonometric equations if we replace x in equations like these with trigonometric functions. If we use $\sin x$ and $\tan \theta$ in the two equations above, we get

$$\sin^2 x - 1 = 0 \qquad \tan^2 \theta + \tan \theta = 0$$

We can factor these equations just as we did above, and we get

$$(\sin x + 1)(\sin x - 1) = 0 \qquad (\tan \theta)(\tan \theta + 1) = 0$$

Now the values for x and θ can be found by setting the individual factors equal to zero. In the next three examples we show how some trigonometric equations can be solved by factoring.

Example 39.A.1 Solve: $\tan^2 \theta - 1 = 0 \qquad 0° \le \theta < 360°$

Solution This trigonometric equation can be solved by factoring and setting the individual factors equal to zero.

$(\tan \theta + 1)(\tan \theta - 1) = 0$		factored
$\tan \theta + 1 = 0$	$\tan \theta - 1 = 0$	set factors equal to zero
$\tan \theta = -1$	$\tan \theta = 1$	solved

The tangent of 45° is 1, and the tangent is positive in the first and third quadrants and negative in the second and fourth quadrants.

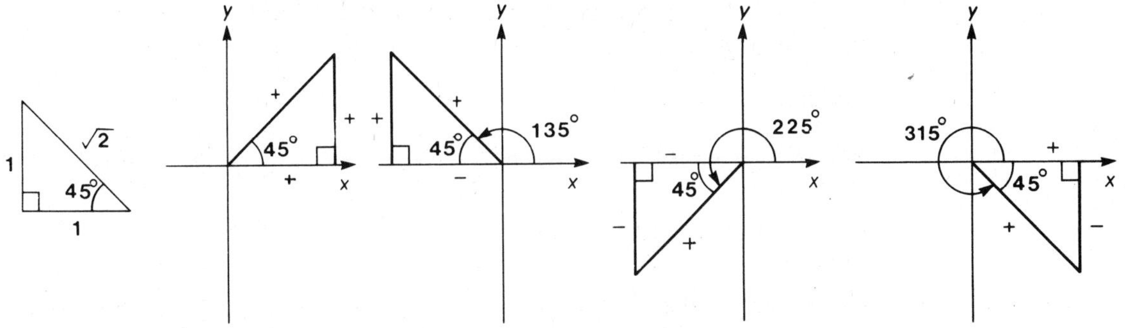

We see that there are four angles that satisfy the equation.

$$\boldsymbol{\theta = 45°, 135°, 225°, 315°}$$

Example 39.A.2 Solve: $\sin^2 \theta - \sin \theta = 0 \qquad 0° \leq \theta < 360°$

Solution We begin by factoring and get

$$(\sin \theta)(\sin \theta - 1) = 0$$

Now we set each of the factors equal to 0 and solve.

$$\sin \theta = 0 \qquad\qquad \sin \theta - 1 = 0$$

Thus, $\theta = 0°, 180°$ $\qquad\qquad \sin \theta = 1$

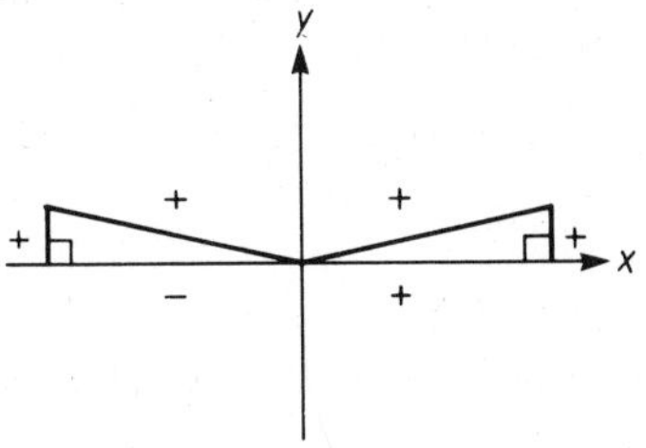

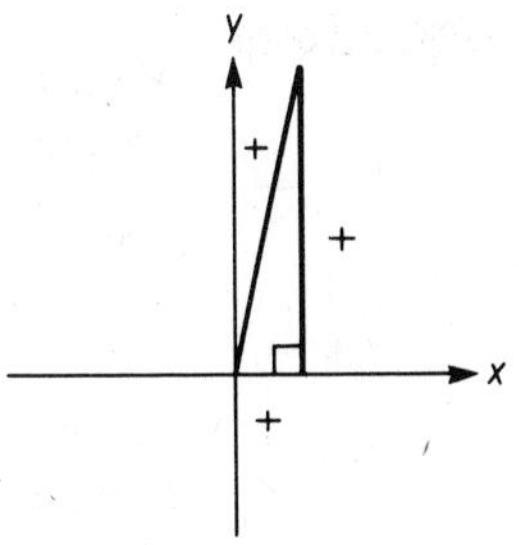

The sine of 0° equals 0 and the sine of 180° = 0 so

$$\boldsymbol{\theta = 0°, 180°}$$

The only angle whose sine is +1 is 90° so

$$\boldsymbol{\theta = 90°}$$

Thus, there are three values of θ that satisfy the given equation.

Example 39.A.3 Solve: $\cos^2 \theta = 1 \qquad 0° \leq \theta < 360°$

Solution First we rearrange the equation and factor.

$$\cos^2 \theta - 1 = 0 \qquad \text{rearranged}$$

$$(\cos \theta - 1)(\cos \theta + 1) = 0 \qquad \text{factored}$$

Now we set each of the factors equal to 0 and solve.

$$\cos \theta - 1 = 0 \qquad\qquad \cos \theta + 1 = 0$$

$$\cos \theta = +1 \qquad\qquad \cos \theta = -1$$

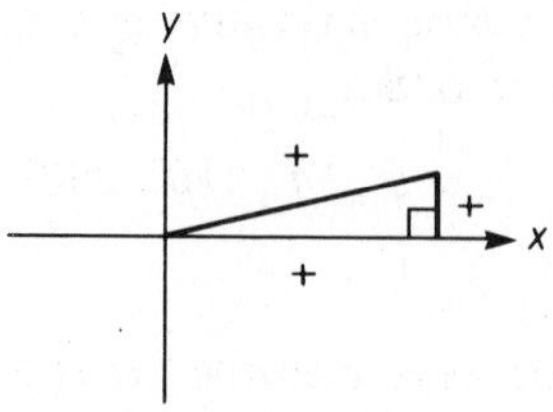

The only angles whose cosine is $+1$ is $0°$.

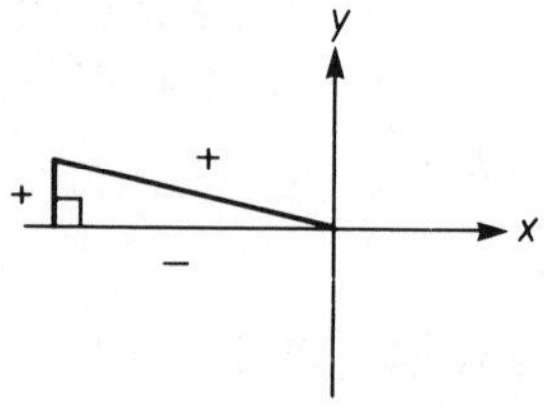

The only angle whose cosine is -1 is $180°$.

Thus, this trigonometric equation has two solutions.

$$\boldsymbol{\theta = 0°, 180°}$$

39.B Loss of roots caused by division

The factor method will yield all the roots of a trigonometric equation and is recommended for this reason. **If an attempt is made to reduce an equation by dividing both sides of the equation by a term containing the unknown, the result may be a defective equation whose solution will not provide all the roots of the original equation.** For example, if we are asked to solve this equation,

$$2 \sin x \cos x = \sin x \qquad 0° \le \theta < 360°$$

we might begin by dividing both sides of the equation by $\sin x$. The result would be the defective equation

$$2 \cos x = 1$$

The roots of this equation are $60°$ and $300°$, but the original equation also has the roots $0°$ and $180°$, as we see when we use the factor method to solve.

Example 39.B.1 Solve: $2 \sin x \cos x = \sin x \qquad 0° \le \theta < 360°$

Solution We rearrange the equation and factor.

$$2 \sin x \cos x - \sin x = 0 \qquad \text{rearranged}$$

$$(\sin x)(2 \cos x - 1) = 0 \qquad \text{factored}$$

Now we set each of the factors equal to 0 and solve.

$$\sin x = 0 \qquad 2 \cos x - 1 = 0$$

$$2 \cos x = 1$$

$$\cos x = \frac{1}{2}$$

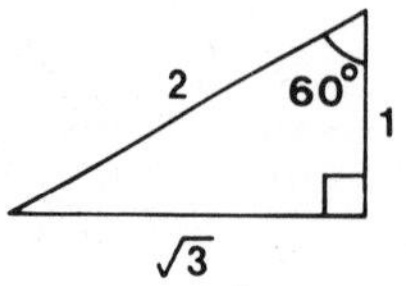

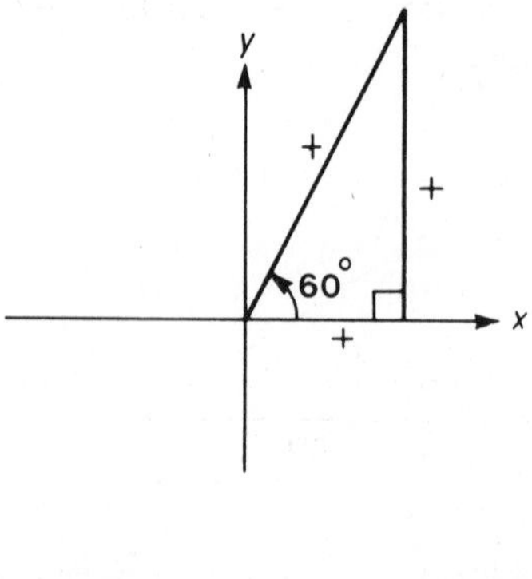

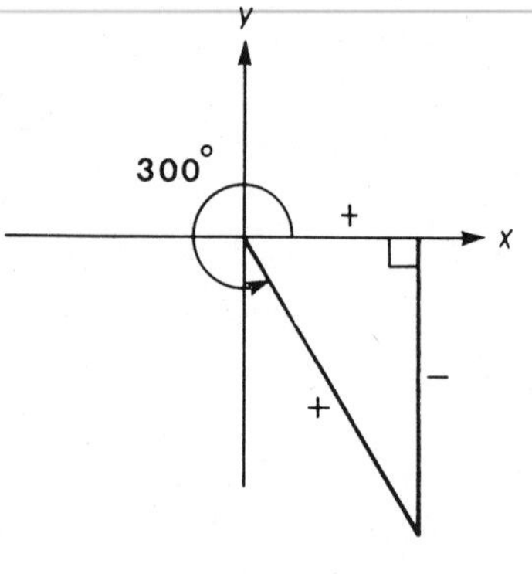

The cosine of 60° is $\frac{1}{2}$, and the cosine is positive in the first and fourth quadrants. The sine of 0° and 180° both equal zero. So:

$$x = 0°, 60°, 180°, 300°$$

Problem set 39

1. The angular velocity of the wheels on the fire engine was 367 radians per second. If the radius of the wheels was 16 inches, what was the linear velocity of the fire engine in miles per hour?
2. The linear velocity of the go-cart was 5 kilometers per hour, but its wheels were only 10 centimeters in diameter. What was the angular velocity of the wheels in radians per minute?
3. The jet could fly at 8 times the speed of the wind and thus could go 1350 miles downwind in 1 hour more than it took to go 700 miles upwind. What was the speed of the jet and what was the speed of the wind?
4. The ratio of the number of reds to the number of whites was 1 to 2. The ratio of the number of greens to the number of whites was 5 to 4. If the total number of reds, whites, and greens was 22, how many were there of each color?
5. Six times the complement of an angle exceeds 2 times the supplement of the same angle by 60°. What is the angle?
6. How many distinguishable ways can the host and 10 guests be seated in a row if three of the guests are identical triplets?
7. How many ways can the letters in the word *came* be arranged if a consonant is in the fourth position?
8. Write a quadratic equation whose roots are $-1 - \sqrt{3}\,i$ and $-1 + \sqrt{3}\,i$.
9. Find the distance between the point $(-4, 6)$ and the line $y = x + 2$.
10. Complete the square to graph $y = 6x + 3x^2$.

Write the equations of the following sinusoids in terms of the cosine function.

11.

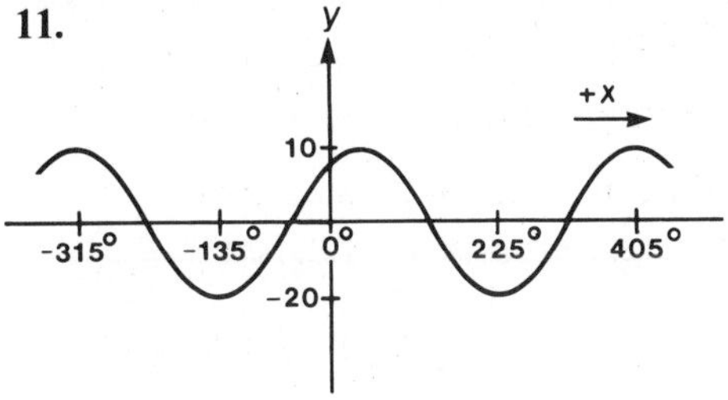

12.

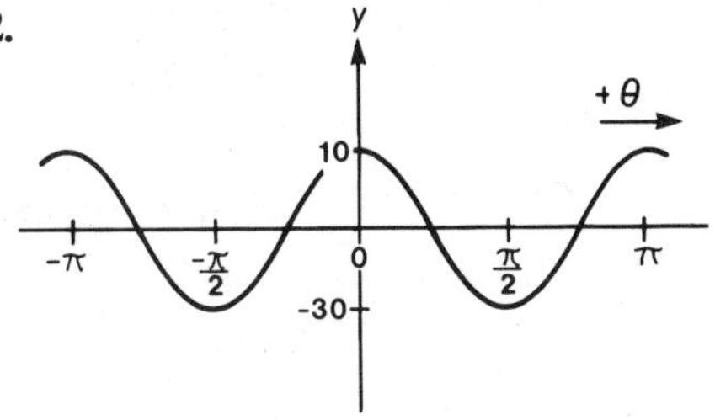

13. Find the area of this triangle in square centimeters. Dimensions are in meters.

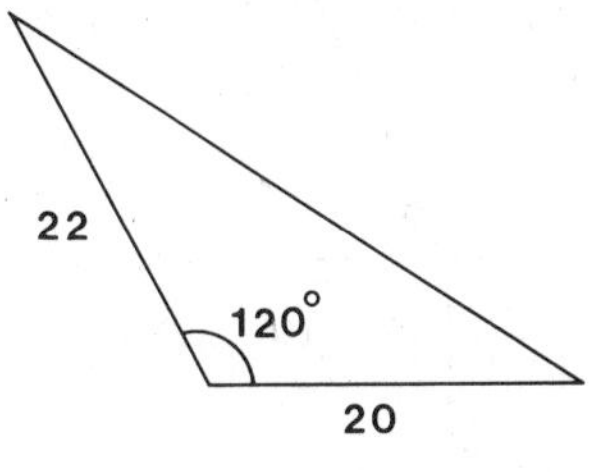

14. Find the area of this trapezoid in square meters. Dimensions are in centimeters.

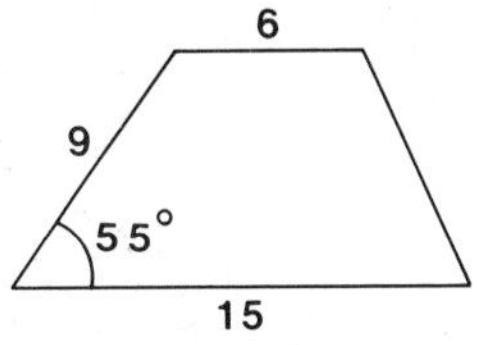

15. The central angle of a sector of a circle is 80°. Find the area of the sector in square centimeters if the radius is 20 centimeters.

16. Find the area in square feet of the segment bounded by an arc of measure 2.4 radians and the chord which joins the endpoints of the arc in a circle of radius 10 inches.

17. Find the standard form of the equation of a circle whose radius is 8 and whose center is (5, 6).

18. Use the locus definition method to find the equation of the line equidistant from $(-2, 4)$ and $(6, -2)$. Write the equation in general form.

19. If the length of a rectangle is $3x + 2y$ and the perimeter is $10x + 6y$, what is the width of the rectangle?

Simplify:

20. $32^{\log_{32} 7}$

21. $3^{\log_3 6 - \log_3 2}$

Solve the following equations given that $(0° \le \theta < 360°)$:

22. $\sin 3\theta - 1 = 0$

23. $\cos^2 \theta - \cos \theta = 0$

24. $\sin^2 \theta - 1 = 0$

Evaluate:

25. $\sin^2 \frac{3\pi}{4} + \cos^2 \frac{3\pi}{4}$

26. $\text{Arcsin}\left(\sin \frac{\pi}{4}\right)$

27. $\cos\left[\text{Arcsin}\left(-\frac{1}{4}\right)\right]$

Solve for x:

28. $3 \log_6 x = \log_6 24 - \log_6 3$

29. $\log_{10} x + \log_{10} (x - 3) = 1$

30. $2 \log_2 x - \log_2 (x - \frac{1}{2}) = -\log_{1/3} 3$

LESSON 40 Data analysis · Multiple variables

40.A Summation notation in data analysis

The summation notation

$$\sum_{x=0}^{3} 3x^2$$

tells us to sum four terms in which the variable x takes on the values 0, 1, 2, and 3.

$$\sum_{x=0}^{3} 3x^2 = 3(0)^2 + 3(1)^2 + 3(2)^2 + 3(3)^2 = 42$$

Sometimes we wish to indicate a sum that does not involve a variable that has a nice succession of whole number values such as 0, 1, 2, 3. This often occurs in statistics problems where the numbers we work with come from measurements of some kind. If we have a list of numbers such as

$$5, 7, 11, 14, 3, -4, 2, -8$$

we can identify the numbers by using a subscripted variable and using counting numbers as subscripts. The letters a, x, y, and t are often used as the variables. If we wish to indicate the sum of the 8 numbers that have been specified in order, we could use the letter

a as a variable and write

$$a_1 + a_2 + a_3 + a_4 + a_5 + a_6 + a_7 + a_8$$

and we can use summation notation to indicate this sum by writing

$$\sum_{i=1}^{8} a_i$$

We note that the variable of summation is *i*, and it identifies the subscript of the variable *a* and does not name the value of the variable. In this problem, a_1 is 5, a_2 is 7, etc., and we have indicated the sum of the 8 numbers being considered.

$$\sum_{i=1}^{8} a_i = 5 + 7 + 11 + 14 + 3 + (-4) + 2 + (-8) = 30$$

There are two forms of summation notation that are sometimes confused by beginners. These two notations have entirely different meanings, as we shall see in the following example.

Example 40.A.1 Using the same list of 8 numbers, evaluate: (*a*) $\sum_{i=1}^{8} (a_i)^2$ (*b*) $\left(\sum_{i=1}^{8} a_i\right)^2$

Solution (*a*) This notation indicates the sum of the squares of the different values of a. In this case, it means

$$\sum_{i=1}^{8} (a_i)^2 = (5)^2 + (7)^2 + (11)^2 + (14)^2 + (3)^2 + (-4)^2 + (2)^2 + (-8)^2 = \mathbf{484}$$

(*b*) This notation means the square of the sum of the different values of a. In this problem, the sum of the values is 30, so the square of the sum is $(30)^2$.

$$\left(\sum_{i=1}^{8} a_i\right)^2 = (30)^2 = \mathbf{900}$$

40.B Multiple variables

Summation notation is often useful when a problem deals with more than two variables. Each set of variables is identified with a different set of subscripted variables. Suppose we have the following two sets of measurements.

$$X = \{4, 3, 5, 2\} \qquad Y = \{2, 6, 3, 4\}$$

We could identify the left set with the variables x_i and the right set with the variables y_i. The following notations have the meanings shown.

$$\sum_{i=1}^{4} x_i y_i = 4 \cdot 2 + 3 \cdot 6 + 5 \cdot 3 + 2 \cdot 4 = 49$$

$$\sum_{i=1}^{4} 7x_i y_i^2 = 7 \cdot 4 \cdot 2^2 + 7 \cdot 3 \cdot 6^2 + 7 \cdot 5 \cdot 3^2 + 7 \cdot 2 \cdot 4^2 = 1407$$

$$\sum_{i=1}^{4} (8x_i + 7y_i) = (8 \cdot 4 + 7 \cdot 2) + (8 \cdot 3 + 7 \cdot 6) + (8 \cdot 5 + 7 \cdot 3) + (8 \cdot 2 + 7 \cdot 4) = 217$$

Example 40.B.1 Given the two ordered sets $X = \{1, 3, 2\}$, $Y = \{2, 2, 3\}$, evaluate $\sum_{i=1}^{3} 2x_i y_i^2$.

Solution

$$\sum_{i=1}^{3} 2x_i y_i^2 = 2 \cdot 1 \cdot 2^2 + 2 \cdot 3 \cdot 2^2 + 2 \cdot 2 \cdot 3^2 = \mathbf{68}$$

Example 40.B.2 Use the values for X and Y from Example 40.B.1 to evaluate $\sum_{i=1}^{3} (2x_i + 3y_i^2)$.

Solution We sum the products of the x values and 2 and sum the products of the squares of the y values and 3.

$$\sum_{i=1}^{3} (2x_i + 3y_i^2) = [2 \cdot 1 + 3(2)^2] + [2 \cdot 3 + 3(2)^2] + [2 \cdot 2 + 3(3)^2] = \mathbf{63}$$

Problem set 40

1. To get there on time, it was necessary to average 40 kilometers per hour. If the wheels had a radius of 14 inches, what should be their average angular velocity in radians per second?

2. The second car had wheels that had a radius of 16 centimeters and the wheels turned at 40 revolutions per second. What was the velocity of the car in miles per hour?

3. Five times Tom's age now exceeds 4 times Lucy's age now by 38. In 5 years, twice Tom's age will only exceed twice Lucy's age by 8. How old will Tom and Lucy be in 13 years?

4. Mike's wages for a 40-hour week came to $200. The next week he got a 30 percent hourly raise but was allowed to work only 38 hours. What was his paycheck for that week?

5. The ratio of the tens digit to the hundreds digit in a three-digit counting number was 2 to 1, and twice the tens digit exceeded 5 times the units digit by 1. What was the number if the sum of the digits was 15?

6. How many ways can a president, a secretary, and a treasurer be chosen from a class of 12 students?

7. How many ways can Tom, Joe, Frank, and Sally sit in a row if Tom refuses to sit next to Sally?

8. Five red marbles, 4 blue marbles, and 2 white marbles are placed in a row. How many ways can they be arranged?

9. Given the ordered set $X = \{3, 1, -1\}$, evaluate $3 \sum_{i=1}^{3} x_i^2 - \left(\sum_{i=1}^{3} x_i\right)^2$.

10. Given the two ordered sets $X = \{2, 3, 4\}$ and $Y = \{1, 2, 3\}$, evaluate $\sum_{j=1}^{3} 3x_j^2 y_j$.

11. Find the distance between the point (2, 4) and the line $y = x - 1$.

12. Complete the square to graph $y - 2x^2 + 4x = -7$.

Write the equations of the following sinusoids in terms of the sine function.

13.

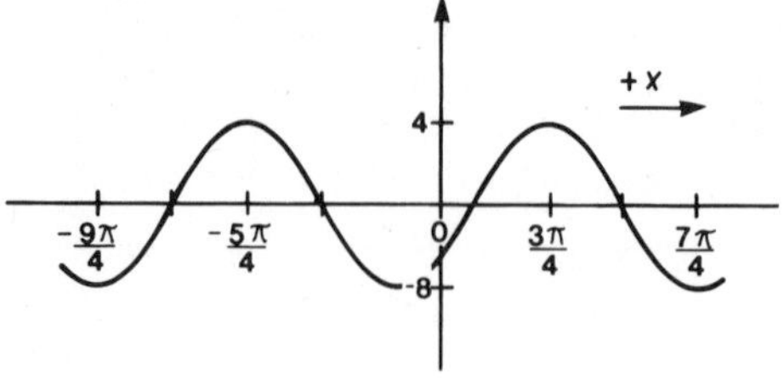

14.

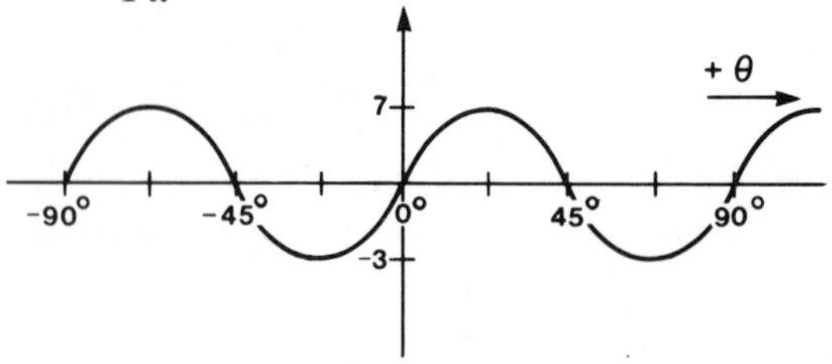

15. Find the area of this triangle in square centimeters.

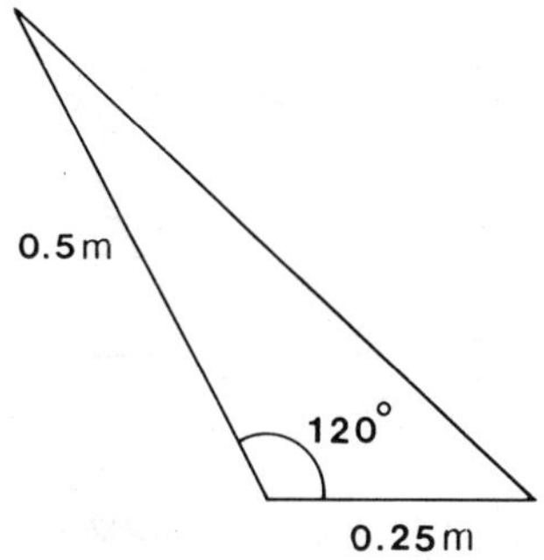

16. The central angle of a sector of a circle is 1.6 radians. Find the area of the sector in square centimeters if the radius of the circle is 1 meter.

17. Find the area in square centimeters of the segment bounded by an arc of measure 150° and the chord which joins the endpoints of the arc in a circle of radius 10 centimeters.

18. Find the standard form of the equation of a circle whose radius is 6 and whose center is (m, n).

19. Use the midpoint formula method to find the equation of the line equidistant from $(-4, 2)$ and $(4, 4)$. Write the equation in slope-intercept form.

20. A boat travels downstream m nautical miles at d knots and then travels back upstream m nautical miles at u knots. What is the average speed for the entire trip? (*Note*: A ***knot*** is a nautical mile per hour.)

21. Simplify: $5^{\log_5 22 - \log_5 2}$

Solve the following equations given that $(0° \le \theta < 360°)$:

22. $\cos 3\theta - \dfrac{\sqrt{2}}{2} = 0$

23. $\cos^2 \theta - \frac{1}{2} \cos \theta = 0$

24. $\sin^2 \theta - \frac{1}{4} = 0$

Evaluate:

25. $2 \sin \dfrac{13\pi}{6} \cos \dfrac{13\pi}{6} - \sin \dfrac{13\pi}{3}$

26. $\cot(-450°) - \dfrac{\cos(-450°)}{\sin(-450°)}$

27. $\sin \left[\text{Arctan} \left(-\dfrac{5}{12} \right) \right]$

Solve for x:

28. $2 \log_5 x = \log_5 16 - \log_5 4$.

29. $\log x + \log (x - 9) = 1$

30. $\log_5 (x + 4) + \log_5 (x - 4) = 2$

LESSON 41 Abstract coefficients · Linear variation

41.A Abstract coefficients

In beginning algebra, we learned that letters can be used in place of unspecified numbers. In this equation

$$2x + 4y = 50$$

the letters x and y are variables. If x takes on the value of 5, then y must equal 10. If x takes on the value of 19, then y equals 3, etc. Thus, while x and y can take on different values in this equation, the symbols 2, 4, and 50 always have the same values, as they represent the constants 2, 4, and 50. At this level of algebra, it is beneficial to begin to place emphasis on problems that use letters to represent constants. If we use a, b, and c in place of the constants 2, 4, and 50 in the equation above, the equation would read

$$ax + by = c$$

Although any letter can be used to represent a constant or a variable, it is customary to use letters from the beginning of the alphabet to represent constants and letters from the end of the alphabet to represent variables. In this lesson we will use letters to represent the constants in systems of linear equations.

Example 41.A.1 Solve for y: $\begin{cases} ax + by = c \\ dx + ey = f \end{cases}$

Solution If we multiply every term in the top equation by d and multiply every term in the bottom equation by $(-a)$, the coefficients of x in the resulting equations will be the same except for the signs. Thus, when we add the equations, the x terms will be eliminated.

$$\begin{array}{lcccr} ax + by = c & \longrightarrow & (d) & \longrightarrow & adx + bdy = \quad cd \\ dx + ey = f & \longrightarrow & (-a) & \longrightarrow & -adx - aey = \quad -af \\ \hline & & & & (bd - ae)y = cd - af \end{array}$$

Note the use of parentheses around $bd - ae$. Now we finish by dividing both sides by $bd - ae$, and we get

$$\boldsymbol{y = \frac{cd - af}{bd - ae}}$$

Example 41.A.2 Solve for x: $\begin{cases} a_1x + b_1y = c_1 \\ a_2x + b_2y = c_2 \end{cases}$

Solution Subscripted constants such as these are standard notation for the general study of equations and will be used extensively in later lessons. To eliminate y, we will multiply as required to make the y coefficients equal but opposite in sign. **Be careful with the subscripts.** It is easy to get them mixed up.

$$\begin{array}{lcccr} a_1x + b_1y = c_1 & \longrightarrow & (b_2) & \longrightarrow & a_1b_2x + b_1b_2y = \quad c_1b_2 \\ a_2x + b_2y = c_2 & \longrightarrow & (-b_1) & \longrightarrow & -a_2b_1x - b_1b_2y = -c_2b_1 \\ \hline & & & & (a_1b_2 - a_2b_1)x = c_1b_2 - c_2b_1 \end{array}$$

To finish, we divide by $a_1b_2 - a_2b_1$ and get

$$\boldsymbol{x = \frac{c_1b_2 - c_2b_1}{a_1b_2 - a_2b_1}}$$

41.B Linear variation

A statement that one variable varies linearly as another variable can sometimes mean the same thing as a statement of direct variation between the two variables. But the two statements may have different meanings, as we explain in the next example.

Example 41.B.1 The total cost varied linearly with the number produced. When 100 were produced, the cost was \$700; and when 400 were produced, the cost was \$2200. Write the equation that gives cost as a function of the number produced.

Solution **When a linear relationship is specified, the intercept may or may not be zero.** The equation implied by this problem is

$$C = mN + b$$

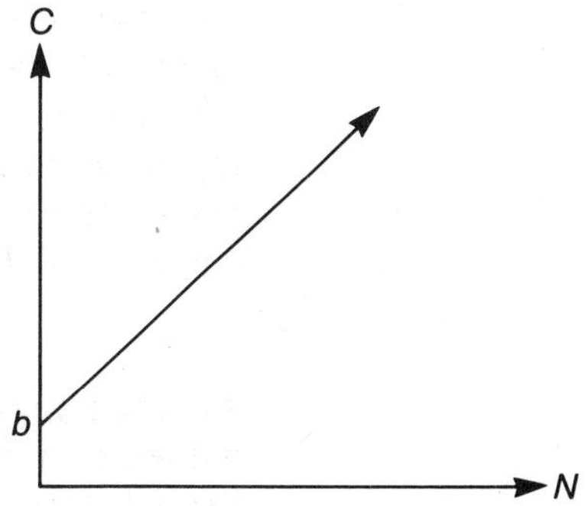

and we have been given the coordinates of two points on the line. We will use 100 for N and 700 for C to get one equation and then will use 400 for N and 2200 for C to get the second equation. Then we will solve the equations for m and b.

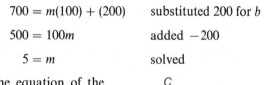

$$\begin{array}{llllll} (a) & 700 = m100 + b & \longrightarrow & (4) & \longrightarrow & 2800 = m400 + 4b \\ (b) & 2200 = m400 + b & \longrightarrow & (-1) & \longrightarrow & \underline{-2200 = -m400 - b} \\ & & & & & 600 = 3b \\ & & & & & 200 = b \end{array}$$

Now we substitute 200 for b in equation (a) and solve for m.

$$\begin{array}{ll} 700 = m(100) + (200) & \text{substituted 200 for } b \\ 500 = 100m & \text{added } -200 \\ 5 = m & \text{solved} \end{array}$$

Now we can write the equation of the line, which, as we see, does have a nonzero intercept.

$$\mathbf{C = 5N + 200}$$

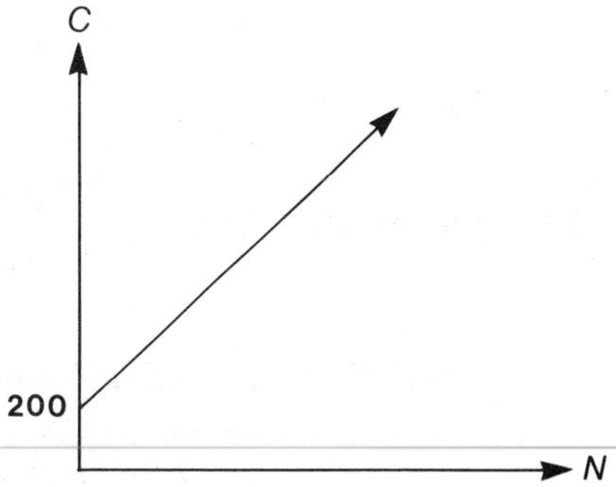

Problem set 41

1. The total cost varied linearly with the number produced. When 200 were produced, the cost was \$2050. When 30 were produced, the cost was \$350. Write an equation that gives cost as a function of the number produced.

2. The wheel had an angular velocity of 723 radians per minute. How fast was the wheel rolling along in feet per second if the radius of the wheel was 20 centimeters?

3. The pressure of a perfect gas varies inversely as the volume if the temperature is held constant. If the temperature is 1500 K, the pressure is 4 atmospheres when

the volume is 500 liters. At the same temperature, what is the pressure when the volume is decreased to 50 liters?

4. The number of reds varied directly as the number of purples and inversely as the number of whites cubed. There were 200 reds when there were 50 purples and 10 whites. How many reds were there when the number of purples was increased to 60 and the number of whites was decreased to 5?

5. Detia could row 12 miles downstream in 1 hour less than she could row 6 miles upstream. What was the speed of the current in the river, and how fast could Detia row in still water if the speed of the current was one-half the speed Detia could row in still water?

6. How many ways can 10 boys sit in 5 chairs that are in 1 row?

7. How many ways can 4 boys and 1 girl be arranged in a row if the girl insists on sitting in the middle?

8. Five red marbles, 4 white marbles, and 2 green marbles are placed in a row. In how many distinguishable ways can they be arranged?

9. Solve for y: $\begin{cases} mx + ny = c \\ dx + ey = f \end{cases}$

10. Given the two ordered sets $X = \{4, 1, 2\}$ and $Y = \{2, 1, 1\}$, evaluate $\sum_{k=1}^{3} (2x_k^2 - y_k)$.

11. Find the distance between the point (3, 1) and the line $y = x - 4$.

12. Complete the square to graph $y = 3x^2 - 12x + 34$.

Write the equations of the following sinusoids in terms of the cosine function.

13.

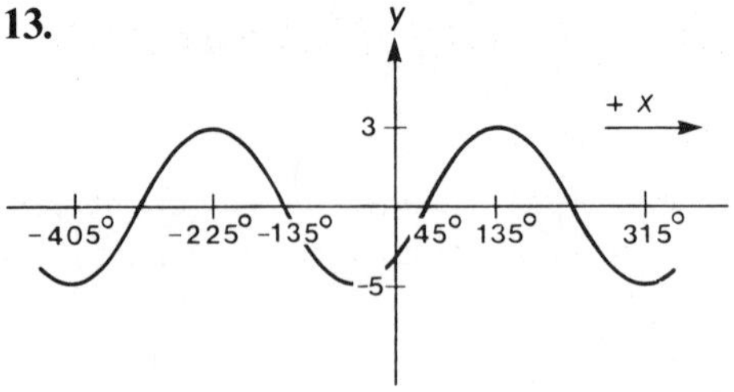

14.

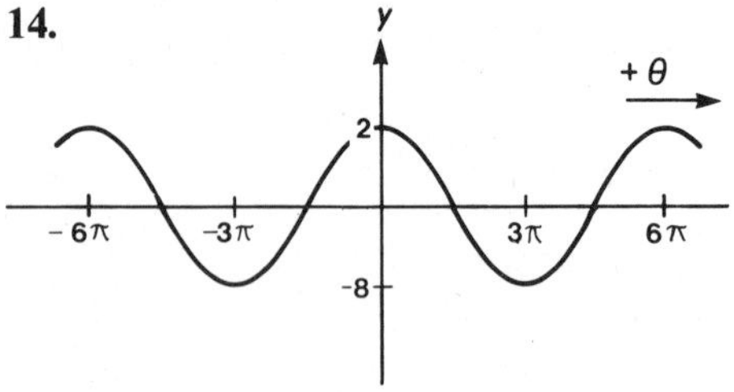

15. Find the area of this trapezoid in square centimeters.

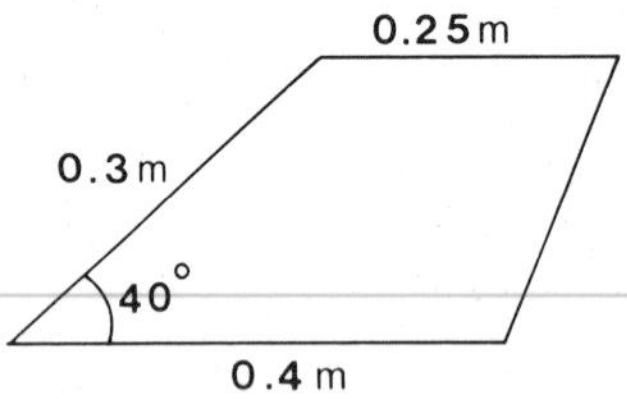

16. The central angle of a sector of a circle is 103°. Find the area of the sector in square centimeters if the radius of the circle is 0.1 meter.

17. Find the area in square centimeters of the segment bounded by an arc of measure 2.44 radians and the chord which joins the endpoints of the arc in a circle whose radius is 8 centimeters.

18. Find the standard form of the equation of a circle whose radius is 4 and whose center is (a, b).

19. Use the locus definition method to find the equation of the line equidistant from $(-4, -4)$ and $(6, 2)$. Write the equation in general form.

20. Solve for a and b.

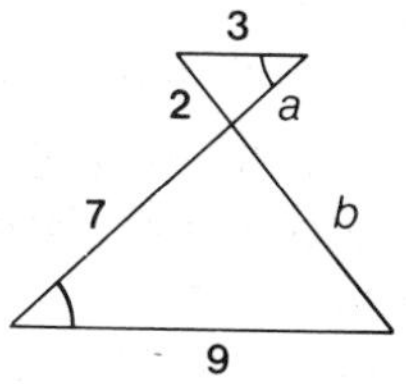

21. Simplify: $6^{2 \log_6 2}$

Solve the following equations given that ($0° \le \theta < 360°$):

22. $\cos 4\theta - 1 = 0$

23. $\sin^2 \theta - \frac{\sqrt{3}}{2} \sin \theta = 0$

24. $\tan^2 \theta = 1$

Evaluate:

25. $2 \sin \frac{19\pi}{6} \cos \frac{19\pi}{6} - \sin \frac{19\pi}{3}$

26. $\tan^2 (-390°) + 1$

27. $\tan \left[\text{Arcsin} \left(-\frac{5}{13} \right) \right]$

Solve for x:

28. $3 \log_6 x = \log_6 16 - \log_6 2$

29. $\log_7 (x + 9) - \log_7 x = \log_7 7$

30. Show why $\log_b (N)^x = x \log_b N$.

LESSON 42 Circles and completing the square

42.A Conics: equations of circles

We review the development of the equation of a circle by using the distance formula to write the equation of a circle of radius 3 whose center is (2, 4).

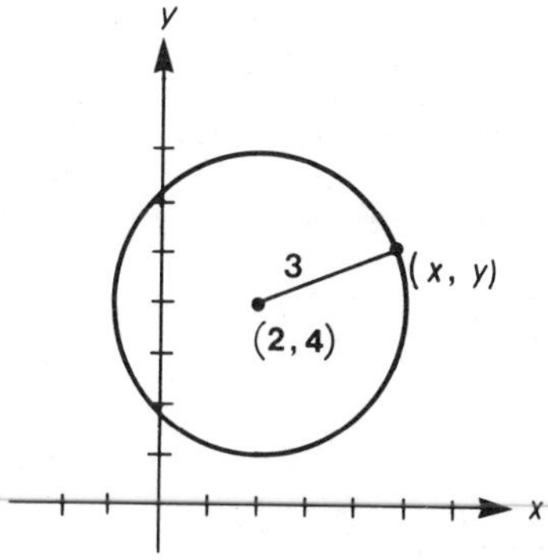

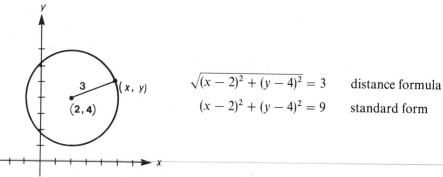

$$\sqrt{(x-2)^2 + (y-4)^2} = 3 \qquad \text{distance formula}$$

$$(x-2)^2 + (y-4)^2 = 9 \qquad \text{standard form}$$

If we do the indicated multiplications and rearrange the terms, we can write the equation of this circle in general form.

$$x^2 - 4x + 4 + y^2 - 8y + 16 = 9 \qquad \text{multiplied}$$

$$x^2 + y^2 - 4x - 8y + 11 = 0 \qquad \text{general form}$$

We note that the standard form is especially useful because, by inspection, we can tell the coordinates of the center of the circle and the length of the radius. If we are given the equation of a circle in general form, we can transform it to standard form by completing the square twice, as we show in the following examples.

Example 42.A.1 The equation $x^2 + y^2 - 6x + 8y + 21 = 0$ is the equation of a circle. Complete the square to change this equation to the standard form and then graph the circle.

Solution We group the x terms and the y terms and move the constant to the other side of the equals sign.

$$(x^2 - 6x \qquad) + (y^2 + 8y \qquad) = -21$$

Now we complete the squares inside the parentheses by inserting +9 and +16. We also add +9 and +16 to the right side as required by the rules for equations.

$$(x^2 - 6x + 9) + (y^2 + 8y + 16) = -21 + 9 + 16$$

Now on the left side we write each term as a quantity squared, and we add on the right side.

$$\mathbf{(x - 3)^2 + (y + 4)^2 = 2^2}$$

This is the equation of a circle of radius 2 whose center is $(3, -4)$, as shown in the figure.

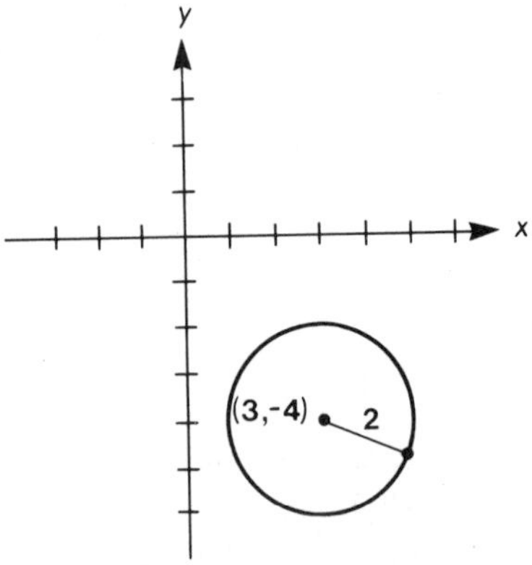

Example 42.A.2 Complete the square to change the form of this equation of a circle, $x^2 + y^2 + 4x - 6y + 6 = 0$, to the standard form, and then graph the circle.

Solution We use parentheses and group the x terms and the y terms.

$$(x^2 + 4x \qquad) + (y^2 - 6y \qquad) = -6$$

Now we add to complete the squares and remember to add the same numbers to the right side of the equation.

$$(x^2 + 4x + 4) + (y^2 - 6y + 9) = -6 + 4 + 9$$

Now we write each grouping on the left side as a squared term and simplify on the right.

$$\mathbf{(x + 2)^2 + (y - 3)^2 = (\sqrt{7})^2}$$

This is the equation of a circle whose center is $(-2, 3)$ and whose radius is $\sqrt{7}$.

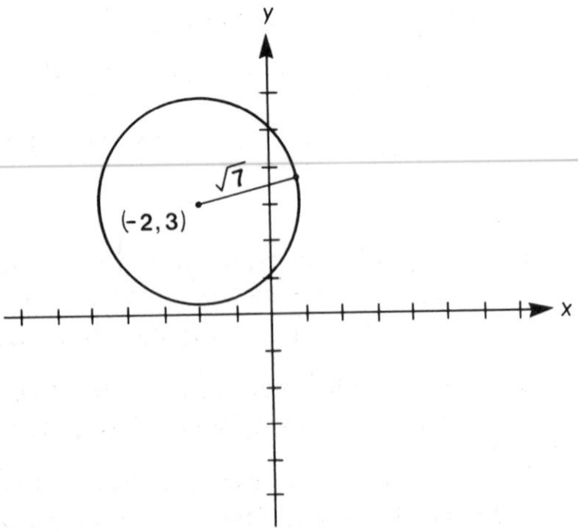

Example 42.A.3 Given the general form of the equation of a circle, $2x^2 + 2y^2 - x + y - 3 = 0$, complete the square to write the standard form of the equation and describe the circle.

Solution We begin by dividing every term by 2 so that the coefficients of x^2 and y^2 are both 1. We get

$$x^2 + y^2 - \frac{1}{2}x + \frac{1}{2}y - \frac{3}{2} = 0$$

Now we rearrange the terms and use parentheses. Then we add as necessary to complete the squares.

$$\left(x^2 - \frac{1}{2}x \qquad\right) + \left(y^2 + \frac{1}{2}y \qquad\right) = \frac{3}{2} \qquad \text{rearranged}$$

$$\left(x^2 - \frac{1}{2}x + \frac{1}{16}\right) + \left(y^2 + \frac{1}{2}y + \frac{1}{16}\right) = \frac{24}{16} + \frac{1}{16} + \frac{1}{16} \qquad \text{completed squares}$$

$$\left(x - \frac{1}{4}\right)^2 + \left(y + \frac{1}{4}\right)^2 = \left(\frac{\sqrt{26}}{4}\right)^2 \qquad \text{simplified}$$

This is the equation of a circle of radius $\sqrt{26}/4$ whose center is $(\frac{1}{4}, -\frac{1}{4})$.

42.B Summation variables and constants

Sometimes we encounter a summation notation in which the variable of summation is increased by a given amount. This variation of summation notation can be used in two different ways, as we show in the next two examples.

Example 42.B.1 Evaluate: $\sum_{i=1}^{3} 2^{i+1}$

Solution In this problem, i takes on the values 1, 2, and 3 and thus the exponents will be $i + 1$ or 2, 3, and 4.

$$\sum_{i=1}^{3} 2^{i+1} = 2^2 + 2^3 + 2^4 = \mathbf{28}$$

Example 42.B.2 Given $X = \{1, 2, 3, 4\}$ and $Y = \{2, 3, 4, 5, 6\}$, evaluate $\sum_{i=1}^{3} (x_i y_{i+1} + y_i)$.

Solution In this case y_{i+1} means that when i equals 1, the second value of y is used. When i equals 2, the third value of y is used, etc.

$$\sum_{i=1}^{3} x_i y_{i+1} + y_i = [(1)(3) + (2)] + [(2)(4) + 3] + [(3)(5) + (4)] = \mathbf{35}$$

Problem set 42

1. The number of reds varied linearly as the number of blues. When there were 2 blues, there were 11 reds. When the blues numbered 8, there were 35 reds. How many reds were there when 6 blues were present?

2. The car rolled merrily along at 60 kilometers per hour. If the radius of its wheels was 12 inches, what was the angular velocity of the wheels in radians per second?

3. The ratio of onlookers to bystanders was 17 to 4. If 1050 natives were gawking at the spectacle, how many were bystanders and how many were onlookers?

4. Marta traveled m miles at a miles per hour, and Kristel traveled the same distance but at a slower rate of b miles per hour. What is the difference in hours between the times of the two girls?

5. Jimbob traveled a miles in b hours and then increased his rate by c miles per hour. How long would it take him to travel 1000 miles at the new rate?

6. How many ways can 3 boys and 2 girls sit in a row if boys cannot sit next to one another?

7. How many ways can the letters of the word *vowel* be arranged if the first letter must be a vowel?

8. How many distinguishable ways can 4 red flags and 3 green flags be arranged in a row?

9. Solve for x: $\begin{cases} ax + by = c \\ mx + ny = f \end{cases}$

10. Given the two ordered sets $X = \{3, 1, -1\}$ and $Y = \{-2, 2, 3, 1\}$, evaluate $\sum_{k=1}^{3} (3x_k^2 - 2y_{k+1})$.

11. Evaluate: $\sum_{i=1}^{3} 2^{i-1}$

12. Find the distance between the point $(-2, 4)$ and the line $y - x + 6 = 0$.

13. Complete the square to graph $y = 2x^2 - 12x + 19$.

Write the equations of the following sinusoids in terms of the sine function.

14.

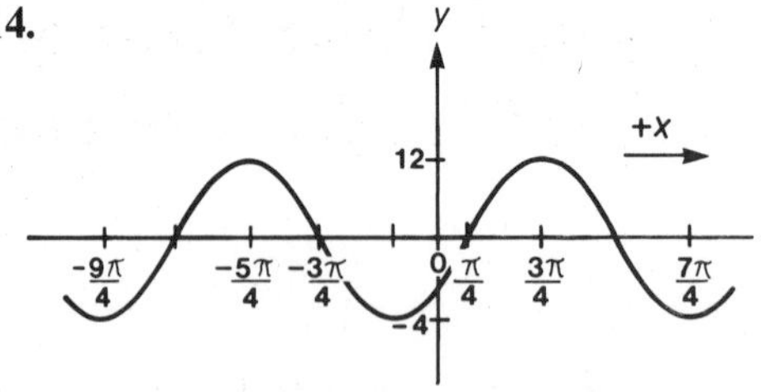

15.

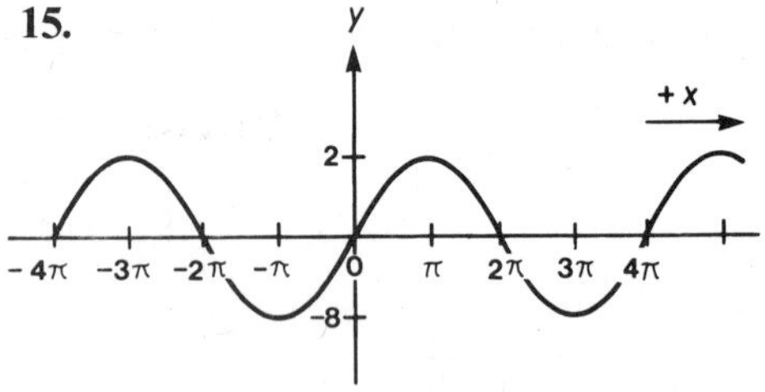

16. Find the area of this triangle in square centimeters.

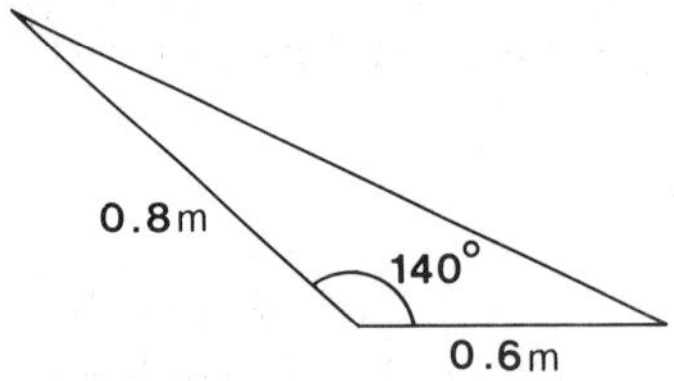

17. The central angle of a sector of a circle is 2.4 radians. Find the area of the sector in square centimeters if the radius of the circle is 0.4 meter.

18. Find the area in square centimeters of the segment bounded by an arc of measure 160° and the chord which joins the endpoints of the arc in a circle whose radius is 10 centimeters.

19. The equation $x^2 + y^2 + 8x - 6y - 11 = 0$ is the equation of a circle. Complete the square to change this equation to standard form and then describe the circle.

20. Complete the square to change the equation of the circle $x^2 + y^2 - 8x + 2y + 13 = 0$ to standard form and then describe the circle.

21. Use the midpoint formula method to find the equation of the perpendicular bisector of the line segment with endpoints $(-4, 2)$ and $(4, 6)$.

22. Solve for a.

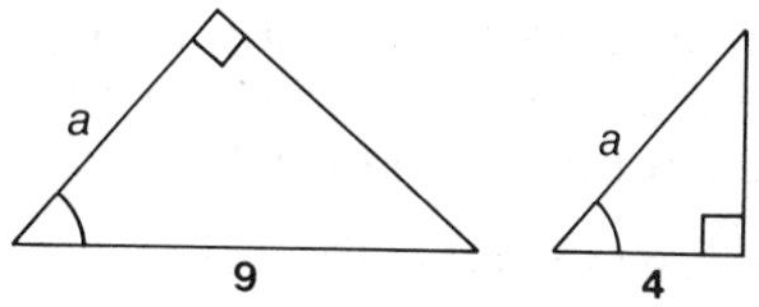

Solve the following equations given that ($0° \le \theta < 360°$):

23. $\cos\theta - 1 = 0$

24. $\cos\theta\sin\theta - \sin\theta = 0$

25. $\cos^2\theta - \frac{1}{4} = 0$

Evaluate:

26. $\sin^2\frac{3\pi}{2} + \cos^2\frac{3\pi}{2}$

27. $\cos^2(-405°) - \sin^2(-405°)$

28. $\sin\left[\text{Arccos}\left(-\frac{5}{6}\right)\right]$

Solve for x:

29. $2\log_8 x = \log_8 6 + \log_8 2 - \log_8 1$

30. $\log_{1/2}(x-3) - \log_{1/2}(x-2) = \log_{1/2} 2$

LESSON 43 The complex plane · Polar form of a complex number · Sums and products of complex numbers

43.A The complex plane

We can graph complex numbers on a rectangular coordinate system if we use the x axis to graph the real part of the number and the y axis to graph the imaginary part of the number. If we do this, the graph of the complex number $-2 - 4i$ will look exactly like the graph of the vector $-2i - 4j$. **This is confusing at first, for i indicates up and down for graphs of complex numbers but indicates right and left for graphs of vectors.**

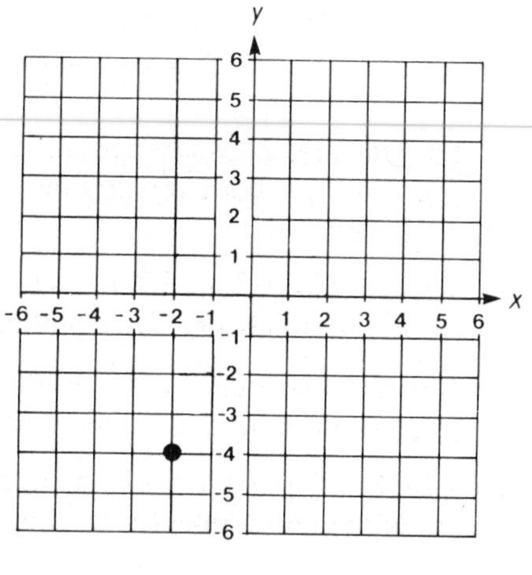

When we graph $-2i - 4j$, we do not need to put the i and j on the graph because we can visually determine directions by looking at the graph. When we graph $-2 - 4i$, we do not need to put an i on the graph because we can remember that we use the y direction to graph the imaginary part of a complex number and the x direction to graph the real part of a complex number.

When we graph vectors, we call the system of coordinates a ***rectangular coordinate system*** or a ***Cartesian coordinate system.*** Often it is called simply a ***coordinate plane.*** When we use the coordinate plane to graph complex numbers, we call the plane the ***complex plane*** or the ***Argand plane.*** Some authors replace the letter y on the vertical axis with the word *imaginary*, and others use y as we have in the past. We will continue to use the letter y on the vertical axis and the letter x on the horizontal axis.

43.B Polar form of a complex number

The notations used for the polar form of a vector and the rectangular form of a vector are familiar. The rectangular and polar forms of the vector in the figure are written to the right of the figure.

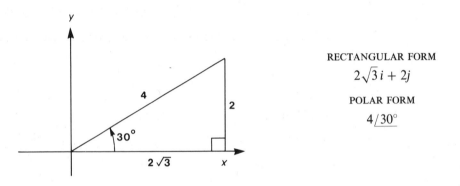

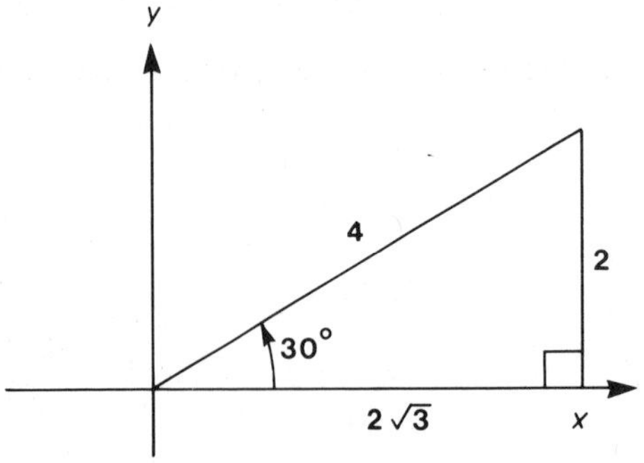

RECTANGULAR FORM

$2\sqrt{3}\,i + 2j$

POLAR FORM

$4\underline{/30^\circ}$

Unfortunately, the polar forms of the corresponding complex number $2\sqrt{3} + 2i$ can be confusing to the beginner. Some authors use an ordered pair (4, 30°) for the polar form of this number, but the notation used more often is

$$4(\cos 30^\circ + i \sin 30^\circ)$$

Since this is a rather cumbersome notation, many people use the notation cis as a shorthand for cos + i sin; and they write the polar form as

$$4 \text{ cis } 30^\circ$$

We will use this notation because it closely resembles the notation

$$4\underline{/30^\circ}$$

used for a vector of the same angle and magnitude. **The length of the hypotenuse of the triangle formed when we graph a complex number is called the *absolute value of the complex number*. So the absolute value of $2\sqrt{3} + 2i$ or 4 cis 30° is the number 4.**

$$|2\sqrt{3} + 2i| = 4$$

	RECTANGULAR FORM	POLAR FORM
Vector	$2\sqrt{3}i + 2j$	$4\underline{/30^\circ}$
Complex number	$2\sqrt{3} + 2i$	4 cis 30°

From time to time, we will use the notation $4(\cos 30^\circ + i \sin 30^\circ)$ instead of 4 cis 30° since the longer notation is used by so many authors.

43.C Sums and products of complex numbers

Complex numbers can be added when they are written in rectangular form by adding real parts to real parts and imaginary parts to imaginary parts. We will demonstrate by adding $(2\sqrt{3} + 2i)$ and $(2 + 2i)$.

$$(2\sqrt{3} + 2i) + (2 + 2i) = 2\sqrt{3} + 2i + 2 + 2i = (2\sqrt{3} + 2) + 4i$$

These numbers cannot be added when they are written in polar form unless the angles are equal or differ by 180°.

$$4 \text{ cis } 30° + 2\sqrt{2} \text{ cis } 45° = \text{cannot be added in this form}$$

Complex numbers can be multiplied in rectangular form or in polar form. To review multiplication of complex numbers in rectangular form, we will multiply $(2\sqrt{3} + 2i)(2 + 2i)$. We will use the vertical format.

$$\begin{array}{l} 2\sqrt{3} + 2i \\ \quad 2 + 2i \\ \hline 4\sqrt{3} + 4i \\ \quad 4\sqrt{3}i + 4i^2 \\ \hline 4\sqrt{3} + 4i + 4\sqrt{3}i - 4 = (4\sqrt{3} - 4) + (4 + 4\sqrt{3})i \end{array}$$

To graph this number, we use a calculator to help us get the decimal number equivalent $2.93 + 10.93i$.

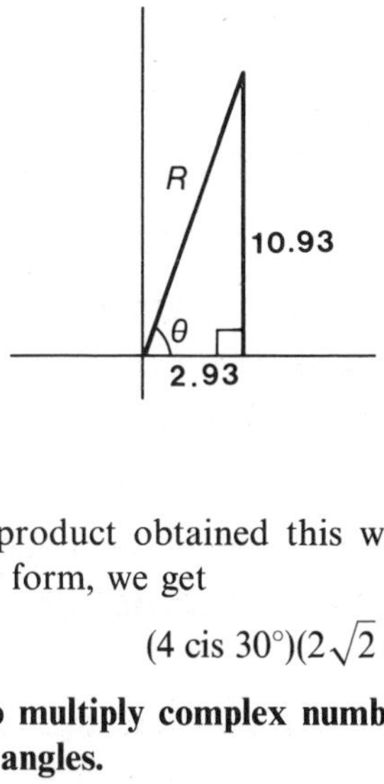

$$\tan\theta = \frac{10.93}{2.93} = 3.73$$

$$\theta = 75°$$

$$R = \sqrt{2.93^2 + 10.93^2} = 11.31$$

So the product obtained this way is **11.31 cis 75°**. If we multiply the same numbers in polar form, we get

$$(4 \text{ cis } 30°)(2\sqrt{2} \text{ cis } 45°) = 8\sqrt{2} \text{ cis } 75° = \mathbf{11.31 \text{ cis } 75°}$$

Thus, to multiply complex numbers in polar form, we multiply the absolute values and add the angles.

Example 43.C.1 Multiply $[5(\cos 20° + i \sin 20°)][6(\cos 42° + i \sin 42°)]$.

Solution First we rewrite the problem using a more familiar notation.

$$(5 \text{ cis } 20°)(6 \text{ cis } 42°)$$

We multiply complex numbers in polar form by multiplying the absolute values and adding the angles.

$$(5 \text{ cis } 20°)(6 \text{ cis } 42°) = \mathbf{30 \text{ cis } 62°}$$

Example 43.C.2 Multiply $(5 \text{ cis } 280°)(7 \text{ cis } 300°)$.

Solution Since the problem is already written in the more familiar notation, we simply multiply the magnitudes and add the angles.

$$(5 \text{ cis } 280°)(7 \text{ cis } 300°) = 35 \text{ cis } 580°$$
$$= \mathbf{35 \text{ cis } 220°}$$

The angles 580° and 220° are coterminal angles, and we normally try to express final results with angles that are between 0° and 360°.

Problem set 43

1. The cost varied linearly with the number of workers employed. When there were 10 workers on the job, the weekly cost was \$15,000. When there were 20 workers on the job, the weekly cost was \$20,000. What was the weekly cost when there were 30 workers on the job?

2. The front wheels had a diameter of 20 inches and they revolved at 75 radians per minute. What was the velocity of the car in kilometers per hour?

3. Maryjo traveled m miles in x hours and then traveled k miles in y hours. If she maintained her overall average rate, how long would it take her to travel 150 miles?

4. The little red car traveled m miles at r miles per hour. The little blue car also traveled m miles but at a slower rate of b miles per hour. How many hours more did it take the blue car to make the trip?

5. Jimmy bought k^2t pencils for d dollars. How many pencils could he buy for \$100?

6. How many three-digit numbers, all of whose digits are odd, are less than 400?

7. How many ways can 4 red marbles and 3 green marbles be arranged in a row?

8. (*a*) Convert $6 + 2i$ to polar form.
   (*b*) Express 5 cis 30° in the form $a + bi$. Use exact numbers.

9. Multiply (6 cis 300°)(2 cis 30°) and express the answer in rectangular form.

10. Multiply (3 cis 70°)(2 cis 110°) and express the answer in rectangular form.

11. Solve for y: $\begin{cases} cx + by = d \\ px + qy = f \end{cases}$

12. Evaluate: $\sum_{i=2}^{3} (2^i - 3^{i-2})(i)$

13. Find the distance between the point $(-4, 6)$ and the line $y - x + 4 = 0$.

Write the equations of the following sinusoids in terms of the cosine function.

14.

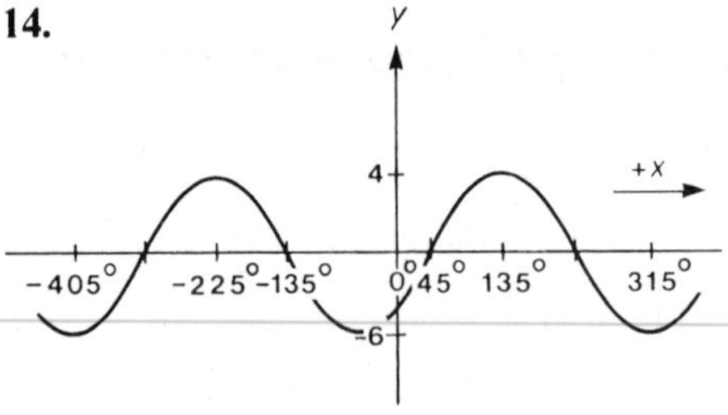

15.

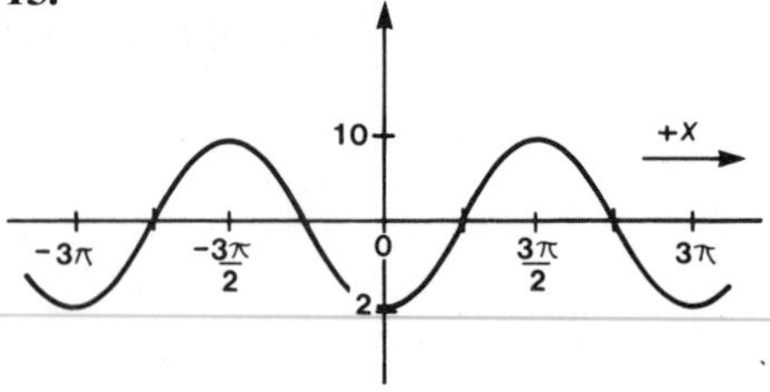

16. Find the area of this trapezoid in square centimeters.

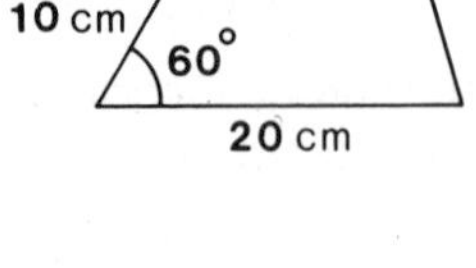

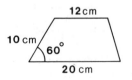

17. Find the area in square centimeters of the segment bounded by an arc of measure 130° and the chord which joins the endpoints of the arc in a circle whose radius is 0.3 meter.

18. The equation $x^2 + y^2 - 4x = 0$ is the equation of a circle. Complete the square to change this equation to standard form and then describe the circle.

19. Complete the square to change the equation of the circle $x^2 + y^2 + 6x - 4y - 9 = 0$ to standard form and describe the circle.

20. Use the locus definition method to find the equation of the perpendicular bisector of the line segment whose endpoints are $(-4, 6)$ and $(6, 8)$.

21. Solve for a and b.

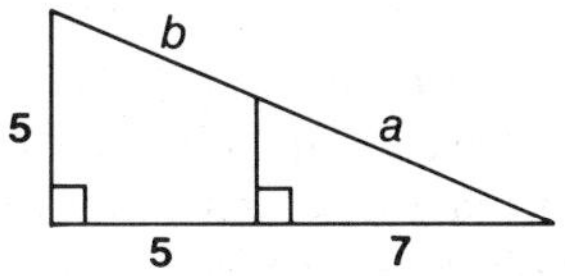

Solve the following equations given that $(0° \le \theta < 360°)$:

22. $\sin\theta - \dfrac{\sqrt{3}}{2} = 0$

23. $\tan\theta \sin\theta - \sin\theta = 0$

24. $\tan^2\theta - 3 = 0$

Evaluate:

25. $\cos^2\dfrac{5\pi}{4} - \sin^2\dfrac{5\pi}{4}$

26. $\tan^3 0° - \cot^2(-405°)$

27. $\sin\left[\text{Arcsin}\left(-\dfrac{8}{9}\right)\right]$

Solve for x:

28. $2\log_8 x = \log_8(2x - 1)$

29. $\log_3(x - 2) + \log_3 x = 1$

30. Simplify: $8^{2\log_8 13}$

LESSON 44 Radicals in trigonometric equations · Graphs of the logarithmic function

44.A Radicals in trigonometric equations

When radicals are encountered in equations, we isolate the radical and raise both sides to the power necessary to eliminate the radical. The equation

$$\sqrt{x-3} - 2 = 0$$

is solved by isolating the radical and then squaring both sides as we show here.

$$\sqrt{x-3} = 2 \qquad \text{isolated radical}$$
$$x - 3 = 4 \qquad \text{squared both sides}$$
$$x = 7 \qquad \text{solved}$$

The same procedure is used when radicals are encountered in trigonometric equations, as we demonstrate in the following example.

Example 44.A.1 Solve: $\sin x - \sqrt{1 - \sin^2 x} = 0$, given that $0° \le x < 360°$.

Solution This equation has a radical that we can eliminate by isolating the radical and squaring both sides.

$$\sin x = \sqrt{1 - \sin^2 x} \qquad \text{isolated radical}$$

$$\sin^2 x = 1 - \sin^2 x \qquad \text{squared both sides}$$

$$2\sin^2 x - 1 = 0 \qquad \text{rearranged}$$

Factoring will be easier if we first divide all terms in the equation by 2.

$$\sin^2 x - \frac{1}{2} = 0 \qquad \text{divided by 2}$$

Now, if we remember that $\frac{1}{2}$ can be written as a product as

$$\frac{1}{2} = \frac{1}{\sqrt{2}} \cdot \frac{1}{\sqrt{2}}$$

we can factor the equation and complete the solution.

$$\left(\sin x - \frac{1}{\sqrt{2}}\right)\left(\sin x + \frac{1}{\sqrt{2}}\right) = 0 \qquad \text{factored}$$

Next we equate both factors to zero and solve.

$$\sin x - \frac{1}{\sqrt{2}} = 0 \qquad\qquad \sin x + \frac{1}{\sqrt{2}} = 0$$

$$\sin x = \frac{1}{\sqrt{2}} \qquad\qquad \sin x = -\frac{1}{\sqrt{2}}$$

The sine of 45° is $1/\sqrt{2}$, and the sine is positive in the first and second quadrants and negative in the third and fourth quadrants.

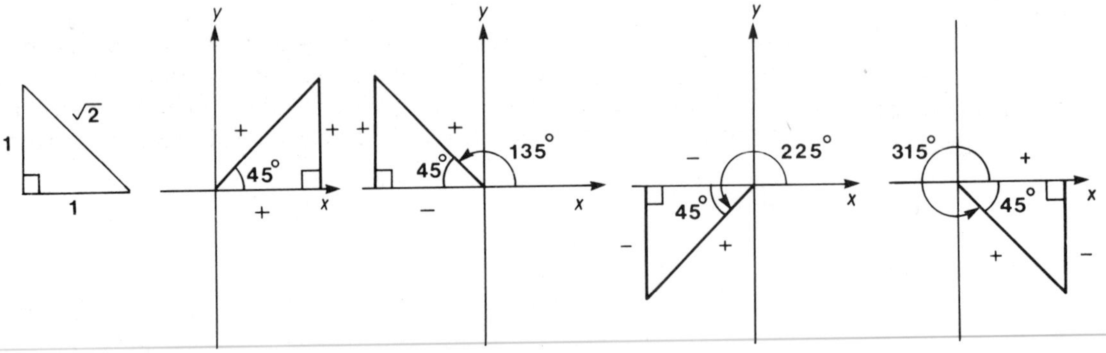

Thus it seems that 45°, 135°, 225°, 315° are solutions. But we must be careful. **In the first step we squared both sides of the equation, and raising both sides of an equation to a power often generates spurious roots in a solution.** If we check all four of these answers, we find that 225° and 315° are not roots of the original equation. We will use a calculator to provide decimal approximations for the values of the functions.

$$\sin 225° \stackrel{?}{=} \sqrt{1 - \sin^2 225°} \qquad\qquad \sin 315° \stackrel{?}{=} \sqrt{1 - \sin^2 315°}$$

$$-0.707 \stackrel{?}{=} \sqrt{1 - (-0.707)^2} \qquad\qquad -0.707 \stackrel{?}{=} \sqrt{1 - (-0.707)^2}$$

$$-0.707 \ne 0.707 \qquad\qquad -0.707 \ne 0.707$$

Thus **45°** and **135°** are the only solutions.

Example 44.A.2 Solve: $(\tan x - \sqrt{3})(\sin x + 1) = 0$, given that $0° \le x < 360°$.

Solution There is no need to eliminate the radical in this equation because there is no variable in the radicand. In fact, this equation is already in factored form so all we have to do is to equate each of the factors to 0 and solve.

$$\tan x - \sqrt{3} = 0 \qquad \sin x + 1 = 0$$
$$\tan x = \sqrt{3} \qquad \sin x = -1$$

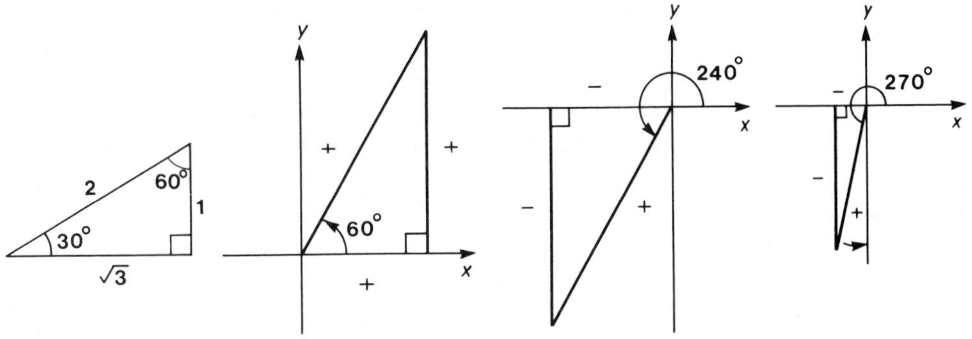

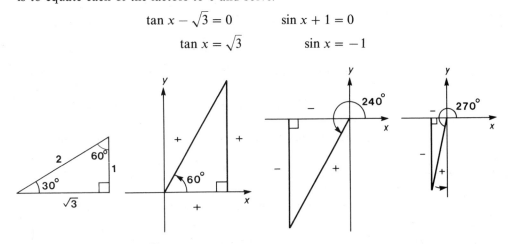

The tangent of 60° is $\sqrt{3}$, and the tangent is positive in the first and third quadrants, so two answers are 60° and 240°. It would seem that the third answer would be 270° because the sine of 270° is -1. But we must be cautious with problems that contain the tangent, cotangent, secant, or cosecant because these functions are not defined for all values of θ. If we try to check our solution by using 270° for θ,

$$(\tan 270° - 3)(\sin 270° + 1) = 0$$

we cannot evaluate the expression because the tangent of 270° is undefined.† Thus there are only two angles that satisfy the stated condition.

$$\mathbf{x = 60°, 240°}$$

44.B Graphs of the logarithmic function

Exponential functions can have as a base any positive number except the number 1. We have been graphing exponential functions whose bases are less than 1 and exponential functions whose bases are greater than 1. We remember that every exponential function can be rewritten as a logarithmic function. Therefore logarithms also can have bases that

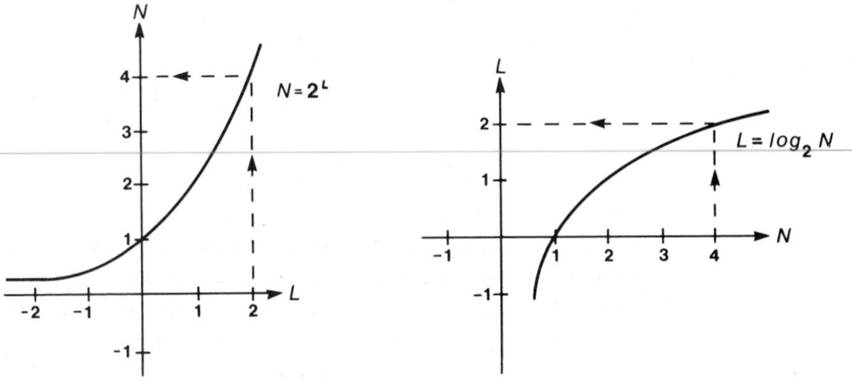

† Expressions such as this are interesting and will be considered further in more advanced courses. We note that as the value of x gets closer and closer to 270°, the absolute value of the first factor gets larger and larger. At the same time, the absolute value of the second term gets closer and closer to zero.

are positive numbers less than 1 or greater than 1. Because logarithms whose bases are less than 1 are rarely encountered, we will restrict our investigation of graphs of logarithmic functions to logarithmic functions whose bases are greater than 1.

When we graph functions, we always graph the independent variable on the horizontal axis and the dependent variable on the vertical axis. In the left-hand figure on page 227, L is the independent variable and N is the dependent variable.

In the right-hand figure on the same page, we graph the same ordered pairs, but change the names of the axes so that N is graphed horizontally and L is graphed vertically. To emphasize that both graphs on page 227 display the same information, we show on the left how the logarithm 2 is paired with the number 4, and on the right we show that the number 4 is paired with the logarithm 2. **Instead of using N and L in the equations, most mathematics books use x and y, and instead of relabeling the axes, they interchange the meaning of x and y on the graphs and in the equations. Thus, in the left-hand graph shown below, x stands for the logarithm, and in the right-hand graph, x stands for the number!**

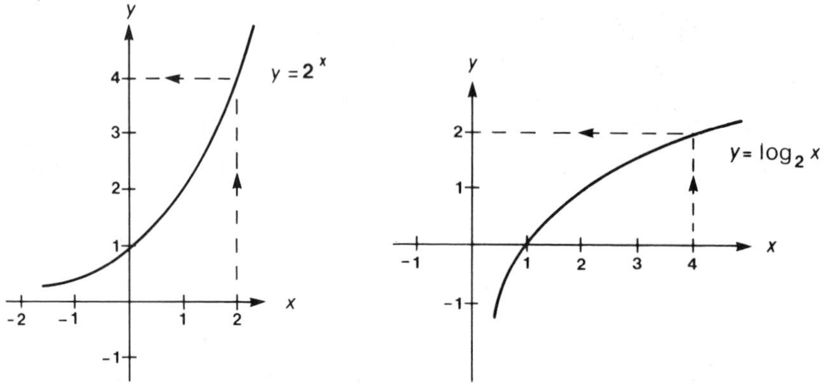

Both graphs present the same information, but because the exponent is the independent variable in the left-hand figure, the graph is considered to be the graph of the exponential function. Since the number is the independent variable in the right-hand figure, this graph is considered to be the graph of the logarithmic function.

If we put both graphs on the same set of axes, we find that the graphs are mirror images about the line $y = x$.

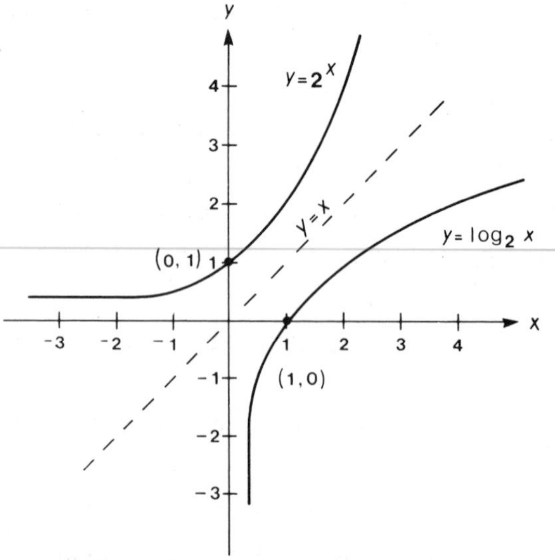

Since we already know how to graph exponentials, we see that we can graph logarithmic functions by graphing the exponential and then drawing its mirror image.

Example 44.B.1 Sketch $y = \log_{3.5} x$.

Solution We could graph the function directly, but we prefer to sketch the graph of the corresponding exponential equation and then sketch the mirror image about the line $y = x$. On the left we interchange x and y, and on the right we write the exponential form of this equation.

$$x = \log_{3.5} y \qquad y = 3.5^x$$

Now on the left we sketch the graph of $y = 3.5^x$, and on the right we repeat the sketch, dash in the line $y = x$, and draw the mirror image about this line, which is the logarithmic function $y = \log_{3.5} x$.

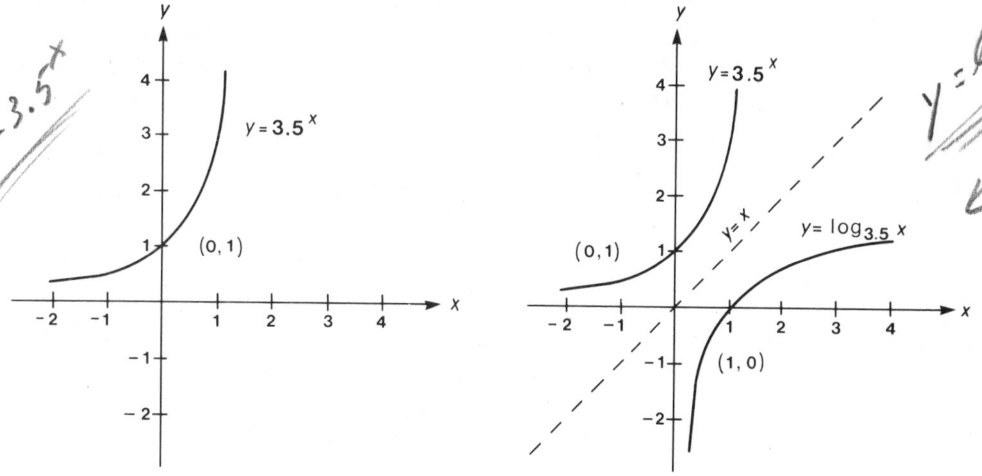

Note how one graph crosses at (0, 1) and the other graph crosses at (1, 0).

Problem set 44

1. The cost of doing business varied linearly with the number of hours the store was open. If the store was open 40 hours a week, the cost was \$1200; but if the store was open only 20 hours, the cost was \$800. What would it cost to keep the store open 30 hours a week?

2. The wheels on the car had a 30-centimeter radius, and the car was traveling at 45 kilometers per hour. What was the angular velocity of the wheels in radians per minute?

3. Sammy traveled m miles in h hours and then traveled x miles in $h + 4$ hours. At the same overall average rate, how long would it take her to travel 50 miles?

4. Peter traveled x miles at p miles per hour. Roger also traveled x miles but at a faster rate of R miles per hour. How many more hours did it take Peter to make the trip?

5. Helen bought $k^2x + m$ pencils for d dollars. How many pencils could she buy for \$500?

6. How many three-digit counting numbers all of whose digits are even are less than 401?

7. How many distinguishable permutations can be formed from the letters in the word *permute*?

8. Graph $y = \log_2 x$.

9. (*a*) Convert $3 + 5i$ to polar form.
   (*b*) Convert 6 cis 60° to rectangular form. Do not use the calculator and give an exact answer.

10. Multiply (5 cis 20°)(6 cis 70°) and express the answer in rectangular form. Give an exact answer.

11. Multiply [6 cis (−30°)](3 cis 90°) and express the answer in rectangular form. Give an exact answer.

12. Solve for x: $\begin{cases} ax + dy = g \\ cx + fy = h \end{cases}$

13. Given the ordered sets $X = \{3, -1, 0, 2\}$ and $Y = \{0, -2, 3\}$, evaluate $\sum_{j=1}^{3} (x_j y_j^2 - x_{j+1}^2)$.

Write the equations of the following sinusoids in terms of the sine function.

14.

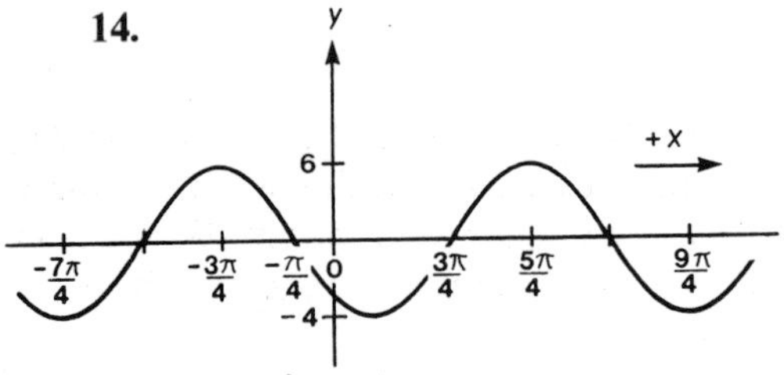

15.

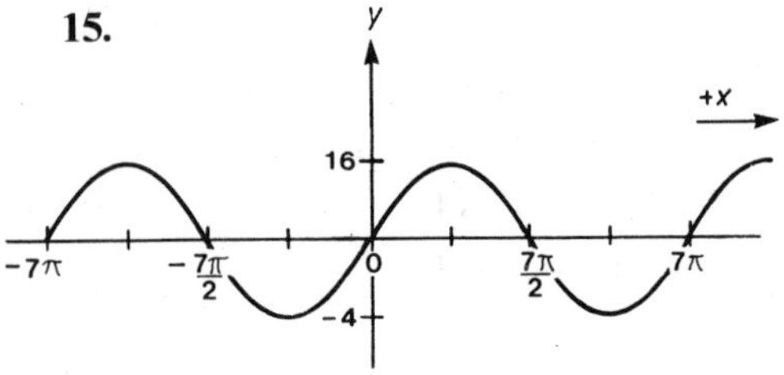

16. Find the area of this triangle in square meters.

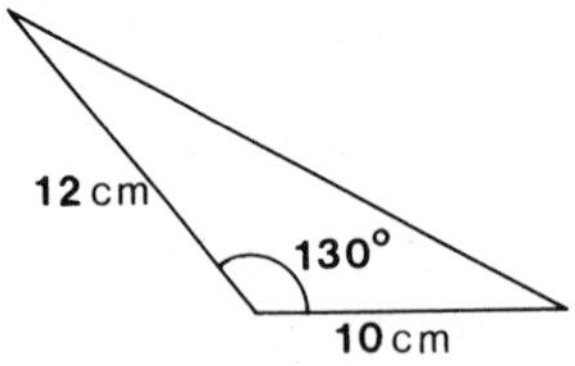

17. Convert 600 kilometers per hour to miles per hour.

18. Prove that vertical angles are equal.

19. The equation $x^2 + y^2 + 10x - 75 = 0$ is the equation of a circle. Change the form of the equation to standard form and give the radius and center of the circle.

20. The latitude of Albany is 42.6° north of the equator. What is the distance from Albany to the equator if the diameter of the earth is 7920 miles?

21. A boat travels downstream x miles at y knots and then travels the same distance upstream at z knots. What is the average speed for the entire trip?

Solve the following equations given that $(0° \le x, \theta < 360°)$:

22. $\left(\sin x - \frac{\sqrt{3}}{2}\right)\left(\sin x + \frac{1}{2}\right) = 0$

23. $\cos x - \sqrt{1 - \cos^2 x} = 0$

24. $\cos 3\theta - \frac{\sqrt{3}}{2} = 0$

Evaluate:

25. $\sin^3 \frac{\pi}{2} - \cos^2 \frac{\pi}{6}$

26. $\sin^2 \frac{19\pi}{6} + \cos^2 \frac{19\pi}{6}$

27. $\cos\left(\text{Arctan } \frac{6}{7}\right)$

Solve for x:

28. $2 \ln x = \ln (6 - x)$

29. $3 \ln x = \ln 8 + 3 \ln 2$

30. Simplify: $7^{2 \log_7 3} + 8^{\log_8 6 - \log_8 3}$

LESSON 45 Formulas for systems of equations · Phase shifts and period changes

45.A Formulas for systems of equations

If we solve a linear system that has abstract coefficients, we can develop formulas that can be used to solve any similar system. To develop a formula for x in a system of two equations and two unknowns, we will solve the system shown below. To solve, we first multiply the top equation by b_2 and the bottom equation by $-b_1$, and then add the resulting equations to eliminate the y terms.

$$\begin{cases} a_1x + b_1y = c_1 & \longrightarrow & (b_2) & \longrightarrow & a_1b_2x + b_1b_2y = \quad b_2c_1 \\ a_2x + b_2y = c_2 & \longrightarrow & (-b_1) & \longrightarrow & -a_2b_1x - b_1b_2y = -b_1c_2 \end{cases}$$
$$(a_1b_2 - a_2b_1)x = b_2c_1 - b_1c_2$$

We finish by dividing both sides of this equation by the coefficient of x.

$$x = \frac{b_2c_1 - b_1c_2}{a_1b_2 - a_2b_1} \qquad \text{(formula)}$$

Now if we are asked to solve the following system for x,

$$\begin{cases} 3x + 2y = 8 \\ 4x - 5y = 3 \end{cases}$$

we can note the correspondence between the coefficients in the two systems of equations. If, in the formula, we use 3, 2, and 8 for a_1, b_1, and c_1, respectively, and use 4, -5, and 3 for a_2, b_2, and c_2, respectively, we can solve for x.

$$x = \frac{b_2c_1 - b_1c_2}{a_1b_2 - a_2b_1} = \frac{(-5)(8) - (2)(3)}{(3)(-5) - (4)(2)} = \frac{-40 - 6}{-15 - 8} = \frac{-46}{-23} = \mathbf{2}$$

Example 45.A.1 Use abstract coefficients to find a formula for y and then use the formula to solve for y in the system shown here.

$$\begin{cases} 3x + 2y = 8 \\ 4x - 5y = 3 \end{cases}$$

Solution To find the formula, we will use the coefficients shown. To solve for y, we will multiply the top equation by $-a_2$ and the bottom equation by a_1.

$$\begin{cases} a_1x + b_1y = c_1 & \longrightarrow & (-a_2) & \longrightarrow & -a_1a_2x - a_2b_1y = -a_2c_1 \\ a_2x + b_2y = c_2 & \longrightarrow & (a_1) & \longrightarrow & a_1a_2x + a_1b_2y = a_1c_2 \end{cases}$$
$$(a_1b_2 - a_2b_1)y = a_1c_2 - a_2c_1$$

so

$$y = \frac{a_1c_2 - a_2c_1}{a_1b_2 - a_2b_1}$$

Now if we use 3, 2, and 8 for a_1, b_1, and c_1, respectively, and use 4, -5, and 3 for a_2, b_2, and c_2, we can solve for y.

$$y = \frac{a_1c_2 - a_2c_1}{a_1b_2 - a_2b_1} = \frac{(3)(3) - (4)(8)}{(3)(-5) - (4)(2)} = \frac{9 - 32}{-15 - 8} = \frac{-23}{-23} = 1$$

45.B Phase shifts and period changes

If the dependent variable y of a trigonometric function completes a full cycle of values as the independent variable θ changes 360°, we say that the period of the function is 360°. Thus, the function $y = \sin \theta$ has a period of 360°. If the dependent variable y completes a full cycle of values as the independent variable θ changes 180°, we say that the period of the function is 180°. Thus, the function $y = \sin 2\theta$ has a period of 180°. This reasoning can be used to show that $y = \sin 3\theta$ has a period of 120° and that $y = \sin \frac{1}{2}\theta$ has a period of 720°. Equations and graphs of sine functions that have periods other than 360° and that also have phase shifts are easier to write and to read if the argument is written in factored form. Here we show two forms of the same equation. Both equations tell us that the function has a period of 180° and a phase angle of +45°.

UNFACTORED ARGUMENT	FACTORED ARGUMENT
$y = \sin (2\theta - 90°)$	$y = \sin 2(\theta - 45°)$

In both forms we can see that θ is multiplied by 2, so the period is 180°, but in the unfactored form it is not easy to see that the phase angle is +45°. For this reason, we will concentrate on the factored form of the argument. To write the argument, we determine the period and the phase angle from the graph. **The coefficient of the argument is 360° divided by the period in degrees or 2π divided by the period in radians.** Thus, if the period is 180°, or π radians, the coefficient is 2.

$$\text{Coefficient} = \frac{360°}{180°} = 2 \qquad \text{or} \qquad \text{Coefficient} = \frac{2\pi}{\pi} = 2$$

We remember that any sinusoid can be expressed either as a sine function with a phase shift or as a cosine function with a phase shift. **The phase angle for a sine function is the angle where the graph of the curve crosses its centerline on the way up. If the curve crosses at +90°, the sine phase angle is +90° and the argument is $C(\theta - 90°)$, where C is the coefficient just defined. The phase angle for a cosine function is the angle for which the value of the function is a maximum. If the maximum value occurs when θ equals +120°, the cosine phase angle is +120° and the cosine argument is $C(\theta - 120°)$.**

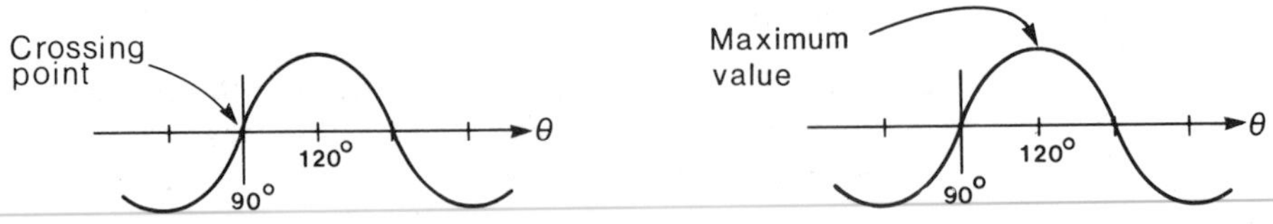

SINE ARGUMENT	COSINE ARGUMENT
$C(\theta - 90°)$	$C(\theta - 120°)$

The general forms of the equations are

$$y = A + B \sin C(\theta - D) \qquad \text{and} \qquad y = A + B \cos C(\theta - D)$$

where A is the value of the centerline, B is the amplitude, C is 360° divided by the period in degrees or 2π divided by the period in radians, and D is the phase angle. We note again that **the argument always displays the negative of the phase angle.**

Example 45.B.1 Write both the sine and cosine equations of this sinusoid.

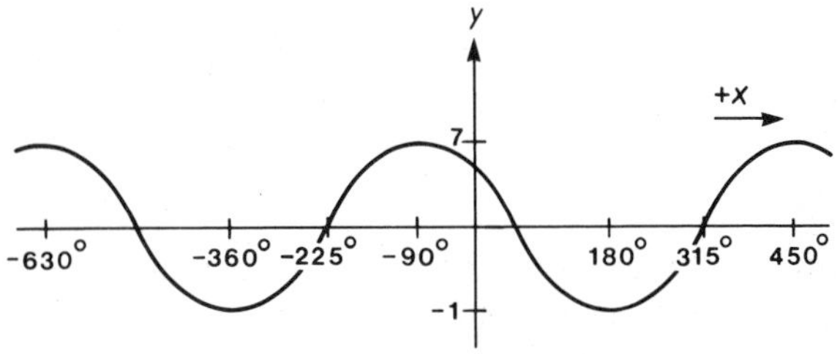

Solution We see that the centerline is $+3$ and that the amplitude is 4. This graph uses x instead of θ, so our equations are

$$y = 3 + 4 \sin C(x - D) \quad \text{and} \quad y = 3 + 4 \cos C(x - D)$$

The period can be measured between any two like points on the curve. We decide to use successive low points and find the distance between $-360°$ and $+180°$ to be $540°$. The coefficient of the argument is $360°$ divided by the period, so

$$\text{Coefficient} = \frac{360°}{540°} = \frac{2}{3}$$

$$\longrightarrow \quad y = 3 + 4 \sin \frac{2}{3}(x - D) \quad \text{and} \quad y = 3 + 4 \cos \frac{2}{3}(x - D)$$

The curve crosses its centerline on the way up when x equals $-225°$ and has a maximum value when x equals $-90°$. The negatives of these angles appear in the arguments, so the equations of this function are

$$\boldsymbol{y = 3 + 4 \sin \frac{2}{3}(x + 225°) \quad \text{or} \quad y = 3 + 4 \cos \frac{2}{3}(x + 90°)}$$

The period for this function is $540°$, so the curve repeats itself every $540°$. Thus the angles in the arguments could be increased or decreased by multiples of $540°$ and still be correct. It is customary to write the phase angle using the angle with the least absolute value, as we did in this example.

Problem set 45

1. The wheels on Danny's Bobcat had a diameter of 26 inches. If he was traveling at 12 miles per hour, what was the angular velocity of the wheels in radians per minute?

2. The cost of the landfill varied linearly with the loads of dirt required. If 10 loads were used, the cost was \$1350. If 20 loads were used, the cost was \$2200. What would a landfill of only 5 loads cost?

3. Ralph traveled k miles in p hours and then traveled z miles in $p + 6$ hours. At the overall average rate, how long would it take Ralph to travel 740 miles?

4. Mumbo traveled m miles at a miles per hour. Jumbo also traveled m miles but at a faster rate of z miles per hour. How much longer did it take Mumbo to make the trip?

5. At the used car sale, Harry purchased p^2k cars for m dollars. How many cars could he have purchased for \$10,000?

6. Theresa arranged 6 blue ones and 3 green ones in a row. How many arrangements were possible?

7. How many different ways can 6 chickens be arranged in a circle?

8. Graph $y = \log_3 x$.

9. (*a*) Convert $4 + 3i$ to polar form.
(*b*) Convert 5 cis 150° to rectangular form. Do not use the calculator and give exact answers.

10. Multiply (3 cis 40°)[2 cis (−50°)] and express the answer in polar form.

11. Multiply [8 cis (−450°)](2 cis 60°) and express the answer in rectangular form. Give an exact answer.

12. Solve for x: $\begin{cases} ax + by = c \\ dx + fy = g \end{cases}$

13. Use the result of Problem 12 to solve for x: $\begin{cases} 3x + 2y = 6 \\ 2x - 4y = 12 \end{cases}$

14. Given the ordered sets $X = \{2, -1, \frac{1}{3}, 4\}$ and $Y = \{\frac{1}{4}, -3, 4\}$, evaluate: $\sum_{i=1}^{3} 2^{i+1} x_{i+1} y_i$

Write the equation of Problem 15 as a sine function and the equation of Problem 16 as a cosine function.

15.

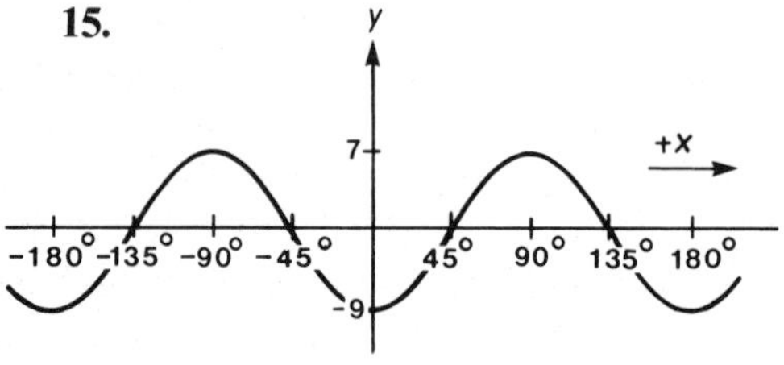

16.

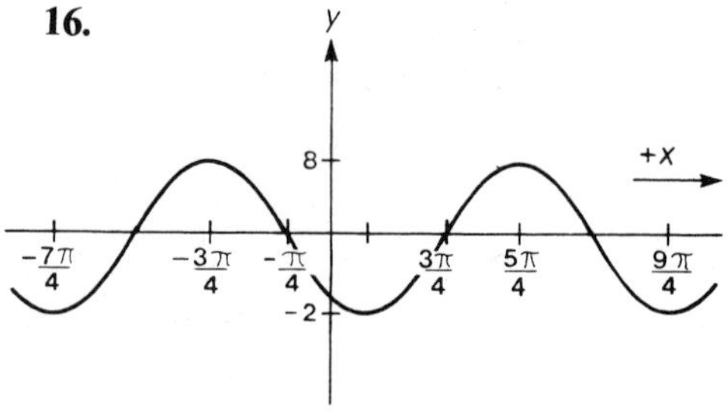

17. Find the area of this trapezoid in square meters.

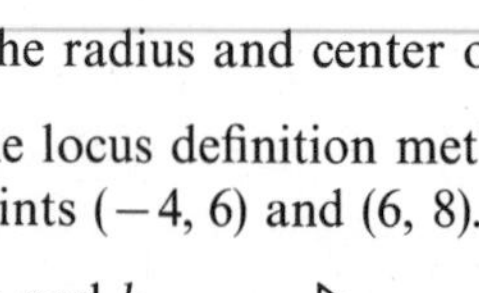

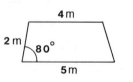

18. Find the area in square centimeters of the segment bounded by an arc of measure 140° and the chord which joins the endpoints of the arc in a circle whose radius is 0.4 meter.

19. $x^2 + y^2 + 6x + 4y + 12 = 0$ is the equation of a circle. Find the radius and center of this circle.

20. Find the radius and center of the circle $x^2 - 8x + y^2 + 6y = -16$.

21. Use the locus definition method to find the equation of the line equidistant from the points (−4, 6) and (6, 8). Express the equation in general form.

22. Find a and b.

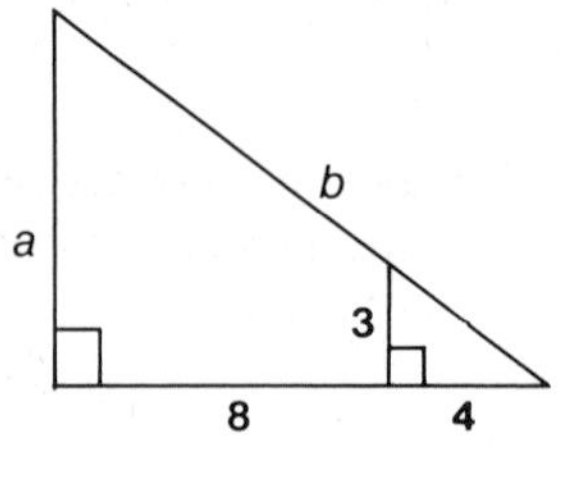

Solve the following equations given that ($0° \le \theta, x < 360°$):

23. $(\cos x - \frac{1}{2})(\sin x + \frac{1}{2}) = 0$

24. $\tan x - \sqrt{1 - 2\tan^2 x} = 0$

25. $\sin 4\theta - \dfrac{1}{2} = 0$

Evaluate:

26. $\cot^2 \dfrac{4\pi}{3} - \tan^2 210°$

27. $\sin^2(-420°) + \sin^2 420°$

28. $\tan\left(\text{Arcsin}\,\dfrac{8}{9}\right)$

Solve for x:

29. $2 \ln x = \ln(6x - 8)$

30. $3 \log_{12} x = \frac{3}{4} \log_{12} 16 + \frac{3}{2} \log_{12} 4$

LESSON 46 Antilogarithms

46.A Antilogarithms

The exponent is the logarithm, and the number is the antilogarithm. If we are given a value and asked for its antilogarithm, we have been given the exponent and asked for the number. The procedure for finding an antilogarithm in base 10 is straightforward, since our number system also has a base of 10. This is the reason that base 10 logarithms have been used historically for calculations. Antilogarithms in base e and bases other than 10 are also useful. We will work with base e and do a lot of estimation for working problems in bases other than 10 since these problems help the development of an understanding of logarithms in general.

Example 46.A.1 If the base is 10, use a table of logarithms to find the antilogarithm of 4.63.

Solution We have been given the exponent 4.63, so we have

$$10^{4.63}$$

Next we write $10^{4.63}$ as $10^{0.63}$ times 10^4:

$$10^{4.63} = 10^{0.63} \times 10^4$$

Now we use the table to find that the number 4.3 is paired with the exponent 0.63, so the antilog is

$$10^{4.63} = 10^{0.63} \times 10^4 = \mathbf{4.3 \times 10^4}$$

Example 46.A.2 Use a table of logarithms to find the base 10 antilogarithm of -4.52.

Solution The expression we wish to evaluate is

$$10^{-4.52}$$

The logarithm table contains only positive decimal numbers, so we must use a trick. We add $+5$ and -5 to the exponent for a net addition of zero. The $+5$ we add to the -4.52 and the -5 we retain.

$$10^{-4.52} = 10^{(-4.52+5)-5} = 10^{0.48} \times 10^{-5}$$

Now we use the log table and find that the number 3.0 is paired with the logarithm 0.48. Thus, we have

$$10^{-4.52} = 10^{0.48} \times 10^{-5} = \mathbf{3.0 \times 10^{-5}}$$

Example 46.A.3 Estimate the base e antilog of 5.6.

Solution We can get a reasonable estimate of

$$e^{5.6}$$

if we approximate e with the number 3. Since 3 is greater than e, we will use an exponent less than 5.6.

$$3^5 = \mathbf{243}$$

This is a reasonable estimate, as the value from a calculator is

$$e^{5.6} = 270.42641$$

Example 46.A.4 Estimate the base e antilog of 7.5.

Solution Again we use 3 as our estimate of e and we use 7 as the exponent.

$$3^7 = \mathbf{2187}$$

This estimate is very rough, as the calculator gives a more exact answer as

$$e^{7.5} = 1808.0424$$

Example 46.A.5 Estimate $\text{antilog}_e\,(-3.2)$.

Solution We need to evaluate

$$e^{-3.2} \qquad \text{which is} \qquad \frac{1}{e^{3.2}}$$

If we use 3^3 as an estimate of $e^{3.2}$, we get

$$\frac{1}{3^3} = \frac{1}{27} = \mathbf{0.037}$$

which is reasonably close to the value we get from a calculator, which is

$$e^{-3.2} = 0.0407622$$

Problem set 46

1. Three dozen eggs and 5 pounds of flour cost \$5.50. Four dozen eggs and 2 pounds of flour cost \$5. What is the price of 1 dozen eggs and what is the cost of 1 pound of flour?

2. The tens digit of a two-digit counting number is 1 greater than the units digit. If the digits are reversed, the new number is smaller than the original number by an amount equal to the original tens digit. What was the original number?

3. The units digit of a two-digit counting number is 1 greater than twice the tens digit. When the digits are reversed, the sum of the new number and the original number is 77. What was the original number?

4. The speed of a boat in still water is 16 miles per hour greater than the speed of the current in the river. The boat can go 48 miles downstream in the same time it takes to go 32 miles upstream. What is the speed of the boat in still water, and what is the speed of the current?

5. Mickmak was 2 kilometers upstream from his starting point when he encountered a log floating downstream. Mickmak rowed upstream 1 more hour and then headed downstream. He got back to the starting point at the same time the log got there. What was the speed of the current in the river? (See the answer in the appendix.)

6. How many three-digit numbers can be formed from the digits 1, 2, 3, 4, and 5 if no digits are repeated in the number?

7. Graph $y = \ln x$.

8. Convert $5 + 12i$ to polar form.

9. Multiply $(4 \text{ cis } 20°)(2 \text{ cis } 40°)$ and express the answer in rectangular form. Give an exact answer.

10. Multiply $[3 \text{ cis } (-200°)](2 \text{ cis } 50°)$ and express the answer in rectangular form. Give an exact answer.

11. Solve for y: $\begin{cases} cx + fy = a \\ dx + gy = b \end{cases}$

12. Use the result of Problem 11 to solve for y: $\begin{cases} 2x - 3y = 5 \\ 3x + 2y = 7 \end{cases}$

13. Given the ordered sets $X = \{-2, 2, \frac{1}{4}, -2\}$ and $Y = \{0, -2, 3\}$, evaluate $\sum_{k=1}^{3} (2^{k-1}x_{k+1} - y_k^2)$.

Write the equation of Problem 14 as a sine function and the equation of Problem 15 as a cosine function.

14.

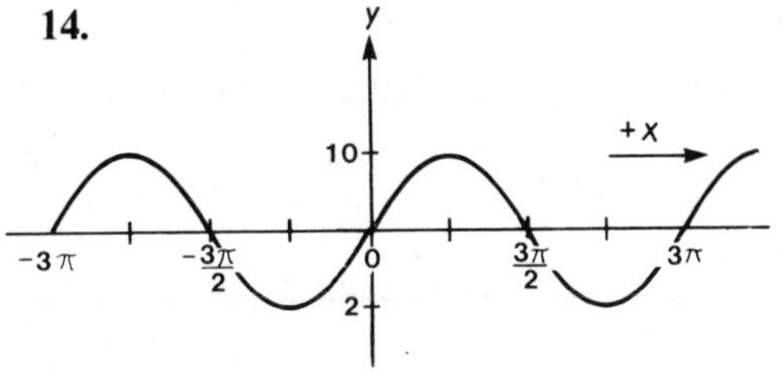

15.

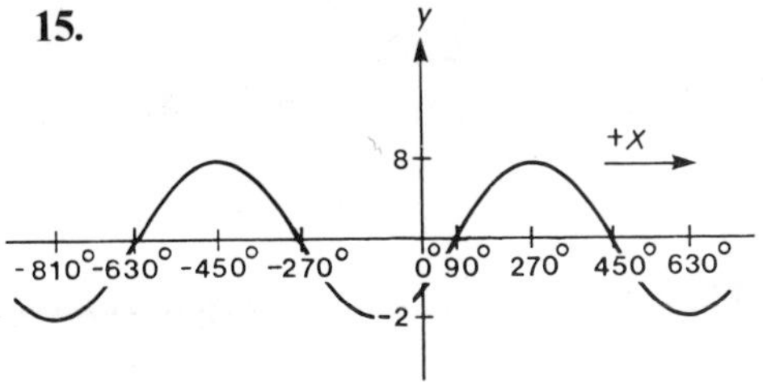

16. Find the area of this triangle in square meters.

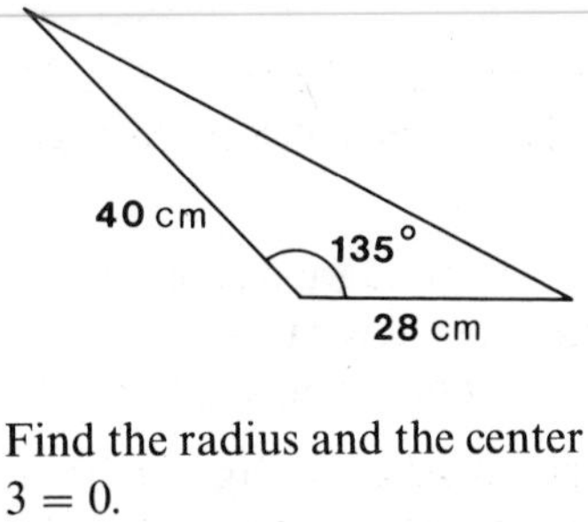

17. Factor $x^2 - 4x + 6$ over the set of complex numbers.

18. Find the radius and the center of the circle whose equation is $x^2 + y^2 - 4x + 6y - 3 = 0$.

19. If $1 < x < 5$ and $1 < y < 5$, compare: *A.* $x - y$ *B.* $y - x$

Solve the following equations given that $(0° \le \theta < 360°)$:

20. $(\tan\theta + 1)(\cos\theta - \frac{1}{2}) = 0$

21. $\sqrt{\sin\theta} - \dfrac{\sqrt{2}}{2} = 0$

22. $\cos 3\theta - \dfrac{1}{2} = 0$

Evaluate:

23. $\tan^2(-405°) - \sec^2(-405°)$

24. $\sin^2\dfrac{13\pi}{6} + \cos^2\dfrac{13\pi}{6}$

25. Arcsin (sin 210°)

Solve for x:

26. $\ln x + \ln x = \ln(4x - 3)$

27. $3\log_7 x = \log_7 16 - \log_7 2$

28. Using the tables only, find $\text{antilog}_{10}(-5.62)$.

29. Estimate $\text{antilog}_e 2$.

30. Estimate $\text{antilog}_e(-2)$.

LESSON 47 Transversals; alternate and corresponding angles · Angles in triangles

47.A Transversals; alternate and corresponding angles

A ***transversal*** is a line that cuts or intersects one or more other lines in the same plane. **When two parallel lines are cut by a transversal, two groups of four equal angles are formed. The four small (acute) angles are equal angles, and the four large (obtuse) angles are equal angles. If the transversal is perpendicular to the parallel lines, all eight angles are right angles.**

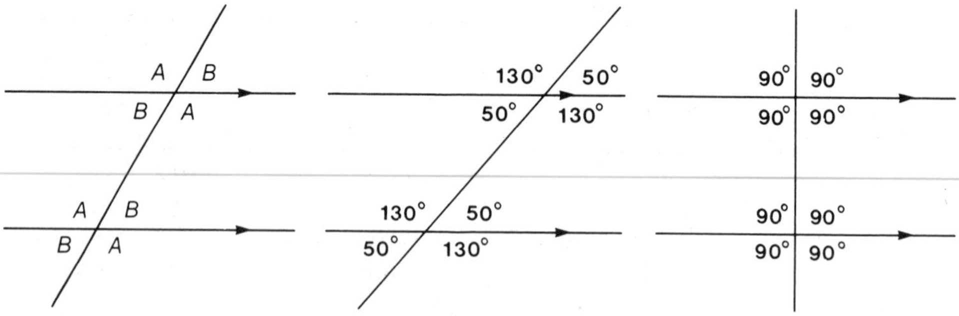

In the figures above, note the use of arrowheads to indicate that lines are parallel. In the left-hand figure, we have named the small angles B and the large angles A. In the center figure, we show a specific example where the small angles are 50° angles, and the large angles are 130° angles. Also, note that **in each case, the sum of a small angle and a large angle is 180° because together the two angles always form a straight line.** The angles have special names that are useful. The four angles between the parallel lines are called ***interior angles***, and the four angles outside the parallel lines are called ***exterior angles.***

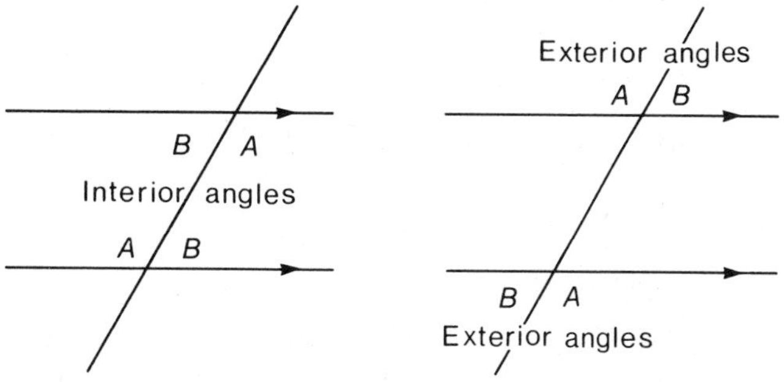

Angles on opposite sides of the transversal are called ***alternate*** angles. It is important to note that **alternate interior angles are equal and that alternate exterior angles are equal.**

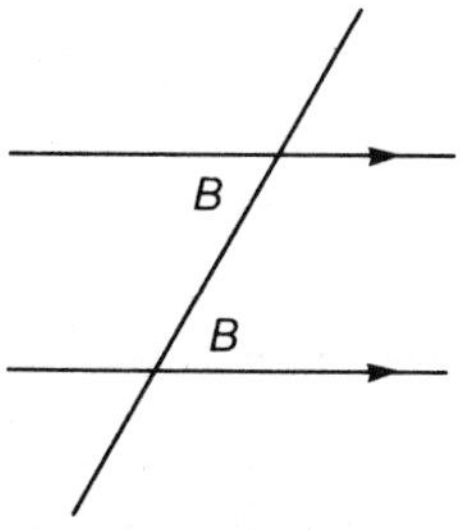

ALTERNATE INTERIOR ANGLES

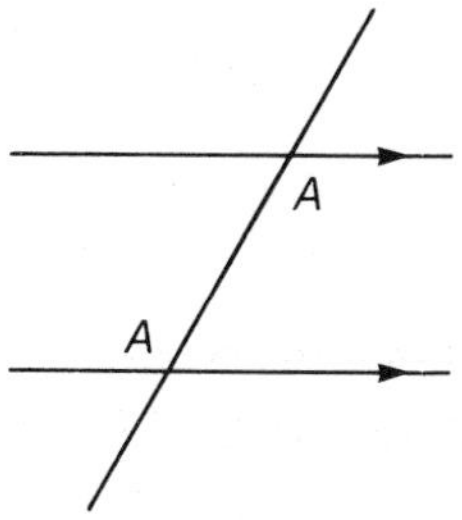

ALTERNATE INTERIOR ANGLES

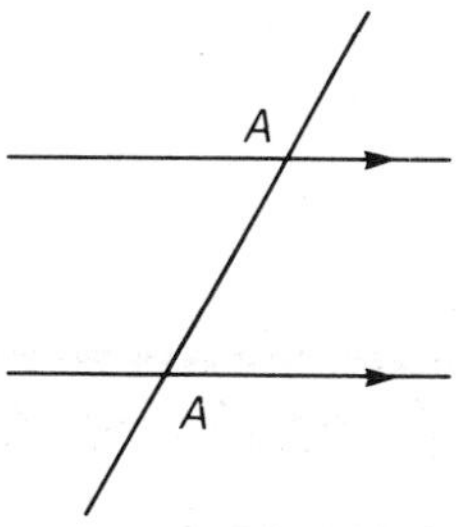

ALTERNATE EXTERIOR ANGLES

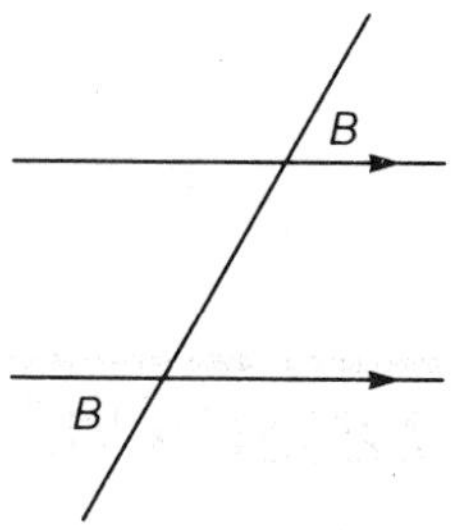

ALTERNATE EXTERIOR ANGLES

We also note that **corresponding angles are equal.** Corresponding angles have corresponding positions in the figure. Thus, the angles above the parallel lines and to the left of the transversal are corresponding, as shown on the left below. There are four pairs of corresponding angles.

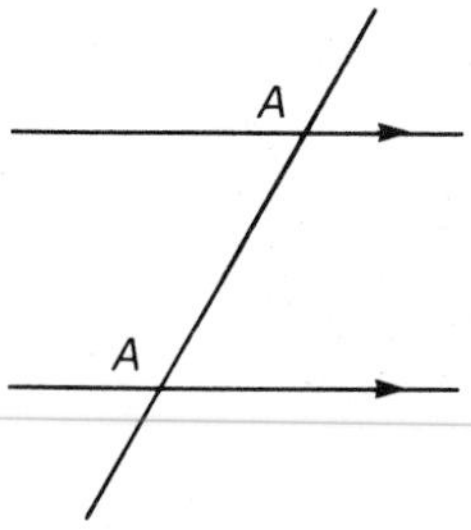

CORRESPONDING ANGLES

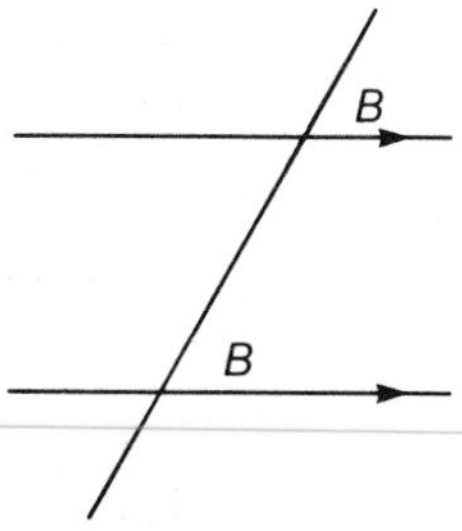

CORRESPONDING ANGLES

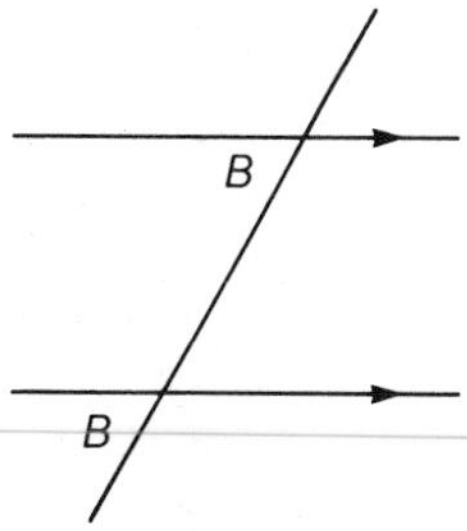

CORRESPONDING ANGLES

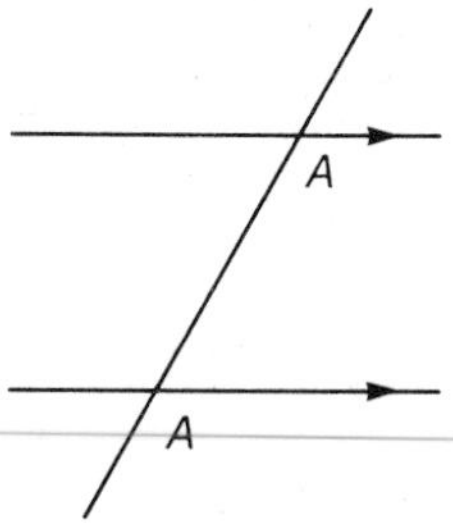

CORRESPONDING ANGLES

It would be nice if we could prove that the four small angles are equal angles and that the four large angles are equal angles. We cannot prove this because we do not have enough facts on which to base a proof. **But if we assume half of what we wish to prove is true, we can then prove that the rest is true.** We must begin by assuming (*a*) that the alternate interior angles are equal, or (*b*) that the alternate exterior angles are equal, or (*c*) that the corresponding angles are equal. As we noted in Lesson 17, an unproven assumption is called a ***postulate.*** We decide to postulate (assume without proof) that when parallel lines are cut by a transversal, the alternate interior angles are equal. We also postulate that if the alternate interior angles are equal, then the lines are parallel. We label the equal angles *A* and *B*.

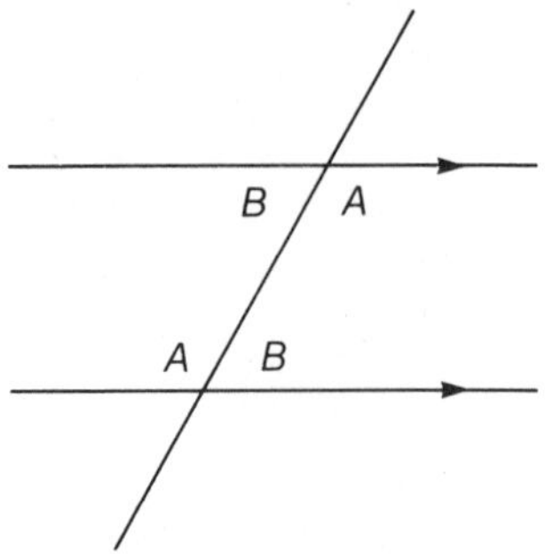

We have already proved that vertical angles are equal, and if we now use this fact, we can label the remaining four angles.

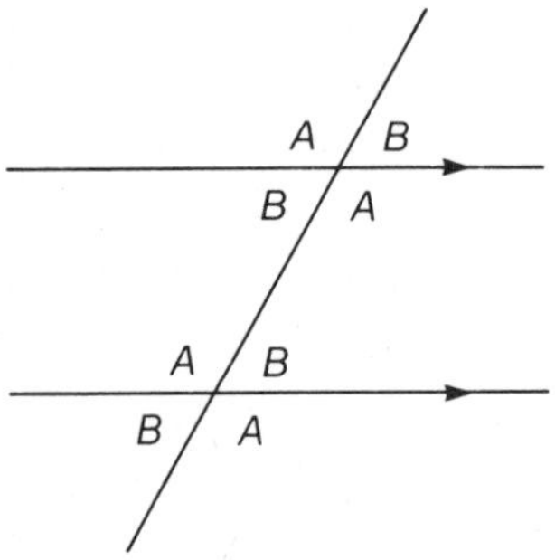

We note that we were forced to postulate most of what we wanted to prove.

Example 47.A.1 Find x, y, a, p, c, and d.

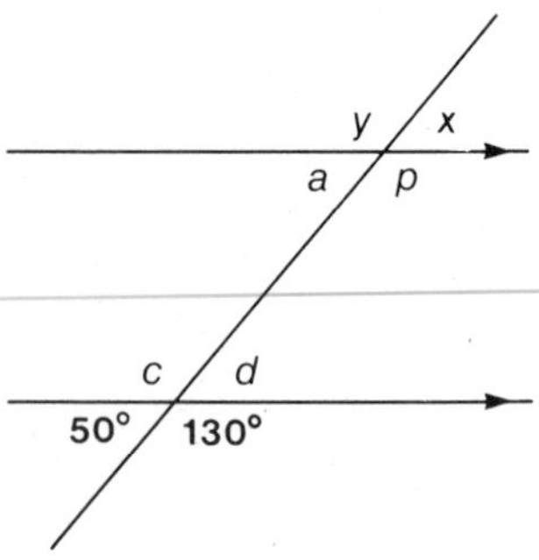

Solution We know that when parallel lines are cut by a transversal, the four small angles are equal and the four large angles are equal. Thus,

$\angle c = \angle p = \angle y = 130°$	large angles are equal
$\angle d = \angle a = \angle x = 50°$	small angles are equal

Example 47.A.2 Given $\angle A = (2x + 3y)^\circ$, $\angle I = 70^\circ$, and $\angle C = (3x + 5y)^\circ$, find x and y.

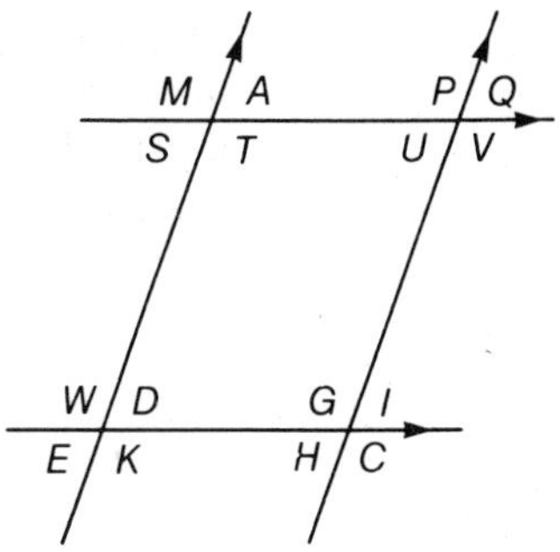

Solution Angle A equals angle D equals angle I because they are corresponding angles.

$$2x + 3y = 70$$

Angle C and angle I sum to 180° (are supplementary), so angle C equals 110°. Thus,

$$3x + 5y = 110$$

We multiply the first equation by -3 and the second equation by $+2$ to solve.

$$\begin{aligned} 2x + 3y &= 70 \longrightarrow (-3) \longrightarrow & -6x - 9y &= -210 \\ 3x + 5y &= 110 \longrightarrow (2) \longrightarrow & 6x + 10y &= 220 \\ & & \hline \mathbf{y} &= \mathbf{10} \end{aligned}$$

Now we solve for x.

$$2x + 3(10) = 70 \longrightarrow 2x = 40 \longrightarrow \mathbf{x = 20}$$

47.B Angles in triangles

We have been using the fact that the sum of the angles in a triangle equals 180°. Now we are in a position to prove this statement.

Example 47.B.1 Prove that the sum of the angles in a triangle is 180°.

Solution We could call this proof the ABC proof because we will use these letters in the proof. On the left we draw a triangle and through one vertex we draw a line parallel to the opposite side. We use arrowheads to indicate that the lines are parallel. We label the top three angles A, B, and C, as shown.

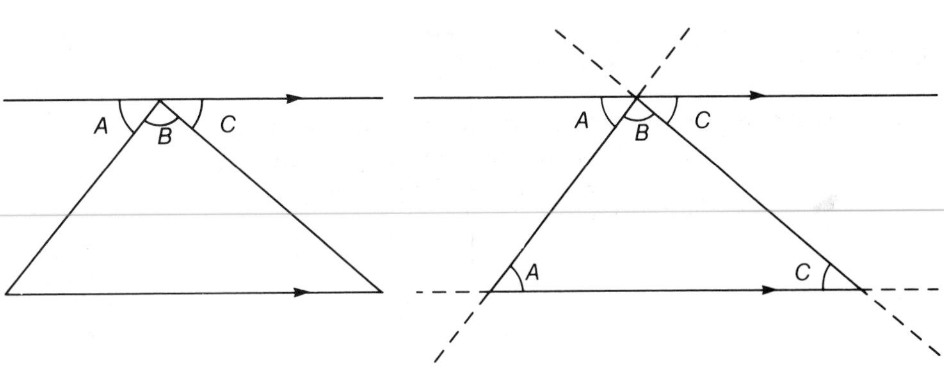

On the right we extend the sides of the triangle and note that we have parallel lines cut by two transversals. We remember that alternate interior angles are equal, and this allows us to label the bottom angles in the triangle A and C as shown. Now the sum of the top angles A, B, and C is 180° because they form a straight angle. Since the three angles in the triangle also have measures A, B, and C, we can see that they also sum to 180°.

Example 47.B.2 Prove that if two angles in one triangle equal two angles in a second triangle, the third angles are equal.

Solution First we draw two triangles that contain the equal angles A and B.

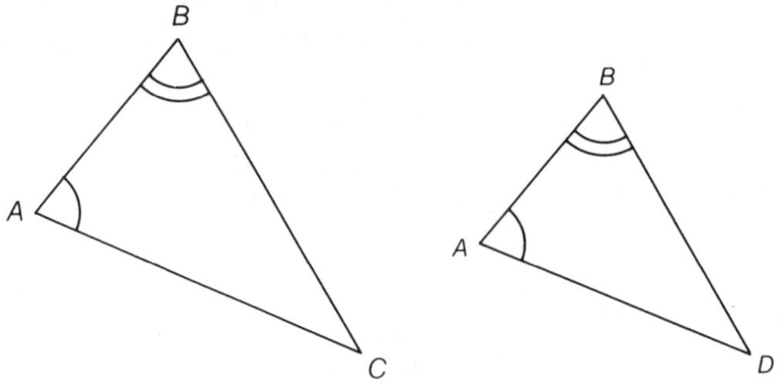

Now we want to prove that angles C and D are equal. If angle C equals angle D, then all three corresponding angles are equal. We will note that each triangle contains 180° and then use substitution to complete the proof.

$\angle A + \angle B + \angle C = 180°$	triangle contains 180°
$\angle A + \angle B + \angle D = 180°$	triangle contains 180°
$\angle A + \angle B + \angle C = \angle A + \angle B + \angle D$	substituted
$\angle C = \angle D$	subtracted $\angle A$ and $\angle B$

Example 47.B.3 Prove that an **exterior angle** of a triangle is equal to the sum of the **remote interior angles.**

Solution An exterior angle of a polygon is the angle formed when any side of the polygon is extended. On the left below we show a triangle with angles A, B, and C. On the right we extend the sides at A to form vertical angle A and exterior angles A' and A'. Angles B and C are on the far side of the triangle from the angles A', so angles B and C are called **remote interior angles.**

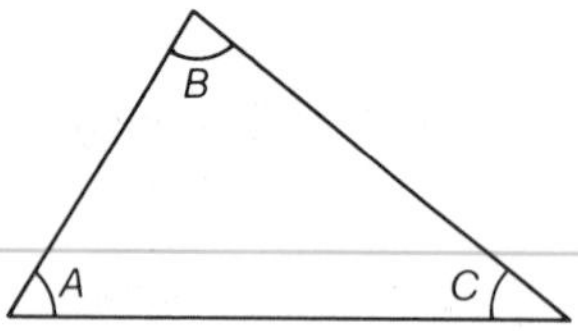

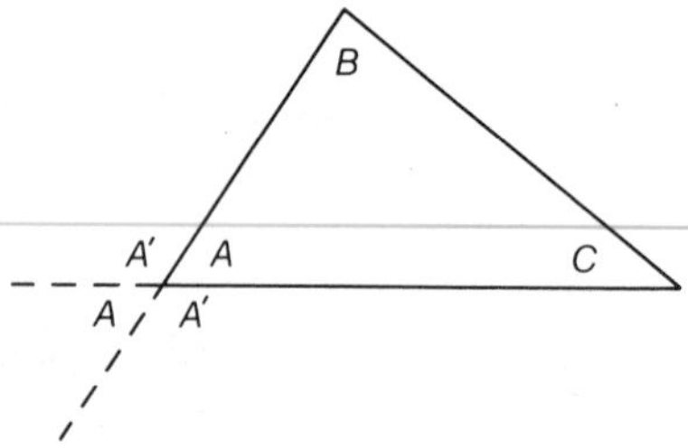

The sum of angles A, B, and C in the triangle is 180°, and the sum of angles A and A' is 180° because they form a **straight angle.**

$\angle A + \angle B + \angle C = 180°$	triangle
$\angle A + \angle A' = 180°$	straight angle

Since both sums equal 180°, they equal each other.

$$\angle A + \angle B + \angle C = \angle A + \angle A'$$

If we add the opposite of $\angle A$ to both sides, we get

$$\begin{array}{rr} \angle A + \angle B + \angle C = & \angle A + \angle A' \\ -\angle A \qquad\qquad\qquad & -\angle A \qquad \\ \hline \angle B + \angle C = & \angle A' \end{array}$$

This finishes the proof and shows that the measure of an exterior angle of a triangle equals the sum of the measures of the remote interior angles.

Example 47.B.4 Find angle A and angle C.

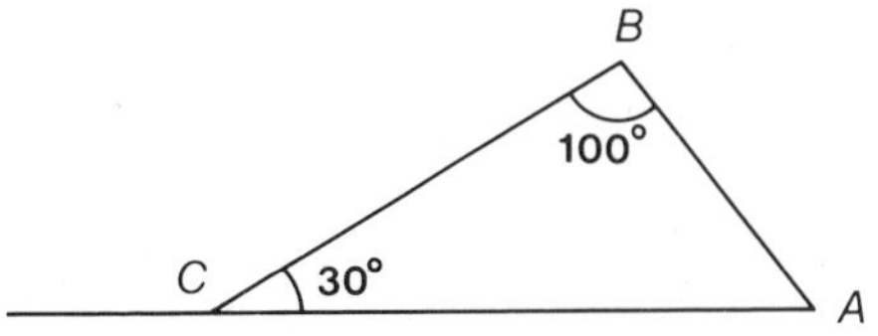

Solution The sum of the angles in a triangle equals 180°, so **angle A must be 50°.**

$$30° + 100° + 50° = 180°$$

The exterior angle equals the sum of the remote interior angles, so angle C equals 150°.

$$\angle C = 100° + 50° = \mathbf{150°}$$

Example 47.B.5 Prove that if the lengths of two sides of a triangle are not equal, then the angles opposite these sides are not equal and the angle opposite the longer side is the larger angle.

Solution We begin with the triangle on the left in which $AC > CB$. Then, in the figure on the right, we locate point X on $\overline{AC}$ and draw $\overline{XB}$ so that the length of $\overline{CX}$ equals the length of $\overline{CB}$.

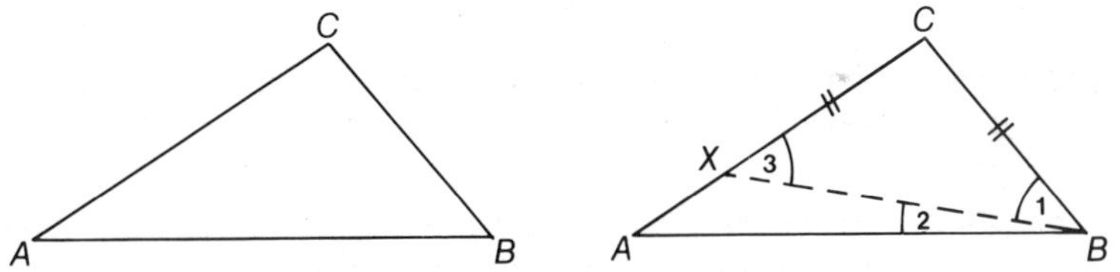

We have postulated that the base angles of an isosceles triangle are equal, so $\angle 3$ equals $\angle 1$. Now, since $\angle 3$ is an exterior angle of triangle AXB, it equals the sum of $\angle A$ and $\angle 2$.

$$\angle 3 = \angle A + \angle 2$$

Thus, $\angle 3$ is greater than $\angle A$, and so $\angle 1$ is greater than $\angle A$.

$$\angle 3 > \angle A$$

$$\angle 1 > \angle A \qquad \text{substitution}$$

Since $\angle ABC$ equals the sum of $\angle 1$ and $\angle 2$, then $\angle ABC$ is greater than $\angle 1$, which is greater than $\angle A$. Thus $\angle ABC$ is greater than $\angle A$.

$$\angle ABC > \angle A$$

We began with the fact that side CA is greater than side CB and showed that this leads to the fact that the angle opposite side CA is greater than the angle opposite side CB.

Example 47.B.6 Prove that, if two angles of a triangle are not equal, then the sides opposite these angles are not equal and the side opposite the larger angle is the longer side.

Solution We draw triangle ABC and are given that angle B is greater than angle A.

$$\angle B > \angle A$$

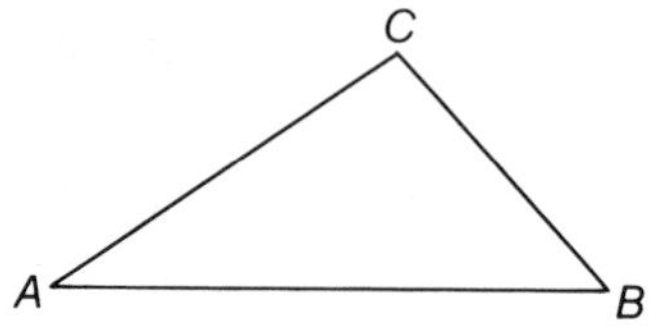

Now side AC is either equal to side CB, less than side CB, or greater than side CB. We will show that it is not equal to or less than, so it must be greater than. This is a type of indirect proof.

1. Suppose $AC = CB$. Then the triangle is isosceles and the base angles A and B are equal. But we are given that the angles are not equal, so we must reject the possibility that $AC = CB$.
2. Suppose $AC < CB$. Then by the preceding proof, angle B is less than angle A. But we are given that angle B is greater than angle A, so we reject this possibility.
3. Thus, side AC must be greater than side CB because that is the only remaining possibility.

Problem set 47

1. Four reds and 3 blues weighed 29 pounds. Five blues and 2 whites also weighed 29 pounds. If 6 reds and 3 whites weighed 51 pounds, how much did each color weigh?

2. The sum of the digits of a three-digit counting number is 11. The units digit is 2 greater than the tens digit. If the hundreds digit and the units digit are interchanged, the sum of the new number and the original number is 1030. What was the original number?

3. If x varies jointly as y and z^2 and inversely as the square root of w, what is the effect on x when y is doubled, z is halved, and w is multiplied by 4?

4. The mad chemist cackled with glee because he had the answer. He had 100 milliliters of a solution that was 70% sugar and had figured out how much water to add so that the resulting solution would be only 40% sugar. How much water did he add?

5. The Big Guy could do 7 jobs in only 2 hours while the Little Guy took 3 hours to do 5 jobs. Working together, how long would it take them to complete 31 jobs?

6. How many distinguishable ways can 3 red marbles, 5 blue marbles, and 2 white marbles be placed in a straight line?

7. Given $\angle C = 105°$. Find $\angle B$ and $\angle A$.

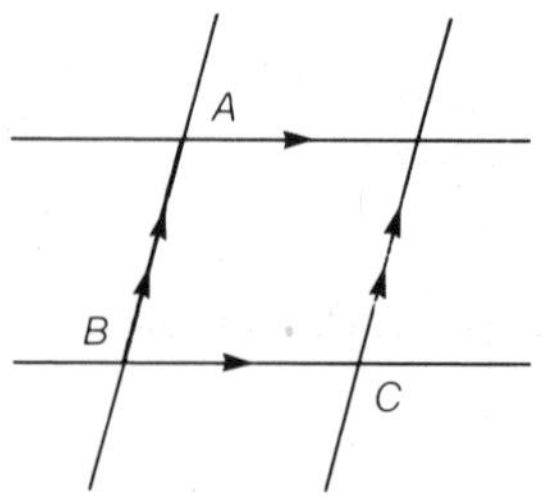

8. Prove that the sum of the angles in a triangle is 180°.

9. Prove that if two angles in one triangle are equal to two angles in another triangle, the third angles are equal.

10. Prove that an exterior angle of a triangle is equal to the sum of the remote interior angles.

11. Using the result of Problem 10, find x.

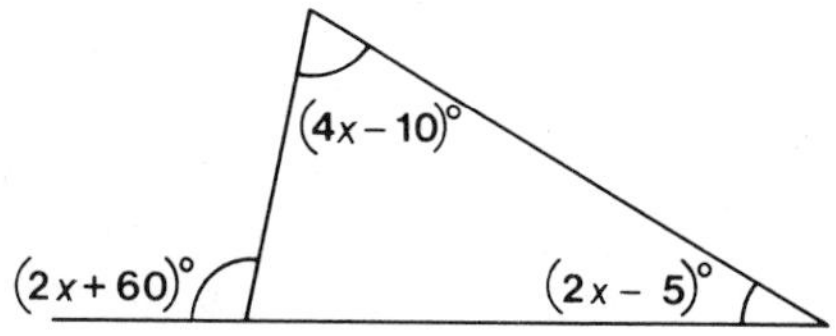

12. Graph $y = \log_{1/2} x$.

13. Convert $6 - 5i$ to polar form.

14. Multiply (4 cis 25°)(3 cis 20°) and express the answer in rectangular form. Give an exact answer.

15. Solve for x: $\begin{cases} hx + gy = a \\ mx + ny = b \end{cases}$

Write the equation of Problem 16 as a sine function and the equation of Problem 17 as a cosine function.

16.

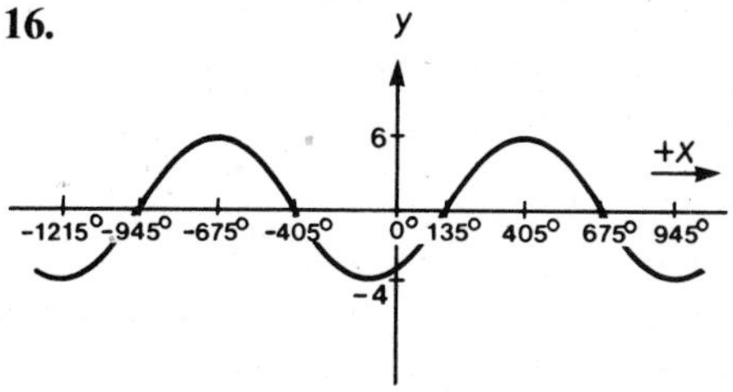

17.

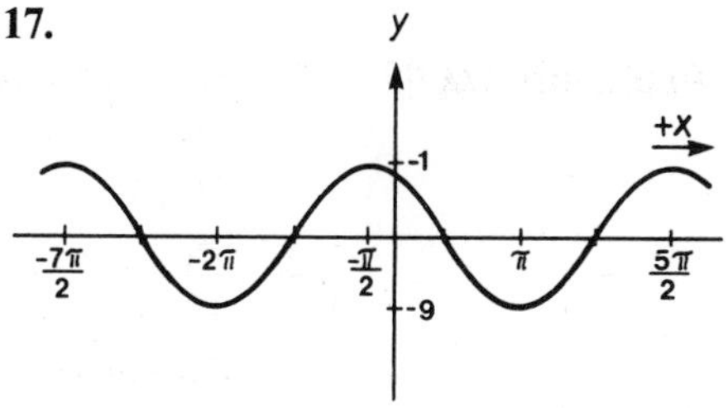

18. Find the area in square centimeters of the triangle shown.

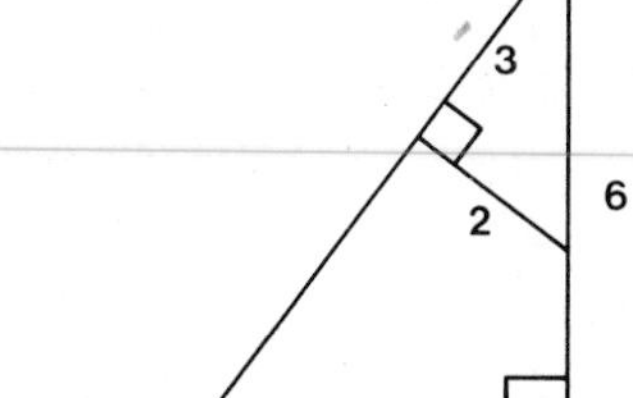

19. Find the radius and center of the circle whose equation is $x^2 + y^2 - 10x + 2y + 22 = 0$.

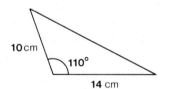

20. Find x.

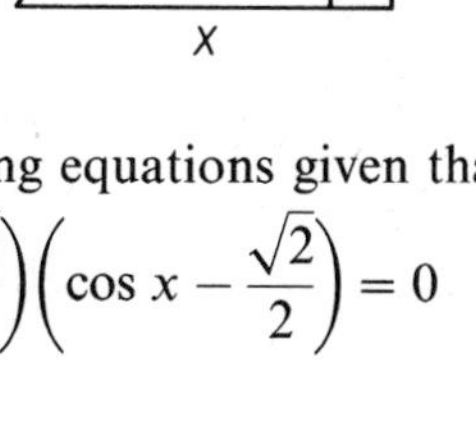

Solve the following equations given that $(0° \le \theta, x < 360°)$:

21. $\left(\sin x - \frac{\sqrt{2}}{2}\right)\left(\cos x - \frac{\sqrt{2}}{2}\right) = 0$

22. $\sqrt{\frac{1 - \cos x}{2}} = 1$

23. $2 \tan 4\theta - \frac{1}{2} = -\frac{1}{2}$

Evaluate:

24. $\tan^2 (-300°) - \sec^2 (-300°)$

25. $\cos \left[\text{Arctan} \left(-\frac{5}{6} \right) \right]$

26. $\tan \left(-\frac{8\pi}{3} \right) \cot \left(-\frac{8\pi}{3} \right)$

27. Solve: $\ln x^3 - \ln x = \ln (2x + 2) + \ln (x + 1)$

28. Simplify: $3^{\log_3 28 - \log_3 4}$

29. Estimate: $\text{antilog}_e\, 3$

30. Using the tables, find $\text{antilog}_{10} (-5.62)$.

LESSON 48 Matrices and determinants

48.A Matrices

A ***matrix*** is a rectangular array of numbers or symbols that stand for numbers.

$$\begin{matrix} 4 & 7 & 5 \\ 2 & 3 & 5 \end{matrix} \qquad \begin{matrix} 4 & 8 \\ 5 & 3 \end{matrix} \qquad \begin{bmatrix} 6 & 1 & 5 & 2 \\ 4 & 2 & 8 & 7 \end{bmatrix} \qquad \begin{bmatrix} 7 & 1 & 8 & 3 & 2 & 5 \\ 5 & 6 & 4 & 3 & 3 & 6 \end{bmatrix}$$

(*a*) (*b*) (*c*) (*d*)

$$\begin{bmatrix} a & b & c \\ d & e & f \\ g & h & i \end{bmatrix} \qquad \begin{bmatrix} 4 \\ 7 \\ 3 \end{bmatrix} \qquad \begin{bmatrix} 5 & 2 & 8 \end{bmatrix} \qquad \begin{bmatrix} 7 & 4 \\ 3 & 5 \\ 8 & 6 \\ 9 & 3 \end{bmatrix} \qquad \begin{bmatrix} 3 \end{bmatrix}$$

(*e*) (*f*) (*g*) (*h*) (*i*)

The individual **entries** of a matrix are called the ***elements*** of the matrix and are always arranged regularly in rows and columns. All rows must have the same number of entries and all columns must have the same number of entries. It is customary but not necessary to use brackets to indicate that an array is being considered as a matrix. The ***dimensions*** (size) of a matrix are given by naming the number of rows and then the number of columns. Thus, (*a*) is a 2×3 (read "two by three") matrix; (*d*) is a 2×6 matrix; and (*h*) is a 4×2 matrix. A matrix can have only one row or one column. We note that (*f*) is a 3×1 matrix, (*g*) is a 1×3 matrix, and (*i*) is a 1×1 matrix.

Two matrices are equal if the entries in one matrix are identical to the entries in the other matrix.

$$\begin{bmatrix} 4 & 7 & 2 \\ 4 & 7 & 2 \end{bmatrix} \qquad \begin{bmatrix} 4 & 7 & 2 \\ 4 & 7 & 2 \end{bmatrix} \qquad \begin{bmatrix} 4 & 2 & 7 \\ 4 & 7 & 2 \end{bmatrix}$$

(*a*) (*b*) (*c*)

Thus, matrices (*a*) and (*b*) are equal matrices, but neither of these is equal to matrix (*c*).

48.B Determinants

If a matrix has the same number of rows as it has columns, the matrix is a ***square matrix***. Every square matrix is associated with one real number called the ***determinant*** of the matrix. **If a matrix is not a square matrix, it does not have a determinant.** The determinant of a matrix is customarily designated by enclosing the matrix within vertical lines.

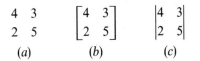

$$\begin{matrix} 4 & 3 \\ 2 & 5 \end{matrix} \qquad \begin{bmatrix} 4 & 3 \\ 2 & 5 \end{bmatrix} \qquad \begin{vmatrix} 4 & 3 \\ 2 & 5 \end{vmatrix}$$

(*a*) (*b*) (*c*)

Array (*a*) is a square matrix. Array (*b*) is also a matrix, and brackets are used to call attention to the fact that it is a matrix. Array (*c*) is the same square matrix, and we have used vertical lines to designate the determinant of the matrix. We find the determinant of a 2×2 square matrix by adding the product of the entries in one diagonal to the negative of the product of the entries in the other diagonal.

$$\text{Determinant} = \begin{vmatrix} a & b \\ c & d \end{vmatrix} \begin{matrix} -cb \\ +ad \end{matrix} = ad - cb$$

Sometimes one forgets which product is positive and which product is negative. As a memory device, we will superimpose the problem on a map of the United States and associate the minus sign with the cold waters of the North Atlantic and associate the plus sign with the sunshine of the islands of the Caribbean.

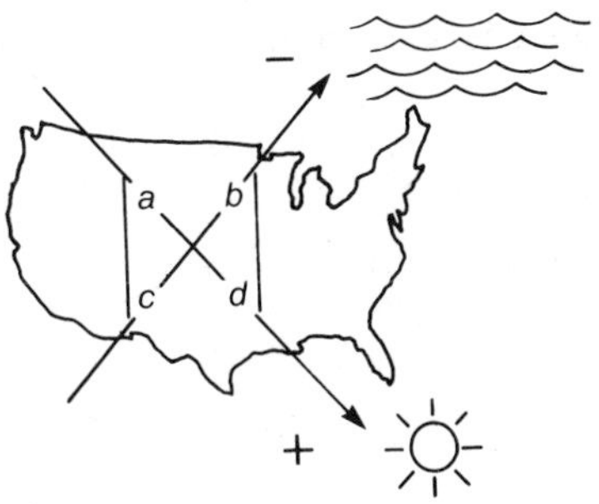

Example 48.B.1 Evaluate: $\begin{vmatrix} -4 & -3 \\ 2 & 7 \end{vmatrix}$

Solution We remember that we use the negative sign with one of the products.

$$\begin{vmatrix} -4 & -3 \\ 2 & 7 \end{vmatrix} = (-4)(7) - (2)(-3) = -28 - (-6) = \mathbf{-22}$$

Example 48.B.2 Evalute: $\begin{vmatrix} -7 & 5 \\ 3 & -4 \end{vmatrix}$

Solution The lower-left to upper-right product is preceded by a minus sign.

$$\begin{vmatrix} -7 & 5 \\ 3 & -4 \end{vmatrix} = (-7)(-4) - (3)(5) = 28 - 15 = \mathbf{13}$$

Example 48.B.3 Find x: $\begin{vmatrix} x+4 & 3 \\ 2 & 4 \end{vmatrix} = 18$

Solution The problem tells us that the value of the determinant is 18 and implies the following equation:

$$(4)(x + 4) - (2)(3) = 18 \quad \text{equation}$$
$$4x + 16 - 6 = 18 \quad \text{multiplied}$$
$$4x = 8 \quad \text{simplified}$$
$$\mathbf{x = 2} \quad \text{divided}$$

Problems such as this one afford practice with the meaning of the determinant notation and are encountered in more advanced courses in mathematics. They are implemented in computer software in a type of problem called *eigenvalue problems.*

Example 48.B.4 Find x: $\begin{vmatrix} x + 4 & 5 \\ 3 & x + 2 \end{vmatrix} = -5$

Solution This is another problem designed to emphasize the meaning of the determinant notation. The equation that results is

$$x^2 + 6x + 8 - 15 = -5 \quad \text{equation}$$

which simplifies to

$$x^2 + 6x - 2 = 0 \quad \text{simplified}$$

We will use the quadratic formula to solve.

$$x = \frac{-6 \pm \sqrt{36 - 4(1)(-2)}}{2} = \frac{-6 \pm \sqrt{44}}{2} = \mathbf{-3 \pm \sqrt{11}}$$

Thus, x is either $-3 + \sqrt{11}$ or $-3 - \sqrt{11}$. If we use $-3 + \sqrt{11}$ for x, we get the determinant on the left. If we use $-3 - \sqrt{11}$ for x, we get the determinant on the right.

$$\begin{vmatrix} 1 + \sqrt{11} & 5 \\ 3 & -1 + \sqrt{11} \end{vmatrix} \qquad \begin{vmatrix} 1 - \sqrt{11} & 5 \\ 3 & -1 - \sqrt{11} \end{vmatrix}$$

Both these determinants have a value of -5.

Problem set 48

1. The variable p varies jointly as the square root of m and as y^2 and varies inversely as x^2. What happens to p when y is doubled, m is quadrupled, and x is halved?

2. Matildabelle ran and ran but got there 20 minutes late. If she ran x miles in k minutes, how fast would she have had to run to get there on time?

3. The trip going was arduous, and it took 2 hours longer to cover the 160 miles than it took to come back. If the total time of the round trip was 6 hours, what was the rate going and what was the rate coming back?

4. If the operation $*$ is defined as $a * b = 2a - b$, and the operation $\#$ is defined as $a \# b = \frac{a}{b} + b$, find the value of $(3 * 2) \# 4$.

5. Each year Darlene got a 20 percent salary increase over what she had been paid the year before. She worked for the company for 3 full years. If her total salary for 3 years was $29,120, how much did she make the first year?

6. Four times the complement of an angle is 40° less than 2 times the supplement of the same angle. What is the angle?

7. Evaluate: $\begin{vmatrix} -4 & 6 \\ 5 & 2 \end{vmatrix}$

8. Solve for x: $\begin{vmatrix} x & 2 \\ 3 & x-1 \end{vmatrix} = 4$

9. Given $\angle A = 110°$, find $\angle B$ and $\angle C$.

10. Prove that the sum of the angles in a triangle is 180°.

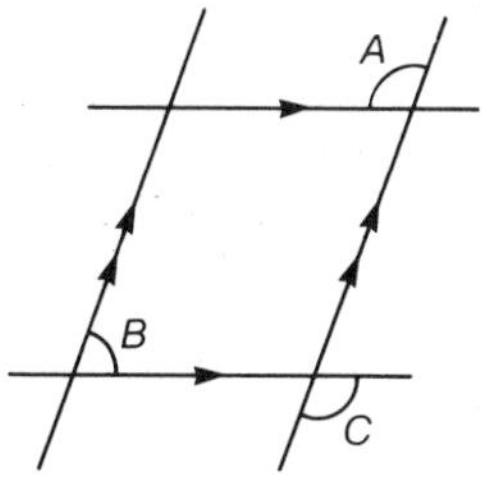

11. Prove that an exterior angle of a triangle is equal to the sum of the remote interior angles.

12. Using the result in Problem 11, find a.

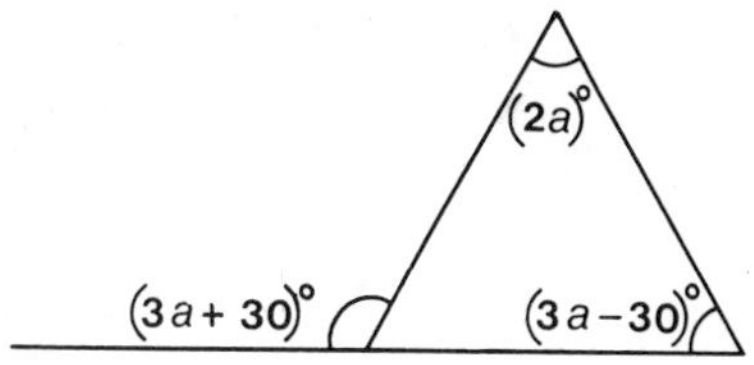

13. Graph $y = \log_{1/3} x$.

14. Multiply (6 cis 35°)(2 cis 25°) and express the answer in rectangular form. Give an exact answer.

15. (*a*) Convert $6 - 2i$ to polar form.

(*b*) Convert 5 cis $\left(-\frac{13\pi}{4}\right)$ to rectangular form. Give an exact answer.

16. Solve for y: $\begin{cases} ax + by = c \\ px + qy = d \end{cases}$

Write the equation of Problem 17 as a cosine function and the equation of Problem 18 as a sine function.

17.

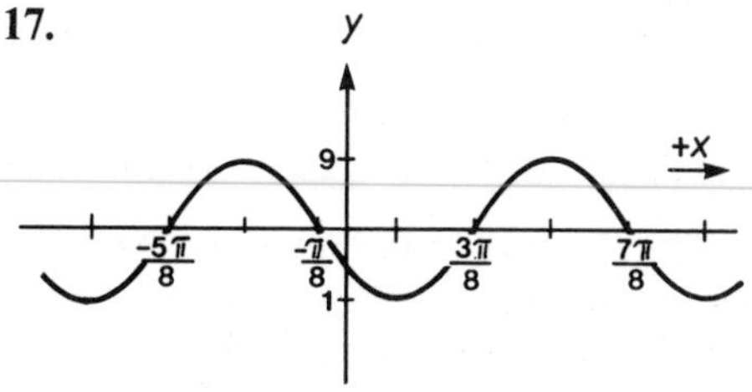

18.

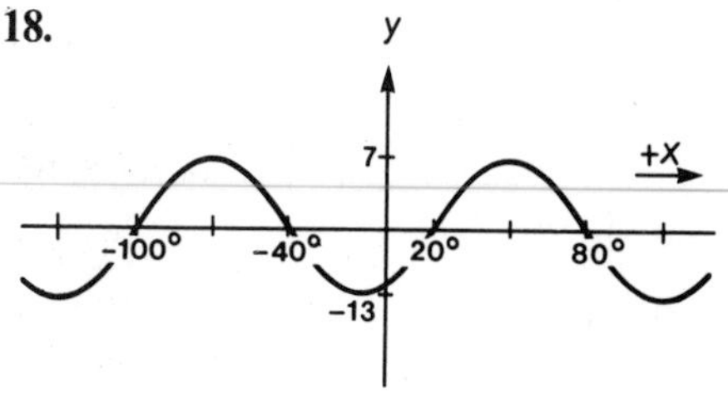

19. Find the area in square centimeters of the segment bounded by an arc of measure 110° and the chord which joins the endpoints of the arc in a circle whose radius is 0.6 meter.

20. Find the radius and center of the circle $x^2 + y^2 + x + y - \frac{7}{2} = 0$.

21. The three triangles shown are similar. Write the necessary proportions and solve for a and b.

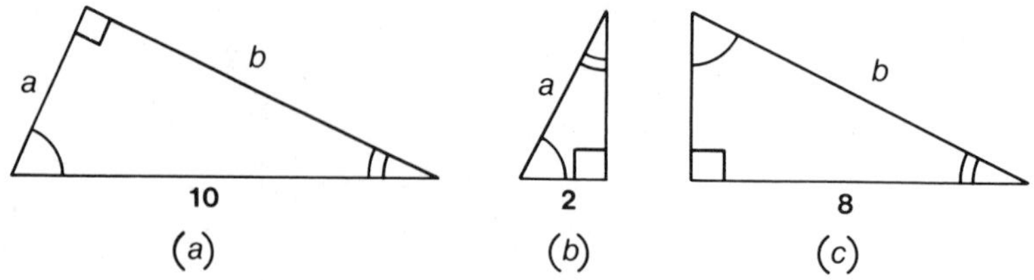

Solve the following equations given that ($0° \le \theta, x < 360°$):

22. $(\tan\theta - \sqrt{3})(\tan\theta + \sqrt{3}) = 0$

23. $\sin x + 2\sin^2 x = 0$

24. $\tan^2 x - 3 = 0$

Evaluate:

25. $\cot^2(-510°) - \csc^2(-510°)$

26. $\sin^2\left(-\frac{3\pi}{4}\right) + \cos^2\left(-\frac{3\pi}{4}\right)$

27. Show why $\log_b \frac{M}{N} = \log_b M - \log_b N$.

28. Solve: $\frac{2}{3}\log_4 8 - 2\log_4 x = \log_4 4$

29. Estimate the value of the base e antilogarithm of -1.

30. Use tables of logarithms to find the base 10 antilogarithm of -8.12.

LESSON 49 The ellipse

49.A The ellipse

A circle is formed when a right circular cone is cut by a plane parallel to the base of the cone. If the plane is tilted slightly, the points of intersection of the figures form an ellipse.

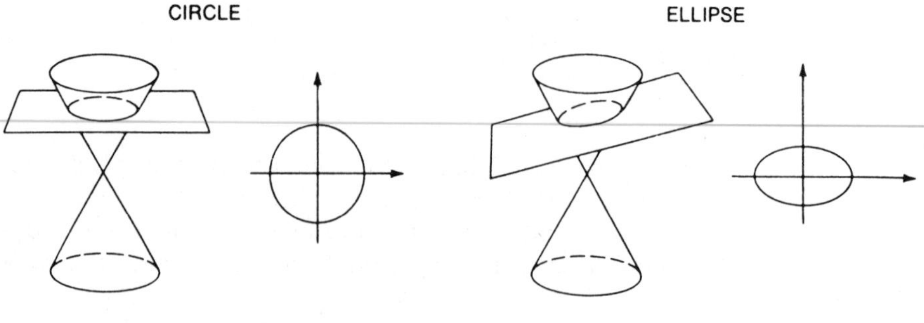

The ellipse can be thought of as a flattened circle. As we see on the next page, the ellipse is formed about two points. Each of the points is called a ***focus*** of the ellipse, and collectively the points are called the ***foci*** of the ellipse. **The ellipse is the locus of points**

such that the sum of the distances from a point on the ellipse to the two foci is a constant. We can draw an ellipse by attaching the ends of a piece of string at F_1 and F_2 and holding the string taut as a pencil is moved around.

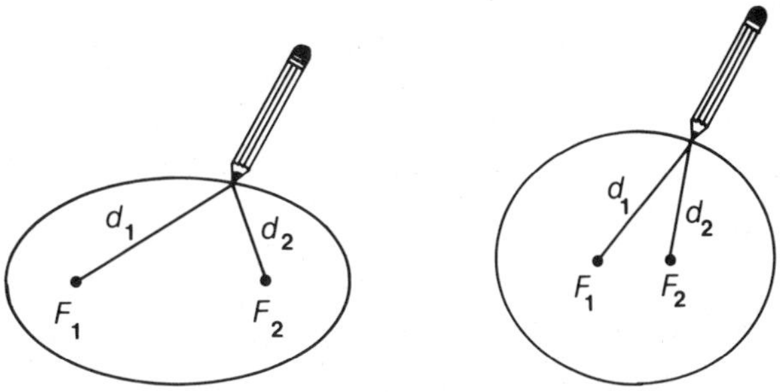

The length of the string is constant. Thus, the lengths d_1 and d_2 change, but their sum always equals the length of the string. The shape of the ellipse can be changed by changing the distance between the foci or by changing the length of the string. As we see in these figures, if we keep the length of the string constant, the ellipse becomes more circular as the foci get closer together, and the ellipse gets narrower as the foci are moved farther apart.

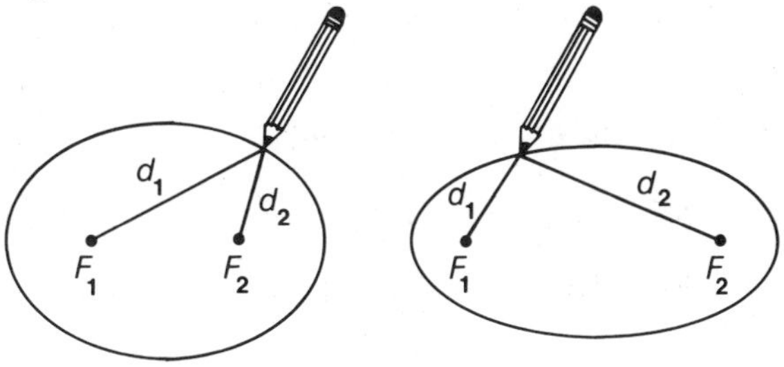

The ellipse has two axes. The axis that passes through the foci is always the longer axis, and it is called the ***major axis.*** The shorter axis is the ***minor axis.*** When graphed on a coordinate plane, the major axis can be horizontal, vertical, or inclined.

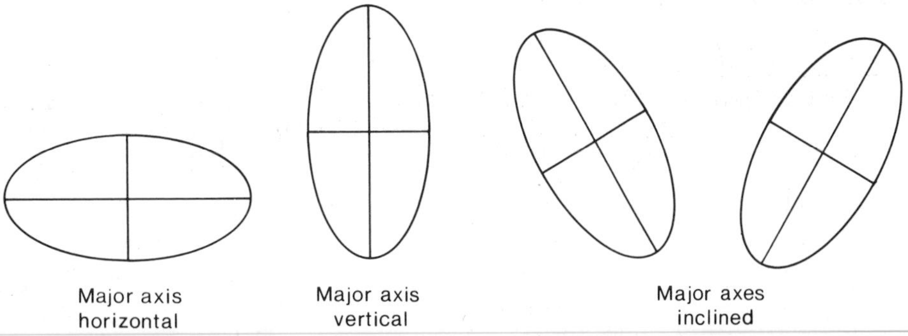

In this book, we will investigate ellipses whose major axes are vertical or horizontal and reserve the study of ellipses with inclined axes for a later course. In a future lesson, we will show that the equation of an ellipse whose major axis is vertical or horizontal and whose center is the origin can be written in **standard form** as

$$\frac{x^2}{a^2} + \frac{y^2}{b^2} = 1 \quad \text{or} \quad \frac{x^2}{b^2} + \frac{y^2}{a^2} = 1$$

The letter *a* is always associated with the major axis. In the left-hand equation above, a^2 is below x^2 so the x axis is the major axis. In the right-hand equation, a^2 is below

y^2 so the y axis is the major axis. **In both equations, the letter *a* represents half the length of the major axis, and the letter *b* represents half the length of the minor axis.** The points $(a, 0)$, $(-a, 0)$, $(0, b)$, and $(0, -b)$ are called the ***vertices*** of the ellipse.

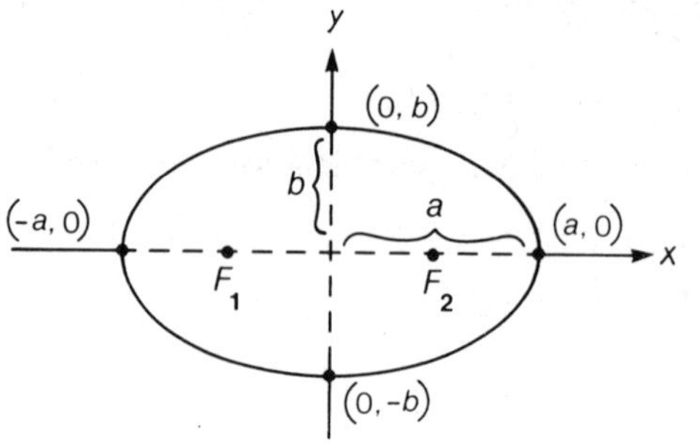

$$\frac{x^2}{a^2} + \frac{y^2}{b^2} = 1$$

Example 49.A.1 Graph the ellipse $\frac{x^2}{25} + \frac{y^2}{9} = 1$.

Solution First we will find the values of y when x equals 0. To do this, we set $x = 0$ and solve for y.

$$\frac{0}{25} + \frac{y^2}{9} = 1$$

$$y^2 = 9$$

$$y = \pm 3$$

Now we let y equal 0 and find the values of x.

$$\frac{x^2}{25} + \frac{0}{9} = 1$$

$$x^2 = 25$$

$$x = \pm 5$$

We have found the coordinates of the vertices, and we can graph the ellipse.

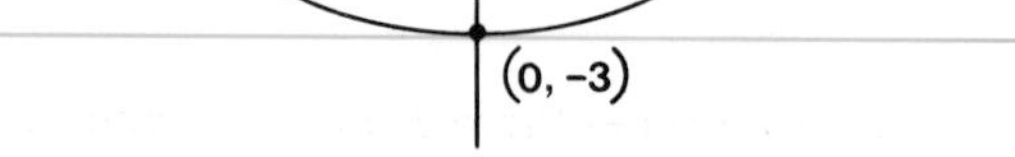

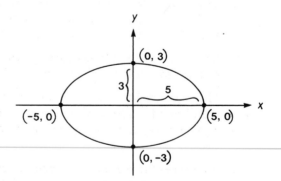

Example 49.A.2 Graph the ellipse $5x^2 + 2y^2 = 15$.

Solution When the ellipse is in standard form, the constant is 1. Thus, we begin by dividing each term by 15, and we get

$$\frac{5x^2}{15} + \frac{2y^2}{15} = 1$$

Now if we let x equal 0, we can solve for y; and if we let $y = 0$, we can solve for x.

LET $x = 0$	LET $y = 0$
$\dfrac{5(0)^2}{15} + \dfrac{2y^2}{15} = 1$	$\dfrac{5x^2}{15} + \dfrac{2(0)^2}{15} = 1$
$y = \pm\sqrt{7.5}$	$x = \pm\sqrt{3}$

We use a calculator to get decimal approximations for ease in graphing.

$$y = \pm\sqrt{7.5} = \pm 2.74 \qquad x = \pm\sqrt{3} = \pm 1.73$$

This time the major axis is vertical.

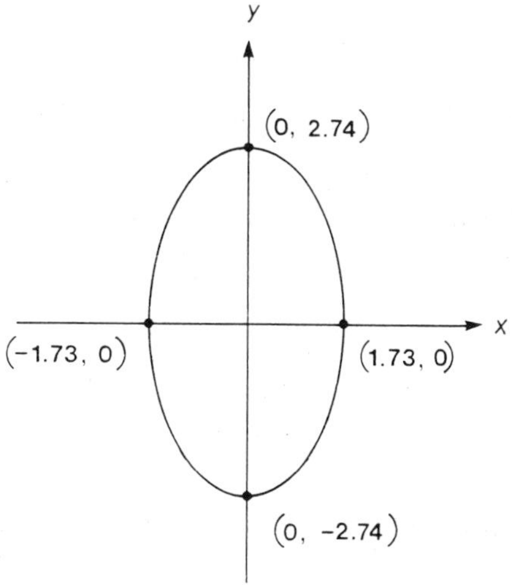

Problem set 49

1. If $a * b$ means $4a - 2b$ and $a \# b$ means $\dfrac{a}{b} - b$, find the value of $(a * b) \# a$ if $a = 8$ and $b = 2$.

2. The sum of the length, width, and height of a rectangular box is 150 centimeters. The length is twice the sum of the width and height, and twice the width is 1 centimeter greater than the height. What are the dimensions of the box?

3. If x varies directly as y^2 and inversely as z and inversely as the square root of w, what happens to x when y is multiplied by 3, z is doubled, and w is quadrupled?

4. The boat could sail at 5 times the speed of the current in the river. Thus, the boat could go 144 miles downstream in 2 hours more than it took to go 64 miles upstream. What was the speed of the boat and how fast was the current in the river?

5. Four times the sum of the number of reds and blues exceeded 3 times the number of whites by 3. Five times the sum of the number of blues and whites exceeded 8 times the number of reds by 13. If there were 5 more whites than blues, how many of each color were there?

6. How many different ways can 5 students sit in 5 chairs in a row if Mark and Ophelia refuse to sit next to each other?

7. Graph the ellipse $\dfrac{x^2}{16} + \dfrac{y^2}{9} = 1$.

8. Graph the ellipse $9x^2 + 4y^2 = 36$.

9. Graph $y = \log_2 x$.

10. Convert $7 + 8i$ to polar form.

11. Multiply $(3 \text{ cis } 40°)[2 \text{ cis } (-70°)]$ and express the answer in rectangular form. Give an exact answer.

12. Solve for x: $\begin{vmatrix} x+1 & 1 \\ 3 & x-1 \end{vmatrix} = 0$

13. Prove that if two angles of one triangle are equal to two angles of another triangle, then the third angles of the triangles are equal.

14. Prove that the exterior angle of a triangle is equal to the sum of the remote interior angles.

15. Using the result in Problem 14, find c.

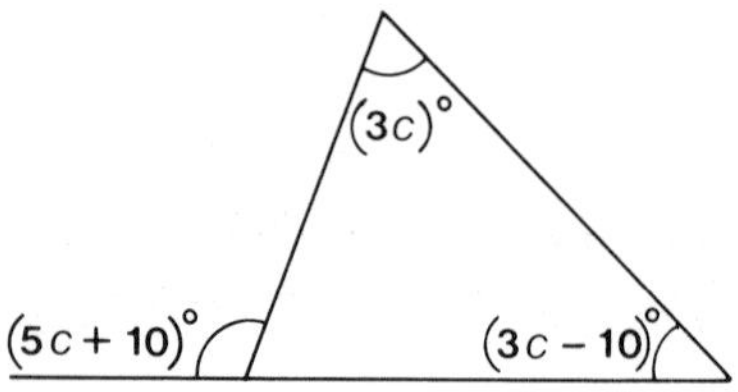

16. Convert 80 kilometers per hour to miles per hour.

Write the equation of Problem 17 as a cosine function and the equation of Problem 18 as a sine function.

17.

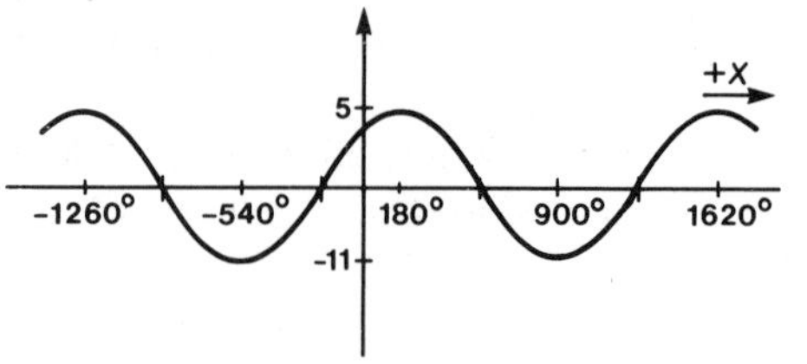

18.

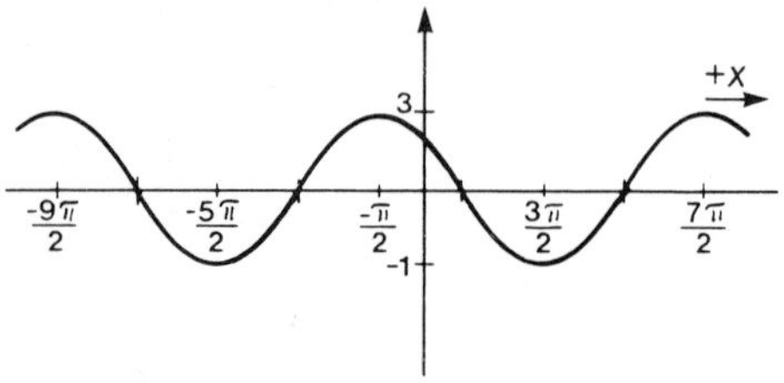

19. Find the area of this triangle in square centimeters.

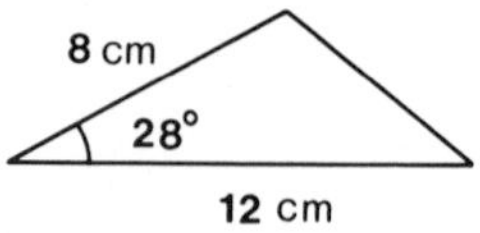

20. Find the radius and the coordinates of the center of the circle whose equation is $x^2 + y^2 + 8x - 12y + 43 = 0$.

21. The three triangles shown are similar. Solve for a and b by writing the appropriate proportions.

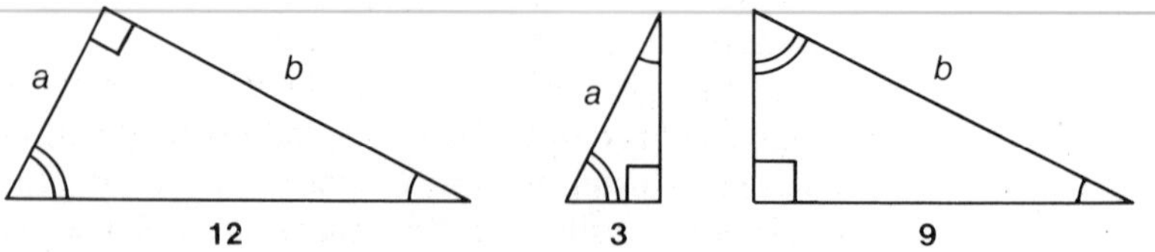

Solve the following equations given that $(0° \le \theta, x < 360°)$:

22. $(2 \cos \theta + 1)(2 \sin \theta + \sqrt{2}) = 0$

23. $\cot^2 x = 3$

24. $\cot^2 x + \cot x = 0$

Evaluate:

25. $\tan^2\left(-\frac{13\pi}{4}\right) - \sec^2\left(-\frac{13\pi}{4}\right)$ **26.** $\sin^2(-480°) + \cos^2(-480°)$

27. Solve: $\frac{3}{4}\log_8 16 + 2\log_8 x = \log_8 x + 1$

28. Simplify: $8^{\log_8 16 - \log_8 2}$

29. Estimate the value of the base e antilogarithm of -2.

30. Find the distance from $(0, -2)$ to $2x - 5y + 4 = 0$.

LESSON 50 One side plus two other parts · Law of sines

50.A One side plus two other parts

The Greek word *gonia* means "angle." *Trigonon* means "three angles," and *metron* means "measure." This is the reason we use the word *trigonometry* to describe the study of the measures of linear geometric figures that have three angles.

Triangles have six principal parts, three sides, and three angles. **If the length of one side and the measures of two other parts are known, it is possible to solve for the measures of the missing parts. We cannot solve for the missing parts if we do not know the length of at least one side.**

Thus, if the triangle is a right triangle, all we need to know is the length of one side and either the measure of a second angle or the length of a second side.

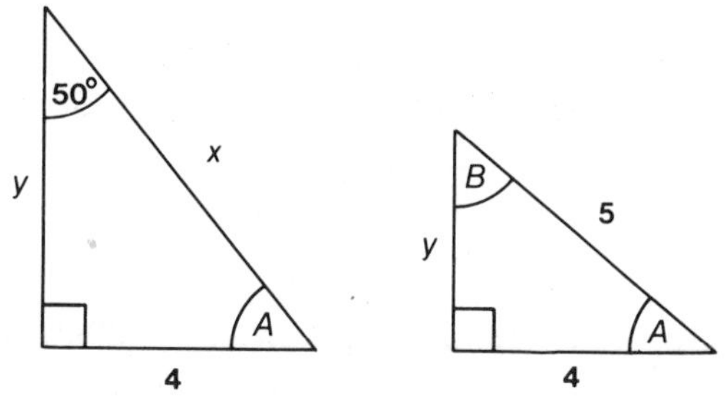

We can solve both of the above right triangles for the missing parts because we know the length of one side and also know the measure of one other part. In the triangle on the left, the other given part is an angle, and in the triangle on the right, the other given part is the length of another side.

A triangle that is not a right triangle is called an ***oblique*** triangle. **Any oblique triangle can be solved if one side and two other parts are known.** Oblique triangles can be solved by using the law of sines or by using the law of cosines. The law we use to solve for the missing parts of a particular oblique triangle depends on which three parts of the triangle are known. In this lesson, we will investigate the use of the law of sines. The derivation of the law of sines is more meaningful after the usefulness of the law of sines has been demonstrated and the statement of the law is familiar. Thus, we will reverse the customary procedure by first learning to use the law of sines and postponing the derivation until a later lesson.

50.B The law of sines (a pair)

A triangle has three sides and three angles. These parts are often labeled by using capital letters for the angles and lowercase letters for the sides opposite the angles, as we show here.

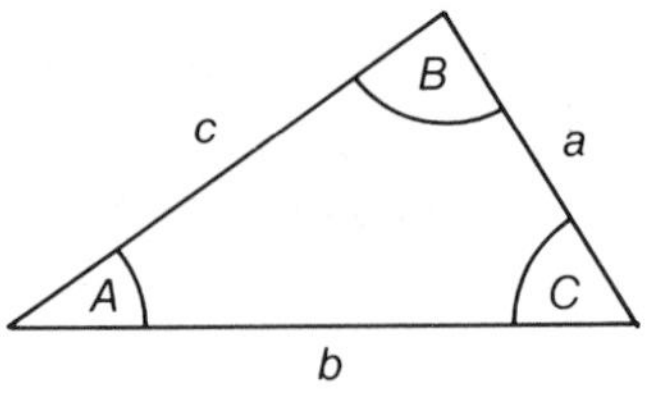

We will consider that an angle and the side opposite the angle constitute **a pair.** The law of sines gives us relationships involving sides and the sines of the paired angles and is normally stated as we show here.

$$\frac{a}{\sin A} = \frac{b}{\sin B} = \frac{c}{\sin C}$$

This statement is confusing to some because only two of these fractions are ever used at the same time. Thus, to use the law of sines, we will use one of the following forms.

$$\frac{a}{\sin A} = \frac{b}{\sin B} \qquad \frac{a}{\sin A} = \frac{c}{\sin C} \qquad \frac{b}{\sin B} = \frac{c}{\sin C}$$

We can solve any triangle if three parts (one must be a side) are known. If two of the parts constitute a pair, we can use the law of sines to solve for the missing parts.

Example 50.B.1 Solve this triangle for the unknown parts.

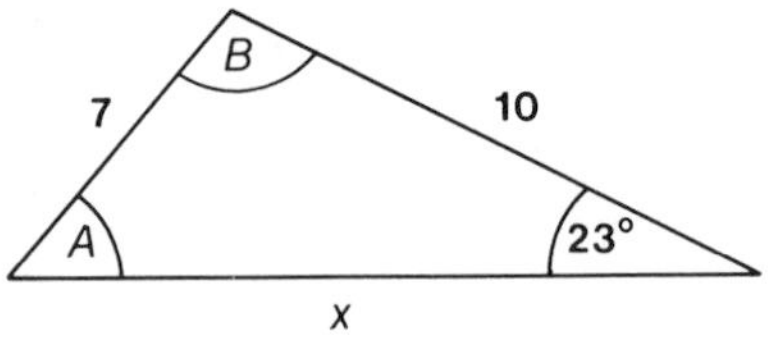

Solution We have **a pair** of knowns and thus can use the law of sines. First, we use the pair to write part of an equation.

$$\frac{7}{\sin 23°} = \frac{\quad}{\quad}$$

Now on the right side, we must also put the length of a side on top and the sine of its **paired angle** below. We will use 10 and angle A.

$$\frac{7}{\sin 23°} = \frac{10}{\sin A}$$

Problems like this one are good problems for getting practice in the use of scientific calculators. First, we solve algebraically for sin A.

$$\sin A = \frac{10 \sin 23°}{7}$$

Then we use the calculator to find a numerical value for sin A.

$$\sin A \approx 0.558$$

There are two angles whose sine is 0.558. One is a first-quadrant angle, and the other is a second-quadrant angle. The calculator will give us the first-quadrant angle.

First-quadrant angle whose sine is $0.558 \approx 33.93°$

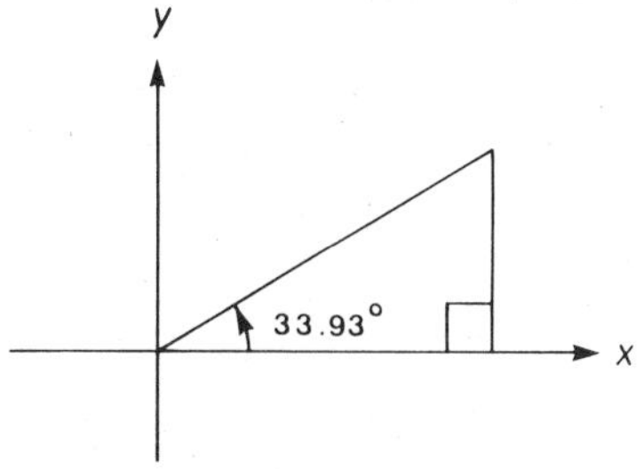

Second-quadrant angle whose sine is $0.558 \approx 180° - 33.93° = 146.07°$

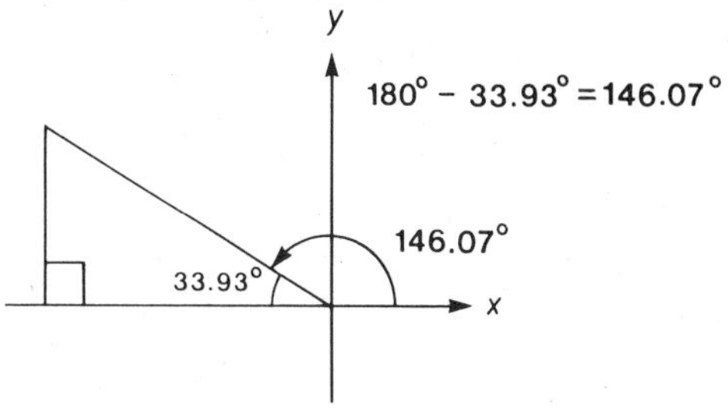

The word *ambiguous* means "capable of being interpreted in two or more ways." **The use of the law of sines to solve for an angle will always result in two possible values for the angle (unless both values are 90°).** Thus we say that this use of the law of sines always produces an ambiguous result. We will discuss the ambiguity that results from this use of the law of sines in more detail in a later lesson. In this triangle, angle A is obviously less than 90°, so we will use the smaller of the two possible values for angle A.

$$\angle A = \mathbf{33.93°}$$

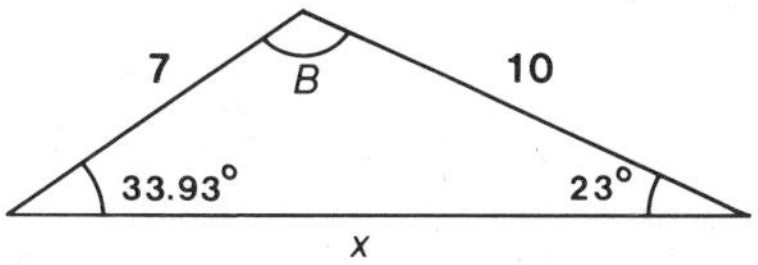

The sum of the angles is 180°, so

$$\angle B = 180° - 23° - 33.93° = \mathbf{123.07°}$$

Now we know angle B, so we can use the law of sines again to find its paired side, which is x.

$$\frac{7}{\sin 23°} = \frac{x}{\sin 123.07°}$$

We solve for x and get

$$x = \frac{7 \sin 123.07°}{\sin 23°} = \mathbf{15.01}$$

We note that there is no ambiguity when the law of sines is used to solve for a missing side.

Example 50.B.2 Solve this triangle for the unknown parts.

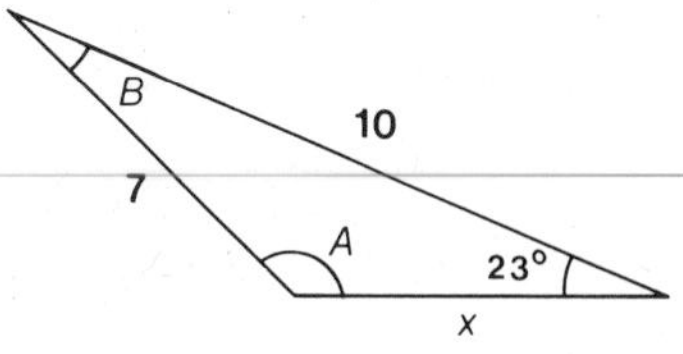

Solution We have **a pair** of known parts so we can use the law of sines. The pair is the side 7 and the 23° angle. We also have the side 10, so we write

$$\frac{7}{\sin 23°} = \frac{10}{\sin A}$$

and we solve for the sine of A.

$$\sin A = \frac{10 \sin 23°}{7} \approx 0.558$$

Again there are two angles that have a sine of +0.558.

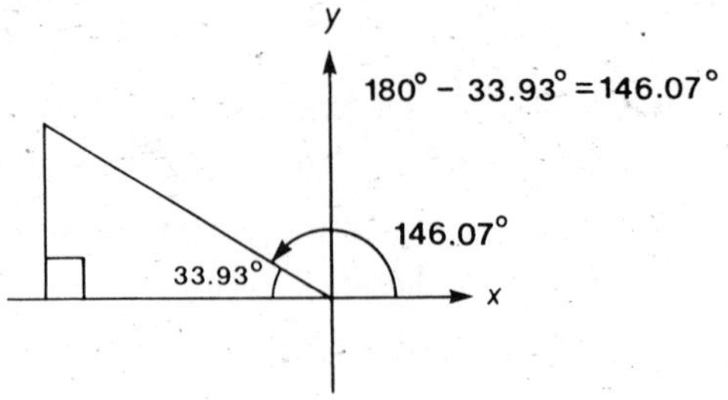

In the triangle of this example, we are looking for the value of an obtuse angle, so angle A has a value of 146.07°.

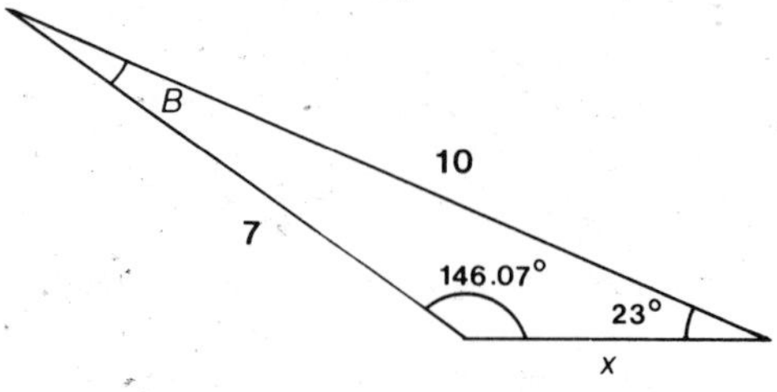

Now we find the value of angle B.

$$\angle \mathbf{B} = 180° - 23° - 146.07° = \mathbf{10.93°}$$

The side x and the 10.93° angle form **a pair,** so we can solve for x.

$$\frac{7}{\sin 23°} = \frac{x}{\sin 10.93°}$$

$$x = \frac{7 \sin 10.93°}{\sin 23°} \approx \mathbf{3.40}$$

Example 50.B.3 Solve this triangle for the unknown parts.

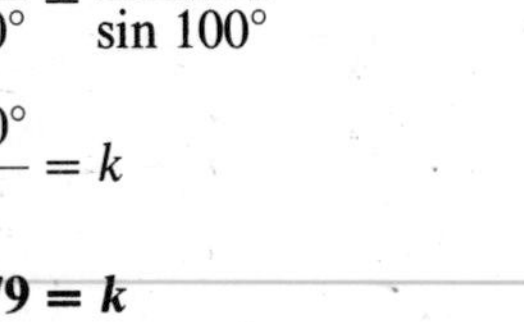

Solution There are 180 degrees in every triangle, so angle A is 100°. Side 7 and the 30° angle constitute **a pair,** so we can use the law of sines to solve for sides m and k.

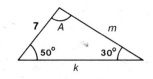

$$\frac{7}{\sin 30°} = \frac{m}{\sin 50°} \qquad \frac{7}{\sin 30°} = \frac{k}{\sin 100°}$$

$$\frac{7 \sin 50°}{\sin 30°} = m \qquad \frac{7 \sin 100°}{\sin 30°} = k$$

$$\mathbf{10.72 = m} \qquad \mathbf{13.79 = k}$$

Problem set 50

1. If $a * b$ means $2a^2 - b$ and $a \# b$ means $\frac{a}{2} - 2b$, what is the value of $a * (a \# b)$ if $a = 4$ and $b = 1$?
2. The ratio of beauties to queens at the fair was 14 to 1. If 2550 women attended the fair and all were either beauties or queens, how many were only beautiful?
3. One of the beauties ran for the exit but got there 2 minutes late. If she ran y yards in m minutes, how fast should she have run to have gotten to the exit on time?

4. The sum of the last two digits of a three-digit counting number is 7. The sum of the first two digits is 5. The middle digit is 4 times the first digit. What is the number?

5. Ten times the complement of the angle exceeds 3 times the supplement of the same angle by 318°. What is the angle?

6. How many distinguishable linear permutations can be made from the letters in the word *calaboose*?

7. Solve this triangle for the unknown parts.

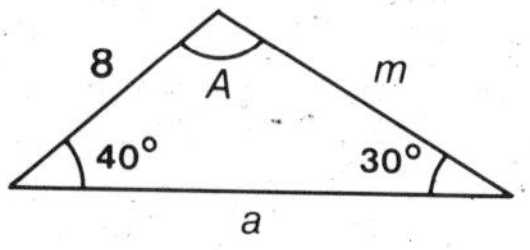

8. Solve this triangle for the unknown parts.

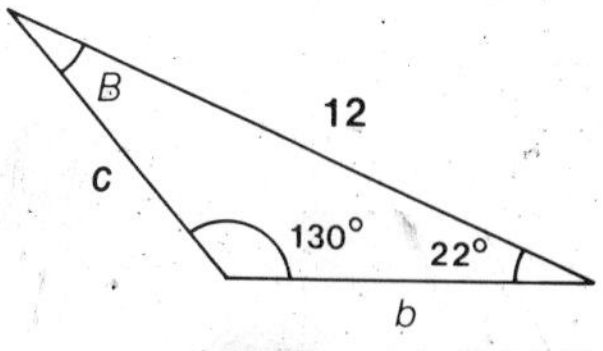

9. Convert $3 + 4i$ to polar form.

10. Graph the ellipse $\frac{x^2}{16} + \frac{y^2}{25} = 1$.

11. Graph the ellipse $4x^2 + 16y^2 = 64$.

12. Graph $y = \log_3 x$.

13. Multiply $(6 \text{ cis } 50°)(3 \text{ cis } 10°)$ and express the answer in rectangular form. Give an exact answer.

14. Solve for a: $\begin{vmatrix} a - 1 & 1 \\ 2 & a \end{vmatrix} = 4$

15. Prove that the sum of the angles of a triangle is 180°.

16. Prove that an exterior angle of a triangle is equal to the sum of the remote interior angles.

17. Using the result of Problem 16, find x.

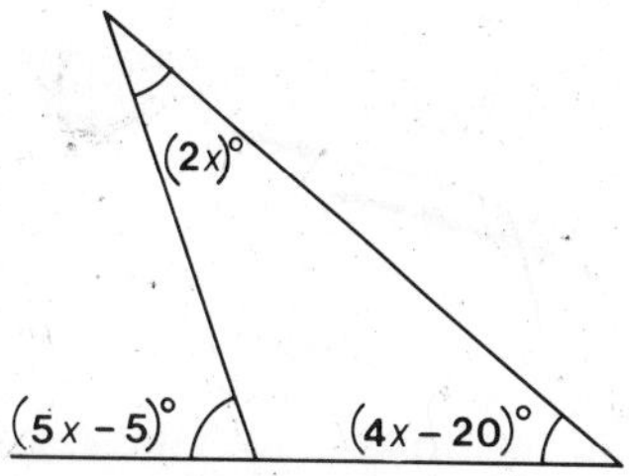

18. Find the area in square centimeters of the segment bounded by an arc of measure 130° and the chord which joins the endpoints of the arc in a circle whose radius is 0.8 meter.

19. Write the equation of the following sinusoid as a cosine function.

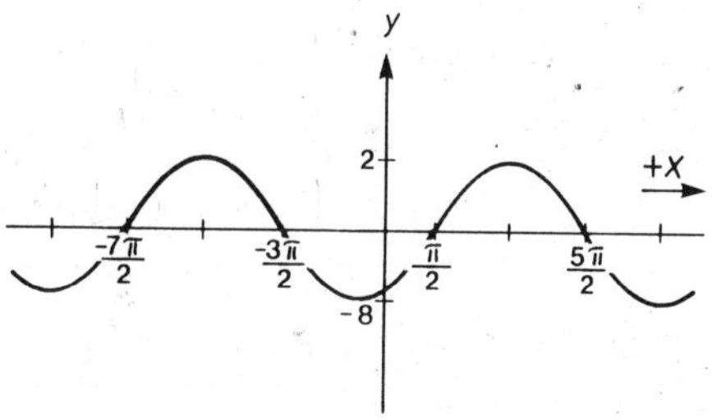

20. Write the equation of the sinusoid whose graph is a sine curve with a centerline value of $y = -10$, an amplitude of 20, and a period of π.

21. Find the radius and center of the circle whose equation is $x^2 + y^2 + 4y = 5$.

22. The three triangles shown are similar. Solve for a and b by writing the appropriate proportions.

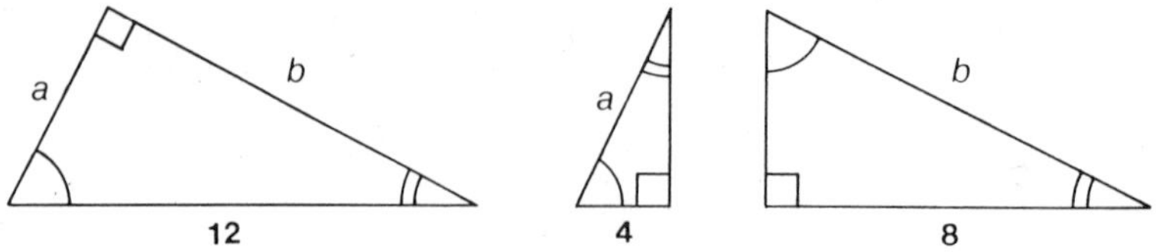

Solve the following equations given that $(0° \le x, t, \theta < 360°)$:

23. $\sin^2 x \cos x = \cos x$

24. $2 \sin^2 t + \sin t - 1 = 0$

25. $\sqrt{3} \tan 3\theta - 1 = 0$

Evaluate:

26. $\sin^2\left(-\frac{2\pi}{3}\right) + \cos^2\left(-\frac{2\pi}{3}\right)$

27. $\cot^3 90° - \sec^2 (-225°) + \csc^2 (150°)$

Solve:

28. $2 \log_7 x + \log_7 49 = 5^{\log_5 2}$

29. $\frac{1}{2} \log_8 16 + \log_8 x = 2 \log_8 (x + 1)$

30. Estimate the base e antilogarithm of 3.

LESSON 51 *Polygons · Areas of regular polygons · Areas of similar figures*

51.A Polygons

Polygons are simple, closed, coplanar geometric figures whose sides are straight lines. These figures are not polygons.

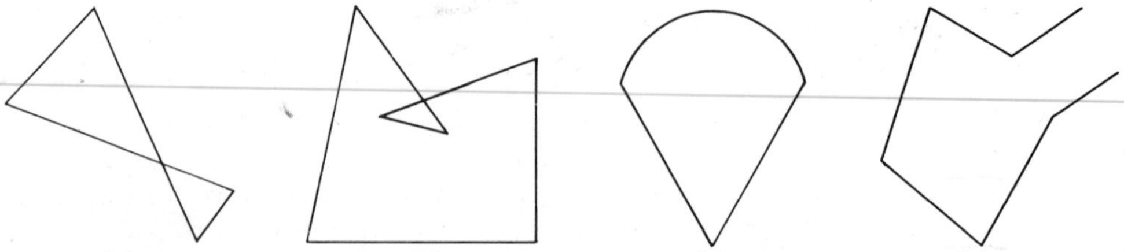

(a) (b) (c) (d)

The sides of the figures (*a*) and (*b*) cross, so these are not simple closed geometric figures. One "side" of (*c*) is not a straight line, and figure (*d*) is not a closed figure. The five figures shown below are all polygons. **Note that in each figure the number of vertices (corners) is the same as the number of sides.**

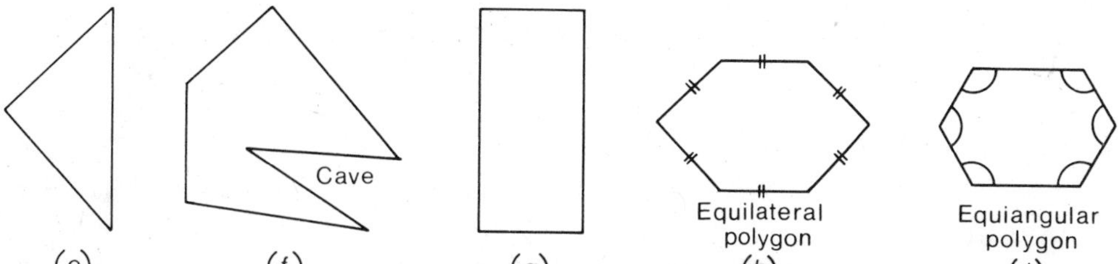

(*e*) (*f*) (*g*) (*h*) (*i*)

Figure (*f*) has an indentation that we can think of as a cave because this polygon is a ***concave polygon.*** Any polygon that does not have a cave is a ***convex polygon.*** Any two points in the interior of a convex polygon can be connected with a line segment that does not cut a side of the polygon.

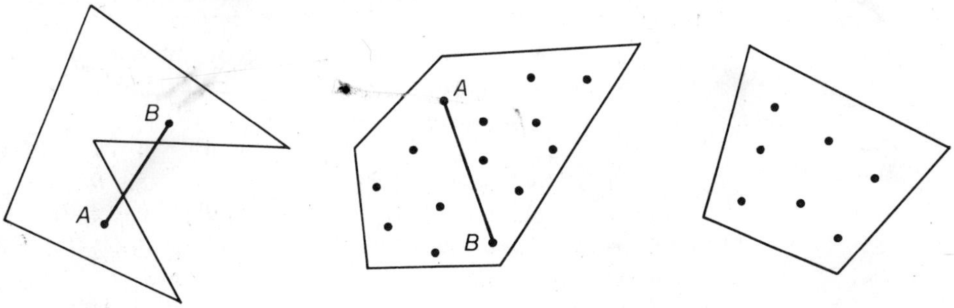

Concave Convex Convex

The sum of the interior angles of any convex polygon depends on the number of sides the polygon has and does not depend on the shape of the polygon. Every convex polygon can be triangulated from one vertex, and the sum of the interior angles of the triangles equals the sum of the interior angles of the polygon.

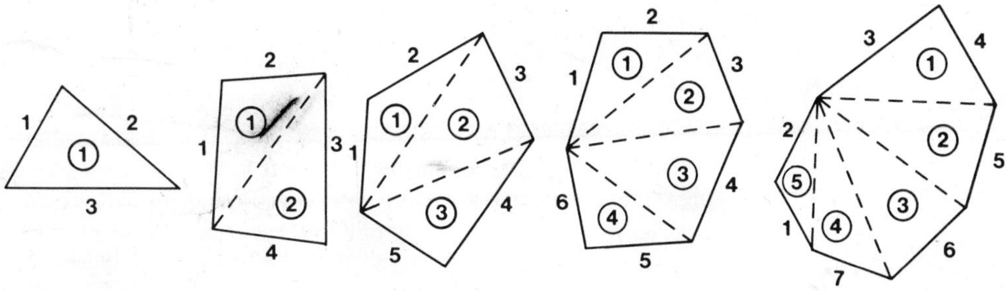

We see that we need at least three sides to form a closed figure, so the triangle is the convex polygon with the fewest sides, and the interior angles of a triangle sum to 180°. The next polygon has four sides and contains two triangles for a sum of 2 × 180°, or 360°. Then comes the five-sided polygon with three triangles and 540°, the six-sided polygon with four triangles, etc.

The number of triangles in the triangulation of a convex polygon is 2 less than the number of sides of the polygon.

Example 51.A.1 Find the sum of the interior angles of a convex polygon that has 16 sides.

Solution Any convex polygon of 16 sides can be triangulated from one vertex into 14 triangles, each of whose angles sum to 180°.

$$\text{Sum of interior angles} = 14 \times 180° = \mathbf{2520°}$$

51.B Regular and irregular polygons; exterior angles

If all the angles of a polygon are equal, and all the sides are equal, the polygon is called a ***regular polygon.*** Polygons that are not regular polygons are called ***irregular polygons.*** The name of a particular polygon is determined by the number of sides of the polygon.

NUMBER OF SIDES	NAME	NUMBER OF SIDES	NAME
3	Triangle	8	Octagon
4	Quadrilateral	9	Nonagon
5	Pentagon	10	Decagon
6	Hexagon	12	Dodecagon
7	Heptagon	n	n-gon

Although these names are useful, we will not concentrate on memorizing them. We note that there is no special name for a polygon of 11 sides or for a polygon of more than 12 sides. When we speak of polygons of more than 12 sides, we use the word *polygon* and tell the number of sides or use the number of sides with the suffix *-gon.* Thus, if a polygon has 143 sides, we would call it a polygon with 143 sides or a 143-gon. The endpoints of one side of a polygon are called ***consecutive vertices,*** and two adjacent sides are called ***consecutive sides.*** A ***diagonal*** of a polygon is the line segment that can be drawn to connect two nonconsecutive vertices.

A polygon has two equal exterior angles at each vertex. Exterior angles are formed by extending one of the sides at the vertex. Here we show one vertex of a polygon and the two equal exterior angles.

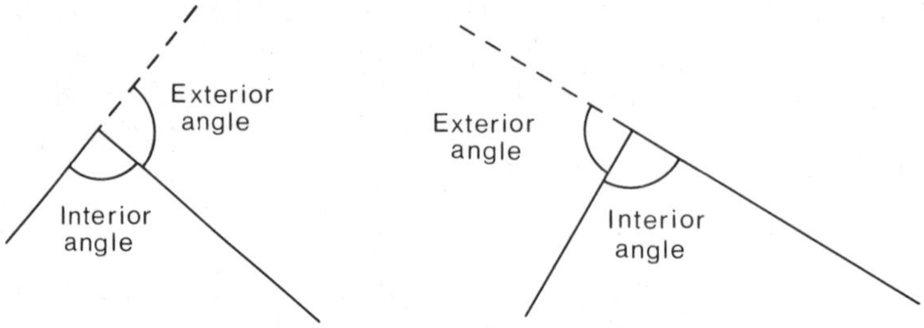

We have just noted that **the sum of the interior angles of a polygon depends on the number of sides the polygon has. Now we note that the sum of the exterior angles (one at each vertex) of any convex polygon is 360° regardless of the number of sides.** The following diagram shows this clearly. If you walk around the polygon shown and turn through the exterior angle at each vertex, at the end of your walk you will be again pointing in the same direction, for you have turned through a full 360°.

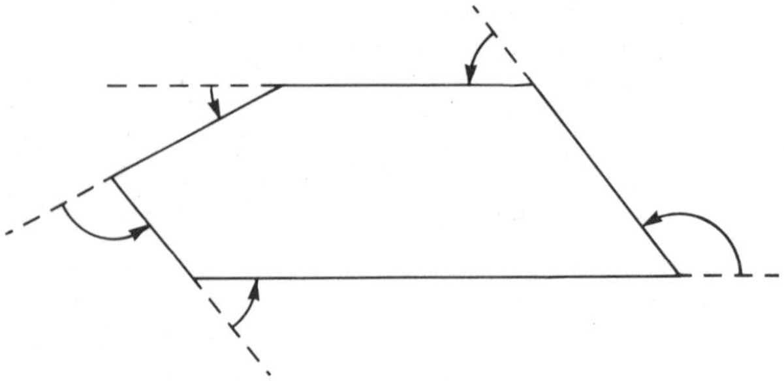

51.C Areas of regular polygons

A regular polygon of any number of sides can be inscribed in a circle. The vertices of the polygon will lie on the circle, and the center of the polygon will also be the center of the circle. The same figure can be obtained by beginning with the regular polygon and drawing a circle that passes through every vertex.

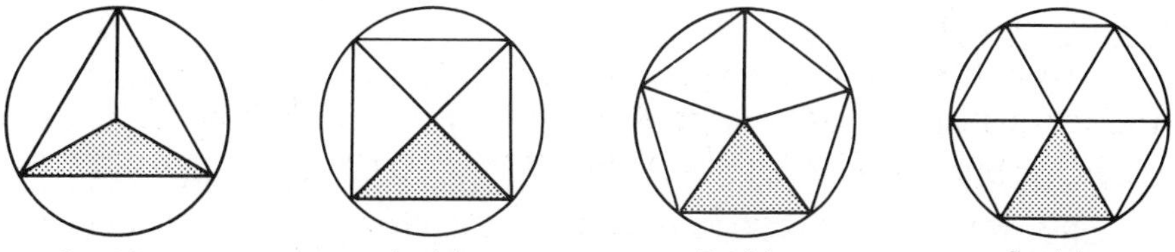

We note that each side of the polygon forms the base of an isosceles triangle whose sides are radii of the circle. The area of the polygon is the sum of the areas of the triangles. The altitude of each of these triangles is called an ***apothem*** of the polygon.

Example 51.C.1 Find the area of a regular pentagon (5 sides) that is inscribed in a circle whose radius is 6 units.

Solution There are 5 sides and 5 triangles. The 360° central angle is divided into 5 angles, each measuring 72°. The apothem bisects this angle (proved in a later lesson), and we have a 36° right triangle whose hypotenuse is 6. We can solve for x and the length of the apothem A.

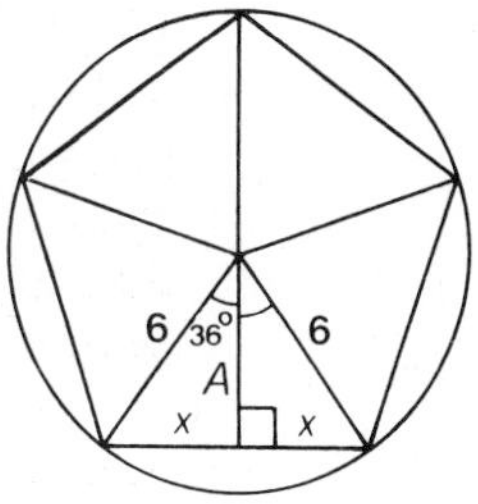

$$x = 6 \sin 36° \qquad A = 6 \cos 36°$$
$$x = 3.53 \qquad A = 4.85$$

The area of each small triangle is half the product of the base and the altitude.

$$\text{Area} = \frac{3.53 \times 4.85}{2} = 8.56 \text{ square units}$$

There are 10 of these small triangles in the figure, so the area of the whole polygon is 10 times the area of one triangle, or

85.6 square units

Example 51.C.2 The perimeter of a regular polygon of 8 sides is 48. Find the area of the polygon.

Solution The central angle is 360° divided by 8, or 45°, and half of 45° is 22.5°. If the perimeter is 48, each side is 6, and half of 6 is 3. We can solve the triangle for the altitude A.

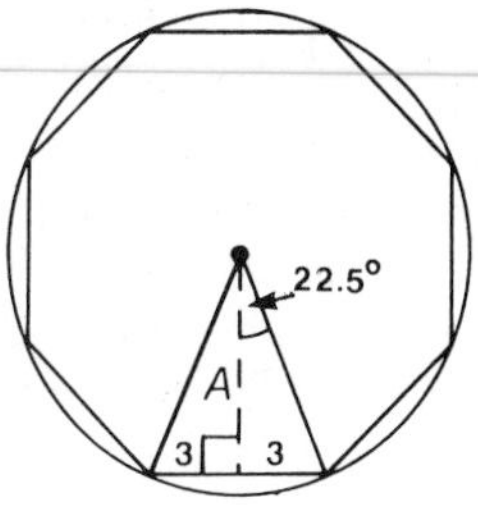

$$A = \frac{3}{\tan 22.5°} = 7.24$$

The area of one small triangle is

$$\frac{3 \times 7.24}{2} = 10.86 \text{ square units}$$

There are 16 of these small triangles, so the total area is

$$16 \times 10.86 = \mathbf{173.8\ square\ units}$$

51.D Areas of similar geometric figures

The ratio of the areas of similar two-dimensional geometric figures equals the square of the scale factor between the figures. This is easy to say but difficult to internalize and to remember. Many people find that specific examples can be a great help in remembering this relationship.

Example 51.D.1 The scale factor between two rectangles is 4. What is the ratio of the areas?

Solution We could use the square of the scale factor, but let's figure it out. On the left we draw a rectangle of dimensions L and W, and on the right we draw a rectangle of dimensions $4L$ and $4W$.

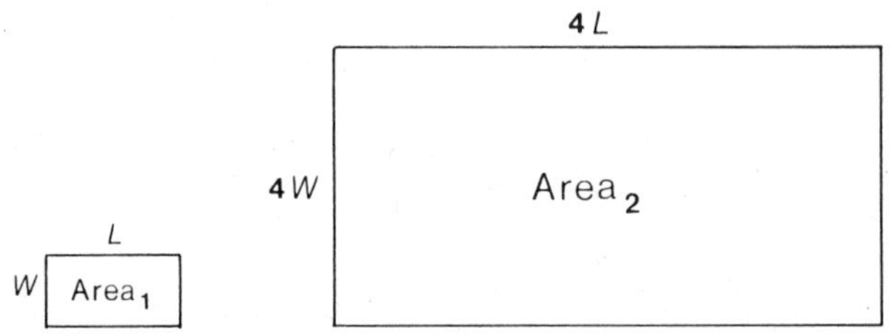

$$\text{Area}_1 = LW \qquad \text{Area}_2 = (4L)(4W) = 16LW$$

$$\frac{\text{Area}_1}{\text{Area}_2} = \frac{LW}{16LW} = \frac{1}{16}$$

Thus, we see that the ratio of the areas is **16 to 1,** or **1 to 16.**

Example 51.D.2 The radius of one circle is R, and the radius of a second circle is $\frac{3R}{5}$. What is the ratio of the area of the first circle to the area of the second circle?

Solution

$$\frac{\text{Area}_1}{\text{Area}_2} = \frac{\pi R^2}{\pi\left(\frac{3R}{5}\right)^2} = \frac{\pi R^2}{\pi\left(\frac{9R^2}{25}\right)} = \mathbf{\frac{25}{9}}$$

We could have tried to use the fact that the ratio of the areas equaled the square of the scale factor but we might have ended up with 9/25. If we work it out each time, we can be accurate and have a better feel for what we are doing.

Problem set 51

1. If $a * b$ means $3a - b$ and $a \# b$ means $\frac{a}{2} + 2b$, evaluate $(x * y) \# y$ if $x = 6$ and $y = 3$.

2. The woman is 3 times as old as her son. If she is half as old as her father, the grandfather is how many times older than the son?

3. M men pledged to contribute a total of \$1000 toward the purchase of playground equipment. If 5 men refused to honor their commitment, how much more did each of the other men have to pay?

4. Son-of-War had h hours of homework to do, but he just worked w hours. What fractional part of his homework remains?

5. If x is an even number, what is the quotient of the next greater even number divided by the next greater odd number?

6. Three were red-headed, two were blondes, and two were brunettes. How many ways could they sit in seven chairs if only the color of the hair was considered?

7. Find the sum of the interior angles of a 7-sided irregular convex polygon.

8. Find the sum of the exterior angles of a 16-sided irregular convex polygon.

9. A six-sided regular polygon is inscribed in a circle whose radius is 6. Find the area of the polygon.

10. The length of a side of an 8-sided regular polygon is 10 units. What is the area of the polygon?

11. Two 12-sided polygons are similar. A side of the larger polygon is 3 times as long as the corresponding side of the smaller polygon. What is the ratio of the area of the larger polygon to the area of the smaller polygon?

12. Solve this triangle for the unknown parts.

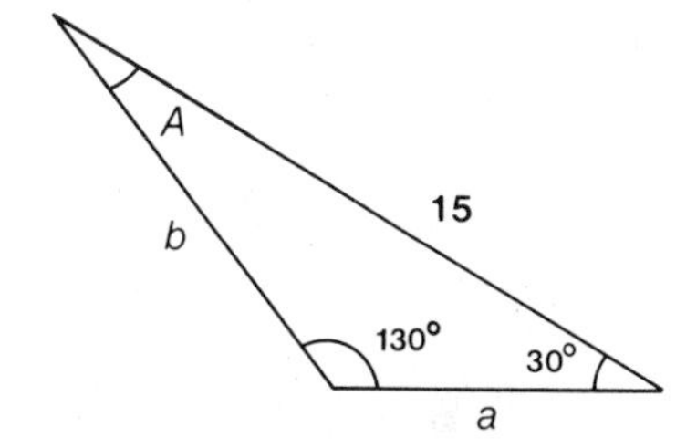

13. Graph the ellipse $9x^2 + 4y^2 = 36$.

14. Graph $y = \log_{1/4} x$.

15. Multiply $(3 \text{ cis } 20°)(4 \text{ cis } 10°)$ and express the answer in rectangular form. Give an exact answer.

16. Solve for b: $\begin{vmatrix} b+2 & 1 \\ -12 & b \end{vmatrix} = 12$

17. Prove that the sum of the angles in a triangle is 180°.

18. Prove that vertical angles are equal.

19. Write the equation of the following sinusoid in terms of the sine function.

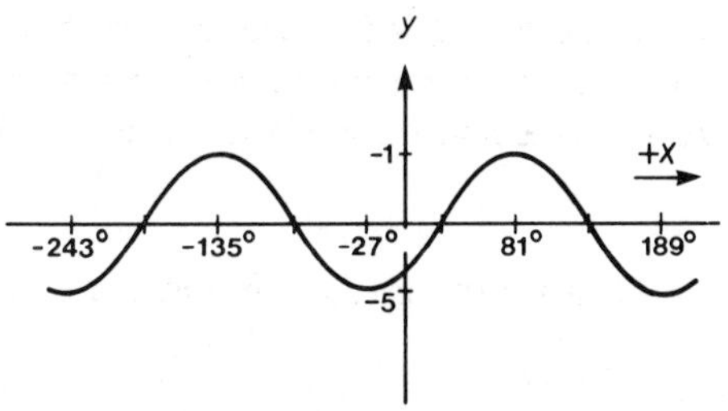

20. Write the equation of the sinusoid whose graph is a sine function with centerline $y = -2$, amplitude of 6, period of 2π, and phase angle of $\pi/4$.

21. Find the radius and the coordinates of the center of the circle whose equation is $x^2 + y^2 + 6x = 0$.

22. The three triangles shown are similar. Solve for x and y by writing the appropriate proportions.

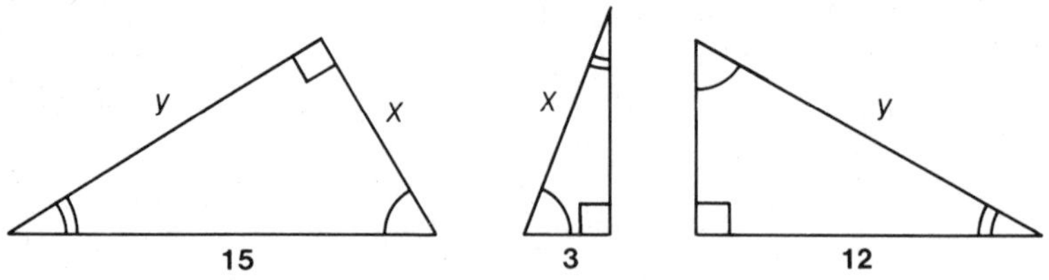

Solve the following equations given that ($0° \le \theta, x < 360°$):

23. $\sin\theta + 2\sin^2\theta = 0$

24. $4\cos^2\theta - 1 = 0$

25. $2\sin^2 x + \sin x - 1 = 0$

Evaluate:

26. $\tan^2(-690°) - \sec^2(-690°)$

27. $\sec^2\dfrac{\pi}{4} + \tan^2\dfrac{\pi}{4}$

Solve:

28. $\dfrac{1}{3}\ln 27 + 2\ln x = \ln(2 - x)$

29. $\log_8(x - 2) - \log_8(x - 3) = 2$

30. Find the base 5 antilogarithm of 3.

LESSON 52 *Cramer's rule*

52.A Cramer's rule

Most mathematicians are intrigued with the study of the patterns that one can obtain from arrays of numbers, and much of the mathematics that we have today is a result of the investigation of these patterns. The study of the patterns of the coefficients in systems of linear equations has evolved into what is known today as linear algebra. The first record we have of these investigations is in a letter to l'Hôpital (French) from Leibniz (German) in 1693. Euler (Swiss) and Maclaurin (Scottish) published works on the subject in 1748, and the opus of Gabrielle Cramer (Swiss) was published in 1750. The English mathematician Cayley is given considerable credit for work he did in the nineteenth century in this area.

One of the most famous patterns of coefficients is named for Cramer and is called ***Cramer's rule.*** It concerns the pattern of the coefficients in the solution of a system of linear equations. We have discovered that we can use elimination to solve a general system of linear equations for x and y, as we show here.

$$\begin{cases} ax + by = e \\ cx + dy = f \end{cases} \begin{matrix} \longrightarrow & (d) & \longrightarrow \\ \longrightarrow & (-b) & \longrightarrow \end{matrix} \begin{aligned} dax + dby &= de \\ -bcx - bdy &= -bf \end{aligned}$$

$$(ad - bc)x = de - bf \longrightarrow x = \frac{de - bf}{ad - bc}$$

$$\begin{cases} ax + by = e \\ cx + dy = f \end{cases} \begin{matrix} \longrightarrow & (-c) & \longrightarrow \\ \longrightarrow & (a) & \longrightarrow \end{matrix} \begin{aligned} -cax - cby &= -ce \\ acx + ady &= af \end{aligned}$$

$$(ad - bc)y = af - ce \longrightarrow y = \frac{af - ce}{ad - bc}$$

If we look carefully at the answers for x and y, we see that the denominators are the same and that the numerators are different. The men mentioned earlier found that these patterns are the same as the patterns we get from the following expressions.

$$x = \frac{\begin{vmatrix} e & b \\ f & d \end{vmatrix}}{\begin{vmatrix} a & b \\ c & d \end{vmatrix}} = \frac{ed - bf}{ad - cb} \qquad y = \frac{\begin{vmatrix} a & e \\ c & f \end{vmatrix}}{\begin{vmatrix} a & b \\ c & d \end{vmatrix}} = \frac{af - ce}{ad - cb}$$

We call this application of the possible patterns from square matrices Cramer's rule. Cramer and the others defined determinants so that the multiplications would produce these patterns. Thus, the rules for determinants were dictated by the requirement that the use of the rules would produce the solutions of the equations. We note that the elements of the determinants in the denominators are the coefficients of x and y in the given equations. **In the determinants in the numerators, the constants replace the coefficients of x when we solve for x, and the constants replace the coefficients of y when we solve for y.**

Example 52.A.1 Use Cramer's rule to solve: $\begin{cases} 3x + 2y = -1 \\ 4x - 3y = 10 \end{cases}$

Solution The denominator determinant for both variables is composed of the coefficients of x and y as they appear in the equations.

$$x = \frac{\begin{vmatrix} \; & \; \\ \; & \; \end{vmatrix}}{\begin{vmatrix} 3 & 2 \\ 4 & -3 \end{vmatrix}} \qquad y = \frac{\begin{vmatrix} \; & \; \\ \; & \; \end{vmatrix}}{\begin{vmatrix} 3 & 2 \\ 4 & -3 \end{vmatrix}}$$

The numerator determinants are the same except that the constants -1 and 10 replace the coefficients of x when we solve for x and replace the coefficients of y when we solve for y.

$$\mathbf{x} = \frac{\begin{vmatrix} -1 & 2 \\ 10 & -3 \end{vmatrix}}{\begin{vmatrix} 3 & 2 \\ 4 & -3 \end{vmatrix}} = \frac{3 - 20}{-9 - 8} = \mathbf{1} \qquad \mathbf{y} = \frac{\begin{vmatrix} 3 & -1 \\ 4 & 10 \end{vmatrix}}{\begin{vmatrix} 3 & 2 \\ 4 & -3 \end{vmatrix}} = \frac{30 + 4}{-9 - 8} = \mathbf{-2}$$

Example 52.A.2 Use Cramer's rule to solve: $\begin{cases} 5x - 3y = 1 \\ 2x - 7y = -17 \end{cases}$

Solution The denominator determinants are the same, and the numerator determinants are different.

$$x = \frac{\begin{vmatrix} 1 & -3 \\ -17 & -7 \end{vmatrix}}{\begin{vmatrix} 5 & -3 \\ 2 & -7 \end{vmatrix}} = \frac{-7-(51)}{-35-(-6)} = \mathbf{2} \qquad y = \frac{\begin{vmatrix} 5 & 1 \\ 2 & -17 \end{vmatrix}}{\begin{vmatrix} 5 & -3 \\ 2 & -7 \end{vmatrix}} = \frac{-85-2}{-35-(-6)} = \mathbf{3}$$

Problem set 52

1. A rod is chopped into 3 pieces. The first piece is 3 times as long as the second piece and the second piece is 3 times as long as the third piece. What fractional part of the rod is the shortest piece?

2. Sambo got $2\frac{1}{2}$ times his regular hourly wage for working on Saturday. On one Saturday he worked $2\frac{1}{2}$ hours and was paid \$16.25. What was his regular hourly wage?

3. Eleanor earned E dollars every month and spent P dollars. What fractional part of her income did she save?

4. A storekeeper sold N items for D dollars and made a profit of P dollars. How much did he pay for each item?

5. A piece of cloth y yards long had f feet cut from one end and n inches cut from the other end. What is the length in inches of the piece that remains?

6. Three times the lesser of two numbers equals 2 times the greater. If the sum of the numbers is 70, what are the two numbers?

Use Cramer's rule to solve:

7. $\begin{cases} 2x - 3y = -4 \\ 4x + 2y = 8 \end{cases}$

8. $\begin{cases} 3x + y = -2 \\ x - 2y = -3 \end{cases}$

9. Find the sum of the interior angles of any 10-sided convex polygon.

10. Find the sum of the exterior angles of an 11-sided regular polygon.

11. A 12-sided regular polygon is inscribed in a circle whose radius is 10 centimeters. Find the area of the polygon.

12. The length of a side of a 6-sided regular polygon is 4 centimeters. What is the radius of the circle which can be circumscribed about this polygon?

13. Two 14-sided polygons are similar. A side of the larger polygon is 4 times as long as the corresponding side of the smaller polygon. What is the ratio of the area of the larger polygon to the area of the smaller polygon?

14. Solve this triangle for the unknown parts.

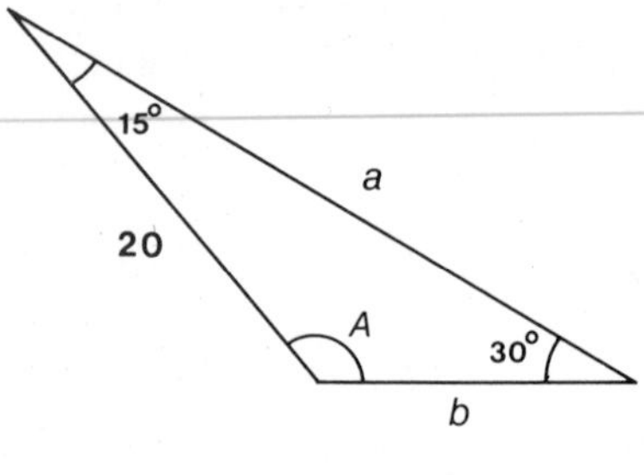

15. Graph the ellipse $25x^2 + 16y^2 = 400$.

16. Multiply $[4 \text{ cis } (-30°)](6 \text{ cis } 90°)$ and express the answer in rectangular form. Give an exact answer.

17. Solve for x: $\begin{vmatrix} x-1 & 5 \\ 3 & x \end{vmatrix} = 5$

18. Prove that if two angles of one triangle are equal to two angles of another triangle, the third angles of both triangles are equal.

19. Prove that the sum of the angles of a triangle is 180°.

20. Write the equation of the following sinusoid as a cosine function.

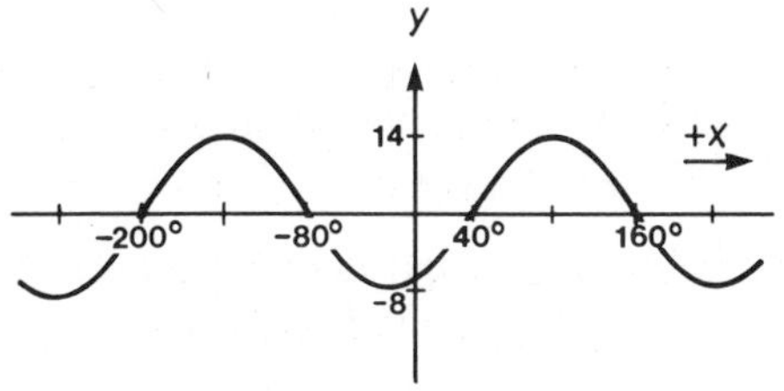

21. Write the equation of the sinusoid whose graph is a sine function with a centerline of $y = -1$, an amplitude of 14, a period of 360°, and a phase angle of $-45°$.

22. Find the radius and center of the circle whose equation is $x^2 + 10x + y^2 - 4y + 20 = 0$.

23. The horse galloped m miles at p miles per hour and then trotted m miles at k miles per hour. What was his average speed for the entire trip?

Solve the following equations given that $(0° \leq t, \theta, x < 360°)$:

24. $4\cos^2 t - 3 = 0$

25. $2\cos 3\theta - 1 = 0$

26. $\sec x - \sqrt{2}\sec x - 1 = 0$

27. Evaluate $\csc^2\left(-\frac{3\pi}{4}\right) - \cot^2\left(-\frac{3\pi}{4}\right)$

28. Solve: $\frac{1}{4}\ln 16 + 2\ln x = \ln(6 - x)$

29. Simplify: $b^{\log_b 24 - \log_b 6}$

30. Estimate the base e antilogarithm of 4.

LESSON 53 Combinations

53.A Combinations

A permutation of 10 objects taken 4 at a time is the number of different **ordered sets** of 4 items that can be selected from a set of 10 items. Any one of the 10 can be first; any one of the 9 remaining can be second; etc. Thus we find that there are

$$P_4^{10} = 10 \cdot 9 \cdot 8 \cdot 7 = 5040$$

5040 permutations. **A *combination* is a selection of items in which order is not considered.** In this case, there are

$$4 \cdot 3 \cdot 2 \cdot 1$$

ways that 4 things can be arranged in order, and if we divide as shown here,

$$\frac{10 \cdot 9 \cdot 8 \cdot 7}{4 \cdot 3 \cdot 2 \cdot 1} = 210$$

we find the number of unordered sets of 10 things taken 4 at a time. **Thus, to find the number of combinations of 10 things taken 4 at a time, we first find the number of permutations of 10 things taken 4 at a time, and then we divide by 4! to remove the effect of order in each collection of items.**

We can write the general expression for the combination of n things taken r at a time as the general expression for the permutation of n things taken r at a time divided by $r!$ to remove the effect of order.

$$_nC_r = \frac{n(n-1)(n-2)(n-3)\cdots(n-r+1)}{r!}$$

The expression for the combination of n things r at a time has the same four forms as do the permutations and has one additional form.

PERMUTATIONS:	$_nP_r$	P_r^n	$P_{n,r}$	$P(n, r)$	
COMBINATIONS:	$_nC_r$	C_r^n	$C_{n,r}$	$C(n, r)$	$\binom{n}{r}$

The last form, in parentheses with the n above the r, is used only for combinations and is almost never used for permutations. Thus, we could write the expression for the number of combinations of 5 things taken 2 at a time in any of the five following forms:

$$_5C_2 \qquad C_2^5 \qquad C_{5,2} \qquad C(5, 2) \qquad \binom{5}{2}$$

At this point, we will note the way most authors use the words ***permutation, arrangement,*** and ***combination.*** The words ***arrangement*** and ***permutation*** are used to designate distinct ordered sets, while the word ***combination*** designates a set or collection without regard to the order of the members of the set.

Example 53.A.1 In how many ways can a committee of 5 students be selected from a group of 12 students?

Solution First we will find the number of permutations of 12 people taken 5 at a time.

$$12 \cdot 11 \cdot 10 \cdot 9 \cdot 8 = 95{,}040$$

Now we divide this product by 5! because there are 5 people in each committee, and order does not count in a committee.

$$\frac{12 \cdot 11 \cdot 10 \cdot 9 \cdot 8}{5 \cdot 4 \cdot 3 \cdot 2 \cdot 1} = \mathbf{792}$$

It is interesting to note that each time we select an unordered set of 5, we leave behind an unordered set of 7. Thus, the number of combinations of 12 things taken 7 at a time should also be 792. It is, as we show here,

$$\frac{12 \cdot 11 \cdot 10 \cdot 9 \cdot 8 \cdot 7 \cdot 6}{7 \cdot 6 \cdot 5 \cdot 4 \cdot 3 \cdot 2 \cdot 1} = 792$$

Example 53.A.2 There are seven points located on a circle as shown. How many different triangles can be drawn using these points as the vertices?

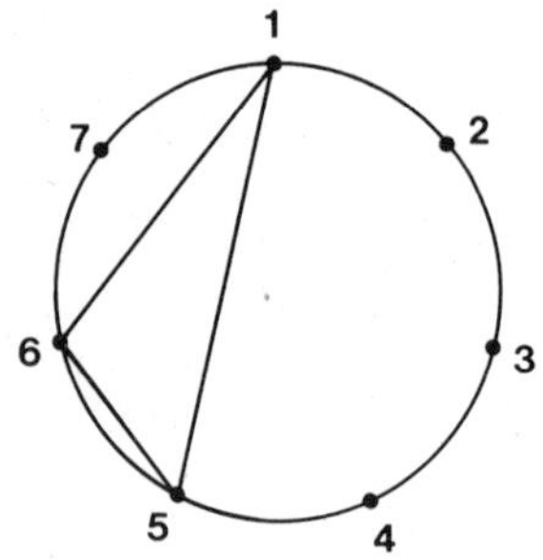

Solution First we will find the number of permutations of 7 things taken 3 at a time.

$$7 \cdot 6 \cdot 5 = 210 \text{ permutations}$$

Every time the same 3 points are used the same triangle results, so the order of the points is not a factor. Thus, we divide by 3! to remove the effect of order.

$$\frac{7 \cdot 6 \cdot 5}{3 \cdot 2 \cdot 1} = \mathbf{35}$$

Thus, it is possible to draw 35 different triangles.

Example 53.A.3 How many different 5-card hands can be dealt from a deck that contains 52 cards?

Solution There are 52 first possibilities, 51 second possibilities, etc., so the following product represents the number of permutations of 52 things taken 5 at a time.

$$52 \cdot 51 \cdot 50 \cdot 49 \cdot 48$$

Now we must divide by 5!, for each combination of 5 cards has 5! possible arrangements or permutations.

$$\frac{52 \cdot 51 \cdot 50 \cdot 49 \cdot 48}{5 \cdot 4 \cdot 3 \cdot 2 \cdot 1} = \mathbf{2{,}598{,}960}$$

There are 2,598,960 possible 5-card hands. We recommend the use of a calculator for calculations like this one.

Problem set 53

1. There were p pupils in the junior class and they decided to spend D dollars on a school project to which all would contribute equally. Then 20 students refused to donate. How much more did each of the rest of the students have to donate?
2. The big car was only averaging 7 miles per gallon of gas so Bo Willy overhauled the carburetor. Now he uses only one-third as much gasoline per mile. How many more miles can he go on 1 gallon of gas?
3. If p varies directly as m squared and inversely as the square root of N, what happens to p if m is multiplied by 4 and N is multiplied by 9?
4. Sarah called Tulsa on the telephone. The cost of the call was \$4.40 for the first 3 minutes and \$1.10 for each additional minute. Sarah talked longer than 3 minutes. In fact, she talked m minutes. What was the cost of her phone call?
5. If 8 points are spaced evenly on a circle, how many different triangles can be drawn using these points as the vertices?
6. How many ways can a committee of 4 people be selected from a group of 8 students?
7. Use Cramer's rule to solve: $\begin{cases} 3x - 4y = -3 \\ 2x + 3y = -4 \end{cases}$
8. Factor $2x^2 - 5x + 6$ over the set of complex numbers.
9. Find the sum of the interior angles of a 13-sided regular polygon.
10. Find the sum of the exterior angles of an 11-sided convex polygon.
11. A 10-sided regular polygon is inscribed in a circle whose radius is 10 cm. Find the area of the polygon.
12. The length of a side of an 8-sided regular polygon is 4 cm. What is the area of the polygon?
13. Two 8-sided convex polygons are similar. A side of the larger polygon is $2\frac{1}{2}$ times as long as the corresponding side of the smaller polygon. What is the ratio of the area of the larger polygon to the area of the smaller polygon?

14. Solve this triangle for the unknown parts.

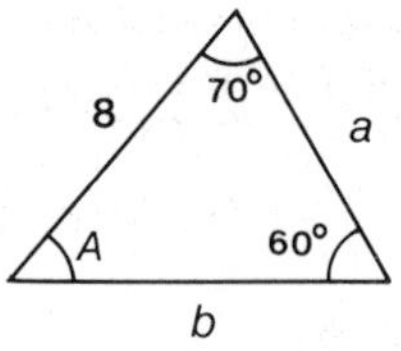

15. Graph the ellipse $5x^2 + 8y^2 = 40$.

16. Multiply $[5 \text{ cis } (-20°)](2 \text{ cis } 80°)$ and express the answer in rectangular form. Give an exact answer.

17. Solve for k: $\begin{vmatrix} 3 & k \\ k+1 & k \end{vmatrix} = 1$

18. Prove that an exterior angle of a triangle equals the sum of the remote interior angles.

19. Prove that the sum of the angles of a triangle is 180°.

20. Write the equation of the following sinusoid in terms of the sine function.

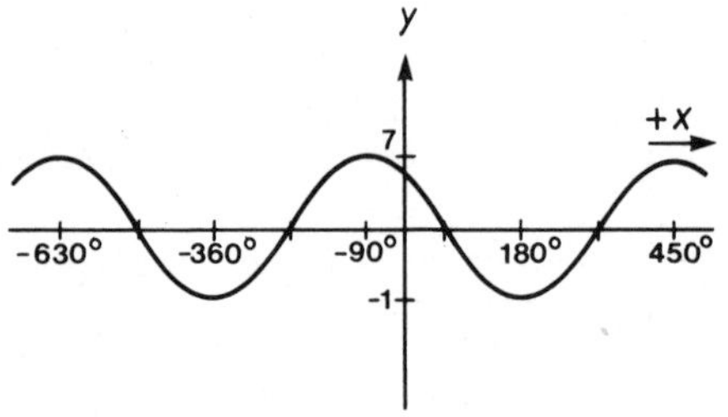

21. Write the equation of the sinusoid whose graph is a sine function with a centerline of $y = 10$, an amplitude of 6, a period of 4π, and a phase angle of $\pi/2$.

22. Find the radius and the coordinates of the center of the circle whose equation is $9x^2 + 9y^2 - 6x + 12y - 31 = 0$.

23. The three triangles shown are similar. Find a and b.

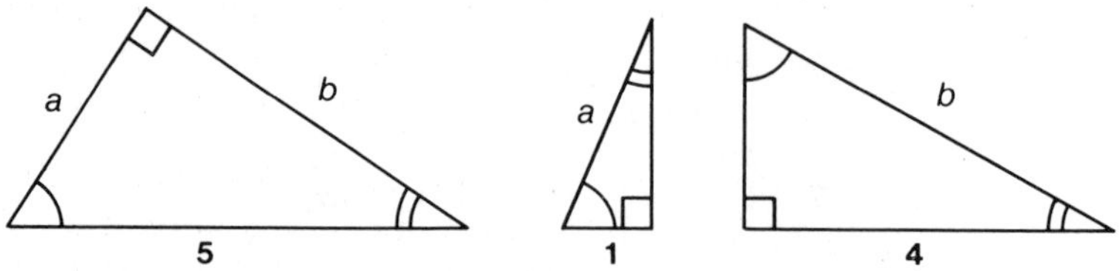

Solve the following equations given that $(0° \leq \theta < 360°)$:

24. $4 \sin^2 \theta - 3 = 0$

25. $2 \sin 3\theta - 1 = 0$

26. $\sin^2 \theta - 4 \sin \theta + 3 = 0$

27. Evaluate: $\cot^2 \frac{14\pi}{3} - \csc^2 \frac{14\pi}{3}$

28. Solve: $\frac{1}{3} \ln 8 + 2 \ln x = \ln(-3x + 2)$

29. Simplify: $h^{3 \log_h 2 - \log_h 2}$

30. Evaluate the base 6 antilogarithm of -2.

LESSON 54 Functions of $(-\theta)$ · Functions of the other angle · Trigonometric identities (1)

54.A Functions of $(-\theta)$

If we look at the triangles that we use to find the values of functions of 30° and −30°, we see that the sine of 30° equals $\frac{1}{2}$ and the sine of −30° equals $-\frac{1}{2}$.

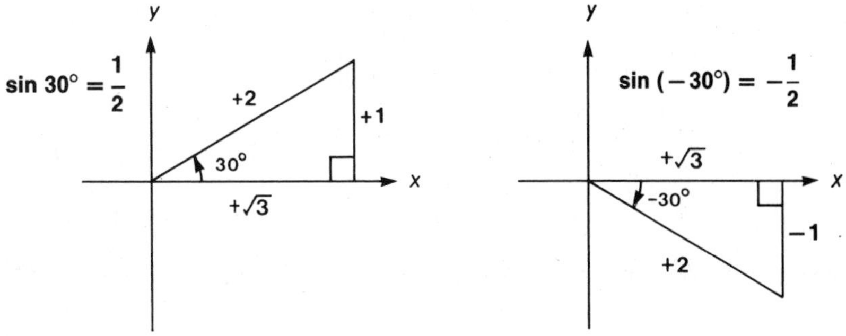

The sine of −30° has the same magnitude as the sine of 30° but has the opposite sign. Thus, we can say that

$$\sin(-30°) = -\sin 30°$$

If we increase θ so that θ is a second-quadrant angle and $-\theta$ is a third-quadrant angle, we get the same relationship between the sines of the angles.

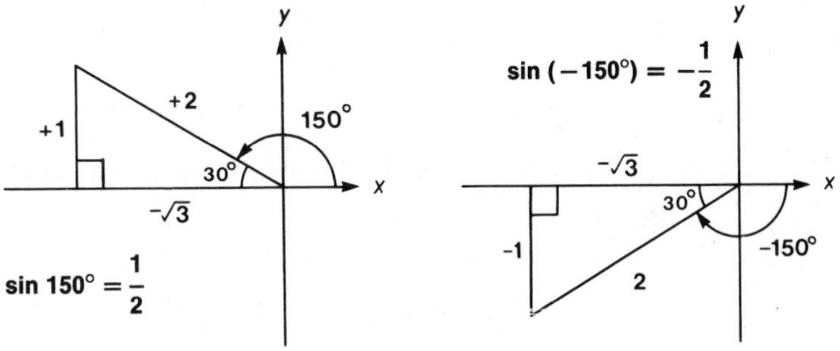

It can be shown that this relationship holds for all values of θ so that, in general, we can say

$$\sin(-\theta) = -\sin\theta$$

We can also see this if we look at the graph of the sine function. If we go a distance θ to the right of 0°, the vertical distance from the axis to the curve represents $\sin\theta$. If we go the same distance to the left of 0°, the vertical distance from the axis to the curve represents the sine of $-\theta$. The vertical distances have the same magnitudes but are measured in opposite directions!

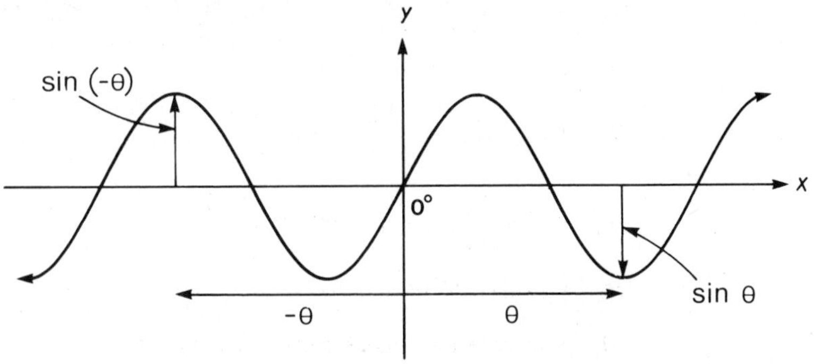

If we go back and look at the four triangles and consider the cosines of $\pm 30°$ and $\pm 150°$, we get

$$\cos 30° = \frac{\sqrt{3}}{2} \qquad \cos(-30°) = \frac{\sqrt{3}}{2}$$

$$\cos 150° = -\frac{\sqrt{3}}{2} \qquad \cos(-150°) = -\frac{\sqrt{3}}{2}$$

Here we see that the cosine of 30° and the cosine of $-30°$ have exactly the same value and that the cosine of 150° and the cosine of $-150°$ are also exactly the same. It can be shown that this relationship holds for any value of the angle and its opposite. In general, we can say

$$\cos(-\theta) = \cos\theta$$

We can also see that $\cos(-\theta) = \cos\theta$ if we look at a graph of the cosine. The distance from the axis to the curve for any value of θ is the same and is in the same direction as it is for $-\theta$.

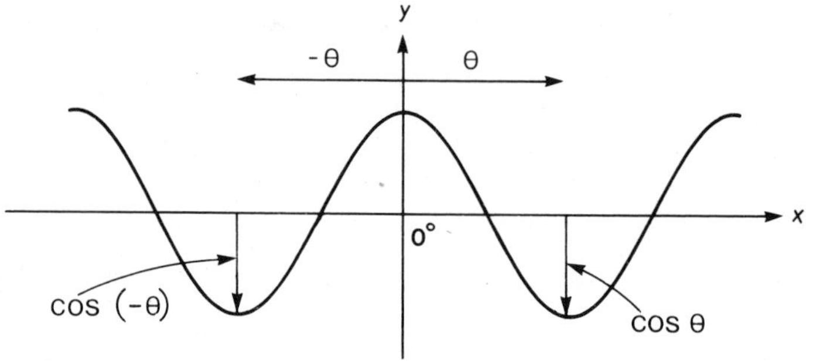

If we go back and look at the four triangles and consider the tangents of the four angles, we get

$$\tan 30° = \frac{1}{\sqrt{3}} \qquad \tan(-30°) = -\frac{1}{\sqrt{3}}$$

$$\tan 150° = -\frac{1}{\sqrt{3}} \qquad \tan(-150°) = \frac{1}{\sqrt{3}}$$

This relationship holds for all values of θ, so we can say

$$\tan(-\theta) = -\tan\theta$$

In a future lesson, when we study the graph of the tangent function, we will be able to see this relationship from the graph. Thus, $\sin(-\theta)$ and $\tan(-\theta)$ have opposite signs from $\sin\theta$ and $\tan\theta$ respectively, but $\cos(-\theta)$ has the same value as $\cos\theta$. Since the cosecant, secant, and cotangent are reciprocal functions, their sign relationships will correspond to those for the sine, cosine, and tangent, as we show here.

$$\sin(-\theta) = -\sin\theta \qquad \cos(-\theta) = \cos\theta \qquad \tan(-\theta) = -\tan\theta$$

$$\csc(-\theta) = -\csc\theta \qquad \sec(-\theta) = \sec\theta \qquad \cot(-\theta) = -\cot\theta$$

54.B Functions of the other angle

The sum of the angles in any triangle is 180°. If the triangle is a right triangle, the right angle equals 90°. Thus, if one acute angle is θ, then the other acute angle must be

$90° - \theta$. If the sum of two angles is $90°$, the angles are called ***complementary angles,*** and thus $90° - \theta$ is often called the complement of θ.

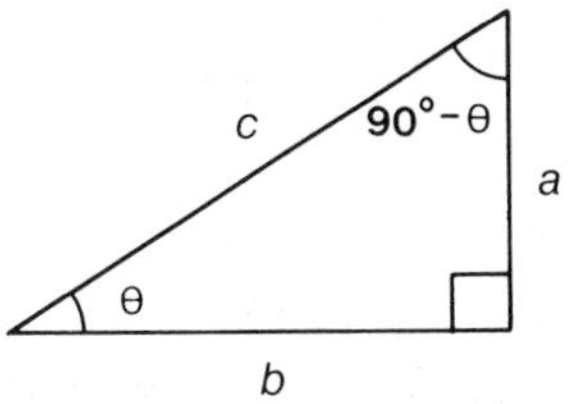

In the right triangle shown here, the sine of θ equals a over c, and the cosine of the other acute angle also equals a over c.

$$\sin \theta = \frac{a}{c} \qquad \cos (90° - \theta) = \frac{a}{c}$$

The cosine of θ equals b over c, and the sine of the other acute angle equals b over c.

$$\cos \theta = \frac{b}{c} \qquad \sin (90° - \theta) = \frac{b}{c}$$

The tangent and cotangent have similar relationships.

$$\tan \theta = \frac{a}{b} \qquad \cot (90° - \theta) = \frac{a}{b}$$

$$\cot \theta = \frac{b}{a} \qquad \tan (90° - \theta) = \frac{b}{a}$$

The secant and cosecant have similar relationships.

$$\sec \theta = \frac{c}{b} \qquad \csc (90° - \theta) = \frac{c}{b}$$

$$\csc \theta = \frac{c}{a} \qquad \sec (90° - \theta) = \frac{c}{a}$$

Thus, the trigonometric functions of θ have the same values as do the trigonometric cofunctions of $(90° - \theta)$. We can remember this if we always think of $(90° - \theta)$ as the other angle.

$(90° - \theta)$ is the other angle

It is interesting to note that the words *co*sine, *co*tangent and *co*secant are abbreviations for the sine of the complementary angle (the other angle), the tangent of the complementary angle (the other angle), and the secant of the complementary angle (the other angle), respectively. Thus

cosine	**means**	**the sine of the other angle**
cotangent	**means**	**the tangent of the other angle**
cosecant	**means**	**the secant of the other angle**

54.C Trigonometric identities (1)

There is a difference between a conditional equation and an identity. A conditional equation is a true equation only for some specific value(s) of the variable(s), while an identity is true for any value(s) of the variable(s). Consider the conditional equation and the identity shown here.

CONDITIONAL EQUATION	IDENTITY
$x + 4 = 7$	$2x - 3 = 3x - x - 3$

This conditional equation can be transformed into a true equation only by replacing x with 3, which we do on the left. No other number will satisfy this equation. The identity will be transformed into a true equation with any replacement value of x. We illustrate this on the right by using -5 as a replacement value for x. Try another number in the identity, for any number will work.

CONDITIONAL EQUATION		IDENTITY	
$(3) + 4 = 7$	used 3 for x	$2(-5) - 3 = 3(-5) - (-5) - 3$	used -5 for x
$7 = 7$	true	$-13 = -13$	true

If we avoid values of the variables that would cause division by zero, the two expressions shown here have identical values.

$$\frac{x}{1 + \dfrac{a}{b + \dfrac{1}{x}}} \qquad \frac{x(bx + 1)}{bx + 1 + ax}$$

For some purposes the form on the left might be preferred, and for other purposes the form on the right might be preferred.

Some algebraic expressions contain combinations of trigonometric functions, and often the solution of a problem will depend on the ability to change the form of one of these trigonometric expressions to an equivalent form that is more useful. The two forms of the expression have identical values and are called ***trigonometric identities.*** Learning to change the forms of these expressions can be thought of as a kind of game or puzzle. The solutions to these puzzles have no immediate applications, but the inability to change trigonometric expressions from one form to another can be a serious liability when you take more advanced courses in mathematics.

54.D Rules of the game

We will be demonstrating that an expression can be changed in form to the form of another expression or that two expressions can be transformed into identical forms. It is customary to eschew the use of the rules for solving equations, so we will not add the same quantity to both expressions nor will we multiply both expressions by the same quantity. Thus, we will restrict ourselves to three procedures. We may:

1. Substitute an equivalent expression for any part of a given expression.
2. Multiply the top and bottom of any expression or the top and bottom of a part of any expression by the same nonzero quantity.
3. Combine terms that have equal denominators.

To begin identities, we remember that the cotangent, secant, and cosecant are reciprocal functions.

$$\cot\theta = \frac{1}{\tan\theta} \qquad \sec\theta = \frac{1}{\cos\theta} \qquad \csc\theta = \frac{1}{\sin\theta}$$

Example 54.D.1 Show that $\dfrac{\cot x}{\csc x} = \cos x$.

Solution A good first step for any trigonometric identity is to replace all tangents, cotangents, secants, and cosecants with equivalent expressions that contain sines and cosines. We will do that, and on the left, we substitute $\sin x$ and $\cos x$ as required and try to algebraically change the left side to $\cos x$.

$$\frac{\cot x}{\csc x} \qquad \text{left side}$$

$$\frac{\dfrac{\cos x}{\sin x}}{\dfrac{1}{\sin x}} \qquad \text{substituted}$$

$$\cos x \qquad \text{simplified}$$

Example 54.D.2 Show that $\sin x \cot x = \dfrac{1}{\sec x}$.

Solution We will work with the left side and replace $\cot x$ with $\cos x$ over $\sin x$.

$$\sin x \cot x \qquad \text{left side}$$

$$\sin x \frac{\cos x}{\sin x} \qquad \text{substituted}$$

$$\cos x \qquad \text{simplified}$$

$$\frac{1}{\sec x} \qquad \text{substituted}$$

Example 54.D.3 Show that $\cos(-\theta) \sin(90° - \theta) = \cos^2 \theta$.

Solution We will work with the left side and replace $\cos(-\theta)$ with $\cos \theta$ and replace $\sin(90° - \theta)$ with $\cos \theta$.

$$\cos(-\theta) \sin(90° - \theta) \qquad \text{left side}$$

$$(\cos \theta)(\cos \theta) \qquad \text{substituted}$$

$$\cos^2 \theta \qquad \text{multiplied}$$

Problem set 54

1. An oak tree is x feet high and is 1 foot higher than $\frac{3}{5}$ the height of a pine tree. Write an expression for the height of the pine tree.

2. The window was marked up 20 percent of cost to get a selling price of \$480. It did not sell so the dealer reduced the markup to 15 percent of cost. What was the new selling price?

3. Mary is 1 year older than Joe. Eight years ago 3 times Mary's age exceeded twice Joe's age by 6. How old will both of them be in 17 years?

4. Pushmataha ran as fast as he could, but he could only cover y yards in m minutes so he got there 15 minutes late. How fast should he have run to have gotten there on time?

5. There were 10 people present. How many committees of 8 could be selected from the 10 people?

6. A club has 10 members and wants them to pose 6 at a time for group pictures. How many groups of 6 can be formed from the 10 people?

7. Show that $\cos x \tan x = \dfrac{1}{\csc x}$.

8. Show that $-\sin(-\theta) \cos(90° - \theta) = \sin^2 \theta$.

9. Show that $\frac{\cot x}{\csc x} = \cos x$.

10. Use Cramer's rule to solve: $\begin{cases} 6x - 4y = 5 \\ 3x + 2y = 6 \end{cases}$

11. Find the sum of the interior angles of a 15-sided irregular convex polygon.

12. Find the sum of the exterior angles of a 15-sided regular polygon.

13. A 5-sided regular polygon (a regular pentagon) is inscribed in a circle whose radius is 12 inches. Find the area of the polygon.

14. The length of a side of an 8-sided regular polygon is 5 inches. What is the radius of the circle which can be circumscribed about this octagon?

15. Two 10-sided convex polygons (decagons) are similar. A side of the larger polygon is $3\frac{1}{3}$ times longer than the corresponding side of the smaller polygon. What is the ratio of the area of the larger polygon to the area of the smaller polygon?

16. Solve this triangle for the unknown parts.

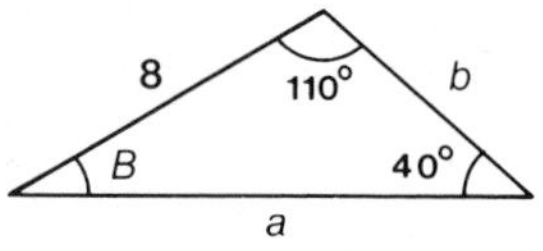

17. Graph the ellipse $6x^2 + 3y^2 = 36$.

18. Multiply $[6 \text{ cis } (-40°)](3 \text{ cis } 100°)$ and express the answer in rectangular form. Give an exact answer.

19. Prove that if an acute angle of one right triangle is equal to an angle of another right triangle, then the other acute angles of both triangles are equal.

20. Write the equation of the following sinusoid as a cosine function.

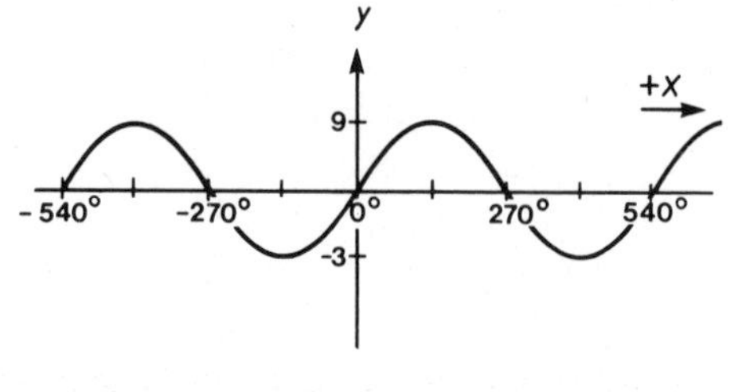

21. Write the equation of the sinusoid whose graph is a sine function with a phase angle of $-30°$, a period of $90°$, and amplitude of $\frac{3}{2}$, and a centerline of $y = -3$.

22. Find the radius and the coordinates of the center of the circle whose equation is $2x^2 + 2y^2 - x + y - \frac{31}{4} = 0$.

23. If $-10 < a < -1$ and $2 < b < 7$, compare: *A.* $a - b$ *B.* $b - a$

Solve the following equations given that $(0° \le x, \theta < 360°)$:

24. $\tan^2 x - 3 = 0$

25. $2 \cos 4\theta - 1 = 0$

26. $2 \cos^2 x + \cos x - 1 = 0$

27. Evaluate: $\tan^2 (-510°) - \sec^2 (-510°)$

Solve:

28. $\log_7 (x + 1) + \log_7 (2x - 3) = \log_7 4x$

29. $\frac{1}{4} \log_{1/2} 16 - 2 \log_{1/2} x = 3$

30. Evaluate the base 5 antilogarithm of -1.

LESSON 55 Binomial expansions (1)

55.A Binomial expansions (1)

In mathematics, we often encounter binomials raised to a nonnegative integral power such as the four expressions shown here.

$$(F + S)^2 \qquad (a + b)^7 \qquad (x + y)^5 \qquad (2x + 3m)^4$$

When we perform the indicated multiplications and write the longer equivalent expressions, we say that we have **expanded the binomials.** If we look at the six expansions shown here we see an interesting pattern.

$(a + b)^0 =$	1	1 term
$(a + b)^1 =$	$1a^1 + 1b^1$	2 terms
$(a + b)^2 =$	$1a^2 + 2ab + 1b^2$	3 terms
$(a + b)^3 =$	$1a^3 + 3a^2b + 3ab^2 + 1b^3$	4 terms
$(a + b)^4 =$	$1a^4 + 4a^3b + 6a^2b^2 + 4ab^3 + 1b^4$	5 terms
$(a + b)^5 =$	$1a^5 + 5a^4b + 10a^3b^2 + 10a^2b^3 + 5ab^4 + 1b^5$	6 terms

We notice that the number of terms in each expansion is 1 greater than the power of the binomial. The expansion of $(a + b)^2$ has 3 terms and the expansion of $(a + b)^5$ has 6 terms, etc. Further, we note that the first and last terms in the expansions contain only 1 variable and that each of these variables has the same exponent as does the binomial. Also, we note that the exponent of one of the variables increases with each term while the exponent of the other variable decreases, and that the sum of the exponents in each term is a constant. If we use a small box $\square$ to represent the coefficient of each term, we can concentrate on the exponents. If we do this for the last line above for the expansion of $(a + b)^5$ and use a^0 and b^0 as necessary to complete the pattern, we get

	$\square a^5b^0 +$	$\square a^4b^1 +$	$\square a^3b^2 +$	$\square a^2b^3 +$	$\square ab^4 +$	$\square a^0b^5$
Exponent of a	5	4	3	2	1	0
Exponent of b	0	1	2	3	4	5

A similar pattern of exponents occurs in every expansion. Now, if we disregard the variables and look only at the coefficients in the expansions, we get the following triangular array.

$(a + b)^0$	1
$(a + b)^1$	1 1
$(a + b)^2$	1 2 1
$(a + b)^3$	1 3 3 1
$(a + b)^4$	1 4 6 4 1
$(a + b)^5$	1 5 10 10 5 1
$(a + b)^6$	1 6 15 20 15 6 1

We note that each number is the sum of the two numbers just above it, as we have indicated in three places. This pattern of coefficients is called ***Pascal's triangle.*** It is easy to reconstruct because the first entry in each row is 1 and the last entry in each row is 1, and there are three 1s at the top.

When we use the patterns just investigated to write the terms of binomial expansions, there is nothing to understand. The same patterns always occur, and it is easier to remember the patterns than it is to perform the indicated multiplications.

Example 55.A.1 Write the fourth term of $(x + y)^6$.

Solution First we write the exponents for x and y in order.

Term	①	②	③	④	⑤	⑥	⑦
For x	6,	5,	4,	3,	2,	1,	0
For y	0,	1,	2,	3,	4,	5,	6

Now from the seventh row of Pascal's triangle, we get the coefficients

Term	①	②	③	④	⑤	⑥	⑦
Coefficient	1	6	15	20	15	6	1

Thus, the fourth term is $\mathbf{20x^3y^3}$.

Example 55.A.2 Write all eight terms of the expansion of $(x + y)^7$.

Solution First we look at the exponents.

For x	7	6	5	4	3	2	1	0
For y	0	1	2	3	4	5	6	7

Now we use the eighth row of Pascal's triangle to write the coefficients and get

1 7 21 35 35 21 7 1

Now we can write the complete expansion.

$$\mathbf{(x + y)^7 = x^7 + 7x^6y + 21x^5y^2 + 35x^4y^3 + 35x^3y^4 + 21x^2y^5 + 7xy^6 + y^7}$$

Problem set 55

1. If x is an odd number, what is the quotient of the next greater odd number divided by the next greater even number?

2. Find three consecutive integers such that the product of the first and the third exceeds the second by 19.

3. The city has an assessed valuation of \$6,400,000. The rate for school taxes is 80 cents per \$100 valuation. If all but 2 percent of the taxes have been collected, how many dollars have not been collected?

4. Twiddybums sell for \$200 each, but students get a 12 percent discount. If students pay cash, the student price is reduced another 6 percent of the original price. What would a student who paid cash have to pay for 4 twiddybums?

5. On a 600-mile trip, the traveler traveled 50 miles per hour for the first one-third of the trip and at 40 miles per hour for the rest of the trip. What was the traveler's average speed for the entire trip?

6. How many different 5-player basketball teams could be formed from 9 players? Assume that anyone can play any position.

7. Write the third term of $(x + y)^7$.

8. Write all five terms of $(x + y)^4$.

9. Show that $\sin x \sec x = \tan x$.

10. Show that $\sin(-\theta)\tan(90° - \theta) = -\cos\theta$.

11. Show that $\sec x \cot x = \csc x$.

12. Use Cramer's rule to solve: $\begin{cases} 4x - 2y = 6 \\ 3x - y = 7 \end{cases}$

13. Find the sum of the interior angles of a 12-sided convex polygon (dodecagon).

14. Find the sum of the exterior angles of a 9-sided convex polygon.

15. What is the radius of the circle that can be circumscribed about a regular 6-sided polygon (hexagon) whose perimeter is 36 centimeters?

16. Two triangles are similar. The ratio of one side of a larger triangle to the corresponding side of a smaller triangle is 4 to 3. What is the ratio of their areas?

17. Solve this triangle for angle A and side a.

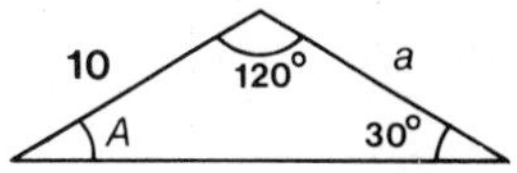

18. Graph the ellipse $8x^2 + 2y^2 = 16$.

19. Multiply $[4 \text{ cis}(-30°)](2 \text{ cis } 90°)$ and express the answer in rectangular form. Give an exact answer.

20. Find the distance from (1, 4) to $3x - 5y + 2 = 0$.

21. Write the equation of the following sinusoid as a sine function.

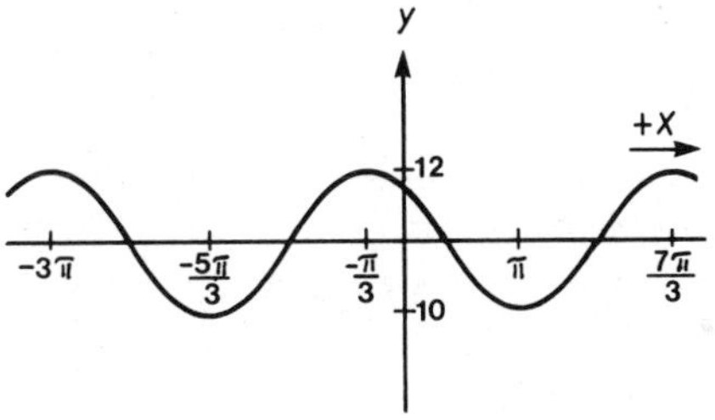

22. Write the equation of the sinusoid whose graph is a sine function with an amplitude of π, a period of 540°, a centerline of $y = \pi/2$, and a phase angle of 60°.

23. Find the radius and center of the circle whose equation is $2x^2 + 2y^2 - 12x + 8y + 24 = 0$.

24. Find x.

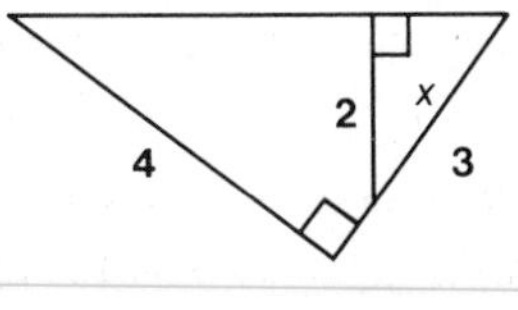

Solve the following equations given that ($0° \le x, \theta < 360°$):

25. $3\tan^2 x - 1 = 0$

26. $\sqrt{3}\tan 3\theta - 1 = 0$

27. Evaluate: $\csc^2 \frac{19\pi}{3} - \cot^2 \frac{19\pi}{3}$

28. Solve: $\log_8(x - 1) - \log_8(x - 2) = 2\log_8 3$

29. Evaluate: $3\log_7 7 + 7^{2\log_7 3 - \log_7 3}$

30. Evaluate the base 6 antilogarithm of 3.

There are five enrichment lessons in the appendix that discuss syllogistic reasoning, matrices, and mathematical induction. Each lesson contains a homework problem set. If these lessons are to be included, the first one should be taught at this point so that the repetitive problems on these topics will be effective. The enrichment problems are in the appendix, and the last entry in each regular problem set will indicate which enrichment problems should be worked. The other four enrichment lessons should be inserted after Lessons 65, 76, 86, and 95.

LESSON 56 Major postulates · Construction

56.A Major postulates

The study of geometry begins with undefined terms, definitions, and postulates. As we have remarked before, postulates are statements that are accepted as true without proof. We try to make as few postulates as possible and then use the postulates and definitions to perform proofs. If an assertion can be proved, we say that it is a ***theorem*** to distinguish it from a postulate, which is an assertion that is not proved. We have made two major postulates thus far. We have postulated that, for triangles, equal angles imply proportional sides and proportional sides imply equal angles. We have postulated that when parallel lines are cut by a transversal, the alternate interior angles are equal. There are other postulates that are made in geometry. The reasonableness of the following postulates can be verified by inspecting the figures shown.

1. The shortest path between two different points is the line segment that connects the points.
2. A line can be drawn through any two different points, and only one line can be drawn through the two points.

3. Through a point not on a given line, one and only one line can be drawn perpendicular to the given line, and one and only one line can be drawn parallel to the given line.

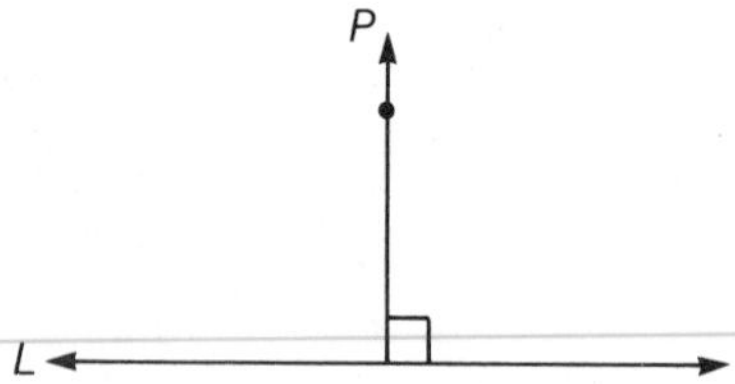

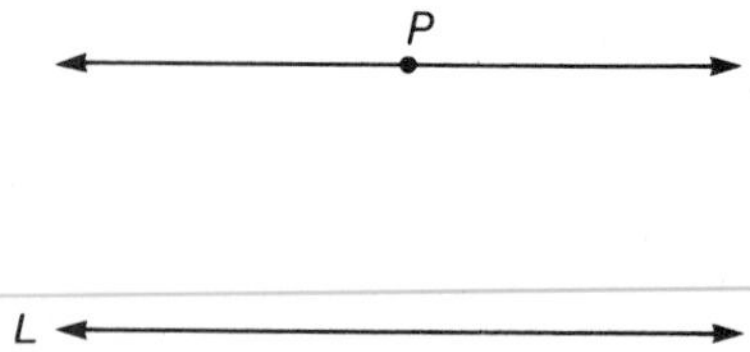

4. The shortest path from a point to a line is along the segment perpendicular to the line. Parallel lines are everywhere equidistant.

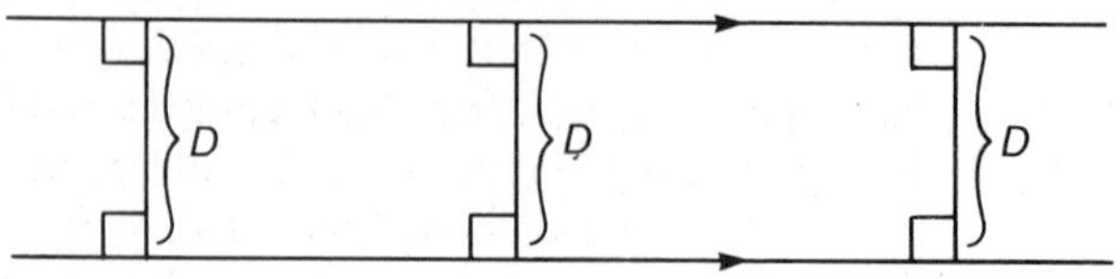

5. Three noncollinear points determine the plane that contains the points.

6. Two lines in the same plane either intersect or they are parallel.

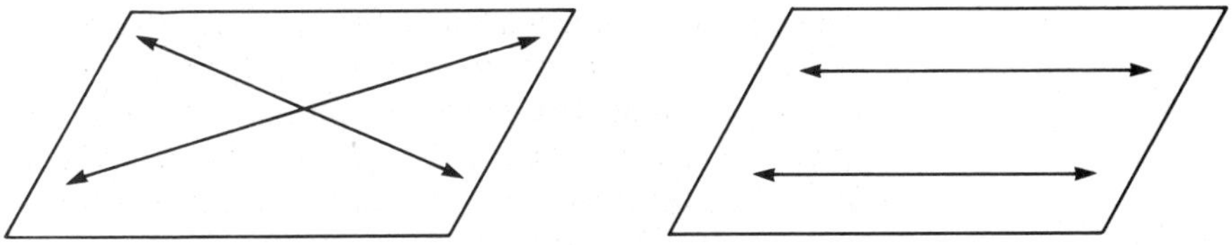

7. The intersection of two planes is a straight line.

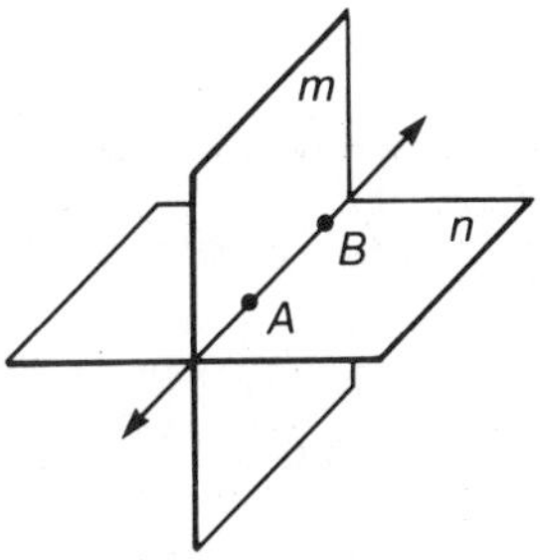

8. A line perpendicular to two lines in a plane is perpendicular to all lines in the plane that pass through the point of intersection.

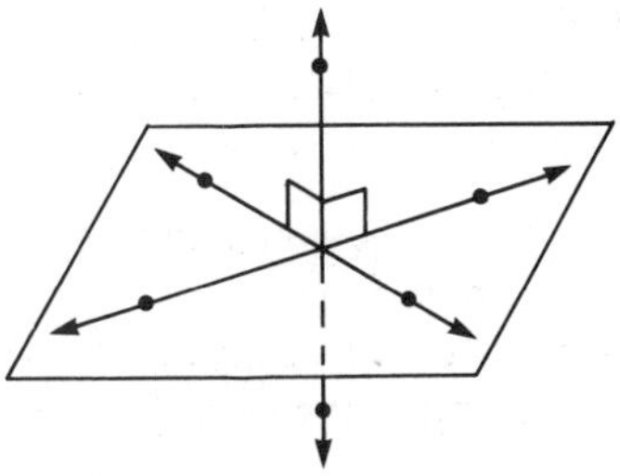

56.B Construction

The tools used for geometric construction by the ancient Greeks were the straightedge and the compass.

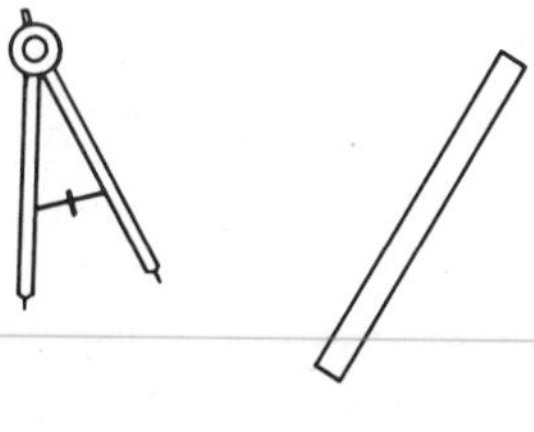

The straightedge of the Greeks did not have markings as do our rulers, so the straightedge could only be used to draw a line segment between or through two points or to extend a given line segment. Sometimes we will use the ruler as a straightedge, and at other times we will use a ruler to measure distances. The modern compass shown above has capabilities that the Greek compasses did not have. We can use a modern compass to copy a given length, to draw a full circle, or to draw an arc (part of a circle).

The most useful constructions are copying line segments, copying angles, bisecting line segments, and bisecting angles. These basic constructions can be used in combination to perform more involved constructions, as we shall see.

Example 56.B.1 Construct a triangle whose sides equal the lengths of these line segments.

Solution We begin by drawing a line segment, marking a beginning point on the line segment, and then using a compass to lay off a length equal to one of the sides. Any one of the sides may be used, and we choose side A.

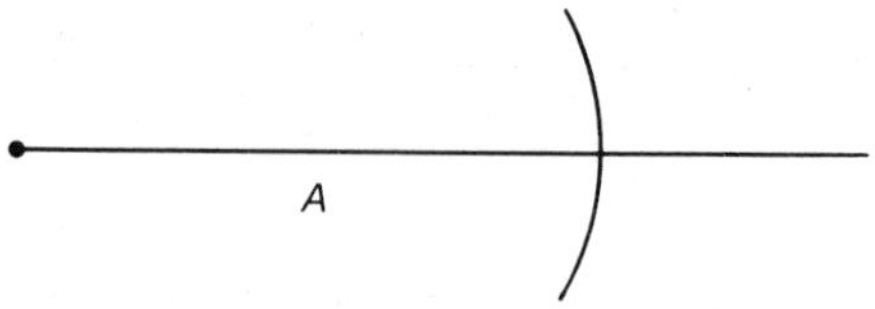

Two of the vertices of the triangle are at the points marked by the dot and the arc. To find the other vertex, we draw an arc of radius B from one end of $\bar{A}$ and an arc of radius C from the other end of $\bar{A}$. The intersection of the arcs marks the other vertex. Then the straightedge is used to connect the vertices.

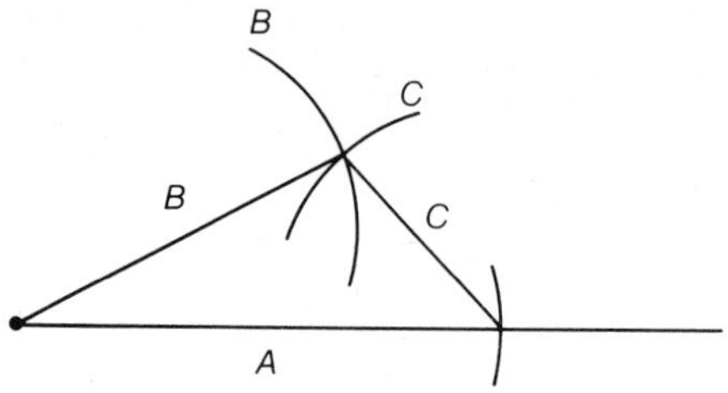

Example 56.B.2 Construct a triangle whose sides equal the lengths of these line segments. Use segment A as the base.

Solution We copy segment A and from each end we lay off arcs whose lengths are B and C.

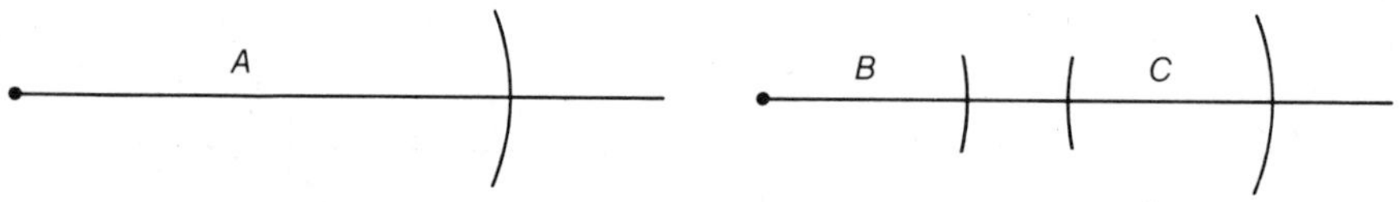

We see that segments B and C are not long enough to meet and form a triangle. **This demonstrates that the sum of the lengths of any two sides of a triangle must exceed the length of the third side.**

Example 56.B.3 Copy the angle shown on the left.

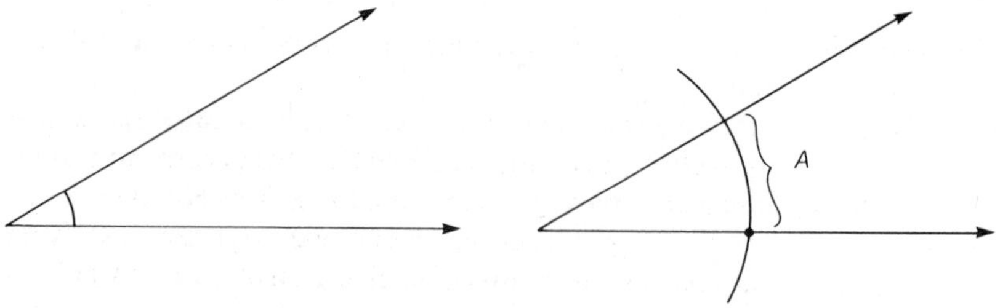

Solution As the first step (on the right on the preceding page), we draw an arc of convenient radius from the vertex of the angle. Next (on the left below), we draw a line segment and draw an arc of the same radius from one endpoint.

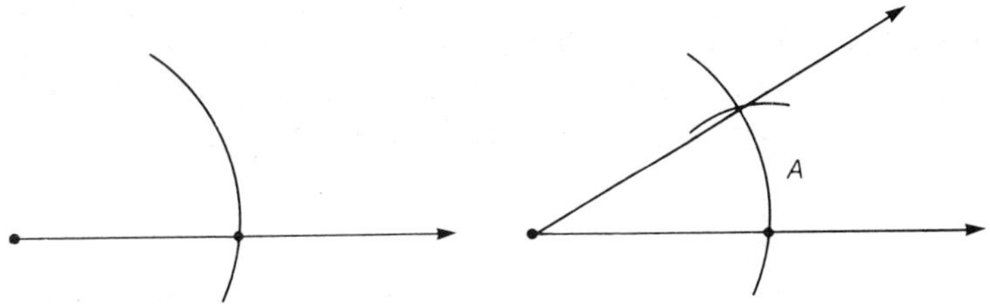

Next we use the compass to measure length A on the preceding page and to draw an arc of radius A as we show on the right. Then we draw the other side of the angle through the intersection of the two arcs.

Example 56.B.4 Construct a line that is parallel to a given line and that passes through a point not on the line.

Solution On the left below, we show the line and the point. The first step is to pick a point X on the line and draw the new line $\overleftrightarrow{PX}$. We do this on the right and call the angle formed angle A.

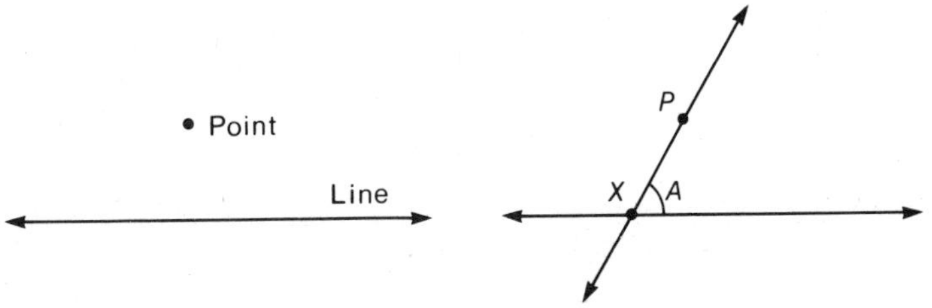

Next we copy angle A at point P.

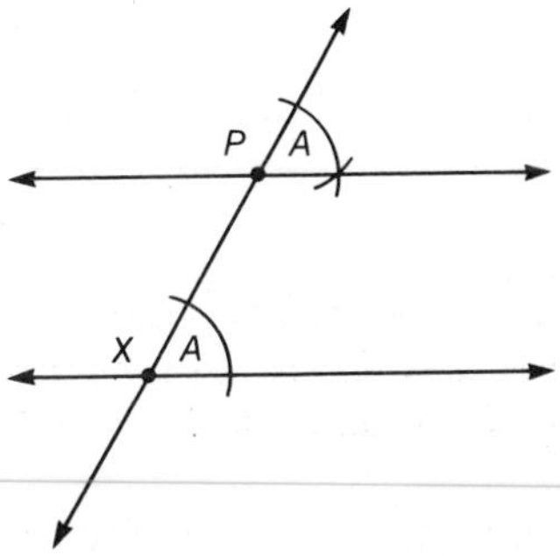

Example 56.B.5 Draw a line segment and then construct a **perpendicular bisector** to the line segment.

Solution A ***bisector*** divides a segment into two equal parts, and the easiest way to construct a bisector is to construct a bisector that is perpendicular to the segment. First we draw the segment and then swing equal arcs from the ends of the segment, as shown on the next page. The radius of the arcs should be greater than half the length of the segment. A line connecting the points of intersection of the arcs will be perpendicular to the segment and will bisect the segment, as every point on this line is equidistant from the ends of the segment. We will prove this statement in a later lesson.

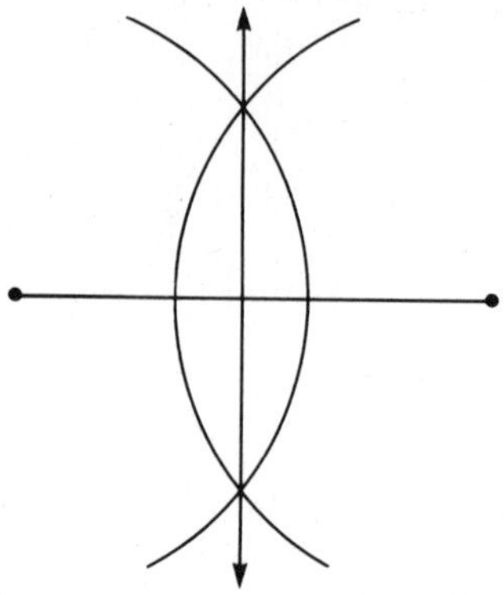

Example 56.B.6 Construct a perpendicular to a line from a point not on the line.

Solution We begin by marking the endpoints of a segment of the line by drawing an arc, using the point as the center.

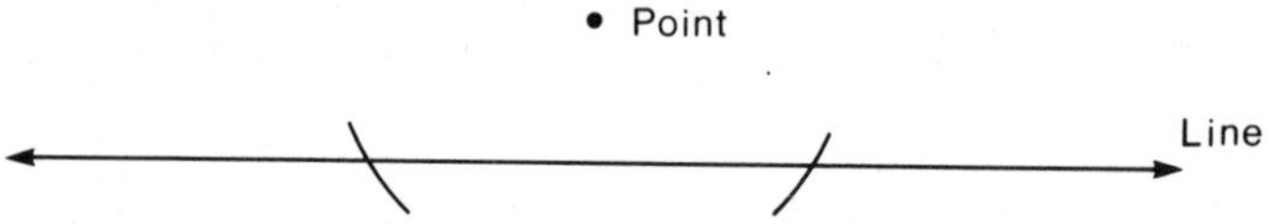

The point lies on the perpendicular bisector of the segment, as it is equidistant from the ends of the segment formed by the arcs. Now, if we construct the perpendicular bisector of the segment, this bisector will pass through the point.

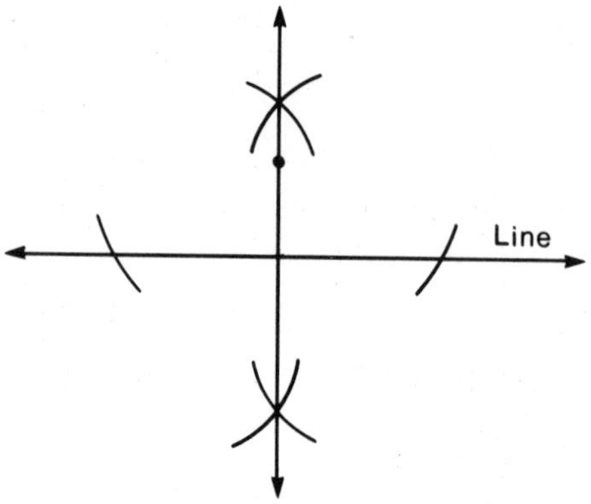

Example 56.B.7 Draw an angle and then bisect the angle.

Solution First we draw the angle and then swing an arc from the vertex of the angle as shown.

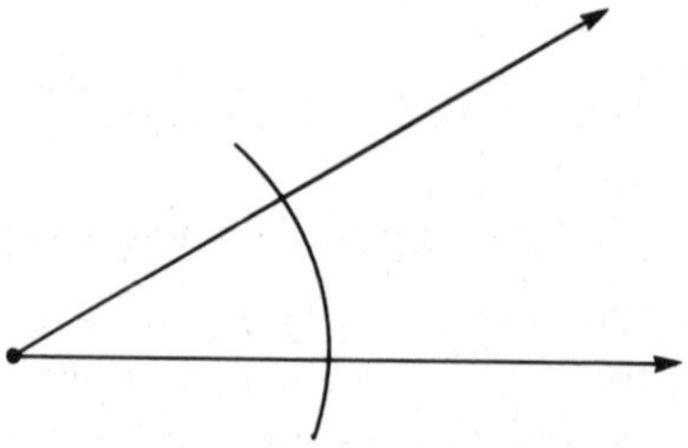

Then from the points where the arc cuts the sides of the angle we swing arcs of equal length. The intersection of these arcs lies on the angle bisector, which we use the straightedge to draw.

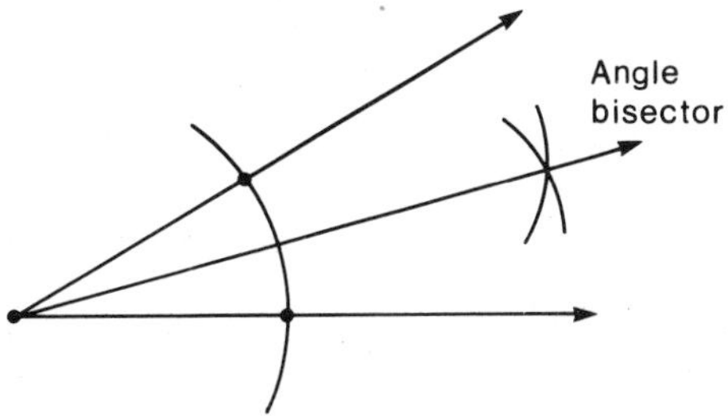

Problem set 56

1. The ratio of whats to hows was 7 to 9. The ratio of hows to ifs was 9 to 5. If the sum of the whats and hows exceeded twice the number of ifs by 12, how many were whats, how many were hows, and how many were ifs?

2. Twice the supplement of an angle exceeded thrice the complement of the angle by 120°. What was the angle?

3. The sum of the digits in a three-digit counting number is 8. If the first and second digit are interchanged, the new number is 180 greater than the original number. If the original units digit exceeds the original tens digit by 1, what is the original number?

4. Reds varied jointly as greens and as whites squared and inversely as blues. Originally there were 80 reds, 2 whites, 2 greens, and 4 blues. How many reds were there when there were 5 greens, 3 whites, and 3 blues?

5. The first 100 cost \$10 each and the next 200 cost \$5 each. How much should Roger pay for the next 100 if the overall average price is to be \$10?

6. How many cheerleading teams of 5 can be selected from 8 cheerleaders?

7. Construct a triangle whose sides measure 6 centimeters, 4 centimeters, and 3 centimeters.

8. Construct a triangle whose sides measure 6 centimeters, 2 centimeters, and 2 centimeters.

9. Draw a line segment 6 centimeters long and construct its perpendicular bisector.

10. Draw a 60° angle, copy the angle, and then bisect the copied angle.

11. Construct a line that is parallel to a given line and that passes through a point not on the line.

12. Write the fourth term of $(a + b)^8$.

13. Write all six terms of $(x + y)^5$.

14. Show that $\tan \theta \sec (90° - \theta) = \sec \theta$.

15. Show that $\dfrac{\csc x}{\sec x} = \cot x$.

16. Use Cramer's rule to solve: $\begin{cases} 3x - 2y = 5 \\ 2x + 5y = 6 \end{cases}$

17. Find the sum of the interior angles of a 4-sided convex polygon (quadrilateral).

18. The perimeter of a regular 9-sided polygon is 36 inches.
    (*a*) What is the length of one of the sides of the polygon?
    (*b*) What is the area of the polygon?

19. Two quadrilaterals are similar. The ratio of one side of the larger quadrilateral to the corresponding side of the smaller quadrilateral is 3 to 2. What is the ratio of their areas?

20. Solve this triangle for the unknown parts.

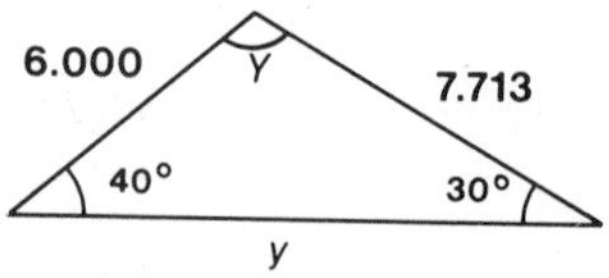

21. Graph the ellipse $3x^2 + 9y^2 = 36$.

22. Multiply $[6 \text{ cis } (-40°)](2 \text{ cis } 100°)$ and express the answer in rectangular form. Give an exact answer.

23. Prove that the exterior angle of a triangle is equal to the sum of the remote interior angles.

24. Write the equation of the following sinusoid as a cosine function.

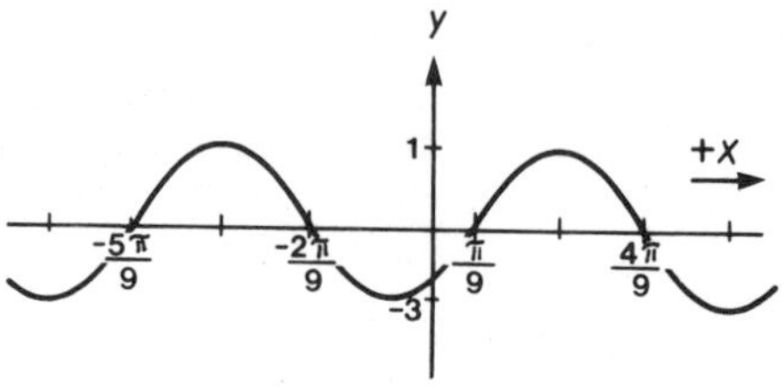

25. Find the radius and the coordinates of the center of the circle whose equation is $3x^2 + 3y^2 - 6x + 2y - 2 = 0$.

26. Find y.

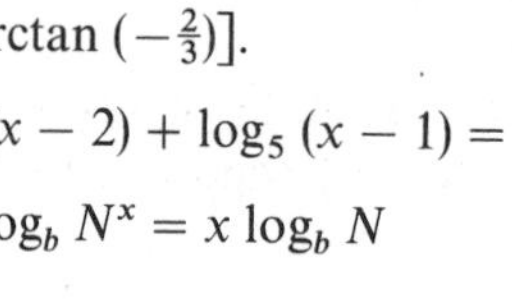

27. Solve, given that $(0° \le x < 360°)$: $2 \sin^2 x - 3 \sin x + 1 = 0$

28. Find $\sin [\text{Arctan } (-\frac{2}{3})]$.

29. Solve: $\log_5 (x - 2) + \log_5 (x - 1) = 2 \log_5 x$

30. Show why $\log_b N^x = x \log_b N$

EP 56.1, 56.2

LESSON 57 The hyperbola

57.A The hyperbola

We remember that the ellipse is the locus of all points such that the **sum of the distances** from any point on the ellipse to two fixed points is a constant. The fixed points are called the foci of the ellipse. The standard form of the equation of an ellipse is shown.

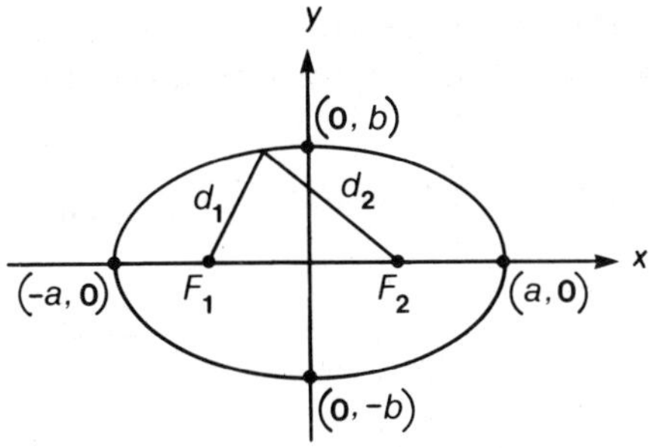

STANDARD FORM
OF THE EQUATION OF AN ELLIPSE
WITH CENTER AT THE ORIGIN:

$$\frac{x^2}{a^2} + \frac{y^2}{b^2} = 1$$

$\text{Distance}_1 + \text{distance}_2 = \text{constant}$

Note that the distance a is one-half the length of the major axis of the ellipse and that the distance b is one-half of the length of the minor axis.

The hyperbola is defined to be the locus of all points such that the **absolute value of the difference of the distances** from any point on the hyperbola to two fixed points is a constant.

$$|\text{Distance}_1 - \text{distance}_2| = \text{constant}$$

A hyperbola is formed from two curves, each the mirror image of the other. In a later lesson, we will show that the equation of a hyperbola whose center is at the origin and whose foci are on the x axis can be written as follows:

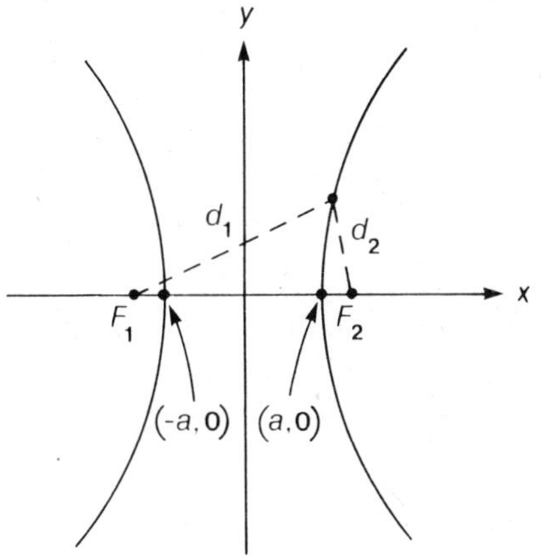

HYPERBOLA WITH
CENTER AT THE ORIGIN:

$$\frac{x^2}{a^2} - \frac{y^2}{b^2} = 1$$

Note that in this equation the minus sign goes with the y^2 term. If the minus sign goes with the x^2 term, as in the next equation, we find that the orientation of the figure is changed.

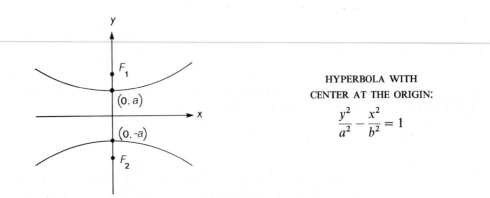

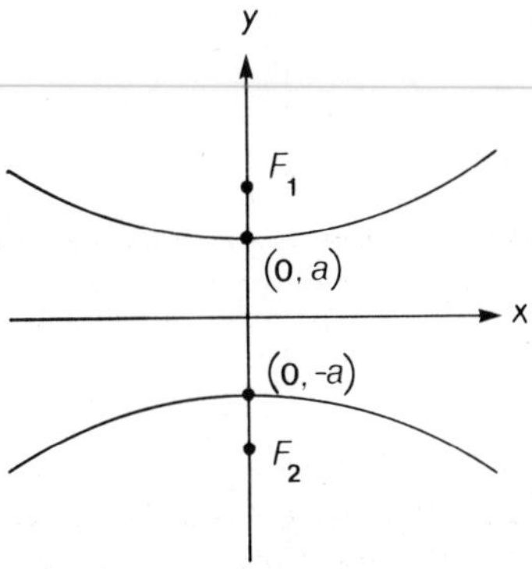

HYPERBOLA WITH
CENTER AT THE ORIGIN:

$$\frac{y^2}{a^2} - \frac{x^2}{b^2} = 1$$

Example 57.A.1 Sketch the hyperbola $\frac{x^2}{9} - \frac{y^2}{4} = 1$, and find the equations of the asymptotes.

Solution We let $y = 0$ and solve for x.

$$\frac{x^2}{9} - \frac{0}{4} = 1$$

$$x^2 = 9$$

$$x = \pm 3$$

Thus, we see that when $y = 0$, x can be either $+3$ or -3, so the hyperbola passes through the points (3, 0) and $(-3, 0)$. From the graph of the hyperbola that we will draw, we will see that these points are the vertices of the hyperbola. Now we let x equal 0 and solve for y.

$$\frac{0}{9} - \frac{y^2}{4} = 1$$

$$y^2 = -4$$

$$y = \pm 2i$$

The points $(0, 2i)$ and $(0, -2i)$ cannot be graphed on a real number rectangular system. Yet, it can be shown that the points $(0, -2)$ and (0, 2) and the points $(-3, 0)$ and (3, 0) can be used to form a rectangle whose diagonals are the asymptotes of the hyperbola. ***Asymptotes*** of a hyperbola are straight lines that the graph of the hyperbola approaches but never quite reaches.

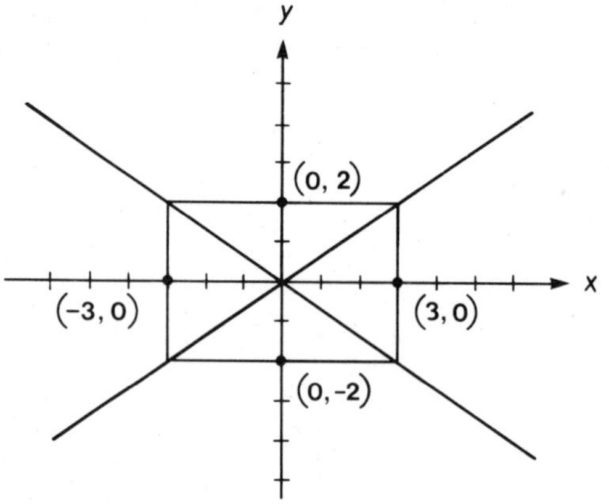

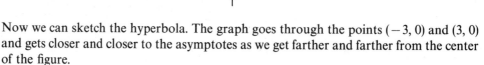

Now we can sketch the hyperbola. The graph goes through the points $(-3, 0)$ and (3, 0) and gets closer and closer to the asymptotes as we get farther and farther from the center of the figure.

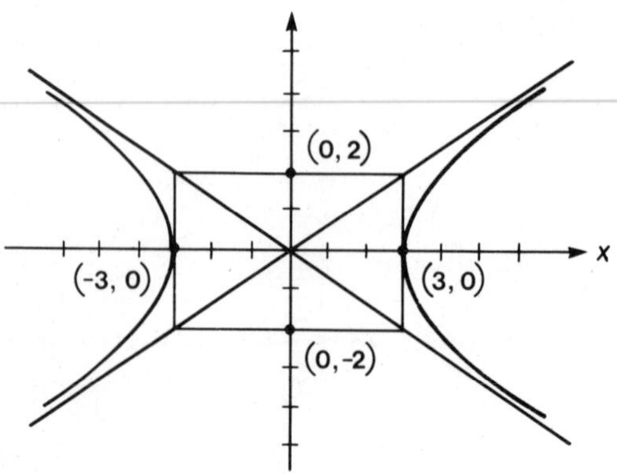

The coordinates of the upper right corner of the rectangle are (3, 2) and the asymptote that passes through this point also passes through the origin. We can use this information to write the equation of this asymptote as $y = \frac{2}{3}x$. The other asymptote passes through the origin and the point $(-3, 2)$. This information allows us to find that the equation of that asymptote is $y = -\frac{2}{3}x$.

Example 57.A.2 Sketch the hyperbola $\frac{y^2}{4} - \frac{x^2}{25} = 1$, and find the equations of its asymptotes.

Solution To find the coordinates of the vertices, we set x equal 0 and solve for y.

$$\frac{y^2}{4} - \frac{0}{25} = 1$$

$$y^2 = 4$$

$$y = \pm 2$$

Thus, the coordinates of the vertices are (0, 2) and $(0, -2)$. To find the coordinates on the other side of the asymptote rectangle, we set $y = 0$ and solve for x.

$$\frac{0}{4} - \frac{x^2}{25} = 1$$

$$x = \pm 5i$$

Thus, the other coordinates on the asymptote rectangle are (5, 0) and $(-5, 0)$. We graph the points, draw the asymptotes, and then sketch the hyperbola.

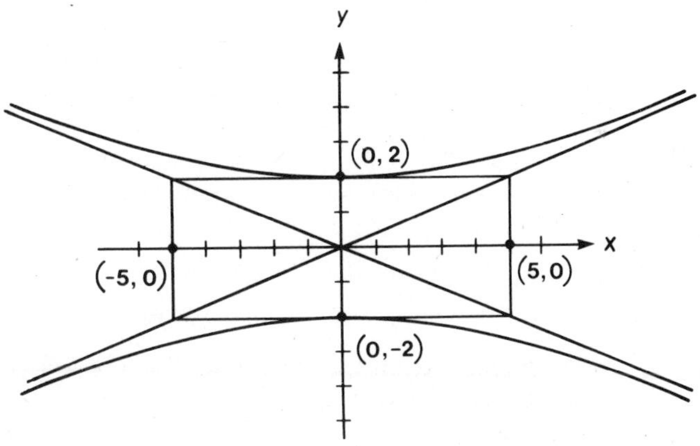

The coordinates of the upper right corner of the rectangle are (5, 2), and the asymptote that passes through this point also passes through the origin. We use this information to write the equation of this asymptote as $y = \frac{2}{5}x$. The other asymptote passes through the point $(-5, 2)$, and thus the equation of the other asymptote is $y = -\frac{2}{5}x$.

Example 57.A.3 Sketch the hyperbola $4y^2 - 9x^2 - 36 = 0$.

Solution The standard form of the equation of any hyperbola has the number 1 as the constant term. Thus, we divide every term by 36 and rearrange to get

$$-\frac{x^2}{4} + \frac{y^2}{9} = 1$$

Now if we let x equal 0, we can solve for y; and if we let $y = 0$, we can solve for x.

LET $x = 0$	LET $y = 0$
$\frac{y^2}{9} - \frac{(0)^2}{4} = 1$	$\frac{(0)^2}{9} - \frac{x^2}{4} = 1$
$y = \pm 3$	$x = \pm 2i$

Thus, the coordinates of two points on the asymptote rectangle are (2, 0) and (−2, 0). We graph the points, draw the asymptotes, and sketch the hyperbola.

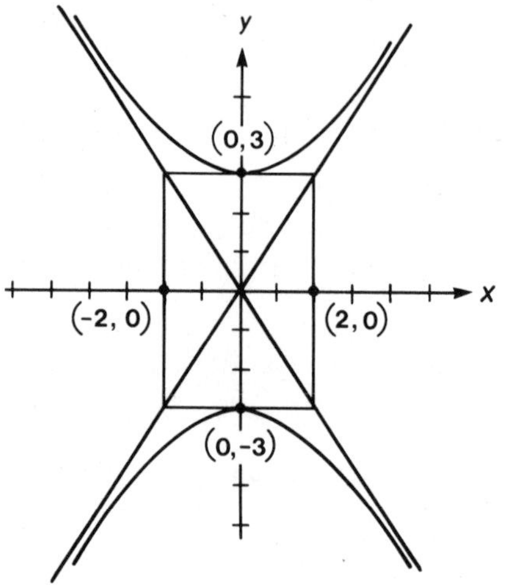

Problem set 57

1. Mark was happy because he had taken 4 tests and still had a 72 average. Then disaster struck because he took the fifth test and his overall average dropped to 70. What grade did he make on the fifth test?

2. Bill put some money in bank A at 6 percent simple yearly interest and put the rest in bank B at 8 percent simple yearly interest. If his total interest after one year was \$220 and the total invested was \$3000, how much money did he put in each bank?

3. Speedy could complete 5 jobs in 3 hours and Slowpoke could complete 2 jobs in 3 hours. Slowpoke worked for 2 hours and then was joined by Speedy. How long did they have to work together if they had to complete a total of 6 jobs?

4. The average temperature for 5 days was 80°. Then the sixth day was so hot that the average temperature for all 6 days was 83°. What was the temperature on the sixth day?

5. Mary bought K articles for a cents each. To pay for the articles, she gave the clerk Q quarters. How many cents did she get in change?

6. How many different committees of 5 can be formed from 3 boys and 6 girls?

7. Sketch the hyperbola $\frac{x^2}{16} - \frac{y^2}{4} = 1$.

8. Sketch the hyperbola $4y^2 - 9x^2 = 36$.

9. Construct a triangle whose sides measure 7 centimeters, 5 centimeters, and 3 centimeters.

10. Draw a line segment 5 centimeters long and construct its perpendicular bisector.

11. Construct a line that is parallel to a given line and which passes through a point not on the line.

12. Write the fifth term of $(a + b)^6$.

13. Write all five terms of $(a + b)^4$.

14. Show that $\sin \theta \csc (90° - \theta) = \tan \theta$.

15. Show that $\sec (90° - \theta) \tan \theta = \sec \theta$.

16. Use Cramer's rule to solve: $\begin{cases} 4x - 3y = 5 \\ 2x - 4y = -3 \end{cases}$

17. Find the sum of the exterior angles of a 9-sided irregular convex polygon.

18. The perimeter of a regular 10-sided polygon (regular decagon) is 50 centimeters.
(*a*) What is the length of one of the sides of the polygon?
(*b*) What is the radius of the circle which can be circumscribed about the polygon?

19. Two convex 5-sided polygons (pentagons) are similar. The ratio of a side of the larger pentagon to a corresponding side of the smaller pentagon is 5 to 3. What is the ratio of the areas of the polygons?

20. Solve this triangle for the unknown parts.

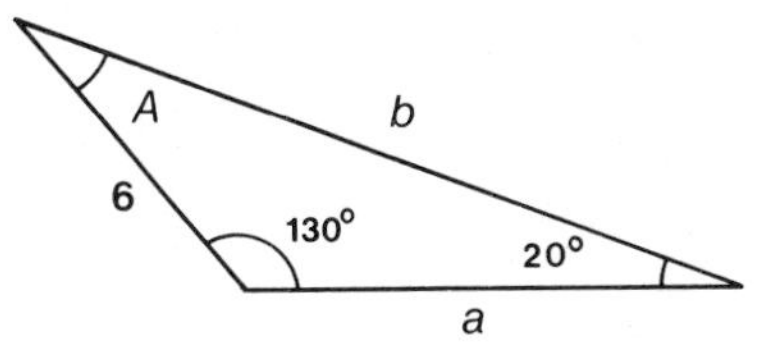

21. Graph the ellipse $49x^2 + 4y^2 = 196$.

22. Multiply $(3 \text{ cis } 20°)(2 \text{ cis } 130°)$ and express the answer in rectangular form. Give an exact answer.

23. Prove that the sum of angles of a triangle is 180°.

24. Write the equation of the sinusoid whose graph is a sine function that has been shifted $3\pi/2$ to the right, that has an amplitude of 4 and a period of 3π, and centerline of $y = 5$.

25. Find the radius and the coordinates of the center of the circle whose equation is $3x^2 + 6x + 6y + 3y^2 + 4 = 0$.

26. Find a and b.

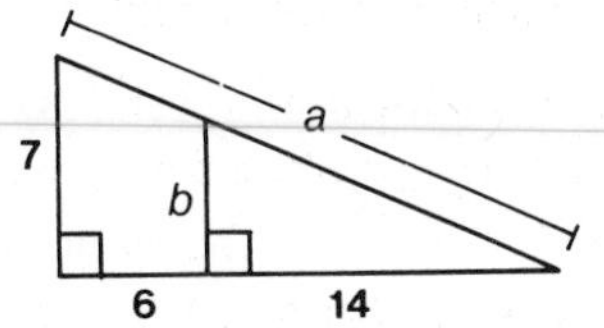

27. Solve, given that $(0° \le \theta < 360°)$: $\sqrt{3} \tan 3\theta - 1 = 0$

28. Evaluate: Arccos (cos 210°)

29. Solve: $2 \ln x - \ln (x - \frac{1}{2}) = \ln 2$

30. Estimate the base e antilogarithm of -3.

EP 57.3

LESSON 58 Roots of complex numbers

58.A Roots of complex numbers

If we use 2 as a factor 3 times, the product is 8.

$$2 \cdot 2 \cdot 2 = 8$$

This is the reason we say that the third root of 8 is 2.

$$\sqrt[3]{8} = 2$$

Because the notation $8^{1/3}$ means the same thing as $\sqrt[3]{8}$, this expression also has a value of 2.

$$8^{1/3} = 2$$

If we use the complex number 2 cis 12° as a factor 3 times, the product is 8 cis 36°

$$(a) \quad (2 \text{ cis } 12°)(2 \text{ cis } 12°)(2 \text{ cis } 12°) = 8 \text{ cis } 36°$$

because we multiply complex numbers in polar form by multiplying the numerical coefficients and adding the angles. Thus, the third root of 8 cis 36° is 2 cis 12°.

$$(8 \text{ cis } 36°)^{1/3} = 2 \text{ cis } 12°$$

There are two other third roots of 8 cis 36°.

$$(b) \quad (2 \text{ cis } 132°)(2 \text{ cis } 132°)(2 \text{ cis } 132°) = 8 \text{ cis } 396° = 8 \text{ cis } (360° + 36°)$$
$$= 8 \text{ cis } 36°$$

$$(c) \quad (2 \text{ cis } 252°)(2 \text{ cis } 252°)(2 \text{ cis } 252°) = 8 \text{ cis } 756° = 8 \text{ cis } (720° + 36°)$$
$$= 8 \text{ cis } 36°$$

In (*b*) the angle of the product is 396°, which is once around (360°) and 36° more. In (*c*) the angle of the product is 756°, which is twice around (720°) and 36° more. Thus, the three third roots of 8 cis 36° are

$$2 \text{ cis } 12° \qquad 2 \text{ cis } 132° \qquad \text{and} \qquad 2 \text{ cis } 252°$$

To get the first root we took the third root of 8 and divided the angle by 3. The angle of the next root is 360°/3 or 120° greater, and the angle of the next root is 2(360°/3) or 240° greater.

$$\sqrt[3]{8 \text{ cis } 36°} = 8^{1/3} \text{ cis } \frac{36°}{3} = 2 \text{ cis } 12°$$

$$= 8^{1/3} \text{ cis} \left(\frac{36°}{3} + 120° \right) = 2 \text{ cis } 132°$$

$$= 8^{1/3} \text{ cis} \left(\frac{36°}{3} + 240° \right) = 2 \text{ cis } 252°$$

If we continue the process, the roots will begin to repeat. The next step would be to add 3 × 120°, or 360°. If we do this, the result is 2 cis 12° again.

$$8^{1/3} \text{ cis} \left(\frac{36°}{3} + 360° \right) = 2 \text{ cis } 372° = 2 \text{ cis } 12°$$

Every complex number except zero has two square roots, three cube roots, four fourth roots, five fifth roots, and, in general, *n nth* roots. The angles of the third roots differ by 360°/3, or 120°. The angles of the fourth roots differ by 360°/4, or 90°. The angles of the fifth roots differ by 360°/5, or 72°; etc. Thus the angles of the *n*th roots differ by 360°/*n*.

Example 58.A.1 Find the four fourth roots of 16 cis 60°. Check the answers by multiplying.

Solution The first root is $16^{1/4}$ cis $(60°/4) =$ **2 cis 15°**. Angles of the fourth roots differ by $360°/4$, or 90°, so the other three roots are

2 cis 105° 2 cis 195° 2 cis 285°

Now we check:

$$(2 \text{ cis } 15°)(2 \text{ cis } 15°)(2 \text{ cis } 15°)(2 \text{ cis } 15°) = 16 \text{ cis } 60°$$

$$(2 \text{ cis } 105°)(2 \text{ cis } 105°)(2 \text{ cis } 105°)(2 \text{ cis } 105°) = 16 \text{ cis } 420°$$
$$= 16 \text{ cis } (60° + 360°) = 16 \text{ cis } 60°$$

$$(2 \text{ cis } 195°)(2 \text{ cis } 195°)(2 \text{ cis } 195°)(2 \text{ cis } 195°) = 16 \text{ cis } 780°$$
$$= 16 \text{ cis } (60° + 720°) = 16 \text{ cis } 60°$$

$$(2 \text{ cis } 285°)(2 \text{ cis } 285°)(2 \text{ cis } 285°)(2 \text{ cis } 285°) = 16 \text{ cis } 1140°$$
$$= 16 \text{ cis } (60° + 1080°) = 16 \text{ cis } 60°$$

Example 58.A.2 Find five fifth roots of i.

Solution **We write a complex number in polar form with a positive coefficient to find the roots.**

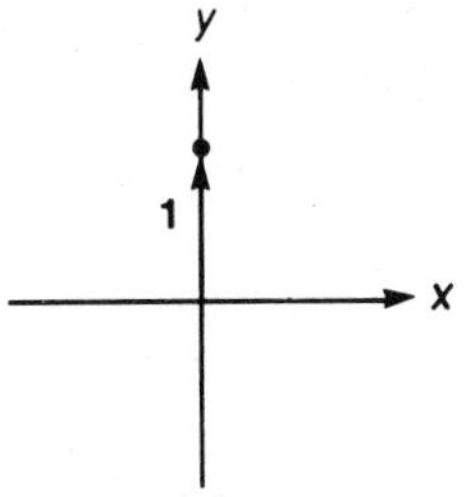

$$0 + i = 1 \text{ cis } 90°$$

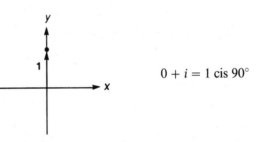

The fifth root of 1 is 1, so we get

$$\sqrt[5]{1 \text{ cis } 90°} = 1^{1/5} \text{ cis } \frac{90°}{5} = \mathbf{1 \text{ cis } 18°}$$

Successive angles of the fifth roots differ by $360°/5$, or 72°, so the other roots are

1 cis 90° 1 cis 162° 1 cis 234° 1 cis 306°

Now we check the angles:

$5 \times 90° = 450° = 90° + 360°$ check

$5 \times 162° = 810° = 90° + 720°$ check

$5 \times 234° = 1170° = 90° + 1080°$ check

$5 \times 306° = 1530° = 90° + 1440°$ check

Example 58.A.3 Find two square roots of 1.

Solution The polar form of $1 + 0i$ is 1 cis 0°.

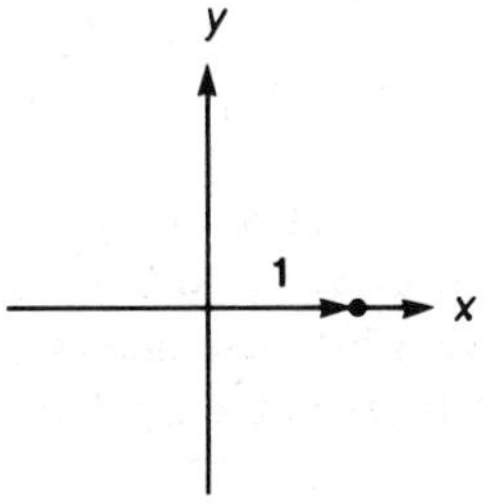

$$1 + 0i$$

The principal square root of 1 is 1, so we get

$$\sqrt{1 \text{ cis } 0^\circ} = 1^{1/2} \text{ cis } \frac{0^\circ}{2} = \mathbf{1 \text{ cis } 0^\circ}$$

The angles of square roots of complex numbers differ by 360°/2, or 180°, so the other square root of 1 cis 0° is **1 cis 180°**. Now we check our answers:

$$(1 \text{ cis } 0^\circ)(1 \text{ cis } 0^\circ) = 1 \text{ cis } 0^\circ$$

$$(1 \text{ cis } 180^\circ)(1 \text{ cis } 180^\circ) = 1 \text{ cis } 360^\circ = 1 \text{ cis } (0^\circ + 360^\circ) = 1 \text{ cis } 0^\circ \qquad \text{check}$$

Of course, if we wish, we could write the answers in rectangular form as 1 and −1.

Example 58.A.4 Find three third roots of −1.

Solution **We always begin by writing the complex number in polar form with a positive coefficient.**

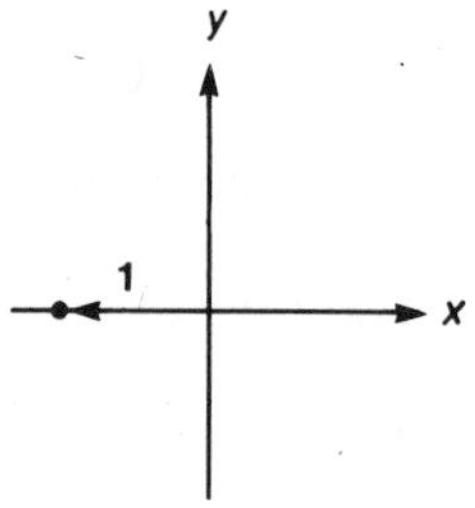

$$-1 + 0i = 1 \text{ cis } 180^\circ$$

The first angle is 180°/3, or 60°. The angles of the third roots differ by 120°, so the three roots are as shown.

$$\sqrt[3]{-1 + 0i} = \sqrt[3]{1 \text{ cis } 180^\circ} = \mathbf{1 \text{ cis } 60^\circ, 1 \text{ cis } 180^\circ, 1 \text{ cis } 300^\circ}$$

These roots can also be written in rectangular form as

$$\mathbf{\frac{1}{2} + \frac{\sqrt{3}}{2}i, \; -1 + 0i, \; \frac{1}{2} - \frac{\sqrt{3}}{2}i}$$

Example 58.A.5 Find the four fourth roots of 42 cis 40°.

Solution We use the root key on the calculator to find that the fourth root of 42 is about 2.55. The angles of the fourth roots differ by 360°/4, or 90°, so our roots are as shown.

$$(42 \text{ cis } 40^\circ)^{1/4} \approx \mathbf{2.55 \text{ cis } 10^\circ, 2.55 \text{ cis } 100^\circ, 255 \text{ cis } 190^\circ, 2.55 \text{ cis } 280^\circ}$$

Problem set 58

1. The still-water speed of the boat was 3 times the speed of the current in the river. If the boat could go 16 miles downstream in 2 hours less than it took to go 32 miles upstream, how fast was the boat and what was the speed of the current in the river?
2. A shelf in the library holds b books. Half of the b books are N inches thick and the rest are $2N$ inches thick. What is the length of the shelf in inches?
3. The cost of finishing the contract varied linearly with the number of men who worked. If 10 men worked, the cost was $5100. If only 5 men worked, the cost was $2600. What would be the cost if only 2 men worked?
4. Four times the complement of an angle was 80° less than twice the supplement of the same angle. What was the angle?

5. A crew of 81 workers can do 1 job in 24 days. In order to finish on time, the contractor increased the size of the work force by one-third. How many days will be saved by adding the additional workers?

6. How many distinguishable ways can 8 animals be lined up along a wall if 2 of the animals are identical twins?

7. Find the four fourth roots of 25 cis 80° and express them in polar form.

8. Find the three cube roots of $16i$ and express them in polar form.

9. Find the two square roots of -1 and express them in rectangular form.

10. Draw a line segment 8 centimeters long and construct its perpendicular bisector.

11. Construct a triangle whose sides measure 8 centimeters, 4 centimeters, and 2 centimeters.

12. Construct a perpendicular to a line from a point not on the line.

13. Write the sixth term of $(a + b)^9$.

14. Write all seven terms of $(x + y)^6$.

15. Show that $\sin (90° - \theta) \sec (90° - \theta) = \cot \theta$.

16. Show that $\dfrac{\tan \theta}{\sec \theta} = \sin \theta$.

17. Use Cramer's rule to solve: $\begin{cases} 5x - 3y = 8 \\ 4x + 2y = 5 \end{cases}$

18. Find the sum of the interior angles of a 16-sided convex polygon.

19. The perimeter of a regular 12-sided polygon is 96 feet.
    (*a*) What is the length of one of the sides of the polygon?
    (*b*) What is the area of the polygon?

20. Solve this triangle for its unknown parts.

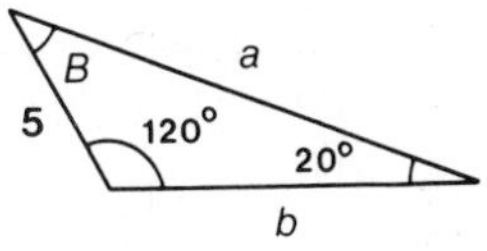

21. Describe the ellipse $16x^2 + 4y^2 = 64$.

22. Graph the hyperbola $\dfrac{x^2}{16} - \dfrac{y^2}{4} = 1$.

23. Find the vertices and asymptotes of the hyperbola $9x^2 - 4y^2 = 36$.

24. Multiply (4 cis 30°)(2 cis 60°) and express the answer in rectangular form. Give an exact answer.

25. Prove that vertical angles are equal.

26. Write the equation of the following sinusoid as a cosine function.

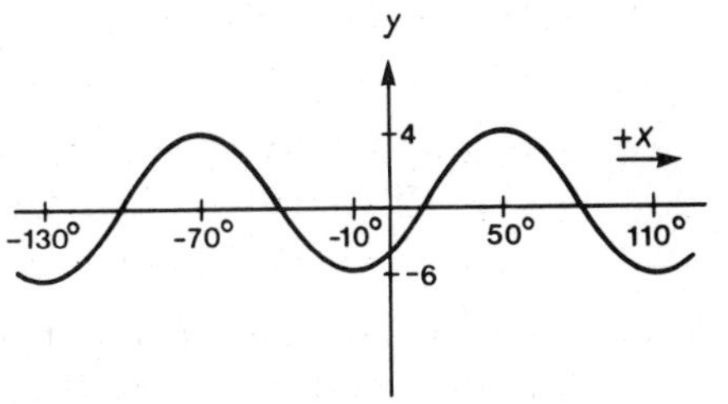

27. Find the radius and the coordinates of the center of the circle whose equation is $2x^2 + 2y^2 - 4y + 2x = 0$.

28. Find x.

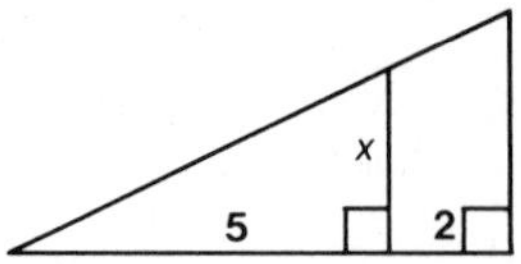

29. Solve, given that $(0° \le \theta < 360°)$: $2 \cos 4\theta - 1 = 0$

30. Solve: $\ln (x - 2) - \ln (3x - 4) = \ln 3$

EP 58.4

LESSON 59 *Trigonometric identities (2)*

59.A Trigonometric identities (2)

To begin this lesson, we list the basic trigonometric relationships that we have used thus far.

$$\sin \theta = \frac{1}{\csc \theta} \qquad \cos \theta = \frac{1}{\sec \theta} \qquad \tan \theta = \frac{1}{\cot \theta}$$

$$\csc \theta = \frac{1}{\sin \theta} \qquad \sec \theta = \frac{1}{\cos \theta} \qquad \cot \theta = \frac{1}{\tan \theta}$$

$$\sin (-\theta) = -\sin \theta \qquad \cos (-\theta) = \cos \theta \qquad \tan (-\theta) = -\tan \theta$$

$$\csc (-\theta) = -\csc \theta \qquad \sec (-\theta) = \sec \theta \qquad \cot (-\theta) = -\cot \theta$$

These relationships are difficult to recall without the use of good mnemonics. The sine, cosine, and tangent can be remembered with "Oscar Had A Hold On Arthur" or with "soh cah toa." The cotangent, secant, and cosecant can be paired reciprocals with the tangent, cosine, and sine, respectively. The last six relationships listed can be developed by drawing triangles in the first and fourth quadrants. It is necessary to devise meaningful long-term memory devices for trigonometric relationships, for there are quite a few whose recall is required. Now we add three more relationships that are most useful.

(*a*) $\sin^2 \theta + \cos^2 \theta = 1$ (*b*) $1 + \cot^2 \theta = \csc^2 \theta$ (*c*) $\tan^2 \theta + 1 = \sec^2 \theta$

We can prove these relationships by using a right triangle and the theorem of Pythagoras.

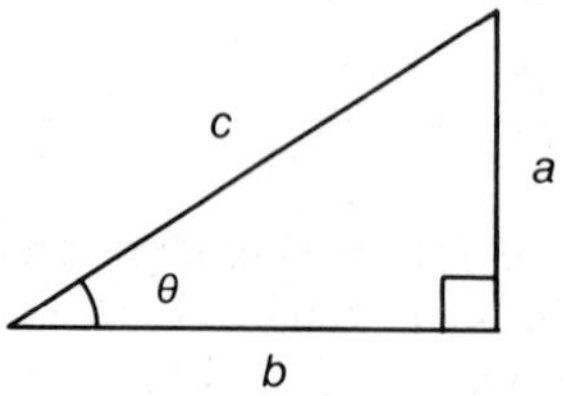

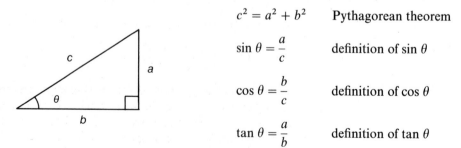

$c^2 = a^2 + b^2$ Pythagorean theorem

$\sin \theta = \dfrac{a}{c}$ definition of $\sin \theta$

$\cos \theta = \dfrac{b}{c}$ definition of $\cos \theta$

$\tan \theta = \dfrac{a}{b}$ definition of $\tan \theta$

To prove (*a*), we write the equation and then substitute for $\sin^2\theta$ and $\cos^2\theta$.

$\sin^2\theta + \cos^2\theta = 1$	equation
$\left(\frac{a}{c}\right)^2 + \left(\frac{b}{c}\right)^2 = 1$	substituted
$\frac{a^2}{c^2} + \frac{b^2}{c^2} = 1$	simplified
$\frac{a^2 + b^2}{c^2} = 1$	added
$\frac{c^2}{c^2} = 1$	$a^2 + b^2 = c^2$
$1 = 1$	check

To prove (*b*) and (*c*), we will use the same procedure and a trick.

TO PROVE (*b*)	TO PROVE (*c*)	
$1 + \cot^2\theta = \csc^2\theta$	$\tan^2\theta + 1 = \sec^2\theta$	equation
$1 + \left(\frac{b}{a}\right)^2 = \left(\frac{c}{a}\right)^2$	$\left(\frac{a}{b}\right)^2 + 1 = \left(\frac{c}{b}\right)^2$	substituted
$\left(\frac{a}{a}\right)^2 + \left(\frac{b}{a}\right)^2 = \left(\frac{c}{a}\right)^2$	$\left(\frac{a}{b}\right)^2 + \left(\frac{b}{b}\right)^2 = \left(\frac{c}{b}\right)^2$	trick; substituted $\frac{b}{b}$ and $\frac{a}{a}$ for 1
$\frac{a^2 + b^2}{a^2} = \frac{c^2}{a^2}$	$\frac{a^2 + b^2}{b^2} = \frac{c^2}{b^2}$	added
$\frac{c^2}{a^2} = \frac{c^2}{a^2}$	$\frac{c^2}{b^2} = \frac{c^2}{b^2}$	$a^2 + b^2 = c^2$

The three equations (*a*), (*b*), and (*c*) have three forms each.

(*a*)	$\sin^2\theta + \cos^2\theta = 1$	$\sin^2\theta = 1 - \cos^2\theta$	$\cos^2\theta = 1 - \sin^2\theta$
(*b*)	$1 + \cot^2\theta = \csc^2\theta$	$\cot^2\theta = \csc^2\theta - 1$	$1 = \csc^2\theta - \cot^2\theta$
(*c*)	$\tan^2\theta + 1 = \sec^2\theta$	$\tan^2\theta = \sec^2\theta - 1$	$1 = \sec^2\theta - \tan^2\theta$

These nine forms are difficult to memorize because they are so similar. If we can remember the form

$$(a)\quad \sin^2\theta + \cos^2\theta = 1$$

we can easily develop the basic form of (*b*) and (*c*). To develop (*b*), we divide every term of (*a*) by $\sin^2\theta$.

$$(b)\quad \frac{\sin^2\theta}{\sin^2\theta} + \frac{\cos^2\theta}{\sin^2\theta} = \frac{1}{\sin^2\theta} \longrightarrow 1 + \cot^2\theta = \csc^2\theta$$

To develop (*c*), we divide every term of (*a*) by $\cos^2\theta$.

$$(c)\quad \frac{\sin^2\theta}{\cos^2\theta} + \frac{\cos^2\theta}{\cos^2\theta} = \frac{1}{\cos^2\theta} \longrightarrow \tan^2\theta + 1 = \sec^2\theta$$

There are no set procedures for proving trigonometric identities, and often there are two or three ways to do the same proof. These problems are standard in all trigonometry books and were contrived to give students practice in transforming trigonometric expressions. We often begin by looking for forms for which we can substitute, such as $\csc^2 x - \cot^2 x$ or $1 + \tan^2 x$. Also, if the expressions contain fractions, it is sometimes helpful to add the fractions.

Example 59.A.1 Show that $\dfrac{\sec^2 x - \tan^2 x}{1 + \cot^2 x} = \sin^2 x$.

Solution We could work with either side. We decide to take the left side and change its form to $\sin^2 x$. First we replace $\sec^2 x - \tan^2 x$ with 1 and replace $1 + \cot^2 x$ with $\csc^2 x$.

$$\frac{\sec^2 x - \tan^2 x}{1 + \cot^2 x} \longrightarrow \frac{1}{\csc^2 x}$$

Now $\csc^2 x$ equals $1/(\sin^2 x)$, so we can write

$$\frac{1}{\csc^2 x} \longrightarrow \frac{1}{\dfrac{1}{\sin^2 x}} \longrightarrow \sin^2 x$$

Now we have changed the left side to $\sin^2 x$ and the identity has been proved.

Example 59.A.2 Show that $\dfrac{1}{\tan A} + \tan A = \sec A \csc A$.

Solution We will work with the left side. We will replace $\tan A$ with $(\sin A)/(\cos A)$.

$$\frac{1}{\dfrac{\sin A}{\cos A}} + \frac{\sin A}{\cos A} \longrightarrow \frac{\cos A}{\sin A} + \frac{\sin A}{\cos A}$$

Next we will find a common denominator and add.

$$\frac{\cos A}{\sin A} \cdot \frac{\cos A}{\cos A} + \frac{\sin A}{\cos A} \cdot \frac{\sin A}{\sin A} \longrightarrow \frac{\cos^2 A + \sin^2 A}{\cos A \sin A}$$

but $\cos^2 A + \sin^2 A = 1$, so we have

$$\frac{1}{\cos A \sin A} \longrightarrow \frac{1}{\cos A} \cdot \frac{1}{\sin A}$$

But these expressions equal $\sec A$ and $\csc A$, so

$$\frac{1}{\cos A} \cdot \frac{1}{\sin A} \longrightarrow \sec A \csc A$$

Example 59.A.3 Show that $\dfrac{1}{1 + \cos A} + \dfrac{1}{1 - \cos A} = 2 \csc^2 A$.

Solution On the left side we have two fractional expressions that can be added. We will begin by adding these fractional expressions.

$$\frac{1 - \cos A}{(1 + \cos A)(1 - \cos A)} + \frac{1 + \cos A}{(1 - \cos A)(1 + \cos A)} \longrightarrow \frac{2}{1 - \cos^2 A}$$

But $1 - \cos^2 A$ equals $\sin^2 A$, which is the reciprocal of $\csc^2 A$.

$$\frac{2}{1 - \cos^2 A} \longrightarrow \frac{2}{\sin^2 A} \longrightarrow 2 \csc^2 A$$

Example 59.A.4 Show that $\dfrac{\cos A}{1 + \sin A} + \dfrac{1 + \sin A}{\cos A} = 2 \sec A$.

Solution Again we will add the fractions.

$$\frac{\cos A}{1 + \sin A} \cdot \frac{\cos A}{\cos A} + \frac{1 + \sin A}{\cos A} \cdot \frac{1 + \sin A}{1 + \sin A} = \frac{\cos^2 A + 1 + \sin A + \sin A + \sin^2 A}{(\cos A)(1 + \sin A)}$$

The top reduces to $2 + 2 \sin A$ because $\cos^2 A + \sin^2 A = 1$.

$$\frac{2 + 2 \sin A}{(\cos A)(1 + \sin A)} \longrightarrow \frac{2(1 + \sin A)}{(\cos A)(1 + \sin A)} = 2 \sec A$$

Problem set 59

1. The pressure was such that 2 hours was required to fill the empty pool to the four-sevenths level. How much more time would it take to fill the pool completely?

2. If M workers can do 50 jobs in 1 day, how many days will it take 10 workers to do 20 jobs?

3. The sum of the digits in a three-digit counting number was 17. The tens digit was 5 less than the hundreds digit. Twice the units digit exceeded 4 times the tens digit by 8. What was the number?

4. Frank and the gang stop for lunch after they have traveled for h hours at m miles per hour. If the total distance to be traveled is 300 miles, how far do they have to go after lunch?

5. Dinah is in a quandary. She has only $\frac{1}{2}$ cup of white sugar, and the recipe calls for $\frac{3}{4}$ cup of white sugar. How much brown sugar must she use if 1 cup of brown sugar is equivalent to $\frac{3}{4}$ cup of white sugar?

6. How many ways can 5 boys sit in a row if Tom insists on sitting in the middle?

7. Find the three cube roots of 27 cis 36° and express them in polar form.

8. Find the four fourth roots of -16 and express them in rectangular form.

9. Construct a triangle whose sides measure 5 centimeters, 4 centimeters, and 3 centimeters.

10. Use a protractor to draw a 40° angle, copy the angle, and then construct the bisector of the copied angle.

11. Write the third term of $(x + y)^6$.

12. Write all four terms of $(a + b)^3$.

13. Show that $\dfrac{\sec^2 x - \tan^2 x}{1 + \cot^2 x} = \sin^2 x$.

14. Show that $\dfrac{\cos A}{1 + \sin A} + \dfrac{1 + \sin A}{\cos A} = 2 \sec A$.

15. Show that $\dfrac{1}{\tan A} + \tan A = \sec A \csc A$.

16. Use Cramer's rule to solve: $\begin{cases} 4x - 2y = 7 \\ 3x + 4y = 9 \end{cases}$

17. Find the sum of the interior angles of a 15-sided convex polygon.

18. The perimeter of a 13-sided regular polygon is 39 inches.
   (*a*) What is the length of one of the sides of the polygon?
   (*b*) What is the area of the polygon?
   (*c*) What is the radius of the circle which can be circumscribed about the polygon?

19. Solve the triangle for its unknown parts.

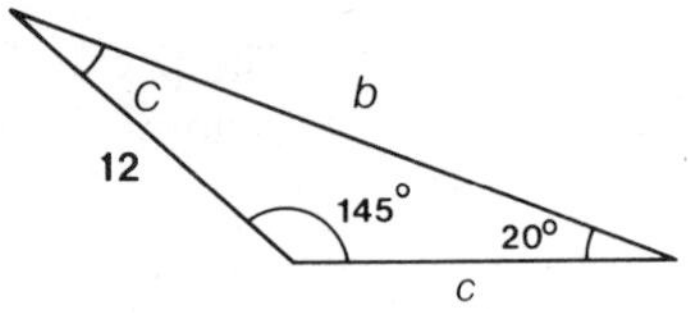

20. Describe the ellipse $9x^2 + 25y^2 = 225$.

21. Find the vertices and asymptotes of the hyperbola $16x^2 - 25y^2 = 400$.

22. Multiply (3 cis 20°)(4 cis 40°) and express the answer in rectangular form. Give an exact answer.

23. Prove that the sum of the angles in a triangle is 180°.

24. Write the equation of the sinusoid whose graph is a cosine function shifted 110° to the left and which has a period of 240°, amplitude of 6, and centerline of $y = -4$.

25. Find the radius and center of the circle whose equation is $3x^2 + 3y^2 + 6x - 12y - 1 = 0$.

26. Find a and b.

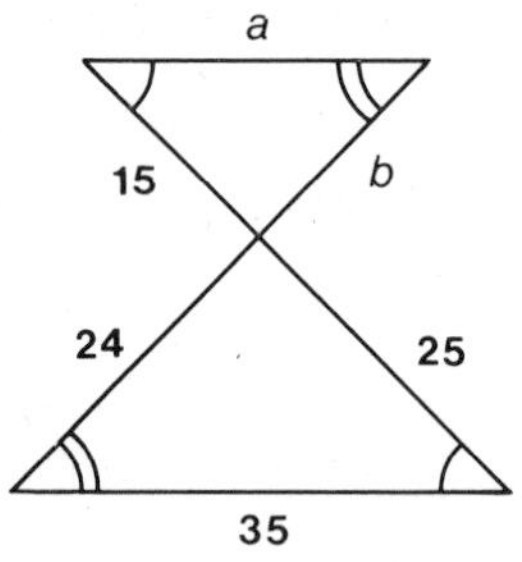

27. Solve, given that $(0° \le \theta < 360°)$: $\sqrt{3}\tan 4\theta - 1 = 0$

28. Find $\tan\left[\text{Arccos}\left(-\frac{3}{5}\right)\right]$.

29. Solve: $\log_7 (2x - 1) - \log_7 (3x + 3) = \log_7 5$

30. Simplify: $2 \log_6 6 + 6^{2 \log_6 3 - \log_6 3}$

EP 59.5

LESSON 60 Law of cosines

60.A Law of cosines

Every triangle has three sides and three angles for a total of six parts. **If we know one side and two other parts, we can solve for the values of the missing parts.**

1. If the triangle is a right triangle, the unknown parts can be found by using the sine, cosine, or tangent.

2. If the triangle is not a right triangle and the **values of a pair** (angle and side opposite) **are known,** the **law of sines** can be used.
3. If the triangle is not a right triangle and the **values of a pair are not known,** then the **law of cosines** can be used.

The proof of the law of cosines is given in detail in the appendix. The law of cosines is normally written in one of the following forms.

$$a^2 = b^2 + c^2 - 2bc \cos A$$

$$b^2 = a^2 + c^2 - 2ac \cos B$$

$$c^2 = a^2 + b^2 - 2ab \cos C$$

The many letters used in these forms can be confusing to the beginner so we will use another form. **We remember that if we had a pair (side and angle opposite), we would use the law of sines. But we do not have a pair, so we use the law of cosines. In the formula, we will use p and P to represent the pair we do not have and a and b to represent the other two sides and write**

$$p^2 = a^2 + b^2 - 2ab \cos P$$

We can remember the law of cosines without difficulty because it looks so much like the Pythagorean theorem with $-2ab \cos P$ attached.

PYTHAGOREAN THEOREM	LAW OF COSINES
$c^2 = a^2 + b^2$	$p^2 = a^2 + b^2 - 2ab \cos P$

The use of a calculator is recommended for finding solutions to problems that are solved by using the law of cosines.

Example 60.A.1 Solve the triangle for the unknown parts.

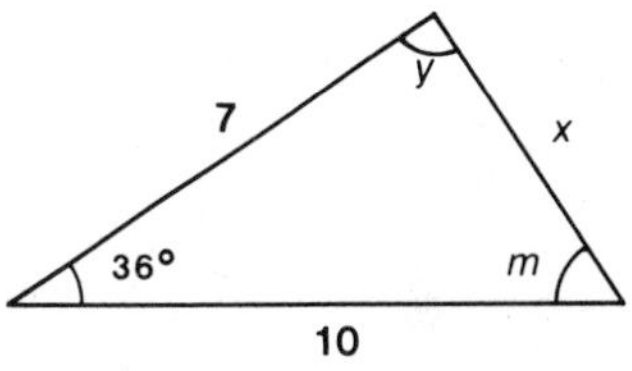

Solution We have one side and two other parts given, but we do not have a pair (angle and side opposite) so we will use the law of cosines.

$$p^2 = a^2 + b^2 - 2ab \cos P$$

The pair we wish we had is side x and the 36° angle, so we replace p with x and P with 36° and use 7 and 10 for the two sides.

$$x^2 = 7^2 + 10^2 - 2(7)(10) \cos 36°$$

$$x^2 = 49 + 100 - 113.26$$

$$x^2 = 35.74$$

$$\mathbf{x = 5.98}$$

Now we have a pair and we can use the law of sines to solve for y and m.

$$\frac{5.98}{\sin 36°} = \frac{10}{\sin y} \qquad \frac{5.98}{\sin 36°} = \frac{7}{\sin m}$$

$$\sin y = \frac{10 \sin 36°}{5.98} \qquad \sin m = \frac{7 \sin 36°}{5.98}$$

$$\sin y = 0.9829 \qquad \sin m = 0.6880$$

so $y = 79.39°$ or $100.61°$ so $m = 43.48°$ or $136.52°$

When we look at the triangle, we see that angle y is greater than 90° and angle m is less than 90°, so

$$\mathbf{y = 100.61°} \qquad \text{and} \qquad \mathbf{m = 43.48°}$$

When we sum the angles, we get 100.61° + 43.48° + 36° = 180.09°. This small difference is a result of rounding off results at several points in the solution.

Example 60.A.2 Solve the triangle for the missing parts.

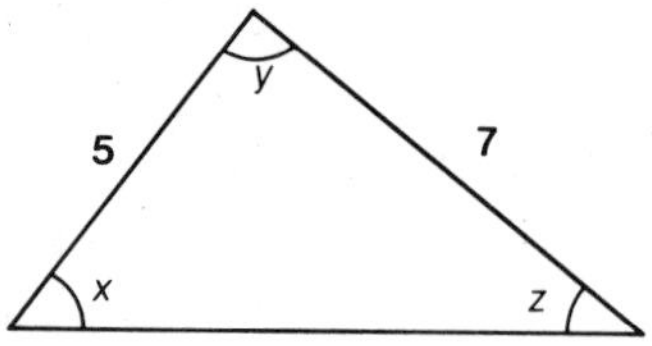

Solution We are given three parts and one of the parts is a side, so the triangle can be solved. **We do not have a pair, so we use the law of cosines.**

$$p^2 = a^2 + b^2 - 2ab \cos P$$

We decide that the pair we wish we had is angle x and side 7. So we replace p with 7 and replace P with x. Then we use 5 and 8 for a and b.

$$7^2 = 5^2 + 8^2 - 2(5)(8) \cos x$$

$$49 = 25 + 64 - 80 \cos x$$

$$40 = 80 \cos x$$

$$0.5 = \cos x$$

so $$x = 60°, 300°$$

From the diagram we see that x is less than 90°; so

$$\mathbf{x = 60°}$$

Now we can use the law of sines to find another angle. We choose to find y.

$$\frac{7}{\sin 60°} = \frac{8}{\sin y}$$

$$\sin y = \frac{8 \sin 60°}{7}$$

$$\sin y = 0.9897$$

so $$y = 81.79° \text{ or } 98.21°$$

From the diagram we see that y is less than 90° so

$$\mathbf{y = 81.79°}$$

Since the angles must add to 180°,

$$180° = 60° + 81.79° + z$$

$$\mathbf{z = 38.21°}$$

Example 60.A.3 Solve the triangle for the missing parts.

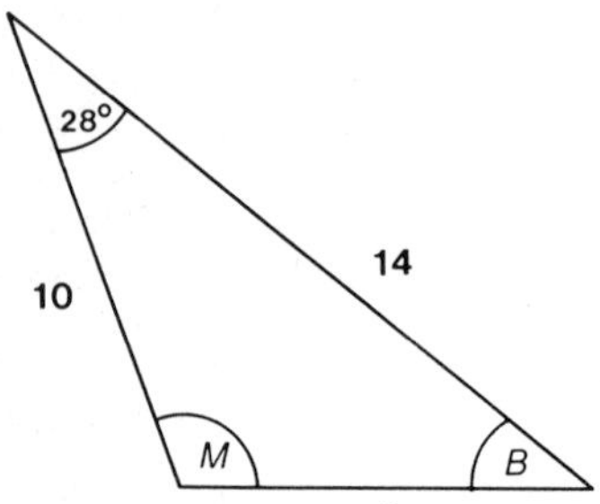

Solution We do not have a pair, so we will use the law of cosines.

$$p^2 = a^2 + b^2 - 2ab \cos P \qquad \text{law of cosines}$$

We will use 10 and 14 for sides a and b and will use 28° and k for the pair we wish we had. We will use a calculator so that the computation can be accomplished quickly and accurately. We must avoid getting bogged down in the arithmetic of these problems.

$k^2 = 10^2 + 14^2 - 2(10)(14)\cos 28°$	substituted
$k^2 = 100 + 196 - 247.23$	simplified
$k^2 = 48.77$	simplified
$\mathbf{k = 6.98}$	root of both sides

Now we have the side that is opposite the 28° angle and thus have the pair necessary for the use of the law of sines.

$$\frac{6.98}{\sin 28°} = \frac{14}{\sin M} \qquad \frac{6.98}{\sin 28°} = \frac{10}{\sin B}$$

$$\sin M = \frac{14 \sin 28°}{6.98} \qquad \sin B = \frac{10 \sin 28°}{6.98}$$

$$\sin M = 0.9416 \qquad \sin B = 0.6726$$

$$M = 70.33° \text{ or } 109.67° \qquad B = 42.27° \text{ or } 137.73°$$

From the diagram of the problem, we see that angle M is greater than 90° and angle B is less than 90°, so

$$\mathbf{M = 109.67°} \qquad \mathbf{B = 42.27°}$$

Now we check the sum of the angles:

$$109.67° + 42.27° + 28° = 179.94° \qquad \text{check}$$

Problem set 60

1. The number 150 was written as the sum of two numbers. The first number was divided by 27. This quotient was added to the second number divided by 23, and the total was 6. What were the two numbers?

2. The sum of the angles in any triangle is 180°. Matildabelle had a triangle in which the second angle was 10° greater than the first angle and the third angle was 25° greater than the second angle. What was the measure of each of the angles of Matildabelle's triangle?

3. Five workers can do three jobs in 2 days. How many workers would it take to do 18 jobs in 10 days?

4. Virginia found that she could buy p pencils for c cents. How many pencils could she buy for \$5?

5. Harry averaged 70 for four straight games and then disaster struck because after the fifth game, his average had dropped all the way to 60. What was his score in the fifth game?

6. The coach had a problem. There are six people on a volleyball team, and he had 10 players. How many different teams could he form from these players? Assume that every player can play any position.

7. Write the four fourth roots of -16 in rectangular form.

8. Write the three cube roots of 8 cis 45° in polar form.

9. Draw a line segment 10 centimeters long and construct its perpendicular bisector.

10. Construct a line that is parallel to a given line and that passes through a designated point that is not on the given line.

11. Write the fourth term of $(x + y)^7$.

12. Write all five terms of $(m + n)^4$.

13. Show that $\dfrac{1 - \cos^2 x}{\sec^2 x - 1} = \cos^2 x$.

14. Show that $\dfrac{1}{1 + \sin A} + \dfrac{1}{1 - \sin A} = 2 \sec^2 A$.

15. Show that $\dfrac{1}{\cot A} + \cot A = \csc A \sec A$.

16. Use Cramer's rule to solve: $\begin{cases} 3x + 6y = 4 \\ 2x - 5y = 1 \end{cases}$

17. Find the sum of the interior angles of a 13-sided convex polygon.

18. The perimeter of a 12-sided regular polygon is 36 inches. What is the area of the polygon?

19. Solve the triangle for its unknown parts.

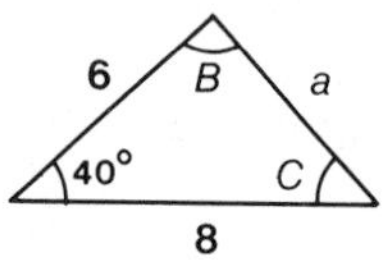

20. Solve the triangle for its unknown parts.

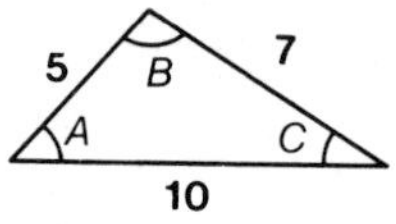

21. Describe the ellipse $4x^2 + 25y^2 = 100$.

22. Describe the hyperbola $4x^2 - 25y^2 = 100$.

23. Multiply $(2 \text{ cis } 30°)[4 \text{ cis } (-90°)]$ and express the answer in rectangular form. Give an exact answer.

24. Prove that an exterior angle of a triangle is equal to the sum of the remote interior angles.

25. Write the equation of the following sinusoid in terms of the sine function.

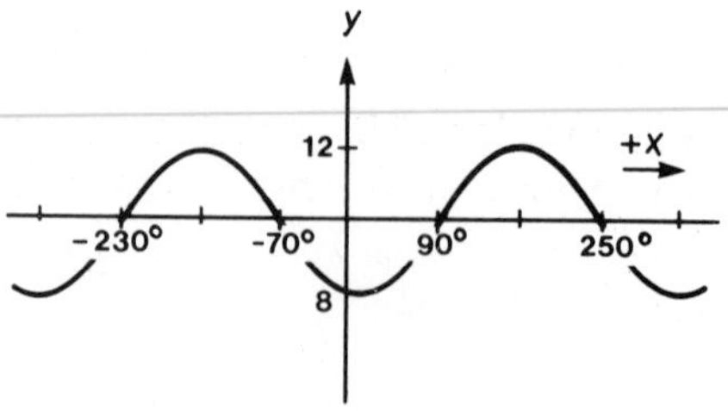

26. Find the radius and the coordinates of the center of the circle whose equation is $2x^2 + 2y^2 - 4x + 8y + 1 = 0$.

27. The three triangles shown are similar. Find x and y.

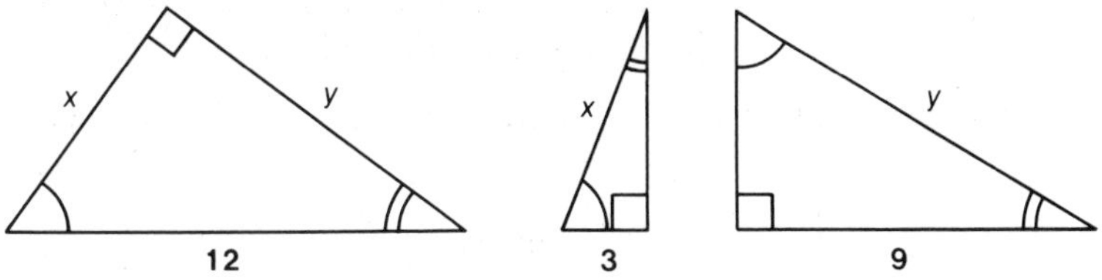

28. Solve, given that ($0° \le \theta < 360°$): $\sqrt{3}\tan 3\theta + 1 = 0$

29. Find $\cos\left[\text{Arcsin}\left(-\frac{4}{5}\right)\right]$.

30. Solve: $\log_{1/2}(3x + 2) - \log_{1/2}(x - 2) = -\log_{1/2} 4$

EP 60.6

LESSON 61 Taking the logarithm of · Exponential equations

61.A Taking the logarithm of

Taking the logarithm of is an operation just as raising to a power is an operation. We can raise the number 100 to the one-half power by writing either

$$(100)^{1/2} \qquad \text{or} \qquad \sqrt{100}$$

and the value of both of these expressions is 10. We can raise x to the one-half power by writing

$$x^{1/2} \qquad \text{or} \qquad \sqrt{x}$$

and, of course, no further simplification is possible unless we have a numerical value for x. **To take the logarithm of a number or an expression, we simply write the abbreviation for the word logarithm in front of the number or the expression.** To take the common logarithm of 100, we write either log or $\log_{10}$ in front of the number.

$$\log 100 \qquad \text{or} \qquad \log_{10} 100$$

When the abbreviation log is used and the base is not indicated, a base of 10 is understood, so the above expressions mean the same thing. Both have a value of 2. To take the common logarithm of x, we would write either

$$\log x \qquad \text{or} \qquad \log_{10} x$$

If we are asked to take the natural logarithm of 100, we would write either

$$\ln 100 \qquad \text{or} \qquad \log_e 100$$

because the letters ln mean that the base is e. The approximate numerical value of both these expressions is 4.605. To take the natural logarithm of x, we would write either

$$\ln x \qquad \text{or} \qquad \log_e x$$

61.B Exponential equations

We remember that expressions that consist of a base and an exponent are called ***powers.*** All the following expressions are powers.

(*a*) $5^{2.3}$ (*b*) $(3y)^4$ (*c*) x^2 (*d*) 2^x (*e*) 3^{2y+4}

The expressions (*d*) and (*e*) are considered to be special forms of powers because in each expression the base is a positive real number (not 1) and the exponent contains a variable. We call these powers ***exponentials*** and call an equation that contains an exponential an ***exponential equation.***

We have been solving logarithmic equations by rewriting them as exponential equations. Thus we can find the value of x in this logarithmic equation

$$\log_{1/2} x = 2$$

by rewriting the equation in exponential form and then solving.

$$\left(\frac{1}{2}\right)^2 = x \qquad \text{exponential form}$$

$$\frac{1}{4} = x \qquad \text{simplified}$$

Now we find that many exponential equations can be solved by taking the logarithm of both sides of the equation and using logarithms to complete the solution. When we work these problems, it is important to remember that $\log_{10} 10^1$ is 1 and $\log_e e^1$ is 1.

Example 61.B.1 Solve $10^{-2x+2} = 8$.

Solution First we take the logarithm of both sides to the base 10. **We remember that, if we write *log* and do not designate a base, the base is understood to be 10.**

$$\log 10^{-2x+2} = \log 8 \qquad \text{log of both sides}$$

On the left-hand side we will use the power rule for logs, and on the right-hand side we will use the calculator (or the table) to find the log of 8.

$$(-2x + 2) \log 10 = 0.90309$$

But log 10 is 1, so we end up with a simple algebraic equation, which we solve.

$$-2x + 2 = 0.90309 \qquad \text{equation}$$

$$-2x = -1.09691 \qquad \text{added } -2$$

$$\mathbf{x = 0.5485} \qquad \text{divided}$$

Example 61.B.2 Solve $e^{-2x+3} = 5$.

Solution This time, because the base is e, we will take the natural logarithm of both sides.

$$\ln e^{-2x+3} = \ln 5 \qquad \ln \text{ of both sides}$$

Now we will use the power rule for logarithms on the left side and use a calculator on the right side to find the natural log of 5.

$$(-2x + 3) \ln e = 1.6094379$$

We remember that the natural logarithm of e (written $\ln e$) is 1. This is the reason that we used base e instead of base 10 in this problem. Thus, we get

$$-2x + 3 = 1.6094379 \qquad \text{simplified}$$

$$-2x = -1.3905621 \qquad \text{added } -3$$

$$\mathbf{x = 0.695281} \qquad \text{divided}$$

Example 61.B.3 Solve $5^{2x-1} = 6^{x-2}$.

Solution We solve exponential equations by taking the logarithm of both sides. In this equation, neither base is 10 or e so there is no advantage to taking either the common logarithm or the natural logarithm. We decide to take the common logarithm.

$$\log 5^{2x-1} = \log 6^{x-2}$$

Next we use the power rule on both sides.

$$(2x - 1)\log 5 = (x - 2)\log 6$$

Now we use a calculator to find log 5 and log 6 and use these values.

$$(2x - 1)(0.69897) = (x - 2)(0.7781513)$$

Since exactness is not required, we will round off the logarithms before we solve.

$$(2x - 1)(0.70) = (x - 2)(0.78)$$

Now we multiply and complete the solution.

$$1.40x - 0.70 = 0.78x - 1.56 \qquad \text{multiplied}$$

$$0.62x = -0.86 \qquad \text{simplified}$$

$$\mathbf{x = -1.39} \qquad \text{divided}$$

Example 61.B.4 Simplify $(1.01)^7$.

Solution We could get the answer by using the y^x key on a calculator, but we will use logarithms and do it the long way. We have found that simple exponential equations can be solved by taking the logarithm of both sides. If we set the given expression equal to y,

$$y = (1.01)^7$$

we have an exponential equation. We solve by taking the common logarithm of both sides and then we use the power rule.

$$\log y = \log (1.01)^7 \qquad \text{log of both sides}$$

$$\log y = 7 \log 1.01 \qquad \text{power rule}$$

$$\log y = 0.0302496 \qquad \text{evaluated}$$

$$\mathbf{y = 1.072} \qquad \text{antilogarithm}$$

Problem set 61

1. The three dimensions of a rectangular box are height, length, and width. The sum of the dimensions is 18 ft. The height equals four-fifths of the sum of the length and the width and equals 4 times the difference of the length and the width. What are the dimensions of the box?

2. Peter had to make a trip of t miles. He got up early and drove at r miles per hour for h hours and then stopped for lunch. How many miles did he have to drive after lunch?

3. Seven women could do 3 jobs in 5 days. How many days would it take for 9 women to do 27 jobs?

4. The first crew could do a jobs in 3 days. The second crew could do 3 jobs in b days. How long would it take both crews working together to do 13 jobs?

5. Ten workers could do p jobs in 5 days. This was too slow so the contractor hired 5 more workers. How many days would it take the new work force to complete k jobs?

6. There were 20 marbles in a line. Ten were red, 6 were blue, and 4 were white. How many distinguishable linear patterns could be formed?

7. Write the three cube roots of -1 in rectangular form.

8. Write the four fourth roots of 16 cis 60° in polar form.

9. Draw a 50° angle, copy the angle, and then construct a bisector of the copied angle.

10. Construct a triangle whose sides measure 6 inches, 2 inches, and 4 inches.

11. Write all six terms of $(p + q)^5$.

12. Show that $\dfrac{\sin A}{1 + \cos A} + \dfrac{1 + \cos A}{\sin A} = 2 \csc A$.

13. Show that $\dfrac{\csc^2 \theta - \cot^2 \theta}{1 + \cot^2 \theta} = \sin^2 \theta$.

14. Show that $\dfrac{\sin x}{\csc x} + \dfrac{\cos x}{\sec x} = 1$.

15. The perimeter of a 14-sided regular polygon is 42. Find the radius of the circle which can be circumscribed about the polygon.

16. Find the sum of the interior angles of a 10-sided convex polygon.

17. Solve this triangle for its unknown parts.

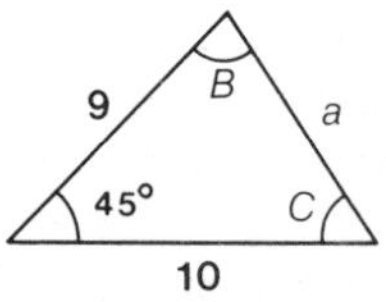

18. Solve this triangle for its unknown parts.

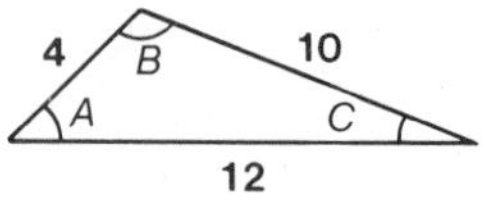

19. Describe the ellipse $9x^2 + 36y^2 = 324$.

20. Describe the hyperbola $9x^2 - 36y^2 = 324$.

21. Multiply (3 cis 20°)[2 cis (−80°)] and express the answer in rectangular form. Give an exact answer.

22. Find the distance from (2, 1) to $2x + y = 3$.

23. Write the equation of the sine curve that is shifted $\pi/8$ to the right, that has a period of $\pi/2$, an amplitude of 9, and a centerline of $y = +2$.

24. Find the radius and the coordinates of the center of the circle whose equation is $2x^2 + 2y^2 - 12y + 4x + 1 = 0$.

25. The three triangles shown are similar. Find a and b.

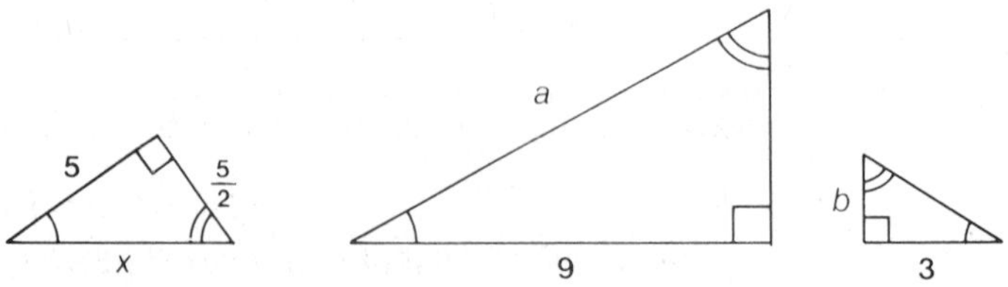

26. Solve, given that $(0° \le x < 360°)$: $4 \sin^2 x - 1 = 0$

27. Solve: $6^{3x+2} = 4^{2x-1}$

28. Solve: $10^{-3x-4} = 5^{2x-1}$

29. Evaluate $(1.02)^8$ by using the logarithm tables.

30. Solve: $\frac{2}{3} \log_7 8 + \log_7 x - \log_7 (x + 2) = \log_7 9$

EP 61.7

LESSON 62 Simple probability · Independent events

62.A Probability

Probability theory had its genesis in the study of games of chance such as rolling dice, drawing cards at random from a deck of cards, or flipping a coin. Problems from games of chance still provide the best models on which to base a study of elementary probability, and we will concentrate on these problems.

The study of probability is based on the study of outcomes that have an equal chance of occurring. A fair coin should come up heads as often as it comes up tails if we flip it enough times. We will assume that our coins are fair coins. A die (singular of dice) has 6 faces. If we roll it enough times, each face should come up approximately one-sixth of the time. We will assume that our dice are fair dice. We will also assume that each card in a deck has the same chance of being selected and that individual marbles have equal chances of being drawn from an urn.

It is customary to call activities such as flipping coins, rolling dice, blindly selecting cards from a deck, or drawing marbles from an urn an ***experiment*** and to call the individual results ***outcomes.*** We will call the **set of equally probable outcomes** of an experiment the ***sample space*** of the experiment, and we will call designated subspaces of the sample space ***events.*** We will define the ***probability of a particular event*** as the number of outcomes that satisfy the requirement divided by the total number of outcomes in the sample space. If we flip a fair coin, it can come up either heads or tails. Thus, our sample space is

H	T

If the event is getting a head, the probability of getting a head is

$$P(\text{H}) = \frac{\text{number of outcomes that are H}}{\text{total number of outcomes in the sample space}} = \frac{1}{2}$$

If we roll a single die, the sample space is

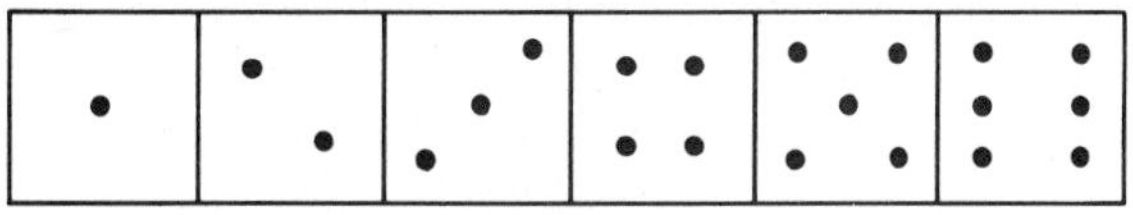

If we define the event as getting a 5, the probability of getting a 5 is

$$P(5) = \frac{\text{number of outcomes that are 5}}{\text{total number of outcomes in the sample space}} = \frac{1}{6}$$

The probability of rolling a number greater than 4 is

$$\frac{\text{Number of outcomes that are greater than 4}}{\text{Total number of outcomes in the sample space}} = \frac{2}{6} = \frac{1}{3}$$

Example 62.A.1 Two dice are rolled. What is the probability of getting (*a*) a 7, (*b*) a number greater than 8?

Solution First we draw a diagram of our sample space. The outcomes are the sums of the values on the individual dice, and there are 36 outcomes in our sample space.

Outcome of second die

Outcome of first die	1	2	3	4	5	6
1	2	3	4	5	6	7
2	3	4	5	6	7	8
3	4	5	6	7	8	9
4	5	6	7	8	9	10
5	6	7	8	9	10	11
6	7	8	9	10	11	12

(*a*) The event is rolling a 7, and we see that 6 of these outcomes are 7, so

$$P(7) = \frac{\text{number of outcomes that equal 7}}{\text{total number of outcomes in the sample space}} = \frac{6}{36}$$

Thus, we find that the probability of rolling a 7 is $\frac{1}{6}$.

(*b*) The event is rolling a number greater than 8, and we see that 10 of these outcomes are greater than 8, so

$$P(>8) = \frac{\text{number of outcomes that are greater than 8}}{\text{total number of outcomes in the sample space}} = \frac{10}{36}$$

Thus, the probability of rolling a number greater than 8 is $\frac{5}{18}$.

62.B Independent events

We have defined probability so that the probability of any event lies between 0 and 1 inclusively.

$$0 \le P(E) \le 1$$

The sample space for the possible outcomes of a single roll of a pair of dice is always the sample space diagrammed in the last problem. If we look at this sample space, we see that there are no outcomes of 146, so the probability of rolling a 146 is 0.

$$P(146) = \frac{\text{number of outcomes that are 146}}{\text{total number of outcomes in the sample space}} = \frac{0}{36} = 0$$

The probability of rolling a number that is less than 146 is 1 because every one of the 36 outcomes is less than 146.

$$P(<146) = \frac{\text{number of outcomes that are less than 146}}{\text{total number of outcomes in the sample space}} = \frac{36}{36} = 1$$

This numerical example demonstrates that the least probability possible for an event is 0 and that the greatest probability possible is 1. Thus, we see that negative probabilities or probabilities greater than 1 are impossible. **Further, we see that a declaration that a probability of a particular event is 4.6 or $-3\frac{1}{2}$ makes no sense because the probability of any event must be a number between 0 and 1 inclusive.**

We say that events that do not affect one another are ***independent events.*** If Danny flips a dime and Paul flips a penny, the outcome of Danny's flip does not affect the outcome of Paul's flip. Thus, we say that these events are independent events. **The probability of independent events occurring in a designated order is the product of the probabilities of the individual events.**

A tree diagram can always be used to demonstrate the probability of independent events occurring in a designated order. This diagram shows the possible outcomes if a coin is tossed three times.

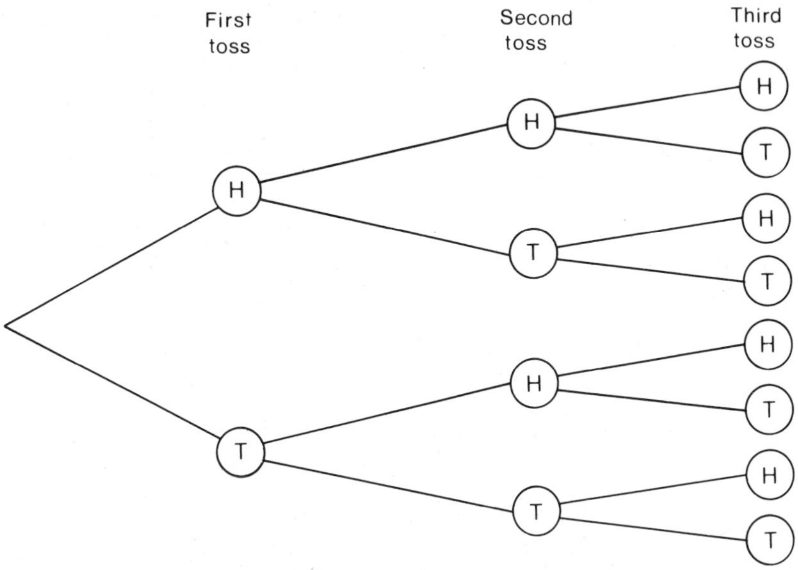

The first toss can be heads or tails and the second and third tosses can be heads or tails. Thus, there are 8 possible ordered outcomes, and the probability of each of these outcomes is $\frac{1}{8}$.

Example 62.B.1 A fair coin is tossed 3 times. What is the probability that it comes up heads every time?

Solution Coin tosses are independent events because the result of one toss has no effect on the result of the next toss. Since the probability of independent events occurring in a designated order is the product of the individual probabilities, we have

$$P(3\text{ heads}) = \frac{1}{2}\cdot\frac{1}{2}\cdot\frac{1}{2} = \mathbf{\frac{1}{8}}$$

Example 62.B.2 A fair coin is tossed 4 times and it comes up heads each time. What is the probability it will come up heads on the next toss?

Solution The results of past coin tosses do not affect the outcome of future coin tosses. Thus, the probability of getting a head on the next toss is $\frac{1}{2}$.

62.C Replacement

When we make successive random selections of cards from a deck or of marbles from an urn, the probability of a certain outcome on the second draw is affected by whether or not the item selected on the first draw is returned before the second draw is made.

Example 62.C.1 An urn contains two black marbles and two white marbles. A marble is drawn and replaced. Then a second marble is drawn. (*a*) What is the probability that both marbles are black? (*b*) If the first marble is not replaced before the second marble is drawn, what is the probability that both marbles are black?

Solution (*a*) The probability of a black marble on the first draw is $\frac{1}{2}$. Since the first marble is replaced, the probability of a black marble on the second draw is also $\frac{1}{2}$, so

$$P(\text{both black}) = \frac{1}{2} \cdot \frac{1}{2} = \mathbf{\frac{1}{4}}$$

(*b*) The probability of a black on the second draw is not the same because the first marble was not replaced. The diagram shows the possibilities:

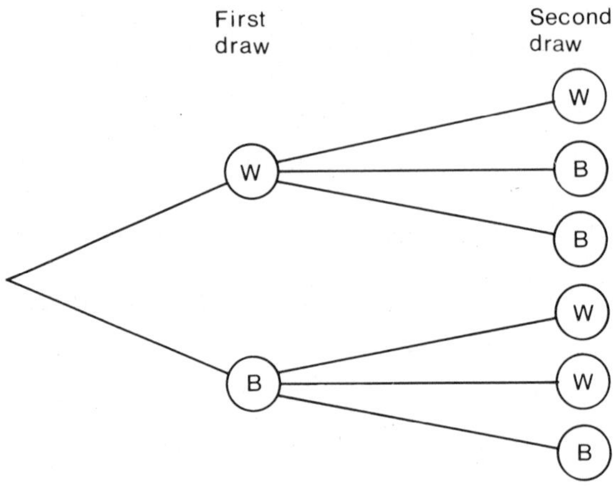

We see that if the first draw was black, then the probability of a black on the second draw is $\frac{1}{3}$ because only 3 marbles remain. Thus, the probability of 2 blacks when there is no replacement between draws is

$$P(\text{both black}) = \frac{1}{2} \cdot \frac{1}{3} = \mathbf{\frac{1}{6}}$$

Example 62.C.2 Two cards are drawn from a 52-card deck without replacement. What is the probability that the first one is red and the second one is black?

Solution The probability of the second draw changes because there is no replacement.

$$P(\text{red then black}) = \frac{26}{52} \cdot \frac{26}{51} = \mathbf{\frac{13}{51}}$$

Problem set 62

1. Two fair dice are rolled. What is the probability of getting a number greater than 9?

2. An urn contains 5 red marbles and 12 white marbles. A marble is drawn and replaced. Then another marble is drawn. What is the probability that the first marble will be red and the second marble will be white?

3. In Problem 2, what is the probability that the first marble will be red and the second will be white if the first marble drawn is not replaced before the second marble is drawn?

4. The radius of the wheel was r inches and the wheel was revolving at 40 revolutions per minute. What was the linear velocity in feet per second of a point on the rim?

5. The cost varied linearly with the number of workers that were employed. When 10 workers were employed the cost was \$450 and when 20 workers were employed, the cost was \$850. What would it cost if only 2 workers were employed?

6. If M men could do J jobs in 1 day, how many days would it take 5 fewer men to do k jobs?

7. Write the five fifth roots of 32 cis 60° in polar form.

8. Draw a 5-centimeter-long line segment and construct its perpendicular bisector, using straightedge and compass.

9. Construct a perpendicular to a line from a point not on the line.

10. Write all seven terms of $(x + z)^6$.

11. Show that $\dfrac{\sin A}{1 - \cos A} + \dfrac{1 - \cos A}{\sin A} = 2 \csc A$.

12. Show that $\dfrac{\sec^2 \theta - \tan^2 \theta}{\tan^2 \theta + 1} = \cos^2 \theta$.

13. Show that $\dfrac{1}{\tan(-x)} + \tan(-x) = -\sec x \csc x$.

14. The perimeter of a 12-sided regular polygon is 96 centimeters. Find the area of the polygon.

15. Find the sum of the exterior angles of a 25-sided convex polygon.

16. Solve this triangle for its unknown parts.

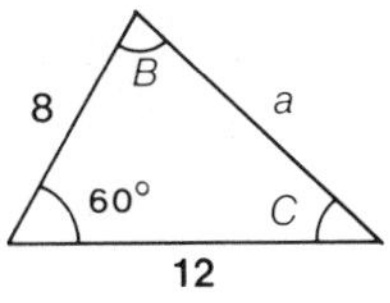

17. Solve this triangle for its unknown parts.

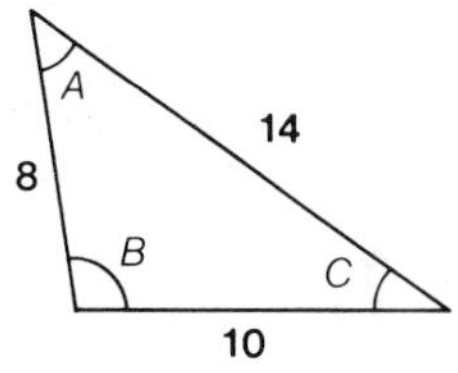

18. Describe the ellipse $16x^2 + 9y^2 = 144$.

19. Describe the hyperbola $9y^2 - 16x^2 = 144$.

20. Multiply $(6 \text{ cis } 30°)[\frac{1}{6} \text{ cis } (-30°)]$ and express the answer in rectangular form. Give an exact answer.

21. Prove that vertical angles are equal.

22. Write the equation of the following sinusoid as a cosine function.

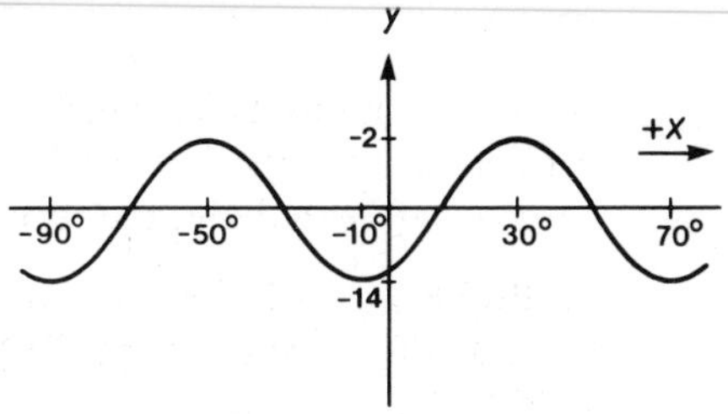

23. Find the radius and the coordinates of the center of the circle whose equation is $y^2 + x^2 + 2x - 6y - 6 = 0$.

24. Find a and b.

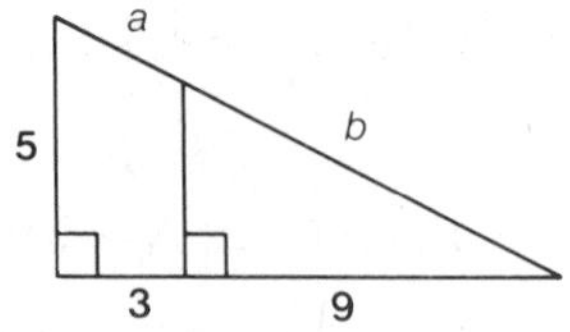

25. Solve, given that $(0° \leq \theta < 360°)$: $\sec^2 \theta + \sec \theta - 2 = 0$

26. Evaluate: $\tan\left[\text{Arccot}\left(-\frac{4}{5}\right)\right]$

27. Solve: $7^{2x-4} = 5^{3x+2}$

28. Solve: $10^{3x-1} = 5^{4x-2}$

29. Evaluate $(1.41)^8$ by using the logarithm tables.

30. Solve: $\log_8 16 - \log_8 4 = x$

EP 62.8

LESSON 63 *Factorable expressions · Sketching sinusoids*

63.A Factorable expressions

Calculus books are rife with problems whose solutions require the factoring of trigonometric expressions such as the ones shown below. Practice with these factorable expressions will improve our ability to change the form of trigonometric expressions and will lessen the intimidation when these expressions are encountered in calculus and in other advanced mathematics courses. For the present, we can consider these problems as puzzles whose solutions have no immediate applications but will be of great value in the future.

EXPRESSION		FACTORED FORM
$\sin^3 x$	$\longrightarrow$	$(\sin x)(\sin^2 x)$
$\tan^2 \theta - 1$	$\longrightarrow$	$(\tan \theta + 1)(\tan \theta - 1)$
$1 - \tan^2 \theta$	$\longrightarrow$	$(1 + \tan \theta)(1 - \tan \theta)$
$\csc^2 x - 1$	$\longrightarrow$	$(\csc x + 1)(\csc x - 1)$
$\sin x - \sin x \cos^2 x$	$\longrightarrow$	$(\sin x)(1 - \cos^2 x)$
$\csc^4 P - \cot^4 P$	$\longrightarrow$	$(\csc^2 P + \cot^2 P)(\csc^2 P - \cot^2 P)$
$1 - 2\sin^2 x + \sin^4 x$	$\longrightarrow$	$(1 - \sin^2 x)(1 - \sin^2 x)$
$\sin^3 x - \cos^3 x$	$\longrightarrow$	$(\sin x - \cos x)(\sin^2 x + \sin x \cos x + \cos^2 x)$

The last two are especially tricky because they must be recognized as having the same form as

$$1 - 2x + x^2 \longrightarrow (1 - x)(1 - x)$$
$$x^3 - y^3 \longrightarrow (x - y)(x^2 + xy + y^2)$$

Look over the forms shown because when one of these forms appears in an identity, it is necessary to recognize that it can be factored.

Example 63.A.1 Show that $\sin x - \sin x \cos^2 x = \sin^3 x$.

Solution First we will factor the left side and get

$$(\sin x)(1 - \cos^2 x) \qquad \text{factored}$$

But $1 - \cos^2 x$ equals $\sin^2 x$, so we have

$$(\sin x)(\sin^2 x) \longrightarrow \sin^3 x$$

Example 63.A.2 Show that $\dfrac{\sec^4 x - \tan^4 x}{\sec^2 x + \tan^2 x} + \tan^2 x = \sec^2 x$.

Solution We begin by factoring $\sec^4 x - \tan^4 x$ and we get

$$\frac{(\sec^2 x + \tan^2 x)(\sec^2 x - \tan^2 x)}{\sec^2 x + \tan^2 x} + \tan^2 x \qquad \text{factored}$$

$$\sec^2 x - \tan^2 x + \tan^2 x = \sec^2 x \qquad \text{canceled and added}$$

Example 63.A.3 Show that $\dfrac{\csc^2 x - 1}{\tan x} = \cot^3 x$.

Solution Factoring won't always work. If we factor in this problem, we get

$$\frac{(\csc x + 1)(\csc x - 1)}{\tan x}$$

and this time factoring did not help. So we remember that $\csc^2 x - 1$ equals $\cot^2 x$ and that $1/(\tan x) = \cot x$. We get

$$\frac{\csc^2 x - 1}{\tan x} = \cot^2 x \cdot \frac{1}{\tan x} = (\cot^2 x)(\cot x) = \cot^3 x$$

63.B Sketching sinusoids

Sinusoids can be sketched quickly and accurately if the curve is drawn first and then the labels added. The crucial label for the sine function is the phase angle, which is the opposite of the angle in the factored argument. The curve crosses its centerline on the way up when θ equals the phase angle. Other crossing points are found by adding or subtracting multiples of half the period to the phase angle. The crucial label for the cosine function is the phase angle, which again is the opposite of the angle in the factored argument. The cosine curve reaches its maximum value when θ equals the phase angle. The values of θ for other extreme values of the curve are found by adding or subtracting multiples of half the period to the phase angle.

Example 63.B.1 Sketch the graph of $y = -10 + 2 \sin 3(x - 45°)$.

Solution As the first step we will sketch a sinusoid, and to the left of the curve we draw a vertical scale on which we indicate the value of the centerline and the maximum and minimum values of the curve.

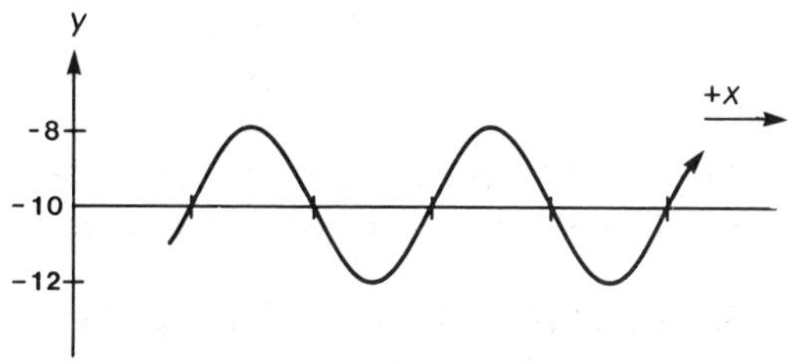

Next, from $(x - 45°)$, we see that the phase angle is $+45°$ because the angle in the argument is the opposite of the phase angle. Thus, one crossing point is the phase angle which is $+45°$. This curve will cross its centerline every half period. The period for this function is 360° divided by 3, or 120°. Half the period is 60°, so we label the other crossing points 60° apart to the left and right of $+45°$.

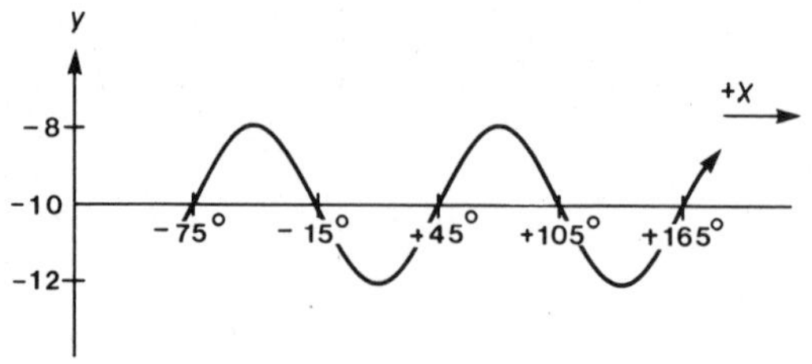

This graph is adequate, but it could be improved slightly by indicating the location of the origin. We note that 0° will lie between $-15°$ and $+45°$, and will be exactly one-fourth of the way from $-15°$ to 45°. We indicate the location of the origin to complete the graph.

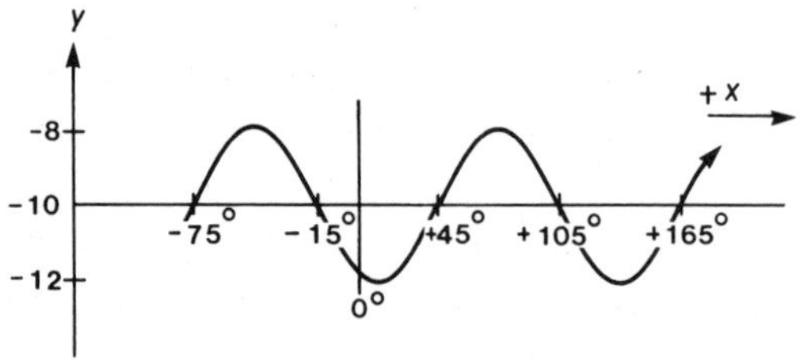

Example 63.B.2 Sketch the graph of $y = -2 + 4 \cos 2\left(x + \frac{2\pi}{3}\right)$.

Solution This time we will begin by determining the values of θ for which the curve is a maximum. The phase angle is $-\frac{2\pi}{3}$, and this is one maximum point. The period is π radians, so the curve will have a maximum value every π radians to the right and the left of this point. We draw a sinusoid, and label the centerline and the maximum and minimum values.

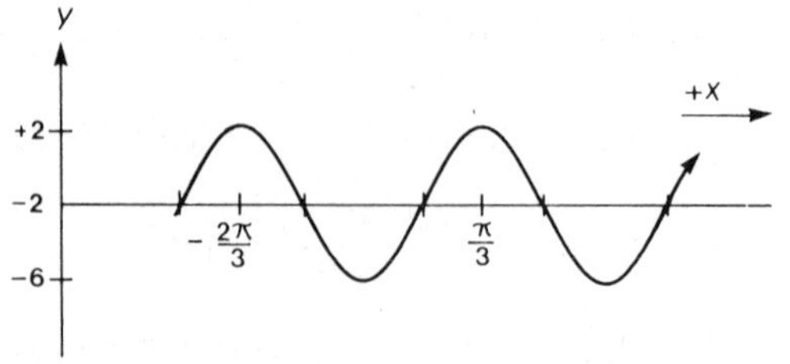

The minimum points occur regularly one-half period, or $\frac{\pi}{2}$ radians, to the right and left of the maximum points. We label the minimum points and locate the position of the origin to complete the graph.

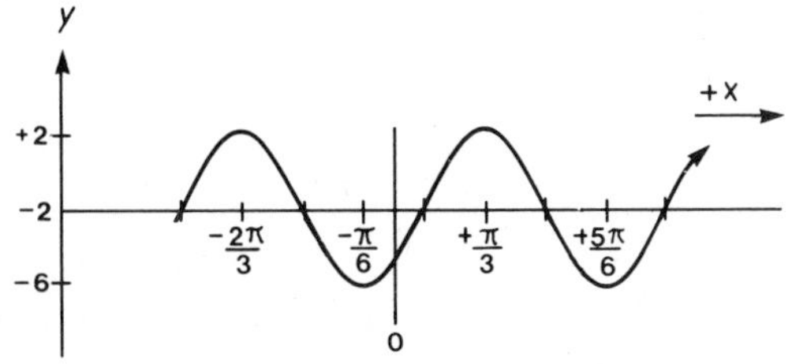

Problem set 63

1. The average temperature for 5 days was 100°, and then it was cold for 1 day. That brought the average down to 90 degrees for the 6-day period. What was the temperature on the sixth day?

2. Frankie ran the k yards in p minutes and got to the party m minutes early. How fast should Frankie have run to get to the party on time?

3. Johnny found that he could do 4 jobs in 3 days. When Johnny worked with Bradley, they found they could finish 11 jobs in 6 days. How many jobs could Bradley complete in 4 days working alone?

4. The general expressions for consecutive multiples of 11 are $11N$, $11(N + 1)$, $11(N + 2)$, etc., where N is an integer. Find three consecutive multiples of 11 such that 4 times the sum of the first and the third is 66 less than 10 times the second.

5. A fair coin was flipped 3 times. What is the probability that the first two tosses come up heads and the third toss then comes up tails?

6. The urn contained 7 marbles. Four were white and 3 were blue. Two marbles were drawn. What is the probability that both were white (*a*) with replacement and (*b*) without replacement?

7. Write the four fourth roots of 16 cis 120° in rectangular form. Give exact answers.

8. Construct a line that is parallel to a given line and that passes through a designated point not on the line.

9. Use a protractor to draw a 60° angle and then construct its bisector.

10. Write all eight terms of $(a + c)^7$.

11. Show that $\frac{\csc^4 x - \cot^4 x}{\csc^2 x + \cot^2 x} + \cot^2 x = \csc^2 x$.

12. Show that $\cos x - \cos x \sin^2 x = \cos^3 x$.

13. Show that $\frac{\sec^2 \theta - 1}{\cot \theta} = \tan^3 \theta$.

14. Show that $\cos(-\theta) \csc(-\theta) = \cot(-\theta)$.

15. The perimeter of a 10-sided regular polygon (regular decagon) is 60 centimeters. Find the radius of the circle which can be circumscribed about the decagon.

16. Solve this triangle for its unknown parts.

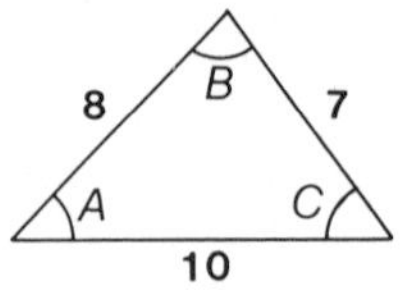

17. Find the area in square centimeters of this triangle.

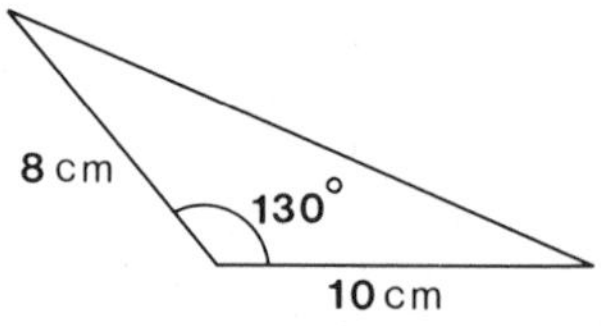

18. Describe the ellipse $4x^2 + 25y^2 = 100$.

19. Find the vertices and the equations of the asymptotes of the hyperbola $4x^2 - 25y^2 = 100$.

20. Prove that the sum of the angles of a triangle equals 180°.

21. Sketch $y = -2 + 4 \cos 2\left(x + \frac{2\pi}{3}\right)$.

22. Sketch $y = -1 + 8 \sin 2(x - 45°)$.

23. Find the radius and the coordinates of the center of the circle whose equation is $x^2 + y^2 + 6x - 4y - 15 = 0$.

24. Find y.

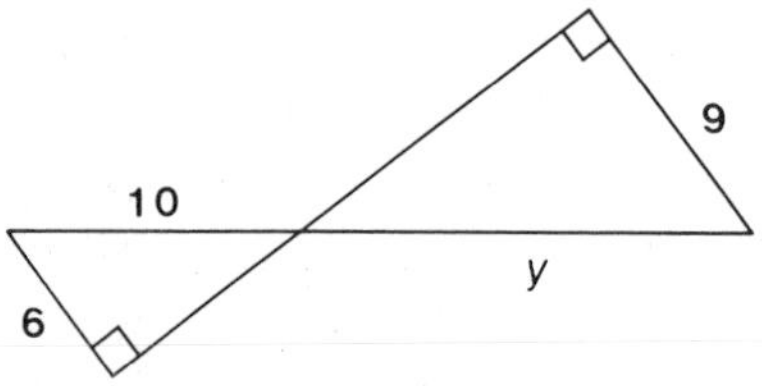

Solve the following equations given that $(0° \le \theta, x < 360°)$:

25. $2 \cos 3\theta - \sqrt{3} = 0$

26. $4 \sin^2 x - 3 = 0$

27. Solve: $8^{3x-1} = 5^{2x+1}$

28. Solve: $10^{2x-3} = 4^{2x+1}$

29. Factor $x^2 + 4x + 6$ over the set of complex numbers.

30. Solve: $\frac{3}{2} \log_8 4 + 2 \log_8 x = \log_8 16$

EP 63.9

LESSON 64 Echelon solutions

64.A Echelon solutions

There are many ways to solve systems of linear equations. In Algebra I we learned to use the substitution method and the elimination method, and we also learned to find the solution by graphing. In this book, we have introduced matrix solutions of these systems by using determinants and Cramer's rule. Now we will look at the use of

echelon matrices to solve systems of linear equations. The word **echelon** is a military word that comes from the Latin word *scalae*, which means "steps" or "stairs." Soldiers or airplanes are said to be in echelon when they are arranged in a regular but staggered formation.

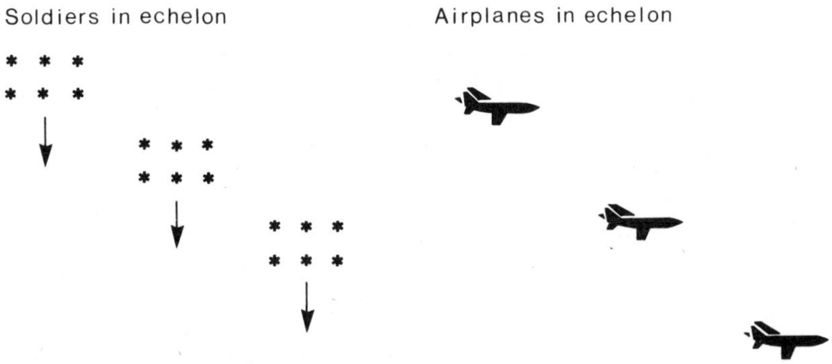

We can solve systems of equations by beginning with the coefficients in a matrix and changing the form of the matrix until it consists of zeros, an echelon of 1s, and a column of constants. If we begin with the system of equations shown on the left, we can end up with the matrix shown on the right.

$$\begin{aligned} 4x + 2y - z &= 18 \\ 2x + 3y + 2z &= 5 \\ 4x - y + 3z &= -7 \end{aligned} \qquad \begin{bmatrix} 1 & 0 & 0 & 2 \\ 0 & 1 & 0 & 3 \\ 0 & 0 & 1 & -4 \end{bmatrix}$$

Then, from the rows in the matrix, we can read that x equals 2, y equals 3, and z equals -4. The echelon matrix method is especially useful, for it lends itself to programming for computer use. We will begin by looking at systems of two equations in two unknowns. We remember that when we use the elimination method of solving equations, we can

1. **Multiply every term on both sides of an equation by the same constant**
2. **Add two equations together**

We will use these rules to solve the following system.

$$\begin{matrix} (a) \\ (b) \end{matrix} \quad \begin{cases} 4x + 3y = 24 \\ 2x - y = 2 \end{cases}$$

We begin by making the coefficient of x in equation (a) equal to 1. We do this by multiplying every term in equation (a) by $\frac{1}{4}$.

$$\begin{matrix} \frac{1}{4}(a) \\ (b) \end{matrix} \quad \begin{cases} x + \frac{3}{4}y = 6 \\ 2x - y = 2 \end{cases}$$

Next we multiply the equation $\frac{1}{4}(a)$ by -2 and add the result to equation (b).

$$\begin{matrix} \frac{1}{4}(a) \\ (b) \end{matrix} \quad \begin{cases} x + \frac{3}{4}y = 6 & \longrightarrow & (-2) & \longrightarrow & -2x - \frac{3}{2}y = -12 \\ 2x - y = 2 & \longrightarrow & (1) & \longrightarrow & 2x - y = 2 \end{cases}$$

$$-\frac{5}{2}y = -10$$

Now we have

$$\begin{array}{rl} \frac{1}{4}(a) & \left\{ \begin{array}{l} x + \frac{3}{4}y = 6 \\ 0 - \frac{5}{2}y = -10 \end{array} \right. \\ (c) & \end{array}$$

We can solve (c) by multiplying both sides by $-\frac{2}{5}$, and now our equations are

$$\begin{array}{rl} \frac{1}{4}(a) & \left\{ \begin{array}{l} x + \frac{3}{4}y = 6 \\ 0 + \ \ y = 4 \end{array} \right. \\ -\frac{2}{5}(c) & \end{array}$$

Now, if we multiply the bottom equation by $-\frac{3}{4}$ and add it to the top equation, we can solve for x.

$$\begin{array}{rlcccl} \text{Top:} & x + \frac{3}{4}y = 6 & \longrightarrow & (1) & \longrightarrow & x + \frac{3}{4}y = \ \ 6 \\ \text{Bottom:} & 0 + \ \ y = 4 & \longrightarrow & \left(-\frac{3}{4}\right) & \longrightarrow & 0 - \frac{3}{4}y = -3 \\ \hline & & & & & x + 0 \ = \ \ 3 \end{array}$$

Now our equations are

$$\begin{cases} x + 0 = 3 \\ 0 + y = 4 \end{cases}$$

and the solution, of course, is (3, 4). Now we repeat the process, using a matrix that has only the numbers but no variables. **We will work down the matrix, forming the 0s in front and forming the echelon of 1s. Then we will work back up, forming the 0s to the right of the echelon.**

$$\begin{bmatrix} 4 & 3 & 24 \\ 2 & -1 & 2 \end{bmatrix}$$ original matrix

(1) $$\begin{bmatrix} 1 & \frac{3}{4} & 6 \\ 2 & -1 & 2 \end{bmatrix}$$ multiplied top row by $\frac{1}{4}$ to get 1 as first entry in the top row

(2) $$\begin{bmatrix} 1 & \frac{3}{4} & 6 \\ 0 & -\frac{5}{2} & -10 \end{bmatrix}$$ multiplied the top row by -2 and added the result to the bottom row to get 0 as the first entry in the bottom row

(3) $$\begin{bmatrix} 1 & \frac{3}{4} & 6 \\ 0 & 1 & 4 \end{bmatrix}$$ multiplied the bottom row by $-\frac{2}{5}$ to get 1 as the second entry in the bottom row

(4) $$\begin{bmatrix} 1 & 0 & 3 \\ 0 & 1 & 4 \end{bmatrix}$$ multiplied the bottom row by $-\frac{3}{4}$ and added the result to the top row to get 0 as the second entry in the top row

The answer is $\boldsymbol{x = 3}$ and $\boldsymbol{y = 4}$.

Example 64.A.1 Use the matrix echelon method to solve: $\begin{cases} 3x + y = 11 \\ 2x - 4y = -2 \end{cases}$

Solution Our original matrix is

$$\begin{bmatrix} 3 & 1 & 11 \\ 2 & -4 & -2 \end{bmatrix}$$

Now we will multiply and add as required in four steps to get matrices of the following forms:

$$\underset{(1)}{\begin{bmatrix} 1 & a & b \\ c & d & e \end{bmatrix}} \longrightarrow \underset{(2)}{\begin{bmatrix} 1 & a & b \\ 0 & f & g \end{bmatrix}} \longrightarrow \underset{(3)}{\begin{bmatrix} 1 & a & b \\ 0 & 1 & h \end{bmatrix}} \longrightarrow \underset{(4)}{\begin{bmatrix} 1 & 0 & i \\ 0 & 1 & h \end{bmatrix}}$$

The first step is to multiply the first row by $\frac{1}{3}$ to make the first entry 1 in this row. We do this and get

(1) $\begin{bmatrix} 1 & \frac{1}{3} & \frac{11}{3} \\ 2 & -4 & -2 \end{bmatrix}$ multiplied by $\frac{1}{3}$

(2) $\begin{bmatrix} 1 & \frac{1}{3} & \frac{11}{3} \\ 0 & -\frac{14}{3} & -\frac{28}{3} \end{bmatrix}$ multiplied the top row by -2 and added the result to the bottom row to get a 0 in the bottom row

(3) $\begin{bmatrix} 1 & \frac{1}{3} & \frac{11}{3} \\ 0 & 1 & 2 \end{bmatrix}$ multiplied the second row by $-\frac{3}{14}$ to get 1 as the second entry in the second row

(4) $\begin{bmatrix} 1 & 0 & 3 \\ 0 & 1 & 2 \end{bmatrix}$ multiplied the second row by $-\frac{1}{3}$ and added the result to the top row to make the second entry 0 in the top row

Now we see that the answers are $\boldsymbol{x = 3}$ and $\boldsymbol{y = 2}$.

In the problem sets, echelon solutions of matrices may be attempted by students in teams of two or three to reduce time loss caused by mistakes in arithmetic.

Problem set 64

1. Kondine drove m miles in h hours. If he doubled his rate, how long would it have required to drive a distance that was 60 miles greater?

2. Find three consecutive integers such that the product of the first two is 14 greater than the third.

3. A fair coin was flipped twice and it came up heads both times. If it is flipped twice more, what is the probability that the next two flips will be heads?

4. A racecourse goes 200 miles up a hill and then 160 miles down the other side. If Marjorie drives up the hill at 50 mph, how fast must she drive down the hill to average 60 mph for the whole race?

5. An urn contains 5 red marbles and 4 blue marbles. Two marbles are drawn. What is the probability that the first will be red and the second blue (a) with replacement, (b) without replacement?

6. The box held bicycle components. There were 10 different types of bicycle bodies, 4 different types of bicycle seats, and 5 different types of handlebars. How many different-looking bicycles could be assembled from these parts?

Use the matrix echelon method to solve:

7. $\begin{cases} 3x - 2y = -1 \\ 2x + 3y = 8 \end{cases}$

8. $\begin{cases} 2x - 3y = 5 \\ x + 2y = 0 \end{cases}$

9. Construct a triangle whose sides measure 4 centimeters, 3 centimeters, and 6 centimeters.

10. Write the three third roots of 8 cis 90° in rectangular form. Give exact answers.

11. Write all 9 terms of $(p + q)^8$.

12. Show that $\sec^2 x - \sec^2 x \cos^2 x = \tan^2 x$.

13. Show that $\dfrac{\sec^4 x - \tan^4 x}{\sec^2 x + \tan^2 x} = 1$.

14. Show that $\cos(-x)\tan(-x)\csc(-x) = 1$.

15. Show that $\dfrac{\sin^2 x + \cos^2 x}{\sec^2 x - 1} = \cot^2 x$.

16. Two 11-sided polygons are similar. The ratio of the length of a side of the larger polygon to the length of the corresponding side of the smaller polygon is 6 to 5. What is the ratio of the area of the larger polygon to the area of the smaller polygon?

17. Solve this triangle for its unknown parts.

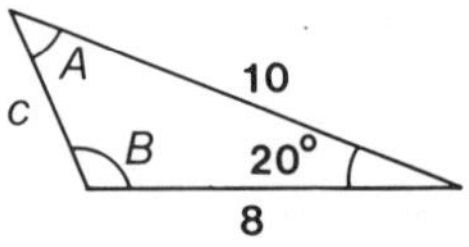

18. Find the area of this trapezoid in centimeters. Dimensions are in meters.

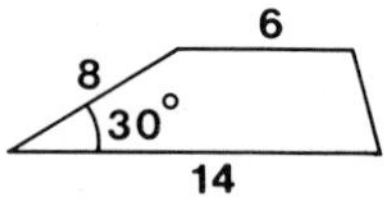

19. Convert 80 miles per hour to kilometers per second.

20. Find the vertices and the equations of the asymptotes of the hyperbola $9x^2 - 16y^2 = 144$.

21. Prove that vertical angles are equal.

22. Find the radius and the coordinates of the center of the circle whose equation is $x^2 + y^2 - 4x = 0$.

23. Sketch $y = 5 + 4 \sin 3(x - 90°)$.

24. Sketch $y = -3 + 4 \sin 2\left(x + \dfrac{\pi}{4}\right)$.

25. Factor $8x^6y^{12} - 27p^9$.

Solve the following equations given that $(0° \le \theta, x < 360°)$:

26. $2 \sin 4\theta - 1 = 0$

27. $(4 \sin^2 x - 1)(\sec x - 2) = 0$

28. Solve: $6^{3x-2} = 5^{2x-1}$

29. Evaluate $(2.02)^5$ by using the logarithm tables.

30. Solve: $\log_{1/2} x = -3$

EP 64.10

LESSON 65 *Advanced trigonometric equations · Clock problems*

65.A Advanced trigonometric equations

We work with trigonometric equations to give us practice with the signs and values of the trigonometric functions in the four quadrants. We can devise trigonometric equations that contain two different trigonometric functions that will also give us practice in using these three identities.

$$\sin^2\theta + \cos^2\theta = 1 \qquad \tan^2\theta + 1 = \sec^2\theta \qquad 1 + \cot^2\theta = \csc^2\theta$$

Example 65.A.1 Solve: $3\tan^2\theta = 7\sec\theta - 5 \qquad 0° \le \theta < 360°$

Solution This equation contains a $\tan^2\theta$ term and a $\sec\theta$ term. If we replace $\tan^2\theta$ with $\sec^2\theta - 1$ from the middle identity above, we will have an equation whose only variable is $\sec\theta$.

$$3(\sec^2\theta - 1) = 7\sec\theta - 5 \qquad \text{substituted}$$
$$3\sec^2\theta - 3 = 7\sec\theta - 5 \qquad \text{multiplied}$$
$$3\sec^2\theta - 7\sec\theta + 2 = 0 \qquad \text{rearranged}$$

This equation has the same form as $3s^2 - 7s + 2 = 0$, which can be factored as $(3s - 1)(s - 2) = 0$. Thus, we can factor the secant variable equation, set each of the factors equal to zero, and solve.

$$(3\sec\theta - 1)(\sec\theta - 2) = 0$$

$$\text{If} \quad 3\sec\theta - 1 = 0 \qquad \text{If} \quad \sec\theta - 2 = 0$$
$$3\sec\theta = 1 \qquad \sec\theta = 2$$
$$\sec\theta = \frac{1}{3}$$

If the secant has a value of $\frac{1}{3}$, the cosine has a value of 3. This is impossible because the cosine is never greater than 1, and thus we discard this solution. If the secant has a value of 2, the cosine equals $\frac{1}{2}$.

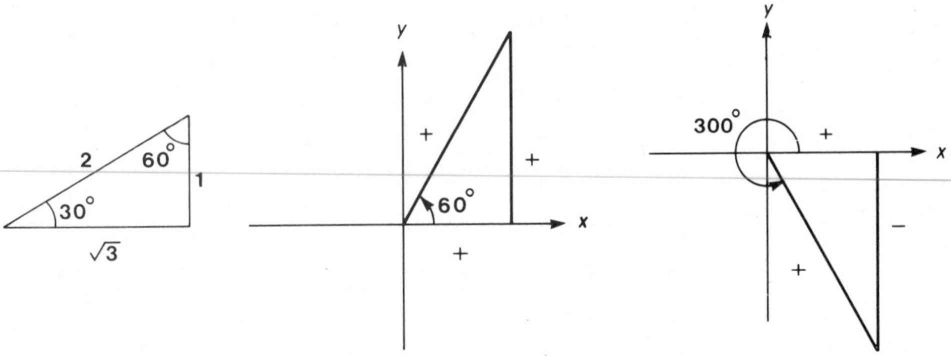

The cosine of 60° is $\frac{1}{2}$, and the cosine is positive in the first and fourth quadrants. Thus, our answers are 60° and 300°.

$$\boldsymbol{\theta = 60°, 300°}$$

Example 65.A.2 Solve: $2\sin^2 x = 3 + 3\cos x$, given that $0° \le x < 360°$.

Solution Since $\sin^2 x + \cos^2 x = 1$, we will replace $\sin^2 x$ in the given equation with $1 - \cos^2 x$.

$$2(1 - \cos^2 x) = 3 + 3\cos x \qquad \text{substituted}$$
$$2 - 2\cos^2 x = 3 + 3\cos x \qquad \text{multiplied}$$
$$2\cos^2 x + 3\cos x + 1 = 0 \qquad \text{rearranged}$$

Now we factor and set each of the factors equal to zero and solve.

$$(2\cos x + 1)(\cos x + 1) = 0$$

If $2\cos x + 1 = 0$ If $\cos x + 1 = 0$

$2\cos x = -1$ $\cos x = -1$

$\cos x = -\frac{1}{2}$

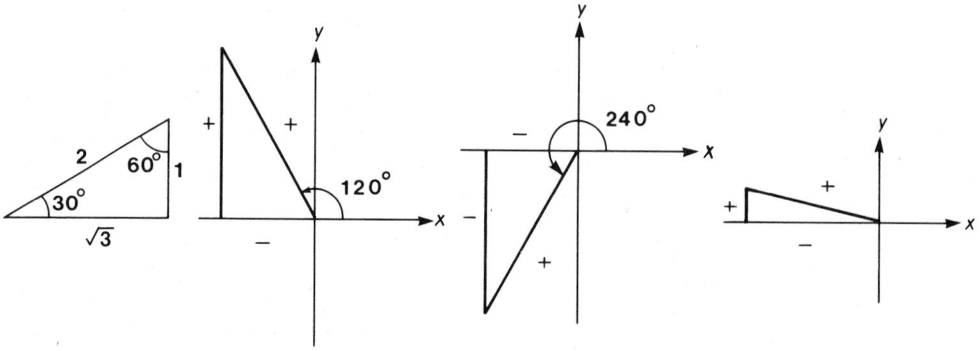

The cosine of 60° is $\frac{1}{2}$, and the cosine is negative in the second and third quadrants. Also, the angle whose cosine is -1 is 180°.

$$\mathbf{x = 120°, 180°, 240°}$$

Example 65.A.3 Solve: $2\tan^2\theta = \sec\theta - 1$, given that $0° \le \theta < 360°$.

Solution We will begin by substituting $\sec^2\theta - 1$ for $\tan^2\theta$.

$$2(\sec^2\theta - 1) = \sec\theta - 1 \qquad \text{substituted}$$
$$2\sec^2\theta - 2 = \sec\theta - 1 \qquad \text{multiplied}$$
$$2\sec^2\theta - \sec\theta - 1 = 0 \qquad \text{rearranged}$$

This equation has the same form as $2x^2 - x - 1 = 0$, which can be factored as $(2x + 1)(x - 1) = 0$. We will factor the secant variable equation and set each of the factors equal to zero and solve.

$$(2\sec\theta + 1)(\sec\theta - 1) = 0$$

If $2\sec\theta + 1 = 0$ If $\sec\theta - 1 = 0$

$2\sec\theta = -1$ $\sec\theta = 1$

$\sec\theta = -\frac{1}{2}$

If the secant equals $-\frac{1}{2}$, then the cosine equals -2. But this is impossible because the values of the cosine lie between -1 and $+1$. Thus, we discard this result. On the right, if the secant equals 1, the cosine also equals 1. The cosine of 0° is 1, so our answer is

$$\theta = 0°$$

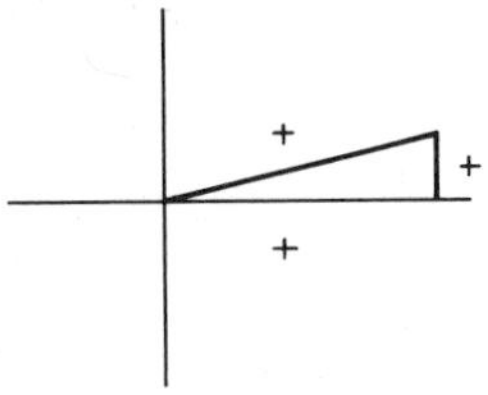

65.B Clock problems

In some rate problems, it is convenient to measure distances in spaces and rate in spaces per unit time. In these problems, rate times time equals spaces. For instance, if one thing moved at 20 spaces per second, it would go 100 spaces in 5 seconds.

$$\text{Rate} \times \text{time} = \text{spaces}$$

$$20\,\frac{\text{spaces}}{\text{sec}} \times 5\ \text{sec} = 100 \text{ spaces}$$

Problems about the hands of a clock fall into this category. The spaces are the 60 one-minute spaces around the face. The rate of the minute hand is 1 space per minute, and the rate of the hour hand is 5 spaces per 60 minutes or $\frac{1}{12}$ space per minute.

Example 65.B.1 The hands of a clock point in the same direction. In how many minutes will they point in opposite directions?

Solution The little hand will move through S spaces and the big hand will move through $S + 30$ spaces so that it will be 30 spaces ahead. The equations are

$$R_L T_L = S \qquad R_B T_B = S + 30 \qquad R_B = 1 \qquad R_L = \frac{1}{12} \qquad T_L = T_B$$

We note that the presence of five unknowns required that we write five equations to get a unique solution. We begin by substituting in the first two equations and get

$$\frac{T_L}{12} = S \qquad T_B = S + 30$$

The right-hand equation tells us that $S = T_B - 30$. We equate the two values of S and eliminate the subscripts on T because the times are equal. Then we solve.

$$\frac{T_L}{12} = T_B - 30 \qquad \text{both equal } S$$

$$\frac{T}{12} = T - 30 \qquad T_L = T_B = T$$

$$T = 12T - 360 \qquad \text{multiplied}$$

$$11T = 360 \qquad \text{simplified}$$

$$\mathbf{T = 32\frac{8}{11}\ min} \qquad \text{solved}$$

Example 65.B.2 It is 3 o'clock. In how many minutes will the two hands of the clock point in the same direction?

Solution The hands are 15 spaces apart, so the little hand will travel S spaces and the big hand will have to travel $S + 15$ spaces to catch up. The equations are

$$R_L T_L = S \qquad R_B T_B = S + 15 \qquad R_L = \frac{1}{12} \qquad R_B = 1 \qquad T_L = T_B$$

Since the times are equal, we can delete the subscripts on T. We begin by substituting into the first two equations and get

$$\frac{T}{12} = S \qquad T = S + 15$$

We solve the right-hand equation for S, substitute, and solve for T.

$$\frac{T}{12} = T - 15 \qquad \text{substituted}$$

$$T = 12T - 180 \qquad \text{multiplied}$$

$$11T = 180 \qquad \text{simplified}$$

$$\mathbf{T = 16\frac{4}{11}\ \textbf{min}} \qquad \text{solved}$$

Problem set 65

1. It is high noon and the crowd is waiting for the time the big hand and the little hand will be pointing in opposite directions. How long will they have to wait?

2. It is 9 o'clock. How long will it be before both hands are pointing in the same direction?

3. Find three consecutive even integers such that the product of the first and the second equals the product of the third and the number 3.

4. The first time Henry made the trip he drove at 10 miles per hour and got there 5 hours late. The next time he drove at 25 miles per hour and got there 1 hour early. How long was the trip? (*Hint:* The distances are equal. The time for the first trip was the correct time plus 5 and the time for the second trip is the correct time minus 1.)

5. An urn contains 4 red marbles and 3 white marbles. Two marbles are drawn and replaced. Both the marbles were red. What is the probability the next marble will be red?

6. Four boys and 2 girls sit in 6 chairs placed in a circle. How many seating arrangements are possible?

7. Use the matrix echelon method to solve: $\begin{cases} 2x - 3y = -5 \\ x + 2y = 8 \end{cases}$

8. Construct a line that is parallel to a given line which passes through a designated point not on the line.

9. Write all 10 terms of $(x + y)^9$.

10. Write the four fourth roots of 16 cis 120° in rectangular form. Give exact answers.

Solve the following equations given that $(0° \le \theta < 360°)$:

11. $3 \tan^2 \theta = 7 \sec \theta - 5$

12. $2 \sin^2 \theta = 3 + 3 \cos \theta$

13. $2 \tan^2 \theta = \sec \theta - 1$

14. Show that $\dfrac{\cos^4 x - \sin^4 x}{\cos^2 x - \sin^2 x} = 1$.

15. Show that $\tan x + \cot x = \sec x \csc x$.

16. Show that $\dfrac{1}{1 + \cos x} + \dfrac{1}{1 - \cos x} = 2 \csc^2 x$.

17. The perimeter of a regular 8-sided polygon (regular octagon) is 32 cm. What is the area of the polygon?

18. Solve this triangle for its unknown parts.

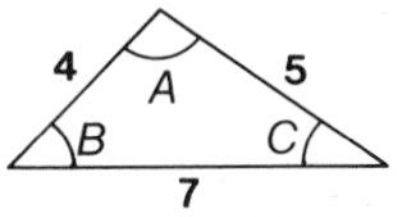

19. Find the area of this triangle.

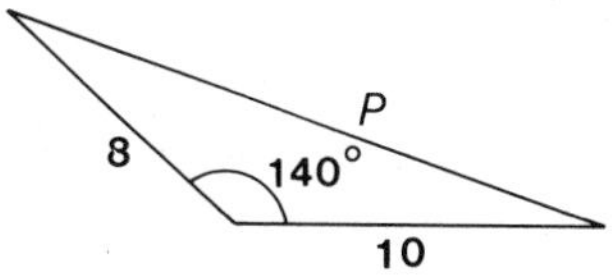

20. Find the sum of the interior angles of a 12-sided convex polygon.

21. Find the area in square centimeters of the segment bounded by an arc of measure 50° and the chord joining the endpoints of the arc in a circle whose radius is 10 centimeters.

22. Prove that the sum of the angles of a triangle equals 180°.

23. Describe the ellipse $9x^2 + 4y^2 = 36$.

24. Find the vertices and the equations of the asymptotes of the hyperbola $4y^2 - 9x^2 = 36$.

25. Sketch $y = -2 + 5 \sin 3\left(x + \dfrac{\pi}{2}\right)$.

26. Sketch $y = 3 + 5 \cos \dfrac{1}{2}(x - 270°)$.

27. If $-4 < a < 2$ and $3 < b < 6$, compare: *A.* $\dfrac{1}{a}$ *B.* $\dfrac{1}{-b}$

28. Solve: $10^{3x-2} = 7^{2x+3}$

29. Solve: $\dfrac{2}{3} \log_3 8 - \log_3 (3x - 2) + \log_3 (x - 2) = \log_3 4$

30. Evaluate $(1.04)^6$ by using the logarithm tables.

EP 65.11

> If the enrichment lessons are being included, the second enrichment lesson should be taught next and should be followed with Lesson 66.

LESSON 66 Proofs of similarity

66.A Proofs of similarity

If the angles of one triangle equal the corresponding angles of another triangle, the triangles are similar, and the lengths of corresponding sides are proportional. In this lesson we will look at the different ways that we can be told that the angles are equal. The first figure we will look at is a figure formed by two intersecting lines.

Example 66.A.1 Given $\angle YXM = \angle ABM$, prove that $\frac{XY}{BA} = \frac{MX}{BM}$.

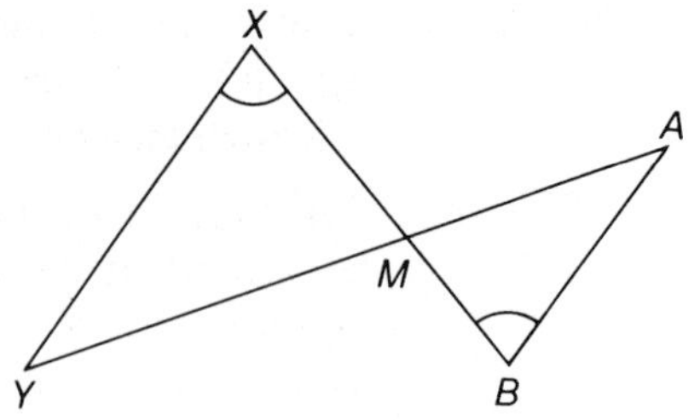

Solution **Usually, when we are asked to prove a proportion, similar polygons are implied because in similar polygons, the lengths of the corresponding sides are proportional.** The first step is to redraw the figure and to use tick marks to indicate what we know.

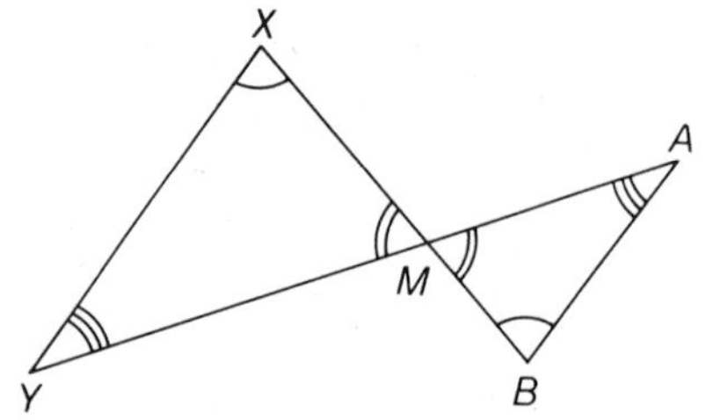

The angles at M are equal because they are vertical angles. We were told that angles X and B were equal. If two angles in each triangle are equal, the third angles are equal. Thus the triangles are similar because all 3 angles are equal. To make the statement of similarity in each triangle, we begin at angle M and then go to the angle with the single tick mark.

$$\triangle MXY \sim \triangle MBA$$

We use this statement of triangle similarity to help us write the desired proportion.

$$\frac{XY}{BA} = \frac{MX}{MB}$$

Example 66.A.2 Given $\overline{XY} \parallel \overline{BA}$, prove that $\frac{XY}{BA} = \frac{XM}{BM}$.

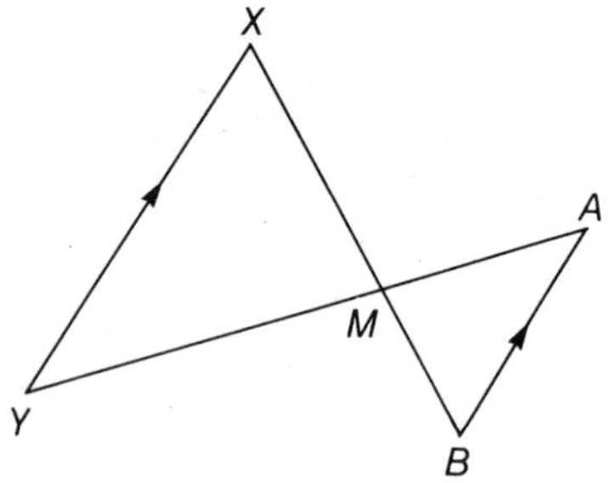

Solution This time the problem is exactly the same except that we were told that the lines were parallel. **Whenever we are given parallel lines, we look for transversals and corresponding angles or alternate interior angles.** Thus, we redraw the figure, extend the lines, and use tick marks to indicate equal angles.

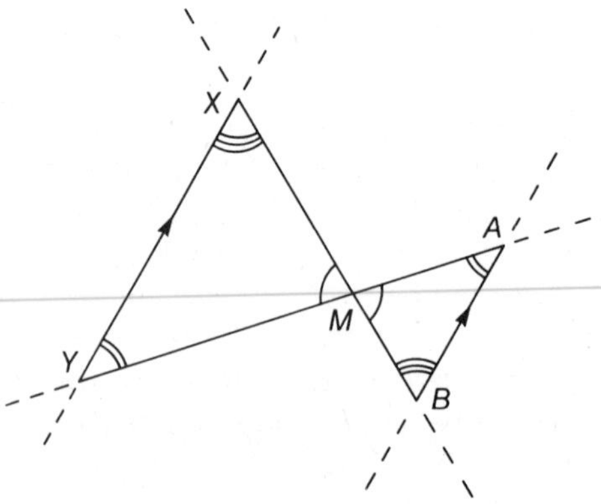

This time we can see at a glance that we have vertical angles equal and two pairs of equal alternate interior angles. Thus, again we can write

$$\triangle MXY \sim \triangle MBA \qquad \text{and so} \qquad \frac{XY}{BA} = \frac{MX}{MB}$$

Example 66.A.3 Prove that the small triangle on the left ($\triangle CBA$) is similar to the large triangle ($\triangle ABD$) and write three proportions.

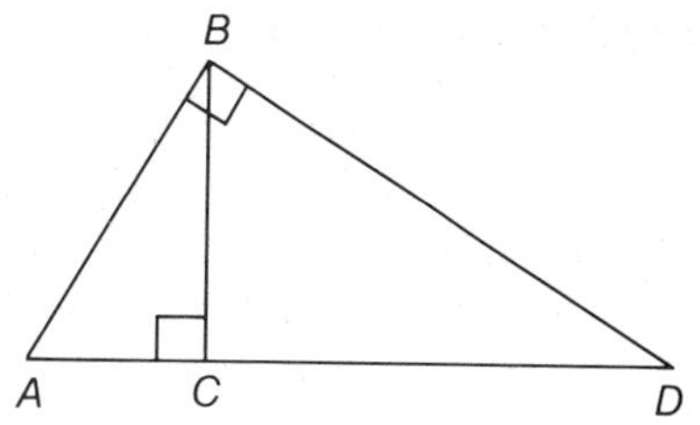

Solution The triangle ACB contains angle A and also contains a right angle. The large triangle ABD contains angle A and also contains a right angle. When two angles in a triangle are equal, the third angles are equal. Thus the triangles are similar. We write the statement of similarity by listing the vertex at A and then the right-angle vertex.

$$\triangle ACB \sim \triangle ABD$$

Now we can write the proportions

$$\frac{AC}{AB} = \frac{CB}{BD} \qquad \frac{AC}{AB} = \frac{AB}{AD} \qquad \frac{CB}{BD} = \frac{AB}{AD}$$

Example 66.A.4 Prove that the small triangle on the right ($\triangle BCD$) is similar to the large triangle ($\triangle ABD$) and write three proportions.

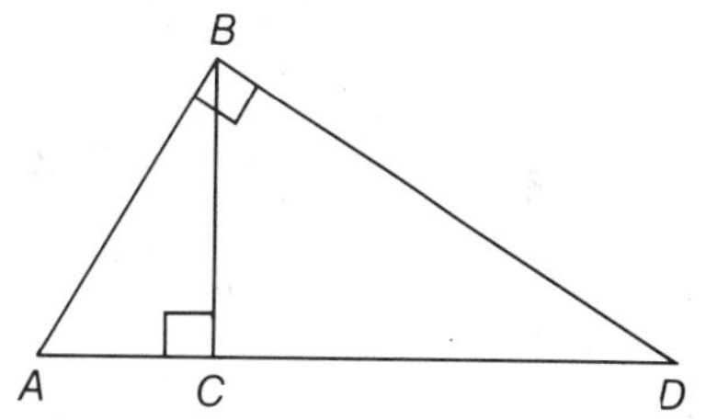

Solution The small triangle on the right is similar to the large triangle because both contain angle D and both have a right angle. Thus, the third angles must be equal and the triangles are similar. We write the statement of similarity beginning at vertex D and then listing the vertex at the right angle.

$$\triangle DBA \sim \triangle DCB$$

Now we can write the three proportions.

$$\frac{DC}{DB} = \frac{CB}{BA} \qquad \frac{DC}{DB} = \frac{DB}{DA} \qquad \frac{CB}{BA} = \frac{DB}{DA}$$

Example 66.A.5 Prove that the two small triangles are similar.

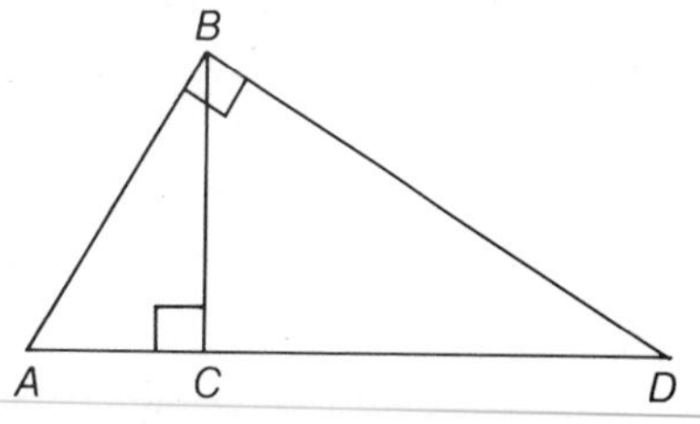

Solution We have proved that the angles in the big triangle equal the angles in the small triangle on the left. Also, we have proved that the angles in the big triangle equal the angles in the small triangle on the right. Since things that equal the same thing are equal to each other, the two small triangles have the same angles and are similar. We write the statement of similarity as

$$\triangle ACB \sim \triangle BCD$$

Whenever the perpendicular from the hypotenuse intersects the right angle, three similar triangles are formed. The proof of this statement is contained in the solution of the preceding three examples.

Example 66.A.6 Find x, y, and z.

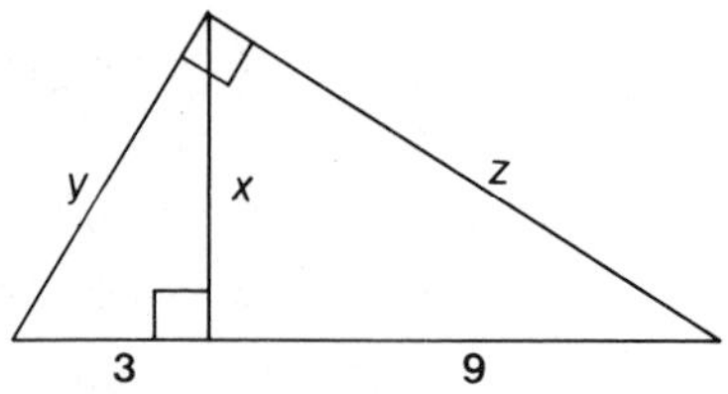

Solution We have just proved that the three triangles in this figure are similar. Deciding which proportions to use is difficult because the figure is confusing. One approach is to write ratios of short sides, ratios of long sides, and ratios of hypotenuses and then see which pairs form productive proportions. We will write a proportion whose first ratio is the ratio of the hypotenuse of the big triangle to the hypotenuse of the left triangle. The other ratio of the proportion compares the short sides in the same order.

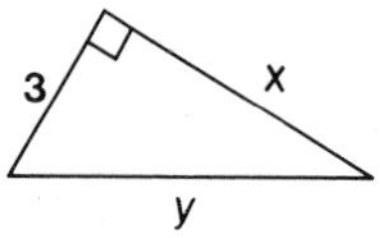

Left triangle

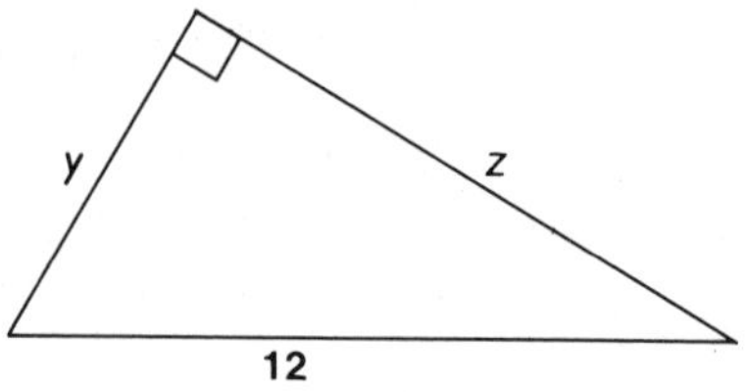

Big triangle

$$\frac{12}{y} = \frac{y}{3} \longrightarrow 36 = y^2 \longrightarrow \mathbf{y = 6}$$

Now, in the left triangle we substitute 6 for y and use the Pythagorean theorem to find x.

$$6^2 = x^2 + 3^2 \longrightarrow x^2 = 27 \longrightarrow \mathbf{x = 3\sqrt{3}}$$

Next, we use the big triangle with 6 substituted for y and solve for z.

$y^2 + z^2 = 12^2$	theorem
$6^2 + z^2 = 12^2$	substituted
$z^2 = 108$	simplified
$\mathbf{z = 6\sqrt{3}}$	solved

Problem set 66

1. It is high noon again and the hands of the clock point in the same direction one more time. How long will the crowd have to wait to see the hands pointing in the same direction again?

2. Armbrister and Trevor found that it was possible to cover m miles in k hours. If they tripled their rate, how long would it take to go $A + 10$ miles?

3. Find three consecutive odd integers such that the product of the first two is 8 greater than the third.

4. The little red plane made the trip at 400 miles per hour and got there 2 hours ahead of time. The next time the pilot reduced his speed 200 miles per hour, and this time the plane was 2 hours late. How long was the trip?

5. A deck of cards has 52 cards. There are 13 spades, 13 clubs, 13 hearts, and 13 diamonds. A card is drawn and replaced. Then another card is drawn. What is the probability that both cards will be clubs?

6. A pair of dice is rolled twice. What is the probability that the first number will be 8 and that the second number will be 7?

7. Use the matrix echelon method to solve: $\begin{cases} 2x - 3y = 5 \\ 3x + 4y = -1 \end{cases}$

8. Draw a line segment 8 centimeters long and construct its perpendicular bisector.

9. What is the sixth term of $(p + q)^8$?

10. Write the three cube roots of 27 cis 180° in rectangular form. Give exact solutions.

Solve the following equations given that ($0° \le \theta < 360°$):

11. $3 \cot^2 \theta = 7 \csc \theta - 5$

12. $2 \cos^2 \theta = 3 + 3 \sin \theta$

13. $2 \tan^2 \theta = \sec \theta - 1$

14. Show that $\dfrac{1}{\sec^2 \theta} + \dfrac{1}{\csc^2 \theta} = 1$.

15. Show that $\sec \theta - \tan \theta \sin \theta = \cos \theta$.

16. Show that $\dfrac{\sec^2 \theta}{\sec^2 \theta - 1} = \csc^2 \theta$.

17. The perimeter of a regular octagon is 40 centimeters. What is the radius of the circle which can be circumscribed about the octagon?

18. Solve this triangle for its unknown parts.

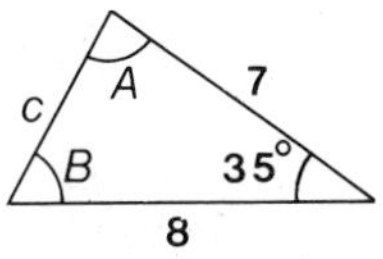

19. Prove that if two angles of one triangle are equal to two angles of another triangle, then the triangles are similar.

20. Given $\overline{XY} \parallel \overline{AB}$, prove that $\dfrac{XY}{BA} = \dfrac{XM}{BM}$.

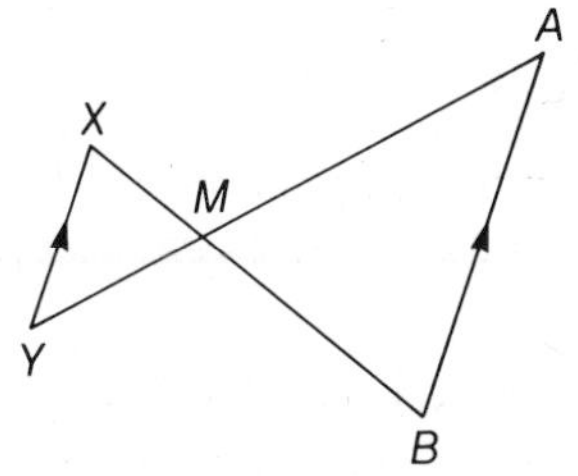

21. Prove that $\triangle CBA$ is similar to $\triangle BDA$ and write the proportions.

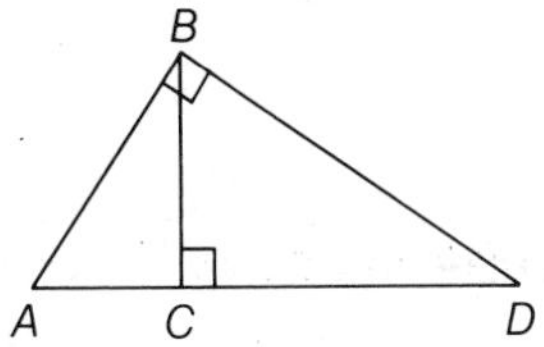

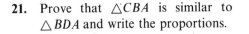

22. Find x, y, and z.

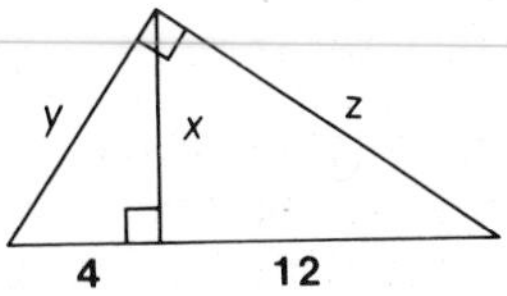

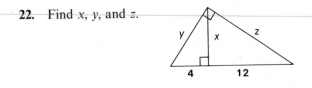

23. Describe the ellipse $16x^2 + 25y^2 = 400$.

24. Find the vertices and the equations of the asymptotes of the hyperbola $16x^2 - 25y^2 = 400$.

Sketch:

25. $y = -1 + 10 \sin \frac{1}{3}(x - 180°)$

26. $y = 2 + \cos \frac{1}{4}\left(x - \frac{9\pi}{4}\right)$

Solve:

27. $12^{2x-3} = 2^{3x+2}$

28. $\frac{3}{4} \log_2 16 + 2 \log_2 x = 2 \log_2 4$

29. Show why $\log_b MN = \log_b M + \log_b N$.

30. Evaluate $(1.02)^3$ by using the logarithm tables.

EP 66.12

LESSON 67 Arithmetic progressions and arithmetic means

67.A Arithmetic progressions and arithmetic means

The English word **sequence** comes from the Latin word *sequi*, which means "to follow." **If a group of numbers is arranged in a definite order so that one number follows another number, we say the numbers have been arranged *sequentially* and that the numbers form a *sequence*.** On the left, we show six numbers in a random pattern. We say that these numbers are arranged nonsequentially. On the right, we show two of the many ways these six numbers can be arranged sequentially.

1
5
8
3
6
2

(*a*) 8, 3, 2, 1, 6, 5
(*b*) 6, 5, 8, 1, 2, 3

If a sequence has a finite number of members, we say that the sequence is a ***finite sequence.*** Sequences (*a*) and (*b*) have six members and are finite sequences. If we indicate that a **patterned sequence** has no end by writing three dots after the last entry,

(*c*) 1, 2, 3, 4, 5, . . .

we have designated an ***infinite sequence.***

Subscripted variables are often used to designate the members of a sequence. The letters most often used for the variables are x, y, a, s, and t. When t is used, the authors often indicate that the letter is an abbreviation for the word *term*. We could use t to indicate the terms of an 8-term sequence by writing

$$t_1, t_2, t_3, t_4, t_5, t_6, t_7, t_8$$

or use the letter a and write

$$a_1, a_2, a_3, a_4, a_5, a_6, a_7, a_8$$

The English word **progression** comes from the Latin word *progredi*, which means "to go forward." In mathematics, we use this word to describe a sequence in which each term depends in some way on the term that precedes it. An ***arithmetic progression*** (arithmetic sequence) is formed by choosing a first term and then adding the same constant to form each succeeding term. Thus, each term in an arithmetic progression is greater (or less) than the one that precedes it by a given amount. We call the difference between terms the ***common difference*****, and any sequence that has a common difference between the terms is an *****arithmetic sequence*****.** Each term in (*a*) is 3 greater than the preceding term. Thus, the **common difference** is +3.

$$(a)\quad 7, \underline{10}, \underline{13}, \underline{16}, \underline{19}, 22$$
$$(b)\quad 7, \underline{3}, \underline{-1}, \underline{-5}, \underline{-9}, \underline{-13}, -17$$

Each term in (*b*) is 4 less than the preceding term, so the common difference is −4. The terms between the end terms in a finite arithmetic sequence are called the ***arithmetic means.*** In (*a*) and (*b*) above the means are underlined. Sequence (*a*) has 6 terms and 4 means, and sequence (*b*) has 7 terms and thus has 5 means. If we look at (*a*) and (*b*), we note that the second term uses the difference once. The third term uses the difference twice, the fourth term uses the difference three times; etc.

$$\begin{array}{llllll} & ① & ② & ③ & ④ & ⑤ \\ (a) & 7, & 7+(3), & 7+(3+3), & 7+(3+3+3), & 7+(3+3+3+3) \\ (b) & 7, & 7+(-4), & 7+(-4-4), & 7+(-4-4-4), & 7+(-4-4-4-4) \end{array}$$

So each term equals the first term plus the difference one fewer times than the number of the term. If we use a_1 for the first term and n for the number of the nth term, we have, in general,

$$\begin{array}{lllllll} ① & ② & ③ & ④ & ⑤ & & (n) \\ a_1, & a_1+d, & a_1+2d, & a_1+3d, & a_1+4d, & \ldots, & a_1+(n-1)d \end{array}$$

Example 67.A.1 Write the first four terms of an arithmetic sequence whose first term is −14 and whose common difference is 10.

Solution We begin with −14 and add 10 to get each succeeding term.

$$\begin{array}{llll} ① & ② & ③ & ④ \\ -14, & -14+(10), & -14+(10+10), & -14+(10+10+10) \end{array}$$

So our sequence is

$$\mathbf{-14, -4, 6, 16, \ldots}$$

Example 67.A.2 Find the twenty-fifth term of an arithmetic sequence whose first term is 12 and whose common difference is −6.

Solution The *first* term is 12. The *second* term is $12+\underline{1}\cdot(-6)$. The *third* term is $12+\underline{2}(-6)$, etc., until the twenty-fifth term will be

$$12+\underline{24}(-6) = \mathbf{-132}$$

Example 67.A.3 Insert three arithmetic means between 2 and −4.

Solution We always draw diagrams of problems when possible because diagrams aid understanding and help prevent mistakes. A useful diagram for this type of problem is to write the sequence twice, once using the given numbers and again using variables. There are 3 means, so each sequence has 5 terms. Often we find that we know enough to equate two pairs of corresponding terms in the two sequences. Then we can solve the resulting equations to find out what we want to know.

$$\begin{array}{lllll} ① & ② & ③ & ④ & ⑤ \\ 2, & \_\_\_, & \_\_\_, & \_\_\_, & -4 \\ a_1, & a_1+d, & a_1+2d, & a_1+3d, & a_1+4d \end{array}$$

From these sequences we see that the first terms imply equation (*a*) and the fifth terms imply equation (*b*).

$$(a) \quad a_1 = 2 \qquad (b) \quad a_1 + 4d = -4$$

We use substitution to solve these equations for *d*.

$$\begin{aligned} 2 + 4d &= -4 && \text{substituted} \\ 4d &= -6 && \text{added } -2 \\ d &= -1.5 && \text{divided by 4} \end{aligned}$$

Now we can find the three means by adding -1.5 progressively to form the terms. Our sequence, with the means underlined, is

$$\mathbf{2, \underline{0.5}, \underline{-1}, \underline{-2.5}, -4}$$

Example 67.A.4 Write the first five terms of an arithmetic sequence in which $a_{17} = -40$ and $a_{28} = -73$.

Solution We begin with a diagram that shows the sequence twice

(1)		(17)		(28)
?	...	-40	...	-73
a_1	...	$a_1 + 16d$	...	$a_1 + 27d$

In this problem we see that our equations will come from the seventeenth and the twenty-eighth terms.

$$\begin{aligned} &(17) \quad a_1 + 16d = -40 \longrightarrow (-1) \longrightarrow && -a_1 - 16d = +40 \\ &(28) \quad a_1 + 27d = -73 \longrightarrow (1) \longrightarrow && a_1 + 27d = -73 \\ & && \overline{11d = -33} \\ & && d = -3 \end{aligned}$$

Now we use -3 for *d* in the top equation to find a_1.

$$\begin{aligned} a_1 + 16(-3) &= -40 && \text{substituted} \\ a_1 - 48 &= -40 && \text{multiplied} \\ a_1 &= 8 && \text{added} \end{aligned}$$

Now we can write the first five terms:

$$\mathbf{8, 5, 2, -1, -4}$$

Example 67.A.5 Find the tenth term of an arithmetic sequence in which the first term is $3x + 2y$ and the sixth term is $8x + 12y$.

Solution We begin with a diagram that shows the sequence twice,

(1)	(2)	(3)	(4)	(5)	(6)		(10)
$3x + 2y$	____	____	____	____	$8x + 12y$	...	____
a_1	$a_1 + d$	$a_1 + 2d$	$a_1 + 3d$	$a_1 + 4d$	$a_1 + 5d$	...	$a_1 + 9d$

In this problem our two equations come from the first and the sixth terms.

$$\begin{aligned} &(1) \quad a_1 = 3x + 2y && \text{equated the first terms} \\ &(6) \quad a_1 + 5d = 8x + 12y && \text{equated the sixth terms} \end{aligned}$$

$$\begin{aligned} (3x + 2y) + 5d &= 8x + 12y && \text{substituted} \\ 5d &= 5x + 10y && \text{added} \\ d &= x + 2y && \text{simplified} \end{aligned}$$

Since the tenth term equals $a_1 + 9d$, we get

$$a_{10} = (3x + 2y) + 9(x + 2y) = \mathbf{12x + 20y}$$

Problem set 67

1. Now it is 6 o'clock. In how many minutes will the little hand and the big hand be at right angles to each other?

2. The output varied linearly with the quality of the input. When the input quality was 10, the output was 45. When the input quality fell to 8, the output only fell to 37. Write a linear equation which describes output as a function of input.

3. Find three consecutive even integers such that the product of the first and the third is 18 greater than the product of -1 and the third.

4. Anne averaged 30 kilometers per hour, but got to the flower market 2 hours late. The next day she increased her average speed to 64 kilometers per hour and got to the flower market on time. How far was it to the flower market?

5. One card is drawn from a deck of 52 cards and not replaced. Then a second card is drawn. What is the probability that the first card will be a spade and the second card will not be a spade?

6. A pair of dice is rolled. What is the probability that the number on the dice is greater than 9?

7. Use the matrix echelon method to solve: $\begin{cases} 2x - 3y = 1 \\ 3x + 4y = 10 \end{cases}$

8. Draw a 45° angle, copy the angle, and then construct the bisector of the copied angle.

9. Write the first five terms of an arithmetic sequence whose first term is -10 and whose common difference is 6.

10. Find the thirtieth term of an arithmetic sequence whose first term is 5 and whose common difference is -4.

11. Insert three arithmetic means between 3 and -13.

12. Write the first five terms of an arithmetic sequence whose tenth term is -30 and whose twentieth term is 40.

13. Find the eighth term of an arithmetic sequence in which the first term is $2x + 3y$ and the sixth term is $7x + 8y$.

14. Write the three cube roots of 8 cis 270° in rectangular form. Give exact solutions.

Solve the following equations given that $(0° \le x, \theta < 360°)$:

15. $2 \sin^2 x + 3 \sin x + 1 = 0$

16. $2 \tan^2 \theta = 3 \sec \theta - 3$

17. $-1 - \sqrt{3} \tan 3\theta = 0$

Show that:

18. $\dfrac{\sec^2 x}{\sec^2 x - 1} = \csc^2 x$

19. $\dfrac{\cos^2 \theta}{\sin \theta} + \sin \theta = \csc \theta$

20. $\dfrac{\cos(-x)}{\sin(-x)\cot(-x)} = 1$

21. Solve this triangle for its unknown parts.

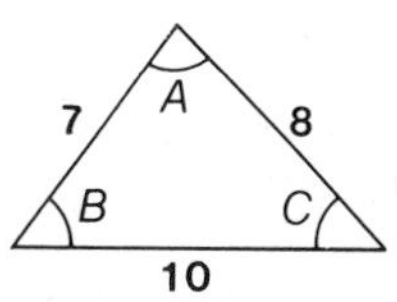

22. Find the distance from the point (0, 0) to the line $x + y = 4$.

23. Given $\angle BAC = \angle CED$, prove that $\dfrac{BC}{CD} = \dfrac{AB}{DE}$.

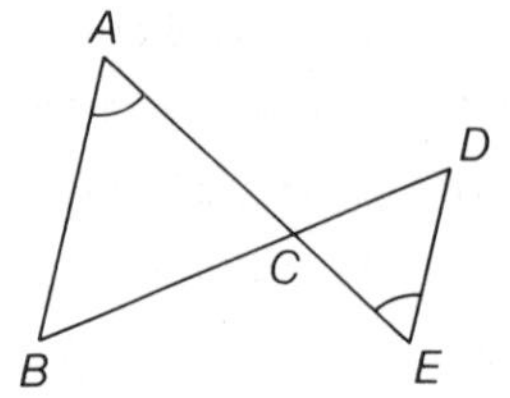

24. Prove that $\triangle BCD$ is similar to $\triangle ACB$ and write three statements of proportionality using the sides of these triangles.

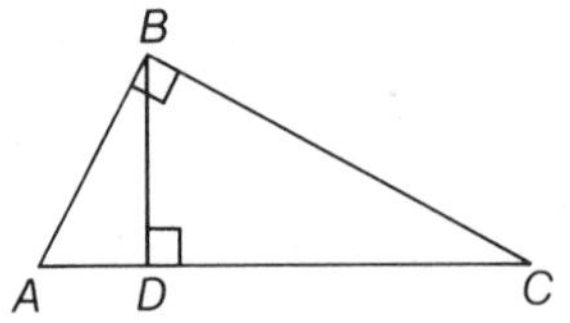

Sketch:

25. $y = 4 + 7 \sin 2\left(x + \dfrac{2}{3}\pi\right)$

26. $y = 1 + 5 \cos \dfrac{1}{3}(x - 405°)$

Solve:

27. $10^{3x-2} = 5^{2x-1}$

28. $\dfrac{2}{3} \log_5 8 - \log_5 (x - 4) = 1$

29. Evaluate $(1.04)^4$ by using the logarithm tables.

30. Find the vertices and the equations of the asymptotes of the hyperbola $16x^2 - 9y^2 = 144$.

EP 67.13

LESSON 68 Sum and difference identities · Tangent identities

68.A Memorizing identities

Unfortunately, the functions of sums and products of angles cannot be determined by adding or multiplying the functions of the individual angles. For example, the values of the sines of 30° and 60° are

$$\sin 30° = \frac{1}{2} \qquad \sin 60° = \frac{\sqrt{3}}{2}$$

But as we show here, the sine of (2 × 30°) is not twice the sine of 30°, and the sine of (30° + 60°) is not the sine of 30° plus the sine of 60°.

$$\sin (2 \times 30°) \neq 2 \times \frac{1}{2} \qquad \text{because} \qquad \sin 60° = \frac{\sqrt{3}}{2}$$

$$\sin (30° + 60°) \neq \frac{1}{2} + \frac{\sqrt{3}}{2} \qquad \text{because} \qquad \sin 90° = 1$$

To find the functions of combinations of angles such as these, it is necessary to use trigonometric identities. There are other uses for trigonometric identities, and there are about 25 trigonometric identities that should be memorized because their use is required in calculus and in other upper-division mathematics courses. The ability to recall and use these identities permits a straightforward solution to problems whose solution is otherwise troublesome. Most people have difficulty remembering the identities because there are so many and because many identities look alike. Fortunately, if a few of the identities are memorized, the rest can be developed quickly and accurately when needed. The six key identities that should be memorized are

$$(a) \quad \sin(A+B) = \sin A \cos B + \cos A \sin B$$
$$(b) \quad \sin(A-B) = \sin A \cos B - \cos A \sin B$$
$$(c) \quad \cos(A+B) = \cos A \cos B - \sin A \sin B$$
$$(d) \quad \cos(A-B) = \cos A \cos B + \sin A \sin B$$
$$(e) \quad \tan\theta = \frac{\sin\theta}{\cos\theta}$$
$$(f) \quad \sin^2\theta + \cos^2\theta = 1$$

The derivations of (*a*), (*b*), (*c*), and (*d*) are difficult to follow unless one is familiar with the identities. So for now, we will concentrate on memorizing these identities and will hold the derivations until later. The identities (*e*) and (*f*) are used often and are easy to remember. To memorize the other four, it is helpful to look for patterns. The first pattern is that in each identity the letters *A* and *B* alternate *A*, *B*, *A*, *B*, *A*, *B* all the way across. The second thing to note is if the left side begins with sin, the right side also begins with sin. In addition, we note that (*b*) is exactly the same as (*a*) except the signs in the middle are different, and that (*d*) is exactly the same as (*c*) except the signs in the middle are different. So if we can memorize the following

$$\sin(A+B) = \sin A \cos B + \cos A \sin B$$
$$(\quad - \quad) = \qquad\qquad - \qquad\qquad$$
$$\cos(A+B) = \cos A \cos B - \sin A \sin B$$
$$(\quad - \quad) = \qquad\qquad + \qquad\qquad$$

and remember that on the left the signs from top to bottom are +, −, +, − and that on the right the middle signs from top to bottom are +, −, −, +, the four key identities can be reproduced. We suggest practicing writing down these identities several times a day and that they be written down as the first step in taking any test that requires the use of trigonometric identities.

Example 68.A.1 Simplify: $\sin\left(\theta + \frac{\pi}{4}\right)$

Solution This is the sine of a sum and requires the use of the identity for $\sin(A+B)$.

$$\sin(A+B) = \sin A \cos B + \cos A \sin B$$

Now we replace A with θ and replace B with $\frac{\pi}{4}$

$$\sin\left(\theta + \frac{\pi}{4}\right) = \sin\theta \cos\frac{\pi}{4} + \cos\theta \sin\frac{\pi}{4}$$

The sine and the cosine of $\pi/4$ equal $1/\sqrt{2}$, so we get

$$\sin\left(\theta + \frac{\pi}{4}\right) = \sin\theta \cdot \frac{1}{\sqrt{2}} + \cos\theta \cdot \frac{1}{\sqrt{2}} = \frac{\sqrt{2}}{2}\sin\theta + \frac{\sqrt{2}}{2}\cos\theta = \mathbf{\frac{\sqrt{2}}{2}(\sin\theta + \cos\theta)}$$

Example 68.A.2 Find cos 15° by using a trigonometric identity and the fact that $60° - 45° = 15°$.

Solution We will use the identity for $\cos(A - B)$.

$$\cos(A - B) = \cos A \cos B + \sin A \sin B$$

Now we replace A with 60° and B with 45°.

$$\cos(60° - 45°) = \cos 60° \cos 45° + \sin 60° \sin 45°$$

$$\cos 15° = \frac{1}{2}\frac{1}{\sqrt{2}} + \frac{\sqrt{3}}{2}\frac{1}{\sqrt{2}} \longrightarrow \frac{1}{2\sqrt{2}} + \frac{\sqrt{3}}{2\sqrt{2}} \longrightarrow \frac{\sqrt{2}}{4} + \frac{\sqrt{6}}{4} \longrightarrow \mathbf{\frac{\sqrt{2}+\sqrt{6}}{4}}$$

Example 68.A.3 Simplify $\cos\left(\theta + \frac{\pi}{2}\right)$.

Solution For this we will use the identity for $\cos(A + B)$.

$$\cos(A + B) = \cos A \cos B - \sin A \sin B$$

We replace A with θ and replace B with $\pi/2$ and get

$$\cos\left(\theta + \frac{\pi}{2}\right) = \cos\theta \cos\frac{\pi}{2} - \sin\theta \sin\frac{\pi}{2}$$

Now $\cos \pi/2$ is 0 and $\sin \pi/2$ is 1, so we get

$$\cos\left(\theta + \frac{\pi}{2}\right) = (\cos\theta)(0) - (\sin\theta)(1) = \mathbf{-\sin\theta}$$

68.B Tangent identities

The tangent of an angle equals the sine of the angle divided by the cosine of the angle.

$$\tan\theta = \frac{\sin\theta}{\cos\theta}$$

The argument does not have to be a single variable. If the argument is $4x - 3\pi$, we can write

$$\tan(4x - 3\pi) = \frac{\sin(4x - 3\pi)}{\cos(4x - 3\pi)}$$

Some people find it helpful to use empty parentheses and to write

$$\tan(\quad) = \frac{\sin(\quad)}{\cos(\quad)}$$

and to remember that the same entry must be made in all three parentheses.

Example 68.B.1 Develop an identity for $\tan(A + B)$.

Solution We know that $\tan(A + B)$ equals $\sin(A + B)$ divided by $\cos(A + B)$.

$$\tan(A + B) = \frac{\sin(A + B)}{\cos(A + B)} = \frac{\sin A \cos B + \cos A \sin B}{\cos A \cos B - \sin A \sin B}$$

There are many forms of tangent identities. We will concentrate on forms in which the first entry in the denominator is the number 1. To change $\cos A \cos B$ to 1, we must divide it by itself. We do this but also divide every other term in the whole expression by cos A cos B so that the value of the expression will be unchanged.

$$\tan(A+B) = \frac{\dfrac{\sin A \cancel{\cos B}}{\cos A \cancel{\cos B}} + \dfrac{\cancel{\cos A}\sin B}{\cancel{\cos A}\cos B}}{\dfrac{\cancel{\cos A}\cancel{\cos B}}{\cancel{\cos A}\cancel{\cos B}} - \dfrac{\sin A \sin B}{\cos A \cos B}}$$

We cancel as shown and end up with

$$\mathbf{\tan(A+B) = \frac{\tan A + \tan B}{1 - \tan A \tan B}}$$

Example 68.B.2 Develop the identity for tan $(A - B)$.

Solution The procedure is the same except we use the identities for $(A - B)$ instead of for $(A + B)$.

$$\tan(A-B) = \frac{\dfrac{\sin A \cancel{\cos B}}{\cos A \cancel{\cos B}} - \dfrac{\cancel{\cos A}\sin B}{\cancel{\cos A}\cos B}}{\dfrac{\cancel{\cos A}\cancel{\cos B}}{\cancel{\cos A}\cancel{\cos B}} + \dfrac{\sin A \sin B}{\cos A \cos B}}$$

We cancel as shown and end up with

$$\mathbf{\tan(A-B) = \frac{\tan A - \tan B}{1 + \tan A \tan B}}$$

Example 68.B.3 Evaluate tan $(\theta + 45°)$.

Solution We will use the identity for tan $(A + B)$.

$$\tan(A+B) = \frac{\tan A + \tan B}{1 - \tan A \tan B}$$

We substitute θ for A and 45° for B and get

$$\tan(\theta + 45°) = \frac{\tan\theta + \tan 45°}{1 - \tan\theta \tan 45°}$$

Now tan 45° equals 1, so we get

$$\tan(\theta + 45°) = \frac{\tan\theta + 1}{1 - (\tan\theta)(1)} = \mathbf{\frac{\tan\theta + 1}{1 - \tan\theta}}$$

Problem set 68

1. Tom looked at his watch when the sun appeared and saw that it was exactly 5 o'clock. He couldn't begin until both hands on his watch pointed in the same direction. How long did he have to wait?

2. Find three consecutive multiples of 3 such that 3 times the sum of the first and the third exceeds 4 times the second by 42.

3. Jimbob averaged 60 kilometers per hour from home to the office, but got there 1 hour late. The next day he increased his speed to 90 kilometers per hour and got there 1 hour early. How far was it from home to the office?

4. The panther ran a distance of x yards in y minutes but arrived k minutes late to the feast. How fast would the panther have had to run to have arrived on time?

5. An urn contains 4 red marbles, 2 white marbles, and 3 green marbles. Two marbles are drawn without replacement. What is the probability that both of them are white?

6. A pair of dice is rolled. What is the probability that the number will be greater than 10 or less than 6?

7. Use the matrix echelon method to solve: $\begin{cases} 4x - 5y = 2 \\ 3x + 2y = -10 \end{cases}$

8. Construct a triangle whose sides measure 4 centimeters, 5 centimeters, and 9 centimeters.

9. Find the tenth term of an arithmetic sequence whose first term is 6 and whose common difference is -3.

10. Find the four arithmetic means between 6 and 106.

11. Write the first four terms of an arithmetic sequence in which the tenth term is 39 and the fourth term is 15.

12. Write the four fourth roots of 16 cis 40° in polar form.

13. Find sin 15° by using a trigonometric identity and the fact that $60° - 45° = 15°$.

14. Simplify $\cos\left(\theta - \frac{\pi}{4}\right)$ by using sum and difference identities.

15. Develop the identity for $\tan(A + B)$ by using the identities for $\sin(A + B)$ and $\cos(A + B)$.

16. Find tan 75° by using a trigonometric identity and the fact that $75° = 30° + 45°$.

Solve the following equations given that $(0° \le x, \theta < 360°)$:

17. $2\cos^2 x + \sin x + 1 = 0$

18. $2\tan^2 x - 3\sec x = -3$

19. $1 + 2\cos 4\theta = 0$

Show that:

20. $\sec x + \sec x \tan^2 x = \sec^3 x$

21. $\frac{\sin^2 x}{\cos x} + \cos x = \sec x$

22. $\frac{\tan(-\theta)\cos(-\theta)}{\sin(-\theta)} = 1$

23. Solve this triangle for its unknown parts.

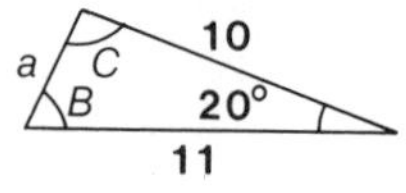

24. Prove that vertical angles are equal.

25. Given $\overline{DE} \parallel \overline{BC}$. Prove that $\frac{AD}{AB} = \frac{AE}{AC}$.

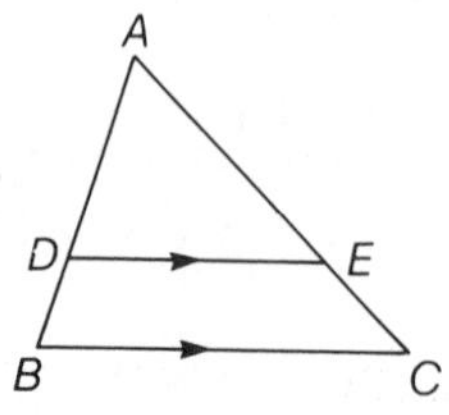

26. Find a, b, and h.

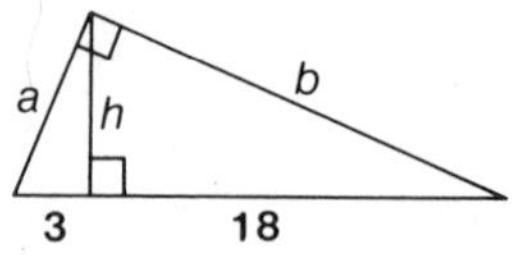

27. Sketch $y = -2 + 3 \sin \frac{2}{3}(x + 90°)$.

Solve:

28. $6^{2x-4} = 10^{3x+1}$

29. $\log_2 (x + 1) + \log_2 (x - 2) = 2$

30. $\log_3 7x + \frac{2}{3} \log_3 27 = 7^{3 \log_7 2 - \log_7 2}$

EP 68.14

LESSON 69 Forms of proportions · Proportional sides · Angle side angle · Hypotenuse leg

69.A Forms of proportions

Here we show two proportions. If the proportion on the left is a true proportion, the proportion on the right is also a true proportion. In other words, the proportion on the left implies the proportion on the right.

$$\frac{a+b}{a} = \frac{c+d}{c} \quad \xrightarrow{\text{implies}} \quad \frac{b}{a} = \frac{d}{c}$$

To see how this is true, we write each of the ratios in the left proportion as the sum of two fractions.

$$\frac{a}{a} + \frac{b}{a} = \frac{c}{c} + \frac{d}{c}$$

Now a over a equals 1 and c over c equals 1, so

$$1 + \frac{b}{a} = 1 + \frac{d}{c}$$

and if we add -1 to both sides, we get

$$\frac{b}{a} = \frac{d}{c}$$

This completes the proof. We will use the fact that one of these proportions implies the other proportion in the next section and in future lessons.

69.B Proportional sides

We can show that a line drawn parallel to a base of a triangle divides the sides it intersects into segments whose lengths are proportional. In the figure shown here, the line divides the sides of the triangle into segments whose lengths are proportional, as indicated by the proportions on the right.

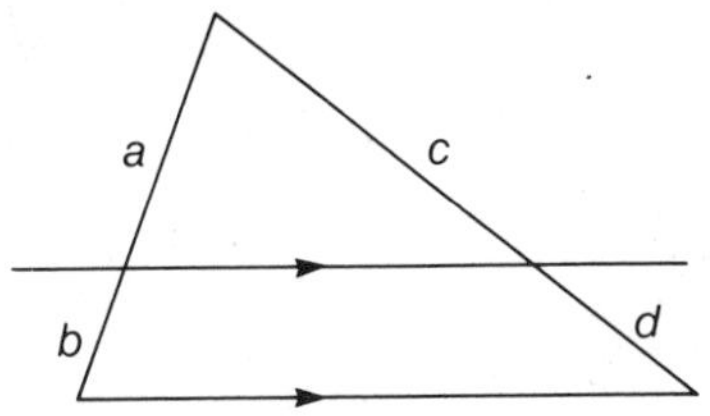

$$\frac{a+b}{a} = \frac{c+d}{c} \quad \xrightarrow{\text{implies}} \quad \frac{b}{a} = \frac{d}{c}$$

Example 69.B.1 In the figure shown, $\overline{BD} \parallel \overline{CE}$. Show that $\frac{BC}{AB} = \frac{DE}{AD}$.

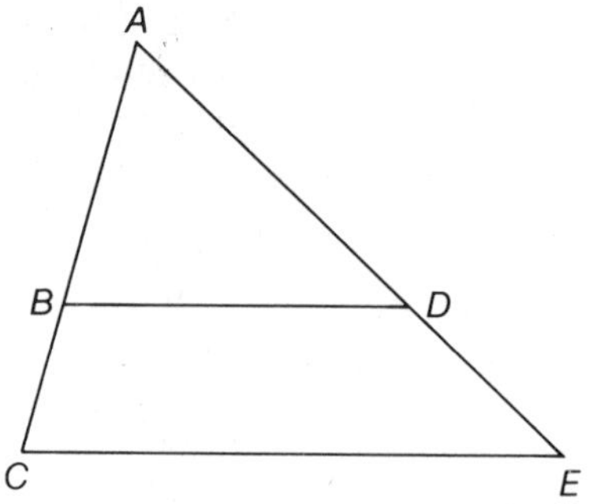

Solution Whenever we are asked to show that a proportion is true, we need to look for similar triangles because the lengths of the sides of similar triangles are proportional. We redraw the figure and mark angles that are equal.

We see that angle A is in both the small triangle and the large triangle. Also, the angles marked with the same tick marks are equal because they are corresponding angles formed by parallel lines and transversals.

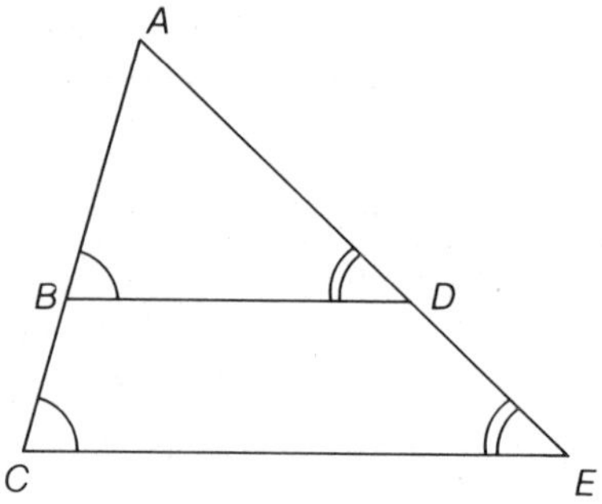

Thus, the angles in the small triangle equal the angles of the large triangle, and so the sides are proportional. Thus,

$$\frac{AC}{AB} = \frac{AE}{AD}$$

Now if we replace AC with $AB + BC$ and replace AE with $AD + DE$, we get

$$\frac{AB + BC}{AB} = \frac{AD + DE}{AD}$$

We can simplify this by noting that the left side can be written as 1 plus a fraction and the right side can be written as 1 plus a fraction.

$$1 + \frac{BC}{AB} = 1 + \frac{DE}{AD}$$

Now if we add -1 to both sides, we get

$$\frac{BC}{AB} = \frac{DE}{AD}$$

69.C Side angle side

We have defined similar polygons to be polygons in which the corresponding angles are equal and in which the corresponding sides are proportional. For triangles we have postulated that if corresponding angles are equal, then corresponding sides are proportional, and if corresponding sides are proportional, then corresponding angles are equal. **Triangles are also similar if the lengths of the sides that form an angle in one triangle are proportional to the lengths of the sides that form an equal angle in another triangle.** This assertion is called the ***side-angle-side (SAS) theorem.*** A close inspection of the two triangles shown here should convince one of the truth of this theorem. The triangles are similar because corresponding angles are equal and the lengths of the corresponding sides are proportional.

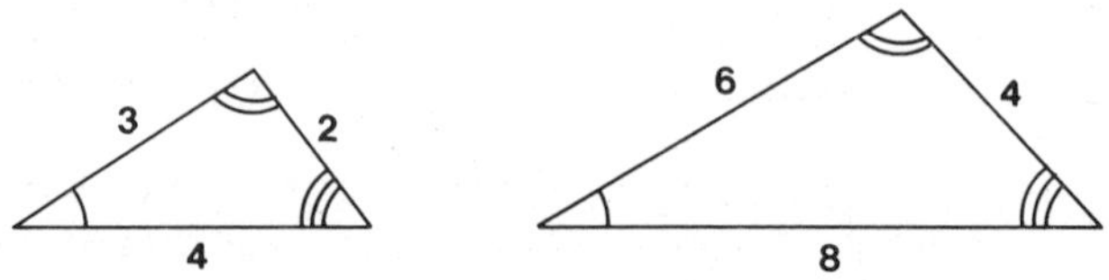

Now if we delete the bottom sides and the tick marks on the bottom angles, we see that nothing can change because the bottom sides must have the same lengths as the sides in the original triangles,

since they must be drawn in the same positions as before. Thus the bottom angles must still have the same measures as before. From this, we see that if equal angles are formed by sides whose lengths are proportional, we know that the triangles formed are similar even though the other three measurements have not been given.

69.D Hypotenuse leg

The next statement of triangle similarity pertains only to right triangles and is a theorem because it also can be proved. If the lengths of one leg and the hypotenuse of one right triangle are proportional to the lengths of a leg and the hypotenuse of another right triangle, the triangles are similar. This theorem is known as the ***hypotenuse-leg (HL) theorem.*** To prove this theorem, we remember that the same scale factor must apply to every pair of corresponding sides. Thus if the triangles shown below are to be similar, then side m must equal ka.

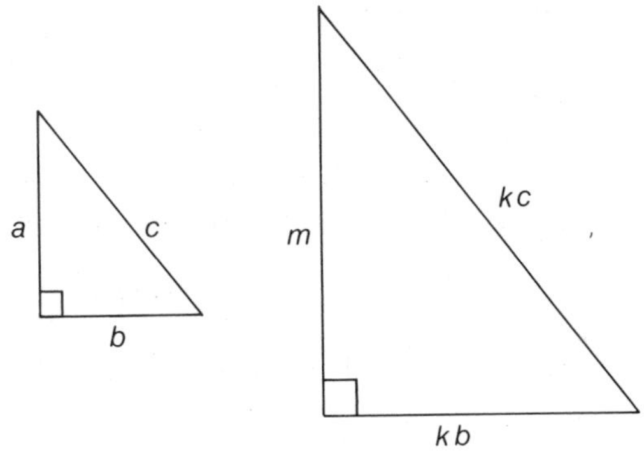

There is more than one way to prove this, and we decide to use an algebraic proof that involves the Pythagorean theorem. We use this theorem for both triangles.

LEFT TRIANGLE		RIGHT TRIANGLE	
$a^2 + b^2 = c^2$	theorem	$m^2 + k^2b^2 = k^2c^2$	theorem
$a^2 = c^2 - b^2$	rearranged	$m^2 = k^2(c^2 - b^2)$	rearranged
$a = \sqrt{c^2 - b^2}$	solved for a	$m = k\sqrt{c^2 - b^2}$	solved for m

We see that m equals $k\sqrt{c^2 - b^2}$, but $\sqrt{c^2 - b^2}$ equals a; so m equals ka. This gives us the last of the ways we can tell if triangles are similar. We have three ways in all.

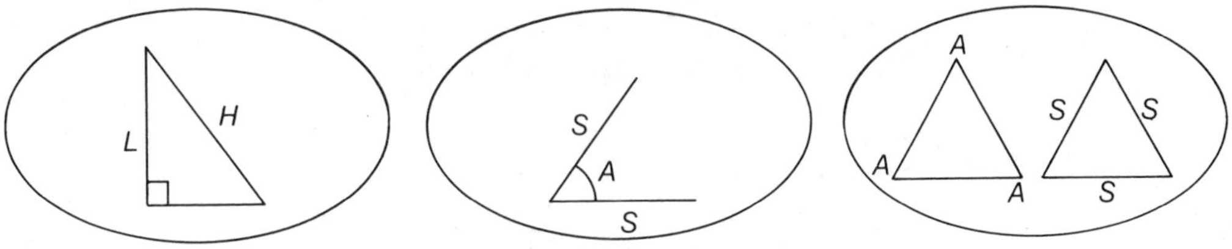

In the figure above, we grouped the AAA (angle-angle-angle) and SSS (side-side-side) statements because these were defined and postulated at the same time. These statements and the SAS statement work for any triangle, while the HL statement is valid only for right triangles. Most geometry books consider the case of two angles and the included side as a special case and note it by writing ASA (angle-side-angle). We remember that if two angles in one triangle equal two angles in another triangle, the third angles are also equal. Thus the ASA case has already been considered when we discussed the AAA case, and it is not necessary to consider it separately.

Problem set 69

1. It is exactly 3 p.m. How long will it take for the big hand to overtake the little hand?

2. Custo and Bob had \$100 between them. If Custo spent one-fourth of his share and Bob spent one-third of his share, they would have \$70 left. How much did each boy have to begin with?

3. The bottle held 4 reds, 4 blacks, and 2 whites. Three marbles were drawn with no replacement between draws. What is the probability that the first two were red and the third was white?

4. A pair of dice was rolled twice. What is the probability that the first roll was not a 7 and the second roll was a 7?

5. The sum of the digits in a two-digit number was 11. If the digits were interchanged, the new number would be 45 greater than the original number. What was the original number?

6. The tens digit in a three-digit counting number is equal to the sum of the other two digits. Four times the units digit exceeds the hundreds digit by 4, and the tens digit is 3 times the units digit. What is the number?

7. Use the matrix echelon method to solve: $\begin{cases} 2x - y = -1 \\ 3x + 2y = 9 \end{cases}$

8. Construct a line that is parallel to a given line and that passes through a designated point that is not on the line.

9. Insert the four arithmetic means between 10 and 25.

10. Write the first four terms of an arithmetic sequence in which the fourth term is -3 and the tenth term is -15.

11. Write the five fifth roots of 32 cis 60° in polar form.

12. Find cos 75° by using a trigonometric identity and the fact that $75° = 30° + 45°$.

13. Simplify $\sin\left(\theta + \frac{\pi}{6}\right)$ by using sum and difference identities.

14. Develop the identity for $\tan(A - B)$, using the identities for $\sin(A - B)$ and $\cos(A - B)$.

Solve the following equations given that $(0° \le x, \theta < 360°)$:

15. $2\sin^2 x + 3\cos x = 0$

16. $2\sin^2\theta + 15\cos\theta - 9 = 0$

17. $3 - 6\sin 4\theta = 0$

Show that:

18. $\csc x + \csc x \cot^2 x = \csc^3 x$

19. $\dfrac{1 - \cos^2\theta}{1 + \tan^2\theta} = \sin^2\theta\cos^2\theta$

20. $\sin^2\theta = (1 - \cos\theta)(1 + \cos\theta)$

21. Solve this triangle for its unknown parts.

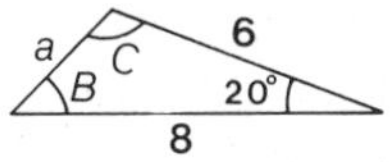

22. In the figure shown, $\overline{BC} \parallel \overline{DE}$. Prove that $\dfrac{AD}{DB} = \dfrac{AE}{EC}$.

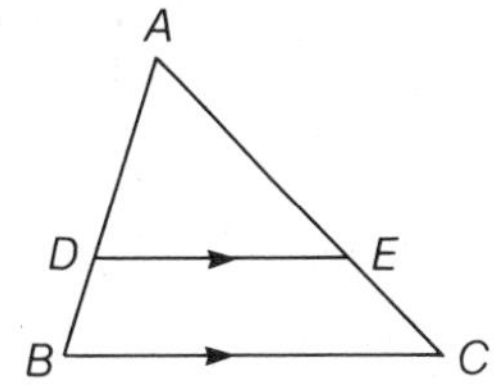

23. Find the length of a if the equal angles are as denoted in the figures below.

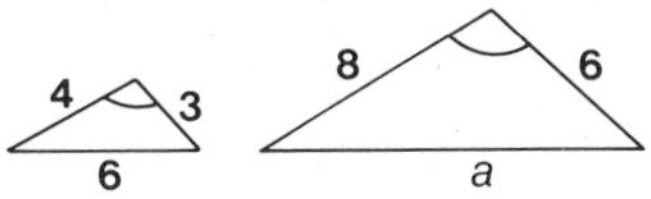

24. Solve for c.

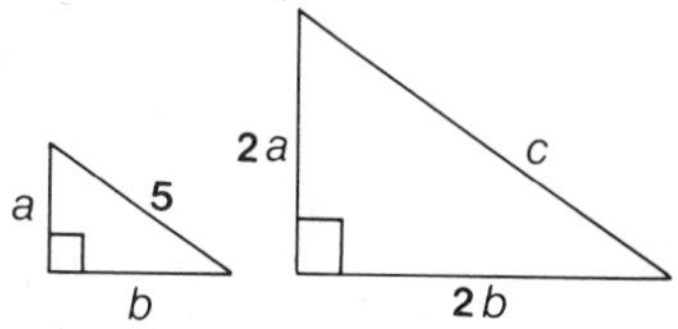

25. Solve for a.

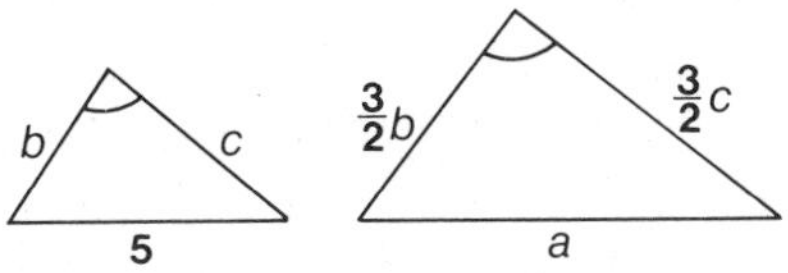

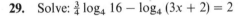

26. Find a, b, and h.

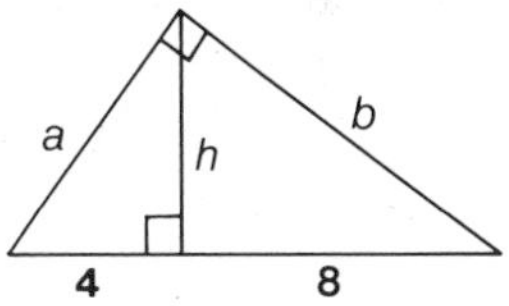

27. Sketch $y = 1 + \cos\left(x - \dfrac{5\pi}{3}\right)$.

28. Solve: $8^{4x+2} = 5^{2x-3}$

29. Solve: $\frac{3}{4}\log_4 16 - \log_4 (3x + 2) = 2$

30. Find the radius and the coordinates of the center of the circle whose equation is $x^2 + y^2 - 4x + 2y + 1 = 0$.

EP 69.15

LESSON 70 Exponential equations

70.A Exponential equations

Exponential equations of the form

$$A_t = A_0 e^{kt}$$

are important because they can be used to help us understand many everyday problems such as the growth of bacteria in biology, the voltage on a capacitor in engineering, radioactive decay in physics, and the growth of money in banking. The independent variable is t and is plotted on the horizontal axis. The dependent variable is A_t and is plotted on the vertical axis. The letters A_0 and k are constants whose values must be determined for each problem. Real-world problems often begin when time equals zero, so negative time has no meaning in these problems. Thus, the graphs begin when t is zero.

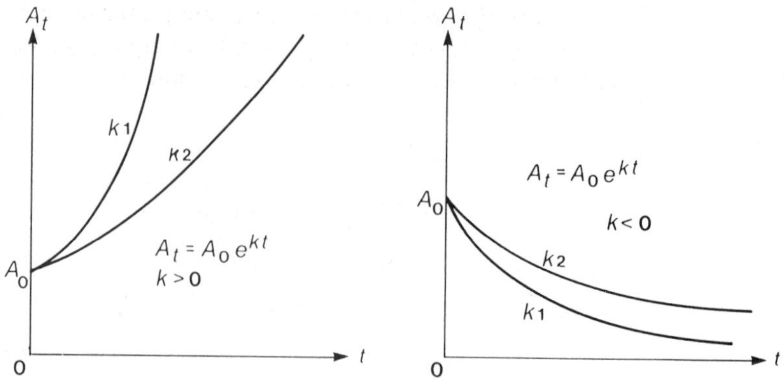

We use A_0 to designate the value of A_t when time is zero and call this value the initial value or the initial amount. In the left-hand figure, A_t equals A_0 when time is zero, and A_t increases as time increases because k is positive. In the right-hand figure, A_t equals A_0 when time is zero and decreases as time increases because k is negative. In each figure, the curves show that the change is faster for k_1 than for k_2. This is true if $|k_1|$ is greater than $|k_2|$.

We remember that direct and inverse variation problems are two-step problems and that the first step is to solve for the value of the constant of proportionality k. Exponential growth or decay problems are also two-step problems in which the first step is to solve for the value of the constant k in the exponent. We will solve for k by taking the logarithm of both sides of the equation. Next we will replace k in the equation with the proper value.

Then we will do the second part of the solution. **If time is given and the amount is the unknown, a simple evaluation is required. If the amount is given and time is the unknown, we must again take the logarithm of both sides to find *t*.** The scientific calculator will enable quick and accurate solutions to these problems.

Example 70.A.1 The number of bacteria present at noon was 400, and 9 hours later the bacteria numbered 800. Assume exponential growth and find the number of bacteria present at noon the next day.

Solution We begin by writing the exponential equation for the number of bacteria present at some time t. We use the symbol A_t to represent this number.

$$A_t = A_0 e^{kt}$$

For this problem time began at noon. The number of bacteria was 400 when time equaled 0 (noon), so A_0 equals 400. Now we have

$$A_t = 400e^{kt}$$

Solving for *k* always requires that we take the natural logarithm of both sides of the equation. To solve for k, we use 9 for t and 800 for A_t. Next we divide both sides of the equation by 400 to isolate the exponential. Then we take the natural logarithm of both sides so we can solve for k. Then we use this value of k in the equation.

$A_t = 400e^{kt}$	equation
$800 = 400e^{9k}$	substituted
$2 = e^{9k}$	divided by 400
$0.693 = 9k$	ln of both sides
$0.077 = k$	solved for k
$A_t = 400e^{0.077t}$	replaced k with 0.077

Now that we have k, we can complete the second part of the solution. We are asked for A_{24}, which is the value of A_t when t equals 24. All that is required is an evaluation of the exponential when t is replaced with 24.

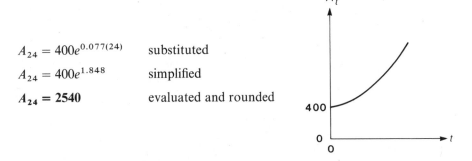

$A_{24} = 400e^{0.077(24)}$	substituted
$A_{24} = 400e^{1.848}$	simplified
$\mathbf{A_{24} = 2540}$	evaluated and rounded

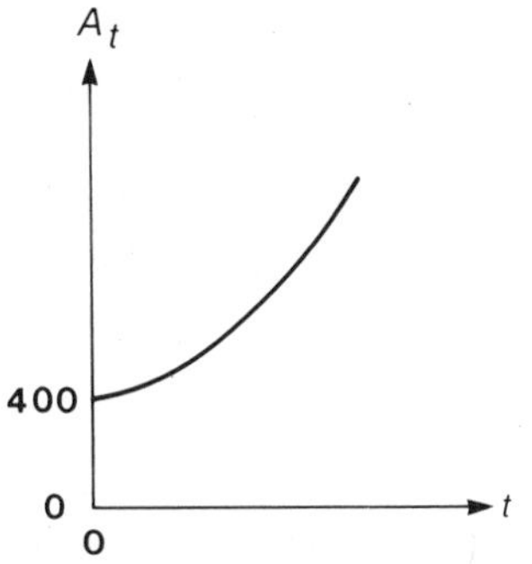

The sketch shown at the right is accurate enough for most purposes. It shows that time is plotted horizontally and the amount is plotted vertically. It also shows the amount when time equals zero and indicates that the amount increases exponentially as time increases.

Example 70.A.2 The number of bacteria present when the experiment began was 1200. After 100 hours there were 2700 bacteria present. Assume exponential growth and find the time required for the number of bacteria to increase to 30,000. Sketch the curve.

Solution First we must find the constant k for this problem and insert this number into the equation in place of k. We begin with the equation and use 1200 for A_0. Next we replace A_t with 2700 and t with 100. Then we divide to isolate the exponential and take the natural logarithm of both sides to solve for k.

$A_t = 1200e^{kt}$	used 1200 for A_0
$2700 = 1200e^{100k}$	substituted
$2.25 = e^{100k}$	divided by 1200
$0.81093 = 100k$	ln of both sides
$0.00811 = k$	solved for k
$A_t = 1200e^{0.00811t}$	substituted

Now that we have the value for k, we can solve for the time when the amount present is 30,000. **To solve for t, we must again take the natural logarithm of both sides of the equation.**

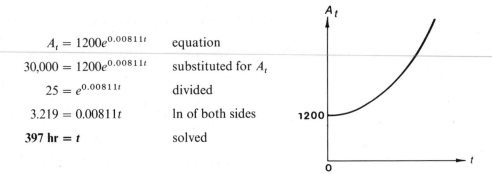

$A_t = 1200e^{0.00811t}$	equation
$30{,}000 = 1200e^{0.00811t}$	substituted for A_t
$25 = e^{0.00811t}$	divided
$3.219 = 0.00811t$	ln of both sides
397 hr $= t$	solved

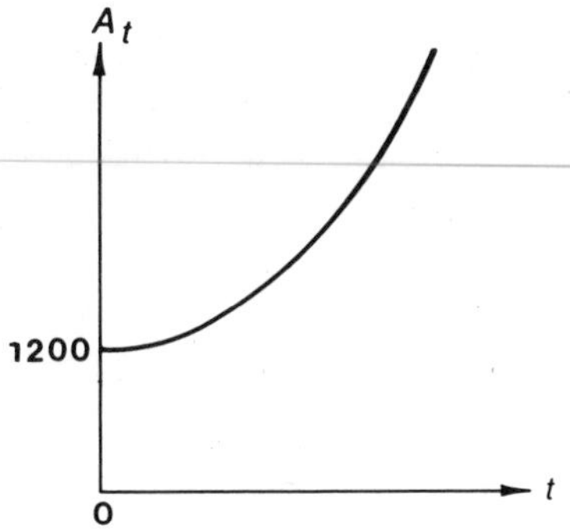

The sketch shown is sufficient. It shows the initial amount and indicates that the amount increases exponentially as time increases.

Example 70.A.3 The amount of substance initially present was 400 grams, and after 90 hours only 380 grams remained. Assume an exponential decrease and determine the half-life of the substance. Make a sketch of the graph.

Solution The ***half-life*** is the time required for the amount to decrease to half the original amount. Thus, we are asked to find the time required for the amount present to decrease from 400 grams to 200 grams. **We begin as always by substituting, isolating the exponential, and then taking the natural logarithm of both sides to find *k*.**

$$A_t = 400e^{kt} \qquad \text{equation}$$
$$380 = 400e^{90k} \qquad \text{substituted}$$
$$0.95 = e^{90k} \qquad \text{divided}$$
$$-0.051 = 90k \qquad \text{ln of both sides}$$
$$-0.00057 = k \qquad \text{solved}$$
$$A_t = 400e^{-0.00057t} \qquad \text{substituted}$$

Now that we have a value for k, we can solve for the time required to have only 200 grams left.

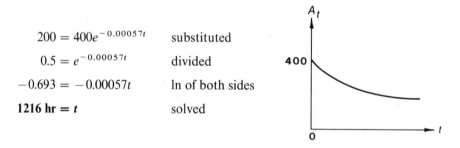

$$200 = 400e^{-0.00057t} \qquad \text{substituted}$$
$$0.5 = e^{-0.00057t} \qquad \text{divided}$$
$$-0.693 = -0.00057t \qquad \text{ln of both sides}$$
$$\mathbf{1216\ hr} = t \qquad \text{solved}$$

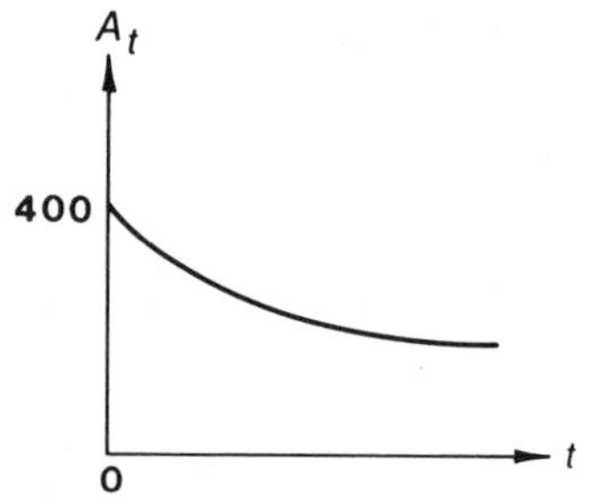

The graph shows all that we want to know. It shows the amount when t equals 0 and indicates that the amount decreases exponentially with time. The amount present always decreases with time when k is a negative number.

Problem set 70

1. The number of bacteria at noon was 400, and 10 hours later the number was 4000. Assume exponential growth and find the values of A_0 and k. Then find the number of bacteria present at midnight. Sketch the graph.

2. There were 40 grams of mixture in the bowl when Linda walked in. Fifty minutes later only 20 grams was left. If the decay was exponential, find the values of A_0 and k and then find the amount remaining after another 50 minutes.

3. At a certain instant 100 grams of a radioactive substance is present. After 4 years, 20 grams remains. Find A_0 and k and then find the half-life of the substance. Sketch the graph.

4. Tommie sees that it is exactly 3 o'clock so it is not yet time to go. It will be time to go the first time the hands are pointing in the same direction. What will the time on the clock be when it is time to go?

5. Two cards are drawn from a full deck without replacement. What is the probability that both cards are red?

6. A pair of dice is rolled twice. What is the probability that both rolls of the dice yield numbers less than 5?

7. Use Cramer's rule to solve: $\begin{cases} 3x - 4y = 2 \\ 2x + 3y = 4 \end{cases}$

8. Draw a line segment 4 centimeters long and construct its perpendicular bisector.

9. Find the twentieth term of an arithmetic sequence whose first term is 2 and whose common difference is -4.

10. Write the first three terms of the arithmetic sequence whose eighth term is -8 and whose tenth term is -12.

11. Write the three cube roots of 27 cis 30° in polar form.

12. Find sin 75° by using a trigonometric identity and the fact that $75° = 45° + 30°$. Use decimal approximations.

13. Simplify $\sin\left(\theta - \frac{\pi}{6}\right)$ by using sum and difference identities. Use exact values.

14. Develop the identity for $\tan(A + B)$ by using the identities for $\sin(A + B)$ and $\cos(A + B)$.

Solve the following equations given that $(0° \le x, \theta < 360°)$:

15. $\sqrt{3}\tan^2 x + 2\tan x - \sqrt{3} = 0$ *Note:* $\sqrt{3}\,x^2 + 2x - \sqrt{3} = (\sqrt{3}\,x - 1)(x + \sqrt{3})$

16. $\tan^2\theta - 5\tan\theta + 6 = 0$

17. $\sec 4\theta = 1$

18. Show that $\dfrac{\cos\theta}{1 - \sin\theta} - \dfrac{\cos\theta}{1 + \sin\theta} = 2\tan\theta$.

19. Show that $\dfrac{\cos^3 x + \sin^3 x}{\cos x + \sin x} = 1 - \sin x \cos x$. *Note:* Factor the numerator by noting that it is the sum of two cubes.

20. Show that $(1 - \sin\theta)(1 + \sin\theta) = \cos^2\theta$.

21. Solve this triangle for a.

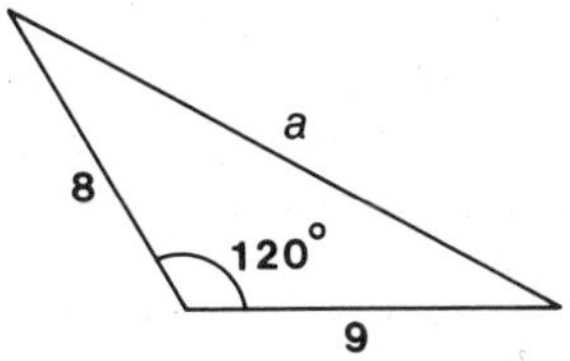

22. In the figure shown, $\overline{BC} \parallel \overline{DE}$. Find the length of $\overline{EC}$.

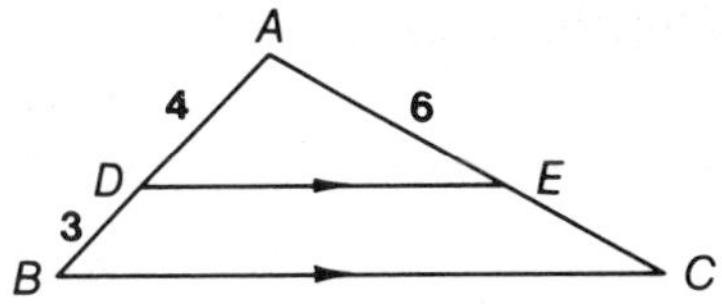

23. Find the length of d if the equal angles are as denoted in the figures below.

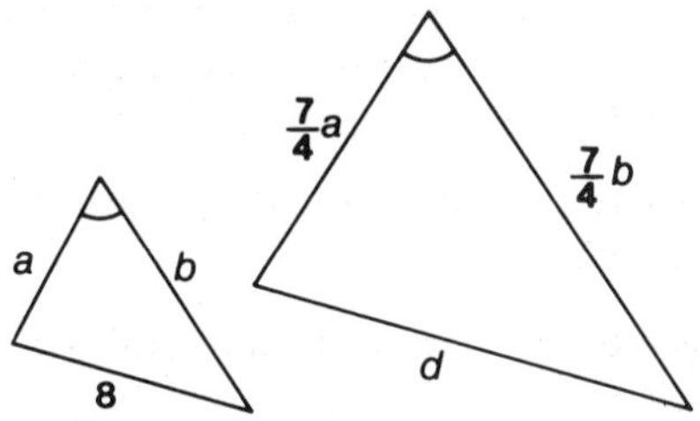

24. Find a, b, and h.

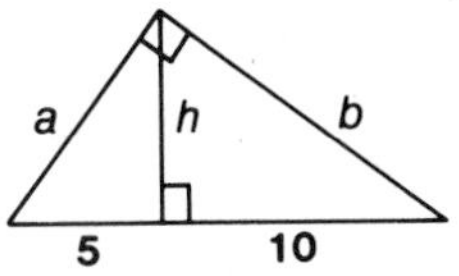

25. The perimeter of a regular pentagon is 30 cm. What is the area of the pentagon?

26. Sketch $y = -7 + 10 \sin \frac{9}{5}x$.

27. Solve: $9^{8x-3} = 5^{2x-3}$

28. Solve: $\frac{2}{3} \log_2 27 + \log_2 (3x + 2) = 2$

29. Simplify: $2^{2 \log_2 3 - \log_2 3}$

30. Prove that an exterior angle of a triangle is equal to the sum of the remote interior angles of the triangle.

EP 70.16

LESSON 71 The ellipse (2)

71.A The ellipse (2)

An ellipse is symmetric about its two axes, as we show in the figure on the left below. On the right we show the standard forms of the equations of an ellipse whose major and minor axes are the coordinate axes. In these equations a is always greater than b. If the major axis (the axis through the foci) is the x axis, a^2 is below x^2, as in the left-hand equation. If the major axis is the y axis, a^2 is below y^2, as in the right-hand equation.

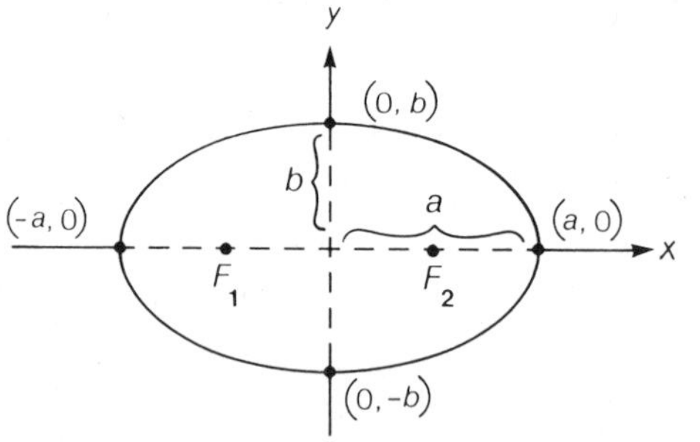

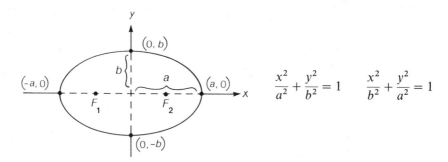

$$\frac{x^2}{a^2} + \frac{y^2}{b^2} = 1 \qquad \frac{x^2}{b^2} + \frac{y^2}{a^2} = 1$$

We remember that the sum of the distances from any point on an ellipse to the two foci is a constant. With the aid of the imaginary piece of string used to draw an ellipse, we can reason that the value of the constant is $2a$, which equals the length of the string and equals the length of the major axis of the ellipse.

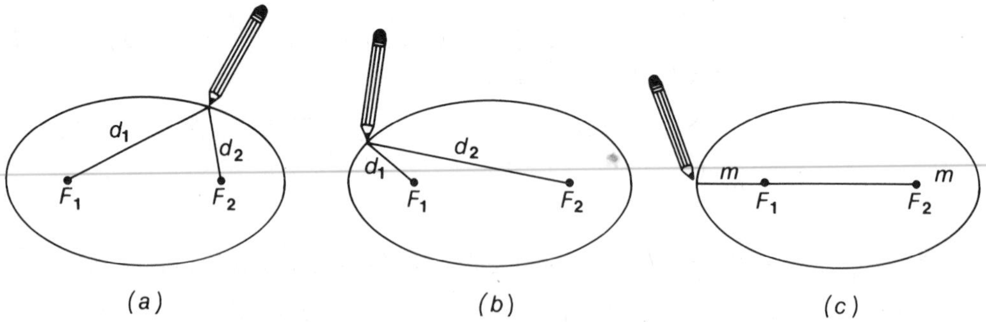

We begin at (a) and trace the ellipse by moving the pencil counterclockwise (b) until we get to the vertex in (c). Now the string goes from F_2 to the pencil and back through distance m to F_1. The string covers the distance m twice. If we mentally remove a piece of string m units long, we can use it to cover the distance m on the right. Thus, our piece of string stretches from vertex to vertex and has a length of $2a$.

Now if we move the pencil to the end of the minor axis, we have the following figure.

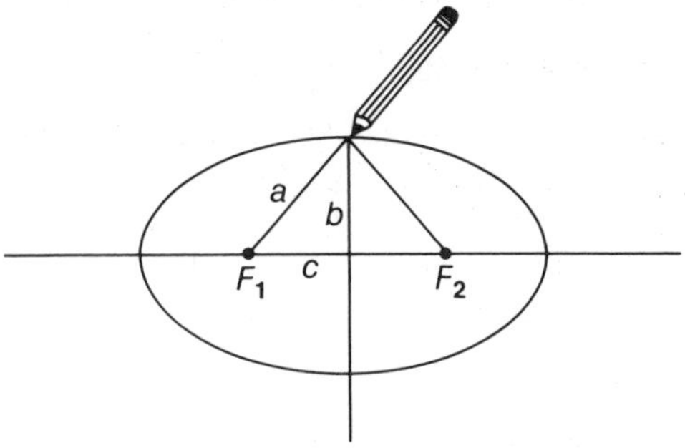

The length of the string is $2a$, so half its length is a. We have formed a right triangle whose hypotenuse is a and whose legs are b and c, as shown. The length of one side is the distance from the origin to the focus, and the length of the other side equals half the length of the minor axis. We can use the theorem of Pythagoras and write

$$a^2 = c^2 + b^2$$

We can use this relationship and the standard form of the equation of an ellipse to solve some interesting problems. In the next example, we are given values for c and a and must solve for b.

Example 71.A.1 Write the standard form of the equation of the ellipse with vertices at $(\pm 5, 0)$ and with foci at $(\pm 4, 0)$.

Solution **We always begin with a diagram.** The foci of an ellipse always lie on the major axis, so the x axis is the major axis.

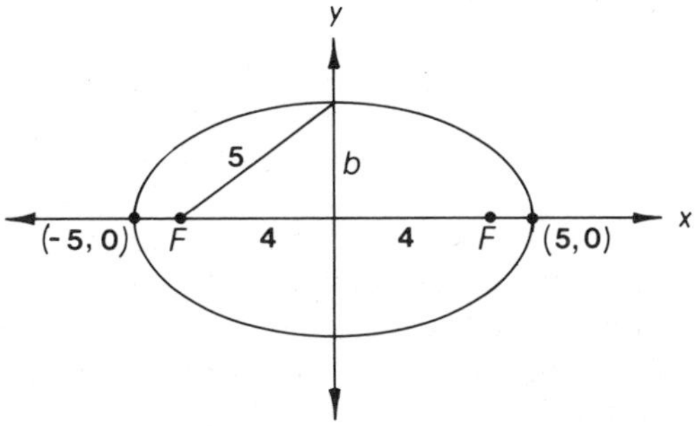

We see that the length of the major axis is 10, so half the major axis is 5. We draw the triangle and get

$$5^2 = 4^2 + b^2$$
$$9 = b^2$$
$$3 = b$$

The equation of an ellipse whose major axis lies along the x axis is

$$\frac{x^2}{a^2} + \frac{y^2}{b^2} = 1$$

Thus, since in this problem $a = 5$ and $b = 3$, the equation for this ellipse is

$$\mathbf{\frac{x^2}{25} + \frac{y^2}{9} = 1}$$

Example 71.A.2 Write the standard form of the equation of the ellipse with vertices at $(0, \pm 6)$ and foci at $(0, \pm 5)$.

Solution **We always begin with a diagram.** We remember that the foci are always on the major axis.

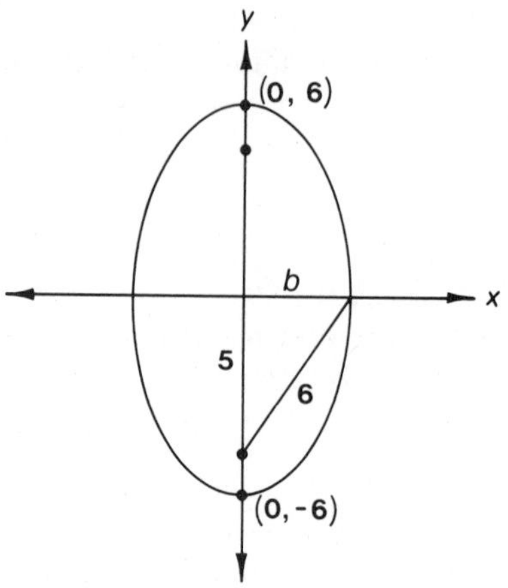

From the triangle, we get

$$6^2 = 5^2 + b^2$$
$$36 = 25 + b^2$$
$$\sqrt{11} = b$$

The length of the minor axis is $2\sqrt{11}$. This time the major axis lies along the y axis, so the equation is

$$\frac{x^2}{b^2} + \frac{y^2}{a^2} = 1$$

Since $a = 6$ and $b = \sqrt{11}$, the equation of the ellipse in standard form is

$$\mathbf{\frac{x^2}{11} + \frac{y^2}{36} = 1}$$

Example 71.A.3 Write the standard form of the equation of the horizontal ellipse whose center is at the origin. The length of the major axis is 10, and the length of the minor axis is 4. What are the coordinates of the foci?

Solution **Again we begin with a diagram.**

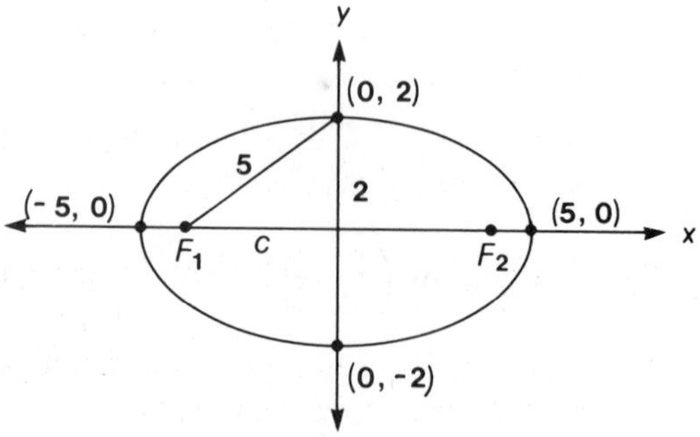

From our diagram, we get

$$5^2 = c^2 + 2^2$$
$$25 = c^2 + 4$$
$$21 = c^2$$
$$\sqrt{21} = c$$

Thus, the coordinates of the foci are $(\sqrt{21}, 0)$ and $(-\sqrt{21}, 0)$, and the equation is

$$\frac{x^2}{25} + \frac{y^2}{4} = 1$$

Problem set 71

1. When the experiment began, there were 40 rabbits. Six years later there were 2000 rabbits. Assume exponential growth and find A_0 and k. Then find the number of rabbits after 8 years. Sketch the graph.
2. When Wilbur walked into the room, there were 40,000. Ten hours later, there were only 30,000. Assume exponential decay and find A_0 and k. Then find the half-life of the things. Sketch the graph.
3. At 8 p.m. things looked just fine because Sir Richard didn't have much longer to wait. He could proceed on his journey when the clock hands pointed in opposite directions. How long did he have to wait?
4. The urn held 4 black marbles and 3 white marbles. A marble was drawn and then replaced. Then a second was drawn and put aside, and then another was drawn. What is the probability that all 3 were white?
5. Three cards were drawn from a deck without replacement. What is the probability that all 3 were black?
6. The sum of the first and the third of three consecutive even counting numbers is 6 greater than the second. What are the numbers?
7. Write an equation of the ellipse with vertices at $(\pm 4, 0)$ and with foci at $(\pm 3, 0)$. Write the equation in standard form.
8. Write an equation of the ellipse with vertices at $(0, \pm 7)$ and foci at $(0, \pm 5)$. Write the equation in general form.
9. Find the equation of a vertical ellipse whose center is the origin, whose major axis is length 10, and whose minor axis is length 4. Write the equation in standard form.
10. Use the matrix echelon method to solve: $\begin{cases} 2x - 3y = -7 \\ 3x + 2y = 9 \end{cases}$
11. Find the sixteenth term of an arithmetic sequence whose first term is 3 and whose common difference is -3.
12. Write the first four terms of the arithmetic sequence whose ninth term is -46 and whose fourth term is -16.
13. Simplify $\sin\left(x - \frac{\pi}{2}\right)$ by using sum and difference identities as required.
14. Find $\tan 75°$ by using sum and difference identities and the fact that $75° = 45° + 30°$. Use decimal approximations.

15. Find tan 15° by using sum and difference identities and the fact that $15° = 60° - 45°$. Use exact values.

Solve the following equations given that $(0° \le x < 360°)$:

16. $\sqrt{3}\cot^2 x + 2\cot x - \sqrt{3} = 0$

17. $3\cos^2 x + 5\cos x - 2 = 0$

18. $\csc 4x - 2 = 0$

Show that:

19. $\dfrac{\sin\theta}{1-\cos\theta} - \dfrac{\sin\theta}{1+\cos\theta} = 2\cot\theta$

20. $\dfrac{\tan^3 x + 1}{\tan x + 1} = \sec^2 x - \tan x$

Hint: First factor the numerator.

21. Solve this triangle for angles A and B.

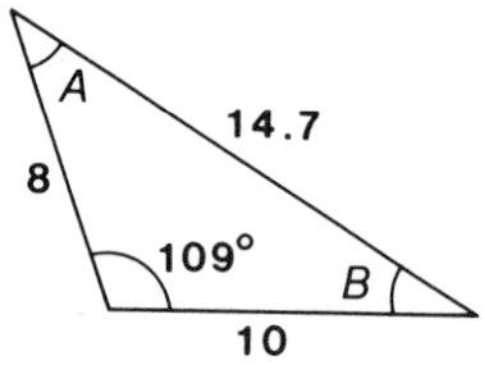

22. In the figure shown, $\overline{BD} \parallel \overline{CE}$. Show that $\dfrac{BC}{AB} = \dfrac{DE}{AD}$.

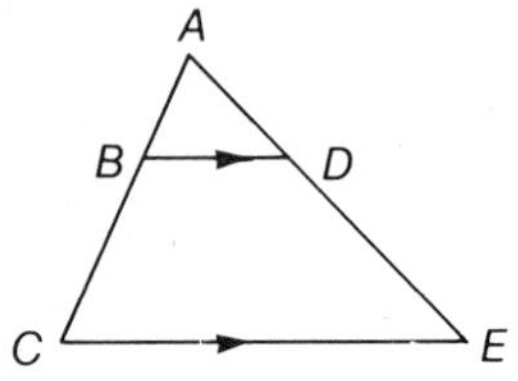

23. Find the length of c.

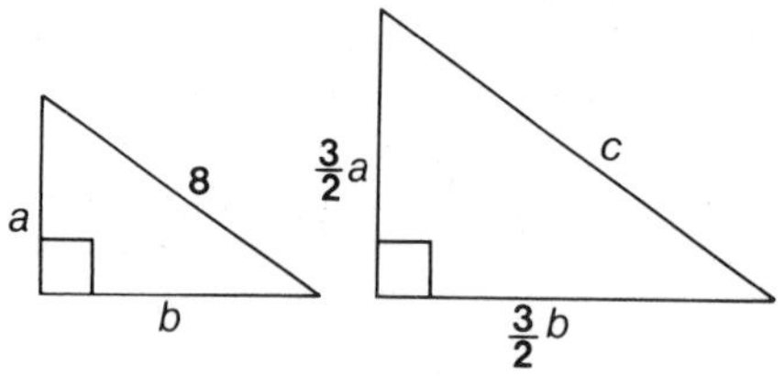

24. Find a, b, and h.

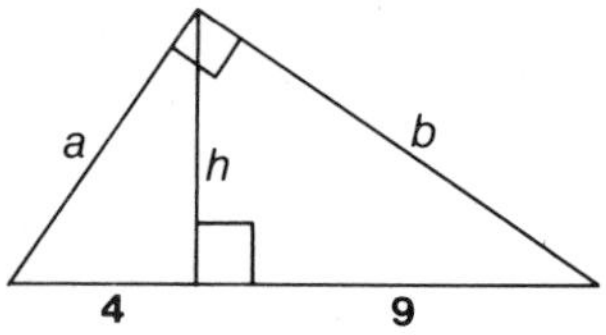

25. What is the sum of the interior angles of a 14-sided convex polygon?

26. Sketch $y = -3 + 10\sin 3(x - 20°)$.

27. Solve: $8^{3x-1} = 4^{2x-1}$

28. Solve: $\frac{3}{4}\ln 16 + 2\ln x = \ln(2x + 1)$

29. Find the base 3 antilogarithm of 4.

30. Prove the sum of the angles of a triangle is 180°.

EP 71.17

LESSON 72 Double-angle identities · Half-angle identities

72.A Double-angle identities

We begin by repeating our key identities. They are the sine and cosine sum and difference identities.

(*a*) $\sin(A + B) = \sin A\cos B + \cos A\sin B$

(*b*) $\sin(A - B) = \sin A\cos B - \cos A\sin B$

(*c*) $\cos(A + B) = \cos A\cos B - \sin A\sin B$

(*d*) $\cos(A - B) = \cos A\cos B + \sin A\sin B$

(e) $\tan \theta = \dfrac{\sin \theta}{\cos \theta}$

(f) $\sin^2 \theta + \cos^2 \theta = 1$

The double-angle identities can be quickly developed from key identities (*a*) and (*c*), as we will show.

Example 72.A.1 Develop the identity for sin 2*A* and cos 2*A*.

Solution (*a*) To develop the identity for sin 2*A*, we write the identity for sin (*A* + *B*).

$$\sin (A + B) = \sin A \cos B + \cos A \sin B$$

Now the trick is to let angle *B* be equal to angle *A*. If *B* equals *A*, then we can replace *B* everywhere with *A*.

$$\sin (A + A) = \sin A \cos A + \cos A \sin A$$

On the left, we have sin 2*A*, and both terms on the right are the product of sin *A* and cos *A*. Thus we have

$$\mathbf{\sin 2A = 2 \sin A \cos A}$$

Now look again at the identity for sin (*A* + *B*) and try to visualize the result of replacing *B* with *A*.

$$\sin (A + B) = \sin A \cos B + \cos A \sin B$$

You should be able to look at this identity and write the expression for sin 2*A* without the intervening steps.

(*b*) A similar procedure is used to develop the identity for cos 2*A*. First we write the identity for cos (*A* + *B*).

$$\cos (A + B) = \cos A \cos B - \sin A \sin B$$

Next we replace *B* with *A* and get

$$\cos (A + A) = \cos A \cos A - \sin A \sin A$$

which simplifies to

$$\mathbf{\cos 2A = \cos^2 A - \sin^2 A}$$

Now look again at the identity for cos (*A* + *B*) and try to visualize the result of replacing *B* with *A*.

$$\cos (A + B) = \cos A \cos B - \sin A \sin B$$

You should be able to look at this identity and write the expression for cos 2*A* without the intervening steps.

We remember that $\sin^2 A + \cos^2 A = 1$. This equation can be written in two other forms.

$$\cos^2 A = 1 - \sin^2 A \qquad \sin^2 A = 1 - \cos^2 A$$

We can use these two equations and substitution to get two other identities for cos 2*A*. To get the first one we use the basic identity for cos 2*A* and replace $\cos^2 A$ with $1 - \sin^2 A$.

$\cos 2A = \cos^2 A - \sin^2 A$	basic identity
$\cos 2A = (1 - \sin^2 A) - \sin^2 A$	substituted
$\mathbf{\cos 2A = 1 - 2 \sin^2 A}$	simplified

We get the third form of cos $2A$ by replacing $\sin^2 A$ with $1 - \cos^2 A$. **We must be careful with the $-$ sign.**

$$\cos 2A = \cos^2 A - \sin^2 A \qquad \text{basic identity}$$

$$\cos 2A = \cos^2 A - (1 - \cos^2 A) \qquad \text{substituted}$$

$$\mathbf{\cos 2A = 2\cos^2 A - 1} \qquad \text{simplified}$$

Example 72.A.2 Begin with the identities for $\sin(A + B)$ and $\cos(A + B)$ and develop the identity for $\tan 2A$.

Solution We begin by developing the identities for $\sin 2A$ and $\cos 2A$. These identities can be memorized but can also be forgotten—especially when they are needed. Practice in developing them now will make the developments automatic later on. We can do both developments in one step.

$$\sin(A + B) = \sin A \cos B + \cos A \sin B$$

and by inspection

$$\sin 2A = 2 \sin A \cos A$$

Also,

$$\cos(A + B) = \cos A \cos B - \sin A \sin B$$

and by inspection

$$\cos 2A = \cos^2 A - \sin^2 A$$

Now the tangent of ( ) equals the sine of ( ) divided by the cosine of ( ). Thus, tan (2A) equals sin ($2A$) divided by cos ($2A$).

$$\tan 2A = \frac{\sin 2A}{\cos 2A} = \frac{2 \sin A \cos A}{\cos^2 A - \sin^2 A}$$

We remember that we concentrate on tangent identities in which the first term in the denominator is the number 1. To get this form, we divide every term above and below by $\cos^2 A$. On top we write $\cos^2 A$ as $(\cos A)(\cos A)$.

$$\tan 2A = \frac{\dfrac{2 \sin A \cos A}{\cos A \cos A}}{\dfrac{\cos^2 A}{\cos^2 A} - \dfrac{\sin^2 A}{\cos^2 A}} \longrightarrow \mathbf{\tan 2A = \frac{2 \tan A}{1 - \tan^2 A}}$$

72.B Half-angle identities

Example 72.B.1 Develop the identities for $\sin \frac{1}{2}x$ and $\cos \frac{1}{2}x$.

Solution This development requires the second and third forms of the identity for cos $2A$. **Rather than trust our memory, we will go back to the basic identity for cos $(A + B)$. We can develop the two forms quickly and accurately, and we try never to depend on memory if it is not necessary.**

$$\cos(A + B) = \cos A \cos B - \sin A \sin B$$

By inspection

$$\cos 2A = \cos^2 A - \sin^2 A$$

Now we can get the other two forms by using $\sin^2 A + \cos^2 A = 1$ and substituting.

USING $\cos^2 A = 1 - \sin^2 A$	USING $\sin^2 A = 1 - \cos^2 A$
$\cos 2A = (1 - \sin^2 A) - \sin^2 A$	$\cos 2A = \cos^2 A - (1 - \cos^2 A)$
$\cos 2A = 1 - 2\sin^2 A$	$\cos 2A = 2\cos^2 A - 1$

Now we have the two forms of $\cos 2A$ that we need. We solve the equation on the left for $\sin^2 A$ and solve the equation on the right for $\cos^2 A$.

$$\cos 2A - 1 = -2\sin^2 A \qquad \cos 2A + 1 = 2\cos^2 A$$

$$-\cos 2A + 1 = 2\sin^2 A \qquad 2\cos^2 A = 1 + \cos 2A$$

$$\boldsymbol{\sin^2 A = \frac{1 - \cos 2A}{2}} \qquad \boldsymbol{\cos^2 A = \frac{1 + \cos 2A}{2}}$$

This intermediate step is in boldface because we have identities for $\sin^2 A$ and $\cos^2 A$ that are sometimes required. To finish the half-angle development requires two steps. The first step is to take the square root of both sides and remember the $\pm$ signs that accrue.

$$\sin A = \pm\sqrt{\frac{1 - \cos 2A}{2}} \qquad \cos A = \pm\sqrt{\frac{1 + \cos 2A}{2}}$$

The final step is to replace A with $x/2$. This type of variable change makes some people uncomfortable when first encountered, but it is a legitimate technique, and it is used whenever it is convenient. When we substitute under the radical, the expression $\cos 2A$ becomes $\cos 2\left(\frac{x}{2}\right)$, or $\cos x$.

$$\boldsymbol{\sin\frac{x}{2} = \pm\sqrt{\frac{1 - \cos x}{2}}} \qquad \boldsymbol{\cos\frac{x}{2} = \pm\sqrt{\frac{1 + \cos x}{2}}}$$

This development will be required in future problem sets because it provides excellent practice in changing the forms of trigonometric expressions.

Problem set 72

1. When the year began, there were only 80, but their growth was exponential. Two years later, there were 400. Find A_0 and k and write the exponential equation that gives the number as a function of time. How long would it take for the number to increase to 2000? Sketch the graph.
2. At the outset, there were 2000 and the decay was exponential. Four years later, there were 500. Write the equation that gives their number as a function of time.
3. Harry flipped a fair coin 3 times. It came up heads every time. What is the probability that the next flip will also come up heads?
4. Ten men, 20 women, and 30 children receive \$3825 for 1 week's work. If 1 man receives as much as 1 woman or 2 children, how much does each man receive for a day's work?
5. One card was drawn from a full deck of 52 cards, and then replaced. Then another card was drawn. What is the probability that both cards were spades?
6. A fair die was rolled 3 times. What is the probability of getting a 6, a 4, and a number greater than 3 in that order?
7. Develop the identity for $\cos 2A$.
8. Develop the identity for $\sin \frac{1}{2}A$.
9. Develop the identity for $\tan 2A$.

10. Write an equation in standard form of the ellipse with vertices at $(\pm 5, 0)$ and with foci at $(\pm 3, 0)$.

11. Write an equation in standard form of the ellipse with vertices at $(0, \pm 8)$ and foci at $(0, \pm 4)$.

12. Find the equation of a horizontal ellipse whose center is the origin and whose major axis is length 12 and whose minor axis is length 4. Write the equation in standard form.

13. Find the eighteenth term of an arithmetic sequence whose first term is 4 and whose common difference is 2.

14. Write the first three terms of the arithmetic sequence whose tenth term is -22 and whose third term is -8.

15. Find sin 105° by using sum and difference identities and the fact that $105° = 60° + 45°$. Use exact values.

16. Find sin 15° by using the half-angle identity for $\sin \frac{1}{2}x$ and letting $x = 30°$. Use decimal approximations.

Solve the following equations given that $(0° \leq y, x < 360°)$:

17. $2 \cos^2 y - 9 \sin y + 3 = 0$

18. $\sec 2x + 2 = 0$

19. Show that $\sec^2 x \sin^2 x + \sin^2 x \csc^2 x = \sec^2 x$.

20. Show that $\sin^2 \theta + \tan^2 \theta + \cos^2 \theta = \sec^2 \theta$.

21. Find angle A.

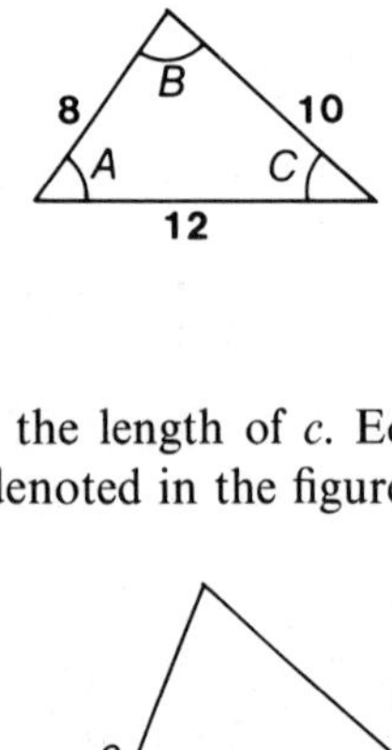

22. Given $\overline{BD} \parallel \overline{CE}$, find the length of $\overline{AB}$.

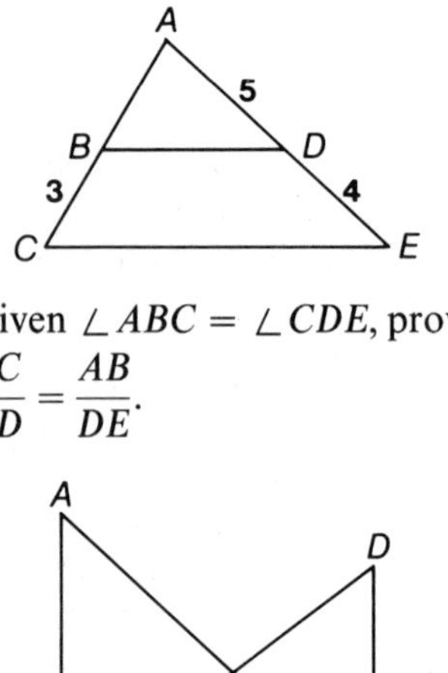

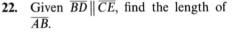

23. Find the length of c. Equal angles are denoted in the figures.

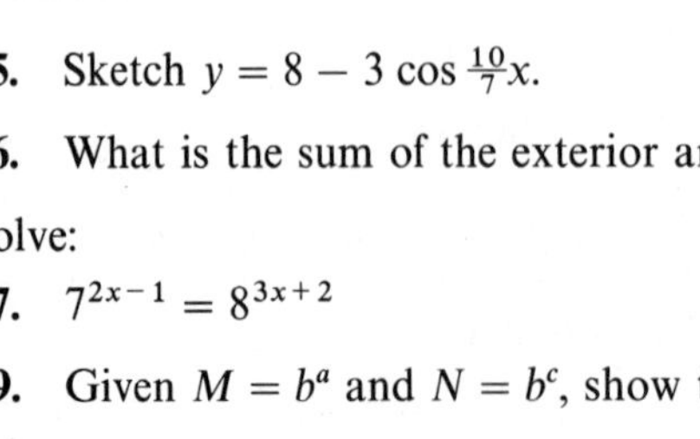

24. Given $\angle ABC = \angle CDE$, prove that $\frac{BC}{CD} = \frac{AB}{DE}$.

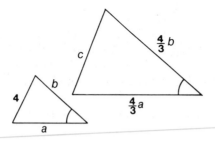

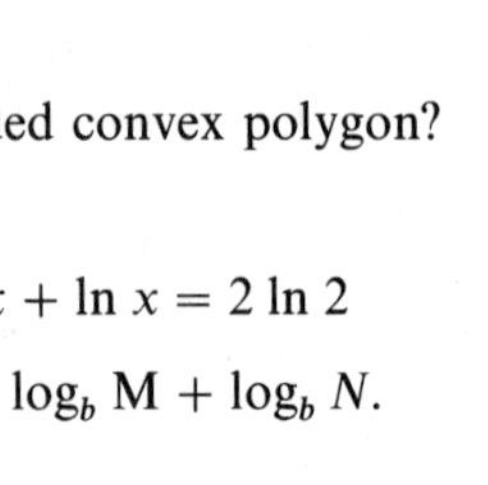

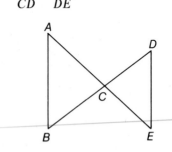

25. Sketch $y = 8 - 3 \cos \frac{10}{7}x$.

26. What is the sum of the exterior angles of a 25-sided convex polygon?

Solve:

27. $7^{2x-1} = 8^{3x+2}$

28. $\ln x + \ln x = 2 \ln 2$

29. Given $M = b^a$ and $N = b^c$, show that $\log_b MN = \log_b M + \log_b N$.

30. Find the base 4 antilogarithm of -1.

EP 72.18

LESSON 73 Geometric progressions

73.A Geometric progressions

We recall that if we begin with a first number and develop a sequence by ***adding*** the same amount to form each succeeding entry, then the sequence is an ***arithmetic sequence*** or an ***arithmetic progression.*** The amount added is called the ***common difference.*** We can tell that this sequence is an arithmetic sequence because each term is 5 greater than the term to its left.

$$-10, -5, 0, 5, 10$$

Thus, the common difference is $+5$. The second term is the sum of the first term and the common difference; the third term is the sum of the first term and two common differences; etc. If we use a_1 for the first term and d for the difference, we can write a general expression for an arithmetic sequence as

$$\underset{①}{a_1}, \quad \underset{②}{a_1 + d}, \quad \underset{③}{a_1 + 2d}, \quad \underset{④}{a_1 + 3d}, \quad \ldots, \quad \underset{ⓝ}{a_1 + (n-1)d}$$

In each entry, we note that the difference is used one fewer times than the number of the term.

If we begin with a number and form the succeeding terms in a sequence by **multiplying by the same factor,** then the sequence formed is called a ***geometric sequence*** or a ***geometric progression.*** The factor used as a multiplier is called the ***common ratio.*** If we begin with 8 and use 2 as a common ratio to form a 5-term sequence, we get

①	②	③	④	⑤
$8,$	$8 \cdot 2,$	$8 \cdot 2 \cdot 2,$	$8 \cdot 2 \cdot 2 \cdot 2,$	$8 \cdot 2 \cdot 2 \cdot 2 \cdot 2$
$8,$	$\underline{16},$	$\underline{32},$	$\underline{64},$	128

We call the terms between the first term and the last term of a finite geometric sequence the ***geometric means*** of the sequence. **If the common ratio is a negative number, the terms in the sequence will alternate in sign.** If we begin with 8 and use -2 as a common ratio to form a 5-term sequence, we get

①	②	③	④	⑤
$8,$	$8(-2),$	$8(-2)(-2),$	$8(-2)(-2)(-2),$	$8(-2)(-2)(-2)(-2)$
$8,$	$\underline{-16},$	$\underline{32},$	$\underline{-64},$	128

The three geometric means between 8 and 128 shown here are not the same as the three geometric means in the example above. **Thus, we see that when we say that geometric means are between 8 and 128, 8 is the first term, 128 is the last term, and the means do not necessarily lie between these numbers on the number line.**

Example 73.A.1 Find the fifth term in a geometric sequence whose first term is -2 and whose common ratio is -3.

Solution The terms are as shown here.

①	②	③	④	⑤
$-2,$	$-2(-3),$	$-2(-3)(-3),$	$-2(-3)(-3)(-3),$	$-2(-3)(-3)(-3)(-3)$

Thus, the fifth term can be written as

$$\mathbf{-2(-3)^4}$$

We note that (-3) was a factor 1 time in the second term, twice in the third term, etc., and, in general, $(n-1)$ times in the nth term. If we use a_1 for the first term and

r for the common ratio, the general expression for the terms in a geometric sequence can be written as

$$\begin{array}{cccccc} ① & ② & ③ & ④ & & (n) \\ a_1, & a_1r, & a_1r^2, & a_1r^3, & \ldots, & a_1r^{n-1} \end{array}$$

and the general expression for the nth term is

$$\boldsymbol{a_n = a_1r^{n-1}}$$

Example 73.A.2 Find three geometric means between 4 and 64.

Solution Making a diagram of the problem enhances understanding and makes memorizing formulas unnecessary. We know that the first term is 4 and the last term is 64.

$$\begin{array}{ccccc} ① & ② & ③ & ④ & ⑤ \\ 4, & \_\_, & \_\_, & \_\_, & 64 \\ a_1, & a_1r, & a_1r^2, & a_1r^3, & a_1r^4 \end{array}$$

We can get one equation (a) from the first terms and one equation (b) from the fifth terms.

$$(a)\quad a_1 = 4 \qquad (b)\quad a_1r^4 = 64$$

Now we use substitution and solve for r.

$$\begin{aligned} (4)r^4 &= 64 && \text{substituted} \\ r^4 &= 16 && \text{divided by 4} \\ r &= \pm 2 && \text{root of both sides} \end{aligned}$$

If $r = 2$, our sequence is

4, <u>8</u>, <u>16</u>, <u>32</u>, 64

If $r = -2$, our sequence is

4, <u>−8</u>, <u>16</u>, <u>−32</u>, 64

and the three geometric means are underlined in each sequence.

Example 73.A.3 Find two geometric means between 2 and $\frac{1}{4}$.

Solution We begin by drawing a diagram of the problem.

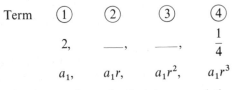

$$\begin{array}{ccccc} \text{Term} & ① & ② & ③ & ④ \\ & 2, & \_\_, & \_\_, & \frac{1}{4} \\ & a_1, & a_1r, & a_1r^2, & a_1r^3 \end{array}$$

This time the first equation comes from the first terms and the other equation comes from the fourth terms.

$$(a)\quad a_1 = 2 \qquad (b)\quad a_1r^3 = \frac{1}{4}$$

We use substitution to solve. Since $a_1 = 2$ and $a_1r^3 = \frac{1}{4}$:

$$\begin{aligned} 2r^3 &= \frac{1}{4} && \text{substitution} \\ r^3 &= \frac{1}{8} && \text{divided by 2} \\ r &= \frac{1}{2} && \text{root of both sides} \end{aligned}$$

The cube root of a positive number is a positive number, so there is only one possible common ratio. Thus, our sequence is

$$\mathbf{2, \underline{1}, \underline{\tfrac{1}{2}}, \tfrac{1}{4}}$$

and the two geometric means are underlined.

Example 73.A.4 Find three geometric means between -16 and -1.

Solution We begin with a diagram of the problem.

①	②	③	④	⑤
-16,	____,	____,	____,	-1
-16,	$-16r$,	$-16r^2$,	$-16r^3$,	$-16r^4$

From the first and fifth terms we see that $a_1 = -16$ and $a_1r^4 = -1$. We combine these equations to get our basic equation.

$$-16r^4 = -1 \qquad \text{equation}$$

$$r^4 = \frac{1}{16} \qquad \text{divided by 16}$$

$$r = \pm\frac{1}{2} \qquad \text{root of both sides}$$

If $r = \frac{1}{2}$, the sequence is

$$\mathbf{-16, \underline{-8}, \underline{-4}, \underline{-2}, -1}$$

If $r = -\frac{1}{2}$, the sequence is

$$\mathbf{-16, \underline{8}, \underline{-4}, \underline{2}, -1}$$

and the geometric means are underlined in each sequence.

Problem set 73

1. When the snow melted, they began to increase exponentially. They began with 30, and in 3 months their number had increased to 900. Find A_0 and k and write the exponential equation that gives the number present as a function of time. Sketch the graph.

2. Initially the mass was 42 grams. After 10 years only 7 grams remained. Assume exponential decay and write the equation that gives the mass remaining as a function of time. How long did it take for the mass to decrease to 30 grams? Sketch the graph.

3. It was exactly 8 o'clock. How long did Mary and Teddy have to wait until the hands of the clock pointed in the same direction?

4. Beaver lost one-eighth of his marbles and then 5000 marbles fell into a hole. Next, half the rest got mislaid so he had only 4500 left. How many marbles did he have when he began?

5. One pipe can fill one cistern in 20 hours and another pipe can fill one cistern in 30 hours. How long will it take to fill one cistern if both pipes are used?

6. A fair die is rolled 3 times. What is the probability of getting a 2, a 5, and a number greater than 2, in that order?

7. Develop an identity for sin $2A$.

8. Develop an identity for cos $\frac{1}{2}A$.

9. Find the sixth term of a geometric sequence whose first term is -4 and whose common ratio is -2.

10. Find two geometric means between 4 and 108.

11. Find three geometric means between 2 and 32.

12. Write an equation of the ellipse with vertices at $(\pm 6, 0)$ and with foci at $(\pm 2, 0)$. Write the equation in standard form.

13. Write an equation of an ellipse whose center is the origin and whose major axis is vertical with length 14 and whose minor axis has length 10. Write the equation in general form.

14. Find the first four terms of the arithmetic sequence whose first term is 6 and whose tenth term is -30.

15. Find $\cos 105°$ by using sum and difference identities and the fact that $105° = 45° + 60°$. Use exact values.

16. Find $\cos 15°$ by using the half-angle identity for $\cos \frac{1}{2}x$ and setting $x = 30°$. Use decimal approximations.

Solve the following equations given that $(0° \leq y, \theta < 360°)$:

17. $2 \sin^2 y - 9 \cos y + 3 = 0$

18. $\sqrt{3} + 2 \cos 3\theta = 0$

Show that:

19. $\dfrac{1 - \cos^2 \theta}{1 + \tan^2 \theta} = \sin^2 \theta \cos^2 \theta$

20. $\csc^2 y \sec^2 y - \sec^2 y = \csc^2 y$

21. Solve this triangle for a and b.

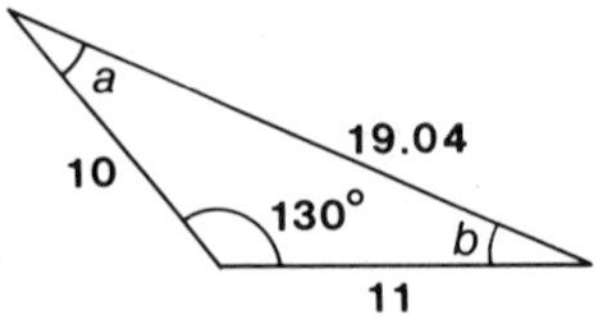

22. Given $\overline{BD} \| \overline{CE}$, show that $\dfrac{AB}{BC} = \dfrac{AD}{DE}$.

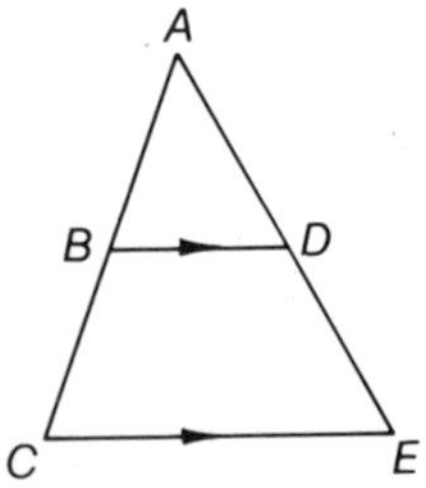

23. Find the length of m.

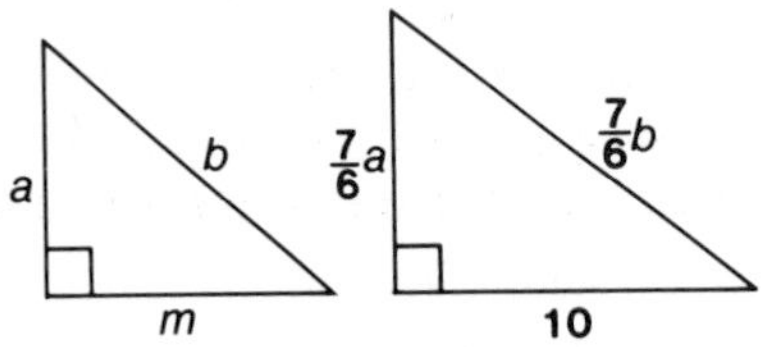

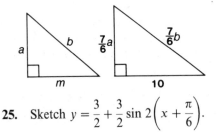

24. Find a, b, and h.

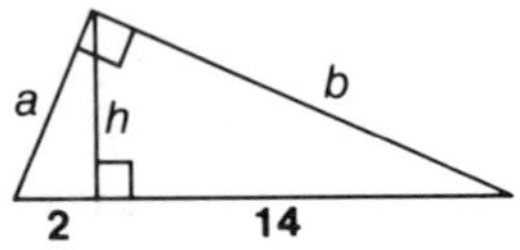

25. Sketch $y = \dfrac{3}{2} + \dfrac{3}{2} \sin 2\left(x + \dfrac{\pi}{6}\right)$.

26. The perimeter of a regular hexagon (6-sided regular polygon) is 48 inches. What is the radius of the circle which can be circumscribed about the hexagon?

Solve:

27. $16^{3x-4} = 4^{2x+1}$

28. $\ln (2x - 3) - \ln 3x = \frac{2}{3} \ln 27$

29. Find the base 4 antilogarithm of -2.

30. Given $M = b^a$ and $N = b^c$, show that $\log_b \dfrac{M}{N} = \log_b M - \log_b N$.

EP 73.19

LESSON 74 *Proofs of congruence*

74.A Proofs of congruence

Congruent polygons are similar polygons whose scale factor is 1. Thus, the corresponding angles in congruent polygons have the same measures, and corresponding sides have the same lengths. To show that two triangles are congruent triangles, we show that they are similar triangles (AAA, SSS, SAS, or HL) and then show that two corresponding sides are equal because this tells us that the scale factor is 1. The statement of the problem will sometimes ask that we prove triangles to be congruent and sometimes ask that we prove that two sides are the same length. Proofs may be in paragraph form or in two-column form. In this book, we will concentrate on paragraph proofs. We will show both a paragraph proof and a two-column proof for the following example. **The proofs in the answers in the back of the book are proof outlines and are not necessarily complete.**

Example 74.A.1 Given: $\overline{RP}$ bisects $\angle QRS$ and $\angle QPS$.
Prove: $RQ = RS$.

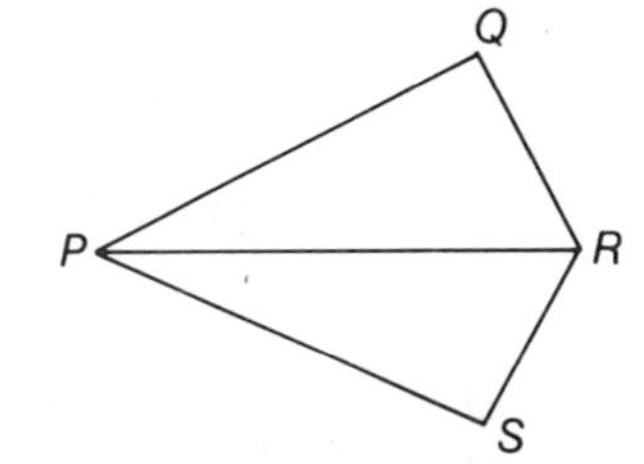

Solution **We want to prove that the lengths of two sides are equal, so we look for two triangles that can be proved to be congruent.** We begin by copying the figure and using tick marks to indicate equal angles. Two pairs of angles are marked equal, so the third pair is also equal. Thus the triangles are similar. We are careful to keep the vertices in order when we write the statement of similarity.

$$\triangle PRQ \sim \triangle PRS$$

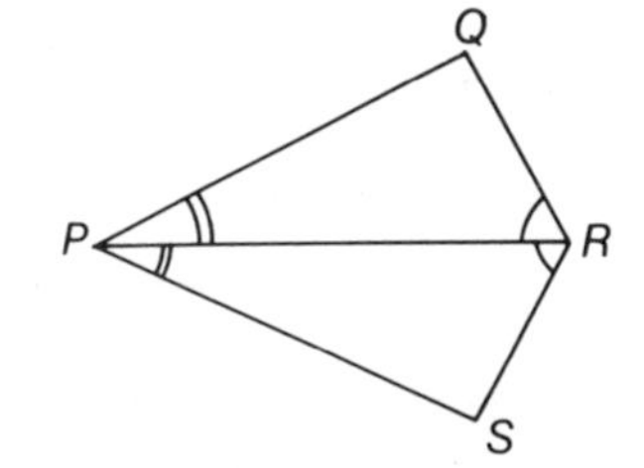

The side PR in one triangle corresponds to side PR in the other triangle, so the scale factor is 1 and the triangles are congruent. We use the symbol $\cong$ to denote congruence.

$$\triangle P\underline{RQ} \cong \triangle P\underline{RS}$$

Thus RQ equals RS because they are the lengths of corresponding sides of congruent triangles. Now we will do the same proof again using the two-column format. The statement is given in the left column and the reason is given in the right column.

STATEMENTS	REASONS
$\angle QPR = \angle SPR$	bisected by RP
$\angle PRQ = \angle PRS$	bisected by RP
$\angle PQR = \angle PSR$	If two angles of one triangle equal two angles of another triangle, the third angles are equal.
$\triangle PQR \sim \triangle PSR$	AAA
$PR = PR$	equals itself
Scale factor = 1	PR and PR corresponding parts
$\triangle PQR \cong \triangle PSR$	similar and scale factor of 1
$RQ = RS$	CPCTE

We know that corresponding parts of congruent triangles have equal measures. The notation CPCTE in the last step is made up of the first letters of the words "*corresponding parts congruent triangles equal.*"

Example 74.A.2 Given: $AO = CO$; $DO = BO$. Prove: $AD = CB$.

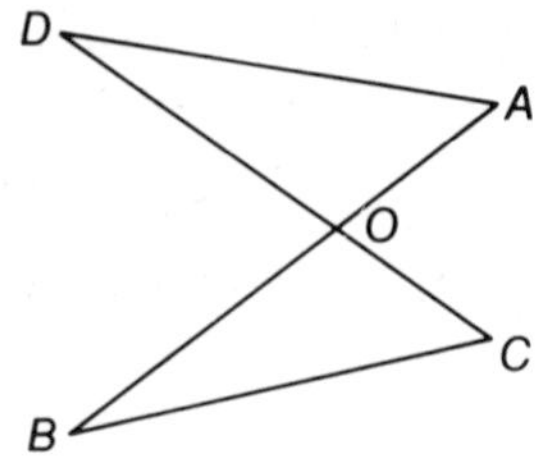

Solution We want to prove that $AD = CB$, so we begin by copying the figure and using tick marks to indicate equal values. The vertical angles are equal and the triangles are similar by side-angle-side with a scale factor of 1. We write the statement of congruence and are careful to list corresponding vertices in the same order.

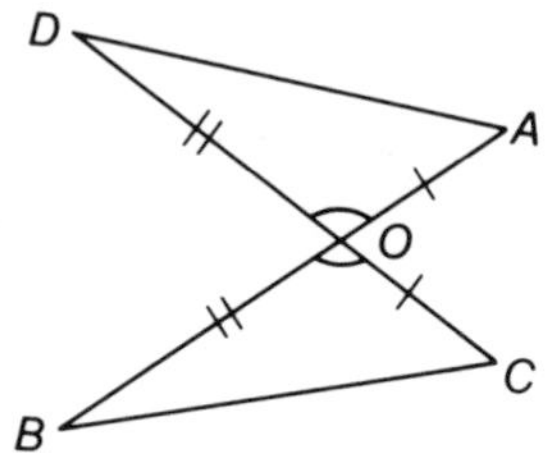

$$\triangle \underline{A}O\underline{D} \cong \triangle \underline{C}O\underline{B}$$

We note in this statement that AD and CB are corresponding sides and thus are equal. For this example, we will do only a paragraph proof.

We are given that side OD equals side OB and side OC equals side OA. The vertical angles DOA and BOC are equal, and the sides of the angles have equal lengths and thus are proportional. Thus, $\triangle DOA \sim \triangle BOC$ by SAS. Since corresponding sides AO and CO are equal, we again note that the scale factor is 1. Thus $\triangle DOA \cong \triangle BOC$ and $DA = CB$ by CPCTE.

Example 74.A.3 Given: $\overline{WX} \perp \overline{UV}$; $UX = VX$. Prove: $UW = WV$.

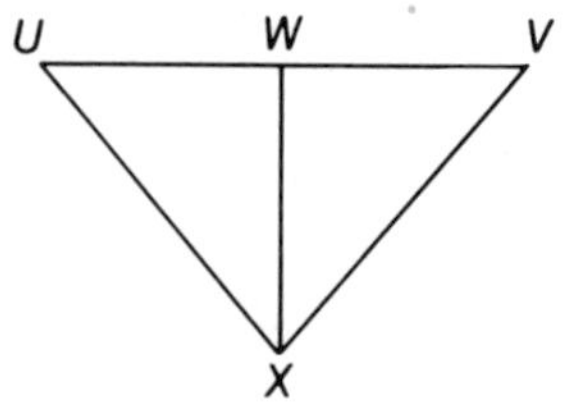

Solution The perpendicular lines form right angles. We copy the figure and indicate equal values. $UX = VX$ and side WX is common, so the right triangles are similar by HL, $\triangle UWX \sim \triangle VWX$. Since corresponding sides WX of $\triangle UWX$ and WX of $\triangle VWX$ are equal, we again note that the scale factor is 1. Thus $\triangle UWX \cong \triangle VWX$ and $UW = WV$ by CPCTE.

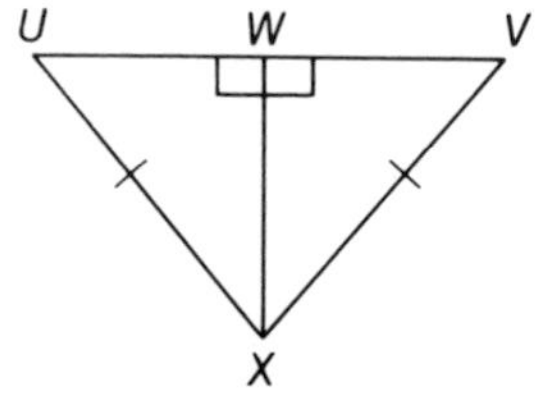

STATEMENT	REASON
$\angle UWX = \angle VWX = 90°$	perpendicular lines form right angles
$UX = VX$	given
$\triangle UWX \sim \triangle VWX$	HL
$WX = WX$	equals itself
$\triangle UWX \cong \triangle VWX$	scale factor is 1
$UW = WV$	CPCTE

In the following example, we see that the figure has three dimensions but recognize that two triangles lie in the same plane.

Example 74.A.4 Given: $\overline{PA}$ and $\overline{QB}$ are perpendicular to plane X; O is the midpoint of $\overline{AB}$; O is the midpoint of $\overline{PQ}$. Prove: $PA = QB$.

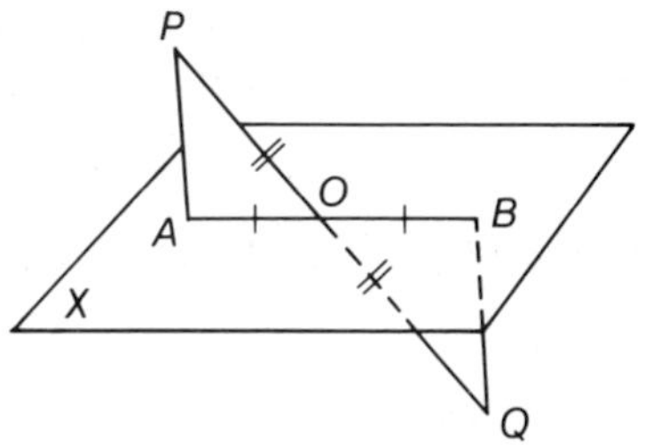

Solution To prove that segments are equal in length requires the proof that $\triangle PAO \cong \triangle QBO$. The triangles are right triangles and the vertical angles at O are equal, so the triangles are similar by AAA. Since $OP = OQ$ and $OA = OB$ by the definition of the midpoint, the lengths of corresponding sides are proportional with a scale factor of 1. Hence the triangles are congruent. Thus, $PA = QB$ because CPCTE.

Problem set 74

1. The substance decayed exponentially. Initially there were 500 grams, but after 100 days only 100 grams remained. Write the exponential equation that gives the mass of the substance as a function of time, and find out how long it would be until 50 grams remained.

2. The fleas increased exponentially. There were only 10 fleas at the outset, but by the end of 3 years there were 2000 fleas. How many fleas would there be 6 years from the outset?

3. All the money was in the pot. Scylla removed \$2 and then removed one-sixth of what was left. Then Charybdis removed one-half of what remained, and now only \$9 remained in the pot. How many dollars had been in the pot in the beginning?

4. The units digit of a two-digit counting number is 2 greater than the tens digit. If the number is increased by 6 and then divided by the sum of the digits, the quotient is 5. What is the number?

5. Fourteen workers could do M jobs in K days. The production supervisor thought this was too slow, and hired 7 more workers. How long would it take the new work force to do F jobs?

6. Given that $\overline{AD}$ bisects $\angle BAC$ and $\angle BDC$, prove $AB = AC$.

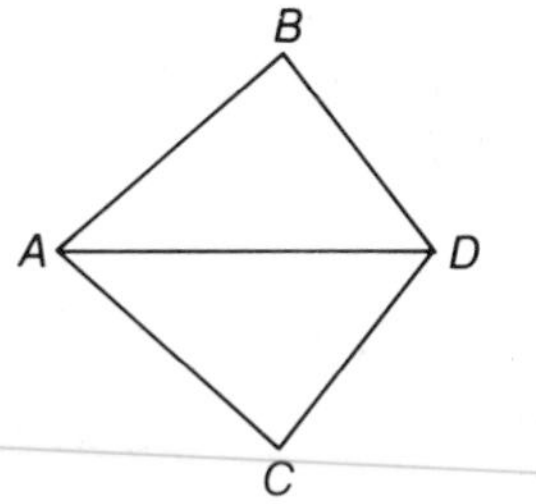

7. Given that $AO = CO$ and $DO = BO$, prove $\angle DAO = \angle OCB$.

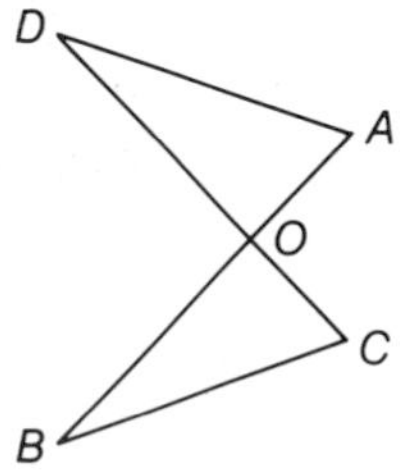

8. Given $\overline{WX} \perp \overline{UV}$, $UW = WV$, prove $UX = XV$.

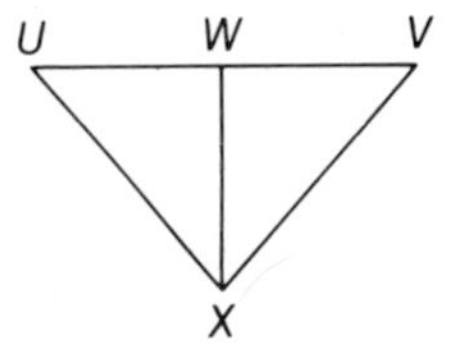

9. Begin with the identities for sin $2A$ and cos $2A$, and develop an identity for tan $2A$.

10. Begin with cos $(A + B)$ and develop the identity for cos $\frac{1}{2}A$.

11. Find the fifth term of a geometric sequence whose first term is -3 and whose common ratio is -2.

12. Find the distance from $(-1, 0)$ to $x - y = 1$.

13. Write an equation in standard form of the ellipse whose vertices are $(0, \pm 5)$ and whose foci are $(0, \pm 2)$.

14. Write the equation in general form of an ellipse whose center is the origin, whose major axis is horizontal of length 16, and whose minor axis has a length of 8.

15. Find the first three terms of the arithmetic sequence whose tenth term is 52 and whose fifteenth term is 82.

16. Find $\tan 105°$ by using the identity for $\tan(A + B)$ and the fact that $105° = 60° + 45°$. Use exact values.

17. Find $\cos 15°$ by using the identity for $\cos \frac{1}{2}x$. Use decimal approximations.

Solve the following equations given that $(0° \le x, \theta < 360°)$:

18. $\tan^2 x - \sec x - 5 = 0$

19. $\sqrt{3} - \tan 4\theta = 0$

Show that:

20. $\dfrac{1 - \sin^2 \theta}{1 + \cot^2 \theta} = \cos^2 \theta \sin^2 \theta$

21. $\sin^2 x \sec^2 x + \sin^2 x \csc^2 x = \sec^2 x$

22. Solve this triangle for a.

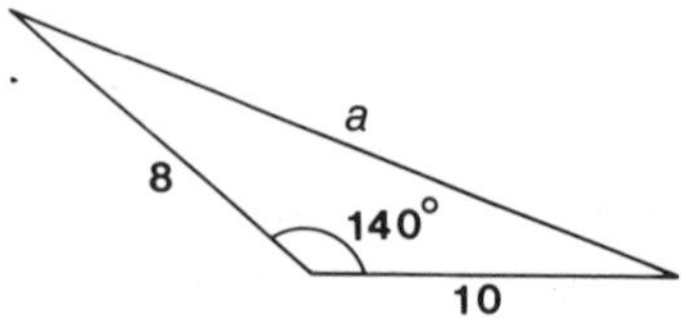

23. Find the length of a given that $\angle A = \angle D$.

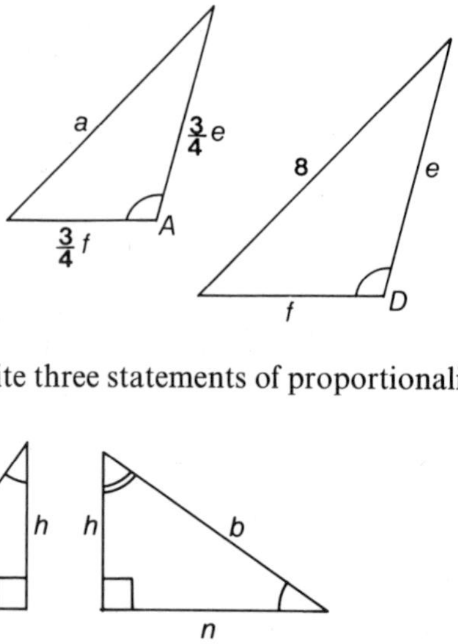

24. The two small right triangles are similar. Write three statements of proportionality.

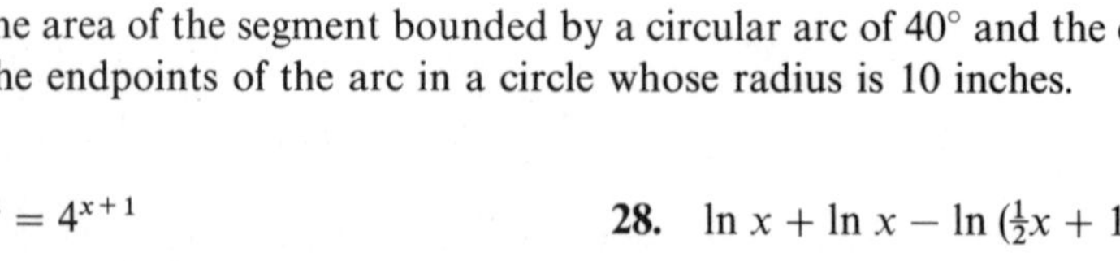

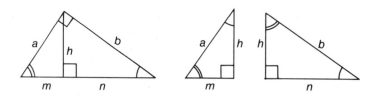

25. Sketch $y = -3 + 2 \cos 3(x - 70°)$.

26. Find the area of the segment bounded by a circular arc of 40° and the chord which joins the endpoints of the arc in a circle whose radius is 10 inches.

Solve:

27. $16^{2x+2} = 4^{x+1}$

28. $\ln x + \ln x - \ln (\frac{1}{2}x + 1) = \ln 2$

29. Find the antilogarithm base 3 of -2.

30. Given $M = b^a$, show that $\log_b M^x = x \log_b M$.

EP 74.20, 74.21

LESSON 75 *Probability of either · Notations for permutations and combinations*

75.A Probability of either

When a coin is flipped and comes up heads, then it does not come up tails. When a red card is drawn from a deck, the card is not black. When a white marble is drawn from an urn, the marble is not green. These events are called ***mutually exclusive events*** because when one event occurs, the other event is excluded or cannot occur. The probability of either of two mutually exclusive events occurring is the sum of the individual probabilities. If we have 3 red marbles, 4 blue marbles, and 6 white marbles in an urn, the probability of drawing a red marble is $\frac{3}{13}$. The probability of drawing a blue marble is $\frac{4}{13}$, and the probability of drawing a white marble is $\frac{6}{13}$.

The probability of drawing a marble that is either red or blue is $\frac{7}{13}$.

$$P(R \text{ or } B) = P(R) + P(B) = \frac{3}{13} + \frac{4}{13} = \frac{7}{13}$$

We often use the word **union** instead of using the word **or,** and we use the symbol $\cup$ to stand for union. Thus,

$$P(R \text{ or } B) = P(R \text{ union } B) = P(R \cup B)$$

In the same way, we often use the word **intersection** instead of using the word **both,** and we invert the union symbol $\cap$ to designate intersection.

$$P(\text{both } R \text{ and } B) = P(R \text{ intersect } B) = P(R \cap B)$$

The probability for both is always zero for mutually exclusive events, as we see in the diagram above, for a marble cannot be both red and blue at the same time.

Some events are not mutually exclusive. As an example, we consider the case of 7 boys and 4 redheads. If we ask for the number who are either boys or who are redheaded, the number is not necessarily 11 because if some of the boys are redheaded, we would have counted them twice. This Venn diagram demonstrates the case of 2 redheaded boys and shows a total of 9 people who either are boys or are redheaded.

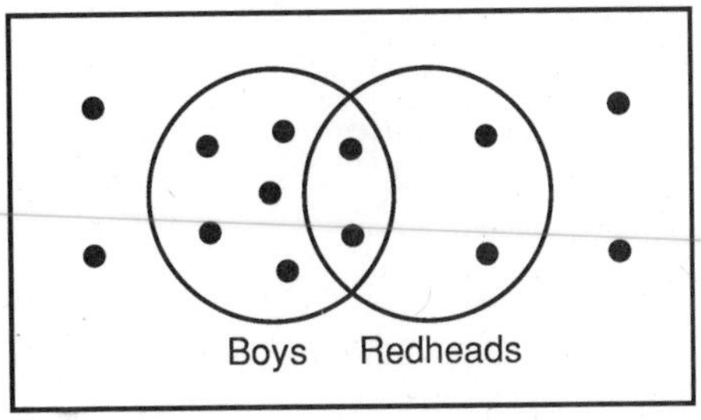

The diagram shows that the events are not mutually exclusive, and the number who either are boys or are redheaded is not the sum of the number of boys and the number of redheads because this procedure counts the redheaded boys twice. To correct for this, we must subtract the number of redheaded boys.

$$N(\text{boys or redheads}) = N(\text{boys}) + N(\text{redheads}) - N(\text{redheaded boys})$$

If we select one person blindly from the above grouping, the probability of a boy is $\frac{7}{13}$, the probability of a redhead is $\frac{4}{13}$, and the probability of a redheaded boy is $\frac{2}{13}$. From this example, we can see that **the probability of a person being either redheaded or a boy is**

$$P(R \cup B) = P(R) + P(B) - P(R \cap B)$$

because we must not consider the redheaded boys twice.

Example 75.A.1 A card is drawn from a full deck. What is the probability that the card is an ace or a black card?

Solution We must not count the two black aces twice, so if A means ace and B means black,

$$P(A \cup B) = P(A) + P(B) - P(B \cap A)$$

$$= \frac{4}{52} + \frac{26}{52} - \frac{2}{52} = \mathbf{\frac{7}{13}}$$

Example 75.A.2 An urn contains 4 white balls and 3 black balls. Two of the white balls are rough and one of the black balls is rough. What is the probability of drawing a ball that is either rough or white?

Solution We must not count the rough white balls twice.

$$P(R \cup W) = P(R) + P(W) - P(R \cap W)$$

$$= \frac{3}{7} + \frac{4}{7} - \frac{2}{7} = \mathbf{\frac{5}{7}}$$

75.B Notations for permutations and combinations

Most books begin the study of permutations and combinations by introducing the following formulas

$${}_nP_r = \frac{n!}{(n-r)!} \qquad {}_nC_r = \frac{n!}{r!(n-r)!}$$

Students are sometimes confused by these notations, and think that they are possibly magic notations that will produce the desired answers. We have delayed the introduction of these notations because they are just a concise way to write what we have been doing and add little to our ability to solve problems.

Example 75.B.1 Take the permutations and the combinations of 7 things taken 3 at a time to do a concrete development of the notations for n things taken r at a time.

Solution The number of permutations of 7 things taken 3 at a time is $7 \cdot 6 \cdot 5$.

$${}_7P_3 = 7 \cdot 6 \cdot 5$$

To use a factorial notation for this problem, we can multiply above and below by 4 factorial and get

$${}_7P_3 = \frac{(7 \cdot 6 \cdot 5) \cdot 4!}{4!}$$

$$= \frac{7!}{4!}$$

But 4 equals 7 − 3, and if we make this replacement, we get

$${}_7P_3 = \frac{7!}{(7-3)!}$$

Now we can get a general expression for ${}_nP_r$ by replacing 7 with n and replacing 3 with r.

$${}_nP_r = \frac{n!}{(n-r)!}$$

To find the combination of 7 things taken 3 at a time, we would divide by 3! to remove the effect of order in the combinations. We show this below on the left. On the right we replace 7 with n and replace 3 with r to write the general expression for the combination of n things taken r at a time.

$${}_7C_3 = \frac{7!}{3!(7-3)!} \qquad {}_nC_r = \frac{n!}{r!(n-r)!}$$

Problem set 75

1. The number who succeeded varied linearly with the number who tried. When 10 tried, 8 succeeded, but when 20 tried, the number of successes rose to 13. How many succeeded when only 8 tried?

2. Under the onslaught of the horde of kids, the pile of cookies decreased exponentially. They decreased from 10,000 to 9000 in only 40 minutes. Write an exponential equation which expresses cookies as a function of time. What is the half-life of the pile of cookies?

3. The number who wanted increased exponentially with the time. In the beginning, only 100 wanted. After 6 months there were 1000 who wanted. Write the exponential equation which expresses the number who wanted as a function of time and find how long it will take for 2000 to want.

4. A card is drawn from a full deck of 52 cards. What is the probability the card drawn will be either a king or a black card?

5. Take the permutations and combinations of 8 things taken 5 at a time to do a concrete development of the expressions for ${}_nP_r$ and ${}_nC_r$.

6. Given that $AB = AC$ and $BD = DC$, prove that $\overline{AD}$ bisects $\angle BAC$ and $\angle BDC$.

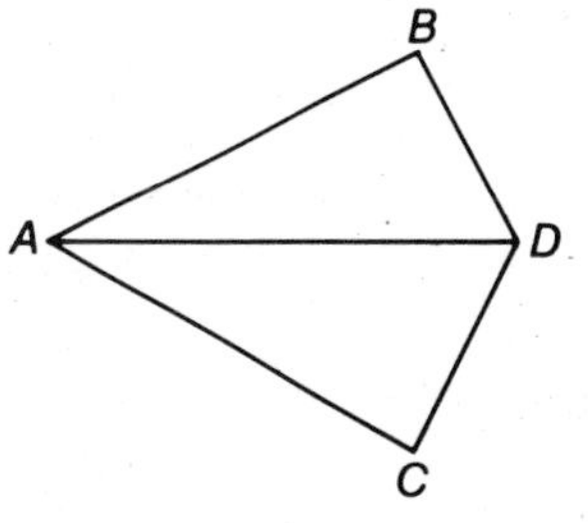

7. Given that $AO = CO$ and $DO = BO$, prove $AD = BC$.

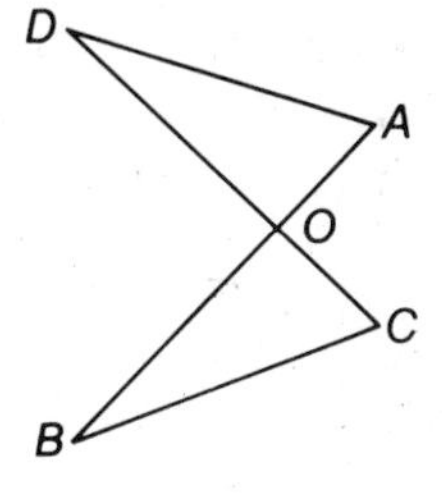

8. Given $UX = VX$ and $\angle UXW = \angle VXW$, prove that $\angle UWX = \angle VWX$.

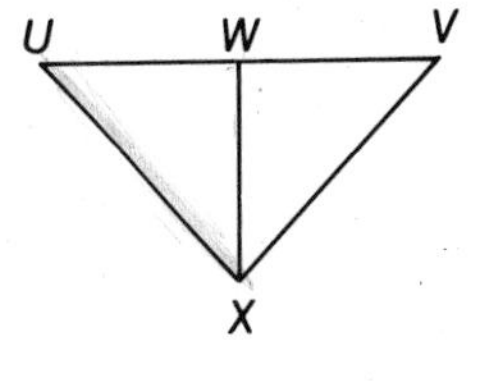

9. Begin with the identity for $\cos(A + B)$ and develop the identity for $\sin \frac{1}{2}A$.

10. Write the four fourth roots of 16 cis 120° in rectangular form. Give exact answers.

11. Find the fourth term of a geometric sequence whose first term is 2 and whose common ratio is $-1/2$.

12. Find two geometric means between 2 and -16.

13. Write an equation in standard form of an ellipse whose center is the origin, whose major axis is vertical of length 10, and whose minor axis is 8 units long.

14. Describe the hyperbola whose equation is $16x^2 - 25y^2 = 400$ and find the equations of the asymptotes.

15. Find the first four terms of the arithmetic sequence whose fourth term is -2 and whose tenth term is 10.

16. Find sin 15° by using the identity for $\sin \frac{1}{2}x$. Use decimal approximations.

17. Use the sum identities as required to find an expression for $\cos\left(x + \frac{\pi}{2}\right)$.

Solve the following equations given that ($0° \le \theta < 360°$):

18. $\tan^2 \theta - \sec \theta - 1 = 0$

19. $\sin 5\theta = 0$

Show that:

20. $\dfrac{\sin^4 \theta - \cos^4 \theta}{\sin^2 \theta - \cos^2 \theta} = 1$

21. $\dfrac{\sec^2 x}{\sec^2 x - 1} = \csc^2 x$

22. Solve this triangle for angles A and B.

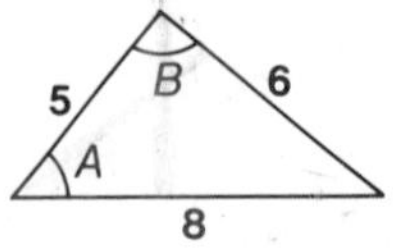

23. Find the length of c.

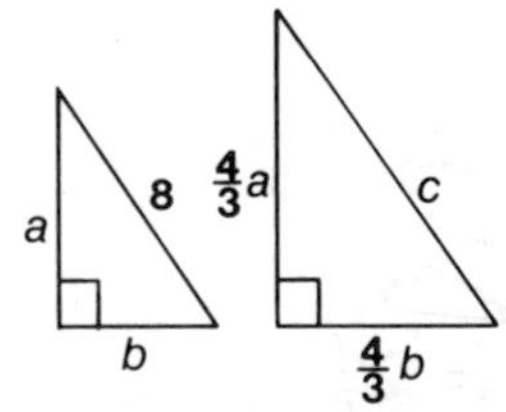

24. Find the lengths of a and b.

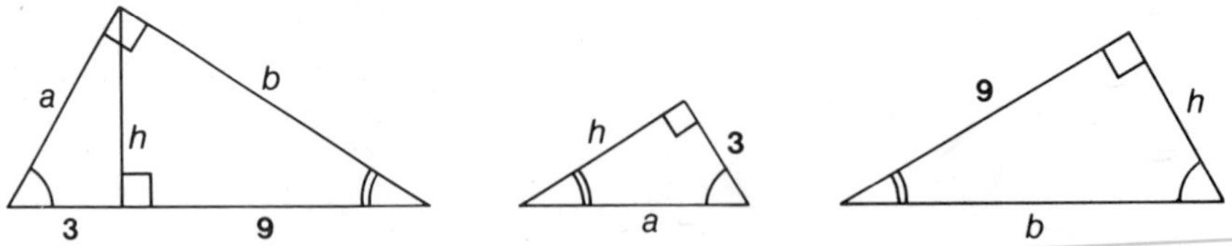

25. Sketch $y = -3 + 5 \cos \frac{1}{2}\left(x - \frac{3}{2}\pi\right)$.

26. The perimeter of a 10-sided regular polygon (regular decagon) is 40 cm. Find the area of this decagon.

Solve:

27. $16^{3x-2} = 2^{4x-1}$

28. $\frac{2}{3} \log_7 8 - \log_7 (x - 1) = 1$

29. Evaluate: $8^{2 \log_8 4 - \log_8 3}$

30. Find the base 4 antilogarithm of -2.

EP 75.22, 75.23

LESSON 76 Advanced trigonometric identities · Proof of the Pythagorean theorem · Triangle inequalities

76.A Advanced trigonometric identities

Many trigonometric identities can be simplified by manipulations that spring from insight or game-playing ability. This ability will increase as more of these problems are worked and as successful thought patterns are practiced.

Example 76.A.1 Show that $\dfrac{1+\sin B}{\cos B} = \dfrac{\cos B}{1-\sin B}$.

Solution We look at cos B on the left and note that if it were $\cos^2 B$, we could replace it with $1 - \sin^2 B$, which can be factored. To get $\cos^2 B$ on the bottom, we multiply above and below by cos B.

$$\frac{\cos B}{\cos B}\cdot\frac{1+\sin B}{\cos B} \longrightarrow \frac{(\cos B)(1+\sin B)}{\cos^2 B}$$

Now we can replace $\cos^2 B$ with $1 - \sin^2 B$.

$$\frac{(\cos B)(1+\sin B)}{1-\sin^2 B}$$

We finish by factoring $1 - \sin^2 B$ and canceling.

$$\frac{(\cos B)(1+\sin B)}{(1-\sin B)(1+\sin B)} \longrightarrow \frac{\cos B}{1-\sin B}$$

Example 76.A.2 Show that $\dfrac{\tan B + 1}{\tan B - 1} = \dfrac{\sec B + \csc B}{\sec B - \csc B}$.

Solution These expressions have the same forms. Two terms are above with a + sign and two terms are below with a − sign. The lower left term in the expression on the left is tan B. We can change tan B to sec B by multiplying it by $1/(\sin B)$.

$$\frac{1}{\sin B}\cdot\tan B \longrightarrow \frac{1}{\sin B}\cdot\frac{\sin B}{\cos B} \longrightarrow \frac{1}{\cos B} \longrightarrow \sec B$$

Let's multiply everything on the left side (both top and bottom) by $1/(\sin B)$ and see if we get the desired changes. First we write tan B as $(\sin B)/(\cos B)$.

$$\frac{\left(\dfrac{\sin B}{\cos B}+1\right)\left(\dfrac{1}{\sin B}\right)}{\left(\dfrac{\sin B}{\cos B}-1\right)\left(\dfrac{1}{\sin B}\right)} \longrightarrow \frac{\dfrac{1}{\cos B}+\dfrac{1}{\sin B}}{\dfrac{1}{\cos B}-\dfrac{1}{\sin B}} \longrightarrow \frac{\sec B + \csc B}{\sec B - \csc B}$$

We were able to change the left expression to the desired form by multiplying each part by $1/(\sin B)$.

Example 76.A.3 Show that

$$(x\sin\theta + y\cos\theta)^2 + (x\cos\theta - y\sin\theta)^2 = x^2 + y^2$$

Solution This problem provides practice in squaring binomials that have two variables and also in factoring and recognizing that $\sin^2\theta + \cos^2\theta = 1$. First we multiply out each squared term:

$$\begin{array}{l} x\sin\theta + y\cos\theta \\ x\sin\theta + y\cos\theta \\ \hline x^2\sin^2\theta + xy\sin\theta\cos\theta \\ \qquad\qquad\qquad xy\sin\theta\cos\theta + y^2\cos^2\theta \\ \hline x^2\sin^2\theta + 2xy\sin\theta\cos\theta + y^2\cos^2\theta \end{array}$$

$$\begin{array}{l} x\cos\theta - y\sin\theta \\ x\cos\theta - y\sin\theta \\ \hline x^2\cos^2\theta - xy\sin\theta\cos\theta \\ \qquad\qquad - xy\sin\theta\cos\theta + y^2\sin^2\theta \\ \hline x^2\cos^2\theta - 2xy\sin\theta\cos\theta + y^2\sin^2\theta \end{array}$$

Now we add:

$$\begin{aligned} &(x^2\sin^2\theta + 2xy\sin\theta\cos\theta + y^2\cos^2\theta) + (x^2\cos^2\theta - 2xy\sin\theta\cos\theta + y^2\sin^2\theta) \\ &\quad = x^2\sin^2\theta + y^2\cos^2\theta + x^2\cos^2\theta + y^2\sin^2\theta \\ &\quad = x^2(\sin^2\theta + \cos^2\theta) + y^2(\sin^2\theta + \cos^2\theta) \\ &\quad = x^2 + y^2 \end{aligned}$$

76.B Proof of the Pythagorean theorem

We remember that the perpendicular from the hypotenuse to the right angle in a right triangle forms two smaller triangles that are similar to the original triangle. We use this figure to prove the Pythagorean theorem. On the left we have the big triangle with sides a, b, and c and note that side c can also be written as $m + x$. On the right we break out the two smaller triangles, and orient them so that the corresponding sides in all three triangles are in the same position.

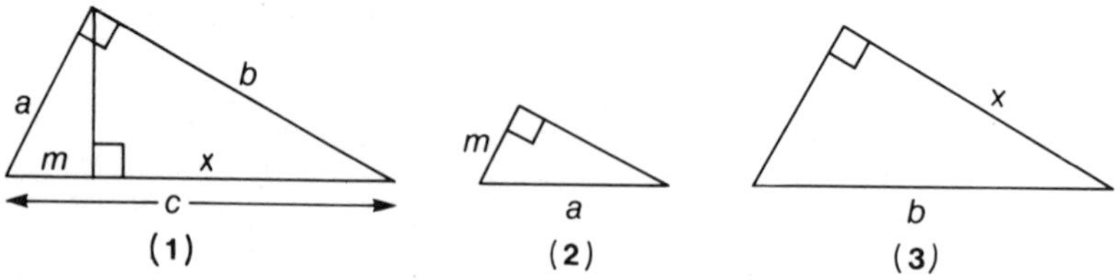

Now on the left below, we equate the ratios of the hypotenuse to the short side in triangle (1) and triangle (2). On the right we equate the ratios of the hypotenuse to the long side in triangle (1) and triangle (3).

$$\frac{c}{a} = \frac{a}{m} \qquad\qquad \frac{c}{b} = \frac{b}{x}$$

Next we cross multiply and get

$$cm = a^2 \qquad\qquad cx = b^2$$

If we add these equations, we get half of what we need.

$$cm + cx = a^2 + b^2$$

Now, on the left-hand side, we factor out c.

$$c(m + x) = a^2 + b^2$$

Then we replace $(m + x)$ with c. Thus the left side becomes c^2 and we have our proof.

$$c(c) = a^2 + b^2 \qquad \text{substituted}$$

$$c^2 = a^2 + b^2 \qquad \text{multiplied}$$

76.C Triangle inequalities

There are several triangle inequalities that should be remembered. They can be justified by inspection and can be proved by using the Pythagorean theorem. In any triangle, the sum of the lengths of any two sides is greater than the length of the third side. We have postulated that the shortest path between two points is the line segment that connects the two points. Thus we have postulated that the shortest path between M and N is segment c, so we can write

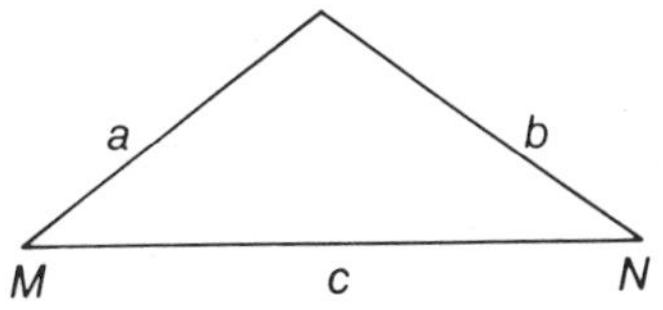

$$c < a + b$$

The other triangle inequalities have to do with the sum of the squares of the lengths of the short sides of a triangle and the square of the length of the longest side of the triangle. On the left below we show right triangle abc. For this triangle, the square of the hypotenuse equals the sum of the squares of the other two sides.

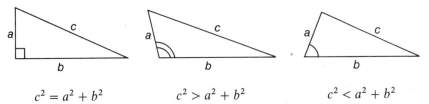

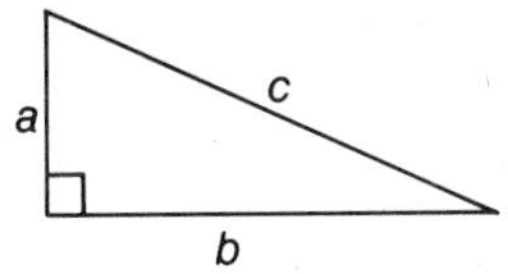

$c^2 = a^2 + b^2$

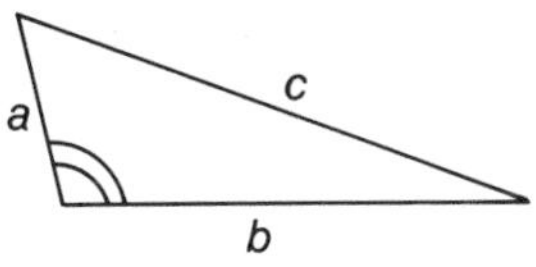

$c^2 > a^2 + b^2$

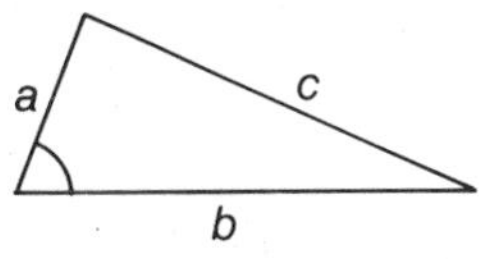

$c^2 < a^2 + b^2$

In the center figure, a and b have the same lengths as before, but the angle formed by a and b is greater than 90°. Thus, c must be longer than the hypotenuse in the right triangle and $c^2 > a^2 + b^2$. In the right figure, a and b have the same lengths as before; but now c is shorter than c in the right triangle, so $c^2 < a^2 + b^2$.

To prove the center inequality shown above, we erect a perpendicular to the base as shown below. Then we use the Pythagorean theorem.

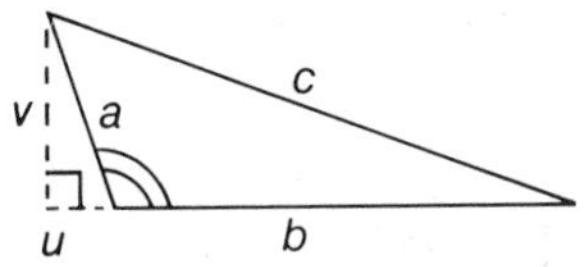

(1)	$c^2 = v^2 + (u + b)^2$	Pyth. thm.
(2)	$c^2 = v^2 + u^2 + 2ub + b^2$	expanded
(3)	$c^2 = a^2 + 2ub + b^2$	substituted
(4)	$c^2 = a^2 + b^2 + 2ub$	rearranged

In step 3 we used the Pythagorean theorem and the small triangle avu to allow us to substitute a^2 for $u^2 + v^2$. From step 4, we see that c^2 is greater than $a^2 + b^2$ by $2ub$. Thus, we are justified in writing for the center triangle

$$c^2 > a^2 + b^2$$

To prove the inequality on the right, we erect a perpendicular as we show here.

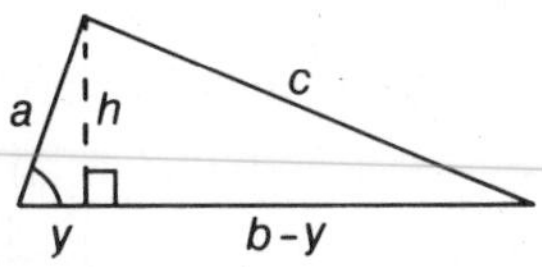

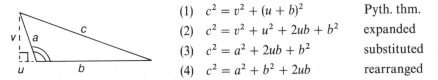

Now we use the Pythagorean theorem on both the small triangles, expand, and add the equations.

$$\begin{array}{rclr}
y^2 + h^2 = a^2 & \longrightarrow & & y^2 + h^2 = a^2 \\
c^2 = h^2 + (b - y)^2 & \longrightarrow & & c^2 = h^2 + b^2 - 2by + y^2 \\
\hline
& & y^2 + h^2 + c^2 = & a^2 + h^2 + b^2 - 2by + y^2
\end{array}$$

Now, if we add $-y^2 - h^2$ to both sides, we get

$$c^2 = a^2 + b^2 - 2by$$

which tells us that c^2 is less than $a^2 + b^2$, so we may write

$$c^2 < a^2 + b^2$$

Example 76.C.1 Is the triangle whose sides are 3, 4, and 5 a right triangle, an acute triangle, or an obtuse triangle?

Solution **If the sum of the squares of the two short sides of a triangle equals the square of the longest side, the triangle is a right triangle. If the sum is less than the square of the longest side, the triangle is an obtuse triangle. If the sum is greater than the square of the longest side, then the triangle is an acute triangle.** In this case, we have

$$3^2 + 4^2 \ ? \ 5^2$$

$$9 + 16 \ ? \ 25$$

$$25 = 25$$

and since the sum equals the square of the long side, the triangle is a **right triangle.**

Example 76.C.2 Classify the triangle whose sides are 4, 7, and 5.

Solution We check the sum of the squares of the two shortest sides.

$$4^2 + 5^2 \ ? \ 7^2$$

$$16 + 25 \ ? \ 49$$

$$41 < 49$$

Since the sum of the squares of the short sides is less than the square of the long side, the triangle is an **obtuse triangle.**

Problem set 76

1. The mother was exasperated because the mess in the kids' room increased exponentially. Only 10 things were out of place at 9 a.m., but 40 minutes later 80 items were out of place. How many items were out of place by 11 a.m.?

2. The sample of the compound disintegrated exponentially. In the beginning there was 400 grams of it in the beaker, but 30 hours later only 300 grams remained. Write an exponential equation which expresses the mass of the compound as a function of time and find the half-life of the compound.

3. Diogenes held his lantern high so he could see clearly. It was between 4 and 5 o'clock, and the big hand was exactly 5 minutes ahead of the little hand. What time was it?

4. There are 4 green marbles and 5 white marbles in an urn. Two of the green marbles have red spots and 3 of the white marbles have red spots. What is the probability of selecting a marble that is green or a marble that has red spots?

5. Take the permutations and combinations of 9 things taken 6 at a time to do a concrete development of the expressions for ${}_nP_r$ and ${}_nC_r$.

6. Prove the Pythagorean theorem, using the figures shown below.

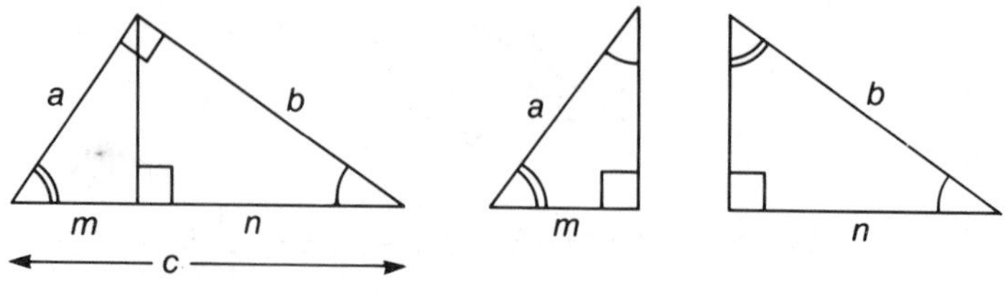

7. Given $AD \perp BC$ and AD bisects $\overline{BC}$, prove that $AB = AC$.

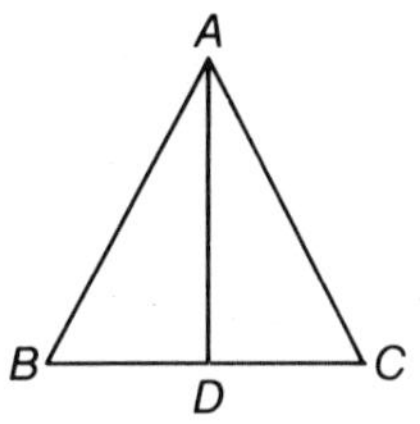

8. Given AD bisects $\angle BAC$ and $AB = AC$, prove $BD = DC$.

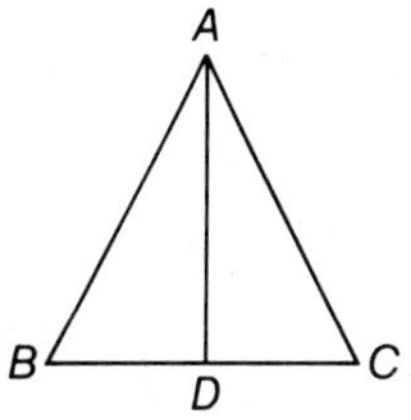

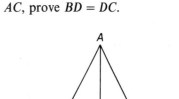

9. Given $AO = CO$ and $BO = DO$, prove that $\angle OAB = \angle OCD$.

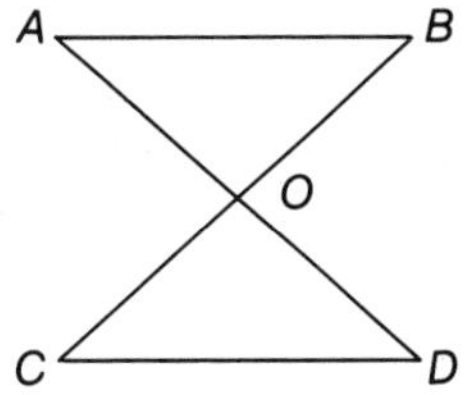

10. Begin with the identity for $\cos(A + B)$, and develop the identity for $\cos 2A$.

11. Write the five fifth roots of 32 cis 20° in polar form.

12. Find three geometric means between 2 and 162.

13. Write the general form of the equation of an ellipse whose center is the origin, whose major axis is vertical of length 8, and whose minor axis has a length of 6.

14. Find the coordinates of the vertices and the equations of the asymptotes of the hyperbola whose equation is $9x^2 - 4y^2 = 36$.

15. Find the first four terms of the arithmetic sequence whose fifth term is 12 and whose thirteenth term is -4.

16. Find sin 285° by using the identity for $\sin(A + B)$ and the fact that $285° = 240° + 45°$. Use decimal approximations.

17. Use a difference identity to find an expression for $\sin\left(x - \frac{\pi}{4}\right)$. Use exact values.

Solve the following equations given that $(0° \leq x < 360°)$:

18. $2\sin^2 x + 7\cos x + 2 = 0$

19. $\sqrt{3}\cot 3x + 1 = 0$

Show that:

20. $\dfrac{1 + \sin B}{\cos B} = \dfrac{\cos B}{1 - \sin B}$

21. $\dfrac{\tan B + 1}{\tan B - 1} = \dfrac{\sec B + \csc B}{\sec B - \csc B}$

22. $(y\sin\theta + x\cos\theta)^2 + (y\cos\theta - x\sin\theta)^2 = x^2 + y^2$

23. Solve this triangle for side a.

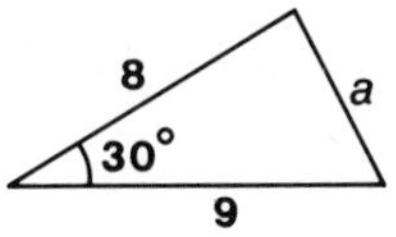

24. Find the length of d.

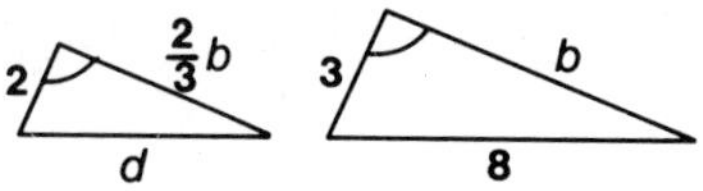

25. Sketch $y = -3 + 5\cos\frac{1}{2}\left(x - \frac{3\pi}{2}\right)$.

26. What is the sum of the interior angles of a 10-sided convex polygon?

Solve:

27. $27^{2x+3} = 3^{x-4}$

28. $\frac{3}{4}\log_8 16 + \log_8 (3x - 2) = 2$

29. Find the base 6 antilogarithm of -2.

30. Given $M = b^a$ and $N = b^c$, show that $\log_b MN = \log_b M + \log_b N$.

EP 76.24, 76.25

> If the enrichment lessons are being included, the third enrichment lesson should be taught next and should be followed with Lesson 77.

LESSON 77 Graphs of secant and cosecant · Graphs of tangent and cotangent

77.A Graphs of secant and cosecant

The sine function and the cosine function are periodic functions, and their graphs are especially useful. The graphs are continuous, and have values for every input value of the independent variable. The cosecant function and the secant function are the reciprocal functions of the sine function and the cosine function, and thus are also periodic functions. Their graphs are not as useful and are seldom encountered because the cosecant and the secant are undefined at values of θ where the sine and cosine have a value of zero. The graphs of these functions are unique and are easily identified because the graphs look like a series of equally spaced U's that alternately open up and down. The equations of these functions can be written with no difficulty if we first sketch and identify the sinusoid which can be drawn by using the given graphs as guides, as we show in the following examples.

Example 77.A.1 Write the equations of these trigonometric functions.

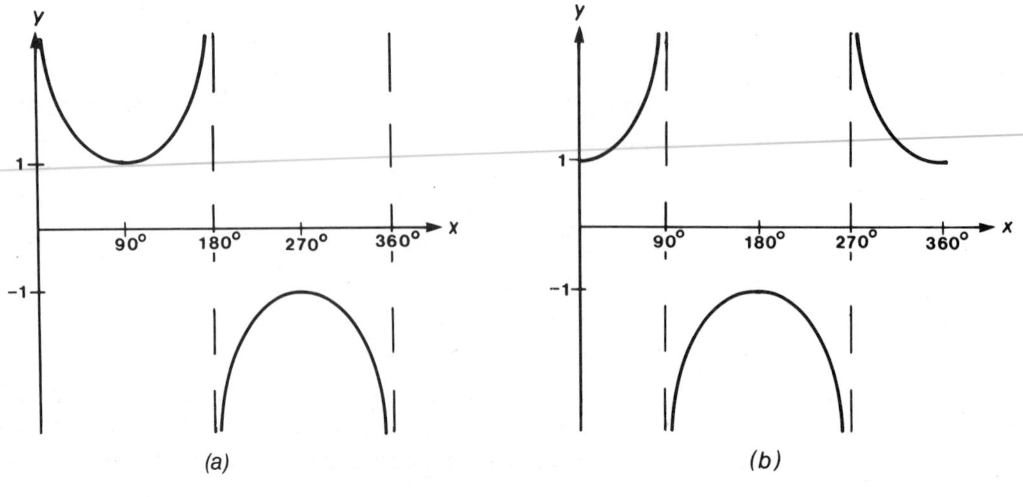

Solution As the first step, we will sketch and identify the sinusoids.

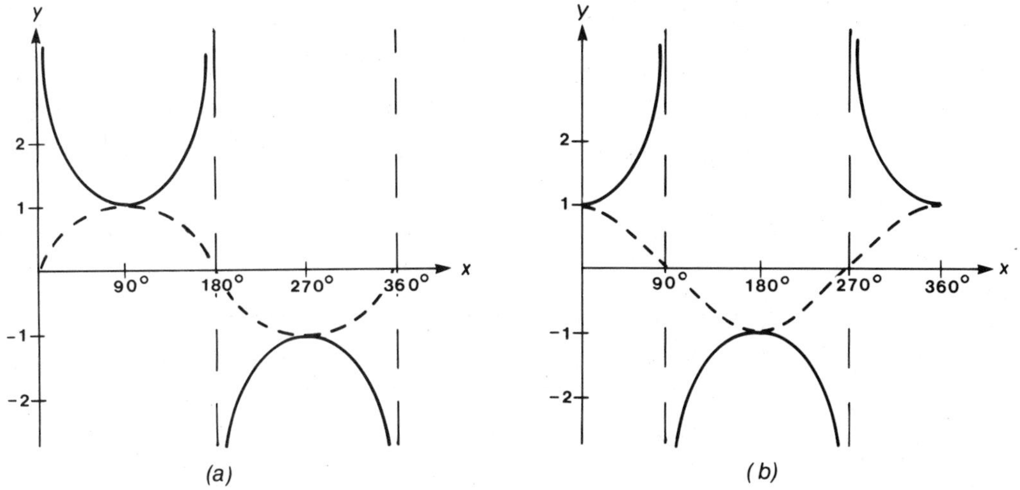

We see that the sinusoid on the left is a sine wave whose equation is $y = \sin\theta$. Thus the equation of the solid curve is

$$\mathbf{y = \csc\theta}$$

The equation of the sinusoid graphed on the right is

$$y = \cos\theta \qquad \text{or} \qquad y = \sin(\theta + 90°)$$

Thus, the equation of the solid curve is

$$\mathbf{y = \sec\theta} \qquad \text{or} \qquad \mathbf{y = \csc(\theta + 90°)}$$

Example 77.A.2 Write the equations of these trigonometric functions.

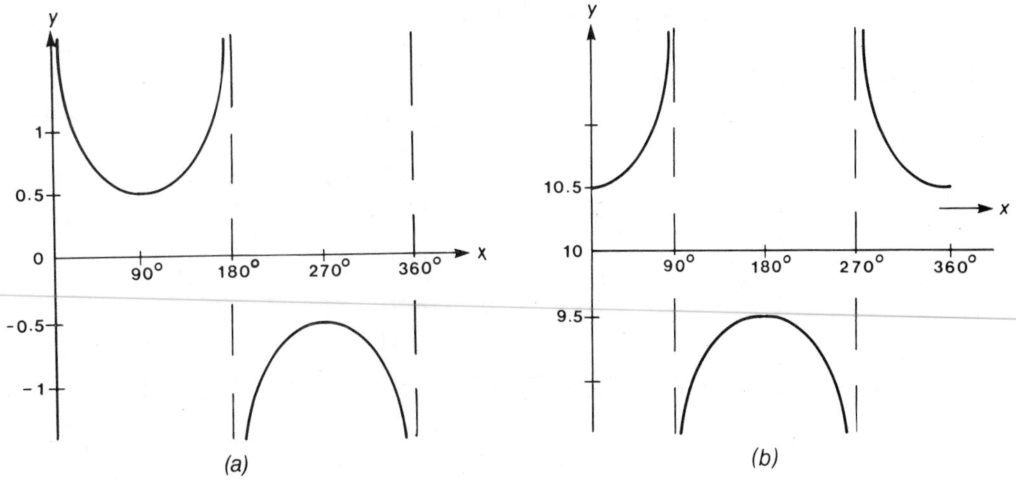

Solution On the next page we draw in the sinusoids whose peak values are the same as the peak values of the solid curves in the graphs above. Then we write the equations of the sinusoids and replace each trigonometric function with its reciprocal function.

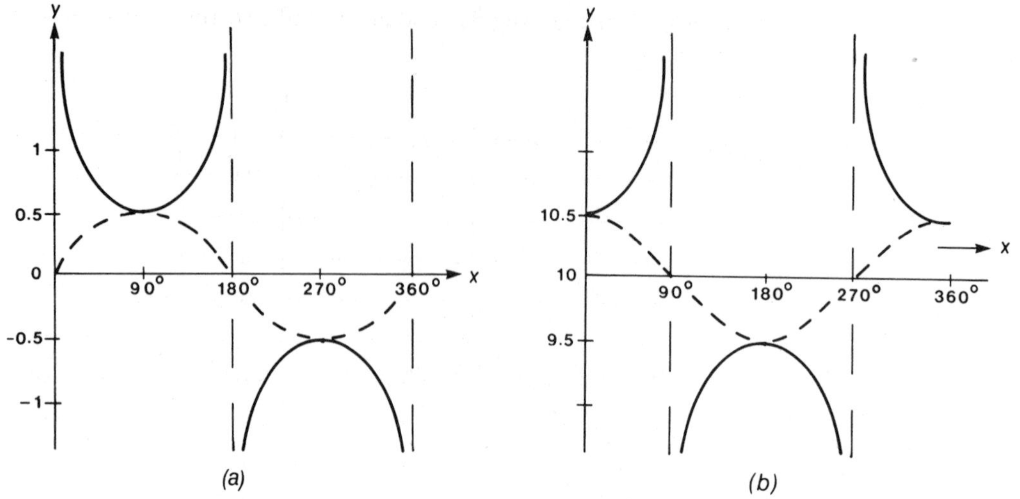

(a) (b)

The sinusoid on the left is

$$y = 0.5 \sin \theta$$

so the graph of the solid curve is

$$\mathbf{y = 0.5 \csc \theta}$$

The sinusoid on the right is

$$y = 10 + 0.5 \cos \theta$$

so the graph of the solid curve is

$$\mathbf{y = 10 + 0.5 \sec \theta}$$

On the left we replaced sin θ with its reciprocal, csc θ, and did not consider the constant 0.5. Note that we did not replace 0.5 sin θ with its reciprocal, which is 2 csc θ. Similarly, on the right we did not consider the constants 10 and 0.5; we simply replaced cos θ with sec θ.

77.B Graphs of tangent and cotangent

The graphs of the tangent function and cotangent function are easy to identify because of their distinctive shapes. These graphs are also seldom encountered because both these functions are undefined every 180°. On the left below we show the graph of the tangent function from 0° to 90°. The value of the tangent of 0° is 0. The value of the tangent of 30° is about 0.58, of 45° is 1, and of 60° is about 1.7. The value increases without limit as 90° is approached. We graph these points and sketch the curve in the figure on the left. An image of this pattern occurs for negative values of θ, as we show in the figure on the right.

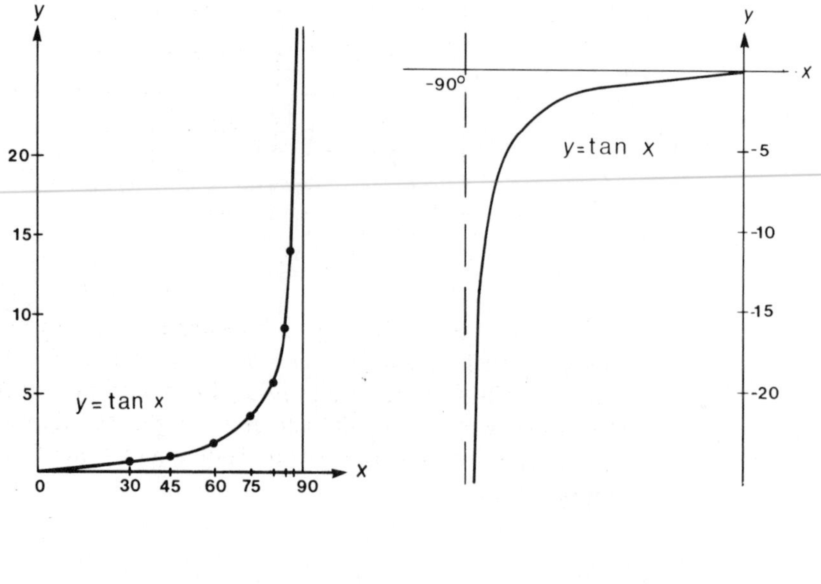

The period of the tangent function is 180°, so this pattern repeats every 180° as we show here.

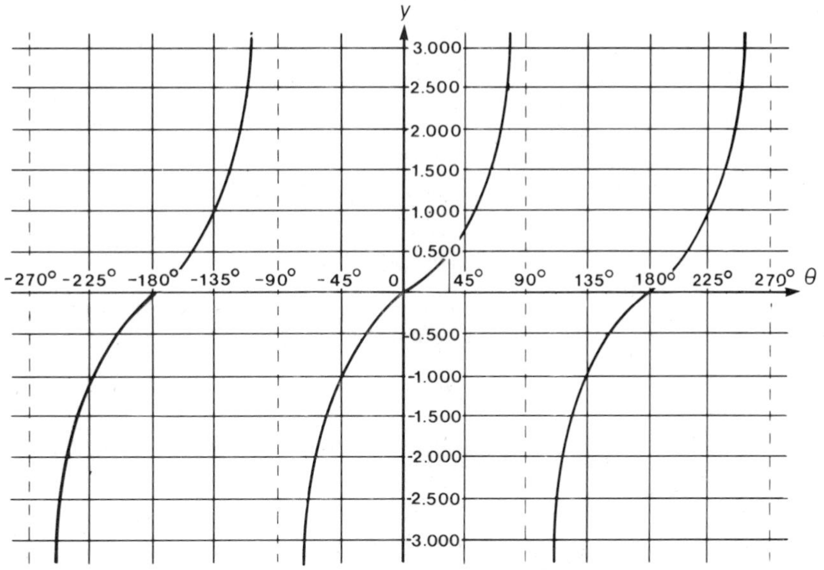

$y = \tan\theta$

The graph of the cotangent function has a similar appearance but the curves flex the other way. The cotangent function is the reciprocal of the tangent function, so the cotangent function has a value of 0 at values of θ where the tangent function is undefined, and is undefined at values of θ where the tangent function equals 0.

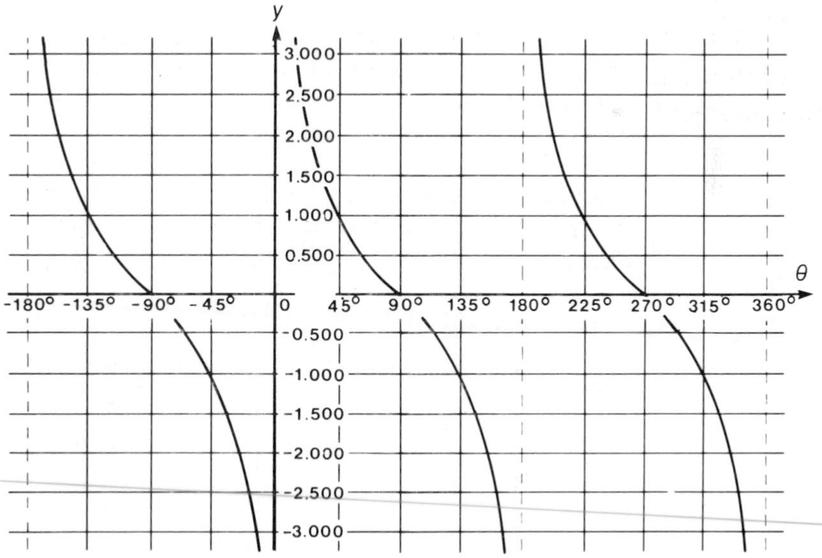

$y = \cot\theta$

It may be interesting to investigate graphs of tangent functions and cotangent functions such as $y = -2\tan\theta$ or $y = \frac{1}{2}\cot(\theta + 30°)$. The sign changes in front of the function will turn the graph upside-down. Adding a constant to the argument will shift the crossing points to the left or the right. Multiplying the argument variable by a constant will change the period. Adding a constant to the function will shift the graph up or down.

Problem set 77

1. Rudolph was observant, as he noted that it took X men 9 days to do P jobs. Then he calculated how long it would take Y men to do 20 jobs. What was his answer?

2. Radium has quite a long half-life. Madame put 1 ounce of radium in the bowl and 100 years later only 0.95817 ounce remained. What is the half-life of radium?

3. Four quick bugs nested in a tree and plotted to increase exponentially. Twenty days later there were 200 quick bugs. Write the exponential equation which expresses the number of quick bugs as a function of time.

4. Four green marbles and 6 red marbles are in an urn. Three green marbles have white spots and 4 red marbles have white spots. What is the probability of drawing a green marble or a marble with white spots?

5. There are 4 boys and 3 girls. How many distinguishable ways can they sit in 7 chairs in a row if the 3 girls are identical in appearance?

6. Graph: (*a*) $y = \tan x$ (*b*) $y = \cot x$

7. Write the equations of these trigonometric functions.

(*a*)

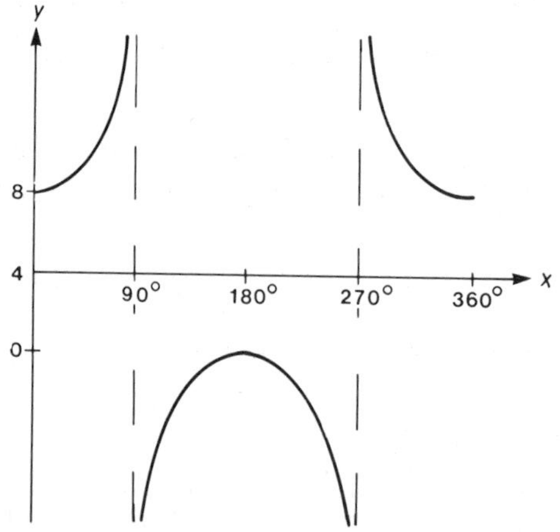

(*b*)

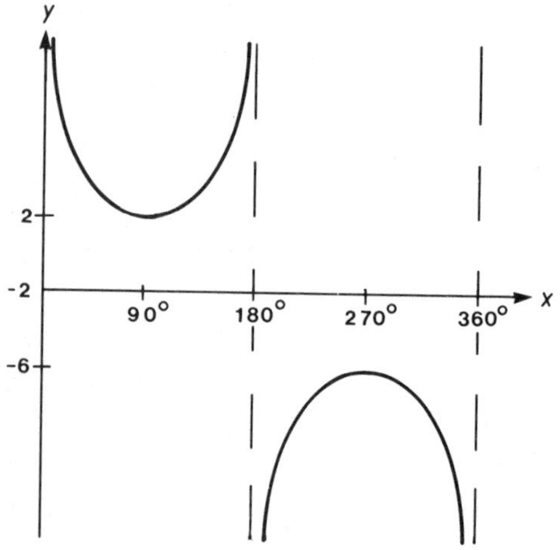

8. Prove the Pythagorean theorem by using the figures shown below.

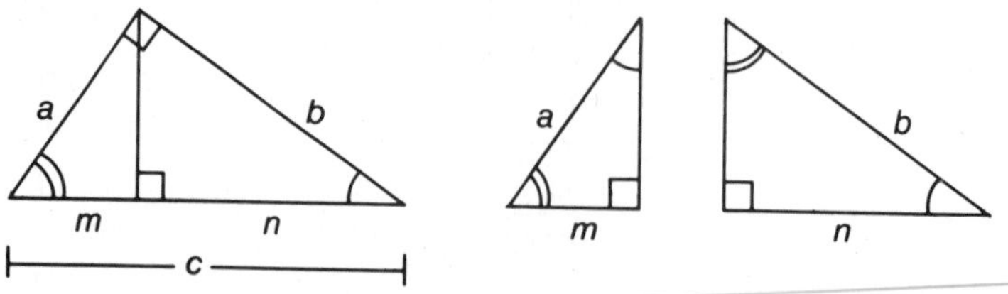

9. Given $\overline{AD}$ is the perpendicular bisector of $\overline{BC}$, prove that $AB = AC$.

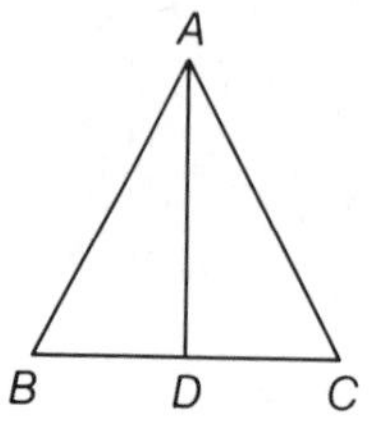

10. Given $\overline{AD}$ is the angle bisector of $\angle A$ and $AB = AC$, prove that $\angle B = \angle C$.

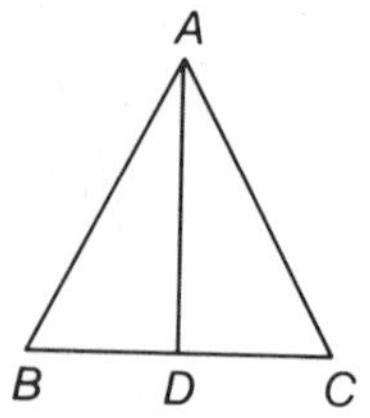

11. Given $AO = CO$ and $BO = DO$, prove $\angle OBA = \angle ODC$.

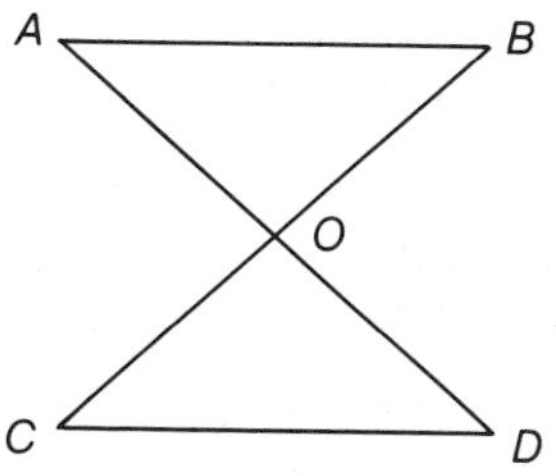

12. Develop the identity for $\tan 2A$ by using the identities for $\cos(A + B)$ and $\sin(A + B)$.

13. Write the four fourth roots of 81 cis 24° in polar form.

14. Find two geometric means between -2 and 16.

15. Write the general form of the equation of an ellipse whose center is the origin, whose major axis is horizontal of length 10, and whose minor axis has a length of 8.

16. Find the first three terms of the arithmetic sequence whose eighth term is 19 and whose tenth term is 25.

17. Find $\cos(-285°)$ by using the identity for $\cos(x + y)$ and the fact $285° = 240° + 45°$ to find $\cos 285°$. Then note that $\cos(-x) = \cos x$. Use exact values.

18. Use a sum identity to find an expression for $\cos\left(x + \frac{\pi}{2}\right)$.

Solve the following equations given that $(0° \leq x < 360°)$:

19. $2\cos^2 x + 7\sin x + 2 = 0$

20. $\sqrt{3}\cot 3x - 1 = 0$

Show that:

21. $\dfrac{1 + \cos x}{\sin x} = \dfrac{\sin x}{1 - \cos x}$

22. $\dfrac{\tan B + 1}{\tan B - 1} = \dfrac{\sec B + \csc B}{\sec B - \csc B}$

23. $(1 + \sin x)^2 + (1 - \sin x)^2 = 4 - 2\cos^2 x$

24. Solve this triangle for side c.

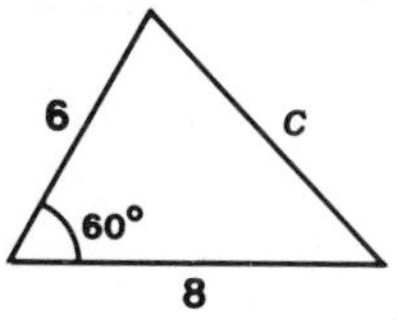

25. Find the length of a.

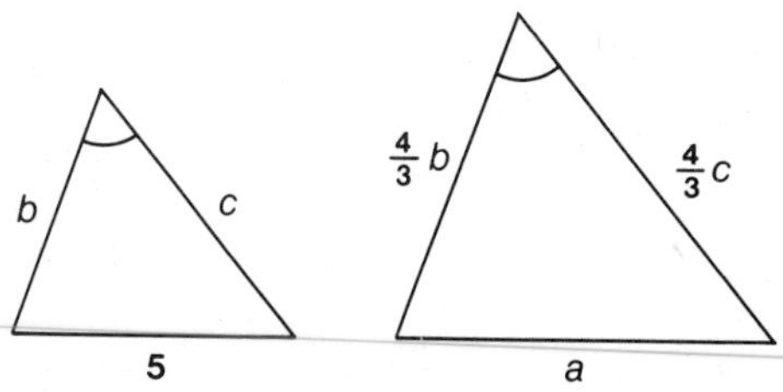

26. Sketch $y = -3 + 2\sin\frac{5}{3}(x - 27°)$.

27. Solve: $12^{2x-2} = 4^{3x+1}$

28. Solve: $\frac{2}{3}\log_3 27 - \log_3(2x - 1) = 1$

29. Find the base 2 antilogarithm of -3.

30. Evaluate: $e^{2\ln 3 - \ln 2}$

EP 77.26, 77.27

LESSON 78 Advanced complex roots

78.A Advanced complex roots

We have restricted finding the roots of complex numbers to problems such as (*a*), where the number is written in polar form, or problems such as (*b*) and (*c*), where the number is either i or the number 1.

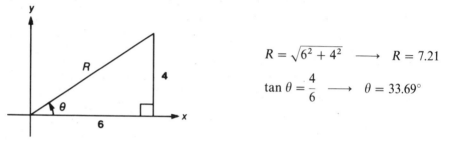

$$(a)\ \sqrt[3]{8\angle 30^\circ} \qquad (b)\ i^{1/4} \qquad (c)\ \sqrt[3]{1}$$

The calculator will permit us to find the roots of any complex number if we remember that the first step is to write the complex number in polar form.

Example 78.A.1 Find the four fourth roots of $6 + 4i$.

Solution **We begin by writing the number in polar form.** We will use the calculator and round off our answers.

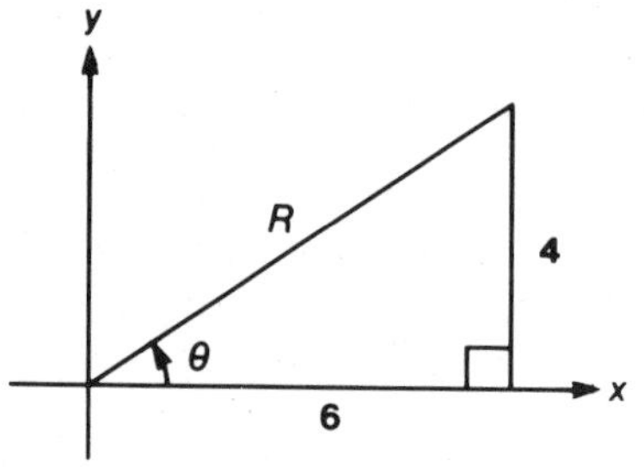

$$R = \sqrt{6^2 + 4^2} \longrightarrow R = 7.21$$

$$\tan\theta = \frac{4}{6} \longrightarrow \theta = 33.69^\circ$$

So we find that $6 + 4i = 7.21 \text{ cis } 33.69^\circ$. Now the first of our fourth roots is $(7.21)^{1/4} \text{ cis } (33.69^\circ/4)$. We use the inverse y^x key or the $\sqrt[x]{y}$ key to find the fourth root of 7.21.

$$(7.21)^{1/4} = 1.64$$

Next we divide 33.69 by 4 to get the angle, so now we have

$$\sqrt[4]{7.21 \text{ cis } 33.69^\circ} = 1.64 \text{ cis } 8.42^\circ$$

Now we add 360°/4 or 90° to get the second root, add 180° to get the third root, and add 270° to get the fourth root; so our four roots are

(*a*) **1.64 cis 8.42°** (*b*) **1.64 cis 98.42°** (*c*) **1.64 cis 188.42°**

and (*d*) **1.64 cis 278.42°**

Example 78.A.2 Find $\sqrt[5]{-17 - 14i}$.

Solution The first step is to write the complex number in polar form.

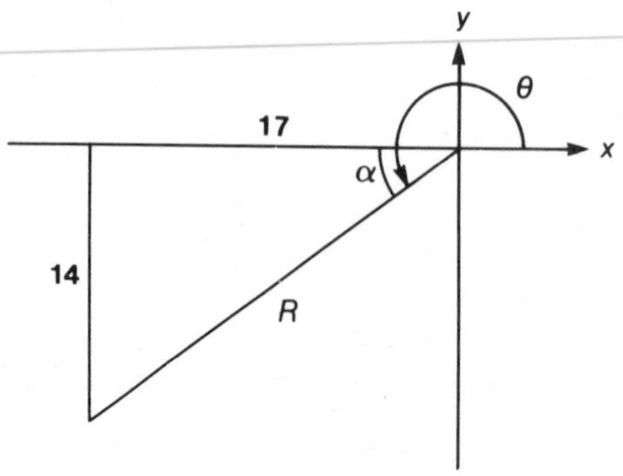

$$R = \sqrt{17^2 + 14^2} \qquad \tan\alpha = \frac{14}{17}$$

$$R = 22.02 \qquad \alpha = 39.47^\circ$$

Therefore,

$$\theta = 180^\circ + 39.47^\circ = 219.47^\circ$$

Now we restate the problem as

$$\sqrt[5]{22.02 \text{ cis } 219.47^\circ} = 22.02^{1/5} \text{ cis } \frac{219.47^\circ}{5} = 1.86 \text{ cis } 43.89^\circ$$

There are four more roots, which we get by adding $\frac{n \cdot 360}{5}$ to 43.89° ($n = 1, 2, 3, 4$).

1.86 cis 43.89° **1.86 cis 115.89°** **1.86 cis 187.89°** **1.86 cis 259.89°**

and **1.86 cis 331.89°**

Problem set 78

1. Rotondo could carry the 140 liters on his back. If the solution was 20% alcohol, how much pure alcohol must he add to get a solution that is 44% alcohol?
2. There were 600 at first, but they increased exponentially. After 60 minutes there were 1000. How many minutes had elapsed before there were 5000?
3. In another room there were also 600, but they decreased exponentially. After 60 minutes, they had decreased in number to only 580. What was the half-life of these creatures?
4. There were 90 people in the room. Half were girls and one-third were redheaded. Two-thirds of the people either were redheaded or were girls. If one person is chosen at random, what is the probability of choosing a redheaded girl?
5. An urn contains 4 green marbles, 3 white marbles, and 3 blue marbles. A marble is drawn and then replaced. Then 2 more marbles are drawn without replacement. What is the probability that all 3 are white?
6. Find the four fourth roots of $3 + 4i$ and express the roots in polar form.
7. Find the three cube roots of $2 + 3i$ and express the roots in polar form.
8. Given C is the midpoint of $\overline{AD}$ and $\overline{BE}$. Prove $AB = ED$.

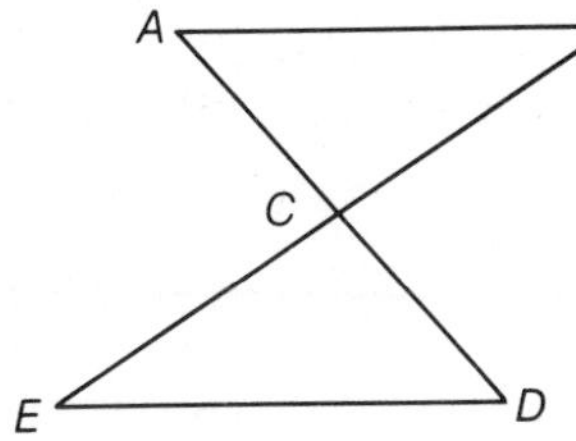

9. Given $\angle B = \angle D$ and $\overline{AD} \parallel \overline{BC}$. Prove $\triangle ABC \cong \triangle CDA$.

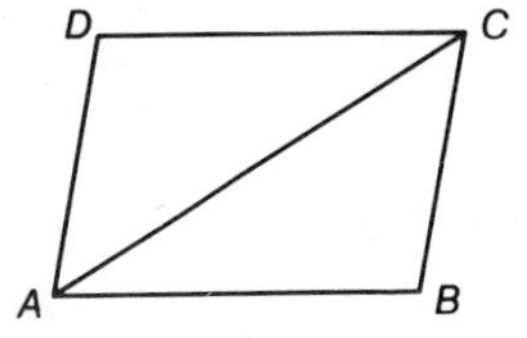

10. Show that $x^2 + y^2 = z^2$, using the figures shown.

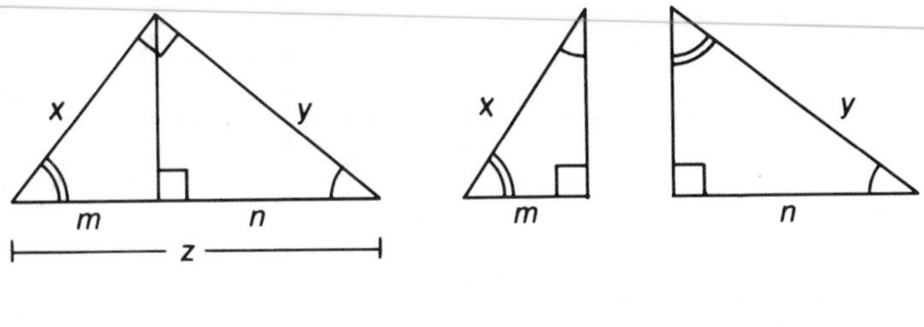

11. Prove that the sum of the angles in a triangle is equal to 180°.
12. Find the two geometric means between 3 and -24.

13. Write the standard form of the equation of an ellipse whose center is the origin, whose major axis is horizontal of length 10, and whose minor axis has a length of 4.

14. Find the coordinates of the vertices and the equations of the asymptotes of the hyperbola $16x^2 - 9y^2 = 144$.

15. Find the first five terms of the arithmetic sequence whose fourth term is 4 and whose thirteenth term is 28.

16. Find cos 285° by using the sum identity for cosine functions and the fact that $285° = 240° + 45°$. Use decimal approximations.

17. Use a sum identity to find an expression for $\sin\left(x - \frac{\pi}{4}\right)$. Use exact values.

Solve the following equations given that $(0° \le x < 360°)$:

18. $3\tan^2 x + 5\sec x + 1 = 0$

19. $-1 + \tan 3x = 0$

Show that:

20. $\dfrac{\sin x}{1 + \cos x} + \dfrac{1 + \cos x}{\sin x} = 2\csc x$

21. $\dfrac{\csc x + \cot x}{\tan x + \sin x} = \cot x \csc x$

22. $\dfrac{\sin^4 x - \cos^4 x}{2\sin^2 x - 1} = 1$

23. Solve this triangle for angle A.

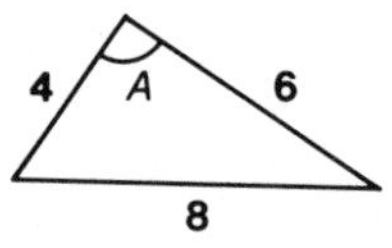

24. Find the length of x.

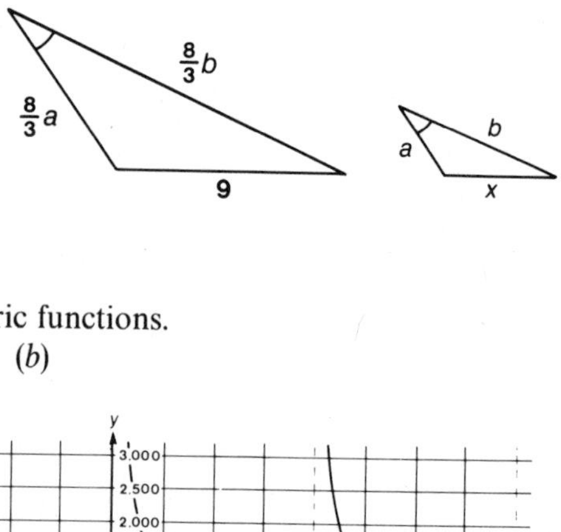

25. Sketch $y = 3 + 11\cos\frac{3}{2}(x - 100°)$.

26. Write the equations of these trigonometric functions.

(a)

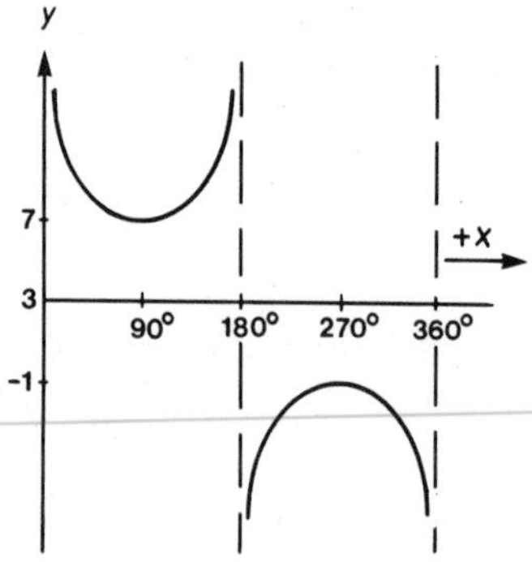

(b)

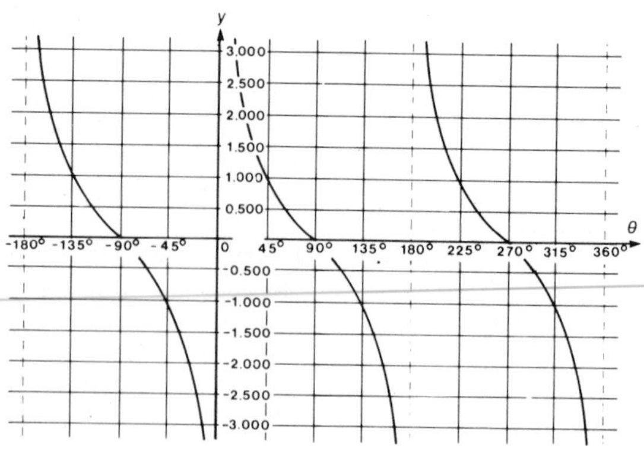

Solve:

27. $9^{3x-2} = 3^{2x-1}$

28. $\frac{1}{3}\log_2 27 - \log_2(2x - 1) = 2$

29. $x = \log_{1/3} 18 - \log_{1/3} 6$

30. Find the base 3 antilogarithm of 3.

EP 78.28, 78.29

LESSON 79 *Double-angle identities · Triangle area formula · Law of sines · Equal angles and proportional sides*

79.A Double-angle identities

We have memorized identities for the sine and cosine of the sums of two angles and have practiced using these identities to write identities for the sine, cosine, and tangent of 2θ. **When we are proving identities, we must remember that these double-angle identities are available and use them whenever the identity contains $\sin 2\theta$, $\cos 2\theta$, or $\tan 2\theta$.**

Example 79.A.1 Show that $(\sin x + \cos x)^2 = 1 + \sin 2x$.

Solution We could work on just one side, but in this proof we will change both expressions to new forms. On the left side we multiply as indicated, and on the right side we replace $\sin 2x$ with $2 \sin x \cos x$.

$$\sin^2 x + 2 \sin x \cos x + \cos^2 x = 1 + 2 \sin x \cos x$$

Now on the left side, we see that we can replace $\sin^2 x + \cos^2 x$ with 1. We make the replacement and have our proof.

$$1 + 2 \sin x \cos x = 1 + 2 \sin x \cos x$$

Example 79.A..2 Show that $\dfrac{\cos^4 x - \sin^4 x}{\cos 2x} = 1$.

Solution We note that the numerator is the difference of two squares and can be factored.

$$\frac{(\cos^2 x + \sin^2 x)(\cos^2 x - \sin^2 x)}{\cos 2x} = 1$$

We remember that there are three identities for $\cos 2x$, and one of these is $\cos^2 x - \sin^2 x$. We make this replacement and find that we have almost completed the proof.

$$\frac{(\cos^2 x + \sin^2 x)\cancel{(\cos^2 x - \sin^2 x)}}{\cancel{\cos^2 x - \sin^2 x}} = 1 \qquad \text{factored}$$

$$\cos^2 x + \sin^2 x = 1 \qquad \text{canceled}$$

$$1 = 1 \qquad \text{simplified}$$

79.B Triangle area formula

The area of any triangle equals half the product of any two sides and the sine of the angle between them. Here we show triangle ABC three times.

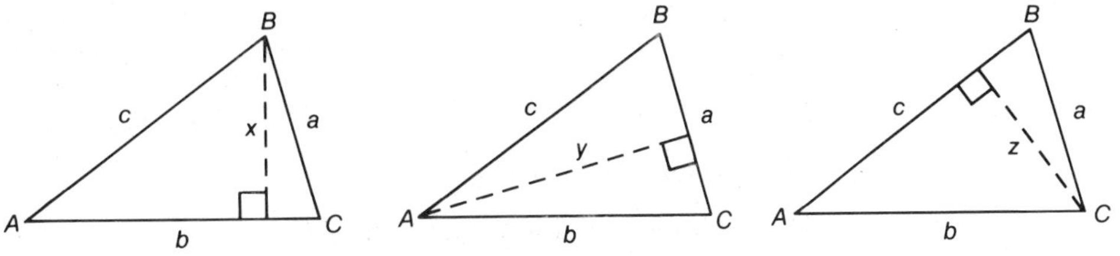

$x = c \sin A$ $\qquad$ $y = b \sin C$ $\qquad$ $z = a \sin B$

In the left-hand figure, we consider side b as the base and show the altitude x. In the center figure, we consider side a as the base and show altitude y. In the right-hand figure, we consider side c as the base and show altitude z. Below each figure we have used the sine of the angle to determine the value of the altitude. We remember that the area of a triangle equals half the product of the base and the altitude. If we substitute the values we have for the base and the altitude for the three triangles on the preceding page, we get

$$\text{Area} = \tfrac{1}{2}(b)(c \sin A) \qquad \text{Area} = \tfrac{1}{2}(a)(b \sin C) \qquad \text{Area} = \tfrac{1}{2}(c)(a \sin B)$$

and if we remove the parentheses we get

$$\text{Area} = \tfrac{1}{2}bc \sin A \qquad \text{Area} = \tfrac{1}{2}ab \sin C \qquad \text{Area} = \tfrac{1}{2}ac \sin B$$

In each case, we see that the area equals one-half the product of two sides and the sine of the angle between them. This proof uses an acute triangle. The same result can be obtained by using an obtuse triangle or a right triangle.

79.C Proof of the law of sines

There are several ways to prove the law of sines. We will prove it by using the area formulas above and using substitution, and then by rearranging the result. We begin with the following two equations.

$$\text{Area} = \tfrac{1}{2}bc \sin A \qquad \text{and} \qquad \text{Area} = \tfrac{1}{2}ab \sin C$$

If we equate these two expressions for the area, we get

$$\tfrac{1}{2}bc \sin A = \tfrac{1}{2}ab \sin C$$

If we divide both sides by $\frac{1}{2}b$, we get the expression

$$c \sin A = a \sin C$$

and we can now get the desired form by dividing both sides by $\sin A \sin C$. Since no angle in a triangle can have a measure of 0° or 180°, we know that neither angle A nor angle C equals 0° or 180°, so neither $\sin A$ nor $\sin C$ equals zero. Thus the division by $\sin A \sin C$ is permissible.

$$\frac{c \sin A}{\sin A \sin C} = \frac{a \sin C}{\sin A \sin C} \longrightarrow \frac{c}{\sin C} = \frac{a}{\sin A}$$

We can get the other equality we need by using the third area equation with either of the others. We do this and get

$$\tfrac{1}{2}ca \sin B = \tfrac{1}{2}ab \sin C$$

This time we will get the desired form in one step by dividing both sides by $\frac{1}{2}a \sin B \sin C$.

$$\frac{\frac{1}{2}ca \sin B}{\frac{1}{2}a \sin B \sin C} = \frac{\frac{1}{2}ab \sin C}{\frac{1}{2}a \sin B \sin C} \longrightarrow \frac{c}{\sin C} = \frac{b}{\sin B}$$

Since all three ratios are equal, we can write the law of sines as

$$\frac{a}{\sin A} = \frac{b}{\sin B} = \frac{c}{\sin C}$$

79.D Equal angles imply proportional sides

Corresponding sides of similar triangles are proportional. This means that the ratio of all pairs of corresponding sides equals the same constant. Given that the triangles shown here are similar triangles,

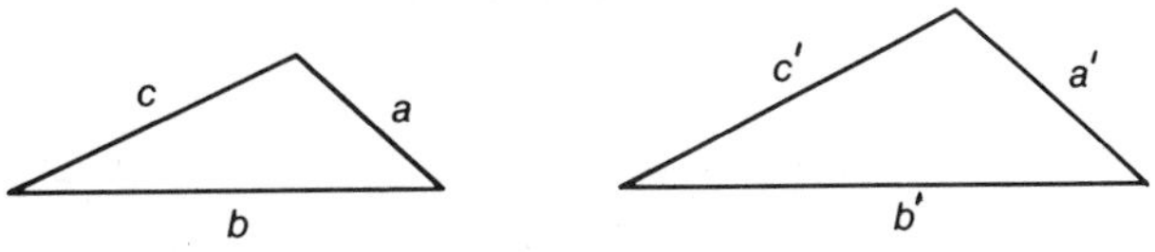

then the ratios of the corresponding sides equal the same constant, which we will call SF for scale factor.

$$\frac{a}{a'} = SF \qquad \frac{b}{b'} = SF \qquad \frac{c}{c'} = SF$$

If we are given two triangles in which corresponding angles are equal, we can use the law of sines to illustrate the fact that the sides are proportional. We remember that the ratio of every side to the sine of the opposite angle is a constant.

$$\frac{a}{\sin A} = \frac{b}{\sin B} = \frac{c}{\sin C} = k$$

If the corresponding angles in the following triangles are equal as indicated, we can use the law of sines to illustrate the fact that the corresponding sides are proportional because we can show that the ratios of corresponding sides all equal the same constant.

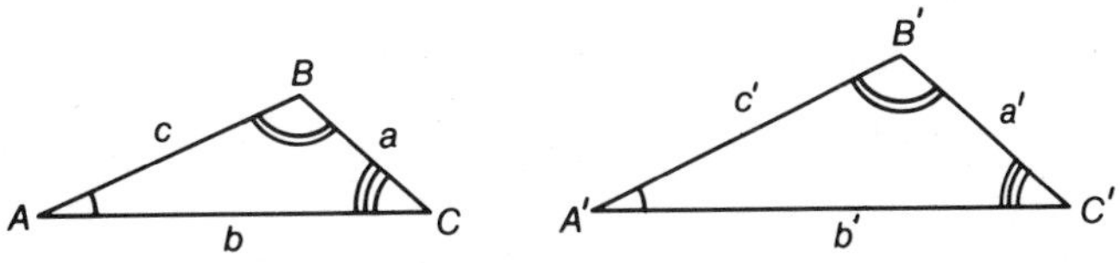

For the left-hand triangle,

$$\frac{a}{\sin A} = k$$

For the right-hand triangle,

$$\frac{a'}{\sin A'} = k'$$

Dividing, we get

$$\frac{\dfrac{a}{\sin A}}{\dfrac{a'}{\sin A'}} = \frac{k}{k'} = P \qquad \text{(another constant)}$$

And, since angle A equals angle A', the sines of the angles are equal. Thus, we can simplify and write

$$\frac{a}{a'} = P$$

If we repeat the procedure for angles B and C, we can get the following

$$\frac{a}{a'} = P \qquad \frac{b}{b'} = P \qquad \frac{c}{c'} = P$$

We have illustrated the fact that the ratios of all corresponding sides equal the same constant, and this implies that the corresponding sides are proportional.

Problem set 79

1. Water flows down the Niger River at 4 mph. If Kunta rows steadily, he can go 27 miles downstream in the same time it takes him to go 3 miles upstream. How fast can Kunta row in still water?

2. There were 500 present initially, and they increased exponentially. If the constant k in the exponent was 0.005, how long did it take them to increase to a total of 4000 present?

3. The number in the stadium decreased exponentially. There were 60,000 when the gun went off, and 5 minutes later only 50,000 remained. How long would it take before only 10,000 remained?

4. It was exactly 4 o'clock when the bell rang. How long did Fred have to wait before the hands on the clock formed a 90° angle?

5. Take the permutation of 8 things taken 3 at a time to do a concrete development of the notation for n things taken r at a time.

6. If the central angle is $\pi/3$ radians in a circle of diameter 12 inches, what is the area of the sector?

7. Find the two square roots of $3 + 4i$ and express the roots in polar form.

8. Given $\overline{AD}$ is perpendicular bisector of $\overline{BC}$, prove that $AB = AC$.

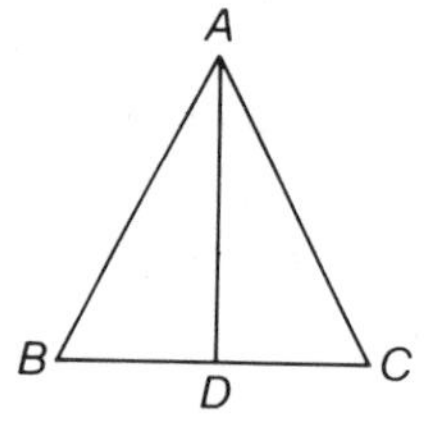

9. Given $\overline{AB} \parallel \overline{DE}$ and $AC = CE$, prove $BC = CD$.

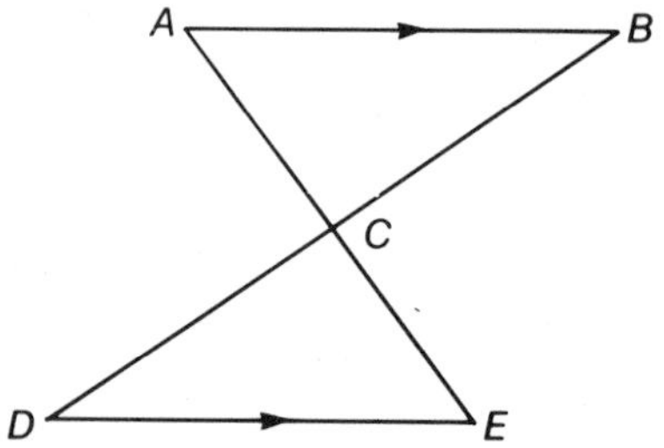

10. Prove the Pythagorean theorem by using the figures shown below.

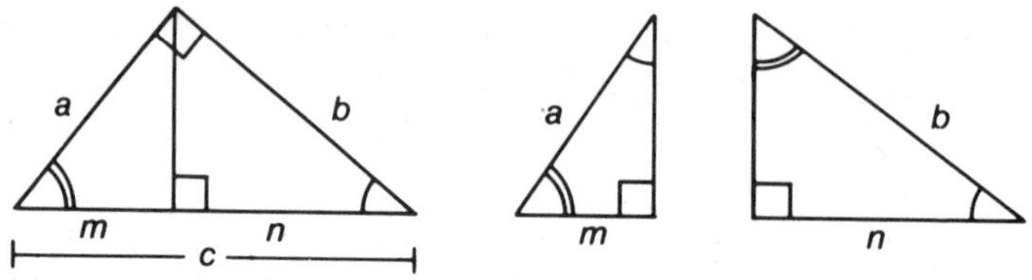

11. Graph $y = \tan x$.

12. Find two geometric means between -2 and 16.

13. Write the general form of the equation of an ellipse whose foci are $(0, \pm 6)$ and whose vertices are $(0, \pm 10)$.

14. Find the coordinates of the vertices and the equations of the asymptotes of the hyperbola $9x^2 - 16y^2 = 144$.

15. Find the first three terms of the arithmetic sequence whose third term is -8 and whose fifth term is 0.

16. Find $\sin(-15°)$ by using the difference identity for the sine function and the fact that $-15° = 30° - 45°$. Use exact values.

17. Use a sum identity to find an expression for $\cos\left(x + \dfrac{\pi}{2}\right)$.

Solve the following equations given that ($0° \le x, \theta < 360°$):

18. $2 \tan^2 x + 3 \sec x = 0$

19. $\sqrt{3} - 2 \sin 3\theta = 0$

Show that:

20. $\dfrac{\cos^4 x - \sin^4 x}{\cos 2x} = 1$

21. $(\sin x + \cos x)^2 = 1 + \sin 2x$

22. $\dfrac{1 - \cos x}{\sin x} = \dfrac{\sin x}{1 + \cos x}$

23. Solve this triangle for angle A.

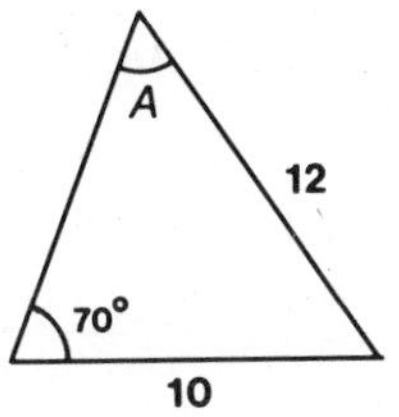

24. Find the length of c.

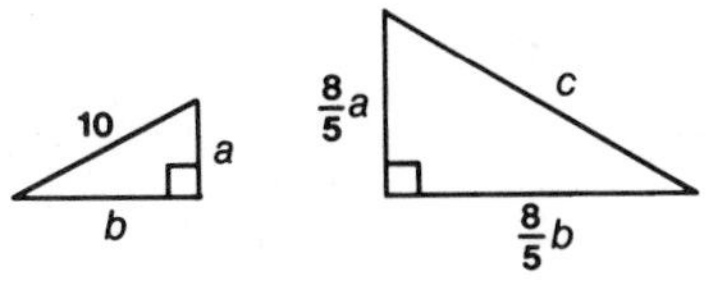

25. Sketch $y = 11 + \sin \frac{3}{4}(x + \pi)$.

26. What is the sum of the exterior angles of a 14-sided convex polygon?

27. Solve: $12^{4x+2} = 8^{2x-3}$

28. Solve: $\frac{2}{3} \log_{12} 8 - \log_{12} (3x + 2) = \frac{1}{2} \log_{12} 10{,}000$

29. Evaluate: $2e^{\ln 2} + e^{2 \ln 8 - \ln 2}$

30. Estimate the base e antilogarithm of 2. Use the approximation $e = 3$.

EP 79.30, 79.31

LESSON 80 The ambiguous case

80.A The ambiguous case

A triangle has three angles and three sides for a total of six primary parts. **When we know the length of one side and know the measures of two other parts, the measures of the three unknown parts can be found.** When we know the values of an angle and the side opposite (a pair), we can use the law of sines for our solution. If our third known value is an angle, then we also know the third angle, and the triangle can be drawn. For instance, if we are given $a = 6$, $A = 30°$, and $B = 70°$, we have a pair (a and A); and we know that angle C equals 80° because the sum of the three angles must be 180°. We know enough to draw the triangle.

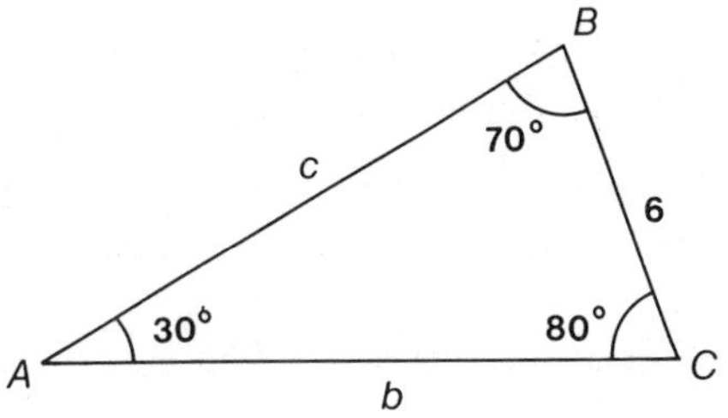

Now we can use the law of sines to find that side b equals 11.28 and side c equals 11.82.

$$\frac{b}{\sin 70°} = \frac{6}{\sin 30°} \qquad \frac{c}{\sin 80°} = \frac{6}{\sin 30°}$$

$$b = \frac{6 \sin 70°}{\sin 30°} = 11.28 \qquad c = \frac{6 \sin 80°}{\sin 30°} = 11.82$$

If we are given the values of a pair, and the third value given is another side and no drawing of the triangle is provided, we have a problem. It might be possible to use the given values to draw one triangle, two triangles, or no triangles. We say that this is an ***ambiguous case,*** because the word *ambiguous* means "capable of two or more interpretations."

Example 80.A.1 Given $A = 40°$, $a = 4$, $b = 9$. Draw the triangle and solve for the values of the other side and angles.

Solution We have been given the measure of angle A, the length of the side opposite this angle, and the length of another side. **We have not been given a figure.** There are five possible figures that can be drawn, and which figure(s) apply depends on the length of side a.

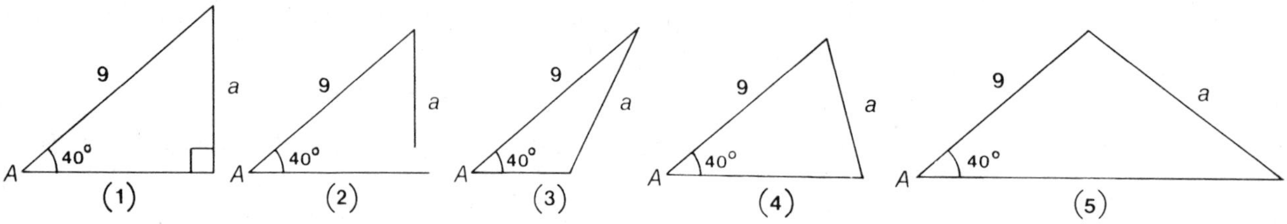

The first step is to use figure (1) to determine the value of the altitude H. If the given length for side a **equals H,** we have a right triangle, (1). If the given length for side a is **less than H,** we do not get a triangle at all, (2). If the given length for side a is **greater than H but less than 9,** two different triangles are possible, (3) and (4). If the given length for side a **is greater than H and greater than 9,** only one triangle is possible, (5). We begin by solving for H.

$$\sin 40° = \frac{H}{9}$$

$$9 \sin 40° = H$$

$$5.79 = H$$

The length we were given for side a was 4, and this length is not as long as H, as we show in figure (2) above, so there is no triangle.

Example 80.A.2 Draw the triangle and find the missing parts if $A = 27°$, $a = 5$, and $b = 7$.

Solution We use the data given to draw the triangle. Now we solve to see how long side H must be for the triangle to be a right triangle.

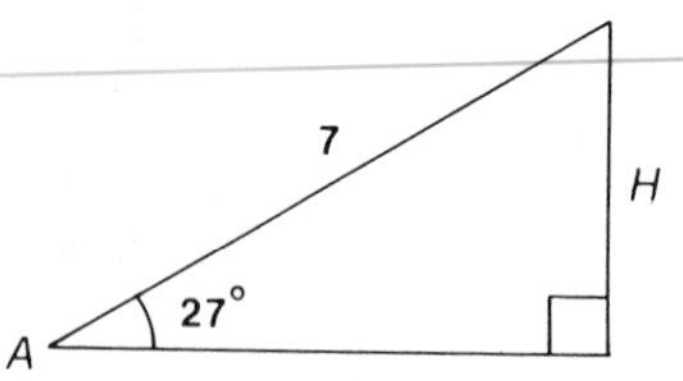

$$\sin 27° = \frac{H}{7} \quad \text{equation}$$

$$7 \sin 27° = H \quad \text{multiplied by 7}$$

$$3.18 = H \quad \text{solved}$$

The length we were given for a is 5, which is greater than 3.18 and less than 7, so there are two possible triangles. We draw them and then solve. We note that the solutions for angle B are the same even though the triangles are different.

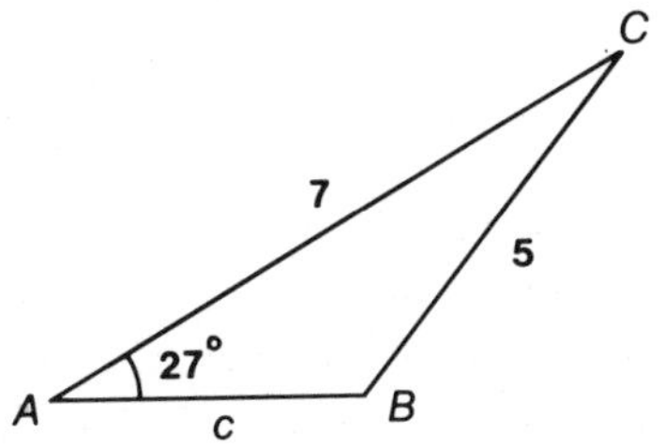

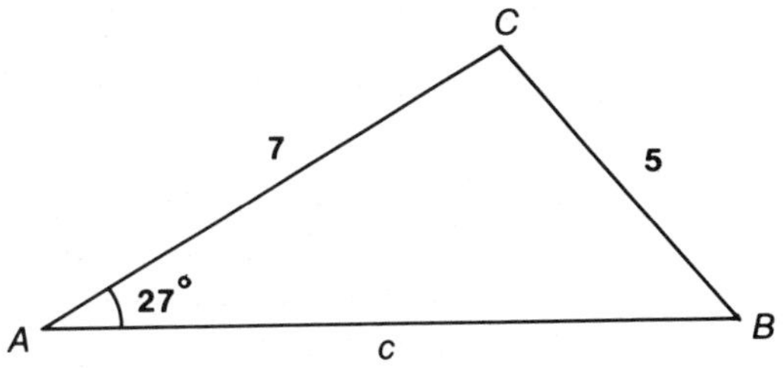

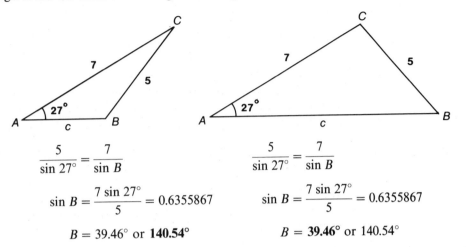

$$\frac{5}{\sin 27°} = \frac{7}{\sin B} \qquad \frac{5}{\sin 27°} = \frac{7}{\sin B}$$

$$\sin B = \frac{7 \sin 27°}{5} = 0.6355867 \qquad \sin B = \frac{7 \sin 27°}{5} = 0.6355867$$

$$B = 39.46° \text{ or } \mathbf{140.54°} \qquad B = \mathbf{39.46°} \text{ or } 140.54°$$

We see that both solutions yield the same answer for angle B. Angle C and the length of side c will be different.

If $B = 140.54°$

$$\angle C = 180° - 27° - 140.54° = 12.46°$$

$$\frac{c}{\sin 12.46°} = \frac{5}{\sin 27°}$$

$$c = \frac{5 \sin 12.46°}{\sin 27°}$$

$$\mathbf{c = 2.38}$$

If $B = 39.46°$

$$\angle C = 180° - 27° - 39.46° = 113.54°$$

$$\frac{c}{\sin 113.54°} = \frac{5}{\sin 27°}$$

$$c = \frac{5 \sin 113.54°}{\sin 27°}$$

$$\mathbf{c = 10.10}$$

Problem set 80

1. The number of horses, sheep, and cows totals 128. One-half the number of sheep plus 12 equals the number of cows, and one-half the number of cows plus 12 equals the number of horses. How many of each kind of animal are there?

2. Their number was only 50 at the beginning, but the increase was exponential. After 30 minutes they numbered 300. How long did it take for them to increase their number to 1500?

3. A card is drawn from a full deck of 52 cards. What is the probability that the card is a 10 or is a spade?

4. The first urn contained 3 red marbles and 4 green marbles. The second urn contained 3 red marbles and 7 green marbles. One marble is drawn from each urn. What is the probability that both marbles are green?

5. A mason built a wall for \$500. If he had received \$5 more per yard, he would have been paid \$750. How many yards of wall did he build?

6. A triangle has a 27° angle. A side adjacent to this angle has length 7 and the side opposite the angle has length 5. Draw the triangle(s) described and find the length(s) of the missing side(s).

7. A triangle has a 40° angle. A side adjacent to the 40° angle has a length of 10, and the side opposite the 40° angle has a length of 5. Draw the triangle(s) described and find the length(s) of the missing side(s).

8. Find the three cube roots of $5 + 8i$ and express the roots in polar form.

9. The central angle of a sector of a circle is 30°. Find the area of the sector in square centimeters if the radius is 5 centimeters.

10. Given $\overline{AB} \parallel \overline{CD}$ and $\overline{AC} \parallel \overline{BD}$, prove that $AC = BD$.

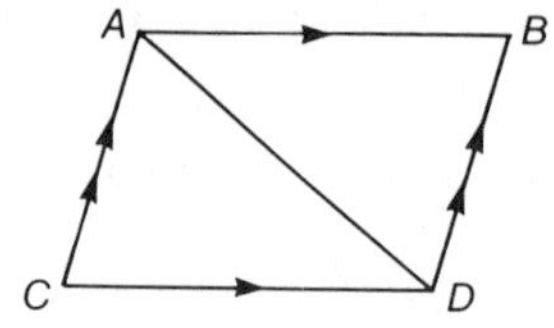

11. Given: $\overline{AB} \parallel \overline{DE}$ and $AB = DE$
Prove: $AC = CE$

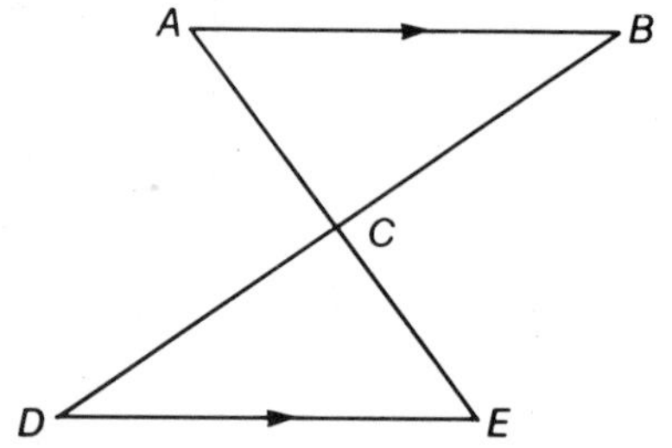

12. Given: $\angle A = \angle B$; $DC = CE$
Prove: $AD = BE$

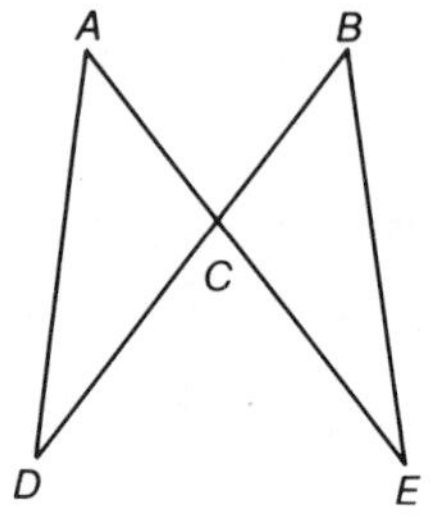

13. Show that $q^2 + r^2 = s^2$ by using the triangles shown.

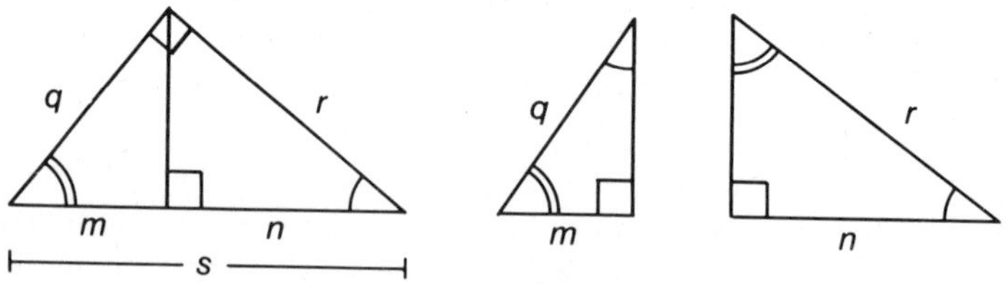

14. Find three geometric means between 2 and 32.

15. Write the general form of the equation of an ellipse whose foci are $(0, \pm 4)$ and whose vertices are $(0, \pm 5)$.

16. Find the coordinates of the vertices and the equations of the asymptotes of the hyperbola $x^2 - y^2 = 4$.

17. Find the first three terms of the arithmetic sequence whose fifth term is 0 and whose eighth term is 9.

18. Find $2 \sin 15° \cos 15°$ by recalling the double-angle identity for the sine function.

Solve the following equations given that $(0° \leq x, \theta < 360°)$:

19. $2 \cos^2 x = 1 - \sin x$

20. $-2 + \sec 3\theta = 0$

Show that:

21. $\cos 2x + 2 \sin^2 x = 1$

22. $\dfrac{\cos x}{1 - \sin x} - \dfrac{\cos x}{1 + \sin x} = 2 \tan x$

23. $\dfrac{2 \sin x}{\sin 2x} = \sec x$

24. Solve this triangle for side c.

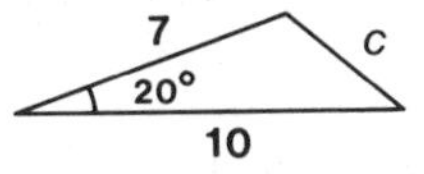

25. Find the length of side c.

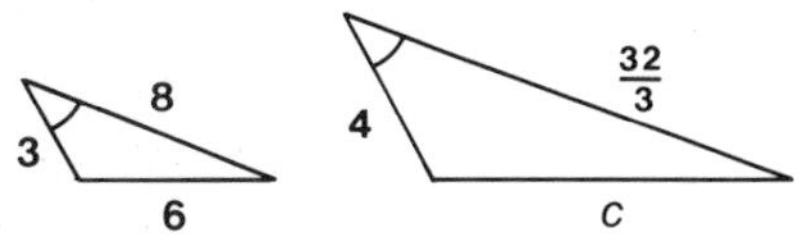

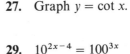

26. Sketch $y = 3 + 4\cos\frac{2}{3}(x + 90°)$.

27. Graph $y = \cot x$.

Solve:

28. $\frac{3}{4}\log_e 16 - \log_e(2x - 4) = \log_e 3$

29. $10^{2x-4} = 100^{3x}$

30. Find the base 6 antilogarithm of -3.

EP 80.32, 80.33

LESSON 81 Isosceles triangles · Angle bisectors · Parallelograms

81.A Isosceles triangles

Isosceles triangles are triangles that have two sides that are equal. We can use congruent triangles to show that the angles opposite these equal sides are equal angles. Also we can go the other way and show that if a triangle has two angles that are equal, then the sides opposite these angles are equal and thus the triangle is an isosceles triangle. We can use the same triangles to show that the bisector of the nonbase angle of an isosceles triangle is the perpendicular bisector of the base, and, conversely, that the perpendicular bisector of the base bisects the nonbase angle. An equilateral triangle has three equal sides and three equal angles, and thus is a special kind of isosceles triangle.

Example 81.A.1 Prove that the base angles of an isosceles triangle are equal and that the bisector of the third angle is the perpendicular bisector of the base.

Solution On the left, we show an isosceles triangle with the length of side $\overline{AB}$ equal to the length of side $\overline{AC}$. On the right we draw the bisector of angle A and note that the two halves of the bisected angle are equal.

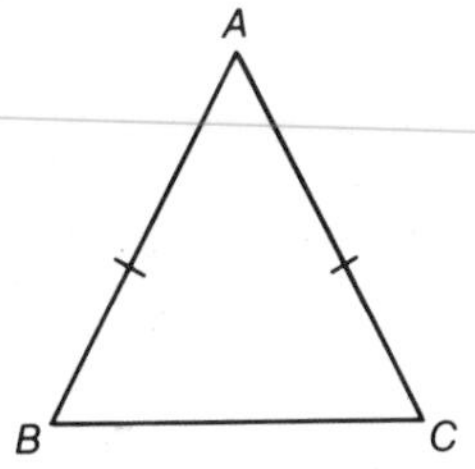

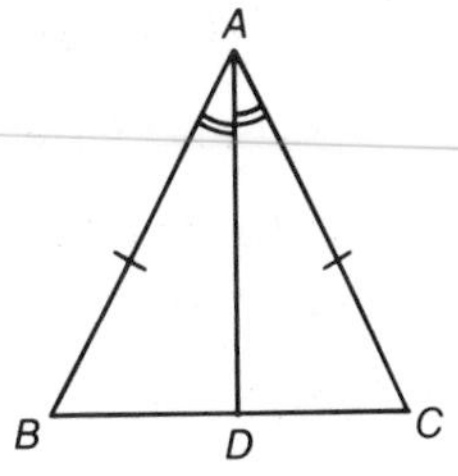

We note that segment $\overline{AD}$ is a side of both triangles BAD and CAD and that these triangles are similar by SAS and congruent because the scale factor is 1.

$$\triangle DBA \cong \triangle DCA$$

Because the triangles are congruent, all pairs of corresponding angles and sides are equal. So the base angles ABD and ACD are equal. Also the lengths of sides BD and DC are equal. Both angles BDA and CDA are right angles because they are equal angles that form a straight angle. Since a line has only one perpendicular bisector, we can also use this proof to state that the perpendicular bisector of the base of an isosceles triangle also bisects the opposite angle.

Example 81.A.2 Find x.

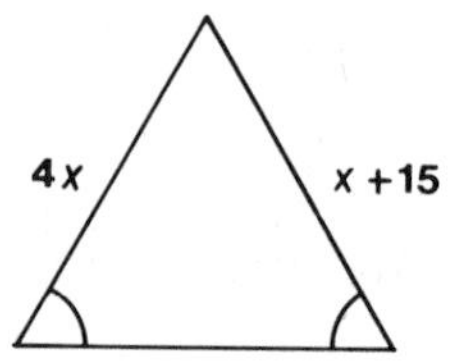

Solution The figure indicates that two angles are equal. ***Sides opposite equal angles in a triangle are always equal.*** Thus, $4x$ is equal to $x + 15$. We write this equation and solve for x.

$$4x = x + 15 \qquad \text{equation}$$
$$3x = 15 \qquad \text{added } -x$$
$$\mathbf{x = 5} \qquad \text{divided}$$

Example 81.A.3 Find x.

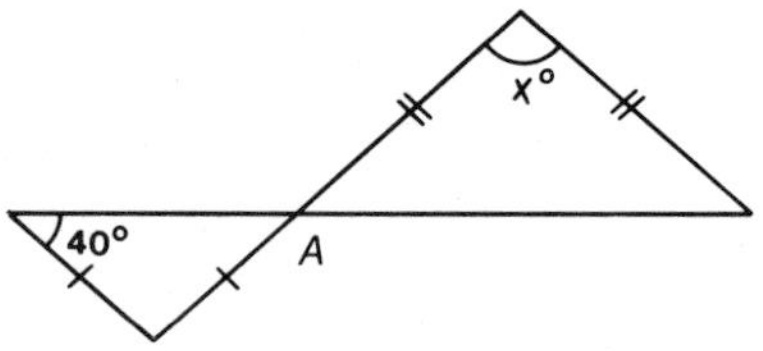

Solution In the left triangle, the ***angles opposite equal sides are equal,*** so one unmarked angle is 40° and the larger angle must be 100°. Thus, both vertical angles equal 40°. Again in the triangle on the right, two sides are equal, so the angles opposite these two sides equal 40° and x equals **100°.**

81.B Angle bisectors

We can use congruent triangles to prove that if a point lies on the bisector of an angle, then it is equidistant from the sides of the angle. Conversely, if the point is equidistant from the sides, then it lies on the angle bisector. When we do this, we remember that we have defined the distance from a point to a line to be equal to the length of the segment perpendicular to the line that connects the point and the line.

Example 81.B.1 Prove that a point on the angle bisector is equidistant from the sides of the angle.

Solution We draw the bisector of an angle, and from a point P on the bisector, we draw lines perpendicular to both sides.

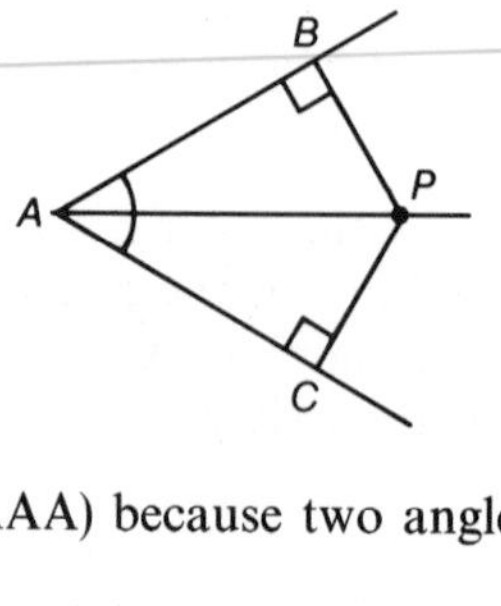

The two triangles are similar (AAA) because two angles are equal, and thus the third angles must be equal. So

$$\triangle PAB \sim \triangle PAC$$

We note that side $\overline{PA}$ is a corresponding side in the two triangles, so the scale factor is 1 and the triangles are also congruent. Thus, sides $\overline{PB}$ and $\overline{PC}$ are equal because they are corresponding parts of congruent triangles, and thus point P is equidistant from the sides.

If we had been told the point was equidistant from the sides and asked to prove that the line bisected the angle, the figure would have been the same. The triangles could have been proved congruent by the hypotenuse-leg method, as the hypotenuse for both triangles is segment AP. Thus, by CPCTE, the two adjacent angles at A are equal angles.

81.C Parallelograms

A ***parallelogram*** is a quadrilateral that has two pairs of parallel sides. All four of these figures are parallelograms.

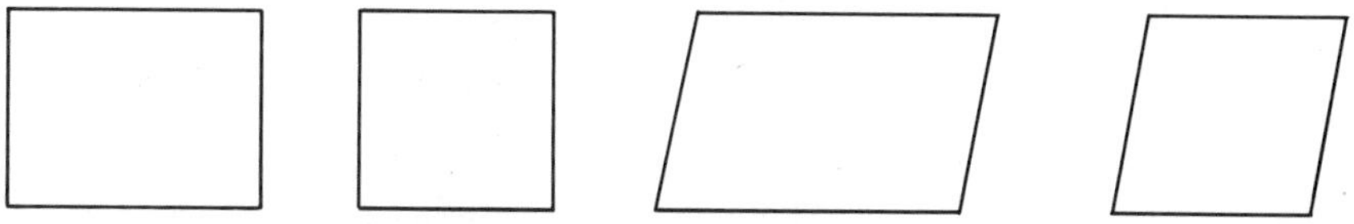

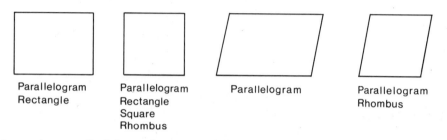

Parallelogram, Rectangle | Parallelogram, Rectangle, Square, Rhombus | Parallelogram | Parallelogram, Rhombus

If the angles are all right angles, a parallelogram is a **rectangle.** If the sides of a rectangle are equal, the rectangle is also a **square** and a **rhombus.** If these figures are "pushed over" to the right, the sides are still parallel, and the **equilateral parallelogram** is no longer a square but is still a rhombus because rhombus is another name for an equilateral parallelogram. If we have a quadrilateral and are given any of the following, we can prove that the quadrilateral is a parallelogram.

1. Both pairs of opposite sides are parallel.
2. Both members of one pair of opposite sides are equal and parallel.
3. Both pairs of opposite sides are equal.
4. Both pairs of opposite angles are equal.
5. The diagonals bisect each other.

We will do these proofs in this lesson and in the homework problem sets that follow. The proof each time will be to show that key triangles are congruent.

Example 81.C.1 Prove that if two sides of a quadrilateral are equal and parallel, then the quadrilateral is a parallelogram.

Solution We draw the quadrilateral shown and draw a diagonal $\overline{PA}$.

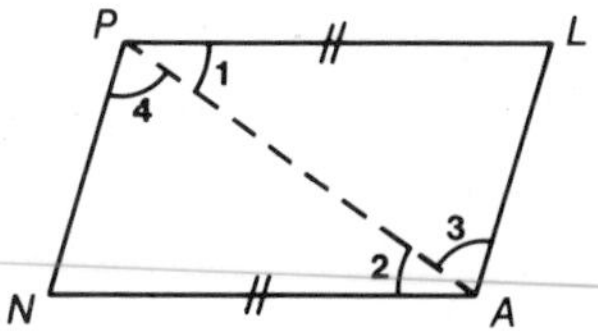

Given: $PL = AN$; $\overline{PL} \parallel \overline{AN}$
Prove: Quadrilateral $PLAN$ is a parallelogram.

We can show that triangles PAN and APL are similar by SAS. The dashed line is a transversal that cuts the parallel lines $\overline{PL}$ and $\overline{NA}$. Angle 2 equals angle 1 because they are alternate interior angles. Side PL is given equal to side NA and side PA equals itself. Thus the triangles are similar with a scale factor of 1.

$$\triangle ANP \cong \triangle PLA$$

Thus, angles 3 and 4 are equal because they are corresponding angles in congruent triangles. This makes $\overline{PN}$ and $\overline{LA}$ parallel because they are lines cut by a transversal and the alternate interior angles are equal. Thus, by the definition of a parallelogram, quadrilateral *PLAN* is a parallelogram because it has two pairs of parallel sides.

Example 81.C.2 Prove that if the diagonals of a quadrilateral bisect each other, then the quadrilateral is a parallelogram.

Solution We draw quadrilateral *DOGS* and draw the diagonals to intersect at *M* as shown. Vertical angles are equal, so the triangle on the left is similar to the triangle on the right by SAS.

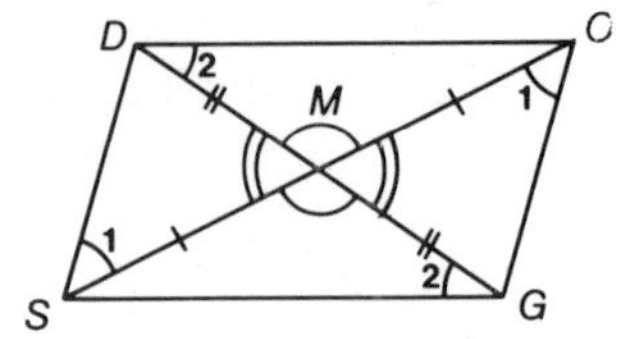

$$\triangle DMS \sim \triangle GMO$$

The angles marked 1 are equal because they are corresponding angles in similar triangles. Thus, $\overline{OG} \parallel \overline{DS}$ because the angles 1 are alternate interior angles and are equal. Also, the upper triangle is similar to the lower triangle by SAS.

$$\triangle GMS \sim \triangle DMO$$

Now the angles marked 2 are equal because they are corresponding angles in similar triangles. Because the angles marked 2 are equal and they are alternate interior angles, the segments $\overline{DO}$ and $\overline{GS}$ are parallel.

The figure is a parallelogram because both pairs of opposite sides are parallel.

Problem set 81

1. A father made a deal with the son. Every day the son worked he was paid \$20, but every day he did not work he was docked \$2. The deal ran for 30 days and then the son was paid \$424. How many days did he work?

2. A pair of fair dice is rolled twice. What is the probability that the first roll will not be a 7 and the second roll will be a 7 in that order?

3. The constant k in the exponential equation was 0.003, and the initial amount was 10. How many units of time had to elapse before the amount increased to 150?

4. If the length of a rectangle is increased by 20 percent and the width is decreased by 20 percent, what happens to the area?

5. Mister Wonderful was paid \$360 for jumping. If he had been paid \$7 more per jump, he would have been paid \$640. How many times did Mister Wonderful jump?

6. Prove that the base angles of an isosceles triangle are equal.

7. Prove that any point on the angle bisector of an angle is equidistant from the sides of the angle.

8. Prove that if one pair of opposite sides of a quadrilateral is equal and parallel, then the quadrilateral is a parallelogram.

9. A triangle has a 30° angle. A side adjacent to this angle has length 6 and the side opposite this angle has length 4. Find the length(s) of the third side.

10. A triangle has a 50° angle. A side adjacent to this angle has length 10 and the side opposite this angle has length 6. Find the length(s) of the third side.

11. A turbine with a radius of 2 feet turns at the rate of 10,000 revolutions per minute. What is the linear velocity of a point on the rim of the turbine?

12. Find the two square roots of $8 + 15i$ and express the roots in polar form.

13. Find three geometric means between 1 and 81.

14. Prove the Pythagorean theorem by using the figures shown below.

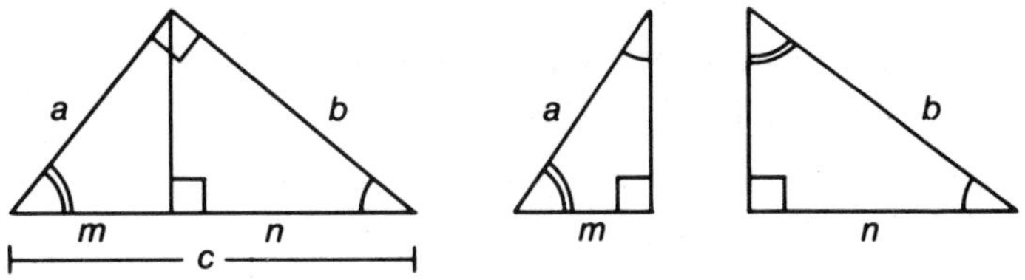

15. Write the standard form of the equation of an ellipse centered at the origin with major axis horizontal of length 10 and minor axis of length 8.

16. Describe the hyperbola whose equation is $16x^2 - 4y^2 = 64$ and find the equations of the asymptotes.

17. Find the twenty-fifth term of an arithmetic sequence whose first term is -6 and whose common difference is 2.

18. Find $2 \sin 30^\circ \cos 30^\circ$ by first recalling the double-angle identity for the sine function. Use exact values.

Solve the following equations given that $(0^\circ \le x, \theta < 360^\circ)$:

19. $\tan x + \sqrt{1 - 2\tan^2 x} = 0$

20. $2 - \csc 3\theta = 0$

Show that:

21. $4\cos^2 x - 2\cos 2x = 2$

22. $\dfrac{2\cos x}{\sin 2x} = \csc x$

23. $\dfrac{\cos x}{\sec x - 1} - \dfrac{\cos x}{\sec x + 1} = 2\cos^3 x \csc^2 x$

24. Solve this triangle for side a.

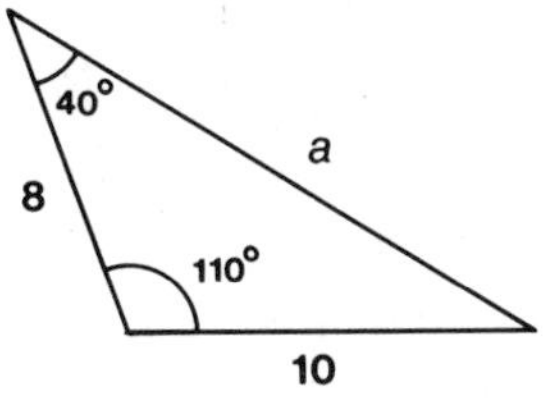

25. Find the length of side a.

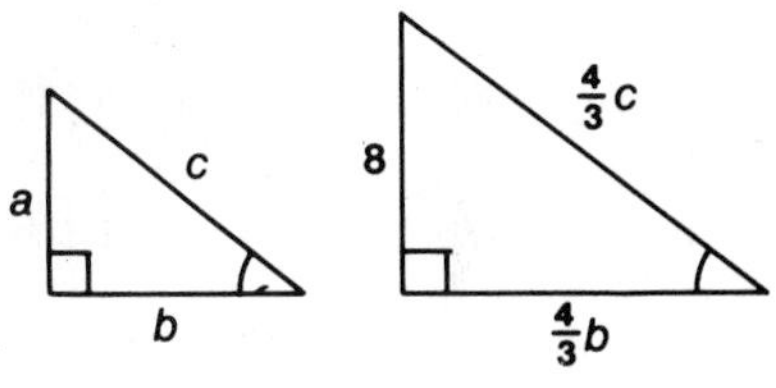

26. Sketch $y = -1 + 2\sin 3\left(x - \dfrac{\pi}{9}\right)$.

27. Write the equations of the following trigonometric functions.

(*a*) (*b*)

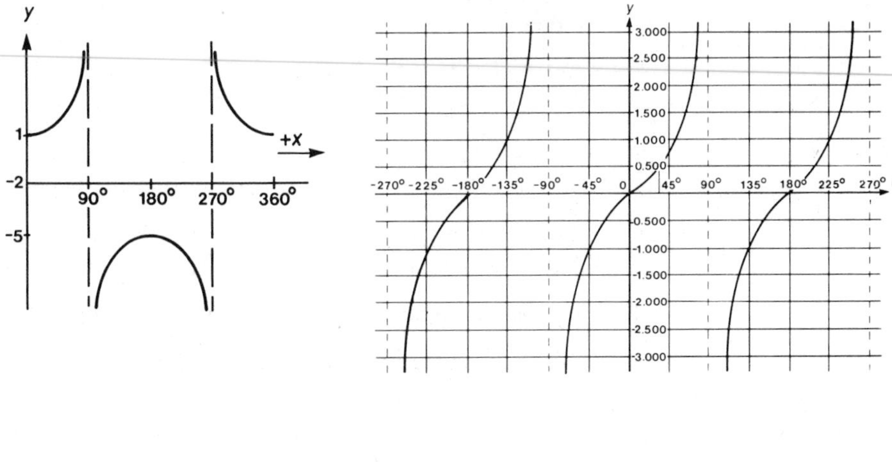

Solve:

28. $\log_{10} x + \log_{10}(x - 3) = 1$

29. $10^{3x+2} = 5^{2x-1}$

30. Find the base 3 antilogarithm of -2.

EP 81.34, 81.35

LESSON 82 Change of base · Contrived logarithm problems

82.A Change of base

We remember that any positive number except 1 can be used as the base for logarithms. Logarithms whose base is 10 are especially useful for involved numerical calculations and historically have been used extensively for this purpose. Logarithms whose base is e possess certain qualities that make them useful in calculus and in other higher mathematics courses. Base e logarithms are studied to prepare for these courses. Many mathematics books have tables of base 10 logarithms and tables of base e logarithms, and most scientific calculators have LOG keys for base 10 logarithms and LN keys for base e logarithms.

Sometimes it is necessary to find a logarithm to a base other than e or 10. Fortunately, this can be done easily if base 10 or base e values are available. There is a formula that can be used to change the base, but it is easy to forget. **We prefer to write the desired change as a logarithmic equation, rewrite the equation as an exponential equation, and then take the logarithm of both sides and solve.** It is a simple procedure and is easy to remember.

Example 82.A.1 Find $\log_5 15$.

Solution We begin by writing a logarithmic equation.

$$y = \log_5 15$$

Now we rewrite this equation as an exponential equation.

$$5^y = 15$$

Next we take the log of both sides. We can use either base 10 or base e. We decide to do both to show that the results would be the same.

USING BASE 10		USING BASE e	
$y \log 5 = \log 15$	took log of both sides	$y \ln 5 = \ln 15$	took ln of both sides
$y = \dfrac{\log 15}{\log 5}$	divided	$y = \dfrac{\ln 15}{\ln 5}$	divided
$y = \dfrac{1.1761}{0.69897}$	log values	$y = \dfrac{2.7081}{1.6094}$	ln values
$y = 1.6826$	divided	$y = 1.6826$	divided

In both examples, we find the same value for the logarithm of 15 to the base 5.

$$\mathbf{\log_5 15 = 1.6826} \qquad \text{which means} \qquad 5^{1.6826} = 15$$

Example 82.A.2 Find $\log_7 82$.

Solution We will write a log equation, change it to an exponential equation, take the $\log_{10}$ of both sides, and solve.

$$y = \log_7 82 \qquad \text{log equation}$$

$$7^y = 82 \qquad \text{exponential equation}$$

$$y \log_{10} 7 = \log_{10} 82 \qquad \text{took log of both sides}$$

$$y = \frac{\log_{10} 82}{\log_{10} 7} \qquad \text{divided by } \log_{10} 7$$

$$y = \frac{1.9}{0.85} = 2.24 \qquad \text{evaluated}$$

Thus, we have

$$\mathbf{\log_7 82 = 2.24} \qquad \text{which means} \qquad 7^{2.24} = 82$$

82.B Contrived logarithm problems

Algebra books contain problems designed to give the reader meaningful practice in fundamental concepts. Some of the problems develop understanding that can be applied directly to real-world problems in science and business. Other problems have no direct applications, but the problems are useful because they provide practice that encourages a more comprehensive understanding of basic concepts. In this lesson, we will investigate some logarithm problems that fall into this category.

We have learned that when a variable is raised to a rational power such as

$$x^{3/2} = 8$$

the solution can be found by raising both sides to the reciprocal of the power. In this example the reciprocal of the power is $\frac{2}{3}$.

$$(x^{3/2})^{2/3} = (8)^{2/3} \longrightarrow x = 4$$

We have learned to recognize that the sum of logarithms or the difference of logarithms means that numbers have been multiplied or divided, respectively.

$$\log (x + 2) + \log (x - 3) \qquad \text{equals} \qquad \log (x + 2)(x - 3)$$

$$\log (x + 2) - \log (x - 3) \qquad \text{equals} \qquad \log \frac{x + 2}{x - 3}$$

The problems discussed in this lesson are designed to help us to remember the following:

1. The logarithm of an exponential equals the exponent times the logarithm of the base of the exponential.

$$\log x^n \qquad \text{equals} \qquad n \log x$$

2. Exponential equations can often be solved by taking the log of both sides. To demonstrate, we solve the following equation for x by taking the log of both sides and then dividing by $\log (n - 4)$.

$$(n - 4)^x = k \longrightarrow x \log (n - 4) = \log k \longrightarrow x = \frac{\log k}{\log (n - 4)}$$

Division by divisors that contain a variable is valid if we exclude values of the variable that cause the divisor to equal zero. Since any nonzero base raised to the zero power has a value of 1, the logarithm of 1 to any nonzero base is 0.

$$b^0 = 1 \qquad \text{therefore} \qquad \log_b 1 = 0$$

The argument of a logarithm can never be negative. In this example, we have the added restriction that the argument cannot equal 1 because this will cause the divisor to equal zero. Thus, n must be greater than 4, and also n cannot equal 5.

$$x = \frac{\log k}{\log (n - 4)} \qquad (n > 4, n \neq 5)$$

3. Logarithmic equations can often be solved by rewriting them as exponential equations. We can rewrite the following logarithmic equation to solve for x as we show here.

$$\log x = 4 \qquad \text{logarithmic equation}$$

$$10^4 = x \qquad \text{exponential form}$$

$$10{,}000 = x \qquad \text{simplified}$$

Example 82.B.1 Solve $\log x^2 = (\log x)^2$.

Solution We will show two different ways to solve this problem. The first way involves division by an expression, $(\log x)$, that contains a variable. **The solution is acceptable if, as the last step, we check the original equation with the value(s) of the variable that would cause the divisor to equal 0.** This last step ensures that we do not inadvertently discard a valid root when we divide by $\log x$. We begin the solution by rewriting $\log x^2$ as $2 \log x$.

$$2 \log x = (\log x)^2 \qquad \text{rewritten}$$

$$2 \log x = (\log x)(\log x) \qquad \text{expanded}$$

Here we wrote $(\log x)^2$ in a more basic form as $(\log x)(\log x)$. Now, if we exclude the possibility that $\log x = 0$, we can divide both sides by $\log x$ and get

$$2 = \log x$$

To finish, we rewrite this log equation as an exponential equation and get

$$10^2 = x \qquad \text{exponential equation}$$

$$\mathbf{100 = x} \qquad \text{solved}$$

As the last step we must see if 1 is a solution to the original equation, because we divided by $\log x$ and $\log x$ has a value of 0 if x equals 1. **This division by $\log x$ is invalid when $\log x$ equals 0, and this division might have caused us to overlook a valid solution.**

$$\log 1^2 = (\log 1)^2 \qquad \text{let } x = 1$$

$$0 = 0 \qquad \text{evaluated}$$

Thus we see that 1 is also a solution, so the equation has two solutions.

$$\mathbf{x = 1 \qquad x = 100}$$

For the second method of solution we begin by writing $\log x^2$ as $2 \log x$, and then we will rearrange the equation and factor to solve.

$$\log x^2 = (\log x)^2 \qquad \text{equation}$$

$$2 \log x = (\log x)^2 \qquad \text{power rule}$$

$$(\log x)^2 - 2 \log x = 0 \qquad \text{rearranged}$$

$$(\log x)(\log x - 2) = 0 \qquad \text{factored}$$

$\log x = 0$	$\log x - 2 = 0$	factors equal zero
	$\log x = 2$	rearranged
$10^0 = x$	$10^2 = x$	exponent form
$\mathbf{1 = x}$	$\mathbf{100 = x}$	solved

We see that the factor method also gives both solutions.

Example 82.B.2 Solve $\log \sqrt{x} = \sqrt{\log x}$.

Solution We will show two different methods of solution. To begin both we replace the radicals with fractional exponents, and then on the left side we rewrite $\log x^{1/2}$ as $\frac{1}{2} \log x$.

$$\log x^{1/2} = (\log x)^{1/2} \qquad \text{replaced radicals}$$

$$\frac{1}{2} \log x = (\log x)^{1/2} \qquad \text{power rule}$$

Next we eliminate the fractional exponent on the right side by squaring both sides, and we get

$$\frac{1}{4}(\log x)^2 = \log x \qquad \text{squared both sides}$$

Now we can complete the solution by dividing both sides by $\log x$ or by factoring.

$$\frac{1}{4} \log x = 1 \qquad \text{divided by } \log x$$

$$\log x = 4 \qquad \text{multiplied}$$

$$10^4 = x \qquad \text{changed form}$$

$$\mathbf{10{,}000 = x}$$

$$\frac{1}{4}(\log x)^2 - \log x = 0 \qquad \text{rearranged}$$

$$(\log x)\left(\frac{1}{4} \log x - 1\right) = 0 \qquad \text{factored}$$

$$\log x = 0 \qquad \log x = 4$$

$$\mathbf{x = 1} \qquad \mathbf{x = 10{,}000} \qquad \text{solved}$$

On the left we divided by $\log x$, and this division is meaningless if $\log x$ equals 0. Since $\log x = 0$ if x is 1, we will check the original equation to see if 1 is a solution.

$$\log \sqrt{1} = \sqrt{\log 1} \qquad \text{substituted}$$

$$0 = 0 \qquad \text{check}$$

This last step tells that 1 is also a solution.

Example 82.B.3 Solve $\log(\log x) = 3$.

Solution We will solve this logarithmic equation by first rewriting it as an exponential equation.

$$10^3 = \log x$$

$$1000 = \log x$$

Now we solve this logarithmic equation by rewriting it as an exponential equation.

$$\mathbf{10^{1000} = x}$$

Example 82.B.4 Solve $x^{\sqrt{\log x}} = 10^8$.

Solution This is an exponential equation, so we will take the log of both sides.

$$\sqrt{\log x}\,\log x = 8 \log 10$$

The right-hand side equals 8 and $(\log x)^{1/2}(\log x)^1 = (\log x)^{3/2}$, so

$$(\log x)^{3/2} = 8$$

Now we raise both sides to the $\frac{2}{3}$ power, and as the last step, we rewrite the logarithmic equation as an exponential equation.

$[(\log x)^{3/2}]^{2/3} = 8^{2/3}$	raised both sides to $\frac{2}{3}$ power
$\log x = 4$	simplified
$10^4 = x$	exponential equation
$\mathbf{10{,}000 = x}$	10^4 equals 10,000

Problem set 82

1. A man working alone could do a job in m hours, and his friend working alone can do the same job in f hours. How long would it take the man and his friend to do the job if they worked together?

2. The amount present was initially 400, but it decreased exponentially. If 300 remained after 60 minutes, how much remained after 3 hours?

3. Rachel roared along for m miles in h hours and proudly arrived 2 hours early. How fast should she have roared along to get there 1 hour late?

4. Robert ran for the March of Dimes and was paid \$1350. If he had been paid \$2 more for each lap, he would have been paid \$2250. How many laps did Robert run?

5. There were 10 people waiting patiently in line to sit in the 5 chairs along the wall. How many different ways can they sit in the chairs?

6. Use a calculator or a table of logarithms to aid in finding $\log_6 81$ to two decimal places.

7. Find the distance from (1, 3) to $2x - 4y + 2 = 0$.

8. Given: $AC = BC$
Prove: $\angle A = \angle B$

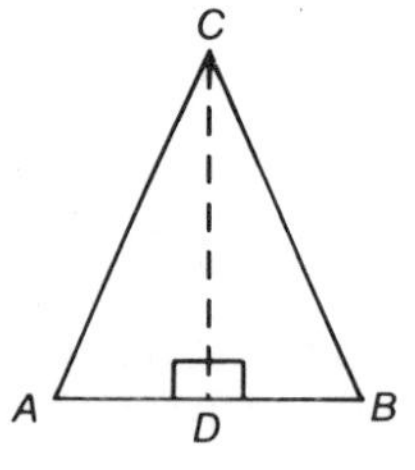

9. Given: $AB = DC$ and $AD = BC$
Prove: $\overline{AB} \parallel \overline{DC}$

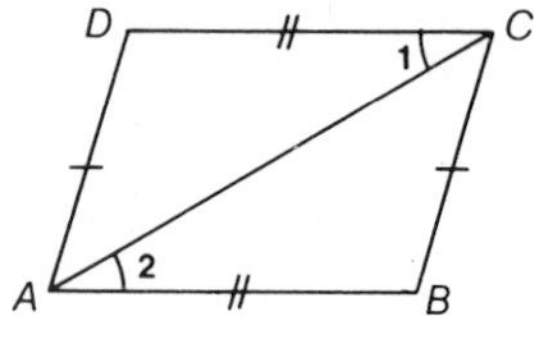

10. Given: $AB = DC$; $\overline{AB} \parallel \overline{DC}$
Prove: $DA = CB$

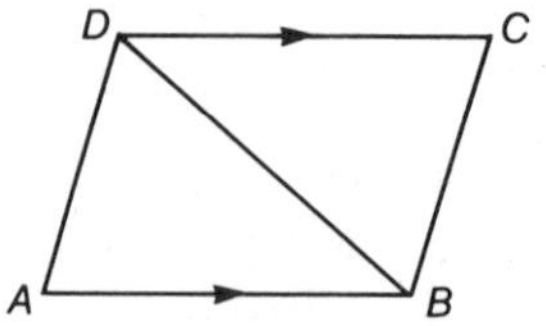

11. A triangle has a 45° angle. A side adjacent to this angle is 8 units long and the side opposite this angle is 4 units long. Find the length(s) of the other side.

12. A triangle has a 20° angle. A side adjacent to this angle has length 10 and the side opposite this angle has length 6. Draw the triangle(s) described and find the measure of the missing side.

13. Find the three cube roots of $6 - 2i$ and express the roots in polar form.

14. Find the fourth term of the geometric sequence whose first term is 2 and whose common ratio is 4.

15. Show that $u^2 + v^2 = w^2$, using the triangles shown.

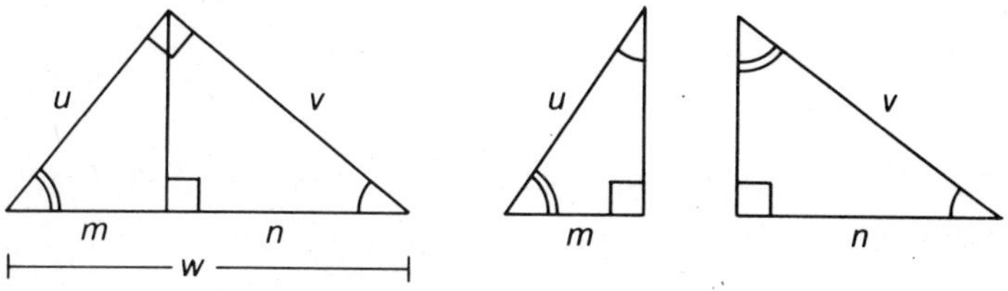

16. Write the general form of the equation of an ellipse centered at the origin with major axis vertical of length 8 and minor axis of length 4.

17. Two pentagons are similar. The ratio of one side of the larger pentagon to the corresponding side of the smaller pentagon is 5 to 4. What is the ratio of their areas?

18. Find $\cos^2 15° - \sin^2 15°$ by using the double-angle identity for the cosine function. Use exact values.

Solve the following equations given that $(0° \le x, \theta < 360°)$:

19. $2\cos^2 x - \sqrt{3}\cos x = 0$

20. $2 - \sqrt{3}\sec 3\theta = 0$

Show that:

21. $\dfrac{2\cos 2x}{\sin 2x} = \cot x - \tan x$

22. $2\csc 2x \cos x = \csc x$

23. $\dfrac{2\tan x}{1 + \tan^2 x} = \sin 2x$

24. Solve this triangle for angle A.

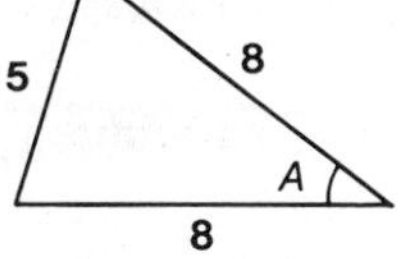

25. Find the length of side c.

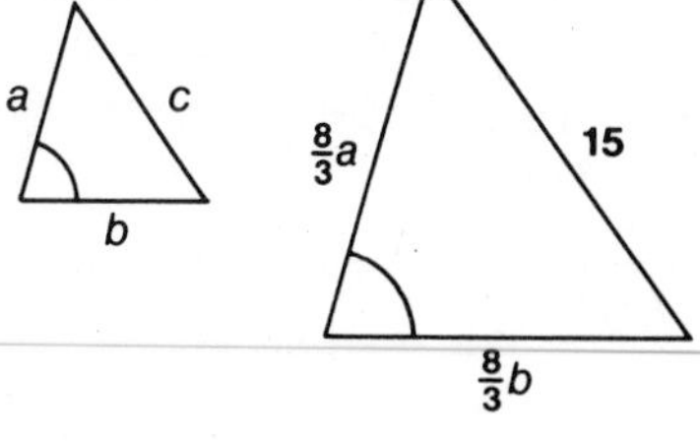

26. Sketch $y = -1 + 5\cos 3(x - 50°)$.

Solve:

27. $\log_2(\log_2 x) = 3$

28. $x^{\sqrt{\log x}} = 10^8$

29. $\log_3 \sqrt{x} = \sqrt{\log_3 x}$

30. Sketch $y = \tan x$.

EP 82.36

LESSON 83 Sequence notations · Advanced sequence problems · The mean

83.A Sequence notations

We have used a_1 for the first term, d for the common difference, and r for the common ratio. Thus, our general expressions for the nth term of an arithmetic progression and the nth term of a geometric progression are

nth TERM (ARITHMETIC)	nth TERM (GEOMETRIC)
$a_n = a_1 + (n-1)d$	$a_n = a_1 r^{(n-1)}$

We note that $n - 1$ appears in both expressions because in the arithmetic progression the difference is used one fewer times than the number of the term, and in the geometric progression the common ratio is used one fewer times than the number of the term. Other authors use other notations. We show several here.

nth TERM (ARITHMETIC)	nth TERM (GEOMETRIC)
$t_n = a + (n-1)d$	$t_n = ar^{n-1}$
$\ell = a + (n-1)d$	$\ell = ar^{n-1}$

83.B Advanced progression problems

Geometric progression problems are straightforward and are easy to solve. We will look at three of them in this lesson. In the first problem, we will use the fact that the common ratio can be found by dividing any term by the term that precedes it. If the geometric progression is $2x^2$, $8x^5$; $32x^8$, we can find the common ratio by dividing the second term by the first term or by dividing the third term by the second term.

$$r = \frac{8x^5}{2x^2} = 4x^3 \qquad \text{also} \qquad r = \frac{32x^8}{8x^5} = 4x^3$$

In general, if the geometric progression is

$$t_1, t_2, t_3, t_4, t_5, t_6, \ldots$$

any fraction formed by dividing a term by the preceding term equals r. Thus, these fractions are equal to each other.

$$r = \frac{t_2}{t_1} = \frac{t_3}{t_2} = \frac{t_4}{t_3} = \frac{t_5}{t_4} = \frac{t_6}{t_5} = \cdots = \frac{t_n}{t_{n-1}}$$

Example 83.B.1 Find the tenth term in the geometric progression that begins $x, \sqrt{2}x^2, 2x^3, \ldots$.

Solution The first term is x, and the common ratio is found by dividing any term by the term that precedes it. In this problem, we can divide the second term by the first term and check by dividing the third term by the second term.

$$r = \frac{\sqrt{2}x^2}{x} = \sqrt{2}x \qquad \text{also} \qquad r = \frac{2x^3}{\sqrt{2}x^2} = \sqrt{2}x$$

Thus x is the first term, and r is $\sqrt{2}x$. Therefore,

$$a_{10} = x(\sqrt{2}x)^9 = \mathbf{2^{9/2}x^{10}}$$

Example 83.B.2 Find the fourth term in the geometric progression that begins $2 + \sqrt{6}$, $6 + 2\sqrt{6}$, $12 + 6\sqrt{6}, \ldots$.

Solution To find r, we will divide the second term by the first term. Then we multiply above and below to rationalize the expression.

$$r = \frac{6 + 2\sqrt{6}}{2 + \sqrt{6}} \cdot \frac{2 - \sqrt{6}}{2 - \sqrt{6}} = \frac{-2\sqrt{6}}{-2} = \sqrt{6}$$

To find the fourth term, we multiply the third term by $\sqrt{6}$.

$$(12 + 6\sqrt{6})(\sqrt{6}) = \mathbf{36 + 12\sqrt{6}}$$

Example 83.B.3 A ball is dropped from a height of 81 inches. On each bounce, the ball rebounds two-fifths of the distance it fell. How far does the ball fall on its sixth fall?

Solution We will draw a picture of the problem (not to scale), and let each term represent the distance the ball fell.

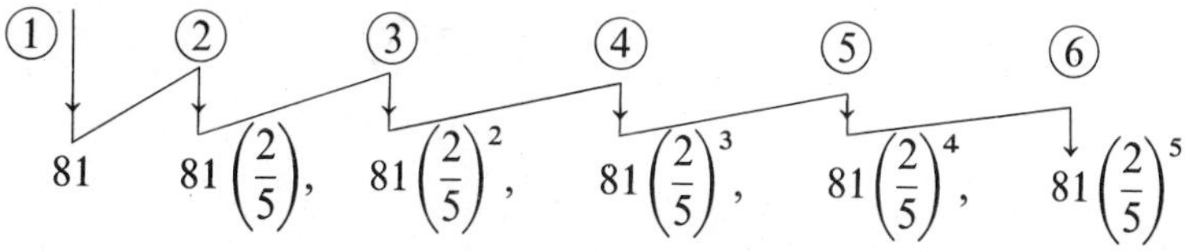

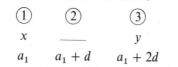

From the diagram we see that on the sixth fall the distance D traveled was

$$D = 81\left(\frac{2}{5}\right)^5 = \mathbf{0.82944\ inch}$$

83.C The mean

We have learned that we can find any counting number of arithmetic and geometric means between two given numbers. Sometimes a problem will ask that we find **the** arithmetic or **the** geometric mean of two numbers. When this happens, we are asked to find *one mean.* **The arithmetic mean** is often called the **average** of the two numbers, and **the geometric mean** is sometimes called the **mean proportional.**

Example 83.C.1 Find the arithmetic mean of x and y.

Solution We want to find **one** arithmetic mean between x and y. A diagram will help.

①	②	③
x	___	y
a_1	$a_1 + d$	$a_1 + 2d$

We see that a_1 is x and $a_1 + 2d$ equals y. We replace a_1 with x and solve for d.

$$x + 2d = y \qquad \text{replaced } a_1 \text{ with } x$$

$$2d = y - x \qquad \text{added } -x$$

$$d = \frac{y - x}{2} \qquad \text{divided}$$

The mean is the first term plus the difference, or

$$x + \frac{y - x}{2}$$

$$\frac{2x}{2} + \frac{y - x}{2} \qquad \text{common denominator}$$

$$\mathbf{\frac{y + x}{2}} \qquad \text{added}$$

We will use this last expression as a general expression for the arithmetic mean. **It is important to note and to remember that the arithmetic mean of two numbers is commonly called the *average* of the two numbers.**

Example 83.C.2 Find the geometric mean (mean proportional) of x and y.

Solution We want to find **one** geometric mean. **A diagram always helps,** so we will use a diagram.

①	②	③
x,	___	y
a_1,	a_1r,	a_1r^2

Our diagram tells us that $a_1 = x$ and $a_1r^2 = y$. We substitute and solve for r.

$$xr^2 = y \qquad \text{equation}$$

$$r^2 = \frac{y}{x} \qquad \text{divided by } x$$

$$r = \pm\sqrt{\frac{y}{x}} \qquad \text{root of both sides}$$

Now the second term is the product of the first term and the common ratio.

$$a_1r \qquad \text{second term}$$

$$x\left(\pm\sqrt{\frac{y}{x}}\right) \qquad \text{substituted}$$

$$\mathbf{\pm\sqrt{xy}} \qquad \text{simplified}$$

We will use this last expression as a general expression for the geometric mean of two numbers. We see that we can have either a positive or a negative geometric mean of two given numbers. **The requirement to recall the expression for the geometric mean occurs from time to time, and it is helpful to commit this expression to memory.**

Example 83.C.3 The positive geometric mean of two numbers is 8, and the difference between the numbers is 30. Find the numbers.

Solution We will use L for the larger number and S for the smaller number. We get two equations.

$$(a)\quad L - S = 30 \qquad (b)\quad \sqrt{LS} = 8$$

First we will square both sides of (b) and then substitute $L - 30$ for S.

$$LS = 64 \qquad \text{squared both sides}$$

$$L(L - 30) = 64 \qquad \text{substituted}$$

$$-30L + L^2 = 64 \qquad \text{multiplied}$$

$$L^2 - 30L - 64 = 0 \qquad \text{simplified}$$

$$L = \frac{+30 \pm \sqrt{900 - 4(1)(-64)}}{2}$$

$$= -2, +32 \qquad \text{solved}$$

Thus we find that both -2 and 32 are solutions for the larger number. If we use these numbers one at a time in equation (a), we find that the smaller numbers are -32 and 2. So the ordered pairs of (L, S) are $\mathbf{(-2, -32)}$, and $\mathbf{(32, 2)}$.

Problem set 83

1. Billy Bob could do m jobs in 4 hours; and when Sally Sue helped, they could do 2 jobs in t hours. What was Sally Sue's rate of doing jobs?

2. After 10 years only 500 remained and after 20 years only 400 remained. What was their half-life?

3. There were 60 people in the room and 20 had blue eyes. Fifty of the people had dyed their hair green, and 10 people who had blue eyes also had dyed green hair. If one person was selected at random, what is the probability of that person having either blue eyes or green hair or both?

4. The value of the purchase varied directly as the square of the satisfaction factor and the square root of the envy factor. What happened to the value when the satisfaction factor was multiplied by 3 and the envy factor was multiplied by 4?

5. Franklin ran the F miles at r miles per hour. If he increased his speed by 4 miles per hour, how long would it take him to run $F + 6$ miles?

6. Use a calculator or a table of logarithms to aid in finding $\log_5 60$ to two decimal places.

7. Use a calculator or a table of logarithms to aid in finding $\log_6 50$ to two decimal places.

8. Given: $\angle A = \angle B$
Prove: $AC = CB$

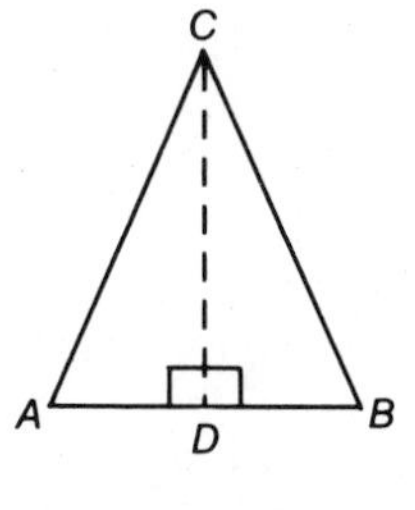

9. Given: $AB = DC$; $AD = BC$
Prove: $\angle A = \angle C$

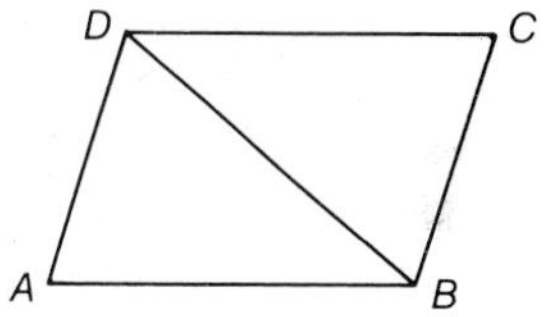

10. Given: $AB = DC$; $\overline{AB} \parallel \overline{DC}$
Prove: $\overline{DA} \parallel \overline{CB}$

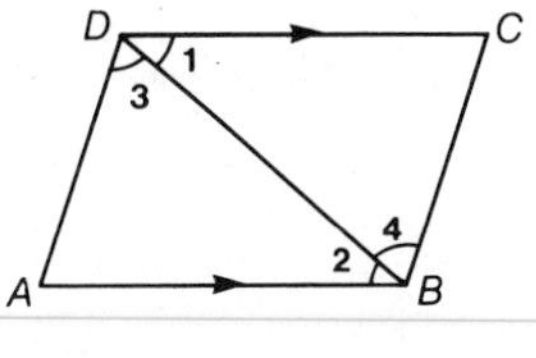

11. A triangle has a 50° angle. A side adjacent to this angle is 10 units long, and the side opposite is 9 units long. How long is the other side?

12. Find four fourth roots of $3 + 2i$ and express the roots in polar form.

13. A ball is dropped from a height of 128 feet. After each bounce, it rebounds one-half of the distance it fell. How far does the ball fall on its fourth fall?

14. The positive geometric mean of two numbers is 9, and the difference of the two numbers is 24. What are the two numbers?

15. Find the fourth term in the geometric progression that begins $1 + \sqrt{2}, 3 + 2\sqrt{2}, \ldots$.

16. Find the arithmetic mean of 8 and 22.

17. Show that $x^2 + y^2 = z^2$, using the figures drawn below.

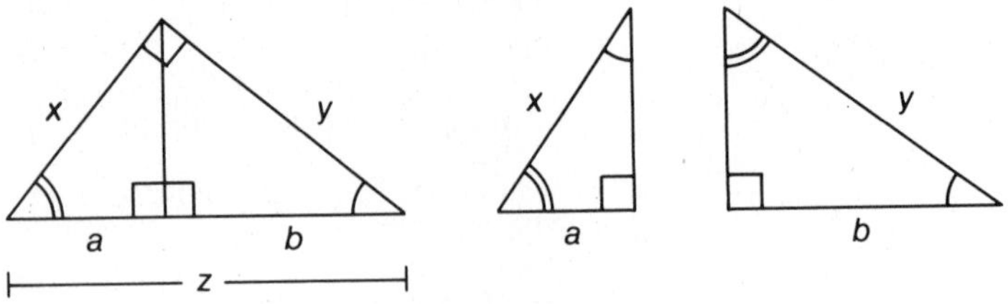

18. Find $2\cos^2 15° - 1$ by using the double-angle identity for the cosine function. Use exact values.

Solve the following equations given that $(0° \le x, \theta < 360°)$:

19. $2\cos^2 x + \sin x - 1 = 0$

20. $2 + \sqrt{3}\sec 3\theta = 0$

Show that:

21. $\dfrac{\cos^3 x - \sin^3 x}{\cos x - \sin x} = 1 + \dfrac{1}{2}\sin 2x$

22. $\dfrac{\cos 2x}{\cos^2 x} = 1 - \tan^2 x$

23. $\tan 2x = \dfrac{2}{\cot x - \tan x}$

24. Solve this triangle for side a.

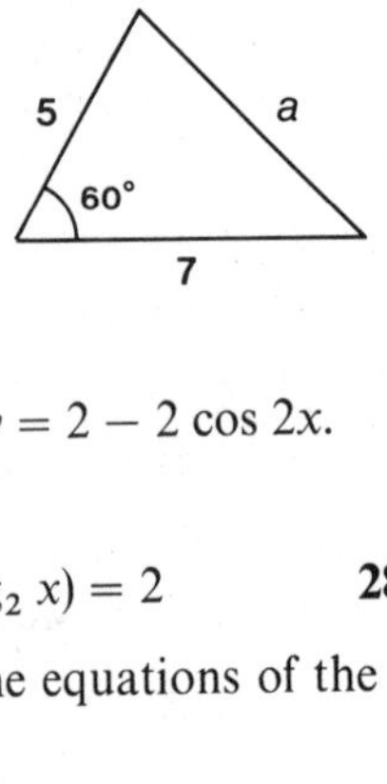

25. Find the length of side y.

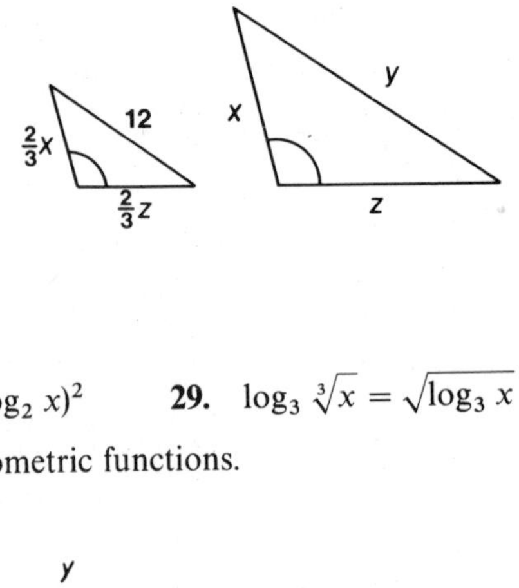

26. Sketch $y = 2 - 2\cos 2x$.

Solve:

27. $\log_2(\log_2 x) = 2$

28. $\log_2 x^2 = 2(\log_2 x)^2$

29. $\log_3 \sqrt[3]{x} = \sqrt{\log_3 x}$

30. Write the equations of the following trigonometric functions.

(*a*)

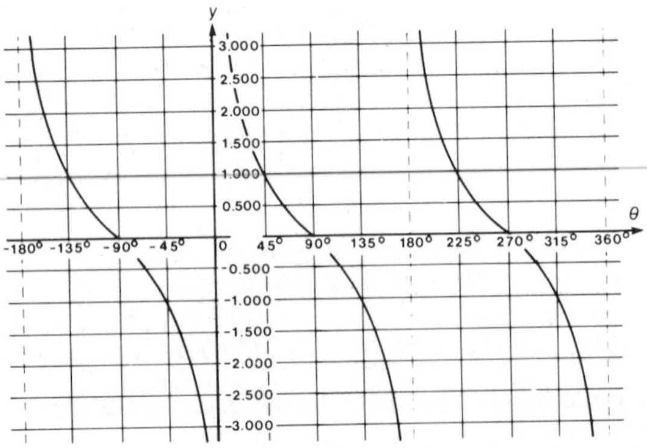

(*b*)

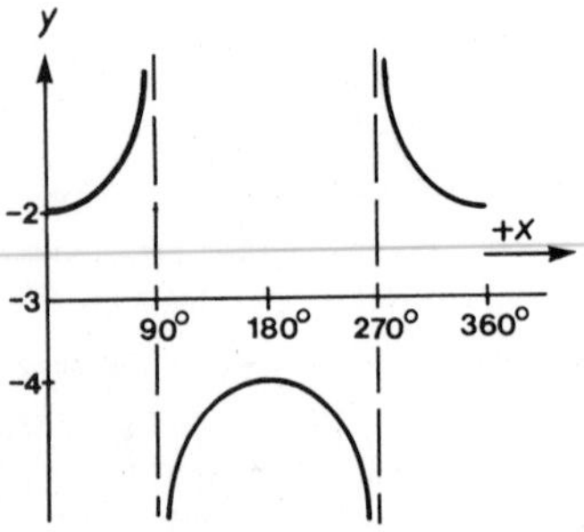

EP 83.37, 83.38

LESSON 84 Product identities · Sum and difference identities

84.A Product identities

There are four identities that involve the products of sines and cosines of angles. The first two are really equivalent, as they involve the product of the sine of one angle and the cosine of another angle. We begin our list with identity (*g*), since identities (*a*) to (*f*) were listed in Lesson 72.

$$(g)\quad \sin A \cos B = \frac{1}{2}[\sin(A+B) + \sin(A-B)]$$

$$(h)\quad \cos A \sin B = \frac{1}{2}[\sin(A+B) - \sin(A-B)]$$

$$(i)\quad \sin A \sin B = \frac{1}{2}[\cos(A-B) - \cos(A+B)]$$

$$(j)\quad \cos A \cos B = \frac{1}{2}[\cos(A+B) + \cos(A-B)]$$

These identities are difficult to memorize and retain because they are so alike. But they can be developed accurately and without effort by looking at the four key identities for the sines and cosines of the sums and differences of angles, as we will show in the following examples.

Example 84.A.1 Develop the identity for $\sin A \cos B$.

Solution **Whenever one of the identities above is required, an excellent first step is to write down all four key identities. By looking at these identities, the necessary identity can be written without error.**

$$(a)\quad \sin(A+B) = \sin A \cos B + \cos A \sin B$$
$$(b)\quad \sin(A-B) = \sin A \cos B - \cos A \sin B$$
$$(c)\quad \cos(A+B) = \cos A \cos B - \sin A \sin B$$
$$(d)\quad \cos(A-B) = \cos A \cos B + \sin A \sin B$$

Now we need an identity for $\sin A \cos B$. We look at the identities (*a*) to (*d*) and see that $\sin A \cos B$ appears in both (*a*) and (*b*). If we add identities (*a*) and (*b*), we get

$$\sin(A+B) + \sin(A-B) = 2\sin A \cos B$$

The $\cos A \sin B$ terms had opposite signs and added to zero. Now we have an expression for $2\sin A \cos B$, and we want only $\sin A \cos B$, so we complete the development by multiplying both sides by $\frac{1}{2}$ and we get the identity we seek.

$$\mathbf{\frac{1}{2}[\sin(A+B) + \sin(A-B)] = \sin A \cos B}$$

Example 84.A.2 Develop the identity for $\cos A \sin B$.

Solution We search the key identities and find $\cos A \sin B$ in identities (*a*) and (*b*), but they have opposite signs. We decide to change the signs in (*b*) so that the result will be positive. To do this, we multiply both sides of (*b*) by -1 and add the equations.

$$\begin{array}{rrl} (a) & \sin(A+B) = & \sin A \cos B + \cos A \sin B \\ -(b) & -\sin(A-B) = & -\sin A \cos B + \cos A \sin B \\ \hline \end{array}$$
$$\sin(A+B) - \sin(A-B) = 2\cos A \sin B$$

Now we complete the development by multiplying both sides by $\frac{1}{2}$, and we get

$$\mathbf{\frac{1}{2}[\sin(A + B) - \sin(A - B)] = \cos A \sin B}$$

Example 84.A.3 Develop the identity for $\cos A \cos B$.

Solution We find $\cos A \cos B$ in key identities (c) and (d), and we begin by adding these identities; the sum is

$$\cos(A + B) + \cos(A - B) = 2\cos A \cos B$$

We finish by multiplying both sides by $\frac{1}{2}$, and we get

$$\mathbf{\frac{1}{2}[\cos(A + B) + \cos(A - B)] = \cos A \cos B}$$

Example 84.A.4 Develop the identity for $\sin A \sin B$.

Solution **This development is a little tricky because of the care that must be taken with the − signs.** We find $\sin A \sin B$ in key identities (c) and (d). If we change the signs in (d), we will end up with $-2\sin A \sin B$ when we add. So we decide to change the signs in (c) by multiplying every term by -1.

$$\begin{array}{rrl} -(c) & -\cos(A + B) = & -\cos A \cos B + \sin A \sin B \\ (d) & \cos(A - B) = & \cos A \cos B + \sin A \sin B \\ \hline \multicolumn{2}{r}{\cos(A - B) - \cos(A + B) =} & 2\sin A \sin B \end{array}$$

We complete the development by multiplying both sides by $\frac{1}{2}$, and we get

$$\mathbf{\frac{1}{2}[\cos(A - B) - \cos(A + B)] = \sin A \sin B}$$

84.B Sum and difference identities

There are four rather involved identities for the sums and differences of sines and cosines of two angles. The appearance of these identities is intimidating, but their development by using the key identities is even easier than the four developments in the preceding section. The identities are as follows:

$$(k) \quad \sin x + \sin y = 2\sin\frac{x + y}{2}\cos\frac{x - y}{2}$$

$$(l) \quad \sin x - \sin y = 2\cos\frac{x + y}{2}\sin\frac{x - y}{2}$$

$$(m) \quad \cos x + \cos y = 2\cos\frac{x + y}{2}\cos\frac{x - y}{2}$$

$$(n) \quad \cos x - \cos y = -2\sin\frac{x + y}{2}\sin\frac{x - y}{2}$$

We note that these identities use the variables x and y rather than the variables A and B. This is because in their development we use a change of variable. We use x to represent $A + B$ and use y to represent $A - B$.

$$A + B = x \qquad A - B = y$$

If we add these equations in their present form, we can solve for A in terms of x and y.

$$\begin{array}{ll} A + B = x & \text{left equation} \\ \underline{A - B = y} & \text{right equation} \\ 2A \quad = x + y & \text{added} \\ A = \dfrac{x+y}{2} & \text{divided} \end{array}$$

If we multiply one of the equations by -1 and add the equations, we can solve for B in terms of x and y.

$$\begin{array}{ll} A + B = x & \text{left equation} \\ \underline{-A + B = -y} & -\text{ right equation} \\ 2B = x - y & \text{added} \\ B = \dfrac{x-y}{2} & \text{divided} \end{array}$$

Example 84.B.1 Develop the identity for $\sin x + \sin y$.

Solution We begin by writing the four key identities. Then over each $A + B$ we write x, and over each $A - B$ we write y. Over each A we write $\dfrac{x+y}{2}$, and over each B we write $\dfrac{x-y}{2}$.

$$(a) \quad \sin(\overbrace{A + B}^{x}) = \sin \overset{\frac{x+y}{2}}{A} \cos \overset{\frac{x-y}{2}}{B} + \cos \overset{\frac{x+y}{2}}{A} \sin \overset{\frac{x-y}{2}}{B}$$

$$(b) \quad \sin(\overbrace{A - B}^{y}) = \sin \overset{\frac{x+y}{2}}{A} \cos \overset{\frac{x-y}{2}}{B} - \cos \overset{\frac{x+y}{2}}{A} \sin \overset{\frac{x-y}{2}}{B}$$

$$(c) \quad \cos(\overbrace{A + B}^{x}) = \cos \overset{\frac{x+y}{2}}{A} \cos \overset{\frac{x-y}{2}}{B} - \sin \overset{\frac{x+y}{2}}{A} \sin \overset{\frac{x-y}{2}}{B}$$

$$(d) \quad \cos(\overbrace{A - B}^{y}) = \cos \overset{\frac{x+y}{2}}{A} \cos \overset{\frac{x-y}{2}}{B} + \sin \overset{\frac{x+y}{2}}{A} \sin \overset{\frac{x-y}{2}}{B}$$

Now we see that we can get $\sin x + \sin y$ by adding the top two equations.

$$\mathbf{\sin x + \sin y = 2 \sin \frac{x+y}{2} \cos \frac{x-y}{2}}$$

Example 84.B.2 Develop the identity for $\sin x - \sin y$.

Solution We see that we can get $\sin x - \sin y$ by adding the negative of identity (*b*) to identity (*a*). We do this mentally and get

$$\mathbf{\sin x - \sin y = 2 \cos \frac{x+y}{2} \sin \frac{x-y}{2}}$$

Example 84.B.3 Develop the identity for $\cos x + \cos y$.

Solution We can get this identity in one step by adding identities (*c*) and (*d*). We do this and get

$$\mathbf{\cos x + \cos y = 2 \cos \frac{x+y}{2} \cos \frac{x-y}{2}}$$

Example 84.B.4 Develop the identity for $\cos x - \cos y$.

Solution The identity can be obtained by adding the negative of identity (d) to identity (c). **Be careful with the signs.** We do this and get

$$\cos x - \cos y = -2 \sin \frac{x+y}{2} \sin \frac{x-y}{2}$$

Of course there are many identities for sums, differences, and products of angles. Problems in the problem sets that refer to *the* identity for a sum, difference, or product of angles are referring to the identities developed above. If the development of these identities is practiced once or twice a day for a period of several weeks, the process will become automatic. Then, in the future, these identities can be developed quickly whenever they are needed.

Problem set 84

1. Joe Willy ran m miles at R miles per hour and got there on time. Then the distance was increased 5 miles. How fast did he have to run to travel the new distance in the same time?

2. The number of greens varied directly as the square root of the number of reds and inversely as the number of whites squared. What happens to the number of greens if the number of reds is multiplied by 16 and the number of whites is doubled?

3. Take the permutations and combinations of 11 things taken 4 at a time to do a concrete development of the general expression of ${}_nP_r$ and ${}_nC_r$.

4. The whistle blew to signal high noon. Rumblat didn't quit because his lunch hour began the next time the clock hands formed a 90° angle. How long did Rumblat have to wait for lunch?

5. Sally Sue bought m of the things for d dollars. If the price was increased k dollars per item, how many could Sally Sue buy for \$14?

6. Develop the identity for $\cos A \cos B$.

7. Develop the identity for $\sin A \sin B$.

8. Develop the identity for $\sin x - \sin y$.

9. Develop the identity for $\cos x - \cos y$.

10. Use a calculator or a table of logarithms to aid in finding $\log_8 50$ to two decimal places.

11. Use a calculator or a table of logarithms to aid in finding $\log_5 60$ to two decimal places.

12. Given: CD is the perpendicular bisector of $\overline{AB}$; $\angle 1 = \angle 2$
Prove: $AC = CB$

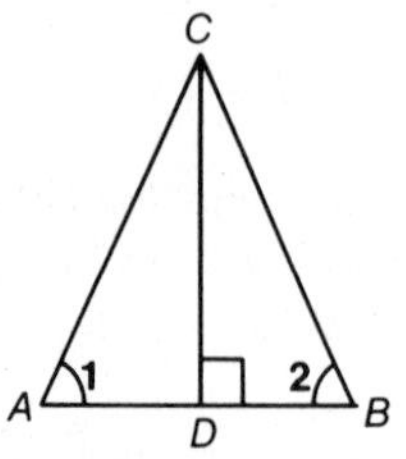

13. Given: $AB = CD$; $\overline{AB} \parallel \overline{CD}$
Prove: $AO = OC$; $DO = OB$
This is the proof that the diagonals of a parallelogram bisect each other.

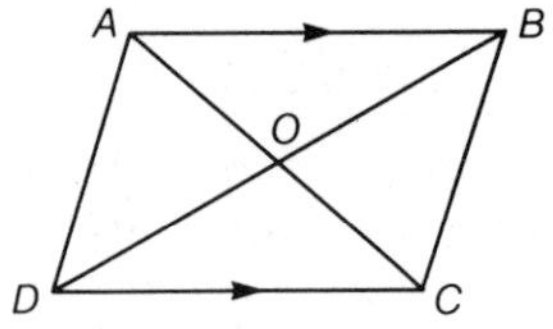

14. A triangle has a 35° angle. A side adjacent to this angle has length 8 and the side opposite this angle has length 4. Draw the triangle(s) described and find the length of the missing side.

15. Find the four fourth roots of $4 - 3i$ and express the roots in polar form.

16. What is the arithmetic mean of 9 and 21?

17. A ball is dropped from a height of 81 feet. After each bounce, it rebounds two-thirds of the distance it fell. How far does the ball fall on its fourth fall?

18. The positive geometric mean of two numbers is 8 and the difference of the two numbers is 12. What are the two numbers?

Solve the following equations given that $(0° \le x, \theta < 360°)$:

19. $2 \sin^2 x + 15 \cos x - 9 = 0$

20. $\sqrt{3} - \cot 2\theta = 0$

Show that:

21. $2 \csc 2x = \cot x + \tan x$

22. $\dfrac{\sin 2x}{\tan x} = 2 \cos^2 x$

23. $(\tan^2 x)(1 + \cot^2 x) = \dfrac{1}{1 - \sin^2 x}$

24. Solve this triangle for angle A.

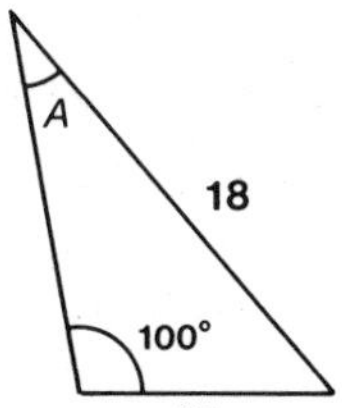

25. Find the length of side x.

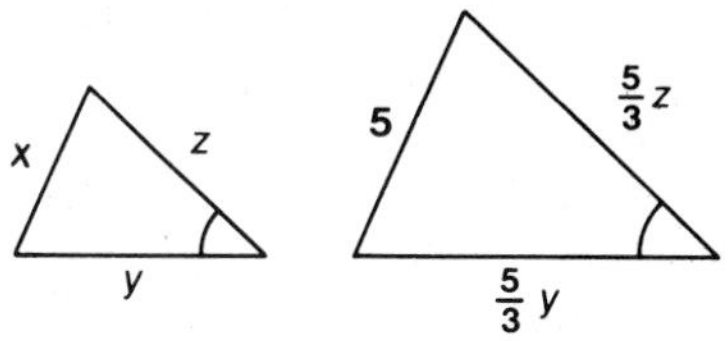

26. Sketch $y = \cot x$.

Solve:

27. $\log_2 (\log_2 x) = 3$

28. $\log_3 x^2 = \log_3 x$

29. $\frac{2}{3} \log_e 8 + \log_e x - \log_e (3x - 2) = \log_e 3$

30. $10^{\log x} = 10^4$

EP 84.39, 84.40

LESSON 85 Zero determinants · 3 × 3 determinants

85.A Zero determinants

We remember that a determinant is a number that is associated with a particular square matrix. A matrix that is not square does not have a determinant.

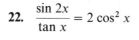

$$\begin{matrix} 4 & 2 \\ 2 & 1 \end{matrix} \qquad \begin{matrix} 8 & 5 & 6 \\ 4 & 7 & 3 \end{matrix}$$

The matrix on the left on the preceding page is a square matrix and has a determinant. The matrix on the right is not square, so it does not have a determinant. While the determinant is a number, we also call the notation

$$\begin{vmatrix} 4 & 2 \\ 2 & 1 \end{vmatrix}$$

a determinant because it represents the number. A determinant can be zero or any other number. The value of the determinant above is 0.

$$\begin{vmatrix} 4 & 2 \\ 2 & 1 \end{vmatrix} = 4 \cdot 1 - 2 \cdot 2 = 0$$

Zero determinants in the denominator when using Cramer's rule tell us that the equations do not have a single common solution. The equations shown here are the equations of parallel lines and thus have no common solution. If we attempt to solve this system by using the elimination method,

$$\begin{cases} 4x + 2y = 8 & \longrightarrow & (1) & \longrightarrow & 4x + 2y = 8 \\ 2x + y = 14 & \longrightarrow & (-2) & \longrightarrow & -4x - 2y = -28 \\ & & & & \overline{0 = -20} \end{cases}$$

the attempt degenerates into the false equation $0 = -20$. If we attempt a solution of the same system by using Cramer's rule,

$$x = \frac{\begin{vmatrix} 8 & 2 \\ 14 & 1 \end{vmatrix}}{\begin{vmatrix} 4 & 2 \\ 2 & 1 \end{vmatrix}} = \frac{-20}{0} \qquad y = \frac{\begin{vmatrix} 4 & 8 \\ 2 & 14 \end{vmatrix}}{\begin{vmatrix} 4 & 2 \\ 2 & 1 \end{vmatrix}} = \frac{40}{0}$$

we see that the denominator determinants are zero. Thus, Cramer's rule cannot be used to solve systems that cannot be solved by using the elimination method because a solution does not exist.

85.B 3 × 3 determinants

If we use the elimination method to solve the following system of equations for x,

$$\begin{cases} a_1x + b_1y + c_1z = k_1 \\ a_2x + b_2y + c_2z = k_2 \\ a_3x + b_3y + c_3z = k_3 \end{cases}$$

the answer will be

$$x = \frac{(k_1b_2c_3 + b_1c_2k_3 + c_1k_2b_3) - (k_3b_2c_1 + b_3c_2k_1 + c_3k_2b_1)}{(a_1b_2c_3 + b_1c_2a_3 + c_1a_2b_3) - (a_3b_2c_1 + b_3c_2a_1 + c_3a_2b_1)}$$

If we are going to use Cramer's rule to solve this system, the solution will be

$$x = \frac{\begin{vmatrix} k_1 & b_1 & c_1 \\ k_2 & b_2 & c_2 \\ k_3 & b_3 & c_3 \end{vmatrix}}{\begin{vmatrix} a_1 & b_1 & c_1 \\ a_2 & b_2 & c_2 \\ a_3 & b_3 & c_3 \end{vmatrix}}$$

Now we must find some system of evaluating these determinants so that we get the same answer that we got when we used elimination. There are many methods that could be used. You could probably invent one of your own. One method is the method of cofactors, and it can be used for any determinant larger than 2 × 2. We will study cofactors in a later lesson. **In this lesson, we will use a method that is applicable only to 3 × 3 determinants.** Given the determinant on the left, we repeat the entries on the right and **repeat the first two columns as columns 4 and 5.**

$$\begin{vmatrix} 3 & -2 & 1 \\ -1 & 4 & 10 \\ 2 & -3 & 5 \end{vmatrix}$$

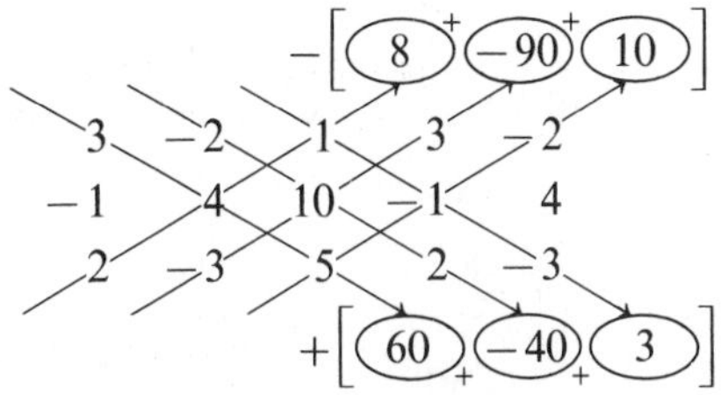

Then we multiply on the diagonals as shown. After we multiply, we sum the products and remember to use the negative of the sum of the upper products.

$$\begin{vmatrix} 3 & -2 & 1 \\ -1 & 4 & 10 \\ 2 & -3 & 5 \end{vmatrix} = (60 - 40 + 3) - (8 - 90 + 10) = \mathbf{95}$$

85.C Determinant solutions of 3 × 3s

Cramer's rule is the same for systems of two equations in two unknowns as it is for three equations in three unknowns. **The denominator determinants are composed of the coefficients of the variables in the equations. In the numerator determinants, the coefficients of x, y, and z are replaced in turn with the constants from the right side of the equations.**

Example 85.C.1 Use Cramer's rule to solve for x, y, and z:

$$\begin{cases} 2x + y + 2z = 7 \\ x + y - z = -2 \\ 3x - y + 2z = 16 \end{cases}$$

Solution First we will evaluate the denominator determinant.

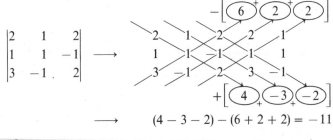

$$\begin{vmatrix} 2 & 1 & 2 \\ 1 & 1 & -1 \\ 3 & -1 & 2 \end{vmatrix} \longrightarrow$$

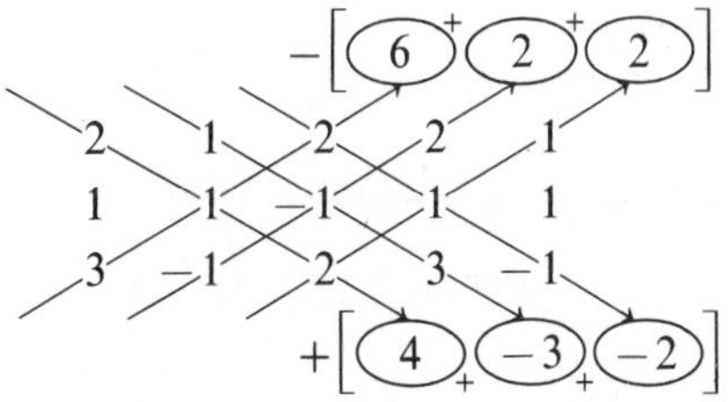

$$\longrightarrow (4 - 3 - 2) - (6 + 2 + 2) = -11$$

Now we solve for x.

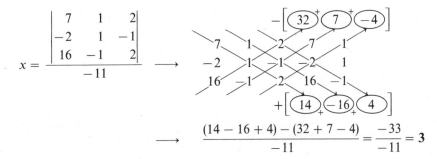

$$x = \frac{\begin{vmatrix} 7 & 1 & 2 \\ -2 & 1 & -1 \\ 16 & -1 & 2 \end{vmatrix}}{-11} \longrightarrow$$

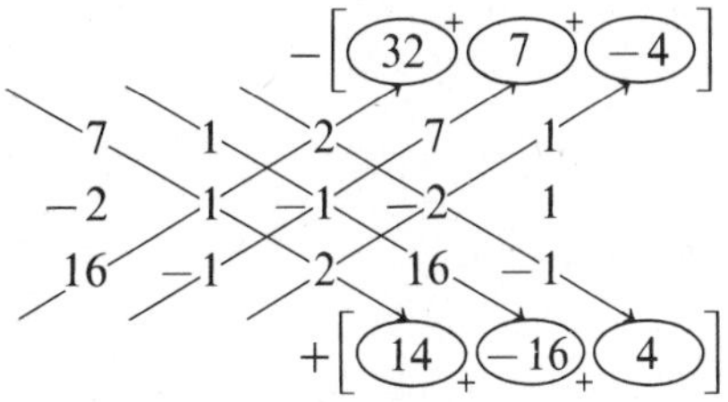

$$\longrightarrow \frac{(14 - 16 + 4) - (32 + 7 - 4)}{-11} = \frac{-33}{-11} = \mathbf{3}$$

Now we solve for y.

$$y = \frac{\begin{vmatrix} 2 & 7 & 2 \\ 1 & -2 & -1 \\ 3 & 16 & 2 \end{vmatrix}}{-11} \longrightarrow$$

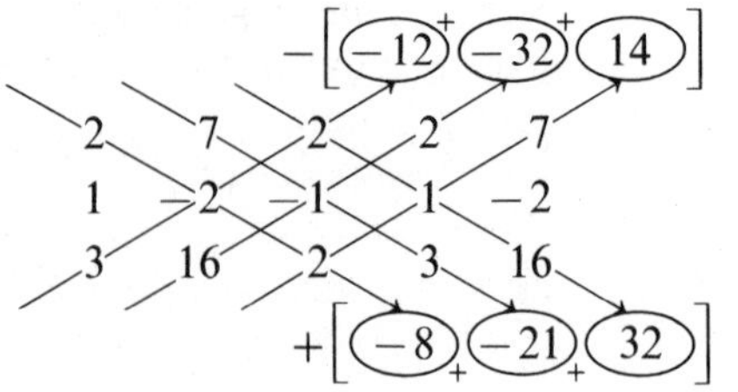

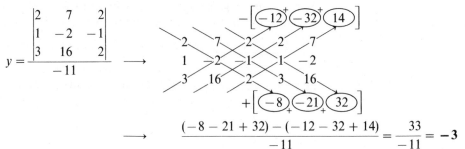

$$\longrightarrow \frac{(-8 - 21 + 32) - (-12 - 32 + 14)}{-11} = \frac{33}{-11} = \mathbf{-3}$$

Now we solve for z.

$$z = \frac{\begin{vmatrix} 2 & 1 & 7 \\ 1 & 1 & -2 \\ 3 & -1 & 16 \end{vmatrix}}{-11} \longrightarrow$$

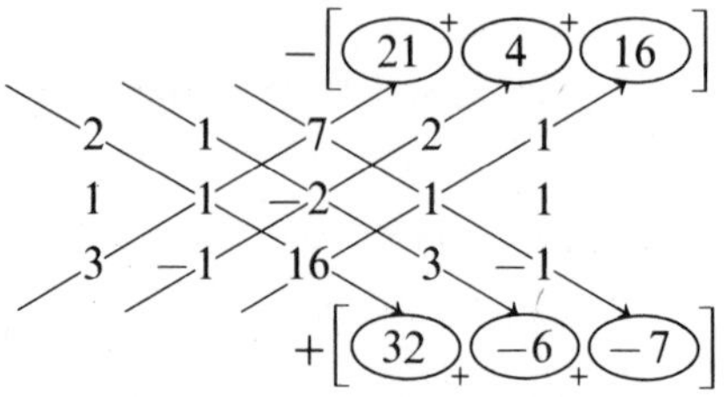

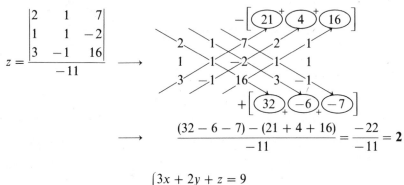

$$\longrightarrow \frac{(32 - 6 - 7) - (21 + 4 + 16)}{-11} = \frac{-22}{-11} = \mathbf{2}$$

Example 85.C.2 Use Cramer's rule to solve for z: $\begin{cases} 3x + 2y + z = 9 \\ 2y + 3z = 14 \\ x + 2y = 3 \end{cases}$

Solution Two of the equations have zeros as coefficients for one variable. This will simplify the solution a little, as we will see.

$$z = \frac{\begin{vmatrix} 3 & 2 & 9 \\ 0 & 2 & 14 \\ 1 & 2 & 3 \end{vmatrix}}{\begin{vmatrix} 3 & 2 & 1 \\ 0 & 2 & 3 \\ 1 & 2 & 0 \end{vmatrix}} \longrightarrow$$

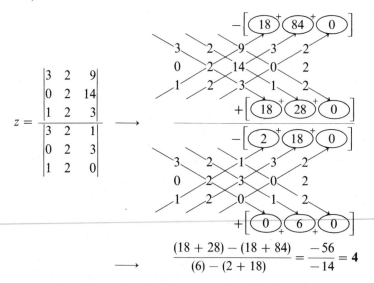

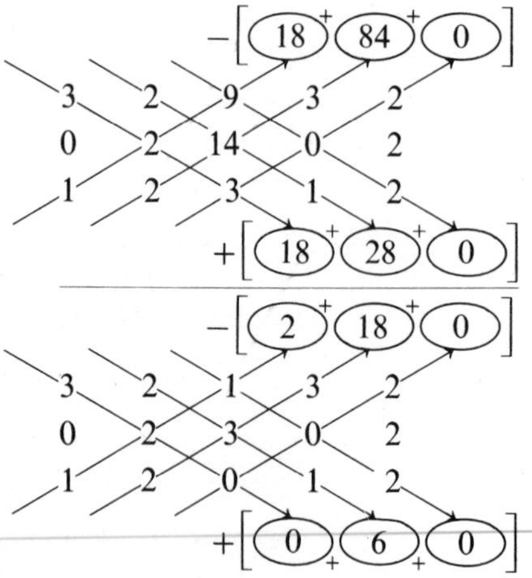

$$\longrightarrow \frac{(18 + 28) - (18 + 84)}{(6) - (2 + 18)} = \frac{-56}{-14} = \mathbf{4}$$

Problem set 85

1. The ratio of reds to greens was 4 to 3, and altogether there were 63 of them lying around the house. How many of them were red?

2. Jimmy counted 800 of the little furry creatures at the outset and after 20 minutes of exponential decay, only 760 of them remained. What was the half-life of the little furry creatures?

3. Two of the three pots contained only brass coins, but one of the pots contained 5 silver coins, 4 gold coins, and 2 alloy coins. Harriet selected a pot and then drew 1 coin. What was the probability that the coin was a gold coin?

4. If $x \# y = 2x - 3y$ and $x * y = x - y$, evaluate $(a \# b) * b$ if $a = 10$ and $b = 2$.

5. The 360-mile trip out was made by car, and the 360-mile trip back was made by plane at twice the speed of the trip out. If the round trip took a total of 9 hours, what was the speed on the trip out?

6. Evaluate: $\begin{vmatrix} 2 & 0 & -1 \\ 0 & 3 & -2 \\ 3 & 4 & -1 \end{vmatrix}$

7. Use Cramer's rule to solve for z: $\begin{cases} 2x + 3y + z = 2 \\ y + 2z = 5 \\ x + 2y = -1 \end{cases}$

Develop the identity for:

8. $\cos A \sin B$

9. $\sin x + \sin y$

10. Use a calculator or a table of logarithms to aid in determining $\log_5 35$.

11. Use a calculator or a table of logarithms to aid in determining $\log_6 40$.

12. Given: $AB = CD$; $AD = BC$
Prove: $\angle ADB = \angle DBC$;
$\angle BAC = \angle ACD$

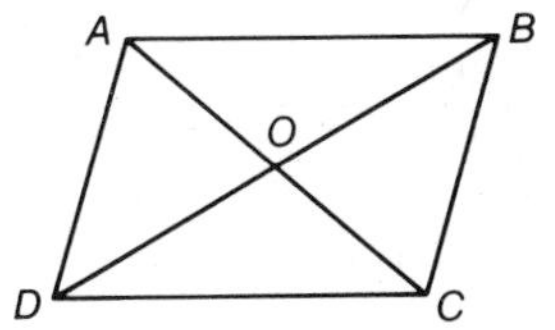

13. Given: E is the midpoint of $\overline{AC}$;
$\overline{AB} \parallel \overline{FC}$
Prove: $DE = EF$

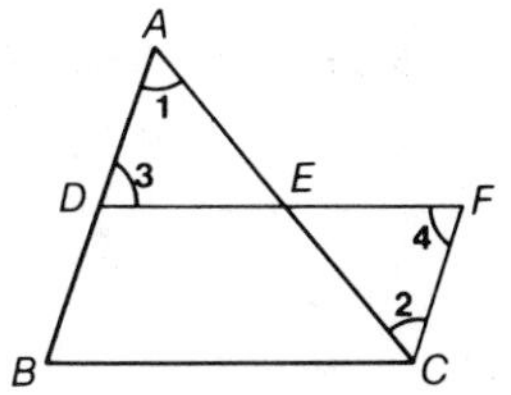

14. A triangle has a 20° angle. A side adjacent to this angle has length 8 and the side opposite this angle has length 4. Draw the triangle(s) described and find the length(s) of the missing side.

15. Find the three cube roots of $4 + 2i$ and express the roots in polar form.

16. A ball is dropped from a height of 256 feet. After each bounce, the ball rebounds three-fourths of the distance it fell. How far does the ball fall on its fifth fall?

17. The positive geometric mean of two numbers is 4 and the arithmetic mean of the two numbers is 5. What are the two numbers?

18. The negative geometric mean of two numbers is -10 and the difference of the two numbers is 15. What are the two numbers?

Solve the following equations given that ($0° \leq x < 360°$):

19. $2 \csc 3x + 4 = 0$

20. $2 \cos^2 x + 15 \sin x - 9 = 0$

Show that:

21. $\dfrac{\sec 2x - 1}{2 \sec 2x} = \sin^2 x$

22. $(\cot^2 x)(1 + \tan^2 x) = \dfrac{1}{1 - \cos^2 x}$

23. $\csc 2x = \frac{1}{2} \cot x \sec^2 x$

24. Find the area of this triangle.

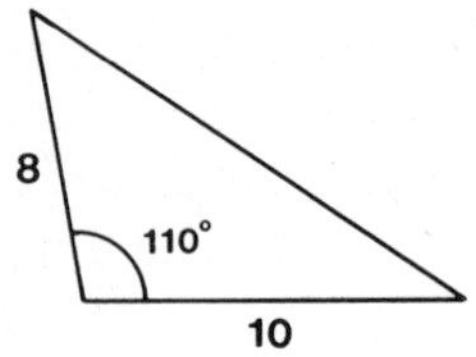

25. Find the sum of the interior angles of a 13-sided convex polygon.

26. Sketch $y = 10 + 2 \sin 4\left(x + \frac{\pi}{6}\right)$.

Solve:

27. $x^{\ln x} = e^4$

28. $\log_4 (x + 3) + \log_4 (x - 3) = 2$

29. $\log_4 \sqrt[4]{x} = \sqrt{\log_4 x}$

30. Find the base 4 antilogarithm of 3.

EP 85.41, 85.42

LESSON 86 Binomial expansions · Overlapping triangles

86.A More binomial expansions

The binomial expansions investigated thus far have involved expressions such as the four shown here.

$$(a + b)^{10} \qquad (m + n)^7 \qquad (x + y)^4 \qquad (p + q)^6$$

The coefficient of each variable is $+1$, and the coefficients in the expansion will be the same as the numbers in Pascal's triangle (see page 279). The exponents of the variables in the binomials are 1, so the exponents in the expansions will increase and decrease in the familiar patterns. When the coefficients and/or the exponents are not 1, the patterns in the expansions will not be so obvious.

Example 86.A.1 Find the fourth term of $(-3x + 2y^2)^4$.

Solution We will replace $-3x$ with F (for first term) and replace $2y^2$ with S (for second term), and then expand $(F + S)^4$. To do this, we need to find the exponents for F and S in the fourth term and the coefficient of the fourth term. We remember the pattern for the exponents, and we get the coefficients from the fifth row of Pascal's triangle.

Term number	①	②	③	④	⑤
Exponents of F	4	3	2	1	0
Exponents of S	0	1	2	3	4
Coefficients	1	4	6	4	1

So the fourth term of $(F + S)^4$ is $4FS^3$. If we replace F with $-3x$ and S with $2y^2$, we get

$$4(-3x)(2y^2)^3 = \mathbf{-96xy^6}$$

Example 86.A.2 Expand $(2a^2 - x^3)^4$.

Solution We will use F to represent the first term $(2a^2)$ in the binomial and will use S to represent the second term $(-x^3)$ in the binomial, and then expand $(F + S)^4$. We look at the exponents of F and S and at the fifth row in Pascal's triangle.

Term number	①	②	③	④	⑤
Exponents of F	4	3	2	1	0
Exponents of S	0	1	2	3	4
Coefficients	1	4	6	4	1

Now we write the expansion of $(F + S)^4$.

$$(F + S)^4 = F^4 + 4F^3S + 6F^2S^2 + 4FS^3 + S^4$$

Now we replace F with $2a^2$ and S with $-x^3$.

$$(2a^2 - x^3)^4 = (2a^2)^4 + 4(2a^2)^3(-x^3) + 6(2a^2)^2(-x^3)^2 + 4(2a^2)(-x^3)^3 + (-x^3)^4$$

and now we simplify every term and get

$$\mathbf{(2a^2 - x^3)^4 = 16a^8 - 32a^6x^3 + 24a^4x^6 - 8a^2x^9 + x^{12}}$$

Example 86.A.3 Find the third term of $(-3x + 2y^2)^5$.

Solution First we will use F for $-3x$ and S for $2y^2$ and write the exponents and the coefficients for $(F + S)^5$.

Term number	①	②	③	④	⑤	⑥
Exponents of F	5	4	3	2	1	0
Exponents of S	0	1	2	3	4	5
Coefficients	1	5	10	10	5	1

The third term of $(F + S)^5$ is $10F^3S^2$, and if we replace F with $-3x$ and S with $2y^2$, we get

$$\text{Third term} = 10(-3x)^3(2y^2)^2$$
$$= \mathbf{-1080x^3y^4}$$

86.B Overlapping triangles

We found that the proof of the Pythagorean theorem was simplified by redrawing the figure so that the triangles of interest were shown separately. We find that proofs concerning figures with overlapping triangles are often made easier if the figure is redrawn with the triangles shown separately. We demonstrate this procedure in the following example.

Example 86.B.1 Given: $WX = ZY$; $WY = ZX$
Prove: $\triangle WXY \cong \triangle ZYX$

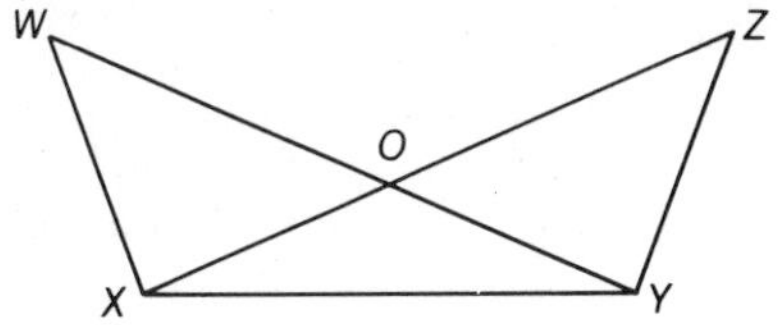

Solution The proof is made easier if we first break out the triangles in which we are interested and mark the equal segments.

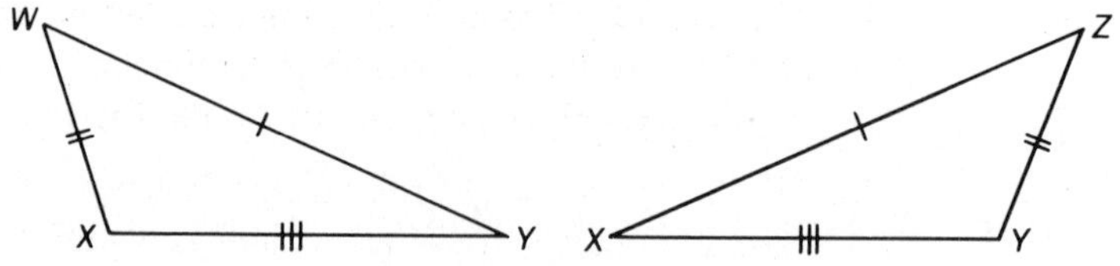

We see that the triangles are congruent because the corresponding sides of the two triangles have the same lengths. Thus they are similar (SSS) and the scale factor is 1.

$$\triangle WXY \cong \triangle ZYX$$

Example 86.B.2 Given: $MN = MP$; $\overline{NY} \perp \overline{MP}$; $\overline{PX} \perp \overline{NM}$
Prove: $YN = XP$

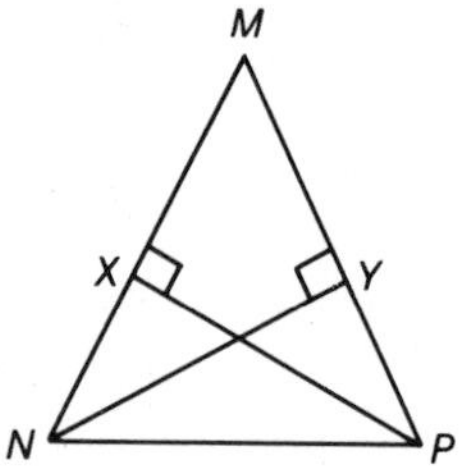

Solution There are four small triangles that have either $\overline{YN}$ or $\overline{XP}$ as sides; and since we are not sure which one to use, we will draw all four separately and use tick marks to identify equal components.

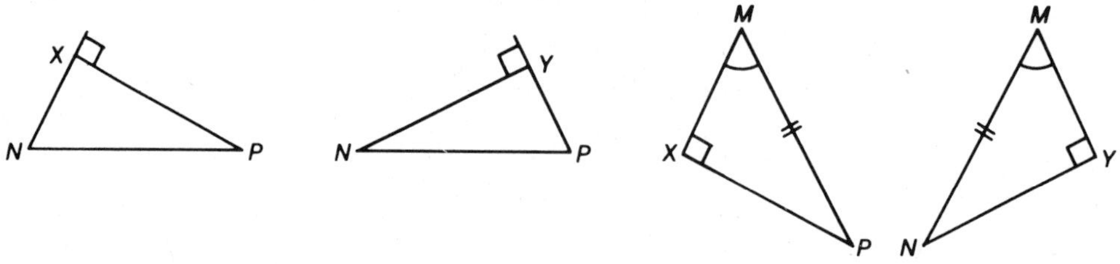

We do not have enough information to use the two triangles on the left, but we see that the two triangles on the right are similar because each one contains a right angle and each one contains angle M. Thus, the third angles are equal and the triangles are similar by AAA.

$$\triangle MXP \sim \triangle MYN$$

Sides $\overline{MP}$ and $\overline{MN}$ are corresponding sides and have equal lengths, so the scale factor is 1 and the triangles are congruent.

$$\triangle MXP \cong \triangle MYN$$

Thus, $YN = XP$ by CPCTE.

Problem set 86

1. Four times the complement of angle 1 is 40° less than the supplement of angle 2. Find the measures of angle 1 and angle 2 if the sum of the two angles is 80°.

2. Wanatobe is 5 times as old as little Pete. Five years ago, Wanatobe's age exceeded 6 times the age of little Pete by 19 years. How old will both of them be in 17 years?

3. Donny peeked around the corner and quickly drew one card from a full deck. He looked at the card and smiled. What was the probability that Donny's card was a 2 or was red or was a red 2?

4. The level of the milk in the magic pitcher increased exponentially. When Greselda first looked, the level was 0.04 centimeter. Twenty seconds later the level was 2.6 centimeters. How long would it take for the level to increase to 16 centimeters?

5. The *Gerta Sue* could huff and puff her way 33 miles down the Old Swampy in 1 hour less than it took her to huff and puff 20 miles up the Old Swampy. If the *Gerta Sue*'s speed was twice the speed of the current, what was the *Gerta Sue*'s speed in still water and what was the speed of the current?

6. Find the fourth term of $(x - y)^7$.

7. Expand $(2a^2 - b^3)^3$.

8. Use Cramer's rule to solve for x: $\begin{cases} 3x - y + z = 0 \\ 3y + 2z = 4 \\ x + 2y = 5 \end{cases}$

9. Develop the identity for $\cos x + \cos y$.

10. Develop the identity for $\cos A \sin B$.

11. Use a calculator or logarithm tables to aid in finding $\log_6 40$.

12. Given: $AB = CD$; $AD = BC$
Prove: $\triangle AOB \cong \triangle COD$

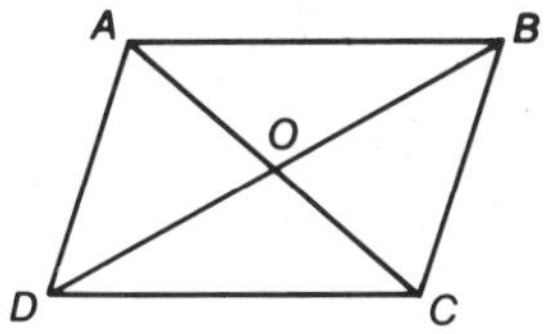

13. Given: D is the midpoint of $\overline{AB}$.
E is the midpoint of $\overline{AC}$.
Prove: $\overline{DE} \parallel \overline{BC}$

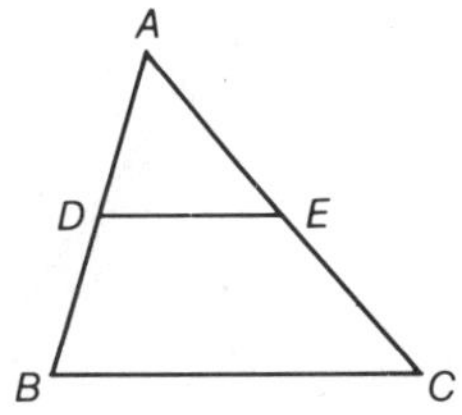

14. A triangle has a 50° angle. A side adjacent to this angle has length 10 and the side opposite this angle has length 9. Draw the triangle(s) described and find the length(s) of the missing side(s).

15. Find the five fifth roots of $-2 + 8i$ and express the roots in polar form.

16. A ball is dropped from a height of 243 feet. After each bounce, the ball rebounds one-third of the distance it fell. How far does the ball fall on its fourth fall?

17. The negative geometric mean of two numbers is -12. The arithmetic mean of the two numbers is 20. Find the two numbers.

18. The perimeter of a regular hexagon is 30. Find the area of the hexagon.

Solve the following equations given that $(0° \le \theta, x < 360°)$:

19. $\cot 3\theta = 0$

20. $3 \tan^2 x + 5 \sec x + 1 = 0$

Show that:

21. $\dfrac{\sin x \tan x}{1 - \cos x} - 1 = \sec x$

22. $\dfrac{\cos 2x}{\sin^2 x} = \cot^2 x - 1$

23. $\dfrac{1 + \sin x}{\cos x} + \dfrac{\cos x}{1 + \sin x} = \dfrac{4 \sin x}{\sin 2x}$

24. Write the equations of the following trigonometric functions.

(*a*)

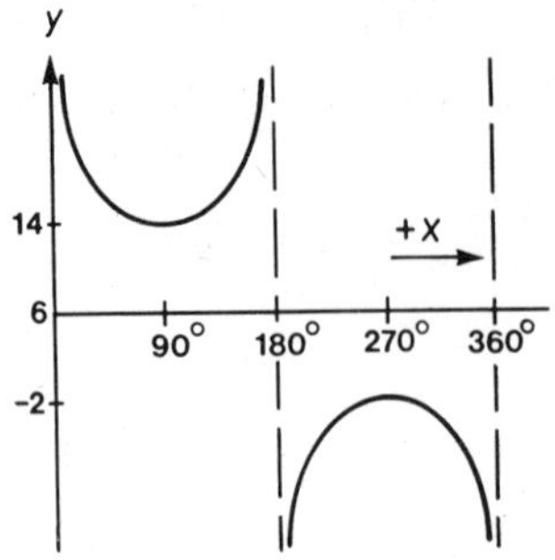

(*b*)

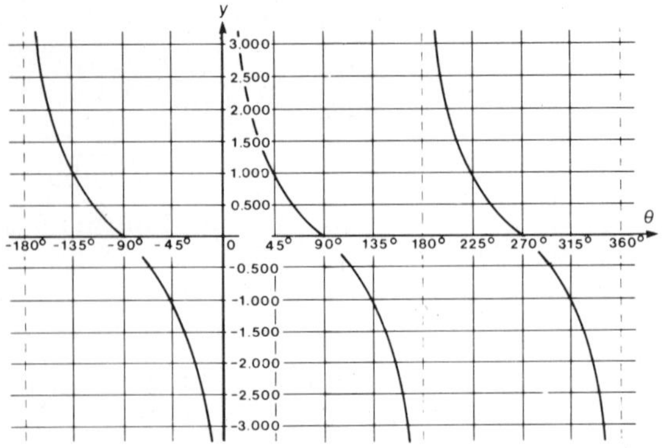

25. Find the sum of the exterior angles of a 15-sided convex polygon.

26. Sketch $y = -2 + 4 \csc x$.

Solve:

27. $\sqrt{\log_{81} x} = 2 \log_{81} x$

28. $\log_2 (x + 1) - \log_2 (x - 1) = 1$

29. $\ln x + \ln (x - 1) = \ln 20$

30. Find the base 4 antilogarithm of 2.

EP 86.43, 86.44

If the enrichment lessons are being included, the fourth enrichment lesson should be taught next. Then Lesson 87 should be taught.

LESSON 87 *Calculations with logarithms · Power of the hydrogen*

87.A Calculations with logarithms

Problems that involve multiplications, divisions, and taking roots can be performed by writing the numbers as powers and using the rules for exponents. For example, we can multiply 10,000 by 100 by writing both numbers as powers of 10:

$$10^4 \cdot 10^2 = 10^6$$

We see that the answer is 10^6, which equals 1 million. When we do this multiplication by using logarithms, we just use the exponents.

$$\log (10{,}000)(100) = \log 10{,}000 + \log 100 = 4 + 2 = 6$$

The antilogarithm of 6 is 1 million, so the answer is the same as the answer above. To take the cube root of 1 million by using exponents, we could write

$$(10^6)^{1/3}$$

This time we will use (*a*) and substitute

$$10^{-7.05} = \text{H}^+ \qquad \text{substituted}$$

$$10^{-7.05+8-8} = \text{H}^+ \qquad \text{added } +8-8$$

$$10^{0.95} \times 10^{-8} = \text{H}^+ \qquad \text{simplified}$$

$$\mathbf{8.9 \times 10^{-8} = H^+} \qquad \text{antilog}$$

Problem set 87

1. The pressure of an ideal gas varies inversely with the volume if the temperature is constant. When the temperature was 500 K, the pressure was 4 atmospheres and the volume was 10 liters. At the same temperature, what was the pressure when the volume was reduced to 2 liters?

2. The onlookers gazed in wonder as the size of the thing decreased exponentially. When it was first observed, it measured 42 cubits. But in only 30 minutes, its measure had decreased to 39 cubits. How long would it take before the thing measured only 12.5 cubits?

3. The fair coin was tossed 4 times. What is the probability that all 4 tosses came up heads?

4. How much pure acid must be added to 180 grams of a 35% acid solution to produce a solution that is 50% acid?

5. Harriet ran k miles in p hours. Then she increased her speed s miles per hour. How long would it take her to cover 12 miles at the new speed?

Use base 10 logs to simplify:

6. $(6300 \times 10^{-12})(50 \times 10^4)$

7. $\dfrac{\sqrt[6]{525{,}000}}{(6300)^{1.5}}$

8. Find the pH of a liquid if the concentration of hydrogen ions (H^+) is 5.3×10^{-5} mole per liter.

9. Find the concentration of hydrogen ions (H^+) in a liquid if the pH of the liquid is 6.5.

10. Find the fifth term of $(x - y)^8$.

11. Expand $(3a^2 - b^3)^4$.

12. Use Cramer's rule to solve for x: $\begin{cases} 2x + y + 3z = -3 \\ 3y + 4z = 5 \\ x + 2y = 3 \end{cases}$

Develop the identity for:

13. $\sin x - \sin y$

14. $\sin A \sin B$

15. Use a calculator or logarithm tables to aid in determining $\log_5 22$.

16. Given: $\overline{AD}$ bisects angle A;
$AB = AC$
Prove: $\angle ADB = \angle ADC = 90°$

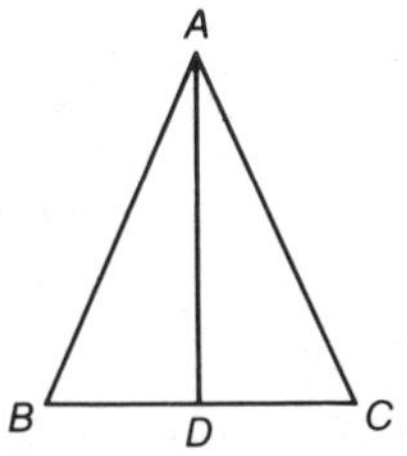

17. Given: D is the midpoint of $\overline{AB}$.
E is the midpoint of $\overline{AC}$.
Prove: $DE = \frac{1}{2}BC$

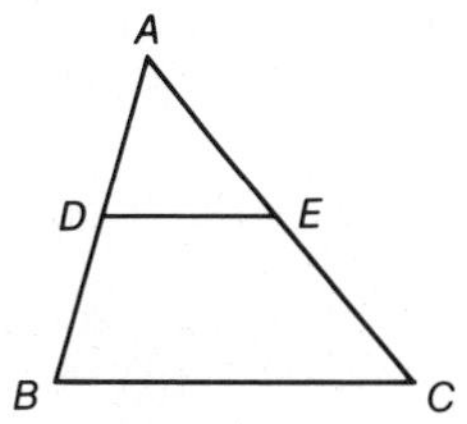

18. A triangle has a 25° angle. A side adjacent to this angle is 8 units long and the side opposite the angle is 5 units long. What is the length of the third side?

19. Find the three cube roots of $-3 + 4i$ and express the roots in polar form.

20. A ball is dropped from a height of 128 feet. On each bounce, the ball rebounds one-fourth of the distance it fell. How far will the ball rebound on the fourth bounce?

21. What is the area of the triangle shown?

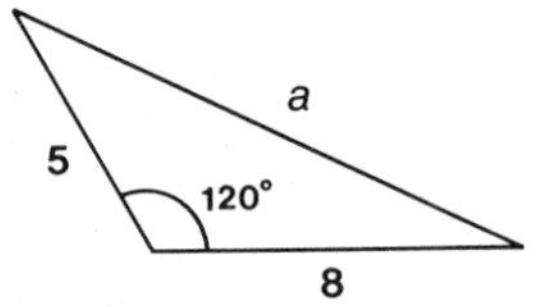

Solve the following equations given that $(0° \leq \theta, x < 360°)$:

22. $2 + \tan 3\theta = 0$

23. $3 \tan^2 x + 5 \sec x + 1 = 0$

Show that:

24. $\dfrac{\cos 2x + 1}{2} = \cos^2 x$

25. $\dfrac{2 \cot x}{\tan 2x} = \csc^2 x - 2$

26. Sketch $y = 4 + 4 \sec x$.

Solve:

27. $\log_5 \sqrt{x^2 + 16} = 1$

28. $\frac{2}{3} \log_4 8 - \log_4 (3x - 2) = 2$

29. $4 \log_3 \sqrt[4]{x} = \log_3 (3x + 1)$

30. $\log_2 (\log_2 x) = 1$

EP 87.45, 87.46

LESSON 88 Arithmetic series · Geometric series

88.A Arithmetic series

A ***series*** **is the indicated sum of a sequence.** Here we show the first 10 terms of an arithmetic sequence whose first term is 11 and whose common difference is 3.

$$\begin{matrix} ① & ② & ③ & ④ & ⑤ & ⑥ & ⑦ & ⑧ & ⑨ & ⑩ & \\ 11, & 14, & 17, & 20, & 23, & 26, & 29, & 32, & 35, & 38, & \ldots \end{matrix}$$

If we put a plus sign between each of the members of this arithmetic sequence, we turn the arithmetic sequence into an arithmetic series.

$$\begin{matrix} ① & & ② & & ③ & & ④ & & ⑤ & & ⑥ & & ⑦ & & ⑧ & & ⑨ & & ⑩ & \\ 11 & + & 14 & + & 17 & + & 20 & + & 23 & + & 26 & + & 29 & + & 32 & + & 35 & + & 38 & + \cdots \end{matrix}$$

Thus, we see that an arithmetic series is the same thing as an arithmetic sequence that has a plus sign between every entry. Sometimes we find it necessary to find the sum of a number of terms in a series. We will indicate the sum by using a subscripted capital S. The subscript tells us how many terms of the series we are adding. We can show the sum of 4, 6, or n terms of this series by writing

$$S_4 = 11 + 14 + 17 + 20 = 62$$

$$S_6 = 11 + 14 + 17 + 20 + 23 + 26 = 111$$

$$S_n = 11 + 14 + 17 + 20 + 23 + 26 + 29 + 32 + \cdots + a_n = ?$$

We can develop a formula for the sum of n terms of an arithmetic series by using a specific series which has **an even number of terms** to get the pattern and then generalizing. Using the first 8 terms of the series S_n at the bottom of the preceding page,

$$(11) + (14) + (17) + (20) + (23) + (26) + (29) + (32)$$

we see that the sum of the first term and the last term is $11 + 32 = 43$. The sum of the second term and the next to the last term is $14 + 29 = 43$. The sum of the other two pairs is also 43. There are 8 terms in all, and thus there are 4 pairs of terms. The value of each pair is the same as the sum of the first term and the eighth term, so the sum of this 8-term series is

$$\text{Sum of all 8 terms} = \frac{8}{2}(\text{first term} + \text{eighth term})$$

If we use n for the number of terms instead of 8 and a_1 for the first term and a_n for the nth term, we get a formula for the sum of n terms.

$$S_n = \frac{n}{2}(a_1 + a_n)$$

A formal proof of this formula will be presented in one of the lessons on mathematical induction. We used a series with an even number of terms to develop this formula. The formula will also work for the sum of an odd number of terms because the value of the middle term equals half the sum of the first term and the last term. To demonstrate, we will find the sum of the 9 terms of this arithmetic series by adding, and then we will use the formula to see if the formula gives the same result.

(1) (2) (3) (4) (5) (6) (7) (8) (9)

$$S_9 = 11 + 14 + 17 + 20 + 23 + 26 + 29 + 32 + 35 = 207$$

Now we will use the formula.

$$S_9 = \frac{9}{2}(11 + 35) \qquad \text{substituted}$$

$$S_9 = (4.5)(46) \qquad \text{simplified}$$

$$S_9 = \mathbf{207} \qquad \text{multiplied}$$

We see that the formula gives us the same result as we get when we add the individual terms.

Formulas are difficult to remember, and putting numbers into formulas to find a numerical answer is a task that brings few rewards. Thus, in the problem sets, we will have problems, such as the next example, which require the development of this formula as well as its use.

Example 88.A.1 An arithmetic sequence has a first term of -10 and a difference of $+20$. Use the first 4 terms of this sequence to write a series and develop the formula. Then use the formula to find the sum of the first 11 terms of the sequence.

Solution First we write the first 4 terms of the sequence and then insert the plus signs to form a series.

	(1)	(2)	(3)	(4)
Sequence	-10	10	30	50
Series	$-10 +$	$10 +$	$30 +$	50

We see that the sum of the first term and the last term is 40 and that the other two terms also sum to 40. There is one-half of four pairs, so our formula for the sum of 4 terms is

$$S_4 = \frac{4}{2}(\text{first} + \text{fourth})$$

If we use n instead of 4 and a_1 and a_n instead of first and fourth, respectively, we get

$$S_n = \frac{n}{2}(a_1 + a_n)$$

In this problem we are told that the first term is -10, and we compute the value of the eleventh term to be 190, which is the sum of the first term and 10 times the difference. Now we can use the formula to find the sum of the first 11 terms.

$$S_{11} = \frac{11}{2}(-10 + 190) = (5.5)(180) = \mathbf{990}$$

88.B Geometric series

A geometric series is formed by placing plus signs between the terms of a geometric sequence. To develop a formula for the sum of a geometric series, we will subtract one series from another to get rid of all terms between the first term and the last term. We begin by writing the general expression for a geometric sequence. Note how we write the general form of the next-to-last term.

$$\begin{array}{cccccccc} (1) & (2) & (3) & (4) & & (n-1) & (n) \\ a_1 & a_1r & a_1r^2 & a_1r^3 & \ldots & a_1r^{n-2} & a_1r^{n-1} \end{array}$$

Now if we place a plus sign between each term, we will have a geometric series. We set this series equal to S_n to indicate the sum of n terms.

$$(a) \quad S_n = a_1 + a_1r + a_1r^2 + a_1r^3 + \cdots + a_1r^{n-2} + a_1r^{n-1}$$

The next step is to multiply each term on both sides by r.

$$(b) \quad rS_n = a_1r + a_1r^2 + a_1r^3 + a_1r^4 + \cdots + a_1r^{n-1} + a_1r^n$$

Now if we multiply both sides of equation (b) by -1 and add the result to equation (a), we can eliminate the middle terms in both equations.

$$\begin{array}{rl} (a) & S_n = a_1 + a_1r + a_1r^2 + a_1r^3 + \cdots + a_1r^{n-2} + a_1r^{n-1} \\ (-1)(b) & -rS_n = \quad - a_1r - a_1r^2 - a_1r^3 - \cdots - a_1r^{n-2} - a_1r^{n-1} - a_1r^n \\ \hline & S_n - rS_n = a_1 \qquad\qquad\qquad\qquad\qquad\qquad - a_1r^n \end{array}$$

Next we factor out S_n on the left side and a_1 on the right side. We finish by dividing both sides by the coefficient of S_n.

$$S_n(1 - r) = a_1(1 - r^n) \qquad \text{factored}$$

$$S_n = \frac{a_1(1 - r^n)}{1 - r} \qquad \text{divided by } 1 - r$$

This is a simple formula, and using it to produce numerical results teaches us little. Thus, the homework problems will request the development of this formula each time its use is required. The development gives practice in the use of sequence and series notation and will be beneficial in later courses.

Example 88.B.1 Develop the formula for the sum of n terms in a geometric series and use the formula to find the sum of the first 9 terms in a geometric series whose first term is -8 and whose common ratio is -2.

Solution The development on the previous page should be repeated to find that

$$S_n = \frac{a_1(1 - r^n)}{1 - r}$$

If we make the required substitutions, we get

$$S_9 = \frac{-8[1 - (-2)^9]}{1 - (-2)}$$

$$S_9 = \frac{-8[1 - (-512)]}{3}$$

$$S_9 = \frac{-4104}{3} = \mathbf{-1368}$$

Example 88.B.2 Find the sum of the first 10 terms of the geometric series in the preceding example.

Solution We will use the formula again, but this time n will be 10.

$$S_n = \frac{a_1(1 - r^n)}{1 - r}$$

$$S_{10} = \frac{-8[1 - (-2)^{10}]}{1 - (-2)}$$

$$S_{10} = \frac{-8(1 - 1024)}{3} = \mathbf{2728}$$

It is interesting to note that the sum of 9 terms of this series is a negative number, and the sum of 10 terms of the same series is a positive number. The terms in the series alternate in sign, and each time another term is included in the sum the sign of the sum changes. This pattern of alternating sign changes of the sum always occurs in a geometric series in which r is a number that is less than -1. It is interesting to note that if r is not zero and is greater than -1, the sum of any number of terms in the series has the same sign as the first term in the series. Take a particular series and see if you can see why this statement is true.

Problem set 88

1. The digits of a two-digit counting number were reversed and the new number was 9 greater than the original number. What was the original number if the sum of its digits was 9?

2. A single card is drawn from a deck of 52 cards. What is the probability that the card is an 8 or is a black card or is a black 8?

3. Sixty percent of the number of blues exactly equaled the number of whites. Five times the number of reds was 10 greater than twice the number of whites. If the total of all three colors was 140, how many were white, how many were red, and how many were blue?

4. The price of gasoline was \$1.40 a gallon plus a federal tax of f cents a gallon and a state tax of s cents a gallon. How many gallons could Beetle purchase for \$42?

5. If $p = \dfrac{14}{a + b}$ then $\dfrac{4}{p + 3} = ?$

6. (*a*) Develop a formula for the sum of an arithmetic series with a_1 as the first term and a_n as the last term.

(*b*) Using the formula developed in (*a*), find the sum of the following arithmetic series: $2 + 4 + 6 + \cdots + 98 + 100$.

7. (*a*) Develop the formula for the sum of n terms of a geometric series whose first term is a and whose common ratio is r.
   (*b*) Using the formula developed in (*a*), find the sum of the first 5 terms of the geometric series whose first term is 2 and whose common ratio is -2.

8. Factor $x^2 + x + 3$ over the set of complex numbers.

9. Use base 10 logs to simplify: $\dfrac{\sqrt[3]{53{,}000}}{(3200)^{2.5}}$

10. Find the pH of a liquid if the concentration of H^+ is 6.2×10^{-4} mole per liter.

11. Find the concentration of hydrogen ions (H^+) in a liquid if the pH of the liquid is 8.5.

12. Find the fourth term of $(x + 2y)^6$.

13. Expand $(x - y)^4$.

14. Use Cramer's rule to solve for x: $\begin{cases} 2x + 3y + z = 0 \\ x + 2z = 4 \\ y - 3z = -4 \end{cases}$

Develop the identity for:

15. $\cos x + \cos y$

16. $\sin x \cos y$

17. Use a calculator or logarithm tables to aid in finding $\log_6 45$.

18. Given: $AB = DC$; $AC = DB$
    Prove: $\triangle ABC \cong \triangle DCB$

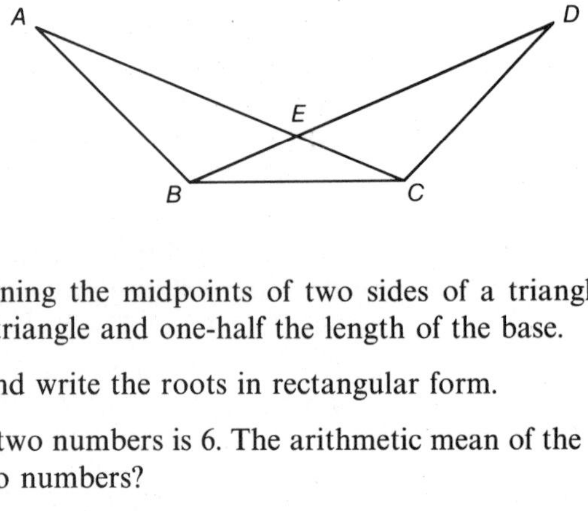

19. Prove that the line segment joining the midpoints of two sides of a triangle is parallel to the third side of the triangle and one-half the length of the base.

20. Find the three cube roots of i and write the roots in rectangular form.

21. The positive geometric mean of two numbers is 6. The arithmetic mean of the two numbers is 10. What are the two numbers?

Solve the following equations given that ($0^\circ \le \theta, x < 360^\circ$):

22. $-1 + \sqrt{2} \sin 3\theta = 0$

23. $2 \tan^2 x + 3 \sec x = 0$

Show that:

24. $\dfrac{1 - \cos 2x}{2} = \sin^2 x$

25. $\dfrac{2 + \cos 2y - 5 \sin y}{3 + \sin y} = 1 - 2 \sin y$

26. Sketch $y = -1 + \sin \frac{1}{2}(x - 90^\circ)$.

Solve:

27. $\sqrt{\log_2 x} = \frac{1}{2} \log_2 x$

28. $\ln x + \ln x - \ln (2x - 2) = \ln 2$

29. $\log_2 (\log_3 x) = 1$

30. Find the base 2 antilogarithm of 3.

EP 88.47, 88.48

LESSON 89 Cofactors · Expansion by cofactors

89.A Cofactors

If we use the elimination method to solve the following system of equations for x

$$a_1x + b_1y + c_1z = k_1$$
$$a_2x + b_2y + c_2z = k_2$$
$$a_3x + b_3y + c_3z = k_3$$

the answer will be the expression shown here.

$$x = \frac{(k_1b_2c_3 + b_1c_2k_3 + c_1k_2b_3) - (k_3b_2c_1 + b_3c_2k_1 + c_3k_2b_1)}{(a_1b_2c_3 + b_1c_2a_3 + c_1a_2b_3) - (a_3b_2c_1 + b_3c_2a_1 + c_3a_2b_1)}$$

We have found that we can get the same result from Cramer's rule by evaluating the following determinants.

$$x = \frac{\begin{vmatrix} k_1 & b_1 & c_1 \\ k_2 & b_2 & c_2 \\ k_3 & b_3 & c_3 \end{vmatrix}}{\begin{vmatrix} a_1 & b_1 & c_1 \\ a_2 & b_2 & c_2 \\ a_3 & b_3 & c_3 \end{vmatrix}}$$

We develop methods of evaluating determinants so we can get the same answer for x by using determinants that we get when we use elimination. How we get the result does not matter so long as the result is the same. Now we will look at the cofactor/minor method to see why it will also give the same result. To do this we will look at the denominator of the fraction above, which is

$$(a_1b_2c_3 + b_1c_2a_3 + c_1a_2b_3) - (a_3b_2c_1 + b_3c_2a_1 + c_3a_2b_1)$$

We begin by removing the parentheses to get

$$a_1b_2c_3 + b_1c_2a_3 + c_1a_2b_3 - a_3b_2c_1 - b_3c_2a_1 - c_3a_2b_1$$

Now we rearrange the terms so that the terms with a_1 are first; then come the terms with a_2 and then the terms with a_3.

$$a_1b_2c_3 - b_3c_2a_1 + c_1a_2b_3 - c_3a_2b_1 + b_1c_2a_3 - a_3b_2c_1$$

Now we factor out a_1 from the first two terms, factor out $-a_2$ from the second and third terms, and factor out a_3 from the last two terms.

$$a_1(b_2c_3 - b_3c_2) - a_2(b_1c_3 - b_3c_1) + a_3(b_1c_2 - b_2c_1)$$

Now this is exactly the same thing as

$$a_1\begin{vmatrix} b_2 & c_2 \\ b_3 & c_3 \end{vmatrix} - a_2\begin{vmatrix} b_1 & c_1 \\ b_3 & c_3 \end{vmatrix} + a_3\begin{vmatrix} b_1 & c_1 \\ b_2 & c_2 \end{vmatrix}$$
$$(M) \qquad\qquad (N) \qquad\qquad (P)$$

If we go back to the original determinant three times,

$$\begin{matrix} \cancel{a_1} & \cancel{b_1} & \cancel{c_1} \\ a_2 & b_2 & c_2 \\ a_3 & b_3 & c_3 \end{matrix} \qquad \begin{matrix} a_1 & b_1 & c_1 \\ \cancel{a_2} & \cancel{b_2} & \cancel{c_2} \\ a_3 & b_3 & c_3 \end{matrix} \qquad \begin{matrix} a_1 & b_1 & c_1 \\ a_2 & b_2 & c_2 \\ \cancel{a_3} & \cancel{b_3} & \cancel{c_3} \end{matrix}$$
$$(Q) \qquad\qquad (R) \qquad\qquad (S)$$

we see that we can get (*M*) from (*Q*) by crossing out the row and column of a_1, (*N*) from (*R*) by crossing out the row and column of a_2, and (*P*) from (*S*) by crossing out the row and column of a_3. Further, we see that the original development of this method required no great insight but did require persistence, patience, and a certain fascination with playing with patterns. One knew the required end pattern and had the starting determinant. The rest was just trial and error.

The advantage of this system is that it can be used to find the determinants of square matrices of any size by breaking them down to expressions which contain smaller square matrices, which can be broken down, etc. When we cross out the row and column of an element, we call the smaller determinant that results the ***minor*** of the element. If the proper sign is appended to the minor, the combination is called the ***cofactor*** of the element. As we saw above, not all cofactor signs are positive. It can be shown that the signs of the cofactors are in the form of a checkerboard matrix of + and − signs in which the sign in the upper left corner is +.

MATRIX OF COFACTOR SIGNS
$$\begin{vmatrix} + & - & + & - & + \\ - & + & - & + & - \\ + & - & + & - & + \\ - & + & - & + & - \\ + & - & + & - & + \end{vmatrix}$$

Example 89.A.1 Find the cofactor of 7 in the following determinant.

$$\begin{vmatrix} 4 & 7 & 3 \\ 2 & 5 & 6 \\ 2 & 1 & 5 \end{vmatrix}$$

Solution To find the minor of 7, we cross out the row and column of 7.

$$\begin{array}{ccc} \not{4} & \not{7} & \not{3} \\ 2 & \not{5} & 6 \\ 2 & \not{1} & 5 \end{array}$$

The minor of the element 7 is thus

$$\begin{vmatrix} 2 & 6 \\ 2 & 5 \end{vmatrix}$$

and the sign of the 7 in the checkerboard pattern is a minus sign

$$\begin{array}{ccc} + & \ominus & + \\ - & + & - \\ + & - & + \end{array}$$

so the cofactor is

$$-\begin{vmatrix} 2 & 6 \\ 2 & 5 \end{vmatrix}$$

89.B Expansion by cofactors

The value of a determinant can be found by summing the products of the elements in any row or column with their respective cofactors. This means that each term in the sum has three factors. The first factor is the element. The second factor is the sign from the checkerboard, and the third factor is the minor of the element.

Example 89.B.1 Use cofactors to evaluate this determinant: $\begin{vmatrix} -4 & 2 & 1 \\ 1 & 3 & -2 \\ -1 & 2 & -3 \end{vmatrix}$

Solution We could expand using any row or any column. We decide to use the third row.

$$\begin{vmatrix} -4 & 2 & 1 \\ 1 & 3 & -2 \\ -1 & 2 & -3 \end{vmatrix} \quad \begin{vmatrix} -4 & 2 & 1 \\ 1 & 3 & -2 \\ -1 & 2 & -3 \end{vmatrix} \quad \begin{vmatrix} -4 & 2 & 1 \\ 1 & 3 & -2 \\ -1 & 2 & -3 \end{vmatrix}$$

There will be three factors in each term. They are the element that is crossed out, the sign from the checkerboard, and the minor of the element.

$$(-1)(+)\begin{vmatrix} 2 & 1 \\ 3 & -2 \end{vmatrix} + (2)(-)\begin{vmatrix} -4 & 1 \\ 1 & -2 \end{vmatrix} + (-3)(+)\begin{vmatrix} -4 & 2 \\ 1 & 3 \end{vmatrix}$$

Now we simplify these expressions and add to evaluate the determinant.

$-[(-4)-(3)] - 2[(8)-(1)] - 3[(-12)-(2)]$	evaluated minors
$= 7 - 14 + 42$	simplified
$= \mathbf{35}$	added

Example 89.B.2 Use cofactors to evaluate: $\begin{vmatrix} -3 & 1 & 2 \\ 2 & -3 & -4 \\ 0 & 4 & -5 \end{vmatrix}$

Solution If an element in a matrix is 0, then the product of this element and its cofactor is 0. Thus, the easiest solution is to expand using the row or column that contains the most 0s. In this problem, we note that there is a 0 in the first column and also in the third row, so we could use either. We decide to use the third row.

$$\begin{matrix} -3 & 1 & 2 \\ 2 & -3 & -4 \\ 0 & 4 & -5 \end{matrix} \qquad \begin{matrix} -3 & 1 & 2 \\ 2 & -3 & -4 \\ 0 & 4 & -5 \end{matrix} \qquad \begin{matrix} -3 & 1 & 2 \\ 2 & -3 & -4 \\ 0 & 4 & -5 \end{matrix}$$

$$(0)(+)\begin{vmatrix} 1 & 2 \\ -3 & -4 \end{vmatrix} + (4)(-)\begin{vmatrix} -3 & 2 \\ 2 & -4 \end{vmatrix} + (-5)(+)\begin{vmatrix} -3 & 1 \\ 2 & -3 \end{vmatrix}$$

and this simplifies as

$0 - 4(12 - 4) + (-5)(9 - 2)$	simplified
$= 0 - 32 + (-35) = \mathbf{-67}$	added

Example 89.B.3 Use cofactors to evaluate: $\begin{vmatrix} -3 & 1 & 2 \\ 2 & -3 & -4 \\ 1 & 4 & 0 \end{vmatrix}$

Solution This time we decide to use the third column for our expansion,

$$2(+)\begin{vmatrix} 2 & -3 \\ 1 & 4 \end{vmatrix} + (-4)(-)\begin{vmatrix} -3 & 1 \\ 1 & 4 \end{vmatrix} + (0)(+)\begin{vmatrix} -3 & 1 \\ 2 & -3 \end{vmatrix}$$

and this simplifies to

$$\begin{aligned} &(2)(+)(8 + 3) + (-4)(-)(-12 - 1) + (0)(+)(9 - 2) \\ &= 22 + (-52) + 0 \\ &= \mathbf{-30} \end{aligned}$$

Problem set 89

1. The number who succeeded varied linearly as the number who tried. When 40 tried, 2 succeeded; but when 80 tried, 12 succeeded. How many succeeded when only 60 tried?

2. The grandfather clock in the hall bonged 7 times for 7 o'clock. How long did Sammy Lee have to wait if he wanted to see the clock hands pointing in opposite directions?

3. When Ida Jane looked the first time, there were 4200 of the things in the bowl; and they were decreasing. She looked again 20 minutes later, and there were only 4100 of them left. If the decrease was exponential, what was the half-life of the things?

4. Paul, Terry, and Audley found that K workers can do 40 jobs in h hours. How many workers would it take to do m jobs in 14 hours?

5. Ten people came out for the tennis team. If there were 6 players on a team, how many different teams could the coach form?

Use cofactors to evaluate:

6. $\begin{vmatrix} -2 & 0 & 1 \\ 3 & 1 & 2 \\ 1 & 1 & 0 \end{vmatrix}$

7. $\begin{vmatrix} -2 & 0 & 3 \\ 0 & 1 & 2 \\ 3 & 1 & -1 \end{vmatrix}$

8. (*a*) Develop a formula for the sum of an arithmetic series with n terms, a_1 as its first term, and a_n as its last term.
   (*b*) Using the formula developed in (*a*), find: $-2 + 4 + 10 + \cdots + 46$

9. (*a*) Develop the formula for the sum of n terms of a geometric series whose first term is a and whose common ratio is r.
   (*b*) Using the formula developed in (*a*), find the sum of the first 6 terms of the geometric series whose first term is 1 and whose common ratio is $-1/2$.

10. Use base 10 logs to simplify: $\dfrac{3300 \times 10^7}{2200 \times 10^3}$

11. Find the distance from $(1, 2)$ to $x - 3y + 5 = 0$.

12. Find the pH of a liquid if the concentration of the H^+ is 4.4×10^{-4} mole per liter.

13. Find the fifth term of $(x - 2y)^6$.

14. Expand $(3x - 2y)^3$.

15. Use Cramer's rule to solve for x: $\begin{cases} 2x + y + z = 0 \\ 2y + 3z = 5 \\ x + 3y = 1 \end{cases}$

16. Develop the identity for $\cos x - \cos y$.

17. Use a calculator or a table of logarithms to aid in finding $\log_5 30$.

18. Given: $AB = DC$; $AC = DB$
    Prove: $\angle A = \angle D$

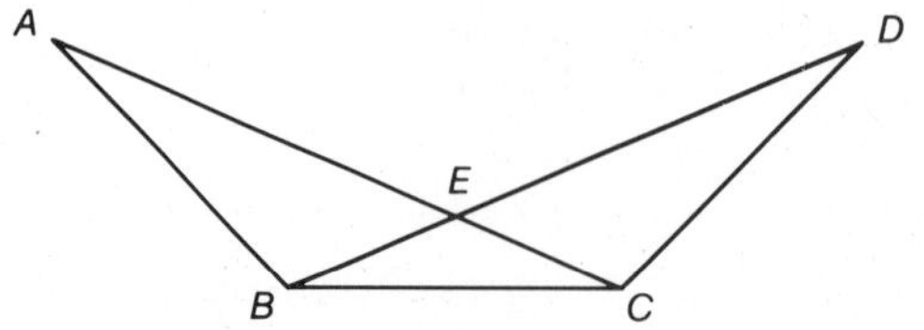

19. Given: $\angle CDA$ and $\angle ABC$ are right angles; $CD = AB$
    Prove: $CB = AD$

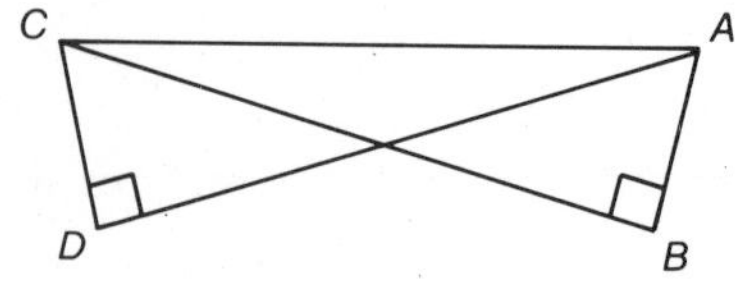

20. Find the three cube roots of -1 and write the roots in rectangular form, using exact numbers.

21. A ball is dropped from a height of 256 feet. On each bounce, the ball rebounds one-fourth of the distance it fell. How far does it rebound after its fourth fall?

Solve the following equations given that ($0° \le x, \theta < 360°$):

22. $1 - \sqrt{2}\cos 3x = 0$

23. $\sec^2\theta = 2\tan\theta + 4$

Show that:

24. $\frac{1}{2}\sin 2x \sec x = \sin x$

25. $\frac{1 + \cos 2x}{\sin 2x} = \cot x$

26. Write the equations of the following trigonometric functions.

(a)

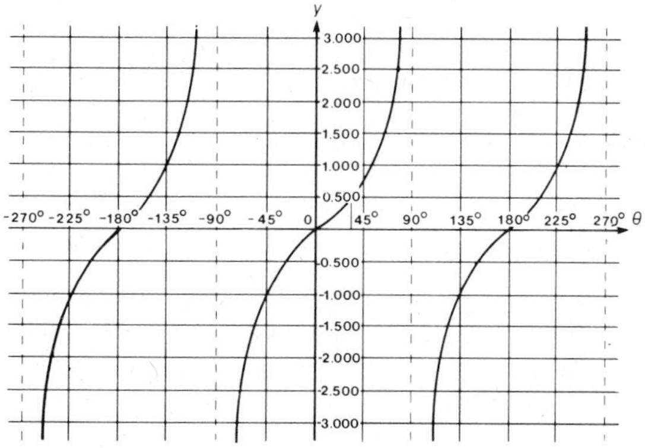

(b)

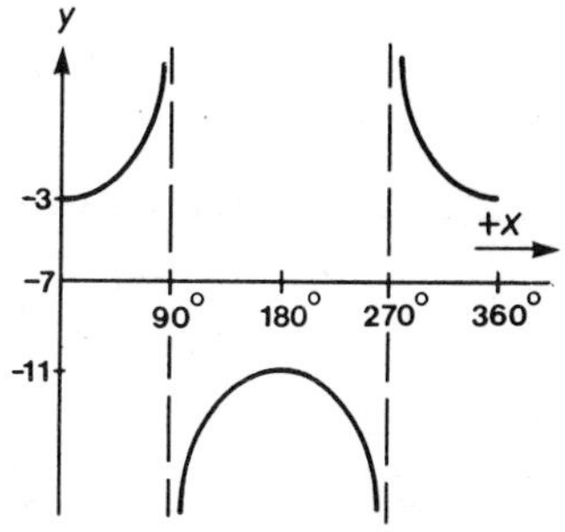

Solve:

27. $\sqrt{\log_3 x} = \frac{1}{2}\log_3 x$

28. $\log_3(\log_2 x) = 1$

29. $\ln(2x + 6) - \ln(x - 3) = \ln x$

30. Find the antilogarithm base 3 of -2.

EP 89.49, 89.50

LESSON 90 Proportional segments · Side ratios and angle bisectors

90.A Proportional segments

In the triangle below, the angles marked with the same tick marks are equal angles because they are corresponding angles formed by parallel lines and a transversal. This allows us to prove that the big triangle is similar to the little triangle, and this similarity permits us to write the proportions shown.

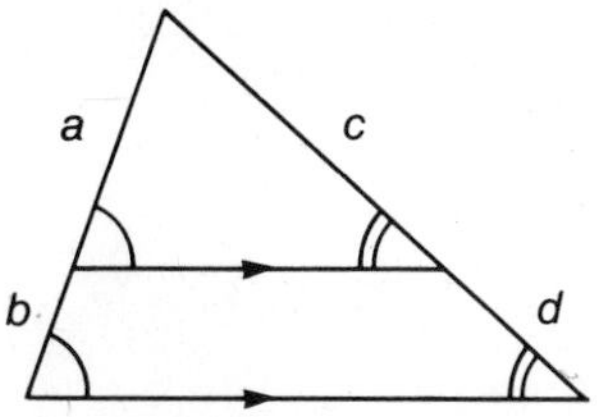

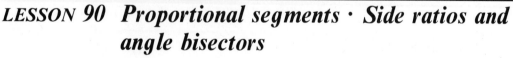

$$\frac{a+b}{a} = \frac{c+d}{c} \quad \xrightarrow{\text{which simplifies to}} \quad \frac{b}{a} = \frac{d}{c}$$

$\frac{a}{a} + \frac{b}{a} = \frac{c}{c} + \frac{d}{c}$

$1 + \frac{b}{a} = 1 + \frac{d}{c}$

$\frac{b}{a} = \frac{d}{c}$

We can use an extension of this development to show that three parallel lines cut proportional segments from pairs of transversals. In the figure on the left below, we show a system of three parallel lines cut by two transversals. The lengths of the corresponding segments of the transversals are proportional. To the right of the figures, we show some of the proportions that we can write.

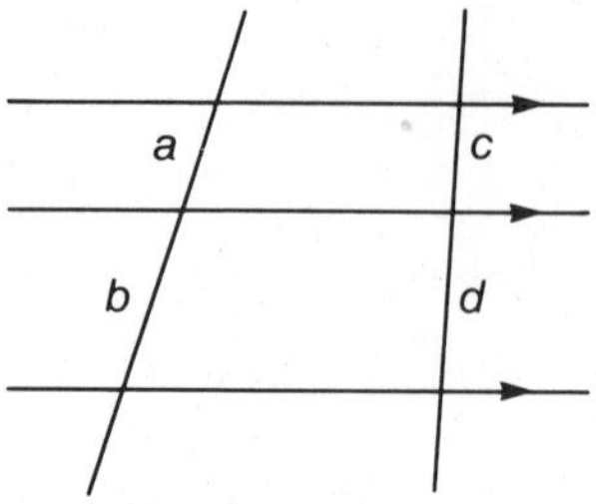

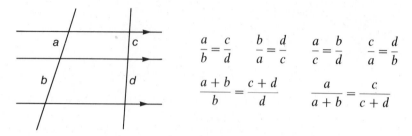

$$\frac{a}{b} = \frac{c}{d} \qquad \frac{b}{a} = \frac{d}{c} \qquad \frac{a}{c} = \frac{b}{d} \qquad \frac{c}{a} = \frac{d}{b}$$

$$\frac{a+b}{b} = \frac{c+d}{d} \qquad \frac{a}{a+b} = \frac{c}{c+d}$$

There are several proofs that are quite straightforward. One way is to draw the auxiliary line shown on the left below. The two segments x and y form the two triangles shown separately on the right.

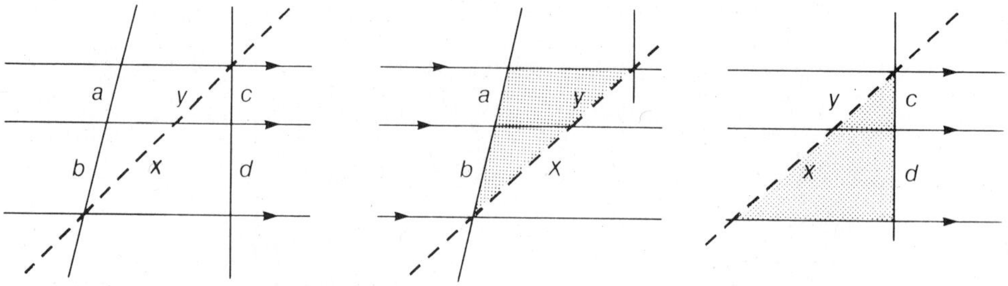

Both of these figures contain parallel lines, a transversal, a big triangle, and a little triangle. These figures are just like the first figure in the lesson. Thus, from the center figure, we can write this ratio,

$$\frac{a}{b} = \frac{y}{x}$$

and from the right-hand figure, we can write this ratio.

$$\frac{y}{x} = \frac{c}{d}$$

Now, since a over b and c over d both equal y over x, they equal each other.

$$\frac{a}{b} = \frac{c}{d}$$

Example 90.A.1 Find x.

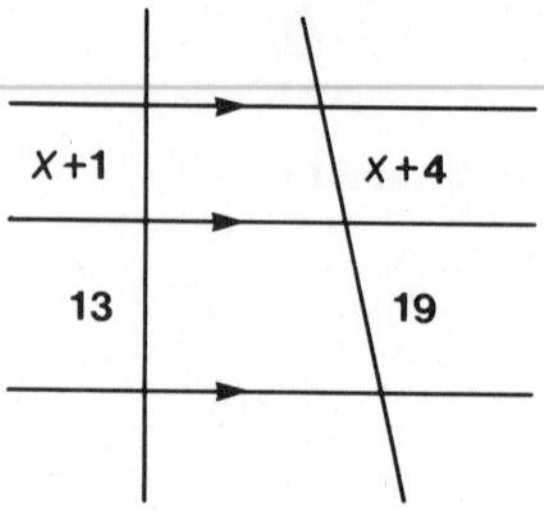

Solution We write the proportion, cross multiply, and solve.

$$\frac{x+1}{13} = \frac{x+4}{19} \qquad \text{proportion}$$

$$19x + 19 = 13x + 52 \qquad \text{multiplied}$$

$$6x = 33 \qquad \text{simplified}$$

$$\mathbf{x = \frac{11}{2}} \qquad \text{solved}$$

90.B Side ratios and angle bisectors

If a ray bisects an angle of a triangle, it also divides the opposite side into segments proportional to the other two sides. This one is not too easy to see.

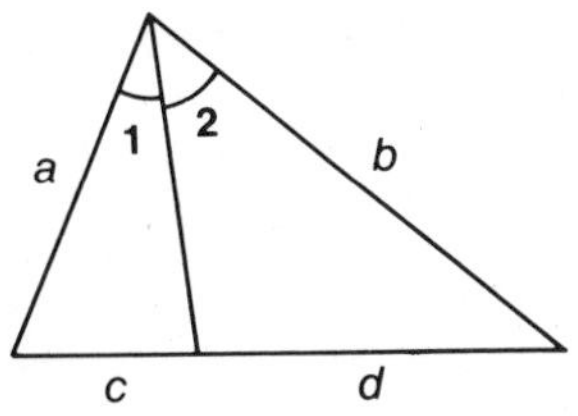

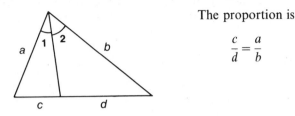

The proportion is

$$\frac{c}{d} = \frac{a}{b}$$

The proof shown here is tricky because it requires that two line segments be added to form another triangle. On the left below, we form this triangle by drawing m as an extension of b and by drawing line segment k parallel to the angle bisector. The angles 1, 2, 3, and 4 are equal. Angle 1 equals angle 2 because they are halves of the bisected angle. Angle 1 equals angle 3 because they are alternate interior angles, and angle 2 equals angle 4 because they are corresponding angles. Using substitution we see that angle 3 equals angle 4.

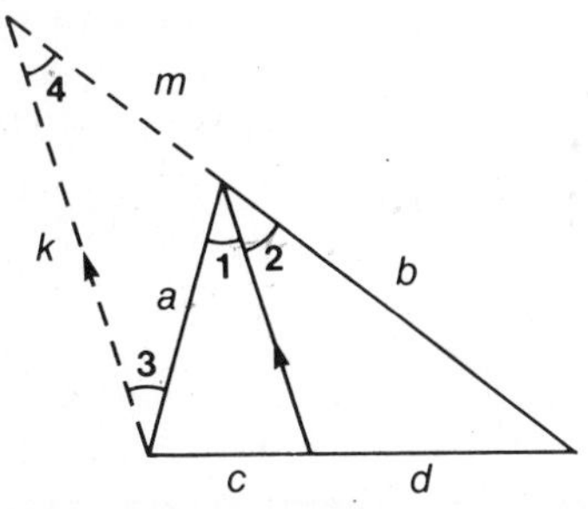

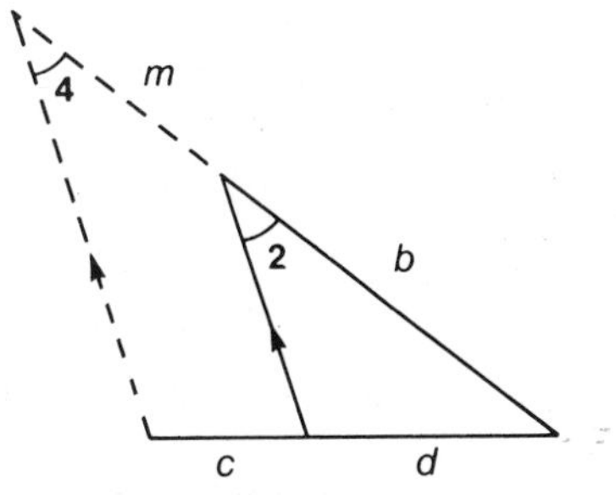

The fact that angle 3 equals angle 4 makes the leftmost triangle an isosceles triangle, so side m equals side a. From the simplified figure on the right, we can write the ratios of the sides. If in these ratios we replace m with a, we get our final result.

$$\frac{c}{d} = \frac{m}{b} \quad \xrightarrow{\text{replace } m \text{ with } a} \quad \frac{c}{d} = \frac{a}{b}$$

Example 90.B.1 Find x.

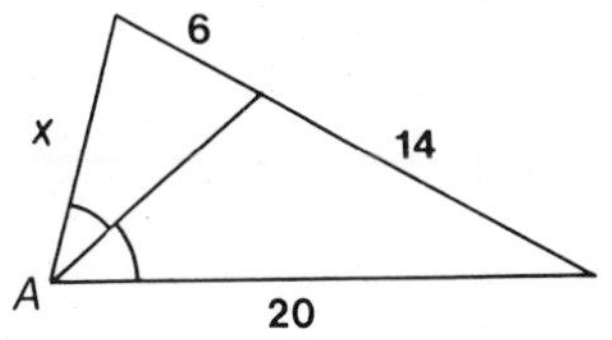

Solution The two adjacent angles at A are shown to be equal, and the angle bisector divides the opposite side into segments proportional to the other two sides.

$$\frac{6}{14} = \frac{x}{20} \qquad \text{proportion}$$

$$120 = 14x \qquad \text{multiplied}$$

$$\mathbf{\frac{60}{7} = x} \qquad \text{solved}$$

Example 90.B.2 Find x.

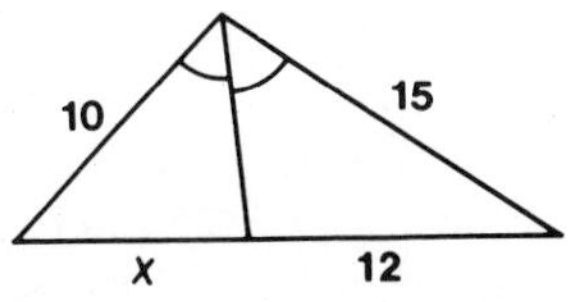

Solution If a ray bisects an angle of a triangle, it also divides the opposite side into segments proportional to the other two sides.

$$\frac{x}{12} = \frac{10}{15} \quad \text{proportion}$$

$$15x = 120 \quad \text{multiplied}$$

$$\boldsymbol{x = 8} \quad \text{solved}$$

Problem set 90

1. Franklin was fascinated to watch the exponential growth. It began with 42, and in only 8 hours was up to 60. What would it be up to in 30 hours?

2. Mary K could do 4 jobs in 5 hours, and Dolly could do 7 jobs in 3 hours. How long would it take both women working together to do 47 jobs?

3. Eight men could do b jobs in c hours. This was too slow so they got d other men to help. How long would it take the new crew to do 9 jobs?

4. There were 10 marbles in a line. Four were red and 6 were black. How many distinguishable linear patterns could be formed with the marbles?

5. The radius of the wheel was 20 inches. How fast was it rolling in miles per hour if its angular velocity was 200 radians per second?

6. Find x.

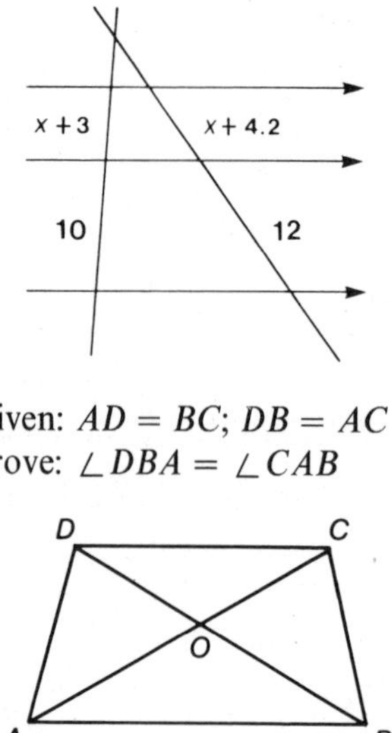

7. Given: $\overline{DE}$ is the angle bisector of $\angle BDC$; $\overline{AB} \parallel \overline{DE}$

Prove: $\dfrac{DC}{DB} = \dfrac{EC}{BE}$

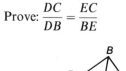

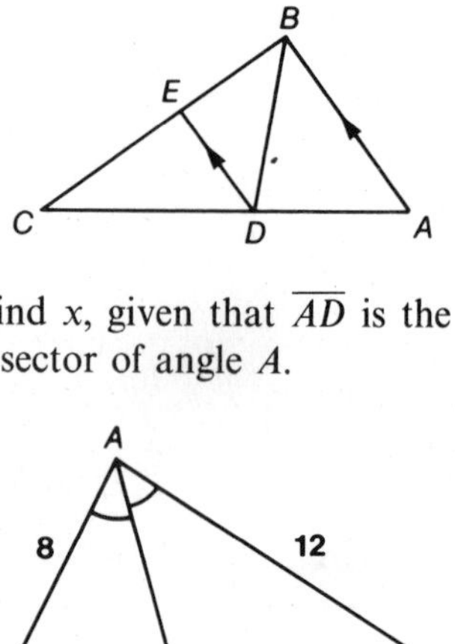

8. Given: $AD = BC$; $DB = AC$
Prove: $\angle DBA = \angle CAB$

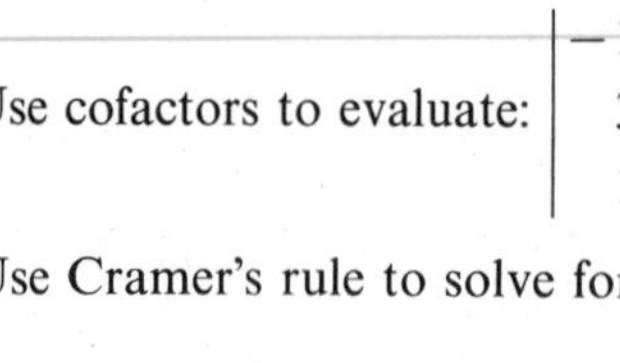

9. Find x, given that $\overline{AD}$ is the angle bisector of angle A.

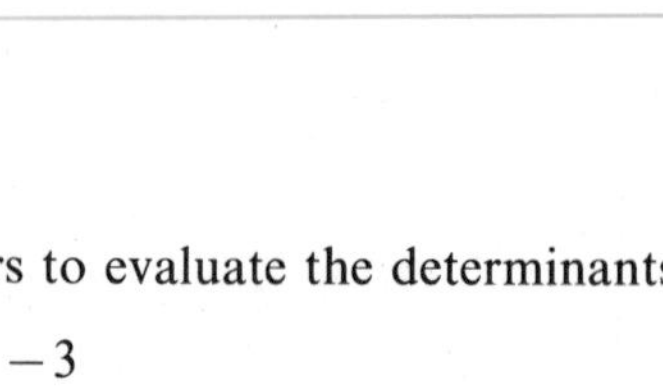

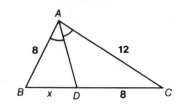

10. Find the fourth term of $(2x - 3y)^4$.

11. Use cofactors to evaluate: $\begin{vmatrix} -1 & 0 & 2 \\ 3 & 2 & 0 \\ 1 & 0 & -2 \end{vmatrix}$

12. Use Cramer's rule to solve for x. Use cofactors to evaluate the determinants:

$$\begin{cases} x + y + 2z = -3 \\ 2x - z = 5 \\ 2y + z = 1 \end{cases}$$

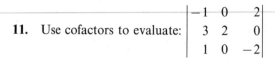

13. (*a*) Develop a formula for the sum of an arithmetic series with n terms, a_1 as its first term, and a_n as its last term.
(*b*) Using the formula developed in (*a*), find: $-4 + 0 + 4 + 8 + \cdots + 36$.

14. (*a*) Develop the formula for the sum of n terms of a geometric series whose first term is a and whose common ratio is r.
(*b*) Using the formula developed in (*a*), find the sum of the first seven terms of the geometric sequence: 5, 15, 45, ...

Use base 10 logs to simplify:

15. $\dfrac{\sqrt[3]{22{,}000}}{(1000)^{1.5}}$

16. $(3600 \times 10^8)(2500 \times 10^{17})$

17. Find the concentration of hydrogen ions (H^+) if the pH of the liquid is 8.5.

18. Develop the identity for $\sin x - \sin y$.

19. Use a calculator or logarithm tables to aid in finding $\log_6 22$.

20. Find the three cube roots of $-5 + 3i$ and write the roots in polar form.

21. The arithmetic mean of two numbers is -10. The negative geometric mean of the same two numbers is -8. What are the two numbers?

Solve the following equations given that ($0° \le x < 360°$):

22. $\sqrt{2} - 2\cos 2x = 0$

23. $\tan x + \sqrt{1 - 2\tan^2 x} = 0$

Show that:

24. $(\cos x - \sin x)(\cos x + \sin x) = \cos 2x$

25. $\dfrac{\tan x + 1}{\tan x - 1} = \dfrac{\sec x + \csc x}{\sec x - \csc x}$

26. Sketch $y = \tan x$.

27. Solve: $\sqrt{\log_4 x} = \frac{1}{2}\log_4 x$

28. Solve: $\log_4(\log_2 x) = 1$

29. Solve: $2\log x^2 = (\log x)^2$

30. Evaluate: $e^{2\ln 3 - \ln 2}$

EP 90.51, 90.52

LESSON 91 Translation of axes · Equations of the ellipse · Equations of the hyperbola

91.A Translation of axes

The equation of a geometric figure is often easier to write if the center of the figure is the origin. For example, the circle shown on the left below has a radius of 3 and is centered at the origin. The circle on the right also has a radius of 3, but because its center is at $(-2, 1)$ the equation is more complicated.

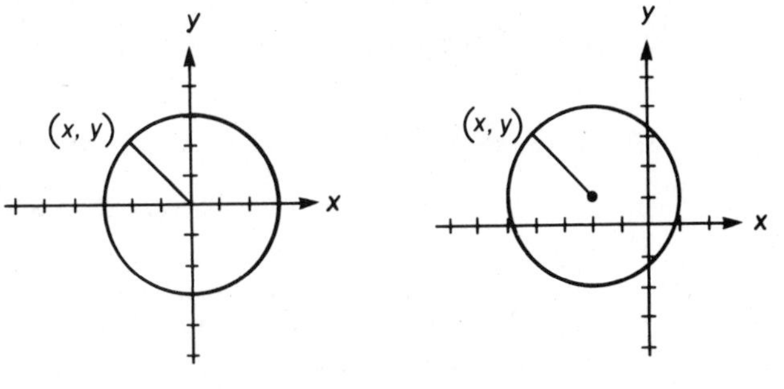

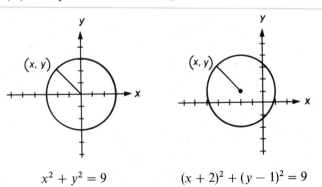

$x^2 + y^2 = 9$ $(x + 2)^2 + (y - 1)^2 = 9$

Thus, we normally find it easier to write the equation of a figure in the simpler form that it has when the figure is centered at the origin and then **translate** (shift horizontally and/or vertically) the coordinate axes. In the figures on the preceding page, when the coordinate system is shifted so that the center of the circle is $(-2, 1)$, we note that x in the equation is replaced with $(x + 2)$ and y is replaced with $(y - 1)$. To see why, we will look at the distance to a point P from two different origins on a number line.

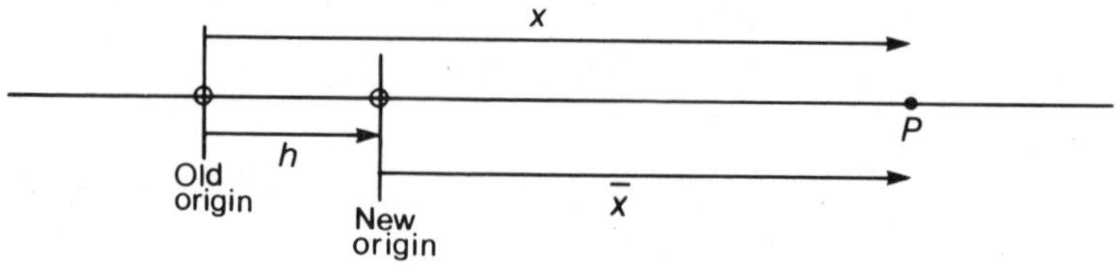

If we use x to designate the distance from the old origin to the point and use $\bar{x}$ to designate the distance from the new origin to the point, we can write the following equations:

$$x = h + \bar{x} \qquad \text{or} \qquad \bar{x} = x - h$$

Thus, we see if the coordinate axes are translated an x distance of h, the new x coordinate of the point will be $x - h$. If we repeat this development for y, we can show that if the coordinate axes are translated a y distance of k, the new y coordinate of the point will be $y - k$. This gives us the two equations that are often called ***equations for translation of rectangular coordinates:***

$$\bar{x} = x - h \qquad \bar{y} = y - k$$

91.B Equations of the ellipse

On the left below we show the standard form of the equation of an ellipse whose center is the origin and whose major axis is horizontal and is 8 units long and whose minor axis is 6 units long. On the right we show the equation of the same ellipse, but this time its center is $(3, -4)$.

$$(a)\quad \frac{x^2}{4^2} + \frac{y^2}{3^2} = 1 \qquad (b)\quad \frac{(x-3)^2}{4^2} + \frac{(y+4)^2}{3^2} = 1$$

To change equation (b) from the standard form to the general form, we first clear the denominators by multiplying every numerator by $16 \cdot 9$.

$$\frac{\cancel{16} \cdot 9(x-3)^2}{\cancel{16}} + \frac{16 \cdot \cancel{9}(y+4)^2}{\cancel{9}} = 16 \cdot 9$$

Next we expand the binomials and get

$$9(x^2 - 6x + 9) + 16(y^2 + 8y + 16) = 144$$

We finish by multiplying and rearranging and get

$$9x^2 + 16y^2 - 54x + 128y + 193 = 0 \qquad \text{general form}$$

In the following example, we show how this process can be reversed by beginning with the general form of an equation and completing the square twice to write the equation in standard form.

Example 91.B.1 Describe the ellipse $3x^2 + 2y^2 - 6x + 8y + 5 = 0$. Begin by writing the equation in standard form.

Solution We rearrange the terms and use parentheses:

$$(3x^2 - 6x \qquad) + (2y^2 + 8y \qquad) = -5$$

Next we factor out a 3 from the first set of parentheses and a 2 from the second set of parentheses:

$$3(x^2 - 2x \qquad) + 2(y^2 + 4y \qquad) = -5$$

Next we complete the square by inserting a 1 in the first set of parentheses and a 4 in the second.

$$3(x^2 - 2x + 1) + 2(y^2 + 4y + 4) =$$

Now on the right, we must add 3 and 8 because we have added 3 and 8 to the left side.

$$3(x^2 - 2x + 1) + 2(y^2 + 4y + 4) = -5 + 3 + 8$$

Now we simplify and get

$$3(x - 1)^2 + 2(y + 2)^2 = 6$$

Now we make the constant term 1 by dividing every term by 6, and we get

$$\frac{3(x-1)^2}{6} + \frac{2(y+2)^2}{6} = \frac{6}{6}$$

or

$$\frac{(x-1)^2}{(\sqrt{2})^2} + \frac{(y+2)^2}{(\sqrt{3})^2} = 1$$

This is the equation of an ellipse whose center is $(1, -2)$, whose major axis is vertical of length $2\sqrt{3}$, and whose minor axis is horizontal of length $2\sqrt{2}$.

91.C Equations of the hyperbola

On the left, we show the standard form of an equation of a hyperbola whose center is the origin. On the right, we show the equation that would result if the center of this hyperbola were shifted to $(-2, 3)$.

$$(a)\quad \frac{x^2}{9} - \frac{y^2}{16} = 1 \qquad\qquad (b)\quad \frac{(x+2)^2}{9} - \frac{(y-3)^2}{16} = 1$$

We can write equation (b) in the general form if we perform the indicated multiplications and multiply every term by $9 \cdot 16$ to clear the denominators.

$$\frac{\cancel{9} \cdot 16(x^2 + 4x + 4)}{\cancel{9}} - \frac{9 \cdot \cancel{16}(y^2 - 6y + 9)}{\cancel{16}} = 1 \cdot 9 \cdot 16$$

Now, if we simplify this expression, we can write the general form of the equation as

$$16x^2 - 9y^2 + 64x + 54y - 161 = 0$$

In the following example, we show how this process can be reversed by beginning with the general equation of a hyperbola and completing the square twice to write the equation in standard form.

Example 91.C.1 Complete the square twice to change the form of $9x^2 - 4y^2 + 18x - 16y - 43 = 0$ to the standard form. Graph the equation with center at the origin and then relabel the axes.

Solution First we rearrange the equation and use parentheses.

$$(9x^2 + 18x \qquad) + (-4y^2 - 16y \qquad) = 43$$

Now we factor out a 9 from the first set of parentheses and a -4 from the second.

$$9(x^2 + 2x \qquad) - 4(y^2 + 4y \qquad) = 43$$

Now we complete the square inside each set of parentheses and add $+9$ and -16 to the right side because we added $+9$ and -16 to the left side.

$$9(x^2 + 2x + 1) - 4(y^2 + 4y + 4) = 43 + 9 - 16$$

Now we simplify the expressions.

$$9(x + 1)^2 - 4(y + 2)^2 = 36$$

Since the right side must equal 1, we divide every term by 36 and get

$$\frac{(x + 1)^2}{4} - \frac{(y + 2)^2}{9} = 1$$

We will graph this equation by first graphing the sister equation.

$$\frac{x^2}{(2)^2} - \frac{y^2}{(3)^2} = 1$$

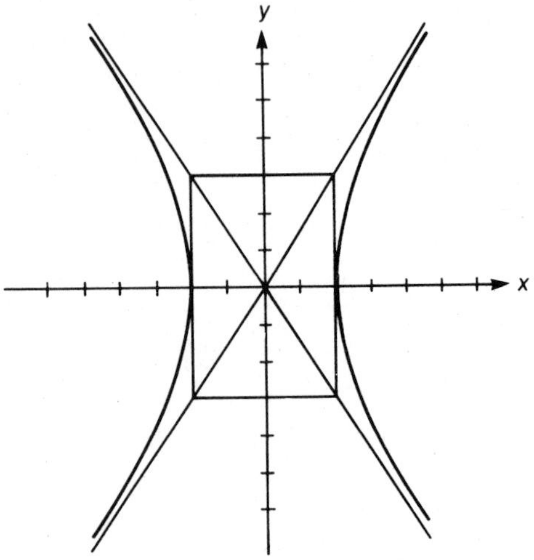

The graph that we need is exactly the same except that its center is $(-1, -2)$ instead of the origin. We merely have to relabel the horizontal and vertical axes and note the coordinates of two corners of the rectangle.

$$\frac{(x + 1)^2}{4} - \frac{(y + 2)^2}{9} = 1$$

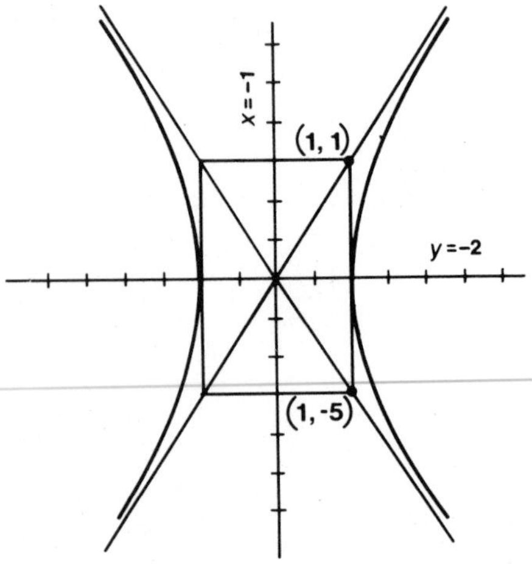

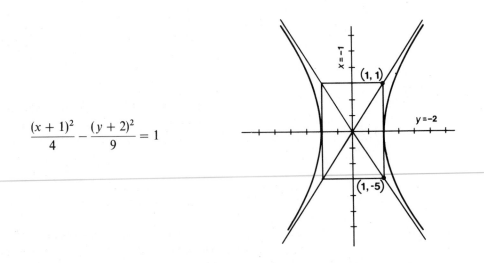

We see that both asymptotes go through the point $(-1, -2)$. We can use the lengths of the sides of the rectangle to find that the coordinates of the upper right corner are $(1, 1)$ and the coordinates of the lower right corner are $(1, -5)$. We can use these points to find the equations of the asymptotes.

$y = \frac{3}{2}x + b$ slope $\frac{3}{2}$

$1 = \frac{3}{2}(1) + b$ used (1, 1)

$-\frac{1}{2} = b$ solved

$y = \frac{3}{2}x - \frac{1}{2}$ asymptote

$y = -\frac{3}{2}x + b$ slope $-\frac{3}{2}$

$-5 = -\frac{3}{2}(1) + b$ used (1, −5)

$-\frac{7}{2} = b$ solved

$y = -\frac{3}{2}x - \frac{7}{2}$ asymptote

Problem set 91

1. Frank Boy owned three-sevenths of the business, and his share of the profits was \$12,600. Julie Girl was not downcast as she owned four twenty-first parts of the business. What was Julie Girl's share of the profits?

2. Binibo bumped out 72 miles and then walked back home at one-third of his bumping speed. If the total time for his trip was 24 hours, how fast could he bump?

3. Susie Bee piled the coals to the fire, but still the things decreased exponentially. At first they numbered 400, but in 20 minutes they numbered only 380. What was their half-life?

4. The wheels whined at 300 radians per minute. Frank hung on for dear life because the radius of the wheels was 1 full meter and Frank was on the rim. What was Frank's speed in miles per minute?

5. How many ways can Arthur, Guinevere, and seven knights be seated at the round table?

6. Write the equation of the circle shown in standard form and in general form.

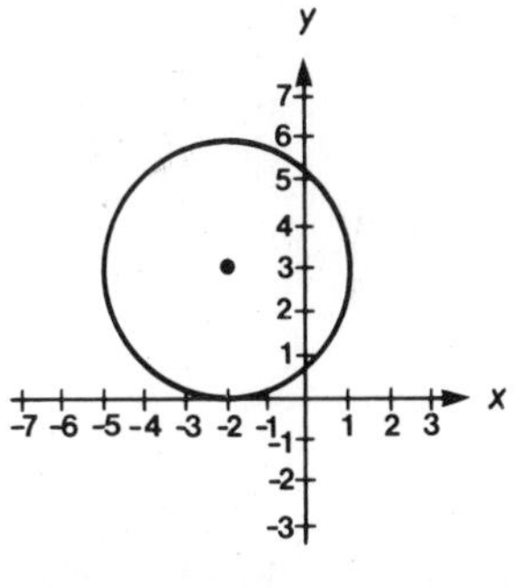

7. $x^2 + 2y^2 - 10x + 8y + 29 = 0$ is the general equation of an ellipse. Write the equation of this ellipse in standard form and give the coordinates of the center, the length of the major axis, and the length of the minor axis.

8. $9x^2 + 4y^2 + 54x - 8y + 49 = 0$ is the general equation of an ellipse. Write the equation of this ellipse in standard form and give the coordinates of the center, the length of the major axis, and the length of the minor axis.

9. $x^2 - y^2 - 2x - 4y - 4 = 0$ is the general equation of a hyperbola. Write the equation of this hyperbola in standard form and give the coordinates of the center, the coordinates of the vertices, and the equations of the asymptotes.

10. $4x^2 - y^2 + 8x - 4y - 4 = 0$ is the general equation of a hyperbola. Write the equation of this hyperbola in standard form and give the coordinates of the center, the coordinates of the vertices, and the equations of the asymptotes.

11. Given: $\overline{DE}$ is the angle bisector of $\angle BDC$; $\overline{AB} \parallel \overline{DE}$

Prove: $\dfrac{DC}{DB} = \dfrac{EC}{BE}$

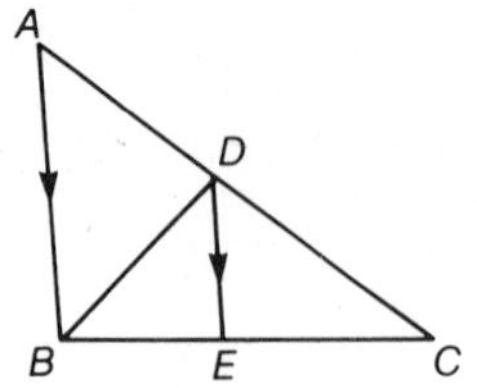

12. Find x.

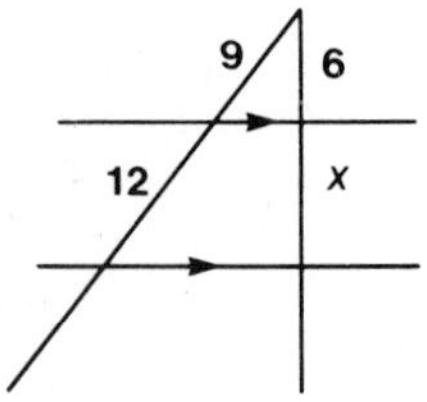

13. Given: $AB = AC$; $\overline{BD} \perp \overline{AC}$; $\overline{EC} \perp \overline{AB}$

Prove: $BD = CE$

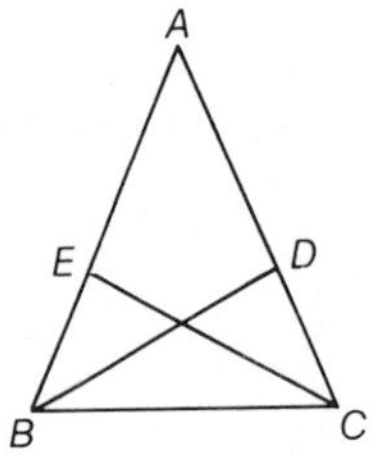

14. Find x, given that $\overline{AD}$ is the angle bisector of angle A.

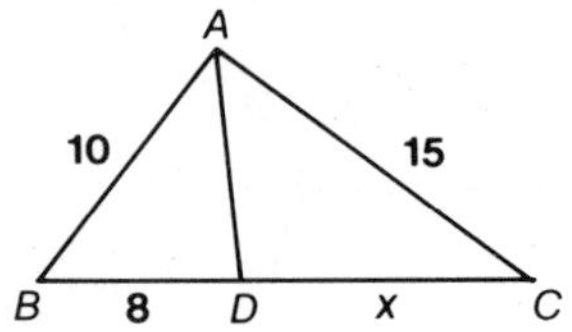

15. Find the third term of $(3x - 2y)^6$.

16. Use Cramer's rule to solve for y. Use cofactors to evaluate the determinants.

$$\begin{cases} 2x + y + 2z = 2 \\ 2y + z = 5 \\ x + 3y = 2 \end{cases}$$

17. (*a*) Develop a formula for the sum of an arithmetic series with n terms, a_1 as its first term, and a_n as its last term.
(*b*) Using the formula developed in (*a*), simplify: $-8 + (-4) + 0 + \cdots + 24$.

18. (*a*) Develop the formula for the sum of n terms of a geometric series whose first term is a and whose common ratio is r.
(*b*) Using the formula developed in (*a*), find the sum of the first 7 terms of the geometric sequence: $4, -8, 16, \ldots$.

19. Use base 10 logs to simplify: $\dfrac{\sqrt[4]{64{,}000}}{(2100)^{1.4}}$

20. The pH of a solution is 3.5. What is the concentration of hydrogen ions in moles per liter of the solution?

21. Develop the identity for $\sin x \cos y$.

22. Use a calculator or a table of logarithms to aid in determining $\log_5 45$.

23. Find the four fourth roots of $-6 + 4i$ and write the roots in polar form.

24. A regular pentagon has perimeter 25 cm. What is the area of the pentagon?

25. Solve, given that $(0° \leq x \leq 360°)$: $2 \sin^2 x + \sqrt{3} \sin x = 0$

Show that:

26. $\dfrac{\sin^3 x + \cos^3 x}{\sin x + \cos x} = 1 - \dfrac{1}{2}\sin 2x$

27. $\dfrac{\cot x + 1}{\cot x - 1} = \dfrac{\csc x + \sec x}{\csc x - \sec x}$

28. Sketch $y = -7 + 4 \sin \dfrac{3}{8}\left(x - \dfrac{2\pi}{3}\right)$.

Solve:

29. $\frac{1}{2} \log_3 25 - \log_3 (2x - 5) = 2$

30. $\log_2 3 = 2 \log_2 x$

EP 91.53, 91.54

LESSON 92 Higher-order echelons

92.A Higher-order echelons

The matrix echelon method of solution can be used to solve any $n \times n$ system of linear equations. In this lesson, we will investigate the use of the echelon method to solve systems of three equations in three unknowns. The coefficients of a system of three equations in three unknowns can be used to form a 3×4 matrix, as we show here.

$$\begin{cases} 3x + 2y + z = 10 \\ x - 3y + 2z = 1 \\ 2x + y - z = 1 \end{cases} \qquad \begin{bmatrix} 3 & 2 & 1 & 10 \\ 1 & -3 & 2 & 1 \\ 2 & 1 & -1 & 1 \end{bmatrix}$$

By using the rules for matrices, we can change this matrix into the echelon matrix on the left

$$\begin{bmatrix} 1 & 0 & 0 & 1 \\ 0 & 1 & 0 & 2 \\ 0 & 0 & 1 & 3 \end{bmatrix} \qquad \text{which can be read as} \qquad \begin{aligned} x &= 1 \\ y &= 2 \\ z &= 3 \end{aligned}$$

When we solve equations by using the elimination method, we can

1. Multiply every term in an equation by the same number
2. Add two equations
3. Change the order in which the equations are written

These rules translate into three of the rules for matrices, which are as follows:

1. Every entry in a row can be multiplied by the same number.
2. The corresponding entries in two rows can be added.
3. Any two rows can be interchanged.

First we work down, forming the echelon of 1s and the 0s that appear to the left of the echelon of 1s. Then we work back up to form the 0s that appear to the right of the echelon of 1s.

Example 92.A.1 Use echelon matrices to solve: $\begin{cases} 3x + 2y + z = 10 \\ x - 3y + 2z = 1 \\ 2x + y - z = 1 \end{cases}$

Solution We begin by writing the ***augmented matrix.*** The first three columns are formed with the coefficients of the variables, and the last column is formed with the constant terms.

$$\begin{bmatrix} 3 & 2 & 1 & 10 \\ 1 & -3 & 2 & 1 \\ 2 & 1 & -1 & 1 \end{bmatrix}$$

We always make the entry in the upper left-hand corner the number 1. We could do this by multiplying every entry in the first row by $\frac{1}{3}$. Instead we just interchange the first two rows. This is the same thing as changing the order in which the first two equations are written.

$$\begin{bmatrix} 1 & -3 & 2 & 1 \\ 3 & 2 & 1 & 10 \\ 2 & 1 & -1 & 1 \end{bmatrix} \quad \text{interchanged the first two rows}$$

Next we will use this 1 to make the two entries below it 0. First, we multiply the top row by -3 and add it to the second row. Then we multiply the top row by -2 and add it to the third row.

$$\begin{bmatrix} 1 & -3 & 2 & 1 \\ 0 & 11 & -5 & 7 \\ 0 & 7 & -5 & -1 \end{bmatrix}$$

Now we want the second 1 in our echelon. We get this by multiplying every entry in the second row by $\frac{1}{11}$.

$$\begin{bmatrix} 1 & -3 & 2 & 1 \\ 0 & 1 & -\frac{5}{11} & \frac{7}{11} \\ 0 & 7 & -5 & -1 \end{bmatrix}$$

Next we use this new 1 to get a 0 as the second entry in the third row. We multiply the second row by -7 and add it to the third row.

$$\begin{bmatrix} 1 & -3 & 2 & 1 \\ 0 & 1 & -\frac{5}{11} & \frac{7}{11} \\ 0 & 0 & -\frac{20}{11} & -\frac{60}{11} \end{bmatrix}$$

Now to get the last 1 in the echelon, we multiply every term in the third row by $-11/20$.

$$\begin{bmatrix} 1 & -3 & 2 & 1 \\ 0 & 1 & -\frac{5}{11} & \frac{7}{11} \\ 0 & 0 & 1 & 3 \end{bmatrix}$$

Now we work back up to change $-\frac{5}{11}$, 2, and -3 to 0. First we multiply the bottom row by $\frac{5}{11}$ and add it to the second row.

$$\begin{bmatrix} 1 & -3 & 2 & 1 \\ 0 & 1 & 0 & 2 \\ 0 & 0 & 1 & 3 \end{bmatrix}$$

Now we multiply the second row by 3 and add it to the top row and get

$$\begin{bmatrix} 1 & 0 & 2 & 7 \\ 0 & 1 & 0 & 2 \\ 0 & 0 & 1 & 3 \end{bmatrix}$$

Now we multiply the bottom row by -2 and add it to the top row and get

$$\begin{bmatrix} 1 & 0 & 0 & 1 \\ 0 & 1 & 0 & 2 \\ 0 & 0 & 1 & 3 \end{bmatrix} \quad \text{so} \quad \begin{aligned} x &= 1 \\ y &= 2 \\ z &= 3 \end{aligned}$$

Mistakes can be minimized in the working of these problems if two people work together.

The echelon matrix method works well on computers. See if you can write a program for this method for solving 3 × 3 systems of equations.

Problem set 92

1. The Formula XI cars averaged 200 miles per hour. If the diameter of the wheels was 0.8 meter, what was the angular velocity of the wheels in radians per minute?

2. Driver number 1 drove at 35 miles per hour for h hours, so he drove farther than driver number 2 who drove at 40 miles per hour for $h - 2$ hours. How much farther did he drive?

3. Nellie Bly rode her bicycle k kilometers in m minutes. Captain Fletcher walked half that distance in 3 times the time. What is Captain Fletcher's rate in kilometers per minute?

4. Sambo ran a miles in b hours and then he ran c miles in d hours. What was his overall average speed, and how long would it take him to go 1000 miles at this speed?

5. The probability that the thing either would be red or would have white spots or would be red with white spots was 0.80. If the probability of being red was 0.62 and the probability of having white spots was 0.35, what was the probability that it was red and also had white spots?

6. Write the equation of the circle shown in standard form and in general form.

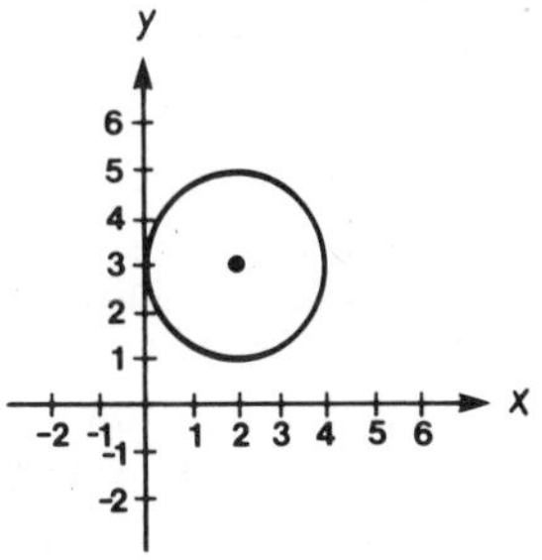

7. $x^2 + 4y^2 + 10x + 24y + 45 = 0$ is the general equation of an ellipse. Write the equation of this ellipse in standard form and give the coordinates of the center, the length of the major axis, and the length of the minor axis.

8. $4x^2 + 9y^2 - 16x + 18y - 11 = 0$ is the general equation of an ellipse whose center is not the origin. Write the equation of this ellipse in standard form and give the coordinates of the center, the length of the minor axis, and the length of the major axis.

9. $4x^2 - y^2 + 16x - 4y - 4 = 0$ is the general equation of a hyperbola. Write the coordinates of the center, the coordinates of the vertices, and the equations of the asymptotes.

10. Write the equation in standard form of the hyperbola whose general equation is $x^2 - y^2 - 2x - 4y - 4 = 0$ and give the coordinates of the center, the coordinates of the vertices, and the equations of the asymptotes.

11. Given: $\overline{DE}$ bisects $\angle BDC$.

Prove: $\dfrac{DC}{DB} = \dfrac{EC}{BE}$

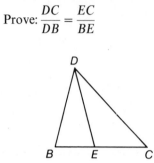

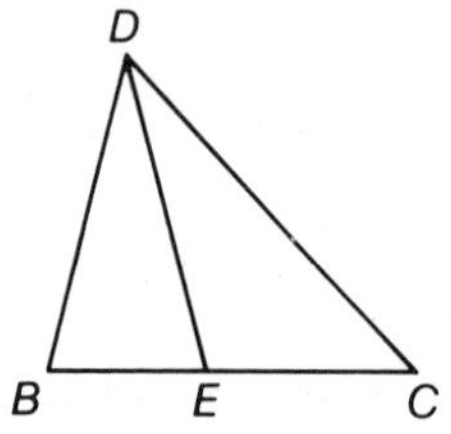

12. Find x.

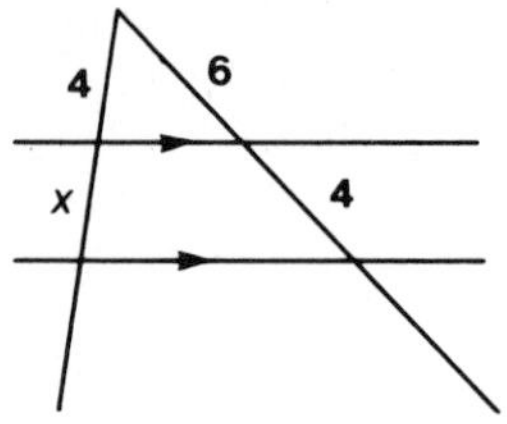

13. Given: $\overline{BD}$ and $\overline{CE}$ are perpendicular to $\overline{AC}$ and $\overline{AB}$ as shown, and $AE = AD$.

Prove: $\triangle ABC$ is an isosceles triangle

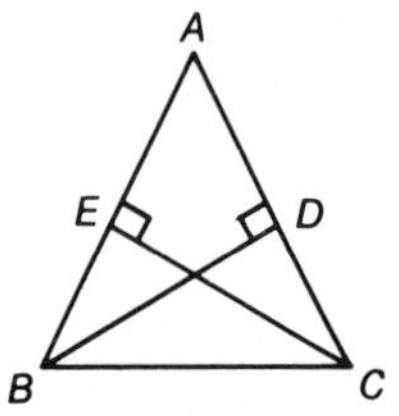

14. Find x given that $\overline{AD}$ is the angle bisector of angle A.

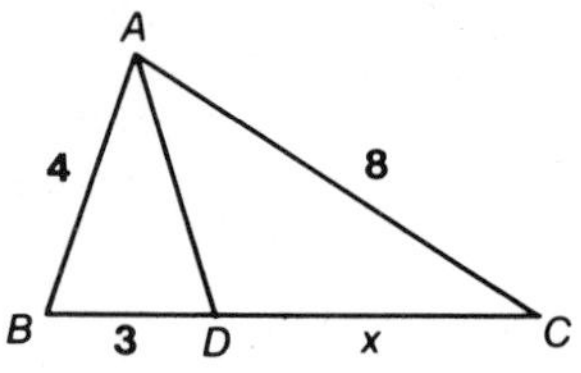

15. Find the fourth term of $(x - 3y)^7$.

16. Use the echelon method to solve this system of equations: $\begin{cases} 2x + y + z = 0 \\ 2y - z = -1 \\ 3x - y = -7 \end{cases}$

17. (*a*) Develop the formula for the sum of n terms of a geometric series whose first term is a and whose common ratio is r.

(*b*) Using the formula developed in (*a*), find the sum of the first 8 terms of the geometric sequence: $-4, 8, -16, \ldots$.

18. (*a*) Develop a formula for the sum of an arithmetic series with n terms, a_1 as its first term, and a_n as its last term.

(*b*) Using the formula developed in (*a*), find $-2 + 2 + 6 + \cdots + 30$.

19. The concentration of hydrogen ions (H^+) in a solution is 6.5×10^{-6} mole per liter. What is the pH of the solution?

20. Use base 10 logs to simplify: $\dfrac{\sqrt[3]{28{,}000}}{(3600)^{0.8}}$

21. Develop the identity for $\sin x \sin y$.

22. Find the two square roots of $-3 + 2i$ and express the roots in polar form.

23. Express $\log_5 60$ in terms of common logarithms. Do not find a numerical answer.

24. What is the sum of the exterior angles of a 25-sided convex polygon?

25. Solve, given that ($0° \le x < 360°$): $2 \sin^2 x + 15 \cos x - 9 = 0$

Show that:

26. $\dfrac{\sin x + \cos x}{\tan^2 x - 1} = \dfrac{\cos^2 x}{\sin x - \cos x}$

27. $\dfrac{2 \cos 2x}{\sin 2x} = \cot x - \tan x$

28. Sketch $y = 4 + 4 \sec x$.

Solve:

29. $\frac{2}{3} \log_4 8 + \log_4 (2x - 3) = -1$

30. $\log_3 (\log_2 x) = 2$

EP 92.55, 92.56

LESSON 93 Altitudes · Medians and overlapping triangles

93.A Altitudes and medians

Any side of a triangle can be designated as the base of the triangle. The ***altitude*** of a triangle is defined as the perpendicular line segment from the base to the other vertex or is defined as the length of this line segment. There are three possible configurations, as we show here.

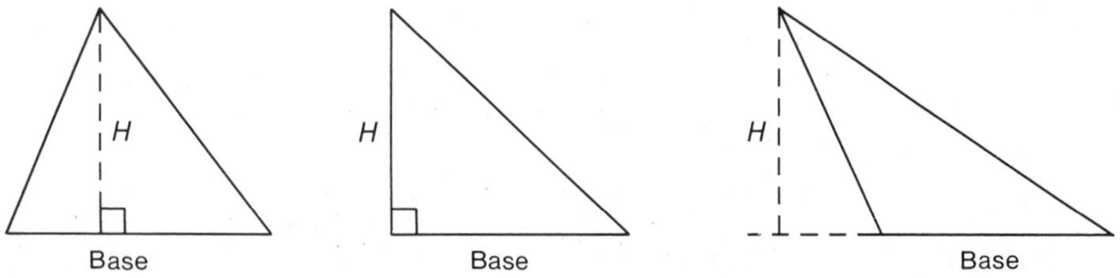

In the left-hand figure, the altitude H is in the interior of the triangle. The center triangle is a right triangle, and the altitude is a leg of the triangle. The base of the triangle on the right had to be extended so that the altitude could be drawn. The following proof involves the altitude and the sides of an isosceles triangle.

Example 93.A.1 Prove that if a point lies on the perpendicular bisector of a segment it is equidistant from the endpoints of the segment.

Solution First we draw segment $\overline{BC}$, construct a perpendicular bisector, and select a point P on the bisector. Then we connect points P, B, and C as shown.

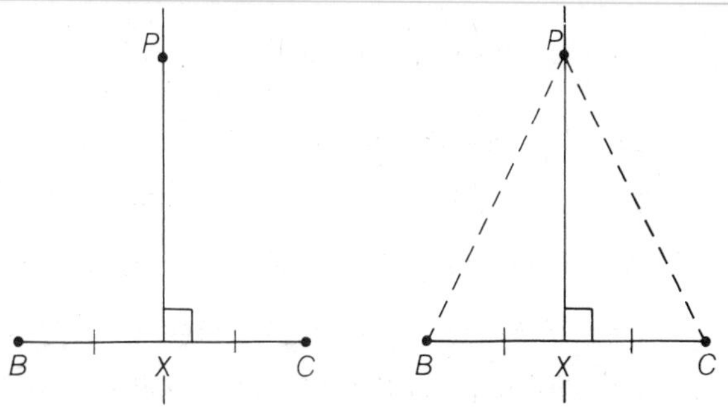

The two triangles are similar by SAS because $BX = XC$, the two angles are right angles, and side PX is common to both triangles. Since the scale factor is 1, the triangles are also congruent.

$$\triangle BPX \cong \triangle CPX$$

Thus, PB and PC are equal because they are corresponding parts of congruent triangles. This proves that the point P is equidistant from the endpoints B and C.

93.B Medians and more complicated geometric figures

A ***median*** of a triangle is a line segment from one vertex to the midpoint of the opposite side. Proofs that involve medians are often made easier if the figure is redrawn with the triangles involved shown separately. We will demonstrate this in the next example.

Example 93.B.1 In the triangle on the left below, $\overline{BN}$ and $\overline{CM}$ are medians and $AB = AC$. Prove $BN = CM$.

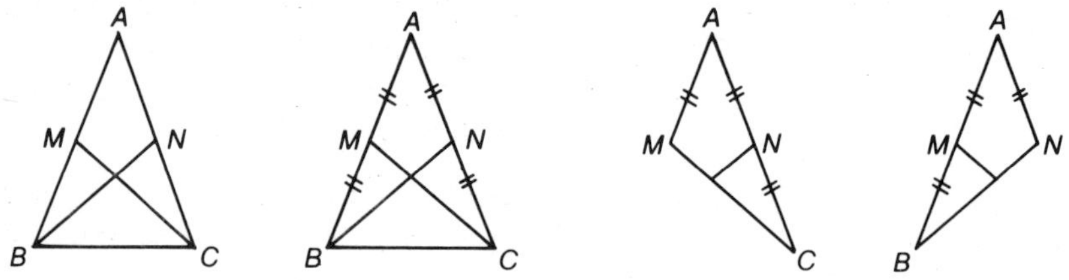

Solution **Whenever we are asked to prove that segments are equal, we look for congruent triangles.** We begin by drawing the second figure and using tick marks to indicate that four segments are equal because $AB = AC$ and M and N are midpoints. Overlapping triangles are sometimes confusing, so on the right we draw separately the two triangles in which we are interested. We see that both triangles contain angle A and that the sides that form this angle are equal. Thus, the triangles are similar by SAS. Since the scale factor is 1, the triangles are also congruent.

$$\triangle AMC \cong \triangle ANB$$

Since corresponding parts of congruent triangles are equal, MC equals BN.

Example 93.B.2 Given: $\overline{SR}$ is the perpendicular bisector of $\overline{QT}$; $\overline{QR}$ is the perpendicular bisector of $\overline{SP}$. Prove: $PQ = ST$.

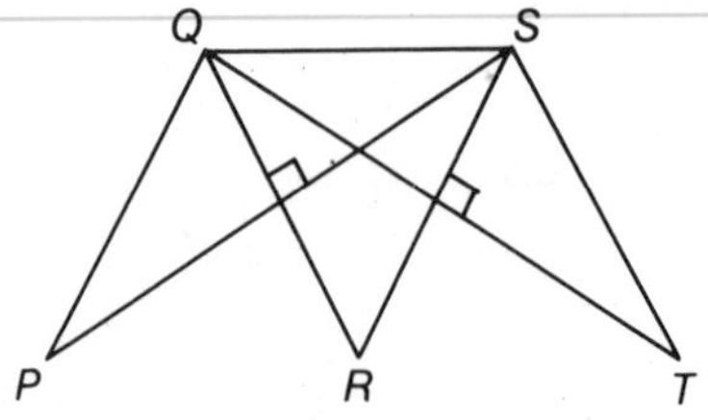

Solution This proof does not involve medians, but the figure is quite involved, and again we find that the proof is easier if we redraw the figure so that the parts of interest are shown with as little confusion as possible. On the left we use small circles to identify the segments we wish to prove equal. Then on the right we break out the two parts of the figure that we will use in the proof.

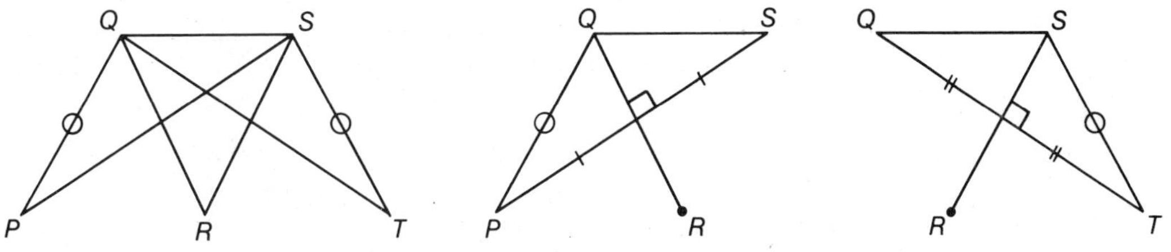

In the center figure, the two right triangles are similar by SAS with scale factor 1. Thus they are congruent, so side PQ equals side QS because CPCTE. In the figure on the right the two right triangles are congruent since they are similar with scale factor 1. Thus side QS equals side ST by CPCTE. Since PQ and ST both equal QS, they are equal to each other.

Problem set 93

1. Karen was perplexed because she had never before been able to observe exponential decay. At the beginning, there were 1440 grams of the substance and after 50 hours only 1360 grams remained. How many hours after the beginning would it be before only 400 grams remained?

2. Four workers could do 15 jobs in d days. To speed things up, w more workers were hired. With this addition, how long would it take to complete 135 jobs?

3. Jocko needed more space in a hurry as the volume of the blob was increasing exponentially. At first it measured 40 cubic units, but after 300 minutes it measured 200 cubic units. The volume of the room was 1800 cubic units. How long did it take for the blob to completely fill the room?

4. After much fumbling and twitching, Harry Bill drew a single card from a full deck. What was the probability that the card he drew was either a queen or a spade or both?

5. Miss Fussbudget was perplexed as she had to appoint a committee of 4 to investigate the alleged peculation. If 7 citizens had volunteered, how many ways could she form a committee of 4?

6. Given: $\overline{SR}$ is the perpendicular bisector of $\overline{QT}$; $\overline{QR}$ is the perpendicular bisector of $\overline{SP}$
   Prove: $PQ = ST$

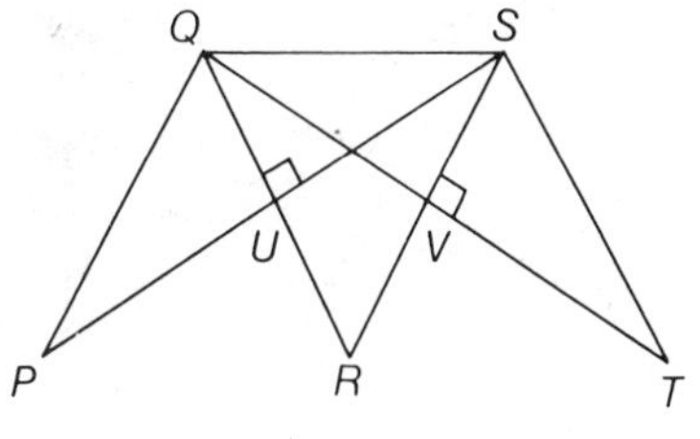

7. Given: Quadrilateral $ABCD$. P is the midpoint of $\overline{AD}$; Q is the midpoint of $\overline{AB}$; R is the midpoint of $\overline{BC}$; and S is the midpoint of $\overline{DC}$
   Prove: $PQ = SR$

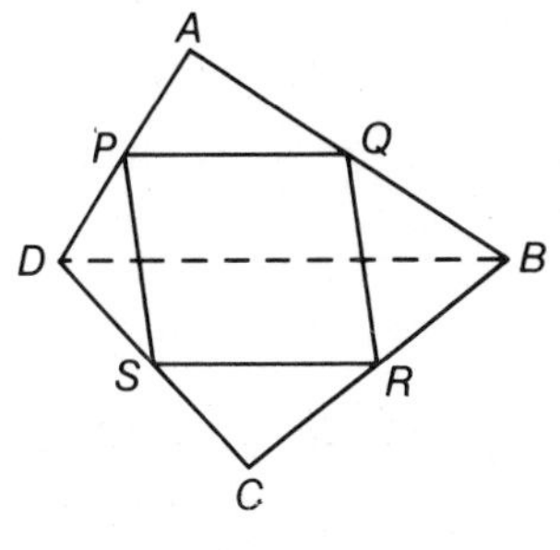

8. Given: $\overline{AD}$ is the angle bisector of angle A

Prove: $\dfrac{AC}{AB} = \dfrac{DC}{DB}$

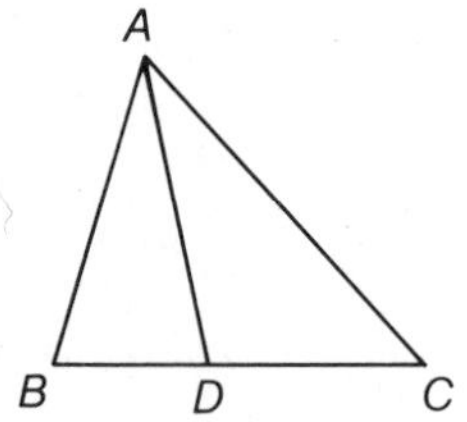

9. Prove that any point which lies on the perpendicular bisector of a segment is equidistant from the endpoints of the segment.

10. $x^2 + 2y^2 - 10x + 8y + 29 = 0$ is the general equation of an ellipse. Write the equation of this ellipse in standard form and give the coordinates of the center, the length of the major axis, and the length of the minor axis.

11. The general equation of a hyperbola is $36x^2 - 9y^2 - 24x + 54y - 113 = 0$. Write the equation of this hyperbola in standard form and give the coordinates of the center, the coordinates of the vertices, and the equations of the asymptotes.

12. Write the equation of the circle shown in standard form and general form.

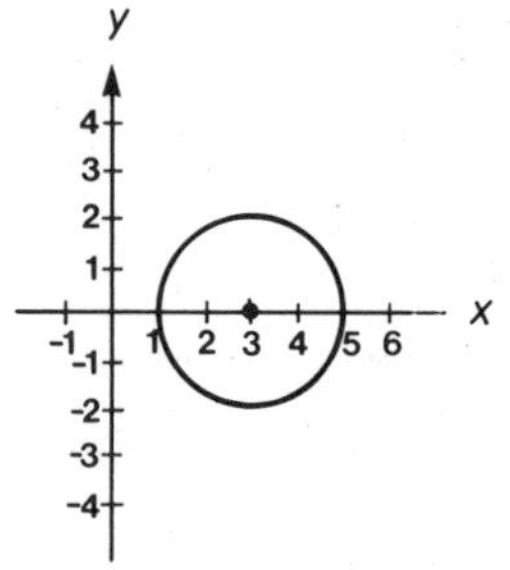

13. Find the three cube roots of $+i$ and write them in rectangular form. Give exact answers.

14. Use Cramer's rule to solve this system of equations. Use the method of cofactors to evaluate the determinants.

$$\begin{cases} x + 2y + z = 0 \\ 2x - y + 3z = 11 \\ 3y + 4z = -2 \end{cases}$$

15. Use the echelon method to solve this system of equations:

$$\begin{cases} 2x + y + z = 3 \\ 3y + 2z = 0 \\ 3x + 2y = -1 \end{cases}$$

16. (*a*) Develop the identity for $\cos x + \cos y$.
(*b*) Find $\cos 75^\circ + \cos 15^\circ$ by using the identity found in (*a*). Use decimal approximations

17. (*a*) Develop the identity for $\cos x - \cos y$.
(*b*) Find $\cos 75^\circ - \cos 15^\circ$ by using the identity found in (*a*). Use exact values.

18. The first term of an arithmetic sequence is 4 and the common difference is -5.
(*a*) What is the tenth term of the arithmetic sequence?
(*b*) What is the sum of the first 10 terms of the arithmetic sequence described?

19. The pH of a solution is 7.6. What is the concentration of hydrogen ions in the solution?

20. Use base 10 logs to simplify: $\dfrac{\sqrt[5]{63{,}900}}{(2100)^{0.4}}$

21. A triangle has a 30° angle. A side adjacent to this angle has length 10, and the side opposite this angle has length 8. Draw the triangle(s) described and find the length(s) of the missing side(s).

22. Express $\log_6 40$ in terms of common logarithms. Do not find a numerical answer.

23. A ball is dropped from a height of 243 feet. After each bounce, the ball rebounds two-thirds of the distance it fell. How far does the ball fall on its fourth fall?

24. Sketch $y = \cot x$.

25. Solve given that $(0° \le x < 360°)$: $4 \sin^2 x \tan x = \tan x$

Show that:

26. $2 \csc 2x \sin x = \sec x$

27. $(\tan\theta - \sec\theta)^2 = \dfrac{1 - \sin\theta}{1 + \sin\theta}$

Solve:

28. $5^{2x-1} = 6^{2x+1}$

29. $\log_2 (x^2 + 3x + 4) = 3^{\log_3 2}$

30. $\log_2 8 - \log_2 4 = x$

EP 93.57, 93.58

LESSON 94 *Convergent geometric series*

94.A Convergent geometric series

We remember that we can derive the formula for the sum of n terms of a geometric series by using only four steps. The first step is to write the general expression for the sum of n terms (a). Then we multiply every term on both sides by $-r$ and add the two equations to get (b). Note how the terms on the right are shifted one place to the right so that like terms can be aligned vertically.

$$\begin{array}{rrl}
 & & \quad\;\; (1) \quad\; (2) \quad\;\; (3) \quad\;\; (4) \qquad\qquad\qquad (n-1) \qquad (n) \\
(a) & S_n = & a_1 + a_1 r + a_1 r^2 + a_1 r^3 + \cdots + a_1 r^{n-2} + a_1 r^{n-1} \\
-r(a) & -rS_n = & \qquad - a_1 r - a_1 r^2 - a_1 r^3 - \cdots - a_1 r^{n-2} - a_1 r^{n-1} - a_1 r^n \\
\hline
(b) & S_n - rS_n = & a_1 \qquad\qquad\qquad\qquad\qquad\qquad\qquad\qquad\qquad\qquad - a_1 r^n
\end{array}$$

Now we factor out S_n on the left side and factor out a_1 on the right side. Then we divide both sides by the coefficient of S_n.

$$S_n(1 - r) = a_1(1 - r^n) \qquad \text{factored}$$

$$S_n = \frac{a_1(1 - r^n)}{1 - r} \qquad \text{divided by } 1 - r$$

Now let's look at the $(1 - r^n)$ on top. If r^n is very, very small, then $(1 - r^n)$ almost equals 1. Let's let r^n be 0.000001. Then we get

$$S_n = \frac{a_1(1 - 0.000001)}{1 - r} \approx \frac{a_1(0.999999)}{1 - r}$$

But 0.999999 is almost the same as 1, and if we let r^n get smaller and smaller, then the value of $1 - r^n$ gets even closer to 1. In calculus, we use the word ***limit*** to say that $1 - r^n$ approaches 1 as a limit as r^n gets smaller. It never is exactly equal to 1, but if we use the value of 1 for $1 - r^n$, our error will be extremely small. If r is a number between -1 and 0 or between 0 and $+1$,

$$-1 < r < 0 \qquad \text{or} \qquad 0 < r < 1$$

as n increases, r^n gets very small. For instance, if r is $\frac{1}{2}$, the value of r^n when n equals 12 is

$$\left(\frac{1}{2}\right)^{12} = \frac{1}{4096} \approx 0.0002441$$

and $(1 - r^n) \approx 0.9997559$, a number very close to 1.

If we use 1 for $1 - r^n$, the formula becomes

$$\mathbf{S_n = \frac{a_1}{1 - r}}$$

We can use this formula to find the exact sum of an infinite geometric series if $|r|$ is less than 1. If $|r|$ is less than 1, we say that the series is a *convergent geometric series.* If $|r|$ is greater than or equal to 1, the series is a *divergent series.* The sum of a divergent series cannot be found.

Example 94.A.1 Find the sum of the infinite geometric series

$$5 + \frac{5}{2} + \frac{5}{4} + \frac{5}{8} + \cdots$$

Solution We see that a_1 is 5 and r is $\frac{1}{2}$. Since $|r|$ is less than 1, the series is a convergent series, and we can find the sum of an infinite convergent series.

$$S_n = \frac{a_1}{1 - r} = \frac{5}{1 - \frac{1}{2}} = \mathbf{10}$$

Thus, the sum of this series gets closer and closer to 10 as the number of terms increases. The sum is never greater than 10 no matter how many terms are used.

Example 94.A.2 A ball is dropped from a height of 12 ft and rebounds two-fifths of the fall distance on each succeeding bounce. (*a*) How far will the ball fall on the tenth fall? (*b*) What will be the total distance the ball will travel?

Solution This problem is used in almost every algebra book. **We always draw a diagram of a problem when we can. Diagrams aid understanding and help prevent mistakes.**

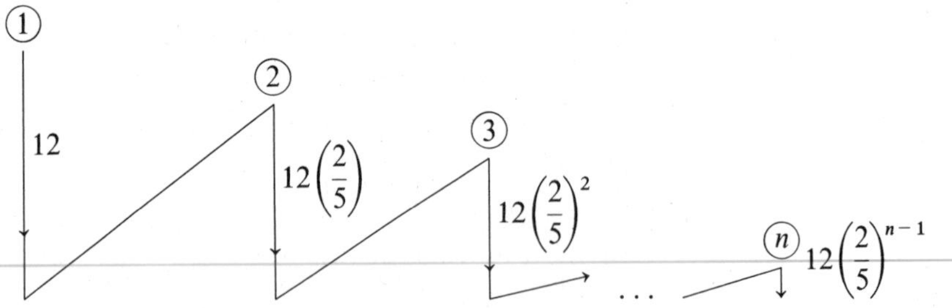

(*a*) The sequence that describes the distance the ball falls is

$$\underset{①}{12}, \quad \underset{②}{12\left(\frac{2}{5}\right)}, \quad \underset{③}{12\left(\frac{2}{5}\right)^2}, \quad \underset{④}{12\left(\frac{2}{5}\right)^3}, \quad \ldots, \quad \underset{(n)}{12\left(\frac{2}{5}\right)^{n-1}}$$

On the second fall, the ball falls $12(\frac{2}{5})$; on the third fall, $12(\frac{2}{5})^2$; and so on the tenth fall:

$$\text{10th fall} = 12\left(\frac{2}{5}\right)^9 = 12(0.0002621) \approx \mathbf{0.00314573\ ft}$$

(*b*) Now we will find the sum of the distances the ball falls,

$$12 + 12\left(\frac{2}{5}\right) + 12\left(\frac{2}{5}\right)^2 + \cdots$$

and we have a formula for the sum of this infinite geometric series.

$$S_n = \frac{a_1}{1 - r} = \frac{12}{1 - \frac{2}{5}} = \frac{12}{\frac{3}{5}} = 20 \text{ ft}$$

This is the sum of the distances the ball fell. It rebounded the distances the ball fell less the distance of the first fall, which was 12 ft.

$$\text{Distance rebounded} = 20 - 12 = 8 \text{ ft}$$

Thus the sum of its ups and downs is 20 ft plus 8 ft = **28 ft.**

Example 94.A.3 A rabbit runs 2 miles in the first minute, 0.8 mile in the next minute, 0.32 mile in the next minute, and 0.4 times this distance in the next minute. How far will the rabbit travel in all if he continues this process indefinitely?

Solution If we divide 0.8 by 2 and divide 0.32 by 0.8, we get 0.4 both times.

$$\frac{0.8}{2} = 0.4 \qquad \frac{0.32}{0.8} = 0.4$$

So we see that we have been asked to find the sum of an infinite geometric series whose first term is 2 and whose common ratio is 0.4.

$$\begin{array}{cccccc} ① & ② & ③ & ④ & & ⓝ \\ a_1 + & a_1r + & a_1r^2 + & a_1r^3 + & \cdots + & a_1r^{n-1} + \cdots \\ 2 + & 2(0.4) + & 2(0.4)^2 + & 2(0.4)^3 + & \cdots + & 2(0.4)^{n-1} + \cdots \end{array}$$

We can find the sum of this infinite series because $|r|$ is less than 1.

$$S_n = \frac{a_1}{1 - r} = \frac{2}{1 - 0.4} = \frac{2}{0.6} = \mathbf{\frac{10}{3}}$$

So the rabbit will run only $\frac{10}{3}$ miles if he runs forever.

Problem set 94

1. Salvatore was amazed at the size of x. The overall average of 1.0, 0.8, 0.2, and x was exactly 0.6. How large was x?

2. The average of two numbers is A. If one of the numbers is m, what is the other number?

3. At the class picnic, the sum of 10 percent of the girls and 20 percent of the boys was 16. If the ratio of girls to boys was 2 to 3, how many boys came to the class picnic?

4. It was exactly 6 p.m. and the hands of the clock pointed in opposite directions. What time would it be the next time both hands pointed in the same direction?

5. If Eric and Tweeters work together, they can complete the job in 2 days. If Eric works alone, he can complete the job in x days. How long would it take Tweeters to complete the job alone?

6. Find the sum of the infinite geometric series: $4 + \frac{4}{3} + \frac{4}{9} + \frac{4}{27} + \cdots$

7. A hare runs 4 miles in the first minute, 2 miles in the next minute, 1 mile in the next minute, and so on. How far will the hare travel in all if he runs forever?

8. Write the equation of the circle shown in standard form and general form.

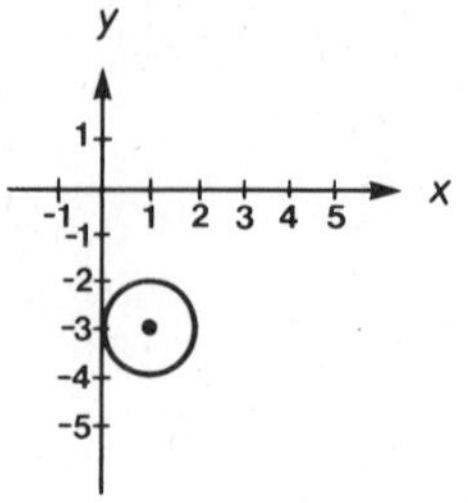

9. Given: $\angle PQR$ and $\angle PSR$ are right angles; $PQ = PS$
Prove: $QO = OS$

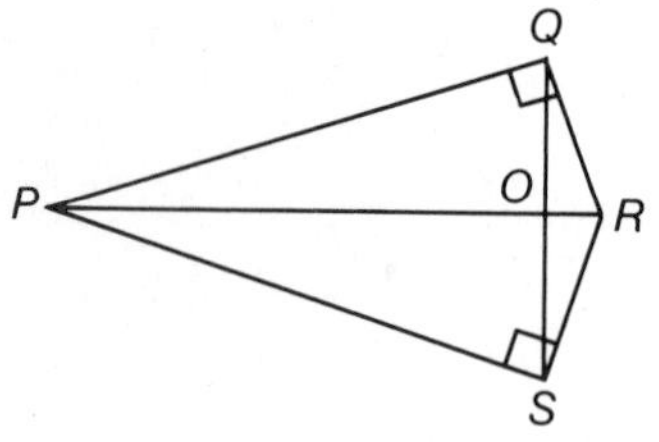

10. Use the figures shown below to prove the Pythagorean theorem.

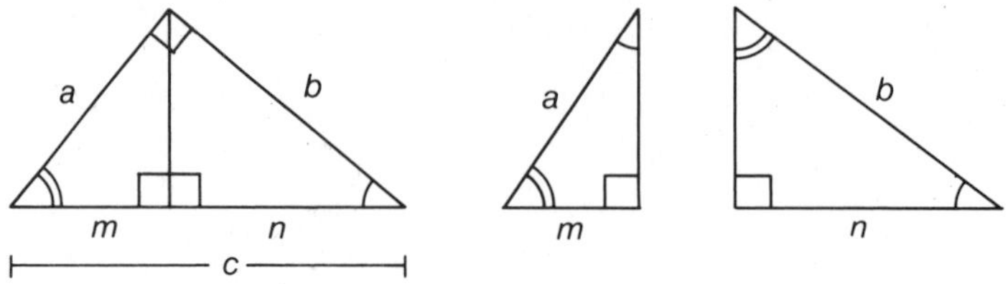

11. Given: Quadrilateral $ABCD$. P, Q, R, S are the midpoints of $\overline{AD}$, $\overline{AB}$, $\overline{BC}$, and $\overline{DC}$, respectively.
Prove: $PS = QR$

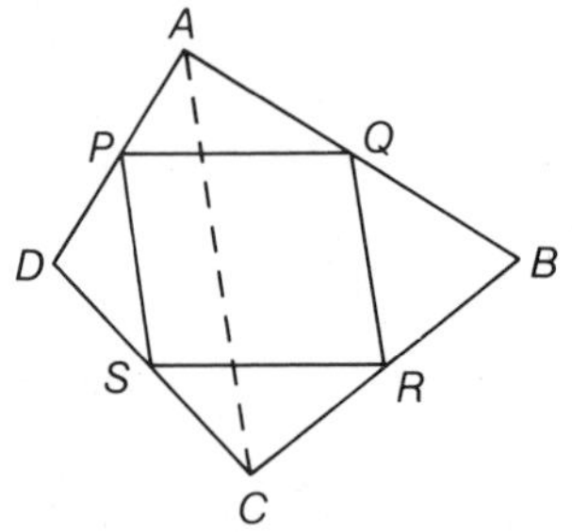

12. $9x^2 + 4y^2 + 54x - 8y + 49 = 0$ is the general equation of an ellipse. Write the equation of this ellipse in standard form and give the coordinates of the center, the length of the major axis, and the length of the minor axis.

13. $x^2 - y^2 - 14x - 8y + 29 = 0$ is the general equation of a hyperbola. Write the equation of this hyperbola in standard form and give the coordinates of the center, the coordinates of the vertices, and the equations of the asymptotes.

14. Use Cramer's rule to solve this system of equations. Use the method of cofactors to evaluate the determinants:

$$\begin{cases} -2x + y - z = 7 \\ 2y + 3z = 1 \\ x - 3y = -8 \end{cases}$$

15. Use the echelon method to solve this system of equations:

$$\begin{cases} 3x + y + z = 4 \\ 2y - z = 2 \\ 2x + y = 1 \end{cases}$$

16. (*a*) Develop the identity for $\sin A \cos B$.
(*b*) Find $\sin 75° \cos 15°$ by using the identity found in (*a*). Use exact values.

17. (*a*) Develop the identity for $\sin x + \sin y$.
(*b*) Find $\sin 15° + \sin 75°$ by using the identity found in (*a*). Use decimal approximations.

18. The pH of a solution is 8.5. What is the concentration of hydrogen ions in the solution?

19. The first term of an arithmetic sequence is a_1 and the common difference is d.
(*a*) What is the nth term of the arithmetic sequence?
(*b*) What is the sum of the first n terms if we use the expression found in (*a*) for the last term of the sequence?

20. Write the three cube roots of $-i$ in rectangular form. Give exact answers.

21. Use base 10 logs to simplify: $\sqrt[4]{42{,}000}\sqrt[3]{2300}$

22. Express ln 22 in terms of common logarithms. Do not find a numerical answer.

23. Sketch $y = 2 + \sin \frac{3}{2}(x + 40°)$.

24. Find the sum of the exterior angles of a 25-sided convex polygon.

25. Construct a line that is parallel to a given line which passes through a point not on the line.

26. Solve, given that $(0° \le \theta < 360°)$: $\sqrt{3}\tan 3\theta - 1 = 0$

Show that:

27. $\sec x - \sin x \tan x = \cos x$

28. $\sec 2x = \dfrac{\sec^2 x}{2 - \sec^2 x}$

29. Solve: $2^{3x-2} = 4$

30. Solve: $\log_6 (x - 1) + \log_6 (x - 2) = 2 \log_6 \sqrt{6}$

EP 94.59, 94.60

LESSON 95 *Prisms and cylinders · Pyramids and cones · Spheres · Diagonals of rectangular solids*

95.A Prisms and cylinders

A *cylindrical surface* is defined to be the surface generated by the movement of a straight line that is always parallel to a fixed straight line. If the cylindrical surface is closed and is cut by two parallel planes that are not parallel to the fixed line, the solid formed is called either a cylinder or a prism. If the figure formed by the intersection of the cylinder and the plane is a polygon, the solid is called a ***prism.*** If the figure is a closed curve, the solid is called a ***cylinder.*** If the sides and bases are perpendicular, the solids are called ***right prisms*** or ***right cylinders.*** If the sides and bases are not perpendicular, the solids are called ***oblique prisms*** or ***oblique cylinders.***

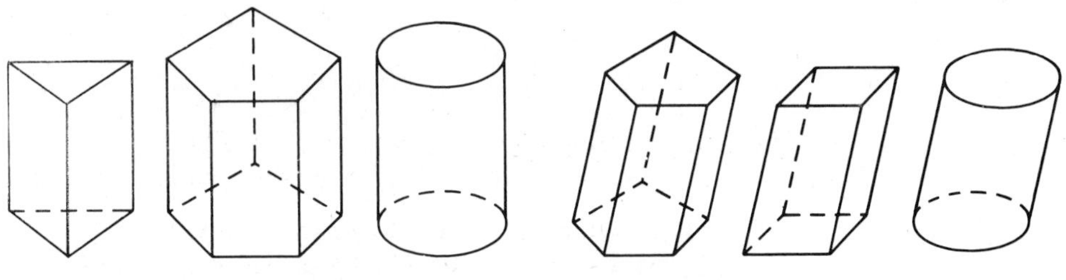

Right prisms and right cylinder   Oblique prisms and oblique cylinder

The volume of any prism or cylinder can be found by multiplying the area of base by the height. This is true for both right and oblique prisms and cylinders. The surface area of a prism or a cylinder is the sum of the areas of the sides (lateral areas) and the areas of both ends (base areas). **The lateral area of a right prism or cylinder equals the perimeter times the height.** Unfortunately, the lateral area of an oblique prism or cylinder is a function of the angle of inclination and cannot be found by using the same rule. We will restrict our surface area investigation to right prisms and cylinders.

Example 95.A.1 Find the volume of this circular cylinder.

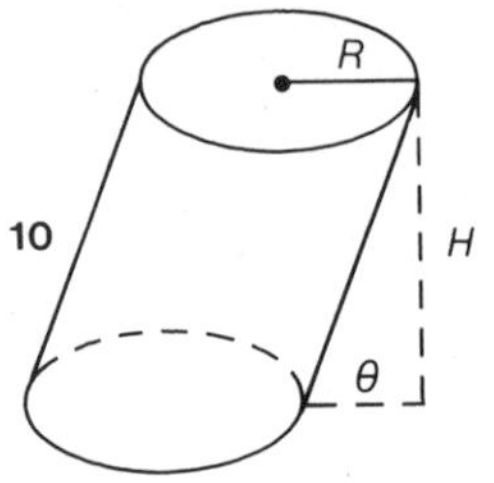

Solution The volume of a cylinder is the area of the base times the height. The area of this base is πR^2, and the height is 10 sin θ, so

$$\text{Volume} = \pi R^2 \cdot 10 \sin \theta$$
$$= \mathbf{10\pi R^2 \sin \theta}$$

Example 95.A.2 Find the surface area of this right prism.

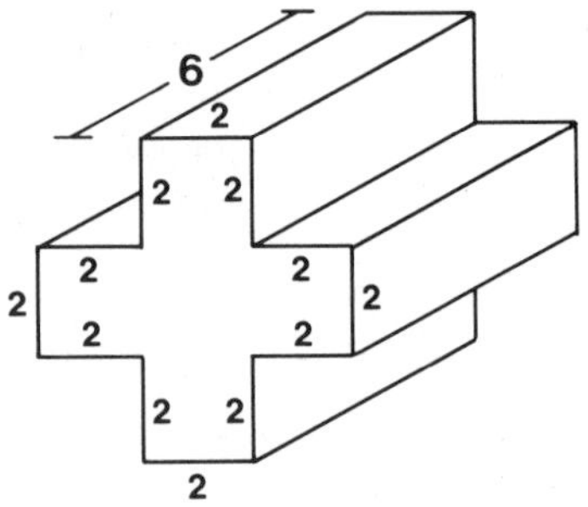

Solution Each base can be divided into 5 squares and the area found by adding the areas of the squares.

$$\text{Area of one base} = 5(2 \times 2)$$
$$= 20 \text{ square units}$$

The lateral area is that of 12 sides that measure 2 × 6.

$$\text{Lateral area} = 12(2 \times 6) = 144 \text{ square units}$$

The total surface area is the area of both bases plus the lateral area.

$$\text{Surface area} = 2 \times 20 + 144 = \textbf{184 square units}$$

For those who like formulas, we remember that the lateral area is the perimeter times the height. The perimeter is 24 units and the height is 6, so we check our lateral area as follows:

$$\text{Lateral area} = 24 \times 6 = 144 \text{ square units}$$

95.B Pyramids and cones

The base of a pyramid is a figure defined by connected line segments (convex polygon), and the base of a cone is a figure defined by a closed curve.

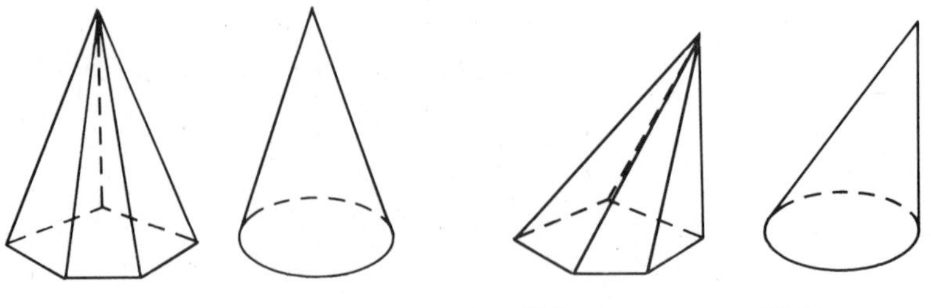

Right pyramid Right cone Oblique pyramid Oblique cone

A ***regular pyramid*** is a pyramid whose base is a regular polygon and whose apex is on the perpendicular through the center of the base. The conical equivalent is a right circular cone whose base is a circle and whose apex is directly "above" the center of the circle.

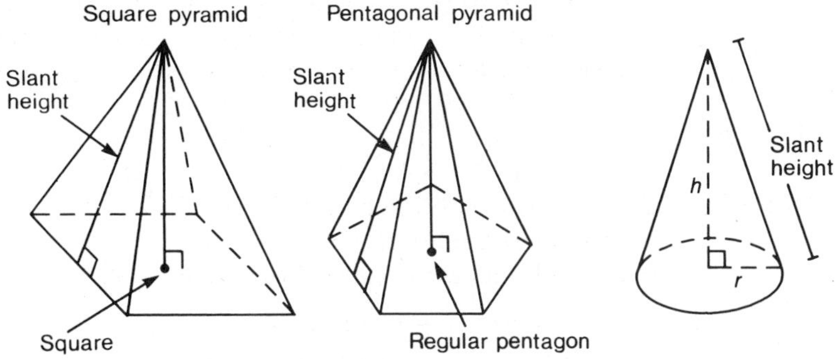

Regular pyramids Right cone

The volume of any pyramid or cone is one-third the product of the area of the base and the height. Since the volume of a prism or a cylinder is the product of the area of the base and the height, the volume of a prism or cylinder is 3 times that of the pyramid or cone with the same base and height. This can be demonstrated with a triangular prism made up of three triangular pyramids, as shown in the following figure.

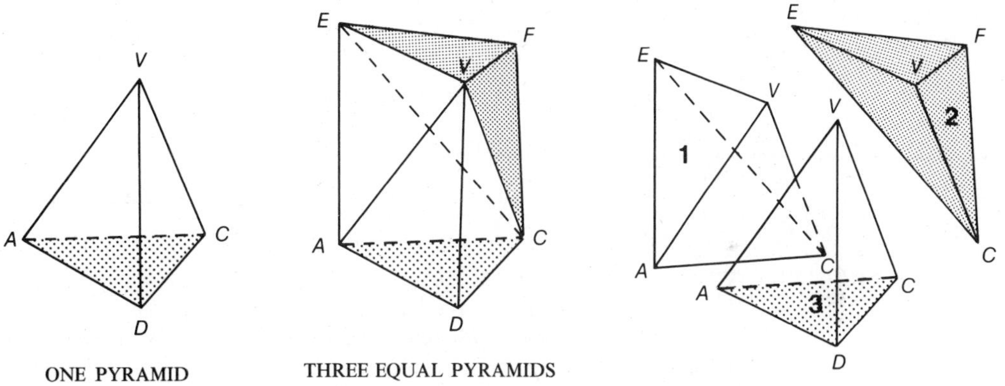

ONE PYRAMID THREE EQUAL PYRAMIDS CAN FORM A PRISM EXPLODED VIEW

The surface area of a pyramid or a cone is the area of the base plus the lateral surface area. The lateral surface area of a cone is the product of π, the radius of the base, and the **slant height** ℓ. The lateral surface area of a pyramid is the sum of the areas of the faces of the pyramid.

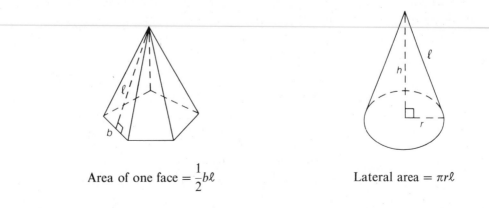

Area of one face $= \frac{1}{2}b\ell$ Lateral area $= \pi r\ell$

If the pyramid on the left were a regular pyramid with 5 lateral faces, the lateral surface area would be 5 times the area of one face. If the pyramid were a regular pyramid of n faces, the lateral surface area would be n times the area of one face.

$$\text{Area of 5 faces} = 5\left(\frac{1}{2}b\ell\right) \qquad \text{Area of } n \text{ faces} = n\left(\frac{1}{2}b\ell\right)$$

$$= \frac{5b}{2}\ell \qquad\qquad = \frac{nb}{2}\ell$$

The value of $nb/2$ is half the perimeter of the base of the pyramid. If we increase the number of faces of the pyramid, the base of the pyramid gets closer and closer to a circle. The perimeter of a circle is πd, or $2\pi r$, and half the perimeter is πr. Thus the formula for the lateral surface area of the right circular cone is $\pi r\ell$.

Example 95.B.1 Find (*a*) the volume and (*b*) the surface area of this right circular cone.

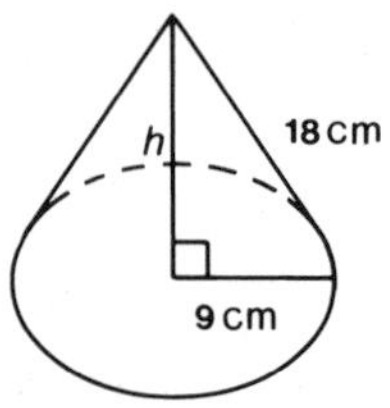

Solution (*a*) The volume V equals one-third the product of the area of the base and the height.

$$V = \frac{1}{3}(\pi \cdot 81)(\sqrt{18^2 - 9^2}) = 243\sqrt{3}\,\pi \text{ cm}^3$$

(*b*) The surface area is the area of the base plus the lateral area.

$$\text{Surface area} = \pi r^2 + \pi r\ell$$

$$\text{Surface area} = \pi(9)^2 + \pi(9)(18) = 243\pi \text{ cm}^2$$

95.C Spheres

A ***circle*** is a figure defined by the set of all points in a ***plane*** that are equidistant from the point called the ***center of the circle.*** **A sphere** is the figure defined by the set of all points in **three-dimensional space** that are equidistant from the point called the ***center of the sphere.***

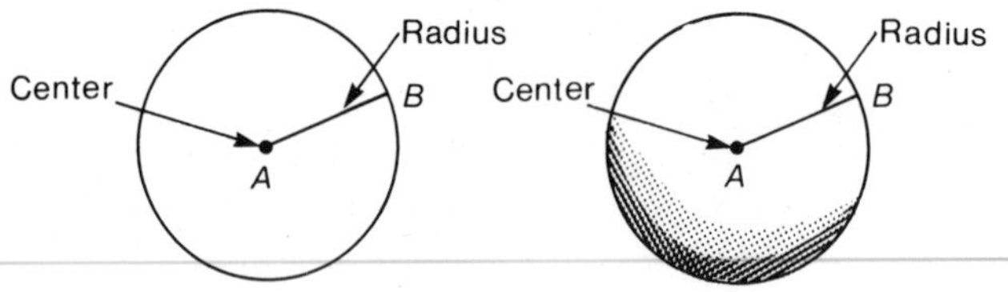

Circle Sphere

The volume and surface area of a sphere can be found by using the following formulas.

$$\text{Volume of a sphere} = \frac{4}{3}\pi r^3 \qquad \text{Surface area of a sphere} = 4\pi r^2$$

Example 95.C.1 Find (*a*) the volume and (*b*) the surface area of a sphere whose radius is 9 cm.

Solution (*a*) $V = \frac{4}{3}\pi r^3$

$= \frac{4}{3}\pi(9)^3$

$= \mathbf{972\pi\ cm^3}$

(*b*) $A = 4\pi r^2$

$= 4\pi(9)^2$

$= \mathbf{324\pi\ cm^2}$

95.D Diagonals of rectangular solids

We can use the Pythagorean theorem twice to find a formula for the length of a diagonal of a rectangular solid, as we show in the following example.

Example 95.D.1 Find the length of the diagonal that connects corners B and G.

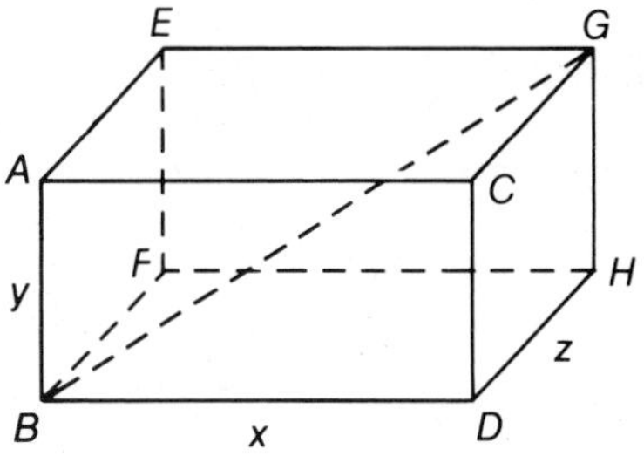

Solution The solution is in two steps. The first step is to find the length of the line segment $\overline{BH}$. To do this we will look at the floor of the solid from above.

$$(BH)^2 = x^2 + z^2$$
$$BH = \sqrt{x^2 + z^2}$$

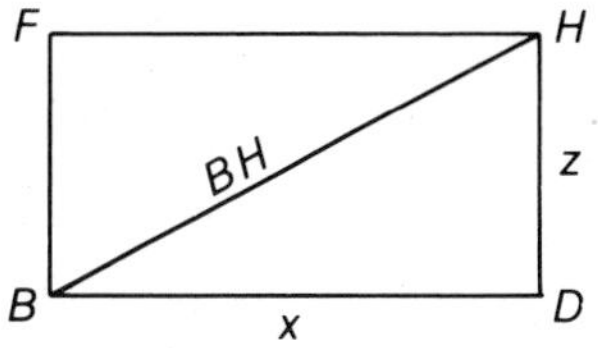

The diagonal $\overline{BG}$, whose length we seek, is the hypotenuse of the triangle whose sides are $\overline{BH}$ and $\overline{GH}$. Now, we know BH, and we can use the Pythagorean theorem to find the length of $\overline{BG}$.

$$(BG)^2 = (\sqrt{x^2 + z^2})^2 + y^2$$
$$(BG)^2 = x^2 + z^2 + y^2$$
$$\mathbf{BG = \sqrt{x^2 + y^2 + z^2}}$$

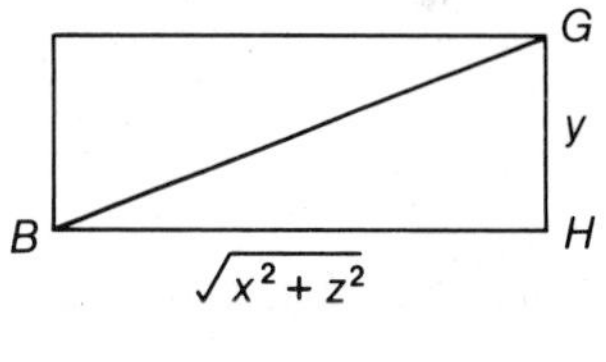

Example 95.D.2 Find the length of the diagonal AC in the rectangular solid shown. Do a two-step development and do not use the formula above.

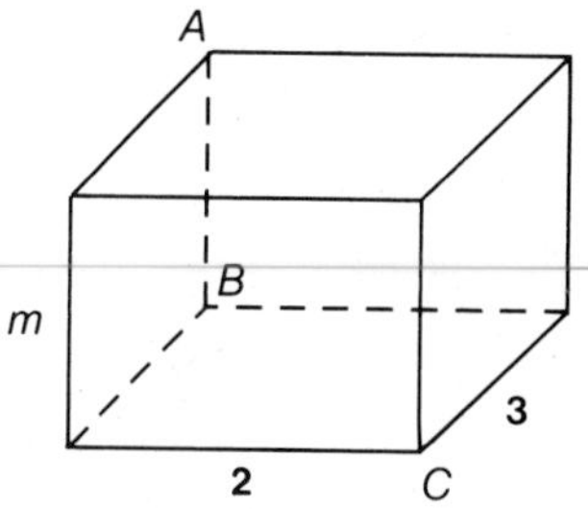

Solution First we find the length of the base diagonal BC.

$(BC)^2 = 2^2 + 3^2$	Pythagorean formula
$(BC)^2 = 13$	added
$BC = \sqrt{13}$	square root of both sides

Now we use this length and length m to find the length of the diagonal AC.

$$(AC)^2 = (\sqrt{13})^2 + m^2$$

$$(AC)^2 = 13 + m^2$$

$$\mathbf{AC = \sqrt{13 + m^2}}$$

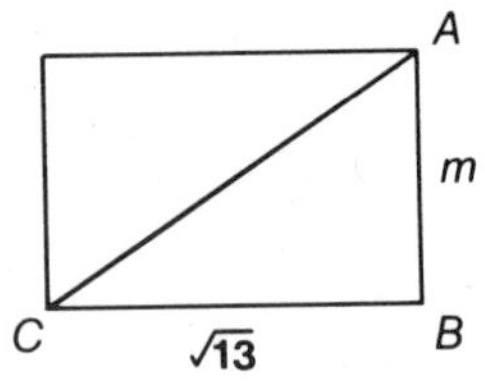

Problem set 95

1. The number who were blue varied linearly with the number who had failed. When 40 had failed, 30 were blue; and when 80 had failed, 40 were blue. How many were blue when only 4 had failed?

2. The success rate varied inversely as the square of the diffidence index. The people who had a diffidence index of 5 had a success rate of 16. What was the success rate of those whose diffidence index was 10?

3. The ratio of the hyper to the insouciant was M to R. If K were being considered, how many were insouciant?

4. Garfield could not believe his eyes. The gauge showed that the oil tank was only one-fifth full. Then the truck pumped 160 gallons into the tank, and the gauge now showed seven-tenths full. How much oil did Garfield's tank hold?

5. What fractional part of a quarter is the sum formed by two pennies, two nickels, and one dime?

6. Two geometric solids are similar. The length of a side of the larger geometric solid is twice as long as the corresponding side of the smaller geometric solid. What is the ratio of the volume of the larger geometric solid to the volume of the smaller geometric solid? (*Hint:* Use a rectangular solid of sides w, l, and h and another with sides $2w$, $2l$, and $2h$ to investigate the general relationship.)

7. The base of a pyramid is a regular hexagon whose perimeter is 24 cm. The height of the pyramid is 10 cm. Find the volume of the pyramid.

8. (*a*) The base of a circular cone has a radius of 10 cm. The height of the cone is 10 cm. Find the volume of the cone.
   (*b*) Assume that the cone referred to in (*a*) is a right circular cone. Find the surface area of the cone.

9. Find the length of the diagonal AC in the rectangular solid shown.

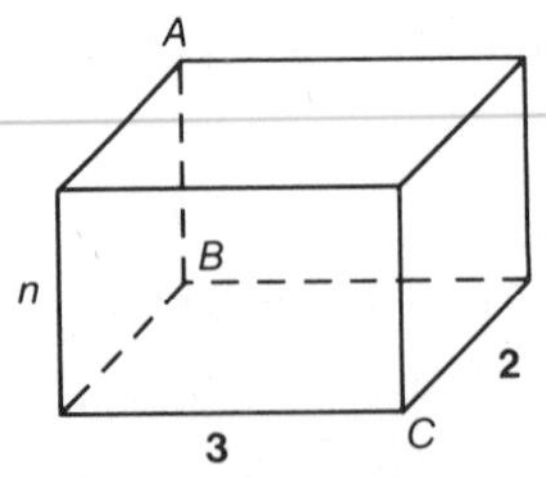

10. A sphere has a radius of 10 cm.
   (*a*) Find the volume of the sphere.
   (*b*) Find the surface area of the sphere.

11. Find the sum of the infinite geometric series: $3 + (-\frac{3}{2}) + (\frac{3}{4}) + (-\frac{3}{8}) + \cdots$.

12. A ball is dropped from a height of 10 feet and rebounds one-half the distance it falls after each bounce. What will be the total distance the ball travels?

13. Given: $\angle PQR$ and $\angle PSR$ are right angles; $\overline{PR}$ is the perpendicular bisector of $\overline{SQ}$.
Prove: $QR = RS$

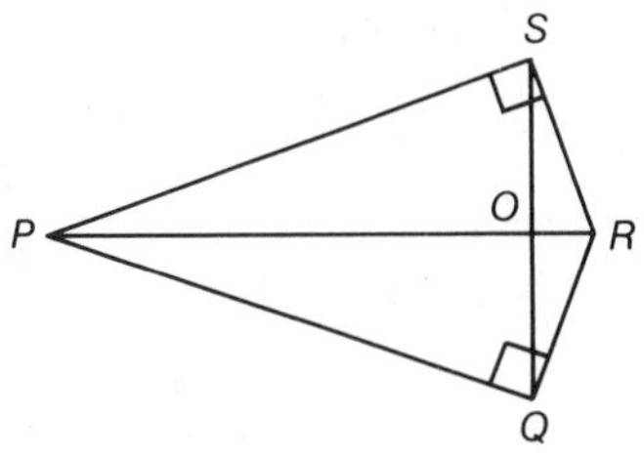

14. The general equation of a hyperbola is $16y^2 - 9x^2 - 64y - 18x - 89 = 0$. Write the equation of this hyperbola in standard form and give the coordinates of the center, the coordinates of the vertices, and the equations of the asymptotes.

15. The general equation of an ellipse is $3x^2 + 4y^2 + 12x - 8y - 176 = 0$. Write the equation of this ellipse in standard form and give the coordinates of the center, the length of the major axis, and the length of the minor axis.

16. Use the echelon method to solve this system of equations: $\begin{cases} 2x - 3y + z = 7 \\ 2y - z = -8 \\ x + y = -5 \end{cases}$

17. (*a*) Develop the identity for $\cos x + \cos y$.
(*b*) Find $\cos 255° + \cos 15°$, using the identity found in (*a*). Use decimal approximations.

18. (*a*) Develop an identity for $\cos A \cos B$.
(*b*) Find $\cos 255° \cos 15°$, using the identity found in (*a*). Use exact values.

19. The first term of an arithmetic sequence is a_1 and the common difference is d.
(*a*) What is the nth term of the arithmetic sequence?
(*b*) What is the sum of the first n terms if we use the expression found in (*a*) for the last term of the sequence?

20. Write the three cube roots of $4 + 5i$ in polar form.

21. Use base 10 logs to simplify: $\sqrt[5]{63{,}000}\,(4500)^{1.5}$

22. Solve this triangle for side a.

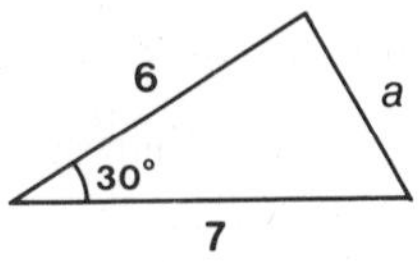

23. Express ln 35 in terms of common logarithms. Do not find a numerical answer.

24. Use a protractor to draw a 40° angle and then construct its bisector, using straightedge and compass.

25. Sketch $y = 5 + 2 \csc x$.

26. Show that: $(\cos 2x)(\sec^2 x) = 1 - \tan^2 x$

27. Solve, given that $(0° \le x < 360°)$: $6 \cos^2 x + 5 \cos x = -1$

28. Show that: $\dfrac{1 + \cos 2x}{\sin 2x} = \cot x$

29. Solve: $3^{2x-4} = 4^{3x-2}$

30. Solve: $\frac{2}{3} \log_4 8 + \log_4 (x - 2) = \log_4 (2x - 3)$

EP 95.61, 95.62

If the enrichment lessons are being included, the fifth enrichment lesson should be taught next and should be followed with Lesson 96.

LESSON 96 *Rational numbers*

96.A Rational numbers

A ***rational number*** is a number that **can be** written as a common fraction. Any terminating decimal number **can be** written as a common fraction. The numbers shown here are terminating decimal numbers

$$(a)\quad 0.023 \qquad (b)\quad 0.0023 \qquad (c)\quad 0.000023$$

and thus **can be** written as a common fraction. We do this by multiplying above and below by the appropriate power of 10. For (*a*), we multiply above and below by 1000.

$$(a)\quad 0.023\left(\frac{1000}{1000}\right) = \frac{23}{1000}$$

For fraction (*b*), we use 10,000 over 10,000 because the decimal point must be moved four places. In (*c*), we must move the decimal point six places, so we multiply by 1,000,000 over 1,000,000.

$$(b)\quad 0.0023\left(\frac{10{,}000}{10{,}000}\right) = \frac{23}{10{,}000} \qquad (c)\quad 0.000023\left(\frac{1{,}000{,}000}{1{,}000{,}000}\right) = \frac{23}{1{,}000{,}000}$$

Decimal numbers whose digits repeat indefinitely in a pattern are also rational numbers because these numbers can be written as common fractions. We use a bar over the repeating digits to indicate that they repeat. Thus,

$$0.00\overline{23} \qquad \text{means} \qquad 0.0023232323\ldots$$

There are several methods that can be used to find a common fraction that has the same value as one of these repeaters. One way is to recognize that these numbers can be expressed as the sum of an infinite geometric series and use the formula for the sum of an infinite series to help find the fraction.

Example 96.A.1 Use an infinite geometric series as an aid in writing $0.00\overline{23}$ as a common fraction.

Solution We always draw the best diagram of the problem that we can. We begin by writing the number expanded.

$$0.0023\ 23\ 23\ 23\ 23\ldots$$

Now we show that this can be written as a sum

$$\begin{array}{ll} 0.0023 & +23 \times 10^{-4} \\ +0.000023 & +23 \times 10^{-4} \times 10^{-2} \\ +0.00000023 & +23 \times 10^{-4} \times 10^{-2} \times 10^{-2} \\ +0.0000000023 & +23 \times 10^{-4} \times 10^{-2} \times 10^{-2} \times 10^{-2} \end{array}$$

This can be written as an infinite geometric series whose first term is 23×10^{-4} and in which r is 10^{-2}.

$$0.0023 + 0.0023(10^{-2}) + 0.0023(10^{-2})^2 + 0.0023(10^{-2})^3 + \cdots$$

Since $|r|$ is less than 1, we can use the formula for the sum of an infinite convergent geometric series.

$$S_n = \frac{a_1}{1 - r}$$

$$= \frac{23 \times 10^{-4}}{1 - 0.01} = \frac{23 \times 10^{-4}}{0.99}$$

To get rid of the 10^{-4}, we multiply above and below by 10^4 and get our fraction of integers.

$$\frac{23 \times 10^{-4}}{0.99} \cdot \frac{10^4}{10^4} = \mathbf{\frac{23}{9900}}$$

Example 96.A.2 Use an infinite geometric series as an aid in showing that $5.\overline{013}$ is a rational number by writing it as a common fraction.

Solution Again we begin by drawing a diagram. First we write the number expanded.

$5.\overline{013}$	means	5.013 013 013 013
$5 + 0.013$		$5 + 0.013$
$+ 0.000013$		$+ 0.013(10^{-3})$
$+ 0.000000013$		$+ 0.013(10^{-3})^2$
$+ 0.000000000013$		$+ 0.013(10^{-3})^3$
$+ \cdots$		$+ \cdots$

This can be written as 5 plus a geometric series whose first term is 0.013 and in which r is 10^{-3}.

$$5 + [0.013 + 0.013(10^{-3}) + 0.013(10^{-3})^2 + 0.013(10^{-3})^3 + \cdots]$$

Now we use $\frac{a_1}{1 - r}$ for the sum of the series.

$$5 + \frac{a_1}{1 - r} \qquad \text{5 plus sum of series}$$

$$5 + \frac{0.013}{1 - 0.001} \qquad \text{substituted}$$

$$5 + \frac{0.013}{0.999} \qquad \text{simplified}$$

$$5 + \frac{13}{999} \qquad \text{simplified}$$

$$\frac{4995}{999} + \frac{13}{999} = \mathbf{\frac{5008}{999}} \qquad \text{added}$$

It seems reasonable to induce from the results of the preceding two examples that when we have 2 repeaters, r is 10^{-2}. When we have 3 repeaters, $r = 10^{-3}$, and thus 4 repeaters will cause r to be 10^{-4}, etc.

Problem set 96

1. Ten years ago, Mary's age exceeded twice Jim's age by 6. Ten years from now, 3 times Mary's age will exceed 4 times Jim's age by 30. How old will Mary and Jim be in 15 years?

2. Jimjoe could do 5 jobs in H hours. When Whortle helped, they could do 10 jobs in 3 hours. What was Whortle's rate in jobs per hour?

3. Twenty hours into the hard part, the exponential decay had reduced their number to 1400. Forty hours into the hard part, their number was found to be only 1300. How many of them would remain 200 hours into the hard part?

4. Marcy sold the first n of them for a total of d dollars. Then she realized she was losing money and increased the price of each one \$3. How many could Patti buy at the new price if Patti had \$400 to spend?

5. The urn contained 4 red marbles and 3 green marbles. Roy drew a marble and did not put it back. Then he drew another marble. What is the probability that both marbles were green?

6. Use an infinite geometric series as an aid for expressing $0.000\overline{31}$ as a common fraction.

7. Use an infinite geometric series as an aid for expressing $6.0\overline{17}$ as a common fraction.

8. Two geometric solids are similar. The ratio of the volume of the larger geometric solid to the volume of the smaller geometric solid is 8 to 1. If a side of the smaller solid is of length 6, what is the length of the corresponding side of the larger solid?

9. The base of a pyramid is a square whose perimeter is 20 cm. The height of the pyramid is 5 cm. Find the volume of the pyramid.

10. Find the length of the diagonal $\overline{AC}$ in the rectangular solid shown.

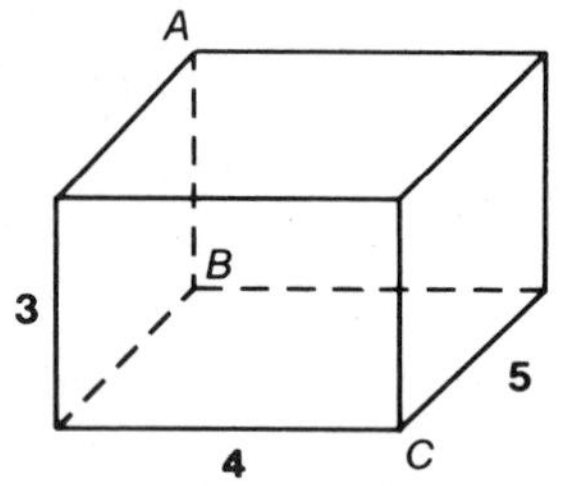

11. (*a*) The base of a circular cone has a radius of 6 cm. The height of the cone is 8 cm. Find the volume of the cone.
    (*b*) Assume that the cone referred to in (*a*) is a right circular cone. Find the surface area of the cone.

12. A sphere has a radius of 6 meters.
    (*a*) Find the volume of the sphere.
    (*b*) Find the surface area of the sphere.

13. A ball is dropped from a height of 132 feet and rebounds one-fourth of the distance it falls after each bounce. What will be the total distance the ball travels?

14. Draw a line segment 4 centimeters long and construct its perpendicular bisector.

15. Given: Quadrilateral $ABCD$. P, Q, R, S are the midpoints of $\overline{AD}$, $\overline{AB}$, $\overline{BC}$, and $\overline{CD}$, respectively.
    Prove: $PQ = SR$; $PS = QR$

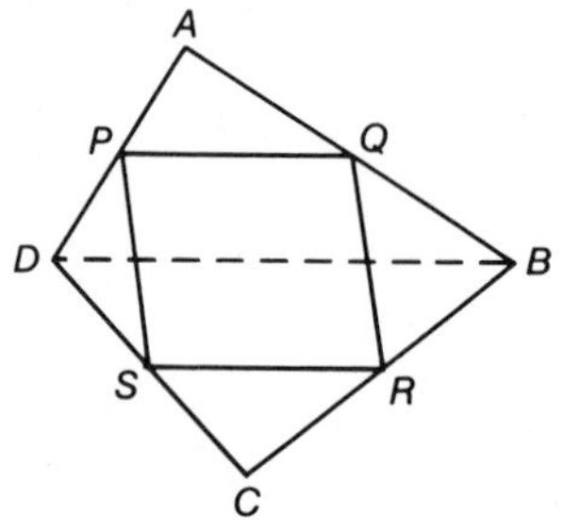

16. Use the figures shown to prove the Pythagorean theorem.

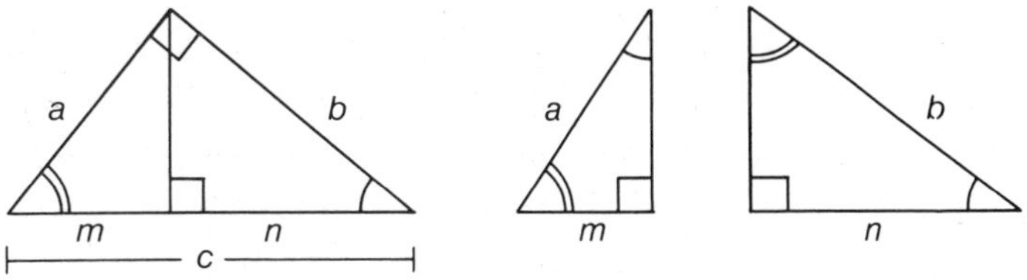

17. Given: $AC = BC$; $DC = EC$
Prove: $\angle AEC = \angle BDC$

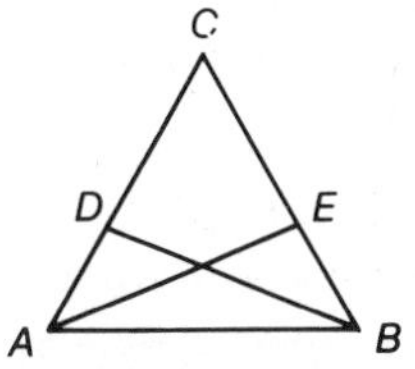

18. $4x^2 - y^2 + 24x + 4y + 28 = 0$ is the general equation of a hyperbola. Write the equation of this hyperbola in standard form and give the coordinates of the center, the coordinates of the vertices, and the equations of the asymptotes.

19. $9x^2 + 25y^2 - 36x + 150y + 260 = 0$ is the general equation of an ellipse. Write the equation of this ellipse in standard form and give the coordinates of the center, the length of the major axis, and the length of the minor axis.

20. (*a*) Develop the identity for $\sin x - \sin y$.
(*b*) Find $\sin 255° - \sin 15°$, using the identity found in (*a*). Use exact values.

21. The first term of a geometric sequence is 2 and the common ratio is -2.
(*a*) What is the twelfth term of the sequence?
(*b*) What is the sum of the first 12 terms?

22. Express ln 42 in terms of common logarithms. Do not find a numerical answer.

23. Solve this triangle for angle A.

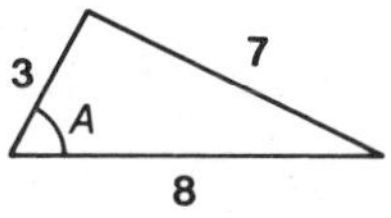

24. Convert 40 miles per hour to kilometers per second.

25. Find the equations of the following trigonometric functions.

(*a*)

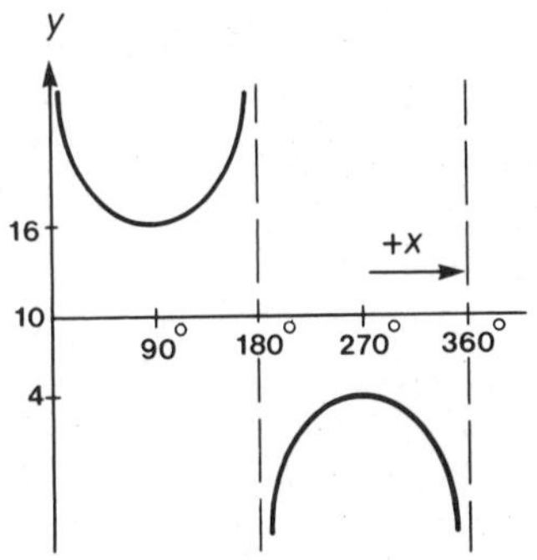

(*b*)

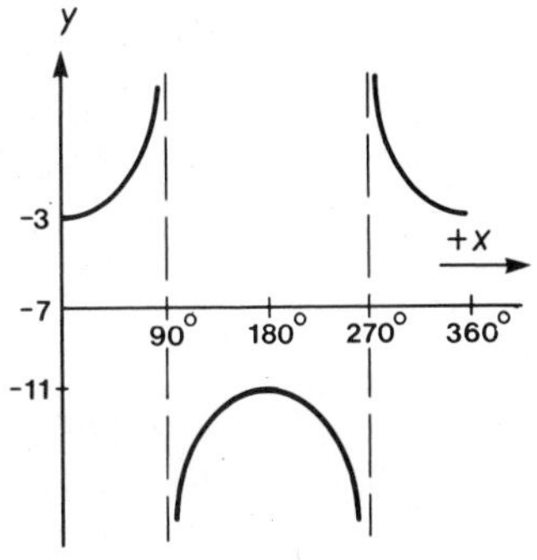

Show that:

26. $(\sin x - \cos x)^2 = 1 - \sin 2x$

27. $\dfrac{\tan^2 x}{\sec x + 1} = \sec x - 1$

28. Solve, given that ($0° \le x < 360°$): $\sqrt{2} - 2\cos 3x = 0$

29. Solve: $\frac{3}{4}\log_5 16 - \log_5 (3x - 2) = -\log_5 (2x + 1)$

30. Find the distance from (0, 2) to $5x + y + 13 = 0$.

EP 96.63, 96.64

LESSON 97 Two-part proofs

97.A Two-part proofs

Some proofs are two-part proofs. The first part is often a proof that two triangles are congruent, and the second part uses the results of the first proof to prove two other triangles are congruent. Often the figures for these proofs are symmetric figures.

Example 97.A.1 Given: $\angle 1 = \angle 2$; $\angle 5 = \angle 6$
Prove: $\overline{AC} \perp \overline{BD}$

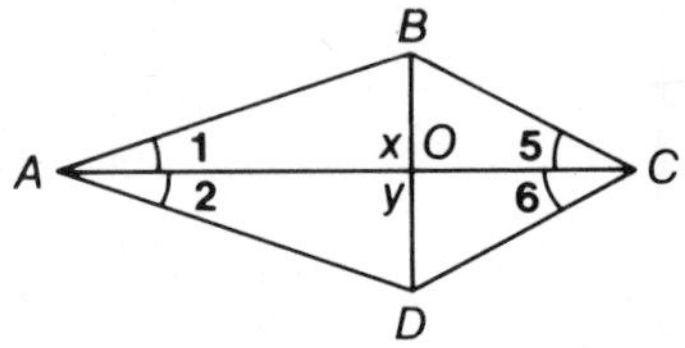

Solution We will prove that angles x and y are equal. Thus each must be a right angle, for their sum is a straight angle. We will begin by proving that the top triangle ABC is congruent to the bottom triangle ADC. On the left we show these two triangles.

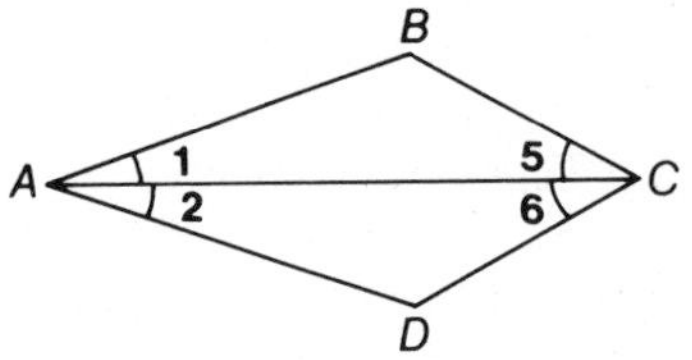

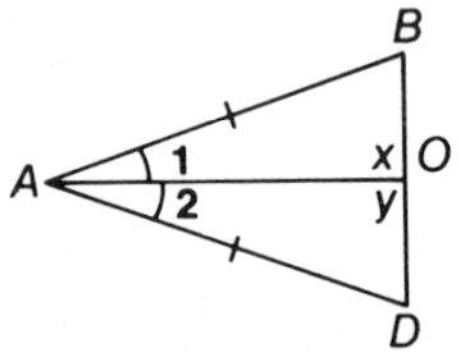

In the left-hand figure, the triangles are similar because we are given $\angle 1 = \angle 2$ and $\angle 5 = \angle 6$. So we know $\angle B = \angle D$ and all three pairs of angles are equal. Thus,

$$\triangle ABC \sim \triangle ADC$$

Side AC is a corresponding side in each triangle, so the scale factor = 1. Thus,

$$\triangle ABC \cong \triangle ADC$$

So $AB = AD$. Now in the right-hand figure the two triangles shown are congruent because they are similar by SAS ($AB = AD$, $AO = AO$, $\angle 1 = \angle 2$), and the scale factor is 1. Thus angle x equals angle y. Since they form a straight angle, each one is 90° and the lines are perpendicular, $\overline{AC} \perp \overline{BD}$.

Example 97.A.2 Given: $\overline{BD}$ and $\overline{KJ}$ bisect each other.
Prove: $AE = CE$

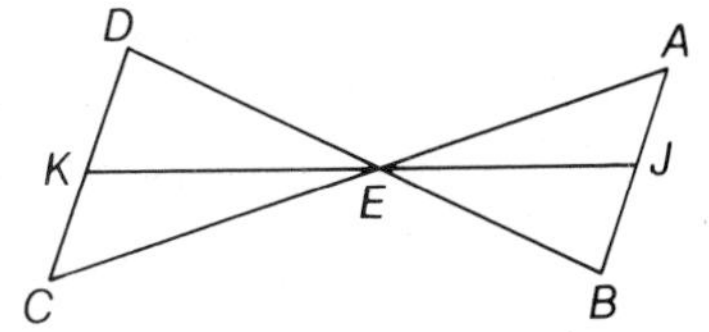

Solution Again we find it helpful to use tick marks to mark equal parts of the figure, and to work with one part of the figure at a time.

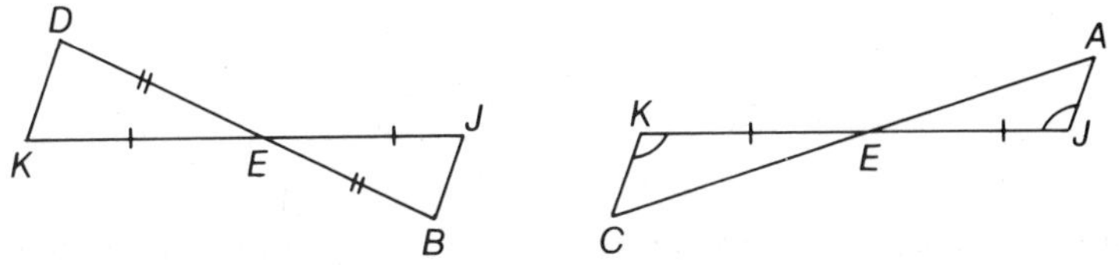

The two triangles on the left are congruent since they are similar by SAS with scale factor = 1, because the vertical angles $\angle KED$ and $\angle JEB$ are equal and because we were given that the sides enclosing the angles are equal. Thus,

$$\triangle KDE \cong \triangle JBE$$

Therefore $\angle DKE = \angle EJB$ by CPCTE. In the triangles on the right, the angles at K and J are equal because supplementary angles of equal angles are equal. The vertical angles $\angle KEC$ and $\angle JEA$ are equal and the triangles are similar by AAA.

$$\triangle KEC \sim \triangle JEA$$

Because the corresponding sides KE and JE are equal, the triangles are also congruent.

$$\triangle KEC \cong \triangle JEA$$

Thus, $EC = EA$ because corresponding sides of congruent triangles are equal in length.

Example 97.A.3 Given the diagram as marked, draw two auxiliary lines and prove $\angle I = \angle M$.

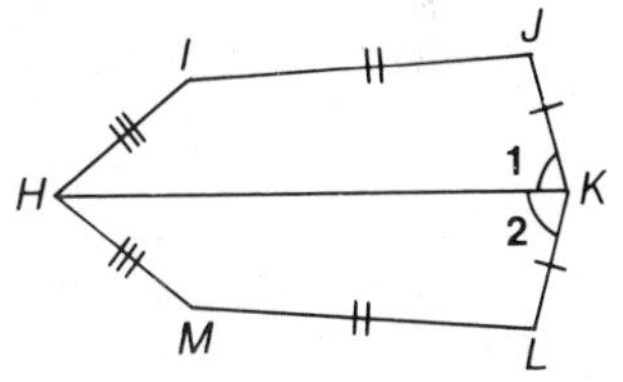

Solution On the left we draw auxiliary lines HJ and HL. Now in the center, we look at the inside triangles. These triangles are congruent because they are similar by SAS with scale factor = 1 since angle 1 equals angle 2 and the sides that include the angles are equal: $JK = KL$, $HK = HK$.

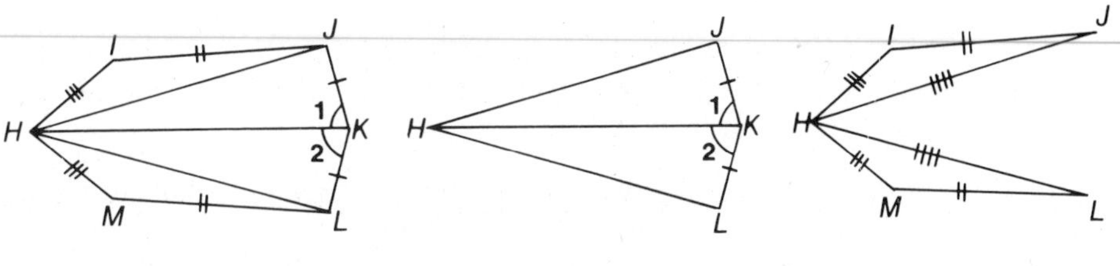

This tells us that $JH = HL$. Now on the right we have marked HJ as equal to HL, and we see that the two triangles are congruent by SSS.

$$\triangle HIJ \cong \triangle HML$$

Thus $\angle I$ equals $\angle M$ because corresponding angles in congruent triangles are equal in measure.

Problem set 97

1. Pharmacist Phillip has two jugs on the shelf. One contains a solution that is 10% key ingredient. A second contains a solution that is 2% key ingredient. How much of each should he use to get 1400 milliliters of a solution that is 6% key ingredient?

2. The number of blues was 4 greater than 3 times the number of reds. There were twice as many blues as whites. If the total of the reds, blues, and whites was 28, how many of each color were there?

3. Twice the supplement of angle A was 200° greater than 4 times the complement of angle B. If the sum of angle A and angle B was 110°, what was the measure of each angle?

4. The ratio of the hundreds digit to the units digit of a three-digit number is 4. If these two digits are reversed, the new number is 297 less than the original number. If the sum of the digits is 13, what is the original number?

5. The *Jewel Ann* can go 60 miles down the river in 1 hour less than it takes her to go 45 miles up the river. If the speed of the *Jewel Ann* in still water is twice the speed of the current, what is the speed of the *Jewel Ann* in still water and how fast is the current?

6. Use an infinite geometric series as an aid in writing $0.000\overline{29}$ as a common fraction.

7. Use an infinite geometric series as an aid in writing $2.0\overline{19}$ as a common fraction.

8. The base of a pyramid is a square whose perimeter is 40 centimeters. The height of the pyramid is 6 centimeters. Find the volume of the pyramid.

9. Two geometric solids are similar. The length of a side of the smaller geometric solid is one-third as long as the corresponding side of the larger geometric solid. What is the ratio of the volume of the larger geometric solid to the volume of the smaller geometric solid?

10. A sphere has a radius of 4 centimeters.
    (*a*) Find the volume of the sphere.
    (*b*) Find the surface area of the sphere.

11. Find the length of the diagonal AB in the rectangular solid shown.

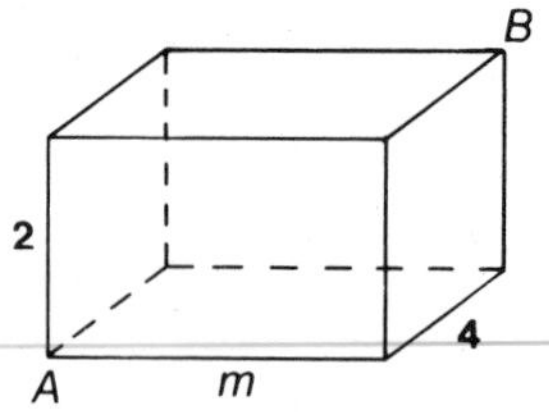

12. (*a*) The base of a circular cone has a radius of 5 cm. The height of the cone is 10 cm. Find the volume of the cone.
    (*b*) Assume that the cone is a right circular cone. Find the surface area of the cone.

13. Find the sum of the following infinite geometric series:

$$\left(\frac{1}{4}\right) + \left(-\frac{1}{8}\right) + \left(\frac{1}{16}\right) + \left(-\frac{1}{32}\right) + \cdots$$

14. Factor $x^2 + 3x + 9$ over the set of complex numbers.

15. Given: $AB = AD$; $BC = CD$
Prove: $\overline{AC} \perp \overline{BD}$

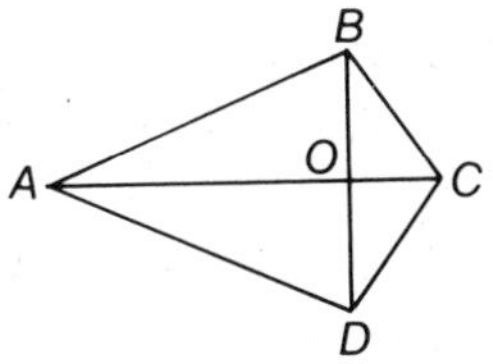

16. Given: $\overline{BD}$ and $\overline{KJ}$ bisect each other.
Prove: $KC = AJ$

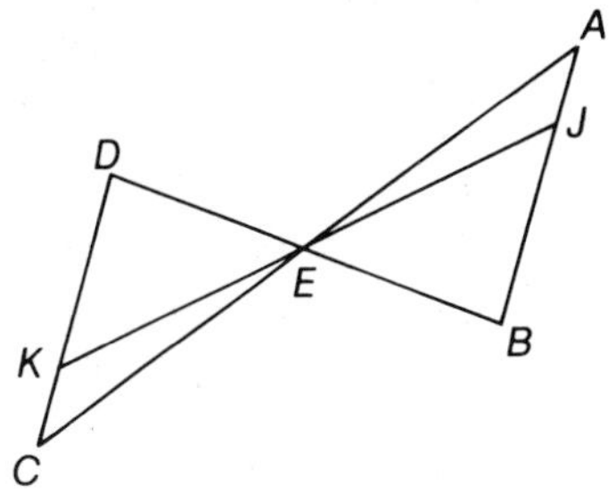

17. Given: The diagram as drawn.
Prove: $\angle IHK = \angle MHK$

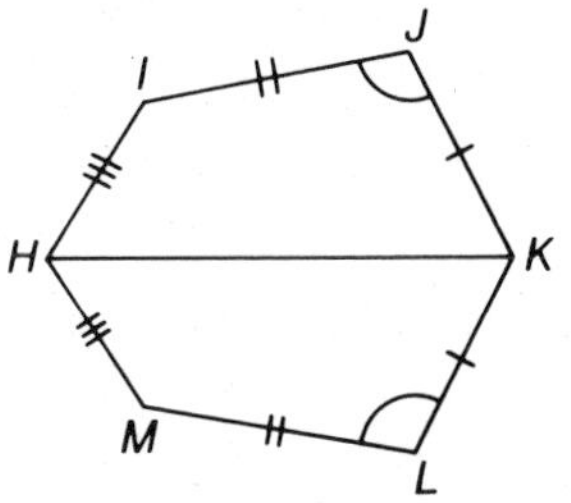

18. The general equation of a hyperbola is $4x^2 - 25y^2 - 8x - 100y - 196 = 0$. Write the equation of the hyperbola in standard form. Give the coordinates of the center, the coordinates of the vertices, and the equations of the asymptotes.

19. The general equation of an ellipse is $25x^2 + 9y^2 + 150x - 36y + 36 = 0$. Write the equation of the ellipse in standard form and give the coordinates of its center, the length of its minor axis, and the length of its major axis, and indicate whether the major axis is horizontal or vertical.

20. (*a*) Develop the identity for $\cos x + \cos y$.
(*b*) Find $\cos 285° + \cos 15°$, using the identity found in (*a*). Use exact values.

21. The first term of an arithmetic sequence is -5 and the common difference is $\frac{2}{5}$.
(*a*) What is the sixteenth term of the arithmetic sequence?
(*b*) What is the sum of the first 16 terms?

22. Solve this triangle for angle B.

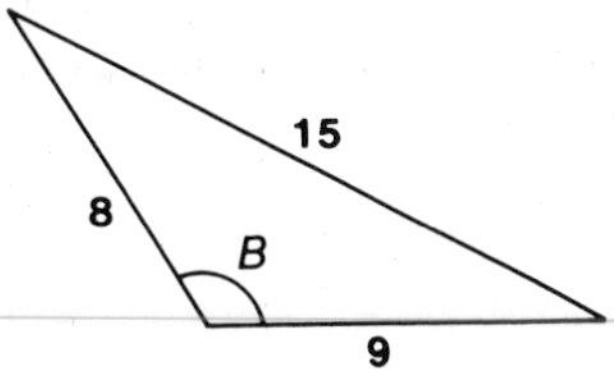

23. Express ln 200 in terms of common logarithms. Do not find a numerical answer.

24. What is the sum of the exterior angles of a 25-sided convex polygon?

25. Write the cube roots of $-i$ in rectangular form. Give exact answers.

Show that:

26. $\sin(-x)\sec(-x) = -\tan x$

27. $\dfrac{\cot x - 1}{1 - \tan x} = \dfrac{\csc x}{\sec x}$

28. Solve, given that $(0° \leq x < 360°)$: $\sin^2 x - \sin x = 0$

29. Solve: $\frac{2}{3} \log_8 8 + \log_8 (4x - 2) = 1$

30. The pH of a solution is 3. What is the concentration of hydrogen ions in moles per liter?

EP 97.65, 97.66

LESSON 98 Trapezoids

98.A Trapezoids

A ***parallelogram*** is a four-sided linear geometric figure in which **both pairs** of opposite sides are parallel. A ***trapezoid*** is a four-sided linear geometric figure which has **exactly one pair** of parallel sides. Both the figures shown below appear to be trapezoids since in the left-hand figure $\overline{AB}$ appears parallel to $\overline{CD}$ and in the right-hand figure $\overline{GE}$ appears parallel to $\overline{HF}$.

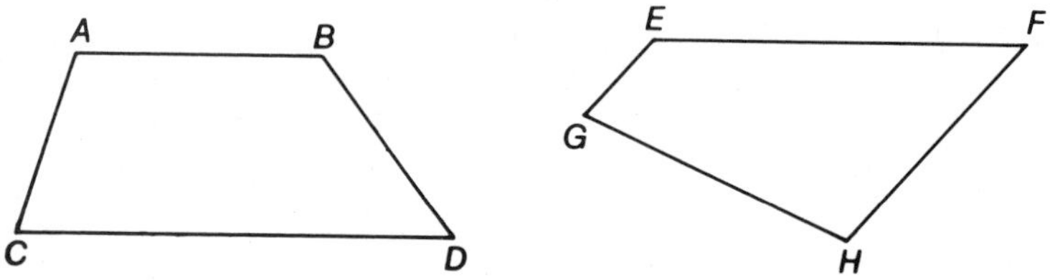

The parallel sides are called the ***bases*** of the trapezoid, and the nonparallel sides are called the ***legs*** of the trapezoid. The line segment that connects the midpoints of the legs of a trapezoid is called the ***median*** of the trapezoid. In the left-hand figure below, line segment $\overline{XY}$ is the median. **An altitude of a trapezoid** is any line segment that connects the bases and is perpendicular to one of the bases. Any number of altitudes can be drawn for a particular trapezoid, and they all have equal lengths. In the center trapezoid below, we show one altitude, and in the trapezoid on the right, we show three altitudes.

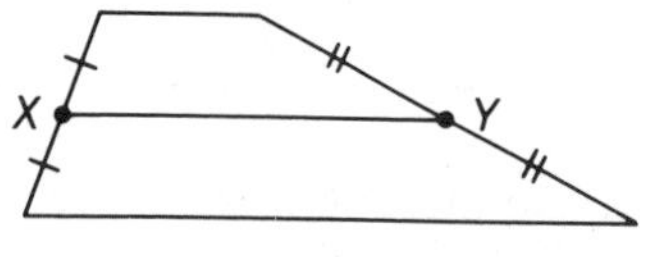

Median

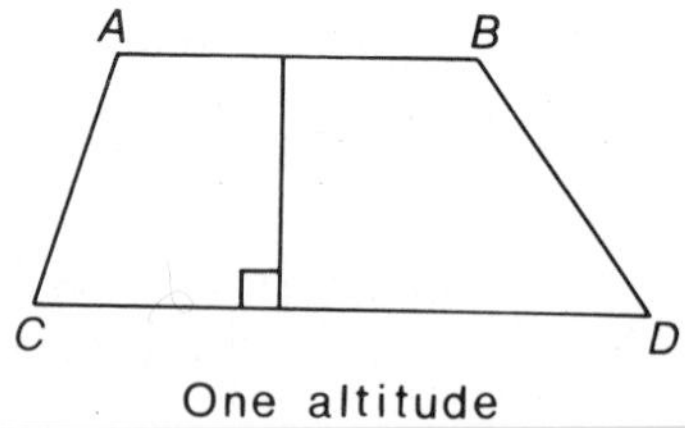

One altitude

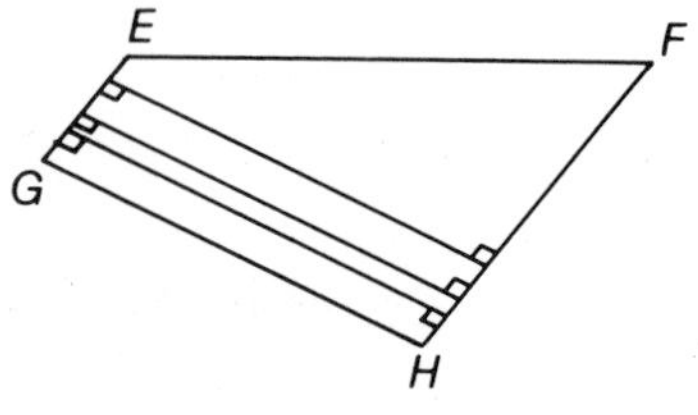

Three altitudes

A trapezoid whose nonparallel sides (legs) have equal length is called an ***isosceles trapezoid*** because *iso* is a Greek prefix that means "equal" and *skelos* is the Greek word for "leg." The angles at each end of a base of an isosceles trapezoid are called a pair of ***base angles.*** An isosceles trapezoid has **two pairs of base angles.**

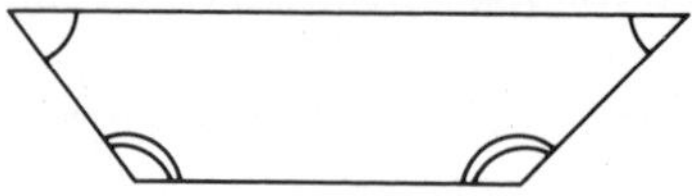
Isosceles trapezoid

Trapezoids have several interesting properties that can be proved.

1. The area of a trapezoid equals one-half the product of the altitude and the sum of the bases.
2. The median of a trapezoid is parallel to its bases, and its length is half the sum of the length of the bases.
3. The base angles of an isosceles trapezoid are equal.
4. The diagonals of an isosceles trapezoid are equal in length.

Example 98.A.1 Derive a general formula for the area of a trapezoid, using the figure shown.

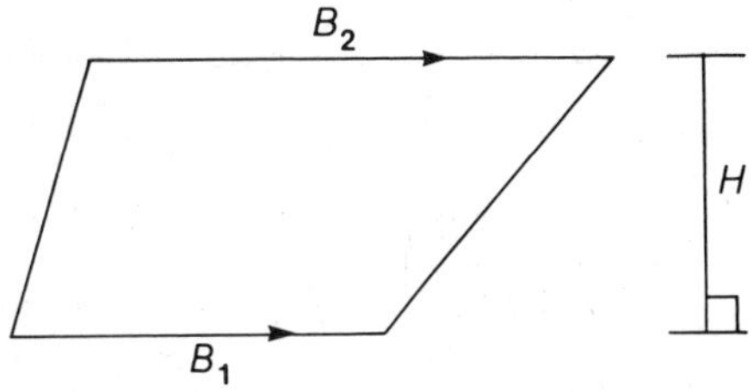

Solution The arrowheads indicate that B_1 is parallel to B_2. The altitude is H. We begin by drawing a diagonal in the left-hand figure below. This divides the trapezoid into the two triangles which we show separately in the center and on the right.

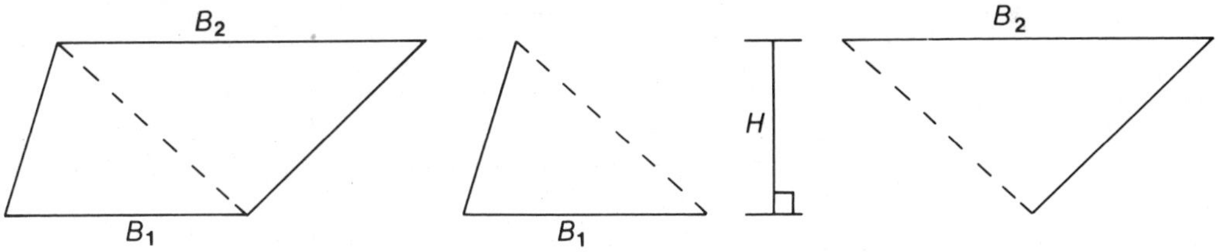

The area of the center triangle is $\frac{1}{2}B_1H$, and the area of the right triangle is $\frac{1}{2}B_2H$. The total area is the sum of these areas, so

$$\text{Area} = \frac{1}{2}B_1H + \frac{1}{2}B_2H \longrightarrow \textbf{Area} = \frac{1}{2}H(B_1 + B_2)$$

Example 98.A.2 The figure shown is a trapezoid whose area is 175 cm^2. Find x.

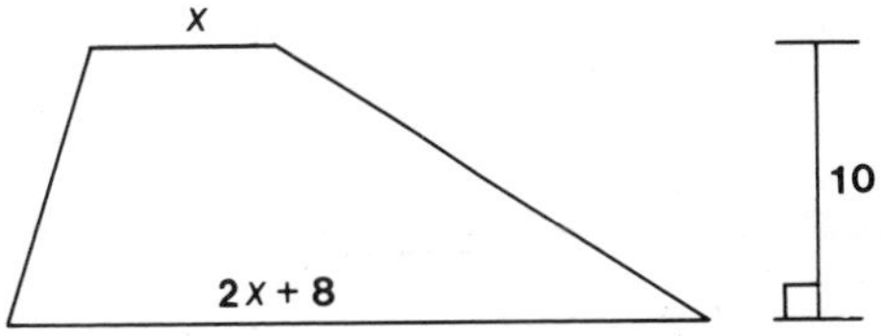

Solution We could use the formula for the area of a trapezoid, but we try to avoid formulas when possible. Thus, we will divide the figure into two triangles and sum the areas.

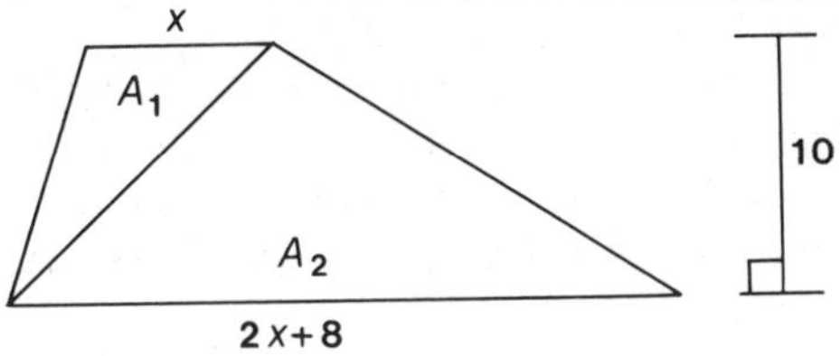

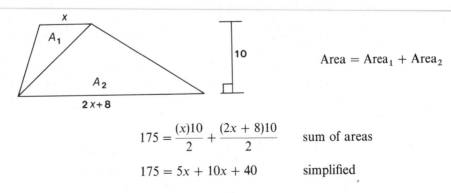

$$\text{Area} = \text{Area}_1 + \text{Area}_2$$

$$175 = \frac{(x)10}{2} + \frac{(2x + 8)10}{2} \qquad \text{sum of areas}$$

$$175 = 5x + 10x + 40 \qquad \text{simplified}$$

$15x = 135$	rearranged
$\mathbf{x = 9}$	divided

Example 98.A.3 Using the figure shown, prove that the median of a trapezoid is parallel to the bases and its length is half the sum of the bases.

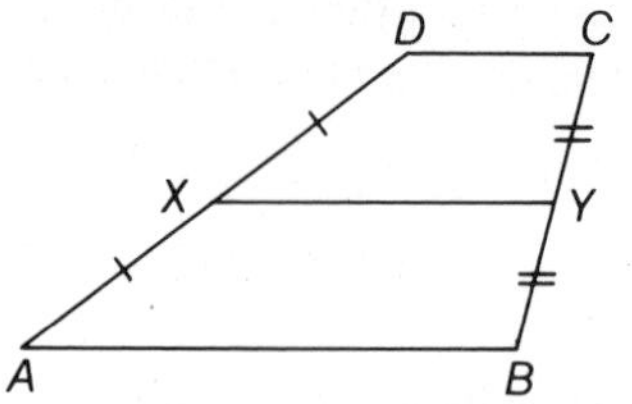

Solution We know that X and Y are midpoints, and so $AX = XD$ and $BY = CY$ as marked. To prove that $\overline{XY}$ is parallel to $\overline{DC}$, we draw segment $\overline{RS}$ parallel to $\overline{CB}$ which passes through X as shown on the left below.

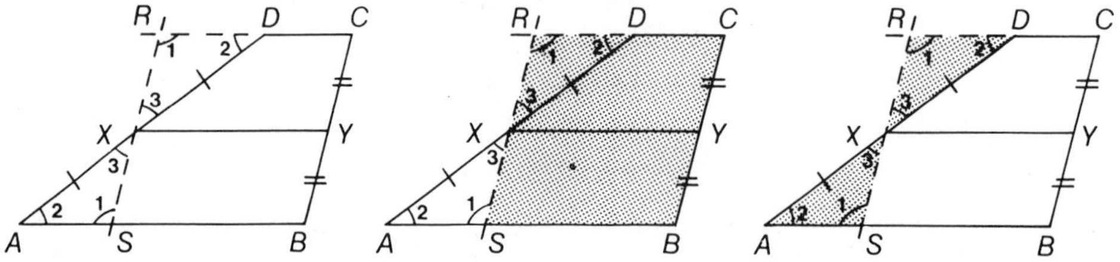

The bases DC and AB of a trapezoid are parallel, so the big quadrilateral $RSBC$ in the center is a parallelogram because both pairs of sides are parallel. The two triangles shaded in the right-hand figure are similar because the angles marked 1 are alternate interior angles, the angles marked 2 are alternate interior angles, and the angles marked 3 are vertical angles. This gives us three pairs of corresponding equal angles. Thus $\triangle RXD \sim \triangle SXA$ by AAA. Since $AX = XD$, and the scale factor = 1, the triangles are congruent. Thus, $RX = XS$ since corresponding parts of congruent triangles are equal.

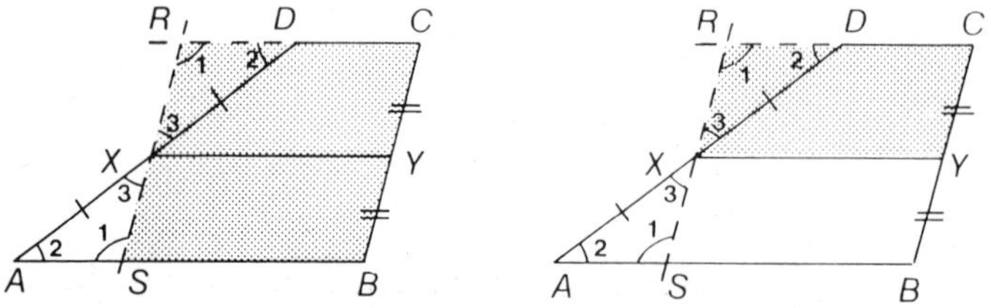

We know that the sides of the parallelogram $RSBC$ are equal and parallel. Because side RX is $\frac{1}{2}$ of RS and side CY is $\frac{1}{2}$ of CB, they are equal to each other. Thus, the small quadrilateral $RXYC$ is a parallelogram because two sides are equal and parallel. To show that the median XY equals one-half the sum of the bases, from the figure we reason as follows.

	$XY = RD + DC$	sides of parallelogram
(a)	$XY = AS + DC$	substituted AS for RD
(b)	$XY = SB$	sides of parallelogram
	$2XY = AS + SB + DC$	added (a) and (b)
	$2XY = DC + AB$	$AS + SB = AB$
	$XY = \frac{1}{2}(DC + AB)$	divided

Example 98.A.4 The figure shown is a trapezoid and $\overline{AB}$ is the median. Find x.

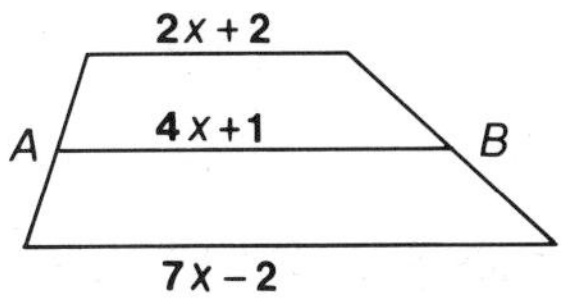

Solution In the preceding example, we proved that the length of the median of a trapezoid equals one-half the sum of the lengths of the bases. This problem requires that we use that fact since we are given each of these lengths in terms of x.

$$\text{Length of the median} = \frac{1}{2}(\text{base}_1 + \text{base}_2)$$

Now we substitute and solve

$$4x + 1 = \frac{1}{2}(2x + 2 + 7x - 2) \qquad \text{substituted}$$

$$4x + 1 = \frac{9x}{2} \qquad \text{simplified}$$

$$8x + 2 = 9x \qquad \text{multiplied by 2}$$

$$\mathbf{2 = x} \qquad \text{solved}$$

Example 98.A.5 Prove that the base angles of an isosceles trapezoid are equal.

Solution An isosceles trapezoid has two sides that are parallel and two nonparallel sides that are equal in length. In the left-hand figure below, we mark the equal sides. In the right-hand figure, we erect two perpendiculars to form two right triangles.

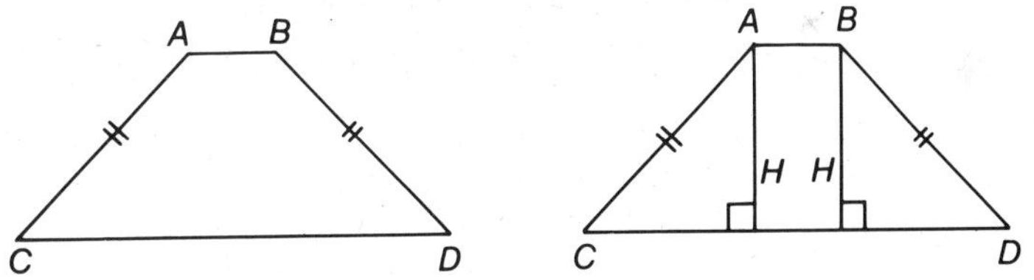

Parallel lines are everywhere equidistant so the sides H are equal, and the right triangles are congruent since they are similar by HL with a scale factor of 1. Thus, angle C equals angle D as they are corresponding parts of congruent triangles.

Example 98.A.6 Prove that the diagonals of an isosceles trapezoid are equal in length.

Solution We draw the isosceles trapezoid $ABDC$. Then we draw the diagonals and shade in two triangles.

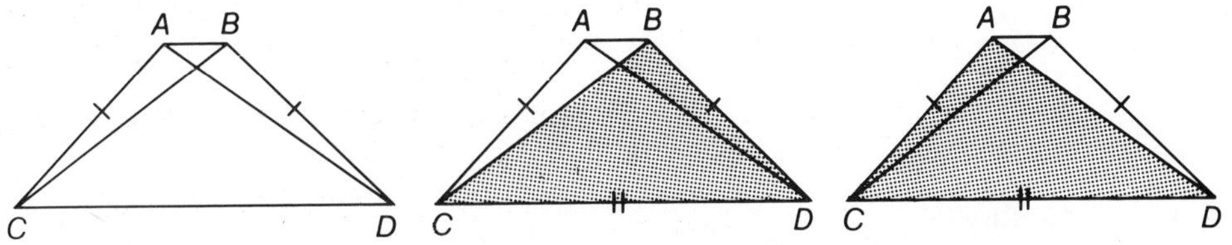

The shaded triangles are congruent since they are similar by SAS with a scale factor of 1. We are given that $AC = BD$, side CD equals itself, and angle ACD equals angle BDC because the base angles of an isosceles trapezoid are equal. Thus, the diagonals $\overline{AD}$ and $\overline{BC}$ are equal because they are corresponding parts of congruent triangles.

Problem set 98

1. The volume of an ideal gas varies directly as the temperature if the pressure is held constant. The pressure of a quantity of gas was 3 atmospheres. The temperature was 4000 K, and the volume was 4 liters. At the same pressure, what was the volume when the temperature was decreased to 2000 K?

2. The ratio of sweets to sours was 7 to 2. If Horatio had 18,000 stashed in a barrel in the basement, how many of them were sour?

3. The young boy discovered that m varied jointly as k and w^2, and inversely as the square root of x. The value of m was multiplied by what when x was multiplied by 8, w was multiplied by 3, and k was multiplied by 2?

4. Arthur sold all m of them for c cents. Then he realized that the price was too low, so he increased the price p cents per item. How many could Walter buy for \$40 at the new price?

5. The gauge on the gas tank showed that it was one-fourth full. When they stopped for gas, it took 14 gallons to fill up the tank. How many gallons did the tank hold?

6. Use a diagram to develop a general formula for the area of the trapezoid with bases B_1 and B_2 and height h.

7. Prove that the median of a trapezoid is parallel to the bases and its length is one-half the sum of the bases.

8. Given: $BD = EC$; $AD = AE$
Prove: $BE = CD$

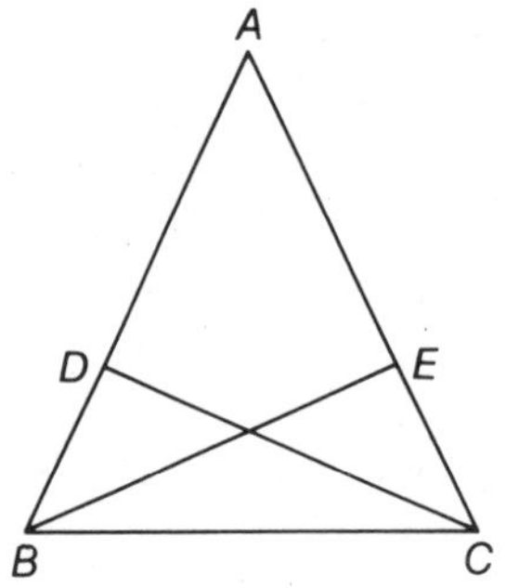

9. Given: $\overline{AB} \parallel \overline{CD}$; $AC = BD$
Prove: $AD = BC$

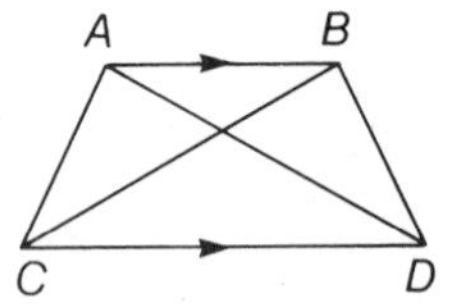

10. Use an infinite geometric series as an aid for expressing $0.00\overline{37}$ as a common fraction.

11. Find the sum of the following geometric series:

$$\frac{2}{3} + \left(-\frac{2}{9}\right) + \left(\frac{2}{27}\right) + \left(-\frac{2}{81}\right) + \cdots$$

12. Find the length of the diagonal $\overline{AB}$ in the rectangular solid shown.

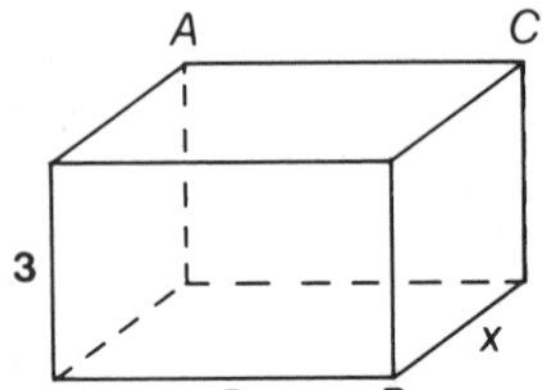

13. The base of a pyramid is a regular pentagon whose perimeter is 30 centimeters. The height of the pyramid is 10 centimeters. Find the volume of the pyramid.

14. Two rectangular boxes are similar. The ratio of the volume of the larger box to the volume of the smaller box is 27 to 1. If the area of a surface of the smaller box is 4 square units, how many square units is the area of corresponding surface of the larger box?

15. A sphere has a radius of 6 centimeters.
(*a*) Find the volume of the sphere.
(*b*) Find the surface area of the sphere.

16. (*a*) The base of a circular cone has a radius of 6 centimeters. The height of the cone is 4 centimeters. Find the volume of the cone.
(*b*) Assume that the cone is a right circular cone. Find the surface area of the cone.

17. The general equation of a hyperbola is $9x^2 - 4y^2 - 54x - 16y - 79 = 0$. Write the equation of the hyperbola in standard form. Give the coordinates of the center, the coordinates of the vertices, and the equations of the asymptotes.

18. The general equation of an ellipse is $25x^2 + 4y^2 - 150x + 32y + 189 = 0$. Write the equation of the ellipse in standard form. Give the coordinates of the center, the length of the major axis, and the length of the minor axis, and indicate whether the major axis is horizontal or vertical.

19. (*a*) Develop the identity for $\sin A \sin B$.
(*b*) Find $\sin 225° \sin 15°$, using the identity found in (*a*). Use exact values.

20. The first term of an arithmetic sequence is 3 and the common difference is 3.
(*a*) What is the seventeenth term of the arithmetic sequence?
(*b*) What is the sum of the first 17 terms?

21. Solve this triangle for angle A.

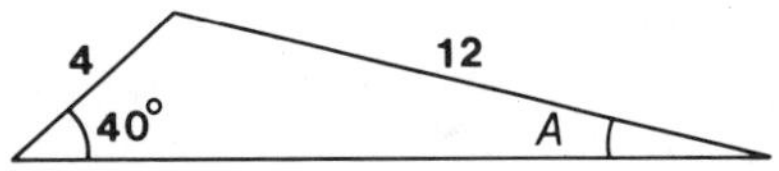

22. Express ln 305 in terms of common logarithms. Do not find a numerical answer.

23. Find the three cube roots of -1 in rectangular form. Give exact answers.

24. Sketch $y = \tan x$.

25. Using the distance formula as required, find the equation of all points which are equidistant from $(-3, -4)$ and $(3, 4)$.

26. Show that: $(1 + \tan x)(1 - \tan x) + 2\tan^2 x = \sec^2 x$

27. Show that: $\dfrac{\sin x}{1 + \cos x} + \dfrac{1 + \cos x}{\sin x} = 2 \csc x$

28. Solve, given that $(0° \leq x < 360°)$: $2 \sin 3x = -1$

29. Solve: $\log (x^2 - 1) - \log (x - 1) = 1$

30. Find the base 2 antilogarithm of -2.

EP 98.67, 98.68

LESSON 99 Graphs of inverse trigonometric relations

99.A Graphs of the arcsine and arccosine

Inverse functions "undo" each other. We know that the sine of 30° is $\frac{1}{2}$ and cos 60° is $\frac{1}{2}$.

$$\sin 30° = \frac{1}{2} \qquad \cos 60° = \frac{1}{2}$$

The inverse functions use the same numbers but in reverse order. They say that an angle whose sine is $\frac{1}{2}$ is 30° and an angle whose cosine is $\frac{1}{2}$ is 60°.

$$\arcsin \frac{1}{2} = 30° \qquad \arccos \frac{1}{2} = 60°$$

Thus, the graph of the arcsine displays the same ordered pairs of θ and sin θ, but in this graph θ is treated as the dependent variable. The values of θ are graphed on the vertical axis, and the values of sine θ are graphed on the horizontal axis. In the same way, the graph of the arccosine has the values of θ graphed vertically, and has the values of cosine θ graphed horizontally. We note from the graph that there are many angles whose sine is 0. These angles are 0°, ±180°, ±360°, ±540°, ±720°, etc. We remember that, for a relationship to be considered a function, there can only be one value of the dependent variable for each value of the independent variable. Thus, when we want to consider the arcsine and arccosine as functions, it is necessary to restrict the values of θ. These restricted values are designated by the heavy lines in the graphs. Note that the values of θ for the sine function are between −90° and 90°, while the values of θ for the cosine function are between 0° and 180°.

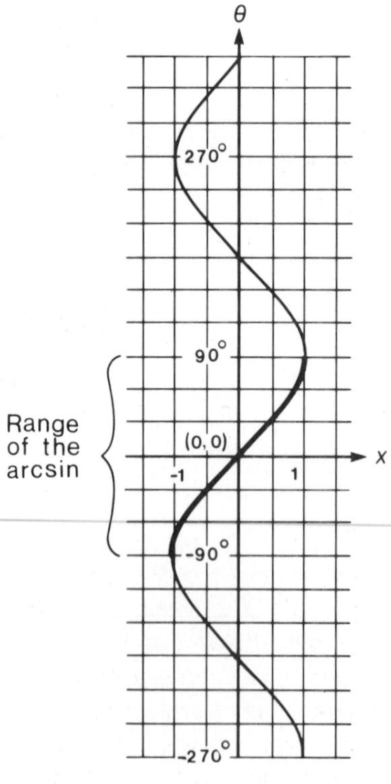

θ = arcsin x

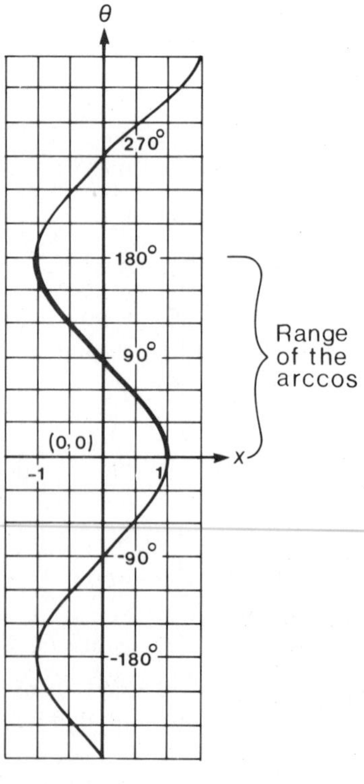

θ = arccos x

99.B Graphs of arcsecant and arccosecant

The graphs of the secant and cosecant are graphs of the ordered pairs of $(\theta, \sec\theta)$, $(\theta, \csc\theta)$ with the first variable plotted on the horizontal axis. The graphs of arcsec θ and arccsc θ are graphs of the same pairs, but with the order reversed, $(\sec\theta, \theta)$, $(\csc\theta, \theta)$. The first variable is again graphed on the horizontal axis, so the curves repeat vertically instead of horizontally as before. To consider these relations as functions, there can be only one image for each value of sec θ and only one image for each value of csc θ. Thus, when arcsec θ is to be considered as a function, the values of θ should be between $0°$ and $180°$, as shown by the heavy lines in the figure on the left below, and $\theta = 90°$ must be excluded. For arccsc θ to be considered as a function, the values of θ should be between $-90°$ and $+90°$, as shown by the heavy lines in the figure on the right, and $\theta = 0°$ must be excluded.

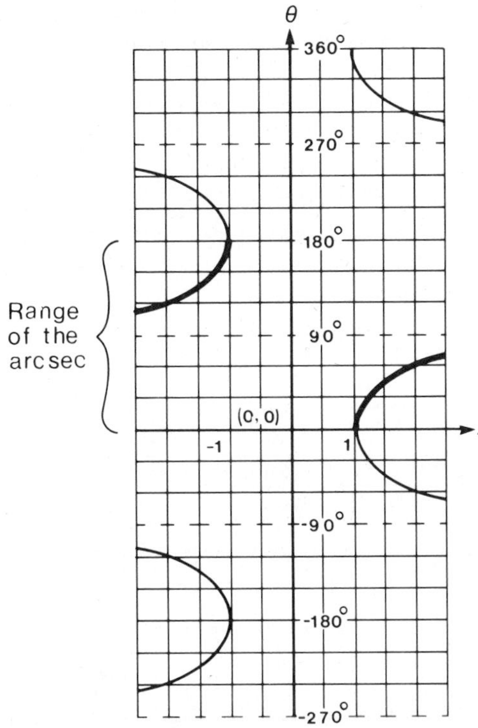

θ = arcsec x

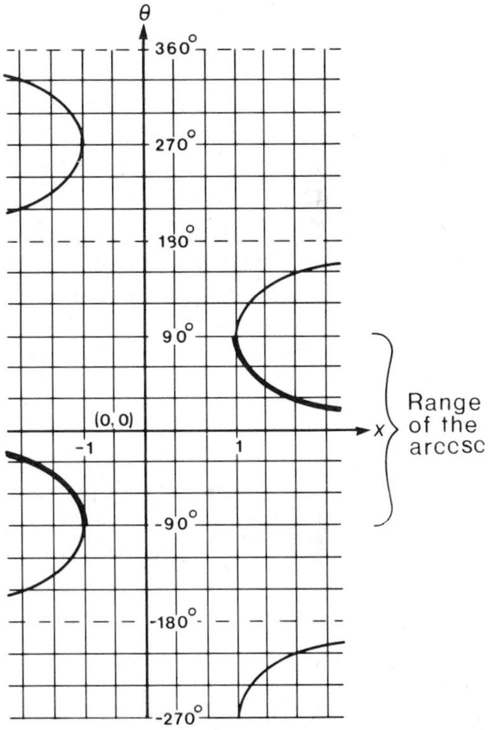

θ = arccsc x

99.C Graphs of the arctangent and arccotangent

The graphs of the arctangent and arccotangent are graphs of the same pairs of coordinates as in the graphs of the tangent and cotangent, but the order is reversed. The values of θ are graphed vertically, and the values of tan θ or cot θ are graphed horizontally, so the curves are horizontal instead of vertical as before. If the pairing is to be a single-valued relationship, there can be only one value of θ for any specified value of tan θ or cot θ; and these values are designated by the heavy lines in the graphs. For arctan θ, the values of θ considered lie between $-90°$ and $+90°$; and for arccot θ, they lie between $0°$ and $180°$.

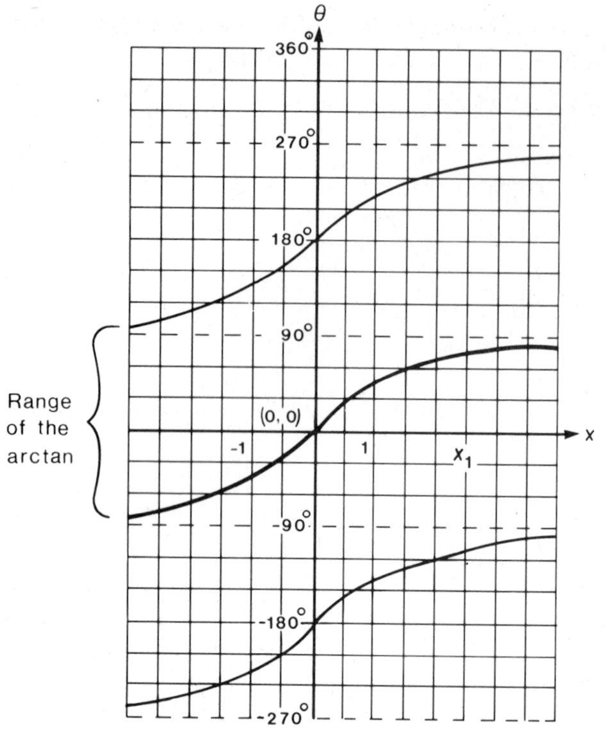

$\theta = \arctan x$

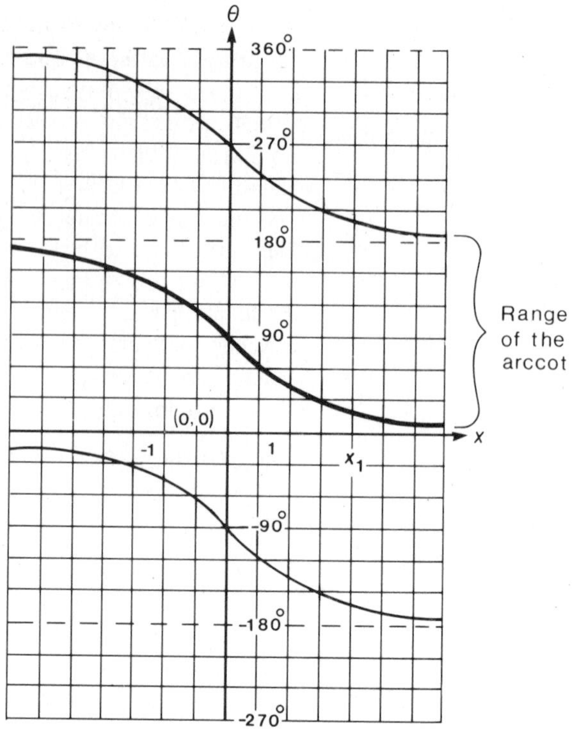

$\theta = \text{arccot}\ x$

Problem set 99

1. One pipe can fill a tank in 10 hours and the second pipe can fill a tank in 8 hours. The first pipe is used for 2 hours, and then the second pipe is also used. How long does it take both pipes to finish filling the tank?

2. The increase was exponential. After 5 hours they numbered 120, and after 10 hours there were 400 of them. How many were there after 30 hours?

3. At 6 a.m. the clock hands pointed in opposite directions. How long would it be before both hands pointed in the same direction?

4. The *Mary Ann* can go 48 miles downstream in 1 hour less than it takes her to go 32 miles upstream. If the speed of the *Mary Ann* in still water is 3 times the speed of the current, what are the speeds of the current and of the *Mary Ann*?

5. Kenny is going to draw a card from a deck of 52 cards. What is the probability that the card will be a queen or will be a black card or both?

6. (*a*) Graph $\theta = \arcsin x$. (*b*) Graph $\theta = \arccos x$. (*c*) Graph $\theta = \arctan x$.

7. Given: $AD = BE$; $DC = EC$
Prove: $\angle A = \angle B$

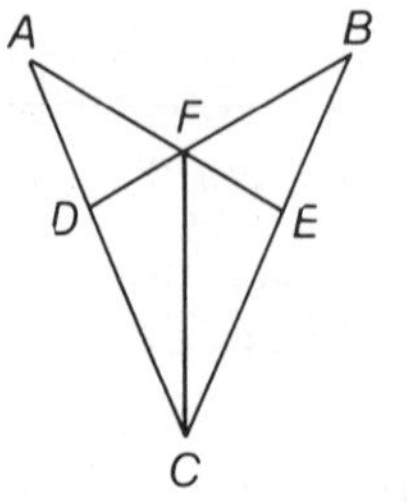

8. Given the following figure, $\overline{RS} \parallel \overline{CB}$, X and Y are the midpoints of $\overline{RS}$ and $\overline{CB}$, respectively.
Prove: $\overline{XY} \parallel \overline{AB}$; $XY = \frac{1}{2}(DC + AB)$

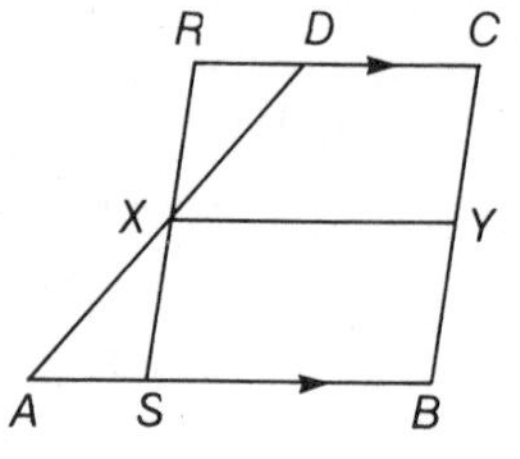

9. Draw a figure to develop a general formula for the area of the trapezoid with bases B_1 and B_2 and height h.

10. Use the figures shown to prove the Pythagorean theorem.

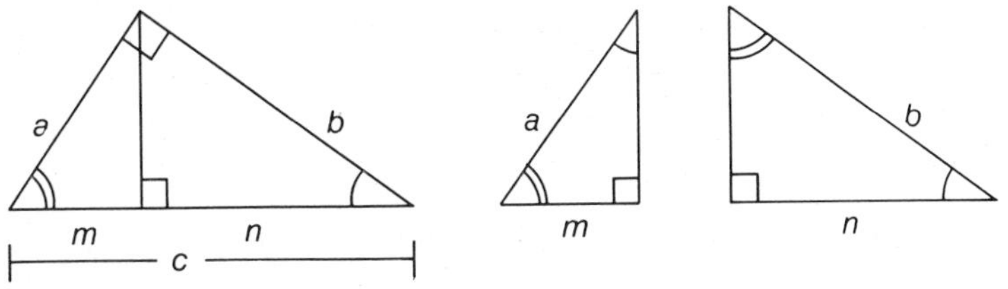

11. Use an infinite geometric series as an aid for expressing $0.00\overline{41}$ as a common fraction.

12. Find the sum of the following geometric series:

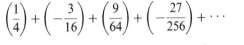

$$\left(\frac{1}{4}\right) + \left(-\frac{3}{16}\right) + \left(\frac{9}{64}\right) + \left(-\frac{27}{256}\right) + \cdots$$

13. Find the length of the diagonal AC in the rectangular solid shown.

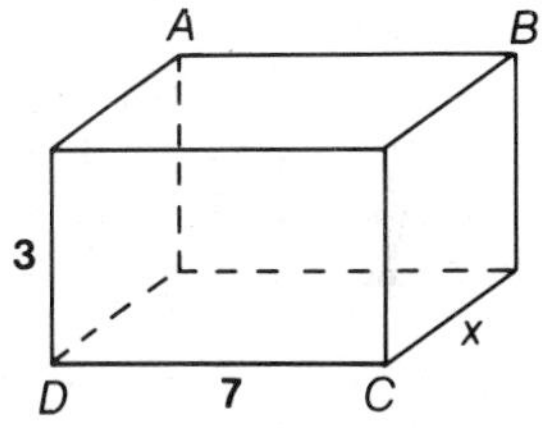

14. The base of a pyramid is an equilateral triangle whose perimeter is 18 centimeters. The height of the pyramid is 10 centimeters. Find the volume of the pyramid.

15. Two geometric solids are similar. The ratio of the volume of the larger geometric solid to the smaller geometric solid is 27 to 8. What is the ratio of the length of a side of the smaller geometric solid to the length of the corresponding side of the larger geometric solid?

16. A sphere has a radius of 10 centimeters.
(*a*) Find the volume of the sphere.
(*b*) Find the surface area of the sphere.

17. (*a*) The base of a circular cone has a radius of 10 centimeters. The height of the cone is 6 centimeters. Find the volume of the cone.
(*b*) Assume that the cone is a right circular cone. Find the surface area of the cone.

18. The general equation of an ellipse is $25x^2 + 9y^2 - 200x + 18y + 184 = 0$. Write the equation of the ellipse in standard form. Give the coordinates of the center, the length of the major axis, and the length of the minor axis, and indicate whether the major axis is horizontal or vertical.

19. The general equation of a hyperbola is $x^2 - 4y^2 + 4x + 32y - 96 = 0$. Write the equation of the hyperbola in standard form. Give the coordinates of the center, the coordinates of the vertices, and the equations of the asymptotes.

20. (*a*) Develop the identity for $\sin x \cos y$.
(*b*) Find $\sin 225° \cos 15°$, using the identity found in (*a*). Use decimal approximations.

21. The first term of a geometric sequence is 4 and the common ratio is 2. What is the fifteenth term of the sequence?

22. Solve this triangle for angle A.

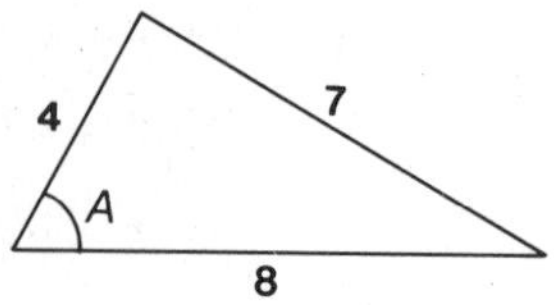

23. Express $\log_4 8$ in terms of common logarithms. Do not give a numerical answer.

24. Find the three cube roots of 1 in polar form. Give exact answers.

25. Sketch $y = -4 + 3 \sin \frac{1}{3}(x - 2\pi)$.

26. Show that: $\frac{1}{2} \sec x \csc(-x) = -\frac{1}{\sin 2x}$

27. Solve, given that $(0° \le x < 360°)$: $-2 \sin 3x = 1$

28. Show that: $\frac{\cos x}{\sec x - 1} - \frac{\cos x}{\sec x + 1} = 2 \cos^3 x \csc^2 x$

29. Solve: $\log \sqrt[3]{x^2} + \log \sqrt[3]{x^4} = \log 2^{-3}$

30. Evaluate: $5^{\log_5 4 - \log_5 2}$

EP 99.69, 99.70

LESSON 100 Advanced logarithmic calculations · Logarithmic inequalities

100.A Advanced logarithmic calculations

We have been using logarithms to perform simple multiplications, divisions, and raising to powers in expressions such as these.

(*a*) $(4327 \times 10^5)(506 \times 10^{-14})$ (*b*) $\frac{4327 \times 10^5}{506 \times 10^{-14}}$ (*c*) $(506 \times 10^{-14})^{3/2}$

A calculator could have been used to get the answers, but we were using these problems to give us practice in using logarithms and to help us understand logarithms. Each of the expressions above emphasizes the use of one of the rules for logarithms. In this lesson, we will look at problems whose solutions require the use of more than one of the rules for logarithms.

Example 100.A.1 Use base 10 logs to simplify: $\sqrt{216}\,\sqrt[3]{4130}$

Solution First, we write each number in scientific notation, replace the radicals with fractional exponents, and write an equation.

$$y = (2.16 \times 10^2)^{1/2}(4.13 \times 10^3)^{1/3}$$

Now we take the logarithm of both sides.

$$\log y = \frac{1}{2}\log(2.16 \times 10^2) + \frac{1}{3}\log(4.13 \times 10^3) \qquad \text{log equation}$$

$$\log y = \frac{1}{2}(0.33 + 2) + \frac{1}{3}(0.62 + 3) \qquad \text{used tables}$$

$\log y = 1.17 + 1.21 = 2.38$ added

$\log y = 0.38 + 2$ simplified

$y = \mathbf{2.4 \times 10^2}$ antilog

Example 100.A.2 Use base 10 logs to simplify: $\dfrac{(\sqrt[3]{406 \times 10^3})^2}{\sqrt{807 \times 10^{17}}}$

Solution First we write the numbers in scientific notation and replace the radicals with fractional exponents. Then we use the variable y and write an equation.

$$y = \frac{(4.06 \times 10^5)^{2/3}}{(8.07 \times 10^{19})^{1/2}}$$

The next step is to take the logarithm of both sides of the equation. Then we solve for the value of y.

$\log y = \frac{2}{3}\log(4.06 \times 10^5) - \frac{1}{2}\log(8.07 \times 10^{19})$ log equation

$\log y = \frac{2}{3}(5.61) - \frac{1}{2}(19.91)$ used tables

$\log y = 3.74 - 9.96 = -6.22$ simplified

$\log y = -6.22 + 7 - 7$ added $+7 - 7$

$\log y = 0.78 - 7$ simplified

$y = \mathbf{6.03 \times 10^{-7}}$ antilog

100.B Logarithmic inequalities: Base greater than 1

Most of the problems that we have worked using logarithms were designed to help us understand the rules for logarithms, and to help us remember that exponential functions and logarithmic functions are two ways to express the same relationships. Sometimes we encounter exercises that are designed to test our knowledge of a single fact. If we recognize this and if we know the fact, then the problems are simple. Most exponential and logarithmic inequality problems fall into this category. First, we will investigate logarithms whose bases are greater than 1. We will use 5 as a base to demonstrate.

$$5^2 = 25 \qquad 5^3 = 125 \qquad 5^4 = 625$$

When the logarithm is 3, the number is 5^3, which is 125. When the logarithm is less than 3, the number is less than 5^3. When the logarithm is greater than 3, the number is greater than 5^3. If we are given the inequality

$$\log_5 N < 3$$

we must carefully consider the meaning of the inequality. Since $\log_5 N$ is an exponent, the inequality says

$$\text{The exponent} < 3$$

Now we investigate the result when the exponent equals 3.

$$\log_5 N = 3 \qquad \text{which says} \qquad 5^3 = N$$

The given inequality says the logarithm (exponent) is less than 3. If this is true, then certainly N will be less than 5^3.

$$N < 5^3$$

Care must be taken with the greater-than symbol, for, of course, it would be incorrect to write

$$5^3 < N \qquad \text{incorrect}$$

Example 100.B.1 Solve for x: $\log_4 (x - 2) < 3$

Solution If the logarithm (exponent) of $x - 2$ is less than 3, then $x - 2$ must be less than 4^3.

$$x - 2 < 4^3 \qquad \text{inequality}$$

$$x < 66 \qquad \text{simplified}$$

But the argument of a logarithm must be a positive number, so $x - 2$ must be greater than zero. This means x must be greater than 2. Thus, the final solution is

$$x > 2 \qquad \text{and} \qquad x < 66$$

which we can express in one compound statement by writing

$$\mathbf{2 < x < 66}$$

100.C Logarithmic inequalities: Base less than 1

To investigate exponentials whose bases are less than 1, we look at three expressions whose bases are $\frac{1}{2}$.

$$\left(\frac{1}{2}\right)^2 = \frac{1}{4} \qquad \left(\frac{1}{2}\right)^3 = \frac{1}{8} \qquad \left(\frac{1}{2}\right)^4 = \frac{1}{16}$$

In the center we see that when the logarithm (exponent) is 3, the number is $\frac{1}{8}$. On the left we see that when the logarithm (exponent) is less than 3, the number is greater than $\frac{1}{8}$. On the right we see that when the logarithm (exponent) is greater than 3, the number is less than $\frac{1}{8}$. Thus, if we look at the inequality

$$\log_{1/2} N < 3$$

we know that if the logarithm is less than 3, the number must be greater than $(\frac{1}{2})^3$.

$$N > (\tfrac{1}{2})^3$$

Example 100.C.1 Solve: $\log_{1/3} (x - 6) > 4$

Solution If the log of $x - 6$ is greater than 4, then $x - 6$ must be less than $(\frac{1}{3})^4$.

$$x - 6 < \left(\frac{1}{3}\right)^4 \qquad \text{equation}$$

$$x - 6 < \frac{1}{81} \qquad \text{expanded}$$

$$x < 6 + \frac{1}{81} \qquad \text{solved}$$

From this we see that x must be less than $6\frac{1}{81}$. Also we remember that the argument of any logarithm must be a positive number (a number greater than 0), so $(x - 6)$ must be greater than 0 and thus x must be greater than 6:

$$x > 6 \qquad \text{and} \qquad x < 6\frac{1}{81}$$

which we can express compactly by writing

$$6 < x < 6\frac{1}{81}$$

Problem set 100

1. Twice the supplement of an angle exceeds 5 times the complement of the angle by 30°. What is the angle?

2. One of the elephants lumbered towards the water hole at f feet per hour for t hours but still got there 2 hours late. How fast should the elephant have lumbered to get to the water hole on time?

3. If $x \# y$ means $2x + 3y$ and $x * y$ means $5x + 4y$, evaluate the expression $2 \# (4 * 3)$.

4. Keeth and Randy were amazed that the first toss of the coin came up heads. What is the probability that the next two tosses will also come up heads?

5. Use the example of 8 things taken 6 at a time to develop an expression for ${}_8P_6$ and ${}_8C_6$.

Use base 10 logs to simplify:

6. $\sqrt{301}\,\sqrt[4]{2600}$

7. $\dfrac{(\sqrt[3]{203 \times 10^4})^2}{\sqrt{804 \times 10^{16}}}$

Solve for x:

8. $\log_3 (x - 2) < 3$

9. $\log_{1/2} (x - 3) > 3$

10. Express $\log_5 6$ in terms of common logarithms.

11. (*a*) Sketch the graph of $\theta = \text{arcsec } x$.
(*b*) Sketch the graph of $\theta = \text{arccsc } x$.

12. Given: $AD = BE$; $DC = EC$
Prove: $AE = BD$

13. Given: The same figure as in Problem 12. $AD = BE$; $DC = EC$
Prove: $\triangle AFD \cong \triangle BFE$

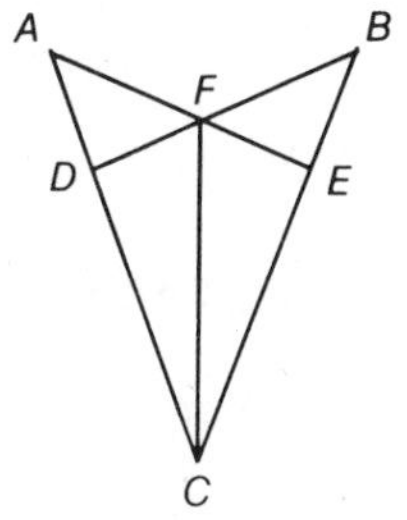

14. Prove that the sum of the angles in a triangle is 180°.

15. Given the figure: Quadrilateral $ABCD$ is a trapezoid with $\overline{DC}$ and $\overline{AB}$ as bases. $\overline{XY}$ is the median.
Prove: $\overline{XY} \parallel \overline{AB}$; $XY = \frac{1}{2}(DC + AB)$

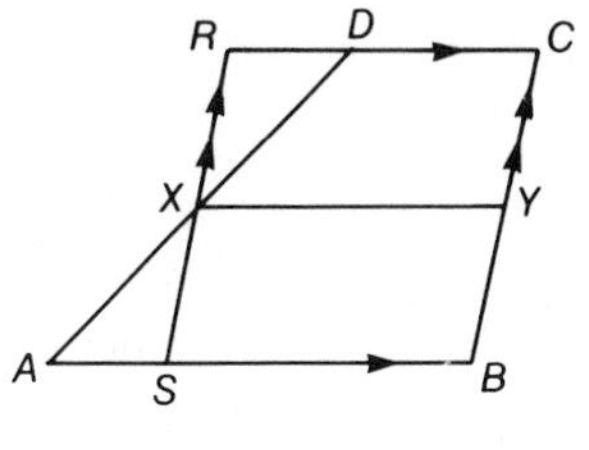

16. Use an infinite geometric series as an aid for expressing $0.00\overline{43}$ as a common fraction.

17. A ball is dropped from a height of 256 feet. After each bounce the ball rebounds three-fourths of the distance it fell. How far will the ball rebound after the fourth bounce?

18. Find the length of the diagonal AB in the rectangular solid shown.

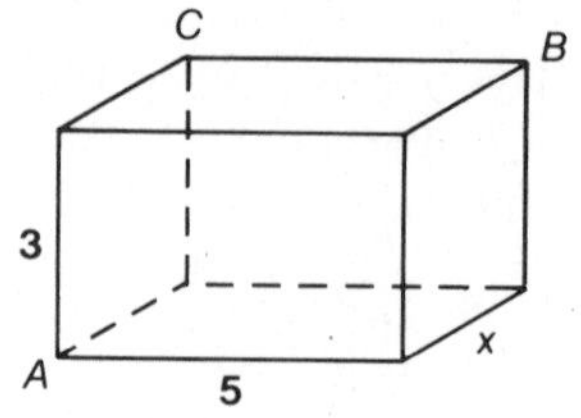

19. The base of a pyramid is a regular octagon whose perimeter is 40 centimeters. The height of the pyramid is 9 centimeters. Find the volume of the pyramid.

20. What is the ratio of the surface area of the smaller sphere to the surface area of the larger sphere if the ratio of the radii is 3 to 5?

21. A sphere has a radius of 9 centimeters.
(*a*) Find the volume of the sphere.
(*b*) Find the surface area of the sphere.

22. (*a*) The base of a circular cone has a radius of 8 centimeters. The height of the cone is 8 centimeters. Find the volume of the cone.
(*b*) Assume that the cone is a right circular cone. Find the surface area of the cone.

23. The general equation of an ellipse is $25x^2 + 9y^2 + 50x - 36y - 164 = 0$. Write the equation of the ellipse in standard form. Give the coordinates of the center, the length of the major axis, and the length of the minor axis, and indicate whether the major axis is horizontal or vertical.

24. The general equation of a hyperbola is $4x^2 - 36y^2 - 40x + 216y - 368 = 0$. Write the equation of the hyperbola in standard form and give the coordinates of the center, the coordinates of the vertices, and the equations of the asymptotes.

25. Find $\cos 255° - \cos 15°$ by using the identity for $\cos x - \cos y$. Use exact values.

26. Solve this triangle for side a.

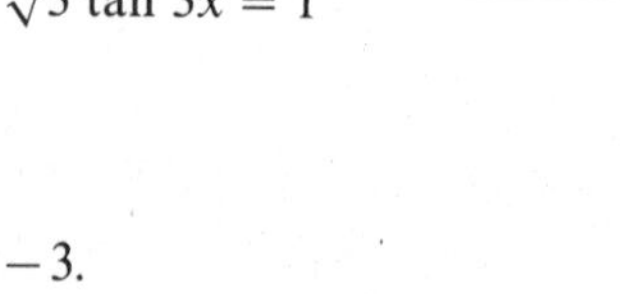

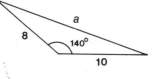

27. Show that $\sec x \csc x = 2 \csc 2x$.

28. Solve, given that $(0° \le x < 360°)$: $\sqrt{3} \tan 3x = 1$

29. Show that: $\dfrac{2 \tan \theta}{1 + \tan^2 \theta} = \sin 2\theta$

30. Find the base 4 antilogarithm of -3.

EP 100.71, 100.72

LESSON 101 Binomial theorem

101.A Binomial theorem

We have been using Pascal's triangle to find the coefficients of the terms of the expansions of expressions such as $(a + b)^n$. Pascal's triangle is satisfactory for expansions when n is a small number such as 4, 5, or 6, but its use is inconvenient when n is a larger number such as 15 or 27 or 50. A triangle of 51 rows with a bottom row of 51 entries would take a long time to construct. An identity called the ***binomial theorem*** allows one to compute the coefficient of any particular term of an expansion without knowing the entries in the row above. The identity can be proved by using mathematical induction. If n is a positive integer, the general form of the expansion of $(a + b)^n$ is as follows.

$$(a+b)^n = a^n + \frac{n}{1}\cdot a^{n-1}b + \frac{n}{1}\cdot\frac{n-1}{2}a^{n-2}b^2 + \frac{n}{1}\cdot\frac{n-1}{2}\cdot\frac{n-2}{3}a^{n-3}b^3 + \cdots$$

$$+\frac{n}{1}\cdot\frac{n-1}{2}\cdot\frac{n-2}{3}\cdots\frac{n-[k-2]}{k-1}a^{n-(k-1)}b^{k-1} + \cdots + b^n$$

In this notation, k represents the number of a particular term in the expansion. If we use factorial notation, the expression for the kth term of an expansion can be written in a form that is easier to remember. Instead of a and b, we will use F for the first term in the binomial and will use S for the second term in the binomial. To use this expression we must say that the value of 0! is 1.

> If n is a positive integer and k is a positive integer less than or equal to n, the kth term of $(F + S)^n$ is
>
> $$\frac{n!}{(n-k+1)!(k-1)!}F^{n-k+1}S^{k-1}$$

The binomial theorem looks complicated, but is especially easy to remember if we can recall that n factorial is the numerator of the coefficient; that the sum of the exponents is n; and that these exponents always appear as factorials in the denominator of the coefficient.

Example 101.A.1 Find the eighth term of the expansion of $(F + S)^{12}$.

Solution The easy way is to begin with the exponent of S. In the first term, the exponent of S is 0, then 1, etc.,

Term:	①	②	③	④	⑤	⑥	...
Exponent of S:	S^0	S^1	S^2	S^3	S^4	...	

so we see that the exponent of S in the eighth term will be 7. Now the exponent of F must add to 7 to make 12, so the exponent of F must be 5. Thus, the variables are

$$F^5S^7$$

Now the numerator of the coefficient is $(5 + 7)!$, which is 12!, and the denominator of the coefficient is 5!7!. Using this information we can write the eighth term of the expansion of $(F + S)^{12}$ as follows:

$$\frac{12!}{5!7!}F^5S^7 = \mathbf{792F^5S^7}$$

If we use the general expression for the kth term given in the box above and use 12 for n and 8 for k, we will get the same result.

$$\frac{n!}{(n-k+1)!(k-1)!}F^{n-k+1}S^{k-1} = \frac{12!}{(12-8+1)!(8-1)!}F^{12-8+1}S^{8-1}$$

$$= \frac{12!}{5!7!}F^5S^7 = \mathbf{792F^5S^7}$$

Example 101.A.2 Find the tenth term of the expansion $(F + S)^{14}$.

Solution We begin by finding the exponent of S for the tenth term.

Term:	①	②	③	④	⑤	...
Exponent of S:	S^0	S^1	S^2	S^3	S^4	...

We see that the exponent of S in the tenth term will be 9. Since the exponent of F must add to 9 to get 14, the exponent of F must be 5. Thus we can write

$$F^5S^9$$

Now we remember that the numerator of the coefficient is $(5 + 9)!$, and the denominator of the coefficient is $5!9!$, so we can write the tenth term of $(F + S)^{14}$ as

$$\frac{14!}{5!9!}F^5S^9 = \mathbf{2002F^5S^9}$$

Example 101.A.3 Find the tenth term of the expansion of $(2x^3 - y)^{15}$.

Solution We will begin by finding the tenth term of the expansion of $(F + S)^{15}$. Then we will replace F with $2x^3$ and replace S with $-y$. The exponent of the variable S in the tenth term is 9, so the exponent of F must be 6.

$$F^6S^9$$

Now we remember the pattern and write the coefficient

$$\text{Tenth term} = \frac{15!}{6!9!}F^6S^9 = 5005\ F^6S^9$$

We finish by replacing F with $2x^3$ and replacing S with $-y$ and then we simplify.

$$5005(2x^3)^6(-y)^9 = 5005[64x^{18}(-y)^9] = \mathbf{-320{,}320x^{18}y^9}$$

Problem set 101

1. Wakulla called Tallahassee on the phone. The cost of the call was \$2.20 for the first 3 minutes and \$0.90 for each additional minute. Wakulla talked longer than 3 minutes. In fact, she talked p minutes. What was the cost of her call?

2. The rug was marked up 80 percent of cost, so its selling price was \$900. It did not sell, so the markup was reduced to 50 percent of cost. What was the new selling price?

3. A city had an assessed valuation of \$8,000,000. The rate for school taxes is 60 cents per \$100 valuation. If all but 4 percent of the taxes had been collected, how many dollars were still owed to the city?

4. The photographer could take a picture of only 3 people at one time. If 7 cheerleaders were to be photographed, how many different groups of three were possible?

5. An urn contains balls and cubes which are either red or green. The probability of choosing a red object is 0.6, the probability of choosing a ball is 0.4, and the probability of choosing a red ball is 0.2. What is the probability of selecting either a ball or a red object?

6. Find the fourth term in the expansion of $(2x^2 - y)^6$.

7. Find the fifth term in the expansion of $(a^2 - 2b)^8$.

8. Use base 10 logs to simplify: $\dfrac{(\sqrt[3]{301 \times 10^4})^2}{\sqrt{901 \times 10^{15}}}$

Solve for x:

9. $\log_5 (x - 2) < 3$

10. $\log_{1/3} (x + 1) < 2$

11. Given: $AD = BE$; $DC = EC$
Prove: $\triangle AFC \cong \triangle BFC$

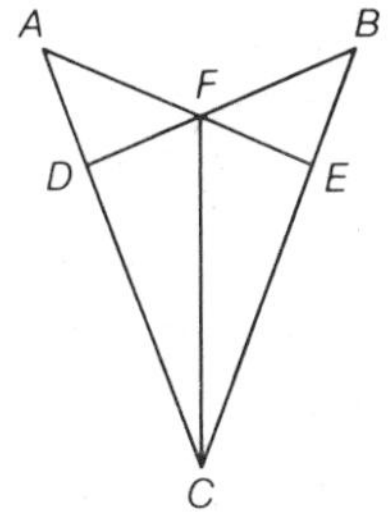

12. Given: $\angle DBC = \angle ACB$; $AE = DE$
Prove: $AB = DC$

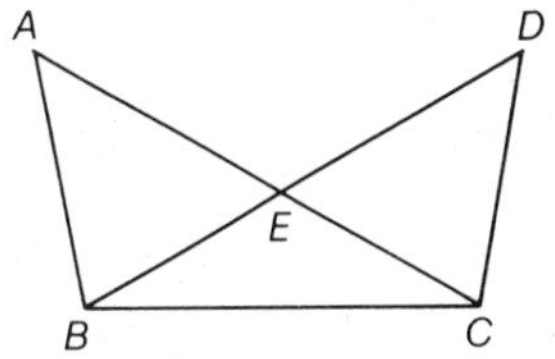

13. Given: $\overline{AD}$ is the angle bisector of $\angle A$.
Prove: $\dfrac{AB}{AC} = \dfrac{BD}{CD}$

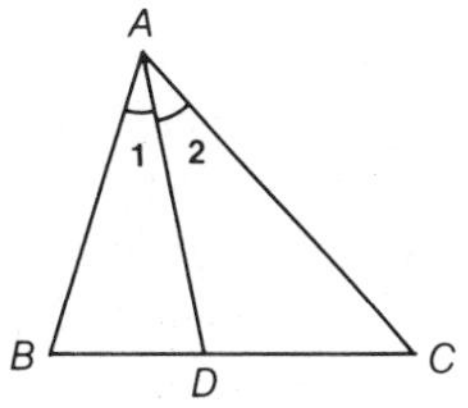

14. Prove that the sum of the angles of a triangle is 180°.

15. (*a*) Sketch the graph of $\theta = \arcsin y$.
(*b*) Sketch the graph of $\theta = \operatorname{arccsc} y$.

16. Use an infinite geometric series as an aid for expressing $0.0\overline{17}$ as a common fraction.

17. A ball is dropped from a height of 128 feet. After each bounce the ball rebounds one-third of the distance it fell. What is the total distance the ball will travel?

18. Find the length of the diagonal AC in the rectangular solid shown.

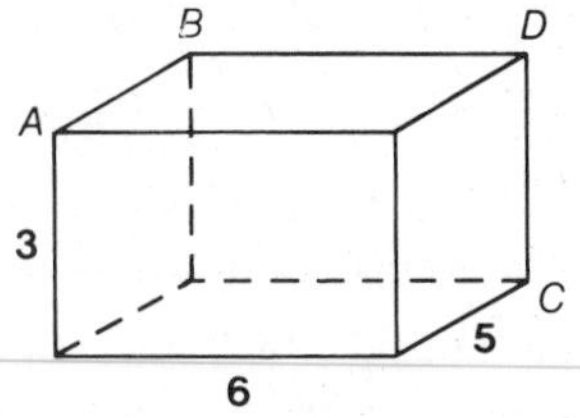

19. The base of a pyramid is a regular hexagon whose perimeter is 36 centimeters. The height of the pyramid is 12 centimeters. Find the volume of the pyramid.

20. A sphere has a radius of 1 centimeter.
(*a*) Find the volume of the sphere.
(*b*) Find the surface area of the sphere.

21. Two geometric solids are similar. The length of a side of the smaller geometric solid is four-fifths the length of the corresponding side of the larger geometric solid.

What is the ratio of the volume of the smaller geometric solid to the volume of the larger geometric solid?

22. (*a*) The base of a circular cone has a radius of 6 centimeters. The height of the cone is 8 centimeters. Find the volume of the cone.
(*b*) Assume the cone is a right circular cone. Find the surface area of the cone.

23. $x^2 - y^2 - 14x - 8y + 37 = 0$ is the equation of a hyperbola. Write the equation of the hyperbola in standard form and give the coordinates of the vertices and the equations of the asymptotes.

24. $16x^2 + y^2 - 128x + 20y + 292 = 0$ is the equation of an ellipse. Write the equation of the ellipse in standard form and give the coordinates of the center, the length of the major axis, and the length of the minor axis, and indicate whether the major axis is horizontal or vertical.

25. Solve this triangle for side *a*.

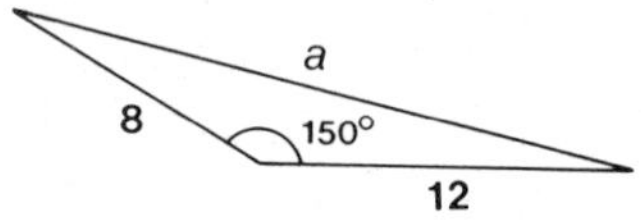

26. Use the identity for $\cos x - \cos y$ to find $\cos 75° - \cos 15°$.

27. Solve, given that $(0° \leq x < 360°)$: $2 \sin^2 x + 3 \sin x = -1$

28. Show that $\tan 2x = \dfrac{2 \tan x}{1 - \tan^2 x}$ by using the double-angle identities for sine and cosine.

29. Show that: $\dfrac{1 + \cos \theta}{\sin \theta} + \dfrac{\sin \theta}{\cos \theta} = \dfrac{\cos \theta + 1}{\sin \theta \cos \theta}$

30. The concentration of hydrogen ions in a solution is 2.3×10^{-4} mole per liter. What is the pH of the solution?

EP 101.73, 101.74

LESSON 102 Circles, chords, secants, and tangents • Arcs and central angles

102.A Circles, chords, secants, and tangents

A ***circle*** is the locus of all points in a plane that are equidistant from a point called the ***center*** of the circle. The ***radius*** of a circle is a line segment that connects a point on the circle to the center or is the length of such a segment. A ***chord*** is a line segment that connects any two points on a circle. A ***diameter*** is a chord that passes through the center of the circle or is the length of such a chord. A ***secant*** is a line that intersects a circle at two points. A ***tangent*** is a line that intersects (touches) a circle at only one point.

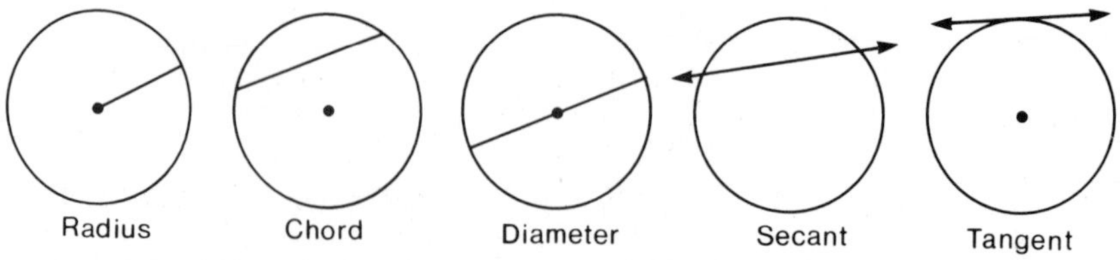

Example 102.A.1 Prove that if a line is tangent to a circle, it is perpendicular to the radius drawn to the point of tangency.

Solution We begin by inspecting the leftmost figure below and postulating that if a line m is in the plane of a circle and contains a point P that lies in the interior of the circle, then the line intersects the circle in two points. Also, since a tangent line t by definition intersects a circle in only one point, then all other points on this tangent line must lie outside the circle, and thus must be farther from the center of the circle than the point of tangency.

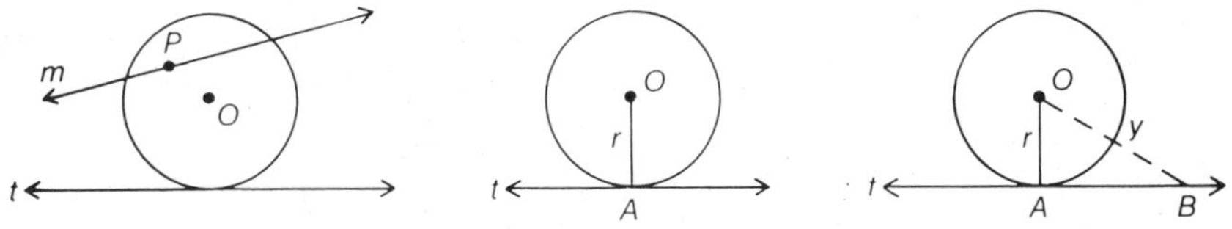

To finish, we will use a type of **indirect proof** called **proof by contradiction.** In this type of proof an assumption is made, and then we show that the assumption leads to a contradiction. Thus the assumption must be false.

If the radius r in the center figure is not perpendicular to the tangent line at A, then there must be some other segment y through point O that is perpendicular to the tangent line at some other point B, as in the figure on the right. But from the postulate above, all points on line t other than point A lie outside the circle. Thus segment y must be longer than radius r. But we remember that the shortest path from a point to a line is measured along the segment perpendicular to the line. Thus the assumption that r is not perpendicular to line t is false. Therefore r must be perpendicular to line t.

Example 102.A.2 Prove that tangents to a circle from a point outside the circle are of equal length.

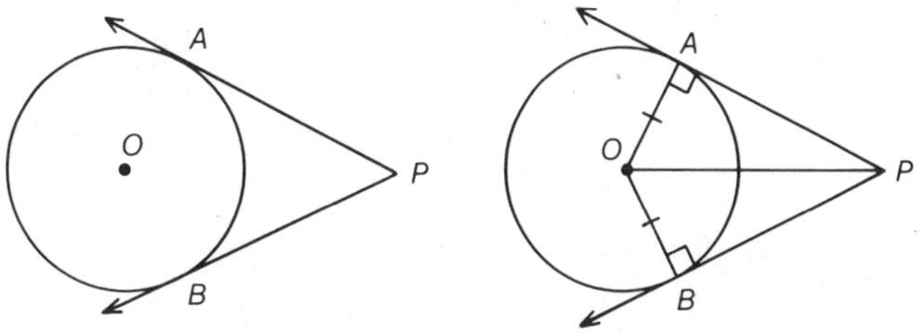

Solution This is an easy proof. In the figure on the left, we show two lines from P that are tangent at A and B. In the right-hand figure, we draw the radii from A and B and connect the center O with point P. The radii are perpendicular at A and B and segment $\overline{OP}$ is the hypotenuse of both triangles. Segments $\overline{OA}$ and $\overline{OB}$ are both radii. Thus, $\triangle OAP$ and $\triangle OBP$ are congruent since they are similar by HL and the scale factor is 1. Thus AP is equal to BP because these segments are corresponding parts of congruent triangles.

102.B Arcs and central angles

An ***arc*** is part of a circle. A ***minor arc*** is an arc that is less than "half" of a circle. A ***semicircle*** is an arc that is half of a circle, and a ***major arc*** is an arc that is more than half of a circle.

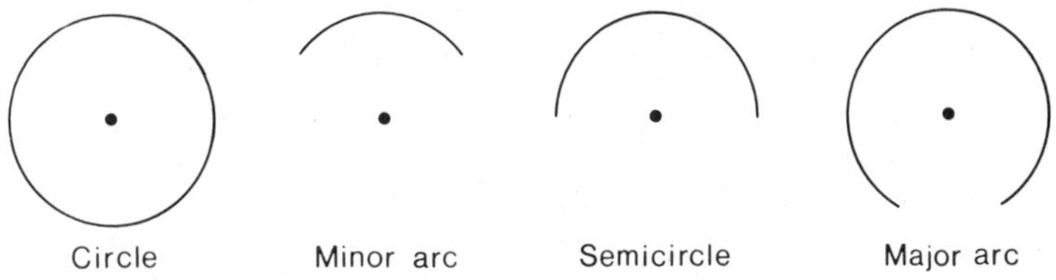

Two points on a circle that are exactly opposite each other lie on a diameter, and are connected by two semicircles. Two points on a circle that are not exactly opposite each other are connected by a major arc and a minor arc, as we show on the next page.

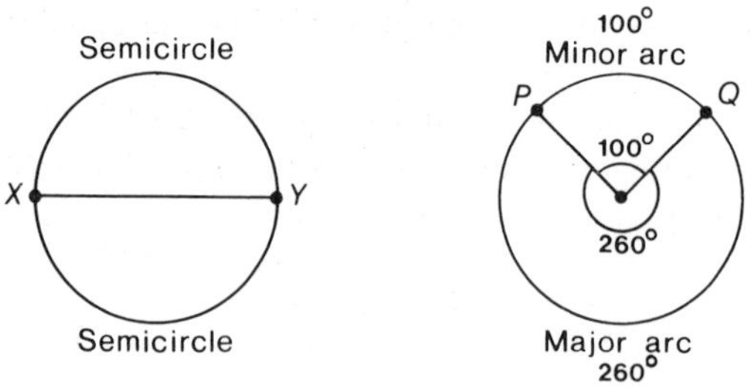

The ***central angle*** of an arc is formed by the radii to the endpoints of the arc. **By definition the angular measure of an arc is the same as the measure of its central angle.** In the figure on the right above the minor arc has a measure of 100° since its central angle has a measure of 100°. The major arc and its central angle both have a measure of 260°. In each case, the measures of the arcs and the measures of the central angles add to 360° because a full circle is divided into 360 degrees.

As we see, two points on a circle determine both a major arc and a minor arc. It is customary to use two letters to designate a minor arc and to use three letters to designate a major arc or a semicircle. The symbol $\overset{\frown}{BC}$ is read "arc BC" and the symbol $\overset{\frown}{ABC}$ is read "arc ABC."

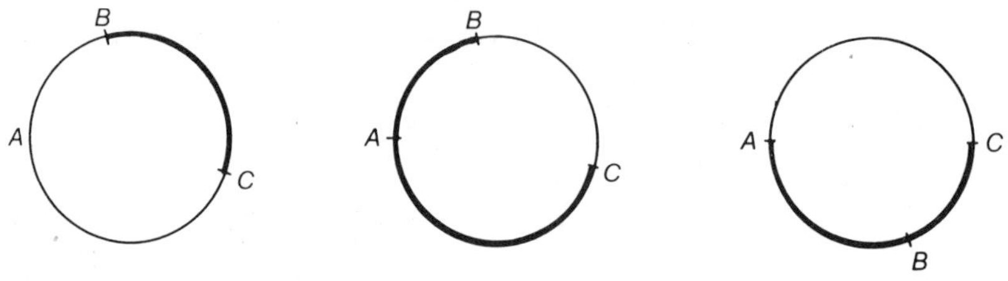

Minor arc *BC* Major arc *BAC* Semicircular arc *ABC*

We will define equal circles to be circles that have equal radii. Equal arcs are arcs of equal circles and are arcs that have the same measure. The notation

$$\overset{\frown}{BD} + \overset{\frown}{DC} = \overset{\frown}{BDC}$$

means that the measure of arc BD plus the measure of arc DC equals the measure of arc BDC.

Example 102.B.1 Prove that in the same circle or in equal circles, equal chords have equal arcs.

Solution Many proofs about circles are easy because the radii of equal circles are always equal. We draw two circles with equal radii and name them circle O and circle P. Next we draw equal chords AB and CD.

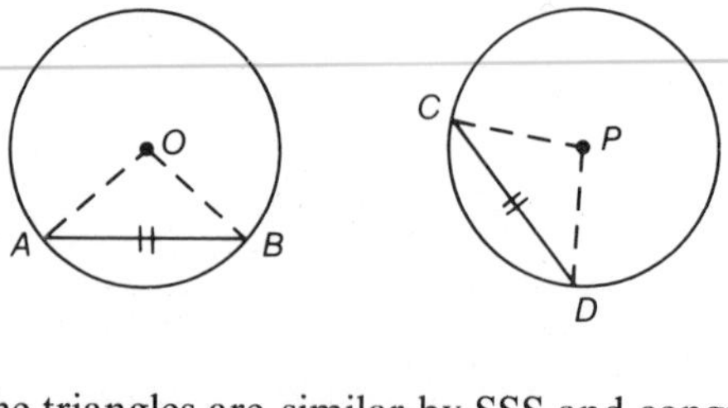

The radii are equal, so the triangles are similar by SSS and congruent because the scale factor is 1. Thus, the central angles AOB and CPD are equal by CPCTE. The arcs AB and CD must then be equal, for their measures are the same as the measures of the central angles.

Example 102.B.2 Prove that in the same circle or in equal circles, equal arcs have equal chords.

Solution We use figures similar to those used in the previous example. We draw two circles with equal radii and name them circle O and circle P. Next we draw the equal arcs AB and CD.

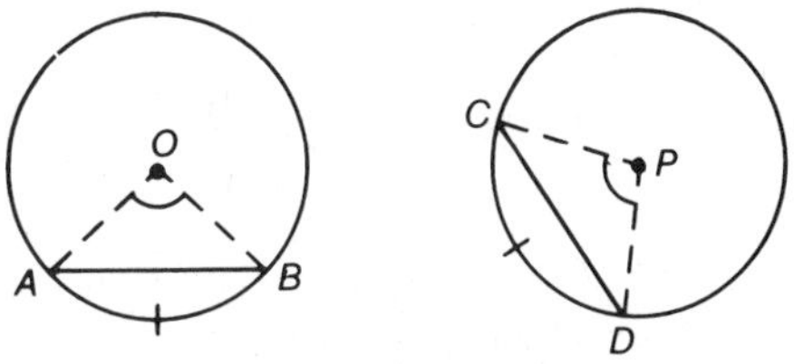

Since arcs AB and CD are equal, the central angles AOB and CPD are equal. The radii are equal, so the triangles AOB and CPD are similar by SAS with scale factor 1. Hence triangles AOB and CPD are congruent and AB and CD are equal since they are corresponding parts of congruent triangles.

Example 102.B.3 Prove that a diameter perpendicular to a chord bisects the chord and its arc.

Solution On the left below, we show circle O, and $\overline{AB} \perp \overline{CD}$. On the right, we connect the radii to the ends of the chord AB to form two triangles. We want to prove that $AZ = BZ$ and that $\overset{\frown}{AD} = \overset{\frown}{BD}$.

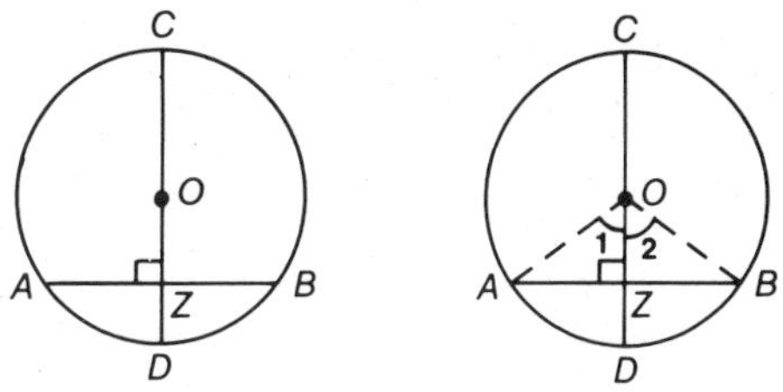

The two triangles are congruent since they are similar by HL and the scale factor equals 1. Thus side AZ equals side ZB. Also, angle 1 and angle 2 are equal, so the arcs AD and BD are equal because their central angles are equal.

Example 102.B.4 Prove that in the same circle or in equal circles, equal chords are equidistant from the center of the circle.

Solution This one is also easy because equal circles have equal radii. On the left below, we show circle O with equal chords AB and CD. On the right, we have drawn the radii to the ends of the chords, and have drawn the perpendicular bisectors of the chords. We want to prove $OX = OY$.

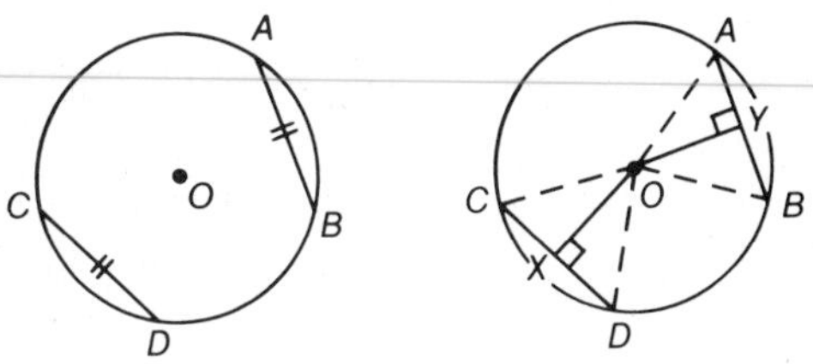

The large triangles ABO and CDO are similar by SSS and congruent because the scale factor is 1. Thus, the angles at A and C are equal by CPCTE. Triangles AYO and CXO are similar by AAA, and since sides AO and CO are equal radii, the triangles are congruent and side XO equals side YO by CPCTE.

Example 102.B.5 Given circle P whose radius is 7. Chord $YZ = 10$. Find PX.

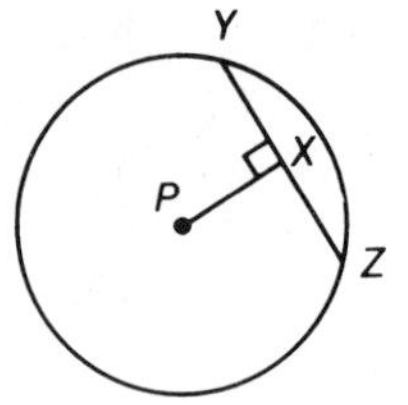

Solution If we draw either radius PY or PZ, we form a right triangle. We know that $\overline{PX}$ bisects $\overline{YZ}$, so $YX = XZ = 5$.

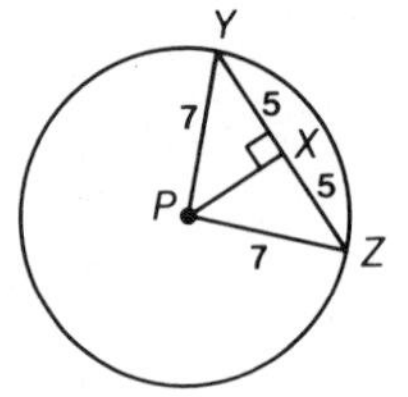

$$(PX)^2 + 5^2 = 7^2$$
$$(PX)^2 = 24$$
$$PX = \sqrt{24}$$
$$PX = \mathbf{2\sqrt{6}}$$

Problem set 102

1. The still-water speed of the boat was 3 times the speed of the current in the river. The boat could go 64 miles down the river in 1 hour less than it took to go 40 miles up the river. How fast was the current in the river and what was the still-water speed of the boat?

2. A crew of 7 workers could do c jobs in d days. How many workers would be needed to do 25 jobs in 11 days?

3. The big man could do 4 jobs in x days while the little man took k days to do m jobs. If they work together, how many jobs can they complete in 14 days?

4. There were w white ones, 4 red ones, and g green ones. How many different ways could they be arranged in a row?

5. The urn contained 5 red marbles and 4 black marbles. If two marbles are drawn without replacement, what is the probability that both are black?

6. Prove that tangents to a circle from a point outside the circle are of equal length.

7. Given: $AD = BE$; $DC = EC$
   Prove: $\angle ACF = \angle BCF$

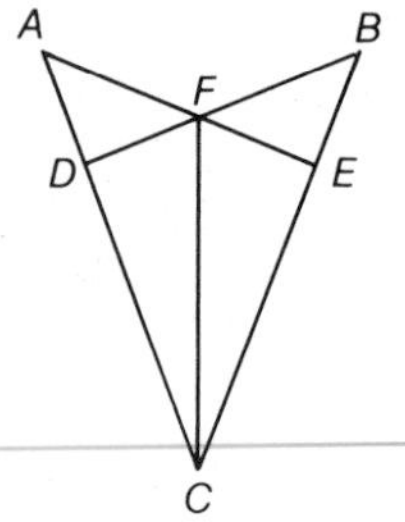

8. Prove that in the same circle or equal circles, equal chords have equal arcs.

9. Given: Diameter CD is perpendicular to chord AB in circle with center O as shown.
   Prove: $AZ = ZB$; $\overset{\frown}{AD} = \overset{\frown}{DB}$

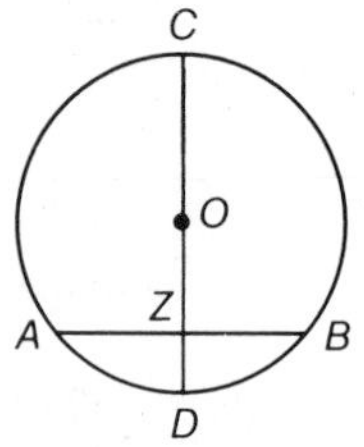

10. Prove that in the same circle or equal circles, equal chords are equidistant from the center of the circle.

11. Find the sixth term in the expansion of $(2x - y^2)^{14}$.

12. Find the fifth term in the expansion of $(2x + y^3)^8$.

13. Use base 10 logs to simplify: $\dfrac{(\sqrt[4]{6200 \times 10^6})^3}{\sqrt{2100 \times 10^4}}$

Solve for x:

14. $\log_3 (x + 2) < 3$

15. $\log_{1/4} (x - 1) < 2$

16. (*a*) Sketch the graph of $\theta = \arccos y$.
(*b*) Sketch the graph of $\theta = \text{arcsec } y$.

17. Use an infinite geometric series as an aid in expressing $0.0\overline{16}$ as a common fraction.

18. A ball is dropped from a height of 81 feet. After each bounce the ball rebounds two-thirds of the distance it fell. What is the total distance the ball will travel?

19. Find the diagonal AD in the rectangular solid shown.

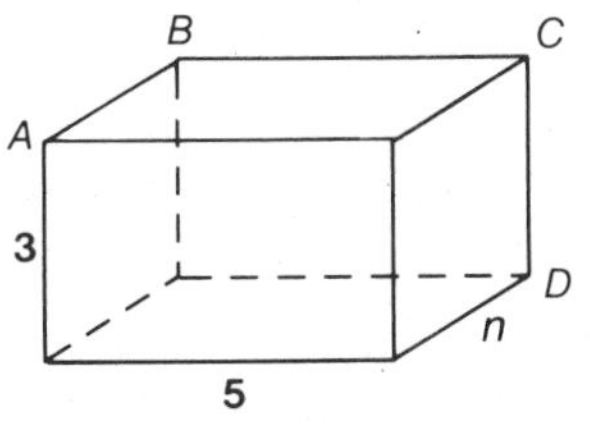

20. The base of a pyramid is a square whose perimeter is 20 centimeters. The height of the pyramid is 10 centimeters. Find the volume of the pyramid.

21. A sphere has a radius of r centimeters.
(*a*) Find the volume of the sphere.
(*b*) Find the surface area of the sphere.

22. What is the ratio of the lengths of the radii of two spheres if the ratio of the volumes of the spheres is 8 to 125?

23. (*a*) The base of a circular cone has a radius of 10 centimeters. The height of the cone is 9 centimeters. Find the volume of the cone.
(*b*) Assume the cone is a right circular cone. Find the surface area of the cone.

24. The equation of a hyperbola is $4x^2 - 9y^2 + 16x + 108y - 344 = 0$. Write the equation of the hyperbola in standard form and give the coordinates of the center, the coordinates of the vertices, and the equations of the asymptotes.

25. The equation of an ellipse is $16x^2 + 25y^2 - 300y + 500 = 0$. Write the equation of the ellipse in standard form. Give the coordinates of the center, the length of the major axis, and the length of the minor axis, and indicate whether the major axis is horizontal or vertical.

26. Solve this triangle for angle A.

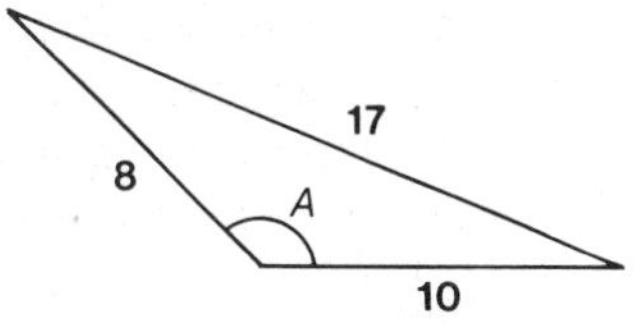

27. Use the identity for $\sin x \cos y$ to find $\sin 15° \cos 285°$. Use exact values.

28. Solve, given that $(0° \le x < 360°)$: $2\cos^2 x + \sqrt{3}\cos x = 0$

29. Show that: $\dfrac{\cot x}{\cot x - 1} - \dfrac{\tan x}{\tan x + 1} = \dfrac{\cot x + \tan x}{\cot x - \tan x}$

30. Solve: $\dfrac{1}{3}\log_2 27 - \log_2 (x - 2) = -\log_2 x$

EP 102.75, 102.76

LESSON 103 *Synthetic division · Zeros and roots*

103.A Synthetic division

In mathematics we use the word **algorithm** to describe a repetitive computational procedure. Thus, the way we do long division can be called a ***long division algorithm.*** On the left below, we use the standard long division algorithm to divide $x^4 + x^2 + 2x - 1$ by $x + 3$. On the right, we repeat the problem, but this time we omit the variables.

$$
\begin{array}{r|l}
 & x^3 - 3x^2 + 10x - 28 \\
\hline
x + 3 & x^4 + 0x^3 + x^2 + 2x - 1 \\
 & \underline{x^4 + 3x^3} \\
 & \quad -3x^3 + x^2 \\
 & \quad \underline{-3x^3 - 9x^2} \\
 & \qquad 10x^2 + 2x \\
 & \qquad \underline{10x^2 + 30x} \\
 & \qquad\quad -28x - 1 \\
 & \qquad\quad \underline{-28x - 84} \\
 & \qquad\qquad 83 \text{ (remainder)}
\end{array}
\qquad
\begin{array}{r|l}
 & 1 - 3 + 10 - 28 \\
\hline
1 + 3 & 1 + 0 + 1 + 2 - 1 \\
 & \underline{\textcircled{1} + 3} \\
 & \quad -3 + 1 \\
 & \quad \underline{\textcircled{-3} - 9} \\
 & \qquad 10 + 2 \\
 & \qquad \underline{\textcircled{10} + 30} \\
 & \qquad\quad -28 - 1 \\
 & \qquad\quad \underline{\textcircled{-28} - 84} \\
 & \qquad\qquad 83 \text{ (remainder)}
\end{array}
$$

We focus our attention on the numbers that have been circled and note that they are repetitions of the numbers in the line directly above them Furthermore, each of the circled numbers is a repetition of the coefficients of the variables in the quotient. These numbers are the keys to this division process. If we omit the number 1 in the divisor and other non-key numbers, we can write the whole process in compact form, as we show on the left.

$$
\begin{array}{r|rrrrr}
3 & 1 & 0 & 1 & 2 & -1 \\
 & & 3 & -9 & 30 & -84 \\
\hline
 & 1 & -3 & 10 & -28 & 83
\end{array}
\qquad\qquad
\begin{array}{r|rrrrr}
-3 & 1 & 0 & 1 & 2 & -1 \\
 & & -3 & 9 & -30 & 84 \\
\hline
 & 1 & -3 & 10 & -28 & 83
\end{array}
$$

(Remainder: 83) (Remainder: 83)

The entries in the bottom line on the left were obtained by subtracting. If we change the sign of the divisor to -3, we can obtain the same bottom line by adding, as we show on the right. This algorithm for division is called ***synthetic division.*** We restrict its use to linear divisors of the form $x \pm a$, where a is a positive real number.

Example 103.A.1 Use synthetic division to divide $-4x^2 + 13 + x^3$ by $-3 + x$.

Solution Before we begin we restate the problem with the polynomials written in descending powers of the variable.

$$x^3 - 4x^2 + 13 \qquad \text{divided by} \qquad x - 3$$

We will use $+3$ as a synthetic divisor because we are dividing by $x - 3$. We record the coefficients of the polynomial and use zero as the coefficient of the missing x term. Then we **bring down** the first coefficient.

$$\begin{array}{r|rrrr} 3 & 1 & -4 & 0 & 13 \\ & & & & \\ \hline & 1 & & & \end{array} \qquad \text{bring down 1}$$

The rest of the steps are **multiply, record,** and **add** steps. We multiply 1 by 3, record under the -4, and add.

$$\begin{array}{r|rrrr} 3 & 1 & -4 & 0 & 13 \\ & & 3 & & \\ \hline & 1 & -1 & & \end{array} \qquad \text{multiply, record, add}$$

Now we multiply -1 by 3, record, and add.

$$\begin{array}{r|rrrr} 3 & 1 & -4 & 0 & 13 \\ & & 3 & -3 & \\ \hline & 1 & -1 & -3 & \end{array} \qquad \text{multiply, record, add}$$

Now we multiply -3 by 3, record, and add.

$$\begin{array}{r|rrrr} 3 & 1 & -4 & 0 & 13 \\ & & 3 & -3 & -9 \\ \hline & 1 & -1 & -3 & 4 \end{array} \qquad \text{multiply, record, add}$$

The first three numbers in the bottom row are the coefficients of the quotient polynomial, and the last number is the remainder. **The quotient polynomial has a degree which is always 1 less than the degree of the original polynomial,** and the quotient polynomial is sometimes called the ***depressed polynomial.*** Thus our result is

$$\frac{x^3 - 4x^2 + 13}{x - 3} = \mathbf{x^2 - x - 3 + \frac{4}{x - 3}}$$

Example 103.A.2 Divide $2x^4 + x^2 + 2x - 1$ by $x + 3$.

Solution First we check to ensure that both polynomials are written in descending powers of the variable. They are, so we record **a synthetic divisor of -3** and remember to write a zero as the coefficient of x^3. **We begin by bringing down** the first coefficient.

$$\begin{array}{r|rrrrr} -3 & 2 & 0 & 1 & 2 & -1 \\ & & & & & \\ \hline & 2 & & & & \end{array} \qquad \text{bring down 2}$$

Now we **multiply, record,** and **add** until the process is complete.

$$\begin{array}{r|rrrrr} -3 & 2 & 0 & 1 & 2 & -1 \\ & & -6 & 18 & -57 & 165 \\ \hline & 2 & -6 & 19 & -55 & 164 \end{array}$$

Thus we get

$$\frac{2x^4 + x^2 + 2x - 1}{x + 3} = \mathbf{2x^3 - 6x^2 + 19x - 55 + \frac{164}{x + 3}}$$

103.B Zeros and roots

The words **zero** and **root** can be confusing because they mean almost the same thing. The word **zero** is used with the word **polynomial,** and the word **root** is used with the word **equation.** On the left below, we show a polynomial, and on the right, we use the same polynomial to write a polynomial equation.

POLYNOMIAL	POLYNOMIAL EQUATION
$x^2 + 5x + 6$	$x^2 + 5x + 6 = 0$

We can write each of the polynomials as a product of factors, as we show here.

$$(x + 3)(x + 2) \qquad (x + 3)(x + 2) = 0$$

If we replace x with either -3 or -2, the expression on the left will equal 0, and the equation on the right will be a true equation. We will demonstrate this by replacing x with -3.

$$(-3 + 3)(-3 + 2) \qquad (-3 + 3)(-3 + 2) = 0$$

$$(0)(-1) \qquad (0)(-1) = 0$$

$$0 \qquad 0 = 0$$

Thus, we say that -3 is a ***zero* of the polynomial** because replacing x with -3 gives the polynomial a value of zero. Also, -3 is a ***root* of the equation** because replacing x with -3 makes the equation a true equality. The difference might seem trivial, but it is not trivial because polynomials do not have roots and equations do not have zeros. It is the other way around.

If we perform the division shown here,

$$\frac{x^2 + 5x + 6}{x + 3} = x + 2$$

we get a quotient of $x + 2$ with no remainder because $x + 3$ is a factor of $x^2 + 5x + 6$, and therefore -3 is a zero of the polynomial. If we use synthetic division to do the division, we see that the remainder is zero.

$$\begin{array}{r|rrr} -3 & 1 & 5 & 6 \\ & & -3 & -6 \\ \hline & 1 & 2 & 0 \end{array} \quad \text{remainder of zero}$$

This zero remainder tells us that -3 is a zero of the polynomial. This demonstrates the way we use synthetic division to see if a given number is a zero of a polynomial.

Example 103.B.1 Use synthetic division to see if -2 is a zero of $x^4 - 2x^3 + 5x - 10$.

Solution We divide by -2.

$$\begin{array}{r|rrrrr} -2 & 1 & -2 & 0 & 5 & -10 \\ & & -2 & 8 & -16 & 22 \\ \hline & 1 & -4 & 8 & -11 & 12 \end{array}$$

The remainder is not zero, so -2 is not a zero of the polynomial.

Example 103.B.2 Use synthetic division to see if -3 is a root of the polynomial equation $2x^4 - 32x = 0$.

Solution The first step is to bring down the coefficient of x^4. Then we repeatedly multiply, record, and add.

$$\begin{array}{r|rrrrr} -3 & 2 & 0 & 0 & -32 & 0 \\ & & -6 & 18 & -54 & 258 \\ \hline & 2 & -6 & 18 & -86 & 258 \end{array}$$

The remainder is not 0, but 258, so -3 is not a root of the polynomial equation.

Problem set 103

1. The trip out was 600 miles. The trip back was also 600 miles, but it took longer because the return speed was only one-third of the outgoing speed. If the round trip took 40 hours, what were the two speeds?

2. After traveling h hours at k miles per hour, the caravan stopped for a rest. If the entire trip was 400 miles, how far did they have to go after they had rested?

3. The half-life of the things was 14 years. If they began with 10,000, how long would it take until only 4000 were still alive?

4. An urn contains 7 red marbles and 4 white marables. Two marbles are drawn without replacement. What is the probability that the marbles are red and white in that order?

5. The radius of the wheel was k inches. The wheel had an angular velocity of r radians per second. What was the velocity of the wheel in meters per hour?

6. Use synthetic division to divide $x^3 - 5x^2 + 12$ by $x - 2$.

7. Use synthetic division to divide $4x^4 - 4x^3 + x^2 - 3x + 2$ by $x + 2$.

8. Use synthetic division to see if -1 is a zero of $x^3 + 2x^2 - 3x - 4$.

9. Use synthetic division to see if -2 is a root of the following polynomial equation: $2x^3 - x^2 + 2x - 4 = 0$

10. Prove that tangents to a circle from a point outside the circle are of equal length.

11. Given: $\angle 1 = \angle 2$; $CD = CE$
Prove: $AF = BF$

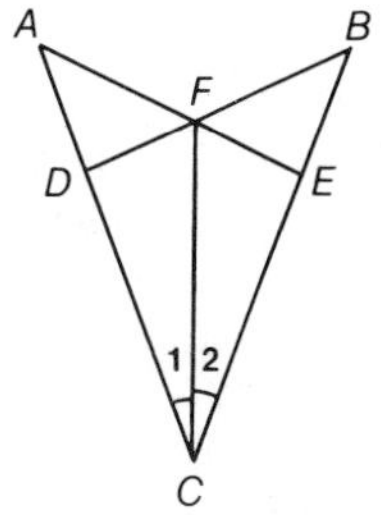

12. Prove that in the same circle or equal circles, equal arcs have equal chords.

13. Using the figure shown, prove that if a diameter bisects an arc, then it is the perpendicular bisector of the chord which joins the endpoints of the arc.

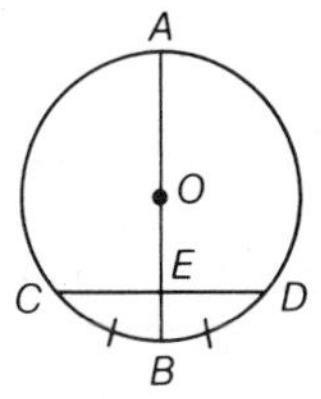

14. Find the fifth term in the expansion of $(2x^2 - y^3)^{15}$.

15. Find the fourth term in the expansion of $(3x^3 - y^2)^8$.

16. Find the distance from $(4, -1)$ to $x + y = 5$.

17. What is the pH of a solution whose concentration of hydrogen ions is 6.3×10^{-4} mole per liter?

Solve for x:

18. $\log_4 (2x - 1) < 2$

19. $\log_{1/3} (2x + 1) < 2$

20. (*a*) Sketch the graph of $\theta = \arcsin y$.
(*b*) Sketch the graph of $\theta = \arccos y$.

21. Use an infinite geometric series as an aid for expressing $0.0\overline{13}$ as a common fraction.

22. (*a*) The base of a circular cone has a radius of 6 centimeters. The height of the cone is 10 centimeters. What is the volume of the cone?
(*b*) Assume the cone is a right circular cone. What is the surface area of the cone?

23. The base of a pyramid is a regular 9-sided polygon whose perimeter is 27 centimeters. If the height of the pyramid is 3 centimeters, what is the volume of the pyramid?

24. What is the sum of the exterior angles of a regular 29-sided polygon?

25. The equation of an ellipse is $36x^2 + 9y^2 = 216x$. Write the equation of the ellipse in standard form. Give the coordinates of the center, the length of the major axis, and the length of the minor axis, and indicate whether the major axis is horizontal or vertical.

26. Use the identity for $\cos x - \cos y$ to find the exact value of $\cos 285° - \cos 15°$.

27. Solve, given that $(0° \leq x < 360°)$: $2 \sin^2 x + \sin x - 1 = 0$

28. Show that: $\dfrac{\tan x}{\tan x - 1} - \dfrac{\cot x}{\cot x + 1} = \dfrac{\tan x + \cot x}{\tan x - \cot x}$

29. Use log tables to find $\log_5 3$.

30. Evaluate: $36^{\log_6 3}$

EP 103.77, 103.78

LESSON 104 The general conic equation

104.A Equations of conics

The general equation of all conic sections is the equation

$$ax^2 + bxy + cy^2 + dx + ey + f = 0$$

If the coefficients a, b, and c are zero and the coefficients d and e are not both zero, then the result is an equation such as

$$4x + 2y + 5 = 0 \qquad \text{STRAIGHT LINE}$$

which is the equation of a straight line. If the coefficients b and c are zero and the coefficients a and e are not zero, then the result is an equation such as

$$x^2 + 4x - y + 1 = 0 \qquad \text{PARABOLA}$$

which is the equation of a parabola. We can change the form of this equation by completing the square and can write the equation in standard form as

$$y = (x + 2)^2 - 3 \qquad \text{PARABOLA}$$

If b equals zero and the constants a and c are equal, we get an equation such as

$$x^2 + y^2 - 8x - 4y + 11 = 0 \qquad \text{CIRCLE}$$

This is the equation of a circle and can be rewritten in standard form. The standard form of this equation is

$$(x + 4)^2 + (y - 2)^2 = 9 \qquad \text{CIRCLE}$$

If $b = 0$, a and c are both positive or both negative, and a is not equal to c, the equation is the equation of an ellipse.

$$4x^2 + 3y^2 + 4x - 2y = 0 \qquad \text{ELLIPSE}$$

If $b = 0$, and a and c have opposite signs, the equation is the equation of a hyperbola. In the following equation, the coefficients 4 and -3 have opposite signs, so the equation is the equation of a hyperbola.

$$4x^2 - 3y^2 + 4x - 3y + 7 = 0 \qquad \text{HYPERBOLA}$$

If b is not zero, the equation will have an xy term. If a conic equation contains an xy term, we know that the graph of the function is inclined to the x and y axes, which is the same thing as saying that the axes of the function have been rotated. The equations of these rotated figures are similar to the equation shown below.

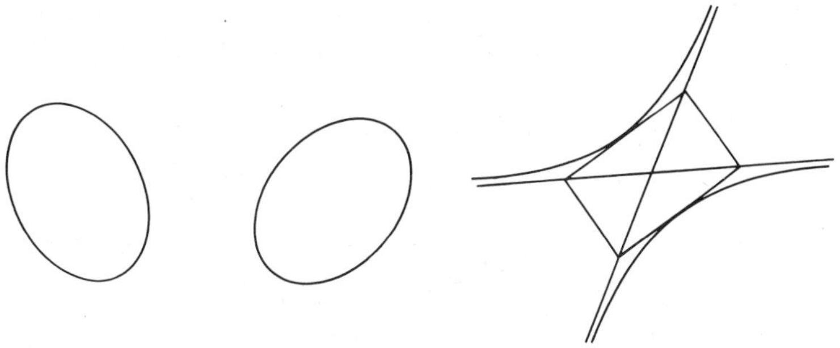

$$3x^2 + 4xy \pm 2y^2 - 4x + 3y + 7 = 0 \qquad \text{ROTATED}$$

With one exception, we will reserve the study of rotated figures until the next course. The exception is the conic whose equation contains only an xy term and a constant such as

$$xy = 5 \qquad \text{and} \qquad xy = -5 \qquad \text{ROTATED}$$

These equations are often encountered. They are equations of hyperbolas that lie in the first and third quadrants or in the second and fourth quadrants. The asymptotes for these hyperbolas are the x and y axes.

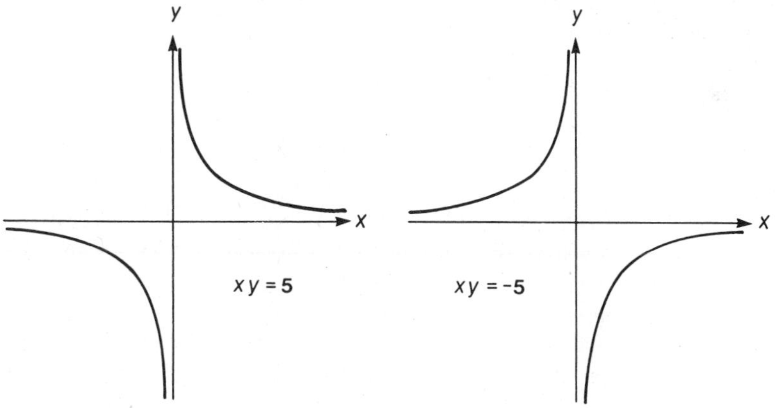

These equations can be graphed quite easily by making a table, selecting values of x, and then solving for the matching values of y.

Example 104.A.1 Graph $xy = -4$.

Solution We recognize this as the equation of a hyperbola which has the x and y axes as asymptotes. We begin by making a table and selecting values of x.

x	1	2	-2	4	-4	-1
y						

Now we use the equation to find the paired values of y.

IF $x = 1$	IF $x = 2$	IF $x = -2$
$(1)y = -4$	$(2)y = -4$	$(-2)y = -4$
$y = -4$	$y = -2$	$y = 2$
IF $x = 4$	IF $x = -4$	IF $x = -1$
$4y = -4$	$(-4)y = -4$	$(-1)y = -4$
$y = -1$	$y = 1$	$y = 4$

We graph these points and sketch the curve.

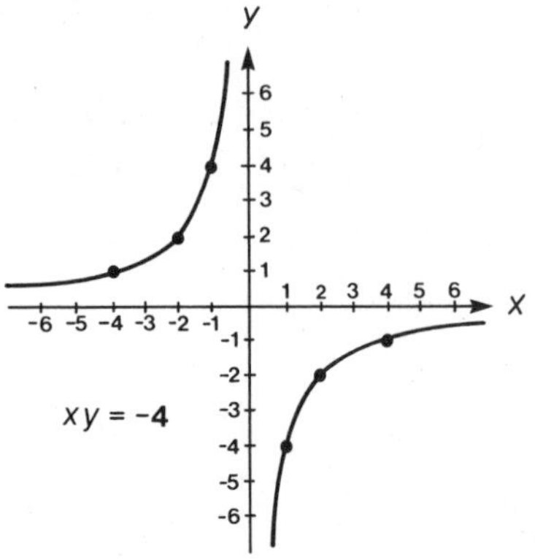

If the equation had been $xy = 4$, the curves would have been graphed in the first and third quadrants. Try a few points and see.

Example 104.A.2 The following equations are the equations of a circle, a parabola, an ellipse, and a hyperbola. Tell which is which and why, and then complete the square on the equation of the ellipse and describe it.

$$(a)\quad x^2 + 2y + 3x + 5 = 0$$
$$(b)\quad 2x^2 + 3x - 2y + 2y^2 + 3 = 0$$
$$(c)\quad 2x^2 - 3y^2 + 7x + 4y + 5 = 0$$
$$(d)\quad 9x^2 + 4y^2 + 36x - 24y + 36 = 0$$

Solution Equation (*a*) is a parabola because it has only one squared term. Equation (*b*) is a circle because there is no xy term and the coefficients of x^2 and y^2 are equal. Equation (*c*) is a hyperbola because the signs of the x^2 term and the y^2 term are different. Equation (*d*) is the equation of an ellipse because the coefficients of the x^2 term and y^2 term have the same sign but different absolute values. We use parentheses to help us complete the square.

$9x^2 + 4y^2 + 36x - 24y + 36 = 0$	equation of an ellipse
$(9x^2 + 36x \quad\;) + (4y^2 - 24y \quad\;) = -36$	rearranged
$9(x^2 + 4x \quad\;) + 4(y^2 - 6y \quad\;) = -36$	factored
$9(x^2 + 4x + 4) + 4(y^2 - 6y + 9) = -36 + 36 + 36$	completed the square twice
$9(x + 2)^2 + 4(y - 3)^2 = 36$	simplified
$\dfrac{(x + 2)^2}{4} + \dfrac{(y - 3)^2}{9} = 1$	divided by 36

This is the equation of an ellipse whose major axis is vertical and has a length of 6, whose minor axis has a length of 4, and whose center is at $(-2, 3)$.

Problem set 104

1. The volume of the hubbub varied linearly with the number who joined in. When 4 joined in, the volume of the hubbub measured 60 units; but it only measured 30 units when 2 joined in. What would the volume of the hubbub measure if 10 joined in?

2. The big container contained a solution that was 10% glycerine. The little container contained a solution that was 40% glycerine. How much should be used from each container to get 300 milliliters of a solution that is 30% glycerine?

3. The sports car was twice as fast as the truck and made the trip in 3 fewer hours than did the truck. If the truck traveled at 50 miles per hour, how long was the trip?

4. Find three consecutive even integers such that the product of the first and the third is 24 less than 9 times the second.

5. Bob's age 10 years ago equaled the current age of John, but 10 years from now 3 times Bob's age will be 16 less than 4 times John's age. How old are both boys now?

6. Graph $xy = 4$.

7. Indicate whether each of the equations represents an ellipse, a hyperbola, a circle, or a parabola.

   (*a*) $x^2 + y^2 - 4x = 0$ (*b*) $4x^2 + 9y^2 = 1$ (*c*) $4x^2 - y^2 = 4$
   (*d*) $x^2 + 2x - 8y - 3 = 0$ (*e*) $x^2 + y^2 + 8x - 6y - 15 = 0$

8. Write equation (*e*) of Problem 7 in standard form and describe the conic section which the equation represents.

9. Use synthetic division to divide $x^4 - 3x^2 - 2x + 1$ by $x - 1$.

10. Use synthetic division to divide $x^3 - 2x^2 + x - 3$ by $x - 2$.

11. Use synthetic division to see if -2 is a root of the following polynomial equation: $x^3 + 2x^2 - 3x - 6 = 0$

12. Use synthetic division to see if -2 is a zero of $x^3 - 2x^2 - 4x + 3$.

13. Given: $\angle 1 = \angle 2$; $CD = CE$
    Prove: $AC = BC$

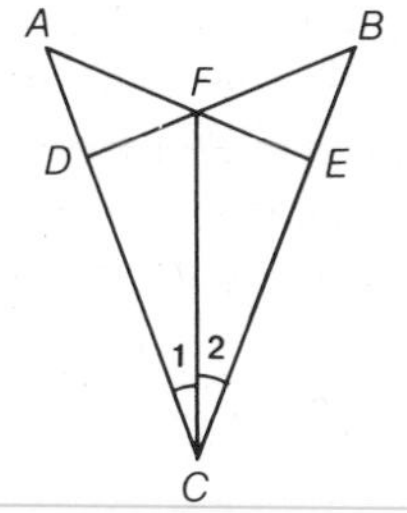

14. Prove that if a diameter of a circle bisects an arc, then it is the perpendicular bisector of the chord which joins the endpoints of the arc.

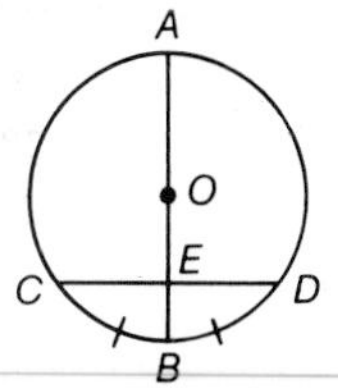

15. Given: P, Q, R, S are midpoints of $\overline{AD}$, $\overline{AB}$, $\overline{BC}$, and $\overline{CD}$, respectively.
    Prove: $PQRS$ is a parallelogram.

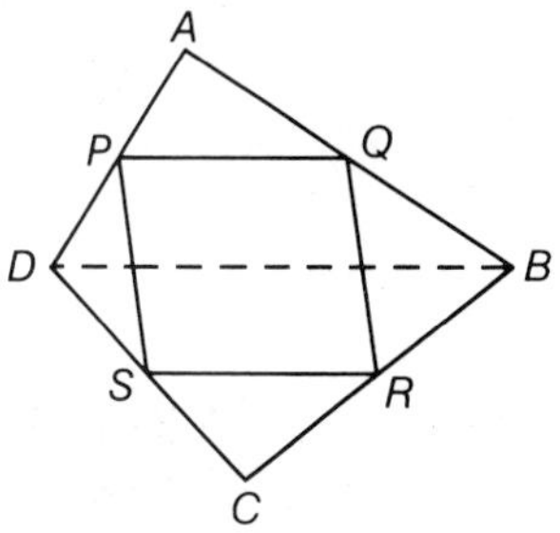

16. Prove that in the same circle or in equal circles, equal chords have equal arcs.

17. Find the fourth term in the expansion of $(2x^2 - y^4)^8$.

18. Use base 10 logs to simplify: $\dfrac{(\sqrt[3]{5100 \times 10^5})^4}{\sqrt{3610 \times 10^4}}$

19. The concentration of hydrogen ions in a solution is 4.3×10^{-4} mole per liter. Find the pH of the solution.

20. Solve for x: $\log_{1/2}(x - 3) < 3$

21. Find the thirteenth term of an arithmetic sequence whose fifth term is 17 and whose tenth term is 42.

22. A sphere has a radius of 8 centimeters.
(*a*) Find the volume of the sphere.
(*b*) Find the surface area of the sphere.

23. Two geometric solids are similar. The length of a side of the larger geometric solid is $2\frac{1}{2}$ times as long as the corresponding side of the smaller geometric solid. What is the ratio of the volume of the larger geometric solid to the volume of the smaller geometric solid?

24. Use the matrix echelon method to solve: $\begin{cases} 2x - 3y - z = 4 \\ x - 2y + 2z = 5 \\ 3x - y + z = 5 \end{cases}$

25. Solve this triangle for side a.

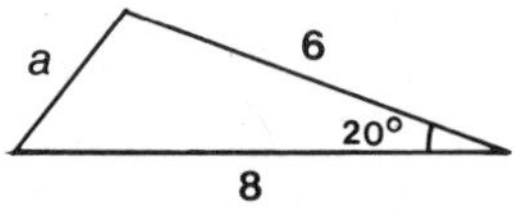

26. Use the identity for $\cos x \cos y$ to find $\cos 315° \cos 15°$. Use exact values.

27. Show that: $\dfrac{\cot^2 x + \sec^2 x + 1}{\cot^2 x} = \sec^4 x$

28. Solve, given that $(0° \le \theta < 360°)$: $-\sqrt{3} - \tan 3\theta = 0$

29. Evaluate: $81^{\log_3 2}$

30. Express $\log_6 5$ in terms of common logarithms. Do not find a numerical answer.

EP 104.79, 104.80

LESSON 105 Inscribed angles

105.A Inscribed angles

An ***inscribed angle*** is an angle whose vertex is on a circle and whose sides are chords of the circle. We can prove that the measure of an inscribed angle is equal to one-half the measure of the arc that it intercepts. To avoid clumsy language, we will often use notations such as

$$\angle X = \widehat{ABC}$$

which states that an angle is equal to an arc. **We emphasize that this notation means that the measure of the angle equals the measure of the arc.** In the three circles shown here, note that the measures of the central angles equal the measures of the intercepted arcs.

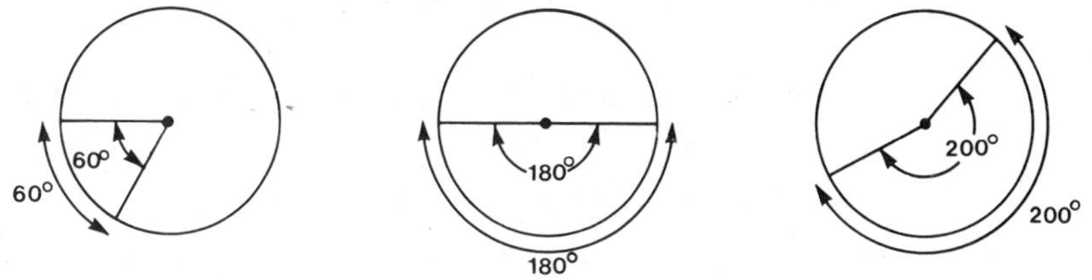

In each of the following circles we show an inscribed angle that intercepts the same arc as does the central angle in the corresponding figure above. **We note that the measure of each inscribed angle is only one-half the measure of the intercepted arc.**

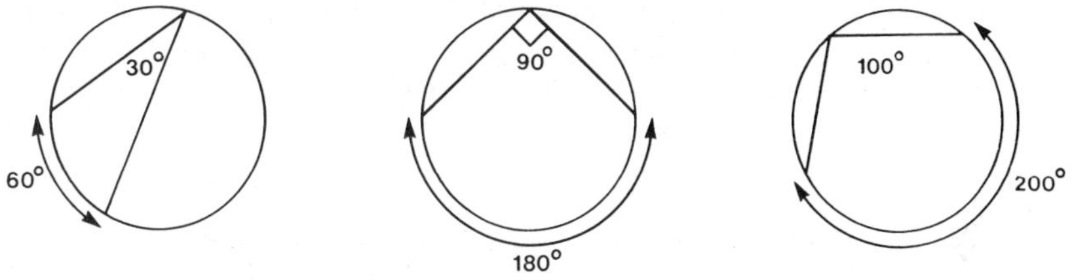

Three different proofs are required for this theorem since the center of the circle can lie on a side of the angle (Case I), the center can lie inside the angle (Case II), or the center can lie outside the angle (Case III).

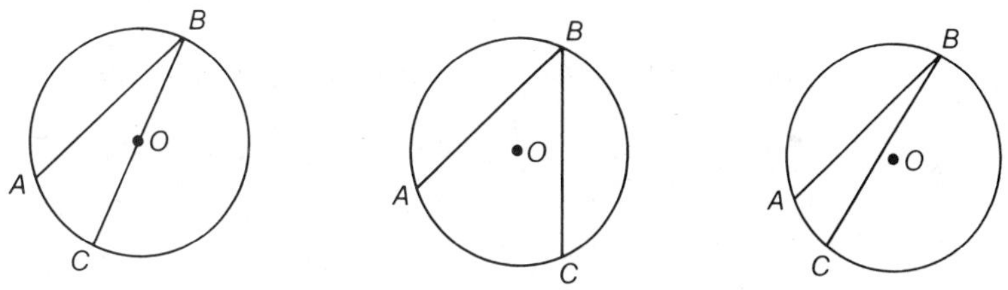

CASE I CASE II CASE III

Example 105.A.1 Prove Case I.

Solution We draw the radius from A and label the angles 1, 2, and 3 as shown. We want to show that $\angle 2 = \frac{1}{2}\overset{\frown}{AC}$.

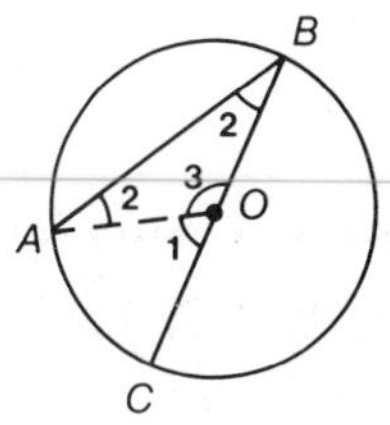

The angles labeled 2 are equal because they are the base angles of an isosceles triangle. These angles and angle 3 sum to 180° (triangle), and angle 3 and angle 1 sum to 180° (straight angle). Thus,

$$\angle 2 = \frac{1}{2}\angle 1 \quad \text{so} \quad \angle 2 = \frac{1}{2}\overset{\frown}{AC}$$

This shows that if one side of an inscribed angle is a diameter, the measure of the angle equals half the measure of the intercepted arc.

Example 105.A.2 Prove Case II.

Solution We want to prove that the measure of angle ABD is one-half the measure of arc AD.

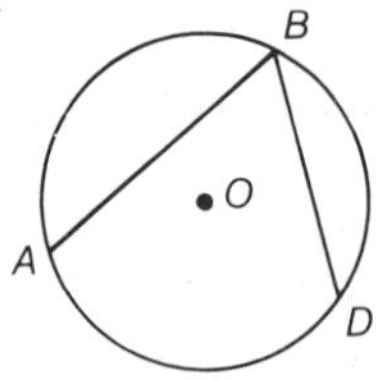

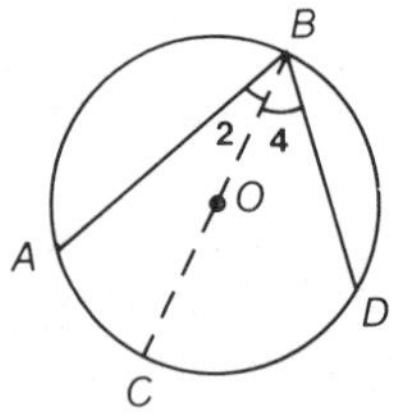

We draw the diameter BC so we can use the result of the proof of Case I. An inscribed angle whose side is a diameter equals half the intercepted arc. Thus

$$\angle 2 = \frac{1}{2}\overparen{AC} \qquad \text{and} \qquad \angle 4 = \frac{1}{2}\overparen{CD}$$

If we add these two equations, we get

$$\angle 2 + \angle 4 = \frac{1}{2}(\overparen{AC} + \overparen{CD}) \qquad \text{added}$$

But angle 2 plus angle 4 equals angle ABD, and $\overparen{AC} + \overparen{CD}$ equals $\overparen{AD}$. If we make these substitutions, we have our proof as we get

$$\angle ABD = \frac{1}{2}\overparen{AD}$$

Example 105.A.3 Prove Case III.

Solution We want to prove that the measure of the angle at B is one-half the measure of arc AC.

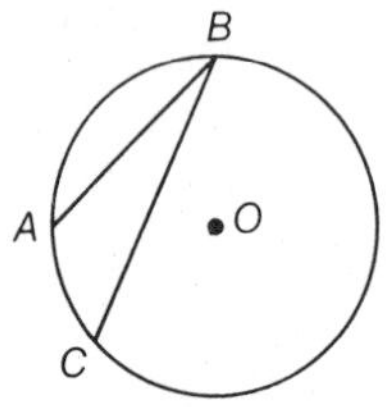

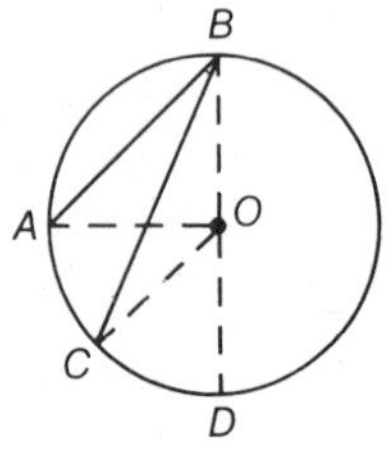

We draw the diameter BD and other lines so we can use the results of Case I. From Case I, we can say

$$\begin{array}{rll} \angle ABD &= \frac{1}{2}\overparen{ACD} & \text{from Case I} \\ \angle CBD &= \frac{1}{2}\overparen{CD} & \text{from Case I} \\ \hline \angle ABD - \angle CBD &= \frac{1}{2}(\overparen{ACD} - \overparen{CD}) & \text{subtracted} \end{array}$$

Since angle ABD minus angle CBD equals angle ABC, and arc ACD minus arc CD equals arc AC, we can make two substitutions and get

$$\angle ABC = \frac{1}{2}\overparen{AC} \qquad \text{substituted}$$

We have proved that an inscribed angle equals half its intercepted arc. This leads to the following corollaries.

1. If two inscribed angles intercept the same arc, then the angles are equal.

Angle 1 equals half of arc BD and angle 2 equals half of arc BD, so angles 1 and 2 are equal angles.

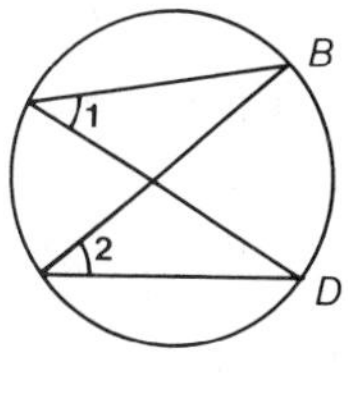

2. If a quadrilateral is inscribed in a circle, the sum of a pair of opposite angles is 180°.

The sides of angles D and F meet at E and G and intercept arcs GDE and GFE, which sum to 360°. Therefore angle D plus angle F equals 180°.

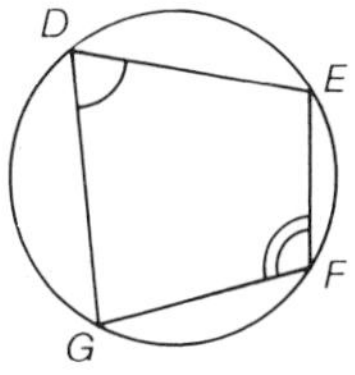

3. An angle inscribed in a semicircle is a right angle.

$\overline{AB}$ is a diameter and thus arcs AXB and AMB both equal 180°. Therefore angles X and M equal 90°.

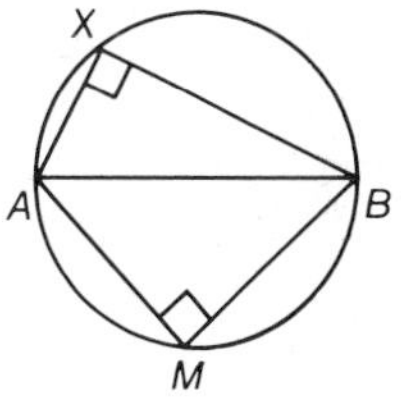

Example 105.A.4 Find x, y, and z.

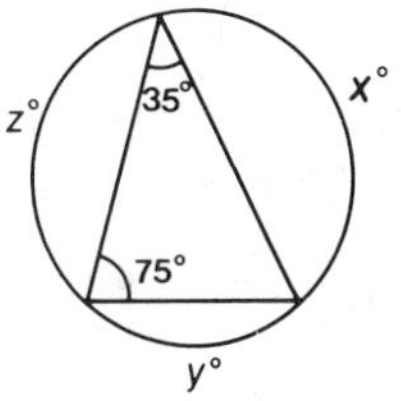

Solution Arc x measures twice the 75° inscribed angle so x equals 150. In the same way, y must equal 70 so x and y sum to 220. Then z makes up the rest of 360° so z equals 140.

Example 105.A.5 Find x, y, and z.

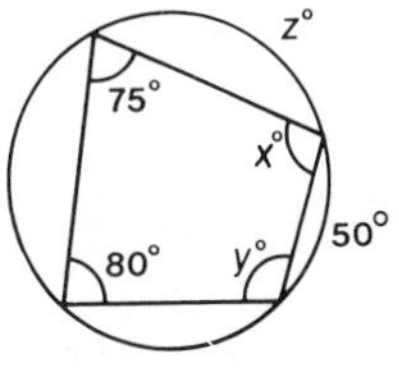

Solution z plus 50 equals 2 times 80.

$$z + 50 = 2 \cdot 80 \longrightarrow z + 50 = 160 \longrightarrow \mathbf{z = 110}$$

Since opposite angles in an inscribed quadrilateral sum to 180°, we can solve for x and y.

$$x + 80 = 180 \qquad y + 75 = 180$$

$$\text{so} \quad \mathbf{x = 100} \qquad \text{so} \quad \mathbf{y = 105}$$

Problem set 105

1. The increase was exponential and 5 hours after the beginning their number had increased to 260. Jim didn't begin to worry until a total of 10 hours after the beginning, when he noted that their number was 380. How long after the beginning would their number be 2000?

2. At noon the hands of the clock pointed in the same direction. What time would it be the next time the hands of the clock pointed in the same direction?

3. Marsha had a great big container that contained 40 liters of a solution that was 5% salt. How many liters of a 20% salt solution should Marsha add to get a 10% salt solution?

4. Prairie Dog trotted for a while at 10 miles per hour and walked the rest of the 152-mile trip at 4 miles per hour. If it took him 20 hours to complete the trip, how far did he trot and how far did he walk?

5. The ratio of the weak to the strong was 7 to 10, and 10 times the number of strong exceeded 4 times the number of weak by 216. When all was said and done, how many were weak and how many were strong?

6. Given: $\angle ABC$ is an inscribed angle as shown.
Prove: $\angle ABC = \frac{1}{2}\overset{\frown}{AC}$

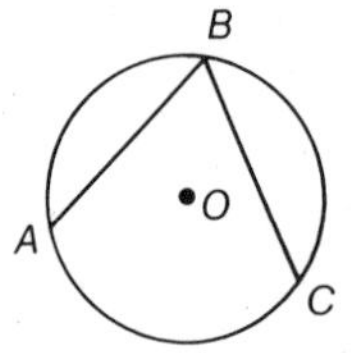

7. Given: The figure as shown.
Prove: $\triangle BAE \sim \triangle DCE$

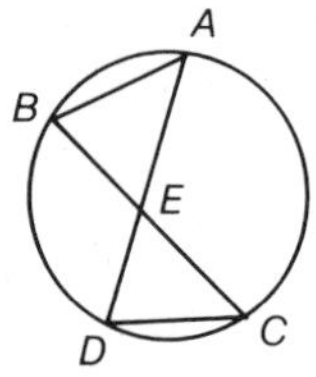

8. Given: $\angle 1 = \angle 2$; $CD = CE$
Prove: $AF = BF$

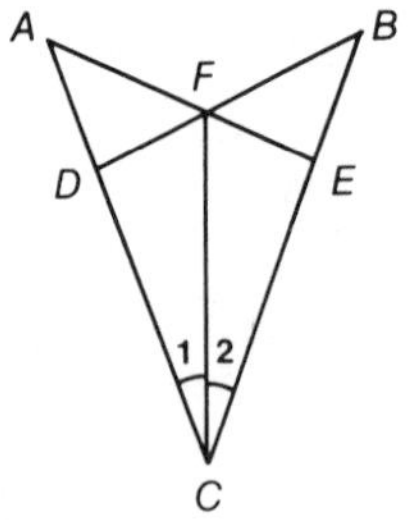

9. Find x, y, and z.

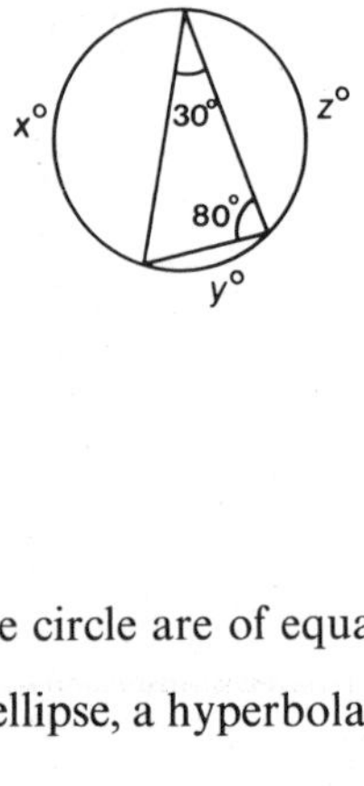

10. Prove that tangents to a circle from a point outside the circle are of equal length.

11. Indicate whether each of these equations represents an ellipse, a hyperbola, a circle, or a parabola.
(a) $x^2 + y^2 + 6x - 4y - 15 = 0$ (b) $x^2 + 6x + 4y + 5 = 0$
(c) $9x^2 - 4y^2 + 54x + 8y + 41 = 0$ (d) $x^2 - 4y^2 = 4$
(e) $16x^2 + 9y^2 = 144$

12. Graph $xy = 8$.

13. Write equation (c) of Problem 11 in standard form and describe the conic section it defines.

14. Use synthetic division to divide $x^5 - 6x^4 - 3x^2 - 2x + 1$ by $x - 2$.

15. Use synthetic division to see if -1 is a zero of $x^3 - 2x^2 + 3x + 6$.

16. Use synthetic division to see if -1 is a root of $x^3 + 2x^2 - 3x - 6 = 0$.

17. Find the fifth term in the expansion of $(x^2 - 2y^3)^9$.

18. Use base 10 logs to simplify: $(\sqrt{6200 \times 10^8})^3(\sqrt[3]{3100})$.

19. The pH of a solution is 9.2. Find the concentration of hydrogen ions in the solution in moles per liter.

20. Find the tenth term of an arithmetic sequence whose thirteenth term is 34 and whose eighth term is 19.

21. Solve for x: $\log_2 (2x - 1) < 1$

22. The base of a pyramid is a square whose perimeter is 16 centimeters. The height of the pyramid is 4 centimeters. What is the volume of the pyramid?

23. (*a*) The base of a circular cone has a radius of 10 centimeters. The height of the cone is 8 centimeters. What is the volume of the cone?
(*b*) Assume the cone is a right circular cone. What is the surface area of the cone?

24. Use Cramer's rule to solve for x. When evaluating the determinants, use the method of cofactors.

$$\begin{cases} -x + y + 2z = 9 \\ 2y - z = -1 \\ 2x + 3y = -1 \end{cases}$$

25. Sketch $y = 2 + 4 \sec x$.

26. (*a*) Develop the identity for $\sin x \sin y$.
(*b*) Find $\sin 315° \sin 15°$. Use exact values.

27. Show that: $\dfrac{\cos^2 x}{1 - \sin x} = \dfrac{1 + \csc x}{\csc x}$

Solve the following equations given that $(0° \le x < 360°)$:

28. $2 \sin^2 x - \sin x = 0$

29. $2 \sin^2 x - 1 = 0$

30. Solve: $\log_3 (\log_2 x) = 1$

EP 105.81, 105.82

LESSON 106 The remainder theorem

106.A The remainder theorem

If we divide the polynomial $x^3 + 4x + 2$ by $x + 1$, we can make some interesting observations that can be generalized. We will use synthetic division.

$$\begin{array}{r|rrrr} -1 & 1 & 0 & 4 & 2 \\ & & -1 & 1 & -5 \\ \hline & 1 & -1 & 5 & -3 \end{array}$$

We note that the remainder is -3. Thus, we can write

$$x^3 + 4x + 2 = (x^2 - x + 5)(x + 1) - 3$$

Now, on the next page, if we replace x on the left with -1, we get the value of $x^3 + 4x + 2$ when $x = -1$. If we replace x on the right side with -1, we will get -3 because $(-1 + 1)$ is zero.

$$(-1)^3 + 4(-1) + 2 = [(-1)^2 - (-1) + 5](-1 + 1) - 3$$
$$-1 - 4 + 2 = [7](0) - 3$$
$$-3 = -3$$

If we use $f(x)$ to designate a polynomial, we use the symbol $f(-1)$ for the value of the polynomial when $x = -1$. We see that this value is -3, the remainder when we used synthetic division. If we use synthetic division to divide by $x - 3$,

$$\begin{array}{r|rrrr} 3 & 1 & 0 & 4 & 2 \\ & & 3 & 9 & 39 \\ \hline & 1 & 3 & 13 & 41 \end{array}$$

we get a remainder of 41. This means that

$$x^3 + 4x + 2 = (x^2 + 3x + 13)(x - 3) + 41$$

Now if we replace x with 3 everywhere on the left side, we get $f(3)$; and the right side equals 41.

$$f(3) = (\text{some number})(3 - 3) + 41$$
$$f(3) = (\text{some number})(0) + 41$$
$$f(3) = 41$$

We can generalize this observation for evaluating a polynomial $P(x)$.

$$P(x) = Q(x)(x - c) + R$$

Now if we replace x everywhere with c, on the left side we get $P(c)$, and on the right side we get R.

$$P(c) = Q(c)(c - c) + R$$
$$P(c) = Q(c)(0) + R$$
$$P(c) = R$$

This means that the remainder of a synthetic division by $(x - c)$ is $P(c)$. This provides us with an expeditious manner of evaluating polynomials. The general development shown here is difficult for some students, but a development using a particular polynomial is more reasonable. Thus, the problem sets will contain requests for the development using a designated polynomial, as in the next example.

Example 106.A.1 Use the polynomial equation $f(x) = x^2 + x + 4$ and a divisor of $x - 3$ to do a specific development of the remainder theorem by showing that in this case the remainder equals $f(3)$.

Solution We begin by dividing $x^2 + x + 4$ by $x - 3$.

$$\begin{array}{r|rrr} 3 & 1 & 1 & 4 \\ & & 3 & 12 \\ \hline & 1 & 4 & 16 \end{array}$$

We can use these results to write

$$f(x) = x^2 + x + 4 = (x + 4)(x - 3) + 16$$

Now if we replace x everywhere with 3, we get

$$f(3) = (3)^2 + (3) + 4 = (3 + 4)(3 - 3) + 16$$
$$f(3) = 16 = (7)(0) + 16$$
$$f(3) = 16 = 16$$

We see that on the left, $f(3)$ is 16, and on the right, the remainder is 16.

Example 106.A.2 Use the remainder theorem to evaluate $2x^3 - 8x^2 + 3x + 5$ when x equals -4.

Solution If we use synthetic division and a "divisor" of -4, the remainder will be $P(-4)$.

$$\begin{array}{r|rrrr} -4 & 2 & -8 & 3 & 5 \\ & & -8 & 64 & -268 \\ \hline & 2 & -16 & 67 & -263 \end{array}$$

Thus, the value of $2x^3 - 8x^2 + 3x + 5$ when x equals -4 is -263, or

$$\boldsymbol{P(-4) = -263}$$

Example 106.A.3 Use the remainder theorem to evaluate $x^7 - 4x^4 + x - 3$ when $x = 2$.

Solution If we use synthetic division and a divisor of 2, the remainder will be $P(2)$.

$$\begin{array}{r|rrrrrrrr} 2 & 1 & 0 & 0 & -4 & 0 & 0 & 1 & -3 \\ & & 2 & 4 & 8 & 8 & 16 & 32 & 66 \\ \hline & 1 & 2 & 4 & 4 & 8 & 16 & 33 & 63 \end{array}$$

The remainder is 63, so

$$\boldsymbol{P(2) = 63}$$

Problem set 106

1. The radius of the wheel was 35 centimeters and the wheel was rolling at 60 feet per second. What was the angular velocity of the wheel in radians per minute?
2. The number of reds exceeded 4 times the number of whites by 2, and 7 times the number of whites was 14 less than 4 times the number of purples. If 4 times the sum of the whites and purples was 6 greater than 3 times the number of reds, how many were there of each color?
3. A card was drawn from a full deck of 52 cards. What is the probability that the card was either a 2 or a spade or was the 2 of spades?
4. Peoria ran as hard as she could but could only average k miles per hour for the m miles. As a consequence, she got there p hours late. How fast should she have run to get there on time?
5. Doray and Smitty had \$200 between them. Doray spent half of his and Smitty spent one-tenth of his, and they still had \$124 left. How much did each boy have when the trip began?
6. Use the polynomial $3x^3 - 9x^2 - 3x + 4$ and a divisor of $x + 2$ to do a specific development of the remainder theorem by showing that the remainder equals $f(-2)$.
7. Use the remainder algorithm to evaluate $x^5 - 3x^4 + 3x - 4$ when $x = 2$.
8. Given: $\angle ABC$ is an inscribed angle as shown.
   Prove: $\angle ABC = \frac{1}{2}\overset{\frown}{AC}$

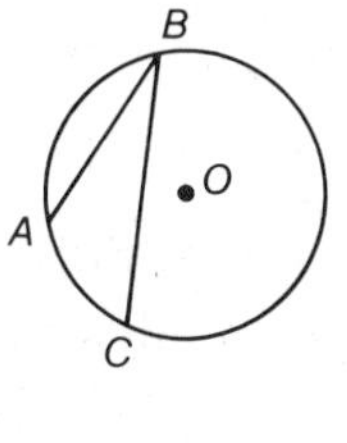

9. Given: Parallelogram $ABCD$
   Prove: Diagonals AC and BD bisect each other.

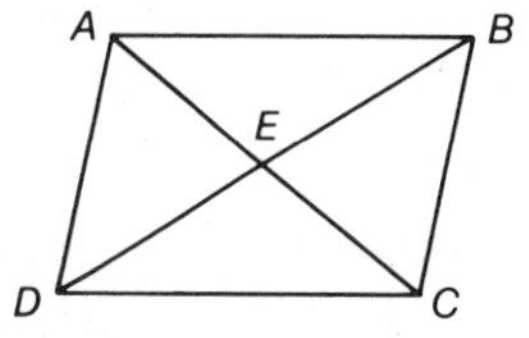

10. Given: The figure as shown.
Prove: $\triangle BAE \sim \triangle DCE$

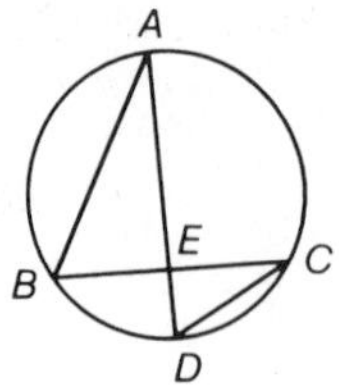

11. Given: Trapezoid $ABDC$ as shown.
M is the midpoint of $\overline{AC}$.
N is the midpoint of $\overline{BD}$.
Prove: $\overline{MN} \| \overline{AB}$; $MN = \frac{1}{2}(AB + CD)$

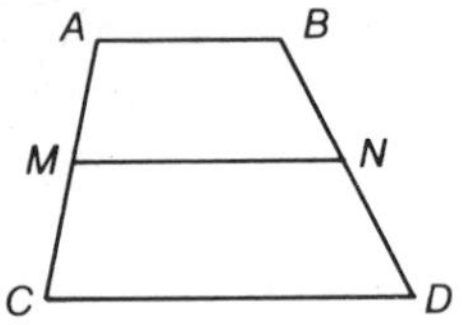

12. Find x, y, and z.

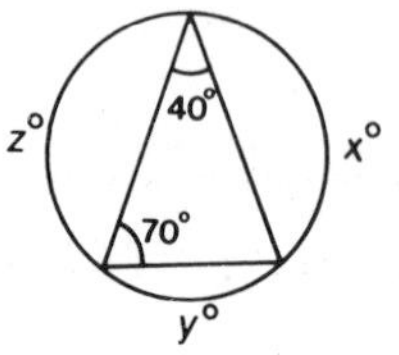

13. Indicate whether each equation given represents an ellipse, a hyperbola, a circle, or a parabola.
(*a*) $5x^2 + 7y^2 = 35$ (*b*) $xy = 4$ (*c*) $4x^2 - y^2 = 4$
(*d*) $x^2 + 6x + 4y + 5 = 0$ (*e*) $x^2 + y^2 - 8y + 2x + 13 = 0$

14. Graph $y = \cot x$.

15. Write equation (*e*) of Problem 13 in standard form and graph the figure it represents.

16. Use synthetic division to see if 2 is a zero of $x^2 - 4x + 6$.

17. Use synthetic division to divide $x^6 - 5x^5 + 4x^3 - 2x + 1$ by $x - 1$.

18. Find the seventh term in the expansion of $(x^4 - y^3)^{10}$.

19. The concentration of hydrogen ions in a solution is 6.5×10^{-4} mole per liter. Find the pH of the solution.

20. Find the sum of the following infinite geometric series:

$$\frac{1}{4} + \frac{2}{12} + \frac{4}{36} + \cdots$$

21. Develop the equation for the sum of the first n terms of an arithmetic sequence whose first term is a and whose common difference is d.

22. Solve for x: $\log_{1/3}(3x - 2) < 1$

23. The base of a pyramid is a regular hexagon whose perimeter is 36 meters. The height of the pyramid is 1 meter. Find the volume of the pyramid.

24. The radius of a sphere is 6 inches.
(*a*) Find the volume of the sphere.
(*b*) Find the surface area of the sphere.

25. Use echelon matrices to solve for x, y, and z: $\begin{cases} 2x + y - z = 0 \\ 2y + 3z = 7 \\ 2x - 3y = 7 \end{cases}$

26. Find the exact value of $\cos 75°$ by using the identity for $\cos(x + y)$ and the fact that $75° = 30° + 45°$.

27. Show that: $\dfrac{\cot x}{\cot x - 1} - \dfrac{\tan x}{\tan x + 1} = \dfrac{\cot x + \tan x}{\cot x - \tan x}$

28. Solve, given that $(0° \le \theta < 360°)$: $\sqrt{2} - 2 \sin 3\theta = 0$

Solve:

29. $\log_2 (\log_3 x) = 2$

30. $\log_2 \sqrt{x} = \sqrt{\log_2 x}$

EP 106.83, 106.84

LESSON 107 One-to-one functions · Inverse functions

107.A One-to-one functions

A ***relation*** is a mapping or a pairing between a set called the ***domain*** and a set called the ***range.*** Some authors define a relation to be the set of ordered pairs themselves. A relation can be defined by an equation. A relation can also be defined by a diagram that indicates the pairings and thus shows the ordered pairs. The three diagrams shown here depict relations.

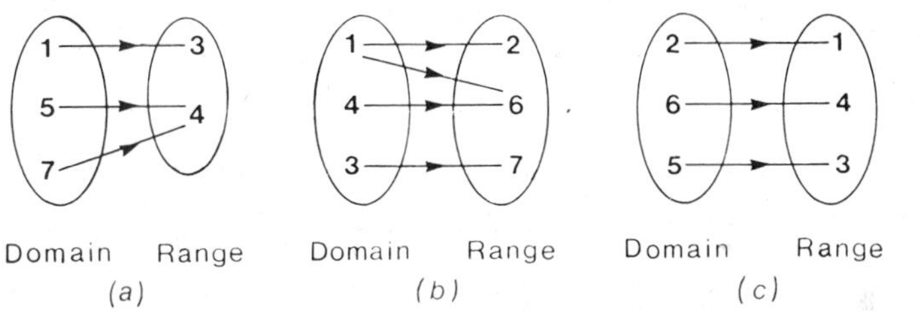

In each of the diagrams, every element of the domain is paired with at least one element in the range. Instead of using diagrams a relation can be designated by using the sets of ordered pairs themselves. If we do this, the same relations can be shown by writing these sets of ordered pairs.

(*a*) (1, 3), (5, 4), (7,4) (*b*) (1, 2), (1, 6), (4, 6), (3, 7) (*c*) (2, 1), (6, 4), (5, 3)

If R is a relation, the ***inverse of R*** (abbreviated R^{-1} and read "R inverse") is the relation obtained by interchanging the elements in each ordered pair. Every relation has an inverse relation. The inverse relations of the relations above are

(a^{-1}) (3, 1), (4, 5), (4, 7) (b^{-1}) (2, 1), (6, 1), (6, 4), (7, 3) (c^{-1}) (1, 2), (4, 6), (3, 5)

A *function* is a relation in which each element in the domain has exactly one image in the range. Thus, in the examples above, (*a*) and (*c*) designate functions. In (*a*) both 5 and 7 have 4 as an image, but this is all right because two elements of the domain can have the same image if each has only one image. In (*b*) the number 1 has two images, and thus this diagram does not depict a function. The function (*c*) is a special function because every element of the domain is paired with only one element in the range, and every element in the range is paired with only one element in the domain. Thus, if we turn function (*c*) around, we still have a function. But if we reverse the order of the elements in function (*a*), the result is not a function because 4 would have two images.

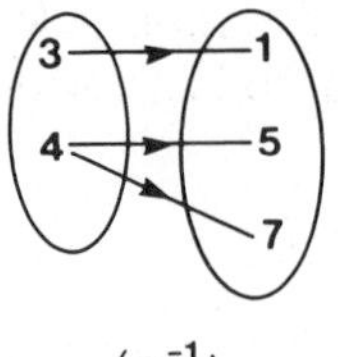

(a^{-1})

(3, 1), (4, 5), (4, 7)

NOT A FUNCTION

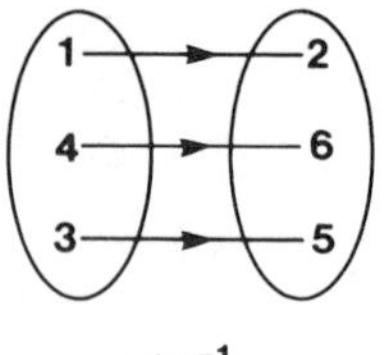

(c^{-1})

(1, 2), (4, 6), (3, 5)

FUNCTION

We call functions like (c) and (c^{-1}) ***one-to-one functions,*** and the original function (c) is said to have an inverse function (c^{-1}).

107.B Inverse functions

The word *inverse* comes from the Latin word *invertere*, which means "to invert" or "reverse the order of." In mathematics, we use the word inverse to describe an "undoing" or a "going back." If we begin with the number 5 and then add 2, the result is 7.

$$5 + 2 = 7$$

If we wish to "undo" the addition of 2 and "get back" to 5, we must add -2.

$$7 + (-2) = 5$$

We call -2 the additive inverse of 2 because adding -2 will allow us to undo the addition of 2. Using the same thought process, we can say that $+2$ is the *additive inverse* of -2 because adding $+2$ will undo the addition of -2.

$$5 + (-2) = 3 \longrightarrow 3 + (+2) = 5$$

We can undo multiplication by multiplying the product by the reciprocal of the multiplier. If we begin again with the number 5 and multiply by 2, we get a product of 10.

$$5 \cdot 2 = 10$$

Now to undo multiplication by 2 and get back to 5, we multiply 10 by $\frac{1}{2}$.

$$10 \cdot \frac{1}{2} = 5$$

We say that $\frac{1}{2}$ is the *multiplicative inverse* of 2 and that 2 is the multiplicative inverse of $\frac{1}{2}$ because multiplying by one of these numbers will undo the effect of multiplying by the other number.

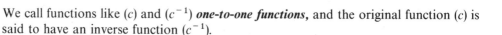

One-to-one functions have inverse functions that will permit us to undo the original transformation and allow us to get back to the original number. Nonconstant linear functions (lines that are not horizontal) belong to the class of one-to-one functions. If we have the equation

$$y = 2x + 3$$

and if we give x a value of 5, we find that the paired value of y is 13.

$$y = 2(5) + 3 \quad \text{substituted}$$
$$y = 10 + 3 \quad \text{multiplied}$$
$$y = 13 \quad \text{added}$$

Now to get back to 5, we need an equation in which an x value of 13 will yield an answer (a y value) of 5. We know that to begin with 13 and go back, we must first undo the addition of 3 by adding -3.

$$(13) - 3 = 10$$

Now we undo the multiplication by 2 by multiplying by $\frac{1}{2}$.

$$\frac{1}{2}[(13) - 3]$$

Now the 13 is the x value in this new equation, and the result is the y value, so we can write

$$y = \frac{1}{2}(x - 3) \qquad \text{equation}$$

$$y = \frac{1}{2}x - \frac{3}{2} \qquad \text{simplified}$$

Now we can use 13 for x in this equation and get back to 5.

$$y = \frac{1}{2}(13) - \frac{3}{2} \qquad \text{substituted}$$

$$y = \frac{13}{2} - \frac{3}{2} \qquad \text{multiplied}$$

$$y = 5 \qquad \text{simplified}$$

In functional notation, we often call the original function $f(x)$ and call the inverse function $f^{-1}(x)$. Note that **this is a special notation for the inverse function, and the -1 is not an exponent.** We can say that the inverse function will always "get you back" by writing

$$f^{-1}[f(x)] = x \qquad \text{for all } x \text{ in the domain of } f$$

This says that if the answer to the f equation, which is $f(x)$, is used for the variable in the f^{-1} equation, the results will be the value of x with which you began. Another way to say the same thing is to say $g(x)$ is an inverse function if

$$g[f(x)] = x \qquad \text{for all } x \text{ in the domain of } f$$

The method of finding the inverse function used in the problem above is slightly involved, and there is a two-step procedure that can be used almost automatically to find inverse functions.

1. **Exchange x and y in the original equation.**
2. **Solve the new equation for y.**

Example 107.B.1 Find the inverse function of $y = 2x + 3$.

Solution This is the same problem that we have just finished, and we will see if the two-step procedure works. First we interchange x and y in the given equation and get

$$x = 2y + 3$$

Now we solve this equation for y.

$$2y = x - 3 \qquad \text{rearranged}$$

$$\boldsymbol{y = \frac{1}{2}x - \frac{3}{2}} \qquad \text{divided by 2}$$

It is interesting to note that the graphs of inverse functions are mirror images about the line $y = x$. Here we show the graph of $y = 2x + 3$ and the graph of $y = \frac{1}{2}x - \frac{3}{2}$.

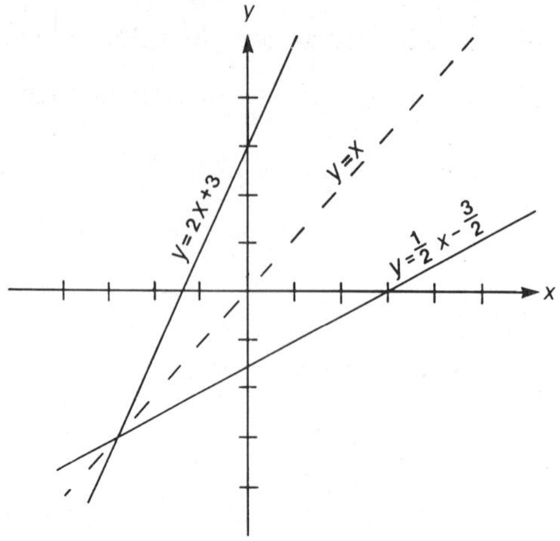

Example 107.B.2 Find the inverse function of $y = \frac{2}{3}x - 5$.

Solution We will use the two-step procedure again. First we interchange x and y in the equation.

$$x = \frac{2}{3}y - 5$$

Now we solve this equation for y.

$$\frac{2}{3}y = x + 5 \qquad \text{rearranged}$$

$$\mathbf{y = \frac{3}{2}x + \frac{15}{2}} \qquad \text{multiplied by } \frac{3}{2}$$

Problem set 107

1. Use the example of 12 things taken 9 at a time to do a concrete development of the expressions for ${}_nP_r$ and ${}_nC_r$.

2. The hundreds digit of a three-digit number is equal to 4 times the units digit, and the tens digit is 5 greater than the units digit. When the units digit and the hundreds digit are interchanged, the new number is 297 less than the original number. What is the original number?

3. This decay was exponential. After 10 minutes there were 480, but after 40 minutes only 470 remained. What was the half-life of the things?

4. Four workers could do k jobs in 5 hours. How long would it take to do 49 jobs if m more workers were added to the work force?

5. The blue man could do 3 jobs in 2 hours, and the green man could do p jobs in h hours. If the blue man and the green man worked together for 10 hours, how many jobs could they complete?

6. Is the relation $\{(1, 4), (2, 3), (4, 6), (5, 2)\}$ a function?

7. Is the relation $\{(1, 5), (6, 2), (5, 3), (1, 8)\}$ a function?

8. Find the inverse function of $y = 3x - 4$.

9. Find the inverse function of $y = \frac{1}{3}x - 4$.

10. Use the polynomial $2x^3 - 9x^2 + 3x - 4$ and a divisor of $x + 2$ to do a specific development of the remainder theorem by showing that the remainder equals $f(-2)$.

11. Use the remainder algorithm to evaluate $x^4 + 4x^3 - 6x^2 - 1$ when $x = -1$.

12. Given: $\angle ABC$ is an inscribed angle as shown.
Prove: $\angle ABC = \frac{1}{2}\overset{\frown}{AC}$

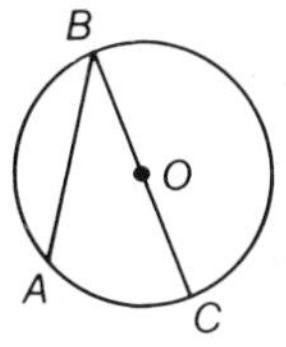

13. Given: $\triangle ABC$, $\overline{BD}$ is the angle bisector of angle B.
Prove: $\dfrac{AB}{BC} = \dfrac{AD}{DC}$

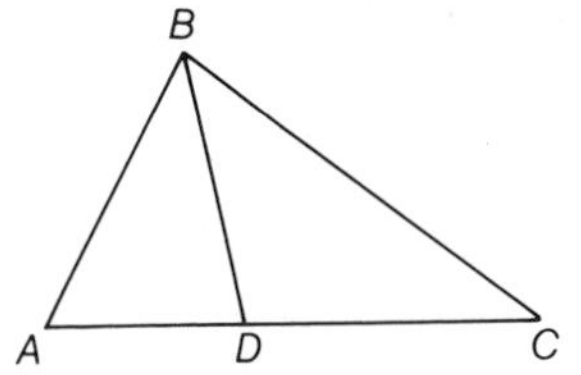

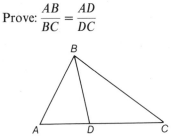

14. Prove that in a circle or in equal circles, equal chords have equal arcs.

15. Given: $AN = NB$; $AD = BC$; $\angle NDC = \angle NCD$
Prove: $AC = BD$

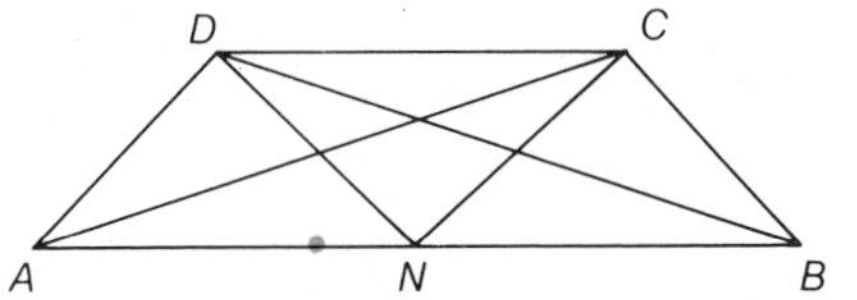

16. Find x, y, and z.

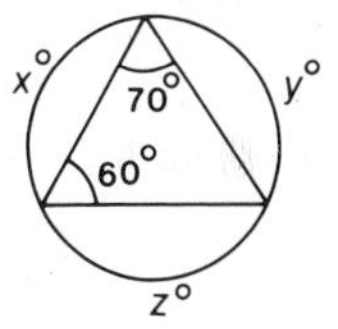

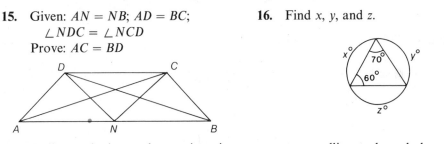

17. Indicate whether each equation given represents an ellipse, a hyperbola, a circle, or a parabola.
(a) $4x^2 + 36y^2 + 40x - 288y + 532 = 0$
(b) $4x^2 - 9y^2 - 16x + 36y - 344 = 0$ (c) $x = \frac{1}{3}y^2 - 2y - 9$
(d) $x^2 + y^2 - 10x + 8y + 5 = 0$ (e) $5x^2 + 8y^2 = 77$

18. Write equation (b) of Problem 17 in standard form and describe as completely as possible the conic section represented by the equation.

19. Find the distance between the point (0, 0) and the line $y - x + 4 = 0$.

20. Use synthetic division to see if 3 is a root of $x^3 - 2x^2 + 2x - 1 = 0$.

21. Use synthetic division to divide $x^5 - 4x^3 + 2x^2 - 3x + 1$ by $x - 2$.

22. What is the sum of the first n terms of an arithmetic sequence whose first term is a and whose common difference is d?

23. Find the fourth term of $(2x^2 - y^3)^9$.

24. The concentration of hydrogen ions in a solution is 8.4×10^{-6} mole per liter. Find the pH of the solution.

25. Three rectangular boxes are similar. The ratio of the surface areas of the boxes is 4 to $9x$ to $60y$. What is the ratio of the lengths of three corresponding sides?

26. Use Cramer's rule to solve for x. When evaluating the determinants, use the method of cofactors.

$$\begin{cases} 2x + 3y + z = -1 \\ 2y + 3z = 8 \\ 3x - y = -10 \end{cases}$$

27. Find sin 75° by using the identity for sin $(x + y)$ and the fact that $75° = 30° + 45°$. Use exact values.

28. Show that $(\sin x - \cos x)^2 = 1 - \sin 2x$.

29. Solve, given that $(0° \le \theta < 360°)$: $\sqrt{2} - 2\cos 2\theta = 0$

30. Solve: $\log_2 \sqrt[3]{x} = (\log_2 x)^2$

EP 107.85, 107.86

LESSON 108 Graphs of polynomial equations

108.A Graphs of polynomial equations

Our experience has shown that first-degree polynomial equations (linear equations) and second-degree polynomial equations (quadratic equations) are easy to graph. There are shortcuts that can be used, but if other approaches fail, these functions can always be graphed point by point by choosing values of x and using the equation to find the paired values of y. The point-by-point method can also be used to graph higher-order polynomial equations.

When we graph higher-order polynomial equations, it is helpful to remember the turning-point theorem which we will use but will not prove. **The turning-point theorem tells us that a polynomial equation has fewer turning points than the degree of the polynomial.** Thus, a third-degree polynomial equation has at most two turning points, and a fourth-degree polynomial equation has at most three turning points, etc. Here we show the graphs of a second-degree, a third-degree, and a fourth-degree polynomial equation and note the number of turning points in each graph.

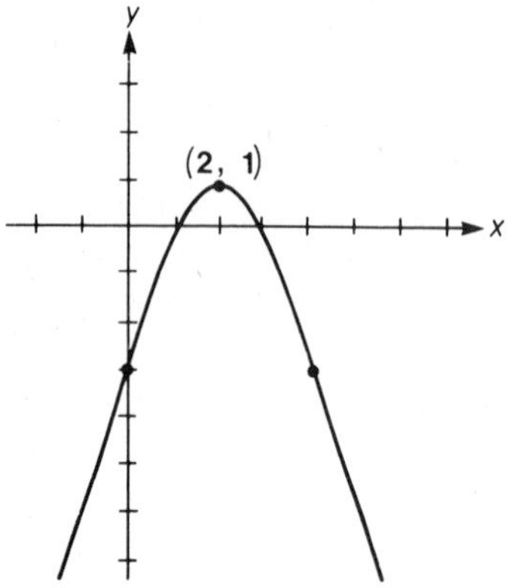

SECOND DEGREE
$y = -x^2 + 4x - 3$

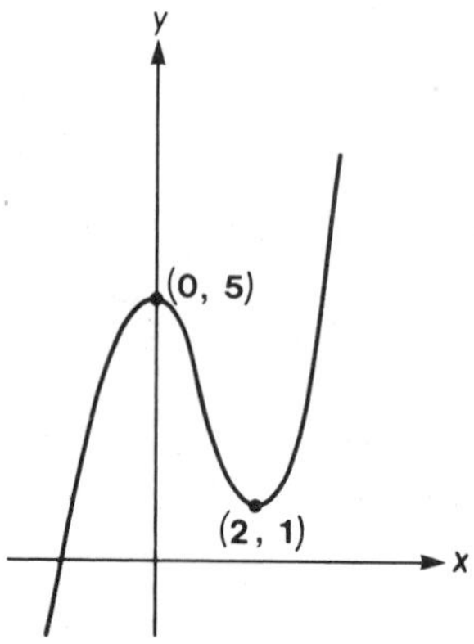

THIRD DEGREE
$y = x^3 - 3x^2 + 5$

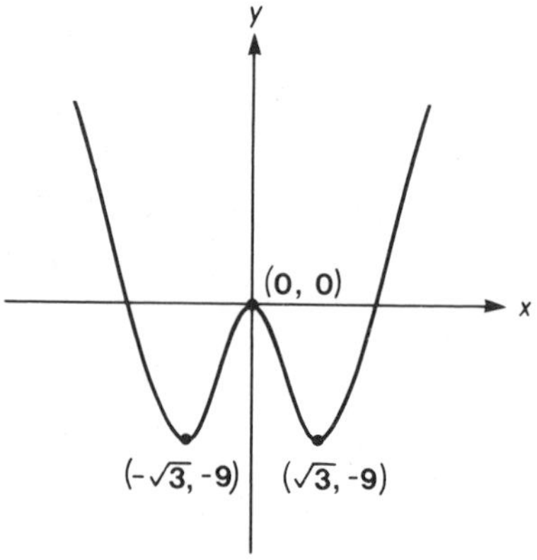

FOURTH DEGREE
$y = x^4 - 6x^2$

The term of highest degree in a polynomial is the dominant term because, for large absolute values of x, the value of the highest-degree term will be greater than the absolute value of the sum of all the other terms in the equation. The greater the absolute value of x, the greater the dominance of the highest-degree term becomes. **Thus, the value of the polynomial for large absolute values of x can be determined by looking at the exponent of the highest-degree term and looking at the sign of the coefficient of this term.** In the graph on the left above, the $-x^2$ term is dominant. Since $-x^2$ is negative for any real value of x, the graph will continue smoothly in the negative y direction as the absolute value of x increases. In the center graph, the dominant term is x^3. This term is negative for negative values of x and positive for positive values of x. In this graph, we see that for large positive values of x, the y values of the function are positive, and for large negative values of x, the y values of the function are negative. The graph will continue to increase and decrease smoothly as shown on the left and the right. The fourth-degree equation has increasingly large values of y in both directions, as we see in the graph on the right, because if x is not zero, x^4 is always positive, and the coefficient of x^4 is $+1$. If the coefficient of x^4 had been negative, then the y values would have increased negatively for large absolute values of x.

108.B The region of interest

We note that each of the graphs above twists and turns through a subset of values of x and then begins to increase or decrease smoothly as the dominance of the term of highest degree becomes more pronounced. We call the spread of values of x in which these changes of direction take place the **region of interest.** We are indeed fortunate that this region can be determined by inspecting the coefficients of the normalized polynomial equation. **To determine the region of interest, we select from the normalized polynomial equation the constant of greatest absolute value and increase this absolute value by 1. If this number is used as the radius of a circle with its center at the origin of the complex plane, the circle will contain on the real axis all x values that are real roots of the equation, all x values of the turning points (maxima or minima), and all x values of all points of inflection. In addition, the circle will contain all those points whose coordinates are the complex roots of the equation.**

To normalize the equation, all terms of the polynomial are divided by the coefficient of the term of highest degree. Here we show two equations (*a*) and (*b*) and the normalized form of each equation (*a*′) and (*b*′).

EQUATION	EQUATION
(*a*) $3x^4 - 11x^3 + 9x^2 + 13x - 10 = 0$	(*b*) $3x^4 + 2x^3 - 2x - 4 = 0$
NORMALIZED FORM	NORMALIZED FORM
(*a*′) $x^4 - \frac{11}{3}x^3 + 3x^2 + \frac{13}{3}x - \frac{10}{3} = 0$	(*b*′) $x^4 + \frac{2}{3}x^3 - \frac{2}{3}x - \frac{4}{3} = 0$

The radii of the region of interest for equations (*a*) and (*b*) are

$$\text{Radius for } (a) = \left(\left|\frac{13}{3}\right| + 1\right) = \frac{16}{3} \qquad \text{Radius for } (b) = \left(\left|-\frac{4}{3}\right| + 1\right) = \frac{7}{3}$$

We use these values of the radius to draw the circle that contains the region of interest for each polynomial.

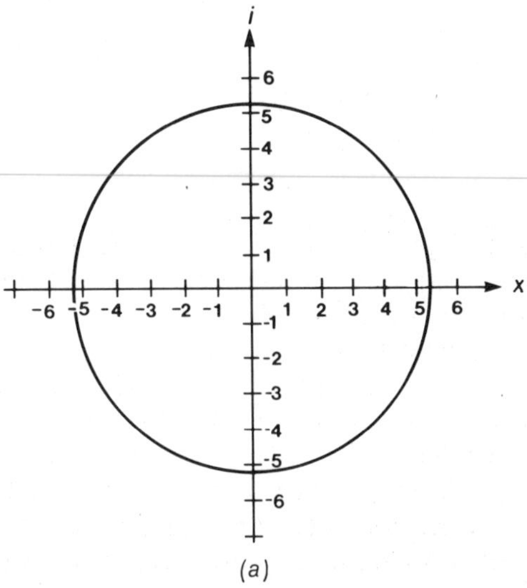

(*a*)

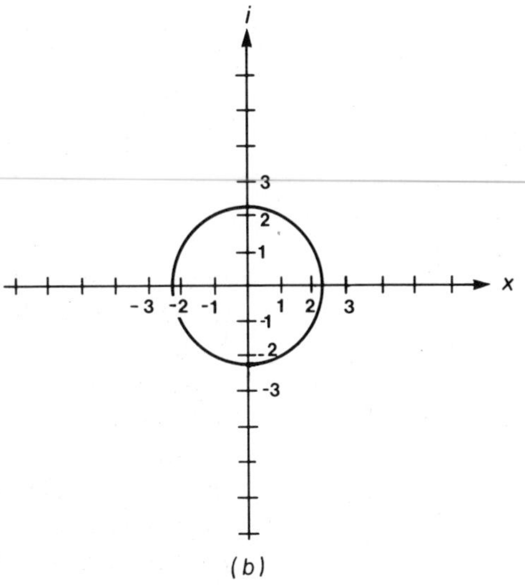

(*b*)

All the roots of equation (a) are contained in circle (a) on the left, and the x values of all turning points and inflection points of the graph of the equation lie between $+\frac{16}{3}$ and $-\frac{16}{3}$. All the roots of equation (b) are contained in circle (b), and the x values of all turning points and inflection points of the graph of the equation lie between $+\frac{7}{3}$ and $-\frac{7}{3}$.

Example 108.B.1 Graph $y = x^3 - 3x^2 + x + 1$.

Solution There are at most two turning points and the x^3 term is the dominant term. For positive values of x, this term has a positive value, so outside the region of interest, y will increase as x increases. For negative values of x, this term is negative, so outside the region of interest, y will increase negatively as x takes on larger negative values. The region of interest is bounded by the x values $\pm(|-3| + 1)$, or ± 4. We will select a few values of x within these limits and use synthetic division and the remainder theorem to find the matching values of y. We decide to use x values of $-2, -1, 0, 1, 2, 3,$ and 4. We begin by letting x equal zero and find that y equals 1. This gives us the point (0, 1). Next we will use synthetic division with the other values of x.

$$\begin{array}{r|rrrr} -2 & 1 & -3 & 1 & 1 \\ & & -2 & 10 & -22 \\ \hline & 1 & -5 & 11 & -21 \end{array} \qquad \begin{array}{r|rrrr} -1 & 1 & -3 & 1 & 1 \\ & & -1 & 4 & -5 \\ \hline & 1 & -4 & 5 & -4 \end{array} \qquad \begin{array}{r|rrrr} 1 & 1 & -3 & 1 & 1 \\ & & 1 & -2 & -1 \\ \hline & 1 & -2 & -1 & 0 \end{array}$$

$$\begin{array}{r|rrrr} 2 & 1 & -3 & 1 & 1 \\ & & 2 & -2 & -2 \\ \hline & 1 & -1 & -1 & -1 \end{array} \qquad \begin{array}{r|rrrr} 3 & 1 & -3 & 1 & 1 \\ & & 3 & 0 & 3 \\ \hline & 1 & 0 & 1 & 4 \end{array} \qquad \begin{array}{r|rrrr} 4 & 1 & -3 & 1 & 1 \\ & & 4 & 4 & 20 \\ \hline & 1 & 1 & 5 & 21 \end{array}$$

The ordered pairs are (0, 1), (−2, −21), (−1, −4), (1, 0), (2, −1), (3, 4), (4, 21). We can graph four of these ordered pairs, as we show on the left below.

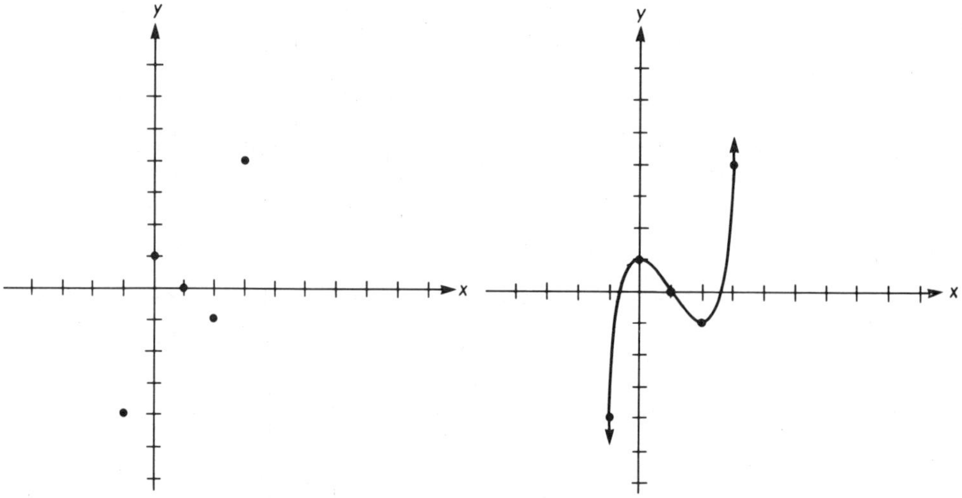

On the right, we connect the points with a smooth curve to complete the graph. We see that this third-degree polynomial equation has two turning points, so all the turning points have been found. The turning points are not necessarily exactly where we show them, but our sketch is a reasonable approximation.

Example 108.B.2 Graph $y = x^3 + 4x^2 + x - 6$.

Solution There are at most two turning points and the x^3 term is the dominant term. From this term, we decide that y has large positive values for large positive values of x and large negative values for large negative values of x. The region of interest is bounded by the x values of $+7$ and -7. If we let x equal 0, we find that the paired value of y is

−6. This gives us the point (0, −6). To find coordinates of other points on the curve, we select x values of −4, −2, 2, and 4 and will use synthetic division and the remainder theorem to find the paired values of y.

−4	1	4	1	−6
		−4	0	−4
	1	0	1	−10

−2	1	4	1	−6
		−2	−4	6
	1	2	−3	0

2	1	4	1	−6
		2	12	26
	1	6	13	20

4	1	4	1	−6
		4	32	132
	1	8	33	126

Now if we try to graph our points, we see that we still don't know much about the shape of the curve.

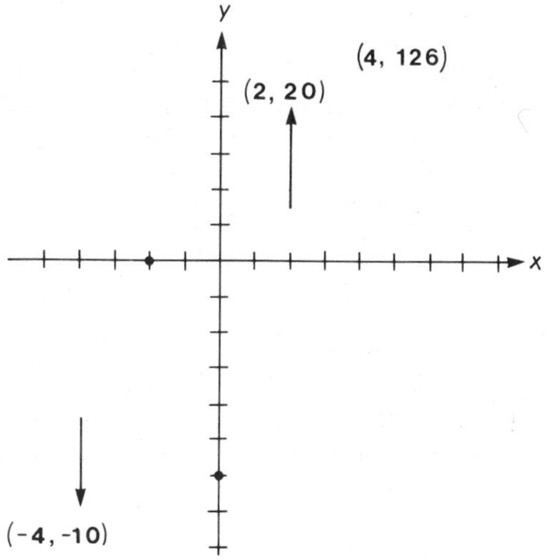

We see that when x equals −4, 2, or 4, we are off the graph, and we can't tell anything from the other two points. So let's set x equal to −3, −1, and 1 and see what happens.

−3	1	4	1	−6
		−3	−3	6
	1	1	−2	0

−1	1	4	1	−6
		−1	−3	2
	1	3	−2	−4

1	1	4	1	−6
		1	5	6
	1	5	6	0

Now we graph these points and make a couple of guesses as to the shape of the curve.

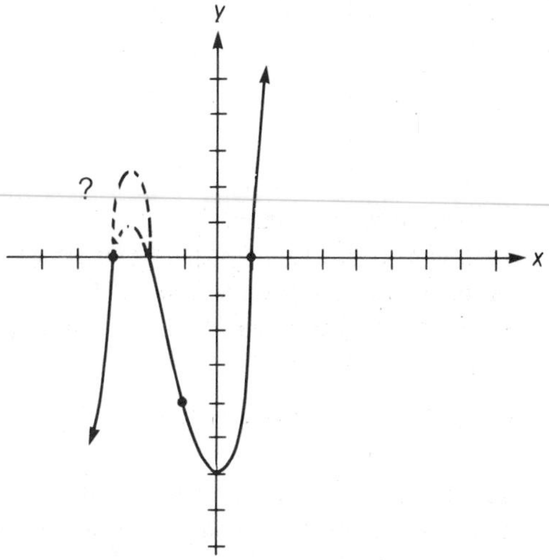

The minimum point is not exactly as shown on the graph, and we still need a point between the x values of -2 and -3. We will let x equal -2.5 and will use a calculator to help with the arithmetic.

-2.5	1	4	1	-6
		-2.5	-3.75	6.875
	1	1.5	-2.75	0.875

It seems that the lower of the two curves is a better guess because the point $(-2.5, 0.875)$ lies on the curve. This method of random selection of x values from the region of interest is rather primitive, but we will use it for a few lessons because of the practice it provides in graphing and in the evaluation of polynomials. This practice will permit appreciation of and understanding of more advanced techniques that will be discussed in later lessons.

Problem set 108

1. At first there were many of them, but after 7 hours of exponential decay, they numbered only 1400. After 24 hours, they numbered only 1300. How many would remain after 60 hours of decay?

2. The race began at 4 o'clock and lasted until the hands on the clock pointed in the same direction. How long did the race last?

3. Five men and w women could do 2 jobs in 7 hours. How long would it take m men and 4 women to do c jobs if the men could work just as fast as the women?

4. The urn contained 6 red marbles and 3 green marbles. Long Sam drew a marble and did not put it back. Then he drew another marble. What is the probability that the first marble was red and that the second marble was green in that order?

5. The number who succeeded varied linearly with the number who gave it a good try. When 20 gave it a good try, 15 succeeded. When 40 gave it a good try, 25 succeeded. How many succeeded when 100 gave it a good try?

6. Is the relation $\{(2, 3), (5, 2), (2, 5), (3, 2)\}$ also a function?

7. Graph $y = x^3 - 2x^2 - 5x + 6$.

8. Graph $y = x^3 + 2x^2 - 5x - 6$.

9. Find the distance from $(1, 5)$ to $y = 3$.

10. Find the inverse function of $y = 4x - 2$.

11. Use synthetic division to divide $x^4 - 3x^3 + 2x^2 - 3x + 4$ by $x - 3$.

12. Given: $\angle ABC$ is an inscribed angle as shown.
Prove: $\angle ABC = \frac{1}{2}\overset{\frown}{AC}$

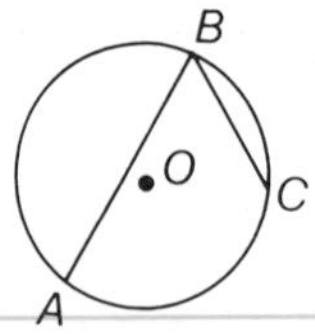

13. Given: $AP = AQ$; $PB = QC$
Prove: $BQ = PC$

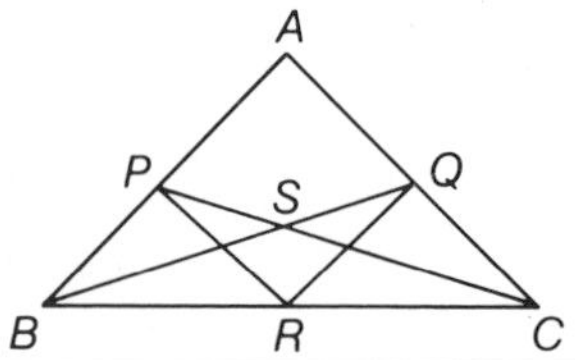

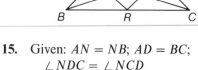

14. Given: $\triangle ABC$. $\overline{BD}$ is the angle bisector of angle B.
Prove: $\dfrac{AB}{BC} = \dfrac{AD}{DC}$

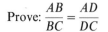

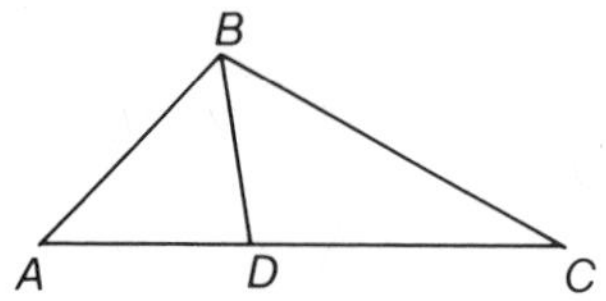

15. Given: $AN = NB$; $AD = BC$; $\angle NDC = \angle NCD$
Prove: $\angle DAB = \angle CBA$; $\angle ADC = \angle BCD$

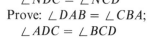

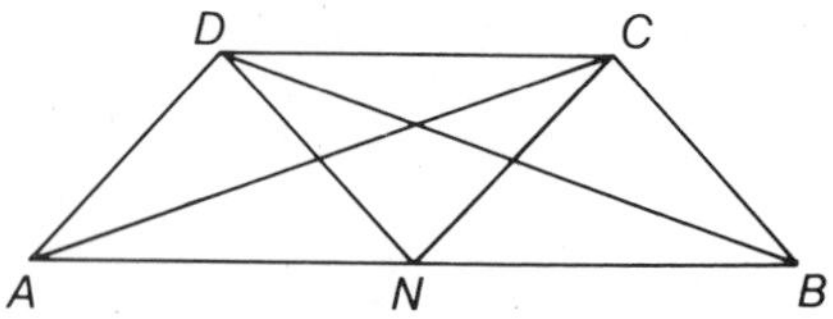

16. Find x, y, and z.

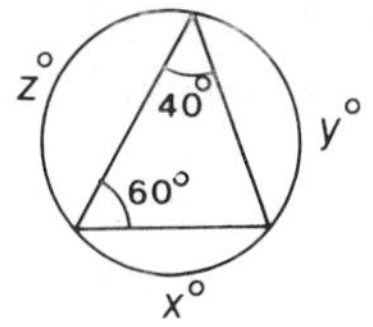

17. Indicate whether each equation shown represents an ellipse, a hyperbola, a circle, or a parabola.
(*a*) $4x^2 + 36y^2 + 40x - 288y + 532 = 0$
(*b*) $25x^2 - 16y^2 - 100x - 96y - 444 = 0$ (*c*) $x^2 + y^2 - 10x - 8y + 16 = 0$
(*d*) $y = -4x^2 + 20x - 16$ (*e*) $x^2 + y^2 - 10x + 8y + 5 = 0$

18. Graph $xy = 8$.

19. Write equation (*e*) of Problem 17 in standard form and describe the conic section represented by the equation.

20. Write the sixth term in the expansion of $(x^3 - 2y^3)^{12}$.

21. Develop the formula for the sum of the first n terms of an arithmetic sequence whose first term is a and whose common difference is d.

22. The pH of a solution is 9.2. What is the concentration of hydrogen ions in moles per liter of the solution?

23. What is the sum of all the terms of the geometric sequence:

$$-\frac{1}{3}, \frac{2}{9}, -\frac{4}{27}, \ldots$$

24. (*a*) The base of a circular cone has a radius of 6 centimeters. The height of the cone is 10 centimeters. What is the volume of the cone?
(*b*) Assume the cone is a right circular cone. What is the surface area of the cone?

25. The radius of a sphere is r inches.
(*a*) Find the volume of the sphere.
(*b*) Find the surface area of the sphere.

26. Use echelon matrices to solve for x, y, and z: $\begin{cases} -x + 2y + z = 9 \\ y - 2z = 0 \\ 2x + 3y = -2 \end{cases}$

27. Find tan 75° by using the identity for tan $(a + b)$ and the fact that $75° = 30° + 45°$. Use exact values.

28. Solve, given that $(0° \le \theta < 360°)$: $-\sqrt{2} - 2 \sin 3\theta = 0$

29. Show that: $\dfrac{\cos^2 x}{1 - \sin x} = \dfrac{1 + \csc x}{\csc x}$

30. Solve: $2 \log_3 x - \log_3 (\frac{2}{3}x - \frac{1}{3}) = 1$

EP 108.87, 108.88

LESSON 109 Chords and tangents

109.A Chords and tangents

We have proved that the measure of an inscribed angle is equal to half the measure of its intercepted arc.

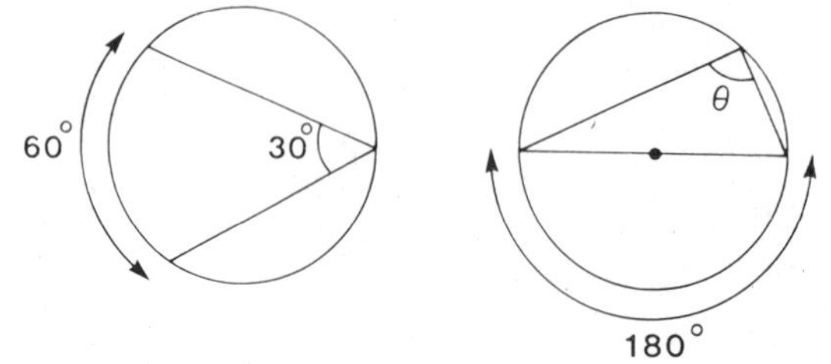

Thus a 30° inscribed angle will intercept an arc of 60°, as we show on the left. On the right we note that any inscribed angle θ that intercepts a diameter must equal 90° because a diameter intercepts an arc of 180°. In the four figures below, from left to right, we note that if we fix one side of an inscribed angle and rotate the other side, the chord formed by the rotated side becomes shorter and shorter. Finally, the ends of the chord (A and C) are almost together and the rotated side is tangent to the circle. From this, we see that the angle formed by a chord and a tangent has the same characteristics as the angle formed by two chords.

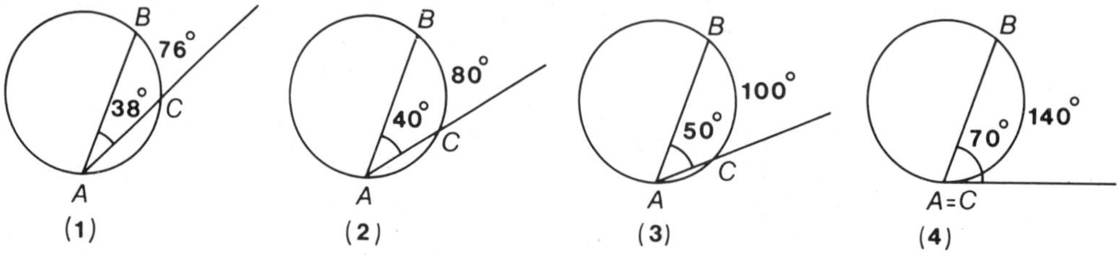

The angle formed by a chord and a tangent ray is equal to half the intercepted arc.

If we treat the case of a chord and a tangent as a separate theorem, there are three possible configurations of the proof, as we see in the following figures. In Case I, the chord intersects the center of the circle; in Case II, the center is included in the angle; and in Case III, the center is outside the angle.

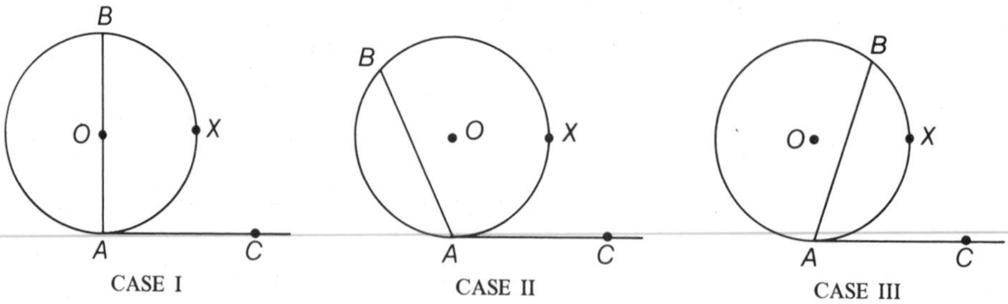

Example 109.A.1 Prove Case I of the chord-tangent theorem.

Solution We use the diagram on the left above. We have proved that a tangent to a circle is always perpendicular to the radius, so tangent AC is perpendicular to radius OA and angle CAO equals 90°. The arc AXB intercepted by the diameter AB measures 180°. Thus, angle CAO measures one-half of arc AXB.

Example 109.A.2 Prove Case II of the chord-tangent theorem.

Solution This proof requires that we draw diameter AOY, as shown in the left figure below.

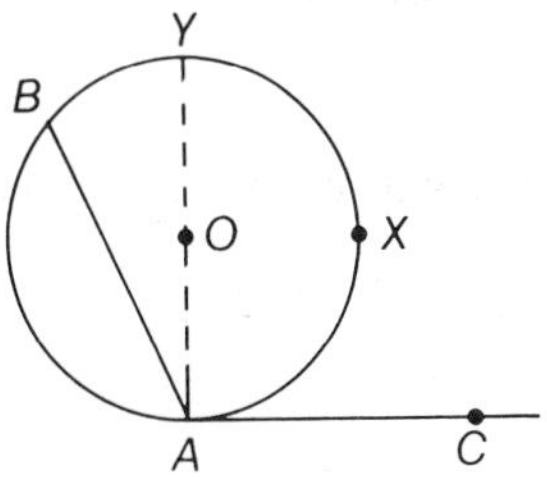

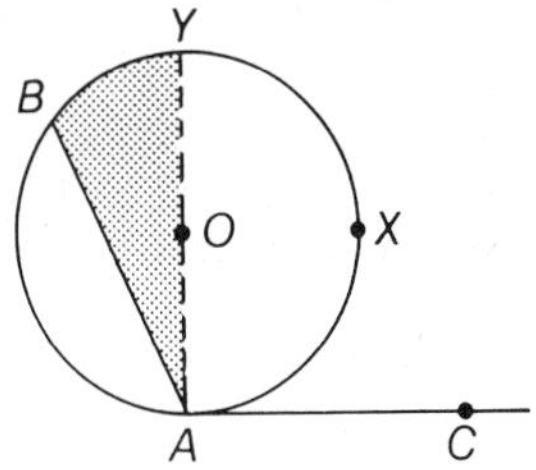

Now, on the right, angle BAY equals one-half of arc BY, and in the same figure, angle YAC equals one-half of arc YXA.

$$\begin{aligned} \angle BAY &= \tfrac{1}{2}\overset{\frown}{BY} \\ \angle YAC &= \tfrac{1}{2}\overset{\frown}{YXA} \\ \hline \angle YAC + \angle BAY &= \tfrac{1}{2}(\overset{\frown}{BY} + \overset{\frown}{YXA}) \end{aligned}$$

Now, $\overset{\frown}{BY} + \overset{\frown}{YXA} = \overset{\frown}{BXA}$ and $\angle BAY + \angle YAC = \angle BAC$, so we have our proof.

$$\angle BAC = \frac{1}{2}\overset{\frown}{BXA}$$

Example 109.A.3 Prove Case III of the chord-tangent theorem.

Solution For this proof, we use the Case III diagram from the preceding page and draw diameter AOY, as we show on the left below.

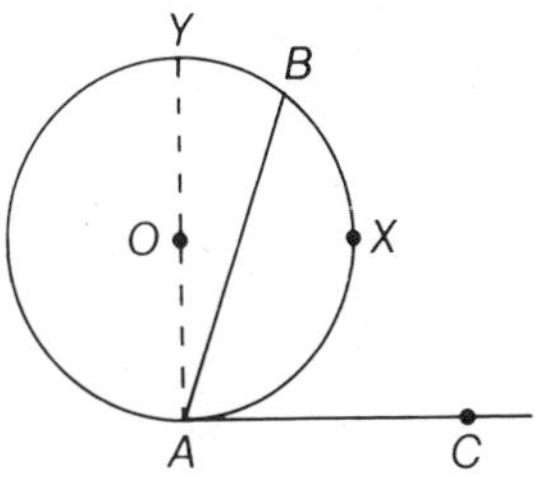

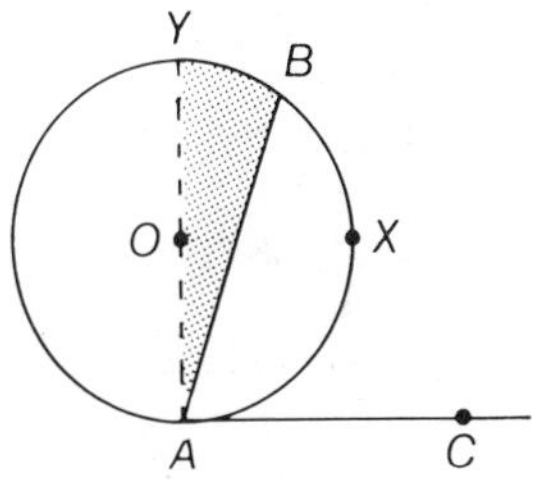

In the right-hand diagram, we see that angle YAB equals one-half arc YB, and in the same figure, we see that angle YAC equals one-half semicircle YXA. This time we subtract instead of adding.

$$\begin{aligned} \tfrac{1}{2}\overset{\frown}{YXA} &= \angle YAC \\ \tfrac{1}{2}\overset{\frown}{YB} &= \angle YAB \\ \hline \tfrac{1}{2}(\overset{\frown}{YXA} - \overset{\frown}{YB}) &= \angle YAC - \angle YAB \end{aligned}$$

But $\overset{\frown}{YXA} - \overset{\frown}{YB} = \overset{\frown}{BXA}$ and $\angle YAC - \angle YAB = \angle BAC$, and our proof is complete.

$$\frac{1}{2}\overset{\frown}{BXA} = \angle BAC$$

Example 109.A.4 Given: CA is tangent to circle O and $\angle CAB = 70°$
Find: $\angle BOA$

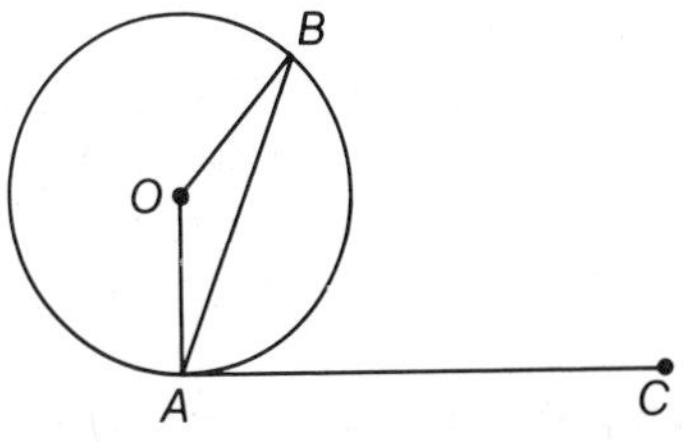

Solution Arc BA is twice angle CAB, so arc BA equals 140°. The central angle equals the intercepted arc, so angle BOA also equals **140°.**

Problem set 109

1. Harry Joe went to the city and met a lot of people. There were s of them from small towns and L of them from larger towns. What fractional part of the people he met were from small towns?

2. Harry Joe's wife also made the trip, and she also met a lot of people. There were s of them from small towns and L of them from larger towns. What percentage of the people she met were from larger towns?

3. The power required to propel a boat varies as the cube of the speed of the boat. If a boat requires 400 units of power at a speed of 10 miles per hour, how many units of power will it require at 20 miles per hour?

4. The volume varied directly as p squared and inversely as the square root of w. What would the volume be multiplied by if p is multiplied by 9 and w is multiplied by 4?

5. Theodosia bought m of them for c cents each. If the grocer increased the price of each item by p cents, how many could Theodosia buy for \$30?

6. Given: $\overline{AC}$ is a tangent to circle O.
   $\overline{BA}$ is a chord of circle O.
   Prove: $\angle BAC = \frac{1}{2}\widehat{BXA}$

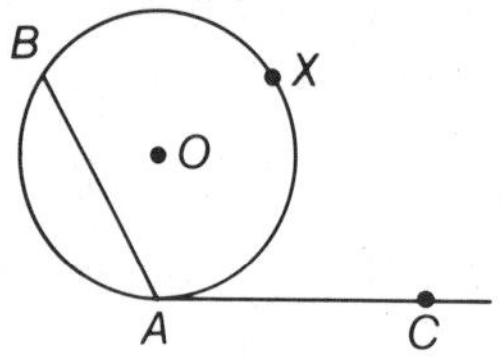

7. Given: $AP = AQ$; $PB = QC$
   Prove: $\angle QBC = \angle PCB$

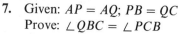

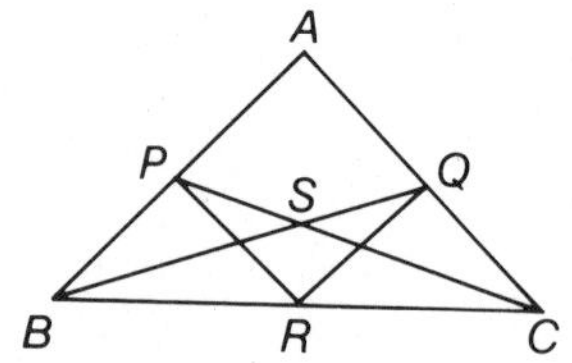

8. Given: $\angle ABC$ is an inscribed angle as shown.

   Prove: $\angle ABC = \frac{1}{2}\widehat{AC}$

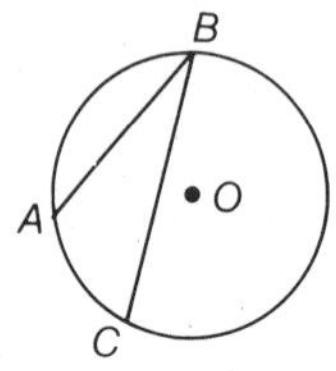

9. Given: The figure as shown.

   Prove: $\dfrac{BE}{AE} = \dfrac{ED}{EC}$

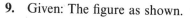

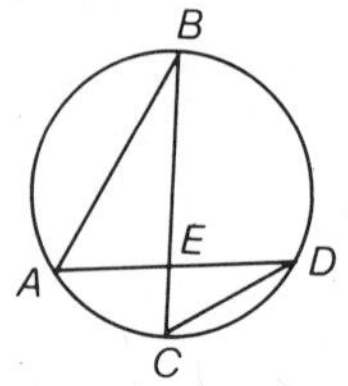

10. Using the figures shown, prove the Pythagorean theorem.

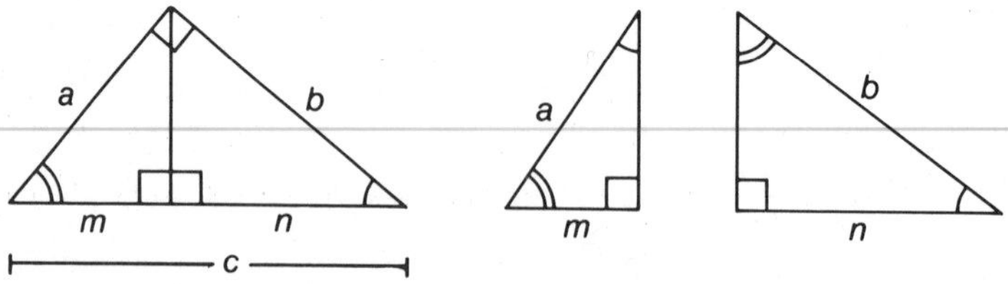

11. Find x, y, and z.

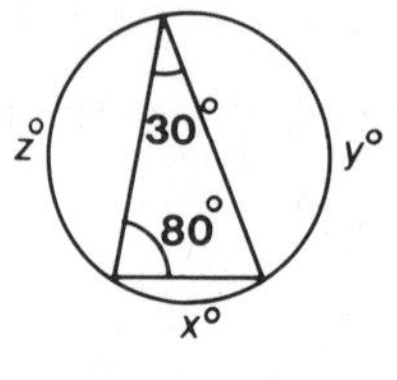

12. Graph $y = -1 + 7 \sin 3(x + 30°)$.

13. Indicate whether each equation is the equation of an ellipse, a hyperbola, a circle, or a parabola.
    (a) $4x^2 + 36y^2 + 40x - 288y + 532 = 0$
    (b) $9x^2 - 54x - 16y - 79 - 4y^2 = 0$ (c) $x - y^2 + 4y - 3 = 0$
    (d) $x^2 + y^2 - 8x + 6y - 56 = 0$ (e) $4x^2 + 36y^2 + 40x - 288y + 532 = 0$

14. Is the relation $\{(1, 4), (-1, 3), (3, 4), (5, 2)\}$ a function?

15. Write equation (b) of Problem 13 in standard form and describe the conic section represented by the equation.

16. Graph $y = x^3 - 4x^2 + x + 6$.

17. Graph $y = x^3 + x^2 - 10x + 8$.

18. Find the inverse function of $y = 3x - 2$.

19. Find the inverse function of $y = \frac{1}{5}x - 6$?

20. Develop the formula for the sum of the first n terms of an arithmetic sequence whose first term is a and whose common difference is d.

21. What is the fourth term in the expansion of $(x^2 - 3y^2)^6$?

22. What is the sum of the first seven terms of the geometric sequence:

$$\frac{1}{2}, -\frac{3}{4}, \frac{9}{8}, \ldots$$

23. The pH of a solution is 7.4. What is the concentration of hydrogen ions in moles per liter of the solution?

24. Find the length of the diagonal AB.

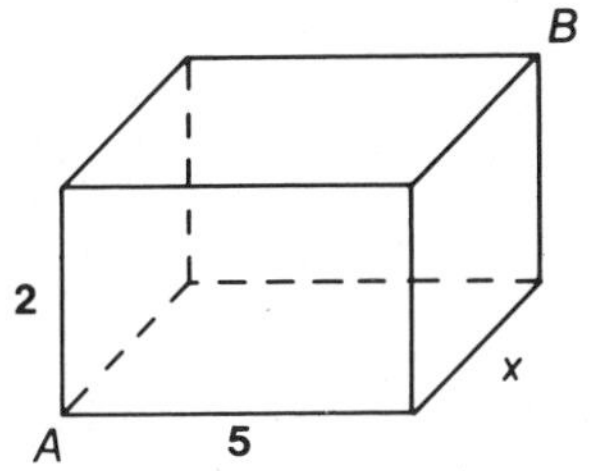

25. The base of a pyramid is a regular hexagon of perimeter 24 inches. The height of the pyramid is 9 inches. What is the volume of the pyramid?

26. Use Cramer's rule to solve for x. Use the method of cofactors to evaluate the determinants.

$$\begin{cases} -2x - y - z = 2 \\ 2y + 3z = 10 \\ 3x + 2y = -5 \end{cases}$$

27. Find sin 15° by using the half-angle identity for the sine. Use decimal approximations.

28. Show that: $\dfrac{\sin^2 x}{1 - \cos x} = \dfrac{1 + \sec x}{\sec x}$

29. Solve, given that $(0 \le x < 360°)$: $3 \tan^2 x + 5 \sec x + 1 = 0$

30. Solve: $\log_2 (\log_3 x) = 2$

EP 109.89, 109.90

LESSON 110 *Graphs of functions · Translations of functions · Piecewise functions · Greatest integer function*

110.A Graphs of functions

A ***function*** can be defined as a set of ordered pairs in which no two pairs have the same first elements and different second elements. A function can also be defined as the pairing or matching between the elements of the ordered pairs subject to the same condition. A graph of a function gives us a visual representation of the sets of ordered pairs. It is customary to lay off the value of the first member x of the ordered pair horizontally and the value of the second member y of the ordered pair vertically. If the convention is followed, the domain of the function is the set of all x values of the points that constitute the function, and the range is the set of all y values of the same points. In the figures below, we show the domain and the range of the function in the graphs. **The value of the function for any value of x is the vertical distance from the horizontal axis to the graph.** The arrow indicates the vertical distance at a value of x that we call x_0. The length of this arrow is $f(x_0)$.

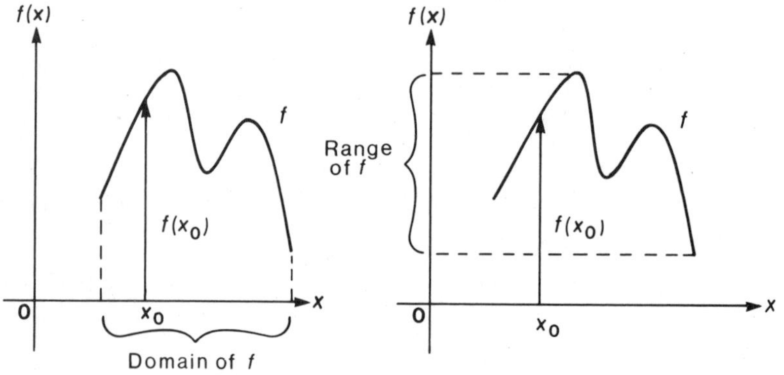

If the domain of a function includes both positive and negative numbers, then the graph of the function will extend both to the left and to the right of the origin. Some functions are symmetric about the y axis, and some functions are symmetric about the origin. **If a function is symmetric about the y axis, the function has the same value at any given distance to the left of the origin as it has at the same distance to the right of the origin. These functions are called *even functions* and possess the quality that for any value of x in the domain of f, $f(-x) = f(x)$.** Here we show the graphs of two even functions.

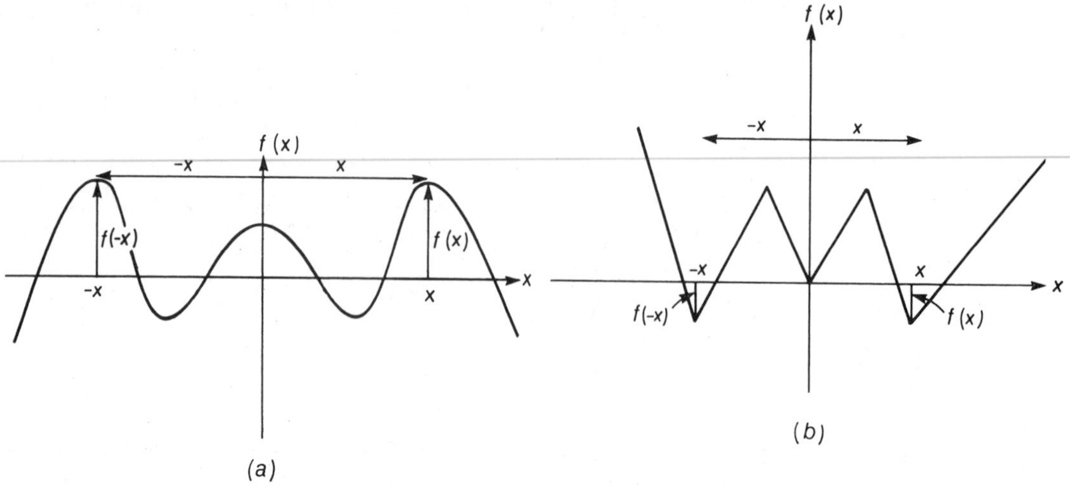

We note that in both graphs, if we go the same distance to the left and right of the y axis, the distances from the x axis to the graphs are equal, and either both are "up" distances or both are "down" distances.

If a function is symmetric about the origin, the function at a distance x to the right of the origin has the negative of the value it has at the same distance to the left of the origin. These functions are called *odd functions*, and in these functions we say that for any value of x in the domain of f, $f(-x) = -f(x)$. Here we show the graphs of two odd functions.

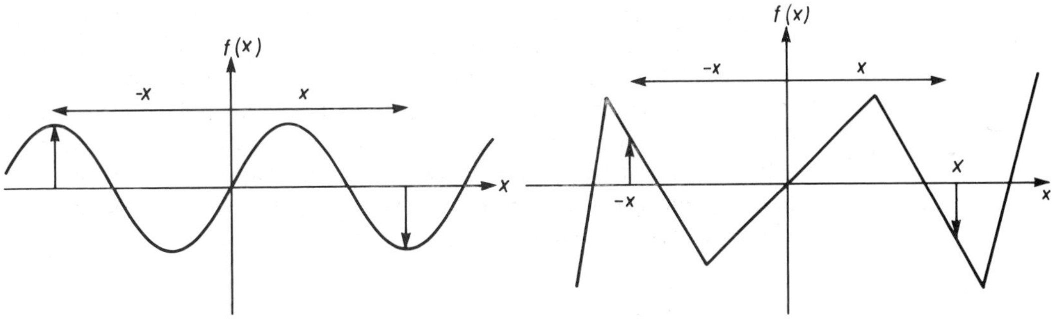

(c) (d)

We note that in both graphs, if we go the same distance to the left and right of the origin, the distance from the x axis to the graph is the same, but on one side you go up and on the other side you go down. Thus an odd function does the same thing on both sides but in different directions.

110.B Absolute value function

We have concentrated our investigation of functions on the functions that are the most useful in higher mathematics and in mathematically based disciplines such as chemistry and physics. Thus, most of our work has been done with polynomial functions with special emphasis on linear and quadratic functions. Examples of these functions are

$$y = 3x + 2 \qquad y = x^2 \qquad 2x + 3y = 5$$

In this book, we have also worked extensively with exponential functions, logarithmic functions, and trigonometric functions, such as

$$y = e^{2t} \qquad y = \log x \qquad y = -\sin 2(x + 30°) \qquad y = \tan x$$

These are important functions because they will be encountered often. There are many other kinds of functions, but they are usually given less emphasis because they are not encountered as often. A function that is discussed in almost every algebra book at this level is the ***absolute value function.***

Example 110.B.1 Graph $f(x) = |x|$.

Solution This is the absolute value function. To graph the function, we make a table to find ordered pairs that satisfy the function.

x	0	2	4	6	-2	-4	-6
$f(x)$	0	2	4	6	2	4	6

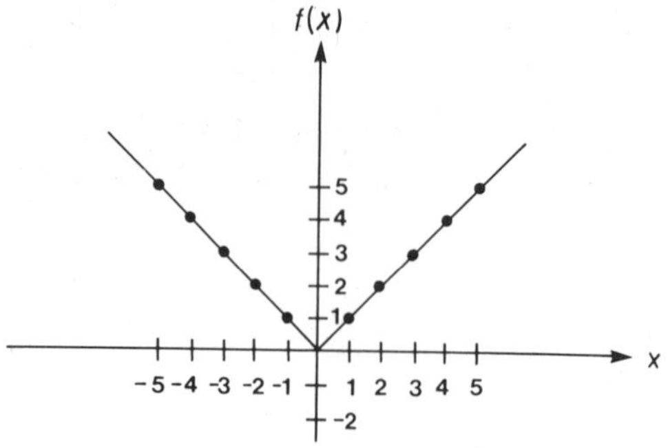

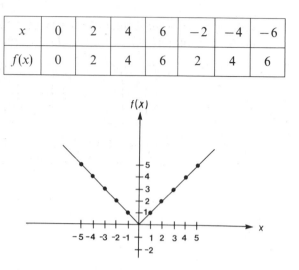

This graph is easy to recognize. There is no number whose absolute value is less than 0, so the least value of $f(x)$ is 0. The absolute value of any positive number is the same as the absolute value of its opposite, so $f(3) = 3$ and $f(-3) = 3$. Thus, if we go out the same distance to the right or the left, we find the value of the function is the same. From the discussion in the preceding section, we see that the absolute value function is an even function.

110.C Translation of functions

In our study of the sine function, we found that the graph of the function can be shifted left or right by adding a constant to the argument, and the shape of the function can be changed by multiplying the argument by a constant. The same procedures apply to the graphs of all functions.

Example 110.C.1 Graph the function $y = |x|$. Then change the equation to shift the graph 3 units to the left and 2 units down. Then graph the new function.

Solution To shift the graph 3 units to the left we add $+3$ to the argument. To shift the graph 2 units down, we add -2 to the function

$y = |x|$ $\qquad$ $y = |x + 3| - 2$

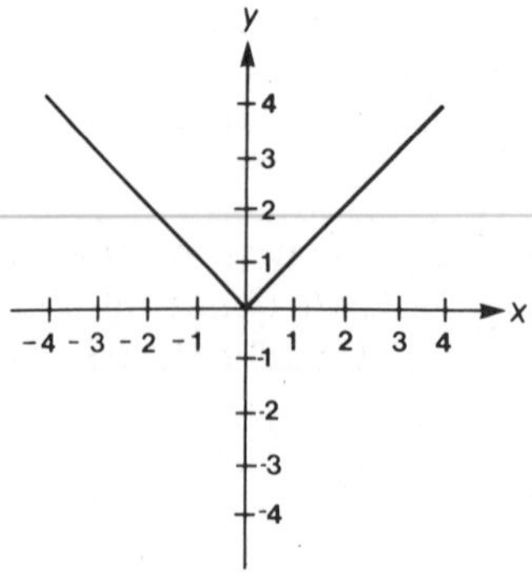

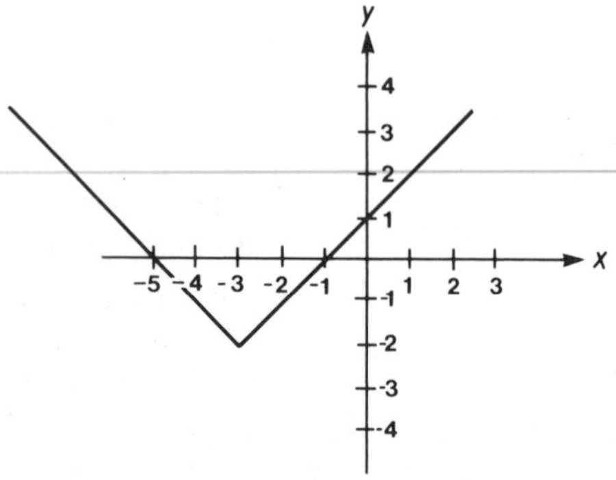

Example 110.C.2 Graph the function $y = \frac{1}{2}x^2$. Then change the equation to shift the curve 3 units to the right and 2 units up. Then graph the new function.

Solution To graph the original function, we make a table, choose values of x, and find corresponding values of y.

x	0	1	2	3	-1	-2	-3
y	0	$\frac{1}{2}$	2	4.5	$\frac{1}{2}$	2	4.5

We show this graph on the left. To shift the graph 3 units to the right, we add -3 to the argument, and we add $+2$ to the function to shift the graph 2 units up.

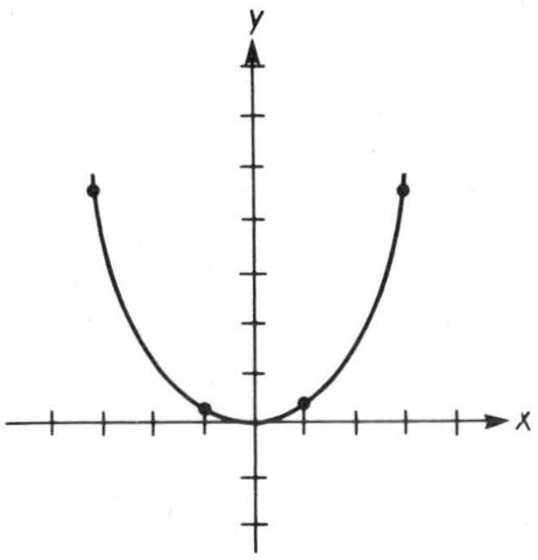

$y = \frac{1}{2}x^2$

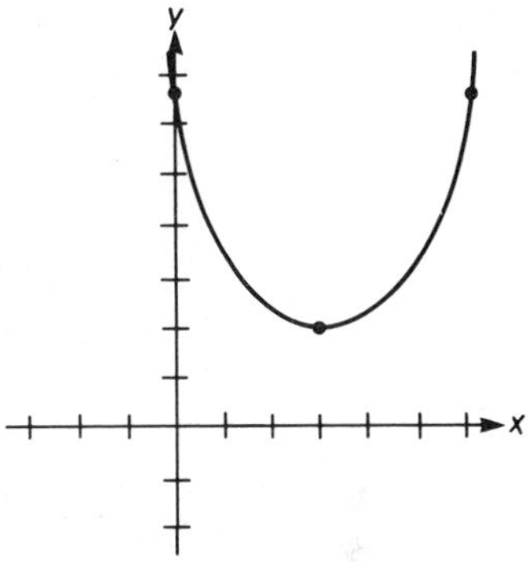

$y = \frac{1}{2}(x - 3)^2 + 2$

Example 110.C.3 Graph the function $y = \frac{1}{2}x$. Then change the equation to shift the graph 2 units to the left and 1 unit down.

Solution On the left we show the graph of $y = \frac{1}{2}x$. In the center, we show the graph of $y = \frac{1}{2}(x + 2)$, which is the original graph shifted 2 units to the left.

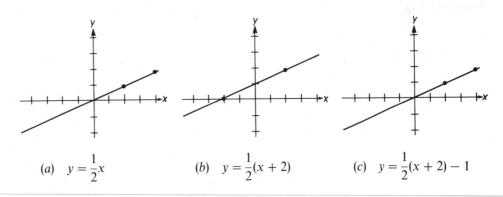

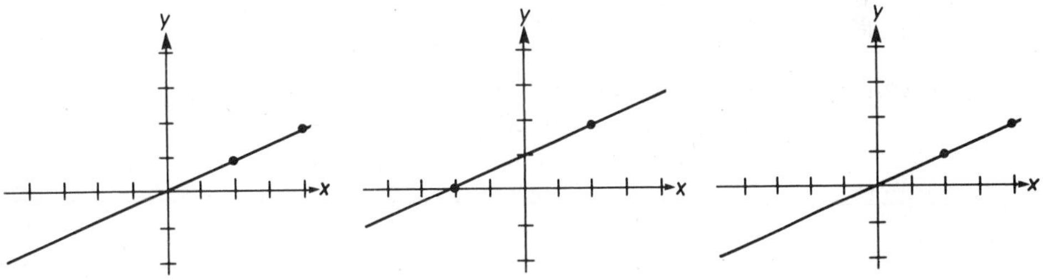

(*a*) $y = \frac{1}{2}x$ (*b*) $y = \frac{1}{2}(x + 2)$ (*c*) $y = \frac{1}{2}(x + 2) - 1$

This example illustrates a peculiarity of linear functions in that a shift left or right has the same effect as a vertical shift. We note that in (*b*), a shift 2 units to the left could be considered to be a vertical shift of $+1$ unit. Thus, (*c*) is the same graph as (*a*).

110.D Piecewise functions

Sinusoidal functions can be described with a single equation that is valid for all values of x. Sometimes, however, we wish to describe functions that are difficult to describe by using a single equation. When this is true, we can often describe the function by using more than one equation and specifying the values of x for which each equation should be used.

Example 110.D.1 Write the equations for this function.

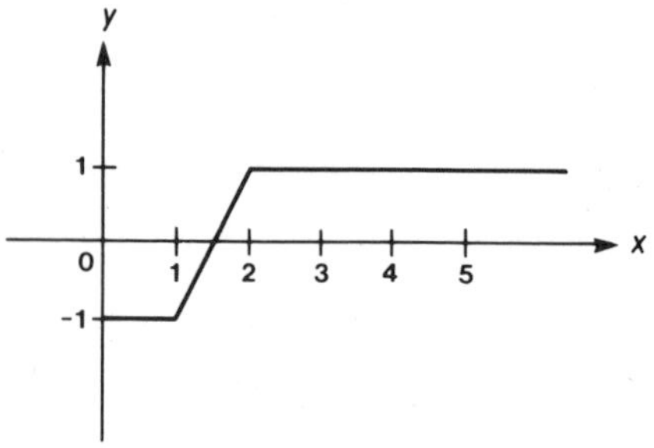

Solution Between $x = 0$ and $x = 1$, the function has a value of -1, so

$$y = -1 \qquad \text{when } 0 \le x \le 1$$

Between $x = 1$ and $x = 2$, the slope is 2 over 1 or 2, and the line $y = 2x$ is shifted $1\frac{1}{2}$ units to the right, so

$$y = 2\left(x - \frac{3}{2}\right) \qquad \text{when } 1 \le x \le 2$$

To the right of $x = 2$, the function has a value of $+1$. So

$$y = 1 \qquad \text{when } x \ge 2$$

Now we will write the three parts of the description:

$$\mathbf{f(x) = -1 \qquad \text{when } 0 \le x \le 1}$$

$$\mathbf{f(x) = 2\left(x - \frac{3}{2}\right) \qquad \text{when } 1 \le x \le 2}$$

$$\mathbf{f(x) = 1 \qquad \text{when } x \ge 2}$$

Example 110.D.2 Write the equations for this function.

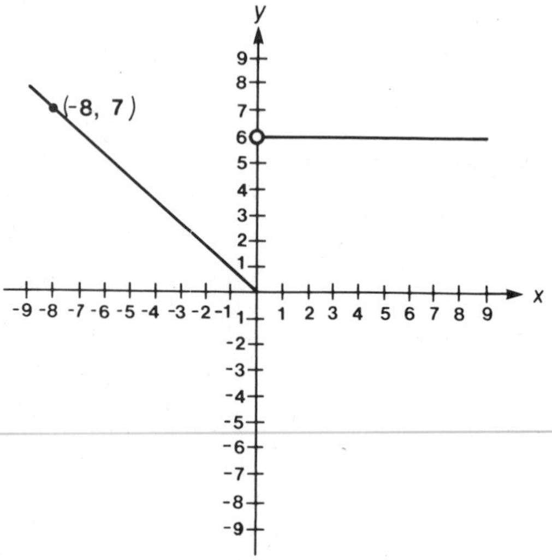

Solution The slope of the first part is $-\frac{7}{8}$ and the intercept is 0, so we can write

$$\mathbf{f(x) = -\frac{7}{8}x \qquad \text{when } x \le 0}$$

And to the right of the origin y equals 6, so

$$\mathbf{f(x) = 6 \qquad \text{when } x > 0}$$

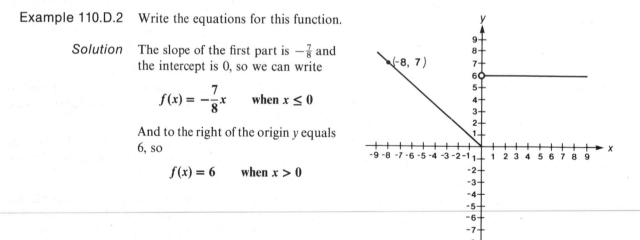

110.E Greatest integer function

The ***greatest integer function*** is a piecewise function for which a notation has been devised. It is

$$f(x) = [x]$$

The value of the function is the value of the greatest integer less than or equal to the value of x. The graph of this function is shown here.

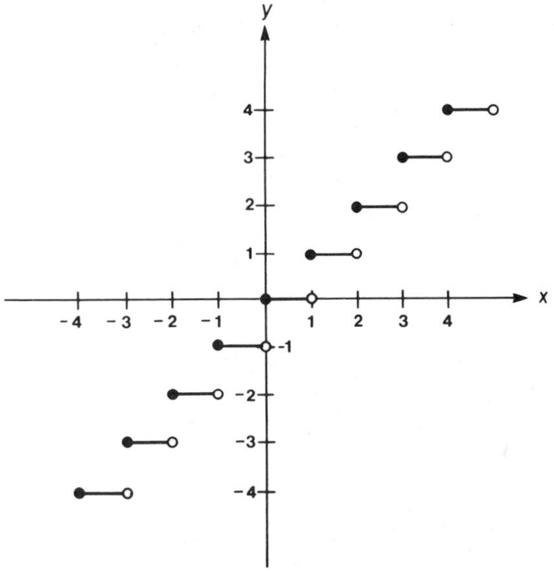

$$f(x) = [x]$$

Let's check a few values. The greatest integer less than or equal to 4 is 4, so 4 has a solid circle. The greatest integer less than or equal to 3.9 is 3, so on the graph from 3 to 4 but not including 4, the value is 3. A check of other values of x will show that the value of y increases only when the value of x gets to the next larger integral value. All functions can be shifted right or left and up or down by changing the equation, and this function is no exception. As an example, we note that the graph could be shifted 40 units to the right by adding -40 to the argument. In addition; the graph could be shifted up 10 units by adding $+10$ to the function. If we do this, we would get

$$y = [x - 40] + 10$$

Problem set 110

1. Reds varied directly as greens and inversely as purples squared. When there were 10 greens and 5 purples, there were 40 reds. How many reds were there when there were 20 greens and 4 purples?

2. The probability of having greens or a cloudy day or both was 0.9. What was the probability of having greens and a cloudy day if the probability of having a cloudy day was 0.7 and the probability of having greens was 0.5?

3. There were not too many of them at first, but the increase was exponential, and 6 hours after the big bang there were 470 in the holding pen. Then 10 hours after the big bang there were 482. How long after the big bang would it be before the number in the holding pen increased to 1460?

4. A rectangular plot of land 200 square feet in area is to be fenced in. The length of the plot is 10 feet longer than the width. What is the length of the fence required to fence in the plot of land?

5. The volume of a circular cylinder is $\pi r^2 h$, and two circular cylinders have equal volumes. The radius of the second cylinder is 2 centimeters greater than that of the first. The height of the second cylinder is one-fourth that of the first. What is the radius of the first cylinder?

6. Sketch:

(*a*) $y = |x|$ (*b*) $y = |x + 2|$ (*c*) $y = |x - 2| + 5$

7. Write the equations for this function.

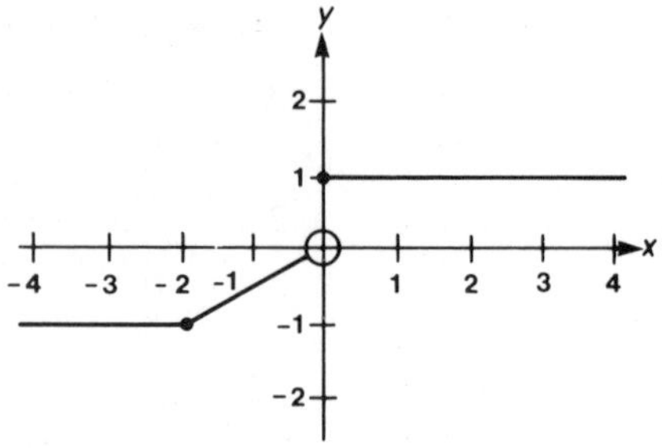

8. Sketch $y = [x]$.

9. Given: $AP = AQ$; $PB = QC$; $BR = RC$
Prove: $\angle BQR = \angle CPR$

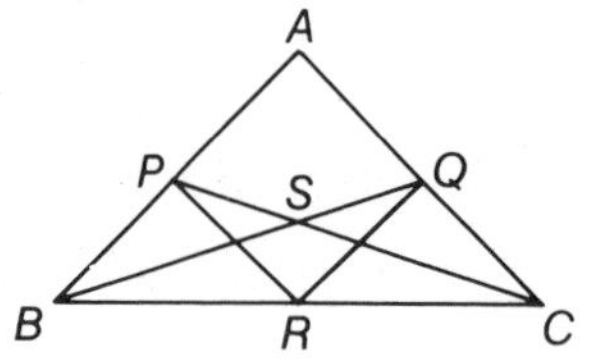

10. Given: $\overline{AC}$ is a tangent to circle O. $\overline{BA}$ is a chord of circle O.
Prove: $\angle BAC = \frac{1}{2}\overset{\frown}{BXA}$

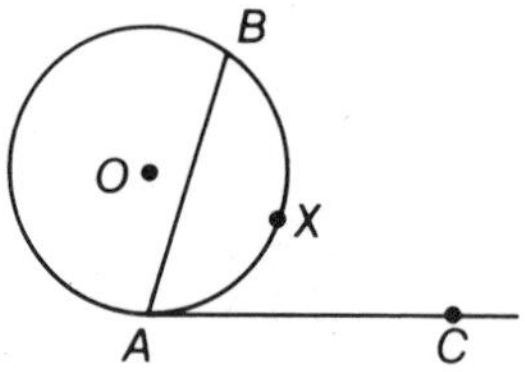

11. Given: The figure as shown.
Prove: $(BE)(EC) = (AE)(ED)$

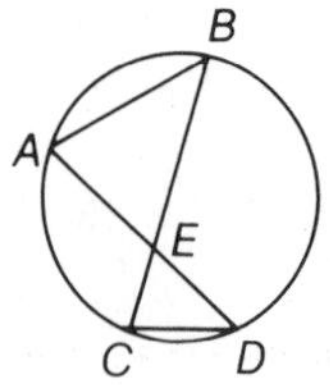

12. Given: $\angle ABC$ is an inscribed angle as shown.
Prove: $\angle ABC = \frac{1}{2}\overset{\frown}{AC}$

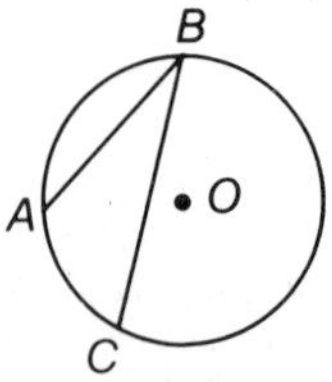

13. Find x, y, and z.

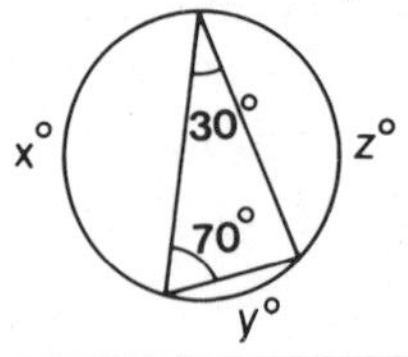

14. Is the relation $\{(2, 4), (4, 2), (1, 2), (2, 1), (1, 3)\}$ a function?

15. Indicate whether each equation shown represents an ellipse, a hyperbola, a circle, or a parabola.

(*a*) $x^2 + 4y^2 + 10x + 24y + 45 = 0$ (*b*) $x^2 + y^2 + 4x - 18y + 69 = 0$

(*c*) $25x^2 - 9y^2 + 300x - 126y + 684 = 0$ (*d*) $x + 5y^2 + 11 + 30y = 0$

(*e*) $4x^2 + 36y^2 + 48x + 216y + 324 = 0$

16. What is the fifth term in the expansion of $(a^2 - 2b^5)^7$?

17. Write equation (*d*) of Problem 15 in a form convenient for graphing and describe the figure the equation represents.

18. Graph $y = x^3 - 2x^2 - 9x + 18$. **19.** Graph $y = x^3 + 2x^2 - 5x - 6$.

20. Find the inverse function of $y = 4x - 2$.

21. Find the inverse function of $y = \frac{1}{3}x + 3$.

22. Develop the formula for the sum of the first n terms of an arithmetic sequence whose first term is a and whose common difference is d.

23. A ball is dropped from a height of 64 feet. After each bounce, the ball rebounds one-half of the distance it fell. How far will the ball have traveled when it strikes the ground for the eighth time?

24. The pH of a solution is 3. What is the concentration of hydrogen ions in moles per liter of the solution?

25. (*a*) The base of a circular cone has a radius of 8 centimeters. The height of the cone is 10 centimeters. What is the volume of the cone?
(*b*) Assume the cone is a right circular cone. What is the surface area of the cone?

26. Use echelon matrices to solve for the unknowns: $\begin{cases} -2x - y + z = -2 \\ x + 2y = 3 \\ 3y + 2z = 2 \end{cases}$

27. Find cos 15° by using the half-angle identity for cosine.

28. Solve, given that $(0° \le x < 360°)$: $2\cos^2 x - 9\sin x + 3 = 0$

29. Show that: $\dfrac{\sec^3 x - 8}{\sec^2 x + \sec x - 6} = \dfrac{\sec^2 x + 2\sec x + 4}{\sec x + 3}$

30. Given that $M = b^a$ and $N = b^c$, show that $\log_b MN = \log_b M + \log_b N$.

EP 110.91, 110.92

LESSON 111 *Intersecting chords · Secants and tangents*

111.A Intersecting chords

Each of the vertical angles formed by intersecting chords is equal to one-half the sum of the intercepted arcs. We illustrate this by noting in the left-hand figure that the sum of the intercepted arcs is 100° and that each of the vertical angles is 50°. In the right-hand figure, the sum of the intercepted arcs is 50° and each of the vertical angles is 25°.

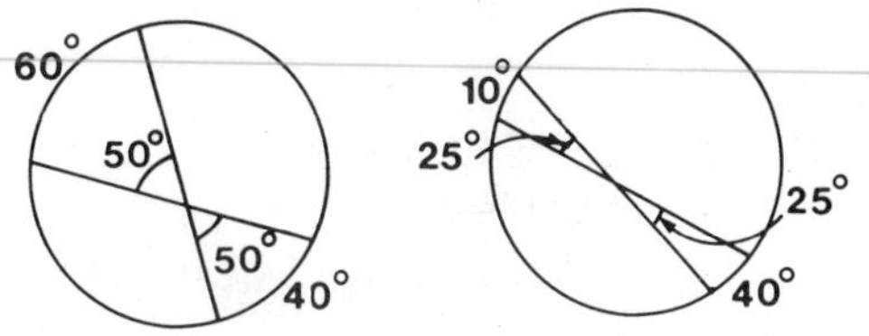

Example 111.A.1 Prove that each of the vertical angles formed by two intersecting chords equals one-half the sum of the intercepted arcs.

Solution On the next page, we draw two intersecting chords in the left-hand figure. In the center and on the right we break out angles 3 and 2.

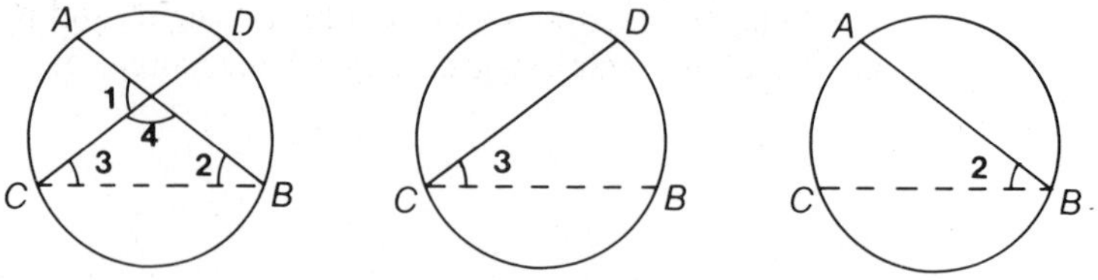

In the left-hand figure, angles 1 and 4 sum to 180° (straight angle); and angle 4 sums with angles 2 and 3 to 180° (triangle). Thus, angle 1 equals the sum of angles 2 and 3.

$$\angle 1 = \angle 2 + \angle 3$$

From the other figures, we see that angle 3 equals $\frac{1}{2}\overset{\frown}{DB}$ and angle 2 equals $\frac{1}{2}\overset{\frown}{CA}$. Now if we substitute, we get

$$\angle 1 = \frac{1}{2}\overset{\frown}{CA} + \frac{1}{2}\overset{\frown}{DB}$$

$$\angle 1 = \frac{1}{2}(\overset{\frown}{CA} + \overset{\frown}{DB})$$

Thus, the vertical angles formed by intersecting chords equal one-half the sum of the intercepted arcs.

111.B Secants and tangents

If two rays originate at a point outside a circle and cut or touch the circle, the angle at the point equals one-half the difference of the arcs intercepted on the circle. This is true if the rays are both tangents, if the rays are both secants, and also if one ray is a tangent and the other is a secant.

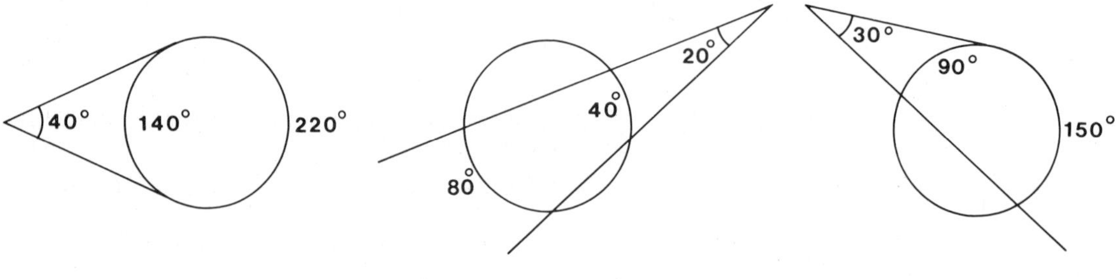

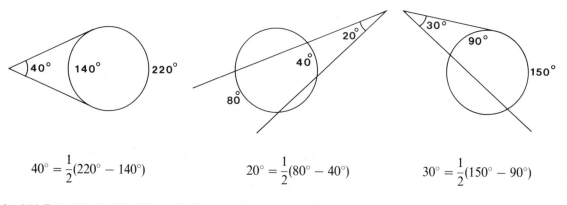

$$40° = \frac{1}{2}(220° - 140°) \qquad 20° = \frac{1}{2}(80° - 40°) \qquad 30° = \frac{1}{2}(150° - 90°)$$

Example 111.B.1 Prove that the angle formed by two secants that intersect outside a circle equals one-half the difference in the intercepted arcs.

Solution On the left we show point P and the two secants. On the right we draw chord AD and label the four angles 1, 2, 3, and 4.

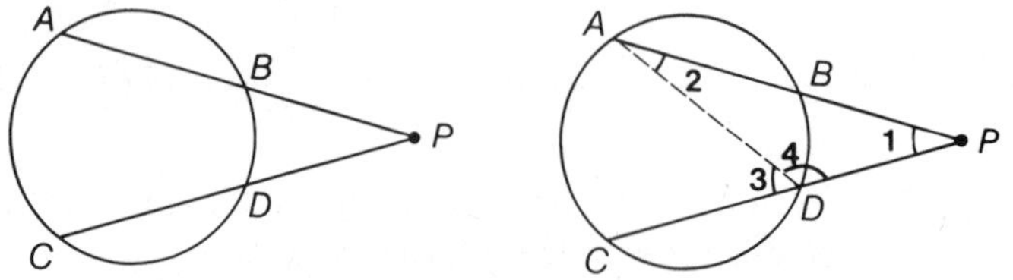

Now angles 1, 2, and 4 sum to 180° (triangle), and angles 3 and 4 sum to 180° (straight angle). Thus, angle 3 equals angle 1 plus angle 2.

$$\angle 1 + \angle 2 = \angle 3 \qquad \text{equation}$$

$$\angle 1 = \angle 3 - \angle 2 \qquad \text{rearranged}$$

Angles 2 and 3 are inscribed angles and are equal to one-half their intercepted arcs.

$$\angle 2 = \frac{1}{2}\overset{\frown}{BD} \qquad \text{inscribed angle}$$

$$\angle 3 = \frac{1}{2}\overset{\frown}{AC} \qquad \text{inscribed angle}$$

Now we substitute these values in the rearranged equation above.

$$\angle 1 = \frac{1}{2}\overset{\frown}{AC} - \frac{1}{2}\overset{\frown}{BD} \qquad \text{substituted}$$

$$\angle 1 = \frac{1}{2}(\overset{\frown}{AC} - \overset{\frown}{BD}) \qquad \text{simplified}$$

Example 111.B.2 Prove that the angle formed by a secant and a tangent that intersect outside the circle equals one-half the difference of the intercepted arcs.

Solution On the left we show the basic figure, and on the right we draw the extra segment AB and label the angles.

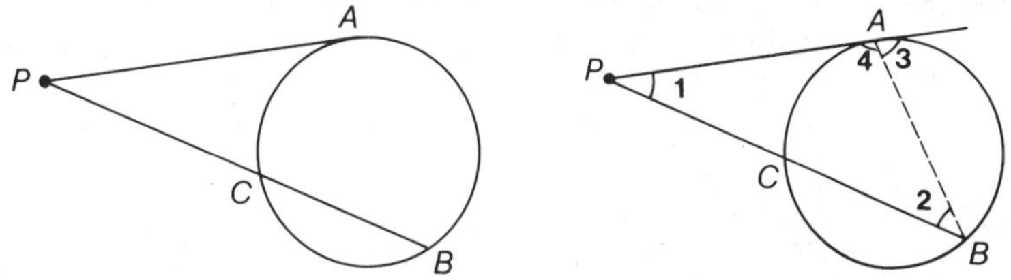

Angles 1, 2, and 4 sum to 180° (triangle), and angles 3 and 4 sum to 180° (straight angle). Thus, angle 3 equals the sum of angles 1 and 2.

$$\angle 1 + \angle 2 = \angle 3 \qquad \text{equation}$$

$$\angle 1 = \angle 3 - \angle 2 \qquad \text{rearranged}$$

Now angle 2 equals half of arc AC and angle 3 equals half of arc AB.

$$\angle 3 = \frac{1}{2}\overset{\frown}{AB} \qquad \text{chord and tangent}$$

$$\angle 2 = \frac{1}{2}\overset{\frown}{AC} \qquad \text{inscribed angle}$$

Now we substitute these values in the rearranged equation above and get

$$\angle 1 = \frac{1}{2}\overset{\frown}{AB} - \frac{1}{2}\overset{\frown}{AC} \qquad \text{substituted}$$

$$\angle 1 = \frac{1}{2}(\overset{\frown}{AB} - \overset{\frown}{AC}) \qquad \text{rearranged}$$

Example 111.B.3 Prove that the angle formed by two tangents intersecting outside a circle equals one-half the difference of the intercepted arcs.

Solution We show the basic figure on the left. On the right we draw chord AB and label the angles.

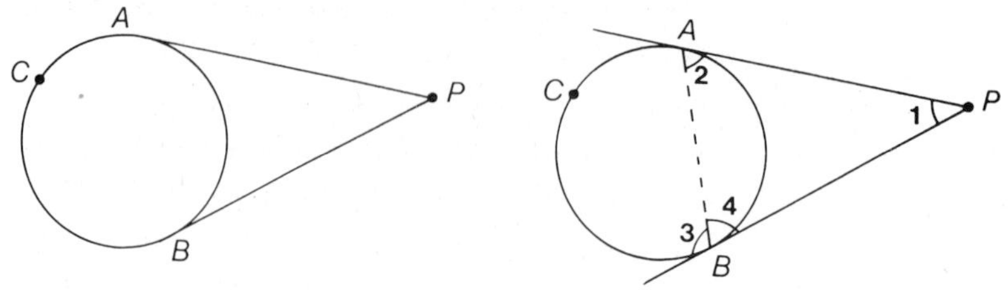

Now the sum of angles 1, 2, and 4 is 180° (triangle), and the sum of angles 3 and 4 is 180° (straight angle). Thus, angle 3 equals the sum of angles 1 and 2.

$$\angle 1 + \angle 2 = \angle 3 \qquad \text{equation}$$

$$\angle 1 = \angle 3 - \angle 2 \qquad \text{rearranged}$$

But we have proved that the angle formed by a chord and a tangent equals one-half the intercepted arc. Thus,

$$\angle 2 = \frac{1}{2}\overset{\frown}{AB} \qquad \angle 3 = \frac{1}{2}\overset{\frown}{BCA}$$

Now we substitute these values in the rearranged equation above.

$$\angle 1 = \frac{1}{2}\overset{\frown}{BCA} - \frac{1}{2}\overset{\frown}{AB} \qquad \text{substituted}$$

$$\angle 1 = \frac{1}{2}(\overset{\frown}{BCA} - \overset{\frown}{AB}) \qquad \text{rearranged}$$

Example 111.B.4 Find angle P.

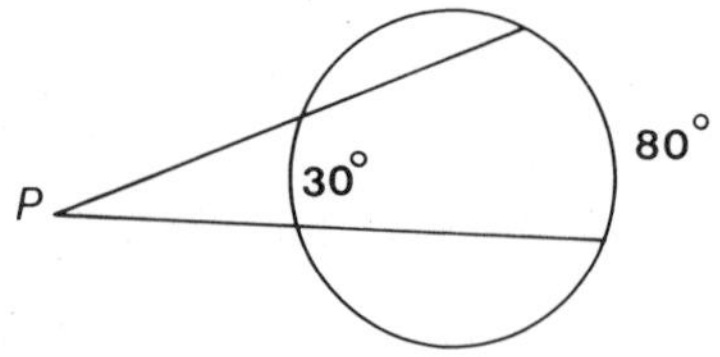

Solution Angle P equals half the difference of the intercepted arcs.

$$P = \frac{1}{2}(80° - 30°) \qquad \text{equation}$$

$$\mathbf{P = 25°} \qquad \text{solved}$$

Example 111.B.5 Find angle A.

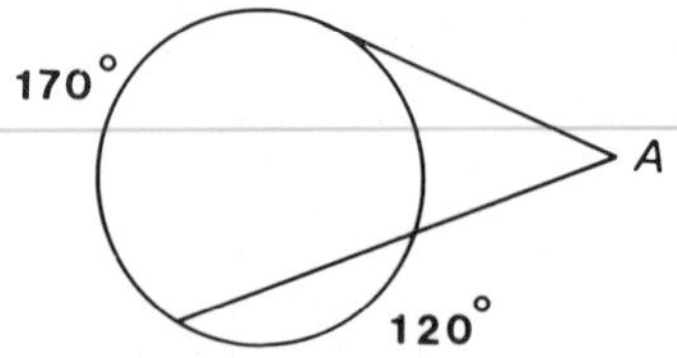

Solution Angle A equals half the difference of the intercepted arcs. One intercepted arc is 170° and we can calculate that the other is 70°.

$$\angle A = \frac{1}{2}(170° - 70°) \qquad \text{equation}$$

$$\mathbf{\angle A = 50°} \qquad \text{solved}$$

Problem set 111

1. A rectangular box has measurements L, W, and H. What happens to the volume of the box if L is multiplied by 6, W is divided by 2, and H is divided by $\sqrt{2}$?

2. The first trip was m miles long and was made in h hours. The second trip was 30 miles longer and had to be made in half the time of the first trip. How fast did Mark have to drive on the second trip?

3. The decay of the substance was exponential, and after 5 hours only 1460 grams remained. After 55 hours, Emily weighed what was left and got a reading of 450 grams. What was the half-life of the substance?

4. The average for the first 19 tosses was A feet. How far did Lucille have to toss it the next time so that the overall average would be exactly 37 feet?

5. Five workers could do k jobs in 3 hours. If 7 more workers were added to the work force, how long would it take them to do $13m$ jobs?

6. Given: $\overline{AP}$ and $\overline{CP}$ intersect at point P as shown.
Prove: $\angle APC = \frac{1}{2}(\overset{\frown}{AC} - \overset{\frown}{BD})$

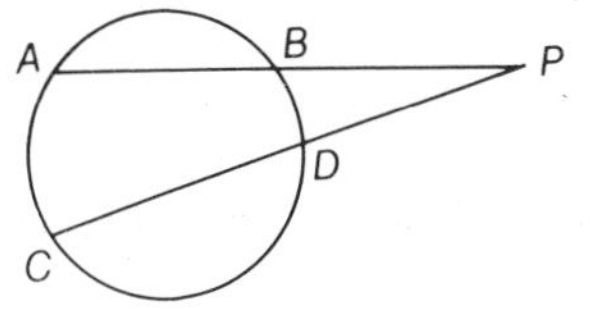

7. Given: $\overline{AB}$ and $\overline{CD}$ intersect at E as shown.
Prove: $\angle AEC = \frac{1}{2}(\overset{\frown}{AC} + \overset{\frown}{DB})$

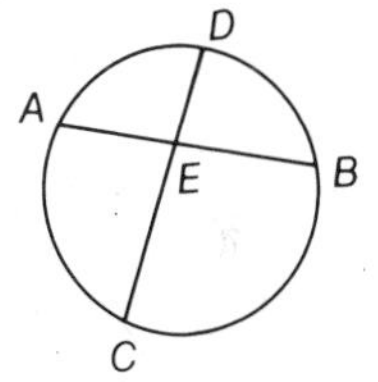

8. Given: Tangent PA and secant PB intersect at P as shown.
Prove: $\angle APB = \frac{1}{2}(\overset{\frown}{AB} - \overset{\frown}{AC})$

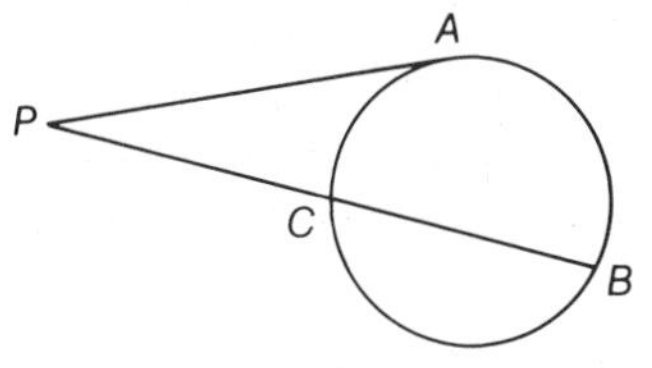

9. Given: Tangents PA and PB intersect at P as shown.
Prove: $\angle APB = \frac{1}{2}(\overset{\frown}{ACB} - \overset{\frown}{AB})$

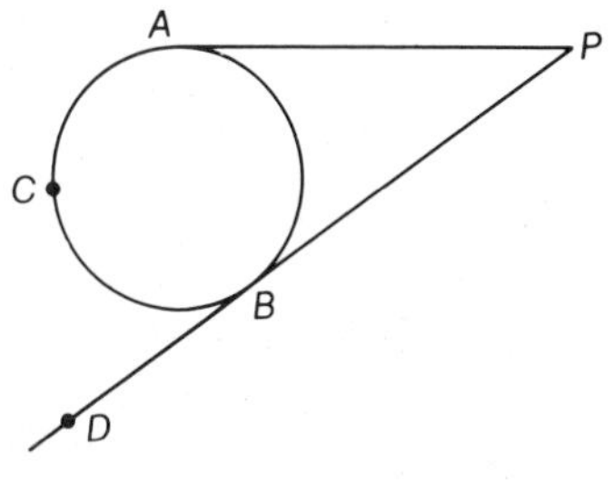

10. Given: $AP = AQ$; $PB = QC$
Prove: $BQ = PC$

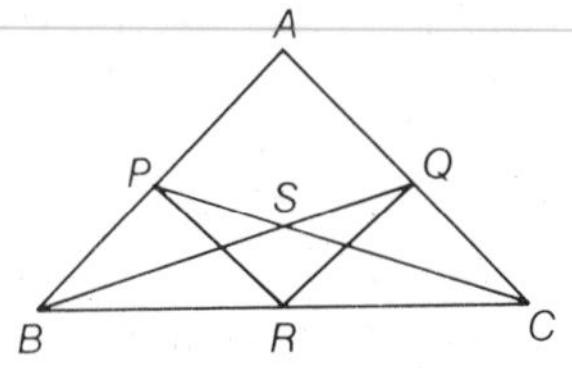

11. Find x, y, and z.

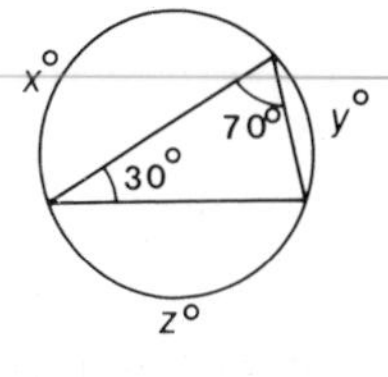

12. Sketch:
(*a*) $y = |x|$ (*b*) $y = 3 + |x|$ (*c*) $y = -3 + |x|$

13. Write the equations for the function shown.

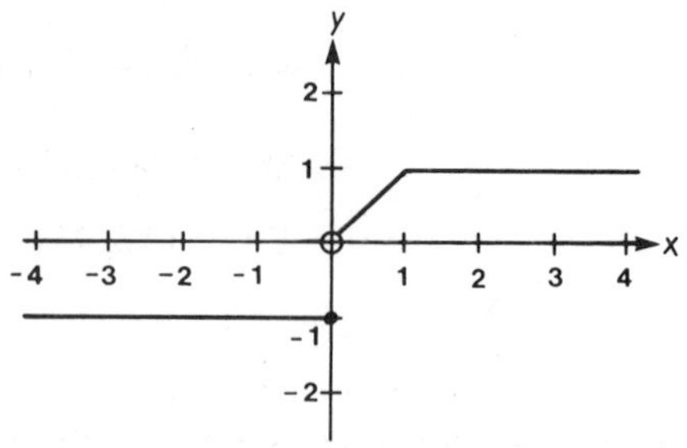

14. Sketch $y = [x]$.

15. Indicate whether each equation shown represents an ellipse, a hyperbola, a circle, or a parabola.

(*a*) $25x^2 - 16y^2 - 100x - 96y - 444 = 0$

(*b*) $4x^2 + 36y^2 + 40x - 288y + 532 = 0$ (*c*) $x^2 + y^2 + 12x - 2y + 21 = 0$

(*d*) $3x = y^2 - 6x - 27$ (*e*) $25x^2 + 9y^2 - 200x + 18y + 184 = 0$

16. Is the relation $\{(0, 2), (2, 0), (3, 1), (1, 3), (1, 1)\}$ a function?

17. Write equation (*a*) of Problem 15 in standard form and describe the properties of the conic section the equation defines.

18. Graph $y = x^3 - x^2 - 10x - 8$.

19. Graph $y = x^3 + 2x^2 - 5x - 6$.

20. Find the inverse function of $y = 2x - 3$.

21. Find the inverse function of $y = \frac{1}{4}x - 4$.

22. The ninth term of an arithmetic sequence is 37 and the fourth term of the same arithmetic sequence is 12. What is the thirteenth term of this arithmetic sequence?

23. The negative geometric mean of two numbers is -12. The arithmetic mean of the two numbers is 20. What are the two numbers?

24. Two geometric solids are similar. If one part of the larger geometric solid is $3\sqrt{2}$ times as long as the corresponding part of the smaller geometric solid, what is the ratio of the volume of the larger geometric solid to the volume of the smaller geometric solid?

25. The concentration of hydrogen ions in a solution is 4.3×10^{-9} mole per liter. What is the pH of the solution?

26. Use Cramer's rule to solve for z. Use the method of cofactors to evaluate the determinants.

$$\begin{cases} 2x - 3y + z = 2 \\ 3x - y = 2 \\ 2y + 3z = 11 \end{cases}$$

27. Solve this triangle for side a.

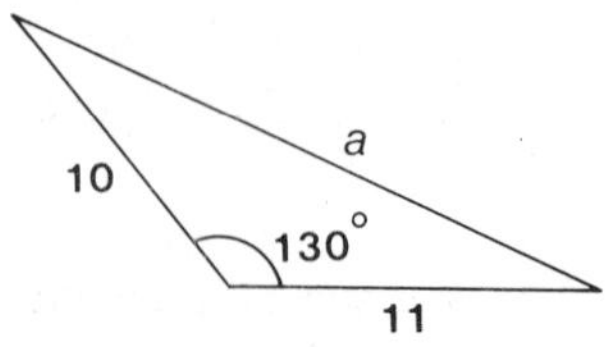

28. Solve, given that ($0° \le x < 360°$): $2 \sin^2 x - 9 \cos x + 3 = 0$

29. Show that: $(\sec x - \tan x)^2 = \dfrac{1 - \sin x}{1 + \sin x}$

30. Express log 6 in terms of natural logarithms. Do not find a numerical answer.

EP 111.93, 111.94

LESSON 112 Primes, relative primes · Rational roots theorem

112.A Primes and relative primes

If a counting number can be composed as the product of two other counting numbers that are both greater than 1, we say that the counting number is a ***composite number.*** The number 6 is a composite number because it can be composed by multiplying 3 and 2.

$$3 \times 2 = 6$$

Some numbers have only themselves and the number 1 as factors and thus cannot be composed as a product of two other counting numbers. These numbers are called ***prime numbers.*** The number 7 is a prime number because 7 and 1 are its only counting number factors.

$$7 \times 1 = 7$$

A fraction is reducible if the numerator and the denominator contain a common prime factor. The fraction $\frac{10}{14}$ is reducible because 10 and 14 both have 2 as a factor.

$$\frac{10}{14} = \frac{\cancel{2} \cdot 5}{\cancel{2} \cdot 7} = \frac{5}{7}$$

A fraction cannot be reduced if the numerator and the denominator do not have a common prime factor. Although the numerator and the denominator of $\frac{10}{21}$ are composite numbers, the fraction cannot be reduced because there are no common factors.

$$\frac{10}{21} = \frac{2 \cdot 5}{3 \cdot 7}$$

We often use the words ***relatively prime*** to describe two counting numbers that do not have common factors other than the number 1. Thus, we could say that 10 and 21 are relatively prime. We normally think of composite numbers when we hear the words *relatively prime.* The numbers do not have to be composite numbers, however, because two different prime numbers do not have common factors other than the number 1. Thus any two different prime numbers are also relatively prime.

Counting numbers have a property that is not immediately obvious. A statement of this property is called the ***fundamental theorem of arithmetic.*** **Each time a counting number is written as a product of prime factors, the same factors must be used.** The order of the factors may be changed, but the factors must be the same. For example, there are three ways that we can write 12 as a product of prime factors,

$$2 \cdot 2 \cdot 3 \qquad 2 \cdot 3 \cdot 2 \qquad 3 \cdot 2 \cdot 2$$

but the same factors must be used each time. This fact is sometimes useful in proofs. For instance, if we have the equation,

$$5(12) = kp$$

we know immediately that kp can be written as $5 \cdot 2 \cdot 2 \cdot 3$ because the prime factors of the left side must be the same as the prime factors on the right side. In the same way, if J is an integer and P and Q have no common factors, and if

$$PJ = -8QQQ$$

then P must be one of the factors of -8.

$$(P)(\text{factors of } J) = (\text{factors of } -8)(\text{factors of } QQQ)$$

All the prime factors of P and J must also appear on the right side because they appear on the left side. Since P and Q have no factors in common, P must be a factor of -8.

112.B Rational roots theorem

Polynomials are classified by the values of the coefficients of the terms of the polynomial. Some polynomials have complex numbers as coefficients and are called ***complex polynomials.*** We will not consider these polynomials and will restrict our observations to polynomials that have real number coefficients. We call a polynomial whose coefficients are real numbers a ***real polynomial.*** A real polynomial equation in which the highest power of the variable is 2 is a quadratic equation. We have learned to solve quadratic equations by factoring, by completing the square, and by using the quadratic formula. Thus, we can find the roots of any quadratic equation quickly and easily. Unfortunately, the search for the roots of higher-order equations such as

$$3x^4 + 9x^2 - 5x + 2 = 0$$

is a task that is considerably more complex. In advanced algebra courses, we will learn to prove theorems that will help us find the solutions. One of these theorems is as follows:

Every real polynomial equation of degree *n* has exactly *n* roots.

This theorem allows us to state that the fourth-degree equation above has exactly four roots. Also, we will learn to prove that

If a real polynomial equation has $a + bi$ as a root, then it has $a - bi$ as a root.

This theorem tells us that complex roots of real polynomial equations always occur in conjugate pairs. If a root of a polynomial equation does not have an imaginary part, then the root is a real number. Every real number is either a rational number or an irrational number.

The ***rational roots theorem*** allows us to say that if the equation

$$3x^4 + 9x^2 - 5x + 2 = 0$$

has a rational root, then this root is one of the possible quotients of an integral factor of 2 divided by an integral factor of 3, as we show here.

INTEGRAL FACTORS		POSSIBLE QUOTIENTS
$\dfrac{\{1, -1, 2, -2\}}{\{1, -1, 3, -3\}}$	$\longrightarrow$	$1, -1, 2, -2, \dfrac{1}{3}, -\dfrac{1}{3}, \dfrac{2}{3}, -\dfrac{2}{3}$

We don't know if one of these numbers is a root, for we don't know if the equation has a rational root. Yet we do know that if the equation has a rational root, then it must be one of these numbers. This is not much information, but it is better than no information at all. It gives us a starting point in our search for roots. If we are given the equation,

$$6x^7 - 3x + 5 = 0$$

we can tell by inspection that if this equation has rational roots, they must be one of the following combinations of an integral factor of 5 divided by an integral factor of 6.

$$1, -1, \frac{1}{2}, -\frac{1}{2}, \frac{1}{3}, -\frac{1}{3}, \frac{1}{6}, -\frac{1}{6}, \frac{5}{2}, -\frac{5}{2}, \frac{5}{3}, -\frac{5}{3}, \frac{5}{6}, -\frac{5}{6}, 5, -5$$

In general, each of the possible rational roots of a polynomial equation whose coefficients are integers is a fraction whose numerator is some integral factor of the constant term divided by some integral factor of the leading coefficient.

$$\frac{\text{an integral factor of the constant}}{\text{an integral factor of the leading coefficient}}$$

The proof is interesting, as you will see in the following example.

Example 112.B.1 Use the polynomial equation $2x^3 + 3x^2 + 2x + 5 = 0$ to develop a specific proof of the rational roots theorem.

Solution We begin by assuming that a solution p/q exists, where p and q do not have a common factor. If so, we can replace x^3 with p^3/q^3, x^2 with p^2/q^2, and x with p/q.

$$2\frac{p^3}{q^3} + 3\frac{p^2}{q^2} + 2\frac{p}{q} + 5 = 0$$

We can eliminate the denominators if we multiply every term by q^3. We do this and get

$$(a) \quad 2p^3 + 3p^2q + 2pq^2 + 5q^3 = 0$$

Now we move $5q^3$ to the right-hand side and factor out a p on the left.

$$p(2p^2 + 3pq + 2q^2) = -5q^3$$

Since p and q are integers, the expression in the parentheses must also be an integer. So we have

$$p(\text{some integer}) = -5qqq$$

All the factors on the left must appear on the right, and since p and q do not have a common factor, p must be a factor of -5. Now we rearrange equation (a) so that all terms on the left have q as a factor.

$$(b) \quad 3p^2q + 2pq^2 + 5q^3 = -2p^3$$

Next we factor out q.

$$q(3p^2 + 2pq + 5q^2) = -2p^3$$

so
$$q(\text{some integer}) = -2p^3$$

Now since p and q do not have a common factor and all the factors on the left must appear on the right, then q must be a factor of -2. Thus we have shown that if a rational root p/q exists, then p must be a factor of -5 and q must be a factor of -2.

Example 112.B.2 List the possible rational roots of the equation $4x^{14} + 3x^8 + 7x + 3 = 0$.

Solution **We do not know if this equation has a rational root, but if it does, it must be one of the following rational numbers:**

$$\pm 1, \pm\frac{1}{2}, \pm\frac{1}{4}, \pm 3, \pm\frac{3}{2}, \pm\frac{3}{4}$$

Problem set 112

1. The probability of reds was 0.4, and the probability of sunshine was 0.7. If the probability of having both reds and sunshine was 0.25, what was the probability of having reds or sunshine or both reds and sunshine?

2. A pair of dice is rolled. What is the probability that the number will be either 7 or 11?

3. Four workers could do k jobs in m hours. If 3 more workers were hired, how long would it take them to do 35 jobs?

4. Sowega ran m miles in h hours. Then he ran k miles in m minutes. At the same overall average rate, how many minutes would it take Sowega to run 30 miles?

5. The wheel rolled merrily along at m miles per hour. If the radius of the wheel was c centimeters, what was the angular velocity in radians per second?

6. Are 136 and 81 relatively prime? If not, what common factor do both numbers share?

7. Are two consecutive positive integers always relatively prime?

8. Use the polynomial $2x^2 + 3x + 5 = 0$ to develop a specific proof of the rational roots theorem.

9. List the possible rational roots of the equation $4x^{15} - 2x^9 + 6x + 3 = 0$.

10. Given: $\overline{AP}$ and $\overline{CP}$ intersect at point P as shown.
Prove: $\angle APC = \frac{1}{2}(\overset{\frown}{AC} - \overset{\frown}{BD})$

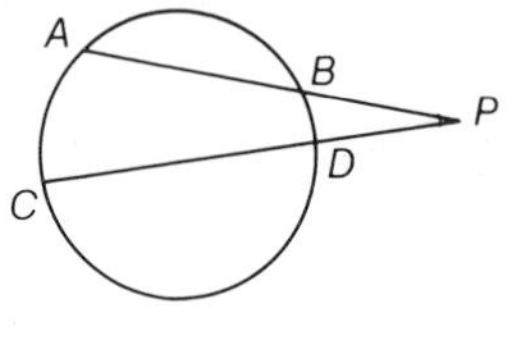

11. Given: Tangent AP and secant PB intersect at point P as shown.
Prove: $\angle APB = \frac{1}{2}(\overset{\frown}{AB} - \overset{\frown}{AC})$

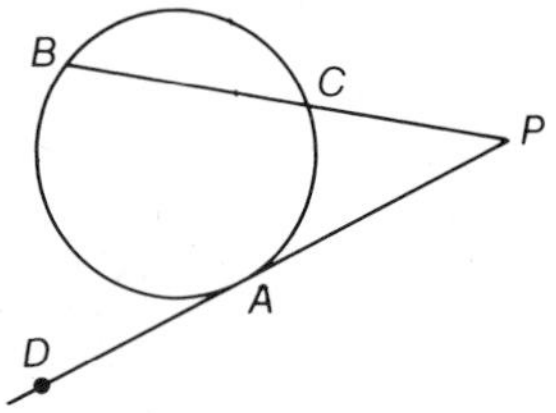

12. Given: $\overline{AB}$ and $\overline{CD}$ intersect at E as shown.
Prove: $\angle AEC = \frac{1}{2}(\overset{\frown}{AC} + \overset{\frown}{DB})$

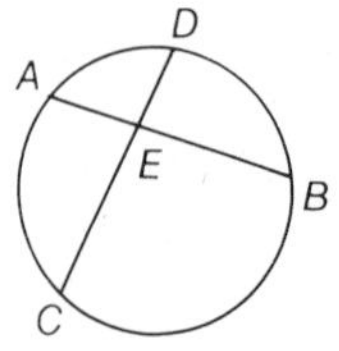

13. Given: Tangents AP and BP intersect at P as shown.
Prove: $\angle APB = \frac{1}{2}(\overset{\frown}{ACB} - \overset{\frown}{AB})$

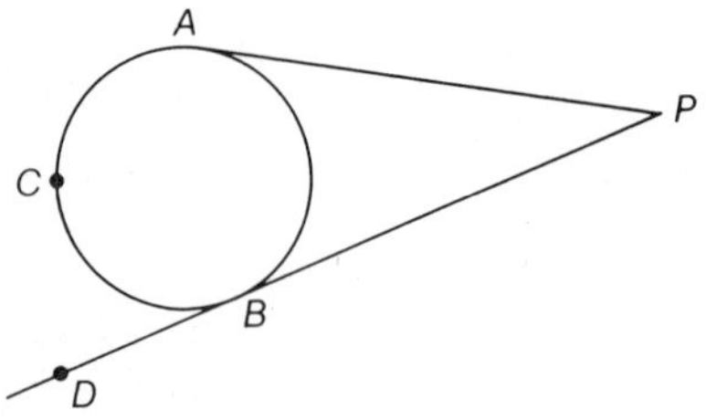

14. Use the figures shown to prove the Pythagorean theorem.

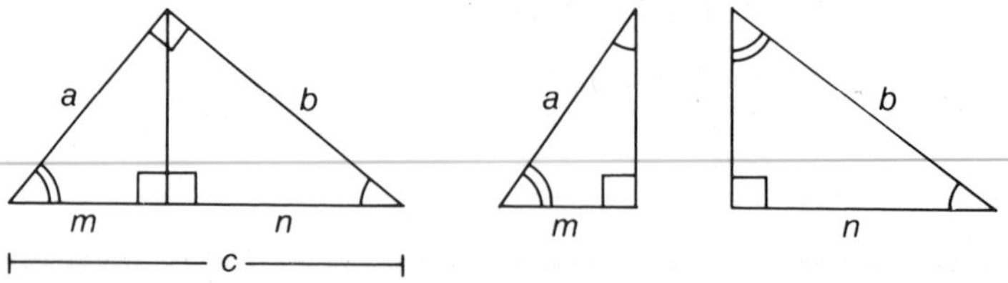

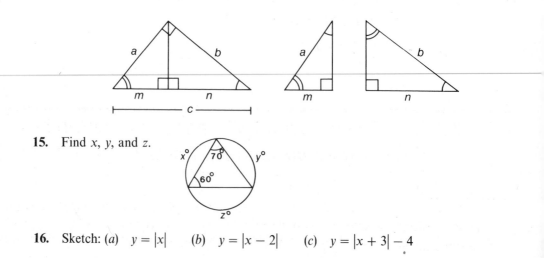

15. Find x, y, and z.

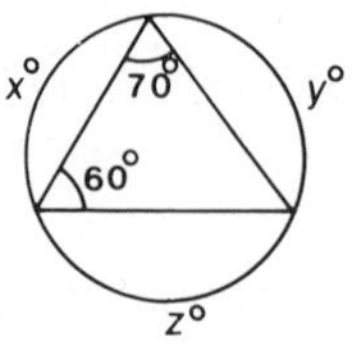

16. Sketch: (a) $y = |x|$ (b) $y = |x - 2|$ (c) $y = |x + 3| - 4$

17. Write the equations of the function shown.

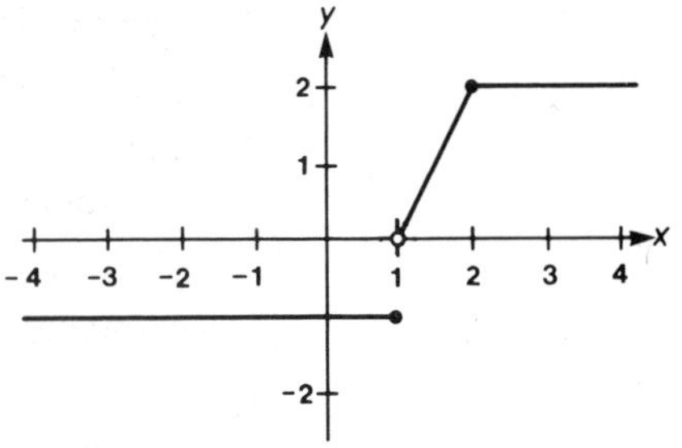

18. Sketch $y = [x] - 2$.

19. Indicate whether each equation shown represents an ellipse, a hyperbola, a circle, or a parabola.

(*a*) $x^2 + y^2 - 10x + 8y + 5 = 0$ (*b*) $12x^2 + y^2 = 48$

(*c*) $4x^2 + 36y^2 + 40x - 288y + 532 = 0$ (*d*) $16x^2 - 9y^2 + 144 = 0$

(*e*) $10x = -y^2$

20. Is the relation $\{(1, 3), (5, 6), (4, 4), (3, 4)\}$ a function?

21. Write equation (*a*) of Problem 19 in standard form and describe the conic section which the equation represents.

22. Factor $x^2 + x + 2$ over the set of complex numbers.

23. Graph $y = x^3 - 3x^2 - x + 3$.

24. The geometric mean of two numbers is 15. The arithmetic mean of the two numbers is 39. Find the two numbers.

25. The base of a pyramid is a regular pentagon with a perimeter of 20 centimeters. What is the volume of the pyramid if its height is 10 centimeters?

26. The concentration of hydrogen ions in a solution is 5.2×10^{-8} mole per liter. What is the pH of the solution?

27. Use echelon matrices to solve for the unknowns: $\begin{cases} 2x - y + z = 4 \\ 2y - z = -3 \\ 3x - 2y = 5 \end{cases}$

28. Show that: $(1 + \tan x)^2 = \sec^2 x + 2 \tan x$

29. Solve: $3 \sec^2 x - 2\sqrt{3} \tan x - 6 = 0$

30. Find the base 2 antilogarithm of -3.

EP 112.95, 112.96

LESSON 113 Horizontal and vertical asymptotes · Lines that contain holes

113.A Horizontal and vertical asymptotes

Every real number can be graphed on a number line, and the relative positions of the graphs of the numbers allow us to visualize the way real numbers are arranged in order. A number is said to be ***greater than*** another number if its graph on a horizontal number line lies to the right of the graph of the other number. The ***absolute value*** of a number is often defined to be the distance of the graph of the number from the origin. We tend to think of the absolute value of a number as designating the quality of bigness of the number. The use of the word *bigness* is frowned upon by some, but we find that the words *big* and *little* (or *large* and *small*) are very helpful when discussing the absolute values of numbers. When we say that a number is a very small negative number, we are saying that the absolute value of this negative number is very small.

VERY SMALL NEGATIVE NUMBER	SMALL POSITIVE NUMBER
-0.0000032	$+0.032$
LARGE NEGATIVE NUMBER	VERY LARGE POSITIVE NUMBER
$-478{,}462$	$+478{,}629{,}413$

Of course, size is relative; and in some cases -0.0000032 would be thought of as a very large negative number.

If the numerator of a fraction is a positive constant and the denominator is a very large positive number, the value of the fraction is a very small positive number. Likewise, if the numerator of a fraction is a positive constant and the denominator is a very large negative number, the value of the fraction is a very small negative number.

$$\frac{4}{1{,}000{,}000} = 0.000004 \qquad \frac{4}{-1{,}000{,}000} = -0.000004$$

If the signs of the numerators of the above fractions are changed, then the values of the fractions change in sign as we show below.

$$\frac{-4}{1{,}000{,}000} = -0.000004 \qquad \frac{-4}{-1{,}000{,}000} = 0.000004$$

To investigate further, we will use the fraction $\frac{4}{x}$. **If x is replaced with very small positive numbers, the value of this fraction becomes very large. The closer the value of x gets to zero, the larger the absolute value of the fraction becomes.**

$$\frac{4}{4} = 1, \quad \frac{4}{2} = 2, \quad \frac{4}{1} = 4, \quad \frac{4}{0.1} = 40, \quad \frac{4}{0.01} = 400, \quad \frac{4}{0.001} = 4000, \quad \frac{4}{0.0001} = 40{,}000$$

If the denominator of this fraction is a very small negative number, the value of this fraction is a very large negative number. The closer the denominator gets to zero, the larger the absolute value of the fraction becomes.

$$\frac{4}{-4} = -1, \quad \frac{4}{-2} = -2, \quad \frac{4}{-1} = -4, \quad \frac{4}{-0.1} = -40, \quad \frac{4}{-0.01} = -400,$$

$$\frac{4}{-0.001} = -4000, \quad \frac{4}{-0.0001} = -40{,}000$$

We can demonstrate how the value of a fraction varies as the value of the denominator changes by graphing the function

$$y = \frac{4}{x}$$

Both large positive and negative values of x cause the value of y to get smaller and smaller, and we say that the value of **y approaches zero.** For x values close to zero the value of y gets very large positive or very large negative. We say that the line $x = 0$ is a ***vertical asymptote*** and that the line $y = 0$ is a ***horizontal asymptote*** for this function. A line is called an ***asymptote*** if the curve approaches the line but does not touch the line as the absolute value of either coordinate becomes very large.

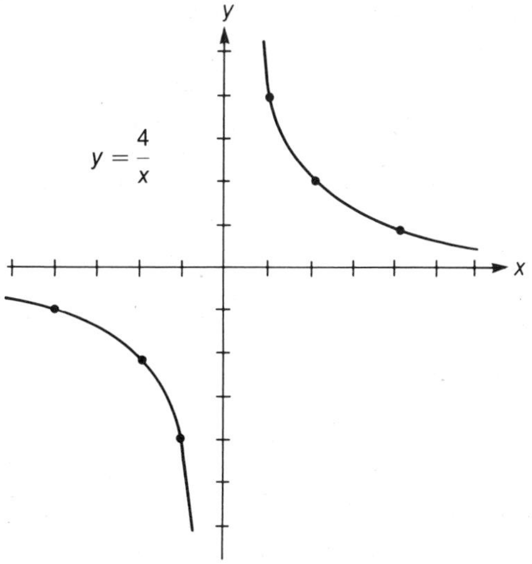

We note that on the positive side of 0 the value of the function increases without limit as x approaches 0 from the right. On the negative side of 0, the value of the function decreases without limit as x approaches 0 from the left. We note that the graph gets closer and closer to the y axis but never touches it.

Example 113.A.1 Sketch the function $y = \dfrac{1}{x - 4}$.

Solution First we look for the horizontal asymptote. If x is a huge positive number (HPN), the denominator is a huge positive number because HPN − 4 is still a huge positive number; and the value of the fraction is very close to zero. If x is a huge negative number (HNN), the denominator is also a huge negative number because HNN − 4 is still a huge negative number.

$$\frac{1}{\text{HPN} - 4} \approx 0 \qquad \frac{1}{\text{HNN} - 4} \approx 0$$

So we see that if x is a huge positive number or a huge negative number, the value of the function is almost zero, so the line $y = 0$ (the x axis) is our horizontal asymptote at both ends.

If x equals $+4$, the denominator equals 0, so the graph could have a vertical asymptote at $x = +4$. Let's check a few values of x to the left and right of 4.

IF $x = +4.5$

$$y = \frac{1}{4.5 - 4} = \frac{1}{0.5} = 2$$

IF $x = 4.1$

$$y = \frac{1}{4.1 - 4} = \frac{1}{0.1} = 10$$

IF $x = 3.5$

$$y = \frac{1}{3.5 - 4} = \frac{1}{-0.5} = -2$$

IF $x = 3.9$

$$y = \frac{1}{3.9 - 4} = \frac{1}{-0.1} = -10$$

The four ordered pairs (4.5, 2), (4.1, 10), (3.5, −2), (3.9, −10) are sufficient to allow us to sketch the graph of the function. **All we want is a rough sketch; a freehand sketch will suffice. We just want an idea of what the graph looks like and don't want to waste a lot of time being more accurate than is necessary.** Thus, we won't even bother to show any values on the graph other than those for a few values of x.

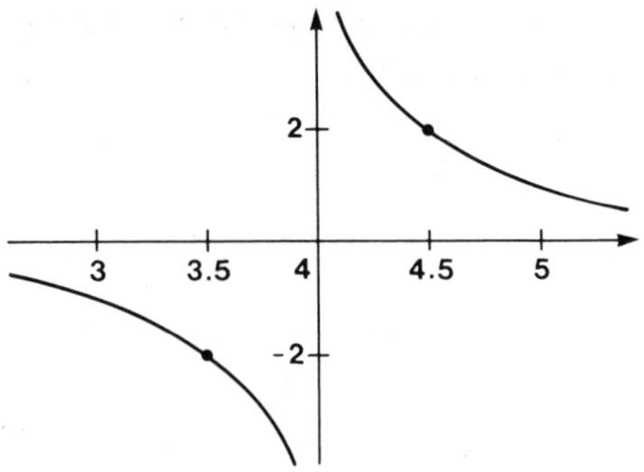

113.B Lines that contain holes

If we are asked to graph the function

$$y = \frac{x^2 - x - 6}{x - 3}$$

the first thing we should note is that the denominator will equal zero if x equals $+3$, so this value of x cannot be used. Next we should try to simplify the function. Let's try to factor the numerator.

$$y = \frac{(x - 3)(x + 2)}{x - 3} = x + 2 \qquad (x \neq 3)$$

We were able to cancel the common factors $(x - 3)$, and the equation reduces to the equation of the line $y = x + 2$. **But the x value of $+3$ still cannot be used because this value of x would cause the original function to have a denominator of zero.** Since division by zero is not permitted, our simplification is not permissible when $x = 3$. We note this by drawing the graph of the line $y = x + 2$ and drawing an empty circle at the x value of $+3$.

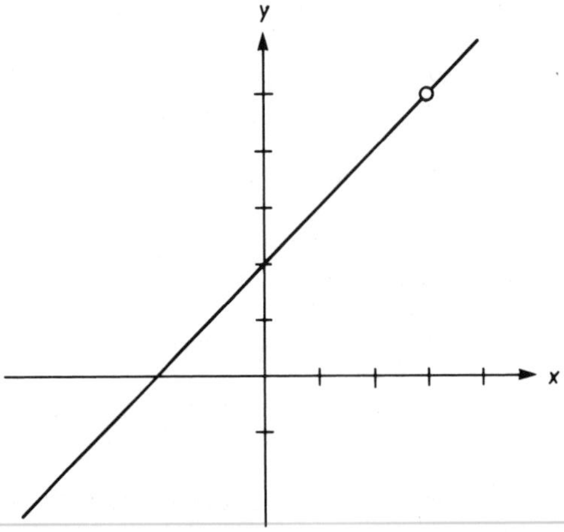

Thus, the graph of this function is not the whole line but a line with a hole in it!

Example 113.B.1 Graph the function $y = \dfrac{-x^2 - 5x - 6}{x + 2}$.

Solution First we note that the function is not defined when x equals -2 because this value of x causes the denominator to equal zero. Next we factor the numerator and cancel.

$$y = \frac{(-1)(x + 3)\cancel{(x + 2)}}{\cancel{x + 2}} \longrightarrow y = -x - 3 \qquad (x \neq -2)$$

Now we graph the function and get a graph of the line $y = -x - 3$ with a hole in it at the x value of -2.

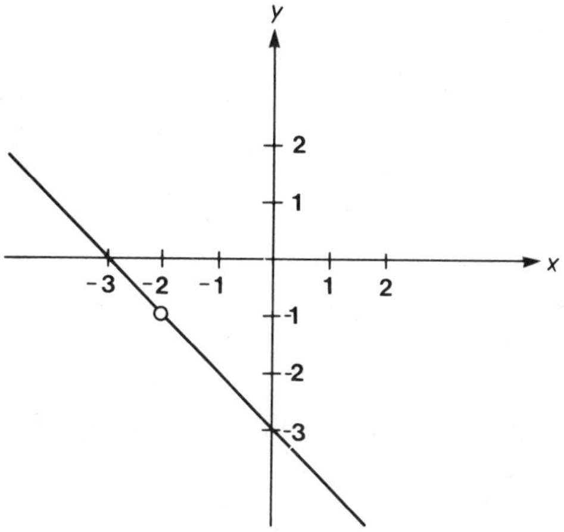

Problem set 113

1. Rotonda could eat p of the things in 6 minutes, while Slim Jim required m minutes to eat just 1 of the things. Jim had a box that contained 12 of the things and he ate for 2 minutes and then was joined by Rotonda. How much more time did it take the two of them to consume the rest of the contents of the box?

2. Seven little shoemakers lived in a hut, but the workroom had room for only 3 of them at a time. How many shoemaking teams were possible?

3. The first leg of m miles was covered in h hours. The second leg was 5 miles longer. If they drove at the same rate, how long did the entire trip take?

4. The cost varied linearly with the number purchased. If 10 were purchased, the cost was \$55; but when 20 were purchased, the cost was \$85. What did it cost if only 1 was purchased?

5. If $d = \dfrac{7}{x + y}$, then $\dfrac{4}{d - 3} = ?$

6. Sketch the function $y = \dfrac{1}{x - 5}$.

7. Graph the function $y = \dfrac{x^2 - 2x - 3}{x + 1}$.

8. Graph $y = [x] + 2$.

9. Graph the function $y = \dfrac{x^2 + 3x + 2}{x + 2}$.

10. Sketch $y = 3 + 2 \sin 2\left(x - \dfrac{\pi}{6}\right)$.

11. Are two prime numbers always relatively prime?

12. Are 144 and 123 relatively prime? If not, what common factor do both numbers share?

13. List the possible rational roots of the equation $5x^{13} - 4x^6 + 2x^2 - 3 = 0$.

14. Given: Tangent AP and secant PB intersect at P as shown.
Prove: $\angle APB = \frac{1}{2}(\overset{\frown}{AB} - \overset{\frown}{AC})$

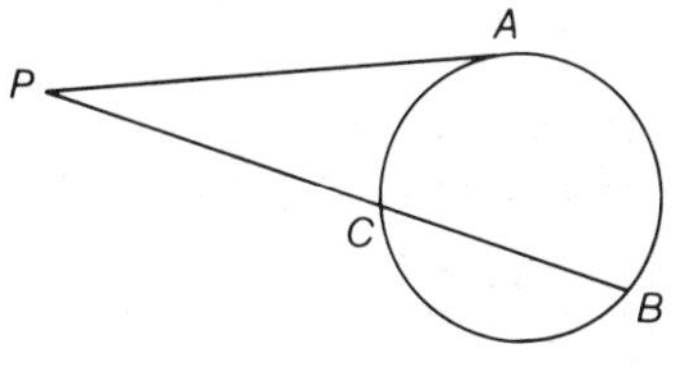

15. Given: Secants AP and CP intersect at point P as shown.
Prove: Show that $\triangle PAD \sim \triangle PCB$.

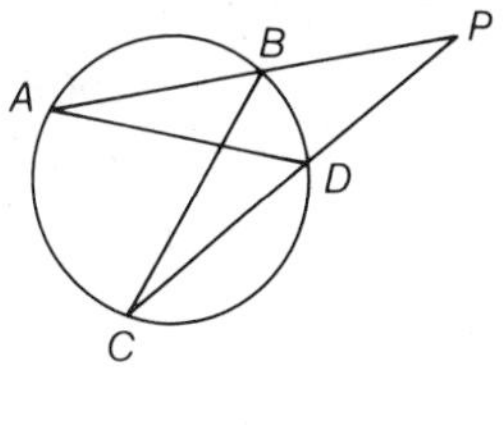

16. Given: Tangents PA and PB intersect at point P as shown.
Prove: $\angle APB = \frac{1}{2}(\overset{\frown}{ACB} - \overset{\frown}{AB})$

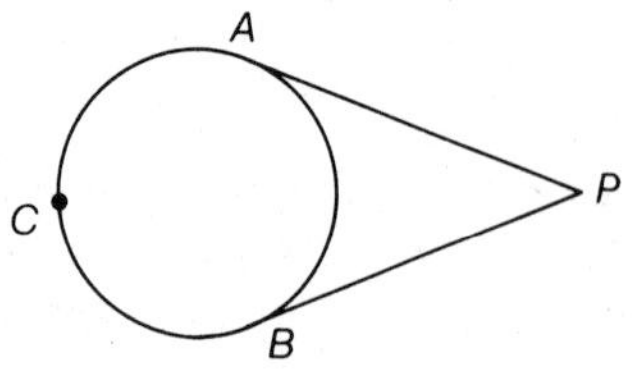

17. Given: $\overline{AB}$ and $\overline{CD}$ intersect at point E as shown.
Prove: $(AE)(EB) = (CE)(ED)$
Hint: Show $\triangle AEC \sim \triangle DEB$.

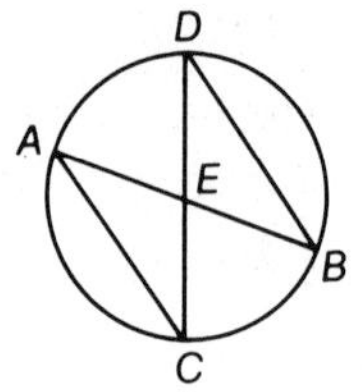

18. Prove that the sum of the angles of a triangle is 180°.

19. Write the equations of the function shown.

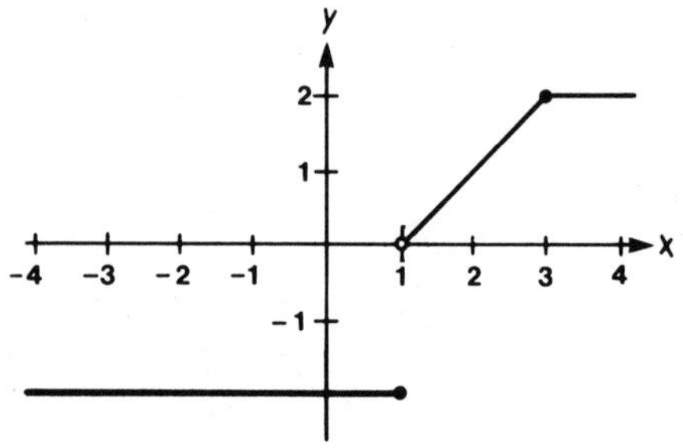

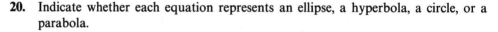

20. Indicate whether each equation represents an ellipse, a hyperbola, a circle, or a parabola.

(*a*) $25x^2 - 144y^2 = 3600$ (*b*) $12x^2 + y^2 = 48$ (*c*) $x^2 + y^2 = 4$
(*d*) $x = -3y^2 - 12y - 5$ (*e*) $9x^2 - y^2 - 90x + 4y + 302 = 0$

21. Complete the square on equation (*d*) of Problem 20 and describe the conic section represented by the equation.

22. Find the distance from (2, 5) to $x + y - 5 = 0$.

23. Find the inverse function of $y = 5x - 3$.

24. Find the sum of the following infinite geometric series:

$$\frac{1}{4} + \left(-\frac{3}{16}\right) + \frac{9}{64} + \cdots$$

25. The base of a pyramid is a square of perimeter 24 centimeters. What is the volume of the pyramid if its height is 8 centimeters?

26. Use Cramer's rule to solve for x. Use the method of cofactors to evaluate the determinants.

$$\begin{cases} 2x + 3y + z = -1 \\ 2y - 3z = -4 \\ 3x + 4y = -5 \end{cases}$$

27. Write the three cube roots of 8 cis 270° in rectangular form. Give exact solutions.

28. Solve, given that $(0° \leq x < 360°)$: $3 \tan^2 x - 1 = 0$

29. Show that: $\sec^2 x = \dfrac{2 \sec 2x}{\sec 2x + 1}$

30. Solve: $\log_2 (x - 1) < 2$

EP 113.97, 113.98

LESSON 114 Products of chord segments · Products of secant segments · Secants and tangents

114.A Products of chord segments

It is interesting to note that if the endpoints of intersecting chords are connected to form triangles, the triangles are always similar. **In the similar triangles shown in the second figure below, the products of the lengths of the segments of each chord are equal.**

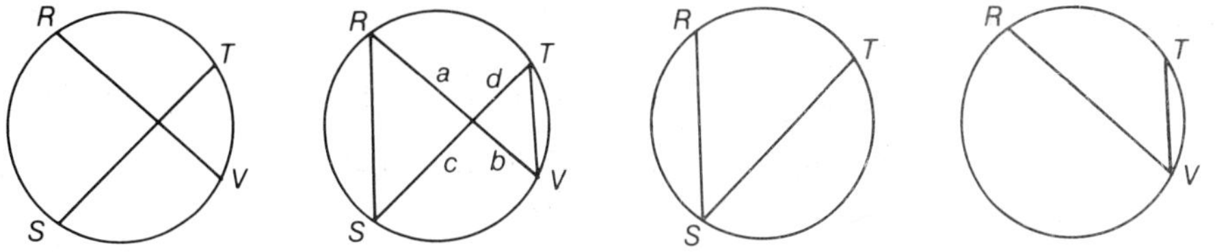

In the left-hand figure, we show the intersecting chords. In the next figure, we connect the endpoints of the chords to form two triangles. These triangles are similar by AAA. First we note that the vertical angles formed by the intersecting chords are equal. Then we break out two figures as shown on the right, and we see that angles S and V are equal because both intercept arc RT. Thus the third angles in the two triangles are equal. If we write the ratios of the sides of the similar triangles, we get

$$\frac{a}{d} = \frac{c}{b}$$

and if we cross multiply, we get two products

$$ab = cd$$

Example 114.A.1 Find x.

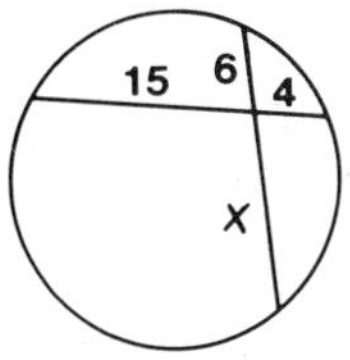

Solution The products of the lengths of the two segments of each chord are equal, so

$6x = 15 \cdot 4$	products of lengths of segments
$\mathbf{x = 10}$	solved

114.B Products of secant segments

We remember that a secant is a line that intersects a circle at two points. For the proofs of this lesson we will call the segment from a point outside the circle to the second point of intersection a ***secant segment*** and the segment from the point outside the circle to the first point of intersection an ***external secant segment***. **We can prove that when two secants are drawn to a circle from a point outside the circle, the product of the length of one secant segment and the length of its external segment equals the product of the length of the other secant segment and the length of its external segment.** The proof requires that we draw intersecting chords.

On the left on the next page, we draw the secants from point P. In the next figure, we draw the intersecting chords; and to the right, we break out the triangles in which we are interested.

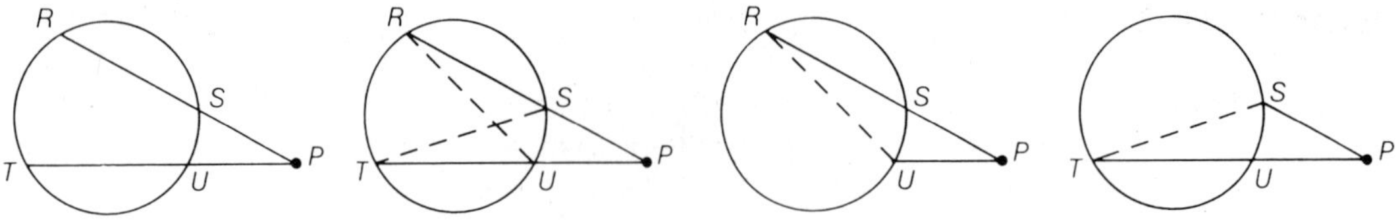

In the triangles on the right, angles R and T are equal because they both intercept arc SU. Both triangles also contain angle P, so the triangles are similar by AAA. We can write the ratios of corresponding sides as

$$\frac{RP}{TP} = \frac{UP}{SP} \qquad \text{corresponding sides}$$

and, if we cross multiply, we get

$$RP \cdot SP = TP \cdot UP$$

Each of these products has two factors. One factor is the length of the secant segment, and the other factor is the length of the external segment of the same secant.

Example 114.B.1 Find x.

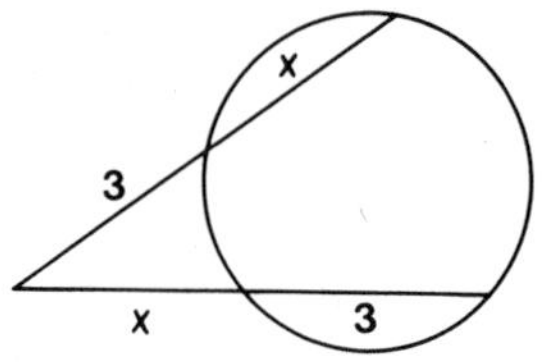

Solution The products of the lengths of the secant segments and the lengths of their external segments are equal.

$(3 + x)3 = (3 + x)x$	equation
$9 + 3x = 3x + x^2$	multiplied
$x^2 - 9 = 0$	rearranged
$\mathbf{x = 3, -3}$	solved

We reject the solution -3 because a length is always represented by a positive number.

114.C Secants and tangents

In the left-hand figure below, the product of the length of one secant segment times the length of its external segment equals the product of the length of the other secant segment times the length of its external segment.

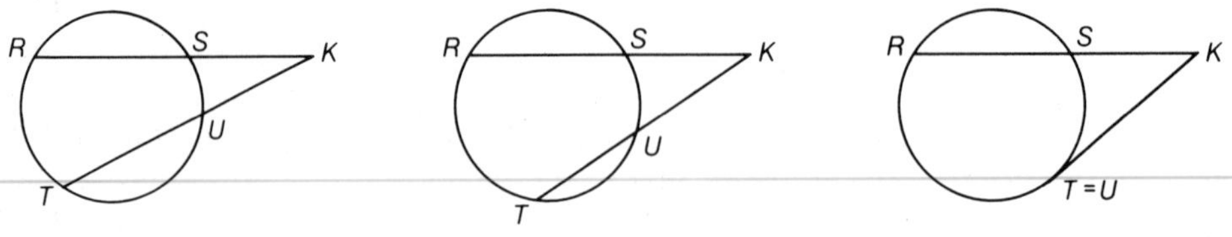

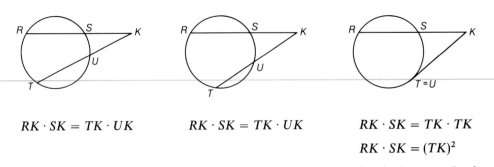

$RK \cdot SK = TK \cdot UK$ $\qquad$ $RK \cdot SK = TK \cdot UK$ $\qquad$ $RK \cdot SK = TK \cdot TK$

$RK \cdot SK = (TK)^2$

In the center figure T and U are closer together, and the equation is the same. In the right-hand figure, the length of the secant segment is the same as the length of the external segment. **So in the case of a tangent and a secant drawn from a point outside the circle, the product of the length of the secant segment and the length of its external segment equals the square of the length of the tangent segment from the point.**

Example 114.C.1 Find x.

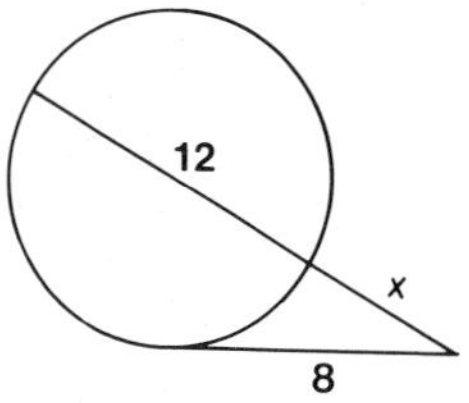

Solution The product of the length of the secant segment and the length of its external segment equals the square of the length of the tangent from the point.

$$(12 + x)x = 8^2 \qquad \text{equation}$$
$$12x + x^2 = 64 \qquad \text{multiplied}$$
$$x^2 + 12x - 64 = 0 \qquad \text{rearranged}$$
$$(x + 16)(x - 4) = 0 \qquad \text{factored}$$
$$\mathbf{x = -16, 4}$$

We reject the negative answer, as a length is always greater than zero.

Problem set 114

1. If $a * y$ means $a - 3y$ and $a \# y$ means $2a + 3y$, evaluate $5 \# (4 * 3)$.

2. Four times the complement of angle A exceeds the supplement of angle B by 70°. Five times the complement of angle B exceeds 3 times the supplement of angle A by $-220°$. What are the measures of angles A and B?

3. We are given that m varies jointly as p and v^3 and inversely as the square root of k. By what number is m multiplied when p is multipled by 3, v is multiplied by 3, and k is multiplied by 4?

4. If the probability of getting red is 0.2 and the probability of having a cloudy day is 0.5, what is the probability of getting red or having a cloudy day or both if the probability of both getting red and having a cloudy day is 0.3?

5. How many 3-letter–4-numeral car tags are possible if all 26 letters and 10 digits can be used but no repetition is permitted? The 3 letters must come first.

6. Find x.

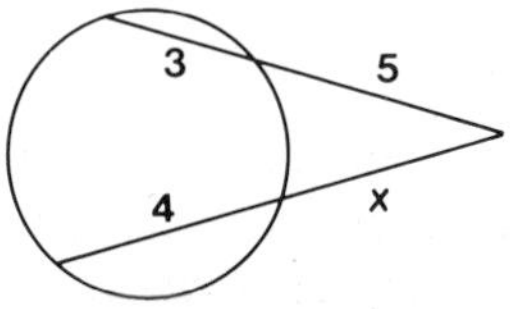

7. Given: $\overline{PR}$ and $\overline{TP}$ are secants which intersect at point P.
Prove: $(PR)(SP) = (TP)(UP)$
Hint: First show $\triangle PRU \sim \triangle PTS$.

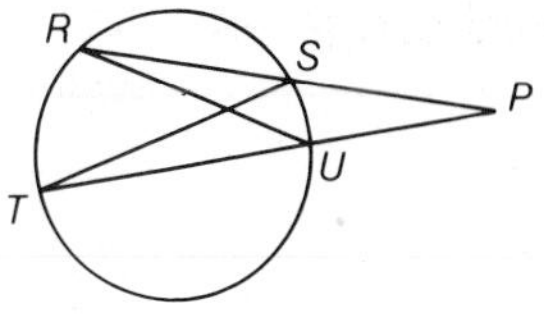

8. Find x, given that $\overline{AD}$ is a tangent to the circle.

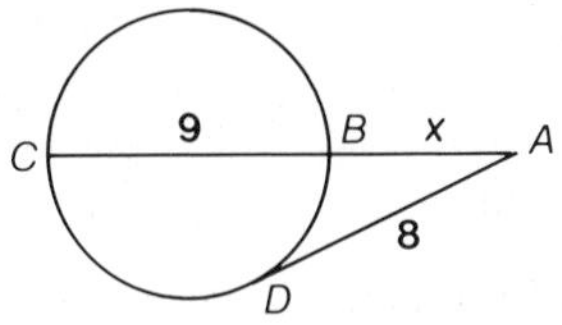

9. Given: $\overline{KT}$ is a tangent and $\overline{KR}$ is a secant.
Prove: $(KT)^2 = (RK)(SK)$
Hint: First show $\triangle KRT \sim \triangle KTS$ and note that $KT/RK = SK/KT$.

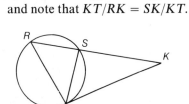

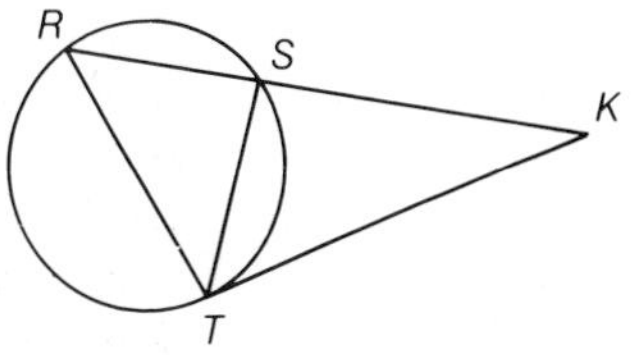

10. Given: Chords AB and CD intersect at E as shown.
Prove: $(AE)(EB) = (CE)(ED)$

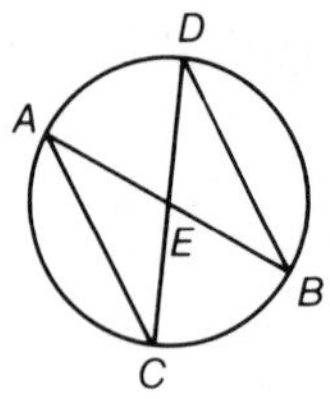

11. Given: Tangents AP and BP intersect at point P as shown.
Prove: $\angle APB = \frac{1}{2}(\overset{\frown}{ACB} - \overset{\frown}{AB})$

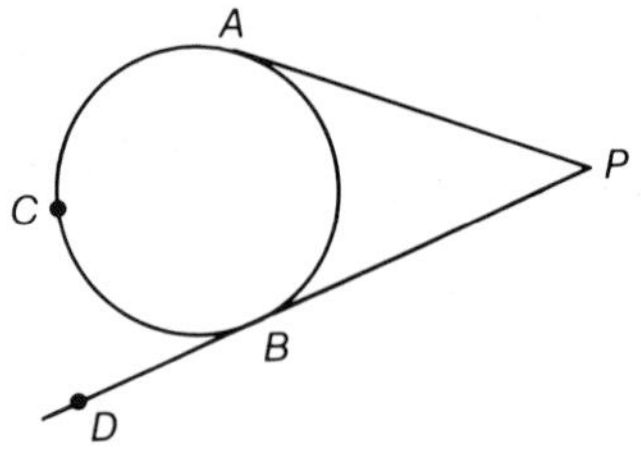

Sketch the function:

12. $y = \dfrac{1}{x}$

13. $y = \dfrac{x^2 - x - 6}{x + 2}$

14. $y = \dfrac{x^2 + x - 6}{x - 2}$

15. Graph $y = [x] - 1$.

16. List the possible rational roots of the equation $6x^{14} - 5x^6 + 8x^4 + 2 = 0$.

17. Are two odd integers always relatively prime? Explain.

18. Sketch $y = \tan x$.

19. Write the equations of the function shown.

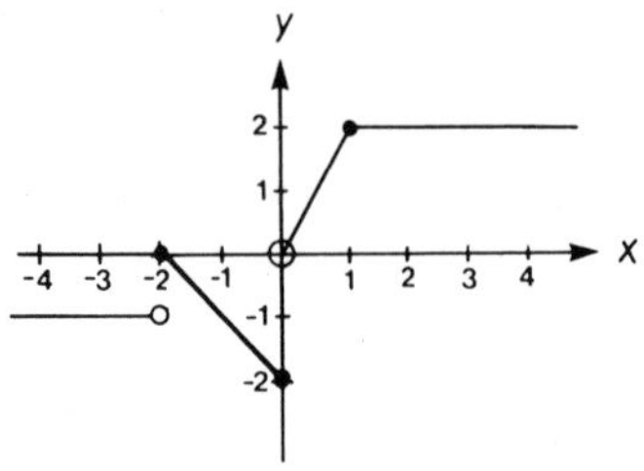

20. Graph $y = x^3 - x^2 - 10x - 8$.

21. A ball is dropped from a height of 256 feet. After each bounce, the ball rebounds three-quarters of the distance it fell. How far has the ball traveled when it bounces for the fifth time?

22. Find the inverse function of $y = 2x + 4$.

23. Indicate whether each equation shown represents an ellipse, a hyperbola, a circle, or a parabola.
(*a*) $x^2 - 4y^2 + 4x + 32y - 96 = 0$ (*b*) $x = -2y^2 + 12y - 10$
(*c*) $x^2 + y^2 - 10x - 8y + 16 = 0$ (*d*) $y = -4x^2 + 20x - 16$
(*e*) $25x^2 + 9y^2 - 200x + 18y + 184 = 0$

24. The base of a pyramid is a square of perimeter 36 m. The height of the pyramid is 4 m. What is its volume?

25. Write equation (*a*) of Problem 23 in standard form and describe the conic section represented by the equation.

26. Use echelon matrices to solve: $\begin{cases} x + 2y + z = 7 \\ 3y - 2z = 0 \\ 2x - y = -2 \end{cases}$

27. Write the three cube roots of $4 + 6i$ in polar form.

28. Show that: $\csc 2x = \frac{1}{2} \cot x \sec^2 x$

29. Solve, given that ($0° \leq x < 360°$): $3 \tan^2 x + 5 \sec x + 1 = 0$

30. Solve: $\sqrt{\log_2 x} = \log_2 \sqrt[3]{x}$

EP 114.99, 114.100

LESSON 115 Point of division formulas

115.A Point of division formulas

We remember that when we move from one point to another point on a number line, the coordinate change is the final coordinate minus the initial coordinate. If we move from 4 to -6, the coordinate change is -10, as we see in the following diagram.

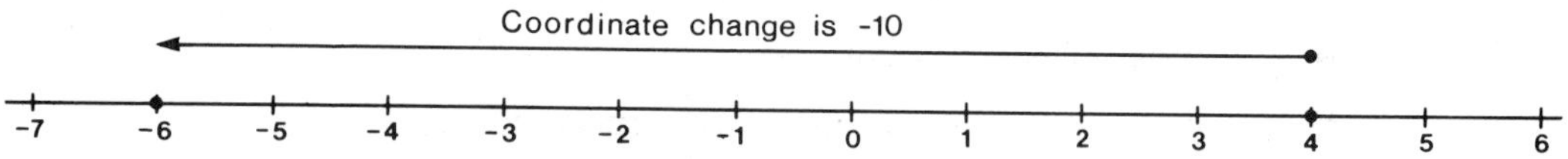

$$\text{Coordinate change} = (\text{final coordinate}) - (\text{initial coordinate})$$
$$= (-6) - (4) = -10$$

If we had moved only $\frac{3}{5}$ of the way from 4 to -6, the coordinate change would have been -6, which is three-fifths of the difference in the two coordinates. From this problem, we can generalize and say that if we move n/d of the way from point (x_1, y_1) to point (x_2, y_2), the coordinate change in x is n/d times $x_2 - x_1$ and the coordinate change in y is n/d times $y_2 - y_1$. We will use the symbol Δx to indicate the change in the x coordinate and the symbol Δy to indicate the change in the y coordinate.

$$\Delta x = \frac{n}{d}(x_2 - x_1)$$

$$\Delta y = \frac{n}{d}(y_2 - y_1)$$

Example 115.A.1 Find general equations for the coordinates of the point F that lies two-fifths of the way from point $P_1(x_1, y_1)$ to $P_2(x_2, y_2)$.

Solution We begin by drawing a diagram.

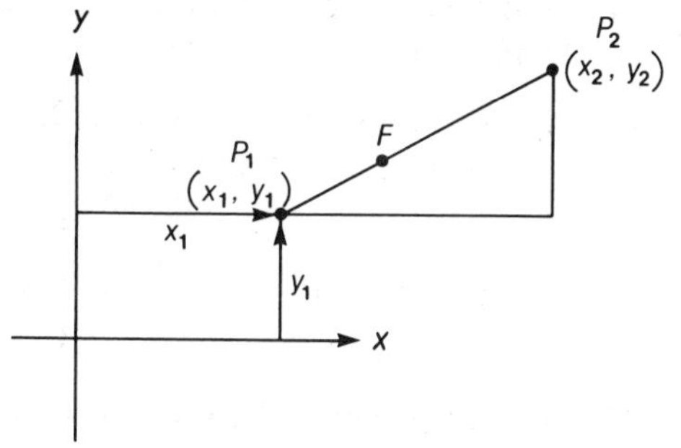

The coordinates of the point F give the total distance and direction from the origin to point F. Thus, the x coordinate is x_1 plus the change in x, and the y coordinate is y_1 plus the change in y.

$$x_F = x_1 + \Delta x \qquad y_F = y_1 + \Delta y$$

$$= x_1 + \frac{2}{5}(x_2 - x_1) \qquad = y_1 + \frac{2}{5}(y_2 - y_1)$$

$$= x_1 + \frac{2}{5}x_2 - \frac{2}{5}x_1 \qquad = y_1 + \frac{2}{5}y_2 - \frac{2}{5}y_1$$

$$\mathbf{x_F = \frac{3x_1 + 2x_2}{5}} \qquad \mathbf{y_F = \frac{3y_1 + 2y_2}{5}}$$

Example 115.A.2 Find general equations for the coordinates of the point F that lies three-sevenths of the way from point P_1 to P_2.

Solution We begin by drawing a diagram.

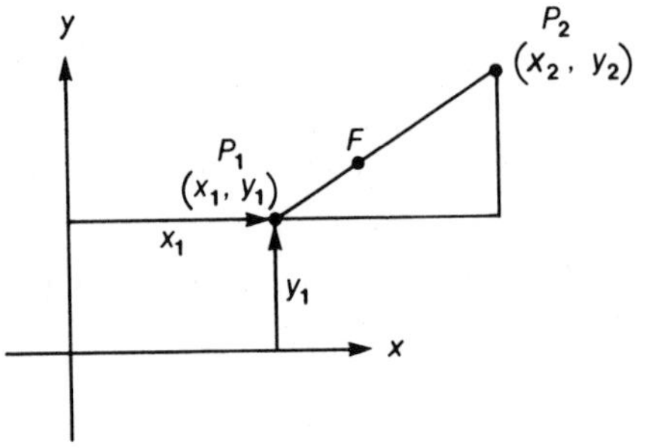

The coordinates x_F and y_F give the total x distance of point F from the origin and the total y distance of point F from the origin. These distances are $x_1 + \Delta x$ and $y_1 + \Delta y$.

$$x_F = x_1 + \Delta x \qquad y_F = y_1 + \Delta y$$

$$= x_1 + \frac{3}{7}(x_2 - x_1) \qquad = y_1 + \frac{3}{7}(y_2 - y_1)$$

$$= x_1 + \frac{3}{7}x_2 - \frac{3}{7}x_1 \qquad = y_1 + \frac{3}{7}y_2 - \frac{3}{7}y_1$$

$$= \frac{4}{7}x_1 + \frac{3}{7}x_2 \qquad = \frac{4}{7}y_1 + \frac{3}{7}y_2$$

$$= \mathbf{\frac{4x_1 + 3x_2}{7}} \qquad = \mathbf{\frac{4y_1 + 3y_2}{7}}$$

Problem set 115

1. The *River Belle* could steam 3 times as fast as the current in the river. She could steam 90 miles down the river in 1 hour less than she could steam 48 miles up the river. What was her speed in still water, and what was the speed of the current in the river?

2. The ratio of reds to blues was 1 to 2, and the greens outnumbered the reds by 7. If the sum of the reds and the blues was 1 greater than the number of greens, how many were there of each color?

3. The pressure of an ideal gas varies inversely as the volume if the temperature is held constant. When the temperature was 400°C, the pressure and volume of an amount of gas were 5 atmospheres and 40 liters, respectively. What would the

pressure be if the volume were decreased to 1 liter and the temperature remained at 400°C?

4. Four times the complement of angle A exceeds twice the supplement of angle B by 40°. If the supplement of angle A exceeds twice the complement of angle B by 70°, find the measure of both angles.

5. The decrease was exponential. After 40 minutes, there were 1460 in the bowl. After 400 minutes, there were only 440 in the bowl. What was the half-life of the things in the bowl?

6. Use a diagram to show that if we move one-fourth of the way from $P_1 = (x_1, y_1)$ to $P_2 = (x_2, y_2)$, the change in the x coordinate will be $\frac{1}{4}(x_2 - x_1)$ and the change in the y coordinate will be $\frac{1}{4}(y_2 - y_1)$.

7. Find the coordinates of the point which lies four-elevenths of the way from $P_1 = (x_1, y_1)$ to $P_2 = (x_2, y_2)$.

8. Find the coordinates of the point which lies one-fourth of the way from (2, 4) to (6, 6).

9. Find a.

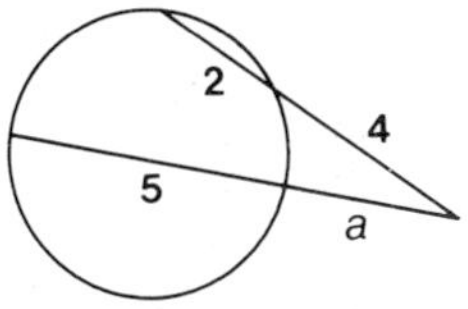

10. Given: $\overline{PR}$ and $\overline{TP}$ are secants that intersect at point P.
Prove: $(RP)(SP) = (PT)(UP)$

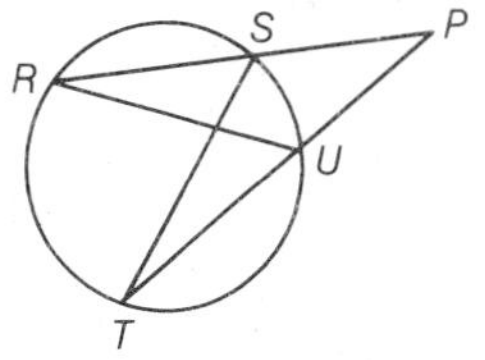

11. Find x if $\overline{PQ}$ is a tangent and $\overline{PR}$ is a secant as shown.

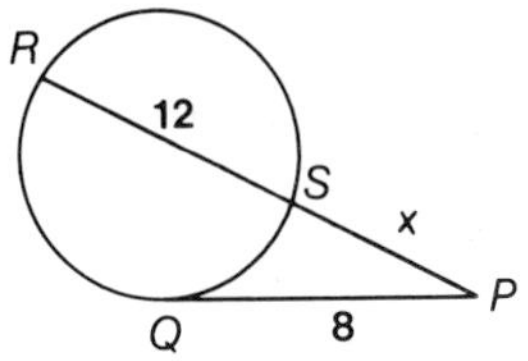

12. Given: $\overline{KT}$ is a tangent and $\overline{KR}$ is a secant which intersect at K.
Prove: $(KT)^2 = (RK)(SK)$

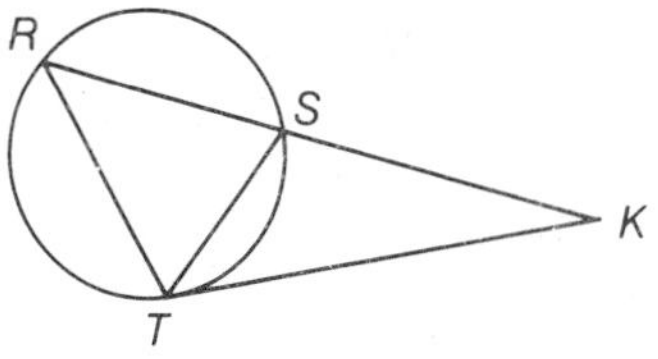

13. Solve for z.

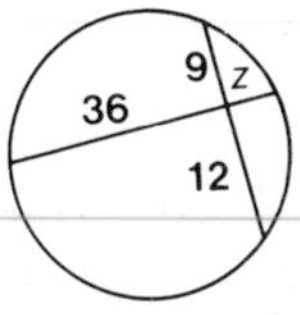

14. Given: Chords AB and CD intersect at E as shown.
Prove: $(AE)(EB) = (CE)(ED)$

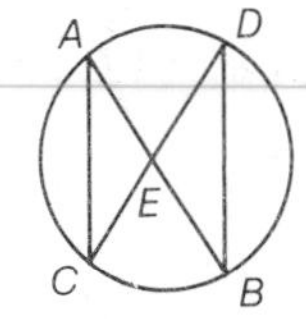

Sketch the function:

15. $y = \dfrac{1}{x + 5}$ **16.** $y = |x - 2|$ **17.** $y = \dfrac{x^2 + x - 2}{x + 2}$

18. Are two nonzero even integers ever relatively prime? Explain.

19. List the possible rational roots of the equation $8x^{12} - 4x^2 + 6x - 5 = 0$.

20. Graph $y = x^3 + 2x^2 - 9x - 18$.

21. Write the equations of the function shown.

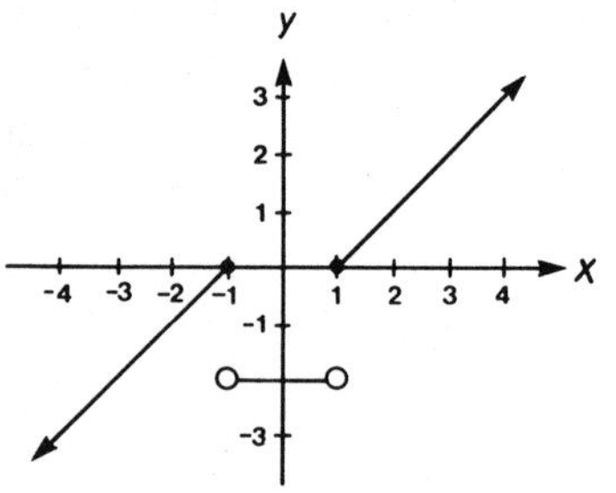

22. Derive a formula for the sum of the first n terms of an arithmetic sequence whose first term is a and whose common difference is d.

23. Indicate whether each equation shown represents an ellipse, a hyperbola, a circle, or a parabola.

(*a*) $x^2 + y^2 - 10x + 8y + 5 = 0$ (*b*) $25x^2 - 16y^2 - 100x - 444 - 96y = 0$

(*c*) $-y^2 + 9x^2 - 90x + 4y + 302 = 0$ (*d*) $x = y^2 - 4y + 3$

(*e*) $16x^2 + 25y^2 + 500 = 300y$

24. Construct a line perpendicular to a given line which passes through a point not on the given line.

25. Write equation (*e*) of Problem 23 in standard form and describe the conic section represented by the equation.

26. The base of a pyramid is a square of perimeter 12 cm. The height of the pyramid is 6 cm. What is its volume?

27. Write the three cube roots of 8 cis 90° in rectangular form. Give exact answers.

28. Solve, given that $(0° \leq \theta < 360°)$: $\sqrt{2}\cos\theta - 1 = 0$

29. Show that: $\dfrac{\sin x}{\tan x + 3\sin x} = \dfrac{1}{\sec x + 3}$

30. Solve: $\sqrt{\log_3 x} = \log_3 \sqrt[4]{x}$

EP 115.101, 115.102

LESSON 116 Asymptotes and holes · Graphs of symmetric rational functions

116.A Asymptotes and holes

We have discussed how the graphs of some functions have asymptotes and the graphs of some functions have holes. Often, we find functions whose graphs have both asymptotes and holes.

Example 116.A.1 Graph the function $y = \dfrac{-5x - 5}{x^2 + 4x + 3}$.

Solution We begin by factoring above and below and get

$$y = \frac{-5\cancel{(x+1)}}{(x+3)\cancel{(x+1)}} = \frac{-5}{x+3} \qquad (x \neq -1, -3)$$

We see the function has a zero denominator when x equals -1 or -3. We cancel the $x + 1$ factors. The remaining function has a horizontal asymptote $y = 0$ and has a vertical asymptote $x = -3$. Also it has a hole in the graph at $x = -1$. To get an idea of what the graph looks like, we find two ordered pairs on the graph on both sides of $x = -3$. Then we sketch the function.

If $x = -3.5$: $\quad y = \dfrac{-5}{-3.5 + 3} \longrightarrow y = \dfrac{-5}{-0.5} \longrightarrow y = +10$

If $x = -5$: $\quad y = \dfrac{-5}{-5 + 3} \longrightarrow y = \dfrac{-5}{-2} \longrightarrow y = +2.5$

If $x = -2.5$: $\quad y = \dfrac{-5}{-2.5 + 3} \longrightarrow y = \dfrac{-5}{0.5} \longrightarrow y = -10$

If $x = -2$: $\quad y = \dfrac{-5}{-2 + 3} \longrightarrow y = \dfrac{-5}{1} \longrightarrow y = -5$

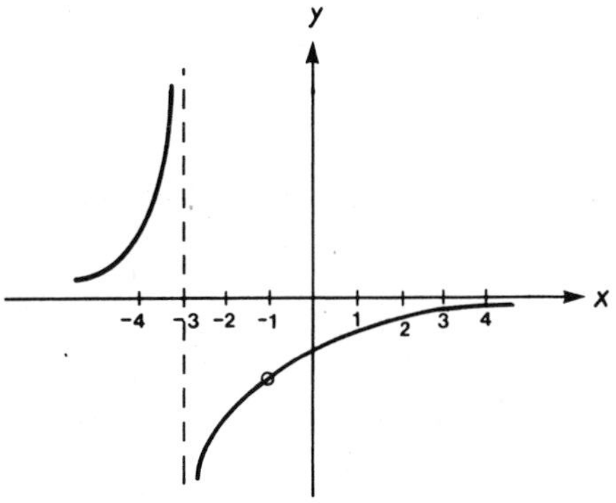

116.B Graphs of symmetric rational functions

The locations of vertical asymptotes in graphs of rational functions whose numerators are a constant are determined by the values of the variable that will cause the denominator to equal 0. Thus, the rational functions

$$y = \frac{4}{x - 2} \quad \text{and} \quad y = \frac{-4}{x - 2}$$

will both have vertical asymptotes at the value of x that makes the denominator equal zero. For both these functions, the equation of the vertical asymptote is $x = 2$. But, because of the difference in signs in the numerator and because of the sign changes in the denominator as x changes values, the graphs of the functions look different.

$$y = \frac{4}{x - 2} \qquad\qquad y = \frac{-4}{x - 2}$$

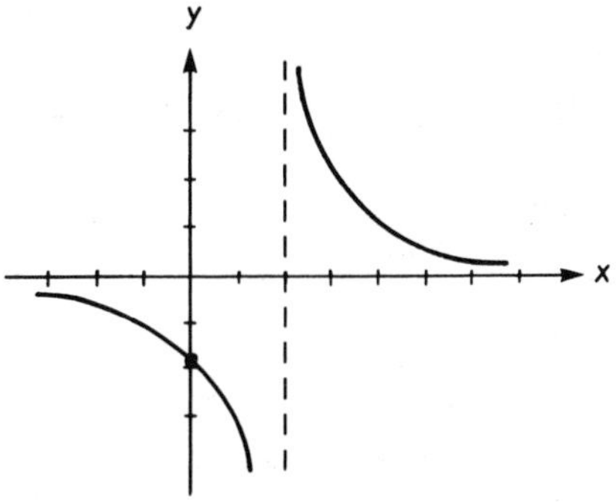

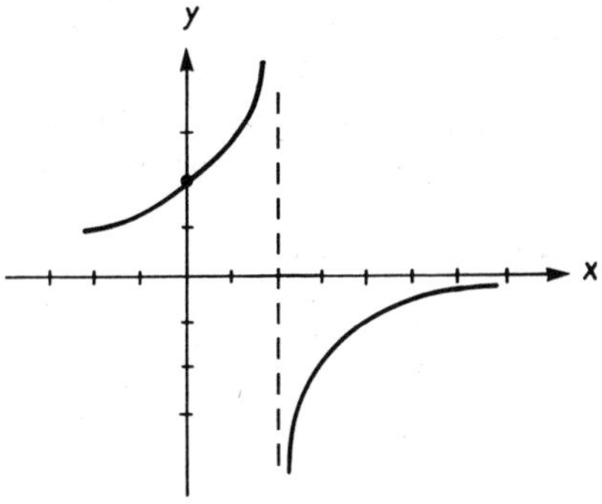

When the denominator of a function is squared and the numerator is a constant, the value of the denominator will be a positive number for all values of x on both sides of the asymptote and the function will be symmetric about the asymptote.

Example 116.B.1 Graph the function $y = \dfrac{4}{(x-3)^2}$.

Solution When x equals 3, the denominator equals zero, so the equation of the vertical asymptote is $x = +3$. To graph the function we choose two x values on both sides of $+3$.

When $x = 4$: $y = \dfrac{4}{(4-3)^2} = \dfrac{4}{1} = 4$

When $x = 6$: $y = \dfrac{4}{(6-3)^2} = \dfrac{4}{9} \approx 0.444$

When $x = 2$: $y = \dfrac{4}{(2-3)^2} = \dfrac{4}{1} = 4$

When $x = 0$: $y = \dfrac{4}{(0-3)^2} = \dfrac{4}{9} \approx 0.444$

We see that the values of y are the same at equal distances to the right and left of the line $x = 3$, so the graph is symmetric about the line $x = 3$.

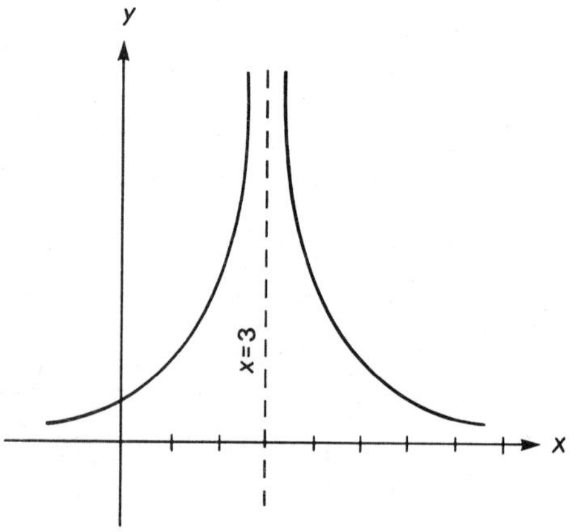

Graphs of some rational functions are more involved than the ones we have studied in this book. In the next book, these more involved graphs will be treated in considerable detail.

Problem set 116

1. Their number was small, but only 6 minutes after the beginning the number had increased to 960. Twenty minutes after the beginning the number was 1100. How long after the beginning was the number 2400 if the increase was exponential?

2. Reds varied directly as greens and inversely as purples squared. When there were 10 greens and 20 purples, there were 25 reds. How many reds were there with 30 greens and two purples?

3. The probability of getting purple or being confused or both was 0.85. If the probability of getting purple was 0.4 and the probability of being confused was 0.7, what was the probability of getting purple and being confused?

4. Use the example of 13 things taken 10 at a time to do a concrete development of the expression for ${}_nP_r$ and ${}_nC_r$.

5. The car was marked up 40 percent of the cost and thus sold for \$2800. There were no buyers so the price was reduced to a 20 percent markup. What was the new selling price?

Sketch the function:

6. $y = \dfrac{1}{x+3}$

7. $y = \dfrac{-2x-6}{x^2+4x+3}$

8. $y = [x] - 3$

9. $y = \dfrac{3}{(x-1)^2}$

10. Sketch $y = -x^3 + x^2 + 10x + 8$.

11. List the possible rational roots of the equation $6x^8 - 3x^3 + 4x^2 - 3x + 5 = 0$.

12. Write the equations of the function shown.

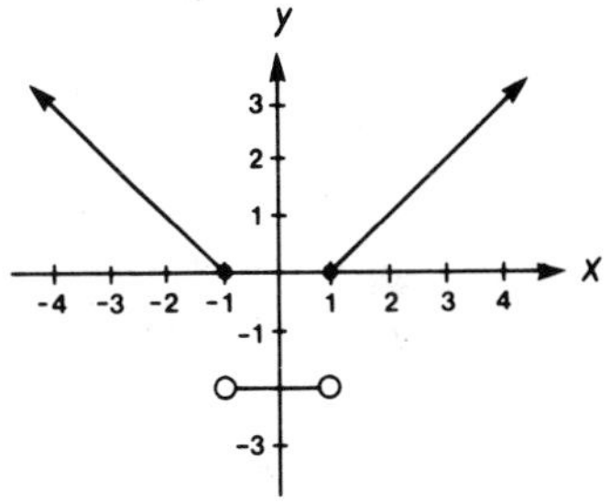

13. A ball is dropped from a height of 100 feet. After each bounce, the ball rebounds one-quarter of the distance it fell. What is the total distance the ball will travel?

14. Find the inverse function of $y = 3x - 4$.

15. Indicate whether each equation shown represents an ellipse, a hyperbola, a circle, or a parabola.

(*a*) $4x^2 + 3y^2 + 40x - 288y + 532 = 0$ (*b*) $100x^2 + 36y^2 = 3600$

(*c*) $-4y^2 + 25x^2 - 200x - 8y + 796 = 0$ (*d*) $5y = x^2 + 10x - 11$

(*e*) $x^2 + y^2 - 10x + 8y + 5 = 0$

16. The base of a circular cone has a radius of 6 inches. The height of the cone is 4 inches.
(*a*) What is the volume of the cone?
(*b*) If the cone is a right circular cone, what is the surface area of the cone?

17. Write equation (*c*) of Problem 15 in standard form and describe the conic section which the equation represents.

18. Find *a*.

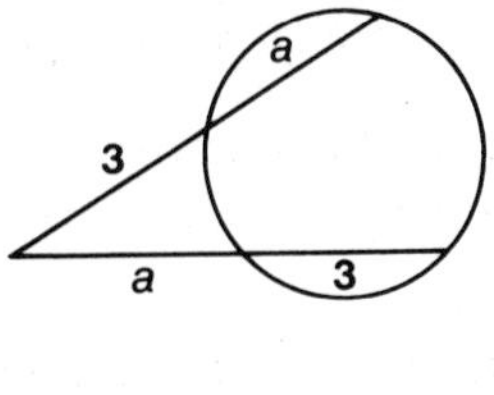

19. Given: $\overline{PR}$ and $\overline{TP}$ are secants which intersect at point P.
Prove: $(RP)(SP) = (PT)(UP)$

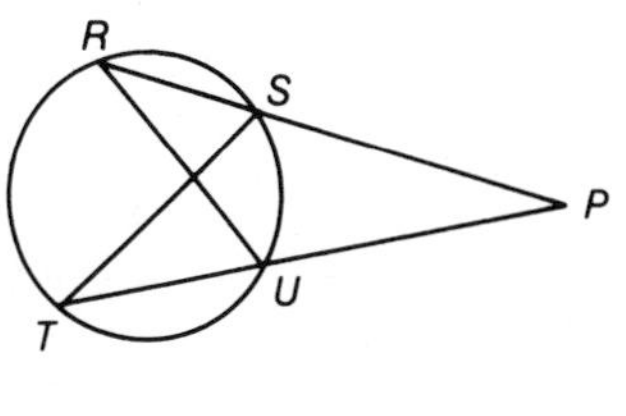

20. Find x, given that $\overline{PS}$ is tangent to the circle.

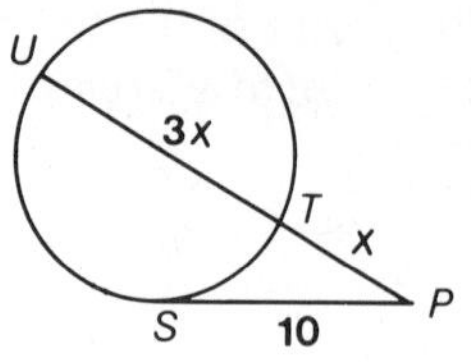

21. Given: $\overline{KT}$ is a tangent and $\overline{KR}$ is a secant as shown.
Prove: $(KT)^2 = (RK)(SK)$

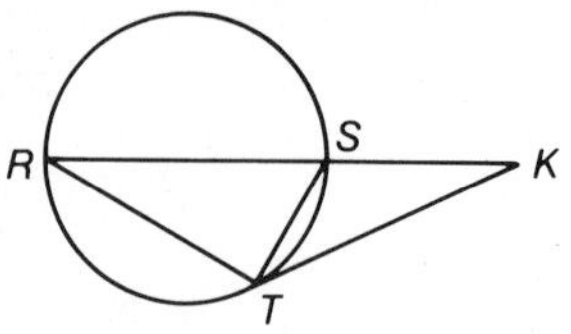

22. Given: Chords AB and CD intersect at E as shown.
Prove: $(AE)(EB) = (CE)(ED)$

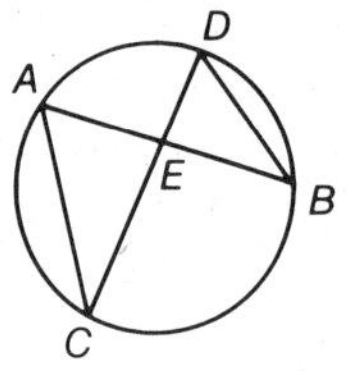

23. Given: $\overline{QS}$ is the perpendicular bisector of $\overline{PR}$; $\overline{RS}$ is the perpendicular bisector of $\overline{QT}$
Prove: $PQ = RT$

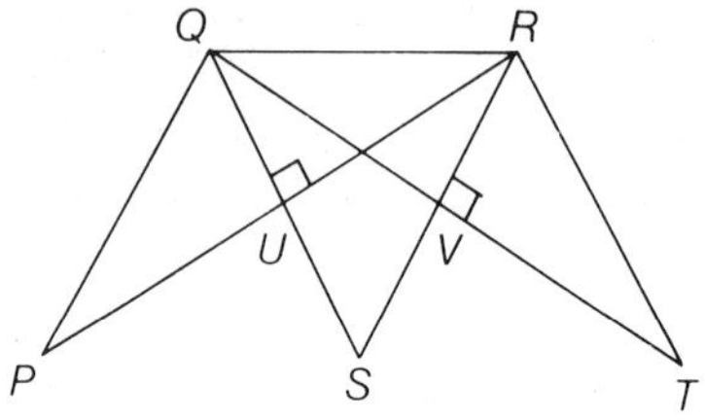

24. The geometric mean of two numbers is 10 and the arithmetic mean of the two numbers is 26. Find the two numbers.

25. Two geometric solids are similar. A side of the smaller geometric solid is one-fourth the length of the corresponding side of the larger geometric solid. What is the ratio of the volume of the larger geometric solid to the volume of the smaller geometric solid?

26. The concentration of hydrogen ions in a solution is 4.5×10^{-6} mole per liter. What is the pH of the solution?

27. Use echelon matrices to solve for the unknowns: $\begin{cases} 2x + y + z = 2 \\ 2y - 3z = -9 \\ 3x - 2z = 4 \end{cases}$

28. Show that: $(\sin^2 x + 1)(\cot^2 x + 1) = 1 + \csc^2 x$

29. Solve, given that $(0° \le x < 360°)$: $2\cos^2 x - 9\sin x + 3 = 0$

30. Find the base 3 antilogarithm of -4.

EP 116.103, 116.104

LESSON 117 Concurrent lines · Equal segments

117.A Concurrent lines

The word *concurrent* is derived from the Latin prefix *com-*, which means "together," and the Latin verb *currere*, which means "to run." Thus, ***concurrent*** means "to run together." If three or more lines "run together" at one point, we say that the lines are concurrent lines. **The bisectors of the angles of a triangle are always concurrent at a point that is equidistant from the sides of the triangle.** As we see here, this point can be used as the center of a circle that is tangent to the sides of the triangle. Such a circle drawn inside a triangle is called an ***inscribed circle*** or ***incircle.*** The center of this circle is called the ***incenter.***

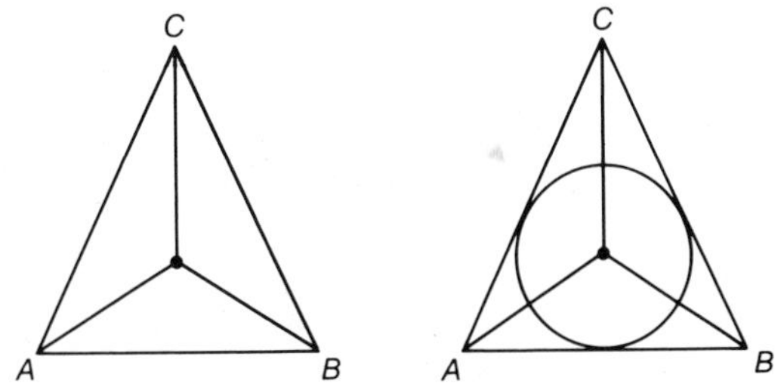

As shown below, the perpendicular bisectors of the sides of a triangle are always concurrent at a point that is equidistant from the vertices of the triangle. This point can be used as the center of a circle that encloses the triangle and passes through each vertex of the triangle. We say that the circle is ***circumscribed*** about the triangle and that the triangle is ***inscribed*** in the circle. This point of concurrency for some triangles can fall outside the triangle, as we show in the right-hand figure below.

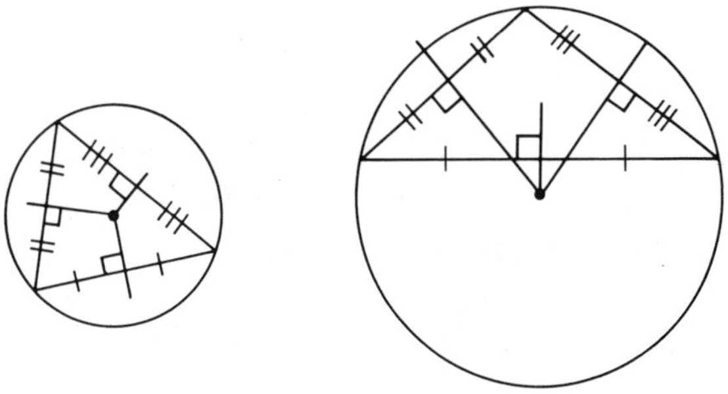

Example 117.A.1 Prove that the angle bisectors of a triangle intersect at a point that is equidistant from the sides of the triangle.

Solution We use the letter I to name the point of intersection of the bisectors of angles A and B. We will prove that this point is equidistant from all three sides. Then since the point is equidistant from the sides of angle C, the bisector of angle C passes through the point.

We begin by drawing perpendiculars from point I to the three sides. In the two figures on the left, we shade in triangles ATI and ARI. We can show that these triangles are congruent. Both are right triangles, and the angles at A are equal because $\overline{AI}$ is the angle bisector. Thus, the third angles are equal and so triangles ATI and ARI are similar. Both triangles share the corresponding side $\overline{AI}$. This gives us congruency because the scale factor is 1. Thus, sides $\overline{TI}$ and $\overline{RI}$ are equal by CPCTE.

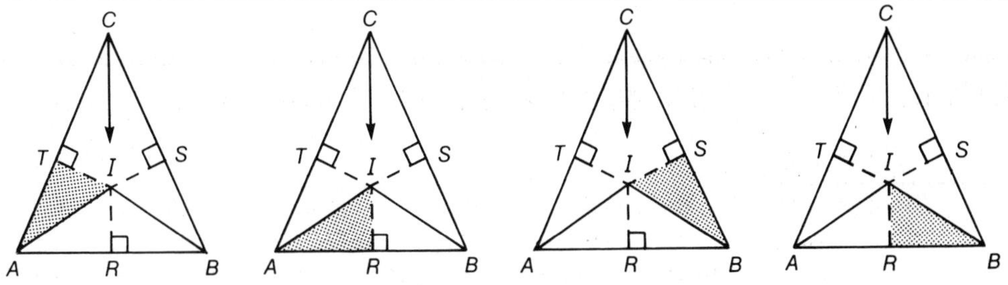

In the two right-hand figures, we shade the triangles BSI and BRI.

These triangles are both right triangles, and the angles at B are equal (angle B is bisected); thus $\triangle BSI$ is similar to $\triangle BRI$ by AAA. Since the triangles share corresponding side $\overline{BI}$, the triangles are congruent. Thus, sides $\overline{RI}$ and $\overline{SI}$ are equal by CPCTE. Since side $\overline{RI}$ is equal to side $\overline{SI}$ and is also equal to side $\overline{TI}$, all three sides are equal.

$$TI = RI = SI$$

Now since point I is equidistant from the sides of angle C, it lies on the bisector of angle C, and the three bisectors are concurrent at I.

Example 117.A.2 Prove that the perpendicular bisectors of the sides of a triangle intersect at a point that is equidistant from the vertices of the triangle.

Solution In the figure on the left below, we show the intersection O of the perpendicular bisectors of sides $\overline{AC}$ and $\overline{BC}$. We want to prove that point O is equidistant from the vertices A, B, and C; and we want to prove that the perpendicular bisector of $\overline{AB}$ also passes through point O. In the figure on the right, we connect O to the three vertices by drawing the segments $\overline{OA}$, $\overline{OB}$, and $\overline{OC}$.

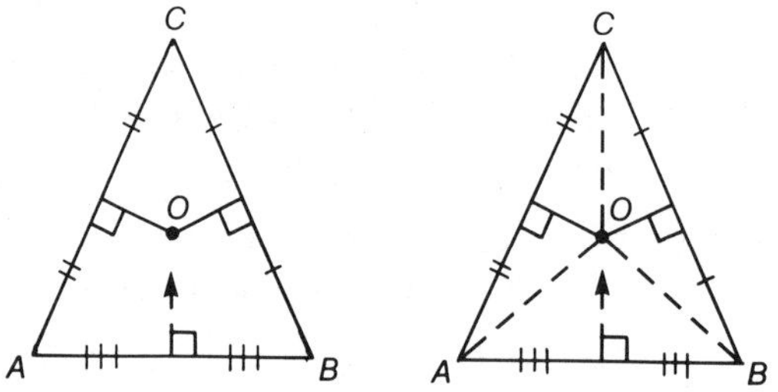

Point O is on the perpendicular bisector of $\overline{CA}$, so it is equidistant from the ends of $\overline{CA}$. Thus OA equals OC. Point O is on the perpendicular bisector of $\overline{CB}$, so it is equidistant from the ends of $\overline{CB}$, and thus OB equals OC. Since OA and OB both equal OC, they equal each other.

$$OA = OB = OC$$

Thus, point O is equidistant from the vertices. We remember also that if a point is equidistant from the ends of a segment, the point lies on the perpendicular bisector of the segment. Thus, point O lies on the perpendicular bisector of $\overline{AB}$ and the three lines are concurrent at O.

117.B Equal segments

We can use construction to divide a line into any number of segments of equal lengths. To illustrate, we will divide a line into three segments of equal lengths. On the left, we show segment AB. On the right we draw ray $\overrightarrow{AP}$ at a convenient angle to $\overline{AB}$.

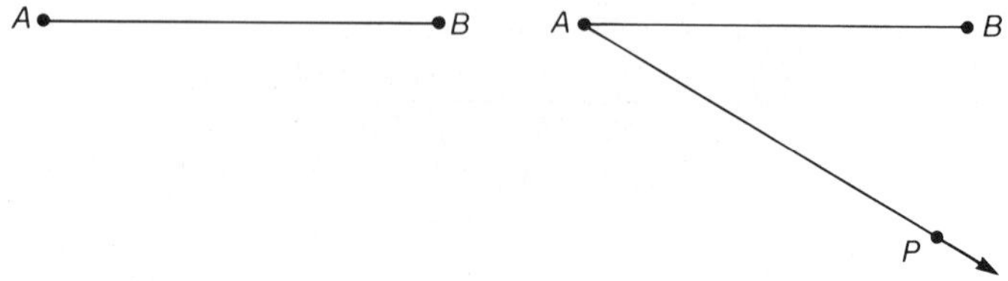

Next on ray $\overrightarrow{AP}$ we use a compass to mark off three equal segments $\overline{AR}$, $\overline{RS}$, and $\overline{ST}$. Lastly, we connect T and B and construct lines parallel to this line from R and S.

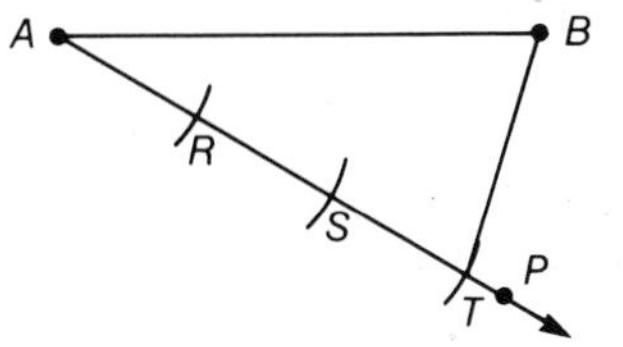

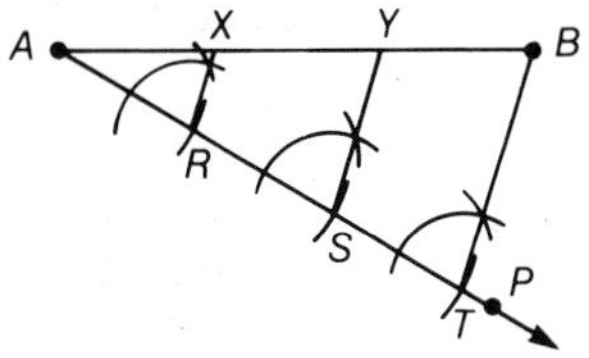

Since parallel lines separate transversals into proportional segments, $AX = XY = YB$. The same procedure could be used to divide $\overline{AB}$ into any desired number of segments of equal lengths by laying off on $\overline{AP}$ the necessary number of equal segments and drawing the required parallel lines.

Problem set 117

1. The decrease was exponential. After 42 minutes, only 1200 grams was left. After 52 minutes, this amount had decreased to 1180 grams. What was the half-life of the substance being considered?

2. Four times the tens digit exceeds twice the units digit by 2. When the two digits are reversed, the new number is 27 greater than the original number. What was the original number?

3. Five workers could do 3 jobs in 7 hours. If k more workers were added to the team, how many jobs could they do in $(p - 2)$ hours?

4. Red could complete 1 job in 2 hours. When he was helped by Greenie, the two of them could complete k jobs in h hours. How many hours would it take Greenie to complete 1 job if he worked alone?

5. Wailer normally got paid \$280 for a 40-hour week. The week of the convention he got a 20 percent hourly raise and was allowed to work 50 hours. How much did he make the week of the convention?

6. Draw a triangle and construct the three perpendicular bisectors of the sides. The intersection of the three perpendicular bisectors is the center of the circle which can be circumscribed about the triangle. Draw this circle.

7. Draw a triangle and construct the three angle bisectors of the vertices. Then construct a line perpendicular to one of the sides which passes through the intersection point of the angle bisectors. The intersection point is the center of the circle which can be inscribed inside a triangle and the line segment which joins the intersection point with one of the sides and is perpendicular to the side is the radius of the circle. Draw this circle.

8. Draw a line segment and divide it into five equal pieces.

9. Find x.

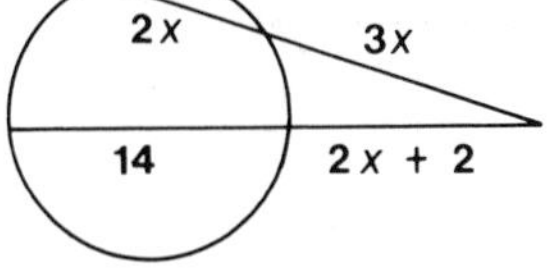

10. Find x, given that $\overline{PQ}$ is a tangent to the circle.

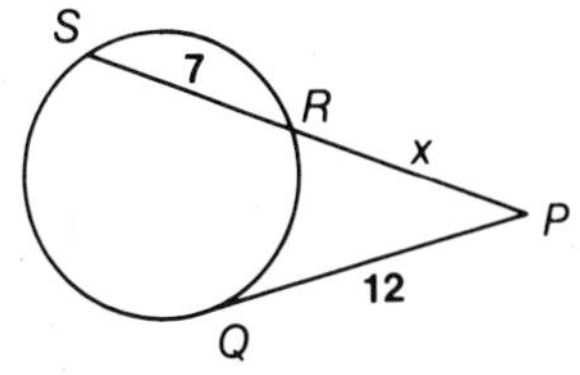

11. Given: $\overline{PR}$ and $\overline{TP}$ are secants which intersect at point P as shown.
Prove: $(TS)(PR) = (RU)(PT)$

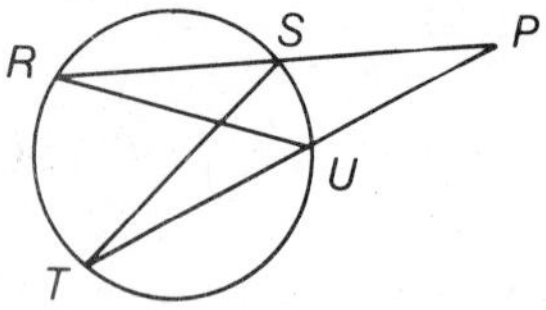

12. Given: Tangents AP and BP intersect at point P as shown.
Prove: $\angle APB = \frac{1}{2}(\widehat{ACB} - \widehat{AB})$

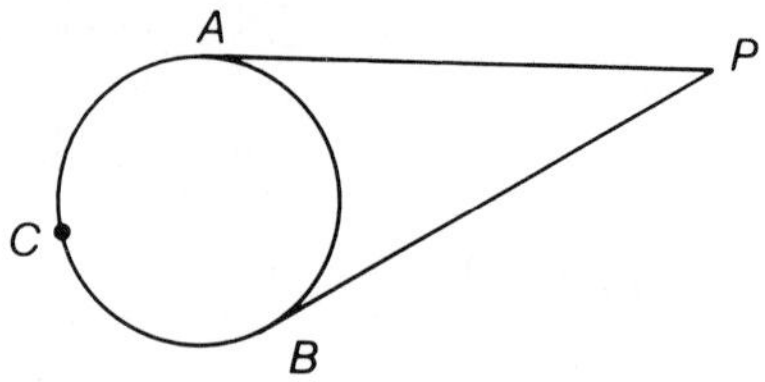

13. Given: $\overline{KT}$ is a tangent and $\overline{KR}$ is a secant which intersect at K as shown.
Prove: $(KR)(TS) = (KT)(RT)$

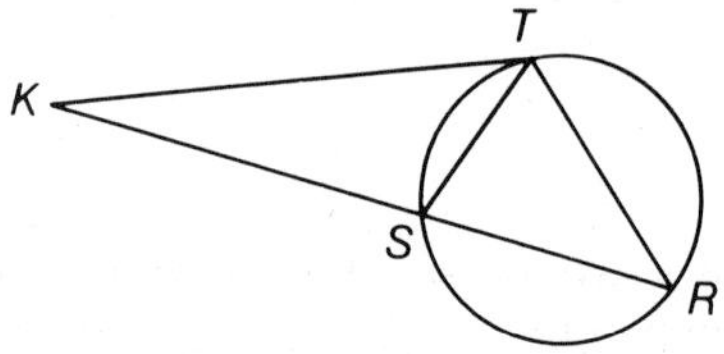

Sketch the function:

14. $y = \dfrac{2}{x - 2}$

15. $y = \dfrac{-2x + 2}{x^2 + 2x - 3}$

16. $y = |x - 2| + 2$

17. $y = \dfrac{2}{(x - 2)^2}$

18. Graph $y = x^3 + x^2 - 36x - 36$.

19. List the possible rational roots of the equation $8x^7 - 4x^3 + 6x^2 - 5x - 3 = 0$.

20. Develop the expression for the sum of the first n terms of an arithmetic sequence whose first term is a and whose common difference is d.

21. Write the equation of the function shown.

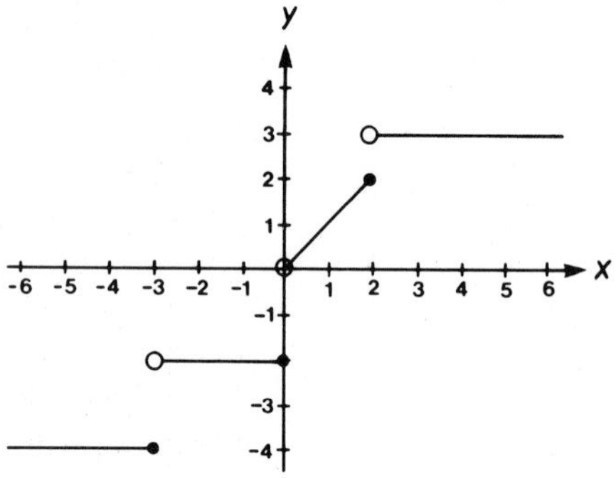

22. Find the coordinates of the point that is two-thirds of the way from $(4, -2)$ to $(-2, -5)$.

23. Indicate whether each equation shown represents an ellipse, a hyperbola, a circle, or a parabola.
(*a*) $x^2 + y^2 + 4x - 18y + 69 = 0$ (*b*) $x^2 + 10x + 24y + 4y^2 = -45$
(*c*) $-y^2 - 90x + 4y + 9x^2 = -302$ (*d*) $y + 41 = -4x^2 + 20x$
(*e*) $4x = y^2$

24. The radius of a sphere is r.
(*a*) What is the volume of the sphere?
(*b*) What is the surface area of the sphere?

25. Complete the square to write equation (*d*) of Problem 23 in a form convenient for graphing, and describe the conic section which the equation represents.

26. Is the relation $\{(2, 3), (3, 4), (4, 5), (5, 2)\}$ a function?

27. Write the four fourth roots of 16 in rectangular form. Give exact answers.

28. Show that: $\dfrac{\cos x}{\cot x + 3 \cos x} = \dfrac{1}{\csc x + 3}$

29. Solve, given that $(0° \leq x < 360°)$: $2 \sin x + 2 \csc x - 5 = 0$

30. Given $M = b^a$ and $N = b^c$, show that $\log_b \dfrac{M}{N} = \log_b M - \log_b N$.

EP 117.105, 117.106

LESSON 118 Roots of polynomial equations

118.A Roots of polynomial equations

Every first-degree polynomial equation has one root. Every second-degree polynomial equation has two roots. Every third-degree polynomial equation has three roots. Every fourth-degree polynomial equation has four roots; and, if n is a counting number, every nth-degree polynomial equation has n roots.

(a) $x^{14} - 3x^5 - 2x = 0$ has 14 roots $\qquad -x^3 + 3 = 0$ has 3 roots $\qquad x^5 - 2x^4 + 6x - 2 = 0$ has 5 roots

To use this statement, we must allow for equal roots as necessary. To illustrate, we will build a third-degree polynomial by multiplying the following three factors.

$$(x + 2)(x + 2)(x - 3) = 0 \qquad \text{factored form}$$

$$x^3 + x^2 - 8x - 12 = 0 \qquad \text{multiplied}$$

The numbers -2 and $+3$ are solutions to the equation. To get the required three roots, we must agree to count -2 as a root twice. Some authors handle this difficulty by saying that a third-degree polynomial equation has **at most** three roots and that this equation has only two roots.

We remember that if we use synthetic division and the remainder theorem and discover a root, the bottom row of numbers in the division will give us the coefficients of a polynomial whose degree is 1 less than that of the original polynomial. To illustrate we will use synthetic division and a synthetic divisor of -2.

$$\begin{array}{r|rrrr} -2 & 1 & 1 & -8 & -12 \\ & & -2 & 2 & 12 \\ \hline & 1 & -1 & -6 & 0 \end{array}$$

The zero tells us that -2 is a root, and the numbers 1, -1, and -6 are the coefficients of the **depressed polynomial** $x^2 - x - 6$. We now can write the original polynomial as a product of the factor $(x + 2)$ and the depressed polynomial.

$$x^3 + x^2 - 8x - 12 = (x + 2)(x^2 - x - 6)$$

Now we can find the zeros of the quadratic polynomial by using the quadratic formula.

$$x = \frac{1 \pm \sqrt{1 - 4(1)(-6)}}{2} = \frac{1 \pm 5}{2} = 3, -2$$

To discuss cubic equations that have complex roots, we decide to construct a polynomial that has $1 + i$ and $1 - i$ as zeros. To do so we use these numbers to write factors and get

$$[x - (1 + i)][x - (1 - i)] = (x - 1 - i)(x - 1 + i) = x^2 - 2x + 2$$

Next we decide to give the polynomial a zero of $+3$ so we use $(x - 3)$ as a factor.

$$(x^2 - 2x + 2)(x - 3) = x^3 - 5x^2 + 8x - 6$$

Now to write an equation we set our polynomial equal to 0.

$$x^3 - 5x^2 + 8x - 6 = 0$$

We have constructed a cubic equation with specified roots. Now we assume we do not know what the roots are and try to go backward and find the roots.

To begin, we use the rational roots theorem to list the possible rational roots as follows:

$$\text{Possible rational roots} = \{\pm 1, \pm 2, \pm 3, \pm 6\}$$

Next we use synthetic division with $+1$, -1, $+2$, -2 as synthetic divisors and get a nonzero remainder each time. Then we try $+3$.

$$\begin{array}{r|rrrr} 3 & 1 & -5 & +8 & -6 \\ & & 3 & -6 & 6 \\ \hline & 1 & -2 & 2 & 0 \end{array}$$

This time we get a remainder of 0, so we know that $+3$ is a root. The bottom row of numbers gives us the coefficients of the depressed polynomial. This allows us to write the cubic in factored form.

$$x^3 - 5x^2 + 8x - 6 = (x - 3)(x^2 - 2x + 2)$$

Now we will use the quadratic formula to find the roots of the quadratic factor.

$$x = \frac{2 \pm \sqrt{(4) - 4(1)(2)}}{2} = \frac{2 \pm \sqrt{-4}}{2} = 1 \pm i$$

Thus, we have found that the roots are **3, 1 + *i*, and 1 − *i*.**

Example 118.A.1 Find the roots of $2x^3 + 3x^2 - 7x - 3 = 0$.

Solution We begin by using the rational roots theorem to make a list of the possible rational roots. The list is

$$+1, -1, +3, -3, +\frac{1}{2}, -\frac{1}{2}, +\frac{3}{2}, -\frac{3}{2}$$

Next we use synthetic division to see if any member of this list is really a root.

$$\begin{array}{r|rrrr} 1 & 2 & 3 & -7 & -3 \\ & & 2 & 5 & -2 \\ \hline & 2 & 5 & -2 & -5 \end{array} \qquad \begin{array}{r|rrrr} -1 & 2 & 3 & -7 & -3 \\ & & -2 & -1 & 8 \\ \hline & 2 & 1 & -8 & 5 \end{array}$$

$$\begin{array}{r|rrrr} 3 & 2 & 3 & -7 & -3 \\ & & 6 & 27 & 60 \\ \hline & 2 & 9 & 20 & 57 \end{array} \qquad \begin{array}{r|rrrr} -3 & 2 & 3 & -7 & -3 \\ & & -6 & 9 & -6 \\ \hline & 2 & -3 & 2 & -9 \end{array}$$

$$\begin{array}{r|rrrr} \frac{1}{2} & 2 & 3 & -7 & -3 \\ & & 1 & 2 & -\frac{5}{2} \\ \hline & 2 & 4 & -5 & -\frac{11}{2} \end{array} \qquad \begin{array}{r|rrrr} -\frac{1}{2} & 2 & 3 & -7 & -3 \\ & & -1 & -1 & 4 \\ \hline & 2 & 2 & -8 & 1 \end{array}$$

$$\begin{array}{r|rrrr} \frac{3}{2} & 2 & 3 & -7 & -3 \\ & & 3 & 9 & 3 \\ \hline & 2 & 6 & 2 & 0 \end{array}$$

Since the remainder of the synthetic division by $\frac{3}{2}$ is 0, we know that $\frac{3}{2}$ is a root of the polynomial equation and that it is not necessary to divide by $-\frac{3}{2}$, for we can use the results of the division by $\frac{3}{2}$ to write the polynomial in factored form as

$$\left(x - \frac{3}{2}\right)(2x^2 + 6x + 2) = 0$$

or
$$\left(x - \frac{3}{2}\right)(2)(x^2 + 3x + 1) = 0$$

Next we will use the quadratic formula to find the roots of the quadratic polynomial equation.

$$x = \frac{-3 \pm \sqrt{9 - 4(1)(1)}}{2}$$

$$x = -\frac{3}{2} \pm \frac{\sqrt{5}}{2}$$

Thus, the roots of the given cubic equation are:

$$+\frac{3}{2}, -\frac{3}{2} + \frac{\sqrt{5}}{2}, -\frac{3}{2} - \frac{\sqrt{5}}{2}$$

Example 118.A.2 Find the roots of $x^3 + 2x^2 + 6x + 5 = 0$.

Solution First, we list the possible rational roots.

$$\pm 1, \pm 5$$

Now we use synthetic division to check these possible roots.

$$\begin{array}{r|rrrr} 1 & 1 & 2 & 6 & 5 \\ & & 1 & 3 & 9 \\ \hline & 1 & 3 & 9 & 14 \end{array} \qquad \begin{array}{r|rrrr} -1 & 1 & 2 & 6 & 5 \\ & & -1 & -1 & -5 \\ \hline & 1 & 1 & 5 & 0 \end{array}$$

The remainder when we use a synthetic divisor of -1 is 0, so we know -1 is a root. It is not necessary to try to use a synthetic divisor of $+5$ and -5, as we can already write the polynomial in factored form as

$$(x + 1)(x^2 + x + 5) = 0$$

Now we use the quadratic formula.

$$x = \frac{-1 \pm \sqrt{1 - 4(1)(5)}}{2}$$

$$x = -\frac{1}{2} \pm \frac{\sqrt{19}}{2} i$$

So the solutions are:

$$-1, -\frac{1}{2} + \frac{\sqrt{19}}{2} i, -\frac{1}{2} - \frac{\sqrt{19}}{2} i$$

Problem set 118

1. The increase was exponential. Fourteen years after the Big Crash there were 400 grams and 40 years after the Big Crash, there were 2800 grams. How many years after the Big Crash would it be before there were 5000 grams?

2. Widlo's speed was 20 miles per hour less than Bridgett's speed. Thus, Widlo could travel 400 miles in one-half the time it took Bridgett to travel 1120 miles. Find the speeds of both and the times of both.

3. Some were fast and the rest were slow. Ten times the number of fast was 180 less than twice the number of slow. Also, one-half the number of slow exceeded 3 times the number of fast by 40. How many were fast and how many were slow?

4. One pipe could fill 2 tanks in 3 hours, and the other pipe could empty 1 tank in 4 hours. If both pipes were used, how long would it take to fill an empty tank?

5. A single die is rolled twice. What is the probability that the first number rolled will be greater than 4 and also that the second number rolled will be less than 4?

Find the roots of:

6. $4x^3 - 4x^2 - 5x + 3 = 0$

7. $4x^3 - 13x + 6 = 0$

Sketch the function:

8. $y = \dfrac{3}{x - 3}$

9. $y = \dfrac{-2x - 6}{x^2 + 5x + 6}$

10. $y = |x - 3| + 3$

11. $y = \dfrac{3}{(x - 3)^2}$

12. Find the inverse function of $y = 2x - 4$.

13. Use the results of Problem 6 as an aid in graphing $y = 4x^3 - 4x^2 - 5x + 3$.

14. Find the coordinates of the point that is two-fifths of the way from (2, 4) to (−5, 2).

15. Given: $\overline{PR}$ and $\overline{TP}$ are secants which intersect at point P.
Prove: $(PS)(RU) = (TS)(PU)$

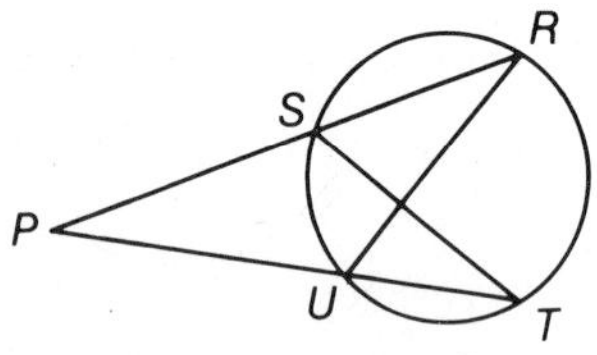

16. Find x.

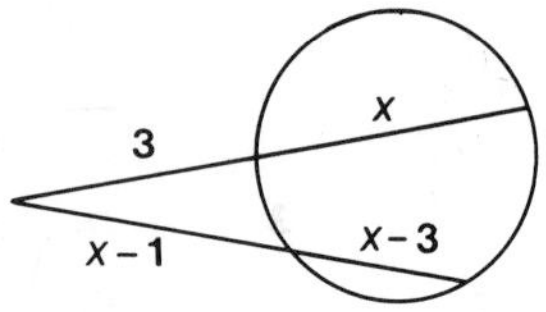

17. Given: $\overline{KT}$ is a tangent and $\overline{KR}$ is a secant which intersect at K as shown.
Prove: $(KT)^2 = (RK)(KS)$

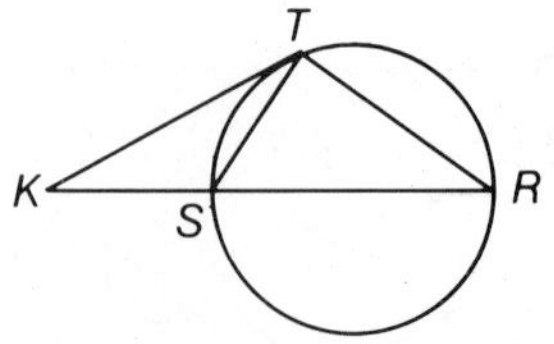

18. Using the figures shown, prove the Pythagorean theorem.

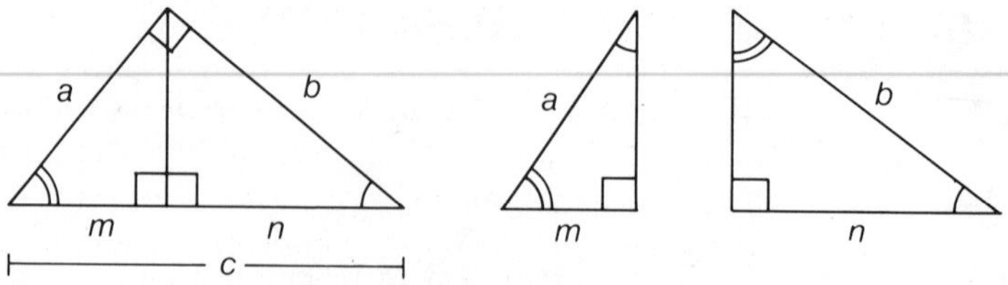

19. Draw a triangle and circumscribe the triangle by constructing the perpendicular bisectors of the sides to find the center of the circle.

20. Draw a triangle and inscribe a circle in the triangle by constructing the angle bisectors of the vertices to find the center of the circle. Draw a perpendicular segment from the center of the circle to one of the sides to construct the radius of the circle.

21. Develop the formula which gives the sum of the first n terms of a geometric sequence whose first term is a_1 and whose common ratio is r.

22. Develop the formula which gives the sum of the first n terms of an arithmetic sequence whose first term is a and whose common difference is d.

23. Write the equations of the function shown.

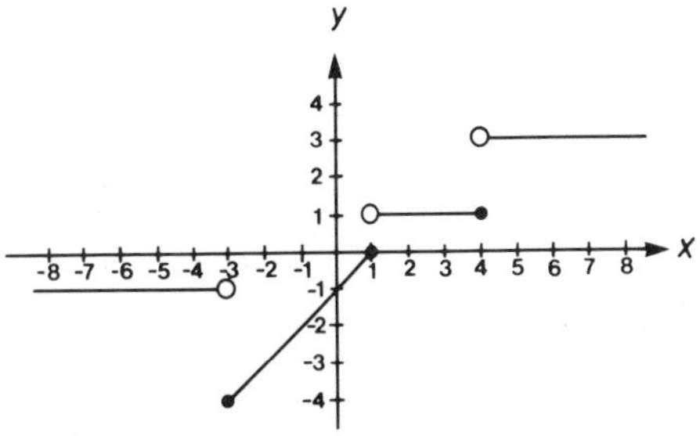

24. The base of a pyramid is a square of perimeter 20 cm. The height of the pyramid is 9 cm. What is the volume of the pyramid?

25. Indicate whether each equation shown represents an ellipse, a hyperbola, a circle, or a parabola.

(*a*) $3x = -2y - 9 + y^2$ (*b*) $y + 4x^2 = 20x - 16$

(*c*) $-y^2 - 90x + 302 + 4y = -9x^2$ (*d*) $4x^2 + 36y^2 - 288y = -40x - 532$

(*e*) $-14y + y^2 + 48 = -x^2$

26. Write equation (*d*) of Problem 25 in standard form and describe the conic section which the equation represents.

27. Write the three cube roots of $-4 + 6i$ in polar form.

28. Show that $\cos 2x + \sin 2x + 2\sin^2 x = (\sin x + \cos x)^2$.

29. Solve, given that $(0° \le x < 360°)$: $2\cot^2 x + 3\csc x = 0$

30. Find $\log_7 10$, using base 10 logarithms.

EP 118.107, 118.108

LESSON 119 Descartes' rule of signs · Upper and lower bound theorem · Irrational roots

119.A Descartes' rule of signs

There is no one direct method of finding the roots of polynomial equations, and the simplest way to find these roots often involves ingenuity as well as skill. The task is simplified somewhat by mustering all the knowledge that we have concerning the roots of these equations. In the preceding lesson, we again noted that every nth-degree equation has exactly n roots. Now we find that the number of positive real roots can be estimated by counting the number of sign changes in the polynomial when the terms of the polynomial are written in descending powers of the variable. We say *estimated* because pairs of complex roots also cause sign changes, and we don't know how many sign changes are caused by the real roots and how many are caused by pairs of complex roots. Thus, three sign changes could indicate three positive real roots or one positive real root, with the other two sign changes caused by a pair of complex roots. If we encounter five sign changes, we could have five positive roots or three positive roots in addition to one pair of complex roots or one positive root in addition to two pairs of complex roots. The same reasoning process tells us that six sign changes would indicate that we have six positive roots, four positive roots, two positive roots, or no positive roots. Since complex roots always occur in pairs, one change in sign tells us that we have one real root and no complex roots. If the factors are $(x + 2)$ and $(x - 3)$, the only positive real root is $+3$. We note that the polynomial equation formed by multiplying these factors and equating the product to zero has one change in sign, indicated below by the symbol ©:

$$x^2 - x - 6 = 0$$
$$+ © - \quad -$$

The polynomial in the following equation

$$x^4 - 2x^3 + 3x^2 + 4x - 7 = 0$$
$$+ © - © + \quad + © -$$

has three changes in sign, so this equation has either three positive real roots or one positive real root. When sign changes are counted, the fact that the term of a particular power is missing is not considered. The next polynomial does not have an x^3 term, but this is not considered. This polynomial

$$x^6 - 4x^5 + 3x^4 - 2x^2 - 3x + 4 = 0$$
$$+ © - © + © - \quad - © +$$

has four sign changes. The four sign changes tell us that there are four positive real roots *or* two positive real roots *or* zero positive real roots. **The number of positive real roots of a polynomial equation equals the number of sign changes in the polynomial $p(x)$, or that number less 2, or less 4, or less 6, etc.**

If we consider the original polynomial to be $p(x)$, then we can find $p(-x)$ by replacing x everywhere with $-x$. The resulting polynomial will be exactly the same as the original polynomial except that the signs of the terms whose exponents are odd will be the opposite of the signs of these terms in $p(x)$.

$$p(x) = x^4 - 2x^3 + 2x - 5 \qquad p(-x) = (-x)^4 - 2(-x)^3 + 2(-x) - 5$$
$$= x^4 + 2x^3 - 2x - 5$$

We see that in this example, $p(-x)$ is the same as $p(x)$ except that the signs of the x^3 term and the x^1 terms are changed. **The number of negative real roots of a polynomial equation equals the number of sign changes in $p(-x)$ or that number less 2, or less 4, or less 6, etc.**

Example 119.A.1 Discuss the number of possible negative real roots of $x^5 - 2x^4 + 3x^3 - 5x^2 + x - 2 = 0$.

Solution To find the number of negative real roots, we count the number of sign changes in $p(-x)$. First we write $p(-x)$, which is the same as $p(x)$ with the signs changed in the terms with odd exponents.

$$p(-x) = -x^5 - 2x^4 - 3x^3 - 5x^2 - x - 2$$
$$- \quad - \quad - \quad - \quad - \quad -$$

There are no sign changes in $p(-x)$, so the given equation has no negative real roots.

Example 119.A.2 Discuss the number of negative real roots of $2x^5 + 3x^4 + 4x^3 + 5x^2 + x + 2 = 0$.

Solution We begin by writing $p(-x)$ and counting the sign changes.

$$p(-x) = -2x^5 + 3x^4 - 4x^3 + 5x^2 - x + 2$$
$$- © + © - © + © - © +$$

We count five sign changes in $p(-x)$, so the original equation has five negative real roots, or three negative real roots, or one negative real root.

119.B Upper and lower bound theorem

The constants in some polynomial equations are such that the region of interest as determined by the method of Lesson 108 is not sufficiently restrictive to be of much use. The equation of the function graphed at the right is $y = x^4 - 13x^2 + 35$. We see that all real roots for this polynomial lie between $+5$ and -5, but the region-of-interest method gives us bounds of $+36$ and -36. We can get more restrictive bounds for this equation by using the upper and lower bound theorem. **To determine an upper bound for real roots of a polynomial equation, we use synthetic division and use positive integers (integers for convenience) as divisors. If every nonzero number in the bottom row is positive or if every nonzero number in the bottom row is negative, there is no real root greater than the positive number used as the divisor.** For the polynomial of this example, we will illustrate by using $+1$, $+3$, and $+4$ as synthetic divisors.

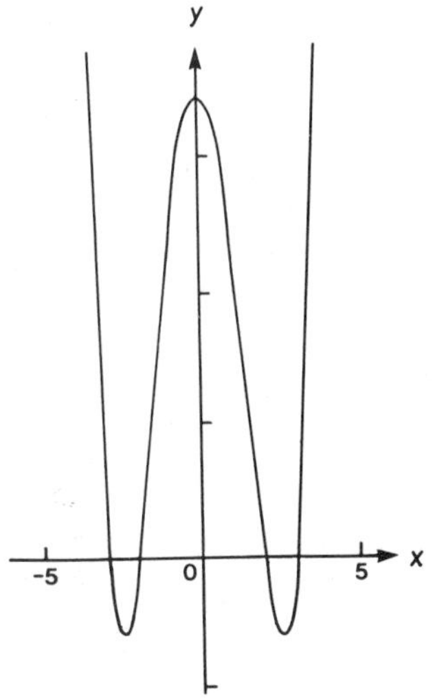

$y = x^4 - 13x^2 + 35$

1	1	0	−13	0	35
		1	1	−12	−12
	1	1	−12	−12	23

3	1	0	−13	0	35
		3	9	−12	−36
	1	3	−4	−12	−1

4	1	0	−13	0	35
		4	16	12	48
	1	4	3	12	83

When we use 1 as a synthetic divisor, we get a remainder of 23 and two sign changes. The nonzero remainder tells us that 1 is not a root, and the sign changes tell us that 1 is probably not an upper bound. When we use 3 as a synthetic divisor, the nonzero remainder tells us that 3 is not a root and the sign change tells us that 3 is not an upper bound. Finally, when we use 4 as a synthetic divisor, we get a nonzero remainder and a bottom row with no sign changes. This tells us that 4 is not a root and that there is no root greater than 4, so 4 is an upper bound.

To determine a lower bound, we again use synthetic division, but use negative numbers as synthetic divisors. For lower bounds we look for alternating signs, because a bottom row of alternating signs tells us that the divisor is a lower bound and that there are no real roots less than this negative divisor. If a zero appears in the bottom row, we can consider the zero to be positive or negative in order to get alternating signs. For the problem under consideration, we will try divisors of -1, -3, and -4.

−1	1	0	−13	0	36
		−1	1	12	−12
	1	−1	−12	12	24

−3	1	0	−13	0	36
		−3	9	12	−36
	1	−3	−4	12	0

−4	1	0	−13	0	36
		−4	16	−12	48
	1	−4	3	−12	84

When we use -1 and -3 as synthetic divisors, we do not get alternating signs, so neither of these numbers is a lower bound. But the synthetic divisor of -4 gives us the alternating signs we seek, and thus we know that there is no real root less than -4.

Example 119.B.1 Use the upper and lower bound theorem to find an upper and a lower bound for real roots of $x^2 - x - 21 = 0$.

Solution **To find an upper bound, we use synthetic division with positive divisors and look for a bottom row in which all nonzero numbers have the same signs.** We will use 1, 2, 3, . . . , as synthetic divisors.

$$\begin{array}{r|rrr} 1 & 1 & -1 & -21 \\ & & 1 & 0 \\ \hline & 1 & 0 & -21 \end{array} \qquad \begin{array}{r|rrr} 2 & 1 & -1 & -21 \\ & & 2 & 2 \\ \hline & 1 & 1 & -19 \end{array} \qquad \begin{array}{r|rrr} 3 & 1 & -1 & -21 \\ & & 3 & 6 \\ \hline & 1 & 2 & -15 \end{array}$$

$$\begin{array}{r|rrr} 4 & 1 & -1 & -21 \\ & & 4 & 12 \\ \hline & 1 & 3 & -9 \end{array} \qquad \begin{array}{r|rrr} 5 & 1 & -1 & -21 \\ & & 5 & 20 \\ \hline & 1 & 4 & -1 \end{array} \qquad \begin{array}{r|rrr} 6 & 1 & -1 & -21 \\ & & 6 & 30 \\ \hline & 1 & 5 & 9 \end{array}$$

The divisor of 6 gives us a row of all positive numbers, so we know there are no real roots greater than 6.

To find a lower bound, we will use negative numbers as divisors and look for a bottom row in which the signs alternate. For synthetic divisors we will use $-1, -2, -3, -4, -5, \ldots$.

$$\begin{array}{r|rrr} -1 & 1 & -1 & -21 \\ & & -1 & 2 \\ \hline & 1 & -2 & -19 \end{array} \qquad \begin{array}{r|rrr} -2 & 1 & -1 & -21 \\ & & -2 & 6 \\ \hline & 1 & -3 & -15 \end{array} \qquad \begin{array}{r|rrr} -3 & 1 & -1 & -21 \\ & & -3 & 12 \\ \hline & 1 & -4 & -9 \end{array}$$

$$\begin{array}{r|rrr} -4 & 1 & -1 & -21 \\ & & -4 & 20 \\ \hline & 1 & -5 & -1 \end{array} \qquad \begin{array}{r|rrr} -5 & 1 & -1 & -21 \\ & & -5 & 30 \\ \hline & 1 & -6 & 9 \end{array}$$

When we use -5 as a divisor, we get a bottom row of alternating signs, so we know there are no real roots less than -5. **Thus, we know that all real roots lie between +6 and −5.**

Example 119.B.2 Use the upper and lower bound theorem to find an upper and a lower bound for real roots for the equation $x^3 - 21x + 20$.

Solution We begin by using a synthetic divisor of $+1$.

$$\begin{array}{r|rrrr} 1 & 1 & 0 & -21 & 20 \\ & & 1 & 1 & \\ \hline & 1 & 1 & -20 & \end{array}$$

This is enough to see that 1 is not an upper bound because the divisor must be large enough to overcome the -21 in the third step to get all positive numbers in the bottom row. For this reason, we decide to skip 2 and 3 and try 4 and 5 as synthetic divisors.

$$\begin{array}{r|rrrr} 4 & 1 & 0 & -21 & 20 \\ & & 4 & 16 & \\ \hline & 1 & 4 & -5 & \end{array} \qquad \begin{array}{r|rrrr} 5 & 1 & 0 & -21 & 20 \\ & & 5 & 25 & 20 \\ \hline & 1 & 5 & 4 & 40 \end{array}$$

We terminated the division by 4 as soon as we got a sign change (-5). **The division by 5 yields all positive numbers in the bottom row, so we know there are no roots of the polynomial that are greater than 5.** For a lower bound, we play a hunch and begin with -4, -5, and -6.

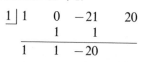

$$\begin{array}{r|rrrr} -4 & 1 & 0 & -21 & 20 \\ & & -4 & 16 & \\ \hline & 1 & -4 & -5 & \end{array} \qquad \begin{array}{r|rrrr} -5 & 1 & 0 & -21 & 20 \\ & & -5 & 25 & -20 \\ \hline & 1 & -5 & 4 & 0 \end{array}$$

$$\begin{array}{r|rrrr} -6 & 1 & 0 & -21 & 20 \\ & & -6 & 36 & -90 \\ \hline & 1 & -6 & 15 & -70 \end{array}$$

We find that -5 is a root and that there are no real roots less than -5 because a zero in the bottom row can be considered as either + or −. We consider this 0 to be − to get a row of alternating signs. We also used -6 as a divisor and note that the last row also contains alternating signs, as we would have predicted.

119.C Irrational roots

We have restricted our investigation of the real roots of polynomial equations to roots that are rational numbers. The list of possible rational roots can be determined by using the rational roots theorem. Unfortunately, there is no similar theorem for finding a list of possible irrational roots, and these roots can only be estimated by using other numerical methods. If the value of a polynomial is positive for some value of x and negative for another value of x, we know that the polynomial will have a value of zero for some x between these two values.

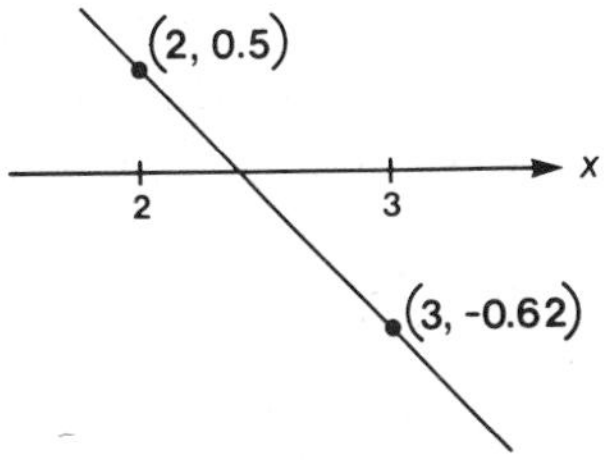

Suppose a polynomial has a y value of 0.5 when x equals 2 and a y value of -0.62 when x equals 3. Then we will know that, for some value of x between 2 and 3, y has a value of zero and the graph crosses the x axis at this point. If the rational zero theorem does not give a possible rational zero between the x values of 2 and 3, we know that the root is an irrational number. This number can be estimated to any accuracy desired by using synthetic division and selecting x values that produce y values closer and closer to zero. The problem of estimating the values of irrational zeros of polynomials can be handled easily by a computer. We suggest you ask your computer teacher for further details on this type of problem.

Problem set 119

1. The decrease was exponential. Five years after the decrease began, Selma found that only 800 remained and to her dismay only 500 remained after 7 years. How many remained after 10 years had gone by?

2. Cordan's speed was 20 miles an hour greater than that of Widla. Thus, Cordan could travel 240 miles in 2 hours less than it took Widla to travel 160 miles. Find the speeds and times of both.

3. Some were red and the rest were blue. Ten times the number of reds exceeded twice the number of blues by 26. If the number of blues exceeded the number of reds by 7, how many were red and how many were blue?

4. One card is drawn from a full deck. What is the probability that the card will be red or will be an ace or will be a red ace?

5. One root of $y = x^3 - 6x^2 + 13x - 10$ is $+2$. What are the other two roots?

6. One root of $y = 3x^3 - x^2 + 2x - 4$ is $+1$. What are the other two roots?

Use Descartes' rule of signs to determine the possible number of:

7. Positive real roots of $x^4 - 2x^3 + 3x^2 + 4x - 7 = 0$

8. Negative real roots of $3x^4 - 4x^3 + 2x^2 + 5x - 2 = 0$

9. Positive real roots of $6x^5 - 17x^4 - 3x^3 + 22x^2 - 7x + 20 = 0$

10. Negative real roots of $2x^5 - 3x^4 - 5x^3 + 11x^2 - 4x + 5 = 0$

Use synthetic division with integers as divisors and the upper and lower bound theorem to find upper and lower bounds for the real roots of the following polynomial equations.

11. $x^3 - 21x + 19 = 0$

12. $x^4 - 2x^3 - 17x + 5 = 0$

Find the roots of the following.

13. $x^3 + 2x^2 - x - 2 = 0$

14. $x^3 - 3x^2 + 4x - 12 = 0$

Sketch the function.

15. $y = \dfrac{4}{x - 4}$

16. $y = |x + 2| - 4$

17. $y = \dfrac{2}{(x - 2)^2}$

18. Find the inverse function of $y = 5x + 6$.

19. Find the coordinates of the point that is one-fourth of the way from (3, 5) to (−4, −3).

20. The base of a pyramid is a square whose perimeter is 28 feet. The height of the pyramid is 12 feet. What is the volume of the pyramid?

21. Write the four fourth roots of $-i$ in polar form.

22. Use base 10 logarithms to find $\log_6 72$.

23. Develop the formula for the sum of the first n terms of a geometric series, given its first term and common ratio.

24. Develop the formula for the sum of the first n terms of an arithmetic sequence whose first term is a and whose common difference is d.

25. Find the number three-fifths of the way from $4\frac{1}{2}$ to $-10\frac{1}{5}$.

ENRICHMENT
LESSON 1

Syllogistic reasoning · Equivalent expressions

EL1.A Syllogistic reasoning

The ancient Greeks formalized the study of logic with their use of ***syllogisms*** in their investigation of deductive reasoning. A ***syllogism*** is a formal reasoning process in which a conclusion is inferred from two statements called ***premises.*** We will look at syllogisms in which the premises are called ***categorical propositions*** because they place things in categories. We will concentrate on premises called ***universal affirmatives*** because these premises affirm that all members of a certain set possess a certain property. This premise is often called the ***major premise.*** The other premise is often called the ***minor premise*** and identifies a member of the set. The conclusion follows that this member has the property possessed by all the members of the set. We demonstrate by using one of the oldest syllogisms known. The first premise is as follows.

1. All men are mortal. (Major premise)

This statement establishes mortality as a property possessed by every member of the set of all men.

2. Aristotle is a man. (Minor premise)

This statement identifies Aristotle as a member of the set of all men.

Aristotle is mortal. (Conclusion)

This conclusion is a logical consequence because if Aristotle is a member of the set of all men, then he possesses the properties possessed by every member of this set. This is the type of reasoning we use in the geometric proofs in this book. Observe:

The sum of the exterior angles of a convex polygon is 360°.
Triangle *ABC* is a convex polygon.

The sum of the exterior angles of triangle *ABC* is 360°.

The major premise identifies a property of every member of the set of convex polygons. The minor premise identifies triangle *ABC* as a member of that set. Thus, triangle *ABC* has all the properties possessed by every member of the set. The entire three-step process is called an ***argument.*** In our investigation of syllogistic reasoning we will concentrate on the argument and will not consider the truth or falsity of the premises. Consider the following syllogism.

All frogs are green.	Major premise
Henry is a frog.	Minor premise
Henry is green.	Valid conclusion

The argument is a valid argument because the major premise stated a property possessed by all frogs (they are green), and the minor premise identified Henry as a member of the set of all frogs. The major premise is false because some frogs are not green and thus Henry might be brown or red or some other color. But, because the argument is a valid argument, we will say that the conclusion is a valid conclusion. **This does not mean that the conclusion is true but means only that the argument is a valid argument.**

The conclusion in the following syllogism is invalid because the argument is faulty, as the minor premise does not identify a member of the set defined by the major premise.

If it rains, I will go to town.	Major premise
It did not rain.	Minor premise
I did not go to town.	Invalid conclusion

The major premise identified the results of the set of days on which rain occurred. It made no statement about the set of days on which there was no rain. Thus, the day in question is not a member of the established set and may or may not possess the property in question.

Example EL1.A.1 Is the following argument a valid argument? Why or why not?

All normal dogs have four legs.
That dog has four legs.
———
That dog is a normal dog.

Solution **The argument is faulty.** The set described is the set of normal dogs. For a valid argument, the minor premise should have stated that a particular dog was a member of this set.

Example EL1.A.2 Is the following argument a valid argument? Why or why not?

All boys are good.
That child is a good child.
———
That child is a boy.

Solution **Invalid.** The major premise made a statement about the set of all boys. The minor premise talked about a member of the set of good children. For a valid argument, the minor premise would have to identify a member of the set of all boys.

Example EL1.A.3 Is the following argument a valid argument? Why?

All chickens have three legs.
Henny Penny is a chicken.
———
Henny Penny has three legs.

Solution **Valid.** All chickens do not have three legs, but we still say that the argument is a valid argument. This does not mean that the conclusion is true. It means that the argument is valid because the major premise identified a property of the set of all chickens and the minor premise identified Henny Penny as a member of the set.

EL1.B The contrapositive

The major premise implies an if-then statement that has two parts called the ***hypothesis*** and the ***conclusion.*** The hypothesis begins with the word *if* and the conclusion begins with the word *then.* When the words *if* and *then* are not written, the premise can be rewritten so that these words are used. For example, the major premise "Rabbits are fast runners" can be written as an if-then statement by writing

HYPOTHESIS	CONCLUSION
If an animal is a rabbit,	then the animal is a fast runner.

Two steps are necessary to form the ***contrapositive*** of a premise. The first step is to replace the **if statement** with the **negative of the then statement.** The second step is to replace the **then statement** with the **negative of the if statement.** Thus, the contrapositive of this premise is

If an animal is **not a fast runner, then** the animal is **not a rabbit.**

If a universal affirmative premise is true, its contrapositive is also true. If a universal affirmative premise is false, its contrapositive is also false. This is easy to see if we use a Venn diagram.

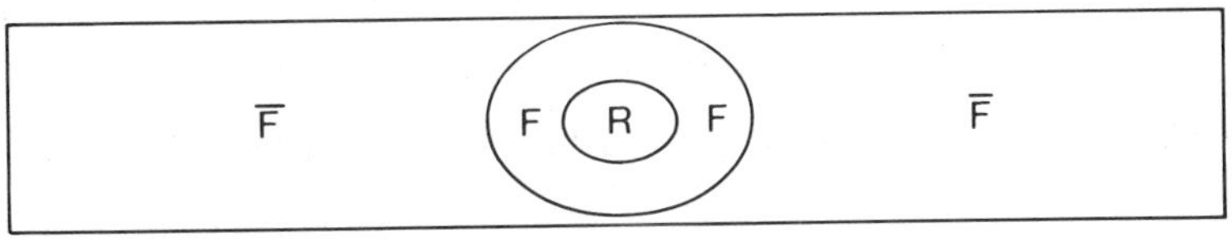

We place all rabbits (R) inside the smaller curve and all fast animals (F) inside the larger curve. This puts all animals who are not fast ($\bar{F}$) outside the larger curve. From this we can see that if an animal is a rabbit, it is also inside the F curve and is a fast runner. Also, we see that if an animal is not a fast runner, it is outside the larger curve and thus cannot be a rabbit.

Example EL1.B.1 Is the following argument valid?

All nonathletes are vegetarians.	Major premise
Jim is a nonvegetarian.	Minor premise
Jim is an athlete.	Conclusion

Solution If we write the contrapositive of the major premise, we get

All nonvegetarians are athletes.	Major premise
Jim is a nonvegetarian.	Minor premise
Jim is an athlete.	Conclusion

This is a **valid argument,** so the original argument is also valid. The conclusion is not necessarily true, but the argument is valid.

EL1.C Equivalent expressions

In later lessons, we will use a process called ***mathematical induction*** to prove some theorems. In these proofs, it will be necessary to prove that if we add one term to one expression, we get the same result as we would get if we replaced k in another expression with $k + 1$. If we practice a few of these now and learn the mechanics, it will be easier to concentrate on the theory when we do the proofs.

Example EL1.C.1 Show that replacing k with $k + 1$ in expression (b) results in an expression equivalent to expression (a).

$$(a)\quad \frac{k(k+1)}{2} + (k+1) \qquad\qquad (b)\quad \frac{k(k+1)}{2}$$

Solution We will multiply the second part of (*a*) by 2 over 2 so the two parts have a common denominator. In (*b*) we replace k with $k + 1$.

$$(a)\quad \frac{k(k+1)}{2} + \frac{2(k+1)}{2} \qquad (b)\quad \frac{(k+1)[(k+1)+1]}{2}$$

Now we simplify the numerator of each term.

$$(a)\quad \frac{k^2 + k + 2k + 2}{2} \qquad (b)\quad \frac{(k+1)(k+2)}{2}$$

We finish by adding and multiplying as required in the numerators.

$$(a)\quad \frac{k^2 + 3k + 2}{2} \qquad (b)\quad \frac{k^2 + 3k + 2}{2}$$

We see that the two expressions are the same.

Example EL1.C.2 Show that replacing k with $k + 1$ in expression (*b*) results in an expression equivalent to expression (*a*).

$$(a)\quad k(3k - 1) + (6k + 2) \qquad (b)\quad k(3k - 1)$$

Solution We simplify in (*a*), and we replace k with $(k + 1)$ in (*b*).

$$(a)\quad 3k^2 - k + (6k + 2) \qquad (b)\quad (k + 1)[3(k + 1) - 1]$$

We finish the simplification on the left and within the brackets on the right.

$$(a)\quad 3k^2 + 5k + 2 \qquad (b)\quad (k + 1)(3k + 2)$$

The expression on the left is in trinomial form. The expression on the right is an equivalent factored form. If we multiply expression (*b*) as indicated,

$$(a)\quad 3k^2 + 5k + 2 \qquad (b)\quad 3k^2 + 5k + 2$$

we see that the two expressions are the same.

Problem set EL1

1. If x is an even integer, what is the quotient of the next greater even integer divided by the next greater odd integer?
2. Find three consecutive integers such that the product of the first and third exceeds the second by 11.
3. The city had an assessed valuation of \$6,400,000. The rate for school taxes is 60 cents per \$100 valuation. If all but 2 percent of the taxes are collected, how many dollars have not been collected?
4. Fiddlesticks sell for \$100 each, but gnomes get a 10 percent discount. If a gnome purchases fiddlesticks in coins instead of dollar bills, the gnome gets 10 percent off of the discount price. What would a gnome who pays in coins have to pay for 5 fiddlesticks?
5. On a 300-mile trip, the traveler traveled 60 miles per hour for the first one-third of the trip and 30 miles per hour for the rest of the trip. What was the traveler's average speed for the entire trip?
6. A deerball team has 9 players playing on the field. How many 9-player deerball teams can be formed from a group of 15 players?
7. Write the fourth term of $(x + y)^6$.
8. Write all six terms of $(x + y)^5$.

9. Is the following argument a valid argument?

All nondogs are not blue.
Jim is a dog.
___
Jim is blue.

10. Is the following argument a valid argument?

1. All authors wear gold watches.
2. John wears a gold watch.
___
3. Thus, John is an author.

11. Show that replacing k with $k + 1$ in expression (b) results in an expression equivalent to expression (a).

(a) $\dfrac{k(k+1)}{2} + (k+1)$ (b) $\dfrac{k(k+1)}{2}$

12. Show that replacing k with $k + 1$ in expression (b) results in an expression equivalent to expression (a).

(a) $k(3k - 1) + (6k + 2)$ (b) $k(3k - 1)$

13. Show that $\cos x \csc x = \cot x$.

14. Use Cramer's rule to solve: $\begin{cases} 2x - 3y = 1 \\ 3x - 2y = 4 \end{cases}$

15. Find the sum of the interior angles of a 7-sided convex polygon.

16. Two triangles are similar. The ratio of the length of one side of the larger triangle to the length of the corresponding side of the other triangle is 5 to 3. What is the ratio of their areas?

17. Solve this triangle for its unknown parts.

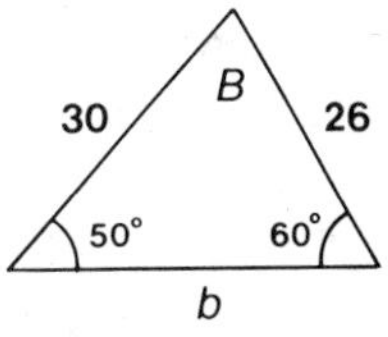

18. Graph the ellipse $4x^2 + 9y^2 = 36$.

19. Multiply $[4 \text{ cis } (-20°)](4 \text{ cis } 20°)$ and express the answer in rectangular form.

20. Prove that an exterior angle of a triangle equals the sum of the remote interior angles.

Write the equations of the following sinusoids in terms of the sine function.

21.

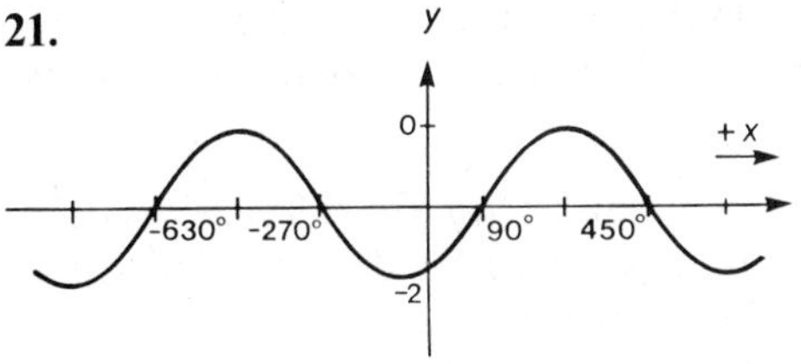

22.

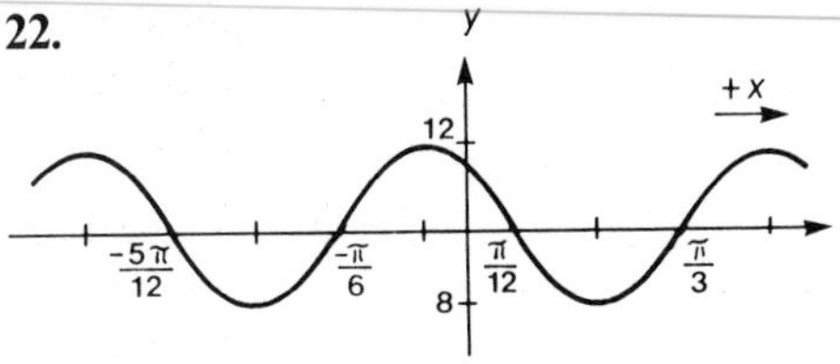

23. Find the radius and center of the circle whose equation is as follows: $x^2 + y^2 - 4x + 2y - 4 = 0$.

24. The three triangles shown are similar. Find a and b.

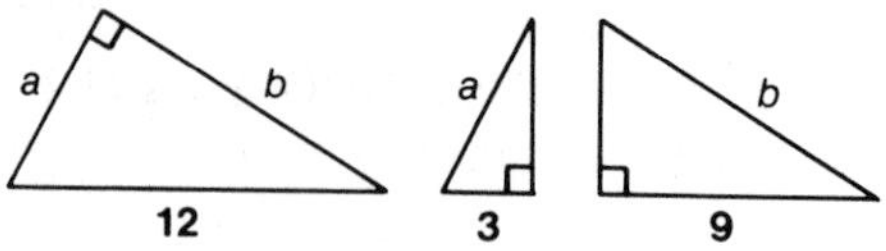

Solve the following equations given that ($0° \le \theta < 360°$):

25. $\sqrt{3}\tan 2\theta - 1 = 0$

26. $2\sin^2\theta - 1 = 0$

27. Evaluate: $\tan^2\left(\frac{16\pi}{3}\right) - \sec^2\left(\frac{16\pi}{3}\right)$

28. Solve: $\log_3(2x - 1) - \log_3(x + 1) = 2\log_3 2$

29. Simplify: $3^{\log_3 6 - \log_3 2}$

30. Evaluate the base 2 antilogarithm of 4.

ENRICHMENT LESSON 2 *More equivalent expressions*

EL2.A More equivalent expressions

Some of the equivalences used in proofs by mathematical induction involve powers or exponentials. The algebraic simplifications in these problems are straightforward but require knowing how to simplify terms that contain exponents.

Example EL2.A.1 Show that replacing k with $k + 1$ in expression (b) results in an expression equivalent to expression (a).

$$(a)\quad 2k^2 + [4(k + 1) - 2] \qquad (b)\quad 2k^2$$

Solution We simplify in (a) and replace k with $k + 1$ in (b).

$$(a)\quad 2k^2 + (4k + 4 - 2) \qquad (b)\quad 2(k + 1)^2$$

Now we simplify within the parentheses on the left and square the expression on the right.

$$(a)\quad 2k^2 + (4k + 2) \qquad (b)\quad 2(k^2 + 2k + 1)$$

Now we add and multiply as indicated and see that (a) and (b) are the same.

$$(a)\quad 2k^2 + 4k + 2 \qquad (b)\quad 2k^2 + 4k + 2$$

Example EL2.A.2 Show that replacing k with $k + 1$ in expression (b) results in an expression equivalent to expression (a).

$$(a)\quad 2^{k+1} - 2 + 2^{k+1} \qquad (b)\quad 2^{k+1} - 2$$

Solution This problem is somewhat involved. First let us note that for the same reason that we can add $2x$ and $2x$ and get $2(2x)$, which equals $4x$, we can add

$$2^{k+1} + 2^{k+1} \qquad \text{and get} \qquad 2(2^{k+1})$$

and that this is 2^1 times 2^{k+1}. Now we can add the exponents 1 and $k + 1$.

$$2^1(2^{k+1}) = 2^{k+2}$$

Now let's work the problem. We add 2^{k+1} and 2^{k+1} in expression (*a*) and replace k with $k + 1$ in expression (*b*), and we get

$$(a)\quad 2(2^{k+1}) - 2 \quad \text{added} \qquad (b)\quad 2^{(k+1)+1} - 2 \quad \text{used } (k+1) \text{ for } k$$

Now we finish by simplifying both expressions and see that (*a*) equals (*b*).

$$(a)\quad 2^{k+2} - 2 \qquad (b)\quad 2^{k+2} - 2$$

Example EL2.A.3 Show that replacing k with $k + 1$ in expression (*b*) results in an expression equivalent to expression (*a*).

$$(a)\quad \frac{k}{k+1} + \frac{1}{(k+1)(k+2)} \qquad (b)\quad \frac{k}{k+1}$$

Solution In (*a*) we multiply the first term by $k + 2$ over $k + 2$ to get a common denominator. In (*b*) we replace k with $k + 1$.

$$(a)\quad \frac{k(k+2)}{(k+1)(k+2)} + \frac{1}{(k+1)(k+2)} \qquad (b)\quad \frac{k+1}{(k+1)+1}$$

We simplify the numerator in (*a*) and simplify the denominator in (*b*).

$$(a)\quad \frac{k^2+2k+1}{(k+1)(k+2)} \qquad (b)\quad \frac{k+1}{k+2}$$

Now the numerator in (*a*) can be factored, and we get the desired result.

$$(a)\quad \frac{\cancel{(k+1)}(k+1)}{\cancel{(k+1)}(k+2)} = \frac{k+1}{k+2} \qquad (b)\quad \frac{k+1}{k+2}$$

Problem set EL2

1. It is 3 p.m. and the crowd is waiting for the time the big hand and the little hand will be pointing in opposite directions. How long do they have to wait?

2. It is 10 a.m. How long will it be before both hands are pointing in the same direction?

3. Find three consecutive even integers such that the product of the first and third is 8 greater than the second.

4. The first time, Cindy drove 10 miles per hour and arrived 5 hours late. The next time, she drove at 20 miles per hour and arrived 2 hours late. How long was the trip?

5. An urn contains 4 red marbles and 3 blue marbles. Two marbles are drawn and replaced. Both the marbles are blue. What is the probability that the next marble drawn will be red?

6. Three boys and 3 girls sit in 6 chairs in a circle. How many seating arrangements are possible?

7. Show that replacing k with $k + 1$ in expression (*b*) results in an expression equivalent to expression (*a*).

$$(a)\quad \tfrac{1}{6}k(k+1)(2k+1) + (k+1)^2 \qquad (b)\quad \tfrac{1}{6}k(k+1)(2k+1)$$

8. Show that replacing k with $k + 1$ in expression (*b*) results in an expression equivalent to expression (*a*).

$$(a)\quad 2^{k+1} - 2 + 2^{k+1} \qquad (b)\quad 2^{k+1} - 2$$

9. Is the following argument valid?

If the switch is not on, then the light is not on.
The light is on.
———
The switch is on.

10. Use the matrix echelon method to solve: $\begin{cases} 2x - y = 4 \\ x + 2y = -3 \end{cases}$

11. Construct a line that is perpendicular to a given line and that passes through a designated point not on the line.

12. Write all six terms of $(x + y)^5$.

13. Write the four fourth roots of 16 cis 240° in rectangular form. Give exact answers.

Solve the following equations given that $(0° \leq x < 360°)$:

14. $\tan^2 x + \tan x = 0$

15. $3 \tan^2 x + 5 \sec x + 1 = 0$

16. Show that: $\dfrac{\tan^2 x - 1}{\tan x} = \tan x - \cot x$

17. Show that $\sec x - \cos x = \sin x \tan x$.

18. The perimeter of a regular 8-sided polygon (regular octagon) is 48 cm. What is the area of the polygon?

19. Solve this triangle for its unknown parts.

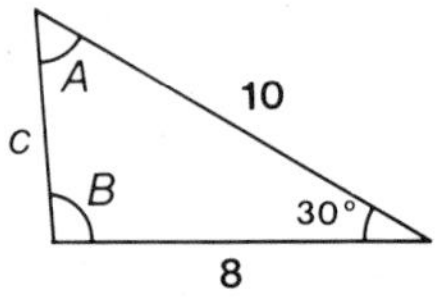

20. Find the sum of the interior angles of a 10-sided convex polygon.

21. Find the area in square centimeters of the segment bounded by an arc of measure 60° and the chord joining the endpoints of the arc in a circle of radius 10 centimeters.

22. Find the radius and center of the circle whose equation is $x^2 - 4x - 5 + y^2 = 0$.

23. Sketch $y = -10 + 20 \cos 2x$.

24. Convert 60 miles per hour to meters per second.

25. Solve for a.

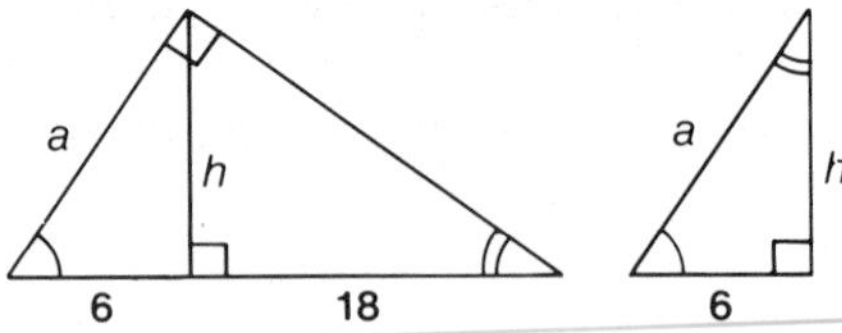

Solve the following equations given that $(0° \leq \theta, x < 360°)$:

26. $2 \sin 2\theta - 1 = 0$

27. $4 \cos^2 x - 1 = 0$

28. Solve: $3^{2x-1} = 4^{3x+2}$

29. Simplify $(1.04)^6$ by using a table of logarithms.

30. Solve: $2 \log_6 x - \dfrac{2}{3} \log_6 27 = \log_6 x$

ENRICHMENT LESSON 3 *Algebra of matrices · Addition of matrices · Associativity and commutativity*

EL3.A Algebra of matrices

We remember that we define a ***matrix*** to be a rectangular array of numbers or symbols that stand for numbers. Thus, all the following arrays can be called matrices.

$$\begin{bmatrix} 4 & 2 \\ 5 & 6 \end{bmatrix} \qquad \begin{matrix} 7 & 4 & 3 & 6 \\ 8 & 9 & 5 & 2 \end{matrix} \qquad \begin{bmatrix} x \\ m \\ p \end{bmatrix} \qquad \begin{bmatrix} 4 \\ 1 \\ 6 \end{bmatrix} \qquad \begin{bmatrix} 2 & 3 & 4 & 5 \end{bmatrix}$$

(*a*) (*b*) (*c*) (*d*) (*e*)

It is customary but not necessary to enclose a rectangular array in brackets when we are considering the array as a matrix. Thus, array (*b*) can be called a matrix even though brackets are not used.

We have already mentioned that the study of matrices arose from the investigation of the solutions of systems of linear equations by considering only the constants in the equations. Cramer's rule was developed, and the rules for determinants were stated. Then, other investigations produced additional insights such as the echelon method of solution. Finally, mathematicians decided that, since we had rules for adding, subtracting, and multiplying real numbers, it would be reasonable to formulate rules for adding, subtracting, and multiplying matrices. Also, since real numbers have inverses and identities for addition and multiplication, why not try to define matrix inverses and matrix identities for addition and multiplication? As a consequence of this effort, rules and definitions have been formulated that permit us to speak of the algebra of matrices in the same way we speak of the algebra of real numbers. Some of the rules and definitions are used more than others, but they are all important because together they define the algebra of matrices.

The size of a matrix is called the ***order*** of the matrix and is defined by indicating the number of rows and then by indicating the number of columns. The following matrix is a 2×3 (read "two by three") matrix because it has 2 rows and 3 columns.

$$\begin{bmatrix} 4 & 3 & 2 \\ 7 & 4 & 6 \end{bmatrix}$$

We say that the order of this matrix is 2×3. Each element of a matrix is called an ***entry,*** and the position of each entry can be identified by using a two-part subscript. The first part gives the row of the entry and the second part gives the column of the entry. We note that the entry in the second row and the first column is a_{21} and that the entry in the second row and the third column is a_{23}.

$$\begin{bmatrix} a_{11} & a_{12} & a_{13} \\ a_{21} & a_{22} & a_{23} \\ a_{31} & a_{32} & a_{33} \end{bmatrix}$$

We read each part of the subscript separately. Thus we read a_{21} as "a two one," and not as "a twenty-one."

Example EL3.A.1 Which entry is called a_{32} in this matrix?

$$\begin{bmatrix} 1 & 2 & 3 & 4 \\ 5 & 6 & 7 & 8 \\ 14 & -7 & -3 & 2 \end{bmatrix}$$

Solution The entry in the third row and second column is -7.

EL3.B Addition of matrices

It is customary to use capital letters such as A, B, and C to designate matrices.

$$A = \begin{bmatrix} 4 & 5 & 7 \\ 2 & 6 & 8 \end{bmatrix} \qquad B = \begin{bmatrix} 9 & 3 & 15 \\ -2 & 2 & -14 \end{bmatrix}$$

If matrices are the same size, they can be added by adding the corresponding entries. Since the matrices shown here have the same number of rows and the same number of columns, they are the same size and can be added. The a_{11} entry in the sum is found by adding the a_{11} entry in A, which is 4, to the a_{11} entry in B, which is 9. Check the other elements in the sum matrix shown here to verify that they were obtained by using the same rule.

$$A + B = \begin{bmatrix} 13 & 8 & 22 \\ 0 & 8 & -6 \end{bmatrix}$$

Matrices D and E shown here can be added because the matrices are the same size. The bottom entries in matrix E are zero, but they do exist.

$$C = \begin{bmatrix} 4 & 1 \\ 3 & 2 \end{bmatrix} \qquad D = \begin{bmatrix} 4 & 1 \\ 3 & 2 \\ 7 & 5 \end{bmatrix} \qquad E = \begin{bmatrix} 5 & 6 \\ 2 & 4 \\ 0 & 0 \end{bmatrix}$$

Matrix C cannot be added to either matrix D or matrix E because there is no rule for adding matrices that are not the same size.

The number 0 is the *identity* for addition of real numbers because if you begin with a particular real number and add 0, the sum is *identically* the particular real number with which you began. In the same way, if we have a matrix

$$F = \begin{bmatrix} 4 & 7 \\ 2 & 5 \\ 3 & 2 \end{bmatrix}$$

and wish to add another matrix and have the result be identical with matrix F, we must add a matrix of the same size whose entries are all zero.

$$\begin{bmatrix} 4 & 7 \\ 2 & 5 \\ 3 & 2 \end{bmatrix} + \begin{bmatrix} 0 & 0 \\ 0 & 0 \\ 0 & 0 \end{bmatrix} = \begin{bmatrix} 4 & 7 \\ 2 & 5 \\ 3 & 2 \end{bmatrix}$$

This may seem trivial, but we are developing the rules for the algebra of matrices and we have defined an identity matrix for matrix addition.

We remember that in the algebra for real numbers, every number has an **opposite** which is also called the ***additive inverse*** of the number. When we add a number and its opposite, the sum is 0, which is the identity for addition. **If we are to have an opposite or an additive inverse for a matrix, the sum of the matrix and its inverse matrix should be the identity matrix.** So how will we define the opposite of a matrix? If we have

$$\begin{bmatrix} 4 & 3 & -2 & 4 \\ 7 & -8 & 6 & -3 \end{bmatrix} + \begin{bmatrix} \text{Inverse} \\ \text{matrix} \end{bmatrix} = \begin{bmatrix} 0 & 0 & 0 & 0 \\ 0 & 0 & 0 & 0 \end{bmatrix}$$

we see that the inverse matrix must be the same size as the given matrix, and every entry must be the negative of the corresponding entry in the given matrix. Thus,

$$\text{Inverse matrix} = \begin{bmatrix} -4 & -3 & 2 & -4 \\ -7 & 8 & -6 & 3 \end{bmatrix}$$

Example EL3.B.1 Given the matrices $A = \begin{bmatrix} 4 & 2 \\ 5 & 3 \end{bmatrix}$ and $B = \begin{bmatrix} 1 & 8 \\ -5 & 4 \end{bmatrix}$, find (*a*) $A + B$, and (*b*) the negative of B.

Solution (*a*) To find $A + B$, we add the corresponding entries and get

$$A + B = \begin{bmatrix} 5 & 10 \\ 0 & 7 \end{bmatrix}$$

(*b*) The additive inverse of matrix B is the same size, but every entry is of the opposite sign.

$$\text{Additive inverse of } B = \begin{bmatrix} -1 & -8 \\ 5 & -4 \end{bmatrix}$$

EL3.C Associativity and commutativity

The order of addition of two real numbers does not affect the sum.

$$2 + 5 = 7 \qquad 5 + 2 = 7$$

The Latin word for exchange is *commutare.* Since we can change the order of the addends, we say that real numbers are ***commutative*** in addition. Likewise, the order of addition of matrices does not affect the sum, so the addition of matrices is also commutative.

$$\begin{bmatrix} 4 & 2 \\ 1 & -3 \end{bmatrix} + \begin{bmatrix} 3 & 5 \\ 7 & 9 \end{bmatrix} = \begin{bmatrix} 7 & 7 \\ 8 & 6 \end{bmatrix} \qquad \text{Also} \qquad \begin{bmatrix} 3 & 5 \\ 7 & 9 \end{bmatrix} + \begin{bmatrix} 4 & 2 \\ 1 & -3 \end{bmatrix} = \begin{bmatrix} 7 & 7 \\ 8 & 6 \end{bmatrix}$$

We say that the addition of real numbers is ***associative,*** for when we add three real numbers, we can associate the first two or the last two.

$$\begin{array}{llll} (a) & (4 + 3) + 5 & (b) & 4 + (3 + 5) \\ & 7 + 5 & & 4 + 8 \\ & 12 & & 12 \end{array}$$

In (*a*) we added 4 and 3 to get 7 and then added 5 for a sum of 12. In (*b*) we got the same result by first adding 3 and 5 to get 8 and then adding 4. Addition of matrices is also associative, as we show in the next example.

Example EL3.C.1 Use the three given matrices to demonstrate that matrix addition is associative.

$$A = \begin{bmatrix} 4 & 1 \\ 3 & 2 \end{bmatrix} \qquad B = \begin{bmatrix} 7 & -5 \\ 2 & 6 \end{bmatrix} \qquad C = \begin{bmatrix} 8 & -3 \\ 0 & 9 \end{bmatrix}$$

Solution First we add $A + B$ and then add C.

$$A + B = \begin{bmatrix} 11 & -4 \\ 5 & 8 \end{bmatrix} \quad \text{so} \quad (A + B) + C = \begin{bmatrix} 11 & -4 \\ 5 & 8 \end{bmatrix} + \begin{bmatrix} 8 & -3 \\ 0 & 9 \end{bmatrix} = \begin{bmatrix} 19 & -7 \\ 5 & 17 \end{bmatrix}$$

Now we add $B + C$ and then add A to see if the result is the same.

$$B + C = \begin{bmatrix} 15 & -8 \\ 2 & 15 \end{bmatrix} \quad \text{so} \quad A + (B + C) = \begin{bmatrix} 4 & 1 \\ 3 & 2 \end{bmatrix} + \begin{bmatrix} 15 & -8 \\ 2 & 15 \end{bmatrix} = \begin{bmatrix} 19 & -7 \\ 5 & 17 \end{bmatrix}$$

The result is the same.

Problem set EL3

1. The number who were skulking on the outskirts increased exponentially. The first time Hilda looked there were 10 skulking on the outskirts. Ten days later she could locate 50 skulkers. How many skulkers could she locate 30 days after the first time?

2. The sample of the compound disintegrated exponentially. In the beginning there were 200 grams of it in the beaker, but 10 hours later only 150 grams remained. What was the half-life of the compound?

3. Ingels and Marianne peered intently at the clock. They noted that it was between 3 o'clock and 4 o'clock and the big hand was exactly 10 minutes ahead of the little hand. What time was it?

4. There are 6 green and 5 purple marbles in an urn. Two of the green marbles have ruby spots and two of the purple marbles have ruby spots. What is the probability of selecting a marble that is green or a marble that has ruby spots or both?

5. Show that replacing k with $k + 1$ in $\frac{k(k+1)}{2}$ yields an expression equivalent to $\frac{k(k+1)}{2} + (k + 1)$.

6. Prove the Pythagorean theorem, using the figures shown.

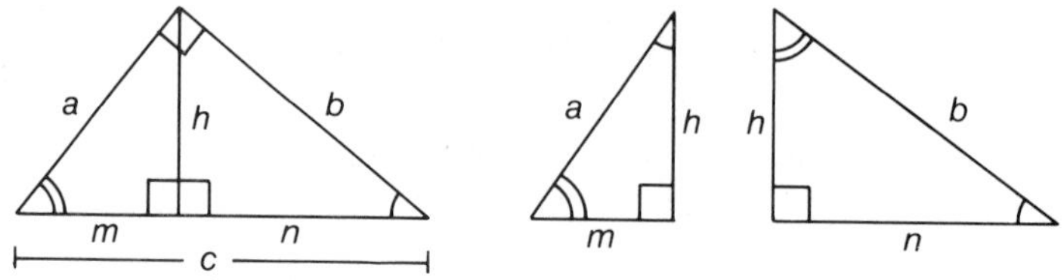

7. Given the matrix shown:
(*a*) Which entry is a_{23}?
(*b*) Which entry is a_{34}?
(*c*) Which entry is a_{32}?

$$\begin{bmatrix} 1 & -2 & 4 & -1 \\ 6 & 3 & -3 & 2 \\ 0 & 4 & 5 & 6 \end{bmatrix}$$

8. Given the matrices shown: $A = \begin{bmatrix} 4 & 3 \\ 2 & 1 \end{bmatrix}$ and $B = \begin{bmatrix} 1 & 4 \\ -3 & 2 \end{bmatrix}$
(*a*) Find $A + B$.
(*b*) Find the additive inverse of matrix A.

9. Write the 3×3 additive identity matrix.

10. Given: $\angle B = \angle C$ and $\overline{AD}$ bisects $\angle A$
Prove: $\triangle ADB \cong \triangle ADC$

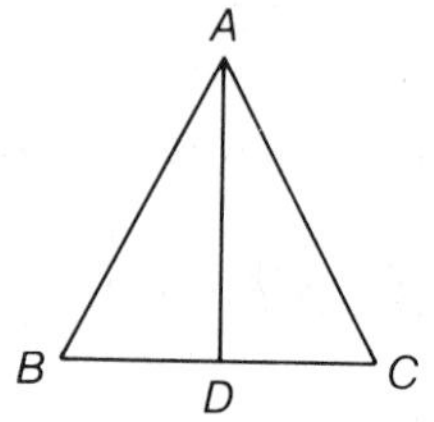

11. Develop the identity for cos $2A$. Begin with the identity for cos $(A + B)$.

12. Write the five fifth roots of 32 cis 30° in polar form.

13. Find two geometric means between 2 and -16.

14. Write the general form of the equation of a horizontal ellipse whose center is the origin and whose major axis is length 8 and whose minor axis is length 6.

15. Find the coordinates of the vertices and the equations of the asymptotes of the hyperbola whose equation is $16x^2 - 9y^2 = 144$.

16. Find the first three terms of the arithmetic sequence whose sixth term is 17 and whose eighth term is 25.

17. Find $\cos 285°$ by using the sum identity for cosine and the fact that $285° = 240° + 45°$.

18. Use the difference identities to find an expression for $\cos\left(x - \frac{\pi}{4}\right)$.

19. Solve $2\cos^2 x + 7\sin x + 2 = 0$, given that $0° \le x < 360°$.

20. Solve, given that $(0° \le \theta < 360°)$: $\sqrt{2}\cos 2\theta = -1$

21. Show that: $(x\sin\theta + y\cos\theta)^2 + (x\cos\theta - y\sin\theta)^2 = x^2 + y^2$

22. Show that: $\dfrac{\cos B}{1 + \sin B} = \dfrac{1 - \sin B}{\cos B}$

23. Solve this triangle for side a.

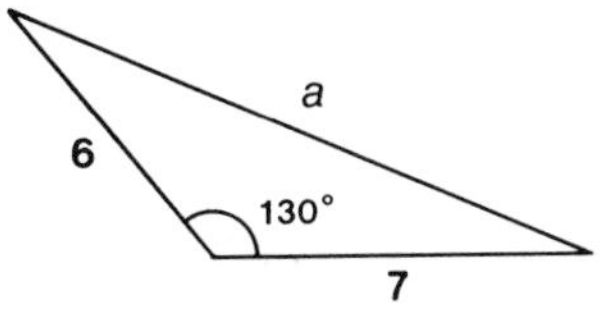

24. Find the length of side a.

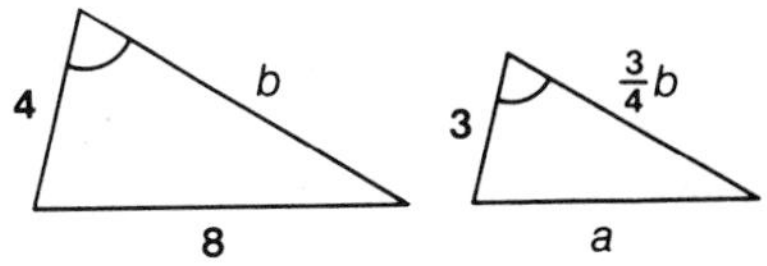

25. Sketch $y = 3 + 5\sin\frac{1}{2}(x - 90°)$.

26. What is the sum of the exterior angles of a 14-sided polygon?

Solve:

27. $6^{3x-2} = 2^{2x+4}$

28. $\frac{1}{4}\log_3 16 - \log_3(2x + 3) = 1$

29. Find the base 3 antilogarithm of -2.

30. Given $M = b^a$ and $N = b^c$, show that $\log_b \dfrac{M}{N} = \log_b M - \log_b N$.

ENRICHMENT LESSON 4 *Simple matrix equations · Matrix multiplication*

EL4.A Simple matrix equations

Real numbers have an identity for addition, and every real number has its own additive inverse, or opposite. We use these ideas when we solve equations using real numbers. For example, the equation

$$x + 5 = 7$$

can be solved by adding the opposite of 5 (additive inverse of 5) to both sides of the equation. The sum of a number and its opposite is 0, and this allows us to isolate the variable x.

$$x + 5 - 5 = 7 - 5 \qquad \text{added } -5$$

$$x + 0 = 2 \qquad \text{simplified}$$

Now 0 is the identity for addition, so x plus 0 is identically x. So

$$x = 2 \qquad \text{identity}$$

Since we have defined the additive inverse for matrices, we can make up matrix equations that can be solved in the same manner. Suppose we have the equation

$$A + \begin{bmatrix} 4 & -3 \\ 7 & 2 \end{bmatrix} = \begin{bmatrix} 5 & 4 \\ 6 & 3 \end{bmatrix}$$

We can solve for A by adding the opposite of the matrix on the left to both sides.

$$A + \begin{bmatrix} 4 & -3 \\ 7 & 2 \end{bmatrix} + \begin{bmatrix} -4 & 3 \\ -7 & -2 \end{bmatrix} = \begin{bmatrix} 5 & 4 \\ 6 & 3 \end{bmatrix} + \begin{bmatrix} -4 & 3 \\ -7 & -2 \end{bmatrix}$$

Now on the left, we have A plus the identity matrix, so we have

$$A + \begin{bmatrix} 0 & 0 \\ 0 & 0 \end{bmatrix} = \begin{bmatrix} 1 & 7 \\ -1 & 1 \end{bmatrix}$$

But matrix A plus the identity matrix is identically matrix A, so we have our solution.

$$A = \begin{bmatrix} 1 & 7 \\ -1 & 1 \end{bmatrix}$$

We have no immediate application for this type of problem, but there is no requirement that everything we study in mathematics have an immediate application. Some things have no applications, but without them we could not form the complete systems that we do find to be useful.

Example EL4.A.1 Solve: $A + \begin{bmatrix} 4 & -2 \\ -3 & 6 \end{bmatrix} = \begin{bmatrix} 5 & 7 \\ 2 & 4 \end{bmatrix}$

Solution We will add the opposite of the left matrix to both sides.

$$A + \begin{bmatrix} 4 & -2 \\ -3 & 6 \end{bmatrix} + \begin{bmatrix} -4 & 2 \\ 3 & -6 \end{bmatrix} = \begin{bmatrix} 5 & 7 \\ 2 & 4 \end{bmatrix} + \begin{bmatrix} -4 & 2 \\ 3 & -6 \end{bmatrix}$$

$$\mathbf{A = \begin{bmatrix} 1 & 9 \\ 5 & -2 \end{bmatrix}}$$

EL4.B Matrix multiplication

There are two kinds of multiplication that involve matrices. The first kind is the multiplication of a matrix by a real number and is called ***scalar multiplication.*** The product is a matrix, each entry of which is the product of the real number and the corresponding entry of the original matrix. Observe.

$$-4\begin{bmatrix} 3 & 2 \\ 7 & -3 \end{bmatrix} = \begin{bmatrix} (-4)(3) & (-4)(2) \\ (-4)(7) & (-4)(-3) \end{bmatrix} = \begin{bmatrix} -12 & -8 \\ -28 & 12 \end{bmatrix}$$

The other kind of multiplication that involves matrices is the multiplication of a matrix by a matrix. **This type of multiplication is called *matrix multiplication* and is defined so that matrices may be multiplied only if the number of columns of the first matrix is the same as the number of rows of the second matrix.** Thus, a $2 \times m$ matrix can be multiplied by an $m \times 3$ matrix because the first has m columns and the second has m rows.

$(2 \times 4 \text{ matrix}) \cdot (7 \times 4 \text{ matrix})$	cannot be multiplied
$(2 \times 4 \text{ matrix}) \cdot (4 \times 7 \text{ matrix})$	can be multiplied

The product of an $n \times m$ matrix and an $m \times p$ matrix is an $n \times p$ matrix. So the product of a 2×4 matrix and a 4×7 matrix is a 2×7 matrix, and the product of a 7×3 matrix and a 3 × 5 matrix is a 7 × 5 matrix. The use of a dot between matrices to indicate multiplication is optional. Let us consider the product of two 2 × 2 matrices, which is another 2 × 2 matrix. To form the upper left-hand entry, c_{11}, of the product of matrix A and matrix B

$$AB = \begin{bmatrix} 4 & 1 \\ 3 & 2 \end{bmatrix} \cdot \begin{bmatrix} 5 & 6 \\ 7 & 8 \end{bmatrix} = C = \begin{bmatrix} c_{11} & c_{12} \\ c_{21} & c_{22} \end{bmatrix}$$

we mentally pull the first row of the matrix on the left (4 and 1) to the right and down the first column of the matrix on the right to get

$$\begin{bmatrix} 4 & 1 \\ * & * \end{bmatrix} \cdot \begin{bmatrix} 4 \cdot 5 & * \\ 1 \cdot 7 & * \end{bmatrix}$$

Now we sum the products indicated.

$$c_{11} = 4 \cdot 5 + 1 \cdot 7 = 27 \longrightarrow C \begin{bmatrix} 27 & * \\ * & * \end{bmatrix}$$

Now to get the upper right-hand entry, c_{12}, we pull the first row of the matrix on the left down the second column of the matrix on the right and sum the indicated products.

$$\begin{bmatrix} 4 & 1 \\ 3 & 2 \end{bmatrix} \cdot \begin{bmatrix} 5 & 4 \cdot 6 \\ 7 & 1 \cdot 8 \end{bmatrix} \qquad 4 \cdot 6 + 1 \cdot 8 = 32 \qquad C \begin{bmatrix} 27 & 32 \\ * & * \end{bmatrix}$$

Now to get the lower left-hand entry, c_{21}, we pull the second row of the matrix on the left down the first column of the matrix on the right

$$\begin{bmatrix} 4 & 1 \\ 3 & 2 \end{bmatrix} \cdot \begin{bmatrix} 3 \cdot 5 & 6 \\ 2 \cdot 7 & 8 \end{bmatrix} \qquad 3 \cdot 5 + 2 \cdot 7 = 29 \longrightarrow C \begin{bmatrix} 27 & 32 \\ 29 & * \end{bmatrix}$$

and to get the last entry, c_{22}, we pull the second row of the matrix on the left down the second column of the matrix on the right.

$$\begin{bmatrix} 4 & 1 \\ 3 & 2 \end{bmatrix} \cdot \begin{bmatrix} 5 & 3 \cdot 6 \\ 7 & 2 \cdot 8 \end{bmatrix} \qquad 3 \cdot 6 + 2 \cdot 8 = 34 \longrightarrow C \begin{bmatrix} 27 & 32 \\ 29 & 34 \end{bmatrix}$$

Example EL4.B.1 Multiply: $\begin{bmatrix} 4 & -2 \\ 3 & -4 \end{bmatrix} \cdot \begin{bmatrix} 2 & 3 \\ 1 & -5 \end{bmatrix}$

Solution We identify the product matrix as

$$\begin{bmatrix} a_{11} & a_{12} \\ a_{21} & a_{22} \end{bmatrix}$$

and find the entries as

$$a_{11} = (4)(2) + (-2)(1) = 6 \qquad a_{12} = (4)(3) + (-2)(-5) = 22$$

$$a_{21} = (3)(2) + (-4)(1) = 2 \qquad a_{22} = (3)(3) + (-4)(-5) = 29$$

Thus, our product is

$$\begin{bmatrix} \mathbf{6} & \mathbf{22} \\ \mathbf{2} & \mathbf{29} \end{bmatrix}$$

Example EL4.B.2 Multiply: $\begin{bmatrix} 2 & 3 \\ 1 & -5 \end{bmatrix} \cdot \begin{bmatrix} 4 & -2 \\ 3 & -4 \end{bmatrix}$

Solution **These matrices are the same matrices we multiplied in the preceding example. The answer will be different this time because the order of multiplication has been changed and,**

as we see, matrix multiplication is not commutative. Again we identify the product matrix as

$$\begin{bmatrix} a_{11} & a_{12} \\ a_{21} & a_{22} \end{bmatrix}$$

and find the entries as

$$a_{11} = (2)(4) + (3)(3) = 17 \qquad a_{12} = (2)(-2) + (3)(-4) = -16$$

$$a_{21} = (1)(4) + (-5)(3) = -11 \qquad a_{22} = (1)(-2) + (-5)(-4) = 18$$

Thus, our product is

$$\begin{bmatrix} \mathbf{17} & \mathbf{-16} \\ \mathbf{-11} & \mathbf{18} \end{bmatrix}$$

Example EL4.B.3 Multiply $\begin{bmatrix} 4 & -2 \\ 3 & -4 \end{bmatrix} \cdot \begin{bmatrix} 1 & 0 \\ 0 & 1 \end{bmatrix}$. Also multiply $\begin{bmatrix} 1 & 0 \\ 0 & 1 \end{bmatrix}\begin{bmatrix} 4 & -2 \\ 3 & -4 \end{bmatrix}$.

Solution The identity for multiplication of real numbers is the number 1 because the product of any real number and 1 is identically the real number itself. The ***identity matrix*** for multiplication of 2 × 2 matrices is the matrix with 0s and 1s shown here because the product of any 2 × 2 matrix and this matrix is identically the 2 × 2 matrix itself. Note that the product is unchanged when the positions of the matrices are switched.

$$a_{11} = (4)(1) + (-2)(0) = 4 \qquad a_{12} = (4)(0) + (-2)(1) = -2$$

$$a_{21} = (3)(1) + (-4)(0) = 3 \qquad a_{22} = (3)(0) + (-4)(1) = -4$$

$$\begin{bmatrix} 4 & -2 \\ 3 & -4 \end{bmatrix}\begin{bmatrix} 1 & 0 \\ 0 & 1 \end{bmatrix} = \begin{bmatrix} 1 & 0 \\ 0 & 1 \end{bmatrix}\begin{bmatrix} 4 & -2 \\ 3 & -4 \end{bmatrix} = \begin{bmatrix} \mathbf{4} & \mathbf{-2} \\ \mathbf{3} & \mathbf{-4} \end{bmatrix}$$

Matrix multiplication is always commutative when one of the two matrices being multiplied is the identity matrix.

Problem set EL4

1. Three times the complement of angle 1 is 100° greater than the supplement of angle 2. Find the measures of angle 1 and angle 2 if the sum of the two angles is 130°.
2. Kristel is twice as old as Marta. Five years ago, Kristel was 3 times as old as Marta. How old are both now?
3. Sly Sam drew a card from a full deck and frowned. What was the probability that Sly Sam's card was an ace or a spade or was the ace of spades?
4. The hole kept on getting bigger. In fact, the depth of the hole grew exponentially. At 8 o'clock in the morning the hole was 5 meters deep. At noon the hole was 15 meters deep. How deep would the hole be at 5 p.m.?
5. Tee Willy could go 30 miles downstream in 4 hours less than it took him to go 30 miles upstream. The still-water speed of his boat was twice the speed of the current in the river. Find the still-water speed of his boat and the speed of the current.
6. Find the third term of $(x - y)^6$.
7. Expand $(2a^2 - b^4)^3$.
8. Use Cramer's rule to solve for x:

$$\begin{cases} 2x - y + z = 7 \\ 2y + 3z = 5 \\ x + 3y = -5 \end{cases}$$

9. Solve for matrix A:

$$A + \begin{bmatrix} 3 & -1 \\ -2 & 2 \end{bmatrix} = \begin{bmatrix} 5 & 0 \\ 6 & -2 \end{bmatrix}$$

10. Multiply: $3\begin{bmatrix} 2 & -1 \\ 6 & 3 \end{bmatrix}$

11. Multiply: $\begin{bmatrix} 2 & -1 \\ 3 & 4 \end{bmatrix}\begin{bmatrix} -3 & -2 \\ 2 & 1 \end{bmatrix}$

12. Develop the identity for $\sin x + \sin y$.

13. Develop the identity for $\sin x \cos y$.

14. Use a calculator or a table of logarithms to aid in determining $\log_5 30$.

15. Given: $AB = CD$; $AD = BC$
Prove: $\triangle AOB \cong \triangle COD$

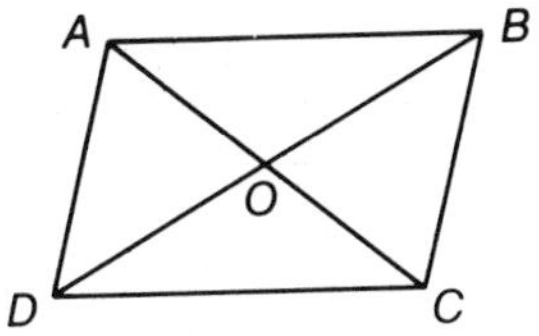

16. Given: D is the midpoint of $\overline{AB}$. E is the midpoint of $\overline{AC}$.
Prove: $DE = \frac{1}{2}BC$

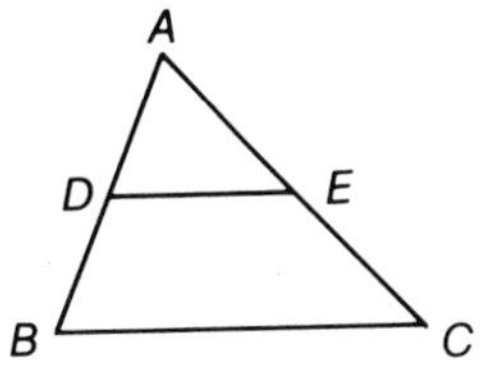

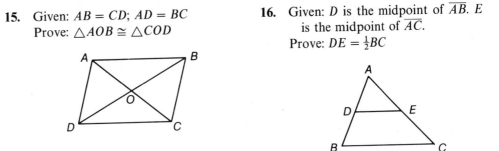

17. A triangle has a 70° angle. A side adjacent to this angle has length 8 and the side opposite this angle has length 5. Draw the triangle(s) described and find the length(s) of the missing side.

18. Find the three cube roots of $-3 + 4i$ and express the roots in polar form.

19. The geometric mean of two numbers is 20. The arithmetic mean of the two numbers is 52. Find the two numbers.

Solve the following equations given that $(0° \le x, \theta < 360°)$:

20. $\tan 2\theta = 0$

21. $2\cos^2 x - 9\sin x + 3 = 0$

Show that:

22. $\dfrac{2\sec 2x}{\sec 2x - 1} = \csc^2 x$

23. $\cot^2 x = \dfrac{1 + \cos 2x}{1 - \cos 2x}$

24. Write the equations of the following graphs in terms of the sine function.

(*a*)

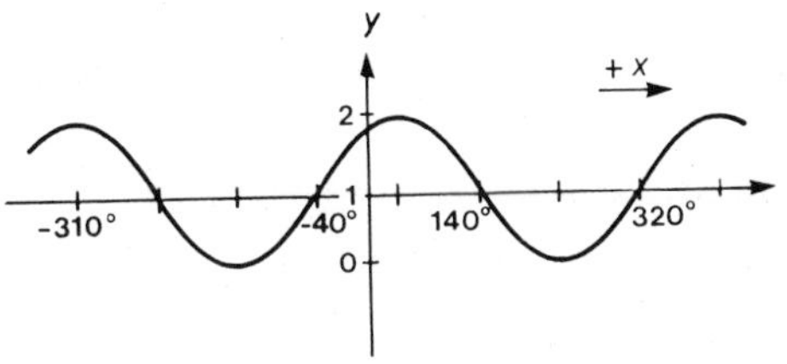

(*b*)

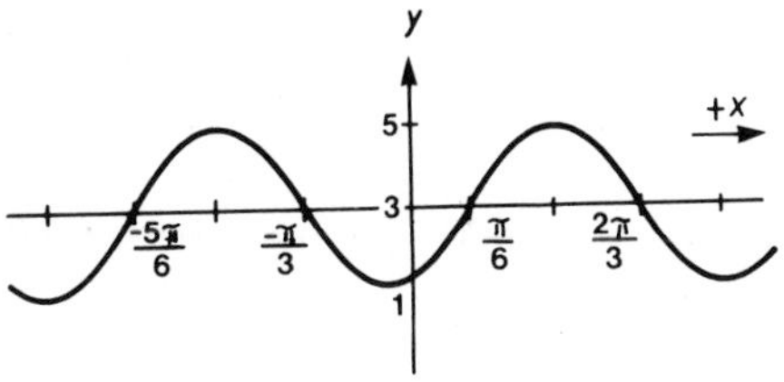

25. Is the following argument valid?

1. If the light is on, then the switch is on.
2. The switch is on.
3. Therefore, the light is on.

26. Sketch $y = 3 - 5\sin\left(x + \dfrac{\pi}{4}\right)$.

27. Solve: $\log_2 \sqrt{x} = 2$

Solve:

28. $\log_2 (2x - 1) - \log_2 (x - 1) = 2$

29. $\ln x + \ln (x + 1) = \ln 6$

30. Find the base 2 antilogarithm of -2.

ENRICHMENT LESSON 5 Mathematical induction

EL5.A Mathematical induction

Suppose we could prove that if something were true for some counting number, then it would be true for the next greater counting number. Then, if we showed that it were true for 1, it would be true for 2. If it were true for 2, then it would be true for 3. If it were true for 3, then it would be true for 4. If it were true for 4, then it would be true for 5, etc. Thus we see that it would be true for every counting number.

A proof that uses this type of reasoning is called a proof by ***mathematical induction.*** Suppose we have a formula that we think is valid for the sum of a series of n terms. We can show that it is valid for the sum of any particular number of terms, but we are not sure that it is valid for the sum of every number of terms. Let's look at a formula that we think is valid for the sum of the first n counting numbers.

$$1 + 2 + 3 + 4 + 5 + \cdots + n = \frac{n(n + 1)}{2}$$

Let's see if it works for four terms.

ADDING	USING THE FORMULA
$1 + 2 + 3 + 4 = 10$	$\frac{4(4 + 1)}{2} = \frac{20}{2} = 10$

Well, it worked for 4. Let's see if it works for nine terms.

ADDING	USING THE FORMULA
$1 + 2 + 3 + 4 + 5 + 6 + 7 + 8 + 9 = 45$	$\frac{9(9 + 1)}{2} = \frac{90}{2} = 45$

It also works for 9, but will it work for 1,062,517 terms and will it work for 7,085,062,103 terms? We think the formula will work for any number of terms, but how can we be sure? To prove that this formula is valid for any number of terms, we will use mathematical induction and begin by observing: **If the formula worked for some number k, the sum would be**

$$1 + 2 + 3 + 4 + 5 + \cdots + k = \frac{k(k + 1)}{2}$$

Now let's add one more term to both sides to see what we would get if the series had one more term.

$$1 + 2 + 3 + 4 + 5 + \cdots + k + \mathbf{(k + 1)} = \frac{k(k + 1)}{2} + \mathbf{(k + 1)}$$

If we simplify the right side we get

$$\frac{k^2 + k}{2} + \frac{2(k + 1)}{2} = \frac{k^2 + 3k + 2}{2}$$

Now if we use $k + 1$ for k in the formula $\frac{k(k + 1)}{2}$, we should get the same result.

$$\frac{(k + 1)[(k + 1) + 1]}{2} = \frac{(k + 1)(k + 2)}{2} = \frac{k^2 + 3k + 2}{2}$$

This proves that the formula will give the correct answer for $(k + 1)$ if the first answer for k was correct. We can show that the first answer was correct for some k by showing that it is correct for $k = 1$.

$$1 + 2 + 3 + 4 + 5 + \cdots + n = \frac{n(n+1)}{2} \qquad \text{original formula}$$

$$1 = \frac{1(1+1)}{2} \qquad n = 1$$

$$1 = 1 \qquad \text{true}$$

Thus, the formula will work for a series of two terms, three terms, four terms, five terms, or any number of terms.

Example EL5.A.1 Use mathematical induction to prove the formula for the sum of an n-term arithmetic series.

$$a_1 + (a_1 + d) + (a_1 + 2d) + \cdots + [a_1 + (n-1)d] = \frac{n[2a_1 + (n-1)d]}{2}$$

Solution The first step is to replace n with k for the kth term, and we get

$$a_1 + (a_1 + d) + (a_1 + 2d) + \cdots + [a_1 + (k-1)d] = \frac{k[2a_1 + (k-1)d]}{2}$$

If this formula is true for the number k, we want to see what we get if we add one more term to both sides.

$$a_1 + \cdots + [a_1 + (k-1)d] + \boldsymbol{a_1 + kd} = \frac{k[2a_1 + (k-1)d]}{2} + \boldsymbol{a_1 + kd}$$

On the right-hand side, we multiply the second term by 2 over 2 and simplify and get

$$\frac{k[2a_1 + (k-1)d] + 2(a_1 + kd)}{2}$$

And we multiply out and get

$$\frac{2ka_1 + k^2d - kd + 2a_1 + 2kd}{2} = \frac{2ka_1 + k^2d + kd + 2a_1}{2}$$

Now we use $k + 1$ for k in the formula and see if we get the same result.

$$\frac{(k+1)\{2a_1 + [(k+1) - 1]d\}}{2} = \frac{(k+1)(2a_1 + kd)}{2} = \frac{2ka_1 + k^2d + 2a_1 + kd}{2}$$

This is the same result! Now we check to see if the formula is valid when k equals 1.

$$a_1 + (a_1 + d) + \cdots + [a_1 + (k-1)d] = \frac{k[2a_1 + (k-1)d]}{2} \qquad \text{formula}$$

$$a_1 = \frac{1[2a_1 + (1-1)d]}{2} \qquad k = 1$$

$$a_1 = a_1 \qquad \text{check}$$

Thus, the formula is correct for two terms, three terms, four terms, or n terms, where n is any counting number.

Example EL5.A.2 Use mathematical induction to prove the formula for the sum of the first n terms of this geometric series:

$$4 + 4r + 4r^2 + 4r^3 + \cdots + 4r^{n-1} = \frac{4(1 - r^n)}{1 - r}$$

Solution First we write the expression for a series of k terms.

$$4 + 4r + 4r^2 + 4r^3 + \cdots + 4r^{k-1} = \frac{4(1 - r^k)}{1 - r}$$

Now if this result is true, we see what the result would be if we add one more term to both sides.

$$4 + \cdots + 4r^{k-1} + \mathbf{4r^k} = \frac{4(1 - r^k)}{1 - r} + \mathbf{4r^k}$$

and we get a common denominator on the right-hand side and simplify.

$$\frac{4(1 - r^k)}{1 - r} + \frac{4r^k(1 - r)}{1 - r} = \frac{4 - 4r^k + 4r^k - 4r^{k+1}}{1 - r} = \frac{4 - 4r^{k+1}}{1 - r}$$

Now let's see the result the formula will give if we replace k with $k + 1$.

$$\frac{4(1 - r^k)}{1 - r} \qquad \text{formula}$$

$$\frac{4(1 - r^{k+1})}{1 - r} = \frac{4 - 4r^{k+1}}{1 - r} \qquad \text{the same result}$$

Now we see if the formula holds for $k = 1$.

$$4 + 4r + 4r^2 + \cdots + 4r^{k+1} = \frac{4(1 - r^k)}{1 - r} \qquad \text{formula}$$

$$4 = \frac{4(1 - r)}{1 - r} \qquad k = 1$$

$$4 = 4 \qquad \text{check}$$

Thus, the formula is correct for two terms, three terms, four terms, or n terms, where n is any counting number.

Problem set EL5

1. The number who were satisfied varied linearly with the number who were paid up. When 80 were paid up, 60 were satisfied. When 50 were paid up, 45 were satisfied. How many were satisfied when only 10 were paid up?
2. The failure rate varied inversely as the square of the indigestion index. The people who had an indigestion of index of 2 had a failure rate of 9. What is the failure rate of people who have an indigestion index of 3?
3. The ratio of the concerned to the indifferent was 3 to 7. If 700 were being considered, how many were indifferent?
4. Peter Cottontail peered into the vat and noted that it was one-fifth full. Peter poured 100 pounds into the vat, and the gauge now showed that the vat was three-fifths full. How many pounds can the vat hold?
5. The steamship could steam 60 miles downstream in 4 hours less than it could steam 60 miles upstream. What was the speed of the water and the speed of the boat if the speed of the boat in still water is twice the speed of the current?
6. Show by mathematical induction that $1 + 2 + 3 + \cdots + n = \frac{1}{2}n(n + 1)$.
7. Use mathematical induction to show that:

$$a + (a + d) + (a + 2d) + \cdots + [a + (n - 1)d] = \tfrac{1}{2}n[2a + (n - 1)d]$$

8. Use mathematical induction to show that:

$$1 + r + r^2 + \cdots + r^n = \frac{1 - r^{n+1}}{1 - r}$$

9. Two geometric solids are similar. The length of a side of the larger geometric solid is 3 times as long as the corresponding side of the smaller geometric solid. What is the ratio of the volume of the larger geometric solid to the volume of the smaller geometric solid?

10. The base of a pyramid is a regular hexagon whose perimeter is 30 centimeters. The height of the pyramid is 6 centimeters. Find the volume of the pyramid.

11. (*a*) The base of a circular cone has a radius of 6 centimeters. The height of the cone is 6 centimeters. Find the volume of the cone.
(*b*) Assume that the cone is a right circular cone. Find the surface area of the cone.

12. Find the length of the diagonal AC in the rectangular solid shown.

13. A sphere has a radius of 6 centimeters.
(*a*) Find the volume of the sphere.
(*b*) Find the surface area of the sphere.

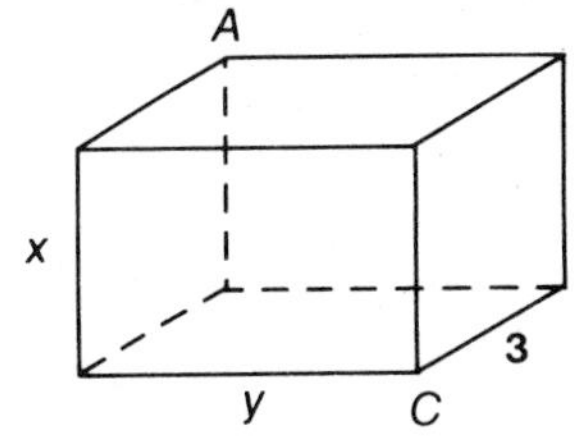

14. Find the sum of the infinite geometric series:

$$2 + \left(-\frac{4}{3}\right) + \left(\frac{8}{9}\right) + \left(-\frac{16}{27}\right) + \cdots$$

15. Given: $\overline{PR}$ is the angle bisector of $\angle P$ and $\angle QRS$.
Prove: $QR = RS$

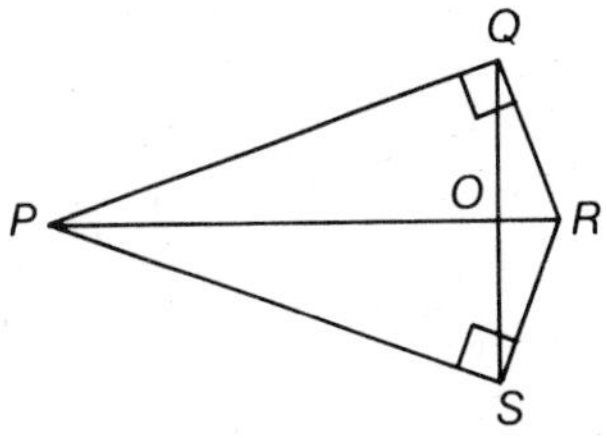

16. $4x^2 - y^2 + 24x + 4y + 28 = 0$ is the equation of a hyperbola. Write the equation of this hyperbola in standard form and give the coordinates of its center, the coordinates of the vertices, and the equations of its asymptotes.

17. $9x^2 + 4y^2 + 54x - 8y + 49 = 0$ is the equation of an ellipse. Write the equation of this ellipse in standard form. Give the coordinates of its center, the length of its major axis, and the length of its minor axis. Indicate whether the major axis is horizontal or vertical.

18. Use the echelon method to solve this system of equations: $\begin{cases} 3x + 2y + z = 5 \\ 3y - 2z = 5 \\ 2x + 3y = 7 \end{cases}$

19. Use the identity for $\sin x + \sin y$ to find $\sin 285° + \sin 15°$.

20. The first term of an arithmetic sequence is a and the common difference is d.
(*a*) What is the nth term of this arithmetic sequence?
(*b*) What is the sum of the first n terms if we use the expression found in (*a*) for the last term of the sequence?

21. Write the three cube roots of $3 + 4i$ in polar form.

22. Solve this triangle for a.

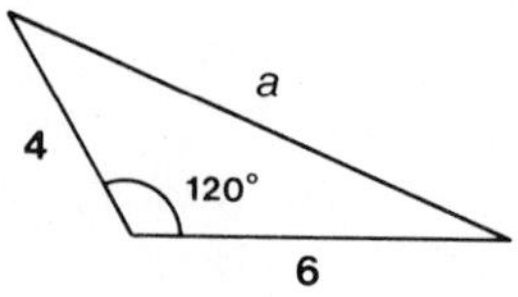

23. Express ln 10 in terms of common logarithms. Do not find a numerical answer.

24. Construct a line parallel to a given line and passing through a given point not on the given line.

25. Sketch $y = -3 + 10 \sin 3(x - 20°)$.

26. Show that: $(\sin 2x)(\sec^2 x) = 2 \tan x$

27. Solve, given that $(0° \leq x < 360°)$: $6 \sin^2 x = -5 \sin x - 1$

28. Solve: $2^{3x-1} = 8^{2x}$

29. Solve: $\frac{3}{2} \log_3 4 - \log_3 (2x + 1) = -\log_3 (x + 1)$

30. Is the following argument valid?

1. If Mark showers, he will smell fresh.
2. Mark smells fresh.
3. Therefore, Mark showers.

Appendixes

APPENDIX 1 Enrichment problems

The following problems are provided to permit a continuing review of the enrichment topics. The first part of the number for each problem designates the problem set to which this problem should be appended.

56.1. Is the following argument valid?

If the switch is on, then the light is not on.
The light is on.
———
Therefore, the switch is on.

56.2. Show that replacing k with $k + 1$ in $\frac{k(k+1)}{2}$ gives an expression equivalent to $\frac{k(k+1)}{2} + (k + 1)$.

57.3. Is the following argument valid?

If the light is on, then the switch is on.
The switch is not on.
———
Therefore, the light is not on.

58.4. Show that replacing k with $k + 1$ in $\frac{k}{k+1}$ gives an expression equivalent to $\frac{k}{k+1} + \frac{1}{(k+1)(k+2)}$.

59.5. Is the following argument valid?

If the switch is not on, the light is not on.
The switch is on.
———
Therefore, the light is on.

60.6. Show that replacing k with $k + 1$ in k^2 gives an expression equivalent to $k^2 + 2k + 1$.

61.7. Is the following argument valid?

If it does not rain, then the game will be played.
The game will not be played.
———
It did not rain.

62.8. Show that replacing k with $k + 1$ in $k(k + 1)$ gives an expression equivalent to $k(k + 1) + 2(k + 1)$.

63.9. Is the following argument valid?

> If it does not rain, the game will take place this Saturday.
> The game took place Saturday.
> ---
> Therefore, it did not rain.

64.10. Show that replacing n with $n + 1$ in n^2 gives an expression equivalent to $n^2 + 2n + 1$.

65.11. Is the following argument valid?

> The computer is protected if the fuse is installed.
> The computer is not protected.
> ---
> The fuse is not installed.

66.12. Show that replacing k with $k + 1$ in $\dfrac{k(k+1)(2k+1)}{6}$ gives an expression equivalent to $\dfrac{k(k+1)(2k+1)}{6} + (k+1)^2$.

67.13. Which of the following asserts the same fact as the following: "If A is irrational, then $1 + A$ is irrational"?
(*a*) If $1 + A$ is irrational, then A is irrational.
(*b*) If $1 + A$ is rational, then A is rational.
(*c*) If A is rational, then $1 + A$ is rational.

68.14. Show that replacing k with $k + 1$ in $\dfrac{5k(k+1)}{2}$ gives an expression that is equivalent to $\dfrac{5k(k+1)}{2} + 5(k+1)$.

69.15. Is the following argument valid?

> If the computer is not protected, then fuse B is not installed.
> Fuse B is installed.
> ---
> Therefore, the computer is protected.

70.16. Show that replacing k with $k + 1$ in $\dfrac{a(1-r^k)}{1-r}$ gives an expression equivalent to $\dfrac{a(1-r^k)}{1-r} + ar^k$.

71.17. Is the following argument valid?

> If Frank studies hard, then he will pass.
> Frank does not study hard.
> ---
> Frank will not pass.

72.18. Show that replacing k with $k + 1$ in $1 - \dfrac{1}{2^k}$ gives an expression equivalent to $1 - \dfrac{1}{2^k} + \dfrac{1}{2^{k+1}}$.

73.19. Is the following argument valid?

The computer is protected if fuse A is installed.
Fuse A is not installed.

Therefore, the computer is unprotected.

74.20. Show that replacing k with $k + 1$ in $\dfrac{k(k+1)(k+2)}{3}$ gives an expression equivalent to $\dfrac{k(k+1)(k+2)}{3} + (k+1)(k+2)$.

74.21. Is the following argument valid?

If Frank studies hard, then he will pass algebra.
Frank does not pass algebra.

Therefore, Frank did not study hard.

75.22. Show that by replacing n with $n + 1$ in the expression $\frac{1}{2}n[2a + (n-1)d]$, we get an expression equivalent to $\frac{1}{2}n[2a + (n-1)d] + a + nd$.

75.23. Is the following argument valid?

All boys are made of frogs, snails, and puppydog tails.
Gale is made of frogs, snails, and puppydog tails.

Thus, Gale is a boy.

76.24. Simplify: $\left(\begin{bmatrix} 2 & 3 \\ 4 & 5 \end{bmatrix} + \begin{bmatrix} 1 & 0 \\ 3 & -2 \end{bmatrix}\right) + \begin{bmatrix} 1 & 1 \\ -1 & 1 \end{bmatrix}$

76.25. Is the following argument valid?

All women with beautiful smiles use Smile toothpaste.
Phyllis uses Smile toothpaste.

Phyllis has a beautiful smile.

77.26. Simplify: $\begin{bmatrix} 1 & -1 \\ 2 & -2 \\ 3 & -3 \end{bmatrix} + \dfrac{1}{6}\begin{bmatrix} -1 & 1 \\ -2 & 2 \\ 3 & 3 \end{bmatrix}$

77.27. Show that replacing k with $k + 1$ in $k(2k - 1) + 1$ gives an expression equivalent to $[k(2k-1) + 1] + (4k + 1)$.

78.28. Simplify: $\begin{bmatrix} 1 \\ -2 \\ 3 \end{bmatrix} + \begin{bmatrix} 3 \\ 2 \\ 1 \end{bmatrix}$

78.29. Is the following argument valid?

All people who are not named Gail are female.
That person is named Gail.

That person is female.

79.30. Simplify: $\begin{bmatrix} -1 & -3 & 4 \\ 2 & 0 & 3 \end{bmatrix} + \begin{bmatrix} 1 & 0 & -1 \\ 0 & 1 & -1 \end{bmatrix}$

79.31. Show that replacing k with $k + 1$ in $2k(k + 1)$ gives an expression equivalent to $2k(k+1) + 4(k+1)$.

80.32. Simplify: $\begin{bmatrix} 1 & -2 & 3 \\ -4 & 6 & -5 \\ 0 & 1 & 0 \end{bmatrix} + \begin{bmatrix} 0 & 0 & 0 \\ 0 & 0 & 0 \\ 0 & 0 & 0 \end{bmatrix}$

80.33. Is the following argument valid?

If fuse A is installed, then the computer is protected.
The computer is protected.
―――――――――――――――
Fuse A is not installed.

81.34. Simplify: $\begin{bmatrix} 2 & 3 \\ 4 & -5 \end{bmatrix} - \begin{bmatrix} 3 & -4 \\ 1 & 0 \end{bmatrix}$

81.35. Show that replacing k with $k + 1$ in $\frac{3(3^k - 1)}{2}$ yields an expression equivalent to $\frac{3(3^k - 1)}{2} + 3^{k+1}$.

82.36. Simplify: $\begin{bmatrix} 2 & 3 \\ 4 & 5 \end{bmatrix} + \left(\begin{bmatrix} 1 & 0 \\ 3 & -2 \end{bmatrix} + \begin{bmatrix} 1 & 1 \\ -1 & 1 \end{bmatrix}\right)$

83.37. Is the following argument valid?

All women with nice smiles use Smile toothpaste.
Valkerina does not have a nice smile.
―――――――――――――――
Valkerina uses Smile toothpaste.

83.38. Simplify: $\begin{bmatrix} 1 & -2 \\ -1 & 2 \end{bmatrix} + 2\begin{bmatrix} 3 & 2 \\ 1 & 0 \end{bmatrix}$

84.39. Is the following argument valid?

All authors are characters.
John is an author.
―――――――――――――――
John is a character.

84.40. Simplify: $\begin{bmatrix} 3 & 2 \\ 1 & 0 \end{bmatrix} + \begin{bmatrix} 1 & -2 \\ -1 & 2 \end{bmatrix}$

85.41. Simplify: $\begin{bmatrix} 6 & 2 \\ 3 & 1 \end{bmatrix} + \begin{bmatrix} -1 & 2 \\ 3 & 4 \end{bmatrix}$

85.42. Show that replacing k with $k + 1$ in $2(2^k - 1)$ yields an expression equivalent to $2(2^k - 1) + 2^{k+1}$.

86.43. Simplify: $\begin{bmatrix} 2 & 0 \\ -1 & 1 \end{bmatrix} + \begin{bmatrix} -1 & 0 \\ 1 & -2 \end{bmatrix}$

86.44. Simplify: $\begin{bmatrix} 2 & 3 \\ 1 & 7 \end{bmatrix} + \begin{bmatrix} 9 & -4 \\ 2 & 0 \end{bmatrix}$

87.45. Simplify: $-2\begin{bmatrix} -4 & 1 \\ 3 & 6 \end{bmatrix} \cdot \begin{bmatrix} 1 & 0 \\ 1 & 1 \end{bmatrix}$

87.46. Show that replacing k with $k + 1$ in $2k^2 + 3k$ yields an expression that is equivalent to $(2k^2 + 3k) + (4k + 5)$.

88.47. Solve: $X - \begin{bmatrix} 2 & 1 \\ -3 & 0 \end{bmatrix} = \begin{bmatrix} -1 & 2 \\ 1 & 0 \end{bmatrix}$

88.48. Is the following argument valid?

Those not wearing colorful clothes are not artists.
Barbary is an artist.

Barbary is wearing colorful clothes.

89.49. Simplify: $\begin{bmatrix} 0 & 1 \\ -5 & 6 \end{bmatrix} \cdot \begin{bmatrix} 3 & -4 \\ 4 & 7 \end{bmatrix}$

89.50. Show that replacing k with $k + 1$ in $\frac{k(3k-1)}{2}$ yields an expression equivalent to $\frac{k(3k-1)}{2} + (3k + 1)$.

90.51. Solve: $\begin{bmatrix} -1 & 2 \\ 4 & -5 \end{bmatrix} - \frac{1}{2}X = \begin{bmatrix} 3 & 4 \\ 2 & -6 \end{bmatrix}$

90.52. Show that replacing k with $k + 1$ in $\frac{k(2k-1)(2k+1)}{3}$ yields an expression equivalent to $\frac{k(2k-1)(2k+1)}{3} + (2k + 1)^2$.

91.53. Show that replacing k with $k + 1$ in $\frac{k}{2k+1}$ yields an expression equivalent to $\frac{k}{2k+1} + \frac{1}{(2k+1)(2k+3)}$.

91.54. Simplify: $\begin{bmatrix} 1 & -2 \\ -1 & 1 \end{bmatrix} \cdot \left(\begin{bmatrix} 2 & 3 \\ -4 & 1 \end{bmatrix} + \begin{bmatrix} -1 & -5 \\ 3 & 1 \end{bmatrix} \right)$

92.55. Simplify: $\begin{bmatrix} 1 & 2 \\ 3 & 4 \end{bmatrix} \cdot \begin{bmatrix} 1 & 0 \\ 0 & 1 \end{bmatrix}$

92.56. Is the following argument valid?

If Mark tries, then he will succeed.
Mark does not succeed.

Mark did not try.

93.57. Simplify: $\begin{bmatrix} -9 & 6 \\ 20 & -5 \end{bmatrix} \cdot \begin{bmatrix} -2 & 1 \\ 2 & -1 \end{bmatrix}$

93.58. Show that replacing k with $k + 1$ in $\frac{k^2(k+1)^2}{4}$ yields an expression that is equivalent to $\frac{k^2(k+1)^2}{4} + (k + 1)^3$.

94.59. Show that replacing k with $k + 1$ in $k^2(2k^2 - 1)$ yields an expression that is equivalent to $k^2(2k^2 - 1) + (2k + 1)^3$.

94.60. Solve: $X + \begin{bmatrix} 1 & 0 \\ 2 & 1 \end{bmatrix} = \begin{bmatrix} -2 & 3 \\ -1 & -2 \end{bmatrix}$

95.61. Simplify: $\begin{bmatrix} 1 & 1 \\ -1 & 1 \end{bmatrix} \cdot \left(\begin{bmatrix} 2 & 3 \\ 4 & -5 \end{bmatrix} + \begin{bmatrix} 1 & 0 \\ 0 & 1 \end{bmatrix} \right)$

95.62. Show that replacing k with $k + 1$ in $\frac{k(k+1)(k+2)}{6}$ yields an expression that is equivalent to $\frac{k(k+1)(k+2)}{6} + \frac{(k+1)(k+2)}{2}$.

96.63. Simplify: $\begin{bmatrix} 1 & 0 \\ 0 & 1 \end{bmatrix} \cdot \begin{bmatrix} 3 & -4 \\ 4 & 7 \end{bmatrix}$

96.64. Prove by induction: $1 + 2 + 3 + \cdots + n = \dfrac{n(n+1)}{2}$

97.65. Prove by induction:

$$\frac{1}{1 \cdot 2} + \frac{1}{2 \cdot 3} + \frac{1}{3 \cdot 4} + \cdots + \frac{1}{n(n+1)} = \frac{n}{n+1}$$

97.66. Is the following argument valid?

Stuntmen are not deaf.
Chesnutt is not deaf.
———
Chesnutt is a stuntman.

98.67. Prove by induction: $1 + 3 + 5 + \cdots + (2n - 1) = n^2$

98.68. Solve: $2X + \begin{bmatrix} 1 & 0 \\ 0 & 2 \end{bmatrix} = \begin{bmatrix} 9 & 4 \\ 8 & 4 \end{bmatrix}$

99.69. Prove by induction: $2 + 4 + 6 + \cdots + 2n = n(n+1)$

99.70. Simplify: $\dfrac{1}{2}\begin{bmatrix} 4 & 6 \\ 2 & -2 \end{bmatrix} \cdot \begin{bmatrix} -2 & 0 \\ 2 & 4 \end{bmatrix}$

100.71. Prove by induction: $1^2 + 2^2 + 3^2 + \cdots + n^2 = \dfrac{n(n+1)(2n+1)}{6}$

100.72. Simplify: $\begin{bmatrix} -1 & 2 \\ 3 & 0 \end{bmatrix} \cdot \left(\begin{bmatrix} 2 & 3 \\ 4 & -5 \end{bmatrix} - \begin{bmatrix} 3 & -4 \\ 1 & 0 \end{bmatrix} \right)$

101.73. Prove by induction: $5 + 10 + 15 + \cdots + 5n = \dfrac{5n(n+1)}{2}$

101.74. Is the following argument valid?

Algebra students do not study hard.
Cheng Lee studies hard.
———
Cheng Lee is not an algebra student.

102.75. Prove by induction:

$$1 \cdot 2 + 2 \cdot 3 + 3 \cdot 4 + \cdots + n(n+1) = \frac{n(n+1)(n+2)}{3}$$

102.76. Simplify: $\begin{bmatrix} 3 & 1 \\ 0 & 2 \end{bmatrix} \cdot \begin{bmatrix} 1 & 0 \\ 1 & 1 \end{bmatrix}$

103.77. Is the following argument valid?

All well-educated people study algebra.
Homer Lee is not well-educated.
———
Homer Lee does not study algebra.

103.78. Simplify: $\begin{bmatrix} \frac{1}{2} & -\frac{1}{3} \\ 2 & \frac{1}{2} \end{bmatrix} \cdot \begin{bmatrix} 6 & 0 \\ 0 & 6 \end{bmatrix}$

104.79. Prove by induction:

$$a + ar + ar^2 + ar^3 + \cdots + ar^{n-1} = \frac{a(1 - r^n)}{1 - r}$$

104.80. Simplify: $\begin{bmatrix} -2 & 3 \\ 4 & -1 \end{bmatrix} \cdot \begin{bmatrix} 1 & x \\ 2 & 4 \end{bmatrix}$

105.81. Simplify: $\begin{bmatrix} 1 & -1 \\ 1 & -2 \end{bmatrix} \cdot \begin{bmatrix} 5 & -5 \\ -5 & 5 \end{bmatrix}$

105.82. Prove by induction:

$$1^2 + 3^2 + 5^2 + \cdots + (2n - 1)^2 = \frac{n(2n - 1)(2n + 1)}{3}$$

106.83. Is the following argument valid?

Those who do not have more fun are not blondes.
Cindy is a brunette.
―――――――――――――――
Cindy does not have more fun.

106.84. Simplify: $\left(\begin{bmatrix} 2 & 3 \\ 4 & -5 \end{bmatrix} - \begin{bmatrix} 3 & -4 \\ 1 & 0 \end{bmatrix}\right) \cdot \begin{bmatrix} -1 & 2 \\ 3 & 0 \end{bmatrix}$

107.85. Prove by induction: $\frac{1}{2^1} + \frac{1}{2^2} + \frac{1}{2^3} + \cdots + \frac{1}{2^n} = 1 - \frac{1}{2^n}$

107.86. Simplify: $\begin{bmatrix} 2 & 1 \\ 0 & 0 \end{bmatrix} \cdot \left(\begin{bmatrix} -1 & 2 \\ -3 & 4 \end{bmatrix} + \begin{bmatrix} 1 & -2 \\ 3 & -4 \end{bmatrix}\right)$

108.87. Is the following argument valid?

Animals with no fleas are not dogs.
Beauregard is a dog.
―――――――――――――――
Beauregard has fleas.

108.88. Solve: $X + \begin{bmatrix} 3 & 5 \\ 2 & 1 \end{bmatrix} \cdot \begin{bmatrix} 0 & 1 \\ -1 & 1 \end{bmatrix} = \begin{bmatrix} 6 & 5 \\ 3 & 2 \end{bmatrix}$

109.89. Prove by induction: $1 + 5 + 9 + \cdots + (4n - 7) + (4n - 3) = n(2n - 1)$

109.90. Simplify: $\left(\begin{bmatrix} 2 & 3 \\ -4 & 1 \end{bmatrix} + \begin{bmatrix} -1 & -5 \\ 3 & 1 \end{bmatrix}\right) \cdot \begin{bmatrix} 1 & -2 \\ -1 & 1 \end{bmatrix}$

110.91. Is the following argument valid?

All well-educated people study algebra.
Lao Tzu studies algebra.
―――――――――――――――
Lao Tzu is well-educated.

110.92. Simplify: $\begin{bmatrix} 3 & 0 \\ 0 & 1 \end{bmatrix} \cdot \begin{bmatrix} 1 & -2 \\ -1 & 2 \end{bmatrix}$

111.93. Prove by induction: $1^3 + 3^3 + 5^3 + \cdots + (2n - 1)^3 = n^2(2n^2 - 1)$

111.94. Simplify: $\left(\begin{bmatrix} 2 & 3 \\ 4 & -5 \end{bmatrix} + \begin{bmatrix} 1 & 0 \\ 0 & 1 \end{bmatrix}\right) \cdot \begin{bmatrix} 1 & -1 \\ 2 & -2 \end{bmatrix}$

112.95. Prove by induction: $4 + 8 + 12 + 16 + \cdots + 4n = 2n(n + 1)$

112.96. Solve: $\begin{bmatrix} 3 & 2 \\ -1 & 1 \end{bmatrix} \cdot \begin{bmatrix} 2 & 1 \\ 0 & -1 \end{bmatrix} + 3X = \begin{bmatrix} 1 & 12 \\ 1 & 6 \end{bmatrix}$

113.97. Solve: $X - \begin{bmatrix} 1 & 3 \\ 2 & 4 \end{bmatrix} = \begin{bmatrix} -1 & -3 \\ 2 & -7 \end{bmatrix}$

113.98. Prove by induction: $3^1 + 3^2 + 3^3 + \cdots + 3^n = \frac{3(3^n - 1)}{2}$

114.99. Prove by induction: $2^1 + 2^2 + 2^3 + \cdots + 2^n = 2(2^n - 1)$

114.100. Simplify: $\begin{bmatrix} x & 2 \\ 2 & 1 \end{bmatrix} \cdot \begin{bmatrix} 2 & -1 \\ 3 & 4 \end{bmatrix}$

115.101. Is the following argument valid?

All spring storms are accompanied by tornadoes.
Last night's storm was accompanied by tornadoes.
———
Therefore, it must be spring.

115.102. Solve: $\begin{bmatrix} 1 & -1 \\ 1 & 0 \end{bmatrix} - X = \begin{bmatrix} 2 & -1 \\ -2 & 1 \end{bmatrix}$

116.103. Prove by induction: $5 + 9 + 13 + \cdots + (4n + 1) = 2n^2 + 3n$

116.104. Is the following argument valid?

Nonstudiers of algebra are not well-educated.
Jim is well-educated.
———
Jim studies algebra.

117.105. Prove by induction: $\frac{1 \cdot 2}{2} + \frac{2 \cdot 3}{2} + \frac{3 \cdot 4}{2} + \cdots + \frac{n(n + 1)}{2} = \frac{n(n + 1)(n + 2)}{6}$

117.106. Is the following argument valid?

All bears are fuzzy.
Fuzzy Wuzzy was a bear.
———
Fuzzy Wuzzy was fuzzy.

118.107. Prove by induction: $1 + 4 + 7 + \cdots + (3n - 2) = \frac{n(3n - 1)}{2}$

118.108. Is the following argument valid?

If A is irrational, $1 + A$ is irrational.
$1 + A$ is irrational.
———
Therefore, A is irrational.

APPENDIX 2 *Tables*

TABLE 1 Values of trigonometric functions

deg	sin	cos	tan	deg	sin	cos	tan	deg	sin	cos	tan
0	.0000	1.000	.0000	6.0	.1045	.9945	.1051	12.0	.2079	.9781	.2126
0.1	.0017	1.000	.0017	6.1	.1063	.9943	.1069	12.1	.2096	.9778	.2144
0.2	.0035	1.000	.0035	6.2	.1080	.9942	.1086	12.2	.2113	.9774	.2162
0.3	.0052	1.000	.0052	6.3	.1097	.9940	.1104	12.3	.2130	.9770	.2180
0.4	.0070	1.000	.0070	6.4	.1115	.9938	.1122	12.4	.2147	.9767	.2199
0.5	.0087	1.000	.0087	6.5	.1132	.9936	.1139	12.5	.2164	.9763	.2217
0.6	.0105	.9999	.0105	6.6	.1149	.9934	.1157	12.6	.2181	.9759	.2235
0.7	.0122	.9999	.0122	6.7	.1167	.9932	.1175	12.7	.2198	.9755	.2254
0.8	.0140	.9999	.0140	6.8	.1184	.9930	.1192	12.8	.2215	.9751	.2272
0.9	.0157	.9999	.0157	6.9	.1201	.9928	.1210	12.9	.2233	.9748	.2290
1.0	.0175	.9998	.0175	7.0	.1219	.9925	.1228	13.0	.2250	.9744	.2309
1.1	.0192	.9998	.0192	7.1	.1236	.9923	.1246	13.1	.2267	.9740	.2327
1.2	.0209	.9998	.0209	7.2	.1253	.9921	.1263	13.2	.2284	.9736	.2345
1.3	.0227	.9997	.0227	7.3	.1271	.9919	.1281	13.3	.2300	.9732	.2364
1.4	.0244	.9997	.0244	7.4	.1288	.9917	.1299	13.4	.2317	.9728	.2382
1.5	.0262	.9997	.0262	7.5	.1305	.9914	.1317	13.5	.2334	.9724	.2401
1.6	.0279	.9996	.0279	7.6	.1323	.9912	.1334	13.6	.2351	.9720	.2419
1.7	.0297	.9996	.0297	7.7	.1340	.9910	.1352	13.7	.2368	.9715	.2438
1.8	.0314	.9995	.0314	7.8	.1357	.9907	.1370	13.8	.2385	.9711	.2456
1.9	.0332	.9995	.0332	7.9	.1374	.9905	.1388	13.9	.2402	.9707	.2475
2.0	.0349	.9994	.0349	8.0	.1392	.9903	.1405	14.0	.2419	.9703	.2493
2.1	.0366	.9993	.0367	8.1	.1409	.9900	.1423	14.1	.2436	.9699	.2512
2.2	.0384	.9993	.0384	8.2	.1426	.9898	.1441	14.2	.2453	.9694	.2530
2.3	.0401	.9992	.0402	8.3	.1444	.9895	.1459	14.3	.2470	.9690	.2549
2.4	.0419	.9991	.0419	8.4	.1461	.9893	.1477	14.4	.2487	.9686	.2568
2.5	.0436	.9990	.0437	8.5	.1478	.9890	.1495	14.5	.2504	.9681	.2586
2.6	.0454	.9990	.0454	8.6	.1495	.9888	.1512	14.6	.2521	.9677	.2605
2.7	.0471	.9989	.0472	8.7	.1513	.9885	.1530	14.7	.2538	.9673	.2623
2.8	.0488	.9988	.0489	8.8	.1530	.9882	.1548	14.8	.2554	.9668	.2642
2.9	.0506	.9987	.0507	8.9	.1547	.9880	.1566	14.9	.2571	.9664	.2661
3.0	.0523	.9986	.0524	9.0	.1564	.9877	.1584	15.0	.2588	.9659	.2679
3.1	.0541	.9985	.0542	9.1	.1582	.9874	.1602	15.1	.2605	.9655	.2698
3.2	.0558	.9984	.0559	9.2	.1599	.9871	.1620	15.2	.2622	.9650	.2717
3.3	.0576	.9983	.0577	9.3	.1616	.9869	.1638	15.3	.2639	.9646	.2736
3.4	.0593	.9982	.0594	9.4	.1633	.9866	.1655	15.4	.2656	.9641	.2754
3.5	.0610	.9981	.0612	9.5	.1650	.9863	.1673	15.5	.2672	.9636	.2773
3.6	.0628	.9980	.0629	9.6	.1668	.9860	.1691	15.6	.2689	.9632	.2792
3.7	.0645	.9979	.0647	9.7	.1685	.9857	.1709	15.7	.2706	.9627	.2811
3.8	.0663	.9978	.0664	9.8	.1702	.9854	.1727	15.8	.2723	.9622	.2830
3.9	.0680	.9977	.0682	9.9	.1719	.9851	.1745	15.9	.2740	.9617	.2849
4.0	.0698	.9976	.0699	10.0	.1736	.9848	.1763	16.0	.2756	.9613	.2867
4.1	.0715	.9974	.0717	10.1	.1754	.9845	.1781	16.1	.2773	.9608	.2886
4.2	.0732	.9973	.0734	10.2	.1771	.9842	.1799	16.2	.2790	.9603	.2905
4.3	.0750	.9972	.0752	10.3	.1788	.9839	.1817	16.3	.2807	.9598	.2924
4.4	.0767	.9971	.0769	10.4	.1805	.9836	.1835	16.4	.2823	.9593	.2943
4.5	.0785	.9969	.0787	10.5	.1822	.9833	.1853	16.5	.2840	.9588	.2962
4.6	.0802	.9968	.0805	10.6	.1840	.9829	.1871	16.6	.2857	.9583	.2981
4.7	.0819	.9966	.0822	10.7	.1857	.9826	.1890	16.7	.2874	.9578	.3000
4.8	.0837	.9965	.0840	10.8	.1874	.9823	.1908	16.8	.2890	.9573	.3019
4.9	.0854	.9963	.0857	10.9	.1891	.9820	.1926	16.9	.2907	.9568	.3038
5.0	.0872	.9962	.0875	11.0	.1908	.9816	.1944	17.0	.2924	.9563	.3057
5.1	.0889	.9960	.0892	11.1	.1925	.9813	.1962	17.1	.2940	.9558	.3076
5.2	.0906	.9959	.0910	11.2	.1942	.9810	.1980	17.2	.2957	.9553	.3096
5.3	.0924	.9957	.0928	11.3	.1959	.9806	.1998	17.3	.2974	.9548	.3115
5.4	.0941	.9956	.0945	11.4	.1977	.9803	.2016	17.4	.2990	.9542	.3134
5.5	.0958	.9954	.0963	11.5	.1994	.9799	.2035	17.5	.3007	.9537	.3153
5.6	.0976	.9952	.0981	11.6	.2011	.9796	.2053	17.6	.3024	.9532	.3172
5.7	.0993	.9951	.0998	11.7	.2028	.9792	.2071	17.7	.3040	.9527	.3191
5.8	.1011	.9949	.1016	11.8	.2045	.9789	.2089	17.8	.3057	.9521	.3211
5.9	.1028	.9947	.1033	11.9	.2062	.9785	.2107	17.9	.3074	.9516	.3230

TABLE 1 Values of trigonometric functions *(continued)*

deg	sin	cos	tan	deg	sin	cos	tan	deg	sin	cos	tan
18.0	.3090	.9511	.3249	24.0	.4067	.9135	.4452	30.0	.5000	.8660	.5774
18.1	.3107	.9505	.3269	24.1	.4083	.9128	.4473	30.1	.5015	.8652	.5797
18.2	.3123	.9500	.3288	24.2	.4099	.9121	.4494	30.2	.5030	.8643	.5820
18.3	.3140	.9494	.3307	24.3	.4115	.9114	.4515	30.3	.5045	.8634	.5844
18.4	.3156	.9489	.3327	24.4	.4131	.9107	.4536	30.4	.5060	.8625	.5867
18.5	.3173	.9483	.3346	24.5	.4147	.9100	.4557	30.5	.5075	.8616	.5890
18.6	.3190	.9478	.3365	24.6	.4163	.9092	.4578	30.6	.5090	.8607	.5914
18.7	.3206	.9472	.3385	24.7	.4179	.9085	.4599	30.7	.5105	.8599	.5938
18.8	.3223	.9466	.3404	24.8	.4195	.9078	.4621	30.8	.5120	.8590	.5961
18.9	.3239	.9461	.3424	24.9	.4210	.9070	.4642	30.9	.5135	.8581	.5985
19.0	.3256	.9455	.3443	25.0	.4226	.9063	.4663	31.0	.5150	.8572	.6009
19.1	.3272	.9449	.3463	25.1	.4242	.9056	.4684	31.1	.5165	.8563	.6032
19.2	.3289	.9444	.3482	25.2	.4258	.9048	.4706	31.2	.5180	.8554	.6056
19.3	.3305	.9438	.3502	25.3	.4274	.9041	.4727	31.3	.5195	.8545	.6080
19.4	.3322	.9432	.3522	25.4	.4289	.9033	.4748	31.4	.5210	.8536	.6104
19.5	.3338	.9426	.3541	25.5	.4305	.9026	.4770	31.5	.5225	.8526	.6128
19.6	.3355	.9421	.3561	25.6	.4321	.9018	.4791	31.6	.5240	.8517	.6152
19.7	.3371	.9415	.3581	25.7	.4337	.9011	.4813	31.7	.5255	.8508	.6176
19.8	.3387	.9409	.3600	25.8	.4352	.9003	.4834	31.8	.5270	.8499	.6200
19.9	.3404	.9403	.3620	25.9	.4368	.8996	.4856	31.9	.5284	.8490	.6224
20.0	.3420	.9397	.3640	26.0	.4384	.8988	.4877	32.0	.5299	.8480	.6249
20.1	.3437	.9391	.3659	26.1	.4399	.8980	.4899	32.1	.5314	.8471	.6273
20.2	.3453	.9385	.3679	26.2	.4415	.8973	.4921	32.2	.5329	.8462	.6297
20.3	.3469	.9379	.3699	26.3	.4431	.8965	.4942	32.3	.5344	.8453	.6322
20.4	.3486	.9373	.3719	26.4	.4446	.8957	.4964	32.4	.5358	.8443	.6346
20.5	.3502	.9367	.3739	26.5	.4462	.8949	.4986	32.5	.5373	.8434	.6371
20.6	.3518	.9361	.3759	26.6	.4478	.8942	.5008	32.6	.5388	.8425	.6395
20.7	.3535	.9354	.3779	26.7	.4493	.8934	.5029	32.7	.5402	.8415	.6420
20.8	.3551	.9348	.3799	26.8	.4509	.8926	.5051	32.8	.5417	.8406	.6445
20.9	.3567	.9342	.3819	26.9	.4524	.8918	.5073	32.9	.5432	.8396	.6469
21.0	.3584	.9336	.3839	27.0	.4540	.8910	.5095	33.0	.5446	.8387	.6494
21.1	.3600	.9330	.3859	27.1	.4555	.8902	.5117	33.1	.5461	.8377	.6519
21.2	.3616	.9323	.3879	27.2	.4571	.8894	.5139	33.2	.5476	.8368	.6544
21.3	.3633	.9317	.3899	27.3	.4586	.8886	.5161	33.3	.5490	.8358	.6569
21.4	.3649	.9311	.3919	27.4	.4602	.8878	.5184	33.4	.5505	.8348	.6594
21.5	.3665	.9304	.3939	27.5	.4617	.8870	.5206	33.5	.5519	.8339	.6619
21.6	.3681	.9298	.3959	27.6	.4633	.8862	.5228	33.6	.5534	.8329	.6644
21.7	.3697	.9291	.3979	27.7	.4648	.8854	.5250	33.7	.5548	.8320	.6669
21.8	.3714	.9285	.4000	27.8	.4664	.8846	.5272	33.8	.5563	.8310	.6694
21.9	.3730	.9278	.4020	27.9	.4679	.8838	.5295	33.9	.5577	.8300	.6720
22.0	.3746	.9272	.4040	28.0	.4695	.8829	.5317	34.0	.5592	.8290	.6745
22.1	.3762	.9265	.4061	28.1	.4710	.8821	.5340	34.1	.5606	.8281	.6771
22.2	.3778	.9259	.4081	28.2	.4726	.8813	.5362	34.2	.5621	.8271	.6796
22.3	.3795	.9252	.4101	28.3	.4741	.8805	.5384	34.3	.5635	.8261	.6822
22.4	.3811	.9245	.4122	28.4	.4756	.8796	.5407	34.4	.5650	.8251	.6847
22.5	.3827	.9239	.4142	28.5	.4772	.8788	.5430	34.5	.5664	.8241	.6873
22.6	.3843	.9232	.4163	28.6	.4787	.8780	.5452	34.6	.5678	.8231	.6899
22.7	.3859	.9225	.4183	28.7	.4802	.8771	.5475	34.7	.5693	.8221	.6924
22.8	.3875	.9219	.4204	28.8	.4818	.8763	.5498	34.8	.5707	.8211	.6950
22.9	.3891	.9212	.4224	28.9	.4833	.8755	.5520	34.9	.5721	.8202	.6976
23.0	.3907	.9205	.4245	29.0	.4848	.8746	.5543	35.0	.5736	.8192	.7002
23.1	.3923	.9198	.4265	29.1	.4863	.8738	.5566	35.1	.5750	.8181	.7028
23.2	.3939	.9191	.4286	29.2	.4879	.8729	.5589	35.2	.5764	.8171	.7054
23.3	.3955	.9184	.4307	29.3	.4894	.8721	.5612	35.3	.5779	.8161	.7080
23.4	.3971	.9178	.4327	29.4	.4909	.8712	.5635	35.4	.5793	.8151	.7107
23.5	.3987	.9171	.4348	29.5	.4924	.8704	.5658	35.5	.5807	.8141	.7133
23.6	.4003	.9164	.4369	29.6	.4939	.8695	.5681	35.6	.5821	.8131	.7159
23.7	.4019	.9157	.4390	29.7	.4955	.8686	.5704	35.7	.5835	.8121	.7186
23.8	.4035	.9150	.4411	29.8	.4970	.8678	.5727	35.8	.5850	.8111	.7212
23.9	.4051	.9143	.4431	29.9	.4985	.8669	.5750	35.9	.5864	.8100	.7239

TABLE 1 Values of trigonometric functions *(continued)*

deg	sin	cos	tan	deg	sin	cos	tan	deg	sin	cos	tan
36.0	.5878	.8090	.7265	42.0	.6691	.7431	.9004	48.0	.7431	.6691	1.1106
36.1	.5892	.8080	.7292	42.1	.6704	.7420	.9036	48.1	.7443	.6678	1.1145
36.2	.5906	.8070	.7319	42.2	.6717	.7408	.9067	48.2	.7455	.6665	1.1184
36.3	.5920	.8059	.7346	42.3	.6730	.7396	.9099	48.3	.7466	.6652	1.1224
36.4	.5934	.8049	.7373	42.4	.6743	.7385	.9131	48.4	.7478	.6639	1.1263
36.5	.5948	.8039	.7400	42.5	.6756	.7373	.9163	48.5	.7490	.6626	1.1303
36.6	.5962	.8028	.7427	42.6	.6769	.7361	.9195	48.6	.7501	.6613	1.1343
36.7	.5976	.8018	.7454	42.7	.6782	.7349	.9228	48.7	.7513	.6600	1.1383
36.8	.5990	.8007	.7481	42.8	.6794	.7337	.9260	48.8	.7524	.6587	1.1423
36.9	.6004	.7997	.7508	42.9	.6807	.7325	.9293	48.9	.7536	.6574	1.1463
37.0	.6018	.7986	.7536	43.0	.6820	.7314	.9325	49.0	.7547	.6561	1.1504
37.1	.6032	.7976	.7563	43.1	.6833	.7302	.9358	49.1	.7559	.6547	1.1544
37.2	.6046	.7965	.7590	43.2	.6845	.7290	.9391	49.2	.7570	.6534	1.1585
37.3	.6060	.7955	.7618	43.3	.6858	.7278	.9424	49.3	.7581	.6521	1.1626
37.4	.6074	.7944	.7646	43.4	.6871	.7266	.9457	49.4	.7593	.6508	1.1667
37.5	.6088	.7934	.7673	43.5	.6884	.7254	.9490	49.5	.7604	.6494	1.1708
37.6	.6101	.7923	.7701	43.6	.6896	.7242	.9523	49.6	.7615	.6481	1.1750
37.7	.6115	.7912	.7729	43.7	.6909	.7230	.9556	49.7	.7627	.6468	1.1792
37.8	.6129	.7902	.7757	43.8	.6921	.7218	.9590	49.8	.7638	.6455	1.1833
37.9	.6143	.7891	.7785	43.9	.6934	.7206	.9623	49.9	.7649	.6441	1.1875
38.0	.6157	.7880	.7813	44.0	.6947	.7193	.9657	50.0	.7660	.6428	1.1918
38.1	.6170	.7869	.7841	44.1	.6959	.7181	.9691	50.1	.7672	.6414	1.1960
38.2	.6184	.7859	.7869	44.2	.6972	.7169	.9725	50.2	.7683	.6401	1.2002
38.3	.6198	.7848	.7898	44.3	.6984	.7157	.9759	50.3	.7694	.6388	1.2045
38.4	.6211	.7837	.7926	44.4	.6997	.7145	.9793	50.4	.7705	.6374	1.2088
38.5	.6225	.7826	.7954	44.5	.7009	.7133	.9827	50.5	.7716	.6361	1.2131
38.6	.6239	.7815	.7983	44.6	.7022	.7120	.9861	50.6	.7727	.6347	1.2174
38.7	.6252	.7804	.8012	44.7	.7034	.7108	.9896	50.7	.7738	.6334	1.2218
38.8	.6266	.7793	.8040	44.8	.7046	.7096	.9930	50.8	.7749	.6320	1.2261
38.9	.6280	.7782	.8069	44.9	.7059	.7083	.9965	50.9	.7760	.6307	1.2305
39.0	.6293	.7771	.8098	45.0	.7071	.7071	1.0000	51.0	.7771	.6293	1.2349
39.1	.6307	.7760	.8127	45.1	.7083	.7059	1.0035	51.1	.7782	.6280	1.2393
39.2	.6320	.7749	.8156	45.2	.7096	.7046	1.0070	51.2	.7793	.6266	1.2437
39.3	.6334	.7738	.8185	45.3	.7108	.7034	1.0105	51.3	.7804	.6252	1.2482
39.4	.6347	.7727	.8214	45.4	.7120	.7022	1.0141	51.4	.7815	.6239	1.2527
39.5	.6361	.7716	.8243	45.5	.7133	.7009	1.0176	51.5	.7826	.6225	1.2572
39.6	.6374	.7705	.8273	45.6	.7145	.6997	1.0212	51.6	.7837	.6211	1.2617
39.7	.6388	.7694	.8302	45.7	.7157	.6984	1.0247	51.7	.7848	.6198	1.2662
39.8	.6401	.7683	.8332	45.8	.7169	.6972	1.0283	51.8	.7859	.6184	1.2708
39.9	.6414	.7672	.8361	45.9	.7181	.6959	1.0319	51.9	.7869	.6170	1.2753
40.0	.6428	.7660	.8391	46.0	.7193	.6947	1.0355	52.0	.7880	.6157	1.2799
40.1	.6441	.7649	.8421	46.1	.7206	.6934	1.0392	52.1	.7891	.6143	1.2846
40.2	.6455	.7638	.8451	46.2	.7218	.6921	1.0428	52.2	.7902	.6129	1.2892
40.3	.6468	.7627	.8481	46.3	.7230	.6909	1.0464	52.3	.7912	.6115	1.2938
40.4	.6481	.7615	.8511	46.4	.7242	.6896	1.0501	52.4	.7923	.6101	1.2985
40.5	.6494	.7604	.8541	46.5	.7254	.6884	1.0538	52.5	.7934	.6088	1.3032
40.6	.6508	.7593	.8571	46.6	.7266	.6871	1.0575	52.6	.7944	.6074	1.3079
40.7	.6521	.7581	.8601	46.7	.7278	.6858	1.0612	52.7	.7955	.6060	1.3127
40.8	.6534	.7570	.8632	46.8	.7290	.6845	1.0649	52.8	.7965	.6046	1.3175
40.9	.6547	.7559	.8662	46.9	.7302	.6833	1.0686	52.9	.7976	.6032	1.3222
41.0	.6561	.7547	.8693	47.0	.7314	.6820	1.0724	53.0	.7986	.6018	1.3270
41.1	.6574	.7536	.8724	47.1	.7325	.6807	1.0761	53.1	.7997	.6004	1.3319
41.2	.6587	.7524	.8754	47.2	.7337	.6794	1.0799	53.2	.8007	.5990	1.3367
41.3	.6600	.7513	.8785	47.3	.7349	.6782	1.0837	53.3	.8018	.5976	1.3416
41.4	.6613	.7501	.8816	47.4	.7361	.6769	1.0875	53.4	.8028	.5962	1.3465
41.5	.6626	.7490	.8847	47.5	.7373	.6756	1.0913	53.5	.8039	.5948	1.3514
41.6	.6639	.7478	.8878	47.6	.7385	.6743	1.0951	53.6	.8049	.5934	1.3564
41.7	.6652	.7466	.8910	47.7	.7396	.6730	1.0990	53.7	.8059	.5920	1.3613
41.8	.6665	.7455	.8941	47.8	.7408	.6717	1.1028	53.8	.8070	.5906	1.3663
41.9	.6678	.7443	.8972	47.9	.7420	.6704	1.1067	53.9	.8080	.5892	1.3713

TABLE 1 Values of trigonometric functions (*continued*)

deg	sin	cos	tan	deg	sin	cos	tan	deg	sin	cos	tan
54.0	.8090	.5878	1.3764	60.0	.8660	.5000	1.7321	66.0	.9135	.4067	2.2460
54.1	.8100	.5864	1.3814	60.1	.8669	.4985	1.7391	66.1	.9143	.4051	2.2566
54.2	.8111	.5850	1.3865	60.2	.8678	.4970	1.7461	66.2	.9150	.4035	2.2673
54.3	.8121	.5835	1.3916	60.3	.8686	.4955	1.7532	66.3	.9157	.4019	2.2781
54.4	.8131	.5821	1.3968	60.4	.8695	.4939	1.7603	66.4	.9164	.4003	2.2889
54.5	.8141	.5807	1.4019	60.5	.8704	.4924	1.7675	66.5	.9171	.3987	2.2998
54.6	.8151	.5793	1.4071	60.6	.8712	.4909	1.7747	66.6	.9178	.3971	2.3109
54.7	.8161	.5779	1.4124	60.7	.8721	.4894	1.7820	66.7	.9184	.3955	2.3220
54.8	.8171	.5764	1.4176	60.8	.8729	.4879	1.7893	66.8	.9191	.3939	2.3332
54.9	.8181	.5750	1.4229	60.9	.8738	.4863	1.7966	66.9	.9198	.3923	2.3445
55.0	.8192	.5736	1.4281	61.0	.8746	.4848	1.8040	67.0	.9205	.3907	2.3559
55.1	.8202	.5721	1.4335	61.1	.8755	.4833	1.8115	67.1	.9212	.3891	2.3673
55.2	.8211	.5707	1.4388	61.2	.8763	.4818	1.8190	67.2	.9219	.3875	2.3789
55.3	.8221	.5693	1.4442	61.3	.8771	.4802	1.8265	67.3	.9225	.3859	2.3906
55.4	.8231	.5678	1.4496	61.4	.8780	.4787	1.8341	67.4	.9232	.3843	2.4023
55.5	.8241	.5664	1.4550	61.5	.8788	.4772	1.8418	67.5	.9239	.3827	2.4142
55.6	.8251	.5650	1.4605	61.6	.8796	.4756	1.8495	67.6	.9245	.3811	2.4262
55.7	.8261	.5635	1.4659	61.7	.8805	.4741	1.8572	67.7	.9252	.3795	2.4383
55.8	.8271	.5621	1.4715	61.8	.8813	.4726	1.8650	67.8	.9259	.3778	2.4504
55.9	.8281	.5606	1.4770	61.9	.8821	.4710	1.8728	67.9	.9265	.3762	2.4627
56.0	.8290	.5592	1.4826	62.0	.8829	.4695	1.8807	68.0	.9272	.3746	2.4751
56.1	.8300	.5577	1.4882	62.1	.8838	.4679	1.8887	68.1	.9278	.3730	2.4876
56.2	.8310	.5563	1.4938	62.2	.8846	.4664	1.8967	68.2	.9285	.3714	2.5002
56.3	.8320	.5548	1.4994	62.3	.8854	.4648	1.9047	68.3	.9291	.3697	2.5129
56.4	.8329	.5534	1.5051	62.4	.8862	.4633	1.9128	68.4	.9298	.3681	2.5257
56.5	.8339	.5519	1.5108	62.5	.8870	.4617	1.9210	68.5	.9304	.3665	2.5386
56.6	.8348	.5505	1.5166	62.6	.8878	.4602	1.9292	68.6	.9311	.3649	2.5517
56.7	.8358	.5490	1.5224	62.7	.8886	.4586	1.9375	68.7	.9317	.3633	2.5649
56.8	.8368	.5476	1.5282	62.8	.8894	.4571	1.9458	68.8	.9323	.3616	2.5782
56.9	.8377	.5461	1.5340	62.9	.8902	.4555	1.9542	68.9	.9330	.3600	2.5916
57.0	.8387	.5446	1.5399	63.0	.8910	.4540	1.9626	69.0	.9336	.3584	2.6051
57.1	.8396	.5432	1.5458	63.1	.8918	.4524	1.9711	69.1	.9342	.3567	2.6187
57.2	.8406	.5417	1.5517	63.2	.8926	.4509	1.9797	69.2	.9348	.3551	2.6325
57.3	.8415	.5402	1.5577	63.3	.8934	.4493	1.9883	69.3	.9354	.3535	2.6464
57.4	.8425	.5388	1.5637	63.4	.8942	.4478	1.9970	69.4	.9361	.3518	2.6605
57.5	.8434	.5373	1.5697	63.5	.8949	.4462	2.0057	69.5	.9367	.3502	2.6746
57.6	.8443	.5358	1.5757	63.6	.8957	.4446	2.0145	69.6	.9373	.3486	2.6889
57.7	.8453	.5344	1.5818	63.7	.8965	.4431	2.0233	69.7	.9379	.3469	2.7034
57.8	.8462	.5329	1.5880	63.8	.8973	.4415	2.0323	69.8	.9385	.3453	2.7179
57.9	.8471	.5314	1.5941	63.9	.8980	.4399	2.0413	69.9	.9391	.3437	2.7326
58.0	.8480	.5299	1.6003	64.0	.8988	.4384	2.0503	70.0	.9397	.3420	2.7475
58.1	.8490	.5284	1.6066	64.1	.8996	.4368	2.0594	70.1	.9403	.3404	2.7625
58.2	.8499	.5270	1.6128	64.2	.9003	.4352	2.0686	70.2	.9409	.3387	2.7776
58.3	.8508	.5255	1.6191	64.3	.9011	.4337	2.0778	70.3	.9415	.3371	2.7929
58.4	.8517	.5240	1.6255	64.4	.9018	.4321	2.0872	70.4	.9421	.3355	2.8083
58.5	.8526	.5225	1.6319	64.5	.9026	.4305	2.0965	70.5	.9426	.3338	2.8239
58.6	.8536	.5210	1.6383	64.6	.9033	.4289	2.1060	70.6	.9432	.3322	2.8397
58.7	.8545	.5195	1.6447	64.7	.9041	.4274	2.1155	70.7	.9438	.3305	2.8556
58.8	.8554	.5180	1.6512	64.8	.9048	.4258	2.1251	70.8	.9444	.3289	2.8716
58.9	.8563	.5165	1.6577	64.9	.9056	.4242	2.1348	70.9	.9449	.3272	2.8878
59.0	.8572	.5150	1.6643	65.0	.9063	.4226	2.1445	71.0	.9455	.3256	2.9042
59.1	.8581	.5135	1.6709	65.1	.9070	.4210	2.1543	71.1	.9461	.3239	2.9208
59.2	.8590	.5120	1.6775	65.2	.9078	.4195	2.1642	71.2	.9466	.3223	2.9375
59.3	.8599	.5105	1.6842	65.3	.9085	.4179	2.1742	71.3	.9472	.3206	2.9544
59.4	.8607	.5090	1.6909	65.4	.9092	.4163	2.1842	71.4	.9478	.3190	2.9714
59.5	.8616	.5075	1.6977	65.5	.9100	.4147	2.1943	71.5	.9483	.3173	2.9887
59.6	.8625	.5060	1.7045	65.6	.9107	.4131	2.2045	71.6	.9489	.3156	3.0061
59.7	.8634	.5045	1.7113	65.7	.9114	.4115	2.2148	71.7	.9494	.3140	3.0237
59.8	.8643	.5030	1.7182	65.8	.9121	.4099	2.2251	71.8	.9500	.3123	3.0415
59.9	.8652	.5015	1.7251	65.9	.9128	.4083	2.2355	71.9	.9505	.3107	3.0595

TABLE 1 Values of trigonometric functions (*continued*)

deg	sin	cos	tan	deg	sin	cos	tan	deg	sin	cos	tan
72.0	.9511	.3090	3.0777	78.0	.9781	.2079	4.7046	84.0	.9945	.1045	9.5141
72.1	.9516	.3074	3.0961	78.1	.9785	.2062	4.7453	84.1	.9947	.1028	9.6768
72.2	.9521	.3057	3.1146	78.2	.9789	.2045	4.7867	84.2	.9949	.1011	9.8448
72.3	.9527	.3040	3.1334	78.3	.9792	.2028	4.8288	84.3	.9951	.0993	10.0187
72.4	.9532	.3024	3.1524	78.4	.9796	.2011	4.8716	84.4	.9952	.0976	10.1988
72.5	.9537	.3007	3.1716	78.5	.9799	.1994	4.9152	84.5	.9954	.0958	10.3854
72.6	.9542	.2990	3.1910	78.6	.9803	.1977	4.9594	84.6	.9956	.0941	10.5789
72.7	.9548	.2974	3.2106	78.7	.9806	.1959	5.0045	84.7	.9957	.0924	10.7797
72.8	.9553	.2957	3.2305	78.8	.9810	.1942	5.0504	84.8	.9959	.0906	10.9882
72.9	.9558	.2940	3.2506	78.9	.9813	.1925	5.0970	84.9	.9960	.0889	11.2048
73.0	.9563	.2924	3.2709	79.0	.9816	.1908	5.1446	85.0	.9962	.0872	11.4301
73.1	.9568	.2907	3.2914	79.1	.9820	.1891	5.1929	85.1	.9963	.0854	11.6645
73.2	.9573	.2890	3.3122	79.2	.9823	.1874	5.2422	85.2	.9965	.0837	11.9087
73.3	.9578	.2874	3.3332	79.3	.9826	.1857	5.2924	85.3	.9966	.0819	12.1632
73.4	.9583	.2857	3.3544	79.4	.9829	.1840	5.3435	85.4	.9968	.0802	12.4288
73.5	.9588	.2840	3.3759	79.5	.9833	.1822	5.3955	85.5	.9969	.0785	12.7062
73.6	.9593	.2823	3.3977	79.6	.9836	.1805	5.4486	85.6	.9971	.0767	12.9962
73.7	.9598	.2807	3.4197	79.7	.9839	.1788	5.5026	85.7	.9972	.0750	13.2996
73.8	.9603	.2790	3.4420	79.8	.9842	.1771	5.5578	85.8	.9973	.0732	13.6174
73.9	.9608	.2773	3.4646	79.9	.9845	.1754	5.6140	85.9	.9974	.0715	13.9507
74.0	.9613	.2756	3.4874	80.0	.9848	.1736	5.6713	86.0	.9976	.0698	14.3007
74.1	.9617	.2740	3.5105	80.1	.9851	.1719	5.7297	86.1	.9977	.0680	14.6685
74.2	.9622	.2723	3.5339	80.2	.9854	.1702	5.7894	86.2	.9978	.0663	15.0557
74.3	.9627	.2706	3.5576	80.3	.9857	.1685	5.8502	86.3	.9979	.0645	15.4638
74.4	.9632	.2689	3.5816	80.4	.9860	.1668	5.9124	86.4	.9980	.0628	15.8945
74.5	.9636	.2672	3.6059	80.5	.9863	.1650	5.9758	86.5	.9981	.0610	16.3499
74.6	.9641	.2656	3.6305	80.6	.9866	.1633	6.0405	86.6	.9982	.0593	16.8319
74.7	.9646	.2639	3.6554	80.7	.9869	.1616	6.1066	86.7	.9983	.0576	17.3432
74.8	.9650	.2622	3.6806	80.8	.9871	.1599	6.1742	86.8	.9984	.0558	17.8863
74.9	.9655	.2605	3.7062	80.9	.9874	.1582	6.2432	86.9	.9985	.0541	18.4645
75.0	.9659	.2588	3.7321	81.0	.9877	.1564	6.3138	87.0	.9986	.0523	19.0811
75.1	.9664	.2571	3.7583	81.1	.9880	.1547	6.3859	87.1	.9987	.0506	19.7403
75.2	.9668	.2554	3.7848	81.2	.9882	.1530	6.4596	87.2	.9988	.0488	20.4465
75.3	.9673	.2538	3.8118	81.3	.9885	.1513	6.5350	87.3	.9989	.0471	21.2049
75.4	.9677	.2521	3.8391	81.4	.9888	.1495	6.6122	87.4	.9990	.0454	22.0217
75.5	.9681	.2504	3.8667	81.5	.9890	.1478	6.6912	87.5	.9990	.0436	22.9038
75.6	.9686	.2487	3.8947	81.6	.9893	.1461	6.7720	87.6	.9991	.0419	23.8593
75.7	.9690	.2470	3.9232	81.7	.9895	.1444	6.8548	87.7	.9992	.0401	24.8978
75.8	.9694	.2453	3.9520	81.8	.9898	.1426	6.9395	87.8	.9993	.0384	26.0307
75.9	.9699	.2436	3.9812	81.9	.9900	.1409	7.0264	87.9	.9993	.0366	27.2715
76.0	.9703	.2419	4.0108	82.0	.9903	.1392	7.1154	88.0	.9994	.0349	28.6363
76.1	.9707	.2402	4.0408	82.1	.9905	.1374	7.2066	88.1	.9995	.0332	30.1446
76.2	.9711	.2385	4.0713	82.2	.9907	.1357	7.3002	88.2	.9995	.0314	31.8205
76.3	.9715	.2368	4.1022	82.3	.9910	.1340	7.3962	88.3	.9996	.0297	33.6935
76.4	.9720	.2351	4.1335	82.4	.9912	.1323	7.4947	88.4	.9996	.0279	35.8006
76.5	.9724	.2334	4.1653	82.5	.9914	.1305	7.5958	88.5	.9997	.0262	38.1885
76.6	.9728	.2317	4.1976	82.6	.9917	.1288	7.6996	88.6	.9997	.0244	40.9174
76.7	.9732	.2300	4.2303	82.7	.9919	.1271	7.8062	88.7	.9997	.0227	44.0661
76.8	.9736	.2284	4.2635	82.8	.9921	.1253	7.9158	88.8	.9998	.0209	47.7395
76.9	.9740	.2267	4.2972	82.9	.9923	.1236	8.0285	88.9	.9998	.0192	52.0807
77.0	.9744	.2250	4.3315	83.0	.9925	.1219	8.1443	89.0	.9998	.0175	57.2900
77.1	.9748	.2233	4.3662	83.1	.9928	.1201	8.2636	89.1	.9999	.0157	63.6567
77.2	.9751	.2215	4.4015	83.2	.9930	.1184	8.3863	89.2	.9999	.0140	71.6151
77.3	.9755	.2198	4.4373	83.3	.9932	.1167	8.5126	89.3	.9999	.0122	81.8470
77.4	.9759	.2181	4.4737	83.4	.9934	.1149	8.6427	89.4	.9999	.0105	95.4895
77.5	.9763	.2164	4.5107	83.5	.9936	.1132	8.7769	89.5	1.000	.0087	114.5887
77.6	.9767	.2147	4.5483	83.6	.9938	.1115	8.9152	89.6	1.000	.0070	143.2371
77.7	.9770	.2130	4.5864	83.7	.9940	.1097	9.0579	89.7	1.000	.0052	190.9842
77.8	.9774	.2113	4.6252	83.8	.9942	.1080	9.2052	89.8	1.000	.0035	286.4777
77.9	.9778	.2096	4.6646	83.9	.9943	.1063	9.3572	89.9	1.000	.0017	572.9571
								90.0	1.000	.0000	

$10^0 = 1$

$\log 1 = 0$

TABLE 2 Common logarithms

n	0	1	2	3	4	5	6	7	8	9
1.0	.0000	.0043	.0086	.0128	.0170	.0212	.0253	.0294	.0334	.0374
1.1	.0414	.0453	.0492	.0531	.0569	.0607	.0645	.0682	.0719	.0755
1.2	.0792	.0828	.0864	.0899	.0934	.0969	.1004	.1038	.1072	.1106
1.3	.1139	.1173	.1206	.1239	.1271	.1303	.1335	.1367	.1399	.1430
1.4	.1461	.1492	.1523	.1553	.1584	.1614	.1644	.1673	.1703	.1732
1.5	.1761	.1790	.1818	.1847	.1875	.1903	.1931	.1959	.1987	.2014
1.6	.2041	.2068	.2095	.2122	.2148	.2175	.2201	.2227	.2253	.2279
1.7	.2304	.2330	.2355	.2380	.2405	.2430	.2455	.2480	.2504	.2529
1.8	.2553	.2577	.2601	.2625	.2648	.2672	.2695	.2718	.2742	.2765
1.9	.2788	.2810	.2833	.2856	.2878	.2900	.2923	.2945	.2967	.2989
2.0	.3010	.3032	.3054	.3075	.3096	.3118	.3139	.3160	.3181	.3201
2.1	.3222	.3243	.3263	.3284	.3304	.3324	.3345	.3365	.3385	.3404
2.2	.3424	.3444	.3464	.3483	.3502	.3522	.3541	.3560	.3579	.3598
2.3	.3617	.3636	.3655	.3674	.3692	.3711	.3729	.3747	.3766	.3784
2.4	.3802	.3820	.3838	.3856	.3874	.3892	.3909	.3927	.3945	.3962
2.5	.3979	.3997	.4014	.4031	.4048	.4065	.4082	.4099	.4116	.4133
2.6	.4150	.4166	.4183	.4200	.4216	.4232	.4249	.4265	.4281	.4298
2.7	.4314	.4330	.4346	.4362	.4378	.4393	.4409	.4425	.4440	.4456
2.8	.4472	.4487	.4502	.4518	.4533	.4548	.4564	.4579	.4594	.4609
2.9	.4624	.4639	.4654	.4669	.4683	.4698	.4713	.4728	.4742	.4757
3.0	.4771	.4786	.4800	.4814	.4829	.4843	.4857	.4871	.4886	.4900
3.1	.4914	.4928	.4942	.4955	.4969	.4983	.4997	.5011	.5024	.5038
3.2	.5051	.5065	.5079	.5092	.5105	.5119	.5132	.5145	.5159	.5172
3.3	.5185	.5198	.5211	.5224	.5237	.5250	.5263	.5276	.5289	.5302
3.4	.5315	.5328	.5340	.5353	.5366	.5378	.5391	.5403	.5416	.5428
3.5	.5441	.5453	.5465	.5478	.5490	.5502	.5514	.5527	.5539	.5551
3.6	.5563	.5575	.5587	.5599	.5611	.5623	.5635	.5647	.5658	.5670
3.7	.5682	.5694	.5705	.5717	.5729	.5740	.5752	.5763	.5775	.5786
3.8	.5798	.5809	.5821	.5832	.5843	.5855	.5866	.5877	.5888	.5899
3.9	.5911	.5922	.5933	.5944	.5955	.5966	.5977	.5988	.5999	.6010
4.0	.6021	.6031	.6042	.6053	.6064	.6075	.6085	.6096	.6107	.6117
4.1	.6128	.6138	.6149	.6160	.6170	.6180	.6191	.6201	.6212	.6222
4.2	.6232	.6243	.6253	.6263	.6274	.6284	.6294	.6304	.6314	.6325
4.3	.6335	.6345	.6355	.6365	.6375	.6385	.6395	.6405	.6415	.6425
4.4	.6435	.6444	.6454	.6464	.6474	.6484	.6493	.6503	.6513	.6522
4.5	.6532	.6542	.6551	.6561	.6571	.6580	.6590	.6599	.6609	.6618
4.6	.6628	.6637	.6646	.6656	.6665	.6675	.6684	.6693	.6702	.6712
4.7	.6721	.6730	.6739	.6749	.6758	.6767	.6776	.6785	.6794	.6803
4.8	.6812	.6821	.6830	.6839	.6848	.6857	.6866	.6875	.6884	.6893
4.9	.6902	.6911	.6920	.6928	.6937	.6946	.6955	.6964	.6972	.6981
5.0	.6990	.6998	.7007	.7016	.7024	.7033	.7042	.7050	.7059	.7067
5.1	.7076	.7084	.7093	.7101	.7110	.7118	.7126	.7135	.7143	.7152
5.2	.7160	.7168	.7177	.7185	.7193	.7202	.7210	.7218	.7226	.7235
5.3	.7243	.7251	.7259	.7267	.7275	.7284	.7292	.7300	.7308	.7316
5.4	.7324	.7332	.7340	.7348	.7356	.7364	.7372	.7380	.7388	.7396
5.5	.7404	.7412	.7419	.7427	.7435	.7443	.7451	.7459	.7466	.7474
5.6	.7482	.7490	.7497	.7505	.7513	.7520	.7528	.7536	.7543	.7551
5.7	.7559	.7566	.7574	.7582	.7589	.7597	.7604	.7612	.7619	.7627
5.8	.7634	.7642	.7649	.7657	.7664	.7672	.7679	.7686	.7694	.7701
5.9	.7709	.7716	.7723	.7731	.7738	.7745	.7752	.7760	.7767	.7774
6.0	.7782	.7789	.7796	.7803	.7810	.7818	.7825	.7832	.7839	.7846
6.1	.7853	.7860	.7868	.7875	.7882	.7889	.7896	.7903	.7910	.7917
6.2	.7924	.7931	.7938	.7945	.7952	.7959	.7966	.7973	.7980	.7987
6.3	.7993	.8000	.8007	.8014	.8021	.8028	.8035	.8041	.8048	.8055
6.4	.8062	.8069	.8075	.8082	.8089	.8096	.8102	.8109	.8116	.8122
6.5	.8129	.8136	.8142	.8149	.8156	.8162	.8169	.8176	.8182	.8189
6.6	.8195	.8202	.8209	.8215	.8222	.8228	.8235	.8241	.8248	.8254
6.7	.8261	.8267	.8274	.8280	.8287	.8293	.8299	.8306	.8312	.8319
6.8	.8325	.8331	.8338	.8344	.8351	.8357	.8363	.8370	.8376	.8382
6.9	.8388	.8395	.8401	.8407	.8414	.8420	.8426	.8432	.8439	.8445
n	0	1	2	3	4	5	6	7	8	9

TABLE 2 Common logarithms (*continued*)

n	0	1	2	3	4	5	6	7	8	9
7.0	.8451	.8457	.8463	.8470	.8476	.8482	.8488	.8494	.8500	.8506
7.1	.8513	.8519	.8525	.8531	.8537	.8543	.8549	.8555	.8561	.8567
7.2	.8573	.8579	.8585	.8591	.8597	.8603	.8609	.8615	.8621	.8627
7.3	.8633	.8639	.8645	.8651	.8657	.8663	.8669	.8675	.8681	.8686
7.4	.8692	.8698	.8704	.8710	.8716	.8722	.8727	.8733	.8739	.8745
7.5	.8751	.8756	.8762	.8768	.8774	.8779	.8785	.8791	.8797	.8802
7.6	.8808	.8814	.8820	.8825	.8831	.8837	.8842	.8848	.8854	.8859
7.7	.8865	.8871	.8876	.8882	.8887	.8893	.8899	.8904	.8910	.8915
7.8	.8921	.8927	.8932	.8938	.8943	.8949	.8954	.8960	.8965	.8971
7.9	.8976	.8982	.8987	.8993	.8998	.9004	.9009	.9015	.9020	.9025
8.0	.9031	.9036	.9042	.9047	.9053	.9058	.9063	.9069	.9074	.9079
8.1	.9085	.9090	.9096	.9101	.9106	.9112	.9117	.9122	.9128	.9133
8.2	.9138	.9143	.9149	.9154	.9159	.9165	.9170	.9175	.9180	.9186
8.3	.9191	.9196	.9201	.9206	.9212	.9217	.9222	.9227	.9232	.9238
8.4	.9243	.9248	.9253	.9258	.9263	.9269	.9274	.9279	.9284	.9289
8.5	.9294	.9299	.9304	.9309	.9315	.9320	.9325	.9330	.9335	.9340
8.6	.9345	.9350	.9355	.9360	.9365	.9370	.9375	.9380	.9385	.9390
8.7	.9395	.9400	.9405	.9410	.9415	.9420	.9425	.9430	.9435	.9440
8.8	.9445	.9450	.9455	.9460	.9465	.9469	.9474	.9479	.9484	.9489
8.9	.9494	.9499	.9504	.9509	.9513	.9518	.9523	.9528	.9533	.9538
9.0	.9542	.9547	.9552	.9557	.9562	.9566	.9571	.9576	.9581	.9586
9.1	.9590	.9595	.9600	.9605	.9609	.9614	.9619	.9624	.9628	.9633
9.2	.9638	.9643	.9647	.9652	.9657	.9661	.9666	.9671	.9675	.9680
9.3	.9685	.9689	.9694	.9699	.9703	.9708	.9713	.9717	.9722	.9727
9.4	.9731	.9736	.9741	.9745	.9750	.9754	.9759	.9763	.9768	.9773
9.5	.9777	.9782	.9786	.9791	.9795	.9800	.9805	.9809	.9814	.9818
9.6	.9823	.9827	.9832	.9836	.9841	.9845	.9850	.9854	.9859	.9863
9.7	.9868	.9872	.9877	.9881	.9886	.9890	.9894	.9899	.9903	.9908
9.8	.9912	.9917	.9921	.9926	.9930	.9934	.9939	.9943	.9948	.9952
9.9	.9956	.9961	.9965	.9969	.9974	.9978	.9983	.9987	.9991	.9996
n	0	1	2	3	4	5	6	7	8	9

Logarithms whose bases are not 10

We can find the logarithm of a number to a base other than 10 by dividing the base 10 logarithm of the number by the appropriate constant. One way to find the entries for a base 15 table of logarithms is to divide the base 10 logarithms of the selected numbers by 1.1761. For a base 7 table we would divide the base 10 logarithms by 0.8451, and for a base 5 table we would divide by 0.6990. To see why, we repeat the development of Lesson 82 by finding the logarithm of 15 to the base 5. First we write the indicated logarithmic equation and then rewrite the equation in exponential form.

$$y = \log_5 15 \quad \xrightarrow{\text{means}} \quad 5^y = 15$$

Next we take the base 10 logarithm of both sides of the exponential equation and solve for y by dividing both sides by log 5.

$$y \log 5 = \log 15 \qquad \text{took log of both sides} \qquad \longrightarrow \qquad y = \frac{\log 15}{\log 5} \qquad \text{divided}$$

The base 10 logarithm of 5 is 0.6990, so we divide log 15 by 0.6990. From this we see that we can find the logarithm of any number to the base 5 by dividing the base 10 logarithm of the number by 0.6990. If we wished to construct a table of base 5 logarithms, we would first decide on the numbers whose logarithms we wished to include. Then we would find the base 5 logarithm of each number by dividing the base 10 logarithm of each number by 0.6990.

A calculator is helpful when constructing a table of logarithms because a calculator will give us the logarithm of any positive number to the base 10. To construct a logarithm table whose base is e, we refer to the example on the preceding page and change 5 to e. If we do this, we get

$$\log_e 15 = \ln 15 = \frac{\log 15}{\log e}$$

The decimal approximation of e is 2.7182818, and the calculator tells us that the base 10 logarithm of this number is approximately 0.43429. Thus a base e table can be constructed by dividing the base 10 logarithm of every number to be included by 0.43429. If we use a calculator to help us find the base e logarithms of 4.6 and 19, we get

$$\ln 4.6 = \frac{\log 4.6}{0.43429} = \frac{0.66276}{0.43429} = \mathbf{1.5261} \qquad \ln 19 = \frac{\log 19}{0.43429} = \frac{1.27875}{0.43429} = \mathbf{2.9444}$$

Logarithms to the base e are sometimes helpful, so a partial table is presented below. If other entries are necessary, they can be calculated by dividing the base 10 logarithm of each new number by 0.43429.

TABLE 3 Natural logarithms

x	$\ln x$	x	$\ln x$	x	$\ln x$	x	$\ln x$	x	$\ln x$
		3.0	1.0986	6.0	1.7918	9.0	2.1972	70	4.2485
0.1	−2.3026	3.1	1.1314	6.1	1.8083	9.1	2.2083	75	4.3175
0.2	−1.6094	3.2	1.1632	6.2	1.8245	9.2	2.2192	80	4.3820
0.3	−1.2040	3.3	1.1939	6.3	1.8405	9.3	2.2300	85	4.4427
0.4	−0.9163	3.4	1.2238	6.4	1.8563	9.4	2.2407	90	4.4998
0.5	−0.6931	3.5	1.2528	6.5	1.8718	9.5	2.2513	95	4.5539
0.6	−0.5108	3.6	1.2809	6.6	1.8871	9.6	2.2618	100	4.6059
0.7	−0.3567	3.7	1.3083	6.7	1.9021	9.7	2.2721	150	5.0106
0.8	−0.2231	3.8	1.3350	6.8	1.9169	9.8	2.2824	200	5.2983
0.9	−0.1054	3.9	1.3610	6.9	1.9315	9.9	2.2925	250	5.5214
1.0	0.0000	4.0	1.3863	7.0	1.9459	10	2.3026	300	5.7038
1.1	0.0953	4.1	1.4110	7.1	1.9601	11	2.3979	350	5.8579
1.2	0.1823	4.2	1.4351	7.2	1.9741	12	2.4849	400	5.9915
1.3	0.2624	4.3	1.4586	7.3	1.9879	13	2.5649	450	6.1092
1.4	0.3365	4.4	1.4816	7.4	2.0015	14	2.6391	500	6.2146
1.5	0.4055	4.5	1.5041	7.5	2.0149	15	2.7081	550	6.3099
1.6	0.4700	4.6	1.5261	7.6	2.0281	16	2.7726	600	6.3969
1.7	0.5306	4.7	1.5476	7.7	2.0142	17	2.8332	650	6.4770
1.8	0.5878	4.8	1.5686	7.8	2.0541	18	2.8904	700	6.5511
1.9	0.6419	4.9	1.5892	7.9	2.0669	19	2.9444	750	6.6201
2.0	0.6931	5.0	1.6094	8.0	2.0794	20	2.9957	1000	6.9078
2.1	0.7419	5.1	1.6292	8.1	2.0919	25	3.2189	1250	7.1309
2.2	0.7885	5.2	1.6487	8.2	2.1041	30	3.4012	1500	7.3132
2.3	0.8329	5.3	1.6677	8.3	2.1163	35	3.5553	1750	7.4674
2.4	0.8755	5.4	1.6864	8.4	2.1282	40	3.6889	2000	7.6009
2.5	0.9163	5.5	1.7047	8.5	2.1401	45	3.8067	2250	7.7187
2.6	0.9555	5.6	1.7228	8.6	2.1518	50	3.9120	2500	7.8240
2.7	0.9933	5.7	1.7405	8.7	2.1633	55	4.0073	2750	7.9193
2.8	1.0296	5.8	1.7579	8.8	2.1748	60	4.0943	3000	8.0064
2.9	1.0647	5.9	1.7750	8.9	2.1861	65	4.1744	5000	8.5172

APPENDIX 3 Proofs

AP3.A

Proof of the law of cosines

To prove the law of cosines we will use the triangle on the left below. On the right we draw a segment from vertex C that is perpendicular to side c.

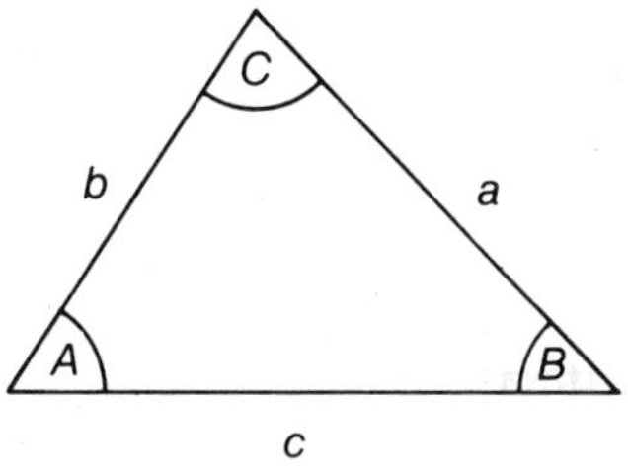

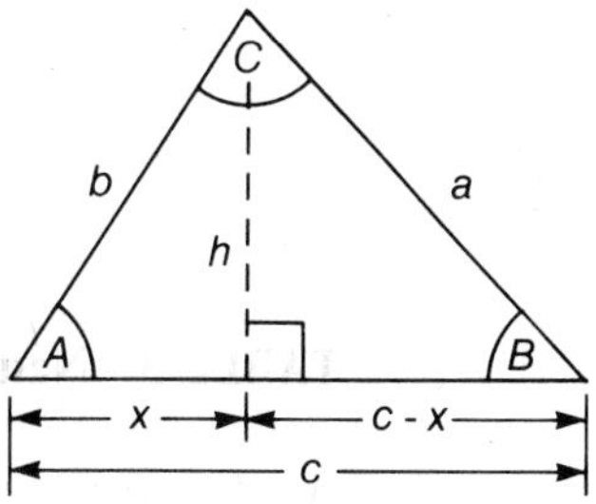

We use the small triangle whose side is x to write the following.

$$\frac{x}{b} = \cos A \quad \longrightarrow \quad x = b \cos A$$

We will use this equivalence for x in the last step. Next we use the Pythagorean theorem in both the small triangles.

$$b^2 = x^2 + h^2 \qquad (c - x)^2 + h^2 = a^2$$

We leave the equation on the left as it is. Then we expand $(c - x)^2$ in the right-hand equation and rearrange this equation to solve for $x^2 + h^2$.

$$b^2 = x^2 + h^2 \qquad c^2 - 2cx + x^2 + h^2 = a^2 \qquad \text{expanded}$$

$$x^2 + h^2 = a^2 - c^2 + 2cx \qquad \text{rearranged}$$

Now we substitute for $x^2 + h^2$ in the left-hand equation

$$b^2 = a^2 - c^2 + 2cx$$

and rearrange

$$a^2 = b^2 + c^2 - 2cx$$

We finish by replacing x with $b \cos A$ in this equation.

$$\mathbf{a^2 = b^2 + c^2 - 2bc \cos A}$$

The proof when one angle is obtuse is similar. This time, in the right-hand figure below, we label the new distance as x.

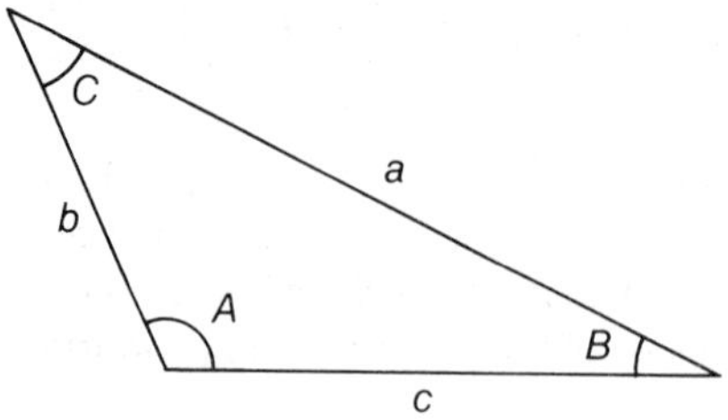

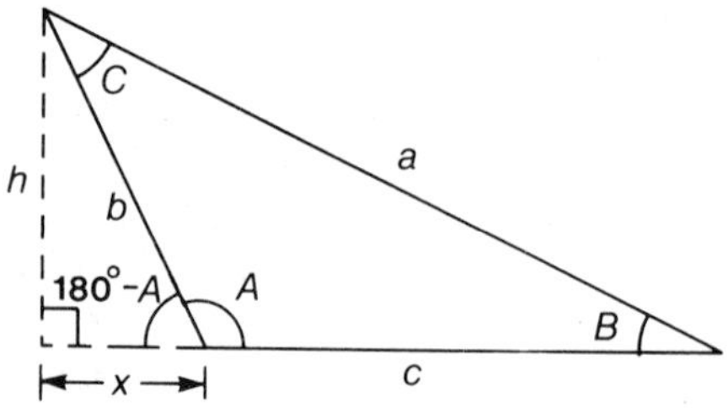

We begin with the small right triangle.

$$\cos(180° - A) = \frac{x}{b} \longrightarrow b\cos(180° - A) = x$$

But $\cos(180° - A) = -\cos A$ so $x = -b\cos A$

Now we use the Pythagorean theorem in both the large right triangle and the small right triangle in the right-hand figure.

$$x^2 + h^2 = b^2 \quad \text{and} \quad (x + c)^2 + h^2 = a^2$$

We leave the left-hand equation as it is and expand and rearrange the right-hand equation.

$$x^2 + h^2 = b^2 \qquad x^2 + 2xc + c^2 + h^2 = a^2 \quad \text{expanded}$$

$$x^2 + h^2 + c^2 + 2xc = a^2 \quad \text{rearranged}$$

Now we substitute b^2 for $x^2 + h^2$ in the right-hand equation and get

$$a^2 = b^2 + c^2 + 2xc \quad \text{substituted}$$

Finally, from the first step, we know that $x = -b\cos A$, so

$$a^2 = b^2 + c^2 - 2bc\cos A \quad \text{substituted}$$

We can use the law of cosines to "prove" that if the sides of one triangle are proportional to the corresponding sides in another triangle, the corresponding angles are equal. We use quotation marks because this "proof" uses circular reasoning in that the definition of the cosine of an angle includes the assumption that the lengths of sides are proportional in two right triangles whose other angles are equal. Note that the word *proof* was avoided on page 389 in a similar development that used the law of sines. Regard the following triangles whose sides are proportional. We use the letter m for the scale factor, or constant of proportionality.

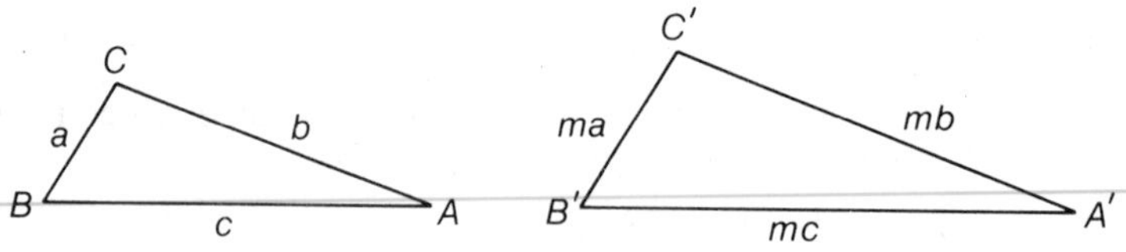

The length of each side in the triangle on the right is m times the length of the corresponding side in the triangle on the left. We would like to show that the corresponding angles are equal. As the first step we write the law of cosines for both triangles, using angles A and A' in the statements.

$$a^2 = b^2 + c^2 - 2bc\cos A \qquad m^2a^2 = m^2b^2 + m^2c^2 - 2mbmc\cos A'$$

Next we rearrange both equations to solve for $\cos A$ and $\cos A'$.

$$\cos A = \frac{b^2 + c^2 - a^2}{2bc} \qquad \cos A' = \frac{m^2b^2 + m^2c^2 - m^2a^2}{2m^2bc}$$

Every term in the expression for cos A' contains m^2. If we factor out m^2, we can cancel and get the same value we got for cos A.

$$\cos A' = \frac{m^2(b^2 + c^2 - a^2)}{m^2(2bc)} = \frac{b^2 + c^2 - a^2}{2bc}$$

Angles A and A' are both positive and less than 180°, and their cosines are equal. This tells us that these angles are equal. The same process can be used to show that angles B and B' are equal and that angles C and C' are also equal. Thus we have shown that if the corresponding sides of two triangles are proportional, then the corresponding angles are equal.

We can also use the law of cosines to illustrate that if two sides of one triangle are proportional to two sides of another triangle, and if the angles included by these sides are equal, then the third sides are also proportional and thus the triangles are similar. In the two triangles shown here,

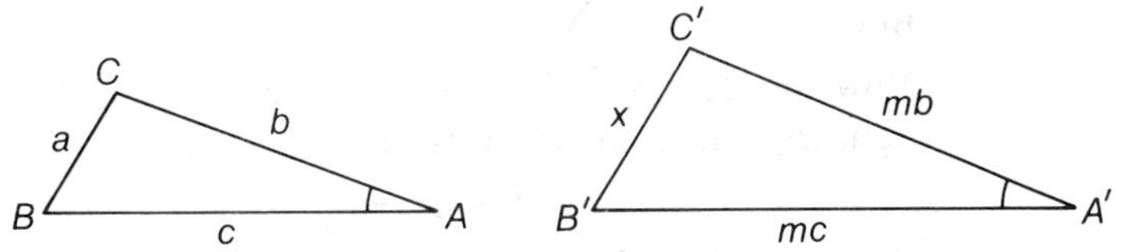

angles A and A' are equal and the scale factor for the sides that form these angles is m. If we can show that side x equals ma, then we have shown that the third sides are also proportional and the triangles are similar. If we write the law of cosines for each triangle, we get

$$a^2 = b^2 + c^2 - 2bc \cos A \qquad x^2 = m^2b^2 + m^2c^2 - 2m^2bc \cos A'$$

If we multiply both sides of the left-hand equation by m^2, we get

$$m^2a^2 = m^2b^2 + m^2c^2 - 2m^2bc \cos A$$

The right side of this equation is exactly the same as the expression for x^2, so we can write

$$x^2 = m^2a^2 \qquad \text{and thus} \qquad x = ma$$

Thus we see that the triangles are similar by SSS. Since the law of cosines is applicable to all triangles, this illustration is also applicable regardless of whether angle A is an acute angle, a right angle, or an obtuse angle.

AP3.B Proof of cos (A − B) and cos (A + B) identities

There are four identities to prove. We will prove them by first proving the identity

$$\cos (A - B) = \cos A \cos B + \sin A \sin B$$

and using this identity to prove the other three identities. We begin by reviewing the fact that the coordinates of a point on a unit circle equal the cosine of the angle and the sine of the angle.

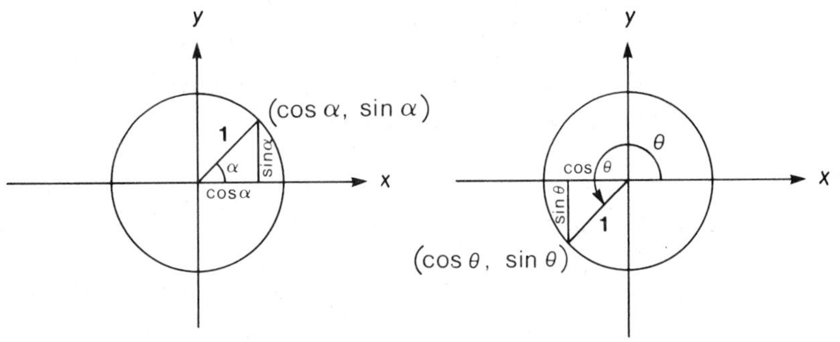

The circles are unit circles, so the length of the hypotenuse of each triangle is 1. The x coordinate of the point on the circle on the left on the preceding page is $\cos \alpha$ and the y coordinate is $\sin \alpha$, so the coordinates of the point are $(\cos \alpha, \sin \alpha)$. The same is true for the circle on the right except this time the angle is θ and thus the x and y coordinates are $(\cos \theta, \sin \theta)$.

In the circle shown below, we show angle α, angle θ, and angle $(\alpha + \theta)$ and indicate the coordinates of the endpoints of the terminal sides of the angles.

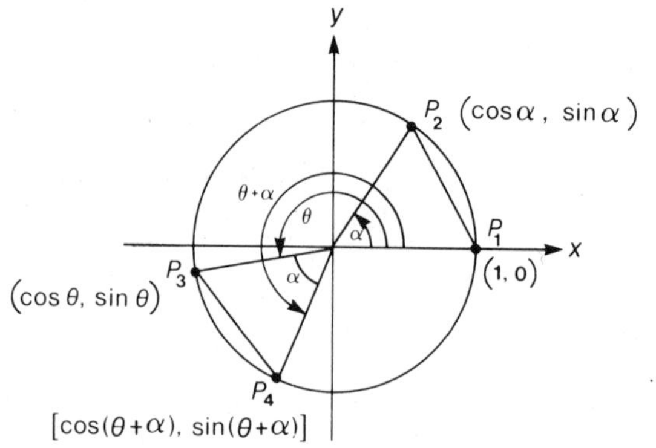

The proof is a little long but involves only the use of the distance formula and a few straightforward algebraic manipulations. The angles marked α are equal, and thus chord $\overline{P_1P_2}$ equals chord $\overline{P_3P_4}$. We use the distance formula to make this statement of equality.

$$\sqrt{(\cos \alpha - 1)^2 + (\sin \alpha - 0)^2} = \sqrt{[\cos (\alpha + \theta) - \cos \theta]^2 + [\sin (\alpha + \theta) - \sin \theta]^2}$$

Now we square both sides to remove the radical signs:

$$(\cos \alpha - 1)^2 + (\sin \alpha - 0)^2 = [\cos (\alpha + \theta) - \cos \theta]^2 + [\sin (\alpha + \theta) - \sin \theta]^2$$

Next the two terms on the left must be squared and the two terms on the right must be squared. We get

$$\cos^2 \alpha - 2 \cos \alpha + 1 + \sin^2 \alpha = \cos^2 (\alpha + \theta) - 2 \cos (\alpha + \theta) \cos \theta + \cos^2 \theta$$
$$+ \sin^2 (\alpha + \theta) - 2 \sin (\alpha + \theta) \sin \theta + \sin^2 \theta$$

We simplify on both sides to get

$$2 - 2 \cos \alpha = 2 - 2 \cos (\alpha + \theta) \cos \theta - 2 \sin (\alpha + \theta) \sin \theta$$

Now we add -2 to both sides to eliminate the constants and get

$$-2 \cos \alpha = -2 \cos (\alpha + \theta) \cos \theta - 2 \sin (\alpha + \theta) \sin \theta$$

Next we divide each term on both sides by -2 and get

$$\cos \alpha = \cos (\alpha + \theta) \cos \theta + \sin (\alpha + \theta) \sin \theta$$

Now we finish by using a change of variable. We let $\alpha = A - B$ and let $\theta = B$, and we get

$$\cos (A - B) = \cos (A - B + B) \cos B + \sin (A - B + B) \sin B$$

which simplifies to

$$\mathbf{\cos (A - B) = \cos A \cos B + \sin A \sin B}$$

Now to get the identity for $\cos (A + B)$, we replace B with $-B$ and get

$$\cos [A - (-B)] = \cos A \cos (-B) + \sin A \sin (-B)$$

If we simplify the left side we get

$$\cos (A + B) = \cos A \cos (-B) + \sin A \sin (-B)$$

Now we remember the basic identities $\cos(-\theta) = \cos\theta$ and $\sin(-\theta) = -\sin\theta$, so we can replace $\cos(-B)$ with $\cos B$ and replace $\sin(-B)$ with $-\sin B$, and we get

$$\cos(A+B) = \cos A \cos B + (\sin A)(-\sin B)$$

$$\mathbf{\cos(A+B) = \cos A \cos B - \sin A \sin B}$$

AP3.C Proof of sin (A + B) and sin (A − B) identities

We begin by restating the identity for $\cos(A - B)$:

$$(d) \quad \cos(A-B) = \cos A \cos B + \sin A \sin B$$

Now to review another basic identity, we draw a right triangle with one angle θ. Since θ and the other angle must sum to 90°, the other angle must be $90° - \theta$.

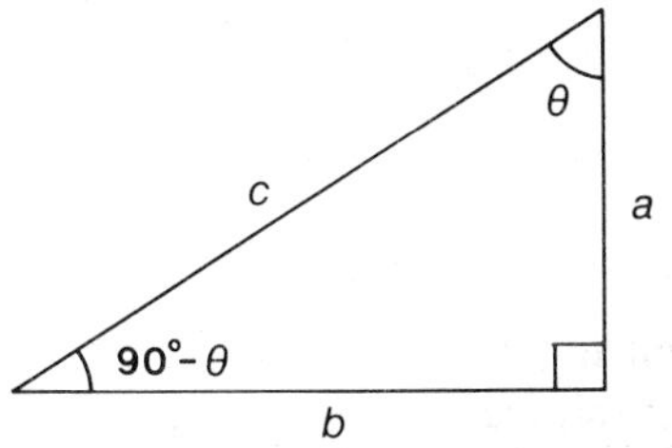

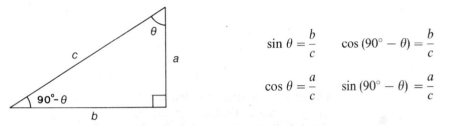

$$\sin\theta = \frac{b}{c} \qquad \cos(90° - \theta) = \frac{b}{c}$$

$$\cos\theta = \frac{a}{c} \qquad \sin(90° - \theta) = \frac{a}{c}$$

Thus, we refresh our memory and recall that $\sin\theta = \cos(90° - \theta)$ and that $\cos\theta = \sin(90° - \theta)$. This figure shows θ to be an acute angle. To show that these formulas are valid for all values of θ, we replace A with 90° and B with θ in equation (d) and get

$$\cos(90° - \theta) = \cos 90° \cos\theta + \sin 90° \sin\theta$$

But the value of cos 90° is 0 and that of sin 90° is 1. So

$$\cos(90° - \theta) = 0 \cdot \cos\theta + 1 \cdot \sin\theta$$

$$\mathbf{\cos(90° - \theta) = \sin\theta \qquad \text{for all } \theta}$$

Now if we replace θ with $(90° - \theta)$, we get

$$\mathbf{\cos\theta = \sin(90° - \theta) \qquad \text{for all } \theta}$$

Next, to prove the identity for $\sin(A + B)$, we replace θ with $(A + B)$.

$$\cos[90° - (A+B)] = \sin(A+B)$$

$$\cos[(90° - A) - B] = \sin(A+B)$$

Now on the left in this equation we use the identity for $\cos(A - B)$, and substitute $(90° - A)$ for A and substitute B for B.

$$\cos(90° - A)\cos B + \sin(90° - A)\sin B = \sin(A+B)$$

But $\cos(90° - A) = \sin A$ and $\sin(90° - A) = \cos A$. Therefore,

$$\mathbf{\sin A \cos B + \cos A \sin B = \sin(A+B)}$$

Now to prove the identity for $\sin(A - B)$, we replace B with $-B$ and get

$$\sin A \cos(-B) + \cos A \sin(-B) = \sin[A + (-B)]$$

but $\cos(-B) = \cos B$ and $\sin(-B) = -\sin B$. Therefore,

$$\sin A \cos B + (\cos A)(-\sin B) = \sin(A - B)$$

and thus

$$\mathbf{\sin A \cos B - \cos A \sin B = \sin(A - B)}$$

APPENDIX 4 Locus development of conics

AP4.A The parabola

A line is the locus of points equidistant from two designated points. The distance formula is used twice to write the equation of a line but is used only once to write the equation of a circle because the definition of a circle involves only one distance.

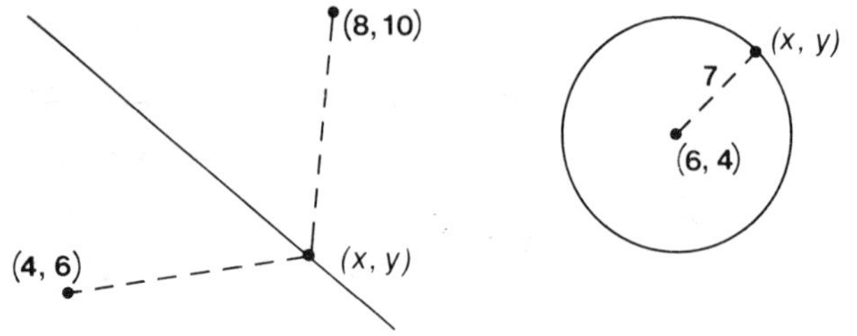

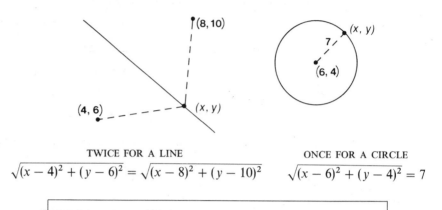

TWICE FOR A LINE

$$\sqrt{(x-4)^2+(y-6)^2}=\sqrt{(x-8)^2+(y-10)^2}$$

ONCE FOR A CIRCLE

$$\sqrt{(x-6)^2+(y-4)^2}=7$$

> **A *parabola* is the locus of all points that are equidistant from a line called the *directrix* and a point called the *focus*.**

Writing the equation of a parabola from the locus definition is another straightforward exercise in the use of the distance formula. Equations of parabolas whose axes of symmetry are not vertical or horizontal have an xy term and are rather involved. We will restrict our investigation to parabolas whose directrix is parallel to the x axis or the y axis.

Example AP4.A.1 Write the equation of the parabola whose focus is (6, 2) and whose directrix is $y = -4$.

Solution As usual, a sketch is very helpful.

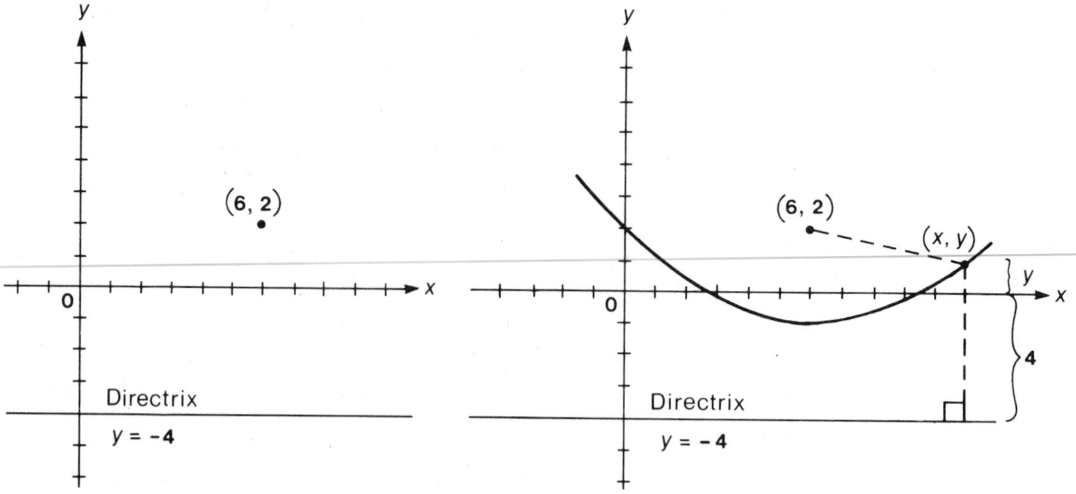

On the left we graph the focus (6, 2) and the directrix $y = -4$. On the right we sketch the parabola and locate a point (x, y) on this curve. The distance from point (x, y) to the directrix is $y + 4$, as we determine by inspection. We equate this distance to the distance from the focus to the point.

$$\sqrt{(x-6)^2 + (y-2)^2} = y + 4$$

This is the finished equation of a parabola in focus-directrix form. To get the general form of the equation, we begin by squaring both sides.

$$(x-6)^2 + (y-2)^2 = y^2 + 8y + 16$$

Now we square the terms on the left as indicated.

$$x^2 - 12x + 36 + y^2 - 4y + 4 = y^2 + 8y + 16$$

Now we add like terms and rearrange to get

$$x^2 - 12x - 12y + 24 = 0 \qquad \text{general form}$$

This is the general form of the equation of a parabola. If we complete the square on the x terms, we can rearrange the equation to get

$$y = \frac{1}{12}(x-6)^2 - 1 \qquad \text{standard form}$$

AP4.B The ellipse

The locus definition of an ellipse is very straightforward.

An *ellipse* is the locus of all points such that the sum of the distances from any one of these points to two fixed points (called *foci*) is a constant.

Example AP4.B.1 Write the equation of the ellipse whose foci are $(-3, 0)$ and $(3, 0)$ and for which the sum of the distances from any point to any point (x, y) on the ellipse is 10.

Solution We begin with a sketch.

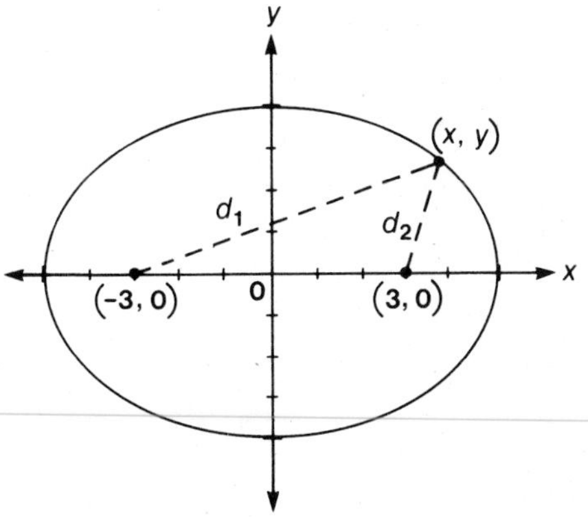

The sum of the distances d_1 and d_2 equals 10. Thus, we must use the distance formula twice.

$$\sqrt{[x-(-3)]^2 + [y-0]^2} + \sqrt{[x-(3)]^2 + (y-0)^2} = 10$$

which we simplify and write as

$$\sqrt{(x+3)^2 + y^2} + \sqrt{(x-3)^2 + y^2} = 10 \qquad \text{two-focus form}$$

The algebraic simplification is straightforward but laborious because we must square the equation twice. First we **isolate the first radical** by moving the second one to the right side.

$$\sqrt{x^2 + 6x + 9 + y^2} = 10 - \sqrt{x^2 - 6x + 9 + y^2}$$

Now we square both sides. This eliminates the radical on the left but not on the right.

$$x^2 + 6x + 9 + y^2 = 100 - 20\sqrt{x^2 - 6x + 9 + y^2} + x^2 - 6x + 9 + y^2$$

Now we rearrange so that the radical with its coefficient is isolated on the right.

$$12x - 100 = -20\sqrt{x^2 - 6x + 9 + y^2} \qquad \text{rearranged}$$

$$3x - 25 = -5\sqrt{x^2 - 6x + 9 + y^2} \qquad \text{divided by 4}$$

Finally, we can eliminate the last radical by squaring both sides.

$$9x^2 - 150x + 625 = 25x^2 - 150x + 225 + 25y^2$$

Then we rearrange to get

$$16x^2 + 25y^2 = 400$$

which we can write in standard form by dividing by 400.

$$\frac{x^2}{25} + \frac{y^2}{16} = 1 \qquad \text{standard form}$$

Example AP4.B.2 Complete the first step of finding the equation of the ellipse whose foci are at (3, 2) and (8, 2) and in which the sum of the distances from any point to the foci is 13.

Solution We begin with a sketch.

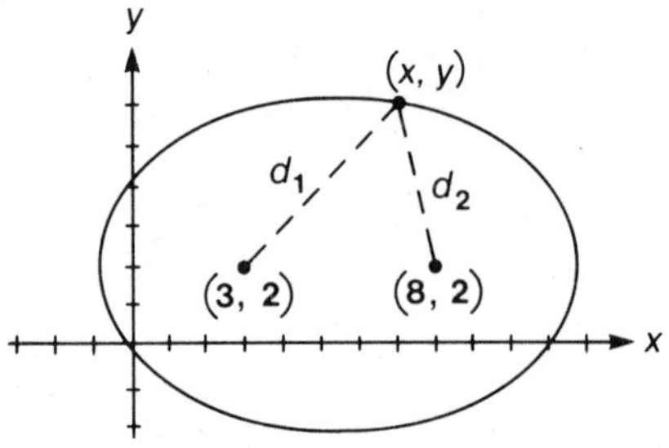

The sum of the distances d_1 and d_2 equals 13. We use the distance formula twice to write

$$\sqrt{(x-3)^2 + (y-2)^2} + \sqrt{(x-8)^2 + (y-2)^2} = 13$$

If further simplification is desired, it is necessary to isolate the radicals one at a time and square both sides each time.

AP4.C The hyperbola

The corresponding locus definition of the hyperbola is also straightforward but involves a difference rather than a sum.

> **A *hyperbola* is the locus of all points such that the absolute value of the difference of the distances from one of these points to the two foci is a constant.**

We will restrict our investigation of hyperbolas to those whose major axes are parallel to either the x or the y axis.

Example AP4.C.1 Find the equation of the hyperbola whose foci are $(-5, 0)$ and $(5, 0)$ and for which the difference of the distances is 6.

Solution We begin by making a sketch.

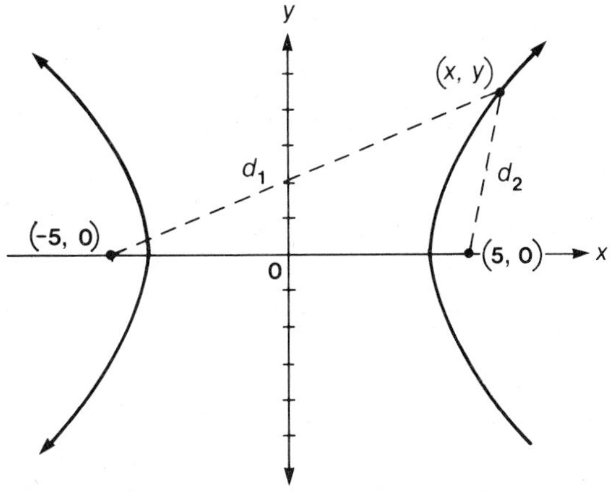

The figure has (x, y) on the right branch and shows that $d_1 - d_2$ will be positive. If (x, y) is on the left branch, $d_1 - d_2$ will be negative. To cover both cases we will use the distance formula to write the equation that says that $d_1 - d_2 = \pm 6$.

$$\sqrt{[x-(-5)]^2 + [y-(0)]^2} - \sqrt{[x-(5)]^2 + [y-(0)]^2} = \pm 6$$

Now we simplify and get

$$\sqrt{(x+5)^2 + y^2} - \sqrt{(x-5)^2 + y^2} = \pm 6$$

To eliminate the radicals, we must isolate them one at a time and square both sides of the equation. First we isolate the left-hand radical.

$$\sqrt{(x+5)^2 + y^2} = \sqrt{(x-5)^2 + y^2} \pm 6$$

If we now square both sides, we can get rid of the left-hand radical but will still have a radical on the right-hand side.

$$(x+5)^2 + y^2 = (x-5)^2 + y^2 \pm 12\sqrt{(x-5)^2 + y^2} + 36$$

Now we simplify outside of the radical, rearrange, and get

$$5x - 9 = \pm 3\sqrt{(x-5)^2 + y^2}$$

Now if we square both sides, we can finally get rid of the ambiguous $\pm$ sign and also the remaining radical.

$$25x^2 - 90x + 81 = 9[(x-5)^2 + y^2]$$

We can finish by expanding and rearranging to get

$$16x^2 - 9y^2 = 144$$

which we put into standard form by dividing every term by 144.

$$\frac{x^2}{9} - \frac{y^2}{16} = 1 \qquad \text{standard form}$$

Example AP4.C.2 Complete the first step of finding the equation of the hyperbola whose foci are at (4, 6) and (4, −2) and for which the difference of the distances is 5.

Solution A sketch always helps.

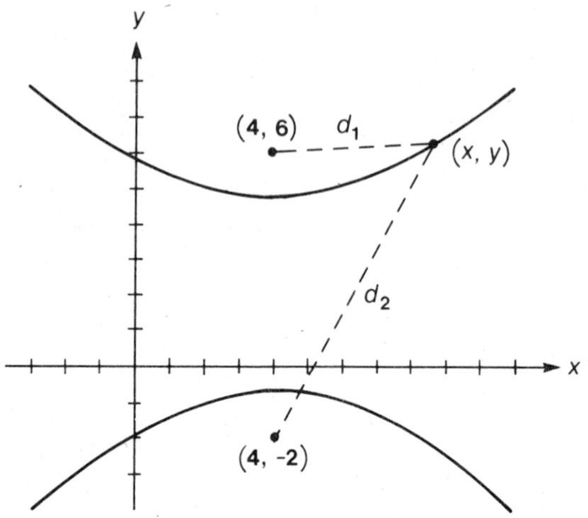

The equation will be

One distance minus the other distance equals ±5

$$\sqrt{(x-4)^2+(y-6)^2}-\sqrt{(x-4)^2+(y+2)^2}=\pm 5$$

The radicals can be eliminated by isolating them one at a time and squaring both sides of the equation. If we study astronomy, we find that comets often travel along hyperbolic paths. One focus for the path of a comet is the sun. In the diagram above the lower focus can represent the position of the sun, and thus the lower branch of the hyperbola represents the path of the comet. The upper branch and the upper focus are not considered for this application.

Answers

Problem set A

1. C **2.** C **3.** A **4.** B **5.** 1775 **6.** 36 **7.** $-\dfrac{6}{23}$ **8.** $\dfrac{40}{7}$ **9.** 19

10. (21, 5) **11.** (9, 10) **12.** 32 **13.** 36 **14.** 16 **15.** (3, 2, 1) **16.** (1, 2, 1)

17. $\left(-\dfrac{1}{2}, 1, 2\right)$ **18.** $(1, -1, 2)$ **19.** (2, 4, 3) **20.** $\left(3, 2, \dfrac{1}{2}\right)$

21. $(x^3y^2)^{1/2}(xy^3)^{1/4} = x^{3/2}yx^{1/4}y^{3/4} = x^{7/4}y^{7/4}$

22. $x^{3/4}(xy)^{1/2}x^{1/2}(x^4)^{1/3} = x^{3/4}x^{1/2}y^{1/2}x^{1/2}x^{4/3} = x^{37/12}y^{1/2}$ **23.** $a^{-7x/2}y^{1+(3x/2)}$

24. $y^{x+3}y^{x/2-1}z^a y^{-(x-a)/2}z^{-(x-a)/3} = y^{x+2+a/2}z^{4a/3-x/3} = y^{(2x+4+a)/2}z^{(4a-x)/3}$ **25.** $4\sqrt{6}$

26. $-\dfrac{73\sqrt{21}}{21}$ **27.** $\sqrt{2} - (1 + \sqrt{2})\sqrt{x} + x$ **28.** $3 + 2\sqrt{3}\sqrt{x} + x$ **29.** $x(\sqrt{6} + \sqrt{2})$

30. $\dfrac{x^2 + y^2}{xy}$

Problem set B

1. 1200 **2.** 119 **3.** $1 - i$ **4.** $(4 - 9\sqrt{2}) + (2\sqrt{3} + 4)i$ **5.** $-3 - 2\sqrt{2}\,i$

6. $(2 + 3\sqrt{2})i$ **7.** $\dfrac{1}{10} + \dfrac{4}{5}i$ **8.** $\dfrac{-17 - 14\sqrt{3}}{23}$ **9.** $\dfrac{2}{5} - \dfrac{2}{5}i$ **10.** $-\dfrac{1}{6} \pm \dfrac{\sqrt{59}}{6}i$

11. $-\dfrac{1}{2} \pm \dfrac{3}{2}i$ **12.** Refer to Review Lesson B **13.** $-\dfrac{1}{3} \pm \dfrac{\sqrt{14}}{3}i$ **14.** $-1, \dfrac{4}{3}$

15. $-\dfrac{3}{4} \pm \dfrac{\sqrt{47}}{4}i$ **16.** A **17.** C **18.** $-\dfrac{22}{13}$ **19.** (12, 10) **20.** $\dfrac{11}{2}$ **21.** $(3, 2, -2)$

22. (1, 2, 4) **23.** (3, 2, 1) **24.** $(2, -1, -1)$

25. $x^{2/3}(x^2)^{1/3}y(x^2y)^{1/5} = x^{2/3}x^{2/3}yx^{2/5}y^{1/5} = x^{26/15}y^{6/5}$

26. $y^{x/2+1}y^{a/2}2y^{2a+3} = 2y^{5a/2+x/2+4}$ **27.** $\dfrac{17\sqrt{6}}{3}$ **28.** $2 + 2\sqrt{2}\sqrt{x} + x$

29. $x + 2x^{1/2}y^{1/2} + y$ **30.** $\dfrac{b + a^2}{ab^2}$

Problem set C

1. $N_G = 80, N_B = 200$ **2.** $N_R = 40, N_B = 100$ **3.** 10,650.27 ft **4.** $4.11\underline{/-41.95^\circ}$

5. $7.68\underline{/108.20^\circ}$ **6.** $0.75i + 8.57j$ **7.** $-5.93i - 4.47j$ **8.** $(\sqrt{6} - 2) + (3 - \sqrt{2})i$

9. $-4 - 2\sqrt{3}$ **10.** $2 + i$ **11.** $-\dfrac{1}{5} + \dfrac{12}{5}i$ **12.** $-\dfrac{1}{4} \pm \dfrac{\sqrt{39}}{4}i$ **13.** $\dfrac{1}{3} \pm \dfrac{\sqrt{22}}{3}$

14. Refer to Review Lesson B **15.** $\frac{1}{4} \pm \frac{\sqrt{39}}{4}i$ **16.** $-\frac{1}{3} \pm \frac{\sqrt{11}}{3}i$ **17.** D **18.** D

19. $\left(\frac{1}{2}, \frac{1}{4}\right)$ **20.** 3 **21.** $(2, -2, 1)$ **22.** $(3, 3, 2)$ **23.** $(3, 4, 4)$ **24.** $(4, 2, 1)$

25. $a^{49/15}b^{23/15}$ **26.** $x^{-3a/2-4}y^{(b-3-a)/2}$ **27.** $\frac{101\sqrt{14}}{14}$ **28.** $x - x^{1/2}y^{-1/2} + x^{1/2}y^{1/2} - 1$

29. $2\sqrt{2} - 2x - \sqrt{2}\sqrt{x} + x\sqrt{x}$ **30.** $\frac{x+y}{y^2}$

Problem set D

1. $\frac{W}{H} = \frac{7}{3}$, $3H = 2W - 40$; $W = 56$, $H = 24$

2. $0.14N_B + 0.2N_G = 54$, $5N_B = 2N_G + 100$, $N_B = 100$, $N_G = 200$ **3.** $\sin 20° = \frac{2000}{d}$; d = 5847.61 ft

4. $y = x + 9$ **5.** $y = \frac{3}{2}x + 8$ **6.** $\frac{xc + bac}{c - ka}$ **7.** $\frac{p(c+b)}{2mc + mb}$ **8.** $\frac{a(pc+m)}{xpc + xm + yc}$

9. $y = \frac{ma}{x} + \frac{mb}{mc} \rightarrow y = \frac{m^2ac + mbx}{xmc} \rightarrow yxmc = m^2ac + mbx \rightarrow yxmc - m^2ac = mbx$

$\rightarrow c(yxm - m^2a) = mbx \rightarrow c = \frac{mbx}{yxm - m^2a} = \frac{bx}{yx - ma}$

10. $\frac{pmya}{byx - pmb}$ **11.** $x^2 + 2x + 4 + \frac{7}{x-2}$ **12.** $8.23\underline{/149.32°}$ **13.** $5.16\underline{/-35.54°}$

14. $-13.59i - 6.34j$ **15.** $31.21i - 28.10j$ **16.** $(1 - \sqrt{2})i$ **17.** $\frac{-21 - 11\sqrt{3}}{104}$

18. $\frac{3}{5} - \frac{16}{5}i$ **19.** $-\frac{1}{6} \pm \frac{\sqrt{71}}{6}i$ **20.** $1 \pm \frac{3\sqrt{2}}{2}$ **21.** Refer to Review Lesson B

22. $\frac{1}{15} \pm \frac{4\sqrt{14}}{15}i$ **23.** C **24.** B **25.** $(3, -3, 2)$ **26.** $(3, 2, 1)$ **27.** $(2, -2, 3)$

28. $a^{8/15}b^{59/15}$ **29.** $x^{(-5a/3)-2}y^{(b-2-2a)/3}$ **30.** $4x^{3/2} - y^{-1}$

Problem set E

1. $N_B = N_W + N_G - 7$, $N_G = 1 + N_B + N_W$, $N_G = 3N_B$; $N_B = 2$, $N_W = 3$, $N_G = 6$

2. $N_Q + N_N + N_D = 20$, $25N_Q + 5N_N + 10N_D = 205$, $N_D = 3N_Q$; $N_N = 8$, $N_D = 9$, $N_Q = 3$

3. $R = \frac{kB}{G^2}$ or $\frac{R_1}{R_2} = \frac{B_1G_2^2}{B_2G_1^2}$; $R = 10$ **4.** $T + U = 13$, $10U + T = 45 + 10T + U$; $N = 49$

5. $0.47(89) + 0.14(P_N) = 0.29(89 + P_N) \rightarrow P_N = 106.8$ oz **6.** $\frac{35}{78}W = 400$, $W = 891.43$ g

7. $y = -\frac{2}{5}x + \frac{11}{5}$ **8.** $\frac{m^2x + 7ya^2}{p^2a - 3x}$ **9.** $\frac{m(d+c)}{ad + ac + bd}$ **10.** $\frac{k(xd+c)}{axd + ac + bd}$

11. $\frac{xkb}{x^2 + akb}$ **12.** $\frac{2pm}{m^2c^2 - ap}$ **13.** $x^2 + 1 - \frac{1}{x^2 - 1}$ **14.** $-6.06i - 2.58j$

15. $-15.06i + 14.22j$ **16.** $-3 + 3i$ **17.** $\frac{-18 - 10\sqrt{3}}{3}$ **18.** $-\frac{21}{17} - \frac{1}{17}i$

19. $-\frac{1}{4} \pm \frac{\sqrt{19}}{4}i$ **20.** $\frac{7}{4}, -1$ **21.** Refer to Review Lesson B **22.** $\frac{1}{3} \pm \frac{\sqrt{11}}{3}i$ **23.** B

24. A **25.** $(2, -1, 3)$ **26.** $(4, 2, -2)$ **27.** $(3, -3, 2)$ **28.** $x^{9/2}y^{1/2}a^2b^{2/3}$

29. $x^{(-5a/2)-3}y^{(b-3)/2-2a/3}$ **30.** $4x^a - y^b$

Problem set F

1. $N_R = N_B + N_W - 11$, $N_W = N_R + N_B - 3$, $N_W = 1 + N_B$; $N_R = 4$, $N_B = 7$, $N_W = 8$
2. $N_N + N_D + N_P = 30$, $5N_N + 10N_D + 1N_P = 135$, $N_P = 2N_D$; $N_N = 15$, $N_D = 5$, $N_P = 10$
3. $B = \dfrac{kG^2}{T}$ or $\dfrac{B_1}{B_2} = \dfrac{G_1^2T_2}{G_2^2T_1}$; 1280 boys 4. $T + U = 5$, $10U + T = 27 + 10T + U$; 14, 41
5. $0.9(P_N) + 0.58(D_N) = 0.78(20)$, $P_N + D_N = 20$; 12.5 liters 90%, 7.5 liters 58%
6. $0.06(370) + 0.135(P_N) = 0.1(370 + P_N)$; $P_N = 422.86$ ml 7. $y = -\dfrac{3}{2}x + 1$
8. $\left(-\dfrac{1}{2} + \dfrac{\sqrt{17}}{2}, \dfrac{1}{2} + \dfrac{\sqrt{17}}{2}\right), \left(-\dfrac{1}{2} - \dfrac{\sqrt{17}}{2}, \dfrac{1}{2} - \dfrac{\sqrt{17}}{2}\right)$ 9. $(1, \pm 2\sqrt{2}), (-1, \pm 2\sqrt{2})$
10. $(-1 + \sqrt{5}, -1 - \sqrt{5}), (-1 - \sqrt{5}, -1 + \sqrt{5})$ 11. $(2x^2y + p)(4x^4y^2 - 2x^2yp + p^2)$
12. $(3x^4y^2 - z^3)(9x^8y^4 + 3x^4y^2z^3 + z^6)$ 13. $\dfrac{\dfrac{n^2a + 7pb^3}{b^3a}}{\dfrac{r^2b^2 - 4a}{b^3a}} = \dfrac{n^2a + 7pb^3}{r^2b^2 - 4a}$
14. $\dfrac{m(2h + g)}{2ch + cg + fh}$ 15. $3k^2bc + \dfrac{18y^3}{d}$ 16. $x^2 - x - 2 - \dfrac{7}{x - 2}$ 17. $-0.88i - 7.32j$
18. $2 + (10 + \sqrt{3})i$ 19. $\dfrac{-99 - 28\sqrt{3}}{382}$ 20. $\dfrac{17}{25} - \dfrac{19}{25}i$ 21. $x = \dfrac{1}{2} \pm \dfrac{\sqrt{39}}{6}i$
22. $-\dfrac{3}{2} \pm \dfrac{3}{2}i$ 23. D 24. B 25. $(1, 1, -1)$ 26. $(2, 1, 3)$ 27. $(4, 2, 1)$
28. $x^6y^{11/6}$ 29. $x^{-5a/3-2}y^{(b-2a)/3-2/3}$ 30. $6x^a - 2x^{a/2}y^{b/3} - 4y^{2b/3}$

Problem set 1

1. $T + U = 12$, $\dfrac{U}{T} = \dfrac{1}{2}$; 84
2. $N_N + N_D + N_Q = 12$, $5N_N + 10N_D + 25N_Q = 155$, $N_N = N_Q + 1$; 4 quarters, 5 nickels, 3 dimes
3. $0.40R + 0.60G = 56$, $\dfrac{R}{G} = \dfrac{1}{4}$; 20 reds, 80 greens
4. $0.2(20) + 1(P_n) = 0.5(20 + P_n)$ or $0.8(20) + 0(P_n) = 0.5(20 + P_n)$; 12 lb
5. $2R = 3B + 8$, $\dfrac{R}{R + B} = \dfrac{5}{7}$; 4 blues, 10 reds
6. $0.035(100) + 0(P_N) = 0.015(100 + P_N)$; $P_N = 133.3$ ounces 7. $y = \dfrac{3}{5}x + \dfrac{6}{5}$
8. $4\sqrt{3}$

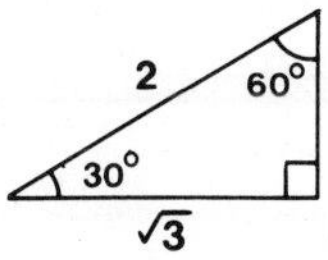

9. $3\sqrt{6}$

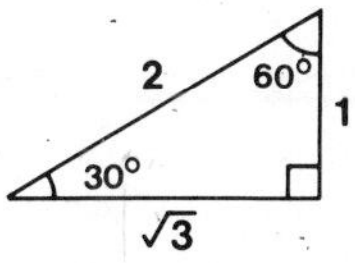

10. $3\sqrt{6}$

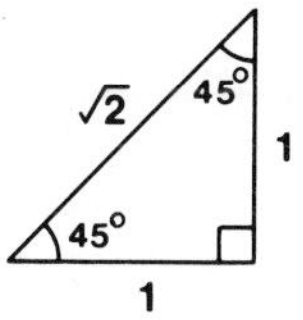

11. $\left(-\dfrac{2}{5} + \dfrac{2\sqrt{11}}{5}, \dfrac{1}{5} + \dfrac{4\sqrt{11}}{5}\right), \left(-\dfrac{2}{5} - \dfrac{2\sqrt{11}}{5}, \dfrac{1}{5} - \dfrac{4\sqrt{11}}{5}\right)$
12. $(3xy^2 + 2p)(9x^2y^4 - 6xy^2p + 4p^2)$ 13. $(2xy^4 - 3z^3)(4x^2y^8 + 6xy^4z^3 + 9z^6)$
14. $\dfrac{n^3a - 7p^2b^3}{s^3b - 5t}$ 15. $\dfrac{x(3t + s)}{6yt + 2ys - 6zt}$ 16. $y = \dfrac{3}{4}s^2df + \dfrac{21x^3}{4g}$ 17. $x^2 + 1 - \dfrac{5}{x^2 - 1}$
18. $1.02i - 5.06j$ 19. $(-12 + 3\sqrt{3} + 2\sqrt{2})i$ 20. $\dfrac{70 + 2\sqrt{6}}{69}$ 21. $\dfrac{1}{10} - \dfrac{7}{10}i$
22. $1 \pm \dfrac{\sqrt{2}}{2}i$ 23. $-\dfrac{5}{6} \pm \dfrac{\sqrt{71}}{6}i$ 24. A 25. A 26. $(1, 2, 3)$ 27. $(1, 3, 2)$
28. $(4, 3, 2)$ 29. $x^{9/2-a/3}y^{-5a/3}$ 30. $6x^{5a/6} - 9z^{2b/3}x^{a/2} - 8z^{b/3}x^{a/3} + 12z^b$

Problem set 2

1. $T + U = 9$, $10U + T = 10T + U - 9$; 54, 45
2. $N_N + N_D + N_S = 35$, $5N_N + 10N_D + 100N_S = 1225$, $N_S = 2N_N$; 10 silver dollars, 5 nickels, 20 dimes
3. $0.73(143) + 0.37(P_N) = 0.51(143 + P_N)$; $P_N = 224.71$ liters
4. $G = R + B + 9$, $B + G = 4R + 1$, $R = 2 + B$; 2 blues, 4 reds, 15 greens

5. $24\frac{15}{16}$ 6. $y = -x + 3$ 7. (a) 0.0168 (b) 2.4414×10^8

8. 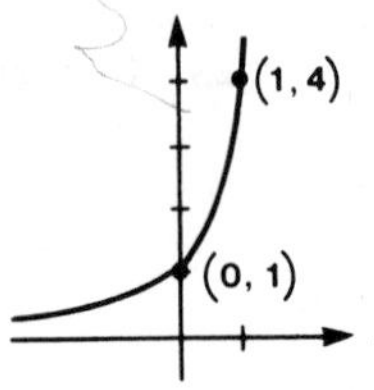

9. 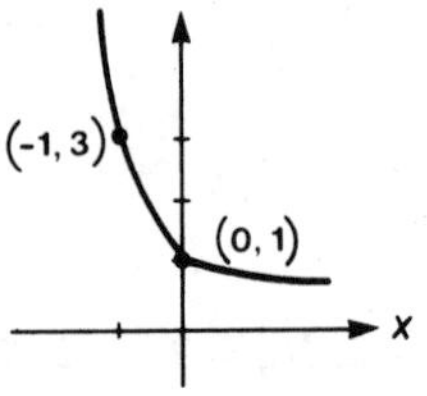

10. $2\sqrt{3}$ 11. 8

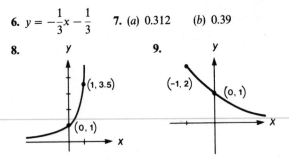

12. $\left(\frac{3+\sqrt{33}}{2}, \frac{-3+\sqrt{33}}{2}\right), \left(\frac{3-\sqrt{33}}{2}, \frac{-3-\sqrt{33}}{2}\right)$ 13. $(4ab^3 - 2p)(16a^2b^6 + 8ab^3p + 4p^2)$

14. $(3b^3a^2 - 4c)(9b^6a^4 + 12b^3a^2c + 16c^2)$ 15. $\frac{a^3y - 6m^2x}{l^2x^2 - 6ty^2}$ 16. $\frac{3x(8l + k)}{32yl + 4ky - 12lz}$

17. $z = \frac{36}{5}ts^2 + \frac{24m}{5n}$ 18. $x^3 + 2x^2 + 4x + 6 + \frac{13}{x - 2}$ 19. $-6.81i - 1.18j$

20. $-6 + (17 + 3\sqrt{3})i$ 21. $\frac{33 - 5\sqrt{3}}{26}$ 22. $1 + 2i$ 23. $\frac{5}{6} \pm \frac{\sqrt{23}}{6}i$ 24. $-\frac{3}{4} \pm \frac{3\sqrt{5}}{4}$

25. A 26. C 27. (1, −1, 3) 28. (5, 2, 4) 29. $a^{7x/2-1}b^{2x+y}$

30. $6x^{3a}y^{2a} - 3x^{5a} - 4y^{5a/2} + 2x^{2a}y^{a/2}$

Problem set 3

1. $T + U = 8$, $10U + T = 10T + U - 36$; 62, 26
2. $N_P + N_N + N_Q = 24$, $N_P + 5N_N + 25N_Q = 160$, $N_N = N_P$; 10 pennies, 10 nickels, 4 quarters
3. $9 + 0(P_n) = 0.25(27 + P_n)$ or $18 + 1(P_n) = 0.75(27 + P_n)$; 9 gal
4. $2(B + G) = R + 4$, $R + B = G + 7$, $R = 2G$; 2 blues, 5 greens, 10 reds 5. $4\frac{1}{2}W = 2\frac{1}{5}$; $\frac{22}{45}$

6. $y = -\frac{1}{3}x - \frac{1}{3}$ 7. (a) 0.312 (b) 0.39

8. 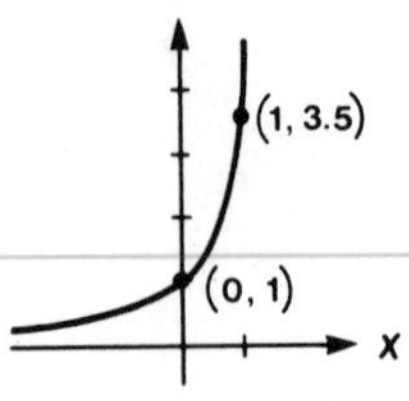

9. 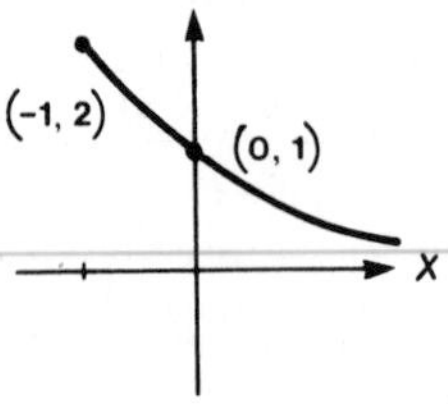

10. $\sqrt{6}$ 11. $2\sqrt{6}$ 12. The two line segments have the same length
13. An angle whose measure is between 0° and 90° 14. (3, 3), (3, −3), (−3, 3), (−3, −3)

15. $(2xb^2 - 3p)(4x^2b^4 + 6xb^2p + 9p^2)$ 16. $\frac{\frac{b^3c - 6m^2a}{a^2c^2}}{\frac{x^3c - 6ya^2}{a^2c^2}} = \frac{b^3c - 6m^2a}{x^3c - 6ya^2}$

17. $\dfrac{3s(l+k)}{2ml+2mk-zl}$

18. $3z = \dfrac{12ms}{nt} - \dfrac{8ml}{nk} \to 3z = \dfrac{12msk - 8mlt}{ntk} \to 3zntk = 12msk - 8mlt \to 3zntk + 8mlt = 12msk$

$\to t(3znk + 8ml) = 12msk \to t = \dfrac{12msk}{3znk + 8ml}$

19. $x^2 - 4x - 11 - \dfrac{21}{x-2}$ **20.** $-8.26i + 0.43j$ **21.** $-10 + (3\sqrt{3} + 26)i$

22. $\dfrac{-78 + 22\sqrt{6}}{15}$ **23.** $\dfrac{4}{3} + 4i$ **24.** $\dfrac{3}{4} \pm \dfrac{\sqrt{11}}{4}i$ **25.** A **26.** D **27.** (2, 4, 1)

28. (4, 6, 1) **29.** $x^{5a+3/2}y^{-2a+4}$ **30.** $36x^3 - 4y$

Problem set 4

1. $N_D = 10$, $N_Q = 2$, $N_H = 2$ **2.** 73, 37

3. $0.0475(176) + 0.035P_N = 0.04(176 + P_N)$; $P_N = 264$ ml **4.** $N_R = 3$, $N_B = 2$, $N_G = 4$

5. $\dfrac{66}{25}$ **6.** $y = \dfrac{3}{5}x - \dfrac{9}{5}$ **7.** (*a*) 1733.25 (*b*) 0.62

8.

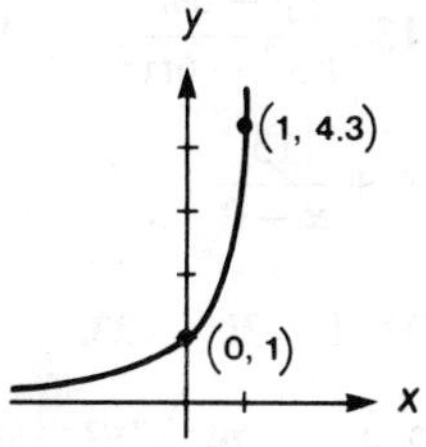

9.

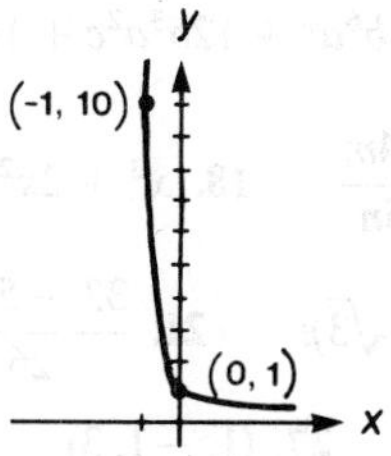

10. $\dfrac{1+\sqrt{2}}{2}$ **11.** $\dfrac{3+2\sqrt{3}}{3}$ **12.** $\dfrac{1+\sqrt{2}}{2}$ **13.** $\dfrac{4+\sqrt{2}}{2}$

14. $\left(\dfrac{2+\sqrt{19}}{5}, \dfrac{1-2\sqrt{19}}{5}\right); \left(\dfrac{2-\sqrt{19}}{5}, \dfrac{1+2\sqrt{19}}{5}\right)$ **15.** $(3a^2b^3 - 2p)(9a^4b^6 + 6a^2b^3p + 4p^2)$

16. $\dfrac{ac^3 - 6m^3xy}{d^2xy^2 - x^3yg}$ **17.** $\dfrac{2z(mt-s)}{mt - s - 3kt}$

18. $4s = \dfrac{3zat^2}{2m} - \dfrac{18z}{h} \to 4s = \dfrac{3zat^2h - 36zm}{2mh} \to 8smh = 3zat^2h - 36zm \to 8smh - 3zat^2h$

$= -36zm \to h(8sm - 3zat^2) = -36zm \to h = \dfrac{36zm}{3zat^2 - 8sm}$

19. $x^3 - x + \dfrac{x-3}{x^2+1}$ **20.** $11.32i + 8.14j$ **21.** $-24 - 22i$ **22.** $\dfrac{-6+3\sqrt{2}}{4}$

23. $-\dfrac{1}{2} - 2i$ **24.** $-\dfrac{1}{5} \pm \dfrac{\sqrt{31}}{5}$ **25.** A **26.** B **27.** $(-1, 2, 2)$ **28.** (10, 4, 2)

29. $a^{3z+6}(b^{3/4})^{3z+2}b^{-3z+2}a^{-4z+3} = a^{-z+9}b^{-3z/4+7/2}$

30. $12 - 6z^{-3/4}x^{-1/2} + 4x^{1/2}z^{1/4} - 2z^{-1/2}$

Problem set 5

1. $O_N - 5 = 2(W_N - 5)$, $O_N + 5 = \dfrac{3}{2}(W_N + 5)$; $O_N = 25$, $W_N = 15$ **2.** $\dfrac{2}{3}T + \dfrac{3}{2}T = 5\dfrac{1}{3}$; $\dfrac{32}{13}$ hr

3. $\dfrac{3}{5} \cdot 3 + R_F \cdot 3 = 3$; $\dfrac{2}{5}\dfrac{\text{sandcastle}}{\text{hr}}$ **4.** $RCD = d$, $\left(\dfrac{1}{6 \cdot 9}\right)C \cdot 5 = 3$; $32\dfrac{2}{5}$ cows **5.** 68

6. $y = \dfrac{1}{2}x - \dfrac{1}{2}$ **7.** (*a*) 133.31 (*b*) 0.16

8. 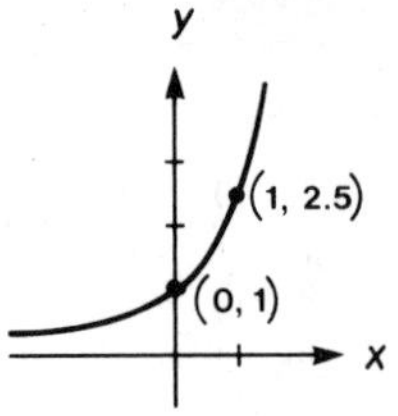

9. 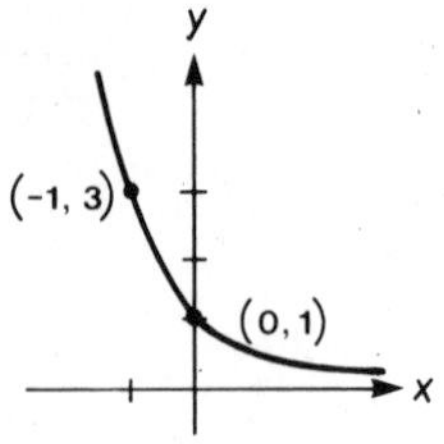

10. $\frac{1-2\sqrt{3}}{2}$ **11.** 0 **12.** 1 **13.** $\frac{3\sqrt{2}-4\sqrt{3}}{6}$

14. $(\sqrt{5}, 2), (\sqrt{5}, -2), (-\sqrt{5}, 2), (-\sqrt{5}, -2)$ **15.** $(2xy^2 - 3a^2b^3)(4x^2y^4 + 6xy^2a^2b^3 + 9a^4b^6)$

16. $\frac{b^2cy - 6m^2x}{mfy^2 + hx^3}$ **17.** $\frac{3s(mr-q)}{2mr - 2q - 6lr}$ **18.** $\frac{18kmt}{5sm^2 + 12k^2}$

19. $x^3 - 4x^2 - x - 2 - \frac{9}{x-2}$ **20.** $10.16i + 10.76j$ **21.** $-6 - 25i$ **22.** $\frac{-48 + 25\sqrt{3}}{11}$

23. $-\frac{2}{3}$ **24.** $-\frac{1}{4} \pm \frac{\sqrt{201}}{12}$ **25.** D **26.** A **27.** $(2, 1, -2)$ **28.** $(9, 4, 2)$

29. $a^{-2z-5}b^{2z+11}$ **30.** $9x - 4z^{1/2}$

Problem set 6

1. $C_N + 10 = 2(E_N + 10), C_N - 5 = 5(E_N - 5); C_N = 30, E_N = 10$ **2.** $\frac{1}{30}T + \frac{1}{40}T = \frac{2}{3}; \frac{80}{7}$ min

3. $RDM = F, \left(\frac{360}{20 \cdot 10}\right) \cdot D \cdot 25 = 360$; 8 days

4. $R_S = R_R - 20, R_RT_R = 325, R_ST_S = 450, T_R = \frac{1}{2}T_S; R_R = 65$ mph, $T_R = 5$ hr, $R_S = 45$ mph, $T_S = 10$ hr

5. 800 liters **6.** 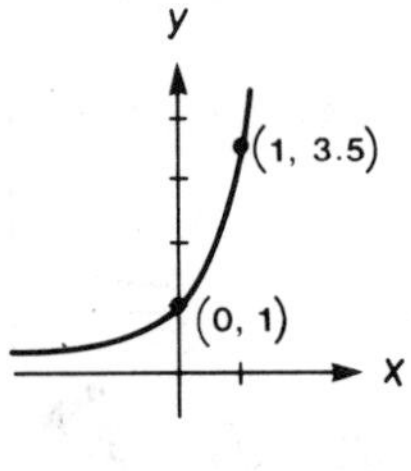

7. 0 **8.** $\frac{\sqrt{2}-2}{2}$ **9.** 0 **10.** 0

11. $k^p = 7$ **12.** $\log_k 7 = p$ **13.** 3 **14.** -3 **15.** 16 **16.** $(1, -1)$

17. $(4x^4y^2 - 3a^2b^3)(16x^8y^4 + 12x^4y^2a^2b^3 + 9a^4b^6)$ **18.** $\frac{cd^2 - 6m^2y^2}{x(mfy + hx)}$ **19.** $\frac{2zr}{3spr + 2q}$

20. $-7.17i + 6.92j$ **21.** $-6\sqrt{3} - 6 - 4i$ **22.** $\frac{-62 + 24\sqrt{3}}{23}$ **23.** $\frac{5}{4} - \frac{3}{4}i$

24. $\frac{3}{4} \pm \frac{\sqrt{73}}{4}$ **25.** D **26.** B **27.** $(6, 2, 1)$ **28.** $(3, 4, 2)$ **29.** $x^{-a+5}b^{2a^2-4a}$

30. $4x - 6z^{1/2}x^{2/3} + 6x^{1/3}z^{1/2} - 9z$

Problem set 7

1. $G_N + 1 = 2(M_N + 1), G_N - 5 = 8(M_N - 5); G_N = 13, M_N = 6$

2. $\frac{1}{10}(4) + R_A(4) = \frac{7}{10} \to R_A = \frac{3}{40}\frac{\text{cakes}}{\text{min}}; \frac{40}{3}$ min

3. $(B + W)3 = 30, (B - W)5 = 30; B = 8$ mph, $W = 2$ mph 4. $\frac{A_1S_1^2}{W_1} = \frac{A_2S_2^2}{W_2}$; 36 acorns

5. $RTW = J, \left(\frac{6}{2 \cdot 3}\right)T \cdot 6 = 6$; 1 day 6.

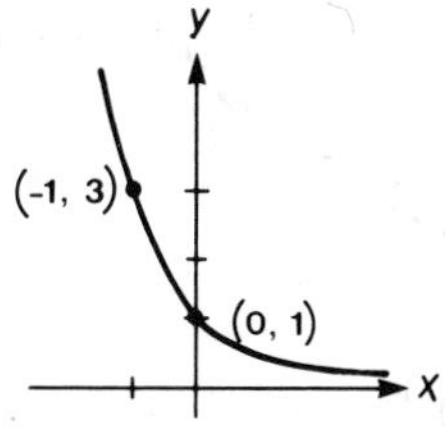

7. $\sqrt{2}$

8. -1 9. 1 10. $\frac{-2+\sqrt{3}}{4}$ 11. $m^n = 8$ 12. $\log_3 7 = k$ 13. 4 14. -3

15. 4 16. $(0, 4), \left(-\frac{12}{5}, -\frac{16}{5}\right)$ 17. $3y^{2n+1}(1 + 4y^{n+1})$ 18. $\frac{abc^2 - c^3d^2a}{mnd - nb^2}$

19. $\frac{3zp}{50tp + k}$ 20. $2.21i + 5.56j$ 21. $-6 + (13 - 6\sqrt{6})i$ 22. $\frac{-27 + 15\sqrt{2}}{31}$

23. $\frac{8}{5} + \frac{16}{5}i$ 24. $\frac{1}{4} \pm \frac{\sqrt{7}}{4}i$ 25. D 26. A 27. $(5, 10, 4)$ 28. $x^{-a/2+13/2}$

29. $-27 - 18z^{1/2}x^{-1/3} + 18x^{1/3}z^{-1/2}$ 30. $y = \frac{2}{3}x - \frac{7}{3}$

Problem set 8

1. $D_N + 7 = 3T_N, D_N = 2T_N; D_N = 14, T_N = 7$

2. $4R_I = \frac{13}{20}; R_I = \frac{13}{80}\frac{\text{missions}}{\text{hr}} \rightarrow \frac{80}{13}$ hr for Irwin to complete the mission alone

3. $R\left(\frac{x}{p} - 2\right) = x; R = \frac{xp}{x - 2p}$ mph 4. $(R + 5)T_{\text{new}} = RT + 20; T_{\text{new}} = \frac{RT + 20}{R + 5}$ hr

5. $RTW = J \rightarrow R = \frac{3}{7.5}$

$RTW = J \rightarrow \left(\frac{3}{7.5}\right)T(6) = 4$

$\rightarrow T = \frac{14}{3}$ days

6.

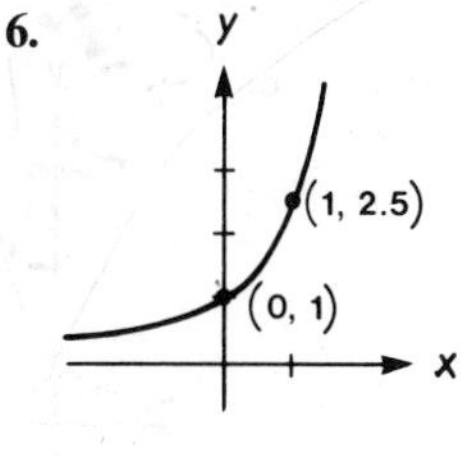

7. $-\frac{3}{2}$

8. $-\sqrt{3}$ 9. $\frac{3\sqrt{3}}{2}$ 10. $\frac{\sqrt{2} - \sqrt{3}}{2}$ 11. $\log_2 9 = k$ 12. 3 13. -4 14. 16

15. 840 16. $10{,}080$ 17. $(2, 0), (-2, 0)$ 18. $4a^{3m}(a - 2)(a + 2)$ 19. $\frac{x^2y - cay^3z}{s^2tca - r^2z}$

20. $\frac{10d}{4k - 3zc}$ 21. $-7.42i - 4.88j$ 22. $6 + 3i$ 23. $\frac{2 - \sqrt{2}}{2}$ 24. $-\frac{3}{10} \pm \frac{\sqrt{111}}{10}i$

25. A 26. D 27. $(6, 2, 5)$ 28. y^{2a-2} 29. $8 - 12b^{-1/2}a^{-3/2} + 4a^{3/2}b^{3/2} - 6b$

30. $x^3 - 2x^2 - 2x - \frac{6}{x - 1}$

Problem set 9

1. $O = 36, L = 40$ 2. $\frac{1}{40}T + \frac{1}{60}T = 3\frac{1}{2}$; $T = 1$ hr 24 min

3. $R\left(\frac{x}{p} - 2\right) = x + 10; R = \frac{p(x + 10)}{x - 2p}$ mph 4. $\left(\frac{6}{30 \cdot 4}\right) \cdot 20 \cdot D = 4; D = 4$ days

5. Since the only multiple of 2 between 6 and 24 that is evenly divisible by $5\frac{1}{2}$ is 22, the builder should order 22-ft lengths to avoid throwing away short pieces of board.

6.

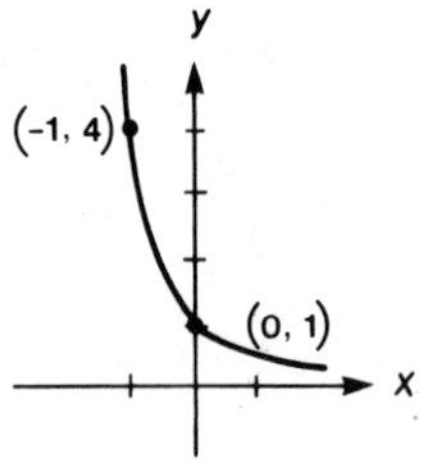

7. $60°$ 8. $\frac{\sqrt{3}}{2}$ 9. $\frac{5\sqrt{41}}{41}$ 10. $\frac{2\sqrt{3}-\sqrt{2}}{2}$

11. $-2\sqrt{2}-\frac{1}{2}$ 12. 6 13. -4 14. 81 15. 126

16. 210 17. $(0, 2), \left(\frac{3}{2}, -\frac{5}{2}\right)$ 18. $2b^{4n+2}(8b+3)$

19. $\frac{2(x+3)}{6bx+18b+3tx}$ 20. $\pm\sqrt{\frac{2sh}{5da}+\frac{4}{a}}$ 21. $+2.86i + 6.33j$ 22. $-\frac{2}{17}+\frac{25}{17}i$

23. $\frac{20-14\sqrt{3}}{47}$ 24. $\frac{1}{6}\pm\frac{\sqrt{5}}{6}i$ 25. D 26. A 27. $(6, 8, 2)$ 28. $z^{3b/2+9/2}$

29. $(2xy^2-3ab^3)(4x^2y^4+6ab^3xy^2+9a^2b^6)$ 30. $y=-\frac{1}{2}x+\frac{5}{2}$

Problem set 10

1. $O = 75, J = 65$ 2. $13R_L = 6\frac{1}{2}$; $R_L = \frac{1}{2}\frac{\text{henway}}{\text{day}}$

3. $3(B+W)=30, 5(B-W)=30$; $B = 8$ mph, $W = 2$ mph

4. $RGD = J, \left(\frac{10}{20\cdot 6}\right)\cdot 30\cdot D = 20$; $D = 8$ days 5. $\left(\frac{g}{x}+p\right)ax = D$; $D = ga + pxa$ miles

6.

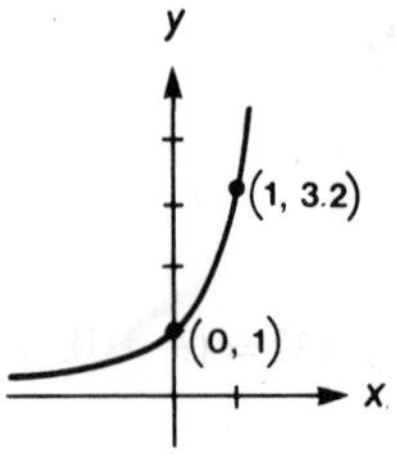

7. $60°$ 8. $\frac{\sqrt{7}}{4}$ 9. $\frac{\sqrt{2}}{2}$ 10. $\frac{3}{2}$ 11. 0 12. 0

13. 7 14. -3 15. 64 16. 10,080 17. 270,270

18. $(3, 1), (3, -1), (-3, 1), (-3, -1)$

19. $(2ab-3c^2d^2)(4a^2b^2+6abc^2d^2+9c^4d^4)$ 20. $\frac{3(z+4)}{2cz+8c+tz}$

21. $\frac{24grt}{drk+18sg}$ 22. $3.24i + 6.62j$ 23. $-5+\frac{1}{6}i$ 24. $-\frac{3}{8}\pm\frac{\sqrt{41}}{8}$ 25. D 26. D

27. $(10, 2, 1)$ 28. $x^{5a/2+7}$ 29. $1-b^{1/2}a^{-2a}+a^{2a}b^{1/2}-b$ 30. 4.27

Problem set 11

1. $(B+W)3 = 45, (B-W)5 = 45$; $B = 12$ mph, $W = 3$ mph

2. $R\left(\frac{100}{m}-1\right) = 100$; $R = \frac{100m}{100-m}$ mph 3. $\frac{100V}{V+W}$ 4. $15R_P = 10$; $T_p = \frac{3}{2}$ hr

5. $RTG = F, \frac{3}{2}\cdot 10\cdot 25 = F$; 375 lb 6.

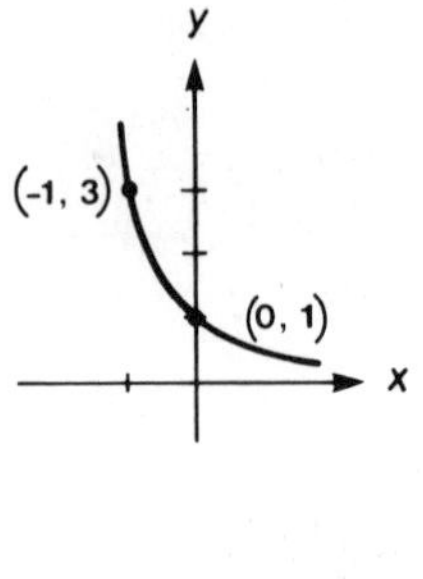

7. $60°$

8. $\frac{\sqrt{3}}{2}$ **9.** $-\frac{3}{4}$ **10.** $-\sqrt{2}$ **11.** $\frac{\sqrt{3}+6}{3}$ **12.** -2 **13.** 12 **14.** $-\frac{40}{3}$ **15.** 4

16. -6 **17.** 8 **18.** 30,240 **19.** (2, 0) **20.** $\frac{a^2b - cfg^2}{x^2yd^2 + cz^3}$ **21.** $\frac{8drs}{hrf - 4sd}$

22. $-0.03i + 3.88j$ **23.** $-\frac{5}{4} + \frac{1}{4}i$ **24.** $-\frac{1}{3} \pm \frac{\sqrt{19}}{3}$ **25.** *C* **26.** *C* **27.** (1, 2, 3)

28. $a^{5b/2 - 3/2}$ **29.** $4a^{x+2}(1 - 3a)$ **30.** $y = -\frac{1}{2}x + 3$

Problem set 12

1. $\frac{R}{B} = \frac{4}{1}; \frac{B}{G} = \frac{2}{1}$, $R + B + G = 55$; 40 reds, 5 greens, 10 blues

2. $RTE = C \rightarrow \left(\frac{20}{5 \cdot 3}\right)T \cdot 5 = 14$; $T = 2.1$ hr **3.** $R\left(\frac{m}{z} - 3\right) = m$; $R = \frac{zm}{m - 3z}$ mph

4. $\frac{17}{30}T = 10$; $T = 17\frac{11}{17}$ hr **5.** $R_B \cdot 16 = 120$, $R_A = \frac{3}{2}R_B$, $R_A \cdot 12 = \frac{3}{2}\left(7\frac{1}{2}\right) \cdot 12 = \$135$

6. $\frac{6}{5}$ **7.** $-\frac{35}{24}$ **8.** $\sqrt{(x-2)^2 + (y+1)^2}$ **9.** 45° **10.** $\frac{3}{4}$ **11.** $\frac{\sqrt{10}}{10}$ **12.** $-\sqrt{2}$

13. $\frac{3}{4}$ **14.** 3 **15.** 21 **16.** -5 **17.** 5 **18.** -5 **19.** 4 **20.** 75,600

21. (3, 1), (3, −1), (−3, 1), (−3, −1) **22.** $\frac{c^2(x^2yd - z^2c)}{gh^2d^2 - fc^3}$ **23.** $\frac{12kszt}{y^2rk + 9sz^2}$

24. $-3.65i - 3.41j$ **25.** $-\frac{5}{4} + \frac{5}{2}i$ **26.** *C* **27.** *C* **28.** (2, 3, 4) **29.** $\frac{3}{4} \pm \frac{\sqrt{57}}{4}$

30. $(2xy^2 - 3a^3b^2)(4x^2y^4 + 6xy^2a^3b^2 + 9a^6b^4)$

Problem set 13

1. $N_R = 10$, $N_W = 25$, $N_B = 30$

2. $P = 5W$, $T_U + \frac{1}{2} = T_D$, $396 = (P + W)T_D$, $132 = (P - W)T_U$; $P = 330$ mph, $W = 66$ mph

3. 500 lb **4.** $\frac{3}{8} \cdot 4 + 4R_J = 6$; $\frac{9}{8}$ jobs per hour **5.** Multiply *L* by 9 **6.** $\frac{21}{5}$

7. $\frac{17}{12}$ **8.** $\sqrt{(x-3)^2 + (y+2)^2}$ **9.** 30° **10.** $-\frac{4}{5}$ **11.** $\frac{2\sqrt{5}}{5}$ **12.** $-\frac{\sqrt{3}}{3}$

13. $\frac{1 - \sqrt{3}}{2}$ **14.** $\frac{2\sqrt{3} + 3\sqrt{2}}{6}$ **15.** $\frac{11}{15}$ **16.** $\frac{49}{4}$ **17.** 4 **18.** -3 **19.** 27

20. 277,200 **21.** (0, 4), $\left(\frac{12}{5}, -\frac{16}{5}\right)$ **22.** $\frac{2(m + x)}{m + x + 3sm}$ **23.** $\frac{48mzks}{4kt^2n - 9mz}$

24. $3.12i - 3.85j$ **25.** $\frac{24}{13} + \frac{3}{13}i$ **26.** *A* **27.** *A* **28.** (1, 1, 4) **29.** 8

30. $x^3 + 3 + \frac{7}{x - 2}$

Problem set 14

1. $P = 4W$, $400 = (P + W)T_D$, $300 = (P - W)T_U$, $T_D = T_U - 1$; $P = 80$ mph, $W = 20$ mph

2. $0.20W = R + 10$, $\frac{3}{5}B = 3R$, $0.10(R + B) = W - 94$; 10 reds, 50 blues, 100 whites

3. $3\sqrt{2} = \frac{2}{\sqrt{6}}x, x = 3\sqrt{3}$ **4.** $x^4 - y^4 = (x^2 + y^2)(x^2 - y^2) = 8$

5. $A = LW, (1.2L)(0.8W) = 0.96LW = 0.96A$; 4% decrease **6.** $y = -x + 2$

7. $y = -5x + 15$ **8.** $\left(\frac{1}{2}, 7\right)$ **9.** $-\frac{12}{7}$ **10.** $-30°$ **11.** $\frac{2\sqrt{10}}{7}$ **12.** $\frac{3\sqrt{10}}{10}$

13. $-\sqrt{3}$ **14.** $\frac{1 + \sqrt{2}}{2}$ **15.** $\frac{5}{4}$ **16.** $\frac{37}{20}$ **17.** 56 **18.** 3 **19.** -6 **20.** $\frac{1}{9}$

21. 210 **22.** $(2\sqrt{6}, 3), (-2\sqrt{6}, 3), (2\sqrt{6}, -3), (-2\sqrt{6}, -3)$ **23.** $\frac{3a^2bc - d^4}{4s^2t - lc^2}$

24. $\frac{4s^2 - h^2}{3}$ **25.** $0.94i - 4.69j$ **26.** $-\frac{7}{6} - \frac{11}{6}i$ **27.** D **28.** $(6, 4, 3)$

29. $(2xy^2 - 3ab^3)(4x^2y^4 + 6xy^2ab^3 + 9a^2b^6)$ **30.** $18a - 3a^{1/2}b^{-1/2} + 6a^{1/2}b^{1/2} - 1$

Problem set 15

1. $W = 20$ mph, $P = 120$ mph **2.** \$384 **3.** $\frac{3}{8}$ **4.** $150R = 6000$; \$4000

5. $R\left(\frac{k}{m} - 2\right) = k + 10$; $R = \frac{m(k + 10)}{k - 2m}$ mph **6.** 625 **7.** 1024 **8.** 24

9. $y = -\frac{7}{5}x - \frac{6}{5}$ **10.** $\left(-\frac{1}{2}, \frac{9}{2}\right)$ **11.** 0 **12.** 60° **13.** $\frac{3}{5}$ **14.** $\frac{\sqrt{5}}{5}$ **15.** $\frac{-1 - \sqrt{2}}{2}$

16. $\frac{2 + \sqrt{2}}{2}$ **17.** $-\frac{\sqrt{6}}{4}$ **18.** 46 **19.** 2 **20.** -4 **21.** 16 **22.** 840

23. $(0, 2), \left(\frac{8}{5}, -\frac{6}{5}\right)$ **24.** $\frac{2(sl - z)}{sl - z + tl}$ **25.** $\frac{(3t + 10k)^2}{5t}$ **26.** $4.71i - 1.53j$ **27.** $\frac{3}{2}i$

28. B **29.** $(3, 2, -1)$ **30.** $x^3 + x + 1$

Problem set 16

1. $G = 4W$, $60 = (G + W)T_D$, $27 = (G - W)T_U$, $T_U + 1 = T_D$; $G = 12$ mph, $W = 3$ mph

2. $r(T + P) = RT + 100$; $r = \frac{RT + 100}{T + P} \frac{\text{mi}}{\text{hr}}$ **3.** 50 mph **4.** 4 liters 90%, 16 liters 75%

5. $2R_S = \frac{2}{5}$; 5 hr **6.** 3125 **7.** 120 **8.** 243 **9.** $y = -\frac{8}{5}x - \frac{1}{2}$ **10.** $\left(\frac{7}{2}, 4\right)$

11. $-\frac{28}{5}$ **12.** 2453.6 mi **13.** $-45°$ **14.** $\frac{2\sqrt{29}}{29}$ **15.** $\frac{\sqrt{7}}{4}$ **16.** $\frac{1}{2}$

17. $\frac{-3\sqrt{2} - 2\sqrt{3}}{6}$ **18.** $-\frac{\sqrt{3}}{2}$ **19.** $-\frac{5}{4}$ **20.** 2 **21.** -4 **22.** 9 **23.** 13,860

24. $(\sqrt{3}, 2), (\sqrt{3}, -2), (-\sqrt{3}, 2), (-\sqrt{3}, -2)$ **25.** $z^{3a/2-1}$ **26.** $\frac{2(s - x_0 - v_0t)}{t^2}$

27. $-2.29i + 4.72j$ **28.** B **29.** $(5, 2, 1)$ **30.** $(2ab^2 - 3x^2y^3)(4a^2b^4 + 6ab^2x^2y^3 + 9x^4y^6)$

Problem set 17

1. $G + F + M = 90$, $3(G + F - 10) = 2(M - 5) + 50$, $F + M + 10 = G + 60$; Gimbel is 20, Farth is 30, Murk is 40. In 175 years they will be 195, 205, and 215.

2. $40R_k + 40R_G = 18$, $R_G = \frac{1}{4}$; $T_k = 5$ hr **3.** 112 **4.** Z becomes $\frac{3}{2}$ times larger

5. Mean = 10, median = 9 **6.** 2520 **7.** 216 **8.** 840 **9.** $b = \frac{9}{2}, a = 6$

10. $\frac{a}{e} = \frac{c}{f}, \frac{c}{f} = \frac{b}{d}, \frac{a}{e} = \frac{b}{d}$ **11.** $y = -\frac{5}{3}x + \frac{8}{3}$ **12.** $\left(\frac{3}{2}, 1\right)$ **13.** $-\frac{1}{7}$ **14.** 2742.5 mi

15. $-30°$ **16.** $\frac{\sqrt{21}}{5}$ **17.** $-\frac{2\sqrt{13}}{13}$ **18.** $\frac{\sqrt{3}}{3}$ **19.** $\frac{3}{2}$ **20.** $\frac{\sqrt{3}-3}{3}$ **21.** 10

22. 3 **23.** -3 **24.** 64 **25.** 220 **26.** $(0, -3), (3, 0)$ **27.** $\frac{3r^2s^2 + h}{3q}$

28. $1.06i - 7.39j$ **29.** $(2, 1, 4)$ **30.** $x^2 + 3 + \frac{10}{x-2}$

Problem set 18

1. $4(90 - A) = 200; A = 40°$ **2.** $3(180 - A) = 450°; A = 30°$

3. $R_T = \frac{D_T}{T_T} \rightarrow 20 = \frac{60 + 20 + 20}{2 + 2 + T_3} \rightarrow T_3 = 1$ hr, $R_3 = 20$ mph

4. $R(s + 10) = 2y; R = \frac{2y}{s + 10}$ yards per second **5.** $\left(\frac{1}{10 \cdot 5}\right) \cdot 2 \cdot T = 1; T = 25$ days

6. 210 **7.** Refer to Lesson 18 **8.** $x = 20, y = 10$ **9.** $x - 2y + 8 = 0$

10. $\frac{x}{-2} + \frac{y}{3} = 1$ **11.** $p = \frac{4}{3}, q = \frac{4}{3}$ **12.** $\frac{CB}{BD} = \frac{AC}{DE}, \frac{AC}{DE} = \frac{AB}{BE}, \frac{AB}{BE} = \frac{CB}{BD}$

13. $y = -\frac{7}{5}x - \frac{6}{5}$ **14.** $\left(2, \frac{9}{2}\right)$ **15.** $\frac{14}{3}$ **16.** 2.1 inches **17.** $-45°$ **18.** $\frac{2\sqrt{6}}{5}$

19. $\frac{-\sqrt{10}}{10}$ **20.** $-\frac{\sqrt{3}}{4}$ **21.** 0 **22.** $\frac{\sqrt{3}+1}{2}$ **23.** $\frac{5}{4}$ **24.** 3 **25.** -3 **26.** 9

27. 9240 **28.** $(3, 2), (3, -2), (-3, 2), (-3, -2)$ **29.** $x^{15a/4 - 13/2}$ **30.** $-2.14i + 5.78j$

Problem set 19

1. $4(90 - A) = (180 - A) + 60; A = 40°$

2. $A = 6W, 700 = (A + W)T_D, 600 = (A - W)T_U, T_D = T_U - 1; A = 120$ mph, $W = 20$ mph

3. $5R = 85, R = 17$ mph **4.** $T + 0.16(410) = 0.18(T + 410); T = 10$ lb **5.** 8

6. $20 \cdot 19 \cdot 18 \cdot 17 \cdot 16 = 1{,}860{,}480$ **7.** Refer to Lesson 18 **8.** $x = 20, y = 10$

9. $x + 3y - 9 = 0$ **10.** $\frac{x}{-5/2} + \frac{y}{5/4} = 1$ **11.** $a = 3, b = \frac{9}{4}$ **12.** 10,461 ft

13. $y = -9x + 7$ **14.** $\left(\frac{3}{2}, 3\right)$ **15.** $\frac{21}{4}$ **16.** 18.32 ft **17.** $-45°$ **18.** $\frac{1}{2}$

19. $\frac{3\sqrt{13}}{13}$ **20.** $\frac{\sqrt{3}}{4}$ **21.** -1 **22.** 1 **23.** $-\frac{16}{3}$ **24.** 14 **25.** 2 **26.** 3

27. 9 **28.** $(2xy^2 - 3ay^3)(4x^2y^4 + 6xy^5a + 9a^2y^6)$ **29.** $\frac{1}{3}(2k + 2p)^2$ **30.** 9

Problem set 20

1. $20°$ **2.** 18 mph **3.** $\left(\frac{1}{10 \cdot 400}\right) \cdot 5 \cdot M = \frac{1}{4}; M = 200$ men

4. $R(h - 3) = m; R = \frac{m}{h - 3}$ mph **5.** $1 + \frac{1}{6}t + \frac{1}{3}t = 4 \rightarrow t = 6$ hr; 9 p.m. **6.** 11,880

7. 154,440 **8.** Refer to Lesson 18 **9.** $x = 15, y = 10$ **10.** $x + 3y - 7 = 0$

11. $\frac{x}{-6/5} + \frac{y}{2} = 1$ **12.** $x = 10, y = 12$ **13.** $\frac{AB}{HG} = \frac{AC}{HF}, \frac{BC}{GF} = \frac{AC}{HF}, \frac{AB}{HG} = \frac{BC}{GF}$

14. $y = 3x + 8$ **15.** $\left(\frac{3}{2}, 1\right)$ **16.** 30.5 ft **17.** $-\frac{3}{4}$ **18.** 150° **19.** $-\frac{3}{5}$ **20.** $\frac{\sqrt{5}}{3}$

21. $2 - \sqrt{3}$ **22.** $\frac{6 - 2\sqrt{3}}{3}$ **23.** -4 **24.** 13 **25.** No solution, $x = -\frac{7}{4}$

26. 3 **27.** 8 **28.** $\frac{g^2z^2 + ts^3}{4}$ **29.** $-5.40i + 2.71j$ **30.** $\frac{6}{25} - \frac{8}{25}i$

Problem set 21

1. $RDM = J, \frac{7}{15} \cdot D \cdot 10 = 14$; 3 days **2.** \$300 **3.** $B = 20$ mph, $W = 5$ mph

4. $\frac{\frac{440}{49}}{\frac{100}{9.8}} = \frac{22}{25}$ **5.** $5R_1 + 5 \cdot \frac{1}{12} = \frac{25}{24} \to R_1 = \frac{3 \text{ jobs}}{24 \text{ hr}} \to$ 16 hr to do 2 jobs **6.** 30,240

7. 25,200 **8.** $(x - 3)^2 + (y - 4)^2 = r^2$

9.

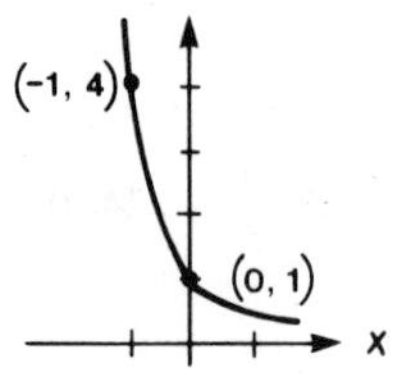

10.

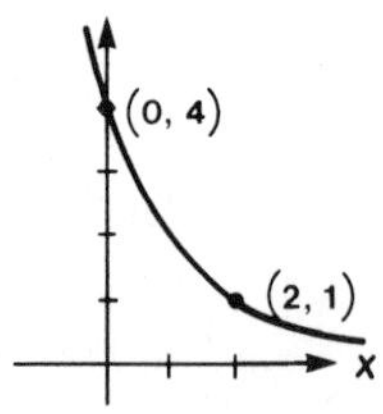

11. Refer to Lesson 18

12. $x = 7, y = 15$

13. $2x + 5y - 13 = 0$

14. $\frac{x}{1/2} + \frac{y}{-3/5} = 1$

15. $a = \frac{32}{3}, b = \frac{28}{3}$ **16.** $\frac{AB}{DE} = \frac{AC}{CE}, \frac{AC}{CE} = \frac{BC}{CD}, \frac{BC}{CD} = \frac{AB}{DE}$ **17.** $y + 2x = 1$ **18.** (2, 5)

19. $\frac{87}{14}$ **20.** 1047 ft **21.** $-60°$ **22.** $\frac{\sqrt{7}}{4}$ **23.** $\frac{3}{5}$ **24.** $\frac{2\sqrt{2} - 1}{2}$ **25.** $-2 + \sqrt{3}$

26. 49 **27.** 6 **28.** 3 **29.** 64 **30.** $x^2 - 2 - \frac{1}{x - 3}$

Problem set 22

1. $RDM = J, \frac{1}{120} \cdot 5 \cdot 8 + \frac{1}{120} \cdot D \cdot 4 = 1$; $D = 20$ days **2.** $S = 31, J = 33$

3. $\frac{S}{F} = \frac{S_x}{X}; S_x = \frac{SX}{F}$ ft **4.** $1.5\left(\frac{56}{35}\right)(H - 40) = 24$; $H = 50$ hr

5. $(130 + f + s)G = 2000, G = \frac{2000}{130 + f + s}$ gal **6.** 13,440 **7.** $y = 5 \sin x$

8. $y = 10 - 6 \cos \theta$ **9.** 0 **10.** $(x + 2)^2 + (y - 3)^2 = r^2$

11.

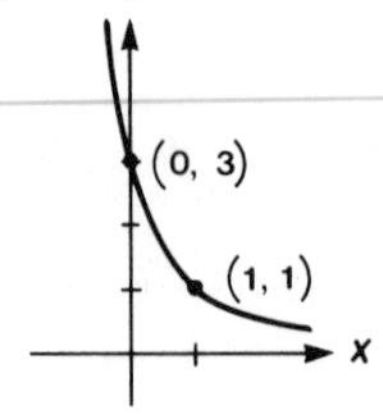

12. Refer to Lesson 18 **13.** $a = 15, b = 20$

14. $x + 4y - 10 = 0$ **15.** $p = \frac{15}{2}, q = \frac{25}{4}$ **16.** B

17. $y = -x$ **18.** $\left(\frac{5}{2}, \frac{1}{2}\right)$ **19.** $-\frac{61}{12}$ **20.** 314 yards

21. 45° **22.** $\frac{3}{5}$ **23.** $\frac{3}{5}$ **24.** $\frac{-2\sqrt{2} + \sqrt{3}}{2}$ **25.** $-\frac{4\sqrt{3}}{3}$ **26.** $\frac{46}{3}$

27. No solution, $x = -\frac{15}{11}$ **28.** 2 **29.** 4 **30.** $\pm\sqrt{\frac{25q^2r^2 + 4s}{3}}$

Problem set 23

1. $R_P + 3R_P \cdot 10 = 3100$, $R_P = 100$ mi/yr; 100 mi

2. $RTM = C$; $\frac{c}{hw}T(w+m) = c$; $T = \frac{hw}{w+m}$ hr

3. $RTC = p$, $\frac{p}{mc}T(c+n) = p$; $T = \frac{mc}{c+n}$ min

4. $RD = \text{cost}$, $\left(\frac{x}{d} - 5\right)D = 100$; $D = \frac{100d}{x - 5d}$ drums

5. $\frac{1}{x} = \frac{y+z}{2}$; $\frac{6}{x} = 3(y+z)$ **6.** $5 \cdot 4 \cdot 3 \cdot 2 = 120$ **7.** $6 \cdot 5 \cdot 4 \cdot 3 = 360$

8. $y = 7 - 3\cos x$ **9.** $y = 4 + 7\sin x$ **10.** 8 **11.** $(x-h)^2 + (y-k)^2 = 25$

12.

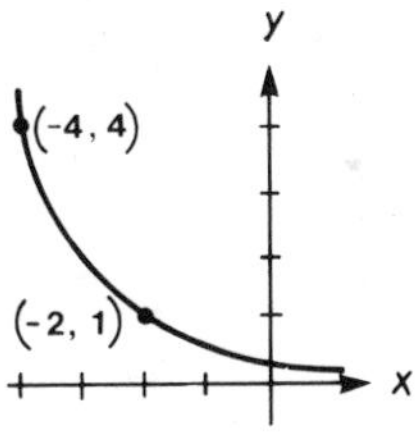

13. Refer to Lesson 18 **14.** $x = 12$, $y = 10$

15. $a = 55$, $b = \frac{95}{2}$ **16.** $\frac{a}{d} = \frac{b}{f}, \frac{c}{e} = \frac{b}{f}, \frac{a}{d} = \frac{c}{e}$

17. $y = -\frac{3}{2}x + \frac{3}{2}$ **18.** $\left(\frac{1}{2}, 3\right)$ **19.** $\frac{35}{9}$

20. 520 or $\frac{500\pi}{3}$ ft **21.** $-30°$ **22.** $-\frac{3}{5}$ **23.** $\frac{3}{5}$ **24.** 0 **25.** $-\sqrt{2}$ **26.** 4

27. 10 **28.** 4 **29.** $\frac{11}{2}$ **30.** 16

Problem set 24

1. $R_O T_O = 24$, $R_B T_B = 24$, $R_B = 2R_O$, $T_O + T_B = 9$; 4 mph going, 8 mph returning, 6 hr going, 3 hr returning

2. $0.92(4000) - A = 0.8(4000 - A)$; $A = 2400$ liters

3. $RTM = A$, $\frac{c}{fk}T(k-x) = c + 10$; $T = \frac{(c+10)fk}{(k-x)c}$ hr

4. $\frac{G}{B} = 2$, $2(B + W) = G + 10$, $B + G + W = 35$; 20 greens, 10 blues, 5 whites

5. $5(m+n)$ **6.** 25 **7.** $2 \cdot 6! \cdot 3! = 8640$ **8.** $y = -10\sin x$ **9.** $y = 3 + 5\cos x$

10. 120 **11.** $(x-h)^2 + (y-k)^2 = 25$

12.

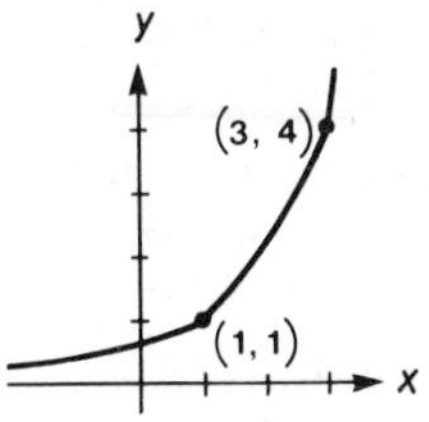

13. Refer to Lesson 18 **14.** $x = 30$, $y = 20$

15. $n = \frac{15}{4}$, $m = 2$ **16.** D **17.** $\frac{x}{-7/6} + \frac{y}{7/5} = 1$

18. $y = -\frac{8}{9}x + \frac{3}{2}$ **19.** $\left(1 - \frac{\sqrt{6}}{2}, 1 + \frac{\sqrt{6}}{2}\right), \left(1 + \frac{\sqrt{6}}{2}, 1 - \frac{\sqrt{6}}{2}\right)$

20. $(xy^2 + p^2z^3)(x^2y^4 - xy^2p^2z^3 + p^4z^6)$ **21.** 2799.2 mi **22.** $\frac{\sqrt{7}}{4}$ **23.** $-\frac{2\sqrt{13}}{13}$

24. $-\frac{2\sqrt{3}}{3}$ **25.** $\frac{3\sqrt{2} + 2\sqrt{3}}{3}$ **26.** 30 **27.** No solution, $x = -\frac{1}{14}$

28. 4 **29.** 3 **30.** (2, 1, 4)

Problem set 25

1. $R_G T_G = 36$, $R_R T_R = 36$, $R_R = 2R_G$, $T_G + T_R = 6$; $R_G = 9$ mph, $R_R = 18$ mph

2. 500 liters **3.** $RTM = F$, $\frac{x}{dy}T(y + 50) = x$, $T = \frac{dy}{y+50}$ days

4. $\frac{R}{E} = 3, \frac{E}{D} = 2, R + E + D = 18$; 2 diamonds, 4 emeralds, 12 rubies **5.** $3(b + c)$

6. $1 \cdot 5 \cdot 5 = 25$ **7.** $2(6!)(4!) = 34{,}560$

8. $(x - 2 + 3i)(x - 2 - 3i) = x^2 - 4x + 13;\ x^2 - 4x + 13 = 0$

9. $\left[x - \left(-\frac{3}{2} + \frac{\sqrt{15}}{2}i\right)\right]\left[x - \left(-\frac{3}{2} - \frac{\sqrt{15}}{2}i\right)\right]$ **10.** $y = 1 - 11 \cos \theta$

11. $y = 3 - 7 \sin x$ **12.** 1680 **13.** $(x - h)^2 + (y - k)^2 = 36$

14.

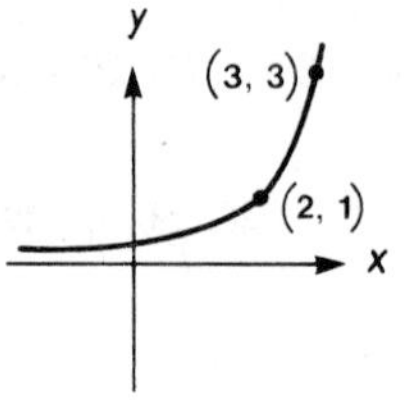

15. Refer to Lesson 18 **16.** $x = 12, y = 2$

17. $n = \frac{3}{2}, m = \frac{9}{8}$ **18.** $\frac{x}{3/2} + \frac{y}{-1/2} = 1$ **19.** $y = -\frac{9}{4}x + \frac{75}{8}$

20. $\frac{35}{9}$ **21.** 628 m **22.** $\frac{\sqrt{119}}{12}$ **23.** $-\frac{5\sqrt{194}}{194}$ **24.** $\sqrt{2}$

25. 0 **26.** $\frac{35}{2}$ **27.** $\frac{2}{9}$ **28.** 8 **29.** 8 **30.** $(-1, -8, 2)$

Problem set 26

1. $F = 4C, (F + C)T_D = 100, (F - C)T_U = 30, T_D = T_U + 1$; current = 10 mph, *Faerie Queen* = 40 mph

2. $RTM = J, \frac{1}{dm}T(40) = 1, T = \frac{dm}{40}$ days **3.** $RTM = I, \frac{x}{dk}T(k - y) = x; T = \frac{dk}{k - y}$ hr

4. $\frac{60}{75} = \frac{4}{5}$ **5.** $RP = \text{cost}, \frac{d}{12}mc = \text{cost}; \frac{dmc}{12}$ dollars **6.** 12 **7.** $9 \cdot 9 \cdot 4 = 324$

8. $y = -5 - 25 \sin x$ **9.** $y = -3 + 7 \cos \theta$ **10.** 5 **11.** $(x - 2)^2 + (y - 1)^2 = 9$

12.

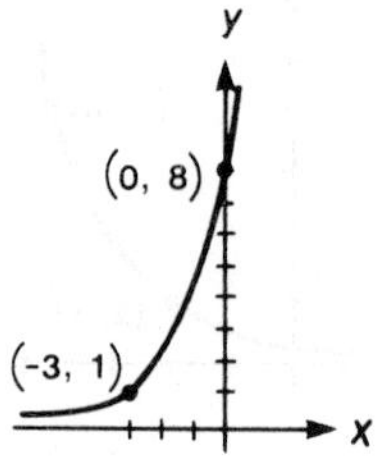

13. $x^2 - 6x + 13 = 0$ **14.** $x = 20, y = 15$

15. $\frac{AB}{AD} = \frac{BE}{CD}, \frac{AE}{AC} = \frac{BE}{CD}, \frac{AB}{AD} = \frac{AE}{AC}$ **16.** $2\sqrt{5}$ **17.** 10 ft

18. $x + y + 1 = 0$ **19.** $(1, 1)$ **20.** $\frac{8}{3}$ **21.** 14 ft

22. $-\frac{3\sqrt{7}}{7}$ **23.** $-45°$ **24.** -1 **25.** 1 **26.** $\frac{15}{4}$ **27.** 3 **28.** 8 **29.** 25

30. $(2xy^2 - 3a^2b^3)(4x^2y^4 + 6xy^2a^2b^3 + 9a^4b^6)$

Problem set 27

1. $R = 4, B = 2, W = 6$ **2.** 450 ml 40%, 150 ml 80%

3. $C_o + C_r = 36, \frac{C_o}{C_r} = 2$, Calories $= 27C_o + 106C_r = 1920$ calories

4. $\frac{1}{m} = \frac{1}{W_1} + \frac{1}{W_2}; m = \frac{W_1W_2}{W_1 + W_2}$ **5.** $\frac{1}{28} \cdot \frac{\$420{,}000}{3} = \$5000$ **6.**

Y	3	2	1	= 6
P	2	2	1	= 4
L	2	2	1	= 4
				14 ways

7. $2 \cdot 8 \cdot 5 = 80$ **8.** $y = -5 - 20 \cos x$ **9.** $y = 6 - 14 \sin \theta$ **10.** 24

11. $(x - 3)^2 + (y - 2)^2 = 16$

12.

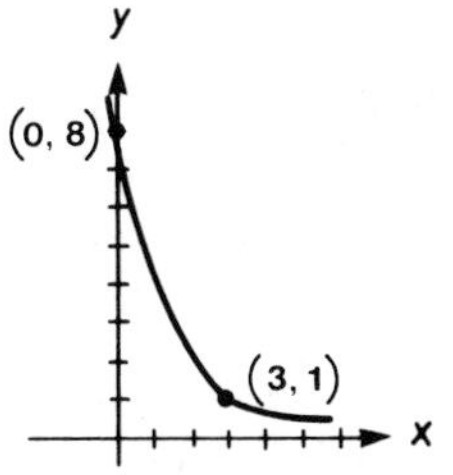

13. $[x - (1 - \sqrt{2}\,i)][x - (1 + \sqrt{2}\,i)]$

14. $\frac{AD}{AC} = \frac{AE}{AB}, \frac{DE}{BC} = \frac{AD}{AC}, \frac{AE}{AB} = \frac{DE}{BC}$ **15.** 6.5 ft

16. $x = 20, y = 5$ **17.** $\frac{x}{7/2} + \frac{y}{-7/4} = 1$

18. $y = \frac{3}{4}x + \frac{5}{4}$ **19.** -1 **20.** $5x + y - 4 = 0$ **21.** 2930 mi **22.** $-\frac{3\sqrt{3}}{8}$

23. 1 **24.** 30° **25.** $\frac{\sqrt{5}}{3}$ **26.** $\frac{7}{3}$ **27.** 0 **28.** 50 **29.** 6

30. $t = \frac{1}{2}[(z^3x - 4)^2 + 3] = \frac{1}{2}(z^6x^2 - 8z^3x + 19)$

Problem set 28

1. $RTM = A, \frac{c}{ba}T(a - d) = c; T = \frac{ba}{a - d}$ hr

2. $\frac{3}{2}D = 72, D = 48$ days; total time = 51 days **3.** \$432

4. $\frac{d}{c}$ dollars/cat, $\frac{8d}{4c}$ dollars/parrot; $\frac{7dp}{4c}$ dollars

5. $RTI = M, \frac{G}{11S}T(S + 14) = K; T = \frac{11KS}{G(S + 14)}$ days

6. $4 \cdot 6 \cdot 4 \cdot 5 = 480$ **7.** $2(4!)(3!) = 288$ **8.** $y = 1 + 5 \sin x$ **9.** $y = 5 - 15 \cos \theta$

10. 420 **11.** $(x + 2)^2 + (y + 3)^2 = 9$ **12.**

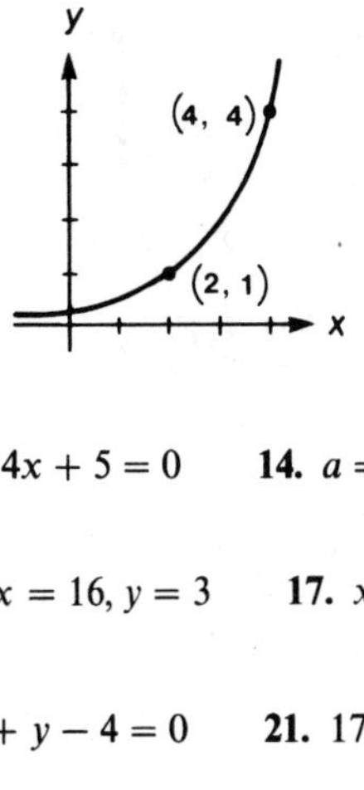

13. $(x - 2 - i)(x - 2 + i) = x^2 - 4x + 5; x^2 - 4x + 5 = 0$ **14.** $a = \frac{7}{5}, b = \frac{7\sqrt{29}}{10}$

15. 72 m **16.** $\frac{3}{2}x + 2y = 30, 4x + 2y = 70; x = 16, y = 3$ **17.** $x + y - 2 = 0$

18. $\frac{x}{-2/5} + \frac{y}{-2/9} = 1$ **19.** -1 **20.** $5x + y - 4 = 0$ **21.** 174 ft **22.** $\frac{\sqrt{2}}{4}$

23. $\frac{1}{3}$ **24.** $\frac{\sqrt{5}}{3}$ **25.** $-\frac{2}{5}$ **26.** $\frac{16}{3}$ **27–29.** Refer to Lesson 28 **30.** 38

Problem set 29

1. $\frac{1}{3}T = 29.5; T = 88.5$ hr **2.** $\frac{1}{4} \cdot 40 + \frac{1}{3} \cdot 12 = 14$; 2 quarts left over

3. $3S = 5J + 15, 2(S + 10) = 4(J + 10) - 20; J = 15, S = 30; J_{15} = 30, S_{15} = 45$

4. $\frac{D}{B} \cdot b = 6, b = \frac{6B}{D}$ **5.** $R(h - 4) = d; R = \frac{d}{h - 4}$ mph **6.** $5 \cdot 4 \cdot 2 = 40$ **7.** 40

8. $y = 5 + 25 \cos x$ **9.** $y = 5 - 15 \cos \theta$ **10.** $7\frac{3}{4}$ **11.** $(x + 2)^2 + (y - 4)^2 = 16$

12.

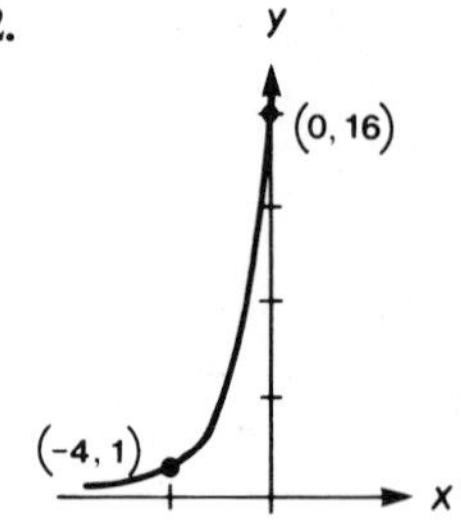

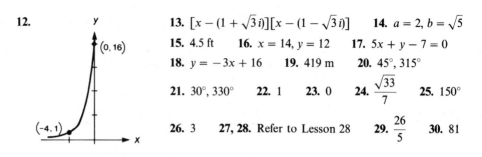

13. $[x - (1 + \sqrt{3}\,i)][x - (1 - \sqrt{3}\,i)]$ **14.** $a = 2, b = \sqrt{5}$
15. 4.5 ft **16.** $x = 14, y = 12$ **17.** $5x + y - 7 = 0$
18. $y = -3x + 16$ **19.** 419 m **20.** 45°, 315°
21. 30°, 330° **22.** 1 **23.** 0 **24.** $\dfrac{\sqrt{33}}{7}$ **25.** 150°
26. 3 **27, 28.** Refer to Lesson 28 **29.** $\dfrac{26}{5}$ **30.** 81

Problem set 30

1. $\frac{7}{3}T + \frac{8}{5}T = 59$; $T = 15$ hr **2.** $3S = 100d$; $S = \dfrac{100d}{3}$ **3.** $\dfrac{F}{S} = \dfrac{69}{S_m}$; $S_m = \dfrac{69S}{F}$ in

4. $\left(\dfrac{16}{3}\right)15 = 80$ oz needed, 8 packages

5. $R(m - 60) = d$, $R = \dfrac{d}{m - 60}$ mi/min $= \dfrac{60d}{m - 60}$ mph **6.** 18

7. $(4 \cdot 5 \cdot 5) + (5 \cdot 5) + 5 = 130$ **8.** $y = 5 + 25 \sin \theta$ **9.** $y = 10 - 20 \cos x$ **10.** 20

11. $(x + 3)^2 + (y - 2)^2 = 25$ **12.**

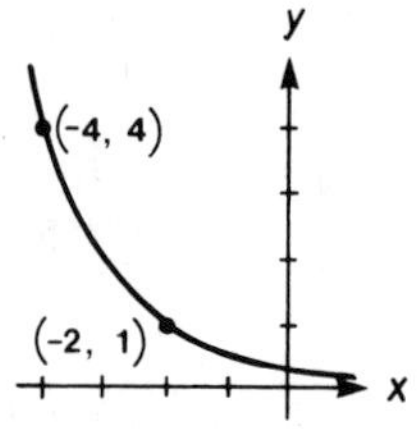

13. $x^2 - 6x + 10 = 0$

14. $\dfrac{AD}{AC} = \dfrac{DE}{BC}, \dfrac{DE}{BC} = \dfrac{AE}{BA}, \dfrac{AD}{AC} = \dfrac{AE}{BA}$ **15.** 20 m **16.** Refer to Lesson 18

17. $6x - 4y - 5 = 0$ **18.** 100π meters **19.** (*a*) 0.5441 (*b*) 1.253 **20.** $e^{8.19}$

21. 240°, 300° **22.** 240°, 300° **23.** 1 **24.** −3 **25.** $-\dfrac{5\sqrt{6}}{12}$ **26.** $\dfrac{\sqrt{7}}{4}$

27, 28. Refer to Lesson 28 **29.** 34 **30.** $\dfrac{8}{9}$

Problem set 31

1. $\frac{5}{4} \cdot 7 + R_B \cdot 7 = 12$, $R_B = \dfrac{13}{28}$, $\dfrac{13}{28}T = 2$, $T = \dfrac{56}{13}$ hr **2.** Current = 5 mph, boy = 10 mph

3. $7(\$30) = \$210$ **4.** $50(60) + 25(56) + 25(R) = 5800$, $R = \$56$

5. $R(S - 120) = D$; $R = \dfrac{D}{S - 120}$ ft/sec **6.** $6 \cdot 6 \cdot 5 \cdot 6 \cdot 1 = 1080$

7.
$$\begin{array}{lll} \text{1 digit} & = & 5 \\ \text{2 digit} = 5 \cdot 5 & = & 25 \\ \text{3 digit} = 2 \cdot 5 \cdot 5 & = & 50 \\ & = & \overline{80} \text{ total} \end{array}$$

8. $y = 4 - 7 \sin \theta$ **9.** $y = 2 - 8 \cos x$ **10.** 25 **11.** $(x - h)^2 + (y - k)^2 = r^2$

12.

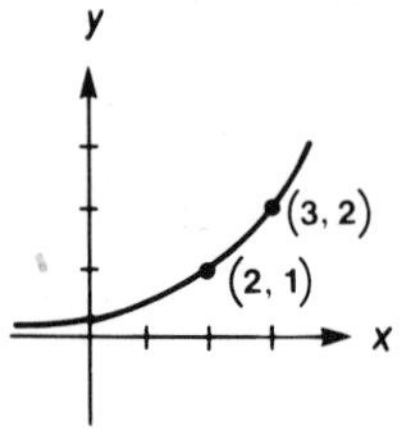

13. $(x + 2 + i)(x + 2 - i)$ **14.** $\dfrac{7}{4}$ **15.** $p = \dfrac{21}{5}$ **16.** 9 m

17. $y = -\frac{1}{5}x + 2$ **18.** 2681.7 mi **19.** (*a*) 1.212 (*b*) 2.791

20. $e^{8.243}$ **21.** 120°, 240° **22.** 15°, 135°, 255°, 75°, 195°, 315°

23. { } because both 480° and 600° > 360° **24.** $\frac{1}{2}$ **25.** $\frac{8}{3}$ **26.** 45°

27, 28. Refer to Lesson 28 **29.** $\frac{20}{9}$ **30.** $\frac{21}{2}$

Problem set 32

1. $\frac{31}{6}T = 31$; $T = 6$ days **2.** $\frac{j}{hm}T(m+p) = j$; $T = \frac{hm}{m+p}$ hr

3. $5(90 - A) = 30 + (180 - A)$; $A = 60°$ **4.** $R(S + 20) = 3Y$; $R = \frac{3Y}{S + 20}$ yd/sec

5. $2800 \text{ francs} \cdot \frac{1 \text{ dollar}}{350 \text{ francs}} \cdot \frac{400 \text{ francs}}{1 \text{ dollar}} = 3200$ francs for a profit of 400 francs

6. $3 \cdot 4 \cdot 5 \cdot 3 = 180$ **7.** $\frac{50(5280)(12)}{(15)(60)(60)(2\pi)} \frac{\text{rev}}{\text{sec}}$ **8.** $y = 1 + 5 \cos x$ **9.** $y = -1 - 7 \cos x$

10. $x^2 + 2x + 9 = 0$ **11.** $(x - h)^2 + (y - k)^2 = 25$ **12.**

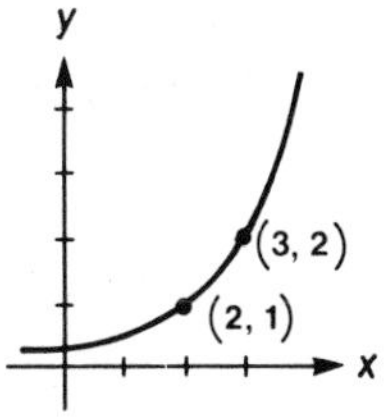

13. $\frac{50(5280)(12)(2.54)}{60} \frac{\text{cm}}{\text{min}}$ **14.** $\frac{30(1000)}{(2.54)^3}$ in^3

15. $a = \frac{65}{4}$, $b = \frac{128}{5}$ **16.** 800 cm

17. $x = 15$, $y = 20$ **18.** $x - \frac{5}{2} = 0$ **19.** 3000π meters **20.** (*a*) $10^{3.792}$ (*b*) $e^{8.732}$

21. 240°, 300° **22.** 0°, 120°, 240° **23.** 180° **24.** $\frac{11}{4}$ **25.** $-\frac{2}{3}$ **26.** $\frac{\sqrt{39}}{8}$

27. Refer to Lesson 28 **28.** $\frac{225}{2}$ **29.** 4 **30.** $z = 4t^4 - 4t^2 + 2$

Problem set 33

1. $\frac{1.5(2\pi)(30)(60)}{5280} \frac{\text{mi}}{\text{hr}}$ **2.** $\frac{30(1000)(100)}{(60)(70)} \frac{\text{rad}}{\text{min}}$ **3.** $R(h - 2) = K$, $R = \frac{K}{h - 2}$ **4.** 20 liters

5. $\frac{1}{8}(2 + h) + \frac{1}{4}(h) = \frac{25}{4}$, $h = 16$ hr **6.** $3 \cdot 3 \cdot 4 = 36$ **7.** $\left(x + \frac{3 + 3\sqrt{5}}{2}\right)\left(x + \frac{3 - 3\sqrt{5}}{2}\right)$

8. $y = 9 - \sin x$ **9.** $y = 6 + 6 \cos \theta$ **10.** $-\frac{25}{6}$ **11.** $(x - 3)^2 + (y - 2)^2 = 36$

12. $y = (x - 3)^2 - 5$ **13.** $y = -(x + 2)^2 + 10$ **14.**

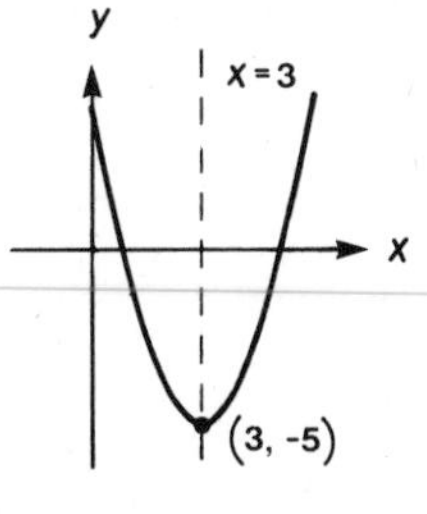

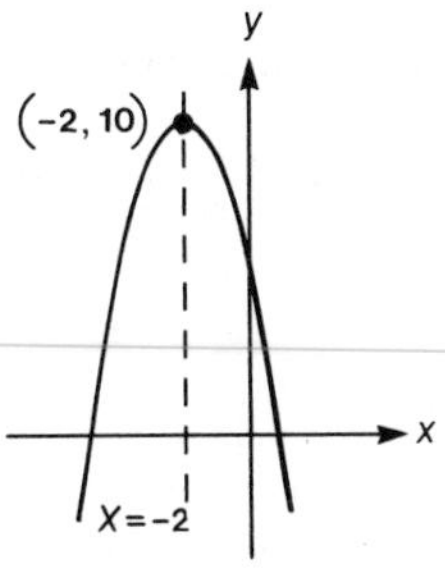

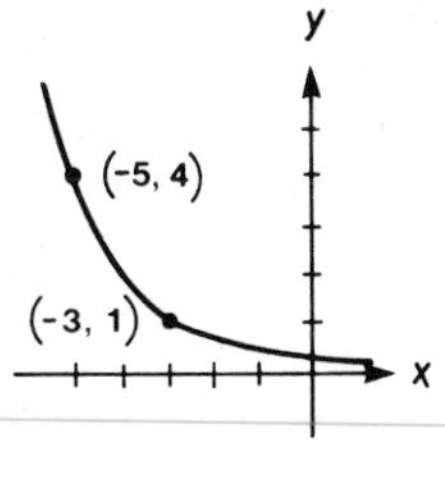

15. $\frac{40(5280)(12)(2.54)}{(60)(60)} \frac{\text{cm}}{\text{sec}}$ **16.** $12(1000)(60)(60)$ cm^3/hr **17.** $x = 6$ **18.** 18 meters

19. $x = 6$, $y = 5$ **20.** $y = 4x + 7$ **21.** (*a*) $10^{3.491}$ (*b*) $e^{8.039}$ **22.** 135°, 225°

23. 10°, 130°, 250°, 50°, 170°, 290° **24.** 0°, 180° **25.** $\frac{16}{3}$ **26.** $-\frac{2}{3}$ **27.** $\frac{\sqrt{7}}{4}$

28. Refer to Lesson 28 **29.** $\frac{1}{6}$ **30.** $\frac{25}{8}$

Problem set 34

1. $\dfrac{10(1000)\text{ rad}}{3(60)(60)\text{ sec}}$ **2.** $\dfrac{40(0.5)(60)}{3(12)}\dfrac{\text{yd}}{\text{min}}$

3. $R_O T_O = 400$, $R_B T_B = 400$, $R_B = 2R_O$, $T_O + T_B = 6$, $R_O = 100$ mph

4. $G = 5$, $R = 6$, $W = 4$ **5.** 10° **6.** $3 \cdot 2 \cdot 1 = 6$ **7.** $\dfrac{8!}{2!2!}$

8. W R W R W R, R W R W R W; 2 ways **9.** $y = 7 + 3 \sin x$

10. $y = 8 - 9 \cos \theta$ **11.** 210 **12.** $(x - h)^2 + (y - k)^2 = r^2$

13. $y = (x - 4)^2 - 18$

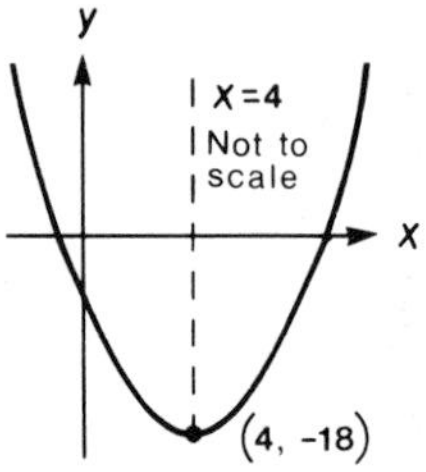

14. $y = -(x + 5)^2 + 29$

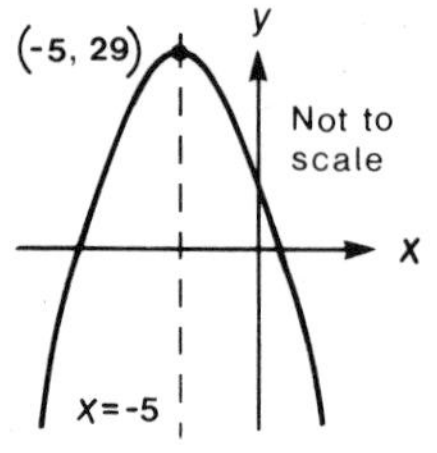

15. $\dfrac{20(100)(60)(60)}{(2.54)(12)(5280)}\dfrac{\text{mi}}{\text{hr}}$

16. $\dfrac{12(1000)}{(2.54)^3(60)}\dfrac{\text{in}^3}{\text{min}}$ **17.** $K = 1.5$

18. $\frac{9}{2}$ ft **19.** $x = 8$, $y = 5$

20. $x + y - 1 = 0$

21. (*a*) $10^{3.763}$ (*b*) $e^{8.666}$

22. 30°, 210° **23.** 10°, 130°, 250°, 70°, 190°, 310° **24.** 45°, 225° **25.** -1 **26.** $\dfrac{3}{4}$

27. $-\dfrac{3}{4}$ **28.** $\left(x - \dfrac{5 + \sqrt{7}i}{2}\right)\left(x - \dfrac{5 - \sqrt{7}i}{2}\right)$ **29.** 6 **30.** 31

Problem set 35

1. $\dfrac{40(2\pi)(10)(2.54)}{60}\dfrac{\text{cm}}{\text{sec}}$ **2.** $\dfrac{260(1000)(100)}{(2.54)(12)(2\pi)(60)}\dfrac{\text{rev}}{\text{min}}$

3. $A = Y + 40$, $A - 10 = 7(Y - 10) + 20$, $A = 53\frac{1}{3}$, $Y = 13\frac{1}{3}$ **4.** $W = (\$16.50)(36) = \$594$

5. 74 **6.** 11! **7.** $\dfrac{9!}{2!3!2!}$ **8.** 125 **9.** $\dfrac{1}{2}(9\text{ m})(4\text{ m})(\sin 55°) = 14.7\text{ m}^2$

10. $\dfrac{1}{2}(9\text{ cm})(5\text{ cm})(\sin 55°) = 18.4\text{ cm}^2$ **11.** $\dfrac{1}{2}(14\text{ m})(\sin 65°)(12\text{ m} + 25\text{ m}) = 234.7\text{ m}^2$

12. 5 m^2 **13.** $\left[\pi(10)^2\left(\dfrac{60°}{360°}\right) - \dfrac{(10)(10)(\sin 60°)}{2}\right][(12)^2(2.54)^2] = 8415.7\text{ cm}^2$

14. $y = 3 - 9 \cos x$ **15.** $(x - 4)^2 + (y - 5)^2 = r^2$

16. $y = (x - 2)^2 + 2$

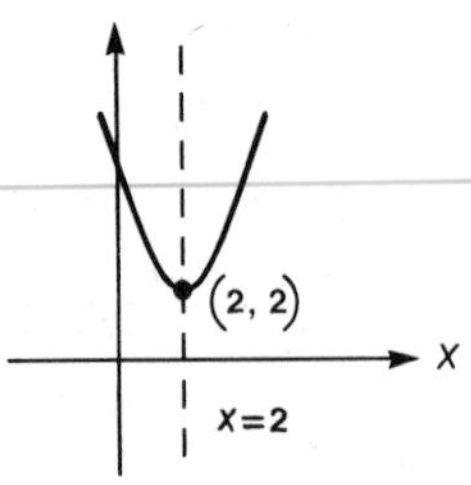

17. $y = -(x + 3)^2 + 17$

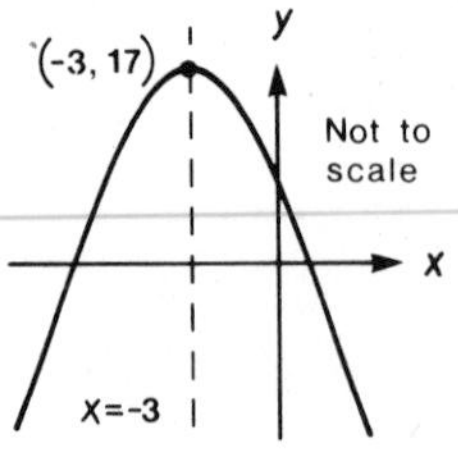

18. $\dfrac{70(1000)(100)}{(2.54)(60)}\dfrac{\text{in}}{\text{min}}$

19. $a = 6$

20. Refer to Lesson 18

21. $x = 7$, $y = 5$

22. $x + 4y + 3 = 0$

23. (*a*) $10^{4.813}$ (*b*) $e^{11.082}$

24. 135°, 315° **25.** 80°, 200°, 320°, 100°, 220°, 340° **26.** 45°, 225° **27.** $\dfrac{11}{3}$

28. $-\dfrac{2\sqrt{13}}{13}$ **29.** Refer to Lesson 28 **30.** $\dfrac{4}{3}$

Problem set 36

1. $v = \omega r = \dfrac{400(4)(60)}{2.54(12)(5280)}$ mph 2. $\omega = \dfrac{v}{r} = \dfrac{40(1000)(100)}{5(60)(60)} \dfrac{\text{rad}}{\text{sec}}$

3. $\dfrac{P_1V_1}{T_1} = \dfrac{P_2V_2}{T_2}, \dfrac{(40)(2)}{400} = \dfrac{P_2(4)}{1000}, P_2 = 50$ atm 4. $\dfrac{N_1}{Q_1} = \dfrac{N_2}{Q_2}, \dfrac{100}{2} = \dfrac{N_2}{40}, N_2 = 2000$

5. $(B + W)T_D = 24, (B - W)T_U = 8, T_D = T_U + 1, B = 3W, W = 2, B = 6$

6. $\dfrac{12!}{6!4!2!} = 13{,}860$ 7. $\dfrac{15!}{3!2!}$ 8. $\left(x - \dfrac{3}{2} + \dfrac{\sqrt{7}}{2}i\right)\left(x - \dfrac{3}{2} - \dfrac{\sqrt{7}}{2}i\right)$ 9. $y = 6 \sin\left(x - \dfrac{\pi}{2}\right)$

10. $y = 10 \sin 2x$ 11. 43.3 cm^2 12. 4 in^2 13. 217.5 ft^2 14. 4.8 m^2 15. 20.57 cm^2

16. $(x - m)^2 + (y - n)^2 = 25$ 17. $y = -(x + 2)^2 + 8$ 18. $\dfrac{100(5280)(12)}{(60)(60)} \dfrac{\text{in}}{\text{sec}}$

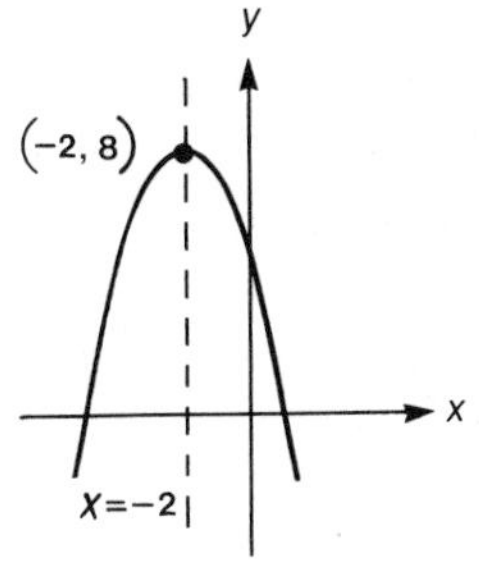

19. $M = \dfrac{20}{9}$ 20. 8021.5 km 21. (a) 10^4 (b) $e^{9.21}$ 22. $y = -\dfrac{4}{7}x + 1$

23. 60°, 300° 24. 20°, 140°, 260°, 100°, 220°, 340° 25. 30°, 150°, 270°, 90°, 210°, 330°

26. 4 27. $\dfrac{\pi}{6}$ 28. Refer to Lesson 28 29. 33 30. No solution, $x = -\dfrac{7}{3}$

Problem set 37

1. $v = \omega r = \dfrac{525(10)(2.54)(60)(60)}{100(1000)} \dfrac{\text{km}}{\text{hr}}$ 2. $\omega = \dfrac{v}{r} = \dfrac{100(5280)(12)(2.54)}{40(60)(60)} \dfrac{\text{rad}}{\text{sec}}$ 3. 3640

4. $\dfrac{25}{7}$ atm 5. $4(6) + 10(4) + 16(\text{avg}) = 30(8)$, avg = 11 6. $\dfrac{5!}{2!2!} = 30$ 7. $\dfrac{9!}{5!4!} = 126$

8. 4! 9. 5.37

10. $y = 2(x - 2)^2 - 3$

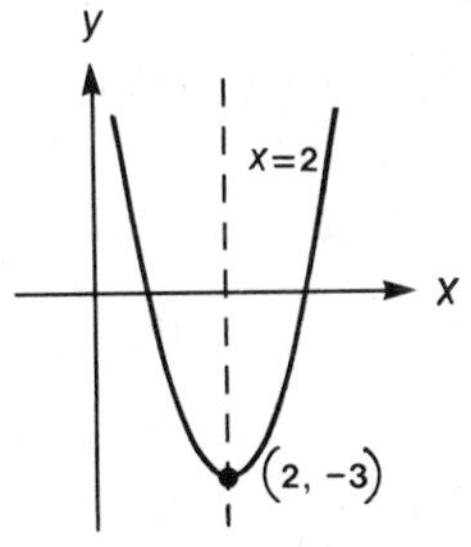

11. $y = -2(x + 2)^2 + 4$

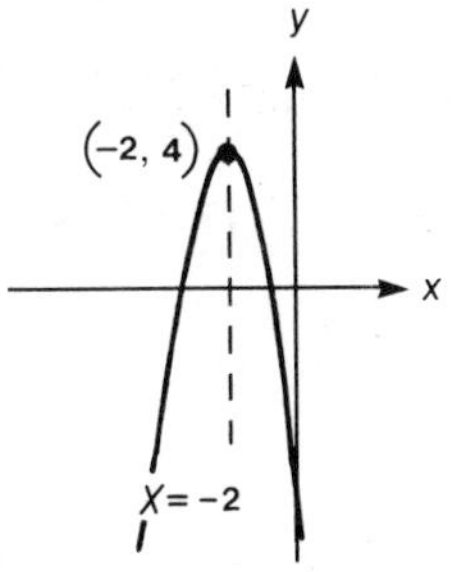

12. $y = -3 + 5 \cos(x - 135°)$

13. $y = 2 + 6 \cos 2\theta$ 14. 34.4 m^2

15. 34.5(100)(100) cm^2

16. 4.05 ft^2 17. 0.12 m^2

18. $(x - h)^2 + (y - k)^2 = r^2$

19. $\dfrac{250(1000)(100)(60)(60)}{2.54(12)(5280)} \dfrac{\text{mi}}{\text{hr}}$ 20. $6\sqrt{3}$ 21. (a) $10^{4.3}$ (b) $e^{9.9}$ 22. $3x + y - 7 = 0$

23. 30°, 330° 24. 6°, 78°, 150°, 222°, 294°, 66°, 138°, 210°, 282°, 354°

25. 15°, 135°, 255°, 75°, 195°, 315° 26. 1 27. 1 28. $\dfrac{\sqrt{15}}{4}$ 29. 1 30. 2

Problem set 38

1. $v = \omega r = 400(1)\dfrac{(60)(60)}{5280}$ mph 2. $\omega = \dfrac{v}{r} = \dfrac{40(1000)(100)}{8(2.54)(60)(2\pi)} \dfrac{\text{rev}}{\text{min}}$

3. $\dfrac{4x + 4}{2y} = \dfrac{N}{10}, N = 20\left(\dfrac{x + 1}{y}\right)$ pencils 4. 30 gal 80%, 20 gal 20% 5. $\dfrac{66}{13}$ days

6. $3!5!$ **7.** $\frac{9!}{2!2!}$ **8.** $9 \cdot 9 \cdot 8 = 648$ **9.** $\frac{2\sqrt{5}}{5}$

10. $y = 3(x - 1)^2 + 2$

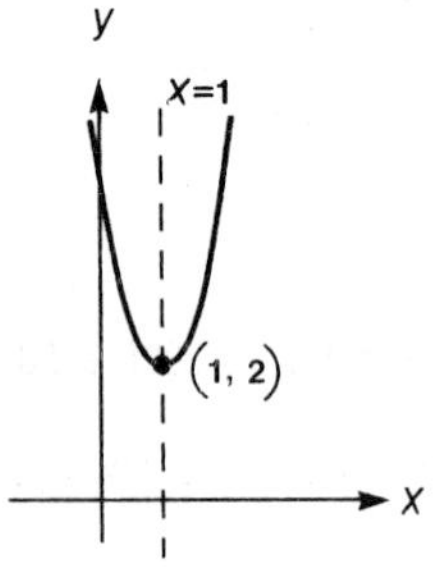

11. $y = 2(x + 1)^2 + 1$

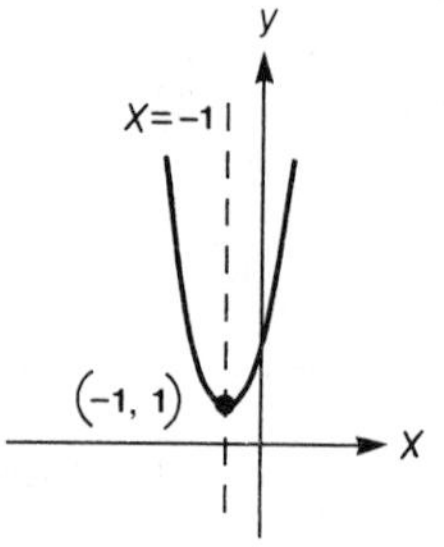

12. $y = 3 + 8 \sin\left(x - \frac{\pi}{4}\right)$

13. $y = 7 + 4 \sin 2\theta$

14. $28.53(100)(100)\ \text{cm}^2$

15. $549.65(100)(100)\ \text{cm}^2$

16. $\left(x - \frac{3}{2} + \frac{\sqrt{7}}{2}i\right)\left(x - \frac{3}{2} - \frac{\sqrt{7}}{2}i\right)$

17. $0.61\ \text{m}^2$ **18.** $(x - 3)^2 + (y - 2)^2 = 100$ **19.** $\frac{30(60)(60)}{100(1000)}\frac{\text{km}}{\text{hr}}$ **20.** $c = 7.5$ **21.** 6

22. 30 **23.** 30°, 210° **24.** 10°, 130°, 250°, 70°, 190°, 310° **25.** 1 **26.** 0

27. $\frac{3}{4}$ **28.** 3 **29.** 2 **30.** $\frac{4}{7}$

Problem set 39

1. $v = \omega r = \frac{367(16)(60)(60)}{12(5280)}\ \text{mph}$ **2.** $\omega = \frac{v}{r} = \frac{5(1000)(100)}{5(60)}\frac{\text{rad}}{\text{min}}$

3. $(A + W)(t_u + 1) = 1350$, $(A - W)t_u = 700$, $A = 8W$; $W = 50$ mph, $A = 400$ mph

4. $R + G + W = 22$, $\frac{R}{W} = \frac{1}{2}$, $\frac{G}{W} = \frac{5}{4}$, $R = 4$, $W = 8$, $G = 10$

5. $6(90 - A) = 2(180 - A) + 60$, $A = 30°$ **6.** $\frac{11!}{3!}$ **7.** 12 **8.** $x^2 + 2x + 4 = 0$ **9.** $4\sqrt{2}$

10. $y = 3(x + 1)^2 - 3$

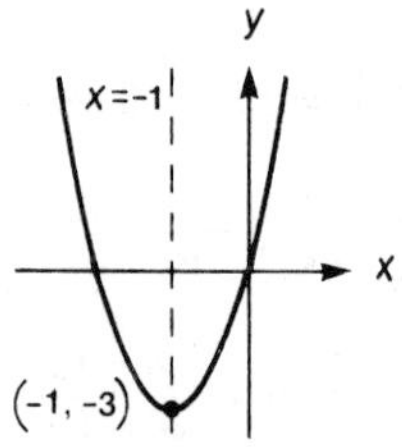

11. $y = -5 + 15 \cos(x - 45°)$ **12.** $y = -10 + 20 \cos 2\theta$

13. $190.5(100)(100)\ \text{cm}^2$ **14.** $\frac{77.4}{100(100)}\ \text{m}^2$ **15.** $279.3\ \text{cm}^2$

16. $\frac{86.2}{12(12)}\ \text{ft}^2$ **17.** $(x - 5)^2 + (y - 6)^2 = 64$

18. $4x - 3y - 5 = 0$ **19.** $2x + y$ **20.** 7 **21.** 3

22. 30°, 150°, 270° **23.** 90°, 270°, 0° **24.** 90°, 270°

25. 1 **26.** $\frac{\pi}{4}$ **27.** $\frac{\sqrt{15}}{4}$ **28.** 2 **29.** 5 **30.** 1

Problem set 40

1. $\omega = \frac{v}{r} = \frac{40(1000)(100)}{14(2.54)(60)(60)}\frac{\text{rad}}{\text{sec}}$ **2.** $v = \omega r = \frac{40(16)(2\pi)(60)(60)}{2.54(12)(5280)}\ \text{mph}$ **3.** $L = 31$, $T = 35$

4. \$247 **5.** $\frac{T}{H} = \frac{2}{1}$, $2T = 5U + 1$, $H + T + U = 15$, $N = 483$ **6.** $12 \cdot 11 \cdot 10$ **7.** 12

8. $\frac{11!}{5!4!2!}$ **9.** 24 **10.** 210 **11.** $\frac{3\sqrt{2}}{2}$

12. $y = 2(x - 1)^2 - 9$

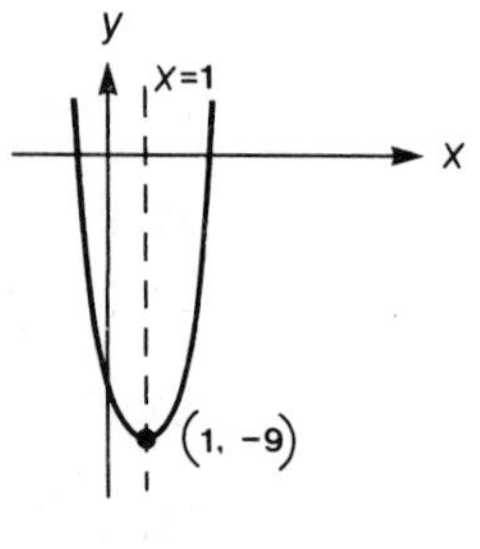

13. $y = -2 + 6 \sin\left(x - \frac{\pi}{4}\right)$ **14.** $y = 2 + 5 \sin 4\theta$

15. $\frac{625\sqrt{3}}{2}\ \text{cm}^2$ **16.** $8000\ \text{cm}^2$

17. $105.90\ \text{cm}^2$ **18.** $(x - m)^2 + (y - n)^2 = 36$

19. $y = -4x + 3$ **20.** $\dfrac{2m}{\dfrac{m}{d} + \dfrac{m}{u}} = \dfrac{2du}{d + u}$ knots **21.** $\dfrac{5^{\log_5 22}}{5^{\log_5 2}} = \dfrac{22}{2} = 11$

22. 15°, 135°, 255°, 105°, 225°, 345° **23.** 90°, 270°, 60°, 300° **24.** 30°, 150°, 210°, 330°

25. 0 **26.** 0 **27.** $-\dfrac{5}{13}$ **28.** 2 **29.** 10 **30.** $\sqrt{41}$

Problem set 41

1. $2050 = m200 + b$, $350 = m30 + b$, $m = 10$, $b = 50$, $C = 10N + 50$

2. $v = \omega r = \dfrac{723(20)}{2.54(12)(60)} \dfrac{\text{ft}}{\text{sec}}$ **3.** 40 atm **4.** 1920 **5.** $W = 2$ mph, $B = 4$ mph

6. $10 \cdot 9 \cdot 8 \cdot 7 \cdot 6$ **7.** 4! **8.** $\dfrac{11!}{5!4!2!}$ **9.** $y = \dfrac{cd - mf}{nd - me}$ **10.** 38 **11.** $\sqrt{2}$

12. $y = 3(x - 2)^2 + 22$ **13.** $y = -1 + 4\cos(x - 135°)$ **14.** $y = -3 + 5\cos\dfrac{\theta}{3}$

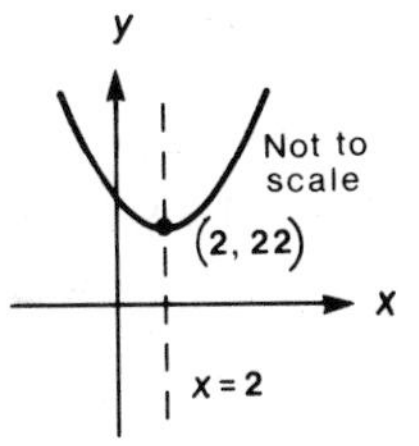

15. 626.7 cm² **16.** 90 cm² **17.** 57.4 cm²

18. $(x - a)^2 + (y - b)^2 = 16$ **19.** $5x + 3y - 2 = 0$

20. $a = \dfrac{7}{3}$, $b = 6$ **21.** 4 **22.** 0°, 90°, 180°, 270°

23. 0°, 180°, 60°, 120° **24.** 45°, 225°, 135°, 315° **25.** 0

26. $\dfrac{4}{3}$ **27.** $-\dfrac{5}{12}$ **28.** 2 **29.** $\dfrac{3}{2}$ **30.** Refer to Lesson 28

Problem set 42

1. $11 = m(2) + b$, $35 = m(8) + b$, $R = 4B + 3$, $R = 27$ **2.** $\omega = \dfrac{v}{r} = \dfrac{60(1000)(100)}{12(2.54)(60)(60)} \dfrac{\text{rad}}{\text{sec}}$

3. $B = 200$, $O = 850$ **4.** $T_M = \dfrac{m}{a}$, $T_K = \dfrac{m}{b}$, $T_K - T_M = \dfrac{m}{b} - \dfrac{m}{a} = \dfrac{ma - mb}{ab}$ hr

5. $\dfrac{1000b}{a + cb}$ **6.** 12 **7.** $2 \cdot 4!$ **8.** $\dfrac{7!}{4!3!}$ **9.** $x = \dfrac{cn - bf}{an - bm}$ **10.** 21 **11.** 7

12. $6\sqrt{2}$ **13.** $y = 2(x - 3)^2 + 1$ **14.** $y = 4 + 8\sin\left(x - \dfrac{\pi}{4}\right)$

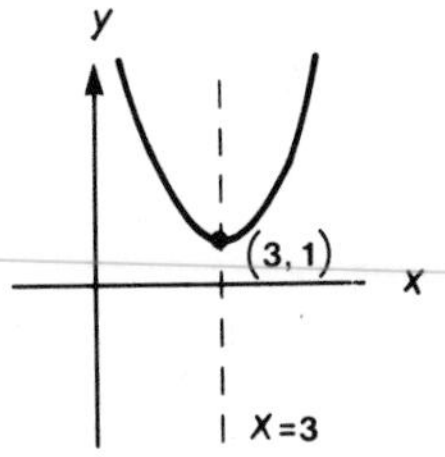

15. $y = -3 + 5\sin\dfrac{x}{2}$ **16.** 1542.7 cm² **17.** 1920 cm² **18.** 122.5 cm²

19. $(x + 4)^2 + (y - 3)^2 = 36$; radius 6, with center $(-4, 3)$

20. $(x - 4)^2 + (y + 1)^2 = 4$; radius 2, with center $(4, -1)$ **21.** $y = -2x + 4$ **22.** 6

23. 0° **24.** 0°, 180° **25.** 60°, 300°, 240°, 120° **26.** 1 **27.** 0 **28.** $\dfrac{\sqrt{11}}{6}$

29. $2\sqrt{3}$ **30.** No solution, $x = 1$

Problem set 43

1. $15{,}000 = m(10) + b$, $20{,}000 = m(20) + b$, $C = 500N + 10{,}000$, $C = \$25{,}000$

2. $v = \omega r = \dfrac{10(75)(2.54)(60)}{100(1000)}\,\dfrac{\text{km}}{\text{hr}}$ **3.** Avg rate $= \dfrac{m+k}{x+y}$, time $= \dfrac{150}{\dfrac{m+k}{x+y}} = \dfrac{150(x+y)}{m+k}$

4. $\dfrac{mr - mb}{br}$ **5.** $\dfrac{k^2t}{d} = \dfrac{N}{100}$, $N = \dfrac{100k^2t}{d}$ **6.** 50 **7.** $\dfrac{7!}{4!3!}$

8. (*a*) 6.3 cis 18.4° (*b*) $\dfrac{5\sqrt{3}}{2} + \dfrac{5}{2}i$ **9.** $6\sqrt{3} - 6i$ **10.** -6 **11.** $\dfrac{dp - cf}{pb - cq}$ **12.** 21

13. $7\sqrt{2}$ **14.** $y = -1 + 5\cos(x - 135°)$ **15.** $y = 6 - 4\cos\dfrac{2}{3}x$ **16.** 138.6 cm^2

17. 676.3 cm^2 **18.** $(x-2)^2 + y^2 = 4$; radius 2 with center (2, 0)

19. $(x+3)^2 + (y-2)^2 = 22$; radius $\sqrt{22}$ with center $(-3, 2)$ **20.** $5x + y - 12 = 0$

21. $a = \dfrac{91}{12}$, $b = \dfrac{65}{12}$ **22.** 60°, 120° **23.** 0°, 180°, 45°, 225° **24.** 60°, 240°, 300°, 120°

25. 0 **26.** -1 **27.** $-\dfrac{8}{9}$ **28.** 1 **29.** 3 **30.** 169

Problem set 44

1. \$1000 **2.** $\omega = \dfrac{v}{r} = \dfrac{45(1000)(100)}{30(60)}\,\dfrac{\text{rad}}{\text{min}}$

3. Avg rate $= \dfrac{m+x}{h+(h+4)}$, time $= \dfrac{50}{\dfrac{m+x}{h+(h+4)}} = \dfrac{50(2h+4)}{m+x}$ hr **4.** $\dfrac{x}{p} - \dfrac{x}{R}$

5. $\dfrac{500(k^2x + m)}{d}$ **6.** 26 **7.** $\dfrac{7!}{2!} = 2520$ **8.**

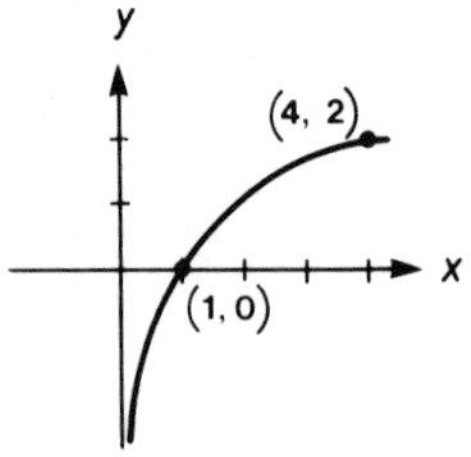

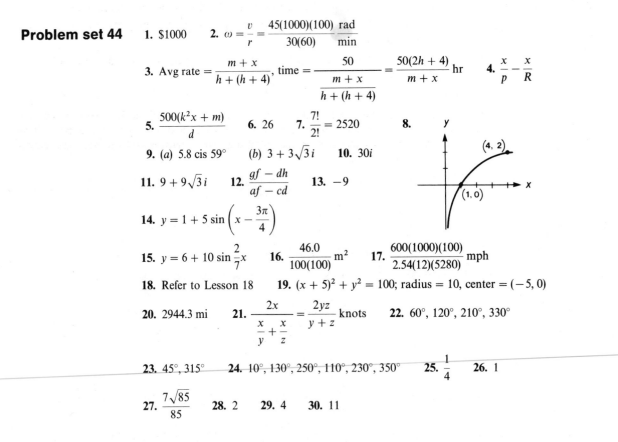

9. (*a*) 5.8 cis 59° (*b*) $3 + 3\sqrt{3}i$ **10.** $30i$

11. $9 + 9\sqrt{3}i$ **12.** $\dfrac{gf - dh}{af - cd}$ **13.** -9

14. $y = 1 + 5\sin\left(x - \dfrac{3\pi}{4}\right)$

15. $y = 6 + 10\sin\dfrac{2}{7}x$ **16.** $\dfrac{46.0}{100(100)}\,\text{m}^2$ **17.** $\dfrac{600(1000)(100)}{2.54(12)(5280)}$ mph

18. Refer to Lesson 18 **19.** $(x+5)^2 + y^2 = 100$; radius = 10, center = $(-5, 0)$

20. 2944.3 mi **21.** $\dfrac{2x}{\dfrac{x}{y} + \dfrac{x}{z}} = \dfrac{2yz}{y+z}$ knots **22.** 60°, 120°, 210°, 330°

23. 45°, 315° **24.** 10°, 130°, 250°, 110°, 230°, 350° **25.** $\dfrac{1}{4}$ **26.** 1

27. $\dfrac{7\sqrt{85}}{85}$ **28.** 2 **29.** 4 **30.** 11

Problem set 45

1. $\omega = \dfrac{v}{r} = \dfrac{12(5280)(12)}{13(60)}\,\dfrac{\text{rad}}{\text{min}}$ **2.** \$925 **3.** $\dfrac{740(2p+6)}{k+z}$ **4.** $\dfrac{m(z-a)}{az}$ **5.** $\dfrac{10{,}000p^2k}{m}$

6. $\frac{9!}{6!3!}$ 7. 5! 8.

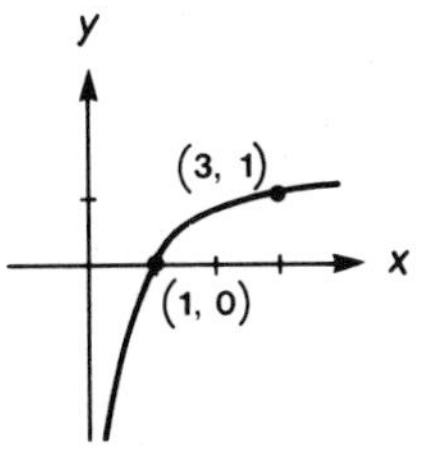

9. (a) 5 cis 36.9° (b) $-\frac{5\sqrt{3}}{2} + \frac{5}{2}i$

10. 6 cis (−10°) 11. $8\sqrt{3} - 8i$ 12. $x = \frac{cf - bg}{af - bd}$ 13. 3 14. 247

15. $y = -1 + 8 \sin 2(x - 45°)$ 16. $y = 3 + 5 \cos\left(x + \frac{3\pi}{4}\right)$ 17. 8.9 m²

18. 1440.5 cm² 19. $(x + 3)^2 + (y + 2)^2 = 1$; radius = 1, center = (−3, −2)

20. Radius = 3, center = (4, −3) 21. $5x + y - 12 = 0$ 22. $a = 9, b = 15$

23. 60°, 300°, 210°, 330° 24. 30°, 210°

25. 7.5°, 97.5°, 187.5°, 277.5°, 37.5°, 127.5°, 217.5°, 307.5° 26. 0 27. $\frac{3}{2}$ 28. $\frac{8\sqrt{17}}{17}$

29. 4, 2 30. 4

Problem set 46

1. $3E + 5F = 5.50$, $4E + 2F = 5.00$, 1 dozen eggs = \$1, flour = 50 cents per pound
2. Orig. no. = $10T + U$, new no. = $10U + T$, $T = U + 1$, $(10U + T) + T = 10T + U$, $T = 9$, $U = 8$, orig. no. = 98
3. Orig no. = $10T + U$, new no. = $10U + T$, $U = 2T + 1$, $(10T + U) + (10U + T) = 77$, $T = 2$, $U = 5$, orig. no. = 25
4. Current = 4 mph, $B = 20$ mph
5. The log drifts at the speed of the water W. Thus $T_L = 2/W$. The distance the boat goes downstream after going upstream is $(B - W)(1) + 2$, and the rate of the boat downstream is $B + W$. Distance downstream divided by rate downstream equals time downstream, which is $2/W - 1$. Thus,

$$\frac{(B - W)1 + 2}{B + W} = \frac{2}{W} - 1 \longrightarrow \frac{B - W + 2}{B + W} + 1 = \frac{2}{W} \longrightarrow \frac{B - W + 2 + B + W}{B + W} = \frac{2}{W}$$

$$\longrightarrow \frac{2B + 2}{B + W} = \frac{2}{W} \longrightarrow \frac{1 + B}{B + W} = \frac{1}{W} \longrightarrow W + BW = B + W$$

$$\longrightarrow B(W - 1) = 0 \longrightarrow W = 1 \text{ kph}$$

6. $5 \cdot 4 \cdot 3 = 60$ 7.

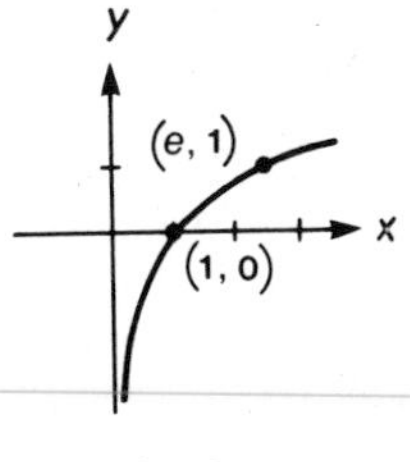

8. 13 cis 67.4° 9. $4 + 4\sqrt{3}\,i$

10. $-3\sqrt{3} - 3i$ 11. $y = \frac{ad - bc}{df - cg}$ 12. $-\frac{1}{13}$ 13. $-\frac{37}{2}$ 14. $y = 6 + 4 \sin \frac{2}{3}x$

15. $y = 3 + 5 \cos \frac{1}{2}(x - 270°)$ 16. $\frac{396.0}{100(100)}$ m² 17. $[x - (2 + \sqrt{2}i)][x - (2 - \sqrt{2}i)]$

18. Radius = 4, center = (2, −3) 19. D 20. 135°, 315°, 60°, 300° 21. 30°, 150°

22. 20°, 140°, 260°, 100°, 220°, 340° 23. −1 24. 1 25. −30° 26. 3, 1 27. 2

28. 2.4×10^{-6} 29. 9 30. $\frac{1}{9}$

Problem set 47

1. $B = 3$ lb, $R = 5$ lb, $W = 7$ lb

2. $H + T + U = 11$, $U = T + 2$, $(100U + 10T + H) + (100H + 10T + U) = 1030$, orig. no. $= 713$

3. $x = \dfrac{k(2y)(\frac{1}{2}z)^2}{\sqrt{4w}} = \dfrac{1}{4} \cdot \dfrac{kyz^2}{\sqrt{w}}$; x is multiplied by $\dfrac{1}{4}$ **4.** 75 ml **5.** 6 hr **6.** $\dfrac{10!}{3!5!2!}$

7. $B = 105°$, $A = 75°$ **8, 9, 10.** Refer to Lesson 47 **11.** 18.75

12.

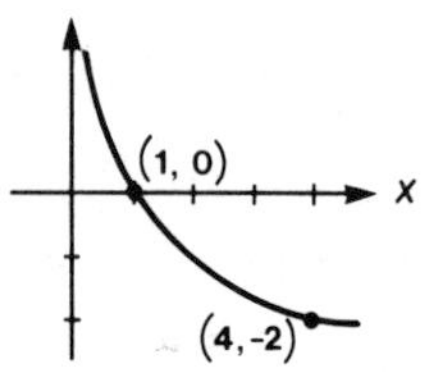

13. 7.8 cis $(-39.8°)$ **14.** $6\sqrt{2} + 6\sqrt{2}\,i$ **15.** $x = \dfrac{an - bg}{hn - gm}$

16. $y = 1 + 5 \sin \frac{1}{3}(x - 135°)$ **17.** $y = -5 + 4 \cos \frac{2}{3}\left(x + \frac{\pi}{2}\right)$

18. 65.8 cm^2 **19.** Center $= (5, -1)$, radius $= 2$ **20.** $x = 4$

21. 45°, 315°, 135° **22.** 180°

23. 0°, 90°, 180°, 270°, 45°, 135°, 225°, 315° **24.** -1 **25.** $\dfrac{6\sqrt{61}}{61}$ **26.** 1

27. No solution, $x = -2 \pm \sqrt{2}$ **28.** 7 **29.** Assume $e \approx 3$, $e^3 \approx 27$

30. 2.4×10^{-6}

Problem set 48

1. p is multiplied by 32 **2.** $\dfrac{x}{k - 20}$ **3.** Rate going, 40 mph; rate back, 80 mph

4. $3 * 2 = 2(3) - 2 = 4$, $(3 * 2) \# 4 = \dfrac{4}{4} + 4 = 5$

5. $S_1 + S_2 + S_3 = 29{,}120$; $S_2 = 0.2S_1 + S_1$, $S_3 = 0.2S_2 + S_2$, $S_1 = \$8000$ **6.** 20°

7. -38 **8.** $\dfrac{1 \pm \sqrt{41}}{2}$ **9.** $\angle B = 70°$, $\angle C = 110°$ **10, 11.** Refer to Lesson 47

12. $a = 30°$ **13.**

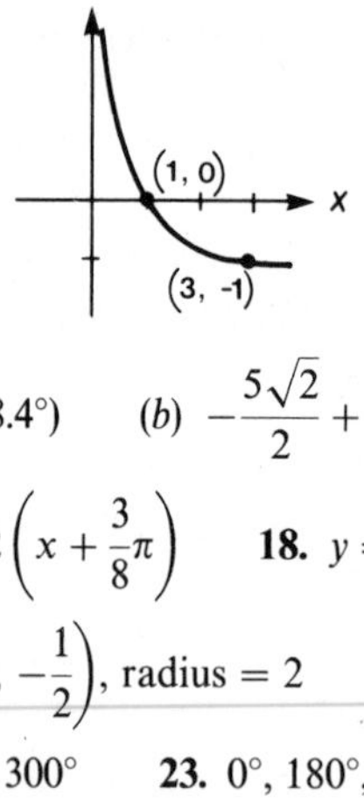

14. $6 + 6\sqrt{3}\,i$

15. (*a*) 6.3 cis $(-18.4°)$ (*b*) $-\dfrac{5\sqrt{2}}{2} + \dfrac{5\sqrt{2}}{2}i$ **16.** $y = \dfrac{ad - cp}{aq - bp}$

17. $y = 5 + 4 \cos 2\left(x + \frac{3}{8}\pi\right)$ **18.** $y = -3 + 10 \sin 3(x - 20°)$ **19.** 1764.3 cm^2

20. Center $= \left(-\frac{1}{2}, -\frac{1}{2}\right)$, radius $= 2$ **21.** $a = 2\sqrt{5}$, $b = 4\sqrt{5}$

22. 60°, 240°, 120°, 300° **23.** 0°, 180°, 210°, 330° **24.** 60°, 240°, 120°, 300°

25. -1 **26.** 1 **27.** Refer to Lesson 28 **28.** 1 **29.** $\dfrac{1}{3}$ **30.** 7.6×10^{-9}

Problem set 49

1. $-\dfrac{9}{2}$ **2.** $w = 17$ cm, $h = 33$ cm, $L = 100$ cm **3.** x is multiplied by $\dfrac{9}{4}$

4. $B = 5W$, $(B - W)T_U = 64$, $(B + W)T_D = 144$, $T_D = T_U + 2$, $B = 20$ mph, $W = 4$ mph

5. $B = 2$, $W = 7$, $R = 4$ **6.** 72

7. 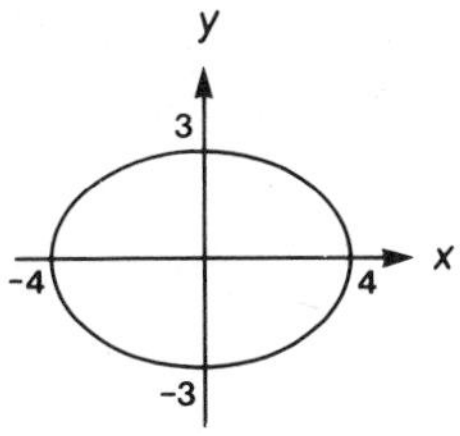

8. 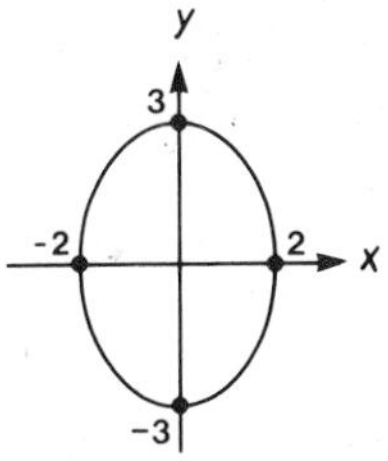

9. 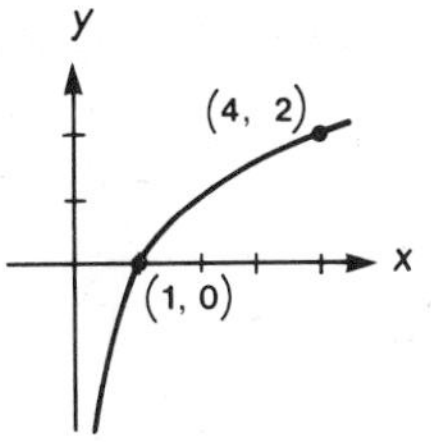

10. 10.6 cis 48.8° **11.** $3\sqrt{3} - 3i$ **12.** ± 2 **13, 14.** Refer to Lesson 47 **15.** $c = 20$

16. $\frac{80(1000)(100)}{2.54(12)(5280)}$ mph **17.** $y = -3 + 8 \cos \frac{1}{4}(x - 180°)$ **18.** $y = 1 + 2 \sin \frac{1}{2}\left(x + \frac{3}{2}\pi\right)$

19. 22.5 cm^2 **20.** Center = (−4, 6), radius = 3 **21.** $a = 6, b = 6\sqrt{3}$

22. 120°, 240°, 225°, 315° **23.** 30°, 210°, 150°, 330° **24.** 90°, 270°, 135°, 315°

25. −1 **26.** 1 **27.** 1 **28.** 8 **29.** Assuming $e \approx 3, e^{-2} \approx \frac{1}{9}$ **30.** 2.599

Problem set 50

1. $4 \# 1 = \frac{4}{2} - 2(1) = 0,\ 4 * (4 \# 1) = 4 * 0 = 2(4)^2 - 0 = 32$ **2.** 2380 **3.** $\frac{y}{m - 2}\frac{\text{yd}}{\text{min}}$

4. 143 **5.** 6° **6.** $\frac{9!}{2!2!}$ **7.** $A = 110°, a = 15.0, m = 10.3$

8. $B = 28°, b = 7.35, c = 5.868$ **9.** 5 cis 53.1°

10. 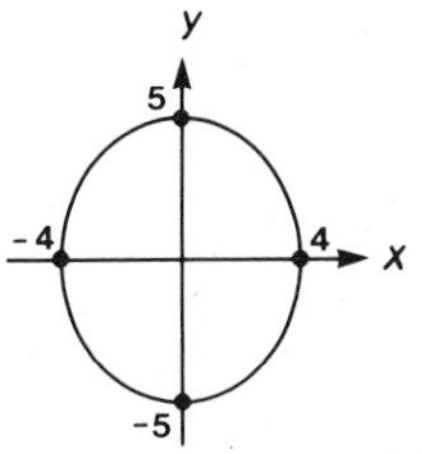

11. 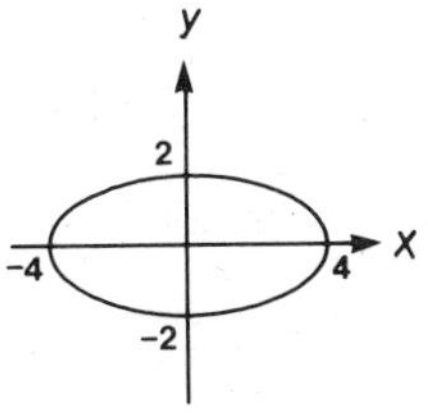

12. 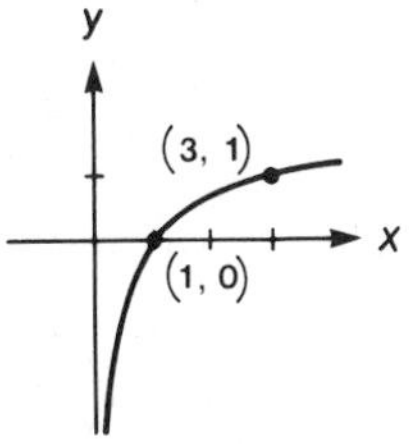

13. $9 + 9\sqrt{3}i$ **14.** 3, −2 **15, 16.** Refer to Lesson 47 **17.** $x = 15$ **18.** 4809.2 cm^2

19. $y = -3 + 5 \cos \frac{1}{2}\left(x - \frac{3\pi}{2}\right)$ **20.** $y = -10 + 20 \sin 2x$

21. Radius = 3, center = (0, −2) **22.** $a = 4\sqrt{3}, b = 4\sqrt{6}$ **23.** 90°, 270°

24. 30°, 150°, 270° **25.** 10°, 130°, 250°, 70°, 190°, 310° **26.** 1 **27.** 2 **28.** 1

29. 1 **30.** Assuming $e \approx 3, e^3 \approx 27$

Problem set 51

1. $\frac{27}{2}$ **2.** $W = 3S,\ W = \frac{1}{2}F = \frac{1}{2}GF,\ GF = 6S$ **3.** $\frac{1000}{M - 5} - \frac{1000}{M} = \frac{\$5000}{M(M - 5)}$

4. Amt of homework remaining = $h - w$, fractional part remaining = $\frac{h - w}{h}$

5. $\frac{x + 2}{x + 1}$ **6.** $\frac{7!}{3!2!2!}$ **7.** 900° **8.** 360° **9.** $54\sqrt{3} = 93.53$ **10.** 482.8 square units

11. 9:1 **12.** $A = 20°, a = 6.7, b = 9.8$ **13.** 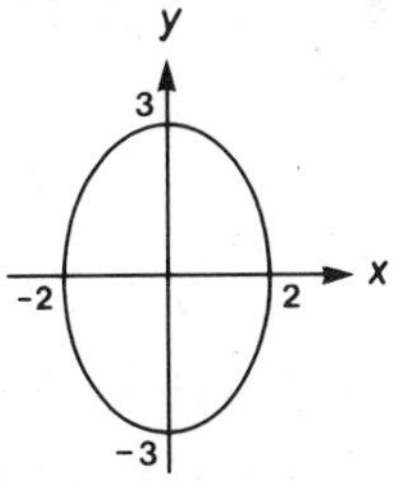

14. 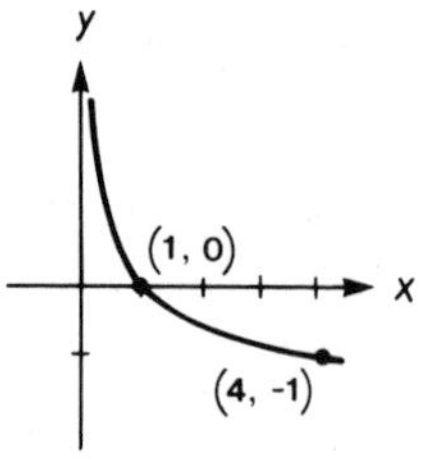

15. $6\sqrt{3} + 6i$ **16.** $0, -2$ **17.** Refer to Lesson 47

18. Refer to Lesson 18 **19.** $y = -3 + 2 \sin \frac{5}{3}(x - 27°)$

20. $y = -2 + 6 \sin \left(x - \frac{\pi}{4}\right)$ **21.** Radius = 3, center = $(-3, 0)$

22. $x = 3\sqrt{5}, y = 6\sqrt{5}$ **23.** 0°, 180°, 210°, 330°

24. 60°, 300°, 120°, 240° **25.** 30°, 150°, 270° **26.** -1 **27.** 3 **28.** $\frac{2}{3}$

29. $\frac{190}{63}$ **30.** 125

Problem set 52

1. $L_1 = 3L_2, L_2 = 3L_3, L_1 = 9L_3, \frac{L_3}{L_1 + L_2 + L_3} = \frac{L_3}{9L_3 + 3L_3 + L_3} = \frac{1}{13}$

2. \$2.60 **3.** $\frac{E - P}{E}$ **4.** $\frac{D - P}{N}$ **5.** y yards $- f$ feet $- n$ inches $= (36y - 12f - n)$ in

6. $L = 28, G = 42$ **7.** $x = 1, y = 2$ **8.** $x = -1, y = 1$ **9.** 1440° **10.** 360°

11. 300 cm^2 **12.** 4 cm **13.** 16:1 **14.** $A = 135°, a = 28.3, b = 10.4$

15. 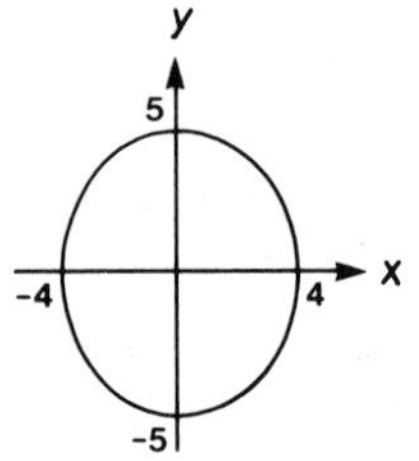

16. $12 + 12\sqrt{3}i$ **17.** $5, -4$ **18, 19.** Refer to Lesson 47

20. $y = 3 + 11 \cos \frac{3}{2}(x - 100°)$ **21.** $y = -1 + 14 \sin (x + 45°)$

22. Center = $(-5, 2)$, radius = 3 **23.** $\frac{2pk}{k + p}$ mph

24. 30°, 330°, 150°, 210° **25.** 20°, 140°, 260°, 100°, 220°, 340°

26. 0° **27.** 1 **28.** $\frac{3}{2}$ **29.** 4 **30.** Assuming $e \approx 3, e^4 \approx 81$

Problem set 53

1. Original contribution $= \frac{D}{p}$ dollars per student, new contribution $= \frac{D}{p - 20}$ dollars per student. Each student must contribute $\left(\frac{D}{p - 20} - \frac{D}{p}\right)$ more dollars.

2. 14 mi **3.** $p = \frac{km^2}{\sqrt{N}}, p = \frac{k(4m)^2}{\sqrt{9N}} = \frac{16km^2}{3\sqrt{N}}$; p is multiplied by $\frac{16}{3}$

4. $C = \$4.40 + \$1.10(m - 3) = \$4.40 + \$1.10m - \$3.30 = \$1.10m + \$1.10 = \$1.10(m + 1)$

5. $\frac{{}_8P_3}{3!} = \frac{8 \cdot 7 \cdot 6}{3 \cdot 2 \cdot 1} = 56$ **6.** $\frac{8 \cdot 7 \cdot 6 \cdot 5}{4 \cdot 3 \cdot 2 \cdot 1}$ **7.** $x = -\frac{25}{17}, y = -\frac{6}{17}$

8. $2\left(x - \frac{5}{4} + \frac{\sqrt{23}}{4}i\right)\left(x - \frac{5}{4} - \frac{\sqrt{23}}{4}i\right)$ **9.** 1980° **10.** 360° **11.** 293.9 cm^2

12. 77.3 cm^2 **13.** $\frac{25}{4}$ **14.** $A = 50°, a = 7.1, b = 8.7$ **15.** 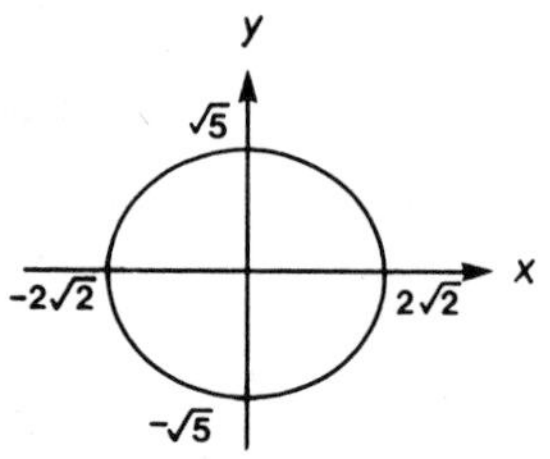

16. $5 + 5\sqrt{3}i$ **17.** 1 **18.** Refer to Lesson 47

19. Refer to Lesson 47 **20.** $y = 3 + 4 \sin \frac{2}{3}(x + 225°)$

21. $y = 10 + 6 \sin \frac{1}{2}\left(x - \frac{\pi}{2}\right)$

22. Center $= \left(\frac{1}{3}, -\frac{2}{3}\right)$, radius $= 2$ **23.** $a = \sqrt{5}, b = 2\sqrt{5}$ **24.** 60°, 120°, 240°, 300°

25. 10°, 130°, 250°, 50°, 170°, 290° **26.** 90° **27.** −1 **28.** $\frac{1}{2}$ **29.** 4 **30.** $\frac{1}{36}$

Problem set 54

1. $x = \frac{3}{5}P + 1, P = \frac{5(x-1)}{3}$ **2.** \$460 **3.** $M = 29, J = 28$

4. $R(m - 15) = y; R = \frac{y}{m - 15} \frac{\text{yd}}{\text{min}}$ **5.** $\frac{10 \cdot 9 \cdot 8 \cdot 7 \cdot 6 \cdot 5 \cdot 4 \cdot 3}{8 \cdot 7 \cdot 6 \cdot 5 \cdot 4 \cdot 3 \cdot 2 \cdot 1} = 45$

6. $\frac{10 \cdot 9 \cdot 8 \cdot 7 \cdot 6 \cdot 5}{6 \cdot 5 \cdot 4 \cdot 3 \cdot 2 \cdot 1} = 210$ **7.** $\cos x \cdot \frac{\sin x}{\cos x} = \sin x = \frac{1}{\csc x}$

8. $-\sin(-\theta)\cos(90° - \theta) = \sin\theta \sin\theta = \sin^2\theta$ **9.** $\frac{\frac{\cos x}{\sin x}}{\frac{1}{\sin x}} = \cos x$ **10.** $x = \frac{17}{12}, y = \frac{7}{8}$

11. 2340° **12.** 360° **13.** 342.4 in^2 **14.** 6.53 in **15.** $\frac{100}{9}$

16. $B = 30°, a = 11.7, b = 6.2$ **17.**

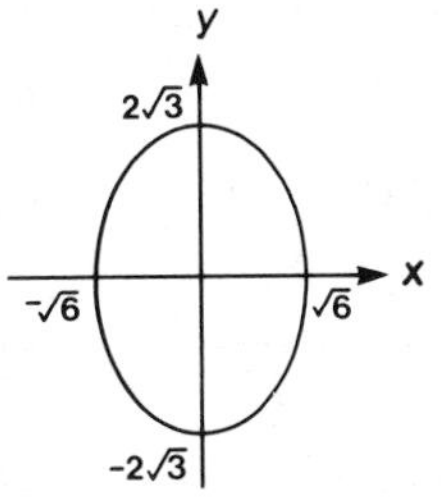

18. $9 + 9\sqrt{3}i$

19. Both triangles have two angles which are equal since both have right angles and a pair of acute angles that are equal. Hence, the third angles are equal.

20. $y = 3 + 6\cos\frac{2}{3}(x - 135°)$ **21.** $y = -3 + \frac{3}{2}\sin 4(x + 30°)$

22. Center $= \left(\frac{1}{4}, -\frac{1}{4}\right)$, radius $= 2$ **23.** B **24.** 60°, 240°, 300°, 120°

25. 15°, 105°, 195°, 285°, 75°, 165°, 255°, 345° **26.** 60°, 300°, 180° **27.** −1 **28.** 3

29. 4 **30.** $\frac{1}{5}$

Problem set 55

1. $\frac{x+2}{x+1}$ **2.** −5, −4, −3 or 4, 5, 6 **3.** \$1024 **4.** \$656

5. 50 mph for 200 mi → 4 hr; 40 mph for 400 mi → 10 hr; average rate $= \frac{600}{14} = \frac{300}{7}$ mph

6. $\frac{9 \cdot 8 \cdot 7 \cdot 6 \cdot 5}{5 \cdot 4 \cdot 3 \cdot 2 \cdot 1} = 126$ **7.** $21x^5y^2$ **8.** $x^4 + 4x^3y + 6x^2y^2 + 4xy^3 + y^4$

9. $\sin x \cdot \frac{1}{\cos x} = \frac{\sin x}{\cos x} = \tan x$

10. $\sin(-\theta)\tan(90° - \theta) = -\sin\theta\cot\theta = -\sin\theta \cdot \frac{\cos\theta}{\sin\theta} = -\cos\theta$

11. $\sec x \cot x = \frac{1}{\cos x} \cdot \frac{\cos x}{\sin x} = \frac{1}{\sin x} = \csc x$ **12.** $x = 4, y = 5$ **13.** 1800° **14.** 360°

15. 6 cm **16.** 16:9 **17.** $A = 30°, a = 10$ **18.**

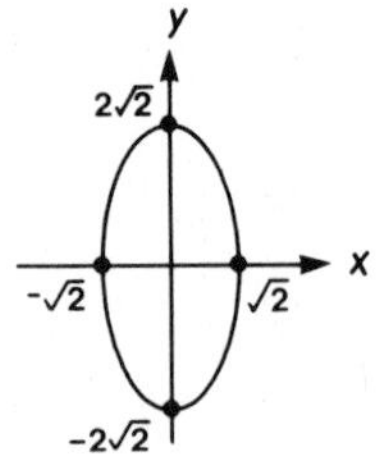

19. $4 + 4\sqrt{3}i$

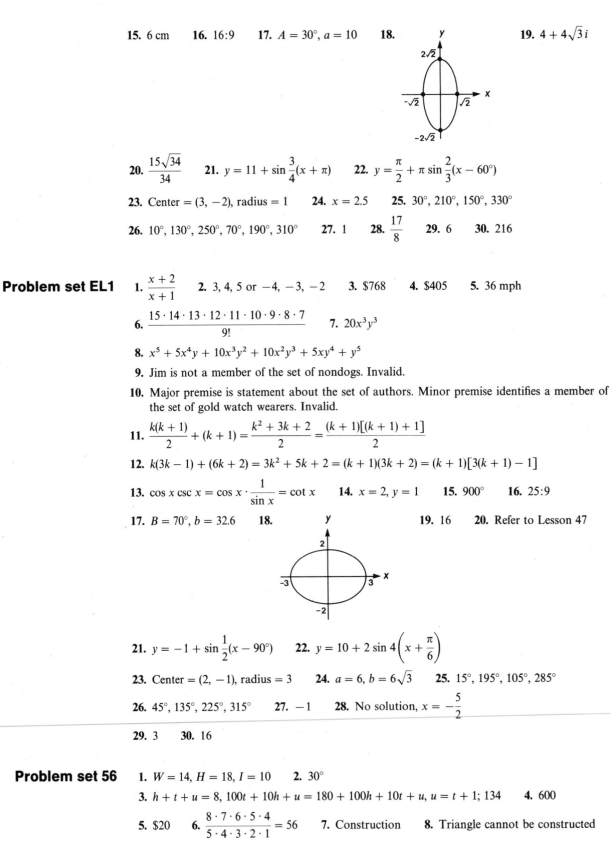

20. $\frac{15\sqrt{34}}{34}$ **21.** $y = 11 + \sin\frac{3}{4}(x + \pi)$ **22.** $y = \frac{\pi}{2} + \pi \sin\frac{2}{3}(x - 60°)$

23. Center $= (3, -2)$, radius $= 1$ **24.** $x = 2.5$ **25.** 30°, 210°, 150°, 330°

26. 10°, 130°, 250°, 70°, 190°, 310° **27.** 1 **28.** $\frac{17}{8}$ **29.** 6 **30.** 216

Problem set EL1

1. $\frac{x + 2}{x + 1}$ **2.** 3, 4, 5 or $-4, -3, -2$ **3.** \$768 **4.** \$405 **5.** 36 mph

6. $\frac{15 \cdot 14 \cdot 13 \cdot 12 \cdot 11 \cdot 10 \cdot 9 \cdot 8 \cdot 7}{9!}$ **7.** $20x^3y^3$

8. $x^5 + 5x^4y + 10x^3y^2 + 10x^2y^3 + 5xy^4 + y^5$

9. Jim is not a member of the set of nondogs. Invalid.

10. Major premise is statement about the set of authors. Minor premise identifies a member of the set of gold watch wearers. Invalid.

11. $\frac{k(k + 1)}{2} + (k + 1) = \frac{k^2 + 3k + 2}{2} = \frac{(k + 1)[(k + 1) + 1]}{2}$

12. $k(3k - 1) + (6k + 2) = 3k^2 + 5k + 2 = (k + 1)(3k + 2) = (k + 1)[3(k + 1) - 1]$

13. $\cos x \csc x = \cos x \cdot \frac{1}{\sin x} = \cot x$ **14.** $x = 2, y = 1$ **15.** 900° **16.** 25:9

17. $B = 70°, b = 32.6$ **18.**

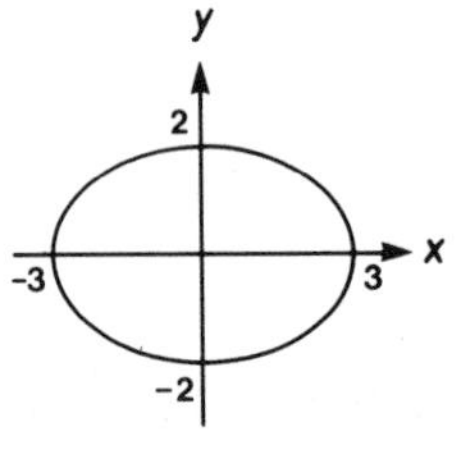

19. 16 **20.** Refer to Lesson 47

21. $y = -1 + \sin\frac{1}{2}(x - 90°)$ **22.** $y = 10 + 2 \sin 4\left(x + \frac{\pi}{6}\right)$

23. Center $= (2, -1)$, radius $= 3$ **24.** $a = 6, b = 6\sqrt{3}$ **25.** 15°, 195°, 105°, 285°

26. 45°, 135°, 225°, 315° **27.** -1 **28.** No solution, $x = -\frac{5}{2}$

29. 3 **30.** 16

Problem set 56

1. $W = 14, H = 18, I = 10$ **2.** 30°

3. $h + t + u = 8, 100t + 10h + u = 180 + 100h + 10t + u, u = t + 1$; 134 **4.** 600

5. \$20 **6.** $\frac{8 \cdot 7 \cdot 6 \cdot 5 \cdot 4}{5 \cdot 4 \cdot 3 \cdot 2 \cdot 1} = 56$ **7.** Construction **8.** Triangle cannot be constructed

9. Construction **10.** Construction **11.** Construction **12.** $56a^5b^3$

13. $x^5 + 5x^4y + 10x^3y^2 + 10x^2y^3 + 5xy^4 + y^5$

14. $\tan\theta \sec(90° - \theta) = \tan\theta \csc\theta = \dfrac{\sin\theta}{\cos\theta} \cdot \dfrac{1}{\sin\theta} = \dfrac{1}{\cos\theta} = \sec\theta$

15. $\dfrac{\csc x}{\sec x} = \dfrac{1}{\sin x} \div \dfrac{1}{\cos x} = \dfrac{\cos x}{\sin x} = \cot x$ **16.** $x = \dfrac{37}{19}, y = \dfrac{8}{19}$ **17.** 360°

18. (*a*) 4 in (*b*) 98.9 in^2 **19.** 9:4 **20.** $Y = 110°$, $y = 11.276$

21.

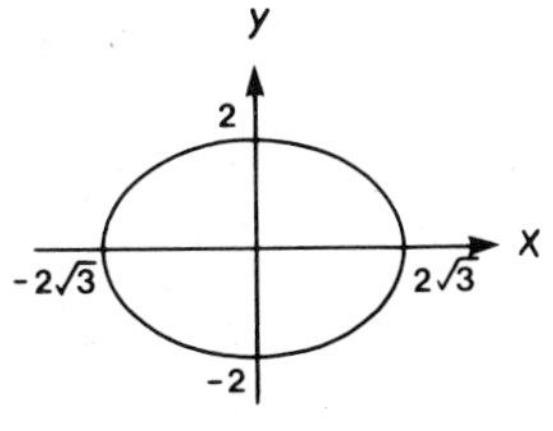

22. $6 + 6\sqrt{3}i$ **23.** Refer to Lesson 47

24. $y = -1 + 2\cos 3\left(x - \dfrac{5\pi}{18}\right)$

25. Radius $= \dfrac{4}{3}$, center $= \left(1, -\dfrac{1}{3}\right)$ **26.** $y = 2$

27. 30°, 150°, 90° **28.** $-\dfrac{2\sqrt{13}}{13}$ **29.** No solution, $x = \dfrac{2}{3}$

30. Refer to Lesson 28 **EP1.** Invalid

EP2. $\dfrac{k(k+1)}{2} + (k+1) = \dfrac{k(k+1) + 2(k+1)}{2} = \dfrac{k^2 + 3k + 2}{2} = \dfrac{(k+1)(k+2)}{2}$

$= \dfrac{(k+1)[(k+1)+1]}{2}$

Problem set 57

1. 62 **2.** \$1000 at 6%, \$2000 at 8% **3.** 2 hr **4.** 98° **5.** $25Q - Ka$

6. $\dfrac{9 \cdot 8 \cdot 7 \cdot 6 \cdot 5}{5 \cdot 4 \cdot 3 \cdot 2 \cdot 1} = 126$

7.

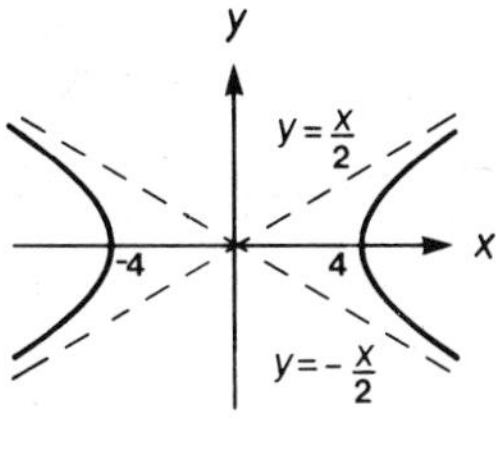

8.

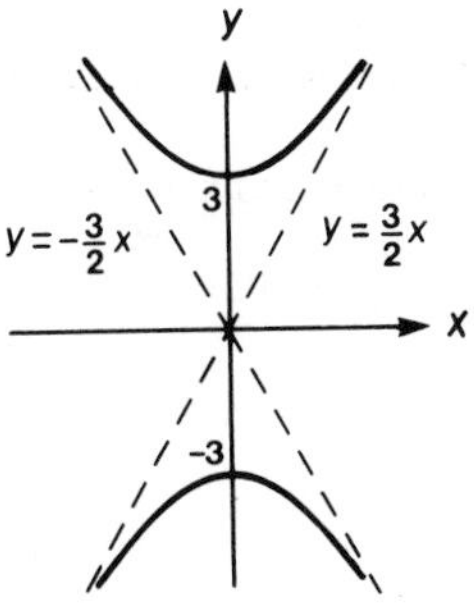

9, 10, 11. Construction **12.** $15a^2b^4$ **13.** $a^4 + 4a^3b + 6a^2b^2 + 4ab^3 + b^4$

14. $\sin\theta \csc(90° - \theta) = \sin\theta \sec\theta = \dfrac{\sin\theta}{\cos\theta} = \tan\theta$

15. $\sec(90° - \theta)\tan\theta = \csc\theta \tan\theta = \dfrac{1}{\sin\theta} \cdot \dfrac{\sin\theta}{\cos\theta} = \dfrac{1}{\cos\theta} = \sec\theta$ **16.** $x = \dfrac{29}{10}, y = \dfrac{11}{5}$

17. 360° **18.** (*a*) 5 cm (*b*) 8.1 cm **19.** 25:9 **20.** $A = 30°$, $a = 8.8$, $b = 13.4$

21.

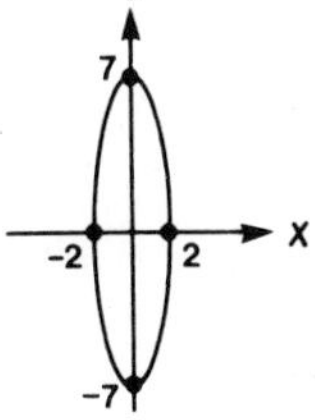

22. $-3\sqrt{3} + 3i$ **23.** Refer to Lesson 47

24. $y = 5 + 4\sin\dfrac{2}{3}\left(x - \dfrac{3}{2}\pi\right)$ **25.** Center $= (-1, -1)$, radius $= \dfrac{\sqrt{6}}{3}$

26. $a = \sqrt{449}, b = \dfrac{49}{10}$ **27.** 10°, 130°, 250°, 70°, 190°, 310°

28. 150° **29.** 1

30. Assuming $e \approx 3$, $e^{-3} \approx \dfrac{1}{27}$ **EP3.** Valid

Problem set 58

1. $C = 6$ mph, $B = 18$ mph **2.** Length $= \frac{b}{2} \cdot N + \frac{b}{2} \cdot 2N = \frac{3bN}{2}$ inches

3. $5100 = 10m + b$, $2600 = 5m + b \to C = 500M + 100$; $C = 500(2) + 100 = \$1100$

4. $40°$ **5.** $RTM = J$, $\left(\frac{1}{24 \cdot 81}\right) T \cdot 108 = 1$, $T = 18$ days for a saving of 6 days

6. $\frac{8!}{2!} = 20{,}160$ **7.** $\sqrt{5}$ cis $20°$, $\sqrt{5}$ cis $110°$, $\sqrt{5}$ cis $200°$, $\sqrt{5}$ cis $290°$

8. $16^{1/3}$ cis $30°$, $16^{1/3}$ cis $150°$, $16^{1/3}$ cis $270°$ **9.** $i, -i$ **10.** Construction

11. Impossible **12.** Construction **13.** $126a^4b^5$

14. $x^6 + 6x^5y + 15x^4y^2 + 20x^3y^3 + 15x^2y^4 + 6xy^5 + y^6$

15. $\sin(90° - \theta)\sec(90° - \theta) = \cos\theta \csc\theta = \cos\theta \cdot \frac{1}{\sin\theta} = \cot\theta$

16. $\tan\theta \cdot \frac{1}{\sec\theta} = \frac{\sin\theta}{\cos\theta}(\cos\theta) = \sin\theta$ **17.** $x = \frac{31}{22}$, $y = -\frac{7}{22}$ **18.** $2520°$

19. (*a*) 8 ft (*b*) 716.6 ft^2 **20.** $B = 40°$, $a = 12.7$, $b = 9.4$

21. Center = (0, 0); major axis is y axis, length = 8; minor axis is x axis, length = 4

22.

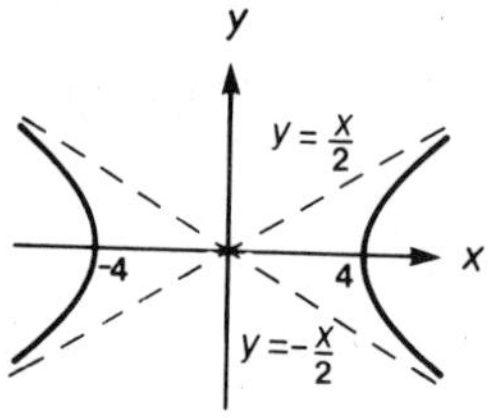

23. Vertices: (2, 0), (−2, 0); asymptotes: $y = \pm\frac{3}{2}x$ **24.** $8i$

25. Refer to Lesson 18 **26.** $y = -1 + 5\cos 3(x - 50°)$

27. Center $= \left(-\frac{1}{2}, 1\right)$, radius $= \frac{\sqrt{5}}{2}$ **28.** $x = \frac{20}{7}$

29. $15°, 105°, 195°, 285°, 75°, 165°, 255°, 345°$ **30.** No solution, $x = \frac{5}{4}$

EP4.
$$\frac{k}{k+1} + \frac{1}{(k+1)(k+2)} = \frac{k(k+2)+1}{(k+1)(k+2)} = \frac{k^2+2k+1}{(k+1)(k+2)} = \frac{(k+1)^2}{(k+1)(k+2)}$$
$$= \frac{k+1}{k+2} = \frac{k+1}{(k+1)+1}$$

Problem set 59

1. $\frac{2}{7}T = \frac{3}{7}$; $T = 1\frac{1}{2}$ hr **2.** $RTM = J$, $\left(\frac{50}{M}\right) \cdot T \cdot 10 = 20$; $T = \frac{M}{25}$ days **3.** 728

4. $300 - hm$ **5.** $\frac{1}{4} = \frac{3}{4}B$; $B = \frac{1}{3}$ cup **6.** $4 \cdot 3 \cdot 1 \cdot 2 \cdot 1 = 24$

7. 3 cis $12°$, 3 cis $132°$, 3 cis $252°$ **8.** $\sqrt{2} + \sqrt{2}i, -\sqrt{2} + \sqrt{2}i, -\sqrt{2} - \sqrt{2}i, \sqrt{2} - \sqrt{2}i$

9, 10. Construction **11.** $15x^4y^2$ **12.** $a^3 + 3a^2b + 3ab^2 + b^3$

13, 14, 15. Refer to Lesson 59 **16.** $x = \frac{23}{11}$, $y = \frac{15}{22}$ **17.** $2340°$

18. (*a*) 3 in (*b*) 118.7 in^2 (*c*) 6.3 in **19.** $C = 15°$, $b = 20.1$, $c = 9.1$

20. Center = (0, 0); major axis is x axis, length = 10; minor axis is y axis, length = 6

21. Vertices = (±5, 0); asymptotes: $y = \pm\frac{4}{5}x$ **22.** $6 + 6\sqrt{3}i$ **23.** Refer to Problem set 47

24. $y = -4 + 6\cos\frac{3}{2}(x + 110°)$ **25.** Center = (−1, 2); radius $= \frac{4\sqrt{3}}{3}$ **26.** $a = 21$, $b = \frac{72}{5}$

27. $7.5°, 97.5°, 187.5°, 277.5°, 52.5°, 142.5°, 232.5°, 322.5°$ **28.** $-\frac{4}{3}$

29. No solution, $x = -\frac{16}{13}$ **30.** 5 **EP5.** Invalid

Problem set 60

1. $F + S = 150, \frac{F}{27} + \frac{S}{23} = 6, F = 81, S = 69$

2. $F = 45°, S = 55°, T = 80°$ 3. $RTM = J, \left(\frac{3}{10}\right) \cdot 10 \cdot M = 18; M = 6$

4. $\frac{500p}{c}$ 5. $\frac{280 + G_5}{5} = 60; G_5 = 20$ 6. $\frac{10 \cdot 9 \cdot 8 \cdot 7 \cdot 6 \cdot 5}{6 \cdot 5 \cdot 4 \cdot 3 \cdot 2 \cdot 1} = C_6^{10} = 210$

7. $\sqrt{2} + \sqrt{2}i, -\sqrt{2} + \sqrt{2}i, -\sqrt{2} - \sqrt{2}i, \sqrt{2} - \sqrt{2}i$ 8. 2 cis 15°, 2 cis 135°, 2 cis 255°

9. Construction 10. Construction 11. $35x^4y^3$ 12. $m^4 + 4m^3n + 6m^2n^2 + 4mn^3 + n^4$

13. $\frac{1 - \cos^2 x}{\sec^2 x - 1} = \frac{\sin^2 x}{\tan^2 x} = \sin^2 x \cdot \frac{\cos^2 x}{\sin^2 x} = \cos^2 x$

14. $\frac{1}{1 + \sin A} + \frac{1}{1 - \sin A} = \frac{1 - \sin A + (1 + \sin A)}{1 - \sin^2 A} = \frac{2}{\cos^2 A} = 2 \sec^2 A$

15. $\frac{1}{\cot A} + \cot A = \frac{1 + \cot^2 A}{\cot A} = \frac{\csc^2 A}{\cot A} = \frac{1}{\sin^2 A} \cdot \frac{\sin A}{\cos A} = \frac{1}{\sin A \cos A} = \csc A \sec A$

16. $x = \frac{26}{27}, y = \frac{5}{27}$ 17. 1980° 18. 100.8 in^2 19. $a = 5.14, B = 91.43°, C = 48.57°$

20. $A = 40.5°, B = 111.8°, C = 27.7°$

21. Center = (0, 0); major axis is x axis, length = 10; minor axis is y axis, length = 4

22. Center = (0, 0); vertices = $(\pm 5, 0)$; asymptotes: $y = \pm\frac{2}{5}x$ 23. $4 - 4\sqrt{3}i$

24. Refer to Lesson 47 25. $y = 10 + 2 \sin \frac{9}{8}(x - 90°)$

26. Center = (1, −2), radius = $\frac{3\sqrt{2}}{2}$ 27. $x = 6, y = 6\sqrt{3}$

28. 50°, 170°, 290°, 110°, 230°, 350° 29. $\frac{3}{5}$ 30. No solution, $x = -\frac{10}{11}$

EP6. $(k + 1)^2 = k^2 + 2k + 1$

Problem set 61

1. $L + W + H = 18, H = \frac{4}{5}(L + W), H = 4(L - W); L = 6$ ft, $W = 4$ ft, $H = 8$ ft

2. $t - rh$ 3. $RTW = J, \left(\frac{3}{5 \cdot 7}\right) \cdot T \cdot 9 = 27; T = 35$ days

4. $\frac{a}{3}T + \frac{3}{b}T = 13; T = \frac{39b}{ba + 9}$ days 5. $\left(\frac{p}{5 \cdot 10}\right) 15t = k \rightarrow t = \frac{10k}{3p}$ days

6. $\frac{20!}{10!6!4!}$ 7. $\frac{1}{2} + \frac{\sqrt{3}}{2}i, -1, \frac{1}{2} - \frac{\sqrt{3}}{2}i$

8. 2 cis 15°, 2 cis 105°, 2 cis 195°, 2 cis 285° 9. Construction

10. Triangle cannot be constructed 11. $p^5 + 5p^4q + 10p^3q^2 + 10p^2q^3 + 5pq^4 + q^5$

12. $\frac{\sin A}{1 + \cos A} + \frac{1 + \cos A}{\sin A} = \frac{\sin^2 A + 1 + 2 \cos A + \cos^2 A}{(\sin A)(1 + \cos A)} = \frac{1 + 1 + 2 \cos A}{(\sin A)(1 + \cos A)}$

$$= \frac{2(1 + \cos A)}{(\sin A)(1 + \cos A)} = \frac{2}{\sin A} = 2 \csc A$$

13. $\frac{\csc^2 \theta - \cot^2 \theta}{1 + \cot^2 \theta} = \frac{1}{\csc^2 \theta} = \sin^2 \theta$ 14. $\frac{\sin x}{\csc x} + \frac{\cos x}{\sec x} = \sin^2 x + \cos^2 x = 1$ 15. 6.7

16. 1440° 17. $B = 74.73°, C = 60.27°, a = 7.33$ 18. $A = 51.3°, B = 110.5°, C = 18.2°$

19. Center = (0, 0); major axis is x axis, length = 12; minor axis is y axis, length = 6

20. Center = (0, 0); vertices = (± 6, 0); asymptotes: $y = \pm\frac{1}{2}x$ **21.** $3 - 3\sqrt{3}\,i$ **22.** $\frac{2\sqrt{5}}{5}$

23. $y = 2 + 9 \sin 4\left(x - \frac{\pi}{8}\right)$ **24.** Center = $(-1, 3)$; radius = $\frac{\sqrt{38}}{2}$ **25.** $a = \frac{9\sqrt{5}}{2}$, $b = \frac{3}{2}$

26. 30°, 150°, 210°, 330°, **27.** -1.9 **28.** -0.75 **29.** 1.17

30. No solution, $x = -\frac{18}{5}$ **EP7.** Invalid

Problem set 62

1. $\frac{1}{6}$ **2.** $\frac{60}{289}$ **3.** $\frac{15}{68}$ **4.** $(2\pi r)(40)\left(\frac{1}{12}\right)\left(\frac{1}{60}\right) = \frac{\pi r}{9}\,\frac{\text{ft}}{\text{sec}}$ **5.** \$130

6. $\frac{J}{M}T(M - 5) = k$; $T = \frac{kM}{J(M - 5)}$ days

7. 2 cis 12°, 2 cis 84°, 2 cis 156°, 2 cis 228°, 2 cis 300° **8, 9.** Construction

10. $x^6 + 6x^5z + 15x^4z^2 + 20x^3z^3 + 15x^2z^4 + 6xz^5 + z^6$

11. $$\frac{\sin A}{1 - \cos A} + \frac{1 - \cos A}{\sin A} = \frac{\sin^2 A + 1 - 2\cos A + \cos^2 A}{(\sin A)(1 - \cos A)} = \frac{2 - 2\cos A}{(\sin A)(1 - \cos A)}$$
$$= \frac{2(1 - \cos A)}{(\sin A)(1 - \cos A)} = \frac{2}{\sin A} = 2 \csc A$$

12. $$\frac{\sec^2 \theta - \tan^2 \theta}{\tan^2 \theta + 1} = \frac{1}{\sec^2 \theta} = \cos^2 \theta$$

13. $$\frac{1}{\tan(-x)} + \tan(-x) = -\frac{1}{\tan x} - \tan x = -\frac{1 + \tan^2 x}{\tan x} = -\frac{\sec^2 x}{\tan x} = \frac{-1}{\cos^2 x} \cdot \frac{\cos x}{\sin x}$$
$$= \frac{-1}{\cos x} \cdot \frac{1}{\sin x} = -\sec x \csc x$$

14. 716.6 cm^2 **15.** 360° **16.** $B = 79.1°$, $C = 40.9°$, $a = 10.6$

17. $A = 44.4°$, $B = 101.5°$, $C = 34.1°$

18. Center = (0, 0); major axis is y axis, length = 8; minor axis is x axis, length = 6

19. Center = (0, 0); vertices = (0, ± 4), asymptotes: $y = \pm\frac{4}{3}x$ **20.** 1

21. Refer to Lesson 18 **22.** $y = -8 + 6 \cos \frac{9}{2}(x - 30°)$ **23.** Center = $(-1, 3)$; radius = 4

24. $a = \frac{13}{4}$, $b = \frac{39}{4}$ **25.** 120°, 240°, 0° **26.** $-\frac{5}{4}$ **27.** -11.75 **28.** -2 **29.** 15.6

30. $\frac{2}{3}$ **EP8.** $k(k + 1) + 2(k + 1) = (k + 1)(k + 2) = (k + 1)[(k + 1) + 1]$

Problem set 63

1. 40° **2.** $R(p + m) = k$; $R = \frac{k}{p + m}\,\frac{\text{yd}}{\text{min}}$

3. $\frac{4}{3} \cdot 6 + R_B \cdot 6 = 11$, $R_B = \frac{1 \text{ job}}{2 \text{ day}} \rightarrow 2$ jobs in 4 days

4. $4[11N + 11(N + 2)] = 10[11(N + 1)] - 66$; 22, 33, 44 **5.** $\frac{1}{8}$ **6.** (*a*) $\frac{16}{49}$ (*b*) $\frac{2}{7}$

7. $\sqrt{3} + i$, $-1 + \sqrt{3}i$, $-\sqrt{3} - i$, $1 - \sqrt{3}\,i$ **8, 9.** Construction

10. $a^7 + 7a^6c + 21a^5c^2 + 35a^4c^3 + 35a^3c^4 + 21a^2c^5 + 7ac^6 + c^7$

11. $\dfrac{\csc^4 x - \cot^4 x}{\csc^2 x + \cot^2 x} + \cot^2 x = \dfrac{(\csc^2 x - \cot^2 x)(\csc^2 x + \cot^2 x)}{\csc^2 x + \cot^2 x} + \cot^2 x$
$= \csc^2 x - \cot^2 x + \cot^2 x = \csc^2 x$

12. $\cos x - \cos x \sin^2 x = (\cos x)(1 - \sin^2 x) = (\cos x)(\cos^2 x) = \cos^3 x$

13. $\dfrac{\sec^2 \theta - 1}{\cot \theta} = \dfrac{\tan^2 \theta}{\cot \theta} = \tan^3 \theta$ 14. $\cos(-\theta)\csc(-\theta) = \cos(-\theta) \cdot \dfrac{1}{\sin(-\theta)} = \cot(-\theta)$

15. 9.7 cm 16. $A = 44.1°$, $B = 83.3°$, $C = 52.6°$ 17. 30.64 cm^2

18. Center = (0, 0), major axis is x axis, length = 10; minor axis is y axis, length = 4

19. Vertices = $(\pm 5, 0)$; asymptotes: $y = \pm\dfrac{2}{5}x$ 20. Refer to Lesson 47

21. Refer to Lesson 63 22. See Lesson 45, Problem 15

23. Center = (−3, 2), radius = $2\sqrt{7}$ 24. $y = 15$ 25. 10°, 130°, 250°, 110°, 230°, 350°

26. 60°, 120°, 240°, 300° 27. 1.2 28. 4.5 29. $[x - (-2 + \sqrt{2}i)][x - (-2 - \sqrt{2}i)]$

30. $\sqrt{2}$ **EP9.** Invalid

Problem set 64

1. $\dfrac{2h}{m}T = m + 60$, $T = \dfrac{h(m + 60)}{2m}$ hr 2. −4, −3, −2, or 4, 5, 6 3. $\dfrac{1}{4}$

4. $60(4 + T) = 360$, $T = 2$ hr to go 160 mi → 80 mph 5. (a) $\dfrac{20}{81}$ (b) $\dfrac{5}{18}$

6. $10 \cdot 4 \cdot 5 = 200$ 7. $x = 1$, $y = 2$ 8. $x = \dfrac{10}{7}$, $y = -\dfrac{5}{7}$ 9. Construction

10. $\sqrt{3} + i$, $-\sqrt{3} + i$, $-2i$

11. $p^8 + 8p^7q + 28p^6q^2 + 56p^5q^3 + 70p^4q^4 + 56p^3q^5 + 28p^2q^6 + 8pq^7 + q^8$

12. $\sec^2 x - \sec^2 x \cos^2 x = (\sec^2 x)(1 - \cos^2 x) = \sec^2 x \sin^2 x = \dfrac{1}{\cos^2 x} \cdot \sin^2 x = \tan^2 x$

13. $\dfrac{\sec^4 x - \tan^4 x}{\sec^2 x + \tan^2 x} = \dfrac{(\sec^2 x - \tan^2 x)(\sec^2 x + \tan^2 x)}{\sec^2 x + \tan^2 x} = \sec^2 x - \tan^2 x = 1$

14. $\cos(-x)\tan(-x)\csc(-x) = (\cos x)(-\tan x) \cdot \dfrac{1}{\sin(-x)} = -\tan x \cdot \dfrac{\cos x}{-\sin x}$
$= -\dfrac{\sin x}{\cos x} \cdot \left(-\dfrac{\cos x}{\sin x}\right) = 1$

15. $\dfrac{\sin^2 x + \cos^2 x}{\sec^2 x - 1} = \dfrac{1}{\tan^2 x} = \cot^2 x$ 16. 36:25 17. $A = 47.8°$, $B = 112.2°$, $c = 3.7$

18. $40(100)(100)\ \text{cm}^2$ 19. $\dfrac{80(5280)(12)(2.54)}{100(1000)(60)(60)} \dfrac{\text{km}}{\text{sec}}$

20. Vertices = $(\pm 4, 0)$, asymptotes: $y = \pm\dfrac{3}{4}x$ 21. Refer to Lesson 18

22. Center = (2, 0), radius = 2

23.

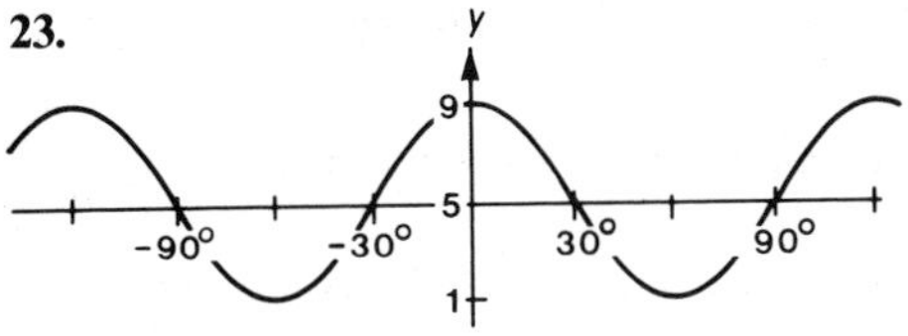

24.

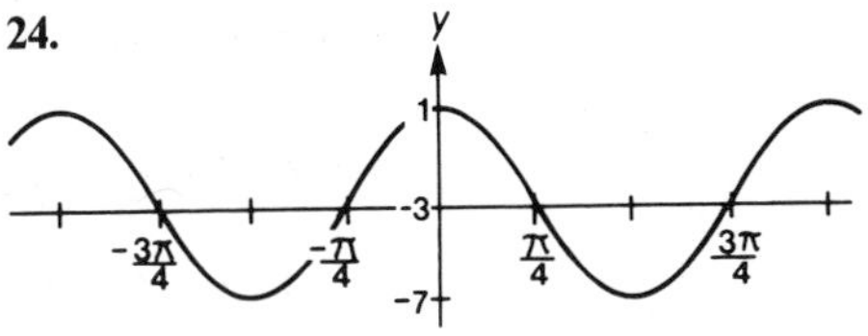

25. $(2x^2y^4 - 3p^3)(4x^4y^8 + 6x^2p^3y^4 + 9p^6)$

26. 7.5°, 97.5°, 187.5°, 277.5°, 37.5°, 127.5°, 217.5°, 307.5° **27.** 30°, 150°, 210°, 330°, 60°, 300°
28. 0.92 **29.** 33.6 **30.** 8 **EP10.** $(n+1)^2 = n^2 + 2n + 1$

Problem set 65

1. $R_L T_L = S,\ R_B T_B = S + 30,\ R_B = 1,\ R_L = \frac{1}{12},\ T_L = T_B;\ T = 32\frac{8}{11}$ min

2. $R_L T_L = S,\ R_B T_B = S + 45,\ R_L = \frac{1}{12},\ R_B = 1,\ T_L = T_B;\ T = 49\frac{1}{11}$ min **3.** 4, 6, 8

4. $10(t+5) = 25(t-1),\ t = 5$; distance = 100 mi **5.** $\frac{4}{7}$ **6.** $5! = 120$

7. $x = 2,\ y = 3$ **8.** Construction

9. $x^9 + 9x^8y + 36x^7y^2 + 84x^6y^3 + 126x^5y^4 + 126x^4y^5 + 84x^3y^6 + 36x^2y^7 + 9xy^8 + y^9$

10. $\sqrt{3} + i,\ -1 + \sqrt{3}i,\ -\sqrt{3} - i,\ 1 - \sqrt{3}i$ **11.** 60°, 300° **12.** 180°, 120°, 240° **13.** 0°

14. $\frac{\cos^4 x - \sin^4 x}{\cos^2 x - \sin^2 x} = \frac{(\cos^2 x + \sin^2 x)(\cos^2 x - \sin^2 x)}{\cos^2 x - \sin^2 x} = \cos^2 x + \sin^2 x = 1$

15. $\tan x + \cot x = \frac{\sin x}{\cos x} + \frac{\cos x}{\sin x} = \frac{\sin^2 x + \cos^2 x}{\sin x \cos x} = \frac{1}{\sin x \cos x} = \sec x \csc x$

16. $\frac{1}{1 + \cos x} + \frac{1}{1 - \cos x} = \frac{2}{1 - \cos^2 x} = \frac{2}{\sin^2 x} = 2\csc^2 x$ **17.** 77.25 cm²

18. $A = 101.5°,\ B = 44.4°,\ C = 34.1°$ **19.** 25.7 **20.** 1800° **21.** 5.3 cm²

22. Refer to Lesson 47

23. Center = (0, 0), major axis: y axis, length = 6; minor axis: x axis, length = 4

24. Vertices: $(0, \pm 3)$; asymptotes: $y = \pm\frac{3}{2}x$

25.

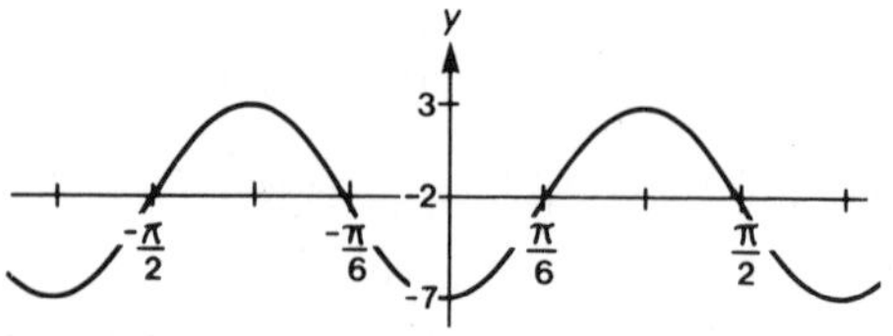

26. See Lesson 46, Problem 15

27. D **28.** 3.46

29. No solution, $x = 0$

30. 1.27 **EP11.** Valid

Problem set EL2

1. $49\frac{1}{11}$ min **2.** $54\frac{6}{11}$ min **3.** 2, 4, 6 **4.** 60 mi **5.** $\frac{4}{7}$ **6.** 5!

7.
$$\begin{aligned}\frac{1}{6}k(k+1)(2k+1) + (k+1)^2 &= (k+1)\left[\frac{1}{6}k(2k+1) + (k+1)\right]\\ &= (k+1)\left[\frac{1}{3}k^2 + \frac{1}{6}k + k + 1\right] = (k+1)\left[\frac{1}{3}k^2 + \frac{7}{6}k + 1\right]\\ &= (k+1)\left(\frac{1}{6}\right)(2k^2 + 7k + 6)\\ &= \frac{1}{6}(k+1)(k+2)(2k+3)\\ &= \frac{1}{6}(k+1)[(k+1)+1][2(k+1)+1]\end{aligned}$$

8. $2^{k+1} - 2 + 2^{k+1} = 2(2^{k+1}) - 2 = 2^{k+2} - 2 = 2^{(k+1)+1} - 2$ **9.** Yes

10. $x = 1,\ y = -2$ **11.** Construction **12.** $x^5 + 5x^4y + 10x^3y^2 + 10x^2y^3 + 5xy^4 + y^5$

13. $1 + \sqrt{3}i,\ -\sqrt{3} + i,\ -1 - \sqrt{3}i,\ \sqrt{3} - i$ **14.** 0°, 180°, 135°, 315° **15.** 120°, 240°

16. $\dfrac{\tan^2 x - 1}{\tan x} = \tan x - \dfrac{1}{\tan x} = \tan x - \cot x$

17. $\sec x - \cos x = \dfrac{1}{\cos x} - \cos x = \dfrac{1 - \cos^2 x}{\cos x} = \dfrac{\sin^2 x}{\cos x} = \sin x \cdot \dfrac{\sin x}{\cos x} = \sin x \tan x$

18. 173.8 cm^2 **19.** $c = 5.04$, $A = 52.5°$, $B = 97.5°$ **20.** 1440° **21.** 9.1 cm^2

22. Center = (2, 0), radius = 3 **23.**

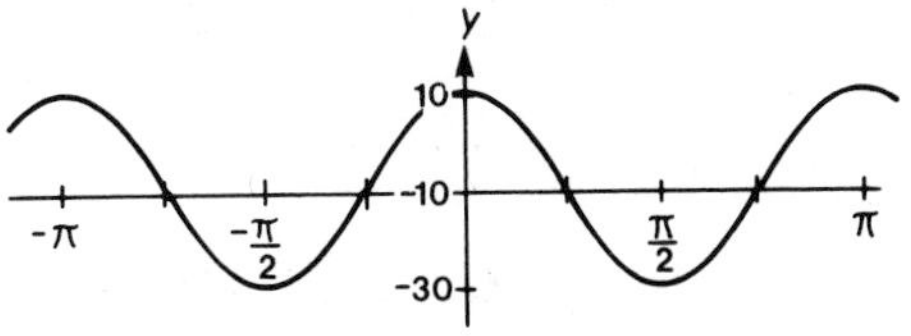

24. $\dfrac{60(5280)(12)(2.54)}{100(60)(60)} \dfrac{\text{m}}{\text{sec}}$

25. 12 **26.** 15°, 195°, 75°, 255°

27. 60°, 300°, 120°, 240° **28.** −1.97 **29.** 1.3 **30.** 9

Problem set 66

1. $R_L T_L = S$, $R_B T_B = S + 60$, $R_L = \dfrac{1}{12}$, $R_B = 1$, $T_L = T_B$; $T = \dfrac{720}{11}$ min **2.** $\dfrac{(A + 10)k}{3m}$

3. 3, 5, 7 **4.** 1600 mi **5.** $\dfrac{1}{16}$ **6.** $\dfrac{5}{216}$ **7.** $x = 1$, $y = -1$ **8.** Construction

9. $56p^3q^5$ **10.** $\dfrac{3}{2} + \dfrac{3\sqrt{3}}{2}i$, -3, $\dfrac{3}{2} - \dfrac{3\sqrt{3}}{2}i$ **11.** 30°, 150° **12.** 270°, 210°, 330°

13. 0° **14.** $\dfrac{1}{\sec^2 \theta} + \dfrac{1}{\csc^2 \theta} = \cos^2 \theta + \sin^2 \theta = 1$

15. $\sec \theta - \tan \theta \sin \theta = \dfrac{1}{\cos \theta} - \dfrac{\sin^2 \theta}{\cos \theta} = \dfrac{1 - \sin^2 \theta}{\cos \theta} = \dfrac{\cos^2 \theta}{\cos \theta} = \cos \theta$

16. $\dfrac{\sec^2 \theta}{\sec^2 \theta - 1} = \dfrac{\sec^2 \theta}{\tan^2 \theta} = \dfrac{1}{\cos^2 \theta} \cdot \dfrac{\cos^2 \theta}{\sin^2 \theta} = \dfrac{1}{\sin^2 \theta} = \csc^2 \theta$ **17.** 6.53 cm

18. $A = 84.4°$, $B = 60.6°$, $c = 4.6$ **19.** Refer to Lesson 47 **20, 21.** Refer to Lesson 66

22. $x = 6.9$, $y = 8$, $z = 13.9$

23. Center = (0, 0); major axis: x axis, length = 10; minor axis: y axis, length = 8

24. Vertices = $(\pm 5, 0)$; asymptotes: $y = \pm\dfrac{4}{5}x$

25.

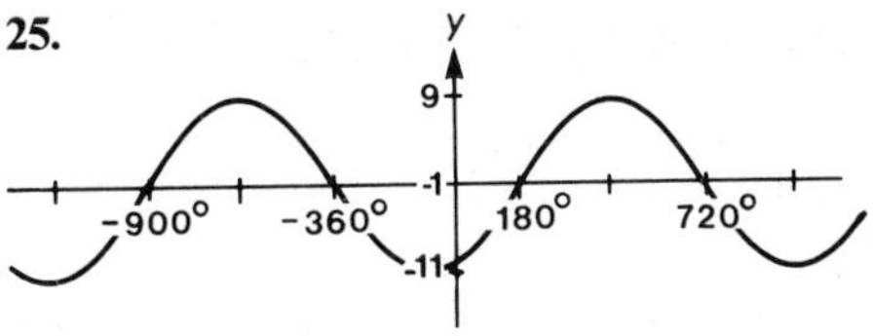

26.

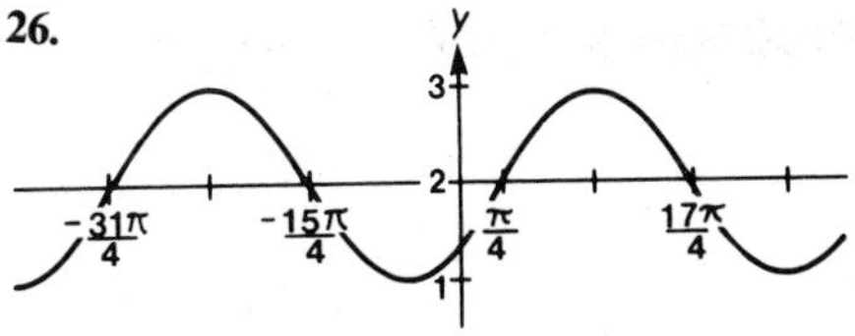

27. 3.06 **28.** $\sqrt{2}$ **29.** Refer to Lesson 28 **30.** 1.06

EP12. $\dfrac{k(k + 1)(2k + 1)}{6} + (k + 1)^2 = \dfrac{k(k + 1)(2k + 1) + 6(k + 1)^2}{6}$

$= \dfrac{(k + 1)[k(2k + 1) + 6(k + 1)]}{6} = \dfrac{(k + 1)[2k^2 + k + 6k + 6]}{6}$

$= \dfrac{(k + 1)(2k^2 + 7k + 6)}{6} = \dfrac{(k + 1)(2k + 3)(k + 2)}{6}$

$= \dfrac{(k + 1)[(k + 1) + 1][2(k + 1) + 1]}{6}$

Problem set 67

1. $R_L T_L = S$, $R_B T_B = S + 15$, $R_B = 1$, $R_L = \frac{1}{12}$, $T_L = T_B$, $T = 16\frac{4}{11}$ min **2.** $O = 4I + 5$

3. 2, 4, 6 **4.** $\frac{1920}{17}$ km **5.** $\frac{13}{68}$ **6.** $\frac{1}{6}$ **7.** $x = 2, y = 1$ **8.** Construction

9. $-10, -4, 2, 8, 14$ **10.** -111 **11.** $a_1 = 3$, $a_1 + 4d = -13$; $-1, -5, -9$

12. $a_1 + 9d = -30$, $a_1 + 19d = 40$; $-93, -86, -79, -72, -65$

13. $(2x + 3y) + 5d = 7x + 8y$; $a_8 = 9x + 10y$ **14.** $2i, -\sqrt{3} - i, \sqrt{3} - i$ **15.** 210°, 330°, 270°

16. 0° **17.** 110°, 230°, 350°, 50°, 170°, 290°

18. $\dfrac{\sec^2 x}{\sec^2 x - 1} = \dfrac{\sec^2 x}{\tan^2 x} = \dfrac{1}{\cos^2 x} \cdot \dfrac{\cos^2 x}{\sin^2 x} = \dfrac{1}{\sin^2 x} = \csc^2 x$

19. $\dfrac{\cos^2 \theta}{\sin \theta} + \sin \theta = \dfrac{\cos^2 \theta + \sin^2 \theta}{\sin \theta} = \dfrac{1}{\sin \theta} = \csc \theta$

20. $\dfrac{\cos(-x)}{\sin(-x)\cot(-x)} = \dfrac{\cos x}{-\sin x\left(-\dfrac{\cos x}{\sin x}\right)} = \dfrac{\cos x}{\cos x} = 1$ **21.** $A = 83.3°$, $B = 52.6°$, $C = 44.1°$

22. $2\sqrt{2}$

23. $\angle BAC = \angle CED$ (given), $\angle ACB = \angle DCE$ (vert. $\angle$'s are equal), $\triangle ACB \sim \triangle ECD$ (2 $\angle$'s of 2 $\triangle$'s are $=$), $\dfrac{BC}{CD} = \dfrac{AB}{DE}$ (corresponding sides proportional)

24. $\angle CDB = \angle ABC$ (both are rt. angles), $\angle C = \angle C$, $\triangle BCD \sim \triangle ACB$ (2 $\angle$'s of 2 $\triangle$'s are $=$), $\dfrac{BC}{AC} = \dfrac{BD}{AB}, \dfrac{BD}{AB} = \dfrac{CD}{CB}, \dfrac{BC}{AC} = \dfrac{CD}{CB}$

25.

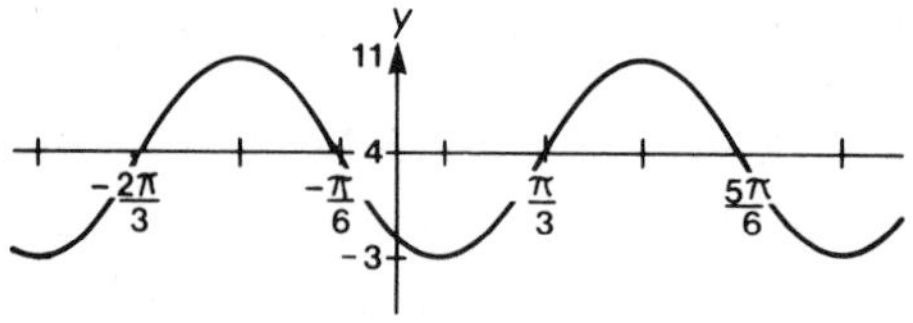

26. See Lesson 47, Problem 16

27. 0.81 **28.** $\frac{24}{5}$ **29.** 1.17

30. Vertices $= (\pm 3, 0)$; asymptotes: $y = \pm\frac{4}{3}x$ **EP13.** *b*

Problem set 68

1. $R_L T_L = S$, $R_B T_B = S + 25$, $R_B = 1$, $R_L = \frac{1}{12}$, $T_L = T_B$, $T = 27\frac{3}{11}$ min

2. Multiples of 3 are $3n$, $3n + 3$, $3n + 6$; $3[(3n) + (3n + 6)] = 4(3n + 3) + 42$; 18, 21, 24

3. $R_L T_L = R_E T_E$, $R_L = 60$, $R_E = 90$, $T_E = T_L - 2$, $D = 360$ km **4.** $\dfrac{x}{y - k}\dfrac{\text{yd}}{\text{min}}$

5. $\frac{2}{9} \cdot \frac{1}{8} = \frac{1}{36}$ **6.** $\frac{13}{36}$ **7.** $x = -2, y = -2$ **8.** Cannot be constructed **9.** -21

10. 26, 46, 66, 86 **11.** 3, 7, 11, 15 **12.** 2 cis 10°, 2 cis 100°, 2 cis 190°, 2 cis 280°

13. $\sin 15° = \sin(60° - 45°) = \sin 60° \cos 45° - \sin 45° \cos 60° = (0.866)(0.707) - (0.707)(0.5) = 0.259$

14. $\cos\left(\theta - \dfrac{\pi}{4}\right) = \cos\theta\cos\dfrac{\pi}{4} + \sin\theta\sin\dfrac{\pi}{4} = \dfrac{\sqrt{2}}{2}\cos\theta + \dfrac{\sqrt{2}}{2}\sin\theta = \dfrac{\sqrt{2}}{2}(\cos\theta + \sin\theta)$

15. Refer to Lesson 68

16. $\tan(30° + 45°) = \dfrac{\tan 30° + \tan 45°}{1 - \tan 30° \tan 45°} = \dfrac{1/\sqrt{3} + 1}{1 - 1/\sqrt{3}} = \dfrac{1 + \sqrt{3}}{\sqrt{3} - 1}$

17. 270° **18.** 0° **19.** 30°, 120°, 210°, 300°, 60°, 150°, 240°, 330°

20. $\sec x + \sec x \tan^2 x = (\sec x)(1 + \tan^2 x) = (\sec x)(\sec^2 x) = \sec^3 x$

21. $\dfrac{\sin^2 x}{\cos x} + \cos x = \dfrac{\sin^2 x + \cos^2 x}{\cos x} = \dfrac{1}{\cos x} = \sec x$

22. $\dfrac{\tan(-\theta)\cos(-\theta)}{\sin(-\theta)} = \dfrac{-\tan\theta\cos\theta}{-\sin\theta} = \dfrac{\sin\theta}{\cos\theta}\cdot\dfrac{\cos\theta}{\sin\theta} = 1$

23. $a = 3.8$, $B = 65°$, $C = 95°$ **24.** Refer to Lesson 18

25. $\angle ADE = \angle ABC$, $\angle AED = \angle ACB$ (since $\overline{DE} \parallel \overline{BC}$), $\triangle ADE \sim \triangle ABC$, $\dfrac{AD}{AB} = \dfrac{AE}{AC}$ (CPCTE)

26. $a = 7.9$, $b = 19.4$, $h = 7.3$ **27.**

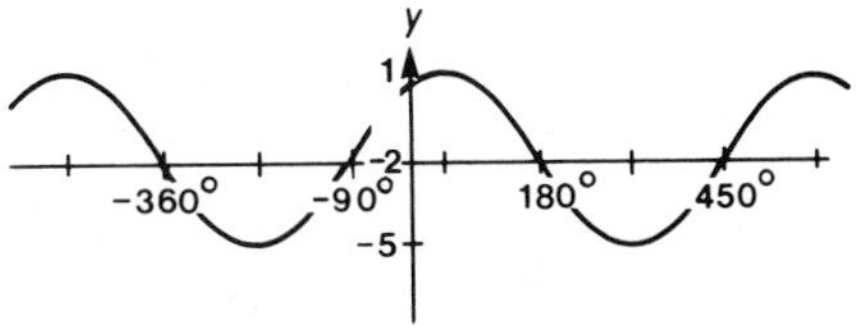

28. -2.85 **29.** 3 **30.** $\dfrac{9}{7}$

EP14. $\dfrac{5k(k+1)}{2} + 5(k+1) = \dfrac{5k^2 + 5k + 10k + 10}{2} = \dfrac{5k^2 + 15k + 10}{2}$

$= \dfrac{5(k^2 + 3k + 2)}{2} = \dfrac{5(k+1)[(k+1)+1]}{2}$

Problem set 69

1. $R_L T_L = S$, $R_B T_B = S + 15$, $R_B = 1$, $R_L = \dfrac{1}{12}$, $T_L = T_B$, $T = 16\dfrac{4}{11}$ min

2. $C + B = 100$, $\dfrac{3}{4}C + \dfrac{2}{3}B = 70$, $C = \$40$, $B = \$60$ **3.** $\dfrac{1}{30}$ **4.** $\dfrac{5}{36}$ **5.** 38 **6.** 462

7. $x = 1$, $y = 3$ **8.** Construction **9.** 13, 16, 19, 22 **10.** 3, 1, -1, -3

11. 2 cis 12°, 2 cis 84°, 2 cis 156°, 2 cis 228°, 2 cis 300°

12. $\cos(30° + 45°) = \cos 30° \cos 45° - \sin 30° \sin 45° = (0.866)(0.707) - (0.5)(0.707) = 0.259$

13. $\sin\left(\theta + \dfrac{\pi}{6}\right) = \sin\theta\cos\dfrac{\pi}{6} + \sin\dfrac{\pi}{6}\cos\theta = \dfrac{\sqrt{3}}{2}\sin\theta + \dfrac{1}{2}\cos\theta$

14. $\tan(A - B) = \dfrac{\tan A - \tan B}{1 + \tan A \tan \mathrm{B}}$ **15.** 120°, 240° **16.** 60°, 300°

17. 7.5°, 97.5°, 187.5°, 277.5°, 37.5°, 127.5°, 217.5°, 307.5°

18. $\csc x + \csc x \cot^2 x = (\csc x)(1 + \cot^2 x) = (\csc x)(\csc^2 x) = \csc^3 x$

19. $\dfrac{1 - \cos^2\theta}{1 + \tan^2\theta} = \dfrac{\sin^2\theta}{\sec^2\theta} = \sin^2\theta\cos^2\theta$ **20.** $\sin^2\theta = 1 - \cos^2\theta = (1 - \cos\theta)(1 + \cos\theta)$

21. $a = 3.1$, $B = 41.0°$, $C = 119.0°$

22. $\angle ADE = \angle ABC$, $\angle AED = \angle ACB$, $\triangle ADE \sim \triangle ABC \rightarrow \dfrac{AB}{AD} = \dfrac{AC}{AE}$

$\rightarrow \dfrac{AD + DB}{AD} = \dfrac{AE + EC}{AE} \rightarrow 1 + \dfrac{DB}{AD} = 1 + \dfrac{EC}{AE} \rightarrow \dfrac{DB}{AD} = \dfrac{EC}{AE} \rightarrow \dfrac{AD}{DB} = \dfrac{AE}{EC}$

23. $a = 12$ **24.** $c = 10$ **25.** $a = \dfrac{15}{2}$ **26.** $a = 6.9$, $b = 9.8$, $h = 5.7$

27.

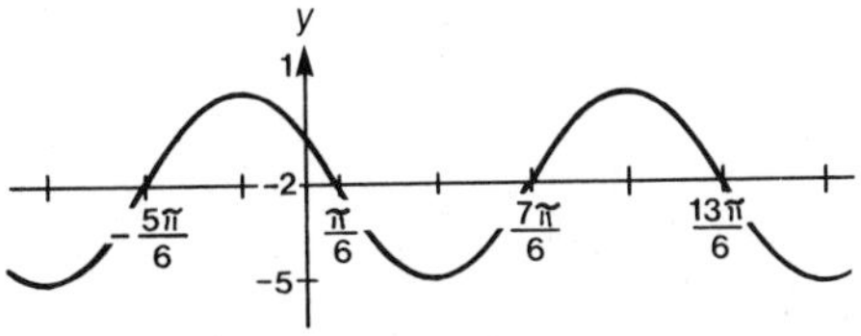

28. -1.76 **29.** $-\dfrac{1}{2}$

30. Center $= (2, -1)$, radius $= 2$

EP15. Valid

Problem set 70

1. $N = 400e^{0.23t}$, 6320 at midnight

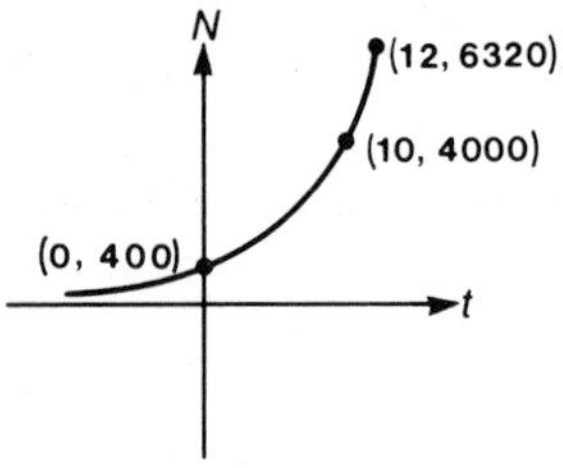

2. $M = 40e^{-0.014t}$, 9.86 g after 100 min

3. $N = 100e^{-0.4t}$, half-life = 1.7 hours

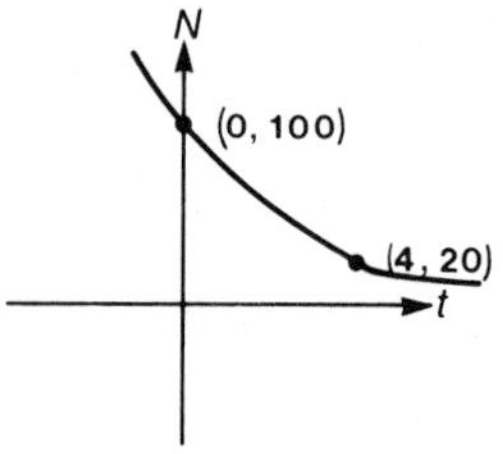

4. $3{:}16\frac{4}{11}$ **5.** $\frac{25}{102}$ **6.** $\frac{1}{36}$

7. $x = \frac{22}{17}, y = \frac{8}{17}$ **8.** Construction

9. -74 **10.** 6, 4, 2

11. 3 cis 10°, 3 cis 130°, 3 cis 250°

12. $\sin(45° + 30°) = \sin 45° \cos 30° + \sin 30° \cos 45° = (0.707)(0.866) + (0.5)(0.707) = 0.966$

13. $\sin\left(\theta - \frac{\pi}{6}\right) = \sin\theta\cos\frac{\pi}{6} - \sin\frac{\pi}{6}\cos\theta = \frac{\sqrt{3}}{2}\sin\theta - \frac{1}{2}\cos\theta$

14. $\tan(A + B) = \dfrac{\tan A + \tan B}{1 - \tan A \tan B}$ **15.** 30°, 210°, 120°, 300°

16. 72°, 252°, 63°, 243° **17.** 0°, 90°, 180°, 270°

18. $\dfrac{\cos\theta}{1 - \sin\theta} - \dfrac{\cos\theta}{1 + \sin\theta} = \dfrac{2\cos\theta\sin\theta}{1 - \sin^2\theta} = \dfrac{2\cos\theta\sin\theta}{\cos^2\theta} = \dfrac{2\sin\theta}{\cos\theta} = 2\tan\theta$

19. $\dfrac{\cos^3 x + \sin^3 x}{\cos x + \sin x} = \dfrac{(\cos x + \sin x)(\cos^2 x - \sin x\cos x + \sin^2 x)}{\cos x + \sin x}$

$= \cos^2 x - \sin x\cos x + \sin^2 x = 1 - \sin x\cos x$

20. $(1 - \sin\theta)(1 + \sin\theta) = 1 - \sin^2\theta = \cos^2\theta$ **21.** $a = 14.7$ **22.** $EC = \frac{9}{2}$ **23.** $d = 14$

24. $a = 8.7, b = 12.2, h = 7.1$ **25.** 61.9 cm² **26.**

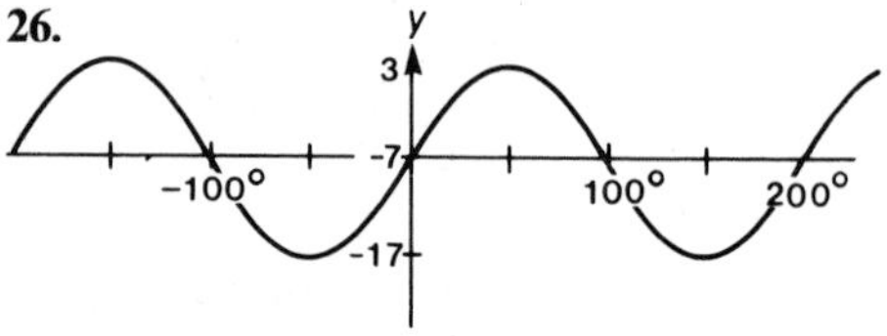

27. 0.12 **28.** $-\frac{14}{27}$ **29.** 3

30. Refer to Lesson 47

EP16. $\dfrac{a(1 - r^k)}{1 - r} + ar^k = \dfrac{a - ar^k}{1 - r} + \dfrac{ar^k(1 - r)}{1 - r} = \dfrac{a - ar^k + ar^k - ar^{k+1}}{1 - r} = \dfrac{a - ar^{k+1}}{1 - r} = \dfrac{a(1 - r^{k+1})}{1 - r}$

Problem set 71

1. $R = 40e^{0.65t}$, after 8 years, 7250.9

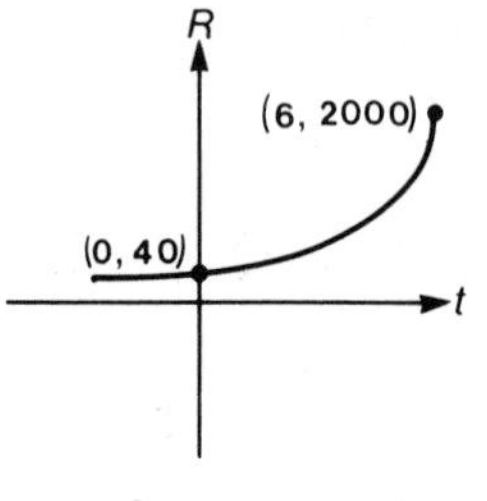

2. $T = 40{,}000e^{-0.029t}$, half-life = 23.9 hours

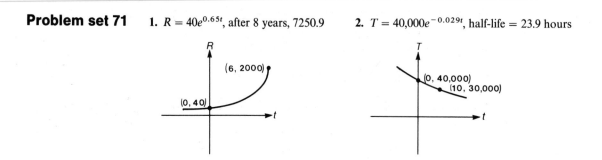

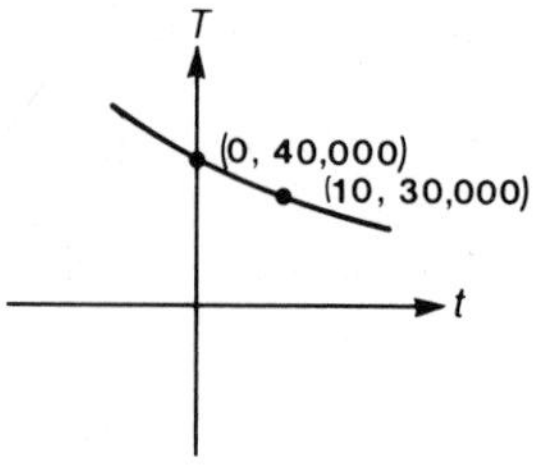

3. $10\frac{10}{11}$ min **4.** $\frac{1}{14}$ **5.** $\frac{2}{17}$ **6.** 4, 6, 8 **7.** $\frac{x^2}{16} + \frac{y^2}{7} = 1$

8. $49x^2 + 24y^2 - 1176 = 0$ **9.** $\frac{x^2}{4} + \frac{y^2}{25} = 1$ **10.** $x = 1, y = 3$ **11.** -42

12. 2, −4, −10, −16 **13.** $\sin\left(x - \frac{\pi}{2}\right) = \sin x \cos \frac{\pi}{2} - \sin \frac{\pi}{2} \cos x = -\cos x$

14. $\tan 75° = \frac{\tan 45° + \tan 30°}{1 - \tan 45° \tan 30°} = \frac{1 + 0.577}{1 - (1)(0.577)} = 3.73$

15. $\tan 15° = \frac{\tan 60° - \tan 45°}{1 + \tan 60° \tan 45°} = \frac{\sqrt{3} - 1}{1 + \sqrt{3}}$ **16.** 60°, 240°, 150°, 330° **17.** 70.5°, 289.5°

18. 7.5°, 97.5°, 187.5°, 277.5°, 37.5°, 127.5°, 217.5°, 307.5°

19. $\frac{\sin\theta}{1 - \cos\theta} - \frac{\sin\theta}{1 + \cos\theta} = \frac{2\sin\theta\cos\theta}{1 - \cos^2\theta} = \frac{2\sin\theta\cos\theta}{\sin^2\theta} = \frac{2\cos\theta}{\sin\theta} = 2\cot\theta$

20. $\frac{\tan^3 x + 1}{\tan x + 1} = \frac{(\tan x + 1)(\tan^2 x - \tan x + 1)}{\tan x + 1} = \tan^2 x + 1 - \tan x = \sec^2 x - \tan x$

21. $A = 40.0°, B = 31.0°$

22. $\angle ABD = \angle ACE$, $\angle ADB = \angle AEC$ (corres. $\angle$'s of $\|$ lines are =) $\rightarrow \triangle ABD \sim \triangle ACE$

$\rightarrow \frac{AC}{AB} = \frac{AE}{AD} \rightarrow \frac{AB + BC}{AB} = \frac{AD + DE}{AD} \rightarrow 1 + \frac{BC}{AB} = \frac{DE}{AD} + 1 \rightarrow \frac{BC}{AB} = \frac{DE}{AD}$

23. $c = 12$ **24.** $a = 7.2, b = 10.8, h = 6$ **25.** 2160° **26.** See Lesson 48, Problem 18

27. 0.2 **28.** $\frac{1}{2}$ **29.** 81 **30.** Refer to Lesson 47 **EP17.** Invalid

Problem set 72

1. $N = 80e^{0.8t}$; 4 years from when year began

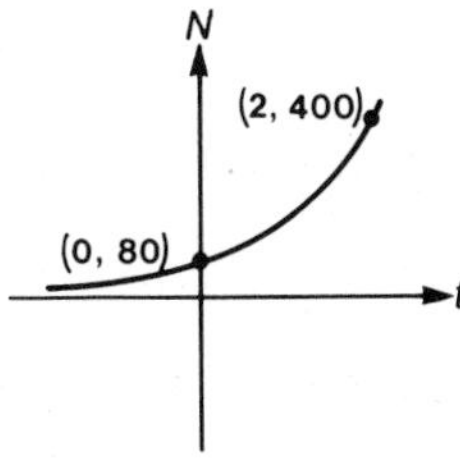

2. $N = 2000e^{-0.35t}$ **3.** $\frac{1}{2}$

4. $10M + 20W + 30C = 3825, M = W, M = 2C, M = 85, \rightarrow \frac{M}{7} = \frac{85}{7} = \$12.14$ per day

5. $\frac{1}{16}$ **6.** $\frac{1}{72}$ **7, 8, 9.** Refer to Lesson 72 **10.** $\frac{x^2}{25} + \frac{y^2}{16} = 1$ **11.** $\frac{x^2}{48} + \frac{y^2}{64} = 1$

12. $\frac{x^2}{36} + \frac{y^2}{4} = 1$ **13.** 38 **14.** −4, −6, −8

15. $\sin(60° + 45°) = \sin 60° \cos 45° + \sin 45° \cos 60° = \frac{\sqrt{6}}{4} + \frac{\sqrt{2}}{4} = \frac{\sqrt{6} + \sqrt{2}}{4}$

16. $\sin 15° = \sqrt{\frac{1 - \cos 30°}{2}} = \sqrt{\frac{1 - 0.866}{2}} = 0.259$

17. 30°, 150° **18.** 60°, 300°, 120°, 240°

19. $\sec^2 x \sin^2 x + \sin^2 x \csc^2 x = (\sin^2 x)(\sec^2 x + \csc^2 x) = (\sin^2 x)\left(\frac{1}{\cos^2 x} + \frac{1}{\sin^2 x}\right)$

$= 1 + \frac{\sin^2 x}{\cos^2 x} = 1 + \tan^2 x = \sec^2 x$

20. $\sin^2\theta + \tan^2\theta + \cos^2\theta = 1 + \tan^2\theta = \sec^2\theta$ **21.** $A = 55.8°$

22. $AB = \frac{15}{4}$ **23.** $c = \frac{16}{3}$

24. $\angle ABC = \angle CDE$ (given), $\angle ACB = \angle DCE$ (vert. $\angle$'s are $=$) $\rightarrow \triangle ACB \sim \triangle ECD$ $\rightarrow \frac{BC}{CD} = \frac{AB}{DE}$

25.

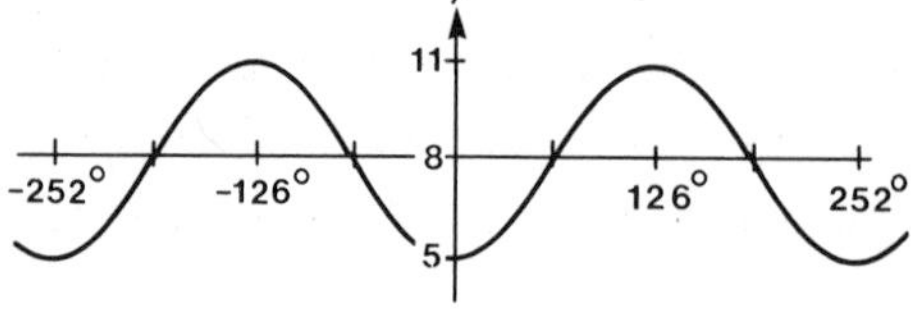

26. 360° **27.** −2.60 **28.** 2

29. Refer to Lesson 28 **30.** $\frac{1}{4}$

EP18. $1 - \frac{1}{2^k} + \frac{1}{2^{k+1}} = 1 - \frac{2}{2}\frac{1}{2^k} + \frac{1}{2^{k+1}} = 1 - \frac{2}{2^{k+1}} + \frac{1}{2^{k+1}} = 1 - \frac{1}{2^{k+1}}$

Problem set 73

1. $N = 30e^{1.13t}$ **2.** $M = 42e^{-0.18t}$, 1.87 years **3.** $43\frac{7}{11}$ min

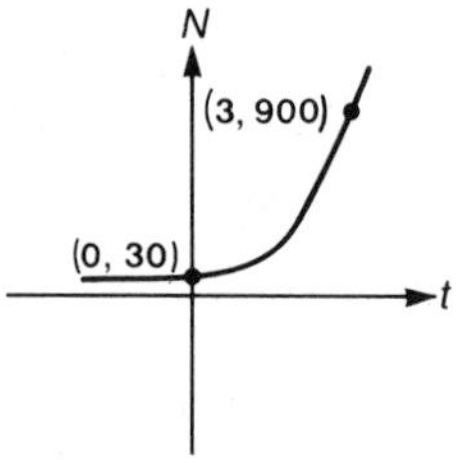

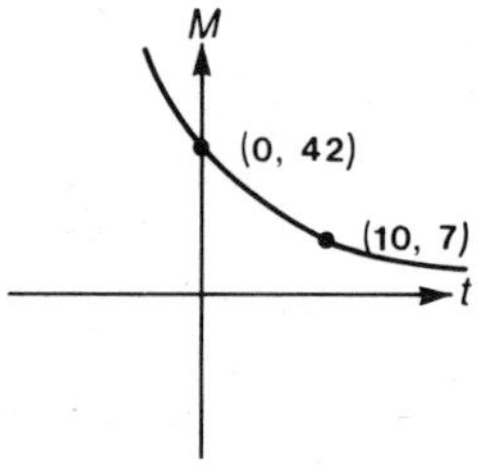

4. $\left(M - \frac{1}{8}M - 5000\right) - \frac{1}{2}\left(M - \frac{1}{8}M - 5000\right) = 4500$, $M = 16{,}000$ **5.** 12 hr

6. $\frac{1}{54}$ **7, 8.** Refer to Lesson 72 **9.** 128 **10.** 12, 36 **11.** 4, 8, 16 and −4, 8, −16

12. $\frac{x^2}{36} + \frac{y^2}{32} = 1$ **13.** $49x^2 + 25y^2 - 1225 = 0$ **14.** 6, 2, −2, −6

15. $\cos(45° + 60°) = \cos 45° \cos 60° - \sin 45° \sin 60° = \frac{\sqrt{2}}{4} - \frac{\sqrt{6}}{4} = \frac{\sqrt{2} - \sqrt{6}}{4}$

16. $\cos 15° = \sqrt{\frac{1 + \cos 30°}{2}} = \sqrt{\frac{1 + 0.866}{2}} = 0.966$ **17.** 60°, 300°

18. 50°, 170°, 290°, 70°, 190°, 310° **19.** $\frac{1 - \cos^2\theta}{1 + \tan^2\theta} = \frac{\sin^2\theta}{\sec^2\theta} = \sin^2\theta\cos^2\theta$

20. $\csc^2 y \sec^2 y - \sec^2 y = (\sec^2 y)(\csc^2 y - 1) = \sec^2 y \cot^2 y = \frac{1}{\cos^2 y} \cdot \frac{\cos^2 y}{\sin^2 y} = \frac{1}{\sin^2 y} = \csc^2 y$

21. $a = 26.3$, $b = 23.7$ **22.** Refer to Example 69.B.1 **23.** $m = \frac{60}{7}$

24. $a = 5.7$, $b = 15.0$, $h = 5.3$ **25.**

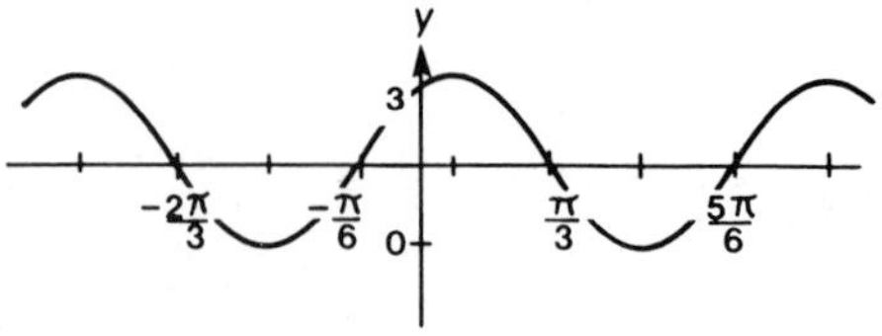

26. 8 inches **27.** $\frac{9}{4}$ **28.** No solution, $x = 1 + \sqrt{3}$ **29.** $\frac{1}{16}$

30. Refer to Lesson 28 **EP19.** Invalid

Problem set 74

1. $S = 500e^{-0.016t}$; 143.9 days **2.** $F = 10e^{1.77(6)} = 409{,}456$; exact answer $= 400{,}000$

3. $(M-2) - \frac{1}{6}(M-2) - \frac{1}{2}\left[(M-2) - \frac{1}{6}(M-2)\right] = 9$, $M = \$23.60$

4. $U = T + 2, \frac{(10T + U) + 6}{T + U} = 5, N = 24$

5. $\frac{M}{14K} \cdot T \cdot 21 = F \rightarrow T = \frac{2KF}{3M}$ days

6. AD bisects $\angle BAC$ and $\angle BDC \rightarrow \angle BAD = \angle CAD, \angle BDA = \angle CDA$
$\rightarrow \triangle ABD \sim \triangle ACD; AD = AD \rightarrow \triangle ABD \cong \triangle ACD \rightarrow AB = AC$

7. $AO = CO, DO = BO$, and $\angle DOA = \angle BOC \rightarrow \triangle AOD \cong \triangle COB$ (SAS) $\rightarrow \angle DAO$
$= \angle OCB$ (CPCTE)

8. $\overline{WX} \perp \overline{UV} \rightarrow \angle UWX = \angle VWX; UW = WV, WX = WX \rightarrow \triangle UWX \cong \triangle VWX$ (SAS)
$\rightarrow UX = VX$ (CPCTE)

9. $\tan 2A = \frac{2 \tan A}{1 - \tan^2 A}$; refer to Lesson 72 **10.** Refer to Lesson 72 **11.** -48

12. $\sqrt{2}$ **13.** $\frac{x^2}{21} + \frac{y^2}{25} = 1$ **14.** $x^2 + 4y^2 - 64 = 0$ **15.** $-2, 4, 10$

16. $\tan(60° + 45°) = \frac{\sqrt{3} + 1}{1 - \sqrt{3}}$
$= -2 - \sqrt{3}$

17. $\cos 15° = \sqrt{\frac{1 + \cos 30°}{2}} = \sqrt{\frac{1 + 0.866}{2}}$
$= 0.966$

18. 71°, 289°, 120°, 240° **19.** 15°, 105°, 195°, 285°, 60°, 150°, 240°, 330°

20. $\frac{1 - \sin^2 \theta}{1 + \cot^2 \theta} = \frac{\cos^2 \theta}{\csc^2 \theta} = \cos^2 \theta \sin^2 \theta$

21. $\sin^2 x \sec^2 x + \sin^2 x \csc^2 x = \sin^2 x \frac{1}{\cos^2 x} + \sin^2 x \frac{1}{\sin^2 x} = \tan^2 x + 1 = \sec^2 x$

22. $a = 16.9$ **23.** $a = 6$ **24.** $\frac{m}{h} = \frac{h}{n}; \frac{h}{n} = \frac{a}{b}; \frac{a}{b} = \frac{m}{h}$

25.

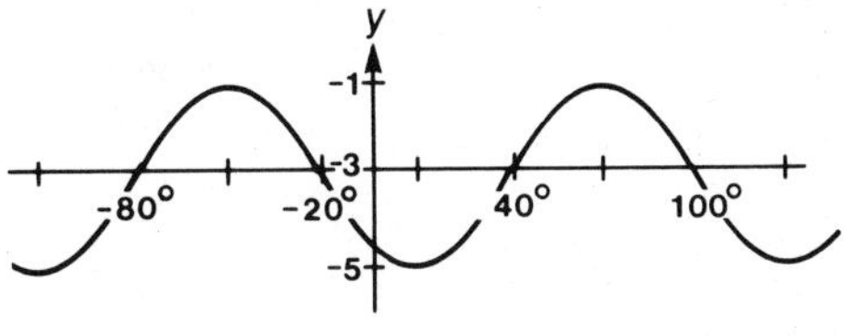

26. 2.8 in^2 **27.** -1 **28.** 2

29. $\frac{1}{9}$ **30.** Refer to Lesson 28

EP20. $\frac{k(k+1)(k+2)}{3} + (k+1)(k+2) = \frac{k(k+1)(k+2) + 3(k+1)(k+2)}{3}$
$= \frac{(k+1)(k+2)(k+3)}{3}$
$= \frac{(k+1)[(k+1)+1][(k+1)+2]}{3}$

EP21. Valid

Problem set 75

1. 7 **2.** $C = 10{,}000e^{-0.0026t}$; 266.6 min **3.** $N = 100e^{0.38t}$; 7.88 months **4.** $\frac{7}{13}$

5. ${}_8P_5 = \frac{8!}{(8-5)!} = 6720; {}_8C_5 = \frac{8!}{5!(8-5)!} = 56$

6. $AB = AC, BD = DC, AD = AD \rightarrow \triangle ABD \cong \triangle ACD \rightarrow \angle BAD = \angle CAD$,
$\angle BDA = \angle ADC \rightarrow AD$ bisects $\angle BAC$ and $\angle BDC$

7. $AO = CO$, $DO = BO$, $\angle AOD = \angle COB \rightarrow \triangle AOD \cong \triangle COB \rightarrow AD = BC$

8. $UX = VX$, $\angle UXW = \angle VXW$, $WX = WX \rightarrow \triangle UWX \cong \triangle VWX \rightarrow \angle UWX = \angle VXW$

9. Refer to Lesson 72 **10.** $\sqrt{3} + i$, $-1 + \sqrt{3}i$, $-\sqrt{3} - i$, $1 - \sqrt{3}i$ **11.** $-\frac{1}{4}$

12. $-4, 8$ **13.** $\frac{x^2}{16} + \frac{y^2}{25} = 1$ **14.** Vertices $= (\pm 5, 0)$; asymptotes: $y = \pm\frac{4}{5}x$

15. $-8, -6, -4, -2$ **16.** $\sin 15° = \sqrt{\frac{1 - \cos 30°}{2}} = \sqrt{\frac{1 - 0.866}{2}} = 0.259$

17. $\cos\left(x + \frac{\pi}{2}\right) = \cos x \cos\frac{\pi}{2} - \sin\frac{\pi}{2}\sin x = -\sin x$ **18.** 60°, 300°, 180°

19. 0°, 72°, 144°, 216°, 288°, 36°, 108°, 180°, 252°, 324°

20. $\frac{\sin^4\theta - \cos^4\theta}{\sin^2\theta - \cos^2\theta} = \sin^2\theta + \cos^2\theta = 1$

21. $\frac{\sec^2 x}{\sec^2 x - 1} = \frac{\sec^2 x}{\tan^2 x} = \frac{1}{\cos^2 x}\cdot\frac{\cos^2 x}{\sin^2 x} = \frac{1}{\sin^2 x} = \csc^2 x$ **22.** $A = 48.5°$, $B = 92.9°$

23. $c = \frac{32}{3}$ **24.** $a = 6$, $b = 10.4$ **25.** See Lesson 49, Problem 18 **26.** 123.1 cm^2

27. $\frac{7}{8}$ **28.** $\frac{11}{7}$ **29.** $\frac{16}{3}$ **30.** $\frac{1}{16}$

EP22. $\frac{1}{2}n[2a + (n - 1)d] + a + nd = na + \frac{1}{2}n(n - 1)d + a + nd$

$$= na + \frac{1}{2}n^2d - \frac{1}{2}nd + a + nd = na + a + \frac{1}{2}n^2d + \frac{1}{2}nd$$

$$= a(n + 1) + \frac{1}{2}nd(n + 1) = \frac{1}{2}(n + 1)(2a + nd) = \frac{1}{2}(n + 1)\{2a + [(n + 1) - 1]d\}$$

EP23. Invalid

Problem set 76

1. 5120 **2.** $M = 400e^{-0.0096t}$; 72.3 hr **3.** $\frac{1}{12}T = S$, $1T = S + 25$, $T = 4{:}27\frac{3}{11}$ **4.** $\frac{7}{9}$

5. ${}_9P_6 = \frac{9!}{(9 - 6)!} = 60{,}480$; ${}_9C_6 = \frac{9!}{6!(9 - 6)!} = 84$ **6.** Refer to Lesson 76

7. $\overline{AD} \perp \overline{BC}$ and $\overline{AD}$ bisects $\overline{BC} \rightarrow \angle ADB = \angle ADC = 90°$, $BD = DC$;
$AD = AD \rightarrow \triangle ADB \cong \triangle ADC$ (SAS) $\rightarrow AB = AC$

8. AD bisects $\angle BAC$, $AB = AC \rightarrow \angle BAD = \angle CAD$; $AD = AD \rightarrow \triangle BAD \cong \triangle CAD \rightarrow BD = DC$

9. $AO = CO$, $BO = DO$ and $\angle AOB = \angle COD \rightarrow \triangle AOB \cong \triangle DOC \rightarrow \angle OAB = \angle OCD$

10. Refer to Lesson 72 **11.** 2 cis 4°, 2 cis 76°, 2 cis 148°, 2 cis 220°, 2 cis 292°

12. 6, 18, 54 and -6, 18, -54 **13.** $16x^2 + 9y^2 - 144 = 0$

14. Vertices $= (\pm 2, 0)$, asymptotes: $y = \pm\frac{3}{2}x$ **15.** 20, 18, 16, 14

16. $\sin(240° + 45°) = \sin 240° \cos 45° + \sin 45° \cos 240° = (-0.866)(0.707) + (0.707)(-0.5)$
$= -0.966$

17. $\sin\left(x - \frac{\pi}{4}\right) = \sin x \cdot \frac{\sqrt{2}}{2} - \frac{\sqrt{2}}{2}\cos x = \frac{\sqrt{2}}{2}(\sin x - \cos x)$ **18.** 120°, 240°

19. 40°, 160°, 280°, 100°, 220°, 340°

20. $\frac{1 + \sin B}{\cos B} = \frac{1 + \sin B}{\cos B}\cdot\frac{1 - \sin B}{1 - \sin B} = \frac{1 - \sin^2 B}{(\cos B)(1 - \sin B)} = \frac{\cos^2 B}{(\cos B)(1 - \sin B)} = \frac{\cos B}{1 - \sin B}$

21. $\dfrac{\tan B + 1}{\tan B - 1} = \dfrac{\dfrac{1}{\sin B}}{\dfrac{1}{\sin B}} \cdot \dfrac{\tan B + 1}{\tan B - 1} = \dfrac{\sec B + \csc B}{\sec B - \csc B}$

22. $(y \sin \theta + x \cos \theta)^2 + (y \cos \theta - x \sin \theta)^2$
$= y^2 \sin^2 \theta + 2yx \sin \theta \cos \theta + x^2 \cos^2 \theta + y^2 \cos^2 \theta - 2yx \sin \theta \cos \theta + x^2 \sin^2 \theta$
$= y^2(\sin^2 \theta + \cos^2 \theta) + x^2(\sin^2 \theta + \cos^2 \theta)$
$= y^2 \cdot 1 + x^2 \cdot 1$

23. $a = 4.5$ 24. $d = \dfrac{16}{3}$ 25. See Lesson 50, Problem 19 26. 1440° 27. -2.6

28. $\dfrac{10}{3}$ 29. $\dfrac{1}{36}$ 30. Refer to Lesson 28 EP24. $\begin{bmatrix} 4 & 4 \\ 6 & 4 \end{bmatrix}$ EP25. Invalid

Problem set EL3

1. 1250 2. 24 hr 3. From 3 o'clock; $\dfrac{T}{12} = S$, $T = S + 25$, $T = 27\dfrac{3}{11}$ min; time $3{:}27\dfrac{3}{11}$

4. $P(G \cup RS) = P(G) + P(RS) - P(G \cap RS) = \dfrac{6}{11} + \dfrac{4}{11} - \dfrac{2}{11} = \dfrac{8}{11}$

5. $\dfrac{k(k+1)}{2} + (k+1) = \dfrac{k^2 + k}{2} + k + 1 = \dfrac{1}{2}k^2 + \dfrac{3}{2}k + 1 = \dfrac{1}{2}(k^2 + 3k + 2)$
$= \dfrac{1}{2}(k+1)(k+2) = \dfrac{1}{2}(k+1)[(k+1)+1]$

6. Refer to Lesson 76 7. (*a*) -3 (*b*) 6 (*c*) 4

8. (*a*) $\begin{bmatrix} 5 & 7 \\ -1 & 3 \end{bmatrix}$ (*b*) $\begin{bmatrix} -4 & -3 \\ -2 & -1 \end{bmatrix}$ 9. $\begin{bmatrix} 0 & 0 & 0 \\ 0 & 0 & 0 \\ 0 & 0 & 0 \end{bmatrix}$

10. AD bisects $\angle A \rightarrow \angle BAD = \angle CAD$, $\angle B = \angle C \rightarrow \triangle ADB \sim \triangle ADC$;
$AD = AD \rightarrow SF = 1 \rightarrow \triangle ADB \cong \triangle ADC$

11. Refer to Lesson 72 12. 2 cis 6°, 2 cis 78°, 2 cis 150°, 2 cis 222°, 2 cis 294°

13. $-4, 8$ 14. $9x^2 + 16y^2 - 144 = 0$ 15. Vertices: $(\pm 3, 0)$; asymptotes: $y = \pm\dfrac{4}{3}x$

16. $-3, 1, 5$

17. $\cos(240° + 45°) = \cos 240° \cos 45° - \sin 240° \sin 45° = \left(-\dfrac{1}{2}\right)\left(\dfrac{\sqrt{2}}{2}\right) - \left(-\dfrac{\sqrt{3}}{2}\right)\left(\dfrac{\sqrt{2}}{2}\right)$
$= \dfrac{\sqrt{6} - \sqrt{2}}{4}$

18. $\cos\left(x - \dfrac{\pi}{4}\right) = (\cos x)\left(\dfrac{\sqrt{2}}{2}\right) + (\sin x)\left(\dfrac{\sqrt{2}}{2}\right) = \left(\dfrac{\sqrt{2}}{2}\right)(\sin x + \cos x)$ 19. 210°, 330°

20. 67.5°, 247.5°, 112.5°, 292.5°

21. $(x \sin \theta + y \cos \theta)^2 + (x \cos \theta - y \sin \theta)^2$
$= x^2 \sin^2 \theta + 2xy \sin \theta \cos \theta + y^2 \cos^2 \theta + x^2 \cos^2 \theta - 2xy \sin \theta \cos \theta + y^2 \sin^2 \theta$
$= x^2(\sin^2 \theta + \cos^2 \theta) + y^2(\sin^2 \theta + \cos^2 \theta)$
$= x^2 + y^2$

22. $\dfrac{\cos B}{1 + \sin B} = \dfrac{\cos B}{1 + \sin B} \cdot \dfrac{1 - \sin B}{1 - \sin B} = \dfrac{(\cos B)(1 - \sin B)}{1 - \sin^2 B} = \dfrac{(\cos B)(1 - \sin B)}{\cos^2 B} = \dfrac{1 - \sin B}{\cos B}$

23. 11.8 24. 6 25. Refer to Problem set 46, Problem 15 26. 360° 27. 1.6

28. $-\dfrac{7}{6}$ 29. $\dfrac{1}{9}$ 30. Refer to Lesson 28

Problem set 77

1. $\frac{180X}{YP}$ days 2. 1622.2 years 3. $N = 4e^{0.196t}$ 4. $\frac{4}{5}$ 5. $\frac{7!}{3!} = 840$

6. (*a*), (*b*) See Lesson 77 7. (*a*) $y = 4 + 4\sec x$ (*b*) $y = -2 + 4\csc x$

8. Refer to Lesson 76

9. $AD = \perp$ bisector $\rightarrow \angle ADB = \angle ADC = 90°, BD = DC; AD = AD$
$\rightarrow \triangle ADB \cong \triangle ADC$ (SAS) $\rightarrow AB = AC$ (CPCTE)

10. $\overline{AD}$ is $\angle$ bisector of $\angle A \rightarrow \angle BAD = \angle CAD; AB = AC, AD = AD$
$\rightarrow \triangle BAD \cong \triangle CAD$ (SAS) $\rightarrow \angle B = \angle C$ (CPCTE)

11. $AO = CO, BO = DO; \angle AOB = \angle COD \rightarrow \triangle AOB \cong \triangle COD$ (SAS) $\rightarrow \angle OBA = \angle ODC$

12. Refer to Lesson 72 13. 3 cis 6°, 3 cis 96°, 3 cis 186°, 3 cis 276°

14. 4, −8 15. $16x^2 + 25y^2 - 400 = 0$ 16. −2, 1, 4

17. $\cos(-285°) = \cos(285°) = \cos(240° + 45°) = -\frac{1}{2}\cdot\frac{\sqrt{2}}{2} - \left(-\frac{\sqrt{3}}{2}\right)\left(\frac{\sqrt{2}}{2}\right) = \frac{\sqrt{6} - \sqrt{2}}{4}$

18. $\cos\left(x + \frac{\pi}{2}\right) = \cos x \cos\frac{\pi}{2} - \sin x \sin\frac{\pi}{2} = -\sin x$ 19. 210°, 330°

20. 20°, 140°, 260°, 80°, 200°, 320°

21. $\frac{1 + \cos x}{\sin x} = \frac{1 + \cos x}{\sin x}\cdot\frac{1 - \cos x}{1 - \cos x} = \frac{1 - \cos^2 x}{(\sin x)(1 - \cos x)} = \frac{\sin^2 x}{(\sin x)(1 - \cos x)} = \frac{\sin x}{1 - \cos x}$

22. $\frac{\tan B + 1}{\tan B - 1} = \frac{\tan B + 1}{\tan B - 1}\cdot\frac{\frac{1}{\sin B}}{\frac{1}{\sin B}} = \frac{\sec B + \csc B}{\sec B - \csc B}$

23. $(1 + \sin x)^2 + (1 - \sin x)^2 = 1 + 2\sin x + \sin^2 x + 1 - 2\sin x + \sin^2 x$
$= 2 + 2\sin^2 x = 2 + 2(1 - \cos^2 x) = 4 - 2\cos^2 x$

24. $c = 7.2$ 25. $a = \frac{20}{3}$ 26. See Lesson 51, Problem 19 27. 7.7 28. 2 29. $\frac{1}{8}$

30. $\frac{9}{2}$ EP26. $\begin{bmatrix} \frac{5}{6} & -\frac{5}{6} \\ 1\frac{2}{3} & -1\frac{2}{3} \\ 3\frac{1}{2} & -2\frac{1}{2} \end{bmatrix}$

EP27. $[k(2k - 1) + 1] + (4k + 1) = 2k^2 + 3k + 2 = (k + 1)(2k + 1) + 1$
$= (k + 1)[2(k + 1) - 1] + 1$

Problem set 78

1. 60 liters 2. 249 min 3. 1226.8 min 4. $\frac{2}{3} = \frac{1}{3} + \frac{1}{2} - P(RG) \rightarrow P(RG) = \frac{1}{6}$

5. $\frac{1}{50}$ 6. 1.5 cis 13.28°, 1.5 cis 103.28°, 1.5 cis 193.28°, 1.5 cis 283.28°

7. 1.5 cis 18.77°, 1.5 cis 138.77°, 1.5 cis 258.77°

8. C is midpoint of AD and $BE \rightarrow AC = CD, BC = CE; \angle ACB = \angle DCE \rightarrow \triangle ACB$
$\cong \triangle DCE$ (SAS) $\rightarrow AB = ED$ (CPCTE)

9. $\overline{AD} \parallel \overline{BC} \rightarrow \angle DAC = \angle ACB; \angle B = \angle D \rightarrow \triangle ABC \sim \triangle CDA;$
$AC = AC \rightarrow$ scale factor $= 1 \rightarrow \triangle ABC \cong \triangle CDA$

10. $\frac{x}{z} = \frac{m}{x}, \frac{y}{z} = \frac{n}{y} \rightarrow x^2 = mz, y^2 = nz \rightarrow x^2 + y^2 = mz + nz = z(m + n) = z^2$

11. Refer to Lesson 47 12. −6, 12 13. $\frac{x^2}{25} + \frac{y^2}{4} = 1$

14. Vertices = $(\pm 3, 0)$; asymptotes: $y = \pm\frac{4}{3}x$ **15.** $-4, -\frac{4}{3}, \frac{4}{3}, 4, \frac{20}{3}$

16. $\cos(240° + 45°) = \cos 240° \cos 45° - \sin 240° \sin 45° = (-0.5)(0.707) - (-0.866)(0.707) = 0.259$

17. $\sin\left(x - \frac{\pi}{4}\right) = \sin x \cos\frac{\pi}{4} - \cos x \sin\frac{\pi}{4} = \frac{\sqrt{2}}{2}\sin x - \frac{\sqrt{2}}{2}\cos x = \frac{\sqrt{2}}{2}(\sin x - \cos x)$

18. 120°, 240° **19.** 15°, 135°, 255°, 75°, 195°, 315°

20. $$\frac{\sin x}{1 + \cos x} + \frac{1 + \cos x}{\sin x} = \frac{\sin^2 x + (1 + \cos x)^2}{(\sin x)(1 + \cos x)} = \frac{\sin^2 x + 1 + 2\cos x + \cos^2 x}{(\sin x)(1 + \cos x)}$$
$$= \frac{2 + 2\cos x}{(\sin x)(1 + \cos x)} = \frac{2(1 + \cos x)}{(\sin x)(1 + \cos x)} = \frac{2}{\sin x} = 2\csc x$$

21. $$\frac{\csc x + \cot x}{\tan x + \sin x} = \frac{\frac{1}{\sin x} + \frac{\cos x}{\sin x}}{\frac{\sin x}{\cos x} + \sin x} = \frac{\frac{1 + \cos x}{\sin x}}{\frac{\sin x + \sin x \cos x}{\cos x}} = \frac{1 + \cos x}{\sin x} \cdot \frac{\cos x}{\sin x + \sin x \cos x}$$
$$= \frac{1 + \cos x}{\sin x} \cdot \frac{\cos x}{(\sin x)(1 + \cos x)} = \frac{\cos x}{\sin x} \cdot \frac{1}{\sin x} = \cot x \csc x$$

22. $$\frac{\sin^4 x - \cos^4 x}{2\sin^2 x - 1} = \frac{(\sin^2 x - \cos^2 x)(\sin^2 x + \cos^2 x)}{2\sin^2 x - (\sin^2 x + \cos^2 x)} = \frac{(\sin^2 x - \cos^2 x)(\sin^2 x + \cos^2 x)}{\sin^2 x - \cos^2 x}$$
$$= \sin^2 x + \cos^2 x = 1$$

23. $A = 104.5°$ **24.** $x = \frac{27}{8}$ **25.** See Lesson 52, Problem 20

26. (*a*) $y = 3 + 4\csc x$ (*b*) $y = \cot\theta$ **27.** 0.75 **28.** $\frac{7}{8}$ **29.** -1 **30.** 27

EP28. $\begin{bmatrix} 4 \\ 0 \\ 4 \end{bmatrix}$ **EP29.** Invalid

Problem set 79

1. 5 mph **2.** $4000 = 500e^{0.005t}$; $t = 415.9$ time units

3. $50{,}000 = 60{,}000e^{K5}$; $K = -0.0365$; $10{,}000 = 60{,}000e^{-0.0365t}$; $t = 49.1$ min

4. $T = S + 5, \frac{1}{12}T = S$; $T = 5\frac{5}{11}$ min **5.** ${}_8P_3 = \frac{8!}{(8-3)!} = 336$ **6.** 18.8 in^2

7. 2.2 cis 26.6°, 2.2 cis 206.6°

8. $\overline{AD}$ is $\perp$ bisector $\rightarrow BD = DC$, $\angle ADB = \angle ADC = 90°$, $AD = AD \rightarrow \triangle ABD \cong \triangle ACD$ (SAS) $\rightarrow AB = AC$ (CPCTE)

9. $\overline{AB} \parallel \overline{DE} \rightarrow \angle ABC = \angle CDE$, $\angle BAC = \angle CED \rightarrow \triangle ABC \sim \triangle EDC$; $AC = CE \rightarrow$ scale factor $= 1 \rightarrow \triangle ABC \cong \triangle EDC \rightarrow BC = CD$

10. Refer to Lesson 76 **11.** Refer to Lesson 77 **12.** 4, -8

13. $25x^2 + 16y^2 - 1600 = 0$ **14.** Vertices = $(\pm 4, 0)$; asymptotes: $y = \pm\frac{3}{4}x$

15. $-16, -12, -8$ **16.** $\sin(30° - 45°) = \frac{1}{2} \cdot \frac{\sqrt{2}}{2} - \frac{\sqrt{3}}{2} \cdot \frac{\sqrt{2}}{2} = \frac{\sqrt{2} - \sqrt{6}}{4}$

17. $\cos\left(x + \frac{\pi}{2}\right) = \cos x \cos\frac{\pi}{2} - \sin x \sin\frac{\pi}{2} = -\sin x$ **18.** 120°, 240°

19. 20°, 140°, 260°, 40°, 160°, 280°

20. $\dfrac{\cos^4 x - \sin^4 x}{\cos 2x} = \dfrac{(\cos^2 x - \sin^2 x)(\cos^2 x + \sin^2 x)}{\cos^2 x - \sin^2 x} = \cos^2 x + \sin^2 x = 1$

21. $(\sin x + \cos x)^2 = \sin^2 x + 2\cos x \sin x + \cos^2 x = 1 + 2\cos x \sin x = 1 + \sin 2x$

22. $\dfrac{1 - \cos x}{\sin x} = \dfrac{1 - \cos x}{\sin x} \cdot \dfrac{1 + \cos x}{1 + \cos x} = \dfrac{1 - \cos^2 x}{(\sin x)(1 + \cos x)} = \dfrac{\sin^2 x}{(\sin x)(1 + \cos x)} = \dfrac{\sin x}{1 + \cos x}$

23. $A = 51.5°$ **24.** $c = 16$ **25.** See Lesson 55, Problem 21 **26.** 360° **27.** −1.94

28. $-\dfrac{49}{75}$ **29.** 36 **30.** 9 **EP30.** $\begin{bmatrix} 0 & -3 & 3 \\ 2 & 1 & 2 \end{bmatrix}$

EP31. $2k(k + 1) + 4(k + 1) = (k + 1)(2k + 4) = (k + 1)(2)(k + 2) = 2(k + 1)[(k + 1) + 1]$

Problem set 80

1. $S = 56, C = 40, H = 32$ **2.** 56.95 min **3.** $\dfrac{4}{13}$ **4.** $\dfrac{2}{5}$

5. $WY = 500, (W + 5)Y = 750, Y = 50$ yd **6.** 2.38 or 10.10 **7.** No such triangle exists

8. 2.1 cis 19.3°, 2.1 cis 139.3°, 2.1 cis 259.3° **9.** 6.54 cm^2

10. $\overline{AB} \parallel \overline{CD}, \overline{AC} \parallel \overline{BD} \rightarrow \angle BAD = \angle ADC, \angle CAD = \angle ADB \rightarrow \triangle ADC \sim \triangle DAB; AD = AD \rightarrow \triangle ADC \cong \triangle DAB \rightarrow AC = BD$ (CPCTE)

11. $\overline{AD} \parallel \overline{DE} \rightarrow \angle BAC = \angle CED, \angle ABC = \angle CDE, \angle ACB = \angle DCE \rightarrow \triangle ACB \sim \triangle ECD; AB = DE \rightarrow SF = 1 \rightarrow \triangle ACB \cong \triangle ECD \rightarrow AC = CE$

12. $\angle A = \angle B, \angle ACD = \angle BCE \rightarrow \triangle ACD \sim \triangle BCE; DC = CE \rightarrow SF = 1 \rightarrow \triangle ACD \cong \triangle BCE \rightarrow AD = BE$

13. $\dfrac{q}{s} = \dfrac{m}{q}, \dfrac{r}{s} = \dfrac{n}{r} \rightarrow q^2 = ms, r^2 = ns \rightarrow q^2 + r^2 = s(m + n) = s^2$

14. 4, 8, 16 and −4, 8, −16 **15.** $25x^2 + 9y^2 - 225 = 0$

16. Vertices = $(\pm 2, 0)$, asymptotes: $y = \pm x$ **17.** −12, −9, −6

18. $2 \sin 15° \cos 15° = \sin 30° = \dfrac{1}{2}$ **19.** 90°, 210°, 330° **20.** 20°, 140°, 260°, 100°, 220°, 340°

21. $\cos 2x + 2\sin^2 x = \cos^2 x - \sin^2 x + 2\sin^2 x = \cos^2 x + \sin^2 x = 1$

22. $\dfrac{\cos x}{1 - \sin x} - \dfrac{\cos x}{1 + \sin x} = \dfrac{2 \sin x \cos x}{1 - \sin^2 x} = \dfrac{2 \sin x \cos x}{\cos^2 x} = \dfrac{2 \sin x}{\cos x} = 2 \tan x$

23. $\dfrac{2 \sin x}{\sin 2x} = \dfrac{2 \sin x}{2 \sin x \cos x} = \dfrac{1}{\cos x} = \sec x$ **24.** $c = 4.2$ **25.** $c = 8$

26. See Lesson 53, Problem 20 **27.** Refer to Lesson 77 **28.** $\dfrac{10}{3}$ **29.** −1 **30.** $\dfrac{1}{216}$

EP32. $\begin{bmatrix} 1 & -2 & 3 \\ -4 & 6 & -5 \\ 0 & 1 & 0 \end{bmatrix}$ **EP33.** Invalid

Problem set 81

1. 22 **2.** $\dfrac{5}{36}$ **3.** 902.7 **4.** Decreased by 4% **5.** 40 **6, 7, 8.** Refer to Lesson 81

9. 2.55 or 7.84 **10.** No such triangle exists **11.** $40{,}000\pi$ ft/min

12. 4.1 cis 30.96°, 4.1 cis 210.96° **13.** 3, 9, 27 and −3, 9, −27 **14.** Refer to Lesson 76

15. $\dfrac{x^2}{25} + \dfrac{y^2}{16} = 1$ **16.** Vertices = $(\pm 2, 0)$; asymptotes: $y = \pm 2x$ **17.** 42

18. $2 \sin 30° \cos 30° = \sin 60° = \dfrac{\sqrt{3}}{2}$ **19.** 150°, 330° **20.** 10°, 130°, 250°, 50°, 170°, 290°

21. $4\cos^2 x - 2\cos 2x = 4\cos^2 x - 2(\cos^2 x - \sin^2 x) = 2\cos^2 x + 2\sin^2 x$
$= 2(\cos^2 x + \sin^2 x) = 2$

22. $\dfrac{2\cos x}{\sin 2x} = \dfrac{2\cos x}{2\sin x\cos x} = \dfrac{1}{\sin x} = \csc x$

23. $\dfrac{\cos x}{\sec x - 1} - \dfrac{\cos x}{\sec x + 1} = \dfrac{2\cos x}{\sec^2 x - 1} = \dfrac{2\cos x}{\tan^2 x} = 2\cos x \cdot \dfrac{\cos^2 x}{\sin^2 x} = 2\cos^3 x\csc^2 x$

24. $a = 14.8$ 25. $a = 6$ 26. See Lesson 56, Problem 24

27. (a) $y = -2 + 3\sec x$ (b) $y = \tan\theta$ 28. 5 29. -1.69 30. $\dfrac{1}{9}$

EP34. $\begin{bmatrix} -1 & 7 \\ 3 & -5 \end{bmatrix}$

EP35. $\dfrac{3(3^k - 1)}{2} + 3^{k+1} = \dfrac{3^{k+1} - 3}{2} + 3^{k+1} = \dfrac{3^{k+1} - 3 + 2(3^{k+1})}{2} = \dfrac{3(3^{k+1}) - 3}{2}$
$= \dfrac{3(3^{k+1} - 1)}{2}$

Problem set 82

1. $\dfrac{1}{m}(t) + \dfrac{1}{f}(t) = 1$, $t = \dfrac{fm}{f + m}$ hr 2. 168.75 3. $\dfrac{m}{h + 3}$ mph 4. 450 laps

5. $P^{10}_5 = \dfrac{10!}{5!} = 30{,}240$ 6. 2.45 7. $\dfrac{4\sqrt{5}}{5}$

8. $\triangle ACD$ and $\triangle CDB$ are right triangles; $AC = CB$, $CD = CD \rightarrow \triangle ACD \cong \triangle BCD$ (HL) $\rightarrow \angle A = \angle B$ (CPCTE)

9. $AB = DC$, $AD = BC$, $AC = AC \rightarrow \triangle DCA \cong \triangle BAC$ (SSS) $\rightarrow \angle 1 = \angle 2 \rightarrow \overline{AB} \parallel \overline{DC}$

10. $AB \parallel DC \rightarrow \angle CDB = \angle DBA$; $AB = DC$, $DB = DB \rightarrow \triangle CDB \cong \triangle ABD$ (SAS) $\rightarrow DA = CB$

11. Triangle cannot be constructed 12. 14.3 or 4.47

13. 1.8 cis 113.86°, 1.8 cis 233.86°, 1.8 cis 353.86° 14. 128

15. $\dfrac{u}{w} = \dfrac{m}{u}$, $\dfrac{v}{w} = \dfrac{n}{v} \rightarrow u^2 = mw$, $v^2 = nw \rightarrow u^2 + v^2 = (m + n)w = w^2$

16. $4x^2 + y^2 - 16 = 0$ 17. 25:16 18. $\cos 30° = \cos^2 15° - \sin^2 15° = \dfrac{\sqrt{3}}{2}$

19. 90°, 270°, 30°, 330° 20. 10°, 130°, 250°, 110°, 230°, 350°

21. $\dfrac{2\cos 2x}{\sin 2x} = \dfrac{2(\cos^2 x - \sin^2 x)}{2\sin x\cos x} = \dfrac{\cos x}{\sin x} - \dfrac{\sin x}{\cos x} = \cot x - \tan x$

22. $2\csc 2x\cos x = \dfrac{2}{\sin 2x}\cos x = \dfrac{2}{2\sin x\cos x}\cos x = \dfrac{1}{\sin x} = \csc x$

23. $\dfrac{2\tan x}{1 + \tan^2 x} = \dfrac{2\tan x}{\sec^2 x} = \dfrac{2\sin x}{\cos x}\cdot\dfrac{\cos^2 x}{1} = 2\sin x\cos x = \sin 2x$ 24. 36.4° 25. $\dfrac{45}{8}$

26. See Lesson 58, Problem 26 27. 256 28. 10,000 29. 81, 1

30. Refer to Lesson 77 EP36. $\begin{bmatrix} 4 & 4 \\ 6 & 4 \end{bmatrix}$

Problem set 83

1. $\dfrac{8 - mt}{4t}\dfrac{\text{job}}{\text{hr}}$ 2. 31 years 3. $\dfrac{20}{60} + \dfrac{50}{60} - \dfrac{10}{60} = 1$ 4. Value is multiplied by 18

5. $(r + 4)T = F + 6$, $T = \dfrac{F + 6}{r + 4}$ hr 6. 2.54 7. 2.18

8. Note that $\overline{CD}$ is $\perp$ to $\overline{AB} \to \angle CDA = \angle CDB = 90°$; $\angle A = \angle B \to \triangle ADC \sim \triangle BDC$; $CD = CD \to SF = 1 \to \triangle ADC \cong \triangle BDC \to AC = CB$

9. $AB = DC$, $AD = BC$, $DB = DB \to \triangle ADB \cong \triangle CBD \to \angle A = \angle C$

10. $\overline{AB} \parallel \overline{DC} \to \angle 1 = \angle 2$; $AB = DC$, $DB = DB \to \triangle DBA \cong \triangle BDC \to \angle 3 = \angle 4 \to \overline{DA} \parallel \overline{CB}$

11. 11.2 or 1.7 **12.** 1.38 cis 8.42°, 1.38 cis 98.42°, 1.38 cis 188.42°, 1.38 cis 278.42°

13. $128\left(\frac{1}{2}\right)^3 = 16$ ft **14.** $\sqrt{xy} = 9$, $x - y = 24$; 3, 27 and -27, -3

15. $a_r = (1 + \sqrt{2})\left(\frac{3 + 2\sqrt{2}}{1 + \sqrt{2}}\right)^3 = (1 + \sqrt{2})(1 + \sqrt{2})^3 = 17 + 12\sqrt{2}$ **16.** $\frac{8 + 22}{2} = 15$

17. $\frac{x}{z} = \frac{a}{x}, \frac{y}{z} = \frac{b}{y} \to x^2 = az, y^2 = bz \to x^2 + y^2 = (a + b)z = z^2$

18. $2\cos^2 15° - 1 = \cos 30° = \frac{\sqrt{3}}{2}$ **19.** 90°, 210°, 330° **20.** 50°, 170°, 290°, 70°, 190°, 310°

21. $\frac{\cos^3 x - \sin^3 x}{\cos x - \sin x} = \frac{(\cos x - \sin x)(\cos^2 x + \cos x \sin x + \sin^2 x)}{\cos x - \sin x}$

$$= \cos^2 x + \cos x \sin x + \sin^2 x = 1 + \frac{1}{2}\sin 2x$$

22. $\frac{\cos^2 x - \sin^2 x}{\cos^2 x} = 1 - \frac{\sin^2 x}{\cos^2 x} = 1 - \tan^2 x$

23. $\tan 2x = \frac{2 \tan x}{1 - \tan^2 x} = \frac{2}{\frac{1}{\tan x} - \tan x} = \frac{2}{\cot x - \tan x}$ **24.** $a = 6.24$ **25.** $y = 18$

26.

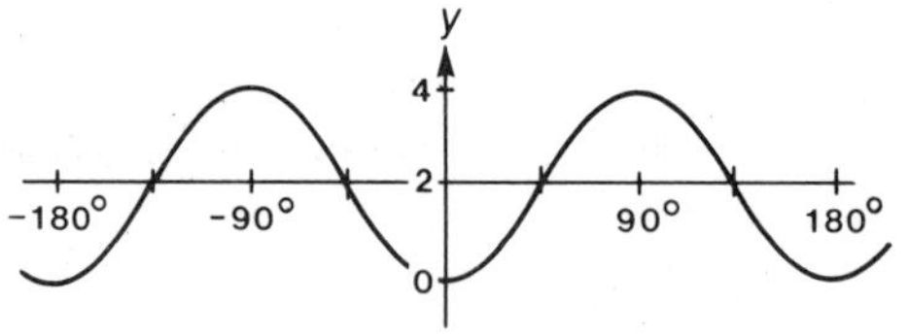

27. 16

28. $2 \log_2 x = 2(\log_2 x)^2 \to (\log_2 x)^2 - \log_2 x = 0 \to (\log_2 x)(\log_2 x - 1) = 0$; $x = 1, 2$

29. 3^9, 1 **30.** (*a*) $y = \cot \theta$ (*b*) $y = -3 + \sec x$ **EP37.** Invalid

EP38. $\begin{bmatrix} 7 & 2 \\ 1 & 2 \end{bmatrix}$

Problem set 84

1. $\frac{m}{R} = \frac{m + 5}{x}$, $x = \frac{R(m + 5)}{m} \frac{\text{mi}}{\text{hr}}$ **2.** The number of greens remains the same.

3. ${}_{11}P_4 = \frac{11!}{(11 - 4)!} = 7920$, ${}_{11}C_4 = \frac{11!}{4!(11 - 4)!} = 330$ **4.** $16\frac{4}{11}$ min

5. $x\left(\frac{d}{m} + k\right) = 14$, $x = \frac{14m}{d + km}$

6, 7, 8, 9. Refer to Lesson 84 **10.** 1.88 **11.** 2.54

12. $\overline{CD}$ is $\perp$ bisector $\to \angle CDA = \angle CDB = 90°$, $\angle 1 = \angle 2 \to \triangle ACD \sim \triangle BCD$; $CD = CD$ $\to SF = 1 \to \triangle ACD \cong \triangle BCD \to AC = CB$

13. $\overline{AB} \parallel \overline{CD} \to \angle ABO = \angle ODC$, $\angle BAO = \angle OCD \to \triangle AOB \sim \triangle COD$; $AB = CD \to SF = 1$ $\to \triangle AOB \cong \triangle COD \to AO = OC$, $DO = OB$

14. No such triangle exists **15.** 1.5 cis 80.78°, 1.5 cis 170.78°, 1.5 cis 260.78°, 1.5 cis 350.78°

16. 15 **17.** 24 ft **18.** 16, 4 or -16, -4 **19.** 60°, 300° **20.** 15°, 195°, 105°, 285°

21. $2\csc 2x = \dfrac{2}{\sin 2x} = \dfrac{2}{2\sin x\cos x} = \dfrac{1}{\sin x\cos x} = \dfrac{\sin^2 x + \cos^2 x}{\sin x\cos x}$

$= \dfrac{\sin x}{\cos x} + \dfrac{\cos x}{\sin x} = \tan x + \cot x$

22. $\dfrac{\sin 2x}{\tan x} = \dfrac{2\sin x\cos x}{\dfrac{\sin x}{\cos x}} = 2\cos^2 x$

23. $(\tan^2 x)(1 + \cot^2 x) = \tan^2 x + \tan^2 x\cot^2 x = \tan^2 x + 1 = \sec^2 x = \dfrac{1}{\cos^2 x} = \dfrac{1}{1 - \sin^2 x}$

24. $A = 33.2°$ **25.** $x = 3$ **26.** Refer to Lesson 77 **27.** 256 **28.** 1 **29.** $\dfrac{6}{5}$

30. 10,000 **EP39.** Valid **EP40.** $\begin{bmatrix} 4 & 0 \\ 0 & 2 \end{bmatrix}$

Problem set 85

1. 36 **2.** $760 = 800e^{-20k} \to k = 0.0026$, $400 = 800e^{-0.0026t} \to t = 270.3$ min **3.** $\dfrac{4}{33}$

4. $(a \# b) * b = (2a - 3b) - b = 2a - 4b = 20 - 8 = 12$ **5.** 60 mph **6.** 19 **7.** 3

8, 9. Refer to Lesson 84 **10.** $\log_5 35 = \dfrac{\log 35}{\log 5} = 2.21$ **11.** 2.06

12. $AB = CD$, $AD = BC$, $DB = DB \to \triangle DAB \cong \triangle BCD \to \angle ADB = \angle DBC$; $AB = CD$, $AD = BC$, $CA = CA \to \triangle DAC \cong \triangle BCA \to \angle BAC = \angle ACD$

13. $\overline{AB} \parallel \overline{FC} \to \angle 1 = \angle 2$, $\angle 3 = \angle 4 \to \triangle ADE \sim \triangle CFE$; E is the midpoint of $AC \to AE = EC \to SF = 1 \to \triangle ADE \cong \triangle CFE \to DE = EF$

14. 10.4 or 4.6 **15.** 1.65 cis 8.86°, 1.65 cis 128.86°, 1.65 cis 248.86° **16.** $256\left(\dfrac{3}{4}\right)^4 = 81$ ft

17. $\sqrt{xy} = 4$, $x + y = 10$; 2, 8 **18.** $-\sqrt{xy} = -10$, $x - y = 15$; 5, 20 or -5, -20

19. 70°, 190°, 310°, 110°, 230°, 350° **20.** 30°, 150°

21. $\dfrac{\sec 2x - 1}{2\sec 2x} = \dfrac{\dfrac{1}{\cos 2x} - 1}{\dfrac{2}{\cos 2x}} = \dfrac{1 - \cos 2x}{2} = \dfrac{1 - (1 - 2\sin^2 x)}{2} = \dfrac{2\sin^2 x}{2} = \sin^2 x$

22. $\cot^2 x\,(1 + \tan^2 x) = \cot^2 x + 1 = \csc^2 x = \dfrac{1}{\sin^2 x} = \dfrac{1}{1 - \cos^2 x}$

23. $\dfrac{1}{2}\cot x\sec^2 x = \dfrac{1}{2}\dfrac{\cos x}{\sin x} \cdot \dfrac{1}{\cos^2 x} = \dfrac{1}{2}\dfrac{1}{\sin x\cot x} = \dfrac{1}{\sin 2x} = \csc 2x$ **24.** 37.6 **25.** 1980°

26.

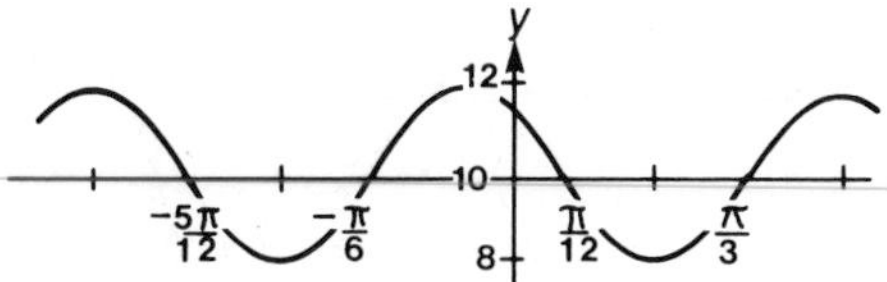

27. e^2, e^{-2} **28.** 5 **29.** 4^{16}, 1

30. 64 **EP41.** $\begin{bmatrix} 5 & 4 \\ 6 & 5 \end{bmatrix}$

EP42. $2(2^k - 1) + 2^{k+1} = 2^{k+1} - 2 + 2^{k+1} = 2(2^{k+1}) - 2 = 2(2^{k+1} - 1)$

Problem set 86

1. $A_1 = 60°$, $A_2 = 20°$ **2.** $W = 47$, $P = 23$ **3.** $\dfrac{7}{13}$ **4.** 28.7 sec

5. $(B - W)T_U = 20$, $(B + W)T_D = 33$, $T_D = T_U - 1$, $B = 2W$, $W = 9$ mph, $B = 18$ mph

6. $-35x^4y^3$ **7.** $8a^6 - 12a^4b^3 + 6a^2b^6 - b^9$ **8.** 1

9, 10. Refer to Lesson 84 **11.** 2.06

12. $AB = CD$, $AD = BC$, $DB = DB \rightarrow \triangle ADB \cong \triangle CBD \rightarrow \angle ABD = \angle BDC$; $AB = CD$, $AD = BC$, $AC = AC$, $\triangle ADC \cong \triangle CBA \rightarrow \angle BAC = \angle ACD \rightarrow \triangle AOB \sim \triangle COD$; $AB = CD \rightarrow SF = 1 \rightarrow \triangle AOB \cong \triangle COD$

13. D is midpoint of $\overline{AB}$, E is midpoint of $\overline{AC} \rightarrow AD = \frac{1}{2}AB$, $AE = \frac{1}{2}AC$, $\frac{AD}{AB} = \frac{AE}{AC} = \frac{1}{2}$, $\angle A = \angle A \rightarrow \triangle ADE \sim \triangle ABC\,(\text{SAS}) \rightarrow \angle ADE = \angle ABC \rightarrow \overline{DE} \parallel \overline{BC}$

14. 11.2 or 1.7 **15.** 1.5 cis 20.8°, 1.5 cis 92.8°, 1.5 cis 164.8°, 1.5 cis 236.8°, 1.5 cis 308.8°

16. 9 ft **17.** 4, 36 **18.** $\frac{75\sqrt{3}}{2}$ **19.** 30°, 150°, 270°, 90°, 210°, 330° **20.** 120°, 240°

21. $$\frac{\sin x \tan x}{1 - \cos x} - 1 = \frac{\sin x \cdot \frac{\sin x}{\cos x}}{1 - \cos x} - 1 = \frac{\sin^2 x}{(\cos x)(1 - \cos x)} - 1$$
$$= \frac{\sin^2 x - \cos x + \cos^2 x}{(\cos x)(1 - \cos x)} = \frac{1 - \cos x}{(\cos x)(1 - \cos x)} = \frac{1}{\cos x} = \sec x$$

22. $$\frac{\cos 2x}{\sin^2 x} = \frac{\cos^2 x - \sin^2 x}{\sin^2 x} = \frac{\cos^2 x}{\sin^2 x} - 1 = \cot^2 x - 1$$

23. $$\frac{1 + \sin x}{\cos x} + \frac{\cos x}{1 + \sin x} = \frac{1 + 2\sin x + \sin^2 x + \cos^2 x}{(\cos x)(1 + \sin x)} = \frac{2 + 2\sin x}{(\cos x)(1 + \sin x)}$$
$$= \frac{2(1 + \sin x)}{(\cos x)(1 + \sin x)} = \frac{2}{\cos x} = \frac{4 \sin x}{2 \sin x \cos x} = \frac{4 \sin x}{\sin 2x}$$

24. (*a*) $y = 6 + 8 \csc x$ (*b*) $y = \cot \theta$ **25.** 360° **26.** Refer to Lesson 77, Problem 7(*b*)

27. 1, 3 **28.** 3 **29.** 5 **30.** 16 **EP43.** $\begin{bmatrix} -2 & 0 \\ 2 & -2 \end{bmatrix}$ **EP44.** $\begin{bmatrix} 11 & -1 \\ 3 & 7 \end{bmatrix}$

Problem set EL4

1. $\angle 1 = 30°$, $\angle 2 = 100°$ **2.** $K = 20$, $M = 10$ **3.** $\frac{4}{13}$ **4.** 59.2 m

5. $B = 10$ mph, $C = 5$ mph **6.** $15x^4y^2$ **7.** $8a^6 - 12a^4b^4 + 6a^2b^8 - b^{12}$

8. $x = 1$ **9.** $\begin{bmatrix} 2 & 1 \\ 8 & -4 \end{bmatrix}$ **10.** $\begin{bmatrix} 6 & -3 \\ 18 & 9 \end{bmatrix}$ **11.** $\begin{bmatrix} -8 & -5 \\ -1 & -2 \end{bmatrix}$

12, 13. Refer to Lesson 84 **14.** 2.1

15. $AB = CD$, $AD = BC$, $DB = DB \rightarrow \triangle ADB \cong \triangle CBD \rightarrow \angle ABO = \angle ODC$, $\angle AOB = \angle DOC \rightarrow AB = DC \rightarrow SF = 1 \rightarrow \triangle AOB \cong \triangle COD$

16. D is midpoint of $\overline{AB}$, E is midpoint of $\overline{AC} \rightarrow AD = \frac{1}{2}AB$, $AE = \frac{1}{2}AC$, $\angle A = \angle A \rightarrow \triangle DAE \sim \triangle BAC$, $SF = 2 \rightarrow DE = \frac{1}{2}BC$

17. No such triangle exists **18.** 1.7 cis 42.3°, 1.7 cis 162.3°, 1.7 cis 282.3°

19. 4, 100 **20.** 0°, 90°, 180°, 270° **21.** 30°, 150°

22. $$\frac{2 \sec 2x}{\sec 2x - 1} = \frac{\frac{2}{\cos 2x}}{\frac{1}{\cos 2x} - 1} = \frac{2}{1 - \cos 2x} = \frac{2}{1 - (1 - 2\sin^2 x)} = \frac{2}{2\sin^2 x}$$
$$= \frac{1}{\sin^2 x} = \csc^2 x$$

23. $$\frac{1 + \cos 2x}{1 - \cos 2x} = \frac{1 + (2\cos^2 x - 1)}{1 - (1 - 2\sin^2 x)} = \frac{2\cos^2 x}{2\sin^2 x} = \cot^2 x$$

24. (*a*) $y = 1 + \sin(x + 40)$ (*b*) $y = 3 + 2\sin 2\left(x - \frac{\pi}{6}\right)$ 25. No

26. Refer to Problem set 45, Problem 16 27. 16 28. $\frac{3}{2}$ 29. 2 30. $\frac{1}{4}$

Problem set 87

1. 20 atm 2. 490.6 min 3. $\frac{1}{16}$ 4. 54 g 5. $\frac{12p}{k + sp}$ 6. 3.15×10^{-3}

7. 1.8×10^{-5} 8. 4.3 9. 3.2×10^{-7} mole/liter 10. $70x^4y^4$

11. $81a^8 - 108a^6b^3 + 54a^4b^6 - 12a^2b^9 + b^{12}$ 12. $-\frac{13}{7}$

13, 14. Refer to Lesson 84 15. 1.92

16. $\overline{AD}$ bisects $\angle A \rightarrow \angle BAD = \angle CAD$, $AB = AC$, $AD = AD \rightarrow \triangle DAB \cong \triangle DAC$ (SAS with $SF = 1$) $\rightarrow \angle ADB = \angle ADC$; $\angle ADB + \angle ADC = 180°$ $\rightarrow \angle ADB = \angle ADC = 90°$

17. D is the midpoint of $\overline{AB}$, E is the midpoint of $\overline{AC} \rightarrow AD = \frac{1}{2}AB$, $AE = \frac{1}{2}AC$;
$\angle A = \angle A \rightarrow \triangle ADE \sim \triangle ABC$ (SAS) $\rightarrow \frac{DE}{BC} = \frac{AD}{AB} = \frac{1}{2} \rightarrow DE = \frac{1}{2}BC$

18. 10.9 or 3.6 19. 1.7 cis 42.3°, 1.7 cis 162.3°, 1.7 cis 282.3° 20. $\frac{1}{2}$ ft

21. 17.3 22. 39°, 159°, 279°, 99°, 219°, 339° 23. 120°, 240°

24. $\frac{\cos 2x + 1}{2} = \frac{2\cos^2 x - 1 + 1}{2} = \cos^2 x$

25. $\frac{2\cot x}{\tan 2x} = \frac{2\cot x}{\frac{\sin 2x}{\cos 2x}} = 2\cot x\frac{\cos 2x}{\sin 2x} = \frac{2\cos x}{\sin x} \cdot \frac{\cos^2 x - \sin^2 x}{2\sin x\cos x}$
$= \frac{\cos^2 x - \sin^2 x}{\sin^2 x} = \cot^2 x - 1 = (\csc^2 x - 1) - 1 = \csc^2 x - 2$

26. Refer to Lesson 77, Problem 7(*a*) 27. ± 3 28. $\frac{3}{4}$ 29. No solution, $x = -\frac{1}{2}$

30. 4 EP45. $\begin{bmatrix} 6 & -2 \\ -18 & -12 \end{bmatrix}$

EP46. $(2k^2 + 3k) + (4k + 5) = 2k^2 + 7k + 5 = 2(k + 1)^2 + 3(k + 1)$

Problem set 88

1. 45 2. $\frac{7}{13}$ 3. $W = 45$, $B = 75$, $R = 20$

4. $140g + fg + sg = 4200$, $g = \frac{4200}{140 + f + s}$ 5. $p + 3 = \frac{14}{a + b} + 3$, so $\frac{4}{p + 3} = \frac{4(a + b)}{14 + 3a + 3b}$

6. (*a*) Refer to Lesson 88; $s = \frac{1}{2}(a_1 + a_n)$ (*b*) 2550

7. (*a*) Refer to Lesson 88; $s = \frac{a - ar^n}{1 - r}$ (*b*) 22

8. $\left(x + \frac{1}{2} + \frac{\sqrt{11}}{2}i\right)\left(x + \frac{1}{2} - \frac{\sqrt{11}}{2}i\right)$ 9. 6.5×10^{-8} 10. 3.21

11. 3.2×10^{-9} 12. $160x^3y^3$ 13. $x^4 - 4x^3y + 6x^2y^2 - 4xy^3 + y^4$ 14. $\frac{8}{3}$

15, 16. Refer to Lesson 84 17. 2.12

18. $AB = DC$, $AC = DB$, $BC = BC \rightarrow \triangle ABC \cong \triangle DCB$

19.

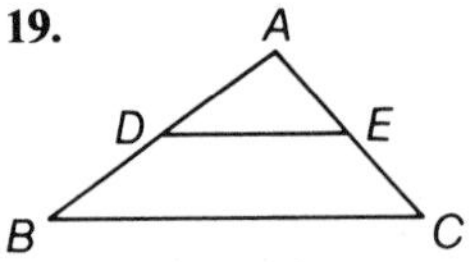

$AD = \frac{1}{2}AB$, $AE = \frac{1}{2}AC$, $\angle A = \angle A \rightarrow \triangle ADE \sim \triangle ABC$
$\rightarrow \angle ADE = \angle ABC \rightarrow \overline{DE} \parallel \overline{BC}; \frac{AD}{AB} = \frac{DE}{BC} \rightarrow \frac{1}{2} = \frac{DE}{BC} \rightarrow DE = \frac{1}{2}BC$

20. $\frac{\sqrt{3}}{2} + \frac{1}{2}i, -\frac{\sqrt{3}}{2} + \frac{1}{2}i, -i$ **21.** 2, 18 **22.** 15°, 135°, 255°, 45°, 165°, 285°

23. 120°, 240° **24.** $\frac{1 - \cos 2x}{2} = \frac{1 - (1 - 2\sin^2 x)}{2} = \frac{2\sin^2 x}{2} = \sin^2 x$

25. $\frac{2 + \cos 2y - 5\sin y}{3 + \sin y} = \frac{2 + (1 - 2\sin^2 y) - 5\sin y}{3 + \sin y} = \frac{-2\sin^2 y - 5\sin y + 3}{3 + \sin y}$
$= \frac{-(2\sin^2 y + 5\sin y - 3)}{3 + \sin y} = \frac{-(2\sin y - 1)(\sin y + 3)}{\sin y + 3} = 1 - 2\sin y$

26.

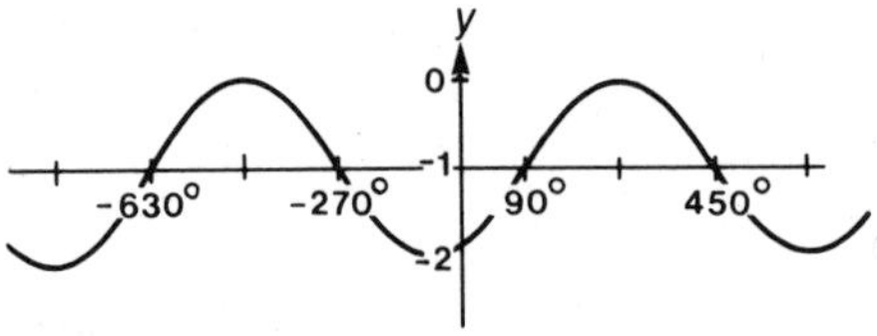

27. 16, 1 **28.** 2 **29.** 9

30. 8 **EP47.** $\begin{bmatrix} 1 & 3 \\ -2 & 0 \end{bmatrix}$ **EP48.** Valid

Problem set 89

1. 7 **2.** $\frac{1}{12}T = S$, $T = S + 5$; $T = 5\frac{5}{11}$ min **3.** 575.3 min

4. $\frac{40}{Kh} \cdot 14M = m$; $M = \frac{mKh}{560}$ men **5.** $C_6^{10} = 210$ **6.** 6 **7.** −3

8. (*a*) Refer to Lesson 88 (*b*) 198 **9.** (*a*) Refer to Lesson 88 (*b*) $\frac{21}{32}$

10. 1.5×10^4 **11.** 0 **12.** 3.4 **13.** $240x^2y^4$ **14.** $27x^3 - 54x^2y + 36xy^2 - 8y^3$

15. $-\frac{16}{17}$ **16.** Refer to Lesson 84 **17.** 2.1

18. $AB = DC$, $AC = DB$, $BC = BC \rightarrow \triangle ABC \cong \triangle DCB \rightarrow \angle A = \angle D$

19. $\triangle CDA$ and $\triangle ABC$ are rt. △'s, $CD = AB$, $CA = CA \rightarrow \triangle CDA \cong \triangle ABC$ (HL) $\rightarrow CB = AD$

20. $\frac{1}{2} + \frac{\sqrt{3}}{2}i, -1, \frac{1}{2} - \frac{\sqrt{3}}{2}i$ **21.** 1 ft **22.** 15°, 135°, 255°, 105°, 225°, 345°

23. 71.6°, 251.6°, 135°, 315° **24.** $\frac{1}{2}\sin 2x \sec x = \frac{1}{2}(2\sin x \cos x)\frac{1}{\cos x} = \sin x$

25. $\frac{1 + \cos 2x}{\sin 2x} = \frac{1 + (2\cos^2 x - 1)}{2\cos x \sin x} = \frac{2\cos^2 x}{2\sin x \cos x} = \frac{\cos x}{\sin x} = \cot x$

26. (*a*) $y = \tan\theta$ (*b*) $y = -7 + 4\sec x$ **27.** 81, 1 **28.** 8 **29.** 6 **30.** $\frac{1}{9}$

EP49. $\begin{bmatrix} 4 & 7 \\ 9 & 62 \end{bmatrix}$

EP50. $\frac{k(3k - 1)}{2} + (3k + 1) = \frac{3k^2 - k + 6k + 2}{2} = \frac{3k^2 + 5k + 2}{2} = \frac{(k + 1)(3k + 2)}{2}$
$= \frac{(k + 1)[3(k + 1) - 1]}{2}$

Problem set 90

1. 160 **2.** 15 hours **3.** $\frac{72c}{b(8+d)}$ hours **4.** $\frac{10!}{4!6!} = 210$

5. $v = \omega r = 200(20)\frac{(60)(60)}{(12)(5280)}\frac{\text{mi}}{\text{hr}}$ **6.** $x = 3$

7. $\overline{AB} \parallel \overline{DE} \to \frac{DC}{AD} = \frac{CE}{EB}$, $\angle EDC = \angle BAD$; $\overline{DE}$ is $\angle$ bisector $\to \angle BDE = \angle EDC$; $\angle BDE = \angle DBA \to \angle DBA = \angle BDE = \angle EDC = \angle BAD$. Thus, $\angle DBA = \angle BAD \to AD = DB \to \frac{DC}{DB} = \frac{EC}{BE}$

8. $AD = BC$, $DB = AC$, $AB = AB \to \triangle ADB \cong \triangle BCA \to \angle DBA = \angle CAB$ **9.** $\frac{16}{3}$

10. $-216xy^3$ **11.** 0 **12.** 1 **13.** (*a*) Refer to Lesson 88 (*b*) 176

14. (*a*) Refer to Lesson 88 (*b*) 5465 **15.** 8.9×10^{-4} **16.** 9×10^{31}

17. 3.16×10^{-9} mole/liter **18.** Refer to Lesson 84 **19.** 1.73

20. 1.8 cis 49.7°, 1.8 cis 169.7°, 1.8 cis 289.7° **21.** −4, −16 **22.** 22.5°, 157.5°, 202.5°, 337.5°

23. 150°, 330° **24.** $(\cos x - \sin x)(\cos x + \sin x) = \cos^2 x - \sin^2 x = \cos 2x$

25. $\frac{\tan x + 1}{\tan x - 1} = \frac{\frac{1}{\sin x}(\tan x + 1)}{\frac{1}{\sin x}(\tan x - 1)} = \frac{\sec x + \csc x}{\sec x - \csc x}$ **26.** Refer to Lesson 77 **27.** 1, 256

28. 16 **29.** 10^4, 1 **30.** $\frac{9}{2}$ **EP51.** $\begin{bmatrix} -8 & -4 \\ 4 & 2 \end{bmatrix}$

EP52.
$$\frac{k(2k-1)(2k+1)}{1} + (2k+1)^2 = \frac{k(2k-1)(2k+1) + 3(2k+1)^2}{3}$$
$$= \frac{(2k+1)[k(2k-1) + 3(2k+1)]}{3}$$
$$= \frac{(2k+1)(2k^2 - k + 6k + 3)}{3}$$
$$= \frac{(2k+1)(2k^2 + 5k + 3)}{3} = \frac{(k+1)(2k+1)(2k+3)}{3}$$
$$= \frac{(k+1)[2(k+1) - 1][2(k+1) + 1]}{3}$$

Problem set 91

1. \$5600 **2.** 12 mph **3.** 270.3 min **4.** $v = \omega r = \frac{300(1)(100)}{2.54(12)(5280)}\frac{\text{mi}}{\text{min}}$ **5.** 8!

6. $(x+2)^2 + (y-3)^2 = 9$, $x^2 + y^2 + 4x - 6y + 4 = 0$

7. $\frac{(x-5)^2}{4} + \frac{(y+2)^2}{2} = 1$, center = (5, −2), major axis = 4, minor axis = $2\sqrt{2}$

8. $\frac{(x+3)^2}{4} + \frac{(y-1)^2}{9} = 1$, center = (−3, 1), major axis = 6, minor axis = 4

9. $(x-1)^2 - (y+2)^2 = 1$, center = (1, −2), vertices = (2, −2), (0, −2); asymptotes: $y = -x - 1$, $y = x - 3$

10. $\frac{(x+1)^2}{1} - \frac{(y+2)^2}{4} = 1$, center = (−1, −2), vertices = (0, −2), (−2, −2); asymptotes: $y = 2x$, $y = -2x - 4$

11. $\overline{DE}$ is $\angle$ bisector of $\angle BDC \to \angle BDE = \angle EDC$. $\overline{AB} \parallel \overline{DE} \to \angle BDE = \angle ABD$, $\angle EDC = \angle BAD$; $\angle ABD = \angle BAD \to AD = DB$. $\overline{AB} \parallel \overline{DE} \to \frac{DC}{AD} = \frac{EC}{BE} \to \frac{DC}{DB} = \frac{EC}{BE}$

12. $x = 8$

13. $\overline{BD} \perp \overline{AC}$, $\overline{EC} \perp \overline{AB} \rightarrow \triangle BDA$ and $\triangle CEA$ are right triangles, $\angle A = \angle A$ $\rightarrow \triangle BDA$ and $\triangle CEA$ are similar. $AB = AC \rightarrow SF = 1 \rightarrow \triangle BDA \cong \triangle CEA \rightarrow BD = CE$

14. $x = 12$ **15.** $4860x^4y^2$ **16.** $\frac{4}{3}$ **17.** (*a*) Refer to Lesson 88, $S = \frac{n}{2}(a_1 + a_n)$ (*b*) 72

18. (*a*) Refer to Lesson 88, $S = \frac{a - ar^n}{1 - r}$ (*b*) 172 **19.** 3.6×10^{-4}

20. 3.16×10^{-4} mole/liter **21.** Refer to Lesson 84 **22.** 2.37

23. 1.6 cis 36.6°, 1.6 cis 126.6°, 1.6 cis 216.6°, 1.6 cis 306.6° **24.** 43 cm^2

25. 0°, 180°, 240°, 300°

26. $$\frac{\sin^3 x + \cos^3 x}{\sin x + \cos x} = \frac{(\sin x + \cos x)(\sin^2 x - \sin x \cos x + \cos^2 x)}{\sin x + \cos x}$$
$$= \sin^2 x - \sin x \cos x + \cos^2 x = 1 - \frac{1}{2}\sin 2x$$

27. $$\frac{\cot x + 1}{\cot x - 1} = \frac{\frac{1}{\cos x}(\cot x + 1)}{\frac{1}{\cos x}(\cot x - 1)} = \frac{\frac{1}{\sin x} + \frac{1}{\cos x}}{\frac{1}{\sin x} - \frac{1}{\cos x}} = \frac{\csc x + \sec x}{\csc x - \sec x}$$

28.

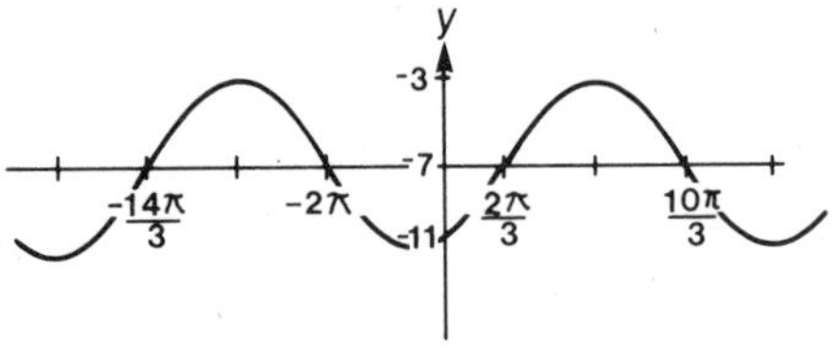

29. $\frac{25}{9}$ **30.** $\sqrt{3}$

EP53. $$\frac{k}{2k + 1} + \frac{1}{(2k + 1)(2k + 3)} = \frac{k(2k + 3) + 1}{(2k + 1)(2k + 3)} = \frac{2k^2 + 3k + 1}{(2k + 1)(2k + 3)}$$
$$= \frac{(2k + 1)(k + 1)}{(2k + 1)(2k + 3)} = \frac{k + 1}{[2(k + 1) + 1]}$$

EP54. $\begin{bmatrix} 3 & -6 \\ -2 & 4 \end{bmatrix}$

Problem set 92

1. $\omega = \frac{v}{r} = \frac{200(5280)(12)(2.54)(2\pi)}{0.4(100)(60)} \frac{\text{rad}}{\text{min}} = 13{,}411.2 \frac{\text{rev}}{\text{min}}$

2. $D = 35h - 40(h - 2)$, $D = (80 - 5h)$ mi **3.** $\frac{k}{6m}$ **4.** Av. speed $= \frac{a + c}{b + d}, \frac{1000(b + d)}{a + c}$ hr

5. 0.17 **6.** $(x - 2)^2 + (y - 3)^2 = 4$, $x^2 + y^2 - 4x - 6y + 9 = 0$

7. $\frac{(x + 5)^2}{16} + \frac{(y + 3)^2}{4} = 1$, center $= (-5, -3)$, major axis $= 8$, minor axis $= 4$

8. $\frac{(x - 2)^2}{9} + \frac{(y + 1)^2}{4} = 1$, center $= (2, -1)$, major axis $= 6$, minor axis $= 4$

9. $\frac{(x + 2)^2}{4} - \frac{(y + 2)^2}{16} = 1$, center $= (-2, -2)$, vertices $= (0, -2), (-4, -2)$;
asymptotes: $y = 2x + 2$, $y = -2x - 6$

10. $(x - 1)^2 - (y + 2)^2 = 1$, center $= (1, -2)$, vertices $= (0, -2), (2, -2)$;
asymptotes: $y = x - 3$, $y = -x - 1$

11. Refer to Lesson 90 **12.** $x = \frac{8}{3}$

13. 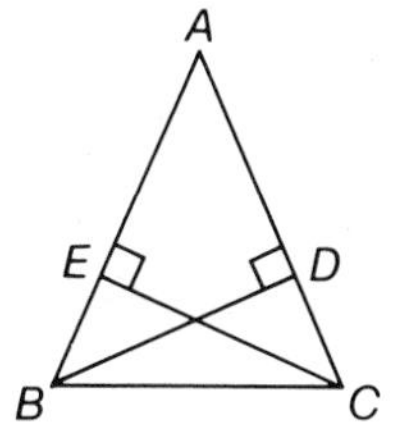

$\triangle ABD$ and $\triangle ACE$ are right triangles. $\angle A = \angle A \rightarrow \triangle ABD \sim \triangle ACE$. $AE = AD \rightarrow \triangle ABD \cong \triangle ACE \rightarrow AB = AC \rightarrow \triangle ABC$ is an isosceles triangle

14. $x = 6$ **15.** $-945x^4y^3$ **16.** $(-2, 1, 3)$

17. (*a*) Refer to Lesson 88, $S = \dfrac{a - ar^n}{1 - r}$ (*b*) 340 **18.** (*a*) Refer to Lesson 88 (*b*) 126

19. 5.19 **20.** 4.3×10^{-2} **21.** Refer to Lesson 84 **22.** 1.9 cis 73.15°, 1.9 cis 253.15°

23. $\dfrac{\log 60}{\log 5}$ **24.** 360° **25.** 60°, 300°

26. $$\frac{\sin x + \cos x}{\tan^2 x - 1} = \frac{\sin x + \cos x}{\dfrac{\sin^2 x}{\cos^2 x} - 1} = \frac{\sin x + \cos x}{\dfrac{\sin^2 x - \cos^2 x}{\cos^2 x}} = \frac{(\cos^2 x)(\sin x + \cos x)}{\sin^2 x - \cos^2 x}$$
$$= \frac{(\cos^2 x)(\sin x + \cos x)}{(\sin x - \cos x)(\sin x + \cos x)} = \frac{\cos^2 x}{\sin x - \cos x}$$

27. $$\frac{2\cos 2x}{\sin 2x} = \frac{2(\cos^2 x - \sin^2 x)}{2 \sin x \cos x} = \frac{\cos x}{\sin x} - \frac{\sin x}{\cos x} = \cot x - \tan x$$

28. Refer to Lesson 77, Problem 7(a) **29.** $\dfrac{49}{32}$ **30.** 512 **EP55.** $\begin{bmatrix} 1 & 2 \\ 3 & 4 \end{bmatrix}$ **EP56.** Valid

Problem set 93

1. 1120.5 hr **2.** $\dfrac{36d}{4 + w}$ days **3.** 709.6 min **4.** $\dfrac{1}{13} + \dfrac{1}{4} - \dfrac{1}{52} = \dfrac{16}{52} = \dfrac{4}{13}$ **5.** $C_4^7 = 35$

6. $\overline{SR}$ is $\perp$ bisector of $QT \rightarrow \triangle QVS$ and $\triangle TVS$ are right triangles, $QV = VT$, $SV = SV \rightarrow \triangle QVS \cong \triangle TVS \rightarrow QS = ST$. QR is $\perp$ bisector of $PS \rightarrow \triangle PUQ$, $\triangle SUQ$ are right triangles, $PU = US$, $QU = QU \rightarrow \triangle PUQ \cong \triangle SUQ \rightarrow PQ = QS$. Thus, $PQ = SQ = ST \rightarrow PQ = ST$.

7. P and Q are midpoints of $\overline{AD}$ and $\overline{AB} \rightarrow PQ = \dfrac{1}{2}DB$ (refer to Problem set 87, Problem 17).

S and R are midpoints of $\overline{DC}$ and $\overline{BC} \rightarrow SR = \dfrac{1}{2}DB$. Thus, $SR = \dfrac{1}{2}DB = PQ \rightarrow SR = PQ$.

8. Refer to Problem set 90, Problem 7

9. 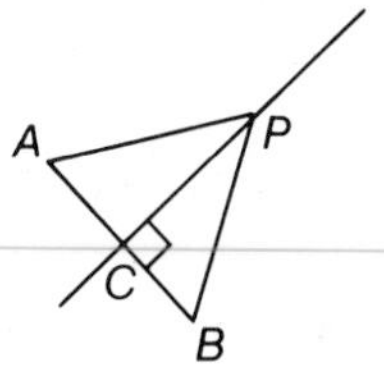

Let P be any point on the $\perp$ bisector of $\overline{AB}$. $\overline{PC}$ is the $\perp$ bisector $\rightarrow \triangle ACP$, $\triangle BCP$ are right triangles, $AC = CB$, $PC = PC \rightarrow \triangle ACP \cong \triangle BCP \rightarrow PA = PB \rightarrow P$ is equidistant from A and B.

10. $\dfrac{(x-5)^2}{4} + \dfrac{(y+2)^2}{2} = 1$, center $= (5, -2)$, major axis $= 4$, minor axis $= 2\sqrt{2}$

11. $\dfrac{(x-\frac{1}{3})^2}{1} - \dfrac{(y-3)^2}{4} = 1$, center $= \left(\dfrac{1}{3}, 3\right)$, vertices $= \left(\dfrac{4}{3}, 3\right), \left(-\dfrac{2}{3}, 3\right)$; asymptotes:

$y = 2x + \dfrac{7}{3}$, $y = -2x + \dfrac{11}{3}$

12. $(x-3)^2 + y^2 = 4$, $x^2 + y^2 - 6x + 5 = 0$ **13.** $\dfrac{\sqrt{3}}{2} + \dfrac{1}{2}i, -\dfrac{\sqrt{3}}{2} + \dfrac{1}{2}i, -i$

14. (3, −2, 1) **15.** (1, −2, 3)

16. (*a*) Refer to Lesson 84 (*b*) $\cos 75° + \cos 15° = 2 \cos 45° \cos 30° = 2(0.707)(0.866) = 1.22$

17. (*a*) Refer to Lesson 84 (*b*) $\cos 75° - \cos 15° = -2 \sin 45° \sin 30° = -\dfrac{\sqrt{2}}{2}$

18. (*a*) −41 (*b*) −185 **19.** 2.51×10^{-8} mole/liter **20.** 0.43 **21.** 14.9 or 2.4

22. $\dfrac{\log 40}{\log 6}$ **23.** $243\left(\dfrac{2}{3}\right)^3 = 72$ ft **24.** Refer to Lesson 77

25. 0°, 180°, 30°, 150°, 210°, 330°

26. $2 \csc 2x \sin x = \dfrac{2}{\sin 2x} \sin x = \dfrac{2 \sin x}{2 \sin x \cos x} = \dfrac{1}{\cos x} = \sec x$

27. $$\frac{1-\sin\theta}{1+\sin\theta} = \frac{1-\sin\theta}{1+\sin\theta}\cdot\frac{1-\sin\theta}{1-\sin\theta} = \frac{1-2\sin\theta+\sin^2\theta}{1-\sin^2\theta} = \frac{1-2\sin\theta+\sin^2\theta}{\cos^2\theta}$$
$$= \sec^2\theta - 2\frac{\sin\theta}{\cos\theta}\cdot\frac{1}{\cos\theta} + \frac{\sin^2\theta}{\cos^2\theta}$$
$$= \sec^2\theta - 2\tan\theta\sec\theta + \tan^2\theta = (\tan\theta - \sec\theta)^2$$

28. −9.3 **29.** 0, −3 **30.** 1 **EP57.** $\begin{bmatrix} 30 & -15 \\ -50 & 25 \end{bmatrix}$

EP58. $$\frac{k^2(k+1)^2}{4} + (k+1)^3 = \frac{k^2(k+1)^2 + 4(k+1)^3}{4} = \frac{(k+1)^2[k^2 + 4(k+1)]}{4}$$
$$= \frac{(k+1)^2(k^2+4k+4)}{4} = \frac{(k+1)^2(k+2)^2}{4} = \frac{(k+1)^2[(k+1)+1]^2}{4}$$

Problem set 94

1. 0.4 **2.** $2A - m$ **3.** $0.10G + 0.20B = 16, \dfrac{G}{B} = \dfrac{2}{3}, B = 60, G = 40$ **4.** $6{:}32\frac{8}{11}$ p.m.

5. $R_T = \dfrac{x-2}{2x}\dfrac{\text{jobs}}{\text{day}} \rightarrow T = \dfrac{2x}{x-2}$ days **6.** 6 **7.** 8 mi

8. $(x-1)^2 + (y+3)^2 = 1, x^2 + y^2 + 4x - 6y + 4 = 0$

9. $\triangle PQR$ and $\triangle PSR$ are right triangles. $PQ = PS, PR = PR \rightarrow \triangle PQR \cong \triangle PSR \rightarrow QR = RS$, $\angle QRP = \angle SRP, OR = OR \rightarrow \triangle RQO \cong \triangle RSO \rightarrow QO = OS$

10. Refer to Lesson 76

11. P, S are midpoints of $\overline{AD}$ and $\overline{DC} \rightarrow PS = \frac{1}{2}AC$; Q, R are midpoints of $\overline{AB}$ and $\overline{CB} \rightarrow QR = \frac{1}{2}AC \rightarrow QR = \frac{1}{2}AC = PS \rightarrow QR = PS$

12. $\dfrac{(x+3)^2}{4} + \dfrac{(y-1)^2}{9} = 1$, center = (−3, 1), major axis = 6, minor axis = 4

13. $\dfrac{(x-7)^2}{4} - \dfrac{(y+4)^2}{4} = 1$, center = (7, −4), vertices = (5, −4), (9, −4); asymptotes: $y = x - 11, y = -x + 3$

14. (−2, 2, −1) **15.** (−1, 3, 4)

16. (*a*) Refer to Lesson 84 (*b*) $\sin 75° \cos 15° = \frac{1}{2}(\sin 90° + \sin 60°) = \frac{1}{2}\left(1 + \frac{\sqrt{3}}{2}\right) = \frac{2+\sqrt{3}}{4}$

17. (*a*) Refer to Lesson 84 (*b*) $\sin 75° + \sin 15° = 2 \sin 45° \cos 30° = 2(0.707)(0.866) = 1.22$

18. 3.16×10^{-9} mole/liter **19.** (*a*) $a + (n-1)d$ (*b*) $\frac{n}{2}[2a + (n-1)d]$

20. $i, -\frac{\sqrt{3}}{2} - \frac{1}{2}i, \frac{\sqrt{3}}{2} - \frac{1}{2}i$ **21.** 188.97 **22.** $\frac{\log_{10} 22}{\log_{10} e}$

23.

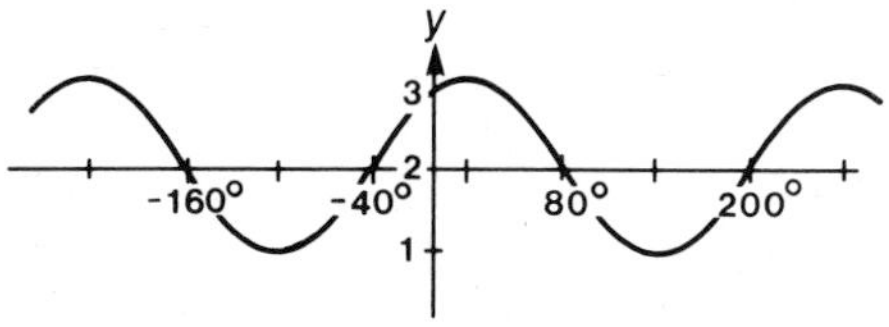

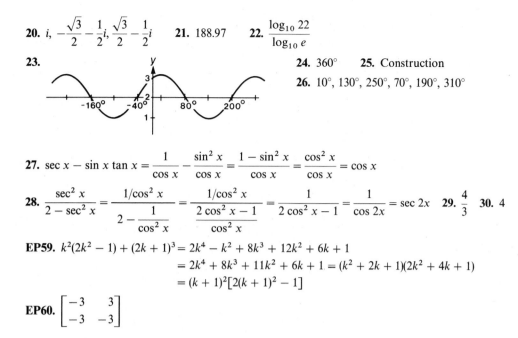

24. 360° **25.** Construction

26. 10°, 130°, 250°, 70°, 190°, 310°

27. $\sec x - \sin x \tan x = \frac{1}{\cos x} - \frac{\sin^2 x}{\cos x} = \frac{1 - \sin^2 x}{\cos x} = \frac{\cos^2 x}{\cos x} = \cos x$

28. $\frac{\sec^2 x}{2 - \sec^2 x} = \frac{1/\cos^2 x}{2 - \frac{1}{\cos^2 x}} = \frac{1/\cos^2 x}{\frac{2\cos^2 x - 1}{\cos^2 x}} = \frac{1}{2\cos^2 x - 1} = \frac{1}{\cos 2x} = \sec 2x$ **29.** $\frac{4}{3}$ **30.** 4

EP59. $k^2(2k^2 - 1) + (2k + 1)^3 = 2k^4 - k^2 + 8k^3 + 12k^2 + 6k + 1$

$= 2k^4 + 8k^3 + 11k^2 + 6k + 1 = (k^2 + 2k + 1)(2k^2 + 4k + 1)$

$= (k + 1)^2[2(k + 1)^2 - 1]$

EP60. $\begin{bmatrix} -3 & 3 \\ -3 & -3 \end{bmatrix}$

Problem set 95

1. 21 **2.** 4 **3.** $\frac{RK}{R + M}$ **4.** 320 gal **5.** $\frac{22}{25}$ **6.** 8:1 **7.** $80\sqrt{3}$ cm^3

8. (*a*) $\frac{1000\pi}{3}$ cm^3 (*b*) $(100\sqrt{2}\pi + 100\pi)$ cm^2 **9.** $\sqrt{13 + n^2}$

10. (*a*) $\frac{4000\pi}{3}$ cm^3 (*b*) 400π cm^2 **11.** $S = \frac{3}{1 - (-\frac{1}{2})} = 2$

12. $D = 10 + \frac{10}{1 - \frac{1}{2}} = 10 + 20 = 30$ ft

13. $\overline{PR}$ is $\perp$ bisector of $\overline{SQ} \rightarrow SO = OQ$, $\triangle SOP$ and $\triangle QOP$ are right triangles. $OP = OP$ $\rightarrow \triangle SOP \cong \triangle QOP \rightarrow PS = PQ$, $PR = PR \rightarrow \triangle PSR \cong \triangle PQR \rightarrow RS = QR$

14. $\frac{(y - 2)^2}{9} - \frac{(x + 1)^2}{16} = 1$; center $= (-1, 2)$; vertices $= (-1, 5), (-1, -1)$; asymptotes: $y = \frac{3}{4}x + \frac{11}{4}$, $y = -\frac{3}{4}x + \frac{5}{4}$

15. $\frac{(x + 2)^2}{64} + \frac{(y - 1)^2}{48} = 1$; center $= (-2, 1)$; major axis $= 16$; minor axis $= 8\sqrt{3}$

16. $(-2, -3, 2)$

17. (*a*) Refer to Lesson 84 (*b*) $2 \cos 135° \cos 120° = 2(-0.707)(-0.5) = 0.707$

18. (*a*) Refer to Lesson 84 (*b*) $\frac{1}{2}(\cos 270° + \cos 240°) = -\frac{1}{4}$

19. (*a*) $a + (n - 1)d$ (*b*) $\frac{1}{2}n[2a + (n - 1)d]$

20. 1.86 cis 17.1°, 1.86 cis 137.1°, 1.86 cis 257.1° **21.** 2,752,243.7 **22.** 3.5 **23.** $\frac{\log_{10} 35}{\log_{10} e}$

24. Construction **25.** Refer to Lesson 77

26. $\cos 2x \sec^2 x = (\cos^2 x - \sin^2 x) \cdot \frac{1}{\cos^2 x} = 1 - \frac{\sin^2 x}{\cos^2 x} = 1 - \tan^2 x$

27. 109.5°, 250.5°, 120°, 240°

28. $\dfrac{1+\cos 2x}{\sin 2x} = \dfrac{1+(2\cos^2 x - 1)}{2\sin x\cos x} = \dfrac{\cos^2 x}{\sin x\cos x} = \dfrac{\cos x}{\sin x} = \cot x$

29. -0.83 **30.** $\dfrac{5}{2}$ **EP61.** $\begin{bmatrix} 7 & -1 \\ 1 & -7 \end{bmatrix}$

EP62. $\dfrac{k(k+1)(k+2)}{6} + \dfrac{(k+1)(k+2)}{2} = \dfrac{k(k+1)(k+2)+3(k+1)(k+2)}{6}$

$= \dfrac{(k+1)(k+2)(k+3)}{6} = \dfrac{(k+1)[(k+1)+1][(k+1)+2]}{6}$

Problem set EL5

1. 25 **2.** 4 **3.** 490 **4.** 250 lb **5.** $B = 20$ mph, $W = 10$ mph

6. $\frac{1}{2}n(n+1) + (n+1) = \frac{1}{2}n^2 + \frac{3}{2}n + 1 = \frac{1}{2}(n+1)(n+2) = \frac{1}{2}(n+1)[(n+1)+1]$

7. $\frac{1}{2}n[2a+(n-1)d] + a + nd = na + \frac{1}{2}n^2d - \frac{1}{2}nd + a + nd = a(n+1) + \frac{1}{2}n^2d + \frac{1}{2}nd$

$= a(n+1) + \frac{1}{2}n(n+1)d = \frac{1}{2}(n+1)(2a+nd)$

$= \frac{1}{2}(n+1)[2a+(n+1-1)d]$

8. $\dfrac{1-r^{n+1}}{1-r} + r^{n+1} = \dfrac{1-r^{n+1}+r^{n+1}-r^{n+2}}{1-r} = \dfrac{1-r^{n+2}}{1-r} = \dfrac{1-r^{(n+1)+1}}{1-r}$

9. 27:1 **10.** $75\sqrt{3}$ cm³ **11.** (*a*) 72π cm³ (*b*) $(36\sqrt{2}\pi + 36\pi)$ cm²

12. $\sqrt{x^2+y^2+9}$ **13.** (*a*) 288π cm³ (*b*) 144π cm² **14.** $\dfrac{6}{5}$

15. $\overline{PR}$ is $\angle$ bisector of $\angle P$ and $\angle QRS \rightarrow \angle QPR = \angle SPR$,
$\angle QRP = \angle SRP \rightarrow \triangle PQR \sim \triangle PSR$; $PR = PR \rightarrow SF = 1$, $\triangle PQR \cong \triangle PSR \rightarrow QR = RS$

16. $\dfrac{(x+3)^2}{1} - \dfrac{(y-2)^2}{4} = 1$, center $= (-3, 2)$, vertices: $(-2, 2)$, $(-4, 2)$;
asymptotes: $y = 2x + 8$, $y = -2x - 4$

17. $\dfrac{(x+3)^2}{4} + \dfrac{(y-1)^2}{9} = 1$, center $= (-3, 1)$; major axis: vertical, 6; minor axis = 4

18. $(-1, 3, 2)$ **19.** $2\sin 150° \cos 135° = -\dfrac{\sqrt{2}}{2}$

20. (*a*) $a + (n-1)d$ (*b*) $\frac{1}{2}n[2a+(n-1)d]$ **21.** 1.7 cis 17.7°, 1.7 cis 137.7°, 1.7 cis 257.7°

22. 8.7 **23.** $\dfrac{1}{\log e}$ **24.** Construction **25.** Refer to Problem set 48, Problem 18

26. $(\sin 2x)(\sec^2 x) = 2\sin x\cos x \dfrac{1}{\cos^2 x} = \dfrac{2\sin x}{\cos x} = 2\tan x$

27. 210°, 330°, 199.5°, 340.5° **28.** $-\dfrac{1}{3}$ **29.** No solution, $x = -\dfrac{7}{6}$ **30.** No

Problem set 96

1. $M = 63$, $J = 41$ **2.** $\dfrac{10H - 15}{3H}\dfrac{\text{jobs}}{\text{hr}}$ **3.** 718.6 **4.** $x\left(\dfrac{d}{n} + 3\right) = 400 \rightarrow x = \dfrac{400n}{d+3n}$

5. $\dfrac{1}{7}$ **6.** $\dfrac{31}{99{,}000}$ **7.** $\dfrac{5957}{990}$ **8.** 12 **9.** $\dfrac{125}{3}$ cm³ **10.** $5\sqrt{2}$

11. (*a*) 96π cm^3 (*b*) 96π cm^2 **12.** (*a*) 288π m^3 (*b*) 144π m^2

13. 220 ft **14.** Construction

15. Draw diagonals $\overline{DB}$ and $\overline{AC}$. P, Q, S, R are midpoints of $\overline{AD}, \overline{AB}, \overline{BC}$, and $\overline{DC}$, respectively $\rightarrow PQ = \frac{1}{2}DB = SR$ and $PS = \frac{1}{2}AC = QR$ (refer to Problem set 87, Problem 17)

16. Refer to Lesson 76

17. $AC = BC, DC = EC, \angle C = \angle C \rightarrow \triangle AEC \cong \triangle BDC \rightarrow \angle AEC = \angle BDC$

18. $\dfrac{(x+3)^2}{1} - \dfrac{(y-2)^2}{4} = 1$, center $= (-3, 2)$, vertices $= (-2, 2), (-4, 2)$;
asymptotes: $y = 2x + 8$, $y = -2x - 4$

19. $\dfrac{(x-2)^2}{\frac{1}{9}} + \dfrac{(y+3)^2}{\frac{1}{25}} = 1$, center $= (2, -3)$, major axis $= \dfrac{2}{3}$, minor axis $= \dfrac{2}{5}$

20. (*a*) Refer to Lesson 84 (*b*) $2 \cos 135° \sin 120° = -\dfrac{\sqrt{6}}{2}$

21. (*a*) -4096 (*b*) -2730 **22.** $\dfrac{\log_{10} 42}{\log_{10} e}$ **23.** 60°

24. $\dfrac{40(5280)(12)(2.54)}{100(1000)(60)(60)} \dfrac{\text{km}}{\text{sec}}$ **25.** (*a*) $y = 10 + 6 \csc x$ (*b*) $y = -7 + 4 \sec x$

26. $(\sin x - \cos x)^2 = \sin^2 x - 2 \sin x \cos x + \cos^2 x = 1 - 2 \sin x \cos x = 1 - \sin 2x$

27. $\dfrac{\tan^2 x}{\sec x + 1} = \dfrac{\sec^2 x - 1}{\sec x + 1} = \dfrac{(\sec x - 1)(\sec x + 1)}{\sec x + 1} = \sec x - 1$

28. 15°, 135°, 255°, 105°, 225°, 345° **29.** No solution, $x = -\dfrac{10}{13}$ **30.** $\dfrac{15\sqrt{26}}{26}$

EP63. $\begin{bmatrix} 3 & -4 \\ 4 & 7 \end{bmatrix}$ **EP64.** For $k = 1$, we get $1 = \dfrac{1(1+1)}{2}$, and also $\dfrac{k(k+1)}{2} + (k+1)$
$= \dfrac{k(k+1)}{2} + \dfrac{2(k+1)}{2} = \dfrac{(k+2)(k+1)}{2} = \dfrac{(k+1)[(k+1)+1]}{2}$

Problem set 97

1. 700 ml 2%, 700 ml 10% **2.** $R = 4, W = 8, B = 16$ **3.** $A = 40°, B = 70°$ **4.** 481

5. $C = 25$ mph, $B = 50$ mph

6. $N = 0.00029 + 0.0000029 + 0.000000029 + \cdots = \dfrac{0.00029}{1 - 0.01} = \dfrac{0.00029}{0.99} = \dfrac{29}{99{,}000}$

7. $N = 2 + 0.019 + 0.00019 + 0.0000019 + \cdots = 2 + \dfrac{0.019}{1 - 0.01} = 2 + \dfrac{0.019}{0.99} = 2 + \dfrac{19}{990} = \dfrac{1999}{990}$

8. 200 cm^3 **9.** 27:1 **10.** (*a*) $\dfrac{256\pi}{3}$ cm^3 (*b*) 64π cm^2 **11.** $\sqrt{20 + m^2}$

12. (*a*) $\dfrac{250\pi}{3}$ cm^3 (*b*) $(25\sqrt{5}\pi + 25\pi)$ cm^2 **13.** $S = \dfrac{\frac{1}{4}}{1 + \frac{1}{2}} = \dfrac{1}{6}$

14. $\left(x + \dfrac{3}{2} - \dfrac{3\sqrt{3}}{2}i\right)\left(x + \dfrac{3}{2} + \dfrac{3\sqrt{3}}{2}i\right)$

15. $AB = AD, BC = CD, AC = AC \rightarrow \triangle ABC \cong \triangle ADC \rightarrow \angle BAO = \angle DAO$;
$AB = AD, AO = AO \rightarrow \triangle ABO \cong \triangle ADO \rightarrow \angle AOB = \angle AOD$;
$\angle AOB + \angle AOD = 180° \rightarrow \angle AOB = \angle AOD = 90°$; $\overline{AC} \perp \overline{BD}$

16. $\overline{BD}$ and $\overline{KJ}$ bisect each other, $KE = EJ, DE = EB, \angle DEK = \angle JEB \rightarrow \triangle DEK \cong \triangle BEJ$
$\rightarrow \angle DKE = \angle BJE \rightarrow \angle CKE = \angle AJE$; $\angle CEK = \angle AEJ \rightarrow \triangle CKE \sim \triangle AJE$;
$KE = EJ \rightarrow SF = 1 \rightarrow \triangle CKE \cong \triangle AJE \rightarrow KC = AJ$

17. Draw $\overline{IK}$ and $\overline{MK}$. $IJ = ML$, $JK = LK$, $\angle IJK = \angle MLK \rightarrow \triangle IJK \cong \triangle MLK \rightarrow IK = MK$; $IH = HM$, $HK = HK \rightarrow \triangle HIK \cong \triangle HMK \rightarrow \angle IHK = \angle MHK$

18. $\dfrac{(x-1)^2}{25} - \dfrac{(y+2)^2}{4} = 1$; center $= (1, -2)$; vertices $= (6, -2), (-4, -2)$;

asymptotes: $y = \frac{2}{5}x - \frac{12}{5}$, $y = -\frac{2}{5}x - \frac{8}{5}$

19. $\dfrac{(x+3)^2}{9} + \dfrac{(y-2)^2}{25} = 1$; center $= (-3, 2)$; major axis, vertical, length 10; minor axis: 6

20. (*a*) Refer to Lesson 84 (*b*) $2 \cos 150° \cos 135° = \dfrac{\sqrt{6}}{2}$

21. (*a*) 1 (*b*) -32 **22.** $B = 123.7°$ **23.** $\dfrac{\log 200}{\log e}$ **24.** 360°

25. $i, -\dfrac{\sqrt{3}}{2} - \dfrac{1}{2}i, \dfrac{\sqrt{3}}{2} - \dfrac{1}{2}i$ **26.** $\sin(-x)\sec(-x) = -\sin x \dfrac{1}{\cos(-x)} = -\dfrac{\sin x}{\cos x} = -\tan x$

27. $$\frac{\cot x - 1}{1 - \tan x} = \frac{\dfrac{\cos x}{\sin x} - 1}{1 - \dfrac{\sin x}{\cos x}} = \frac{\dfrac{\cos x - \sin x}{\sin x}}{\dfrac{\cos x - \sin x}{\cos x}} = \frac{\cos x - \sin x}{\sin x} \cdot \frac{\cos x}{\cos x - \sin x} = \frac{\cos x}{\sin x}$$
$$= \frac{\dfrac{1}{\sin x}}{\dfrac{1}{\cos x}} = \frac{\csc x}{\sec x}$$

28. 0°, 180°, 90° **29.** 1 **30.** 1×10^{-3}

EP65. For $k = 1$, we get $\dfrac{1}{1 \cdot 2} = \dfrac{1}{1+1}$, and $\dfrac{k}{k+1} + \dfrac{1}{(k+1)(k+2)} = \dfrac{k(k+2)+1}{(k+1)(k+2)}$
$$= \frac{k^2 + 2k + 1}{(k+1)(k+2)} = \frac{(k+1)^2}{(k+1)(k+2)} = \frac{k+1}{k+2} = \frac{k+1}{(k+1)+1}$$

EP66. Invalid

Problem set 98

1. 2 liters **2.** 4000 **3.** $\dfrac{9\sqrt{2}}{2}$ **4.** $\dfrac{4000m}{c + pm}$ **5.** $\dfrac{56}{3}$ gal **6.** Refer to Lesson 98

7. Refer to Lesson 98

8. $BD = EC$, $AD = AE$, $BD + AD = AE + EC \rightarrow AB = AC$; $\angle A = \angle A$, $\triangle AEB \cong \triangle ADC$ (SAS) $\rightarrow BE = CD$

9. Trapezoid $ABDC$ is an isosceles trapezoid $\rightarrow \angle ACD = \angle BDC$; $AC = BD$, $CD = CD \rightarrow \triangle ACD \cong \triangle BDC \rightarrow AD = BC$

10. $\dfrac{37}{9900}$ **11.** $\dfrac{1}{2}$ **12.** $\sqrt{34 + x^2}$ **13.** 206.5 cm^3 **14.** 36 square units

15. (*a*) $288\pi \text{ cm}^3$ (*b*) $144\pi \text{ cm}^2$ **16.** (*a*) $48\pi \text{ cm}^3$ (*b*) $(12\sqrt{13}\pi + 36\pi) \text{ cm}^2$

17. $\dfrac{(x-3)^2}{16} - \dfrac{(y+2)^2}{36} = 1$; center $= (3, -2)$; vertices $= (7, -2), (-1, -2)$;

asymptotes: $y = \frac{3}{2}x - \frac{13}{2}$, $y = -\frac{3}{2}x + \frac{5}{2}$

18. $\dfrac{(x-3)^2}{4} + \dfrac{(y+4)^2}{25} = 1$; center $= (3, -4)$; major axis: vertical, length 10; minor axis: 4

19. (*a*) Refer to Lesson 84 (*b*) $\frac{1}{2}(\cos 210° - \cos 240°) = \frac{1 - \sqrt{3}}{4}$

20. (*a*) 51 (*b*) 459 **21.** $A = 12.4°$ **22.** $\frac{\log 305}{\log e}$

23. $\frac{1}{2} + \frac{\sqrt{3}}{2}i, -1, \frac{1}{2} - \frac{\sqrt{3}}{2}i$ **24.** Refer to Lesson 77 **25.** $y = -\frac{3}{4}x$

26. $(1 + \tan x)(1 - \tan x) + 2\tan^2 x = 1 - \tan^2 x + 2\tan^2 x = 1 + \tan^2 x = \sec^2 x$

27. $$\frac{\sin x}{1 + \cos x} + \frac{1 + \cos x}{\sin x} = \frac{\sin^2 x + 1 + 2\cos x + \cos^2 x}{(\sin x)(1 + \cos x)} = \frac{2 + 2\cos x}{(\sin x)(1 + \cos x)}$$
$$= \frac{2(1 + \cos x)}{(\sin x)(1 + \cos x)} = \frac{2}{\sin x} = 2 \csc x$$

28. 70°, 190°, 310°, 110°, 230°, 350° **29.** 9 **30.** $\frac{1}{4}$

EP67. For $k = 1$, we get $1 = (1)^3$, and also $k^2 + (2k + 1) = (k + 1)^2$ **EP68.** $\begin{bmatrix} 4 & 2 \\ 4 & 1 \end{bmatrix}$

Problem set 99

1. $\frac{32}{9}$ hr **2.** 49,382.7 **3.** $\frac{T}{12} = S$, $T = S + 30$; $T = 32\frac{8}{11}$ min

4. $B = 12$ mph, $W = 4$ mph **5.** $\frac{7}{13}$ **6.** Refer to Lesson 99

7. $AD = BE$, $DC = EC \rightarrow AD + DC = BE + EC \rightarrow AC = BC$, $\angle C = \angle C \rightarrow \triangle ACE \cong \triangle BCD$ $\rightarrow \angle A = \angle B$

8. $\overline{RC} \| \overline{AB} \rightarrow \angle DRX = \angle XSA$, $\angle RXD = \angle AXS \rightarrow \triangle XRD \sim \triangle XSA$; $RX = XS \rightarrow SF = 1$. $\triangle XRD \cong \triangle XSA \rightarrow RD = SA$. $RSBC$ is a parallelogram since $\overline{RC} \| \overline{SB}$, $\overline{RS} \| \overline{CB} \rightarrow RS = CB$; X, Y midpoints $\rightarrow XS = \frac{1}{2}RS = \frac{1}{2}CB = YB$. $XS = YB$, $\overline{XS} \| \overline{YB} \rightarrow XSBY$ is a parallelogram $\rightarrow \overline{XY} \| \overline{SB}$. $XY = RD + DC$, $AS = RD \rightarrow XY = AS + DC$. $XY = SB \rightarrow 2XY = AS + DC + SB \rightarrow 2XY = DC + AB \rightarrow XY = \frac{1}{2}(DC + AB)$; $\overline{RC} \| \overline{XY} \| \overline{AB}$

9. Refer to Lesson 98 **10.** Refer to Lesson 76

11. $N = 0.0041 + 0.000041 + 0.00000041 + \cdots = \frac{0.0041}{1 - 0.01} = \frac{41}{9900}$ **12.** $\frac{\frac{1}{4}}{1 + \frac{3}{4}} = \frac{1}{7}$

13. $\sqrt{58 + x^2}$ **14.** $30\sqrt{3}$ cm³ **15.** 2 to 3 **16.** (*a*) $\frac{4000}{3}\pi$ cm³ (*b*) 400π cm²

17. (*a*) 200π cm³ (*b*) $(20\sqrt{34}\pi + 100\pi)$ cm²

18. $\frac{(x - 4)^2}{9} + \frac{(y + 1)^2}{25} = 1$, center $= (4, -1)$; major axis $= 10$, vertical axis; minor axis $= 6$

19. $\frac{(x + 2)^2}{36} - \frac{(y - 4)^2}{9} = 1$, center $= (-2, 4)$, vertices $= (4, 4), (-8, 4)$;

asymptotes: $y = \frac{1}{2}x + 5$, $y = -\frac{1}{2}x + 3$

20. (*a*) Refer to Lesson 84 (*b*) $\frac{1}{2}(\sin 240° + \sin 210°) = \frac{1}{2}(-0.866 - 0.5) = -0.683$

21. 65,536 **22.** $A = 61.0°$ **23.** $\frac{\log 8}{\log 4}$

24. $1, -\frac{1}{2} + \frac{\sqrt{3}}{2}i, -\frac{1}{2} - \frac{\sqrt{3}}{2}i$ **25.**

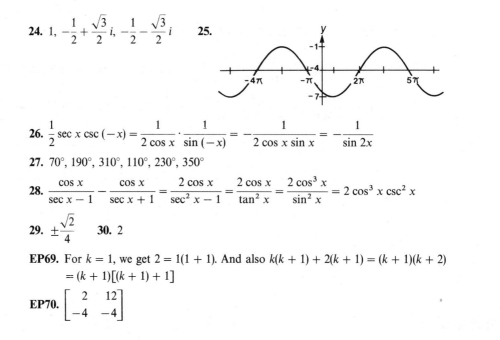

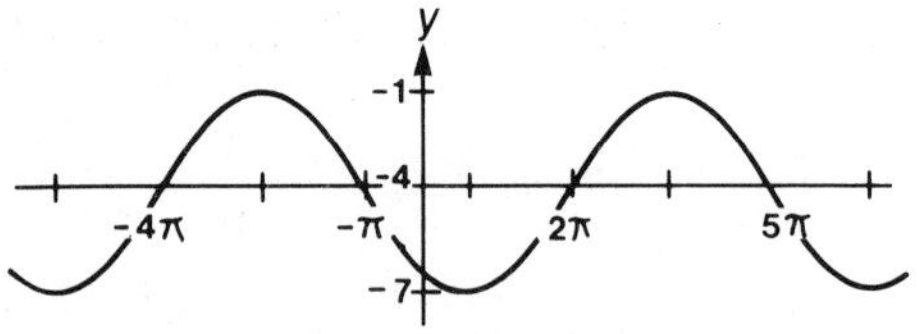

26. $\frac{1}{2} \sec x \csc(-x) = \frac{1}{2 \cos x} \cdot \frac{1}{\sin(-x)} = -\frac{1}{2 \cos x \sin x} = -\frac{1}{\sin 2x}$

27. 70°, 190°, 310°, 110°, 230°, 350°

28. $\frac{\cos x}{\sec x - 1} - \frac{\cos x}{\sec x + 1} = \frac{2 \cos x}{\sec^2 x - 1} = \frac{2 \cos x}{\tan^2 x} = \frac{2 \cos^3 x}{\sin^2 x} = 2 \cos^3 x \csc^2 x$

29. $\pm\frac{\sqrt{2}}{4}$ **30.** 2

EP69. For $k = 1$, we get $2 = 1(1 + 1)$. And also $k(k + 1) + 2(k + 1) = (k + 1)(k + 2)$
$= (k + 1)[(k + 1) + 1]$

EP70. $\begin{bmatrix} 2 & 12 \\ -4 & -4 \end{bmatrix}$

Problem set 100

1. 40° **2.** $\frac{ft}{t - 2}\ \frac{\text{ft}}{\text{hr}}$ **3.** 100 **4.** $\frac{1}{4}$ **5.** ${}_8P_6 = \frac{8!}{(8-6)!} = 20{,}160; {}_8C_6 = \frac{8!}{6!(8-6)!} = 28$

6. 123.9 **7.** 5.7×10^{-6} **8.** $2 < x < 29$ **9.** $3 < x < \frac{25}{8}$ **10.** $\frac{\log 6}{\log 5}$

11. Refer to Lesson 99

12. $AD = BE, DC = EC \rightarrow AD + DC = BE + EC \rightarrow AC = BC,$
$\angle DCE = \angle DCE \rightarrow \triangle AEC \cong \triangle BDC \rightarrow AE = BD$

13. $AD = BE, DC = EC \rightarrow AD + DC = BE + EC \rightarrow AC = BC,$
$\angle DCE = \angle DCE \rightarrow \triangle AEC \cong \triangle BDC \rightarrow \angle A = \angle B, \angle AFD = \angle BFE \rightarrow \triangle AFD \sim \triangle BFE,$
$AD = BE \rightarrow SF = 1 \rightarrow \triangle AFD \cong \triangle BFE$

14. Refer to Lesson 47

15. $\overline{RS} \parallel \overline{CB}, \angle XRD = \angle XSA, \angle RXD = \angle AXS \rightarrow \triangle RXD \sim \triangle SXA; AX = XD \rightarrow SF = 1$
$\rightarrow \triangle RXD \cong \triangle SXA \rightarrow RX = XS$. $RCBS$ is a parallelogram since $\overline{RC} \parallel \overline{AB}, \overline{RS} \parallel \overline{CB}$
$\rightarrow RS = CB$. $XS = \frac{1}{2}RS = \frac{1}{2}CB = YB, \overline{XS} \parallel \overline{YB} \rightarrow XSBY$ is a parallelogram $\rightarrow \overline{XY} \parallel \overline{AB}$.
$XY = RD + DC, XY = SB \rightarrow 2XY = RD + DC + SB, AS = RD$
$\rightarrow 2XY = AS + SB + DC = DC + AB \rightarrow XY = \frac{1}{2}(DC + AB)$

16. $\frac{43}{9900}$ **17.** 81 ft **18.** $\sqrt{34 + x^2}$ **19.** 362.1 cm³ **20.** 9 to 25

21. (*a*) 972π cm³ (*b*) 324π cm² **22.** (*a*) $\frac{512}{3}\pi$ cm³ (*b*) $(8\sqrt{2}\pi + 64\pi)$ cm²

23. $\frac{(x + 1)^2}{9} + \frac{(y - 2)^2}{25} = 1$; center $= (-1, 2)$; major axis: vertical, 10; minor axis = 6

24. $\frac{(x - 5)^2}{36} - \frac{(y - 3)^2}{4} = 1$; center $= (5, 3)$; vertices: $(11, 3), (-1, 3)$;
asymptotes: $y = \frac{1}{3}x + \frac{4}{3}, y = -\frac{1}{3}x + \frac{14}{3}$

25. $-2\sin 135^\circ \sin 120^\circ = -\frac{\sqrt{6}}{2}$ **26.** $a = 16.9$

27. $\sec x \csc x = \frac{1}{\cos x}\frac{1}{\sin x} = \frac{2}{\sin 2x} = 2\csc 2x$ **28.** 10°, 130°, 250°, 70°, 190°, 310°

29. $\frac{2\tan\theta}{1+\tan^2\theta} = \frac{2\tan\theta}{\sec^2\theta} = \frac{2\sin\theta}{\cos\theta}\cdot\cos^2\theta = 2\sin\theta\cos\theta = \sin 2\theta$ **30.** $\frac{1}{64}$

EP71. For $k = 1$, we get $1^2 = \frac{1(1+1)(2+1)}{6}$; $1 = \frac{(2)(3)}{6}$. And also $\frac{k(k+1)(2k+1)}{6} + (k+1)^2$

$= \frac{k(k+1)(2k+1) + 6(k+1)^2}{6} = \frac{(k+1)[k(2k+1) + 6(k+1)]}{6} = \frac{(k+1)(2k^2+7k+6)}{6}$

$= \frac{(k+1)[(k+2)(2k+3)]}{6} = \frac{(k+1)[(k+1)+1][2(k+1)+1]}{6}$

EP72. $\begin{bmatrix} 7 & -17 \\ -3 & 21 \end{bmatrix}$

Problem set 101

1. $(0.9p - 0.5)$ dollars **2.** \$750 **3.** \$1920 **4.** $C^7_3 = 35$

5. $P(B \cup R) = 0.4 + 0.6 - 0.2 = 0.8$ **6.** $\frac{6!}{3!3!}(2x^2)^3(-y)^3 = -160x^6y^3$

7. $\frac{8!}{4!4!}(a^2)^4(-2b)^4 = 1120a^8b^4$ **8.** 2.2×10^{-5} **9.** $0 < x - 2 < 5^3 \rightarrow 2 < x < 127$

10. $x + 1 > \frac{1}{9} \rightarrow x > -\frac{8}{9}$

11. $AD = BE, DC = EC \rightarrow AD + DC = BE + EC \rightarrow AC = BC; \angle C = \angle C \rightarrow \triangle AEC \cong \triangle BDC$
$\rightarrow \angle A = \angle B, \angle AFD = \angle BFE \rightarrow \triangle AFD \sim \triangle BFE; AD = BE \rightarrow SF = 1$
$\rightarrow \triangle AFD \cong \triangle BFE \rightarrow AF = BF, AC = BC, FC = FC \rightarrow \triangle AFC \cong \triangle BFC$

12. $\angle DBC = \angle ACB \rightarrow BE = EC; AE = ED, \angle AEB = \angle DEC \rightarrow \triangle AEB \cong \triangle DEC \rightarrow AB = DC$

13.

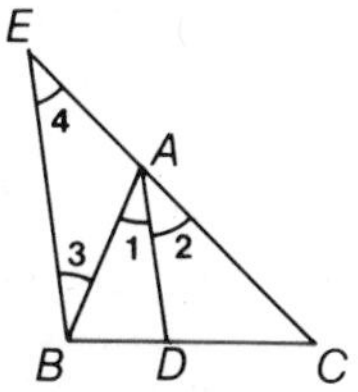

Draw $\overline{BE} \parallel \overline{AD}$ where E is on an extension of AC. $\overline{AD} \parallel \overline{EB}$
$\rightarrow \angle 2 = \angle 4, \angle 1 = \angle 3, \frac{AE}{AC} = \frac{BD}{DC}$. $\overline{AD}$ is $\angle$ bisector $\rightarrow \angle 1 = \angle 2$
$\rightarrow \angle 3 = \angle 4 \rightarrow AE = AB \rightarrow \frac{AB}{AC} = \frac{BD}{DC}$

14. Refer to Lesson 47 **15.** Refer to Lesson 99 **16.** $\frac{17}{990}$

17. $128 + \frac{\frac{256}{3}}{1 - \frac{1}{3}} = 128 + 128 = 256$ ft **18.** $\sqrt{70}$ **19.** $216\sqrt{3}$ cm³

20. (*a*) $\frac{4}{3}\pi$ cm³ (*b*) 4π cm² **21.** 64:125 **22.** (*a*) 96π cm³ (*b*) 96π cm²

23. $\frac{(y+4)^2}{4} - \frac{(x-7)^2}{4} = 1$; center = (7, −4); vertices = (7, −2), (7, −6);
asymptotes: $y = x - 11$, $y = -x + 3$

24. $\frac{(x-4)^2}{4} + \frac{(y+10)^2}{64} = 1$; center = (4, −10); major axis: vertical, 16; minor axis: 4

25. $a = 19.3$ **26.** $-2\sin 45^\circ \sin 30^\circ = -\frac{\sqrt{2}}{2}$ **27.** 210°, 330°, 270°

28. $\tan 2x = \dfrac{\sin 2x}{\cos 2x} = \dfrac{2\sin x\cos x}{\cos^2 x - \sin^2 x} = \dfrac{\frac{1}{\cos^2 x}(2\sin x\cos x)}{\frac{1}{\cos^2 x}(\cos^2 x - \sin^2 x)} = \dfrac{\frac{2\sin x}{\cos x}}{1 - \frac{\sin^2 x}{\cos^2 x}} = \dfrac{2\tan x}{1 - \tan^2 x}$

29. $\dfrac{1+\cos\theta}{\sin\theta} + \dfrac{\sin\theta}{\cos\theta} = \dfrac{\cos\theta + \cos^2\theta + \sin^2\theta}{\sin\theta\cos\theta} = \dfrac{1+\cos\theta}{\sin\theta\cos\theta}$ **30.** 3.6

EP73. For $k = 1$, we get $5 = \dfrac{5\cdot 1(1+1)}{2}$. And also $\dfrac{5k(k+1)}{2} + 5(k+1) = \dfrac{5k(k+1) + 10(k+1)}{2}$

$= \dfrac{5(k+1)(k+2)}{2} = \dfrac{5(k+1)[(k+1)+1]}{2}$

EP74. Valid

Problem set 102

1. $C = 4, B = 12$ **2.** $\dfrac{175d}{11c}$ workers **3.** $\dfrac{56k + 14mx}{kx}$ jobs **4.** $\dfrac{(w+4+g)!}{w!4!g!}$ **5.** $\dfrac{1}{6}$

6. Refer to Lesson 102

7. $AD = BE$, $DC = EC \rightarrow AC = AD + DC = BE + EC = BC$; $\angle C = \angle C \rightarrow \triangle AEC \cong \triangle BDC$ $\rightarrow \angle A = \angle B$, $\angle AFD = \angle BFE \rightarrow \triangle AFD \sim \triangle BFE$; $AD = BE \rightarrow SF = 1$, $\triangle AFD \cong \triangle BFE$ $\rightarrow AF = FB$, $FC = FC$, $AC = BC \rightarrow \triangle AFC \cong \triangle BFC \rightarrow \angle ACF = \angle BCF$

8. Refer to Lesson 102

9. Draw $\overline{OA}$ and $\overline{OB}$. $OA = OB$, $OZ = OZ$, $\triangle OAZ$ and $\triangle OBZ$ are right triangles $\rightarrow \triangle OZA \cong \triangle OZB \rightarrow AZ = ZB$, $\angle AOD = \angle BOD \rightarrow \overset{\frown}{AD} = \overset{\frown}{DB}$

10. Refer to Lesson 102 **11.** $-1{,}025{,}024x^9y^{10}$ **12.** $1120x^4y^{12}$ **13.** 4.8×10^3

14. $-2 < x < 25$ **15.** $\dfrac{17}{16} < x$ **16.** Refer to Lesson 99 **17.** $\dfrac{8}{495}$ **18.** 405

19. $\sqrt{34 + n^2}$ **20.** $\dfrac{250}{3}$ cm^3 **21.** (*a*) $\dfrac{4}{3}\pi r^3$ cm^3 (*b*) $4\pi r^2$ cm^2 **22.** 2:5

23. (*a*) 300π cm^3 (*b*) $(10\sqrt{181}\,\pi + 100\pi)$ cm^2

24. $\dfrac{(x+2)^2}{9} - \dfrac{(y-6)^2}{4} = 1$; center $= (-2, 6)$; vertices $= (1, 6), (-5, 6)$;

asymptotes: $y = \dfrac{2}{3}x + \dfrac{22}{3}$, $y = -\dfrac{2}{3}x + \dfrac{14}{3}$

25. $\dfrac{x^2}{25} + \dfrac{(y-6)^2}{16} = 1$; center $= (0, 6)$; major axis: horizontal, 10; minor axis: 8 **26.** $A = 141.4°$

27. $\dfrac{1}{2}[\sin 300° + \sin(-270°)] = \dfrac{-\sqrt{3} + 2}{4}$ **28.** 90°, 270°, 150°, 210°

29. $\dfrac{\cot x}{\cot x - 1} - \dfrac{\tan x}{\tan x + 1} = \dfrac{\cot x\tan x + \cot x - \tan x\cot x + \tan x}{\cot x\tan x - \tan x + \cot x - 1} = \dfrac{\cot x + \tan x}{\cot x - \tan x}$

30. No solution

EP75. For $k = 1$, we get $1\cdot 2 = \dfrac{1(1+1)(1+2)}{3}$; $2 = \dfrac{(2)(3)}{3}$. And also

$\dfrac{k(k+1)(k+2)}{3} + (k+1)(k+2) = \dfrac{k(k+1)(k+2) + 3(k+1)(k+2)}{3}$

$= \dfrac{(k+1)(k+2)(k+3)}{3} = \dfrac{(k+1)[(k+1)+1][(k+1)+2]}{3}$

EP76. $\begin{bmatrix} 4 & 1 \\ 2 & 2 \end{bmatrix}$

Problem set 103

1. Trip out = 60 mph; trip back = 20 mph **2.** $400 - hk$ **3.** 18.5 years **4.** $\frac{14}{55}$

5. $v = kr\frac{2.54(60)(60)}{100}\frac{\text{m}}{\text{hr}}$ **6.** $x^2 - 3x - 6$ **7.** $4x^3 - 12x^2 + 25x - 53 + \frac{108}{x+2}$ **8.** Yes

9. No **10.** Refer to Lesson 102

11. $\angle 1 = \angle 2$, $CD = CE$, $FC = FC \rightarrow \triangle DFC \cong \triangle EFC \rightarrow DF = FE$, $\angle FDC = \angle FEC$
$\rightarrow \angle ADF = \angle BEF$, $\angle AFD = \angle BFE \rightarrow \triangle AFD \cong \triangle BFE \rightarrow AF = BF$

12. Refer to Lesson 102

13. Draw $\overline{OC}$ and $\overline{OD}$. $\overset{\frown}{CB} = \overset{\frown}{BD} \rightarrow \angle COB = \angle DOB$, $OC = OD$, $OE = OE \rightarrow \triangle COE \cong \triangle DOE$
$\rightarrow CE = ED$, $\angle OEC = \angle OED = 90°$

14. $\frac{15!}{11!4!}(2x^2)^{11}(-y^3)^4 = 2{,}795{,}520x^{22}y^{12}$ **15.** $-13{,}608x^{15}y^6$ **16.** $\sqrt{2}$ **17.** 3.2

18. $0 < 2x - 1 < 16, \frac{1}{2} < x < \frac{17}{2}$ **19.** $2x + 1 > \frac{1}{9}, x > -\frac{4}{9}$ **20.** Refer to Lesson 99

21. $\frac{13}{990}$ **22.** (*a*) 120π cm^3 (*b*) $12\sqrt{34}\pi + 36\pi$ cm^2 **23.** 55.63π cm^3 **24.** 360°

25. $\frac{(x-3)^2}{9} + \frac{y^2}{36} = 1$; center = (3, 0); major axis: vertical, 12; minor axis = 6

26. $-2\sin 150° \sin 135° = -\frac{\sqrt{2}}{2}$ **27.** 30°, 150°, 270°

28. $$\frac{\tan x}{\tan x - 1} - \frac{\cot x}{\cot x + 1} = \frac{\cot x \tan x + \tan x - \cot x \tan x + \cot x}{\tan x \cot x - \cot x + \tan x - 1} = \frac{\tan x + \cot x}{\tan x - \cot x}$$

29. 0.683 **30.** 9 **EP77.** Invalid **EP78.** $\begin{bmatrix} 3 & -2 \\ 12 & 3 \end{bmatrix}$

Problem set 104

1. 150 **2.** 100 ml 10%, 200 ml 40% **3.** 300 miles **4.** 2, 4, 6 **5.** $B = 46$, $J = 36$

6.

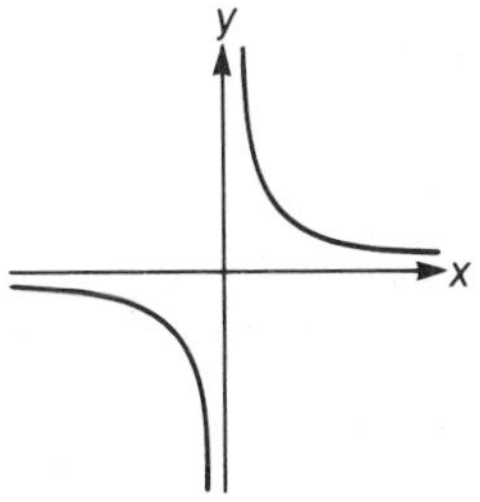

7. (*a*) Circle (*b*) Ellipse (*c*) Hyperbola (*d*) Parabola (*e*) Circle

8. $(x + 4)^2 + (y - 3)^2 = 40$, center = $(-4, 3)$, radius = $2\sqrt{10}$ **9.** $x^3 + x^2 - 2x - 4 - \frac{3}{x-1}$

10. $x^2 + 1 - \frac{1}{x-2}$ **11.** Yes **12.** No

13. $CD = CE$, $\angle 1 = \angle 2$, $FC = FC \rightarrow \triangle FDC \cong \triangle FEC \rightarrow DF = FE$; $\angle CDF = \angle CEF$
$\rightarrow \angle ADF = \angle BEF$, $\angle AFD = \angle BFE \rightarrow \triangle AFD \sim \triangle BFE$; $DF = FE \rightarrow SF = 1$
$\rightarrow \triangle AFD \cong \triangle BFE$; $AD = BE$, $CD = CE \rightarrow AC = AD + CD = BE + CE = BC$

14. Draw radii OC and OD. $\overset{\frown}{CB} = \overset{\frown}{BD} \rightarrow \angle COB = \angle BOD$; $OE = OE \rightarrow \triangle COE \cong \triangle DOE$
$\rightarrow CE = EC$, $\angle OEC = \angle OED = 90°$

15. P and Q are midpoints of $\overline{AD}$ and $\overline{AB} \to AP = \frac{1}{2}AD$, $AQ = \frac{1}{2}AB$, $\angle A = \angle A$ $\to \triangle APQ \sim \triangle ADB$ with $SF = 2$; $\angle APQ = \angle ADB$, $\overline{PQ} \parallel \overline{DB}$, $PQ = \frac{1}{2}DB$. Similarly, $SR = \frac{1}{2}DB$, $\overline{SR} \parallel \overline{DB}$. Thus, $\overline{PQ} \parallel \overline{SR}$, $PQ = SR \to PQRS$ is a parallelogram.

16. Refer to Lesson 102 **17.** $-1792x^{10}y^{12}$ **18.** 6.8×10^7 **19.** 3.4 **20.** $x > \frac{25}{8}$

21. 57 **22.** (*a*) $\frac{2048}{3}\pi \text{ cm}^3$ (*b*) $256\pi \text{ cm}^2$ **23.** $\frac{125}{8}:1$ **24.** $(1, -1, 1)$ **25.** $a = 3.1$

26. $\frac{1}{2}(\cos 330° + \cos 300°) = \frac{1 + \sqrt{3}}{4}$

27. $$\frac{\cot^2 x + \sec^2 x + 1}{\cot^2 x} = \frac{\csc^2 x + \sec^2 x}{\cot^2 x} = \frac{\frac{1}{\sin^2 x} + \frac{1}{\cos^2 x}}{\cot^2 x} = \frac{\frac{\cos^2 x + \sin^2 x}{\sin^2 x \cos^2 x}}{\cot^2 x}$$
$$= \frac{1}{\sin^2 x \cos^2 x} \cdot \frac{\sin^2 x}{\cos^2 x} = \frac{1}{\cos^4 x} = \sec^4 x$$

28. 100°, 220°, 340°, 40°, 160°, 280° **29.** 16 **30.** $\frac{\log 5}{\log 6}$

EP79. For $k = 1$, we get $a = \frac{(1 - r^1)a}{1 - r}$. And also $\frac{a(1 - r^k)}{1 - r} + ar^k = \frac{a(1 - r^k) + ar^k(1 - r)}{1 - r}$
$$= \frac{a - ar^k + ar^k - ar^{k+1}}{1 - r} = \frac{a(1 - r^{k+1})}{1 - r}$$

EP80. $\begin{bmatrix} 4 & -2x + 12 \\ 2 & 4x - 4 \end{bmatrix}$

Problem set 105

1. 31.9 hr **2.** $1{:}05\frac{5}{11}$ p.m. **3.** 20 liters **4.** $D_T = 120$ mi, $D_W = 32$ mi

5. $W = 21$, $S = 30$ **6.** Refer to Lesson 105

7. $\angle ABC = \frac{1}{2}\overset{\frown}{AC}$, $\angle ADC = \frac{1}{2}\overset{\frown}{AC} \to \angle ABC = \angle ADC$, $\angle BEA = \angle DEC \to \triangle BAE \sim \triangle DCE$

8. $\angle 1 = \angle 2$, $CD = CE$, $FC = FC \to \triangle FDC \cong \triangle FEC \to DF = FE$, $\angle CDF = \angle CEF$ $\to \angle ADF = \angle BEF$, $\angle AFD = \angle BFE \to \triangle AFD \sim \triangle BFE$; $DF = FE \to SF = 1$ $\to \triangle AFD \cong \triangle BFE \to AF = FB$

9. $x = 160°$, $y = 60°$, $z = 140°$ **10.** Refer to Lesson 102

11. (*a*) Circle (*b*) Parabola (*c*) Hyperbola (*d*) Hyperbola (*e*) Ellipse

12.

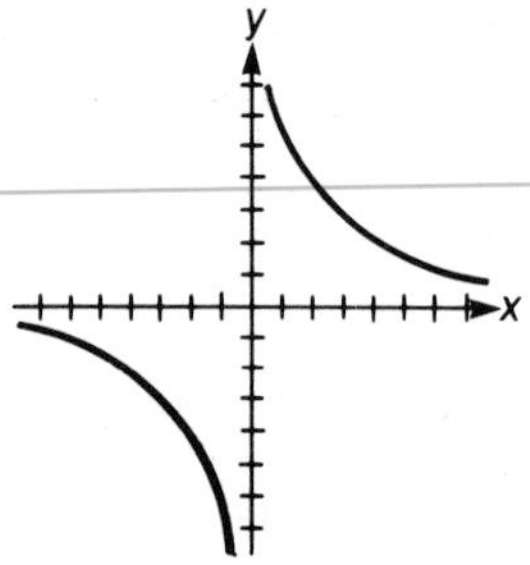

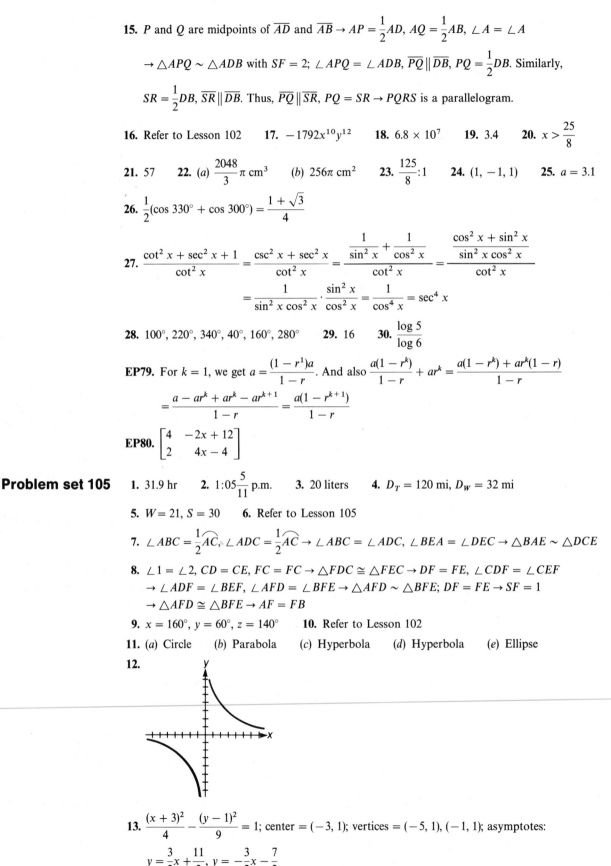

13. $\frac{(x + 3)^2}{4} - \frac{(y - 1)^2}{9} = 1$; center $= (-3, 1)$; vertices $= (-5, 1), (-1, 1)$; asymptotes:
$y = \frac{3}{2}x + \frac{11}{2}$, $y = -\frac{3}{2}x - \frac{7}{2}$

14. $x^4 - 4x^3 - 8x^2 - 19x - 40 - \dfrac{79}{x-2}$ **15.** Yes **16.** No **17.** $2016x^{10}y^{12}$

18. 7.1×10^{18} **19.** 6.3×10^{-10} **20.** 25 **21.** $0 < 2x - 1 < 2; \dfrac{1}{2} < x < \dfrac{3}{2}$ **22.** $\dfrac{64}{3}$ cm^3

23. (*a*) $\dfrac{800}{3}\pi$ cm^3 (*b*) $(20\sqrt{41}\,\pi + 100\pi)$ cm^2 **24.** $(-2, 1, 3)$ **25.** Refer to Lesson 77

26. (*a*) Refer to Lesson 84 (*b*) $\dfrac{1}{2}(\cos 300° - \cos 330°) = \dfrac{1-\sqrt{3}}{4}$

27. $\dfrac{\cos^2 x}{1 - \sin x} = \dfrac{1 - \sin^2 x}{1 - \sin x} = \dfrac{(1 - \sin x)(1 + \sin x)}{1 - \sin x} = 1 + \sin x = 1 + \dfrac{1}{\csc x} = \dfrac{\csc x + 1}{\csc x}$

28. 0°, 180°, 30°, 150° **29.** 45°, 135°, 225°, 315° **30.** 8 **EP81.** $\begin{bmatrix} 10 & -10 \\ 15 & -15 \end{bmatrix}$

EP82. For $k = 1$, we get $1^2 = \dfrac{1(2-1)(2+1)}{3}$; $1 = \dfrac{1(3)}{3}$. And also $\dfrac{k(2k-1)(2k+1)}{3} + (2k+1)^2$

$$= \frac{k(2k-1)(2k+1) + 3(2k+1)^2}{3} = \frac{(2k+1)[k(2k-1) + 3(2k+1)]}{3}$$

$$= \frac{(2k+1)(2k^2 + 5k + 3)}{3} = \frac{(2k+1)[(2k+3)(k+1)]}{3}$$

$$= \frac{(k+1)[2(k+1) - 1][2(k+1) + 1]}{3}$$

Problem set 106

1. $\omega = \dfrac{v}{r} = \dfrac{60(12)(2.54)(60)}{35} \dfrac{\text{rad}}{\text{min}}$ **2.** $R = 10$, $W = 2$, $P = 7$ **3.** $\dfrac{4}{13}$ **4.** $\dfrac{m}{\dfrac{m}{k} - p} = \dfrac{mk}{m - pk}$

5. $D = 140$, $S = 60$ **6.** $f(-2) = -50$ **7.** -14 **8.** Refer to Lesson 105

9. $ABCD$ is a parallelogram $\rightarrow \overline{AB} \parallel \overline{DC}$, $AB = DC \rightarrow \angle ABE = \angle EDC$, $\angle BAE = \angle ECD$ $\rightarrow \triangle AEB \sim \triangle CED$; $AB = DC \rightarrow SF = 1 \rightarrow \triangle AEB \cong \triangle CED \rightarrow AE = CE$, $BE = ED$

10. $\angle ABC = \dfrac{1}{2}\overset{\frown}{AC}$, $\angle ADC = \dfrac{1}{2}\overset{\frown}{AC} \rightarrow \angle ABC = \angle ADC$, $\angle AEB = \angle DEC \rightarrow \triangle BAE \sim \triangle DCE$

11. Refer to Lesson 98 **12.** $x = 140°$, $y = 80°$, $z = 140°$

13. (*a*) Ellipse (*b*) Hyperbola (*c*) Hyperbola (*d*) Parabola (*e*) Circle

14. Refer to Lesson 77 **15.** $(x+1)^2 + (y-4)^2 = 4$, center $= (-1, 4)$, radius $= 2$

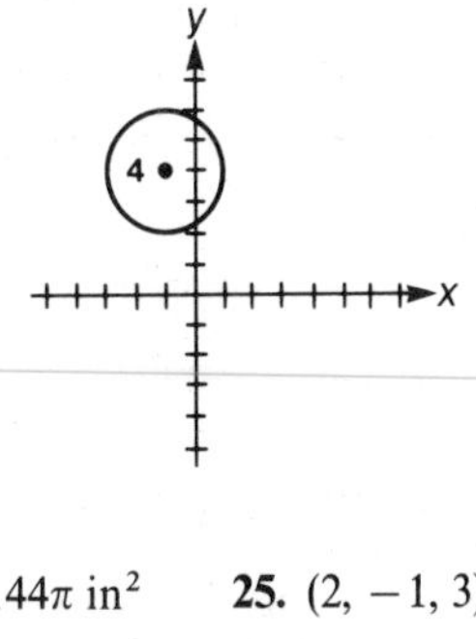

16. No

17. $x^5 - 4x^4 - 4x^3 - 2 - \dfrac{1}{x-1}$

18. $210x^{16}y^{18}$ **19.** 3.2 **20.** $\dfrac{3}{4}$

21. $\dfrac{1}{2}n[2a + (n-1)d]$ **22.** $x > \dfrac{7}{9}$

23. $18\sqrt{3}$ m^3 **24.** (*a*) 288π in^3 (*b*) 144π in^2 **25.** $(2, -1, 3)$ **26.** $\dfrac{\sqrt{6}-\sqrt{2}}{4}$

27. $\dfrac{\cot x}{\cot x - 1} - \dfrac{\tan x}{\tan x + 1} = \dfrac{\cot x \tan x + \cot x - \cot x \tan x + \tan x}{\cot x \tan x - \tan x + \cot x - 1} = \dfrac{\cot x + \tan x}{\cot x - \tan x}$

28. 15°, 135°, 255°, 45°, 165°, 285° **29.** 81 **30.** 1, 16 **EP83.** Invalid

EP84. $\begin{bmatrix} 22 & -2 \\ -18 & 6 \end{bmatrix}$

Problem set 107

1. See Lesson 75 **2.** 461 **3.** 987.7 min **4.** $\dfrac{980}{k(m+4)}$ hr **5.** $\dfrac{15h+10p}{h}$ jobs

6. Yes **7.** No **8.** $y = \frac{1}{3}x + \frac{4}{3}$ **9.** $y = 3x + 12$

10. $\begin{array}{r|rrrr} -2 & 2 & -9 & 3 & -4 \\ & & -4 & 26 & -58 \\ \hline & 2 & -13 & 29 & -62 \end{array}$ $f(-2) = -62$

11. $\begin{array}{r|rrrrr} -1 & 1 & 4 & -6 & 0 & -1 \\ & & -1 & -3 & 9 & -9 \\ \hline & 1 & 3 & -9 & 9 & -10 \end{array}$ $f(-1) = -10$

12. Draw $\overline{AO}$. $AO = OB \rightarrow \angle OBA = \angle OAB$; $\angle AOC = \angle OBA + \angle OAB = 2\angle OBA \rightarrow \frac{1}{2}\angle AOC = \angle OBA \rightarrow \frac{1}{2}\angle AOC = \angle ABC$, $\angle AOC = \overset{\frown}{AC} \rightarrow \angle ABC = \frac{1}{2}\overset{\frown}{AC}$

13. Refer to Lesson 90 **14.** Refer to Lesson 102

15. $\angle NDC = \angle NCD \rightarrow \triangle NDC$ is an isosceles $\triangle \rightarrow ND = NC$, $AD = BC$, $AN = NB \rightarrow \triangle ADN \cong \triangle BCN \rightarrow \angle DAN = \angle CBN$, $AD = BC$, $AB = AB \rightarrow \triangle ADB \cong \triangle BCA \rightarrow DB = AC$

16. $x = 100$, $y = 120$, $z = 140$

17. (*a*) Ellipse (*b*) Hyperbola (*c*) Parabola (*d*) Circle (*e*) Ellipse

18. $\dfrac{(x-2)^2}{81} - \dfrac{(y-2)^2}{36} = 1$; vertices at (11, 2), (−7, 2); center = (2, 2); asymptotes: $y = \frac{2}{3}x + \frac{2}{3}$, $y = -\frac{2}{3}x + \frac{10}{3}$

19. $2\sqrt{2}$ **20.** No **21.** $\begin{array}{r|rrrrrr} 2 & 1 & 0 & -4 & 2 & -3 & 1 \\ & & 2 & 4 & 0 & 4 & 2 \\ \hline & 1 & 2 & 0 & 2 & 1 & 3 \end{array} \rightarrow x^4 + 2x^3 + 2x + 1 + \dfrac{3}{x-2}$

22. $\frac{n}{2}[2a + (n-1)d]$ **23.** $-5376x^{12}y^9$ **24.** 5.1 **25.** $2:3\sqrt{x}:2\sqrt{15y}$ **26.** −3

27. $\dfrac{\sqrt{2}+\sqrt{6}}{4}$ **28.** $(\sin x - \cos x)^2 = \sin^2 x + \cos^2 x - 2\sin x\cos x = 1 - \sin 2x$

29. 22.5°, 202.5°, 157.5°, 337.5° **30.** 1, $\sqrt[3]{2}$

EP85. For $k = 1$, we get $\frac{1}{2^1} = 1 - \frac{1}{2^1}$. And also $1 - \frac{1}{2^k} + \frac{1}{2^{k+1}} = 1 - \frac{2}{2}\frac{1}{2^k} + \frac{1}{2^{k+1}}$
$= 1 - \frac{2}{2^{k+1}} + \frac{1}{2^{k+1}} = 1 - \frac{1}{2^{k+1}}$

EP86. $\begin{bmatrix} 0 & 0 \\ 0 & 0 \end{bmatrix}$

Problem set 108

1. 1111.2 **2.** $21\frac{9}{11}$ **3.** $\dfrac{7c(5+w)}{2(m+4)}$ hr **4.** $\frac{1}{4}$ **5.** 55 **6.** No

7.

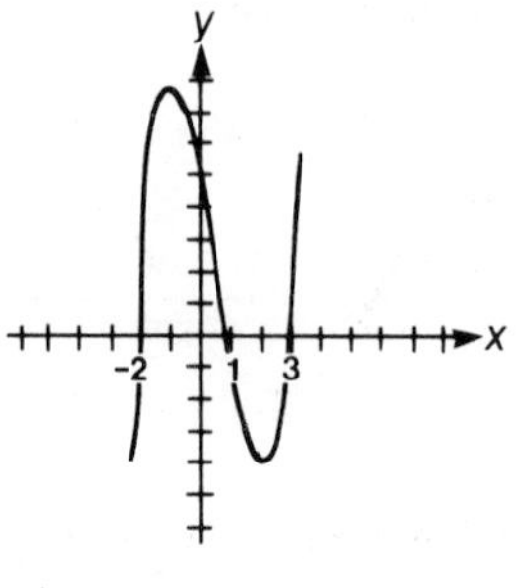

8.

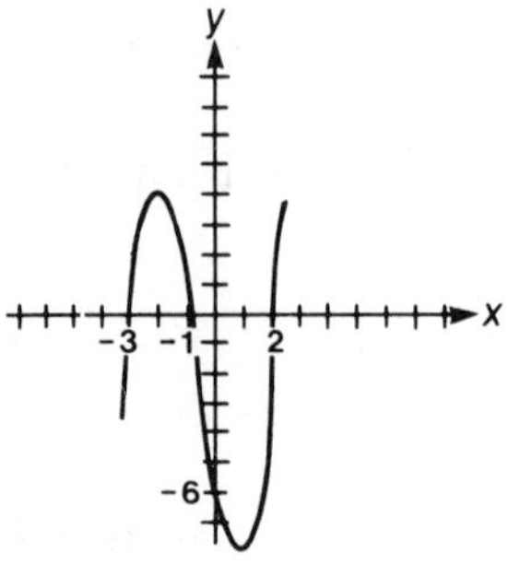

9. 2 **10.** $y = \frac{1}{4}x + \frac{1}{2}$ **11.** $x^3 + 2x + 3 + \frac{13}{x - 3}$ **12.** Refer to Lesson 105

13. $AP = AQ$, $PB = QC \rightarrow AB = AP + PB = AQ + QC = AC$, $\angle A = \angle A \rightarrow \triangle ABQ \cong \triangle ACP \rightarrow BQ = PC$

14. Refer to Lesson 90

15. $\angle NDC = \angle NCD \rightarrow \triangle DNC$ is isosceles $\rightarrow DN = CN$, $AD = CB$, $AN = NB$ $\rightarrow \triangle ADN \cong \triangle BCN \rightarrow \angle DAB = \angle CBA$, $\angle ADN = \angle NCB$, $\angle NDC = \angle NCD$, $\rightarrow \angle ADN + \angle NDC = \angle NCB + \angle NCD \rightarrow \angle ADC = \angle BCD$

16. $x = 80$, $y = 120$, $z = 160$

17. (*a*) Ellipse (*b*) Hyperbola (*c*) Circle (*d*) Parabola (*e*) Circle

18.

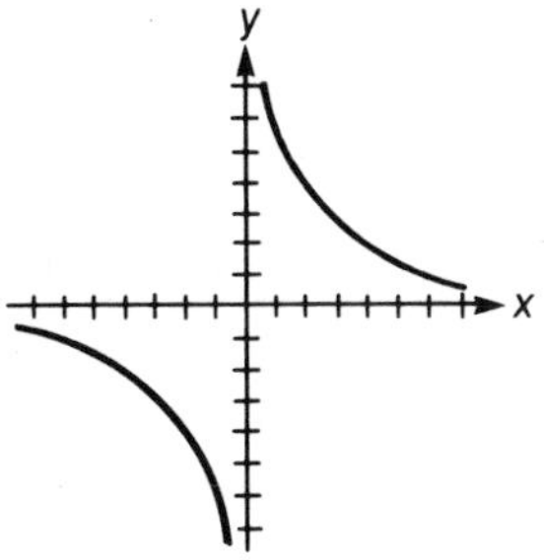

19. $(x - 5)^2 + (y + 4)^2 = 36$, center $= (5, -4)$, radius $= 6$

20. $-25{,}344x^{21}y^{15}$ **21.** $\frac{n}{2}[2a + (n - 1)d]$

22. 6.3×10^{-10} mole/liter **23.** $-\frac{1}{5}$

24. (*a*) 120π cm^3 (*b*) $(12\sqrt{34}\pi + 36\pi)$ cm^2

25. (*a*) $\frac{4}{3}\pi r^3$ in^3 (*b*) $4\pi r^2$ in^2

26. $(-4, 2, 1)$ **27.** $2 + \sqrt{3}$ **28.** 75°, 195°, 315°, 105°, 225°, 345°

29. $\frac{\cos^2 x}{1 - \sin x} = \frac{1 - \sin^2 x}{1 - \sin x} = \frac{(1 - \sin x)(1 + \sin x)}{1 - \sin x} = 1 + \sin x = \frac{1}{\csc x} + 1 = \frac{1 + \csc x}{\csc x}$

30. 1 **EP87.** Valid **EP88.** $\begin{bmatrix} 11 & -3 \\ 4 & -1 \end{bmatrix}$

Problem set 109

1. $\frac{s}{s + L}$ **2.** $\frac{100L}{s + L}$ **3.** 3200 **4.** $V = \frac{kp^2}{\sqrt{w}}, \frac{k(9p)^2}{\sqrt{4w}} = \frac{81kp^2}{2\sqrt{w}}$; V is multiplied by $\frac{81}{2}$

5. $\frac{3000}{c + p}$ **6.** Refer to Lesson 109

7. $AP = AQ$, $PB = QC \rightarrow AB = AP + PB = AQ + QC = AC$, $\angle A = \angle A \rightarrow \triangle ABQ \cong \triangle ACP \rightarrow \angle ABQ = \angle ACP$; $AB = AC \rightarrow \triangle ABC$ is an isosceles $\triangle \rightarrow \angle ABC = \angle ACB \rightarrow \angle ABC - \angle ABQ = \angle ACB - \angle ACP \rightarrow \angle QBC = \angle PCB$

8. Refer to Lesson 105

9. $\angle BAD = \frac{1}{2}\overset{\frown}{BD}$, $\angle BCD = \frac{1}{2}\overset{\frown}{BD} \rightarrow \angle BAD = \angle BCD$; $\angle AEB = \angle CED \rightarrow \triangle AEB \sim \triangle CED$ $\rightarrow \frac{BE}{AE} = \frac{ED}{EC}$

10. $\frac{a}{c} = \frac{m}{a}, \frac{b}{c} = \frac{n}{b} \rightarrow a^2 = mc$, $b^2 = nc \rightarrow a^2 + b^2 = c(m + n) = c^2$

11. $x = 60°$, $y = 160°$, $z = 140°$ **12.**

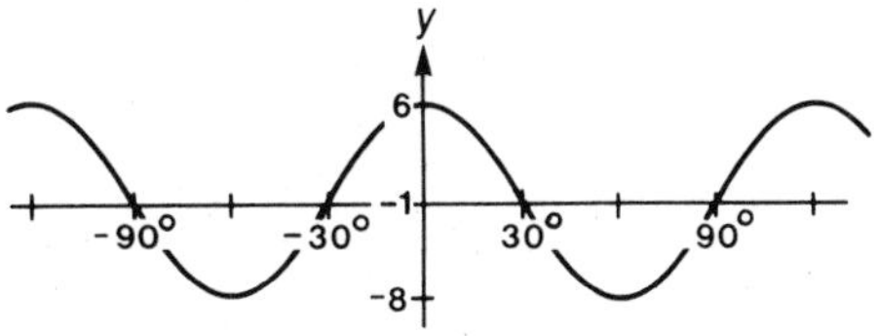

13. (*a*) Ellipse (*b*) Hyperbola (*c*) Parabola (*d*) Circle (*e*) Ellipse **14.** Yes

15. $\frac{(x-3)^2}{16} - \frac{(y+2)^2}{36} = 1$, center $= (3, -2)$; vertices $= (7, -2), (-1, -2)$, asymptotes:
$y = \frac{3}{2}x - \frac{13}{2}$, $y = -\frac{3}{2}x + \frac{5}{2}$

16.

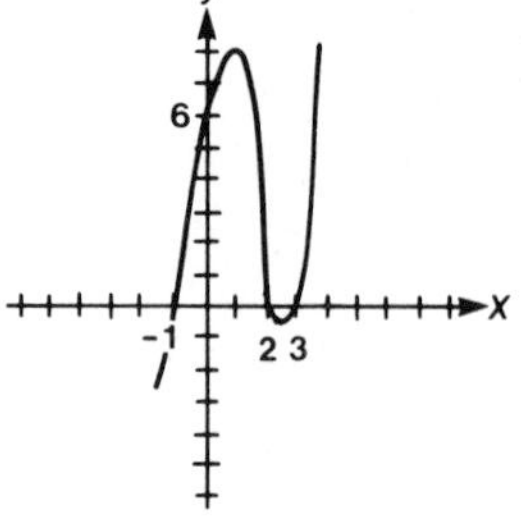

17.

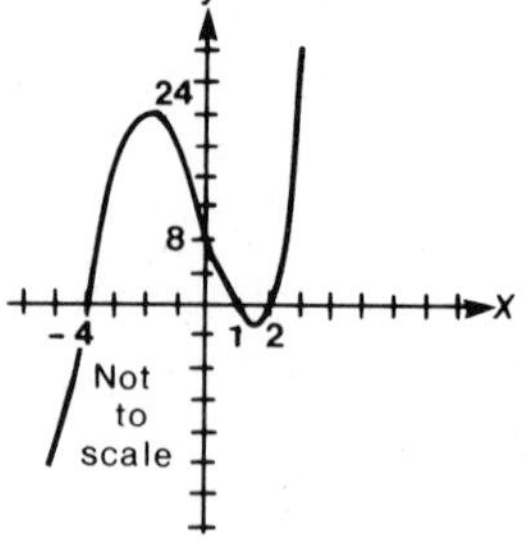

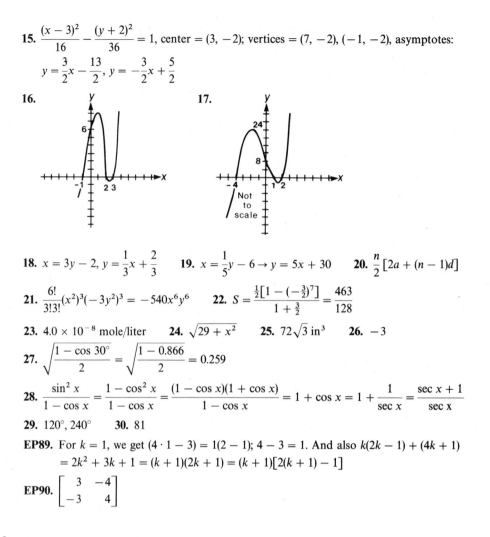

18. $x = 3y - 2$, $y = \frac{1}{3}x + \frac{2}{3}$ **19.** $x = \frac{1}{5}y - 6 \rightarrow y = 5x + 30$ **20.** $\frac{n}{2}[2a + (n-1)d]$

21. $\frac{6!}{3!3!}(x^2)^3(-3y^2)^3 = -540x^6y^6$ **22.** $S = \frac{\frac{1}{2}[1 - (-\frac{3}{2})^7]}{1 + \frac{3}{2}} = \frac{463}{128}$

23. 4.0×10^{-8} mole/liter **24.** $\sqrt{29 + x^2}$ **25.** $72\sqrt{3}$ in^3 **26.** -3

27. $\sqrt{\frac{1 - \cos 30°}{2}} = \sqrt{\frac{1 - 0.866}{2}} = 0.259$

28. $\frac{\sin^2 x}{1 - \cos x} = \frac{1 - \cos^2 x}{1 - \cos x} = \frac{(1 - \cos x)(1 + \cos x)}{1 - \cos x} = 1 + \cos x = 1 + \frac{1}{\sec x} = \frac{\sec x + 1}{\sec x}$

29. 120°, 240° **30.** 81

EP89. For $k = 1$, we get $(4 \cdot 1 - 3) = 1(2 - 1)$; $4 - 3 = 1$. And also $k(2k - 1) + (4k + 1)$
$= 2k^2 + 3k + 1 = (k + 1)(2k + 1) = (k + 1)[2(k + 1) - 1]$

EP90. $\begin{bmatrix} 3 & -4 \\ -3 & 4 \end{bmatrix}$

Problem set 110

1. 125 **2.** 0.3 **3.** 185.8 hr **4.** 60 ft

5. $\pi r^2 h = \pi(r + 2)^2\left(\frac{1}{4}h\right) \rightarrow 4r^2 = r^2 + 4r + 4 \rightarrow (3r + 2)(r - 2) = 0 \rightarrow r = 2$

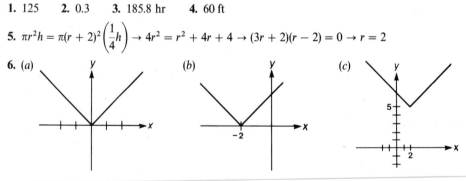

6. (*a*)

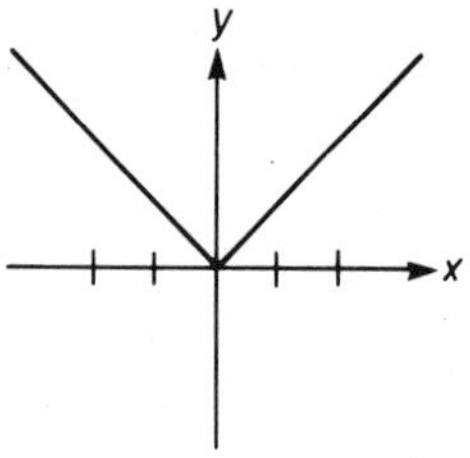

(*b*)

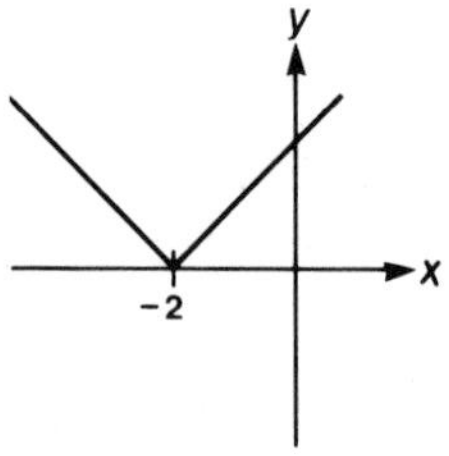

(*c*)

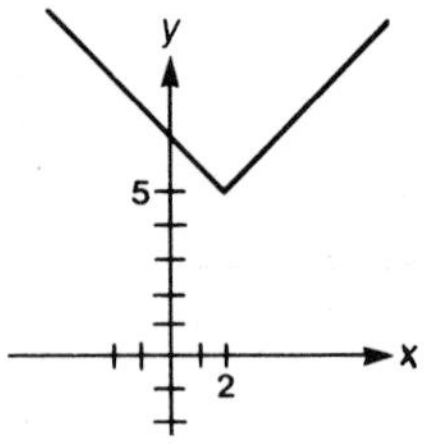

7. $x \le -2$, $y = -1$; $-2 \le x < 0$, $y = \frac{1}{2}x$; $x \ge 0$, $y = 1$ **8.**

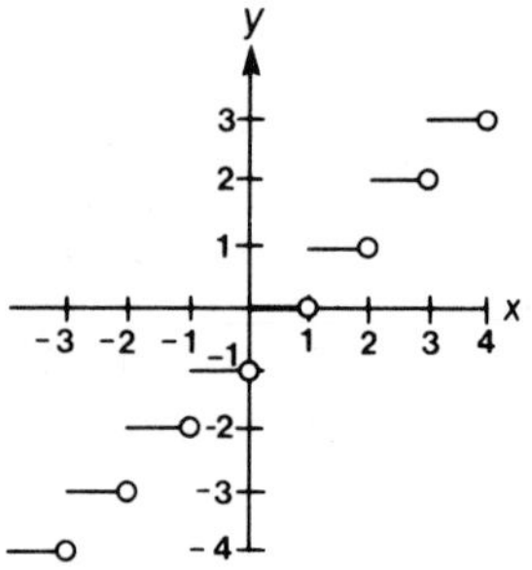

9. $AP = AQ$, $PB = QC \rightarrow AB = AP + PB = AQ + QC = AC$; $\angle A = \angle A \rightarrow \triangle ABQ \cong \triangle ACP \rightarrow BQ = CP$, $\angle ABQ = \angle ACP$. $AB = AC \rightarrow \triangle ABC$ is an isosceles $\triangle \rightarrow \angle ABC = \angle ACB \rightarrow \angle ABC - \angle ABQ = \angle ACB - \angle ACP \rightarrow \angle QBC = \angle PCB$; $BQ = PC$, $\angle QBC = \angle PCB$, $BR = RC \rightarrow \triangle BQR \cong \triangle CPR \rightarrow \angle BQR = \angle CPR$

10. Refer to Lesson 109

11. $\angle BAD = \frac{1}{2}\overset{\frown}{BD}$, $\angle BCD = \frac{1}{2}\overset{\frown}{BD} \rightarrow \angle BAD = \angle BCD$, $\angle BEA = \angle CED$

$\rightarrow \triangle AEB \sim \triangle CED, \frac{BE}{ED} = \frac{AE}{EC} \rightarrow (BE)(EC) = (AE)(ED)$

12. Refer to Lesson 105 **13.** $x = 160°$, $y = 60°$, $z = 140°$ **14.** No

15. (*a*) Ellipse (*b*) Circle (*c*) Hyperbola (*d*) Parabola (*e*) Ellipse

16. $560a^6b^{20}$

17. $x = -5(y + 3)^2 + 34$, parabola, vertex $= (34, -3)$, axis of symmetry: $y = -3$; opens to left

18.

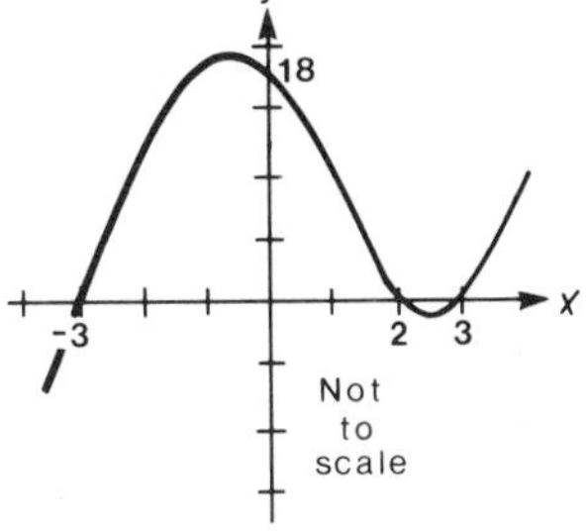

19.

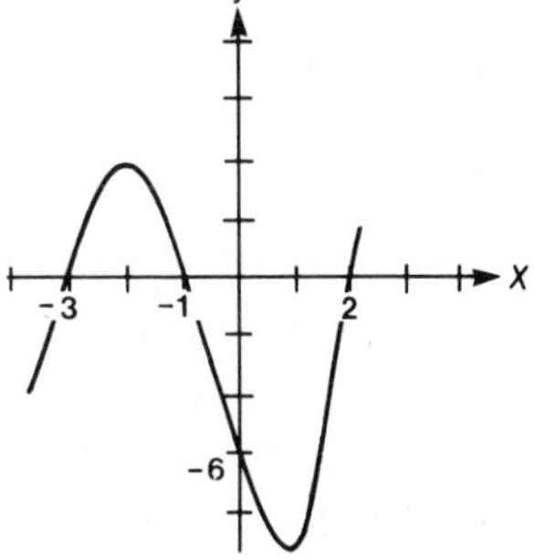

20. $y = \frac{1}{4}x + \frac{1}{2}$ **21.** $y = 3x - 9$ **22.** $\frac{n}{2}[2a + (n - 1)d]$ **23.** 191 ft

24. 1×10^{-3} mole/liter **25.** (*a*) $\frac{640}{3}\pi$ cm³ (*b*) $(16\pi\sqrt{41} + 64\pi)$ cm²

26. $(-1, 2, -2)$ **27.** $\frac{\sqrt{2 + \sqrt{3}}}{2}$ **28.** 30°, 150°

29. $\frac{\sec^3 x - 8}{\sec^2 x + \sec x - 6} = \frac{(\sec x - 2)(\sec^2 x + 2\sec x + 4)}{(\sec x + 3)(\sec x - 2)} = \frac{\sec^2 x + 2\sec x + 4}{\sec x + 3}$

30. Refer to Lesson 28 **EP91.** Invalid **EP92.** $\begin{bmatrix} 3 & -6 \\ -1 & 2 \end{bmatrix}$

Problem set 111

1. Volume is multiplied by $\frac{3\sqrt{2}}{2}$ **2.** $R \cdot \frac{h}{2} = m + 30$, $R = \frac{2(m + 30)}{h}$ mph

3. 29.4 hr **4.** $[20(37) - 19A]$ ft **5.** $\frac{65m}{4k}$ hr **6.** Refer to Lesson 111

7. Draw $\overline{CB}$. $\angle \overset{\frown}{DCB} = \frac{1}{2}\overset{\frown}{DB}$, $\angle ABC = \frac{1}{2}\overset{\frown}{AC}$. $\angle AEC = \angle DCB + \angle \overset{\frown}{ABC}$

$= \frac{1}{2}(\overset{\frown}{DB} + \overset{\frown}{AC})$

8. Refer to Lesson 111

9. Draw $\overline{AB}$. $\angle ABD = \frac{1}{2}\overset{\frown}{ACB}$, $\angle BAP = \frac{1}{2}\overset{\frown}{AB}$, $\angle ABD = \angle BAP + \angle APB \rightarrow \frac{1}{2}\overset{\frown}{ACB}$

$= \frac{1}{2}\overset{\frown}{AB} + \angle APB \rightarrow \angle APB = \frac{1}{2}(\overset{\frown}{ACB} - \overset{\frown}{AB})$

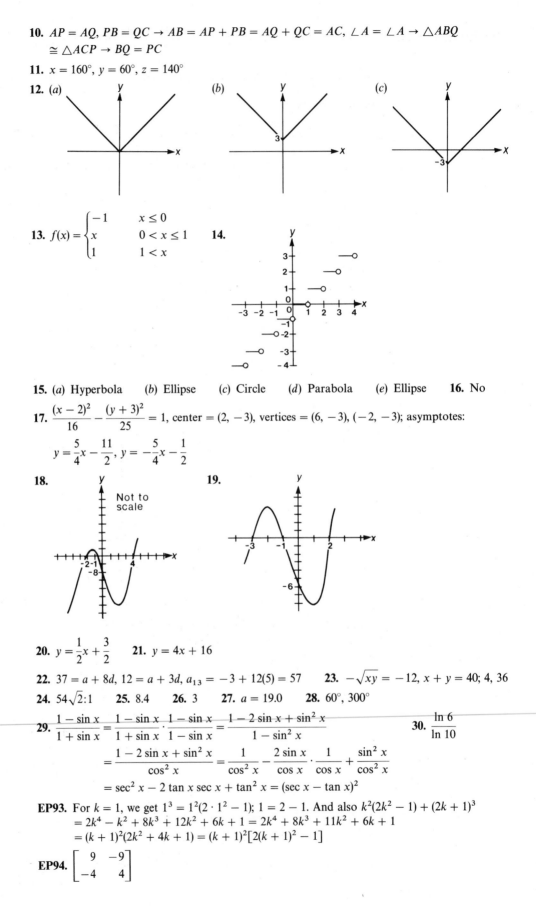

10. $AP = AQ$, $PB = QC \to AB = AP + PB = AQ + QC = AC$, $\angle A = \angle A \to \triangle ABQ \cong \triangle ACP \to BQ = PC$

11. $x = 160°$, $y = 60°$, $z = 140°$

12. (*a*)

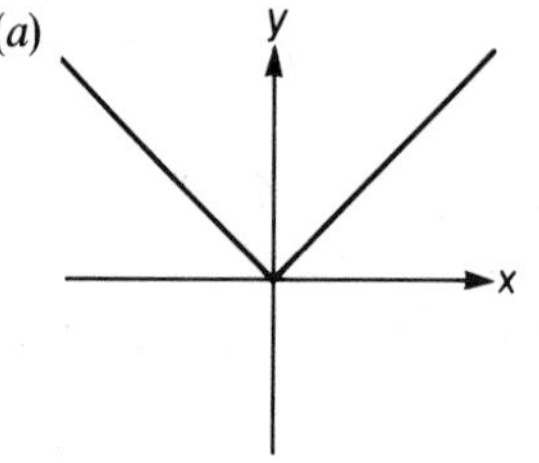

(*b*)

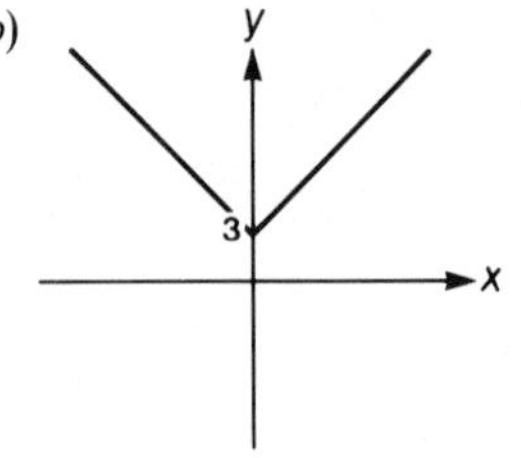

(*c*)

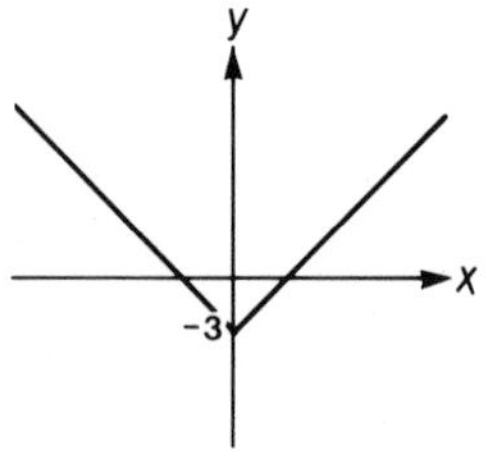

13. $f(x) = \begin{cases} -1 & x \le 0 \\ x & 0 < x \le 1 \\ 1 & 1 < x \end{cases}$

14.

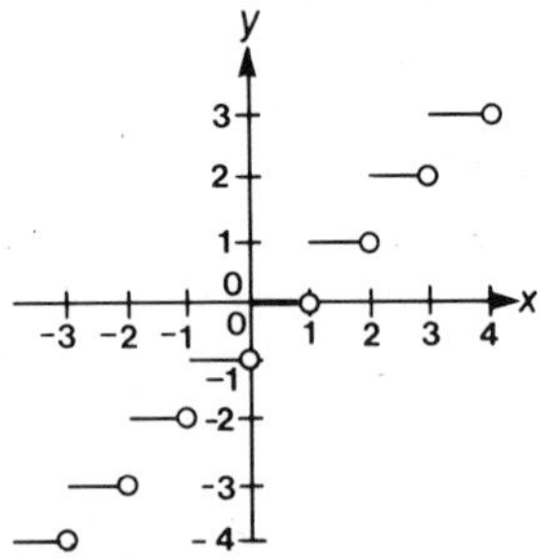

15. (*a*) Hyperbola (*b*) Ellipse (*c*) Circle (*d*) Parabola (*e*) Ellipse **16.** No

17. $\dfrac{(x-2)^2}{16} - \dfrac{(y+3)^2}{25} = 1$, center $= (2, -3)$, vertices $= (6, -3), (-2, -3)$; asymptotes: $y = \dfrac{5}{4}x - \dfrac{11}{2}$, $y = -\dfrac{5}{4}x - \dfrac{1}{2}$

18.

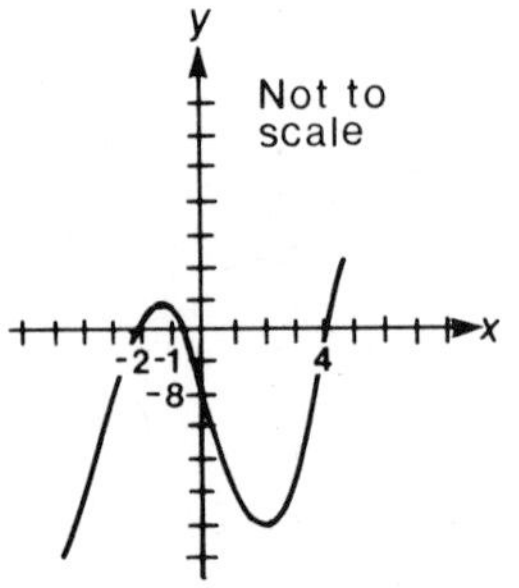

19.

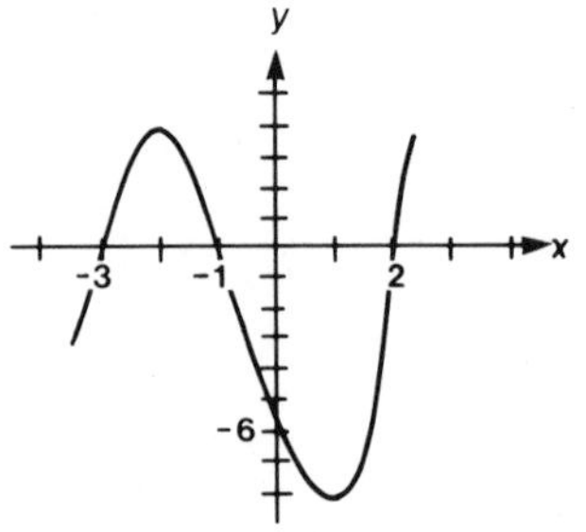

20. $y = \dfrac{1}{2}x + \dfrac{3}{2}$ **21.** $y = 4x + 16$

22. $37 = a + 8d$, $12 = a + 3d$, $a_{13} = -3 + 12(5) = 57$ **23.** $-\sqrt{xy} = -12$, $x + y = 40$; 4, 36

24. $54\sqrt{2}:1$ **25.** 8.4 **26.** 3 **27.** $a = 19.0$ **28.** 60°, 300°

29. $\dfrac{1 - \sin x}{1 + \sin x} = \dfrac{1 - \sin x}{1 + \sin x} \cdot \dfrac{1 - \sin x}{1 - \sin x} = \dfrac{1 - 2\sin x + \sin^2 x}{1 - \sin^2 x}$

$= \dfrac{1 - 2\sin x + \sin^2 x}{\cos^2 x} = \dfrac{1}{\cos^2 x} - \dfrac{2\sin x}{\cos x} \cdot \dfrac{1}{\cos x} + \dfrac{\sin^2 x}{\cos^2 x}$

$= \sec^2 x - 2\tan x \sec x + \tan^2 x = (\sec x - \tan x)^2$

30. $\dfrac{\ln 6}{\ln 10}$

EP93. For $k = 1$, we get $1^3 = 1^2(2 \cdot 1^2 - 1)$; $1 = 2 - 1$. And also $k^2(2k^2 - 1) + (2k + 1)^3$
$= 2k^4 - k^2 + 8k^3 + 12k^2 + 6k + 1 = 2k^4 + 8k^3 + 11k^2 + 6k + 1$
$= (k + 1)^2(2k^2 + 4k + 1) = (k + 1)^2[2(k + 1)^2 - 1]$

EP94. $\begin{bmatrix} 9 & -9 \\ -4 & 4 \end{bmatrix}$

Problem set 112

1. 0.85 **2.** $\frac{2}{9}$ **3.** $\frac{20m}{k}$ hr **4.** $\frac{30(60h + m)}{m + k}$ min **5.** $\omega = \frac{v}{r} = \frac{m(5280)(12)(2.54)}{c(60)(60)} \frac{\text{rad}}{\text{sec}}$

6. Yes **7.** Yes **8.** Refer to Lesson 112 **9.** $\pm 1, \pm 3, \pm\frac{1}{2}, \pm\frac{1}{4}, \pm\frac{3}{2}, \pm\frac{3}{4}$

10. Refer to Lesson 111

11. Draw $\overline{AC}$ and $\overline{AB}$. $\angle DAB = \frac{1}{2}\overset{\frown}{AB}$, $\angle ABC = \frac{1}{2}\overset{\frown}{AC}$, $\angle DAB = \angle ABP + \angle APB$

$\rightarrow \frac{1}{2}\overset{\frown}{AB} = \frac{1}{2}\overset{\frown}{AC} + \angle APB \rightarrow \angle APB = \frac{1}{2}(\overset{\frown}{AB} - \overset{\frown}{AC})$ **12.** Refer to Lesson 111

13. Draw $\overline{AB}$. $\angle ABD = \frac{1}{2}\overset{\frown}{ACB}$, $\angle BAP = \frac{1}{2}\overset{\frown}{AB}$, $\angle ABD = \angle BAP + \angle APB$, $\frac{1}{2}\overset{\frown}{ACB}$

$= \frac{1}{2}\overset{\frown}{AB} + \angle APB \rightarrow \angle APB = \frac{1}{2}(\overset{\frown}{ACB} - \overset{\frown}{AB})$

14. Refer to Lesson 76 **15.** $x = 100°$, $y = 120°$, $z = 140°$

16. (*a*)

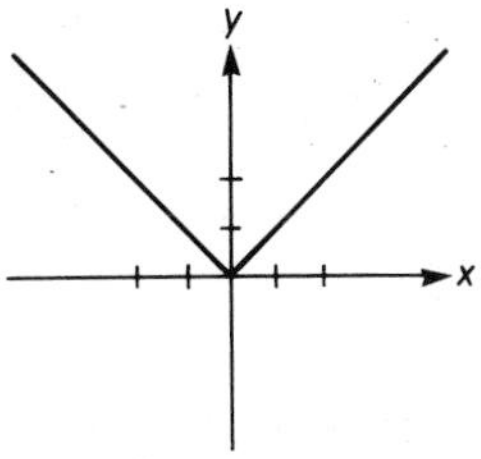

(*b*)

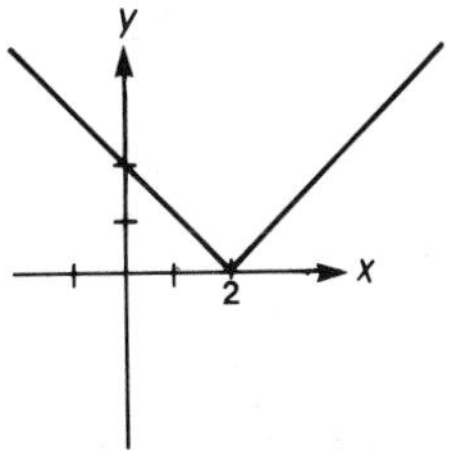

(*c*)

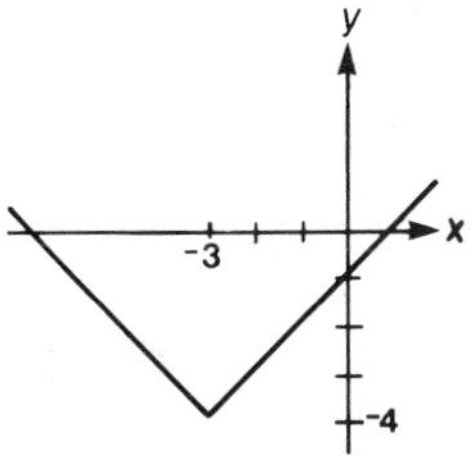

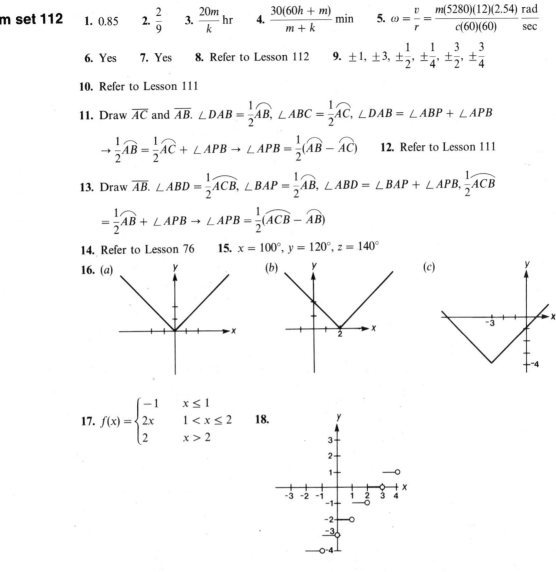

17. $f(x) = \begin{cases} -1 & x \le 1 \\ 2x & 1 < x \le 2 \\ 2 & x > 2 \end{cases}$ **18.**

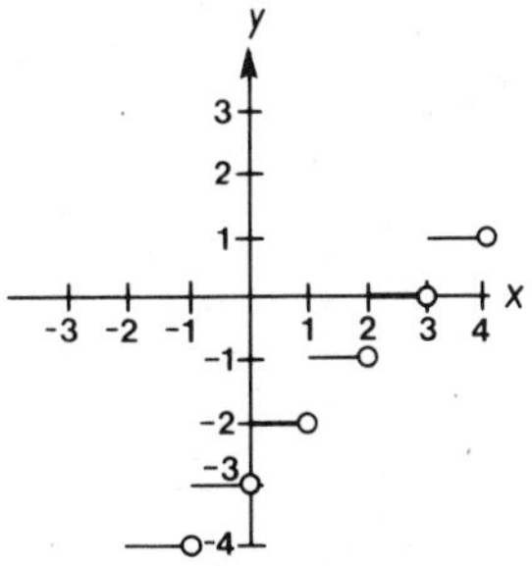

19. (*a*) Circle (*b*) Ellipse (*c*) Ellipse (*d*) Hyperbola (*e*) Parabola **20.** Yes

21. $(x - 5)^2 + (y + 4)^2 = 36$; center $= (5, -4)$, radius $= 6$

22. $\left(x + \frac{1}{2} + \frac{\sqrt{7}}{2}i\right)\left(x + \frac{1}{2} - \frac{\sqrt{7}}{2}i\right)$ **23.**

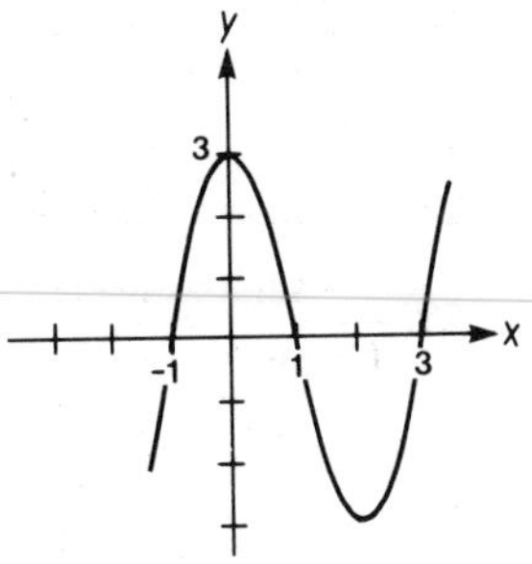

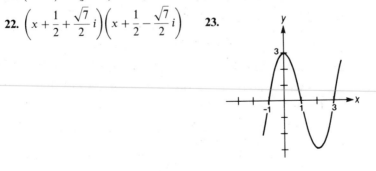

24. 3, 75 **25.** 91.8 cm^3 **26.** 7.3 **27.** $(1, -1, 1)$

28. $(1 + \tan x)^2 = 1 + 2\tan x + \tan^2 x = \sec^2 x + 2\tan x$

29. $(3\tan x + \sqrt{3})(\tan x - \sqrt{3}) = 0 \rightarrow x = 150°, 330°, 60°, 240°$ **30.** $\frac{1}{8}$

EP95. For $k = 1$, we get $4 = 2 \cdot 1(1 + 1)$; $4 = 2(2)$. And also $2k(k + 1) + 4(k + 1)$
$= 2(k + 1)(k + 2) = 2(k + 1)[(k + 1) + 1]$

EP96. $\begin{bmatrix} -\frac{5}{3} & \frac{11}{3} \\ 1 & \frac{8}{3} \end{bmatrix}$

Problem set 113

1. $\dfrac{6(12m - 2)}{mp + 6}$ min **2.** $C_3^7 = 35$ **3.** $\dfrac{hm + h(m + 5)}{m}$ hr **4.** \$28 **5.** $\dfrac{4(x + y)}{7 - 3(x + y)}$

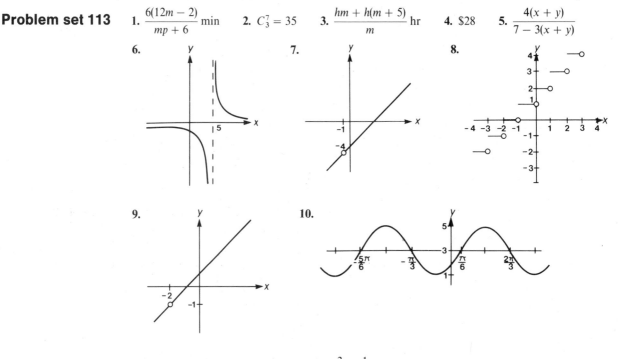

6.

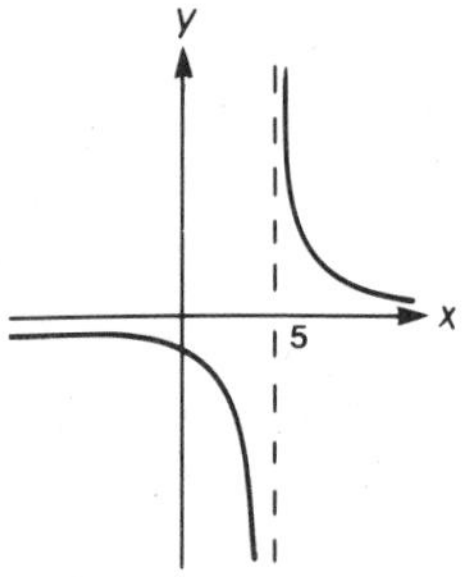

7.

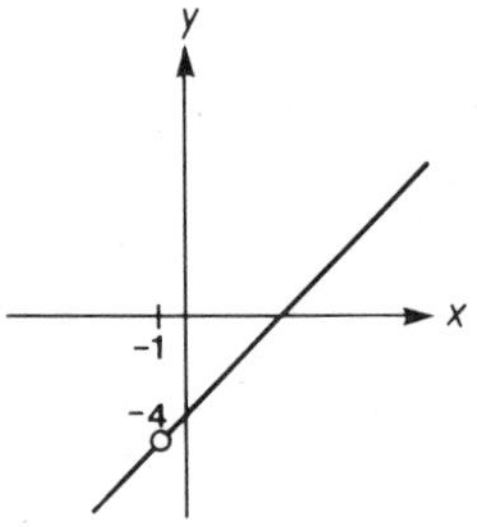

8.

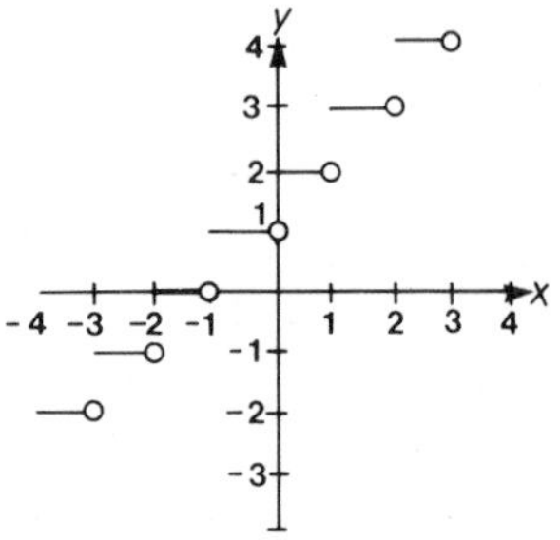

9.

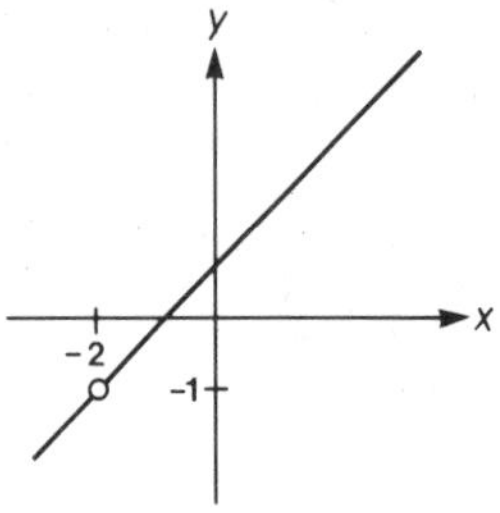

10.

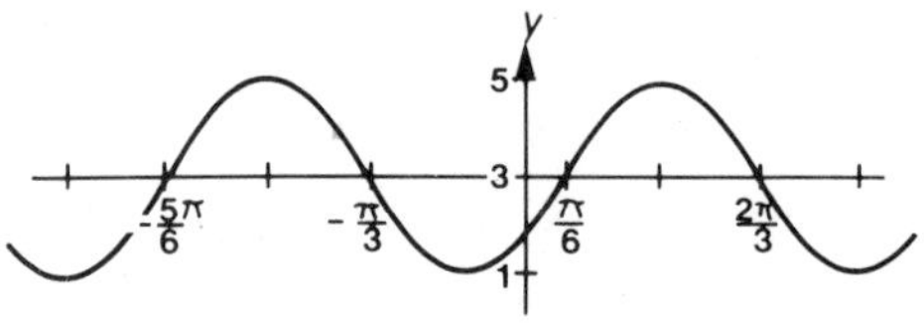

11. Yes **12.** No, 3 **13.** $\pm 1, \pm 3, \pm\frac{3}{5}, \pm\frac{1}{5}$ **14.** Refer to Lesson 111

15. $\angle BAD = \frac{1}{2}\overset{\frown}{BD}$, $\angle BCD = \frac{1}{2}\overset{\frown}{BD} \rightarrow \angle BAD = \angle BCD$, $\angle P = \angle P \rightarrow \triangle PAD \sim \triangle PCB$

16. Refer to Lesson 111

17. $\angle ACD = \frac{1}{2}\overset{\frown}{AD}$, $\angle ABD = \frac{1}{2}\overset{\frown}{AD} \rightarrow \angle ACD = \angle ABD$, $\angle AEC = \angle DEB \rightarrow \triangle AEC \sim \triangle DEB$
$\rightarrow \dfrac{AE}{CE} = \dfrac{ED}{EB} \rightarrow (AE)(EB) = (CE)(ED)$

18. Refer to Lesson 47 **19.** $f(x) = \begin{cases} -2 & x \leq 1 \\ x & 1 < x \leq 2 \\ 2 & x > 3 \end{cases}$

20. (*a*) Hyperbola (*b*) Ellipse (*c*) Circle (*d*) Parabola (*e*) Hyperbola

21. $x = -3(y + 2)^2 + 7$; parabola, vertex $= (7, -2)$; axis of symmetry: $y = -2$; opens to left

22. $\sqrt{2}$ **23.** $y = \frac{1}{5}x + \frac{3}{5}$ **24.** $\frac{1}{7}$ **25.** 96 cm^3 **26.** -3 **27.** $2i, -\sqrt{3} - i, \sqrt{3} - i$

28. 30°, 210°, 150°, 330°

29. $$\frac{2 \sec 2x}{\sec 2x + 1} = \frac{\dfrac{2}{\cos 2x}}{\dfrac{1}{\cos 2x} + 1} = \frac{2}{1 + \cos 2x} = \frac{2}{1 + 2\cos^2 x - 1} = \frac{2}{2\cos^2 x} = \frac{1}{\cos^2 x} = \sec^2 x$$

30. $1 < x < 5$ **EP97.** $\begin{bmatrix} 0 & 0 \\ 4 & -3 \end{bmatrix}$

EP98. For $k = 1$, we get $3^1 = \frac{3(3^1 - 1)}{2}$; $3 = \frac{3(2)}{2}$.

And also $\frac{3(3^k - 1)}{2} + 3^{k+1} = \frac{3^{k+1} - 3 + 2(3^{k+1})}{2} = \frac{3(3^{k+1}) - 3}{2} = \frac{3(3^{k+1} - 1)}{2}$

Problem set 114

1. -5 **2.** $A = 40°, B = 50°$ **3.** $\frac{81}{2}$ **4.** 0.4 **5.** $P_3^{26}P_4^{10}$ **6.** $-2 + 2\sqrt{11}$

7. $\angle SRU = \frac{1}{2}\overset{\frown}{SU}$, $\angle STU = \frac{1}{2}\overset{\frown}{SU} \rightarrow \angle SRU = \angle STU$, $\angle P = \angle P \rightarrow \triangle RPU \sim \triangle TPS$

$\rightarrow \frac{PR}{TP} = \frac{UP}{SP} \rightarrow (PR)(SP) = (TP)(UP)$

8. $\frac{-9 + \sqrt{337}}{2}$

9. $\angle TRS = \frac{1}{2}\overset{\frown}{TS}$, $\angle STK = \frac{1}{2}\overset{\frown}{TS} \rightarrow \angle TRS = \angle STK$, $\angle K = \angle K \rightarrow \triangle RKT \sim \triangle TKS$

$\rightarrow \frac{KT}{RK} = \frac{KS}{KT} \rightarrow (KT)^2 = (KS)(RK)$

10. $\angle C = \frac{1}{2}\overset{\frown}{AD} = \angle B$, $\angle AEC = \angle DEB \rightarrow \triangle AEC \sim \triangle DEB \rightarrow \frac{AE}{ED} = \frac{CE}{EB} \rightarrow (AE)(EB)$

$= (CE)(ED)$

11. Draw AB. $\angle ABD = \frac{1}{2}\overset{\frown}{ACB}$, $\angle BAP = \frac{1}{2}\overset{\frown}{AB}$, $\angle ABD = \angle BAP + \angle APB \rightarrow \frac{1}{2}\overset{\frown}{ACB}$

$= \frac{1}{2}\overset{\frown}{AB} + \angle APB \rightarrow \angle APB = \frac{1}{2}(\overset{\frown}{ACB} - \overset{\frown}{AB})$

12.

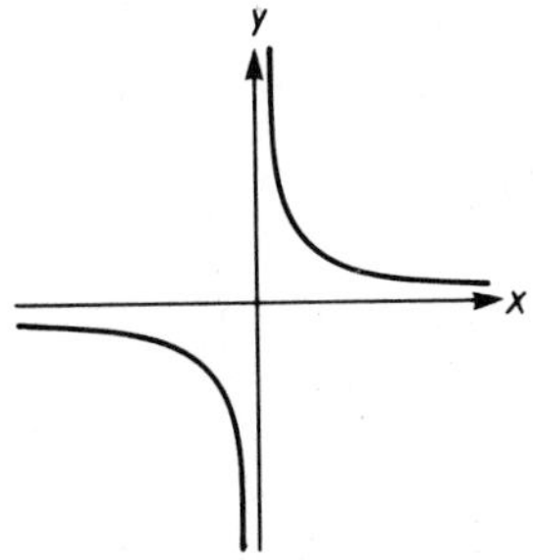

13.

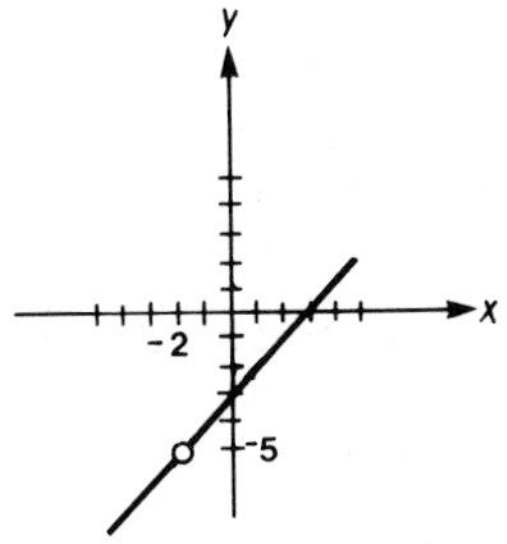

14.

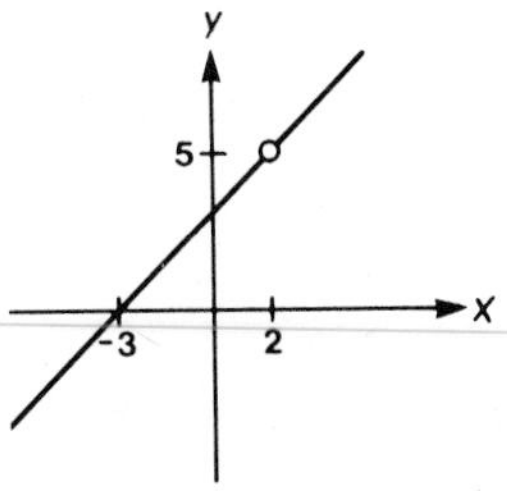

15.

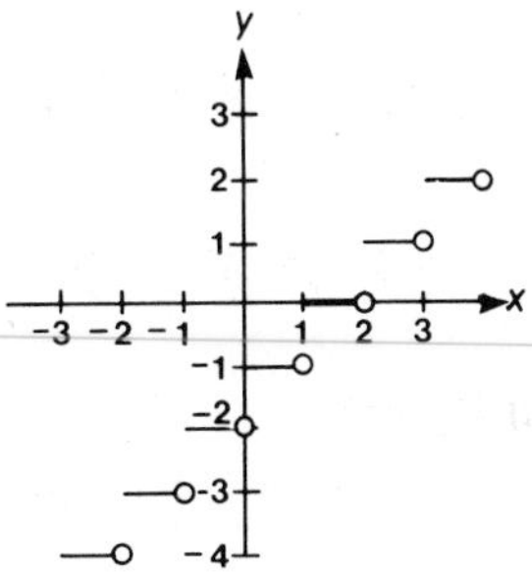

16. $\pm 1, \pm 2, \pm\frac{1}{3}, \pm\frac{1}{6}, \pm\frac{1}{2}, \pm\frac{2}{3}$ **17.** No **18.** Refer to Lesson 77

19. $f(x) = \begin{cases} -2 & x \le -2 \\ -x - 2 & -2 < x \le 0 \\ 2x & 0 < x \le 1 \\ 2 & x > 1 \end{cases}$

20.

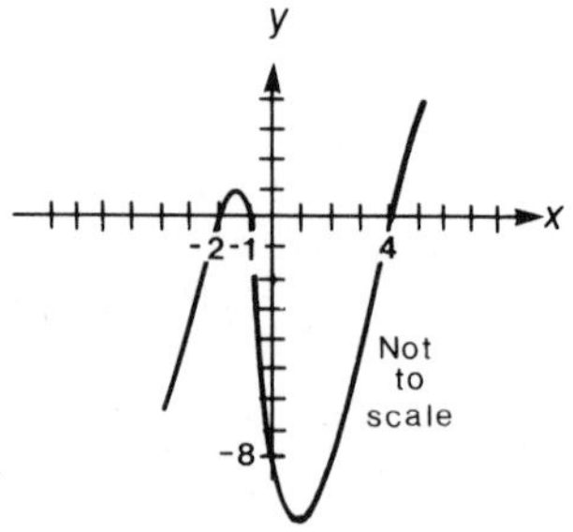

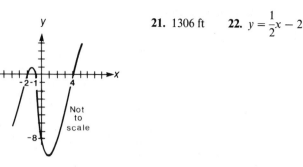

21. 1306 ft **22.** $y = \frac{1}{2}x - 2$

23. (*a*) Hyperbola (*b*) Parabola (*c*) Circle (*d*) Parabola (*e*) Ellipse

24. 108 m^3

25. $\frac{(x+2)^2}{36} - \frac{(y-4)^2}{9} = 1$; center $= (-2, 4)$; asymptotes: $y = \frac{1}{2}x + 5$, $y = -\frac{1}{2}x + 3$

26. (0, 2, 3) **27.** 1.9 cis 18.8°, 1.9 cis 138.8°, 1.9 cis 258.8°

28. $\frac{1}{2}\cot x \sec^2 x = \frac{1}{2}\frac{\cos x}{\sin x} \cdot \frac{1}{\cos^2 x} = \frac{1}{2\sin x \cos x} = \frac{1}{\sin 2x} = \csc 2x$

29. 120°, 240° **30.** 1, 2^9

EP99. For $k = 1$, we get $2^1 = 2(2^1 - 1)$. And also $2(2^k - 1) + 2^{k+1} = 2(2^{k+1}) - 2 = 2(2^{k+1} - 1)$

EP100. $\begin{bmatrix} 2x+6 & -x+8 \\ 7 & 2 \end{bmatrix}$

Problem set 115

1. $B = \frac{9}{2}$ mph, $C = \frac{3}{2}$ mph **2.** $R = 4$, $B = 8$, $G = 11$ **3.** 200 atm **4.** $A = 10°$, $B = 40°$

5. 208 min **6.** Refer to Lesson 115 **7.** $\left(\frac{7x_1 + 4x_2}{11}, \frac{7y_1 + 4y_2}{11}\right)$ **8.** $\left(3, \frac{9}{2}\right)$ **9.** 3

10. $\angle SRU = \angle STU = \frac{1}{2}\overset{\frown}{SU}$, $\angle P = \angle P \rightarrow \triangle PRU \sim \triangle PTS \rightarrow \frac{RP}{PT} = \frac{UP}{SP}$
$\rightarrow (RP)(SP) = (PT)(UP)$

11. $x = 4$

12. $\angle TRS = \frac{1}{2}\overset{\frown}{ST}$, $\angle STK = \frac{1}{2}\overset{\frown}{ST}$, $\angle K = \angle K \rightarrow \triangle TRK \sim \triangle STK \rightarrow \frac{KT}{RK} = \frac{SK}{KT}$
$\rightarrow (KT)^2 = (RK)(SK)$

13. $z = 3$

14. $\angle ACD = \angle ABD = \frac{1}{2}\overset{\frown}{AD}$, $\angle AEC = \angle DEB \rightarrow \triangle AEC \sim \triangle DEB \rightarrow \frac{AE}{ED} = \frac{CE}{EB}$
$\rightarrow (AE)(EB) = (CE)(ED)$

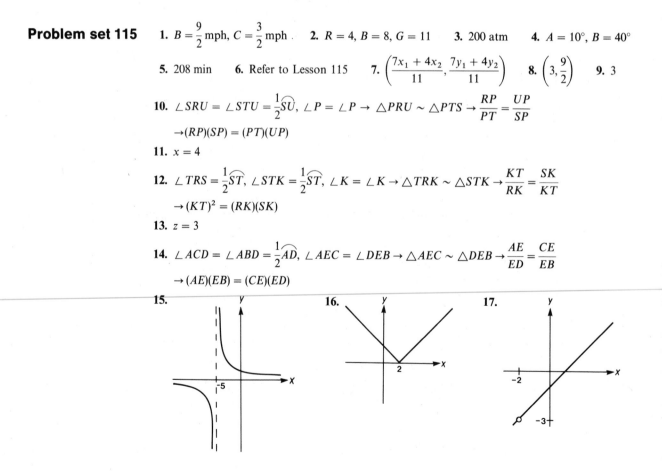

15.

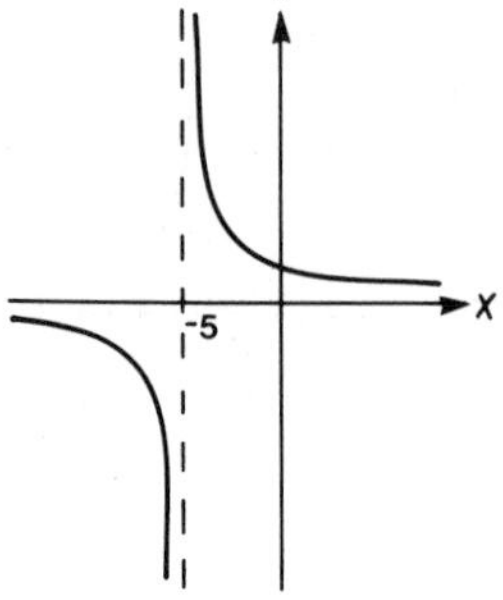

16.

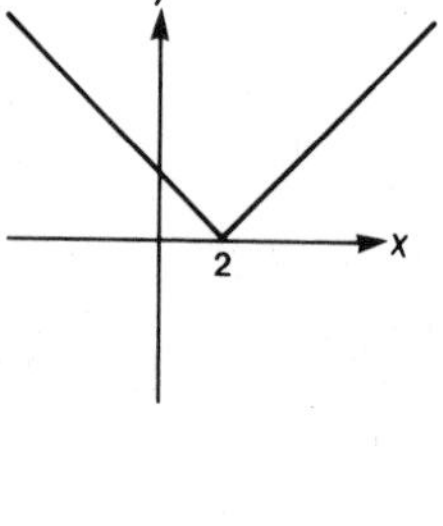

17.

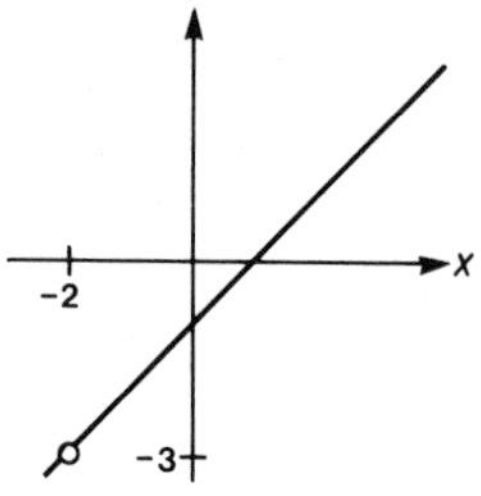

18. No. All nonzero even integers have a factor of 2.

19. $\pm 1, \pm 5, \pm\frac{1}{2}, \pm\frac{5}{2}, \pm\frac{1}{4}, \pm\frac{5}{4}, \pm\frac{1}{8}, \pm\frac{5}{8}$

20.

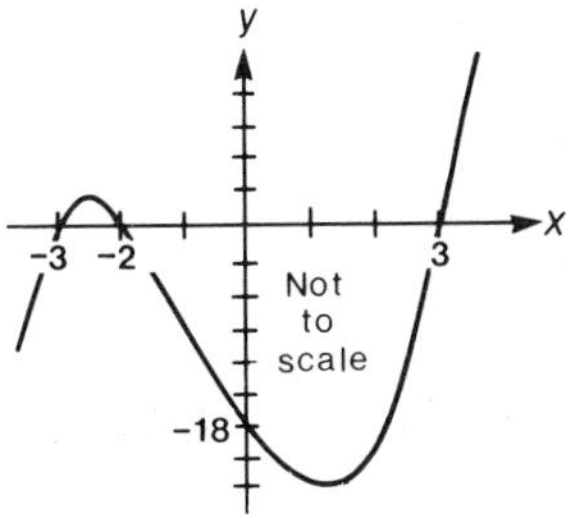

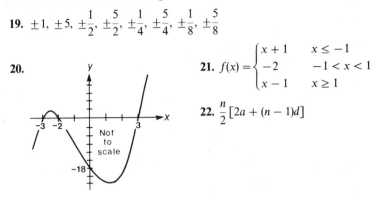

21. $f(x) = \begin{cases} x + 1 & x \leq -1 \\ -2 & -1 < x < 1 \\ x - 1 & x \geq 1 \end{cases}$

22. $\frac{n}{2}[2a + (n - 1)d]$

23. (*a*) Circle (*b*) Hyperbola (*c*) Hyperbola (*d*) Parabola (*e*) Ellipse

24. Construction

25. $\frac{x^2}{25} + \frac{(y - 6)^2}{16} = 1$, center (0, 6); major axis: horizontal, 10; minor axis = 8

26. 18 cm^3 **27.** $\sqrt{3} + i, -\sqrt{3} + i, -2i$ **28.** 45°, 315°

29. $\frac{\sin x}{\tan x + 3 \sin x} = \frac{\frac{1}{\sin x}}{\frac{1}{\sin x}} \cdot \frac{\sin x}{\frac{\sin x}{\cos x} + 3 \sin x} = \frac{1}{\frac{1}{\cos x} + 3} = \frac{1}{\sec x + 3}$

30. 1, 3^{16} **EP101.** Invalid **EP102.** $\begin{bmatrix} -1 & 0 \\ 3 & -1 \end{bmatrix}$

Problem set 116

1. 100.2 min **2.** 7500 **3.** 0.25 **4.** See Lesson 75 **5.** \$2400

6.

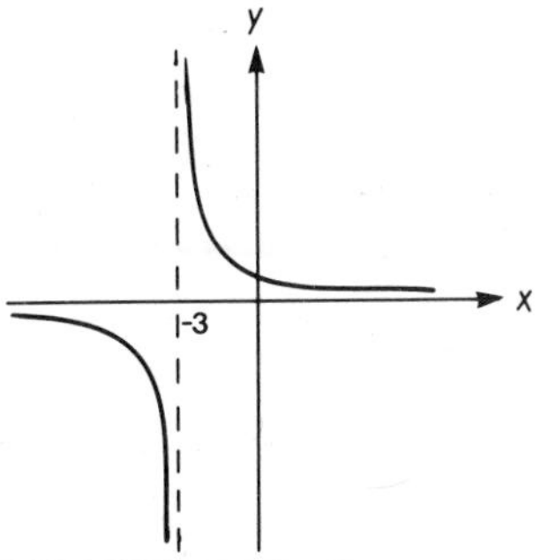

7.

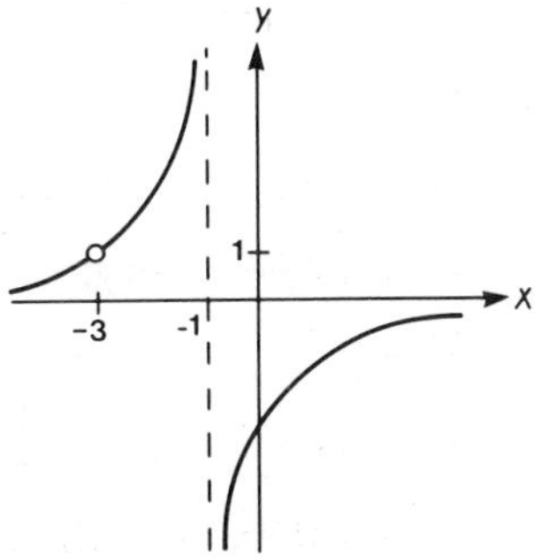

8.

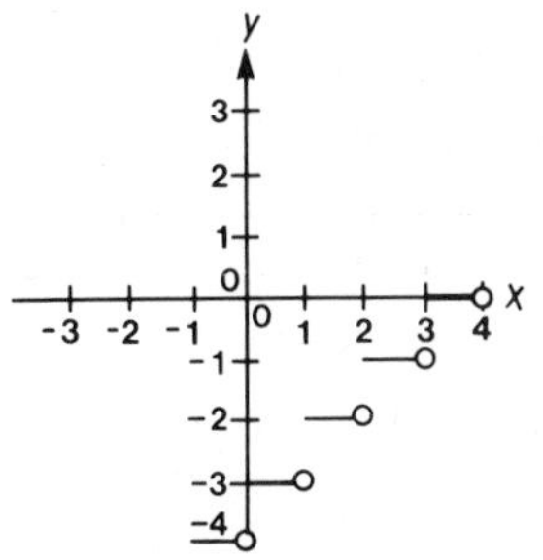

9.

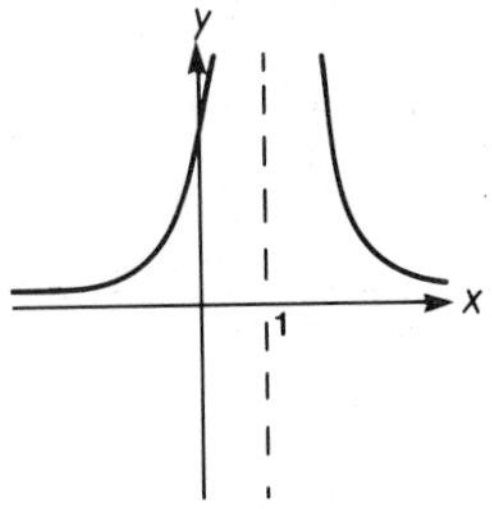

10.

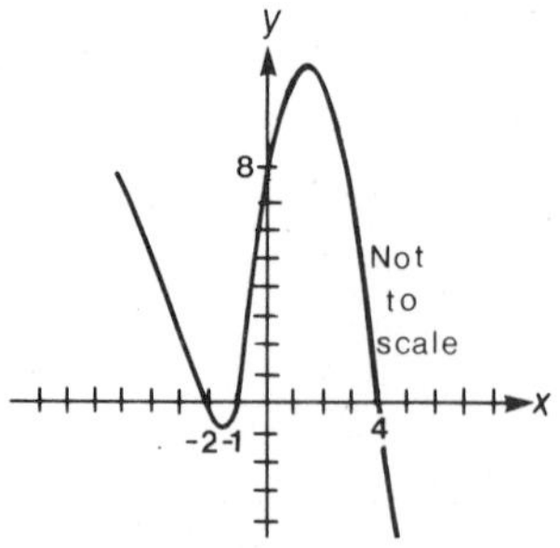

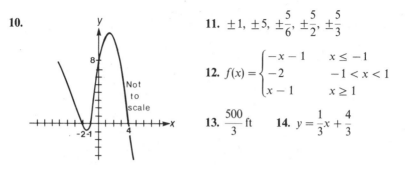

11. $\pm 1, \pm 5, \pm\frac{5}{6}, \pm\frac{5}{2}, \pm\frac{5}{3}$

12. $f(x) = \begin{cases} -x - 1 & x \le -1 \\ -2 & -1 < x < 1 \\ x - 1 & x \ge 1 \end{cases}$

13. $\frac{500}{3}$ ft **14.** $y = \frac{1}{3}x + \frac{4}{3}$

15. (*a*) Ellipse (*b*) Ellipse (*c*) Hyperbola (*d*) Parabola (*e*) Circle

16. (*a*) 48π in^3 (*b*) $12\sqrt{13}\,\pi + 36\pi$ in^2

17. $\frac{(y+1)^2}{100} - \frac{(x-4)^2}{16} = 1$, center $= (4, -1)$; vertices $= (4, 9), (4, -11)$ asymptotes: $y = \frac{5}{2}x - 11, y = -\frac{5}{2}x + 9$

18. $a = 3$

19. $\angle SRU = \angle STU = \frac{1}{2}\overset{\frown}{SU}, \angle P = \angle P \to \triangle PRU \sim \triangle PTS \to \frac{RP}{UP} = \frac{PT}{SP} \to (RP)(SP) = (UP)(PT)$

20. $x = 5$

21. $\angle SRT = \frac{1}{2}\overset{\frown}{ST}, \angle STK = \frac{1}{2}\overset{\frown}{ST}, \angle K = \angle K \to \triangle KRT \sim \triangle KTS \to \frac{KR}{KT} = \frac{KT}{SK} \to (KT)^2 = (KR)(SK)$

22. $\angle ACD = \angle ABD = \frac{1}{2}\overset{\frown}{AD}, \angle AEC = \angle DEB \to \triangle AEC \sim \triangle DEB \to \frac{AE}{CE} = \frac{ED}{EB} \to (AE)(EB) = (CE)(ED)$

23. $\overline{QS}$ is $\perp$ bisector of $\overline{PR} \to PU = UR$, $\triangle QUP$ and $\triangle QUR$ are right $\triangle$'s, $QU = QU \to \triangle PQU \cong \triangle RQU$. $\overline{RS}$ is $\perp$ bisector of $\overline{QT} \to QV = VT$, $\triangle QVR$ and $\triangle RVT$ are right $\triangle$'s, $RV = RV \to \triangle QVR \cong \triangle TVR$. $\triangle PQU \cong \triangle RQU \to PQ = QR$, $\triangle QVR \cong \triangle TVR \to QR = RT \to PQ = RT$ by substitution

24. 2, 50 **25.** 64:1 **26.** 5.3 **27.** $(2, -3, 1)$

28. $\sin^2 x \cot^2 x + \cot^2 x + \sin^2 x + 1 = \cos^2 x + \sin^2 x + \cot^2 x + 1 = 1 + \csc^2 x$

29. 30°, 150° **30.** $\frac{1}{81}$

EP103. For $k = 1$, we get $(4 \cdot 1 + 1) = 2 \cdot 1^2 + 3 \cdot 1$; $5 = 2 + 3$. And also $2k^2 + 3k + (4k + 5) = (2k^2 + 4k + 2) + (3k + 3) = 2(k+1)^2 + 3(k+1)$.

EP104. Valid

Problem set 117

1. 412.4 min **2.** 47 **3.** $\frac{3(5+k)(p-2)}{35}$ jobs **4.** $\frac{2h}{2k-h}$ hr **5.** \$420

6. Construction **7.** Construction **8.** Construction **9.** $x = 4$ **10.** $x = 9$

11. $\angle SRU = \angle STU = \frac{1}{2}\overset{\frown}{SU}, \angle P = \angle P \to \triangle PRU \sim \triangle PTS \to \frac{PR}{PT} = \frac{RU}{TS} \to (TS)(PR) = (RU)(PT)$

12. Refer to Lesson 111

13. $\angle TRS = \angle STK = \frac{1}{2}\overset{\frown}{ST},\ \angle K = \angle K \to \triangle TSK \sim \triangle RTK \to \frac{KR}{KT} = \frac{RT}{TS}$
$\to (KR)(TS) = (KT)(RT)$

14.

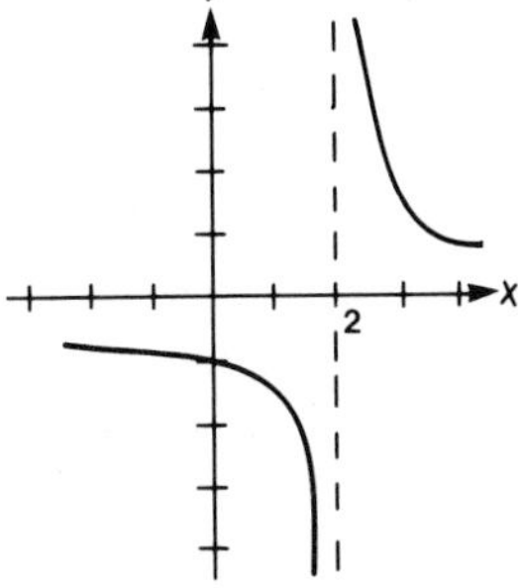

15.

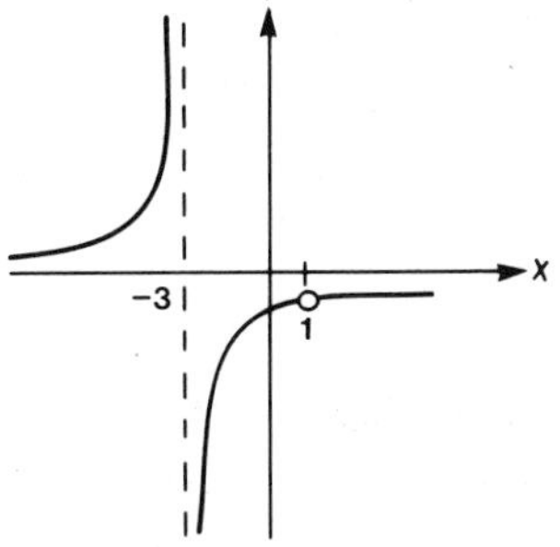

16.

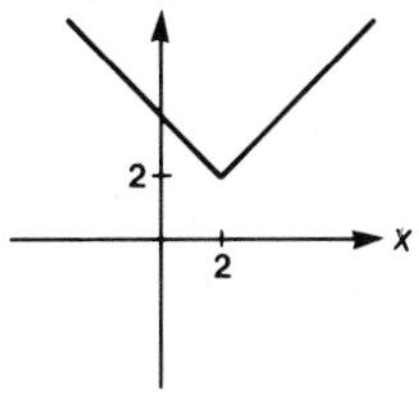

17.

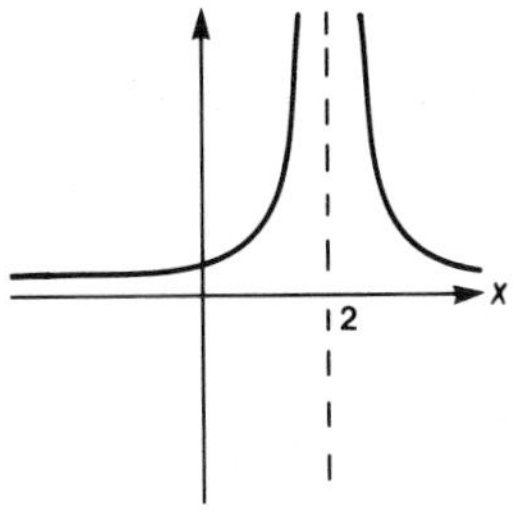

18.

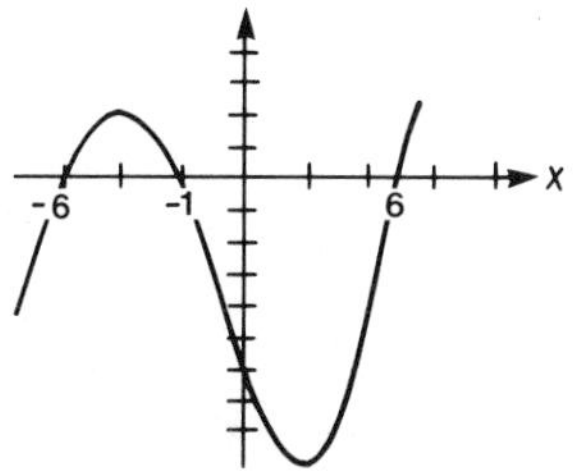

19. $\pm 1, \pm 3, \pm\frac{1}{2}, \pm\frac{3}{2}, \pm\frac{1}{4}, \pm\frac{3}{4}, \pm\frac{1}{8}, \pm\frac{3}{8}$ **20.** $\frac{n}{2}[2a + (n - 1)d]$

21. $f(x) = \begin{cases} -4 & x \le -3 \\ -2 & -3 < x \le 0 \\ x & 0 < x \le 2 \\ 3 & x > 2 \end{cases}$ **22.** $(0, -4)$

23. (*a*) Circle (*b*) Ellipse (*c*) Hyperbola (*d*) Parabola (*e*) Parabola

24. (*a*) $\frac{4}{3}\pi r^3$ (*b*) $4\pi r^2$

25. $y = -4\left(x - \frac{5}{2}\right)^2 - 16$, parabola, vertex $= \left(\frac{5}{2}, -16\right)$; axis of symmetry: $x = \frac{5}{2}$; opens downward

26. Yes **27.** $2, 2i, -2, -2i$

28. $\frac{\cos x}{\cot x + 3\cos x} = \frac{\frac{1}{\cos x}}{\frac{1}{\cos x}} \cdot \frac{\cos x}{\frac{\cos x}{\sin x} + 3\cos x} = \frac{1}{\frac{1}{\sin x} + 3} = \frac{1}{\csc x + 3}$

29. 30°, 150° **30.** Refer to Lesson 28

EP105. For $k = 1$, we get $\frac{1 \cdot 2}{2} = \frac{1(1+1)(1+2)}{6}; \frac{2}{2} = \frac{(2)(3)}{6}$. And also

$$\frac{k(k+1)(k+2)}{6} + \frac{(k+1)(k+2)}{2} = \frac{k(k+1)(k+2) + 3(k+1)(k+2)}{6}$$
$$= \frac{(k+1)(k+2)(k+3)}{6} = \frac{(k+1)[(k+1)+1][(k+1)+2]}{6}$$

EP106. Valid

Problem set 118

1. 47.7 years **2.** $T_B = 16$ hr, $R_B = 70$ mph, $T_W = 8$ hr, $R_W = 50$ mph

3. $F = 10, S = 140$ **4.** $\frac{12}{5}$ hr **5.** $\frac{1}{6}$ **6.** $-1, \frac{1}{2}, \frac{3}{2}$ **7.** $-2, \frac{1}{2}, \frac{3}{2}$

8.

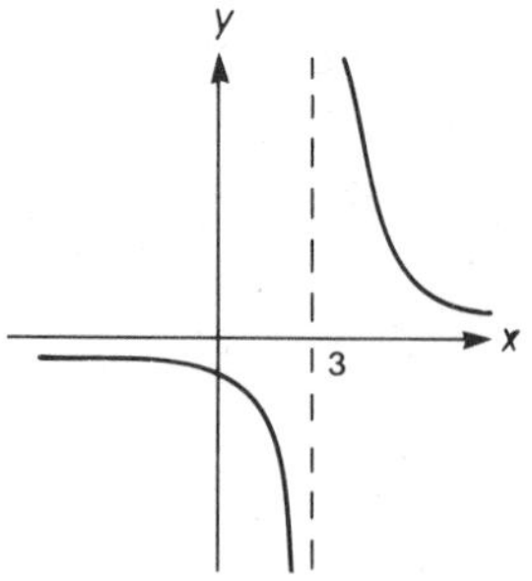

9.

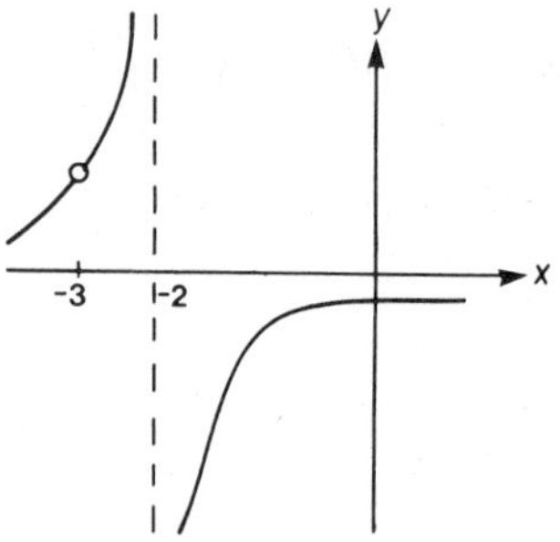

10.

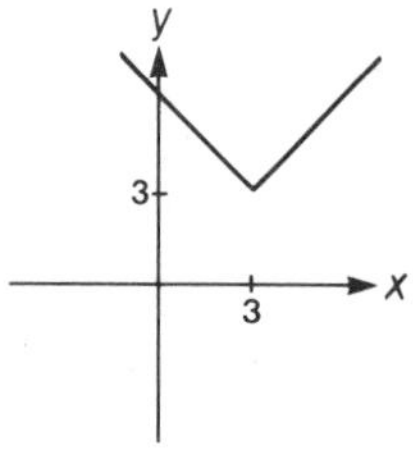

11.

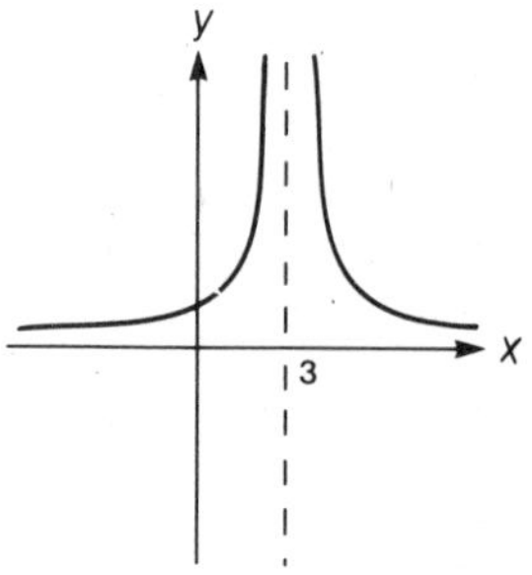

12. $y = \frac{1}{2}x + 2$

13.

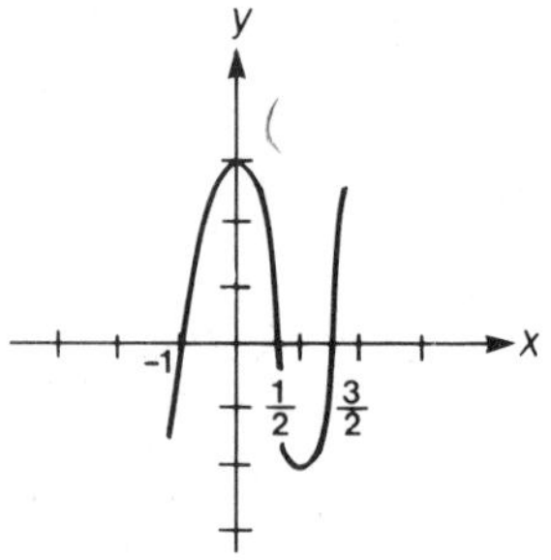

14. $\left(-\frac{4}{5}, \frac{16}{5}\right)$

15. $\angle SRU = \angle STU = \frac{1}{2}SU,\ \angle P = \angle P \rightarrow \triangle PRU \sim \triangle PTS \rightarrow \frac{PS}{PU} = \frac{ST}{RU}$
$\rightarrow (PS)(RU) = (PU)(ST)$

16. $x = 5$

17. $\angle TRS = \angle STK = \frac{1}{2}\overset{\frown}{ST},\ \angle K = \angle K \rightarrow \triangle RKT \sim \triangle TKS \rightarrow \frac{KT}{KS} = \frac{RK}{KT}$
$\rightarrow (KT)^2 = (RK)(KS)$

18. Refer to Lesson 76 **19.** Construction **20.** Construction **21.** See Lesson 88

22. See Lesson 88 **23.** $f(x) = \begin{cases} -1 & x < -3 \\ x - 1 & -3 \le x \le 1 \\ 1 & 1 < x \le 4 \\ 3 & x > 4 \end{cases}$ **24.** 75 cm^3

25. (*a*) Parabola (*b*) Parabola (*c*) Hyperbola (*d*) Ellipse (*e*) Circle

26. $\frac{(x+5)^2}{36} + \frac{(y-4)^2}{4} = 1$, center $= (-5, 4)$, major axis: horizontal, 12; minor axis $= 4$

27. 1.9 cis 41.2°, 1.9 cis 161.2°, 1.9 cis 281.2°

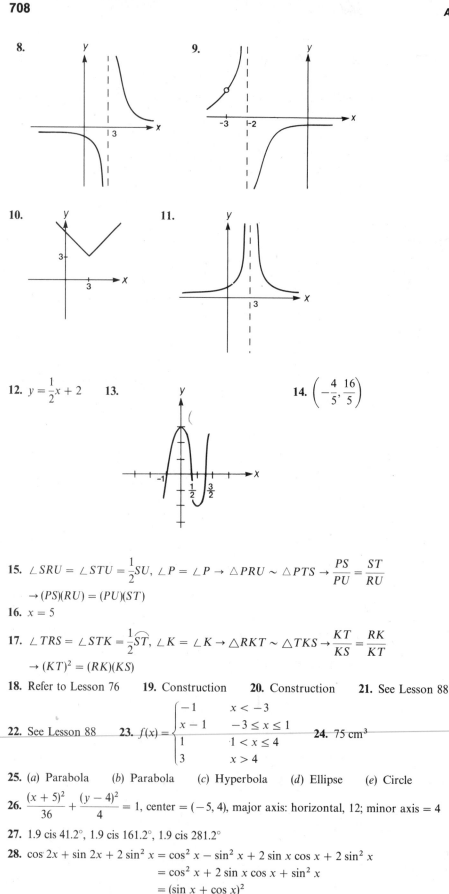

28.
$$\begin{aligned} \cos 2x + \sin 2x + 2\sin^2 x &= \cos^2 x - \sin^2 x + 2\sin x \cos x + 2\sin^2 x \\ &= \cos^2 x + 2\sin x \cos x + \sin^2 x \\ &= (\sin x + \cos x)^2 \end{aligned}$$

29. 330°, 210° **30.** $\dfrac{1}{\log 7}$

EP107. For $k = 1$, we get $(3 \cdot 1 - 2) = \dfrac{1(3 \cdot 1 - 1)}{2}$; $(3 - 2) = \dfrac{(3-1)}{2}$. And also

$$\frac{k(3k-1)}{2} + (3k+1) = \frac{k(3k-1) + 2(3k+1)}{2} = \frac{3k^2 + 5k + 2}{2}$$

$$= \frac{(k+1)(3k+2)}{2} = \frac{(k+1)[3(k+1) - 1]}{2}$$

EP108. Invalid

Problem set 119

1. 247 **2.** $R_w = 20$, $R_c = 40$, $T_w = 8$, $T_c = 6$ **3.** $N_R = 5$, $N_B = 12$

4. $\dfrac{1}{2} + \dfrac{1}{13} - \dfrac{1}{26} = \dfrac{7}{13}$ **5.** $2 + i$, $2 - i$ **6.** $-\dfrac{1}{3} + \dfrac{\sqrt{11}}{3}i$, $-\dfrac{1}{3} - \dfrac{\sqrt{11}}{3}i$ **7.** 3 or 1 **8.** 1

9. 4, 2, or 0 **10.** 1 **11.** +5 and −5 **12.** 4, 0 **13.** −1, −1, −2 **14.** 3, $2i$, $-2i$

15.

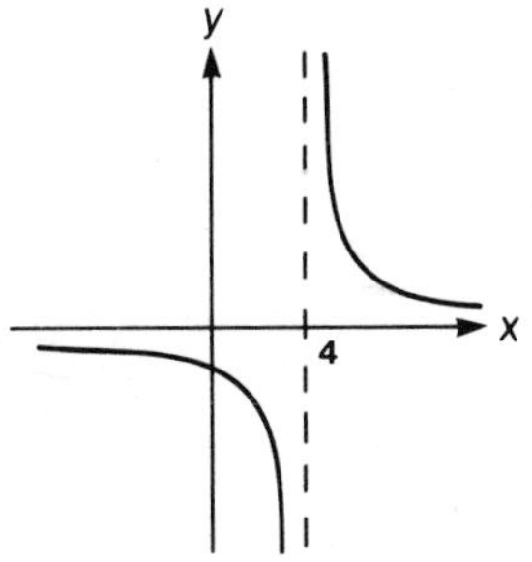

16.

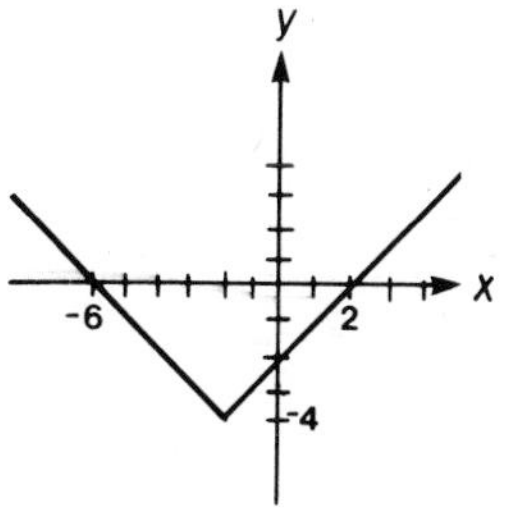

17.

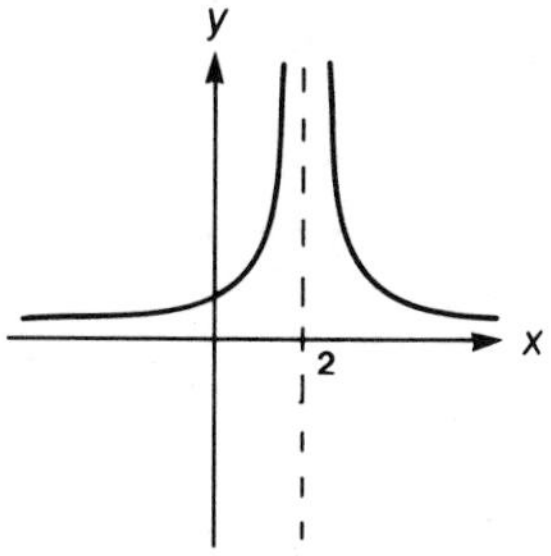

18. $y = \dfrac{1}{5}x - \dfrac{6}{5}$ **19.** $\left(\dfrac{5}{4}, 3\right)$ **20.** 196 ft^3

21. 1 cis 67.5°, 1 cis 157.5°, 1 cis 247.5°, 1 cis 337.5° **22.** 2.387 **23.** See Lesson 88

24. $\dfrac{n}{2}[2a + (n-1)d]$ **25.** $-\dfrac{108}{25}$

Index